THE INDIGENOUS LANGUAGES OF THE AMERICAS

The Indigenous Languages of the Americas

HISTORY AND CLASSIFICATION

Lyle Campbell

OXFORD
UNIVERSITY PRESS

Oxford University Press is a department of the University of Oxford. It furthers the University's objective of excellence in research, scholarship, and education by publishing worldwide. Oxford is a registered trade mark of Oxford University Press in the UK and certain other countries.

Published in the United States of America by Oxford University Press
198 Madison Avenue, New York, NY 10016, United States of America.

© Oxford University Press 2024

All rights reserved. No part of this publication may be reproduced, stored in a retrieval system, or transmitted, in any form or by any means, without the prior permission in writing of Oxford University Press, or as expressly permitted by law, by license, or under terms agreed with the appropriate reproduction rights organization. Inquiries concerning reproduction outside the scope of the above should be sent to the Rights Department, Oxford University Press, at the address above.

You must not circulate this work in any other form
and you must impose this same condition on any acquirer.

Library of Congress Cataloging-in-Publication Data
Names: Campbell, Lyle, author.
Title: The indigenous languages of the Americas : history and classification / Lyle Campbell.
Description: New York, NY : Oxford University Press, 2024. |
Includes bibliographical references and index.
Identifiers: LCCN 2023033270 (print) | LCCN 2023033271 (ebook) |
ISBN 9780197673461 (hardback) | ISBN 9780197673485 (epub)
Subjects: LCSH: Indians—Languages—History. | Indians—Languages—Classification.
Classification: LCC PM109 .C36 2023 (print) | LCC PM109 (ebook) |
DDC 497—dc23/eng/20230906
LC record available at https://lccn.loc.gov/2023033270
LC ebook record available at https://lccn.loc.gov/2023033271

DOI: 10.1093/oso/9780197673461.001.0001

Printed by Integrated Books International, United States of America

Contents

List of Illustrations ix
Preface xi
Acknowledgments xiii
Phonetic Symbols xv
Abbreviations xvii

1. Introduction 1
    1.1. Introduction 1
    1.2. Names and Naming 2
    1.3. Terminology 9
    1.4. Loss of Diversity and the Status of Indigenous Languages of the Americas 10
    1.5. Historical Overview of Attempts to Classify the Languages of the Americas 12
    1.6. Origins of the American Indian Languages 13
    1.7. Methods 21
    1.8. Conventions Used in This Book 23

2. North American Indian Languages North of Mexico 28
    2.1. Introduction 28
    2.2. Classification and History of North American Indian Languages 28

3. Middle American Languages (Mexico and Central America) 146
    3.1. Introduction 146
    3.2. Classification and History of Middle American Languages 147
    3.2.1. Mesoamerican Languages 148
    3.2.2. Non-Mesoamerican Language Families of Middle America 170
    3.3. Mesoamerican Linguistic Prehistory 174

4. *Indigenous Languages of South America* 182
    4.1. Introduction 182
    4.2. Classification and History of South American Indigenous Languages 183
    4.2.1. Larger Language Families 185
    4.2.2. Small Language Families 185
    4.2.3. Language Isolates 186
    4.3. South American Language Families (Including Language Isolates) 188
    4.4. Wrap-Up 275

5. *Unclassified and Spurious Languages* 280
    5.1. Introduction 280
    5.2. Unclassified Languages of North America 281
    5.3. Unclassified Languages of Middle America (Mexico and Central America) 288
    5.4. Unclassified Languages of South America 295
    5.5. Phantom, False, and Spurious Languages 330
    5.5.1. Phantom, False, and Spurious Languages of North America 330
    5.5.2. Phantom, False, and Spurious Languages of Middle America 331
    5.5.3. Phantom, False, and Spurious Languages of South America 333
    5.5.4. Other Language Fakes 335

6. *Distant Linguistic Relationships* 339
    6.1. Introduction 339
    6.2. Recent Success Stories 340
    6.3. Terms and Methods 340
    6.4. Historical Attempts to Classify the Languages of the Americas: A Case Study 342
    6.5. Proposals of Distant Genetic Relationships 345
    6.5.1. The Hokan Hypothesis 345
    6.5.2. Penutian 354
    6.5.3. Yok-Utian 358
    6.5.4. Amerind 358
    6.5.5. Dene-Yeniseian 361
    6.5.6. Mayan-MixeZoquean 366
    6.5.7. Chitimacha-Totozoquean 366
    6.5.8. Macro-Jê Sensu Lato 369
    6.5.9. The Tupían-Cariban and Tupían-Cariban-Jê hypotheses 370
    6.5.10. Macro-Guaicurúan 371
    6.5.11. Quechumaran 372

Appendix 1: A Closer Look at Greenberg's Macro-Panoan Hypothesis 373
Appendix 2: List of Distant Genetic Relationship Proposals 381

7. *Linguistic Areas of the Americas* 388
- 7.1. Introduction 388
- 7.2. North American Linguistic Areas 388
  - 7.2.1. Northwest Coast Linguistic Area 389
  - 7.2.2. Northern Northwest Coast Linguistic Area 392
  - 7.2.3. Plateau Linguistic Area 393
  - 7.2.4. Northern California Linguistic Area 396
  - 7.2.5. Northwest California 398
  - 7.2.6. Clear Lake Linguistic Area 398
  - 7.2.7. South Coast Range and Greater South Coast Range Linguistic Areas 399
  - 7.2.8. Central California Linguistic Area 399
  - 7.2.9. Southern California–Western Arizona Linguistic Area 400
  - 7.2.10. Great Basin Linguistic Area 401
  - 7.2.11. Pueblo Linguistic Area 403
  - 7.2.12. Plains Linguistic Area 405
  - 7.2.13. Northeast Linguistic Area 407
  - 7.2.14. Southeast Linguistic Area 409
- 7.3. Mesoamerican Linguistic Area 413
- 7.4. Linguistic Areas of South America 422
  - 7.4.1. Proposals of Macro-linguistic Areas in South America 423
  - 7.4.2. Amazonia as a Linguistic Area? 424
  - 7.4.3. The Colombian-Central American Linguistic Area 426
  - 7.4.4. Northern Amazonia Linguistic Areas 426
    - 7.4.4.1. The Vaupés (Vaupés-Içana) Linguistic Area 426
    - 7.4.4.2. The Caquetá-Putumayo Linguistic Area 428
    - 7.4.4.3. The Venezuelan-Antillean Linguistic Area 429
    - 7.4.4.4. Southern Guiana (Northeastern Amazonian) Linguistic Area 429
  - 7.4.5. Southern Amazonia Linguistic Areas 430
    - 7.4.5.1. Guaporé-Mamoré Linguistic Area 430
    - 7.4.5.2. Tocantins-Mearim Interfluvium Linguistic Area(?) 430
    - 7.4.5.3. The Upper Xingu Linguistic Area 432
  - 7.4.6. Highlands (West) Linguistic Areas 432
    - 7.4.6.1. The Andean Area, Central Andean Linguistic Area 432
    - 7.4.6.2. The Ecuadoran-Colombian Subarea 436
  - 7.4.7. The Gran Chaco Linguistic Area(?) 436

7.4.8. Southern Region Linguistic Areas 438
7.4.8.1. The Southern Cone Linguistic Area(?) 438
7.4.8.2. "Fuegian" Linguistic Area(?) 438

8. *Contact Languages* 441
    8.1. Introduction 441
    8.2. Pidgins 441
    8.2.1. Indigenous Pidgins of North America 441
    8.2.2. Indigenous Pidgins in South America 445
    8.2.3. *Línguas Gerais* of Brazil 446
    8.3. Lingua Francas of the New World 448
    8.3.1. North American Indigenous Lingua Francas 448
    8.3.2. Lingua Francas in Latin America 449
    8.4. Mixed Languages 451
    8.5. Socio-cultural-political Factors in South America Language Contact 455
    8.5.1. Marriage Patterns, Multilingualism, Linguistic Exogamy 455

9. *Loanwords and Other New Words in the Indigenous Languages of the Americas* 460
    9.1. Introduction 460
    9.2. *Wanderwörter* 460
    9.3. Other Loanwords among Indigenous Languages 464
    9.4. Loanwords from Indigenous Languages into European Languages 467
    9.5. Loanwords from European Languages into Indigenous American Languages 467
    9.6. Calquing 468
    9.7. Taboo and Multilingual Obscenity Avoidance 468
    9.8. Reticence toward Loanwords 469
    9.9. New Words that Rely on Native Resources 470

REFERENCES 473
INDEX OF LANGUAGES 559
INDEX OF PERSONAL NAMES 597
SUBJECT INDEX 603

List of Illustrations

CHART

Chart 3.1　Pipil (Nawat) traits shared with Central and with Peripheral Nahua groups 164

MAPS

Map 2.1.　North American Indian languages (overview) 30
Map 2.2.　Eskimo-Aleut languages 32
Map 2.3.　Na-Dene languages 37
Map 2.4.　Salishan languages 48
Map 2.5.　Utian languages 62
Map 2.6.　Languages of California (pre-contact) 66
Map 2.7.　Uto-Aztecan languages (pre-contact distribution) 81
Map 2.8.　Siouan-Catawban languages (pre-contact) 100
Map 2.9.　Iroquoian languages 116
Map 2.10.　Algonquian languages 123
Map 3.1.　Mayan languages 151
Map 3.2.　Mixe-Zoquean languages 156
Map 3.3.　Branches of the Otomanguean language family 161
Map 4.1.　Languages of the Arawakan family 193
Map 4.2.　Languages of the Cariban language family 204
Map 4.3.　Chibchan languages 208
Map 4.4.　Macro-Jê Sensu Stricto languages 233
Map 4.5.　Pano-Takanan languages 246
Map 4.6.　Tupían Language Family Branches 263
Map 4.7.　Distribution of Tupían, Cariban, and Macro-Jê language families 267

Map 7.1. Languages of the Northwest Coast Linguistic Area 390
Map 7.2. Languages of the Plateau Linguistic Area 394
Map 7.3. Languages of the Great Basin Linguistic Area 402
Map 7.4. Languages of the Pueblo Linguistic Area 403
Map 7.5. Languages of the Plains Linguistic Area 406
Map 7.6. Languages of the Northeast Linguistic Area 408
Map 7.7. Languages of the Southeast Linguistic Area 409
Map 7.8. Languages of the Mesoamerican Linguistic Area (c. 1500) 414
Map 7.9. Languages of the Vaupés Linguistic Area 427
Map 7.10. Languages of the Guaporé-Mamoré Linguistic Area 431
Map 7.11. Languages of the Andes Area 433
Map 7.12. Languages of the Chaco (present day) 437

Preface

IN BOOK PREFACES authors often confess things, like why they decided to write the book and what motivated them to do it. They may refer to challenges and opportunities encountered in the writing, and they sometimes contrast their book with other works or with earlier developments in the field. For me, the primary motivation for writing this book was to update the history and classification of the Indigenous languages of the Americas—much needed. Research on American Indian languages is vibrant and fast-moving, with many advances and discoveries in recent years. Another motivation was to contribute further and to resolve or at least clarify issues, and to address more concertedly some topics not given enough attention in earlier works.

The challenge was, I confess, that I did not want to write the book. I had written a related book a quarter of a century earlier, and it took years to complete; I did not want to face that again. Nevertheless, developments since that book have made this one necessary. I wrote *American Indian Languages: The Historical Linguistics of Native America* in 1997 (Oxford University Press). It got a lot of attention; it won some prizes, including the prestigious Leonard Bloomfield Award from the Linguistic Society of America for the best book in linguistics for the previous two years; and it is very frequently cited. However, I confess also that the continued frequent citations of that earlier book were a large factor motivating me to write this one—it disappointed me to see that earlier book still cited now, for example in hundreds of entries in Wikipedia and elsewhere, as the authoritative contemporary source even on matters no longer accurate, given the advances in the field since the 1997 book appeared.

As for comparison with other works and earlier developments in the field, I very much hope that the updated and more accurate information provided here will come to replace the dated information of the earlier book so frequently cited.

I rush to make clear that this book is not a second edition of the 1997 book. Much in that book is still accurate and I believe valuable; there are things treated in that book that are not repeated here. Rather, this book gives prominence to the new discoveries and developments since 1997 and to topics and issues that received too little attention back then.

I hope readers will find this book useful and interesting, an ample and dependable basic reference on the current state of knowledge about the history and classification of the Indigenous languages of the Americas.

Acknowledgments

OVER THE YEARS I have asked many people questions, both small and large, about various things talked about in this book. I do not remember them all now, nor what I asked nor whether or how their answers may be reflected in what is presented here. I rely on them to remember who they are and what was asked, and to know that I am truly grateful to them for their information and help. I also thank my teachers, colleagues, students, friends, and Indigenous language consultants who have inspired my interest and helped me to learn about the Indigenous languages in the Americas.

In particular, I am grateful to the following individuals for information small and large and advice of various sorts in recent years: Willem F. H. Adelaar, Carolina Coelho Aragon, Rosemary Bean de Azcona, Claire Bowern, Joshua Birchall, Ana Suelly Arruda Câmara Cabral, Thiago Chacon, Mily Crevels, John Elliott, Patience Epps, Andrew Garrett, Spike Gildea, Ives Goddard, Victor Golla, Anthony P. Grant, Harald Hammarström, Raina Heaton, Terrence Kaufman, Carolyn J. MacKay, Jack Martin, Lev Michael, Marianne Mithun, Pieter Muysken, Colleen O'Brien, Sanderson Oliveira, Keren Rice, Richard Rhodes, Chris Rogers, J. Pedro Viegas Barros, Wilson de Lima Silva, Sarah Thomason, Matthias Urban, and Raoul Zamponi.

I am very grateful to the editorial team at Oxford University Press for their unfailing help and advice and work throughout the production of this book.

I thank George Pertix for the huge effort of preparing the maps.

Phonetic Symbols

THE PHONETIC SYMBOLS that appear in this book are identified in this chart. Examples are often given with the symbols used in the sources cited. In American Indian linguistics, the Americanist phonetic symbols are the most commonly used, though many linguists use the International Phonetic Alphabet (IPA) in their representations. Both are listed here, with IPA first and the Americanist symbols in brackets following their IPA equivalents. The more common sounds are given first in chart-like form. Less common, more unusual sounds are listed below this.

	Bilabial	Labiodental	Dental	Alveolar	Postalveolar	Retroflex	Palatal	Velar	Uvular	Pharyngeal	Glottal
Voiceless stops	p			t		ʈ [ṭ]	c	k	q		ʔ
Voiced stops	b			d				g			
Voiceless affricates				ts	tʃ [č]						
Voiced affricates				dz	dʒ [ǰ]						
Voiceless fricatives	ɸ	f	θ	s	ʃ [š]	ʂ [ṣ]	ç	x	χ	ħ	h
Voiced fricatives	β	v	ð	z	ʒ [ž]	ʐ [ẓ]		ɣ	ʁ	ʕ	
Nasals	m			n		ɳ [ṇ]	ɲ [ñ]	ŋ	ɴ		
Approximants	w			ɹ [r]			j [y]				
Laterals				l							

Phonetic Symbols

		Front	Central	Back
High				
	close (tense)	i	ɨ	u
	open (lax)	ɪ		ʊ
Mid				
	close (tense)	e	ə	o
	open (lax)	ɛ		ɔ
Low		æ	a	ɑ

Diacritics and other phonetic symbols used:

C	consonant
V	vowel
Cʰ	aspirated consonant
C̪	dental consonant
C'	glottalized consonant
Cʷ	labialized consonant
Cʸ, Cʲ	palatalized consonant (IPA [Cʲ])
C̥	voiceless consonant
C̣	retroflex consonant
ɓ	Voiced bilabial imploded stop
ɗ	Voiced alveolar imploded stop
qʕ	Voiceless uvular imploded stop
tł	voiceless lateral affricate (IPA [tɬ])
tł'	voiceless glottalized lateral affricate (IPA [tɬ'])
ł, ɬ	voiceless lateral approximant
š, ʃ	voiceless postalveolar (alveopalatal) fricative (IPA [ʃ])
č, tʃ	voiceless postalveolar (alveopalatal) affricate (IPA [tʃ])
ǰ, dʒ	voiced postalveolar (alveopalatal) affricate (IPA [dʒ])
ž, ʒ	voiced postalveolar (alveopalatal) fricative (IPA [ʒ])
ṣ̌	voiceless laminal retroflex fricative (IPA has no equivalent)
č̣	voiceless laminal retroflex affricate (IPA has no equivalent)
r, r̃	voiced alveolar trill (IPA [r])
lʲ, lʸ	voiced palatalized alveolar lateral approximant (IPA [lʲ])
ḷ	voiced retroflex lateral approximate (IPA [ɭ])
ħ, ḥ	voiceless pharyngeal fricative (IPA [ħ])
nʲ, nʸ, ñ	palatalized alveolar nasal; palatal nasal (IPA [ɲ])
V̥	voiceless vowel
Ṽ, Ṿ	nasalized vowel
V:, V·	long vowel (vowel length)
ü	high front rounded vowel (IPA [y])
ɯ	high back unrounded vowel

Abbreviations

ACC	accusative
BEN	benefactive
C	consonant
CLASS	class, classifier
ESALA	Eastern South American Linguistic Area
MZ	Mixe-Zoquean
MLP	Misión la Paz, Argentina
NMLZ	nominalization
OSV	Object-Subject-Verb (word order)
OVS	Object-Verb-Subject (word order)
PL	plural
PMZ	Proto-Mixe-Zoquean
POSS	possessive
PROG	progressive
SA	South America, South American
SG	singular
SVO	Subject-Verb-Object (word order)
V	vowel
VOS	Verb-Object-Subject (word order)
VSO	Verb- Subject-Object (word order)
WSALA	Western South American Linguistic Area

1
Introduction

1.1. INTRODUCTION

This book is about the American Indian languages, the Indigenous languages of the Americas. To begin we might ask, did you know that American Indian Languages are spoken from Siberia to Greenland and from the Arctic to Tierra del Fuego? They include the southernmost language of the world (Yagan [alias Yámana], in Argentina and Chile) and some of the northernmost languages (Eskimoan). Did you know that over a thousand languages were spoken in the Americas at the time of first European contact and that almost 600 are still spoken? Did you know that there are far more language families in the Americas than anywhere else in the world? There are about 170 independent language families (including language isolates) on the American continents; they make up 43 percent of the linguistic diversity of the world, calculated in terms of language families. The Americas were the last major land mass to be occupied by humans, and yet they have a greater number of language families than any other land mass. Have you perhaps wondered how these languages are related to one another, if they are, and how they differ? What about the histories of these languages and what they tell us about the past of the peoples who speak them? Did you know that all the Indigenous languages of the Americas are endangered to one degree or another, many of them severely so?

Answers to questions such as these are the concerns of this book. From time to time, as Morris Swadesh (1954a, 306), well-known specialist in American Indian linguistics, advised, it is good to reexamine "broad questions in light of accumulated data and understanding, so that we may be better guided in our work." A major aim of this book is to do just that. This book takes stock of what is known currently about the history of the Indigenous languages of the Americas while attempting also to make further contributions of its own. The need for such stocktaking is clear, given, for example, that there is not a consensus among experts even on how many American Indian languages there are. Estimates from respected scholars have ranged from as few as 400 to over 2,000 languages. It is assumed, not without reason, that masses of languages have disappeared without a trace, and indeed a great many have ceased to be spoken since first European contact (see Chapter 5). Many others currently are critically endangered and will certainly cease to be spoken in the near future, unless revitalization efforts prove effective. When it comes to the number of independent language families (including language isolates) in the Americas, hypotheses range from only one to nearly 200. The methods for classifying the languages have themselves been the subject both of much misunderstanding and at times of heated disputes.

The typological structure of the Indigenous languages of the Americas has played a role in the history of their classification; however, opinion has varied from assumptions that there is only one structural type shared by all American Indian languages that unites them typologically and genetically (see Campbell 1997a, 39–40, 93), to opinions that there is greater typological diversity in the Americas than in the rest of the world combined (see Ibarra Grasso 1958, 12; McQuown 1955, 501). Edward Sapir and Morris Swadesh (1946, 110) felt that "it is safe to say that any grammatical category to be found elsewhere in the world is sure to have a near analog somewhere in the native languages of the new world." This is overstated, but not by much.

Opinions about the number of "migrations" that brought languages to the New World and the dates when they took place vary widely (see below).

The goals of this book, then, are (1) to survey what is known about the history and classification of the Indigenous languages of the Americas, (2) to put into perspective some of the gaps in knowledge and to assess differences of opinion, and (3) hopefully to resolve some issues and to make some new contributions.

In the remainder in this chapter, matters involving the names of the languages are clarified, terminology is explained, and views concerning the origin of the Indigenous languages of the Americas are examined. As background to the history and classification of the languages, a brief overview of the history of their classification is given. Also conventions utilized in this book are explained and the methods employed are clarified.

1.2. NAMES AND NAMING

There is often sensitivity and sometimes confusion concerning the names used to talk about languages and ethnic groups. For example, some people avoid the word "Indian" and instead prefer "Native American" or "First Nations" or "First Peoples," or just "Indigenous People." However, at the same time, there are members of these groups who prefer to be called "Indians" or "American Indians"; some are offended by alternatives that have been proposed. In this book "Indian" is mostly avoided but is written occasionally in contexts where the people involved prefer "Indian" or where "Indian" is used in the sources cited. "Indian" is found in the official names of many Native American tribes and of their reservations, and it is used by the US Bureau of Indian Affairs and other government agencies. These things make it difficult to avoid "Indian" entirely.

One difficulty with the terms "American Indian" and "American Indian language" is that traditionally in linguistic and anthropological literature they were used unhesitatingly to refer to all Indigenous peoples or languages of the Americas, but today it is not uncommon for "American Indian" to be thought of as applying only to languages and ethnolinguistic groups in North America and not necessarily to the indigenous languages and their speakers in Latin America. Also, many of the Indigenous peoples of Alaska do not consider themselves or their languages to be "American Indian." They are officially Alaska Natives, speakers of Alaska Native languages. Because of this, it might seem convenient to use "Native" as a cover term for all Indigenous peoples and languages in the Americas (as in "Native American"), but unfortunately for some the word "native" is offensive. Another difficulty is that some non-indigenous persons born in North American also at times say they are "native" Americans because of being born here, leaving "Native American" either unclear or weakened and ambiguous as a designation for the Indigenous peoples of North America or of the Americas as a whole.

Other options could be *First Peoples* or *First Nations* or *Aboriginal*, but those terms mostly lack traction outside of Canada. *Amerind* (also *Amerindian*) was controversial and rejected by several Native American groups already when it was first coined at the beginning of the 1900s. It is used today more often in writings from scholars outside of linguistics and from a few non–North American linguists. Many linguists avoid the term (some passionately) in order to escape confusion with or even contamination from Joseph H. Greenberg's (1987) highly criticized and now essentially rejected "Amerind" language classification (see Chapter 6).

In this book, *Indigenous* is frequently used in reference to the peoples and languages of the Americas. It is probably the least objectionable of terms, and yet even it is not without difficulties. To be completely accurate, it would have to specify in some way that it is intended not to include Hawaiian (or Samoan, in American Samoa), but an appellation of *Indigenous Languages of Continental America* or some such thing would be by far too cumbersome and also inaccurate to the extent that it would also exclude erroneously the various American Indian languages spoken on islands closer to the shores of the Americas and in the Caribbean and would not include the speakers of the Eskimoan languages of Siberia and Greenland. Also, *Indigenous* is seen as odd (or pedantic) and is not in use by most ethnolinguistic groups of North America to refer to themselves, and because of this, some find it an objectionable term, though usually not particularly offensive, at least not yet.

In this context a couple of other matters should be mentioned. One is about spellings with or without capitalization of *Indigenous/indigenous* (and *Aboriginal/aboriginal*). Until recently *indigenous* generally occurred without capitalization, but it has been vigorously argued that in reference to peoples, cultures, or languages, it should be capitalized out of respect and to be consistent with capitalization of, for example, *Indian*, *Native American*, and other names. Another matter involves the terms "tribe" and "nation" in reference to Indigenous American groups. Though *tribe* is official in many US government documents and *nation* is frequently used in reference to various peoples, many of the Indigenous groups in the Americas have never considered themselves tribes or nations, not even in North America, and indeed some people feel uncomfortable or offended to be referred to by the term "tribe."[1]

Given that no term is satisfactory to everyone in all contexts, it is important to make it clear that no term used in this book is meant to be disrespectful of anyone, especially not of the people or language referred to. Here most often I just use *Indigenous* (capitalized) when talking about people or languages, alternating sometimes also with *American*

Indian and *Native American*. Given that there is no unobjectionable term that covers all the Indigenous languages of the Americas, sometimes I also use *American Indian* to refer to all of the languages of the Americas together, as in many academic writings, although as mentioned it is not ideal for inclusion of Alaska Native languages and languages of Latin America. The intention is to avoid terms that might be considered objectionable, disrespectful, or offensive.

There is also frequent sensitivity and confusion involving the names of particular languages. Unfortunately there are difficulties of several sorts concerning language names. In recent times, members of a good number of language communities have advocated strongly for adoption of their own names, their self-designations, the community-preferred names, the name of the language in the language itself—called autonyms. The conventional names for languages and the names preferred by members of the language communities often do not match. In a number of cases, these community-recommended autonyms have become generally accepted and are now in common use, for example, O'odham for Papago (and Pima), Diné for Navajo, Kwak'wala for Kwakiutl, Nuu-chah-nulth for Nootka, Ohlone for Costanoan, Purépecha for Tarascan, Tlahuica for Ocuilteco, and Mapudungun for older Araucanian, among many others. In some cases, other names are advocated but are not yet generally known. Examples of both sorts are seen throughout this book.

The desire to promote the interests and rights of the Indigenous groups involved and to respect their wishes and sensitivities calls for the use of the community-preferred names. On the other hand, the traditional names are so entrenched in the literature that it would be impossible to avoid mentioning them if current reference is to be related to past discussions of these languages. I use indigenous groups' own language names whenever I am aware of them, though the alternative, conventional names by which languages have been widely known are also included, usually given in parentheses, so that readers can recognize them or search for them if they are not familiar with newer names.

In many cases, American Indian groups have no particular distinct name of their own for their language other than an equivalent of "our language," "the language," or "the true speech." For example speakers of Kaqchikel (a Mayan language of Guatemala) call their language *qach'ab'al*, literally 'our language', *qa-* 'our' + *ch'ab'al* 'language, speaking'. The names by which Indigenous languages have come to be known conventionally were typically given to them by outsiders; several of these exonyms, as they are called, have pejorative origins or are today considered offensive, and they should no longer be used.[2]

Another source of some misunderstanding is the mismatch between the name for a language and the name for the ethnic group that speaks the language. For example, Wichí is a Matacoan language of Argentina and Bolivia. Its previous name (an exonym) was *Mataco*, but some people were uncomfortable with that name because it sounded to them like Spanish *matar* 'to kill', and in the region it had taken on pejorative connotations in local Spanish. As a result, the name was changed to *Wichí*. It is based on the Wichí word /wikʔi/, which is the name used to refer to an ethnic group—and not the name of the language itself. The Wichís' own name (their autonym) for their language is *Lhamtes*, literally 'the language', or *Wikʔi lhamtes* 'the language of the Wichí' (Terraza 2008, 8). *Wichí* is meant to be an autonym for the people; when used as a name for the language it feels like another exonym, though now widely accepted almost as an autonym.

The names preferred by some speakers sometimes are not generally accepted or recognized by other members of the community, but rather are favored (even invented) for particular non-linguistic purposes. For example, some recognized that *Kaqchikel* (Cakchiquel), mentioned above, was not a recognized autonym for the language, and they suggested instead *Kaqchikel ch'ab'al*, replacing the ethnonym *Kaqchikel* and leaning toward the true autonym *qach'ab'al* 'our language'.[3] Sometimes there is also disagreement about which spelling of a name should be used, or which script or orthography should be employed—the spelling of *Kaqchikel* vs. *Cakchiquel* is a good example of this.

It has not been that uncommon for members of a language community to adopt an ethnonym given to them by outsiders when dealing with outsiders in their area. For example, in Central America, several language communities have come to be known in Spanish by whatever names non-indigenous people tell the Indigenous people that their language is called. For instance, speakers of Teco (Tektiteko, a Mayan language) were told by schoolteachers and missionaries that they spoke Kaqchikel. That is, these outsiders recognized that the Teco people did not speak Mam, a large, related Mayan language found in the region, and so they just assumed erroneously that it must be Kaqchikel, although true Kaqchikel is a large language from a different Mayan subgroup and from an entirely different region. Locals commonly called Cacaopera (of the Misumalpan family) in El Salvador *Lenca*, though Lenca is an unrelated language that was spoken nearby. This came from schoolteachers assigned to work in the town of Cacaopera who had read about the nearby Lenca and just assumed that what was spoken in Cacaopera was also Lenca.

Mistaken linguistic identifications of these sorts have at times led to errors in language classification. For example, some early language classifications in western North America were based on older Spanish documents or on early explorer and military reports that asserted erroneously, for instance, that Seri (a language isolate) and Yaqui (Uto-Aztecan) were identical, that the Yuma (a.k.a. Quechan, a Yuman language) spoke "Pima" (a Uto-Aztecan language), and that Comanche (also Uto-Aztecan) and Kiowa (Kiowa-Tanoan) were the same language (Gursky 1966a, 404). One striking case is the long-surviving and often repeated erroneous classification of Uru-Chipaya as related to "Puquina." Puquina, a language isolate, is a once culturally important but now long dormant language in the Andes (see Chapter 4 for details). This error stemmed from the fact Uru and Chipaya each have often been called "Puquina" in the Andes region, and the Uru even claimed that their language was Puquina (Zariquiey 2020, 254). Although the differences between Puquina versus Uru and Chipaya were clearly shown and the error pointed out and corrected long ago and repeatedly (for example by Chamberlain 1910; Mason 1950, 224–225; Ibarra Grasso 1958, 10; 1964, 37–33; Olson 1964, 314; Adelaar 1989; Adelaar and Muysken 2004, 43, 175, 252; cf. Campbell 1997a, 189, 210), this error persisted and was repeated many times in classifications of South American languages, for example, by Créqui-Montfort and Rivet (1925–1927), Greenberg (1987, 84, 384), Noble (1965), Tovar (1961, 47–49), and so on (see Chapter 4).

The naming of many indigenous languages in the Americas is complicated on the one hand by the many instances where a single language has been known by a variety of names and on the other hand by the many cases where a single name has been used to refer to multiple languages. For example, Atsina (Algonquian) is commonly called *Gros Ventre*, but then Hidatsa (Siouan) has also been called *Gros Ventre*; at the same time both of these languages have been known by multiple names, the former as *Gros Ventre* and *Atsina*, and the latter as *Hidatsa, Gros Ventre, Minitari*, and *Duan*. The confusion regarding the name *Gros Ventre* apparently stems from the fact that the signs for the two tribes in Plains Indian Sign Language are similar. The name *Montagnais* has been applied both to Chipewyan (Athabaskan) and to multiple Algonquian languages. Linguists now attempt to restrict the reference of *Montagnais* to Innu (Montagnais, Montagnais-Naskapi) and Cree-Montagnais (see Chapter 2).

That multiple names can be associated with a single language presents a serious challenge. In this book languages are identified by a primary name followed by alternative names given in parentheses. A few other examples from North America of languages with multiple names are: Kiowa Apache (also called Oklahoma Apache, Plains Apache), Kwak'wala (Kwakiutl, Kwakwaka'wakw), Lakota (Sioux), Mikasuki (Hitchiti, Mikasuki Seminole, Miccosukee), Meskwaki-Sauk (Fox, Mesquakie, Meskwakie), and Unami (Lenape, Lenni-Lenape, Oklahoma Delaware) (for others see Chapter 2).

In Mexico and Central America *Nahuatl* (a Uto-Aztecan language) has also been known as Aztec, Mejicano (Mexicano), and Nahua. There are a number of languages that have been called *Chontal*, for example, Chontal of Tabasco (Mayan) and Chontal of Oaxaca (Tequistlateco in the Tequistlatecan family), and several called *Popoloca, Popoluca*, or *Pupuluca*, such as *Popoloca* (Otomanguean), *Sierra Popoluca, Sayula Popoluca, Oluta Popoluca* (all Mixe-Zoquean), *Pupuluca of Conguaco* (affinity unknown), and others. These names stem respectively from the Nahuatl terms *čontal-* 'foreigner' and *popoloka* 'to babble, speak unintelligibly, speak language badly' (see Brinton 1892a).

Most South American languages have or have had more than one name. For example, Iaté (Fulniô) (language isolate of Brazil) is also called Fornio, Carnijó, and Yathe (Yaathé). Nivaclé (Matacoan family, Argentina and Paraguay) is also called Chulupí and Ashluslay (each with many variant spellings) and has variously been called also Etehua, Choropí (Tšoropí), Chunupí, Güentusé (Wentusix), Mathlela, Sogciagay (Sotygraik, Sotegraik, Sotegai, Sotsiagay, Chotiagagais, Sotiagay), Sówa, Suhín (Sujín, Súxen, Suhin-Chunupi), and "Tapiete" (erroneously so) (Campbell et al. 2020, 1–3). On the other hand, the name Chunupí has been used to refer also to Vilela (of the unrelated Lule-Vilela family, Argentina), not without confusion.[4] For many other examples, see Chapter 4.

J. Alden Mason's (1950, 163) perspectives on the nomenclature of South American languages remain insightful:

> The situation is further complicated by the fact that, in a large number of instances, the same or a very similar name was applied by colonists to several groups of very different linguistic affinities. This may be a descriptive name of European derivation, such as *Orejón*, [Spanish] "Big Ears"; *Patagón*, [Spanish] "Big Feet"; *Coroado*, [Portuguese] "Crowned" or "Tonsured"; *Barbados*, [Portuguese] "Bearded"; *Lengua*, [Spanish] "Tongue, [Language]". Or it may be an Indian word applied to several different groups in the same way that . . . the rustic natives of Puerto Rico and Cuba "*Gíbaros*" [cf. Jívaro] and "*Goajiros*" [cf. Guajiro], respectively. Thus, "*Tapuya*", the Tupí word for "enemy," was applied by them to almost all non-Tupí groups, "*Botocudo*" to wearers of large lip-plugs, etc. Among other names applied to groups of different languages,

sometimes with slight variations, are *Apiacá, Arará, Caripuna, Chavanté, Guaná, Guayaná, Canamarí, Carayá, Catawishi, Catukina, Cuniba, Jívaro, Macú, Tapieté*, not to mention such easily confused names as *Tucano, Tacana* and *Ticuna*. Many mistakes have been made due to confusion of such names.

Other names of this sort applied to various languages include: *Auca* (see Sabela, Mapudungun, etc.), from Quechua *awqa* 'enemy, savage'; *Bugre*; *Cabiji* (*Cabixi*); *Tapiete*, from a Guaraní word meaning 'enemy, rebel'; *Motilón*, from Spanish meaning 'hairless' (shaven hair), given to, for example Yukpa (Cariban) and Barí (Chibchan); and *Baniwa* (*Baníva*), from a Tupí-Guaraníian term for 'bitter manioc', seen in Baniwa of Içana (Kurripako) (Arawakan), Baniwa of Guainia (Baniva, Avani, Abane) (Arawakan), Baniwa (Baniva, Karutana-Baniwa) (Arawakan), Baniva (Baniwa-Yavitero) (Arawakan), and Banawá (Baniva, Baniwa) (Arawan).

Several language families have also been known by multiple names and many of them with multiple spellings too. For example, Miwok-Costanoan and Utian refer to the same language family. Matacoan is also sometimes called Mataguayan or Mataco-Mataguayan; Enlhet-Enenlhet is (or was) also known as Mascoyan (Maskoyan); Nadahup for a long time was of uncertain classification, but languages of the family had been known under the language family labels of Makúan (Macuan),[5] Puinavean, and Vaupés-Japura (Uapés-Japura). Arawakan has also been called Maipurean (Maipuran). (See discussion of these language family names in the Chapters 2, 3, and 4 for details concerning these names.)

Also not to be confused are the similar but nevertheless different names such as *Chon* (Chonan family) with *Chono* (an unrelated language isolate), or *Aushiri* (*Awshiri*, a.k.a. Tequiraca, a language isolate) with *Auishiri* (*Awishiri*, a.k.a. Waorani or Sabela, another language isolate). (See Chapter 4 for other examples and for details.)

While these language names can be confusing, knowing a language's geographical location and the family to which it belongs helps to reduce misunderstandings.

Another recurrent difficulty with names is lack of sufficient information in a number of instances to determine whether what a name refers to is merely a dialect of a single language or whether separate but closely related languages are involved. This is often a difficult question. Terrence Kaufman (1990a, 1994, 2007) spoke of "language areas" and "emergent languages," which he defined as:

> Two or more sets of communities each have a well-defined set of local linguistic traits; there are clear boundaries between one set of communities and another, yet there is a high degree of mutual intelligibility (to the untutored) across these well-defined boundaries. There is a percentage of cognates on Swadesh's 100-word list ranging between 76 and 84, which correlates with an internal time depth of between 600 and 900 years. These sets of communities constitute a language area; its constituent members are emergent languages. (Kaufman 2007, 45)

Kaufman spoke of "emergent languages" as being "made up of entities that are, in my judgment, almost but not quite distinct languages" (Kaufman 2007, 63). Since the term "language area" is easily confused with "linguistic area" (see Chapter 7), I speak mostly of "emergent languages" instead and where relevant of "dialect continua" or "dialect clusters."

The identification of names is further complicated by the fact that many individual languages are known by the name of the river where they are located or by other salient geographical features, such as names of mountains or islands where they are found. Often the Indigenous group and its language are named after the name of the river or some other geographical name. Sometimes, however, the geographical name has been assigned based on the name of the people who live there. A few examples from North America include: *Copper Island Aleut* (Mednyj Aleut); *Eel River* (Athabaskan); *Columbian* (Salishan), named for the Columbia River; *Galice-Applegate* (along Galice Creek and Applegate River); *Ineseño* (Chumash), on the Santa Ynez River; *Laurentian* (Iroquoian), along the St. Lawrence River in Quebec; *Lillooet* (St'at'imcets) (Salishan), Lillooet River; *Lower Chehalis* and *Upper Chehalis* (Salishan), Chehalis River; *Mattole* (Athabaskan), Mattole River; *Nottoway* (Iroquoian), along the Nottoway River; *Susquehannock* (Iroquoian), along the Susquehanna River; *Thompson* (Nłeʔkepmxcin) (Salishan), Thompson River; *Upper Umpqua* (Athabaskan), in the upper drainage of the Umpqua River (*Lower Umpqua* is a dialect of unrelated Siuslaw). (Other examples are seen in Chapters 2 and 4.)

This is especially true also of many language names in South America. I mention here just a few examples from the immense number of cases. Several different languages bear names similar to the Canamarí River: *Kanamaré* [Canamaré] (Arawakan), *Kanamarí* [Kanamaré] (Katukinan), and *Canamari* [Taverí, Matoinahã] (Panoan); *Cofán* (A'ingae, language isolate) for the Cofanes River (Colombia and Ecuador); and *Yurumanguí* (Yurimanguí) (language isolate) for the Yurimanguí River (Colombia). Phillip Harms (1994, 2) pointed out that "the languages and dialects of the Chocó[an] family are often referred to by linguists using the names of the rivers along which they are spoken." (For numerous other examples in South America, see Chapter 4.)

Because the profusion of overlapping names can be confusing, this means that one must take extra care to make certain to which language a name refers in any given instance.

Another matter that bears mentioning is the spellings of the language names. It is not uncommon, particularly in Latin America, for language names to appear in more than one, and sometimes several, alternate spellings. In South America many language names are known in versions that reflect both Spanish and Portuguese orthographic conventions, and some in spellings influenced by English, in variant spellings such as *Shoco/Xoko*, *Capanahua/Kapanawa*, and *Gê/Jê/Yê/Je*. Terrence Kaufman (1990a, 1994, 2007, and elsewhere), in attempting to eliminate such variation and the confusion that comes with it, followed a spelling convention that roughly transliterates Spanish and Portuguese orthographic representations of names to English-like spellings. However, Kaufman's spellings have not been generally adopted, and most linguists and others prefer the more conventional spellings, believing that Kaufman's spellings add a further level of confusion. For the names of Mayan languages spoken in Guatemala, native Mayan linguists have chosen renditions that reflect Kaufman's orthography for Mayan languages (for example, *K'iche'* rather than *Quiché*, *Kaqchikel* instead of *Cakchiquel*, and so on). These spellings, which came to be preferred by native Mayan groups, have been given official status by the Guatemalan government, and are now in general use for languages of Guatemala, although the conventional spellings are retained for the names of Mayan languages spoken in Mexico, such as, for example, *Huastec*, not *Wasteko*.

1.3. TERMINOLOGY

In addition to language names, the terms linguists use to designate levels of relatedness within their classifications can be confusing; the terms are not always used consistently and there is often controversy concerning the validity of the units that some labels are intended to identify. It is important here at the outset to clarify this terminology and to specify how such terms are used in this book. We need clear terminology for a range of entities, each more inclusive than the level below it—something akin to, but clearer than, Rasmus Rask's *dialect-language-branch-stock-class-race* hierarchy (Benediktsson 1980, 22) and more utilitarian than Sydney Lamb's (1959, 41) too finely segmented *phylum-class-order-stock-family-genus-language-dialect* ranking. I employ the following terms.

Dialect means only a variety (regional or social) of a language, mutually intelligible (however difficult this concept may be to define or apply in practice) with other dialects/varieties of the same language. Dialect does not mean here, as it does in the usage of some historical linguists, especially in the past, a daughter language in a language family. **Language** means any distinct linguistic entity that is mutually unintelligible with other languages. A **language family** is a group of genealogically related languages, a group of languages that share a linguistic kinship by virtue of having developed from a common earlier ancestor. In this book, language families are normally designated with the suffix *-an* (as in Algonqui**an**, Uto-Aztec**an**, etc.). The term "language family" here includes also **language isolates**, language families that have only a single member, that is, languages that have no known relatives.

However, language families can be of different magnitudes—that is, they can have different time depths, with some larger-scale families including smaller-scale families (i.e., subfamilies) as their members or branches. Unfortunately, a number of confusing terms have at times been used to attempt to distinguish more inclusive from less inclusive family groupings. The term **subgroup** (or **subfamily**, **branch**) means a group of languages within a well-defined language family that are more closely related to one other than they are to other languages of that family—that is, they constitute a branch of that family. As a proto language (for example, Proto-Indo-European) diversifies, it develops daughter languages (for example, Germanic, Celtic); if a daughter (for example, Proto-Germanic) then subsequently splits up and develops daughter languages of its own (such as English, German), then the descendants (English, German) of that daughter language (Proto-Germanic) constitute members of a subgroup (Germanic languages), and the original daughter language (Proto-Germanic) becomes, in effect, an intermediate proto language, that is, a descendant of the original proto language (Proto-Indo-European), but with daughters of its own (for example, English, German).

Terms that have been used for postulated but unproven higher-order, more inclusive families (proposed distant genetic relationships) include *stock*, *phylum*, and *macro-family* and the compounding element *macro-* (as in Macro-Siouan, Macro-Mayan, etc.). These terms have proven confusing and controversial, as might be expected when proposed names for entities that are not fully agreed to exist are at stake. *Stock* is ambiguous in that in older usage it was equivalent to "language family" (a direct transfer of the common German linguistic term *Stamm* or *Sprachstamm*); however, the term *stock* has often been used in America in the sense of a postulated but unconfirmed larger long-range grouping that would include more than one language family. If such a postulated larger grouping were confirmed, it would simply become a language family, and the families that are its constituents would become *subgroups* of the more inclusive family. The term *family* is both sufficient and non-controversial. The entities called "stock," "phylum," and "macro-" would be bona fide language families if they were established as really related genetically and will not be families if the proposals concerning them fail to hold up. Therefore, I speak of them simply in terms of "proposed distant genetic relationship," "postulated family," "hypothesized remote affinity," and the like.

Another terminological clarification is also needed. Most linguists and many Indigenous people today who work with endangered languages and languages that no longer have any native speakers avoid the word *extinct* when talking about languages, especially ones that have lost their last fluent native speaker in recent years. Instead they say "dormant" or "sleeping." Use of "extinct" and "extinction" in this context is also avoided in this book. Sadly, "extinct language" is often misinterpreted, thought to mean that the people whose heritage language it is are also "extinct," though in most cases the people survive, having shifted to another language. Many of these groups today are trying to revive their languages based on whatever documentary materials may be available, and unfortunately the word "extinct" has a dampening impact on learning their heritage language. Calling it "dormant" or "sleeping" is less negative, suggesting that the work to learn it can help bring it back, hence the many "awakening language" projects now underway to recover these "dormant" languages, no longer called "extinct." The dormant languages, those that have no known native speakers, are marked in the classifications in this book by an asterisk (*) before the name of the language.

With languages becoming dormant at an ever faster and alarming rate and with so many in threat of imminent loss, it is easy to comprehend the sense of urgency linguists feel for language documentation. That is generally recognized as the most compelling and urgent task for linguists right now and into the future. It is difficult to overstate the seriousness and severity of the language endangerment crisis. (See Rehg and Campbell 2018; Campbell and Belew 2018; and *The Catalogue of Endangered Languages* [www.endangeredlanguages.com].)

1.4. LOSS OF DIVERSITY AND THE STATUS OF INDIGENOUS LANGUAGES OF THE AMERICAS

The account of the languages treated in this book starts at the time of first European contact, at roughly 1500 CE, because we have almost no significant written history concerning most of the languages before then.[6] Since that time, a massive number of languages have disappeared without a trace, and many for which we do have some historical information have ceased to be spoken, some long ago. Many of them are among the over 500 unclassified or spurious languages, of which over 400 are in South America, discussed in Chapter 5. That is, the number of indigenous languages spoken in the Americas has changed constantly from the beginning of recorded history and continues changing now, with the rate of language loss highly accelerated in recent years (see Campbell and Belew 2018, and the *Catalogue of Endangered Languages* [www.endangeredlanguages.com]).

All indigenous languages of the Americas are endangered, many severely so (see the *Catalogue of Endangered Languages*). Many are currently critically endangered and will certainly cease to be spoken in the near future. Some 70 still-spoken Indigenous languages in the Americas have 10 or fewer speakers. Of them, 26 are in North America, 4 in Middle America, and 40 in South America. Several others will soon find themselves with fewer than 10 speakers. There are 162 Indigenous languages in the Americas that have fewer than 100 speakers. Nearly all of them will become dormant in the next few years unless revitalization efforts for some of them succeed. The situation is indeed dire.

When Europeans arrived in North America, they encountered some 314 languages spoken in what is now the United States and Canada, belonging to 54 independent language families. Of these, 150 languages are dormant, with no known native speakers (48%). Of 280 languages at that time in territory now in the United States, only 111 are still spoken (60% no longer have any known native speakers).

Mexico and Central America together are the home of circa 221 Indigenous languages, with circa 200 still spoken.[7] They fall into 15 language families, 4 of which are language isolates. South America is home to 100 language families (including isolates)—there are 47 language families and 53 language isolates. These numbers, however, are misleading, since there are hundreds of unclassified languages in the Americas, most long dormant with little or no attestation (see Chapter 5, Campbell 2012a, 115–130). With circa 397 language families (including language isolates) known in the world, South America's 100 language families constitute a quarter of the world's linguistic diversity (25%), calculated in terms of language families.

Of the 54 language families (including isolates) in North America, 28 are now dormant (59%)—there is no known native speaker of any language belonging to any of these 28 language families. Of the 24 language isolates, 18 are dormant; only 6 survive (3 of them are severely endangered); and all the languages of 13 of the 16 minor families are dormant. In addition, several major branches of larger families have lost all their native speakers: Eyak in Na-Dene, Southern New England Algonquian within Algonquian (Algic), Tsamosan within Salishan, Costanoan within Utian, and Catawban within Siouan-Catawban. Four of the 15 language families in Mexico and Central America are dormant; 24 languages with documentation are dormant and there was a large, indeterminate number of other dormant languages that are barely known at all (listed in Chapter 5). In South America there are about 210 dormant languages about which we actually know something and c.380 names of unclassified and mostly dormant languages, nearly 600 dormant languages in total, nearly twice as many no longer spoken tongues as the circa 330 languages still spoken today. (See Chapters 4 and 5 for details.)[8]

The loss of diversity will almost certainly accelerate in the near future, since several of the surviving languages have extremely few speakers, all of them elderly. The loss of any of these languages that are undocumented or only poorly attested will be tragic for historical linguistics, since without information on them we cannot classify them nor understand their histories, ever, and the peoples involved can do nothing to recover their languages.

For numbers of speakers, details of location, and information on vitality status of the still spoken and recently dormant languages, consult the *Catalogue of Endangered Languages* (www.endangeredlanguages.com).

1.5. HISTORICAL OVERVIEW OF ATTEMPTS TO CLASSIFY THE LANGUAGES OF THE AMERICAS

The first comprehensive classification of North American languages was that of John Wesley Powell (1891), in which 58 families were distinguished. (For the history of classification of American Indian language before Powell and more detail of the post-Powell classifications, see Goddard 1996b and Campbell 1997, 26–89; 2021.) An objective was to reduce the vast linguistic diversity of the Americas to manageable genealogical schemes, to bring order to the "bewilderingly large number of languages" (Langdon 1974, 4). A frenzy to reduce further the number of language families in North America began soon after Powell's classification was published. Dixon and Kroeber (1913a, 1913b) announced that they had reduced Powell's 22 California stocks to 12, based on a superficial scanning of vocabularies. Edward Sapir soon joined the "reductionist frenzy," followed by many others. The result was many proposals of distant genetic relationship, offered initially with a minimum of supporting evidence as hunches, as tentative preliminary hypotheses for further investigation. Sapir (1929a) presented his extremely influential six-group classification of the North American Indian languages in his famous *Encyclopaedia Britannica* article (see also Sapir 1921a). He described his rationale for offering the tentative proposals in a letter to Frank Speck (October 2, 1924) as "more intuitive and, even when the evidence is not as full or theoretically unambiguous as it might be, is prepared to throw out [offer] tentative suggestions and to test as it goes along" (quoted in Darnell 1969, 324). Later, Alfred Kroeber (1940b, 466) described this period and Sapir's "preliminariness" of proposals:

> From one point of view such a procedure is nothing less than forecasting. From another, it amounts to a defining of problems which are worthy of attack because they hold out some hope of yielding positive productive results. The procedure has therefore a certain justification and value, provided it is understood for what it really is ... It is in no sense whatever a definable or controllable method of science or scholarship.
>
> The danger of the procedure is that its prophecies may be mistaken, especially by non-linguists, for proved or probable findings. Tremendous havoc can be worked when archaeologists or ethnologists begin to build structures of inference on Sapir's brilliant but flimsy gossamer web of prophecies as if it were a solid foundation.

Sapir (1929a) had tentatively grouped the languages of North America into six "superstocks": Eskimo-Aleut, Na-Dene (including Haida), Algonkin-Wakashan, Hokan-Siouan, Penutian, and Aztec-Tanoan. He considered his classification as "suggestive but far from demonstrable in all its features" (Sapir 1929a, 137).[9]

Much subsequent research continued the "lumping" tradition as it has been called, seeking broader relationships among groups of American Indian languages. Voegelin and Voegelin's (1965) revised version of Sapir's scheme brought these proposals together.

Later, scholars came increasingly to recognize that many of these hypotheses of remote kinship among these language groups could not be validated on the basis of the evidence available, and the pendulum began to swing back toward recognition of a larger number of distinct families based on more reliable data and methods (begun by the papers in Campbell and Mithun 1979).

In spite of trends now away from the reductionism ("lumping") of earlier times, new proposals of remote relationship continued to appear, some also in relatively recent times (see Chapter 6). In some cases, initial hypotheses of distant kinship among languages have been strengthened, as, for example, in the evidence presented by Mary Haas (1958a), Karl Teeter (1964a), Ives Goddard (1975), and Howard Berman (1990b), which helped to confirm the Algic hypothesis (the relationship among Algonquian, Yurok, and Wiyot), and the convincing evidence for the Plateau (Plateau Penutian) hypothesis (with Klamath-Modoc, Sahaptian, and Molala) (see Berman 1996; DeLancey 2018; DeLancey and Golla 1997; Golla 2011, 128–129; see Chapter 2).

Most of the proposals for more inclusive groupings are summarized and evaluated in Campbell (1997a, 66–80), Campbell and Poser (2008), Goddard (1996a, 308–323), and Mithun (1999, 301–310). Few of the newer proposals have withstood scrutiny well. The more visible proposals of remote linguistic kinship involving Indigenous languages in the Americas since those evaluations are assessed in Chapter 6.

1.6. ORIGINS OF THE AMERICAN INDIAN LANGUAGES

As mentioned above, the Americas were the last major land mass to be reached by humans. When and how the founding population or populations arrived, and who they were, are debated. Whatever the date of earliest arrival, there is extensive linguistic diversity among the Indigenous languages of the Americas, in terms of both the numbers of language families and the typology (structural properties) of these languages. A frequent question is what this linguistic picture can contribute to understanding of the earliest peopling of the Americas, to answering the following sorts of questions: Who were the first people to come into the Americas? Were the first "immigrants" part of a single or a continuous movement, or did people arrive in multiple waves? Were there incentives to come—were people "pulled" or were they "pushed" to leave the Old World? Where did they come from, and how did they arrive? Did different groups influence one another, displace one another, or repel or attract one another as they entered the new environment, or was arrival in the Western Hemisphere just an accident? When did human populations arrive in the Americas, and how did they disperse throughout the two "virgin," previously humanless American continents? The answers to such questions that have been offered based on linguistic evidence, as we shall see, have been both controversial and largely disappointing.

The classification of the Indigenous languages of the Americas has played a role in the research on the origin and dispersal of the earliest peoples in the New World right from the beginning of interest in these questions. However, the linguistic picture is compatible with most hypotheses about the founding population(s) in the Americas (more on this below). Therefore extra care must be exercised regarding any claims about the earliest people in the Americas based on American Indian languages.

Comparison of the linguistic situation with information from human genetics and archaeology reveals the potential matches and mismatches from these different sources of information relevant for interpreting the earliest Americans and their languages. A massive amount of work in genetics and archaeology on the origins of the Indigenous peoples of the Americas has been published in the last few years. Unfortunately, there is very little that is not disputed or controversial. The difficulties of reconciling findings and interpretations across scientific disciplines are well known. Concerning the origins and dispersal of the peoples of the Americas, there are also striking differences of opinion among scholars of the same field, at times even among researchers who share the same principles and ostensibly utilize the same methods. Thus we have different views among archaeologists, among geneticists, and among linguists. As Jenifer Raff (2022, 27) tells us, "at present, it's difficult to find two archaeologists who agree on exactly how the Americas were peopled; they differ on which kinds of evidence they find most convincing in accepting or rejecting the validity of ancient sites, how different sites relate to one another, and how archaeological evidence should be integrated with genetic data." Also, the diversity of the archaeological record in some important regions leads to multiple competing interpretations. The number and kinds of differences of interpretation in human genetics can leave the heads of non-experts spinning. Human population genetics is an extremely fast-moving and volatile field. "New results . . . are piling up at a rate so fast it's hard even for experts to keep up with each new discovery" (Raff 2022, preface), and the insights coming from the research labs are changing understanding so quickly that information becomes out of date at a shockingly accelerated rate (see Raff 2020, 276). All of this makes integrating possible contributions from linguistics to answering the questions about origins of the first people(s) to enter the Americas exceedingly difficult.

For much of the twentieth century the dominant view had it that the earliest people in the Americas came from Siberia to Alaska some 12,000 years ago, across the Bering Land Bridge (subsequently flooded) at the end of the last ice age. These people moved through an ice-free corridor between the Laurentide and Cordilleran ice sheets that began to recede at the end of the last ice age, whence they eventually came to occupy all regions of the Americas. They were associated with Clovis culture with its distinctive stone tools.[10] Some scholars believed in another entrance associated with Na-Dene, and many believed also in another later entry, associated with Eskimo-Aleuts (sometimes called the three-wave model). Most now abandon that circa 12,000 BP date, opting for pre-Clovis entry of some few thousands of years earlier, with many favoring a Pacific costal migration rather than just movement through an ice-free inland corridor. Several archaeological sites south of the continental ice sheets dated to pre-Clovis times, showing up by around 15,500 years ago, are now widely accepted (Willerslev and Meltzer 2021, 357; see below).

By the late 1990s, almost all geneticists had rejected the Clovis-First hypothesis (Raff 2022, 71). Starting in the late 1980s most geneticists were attempting to integrate their evidence into the three-wave migration hypothesis. It "became the standard model that all genetics studies of peoples in the Americas tested with new evidence for decades. Between 1987 and 2004, 80 out of the 100 papers published on genetic variation in Native American populations were influenced by (or mentioned) this model" (Raff 2022, 76; see also Bolnick et al. 2004). Around 1990 human genetics imported tools from molecular biology that radically changed the field (Raff 2022, 42), and the results of investigations of mitochondrial and Y chromosome DNA did not agree with the three-wave model that relied substantially on Joseph Greenberg's (1987) three linguistic groupings in the Americas, Amerind, Na-Dene, and Eskimo-Aleut (see Chapter 6). However, "the mitochondrial and Y chromosome sequences gave only a limited glimpse of history; it took the genomic revolution to start filling in the missing pieces, and we are still only partway there" (Raff 2022, 52)—"the [three-wave] hypothesis has been utterly falsified by genomics data" (Raff 2022, 76).

The story begins in East Asia and Siberia at an earlier date, where genomes from Indigenous peoples of the Americas and their ancestors show "formation of the gene pool that gave rise to Native Americans between about 43,000 and 25,000 years ago . . . the group or groups that were directly ancestral to Native Americans" (Raff 2022, 176). Raff (2022, 177) asserts that "two populations . . . served as their antecedents: the ancestral East Asians and the Ancient Northern Siberians." Then, "around 36,000 years ago, a small group of people living in East Asia began to break off from the larger ancestral East Asian population" (Raff 2022, 181), and "by about 25,000 years ago, gene flow with the broader East Asian population stopped completely" (Raff 2022, 181). "Both mitochondrial and nuclear genomes of Native Americans show us that they had been isolated from all other populations for a prolonged period of time, during which they developed the genetic traits found only in Native American populations" (Raff 2022, 190).

In summary of this early period:

> Most scholars agree that the ancestors of the First Peoples came from Upper Paleolithic populations in Siberia and East Asia. The precise whereabouts of these ancestors during the LGM [Last Glacial Maximum]—whether in Beringia, eastern Eurasia, the Siberian Arctic Zone, or even in North America south of the Ice Wall—are currently a matter of ongoing research and debate. Ancient DNA shows us that during the LGM, these ancestors remained isolated from other groups in Eurasia and split into several groups, some of which gave rise to the First Peoples south of the Ice Wall. (Raff 2022, 274)

So, several geneticists see the ancestors of the Native Americas as separated and isolated from the Siberian (Asian) population for around 2,000 years in Beringia (the land mass at the Bering Strait when sea levels were low). This small, isolated population did not diversify significantly for some thousands of years, called the Beringian standstill (the Beringian incubation model, the Beringian Pause) (Tamm et al. 2020), until there was a population expansion at round 16,000 years ago, likely the time of first movements of people southwards into the Americas (see Llamas et al. 2016; Skoglund and Reich 2016; Ribeiro-dos-Santos et al. 2020, 1; de la Fuente et al. 2021, 33).

The Bering land bridge connected Siberia and North America from about 50,000 to 11,000 years ago, after which it was flooded. To call it a bridge may be misleading; the Beringia "land bridge" was twice the size of Texas (Raff 2022, 191,192). As Raff (2022, 192) puts it, "Beringia wasn't a crossing point, but a homeland, a place where people lived for many generations, sheltering from an inhospitable climate and slowly evolving the genetic variation unique to their Native American descendants."

It is hypothesized that the isolated population during the Beringian standstill survived in one or more relatively ice-free refugia. There were "some places in or near Beringia that could have served as . . . refugia for both humans and animals" (Raff 2022, 191).[11] "Between about 26,000 to 19,000 years ago, glacial ice would have prevented travel out of Beringia . . . people could only have migrated before 26,000 years ago or after 19,000 years ago" (Raff 2022, 93).[12] In Raff's (2022, 78) summary, the opinions about dates by which humans had reached the Americans were, by the most conservative estimate, 15,000–14,000 years ago, "and more likely between 17,000 and 16,000 and perhaps even as early as 30,000–20,000 years ago."

This lack of agreement about the dates is notable. She says that "all mitochondrial lineages commonly found in populations below the Arctic Circle share common ancestors between about 18,400 and 15,000 years ago. The close agreement suggests that they were all present in the initial founder population(s)" (Raff 2022, 44), though this does not reveal when they actually arrived in the Americas.

As mentioned, in the last ten to twenty years, much evidence both from archaeology and genetics has appeared that challenges the Clovis-first hypothesis. A significant number of pre-Clovis sites have been proposed.[13] According to Raff (2022, 127), "many archaeologists believe that people entered the Americas after the LGM [Last Glacial Maximum] as soon as a route was opened along the west coast of Alaska, perhaps as early as 17,000 to 16,000 years ago." They must have passed through Alaska; however, even with intense archaeological interest in the area, the results of archaeological research there led to "wildly different interpretations of how the Americas were initially peopled," and do not fit geneticists' interpretations well (Raff 2022, 100). The Cordilleran ice sheet melted back from the Pacific coast around 17,000 years ago (Raff 2022, 84), allowing for possible travel out of Beringia. This deglaciation on the Pacific Northwest coastal corridor, before the availability of the inland ice-free corridor, is linked with the coastal entry theory, sometimes called the "Kelp Highway hypothesis," now accepted by a good number of scholars.[14] For example, Clark et al. (2022) argue strongly from extensive geochronological data (cosmogenic nuclide exposure ages) that the opening of the ice-free corridor happened well after pre-Clovis people had entered the New World, that the ice-free corridor was not available for them to enter the Americas until after the Last Glacial Maximum, but that the data from the Pacific coast show that a coastal migration route was availability earlier.

Some genomic investigations have been interpreted as indicating that a single original population peopled the Americas, followed much later by small migrations into the Arctic and northern Canada (see O'Neill 2019; Willerslev and Meltzer 2021; de la Fuente et al. 2021, 40–41), though this is not the only view.

As for various more far-flung hypotheses about early Native American populations reflecting peoples arriving from Europe, Africa, or the Pacific, "all ancient individuals from whom we have DNA, are genetically most closely related to present-day Indigenous peoples of the Americas" (Raff 2022, 251), and "no skeletal remains that look even remotely like an early human have been found in the Americas" (Raff 2022, 92). (More on this below.)

In summation:

> There are currently several basic models for how, when, and where people first entered the Americas. The most conservative model resembles a new version of Clovis First: a migration of people . . . in Siberia across the Bering Land Bridge sometime between 16,000 and 14,000 years ago, and south of the Ice Wall—probably down an ice-free corridor—after the LGM [Last Glacial Maximum]. This model is based predominantly on an emphasis of the early Alaskan archaeological record, but does not account for pre-Clovis sites or match the genetic record well. (Raff 2022, 274)

> [Another] model] posits an entry into the Americas sometime after the first traces of people in Siberia . . . around 30,000 years ago . . . the majority of scholars agree that people were present in the Americas by at least 14,000 years ago. Some favor 18,000

to 15,000 years ago to account for the majority of the pre-Clovis sites and genetic evidence, and still others argue for a pre-LGM [Last Glacial Maximum] peopling based on archaeological evidence ... and genetic evidence ... First Peoples most likely traveled by boat along the west coast of North America, reaching South America fairly rapidly. (Raff 2022, 275)

To see how the Native American languages relate to these origin questions, it is important to have some basic information in mind about the linguistic diversity of the Americas, about what it is that we are able to work with when it comes to what linguistics can offer toward answering these questions concerning the first peoples in America.

In the view of the linguistic mainstream, there are about 170 independent language families (including language isolates) in the Americas: 54 in North America, 15 in Middle America (Mexico and Central America), and 100 in South America. Linguists believe that many, perhaps most, of these independent language families could be phylogenetically related to other language families, but that this cannot be demonstrated because of the amount of change that the languages have undergone in the great amount of time since the first settlement of the Americas.[15] This means that several scenarios are possible for the origins of the languages of the Americas based on this linguistic picture.

(1) A single entry across the Bering Strait into North America with speakers of a single language. This view is not favored by linguists. It would imply that all the indigenous languages of the Americas are phylogenetically related, all descended from that first immigrant language. Such a view, however, has been favored by some geneticists. For example, Raghavan et al. (2015), using ancient and modern genome-wide data, concluded that "the ancestors of all present-day Native Americans, including Athabascans and Amerindians, entered the Americas as a single migration wave from Siberia." (See also Fagundes et al. 2008; González-José et al. 2008; Tarazona-Santos and Santos 2008; Skoglund and Reich 2016; O'Neill 2019; de la Fuente et al. 2021, 40–41; Fehren-Schmitz 2020, 53; Willerslev and Meltzer 2021; Raff 2022, 251.)

(2) Two or three (or a few) linguistically distinct migrations entered the Americas. Many linguists believe this is plausible, perhaps even probable, but that the linguistic evidence is insufficient to demonstrate it. This view has been favored by a number of geneticists. As mentioned above, for some time many geneticists followed the three-wave model. Reich et al. (2012, 370) claimed to "show that Native Americans descend from at least three streams of Asian gene flow." (See also Ribeiro-dos-Santos et al. 2020, 1.) Willerslev and Meltzer (2021, 359) survey several sources that conclude that with the exception of the later arriving Palaeo-Inuit and Inuit Thule groups, "all ancient human genomes from the Americas have closer affinities to contemporary Native American peoples than to any other present-day populations worldwide." Rowe et al. (2022, 18) argue for "at least two founding populations for the Americas." In their view, "the first human arrival in North America, whether overland or via a coastal route, occurred well before 37,000 years ago." They see a "Native American clade" from circa 16,000 years ago, intersecting with much "earlier

human occupants of the Americas," representatives of Population Y (see below). Others report that "nearly all Native Americans belong to only a small number of identified mitochondrial and Y-chromosome founding haplotypes... Most of their mitochondrial diversity derives from only four major ancestral lineages... These lineages are widely found throughout the Americas, but there is a great deal of variation in their relative frequencies in different populations and geographic regions." "In Y-chromosome DNA, meanwhile, most male Native Americans belong to two principal founding haplogroups" (Fehren-Schmitz 2020, 52).

(3) Multilingual migrations: a single migration with more than one language, or a number of such multiple-language migrations. Though such a scenario is possible, it is not discussed much in the literature.

(4) There are also a number of less plausible notions, some mentioned above. They include claims of early immigration bringing languages with them to the Americas from Africa, Australia, China, India, Japan, or Polynesia, and claims of migrations to the Americas involving Egyptians, Phoenicians, Greeks, Romans, Welsh, Irish, Vikings, and the lost tribes of Israel, among others. There is no reliable linguistic evidence to support any of these, and linguists in general reject them all. Nevertheless, some geneticists have favored some views that would involve pre-Columbian genetic contributions to some Native American populations from the Old World that did not arrive by crossing the Bering Strait.[16]

Others found evidence that seems to suggest that "some Amazonian Native Americans descend partly from a Native American founding population that carried ancestry more closely related to indigenous Australians, New Guineans and Andaman Islanders than to any present-day Eurasians or Native Americans" (Skoglund et al. 2015, 104). Recent reports identify an Australasian signal in genomic data from several South American groups (Raghavan et al. 2015; Skoglund et al. 2015; Skoglund and Reich 2016; Fehren-Schmitz 2020, 54; Ribeiro-dos-Santos et al. 2020; Castro et al. 2021; Rowe et al. 2022). Skoglund et al. (2015) found that the genomes from these populations did not descend from a homogenous group, that a small number of contemporary populations in the Amazon region—Suruí, Karatiana, Xavante, Piapoco, Guaraní—shared a small but significant number of alleles with contemporary Australasians populations, including Indigenous Australians, New Guineans, Papuans, and the Onge from the Andaman Islands. They called it the Ypykuéra population, or Population Y for short. (See Raff 2022, 215; Castro et al. 2021.) Rowe et al. (2022, 19) report that more recent genomic studies reveal a signal of Population Y "in every major linguistic group [in South America], making it geographically widespread."

The genetic signal, however, is not strong, and it is hard at this point to know what to make of it. The Australasian populations in these studies include Andaman, Australian, Papuan New Guinea, Bougainvillean, Dusun, Igorot, and Māori.

Jenifer Raff's (2022, 216) take on it is:
the overall proportion of the genomes of contemporary South Americans with this [Population Y] ancestry is quite low, and people within the same populations who carry it have extremely variable amounts of it. It is also quite old, and it seems to

predate the split between those populations who lived along the coast and those who eventually moved into the Amazonian region. This is not the genetic pattern we would expect to see if there had been a post-LGM migration across the Pacific from Australia and Melanesia.

In addition, the same genetic signal was found in an individual from the Tianyuan Cave site in China dated to 40,000 years ago; he was related to Amazonian populations and Australasian populations. To Pontus Skogund and other researchers, the most likely explanation for these results is not that there was a trans-Pacific migration, but instead that **there was once an ancient population in mainland Asia that contributed ancestry to both contemporary Australasians and the ancestors of the First Peoples before they left Beringia** . . . Another possibility is that people with Population Y ancestry were present in South America before the First Peoples arrived. (p. 217, emphasis added, LRC)

Rowe et al. (2022, 19) also report a hypothesis that:
Population Y contributed ancestry to the Native American clade before its dispersal south from Beringia. Some of the Native Americans then carried this ancestry as they dispersed down the west coast and into South America. In other words, Population Y predated dispersal but did not live in the Americas, and its descendants now solely exist there and in Australasia. (See Skoglund et al. 2015.)

They say that this hypothesis has been favored because it is consistent with the view that Native Americans were the first people to enter the Americas 16,000 years ago (p.19).

Rowe et al. (2022:19) also report a second hypothesis:
Unmixed descendants of Population Y dispersed directly to the Americas during pre-LGM time, predating the Native American arrival by millennia . . . This early population was later displaced by the Native Americans except in South America, where it mixed with Native Americans and left a discernable signal in every major living linguistic group.

Rowe et al. (2022, 19) say that this seems "more likely, because the first hypothesis alone fails to explain archeological sites that predate Native American arrival."

A seeming problem, however, is the absence of a Population Y signal in North America. Rowe et al. say also that "it is technically possible that the older American sites represent entirely separate, unrecognized pre-LGM lineage(s) that became extinct without leaving a discernable genetic trace in younger populations" (p.19) (see Raff 2022).

There has long been speculation and controversy about whether Polynesians made it beyond Rapa Nui (Easter Island) to South America. It had been claimed that there was Native American admixture with people of Rapa Nui from a time before contact with Europeans (Moreno-Mayar et al. 2014). However, recent investigations have dismissed any Native American ancestry on Rapa Nui (Willerslev and Meltzer 2021, 361). As Willerslev and Meltzer (2021, 361) tell it:

The possibility of contact with Pacific peoples has returned with a recent study of several hundred present-day Indigenous peoples who occupy islands in the Pacific Ocean and along the coast of Mesoamerica and South America. Polynesian individuals with Native American admixture most closely related to the Zenu of Colombia are found on half a dozen widely separated eastern Pacific islands. The admixture event is estimated to have occurred in the thirteenth century, far earlier than a European presence in the Pacific, and about the time many of these islands were first settled. It is proposed that this represents the dispersal of Native American individuals into the eastern Pacific, but a more likely scenario . . . is that Native American ancestry on these islands is a result of Pacific peoples having visited South America and admixed or returned with Native American individuals.[17]

However, it is important to keep in mind that regardless of what the real story of these possibly Polynesian or other Australasian genes in American populations may turn out to be, there is no credible linguistic evidence of any linguistic genealogical relationship or significant language contact between any language of the Old World and any Indigenous language of the New World, except for Siberian varieties of Yupik Eskimo, the result of recent back-migration across the Bering Strait, and Greenlandic Eskimo groups, also relatively recent arrivals there from North America. There is nothing linguistic in any American Indian language or group of languages that provided legitimate evidence to support the introduction of any language from outside the Americas in times predating the arrival of Columbus.[18]

Unfortunately, the linguistic evidence does not allow us to eliminate any of these possible scenarios for the peopling of the Americas. There are about 170 independent Indigenous language families (including isolates) in the Americas, and we are not able to reduce this number by any significant extent utilizing adequate methods and reliable linguistic evidence. Today's circa 170 families could be the descendants of a single original language that diversified after arrival in the Americas and then underwent so much change that any past kinship among them is no longer detectable. Or similarly, two or three or a few groups with their own languages or multilingual groups may have entered, but from the linguistic diversity we see today and from the lack of evidence to unite the circa 170 language families further, we cannot argue for or against such a scenario. The current linguistic diversity is also consistent with this scenario. As for the various less plausible hypotheses, we can, of course, suspect them being unlikely and probably eliminate most of them on other grounds, but based on the American Indian languages themselves, not even the far-out, fringe ideas can conclusively be eliminated. In short, the linguistic evidence will not play a decisive role in answering questions about how and when the first peoples arrived in the New World and who they were and what their language or languages may have been. The circa 170 independent language families is not inconsistent with any of a large number of possible hypotheses about the possible first peoples in the Americas.

Lying behind all this is a significant but unanswered, probably unanswerable, question: could so much linguistic diversity develop in the amount of time that elapsed since the first people(s) entered the Americas? Or, how could so much diversity have developed in that length of time? For language classification, the date of arrival is not particularly relevant. Linguists have no reliable means of dating the age of language diversifications. For the classification of the languages of the Americas it matters not at all whether the earliest inhabitants arrived a few thousand years earlier or later—we are still stuck with circa 170 at-present unrelated language families, unique linguistic lineages, and all that is relevant is whether enough change could have taken place since the speakers of the earliest language or languages arrived to result in the current picture of the linguistic diversity. Over time languages undergo more and more changes, losing or replacing many things and changing others beyond recognition, meaning that traces of common ancestry fade until ultimately it is no longer possible to show a phylogenetic relationship shared by these languages.

We simply do not know how much time might be required to produce the amount of linguistic diversity found in the Americas, particularly for groups arriving on previously uninhabited continents. We only know that the oldest language families anywhere that we are able to confirm with the methods and data available extend back in time only some 6,000 years, some might say perhaps as far as 8,000, according to our best estimates. Add another several thousand years on top of that for the arrival of the first inhabitants of the New World and languages that indeed are descended from an original common ancestor may retain essentially no cognate material that has not been replaced or that has not been changed beyond recognition.

Linguistics is, however, not utterly powerless to contribute here. We linguists can, on the basis of what is known of the languages, eliminate some unproductive claims. For example, a massive number of studies in the genetics literature have attempted to correlate Joseph Greenberg's (1987) hypothesis with human genetics, with interpretations for arrival and dispersal of the earliest humans in the New World (see Bolnick et al. 2004). Greenberg's view was that all Native American languages, except the Na-Dene and Eskimo-Aleut languages, belong to a single macro-family, "Amerind." The Amerind hypothesis failed for many reasons and has been rejected by almost all linguists (see Chapter 6 for details). Geneticists and other non-linguists need to be aware that "Amerind" is a dead end for their research interests.

1.7. METHODS

The history and classification of the native languages of the Americas involve all the various methods historical linguists have for finding out about a language's past and discovering its relatives (Campbell 2020a). Much of what is dealt with in this book concerns the classification of the languages, which involves how the language families are established and how the languages within the families are related to one another. In both instances, the comparative method is primary and standard in historical linguistics, and much of the information in this book comes from and relies on applications of the comparative method, and on how it can be used to sort out loanwords from inherited vocabulary, to establish the subgrouping (internal classification) of languages within a language family, to determine impacts from language contact, to detect accidental similarities,[19] to find and evaluate cognates, and much more (see Campbell 2020a).

In recent years, computational phylogenetic methods, inspired by methods in evolutionary biology, have been applied to historical linguistic questions involving Indigenous languages of the Americas, especially to the internal classifications of languages within their language families (i.e., to language family trees). Results of studies that utilize the computational phylogenetic methods are reported here for several language families (for example for

Chapakuran Birchall et al. 2016; for Tupí-Guaraníán Michael et al. 2015 and Gerardi et al. 2023; for Uto-Aztecan Greenhill et al. 2023; etc.). It will be helpful to clarify the differences and similarities among these approaches.

Importantly, most of the more useful computational approaches rely on careful cognate coding. Correct identification of cognates distinguishes inherited forms from loanwords and chance resemblances. That is, these particular quantitative approaches employ and rely on the results of the comparative method, as do standard historical linguistic procedures. A major difference is in the kind and amount of data dealt with and how it is treated.

The standard methods of historical linguistics make use of a wide gamut of linguistic data, while most of the recent quantitative approaches rely only on lexical data. The computational models do not take into account many aspects of language that are known to be important for understanding linguistic change: analogical changes, chain shifts, directionality of changes, semantic change and neologisms, avoidance of homophony, grammaticalization, impacts of language contact, the interdependence of elements in language subsystems (how some elements of a language depend on and are intertwined with other elements in subsystems of the grammar), reanalysis, sociolinguistic conditioning of change, and so on. (See Campbell 2020a for information on these things.)

Many publications based on computational phylogenetic methods rely on cognates that have been established by linguists, where loanwords and accidental similarities have already been eliminated using the standard methods. Dealing with data based on cognates that require the prior work of linguistic experts can lose sight of what historical linguists have to do to establish the cognates: discover sound correspondences, find the sound changes, take the directionality of change into account, determine the shared innovations (needed for subgrouping), recognize plausible semantic changes, identify loanwords and changes due to language contact, eliminate forms that are similar due to analogical changes, and so on.

Most phylogenetic studies rely exclusively on lexical data taken from Swadesh's basic vocabulary lists.[20] Some scholars have attempted to introduce also other kinds of characters, based on sound changes, morphology, or typological traits, and many scholars profess interest in moving in that direction. Linguists have recommended that these approaches take phonological and morphosyntactic data and the various other things necessary for fuller understanding of how language change affects the data into account, as well as that things due to contact-induced language change be avoided. When phonological and morphological characters are included, the results may improve significantly. However, this can introduce new problems, such as the charge of bias in character selection, that the investigator may select characters (traits) to skew the results toward expected or desired outcomes. Linguists have also asked that more standard linguistic criteria for subgrouping be taken into account, for example requiring shared innovations be part of the picture without retentions or only superficially similar things. Linguists distrust lexical evidence alone for language classification—lexical items are the least integrated into the structure of a language and they change very easily for sociocultural, non-linguistic reasons. This contrasts markedly with the confidence that quantitative researchers have had that the sort of lexical data they deal with is sufficient to answer their questions, adequate to provide worthwhile classifications of the languages.[21]

Computational phylogenetic methods for classifying languages fall into two major classes: character-based methods and distance-based ones. Character-based methods produce classifications by evaluating how well different trees account for the distribution of a set linguistic features (e.g., how the data fit in different cognate sets) among a group of genealogically related languages. Rooting phylogenetic trees results in classifications based on shared innovations, making character-based phylogenetic methods roughly compatible with the comparative method (Michael and Chousou-Polydouri 2019). Distance-based methods have proven much less successful; they do not rely on the comparative method for judgments of cognacy. They classify languages based on overall similarity metrics, not distinguishing shared innovations, shared retentions, and parallel independent innovations, meaning that these distance-based classifications cannot render adequate genealogical classifications. For critiques, see for example Carvalho (2020a), Michael (2021), and Michael and Chousou-Polydouri (2019).

Obviously, the application of techniques developed in evolutionary biology to linguistic classification will be to some extent inadequate, since there are important differences between languages and biological species and in how they change. Languages undergo many types of changes that do not affect biological species, changes that have no biological basis, but are motivated by social and cognitive factors. Furthermore, biological diversification (speciation) and linguistic diversification occur on very different time scales, and a language is not inherited biologically, it is learned. As mentioned above, the models adopted from biology do not take into account many aspects of linguistic change that are known to be important for understanding it.

It is significant that in many of the cases cited in this book that employ computational phylogenetic methods the authors mention as an indication of the reliability of their results that they match well the classifications of historical linguists who used the comparative method and standard linguistic methods. Birchall et al. (2016, 281) conclude with, "through this example [Chapakuran classification] we have shown that the comparative method and Bayesian phylogenetic inference are complementary, and that both together can and should be part of the toolbox of historical linguistics."

Problems with the ASJP (Automated Similarity Judgment Program) approach are discussed in Chapter 6.

1.8. CONVENTIONS USED IN THIS BOOK

In the chapters that follow, the alternative names by which a language has been known are given in parentheses after the principal name of that language (see above about names).

In linguistics when languages belong to the same language family, that is, when they descend from a common ancestor, they are said to be genetically related. Unfortunately, that can get confused with uses of the word *genetic* in biology. In this book I use *genetically related* and *genetic relationship* when genealogical relationship, phylogenetic relationship, linguistic kinship among languages is involved. I sometimes also use these other designations to talk about languages that are genetically related to one another, particularly in contexts where confusion with biological genetics could occur.

As mentioned above, the word "extinct" when applied to languages is avoided in this book, and "dormant" is used in its place.

Instead of figures with family-tree diagrams, the subgrouping relationships among the languages of the language families are indicated here by the degree of indentation in the classification lists. Language group headings found more to the left include as their members (descendants) all the groups and languages under them that are indented farther toward the right. Greater degrees of indentation thus reflect hierarchically the degrees of relatedness in the family trees, that is, their branches, subgroups.

Finally, translations of material quoted from languages other than English are my own unless otherwise indicated.

In the next three chapters we move on to the classification and history of the languages of North America, Middle America, and South America. This is followed by a chapter on the unclassified and spurious languages of the Americas and another on proposed but unconfirmed hypotheses of distant genetic relationship. After that comes three chapters dealing with the consequences of language contact: on linguistic areas, contact languages (pidgins, mixed languages, and lingua francas), and loanwords.

NOTES

1. There is an extensive literature about these names, about which should be preferred and about what is wrong with various ones. An informative example is Yellow Bird (1999), one of many.

2. In some cases, an exonym has become the common name used by and sometimes preferred by community members to refer to their ethnic group or to their language. An exonym can gain so much importance that it in effect becomes the autonym, the name that the group uses and prefers to refer to themselves or to their language.

In a few cases there is more than one preferred language name among speakers of a particular language. Sometimes names representing just one dialect or region or clan have been promoted to represent the language as a whole for some non-linguistic reason, especially by some faction in the group. This has at times led to conflict among different people who speak the same language. Some, insisting on an autonym that actually only refers to a particular variety (dialect), have attempted in this way to get official recognition for the dialect as a separate language, often for political motives. To cite one example, a user-submitted recommendation to the *Catalogue of Endangered Languages* (at www.endangeredlanguages.com) suggested that the name *Senćoten* should be changed to *Northern Straits Salish*, since *Senćoten*, traditionally called *Saanich*, is the name of just one of several dialects of the Northern Straits Salish language. In addition to Senćoten (Saanich), the dialects Samish (*Si, Náməś, Siʔnəməš*), Lummi (*Xwlemi*), Songish (*Lekwungen*), Sooke (*T'sou-ke*), and Semiahmoo (*Semyome*) are also included in Northern Straits Salish.

3. Even more precisely, it is composed of *-ch'a* 'say' + *-b'* 'instrument' + *-al* 'location/abstract noun'. What is spelled *qach'ab'al* is pronounced [qačʼaɓɨɬ], phonetically.

4. Chulupí was a very frequently used name, but is now being abandoned because *chulupí* means 'cockroach' in the Spanish of Bolivia and parts of Paraguay. *Nivaclé* is the autonym, from /niwaklé/ 'man, person', 'Nivaclé person', 'Nivaclé language'.

5. The names Makú and Makúan are now avoided. "Makú" is used to refer to 'wild forest Indian' in the region, irrespective of ethnic, linguistic, or political affiliation; it is very strongly pejorative (see Epps and Bolaños 2017, 470).

6. Native oral traditions do not take us much further back in time and can be very difficult to interpret. A few languages of Mesoamerica were recorded in pre-Columbian writing systems; these provide invaluable information about the structure of those languages and sometimes about changes that they underwent, but the historical information obtainable from the texts tends to be limited with respect to the broader history about these languages.

7. There are also three indigenous sign languages in this region.

8. The exact number of distinct currently spoken languages and language families in South America is just not known. For example, in South America there are around 100 indigenous groups that live in isolation (see, for example, https://en.wikipedia.org/wiki/Uncontacted_peoples, accessed June 30, 2023). In Brazil alone there are officially at least 40 "uncontacted" isolated indigenous groups. For some of these uncontacted groups, it is not known whether they speak an already identified language, a language currently unknown but that belongs to a known language family, or perhaps a language that represents an as yet unknown language family or language isolate. In some cases we do not yet know whether a certain named entity refers to some independent language or is just a dialect of a language known by another name.

9. In spite of his classification's heavy leaning on morphological and typological considerations, Sapir also felt that he had both morphological and lexical evidence for the groupings, and he believed that in the future more rigorous comparison with phonological evidence would support his preliminary proposals. Sapir, however, insisted on sound correspondences for definitive proof of genetic relationship: "there may be some evidence for considering distinct languages related—for example, the general form of their grammar may seem to provide such evidence—but the final demonstration can never be said to be given until comparable words can be shown to be but reflexes of one and the same prototype by the operation of dialectic phonetic laws" (Sapir 1949[1931], 74).

10. Today the earliest Clovis sites are dated to between 13,200 and 12,900 years ago (Raff 2022, 98).

11. One was the region of Eastern Beringia (in present-day Alaska), which remained unglaciated throughout the LGM (Last Glacial Maximum), an ice-free cul-de-sac at the end of the Bering Land Bridge; another was the southern portion of central Beringia; and another that perhaps could have served as a refuge was the Northwest Beringian Plain (Raff 2022, 101, 191, 192).

12. Several geneticists are open to the possibility that people could have been in the Americas during or even prior to the Last Glacial Maximum (Raff 2022, 94).

13. For example, Meadowcroft Rockshelter (16,000 BP, possibly as early as 19,000 BP) in Pennsylvania, Paisley Caves (c. 14,000 years ago) in Oregon, Page-Ladson (c. 14,500 years ago) in Florida, the Manis mastodon kill site (c. 14,000 years ago) in Washington, Huaca Prieta (c. 14,5000–13,500 years ago) in Peru, the Buttermilk Creek complex sites (c. 15,000 years ago) in Texas, the Schaefer and Hebior sites (c. 14,500 years ago) in Wisconsin, the Cactus Hill site (c. 16,900–15,000 years ago) in Virginia, the Cooper's Ferry site (c. 16,000 years ago) in Idaho, and the Taima-Taima site (c. 14,000 years ago) in Venezuela. Several of these are now widely accepted, others less so. Monte Verde shows that people must have made it to southern South America by 14,600 years ago. Monte Verde in Chile is now generally believed to have been reliably dated to 14,800–13,800 years ago, though various radiocarbon dates ranging from 33,000 BP to 18,900 BP to 13,500 BP had been reported for the site.

Rowe et al. (2022, 17) report the following as "other recent archeological discoveries placing humans in the Americas during or before the Last Glacial Maximum (LGM)":

> multiple in situ human footprints from New Mexico that date from 22,860 to 21,130 cal BP . . . and footprints from Argentina that date to 30,000 cal BP . . . Simple stone tools

discovered in Chiquihuite Cave, Mexico, date from 26,500 to 19,000 cal BP and represent a previously unknown tradition ... At Coxcatlan Cave, Mexico, re-dating butchered small mammals associated with minimally worked stone tools established a 33,448 to 28,279 cal BP date for the site's lowest cultural level ... Simple flaked stone artifacts are known from numerous ancient South American sites. These include Toca da Tira Peia, Brazil, which dates to 20,000 cal BP ... and Vale da Pedra Furada, Brazil, which dates to 24,000 cal BP ...; older artifacts dating to 32,000 cal BP are also reported from this site ... At Toca do Serrote das Moendas, Brazil, faunal remains associated with human bones were dated to between 29,000 and 24,000 cal BP ... And at Arroyo del Vizcaíno, Uruguay, a fossil-rich 30,000 years old megafaunal locality with cut-marked bones ... adds to a growing record of probable human occupation sites in the Americas that predate arrival of the Native American clade by millennia.

14. Potter et al. (2018), however, argue against incautious acceptance of the coastal route hypothesis.

15. For example, Terrence Kaufman (1990, 25) wrote that "Other scholars (Mary Haas, Victor Golla, myself) have opined that this may well be true [that all the indigenous languages of the New World (except Na-Dené and Eskimo-Aleut) are genetically related to each other], allowing for a reasonable number of languages unclassified for various reasons. I do not, however, think that this can be proven by the comparative method."

16. For example, Malaspinas et al. (2014) claimed to have found human genetic evidence to support Botocudo-Polynesian connections. This was apparently due to a museum error that was later discovered: two Polynesian skulls had been misplaced in the Botocudo (Krenak) box.

17. Note that Zenú (Sinú) of Colombia has been dormant for more than 200 years. It is unclassified and nothing is known of it. There has been speculation of possible Chocóan connections, but this is based on no linguistic evidence. There are people today who identify with Sinú (Zenú) in the Columbian census, but what this means is difficult to interpret. (See Chapter 5.)

18. There is well-known clear evidence of some contact between Polynesia and western South America in the form of at least one loanword, the word for 'sweet potato' borrowed from Quechua *kumar*, seen widely in the Pacific (see Roulliera et al. 2013), for example in Fijian *kumala*, Kiribati (Gilbertese) *kumara*, Rapa Nui (Easter Island) *kumara*, Samoan *'umala*, Tahitian *'umara*, including even *kumara* of New Zealand English, borrowed from Māori *kūmara* (*Polynesian Lexicon Project Online* https://pollex.eva.mpg.de/search/?query=sweet+potato&field=entry). However, this loanword in these languages is not evidence that a viable language from the Pacific or elsewhere was established in the Americas in pre-Columbian times or had any significant impact on any Native American tongue.

19. In connection with accidental similarity, it will be helpful here, near the beginning, to call attention to the criterion of avoiding "short forms" in attempts to demonstrate a genetic relationship between languages not yet shown to be related to one another. This criterion is referred to a number of times in the book. It is generally recognized that very short forms that are similar across languages may owe their similarity to pure accident (chance) and not to inheritance from a common ancestor, and that therefore, such similarity in short forms should not be relied on as useful evidence of a shared kinship. Short forms are generally understood to be words or morphemes of the shape CV, VC, or V. Don Ringe (1999) has shown in his computational historical linguistic work that even for CVC forms it is remarkably easy to find matches across unrelated languages. Since bound morphemes tend to be quite short (C, V, CV, or VC in shape), in isolation they usually provide no trustworthy evidence of distant genetic relationship. Moreover, though

short forms are avoided in argumentation for relatedness among languages, it should be borne in mind that longer forms, too, can be accidentally similar, though far less frequently. That is why systematic, recurring sound correspondences are so helpful and desired, to help eliminate things that are only accidentally similar.

20. It is assumed that the basic vocabulary tends to resist borrowings, but, although less frequent, borrowings in the basic vocabulary are not uncommon. In English, from Swadesh's list of 100 words, the following are loanwords: *die, egg, grease, mountain, person,* and *skin*.

21. Assumptions shared by computational phylogenetic methods include:

There are significant similarities between linguistic change and biological evolution that allow the application of the same methods to determine phylogenetic relationships.

Loanwords is rare (in basic vocabulary, their data sets).

The distribution of cognates among the compared languages can be used to model linguistic evolution (linguistic change) in a phylogenetic tree.

Linguistic characters (traits) generally develop without homoplasia—that is, without independent parallel development (convergent evolution), without acquisition of the same trait in unrelated lineages (branches), although cases of such linguistic change are not rare.

2

North American Indian Languages North of Mexico

2.1. INTRODUCTION

This chapter is about the Indigenous languages of North America (north of Mexico), about their history and classification. As mentioned in Chapter 1, when Europeans arrived in North America they encountered some 314 languages, belonging to 54 independent language families. These include 14 larger language families, 16 smaller language families, and 24 language isolates (languages with no known relatives, language families with only a single member language). All of these languages are now endangered, and 150 of them are dormant, with no known remaining native speakers (48%).

2.2. CLASSIFICATION AND HISTORY OF NORTH AMERICAN INDIAN LANGUAGES

The classification presented here is an updated version the so-called Consensus Classification (Campbell 1997a; Goddard 1996a; Mithun 1999; Golla et al. 2008) and relies heavily but not entirely on the classification in Campbell, Goddard, Golla, and Mithun (in press). It contains:

14 major language families, made up of a sizeable number of languages with significant subgrouping: Algic, Caddoan, Cochimí-Yuman, Eskimo-Aleut, Iroquoian, Kiowa-Tanoan, Muskogean, Na-Dene, Plateau, Salishan, Siouan-Catawban, Utian, Uto-Aztecan, and Wakashan.

16 minor language families, made up of a small number of relatively closely related (usually geographically contiguous) languages: Chimakuan, Chinookan, Chumashan, Comecrudan, Coosan, Kalapuyan, Keresan, Maiduan, Palaihnihan, Pomoan, Salinan, Shastan, Tsimshianic, Wintuan, Yokutsan, and Yukian.

24 language isolates: Adai, Alsea, Atakapa, Beothuk, Cayuse, Chimariko, Chitimacha, Coahuilteco, Cotoname, Esselen, Haida, Karankawa, Karuk, Kootenai, Natchez, Siuslaw, Takelma, Tonkawa, Timucua, Tunica, Washo, Yana, Yuchi, and Zuni.

Names of language families are given in boldface, listed roughly from north to south and west to east. (Dormant languages have an asterisk before their names.)

See Map 2.1 for an overview of North American Indian Languages.

Eskimo-Aleut
Eskimoan[1]
    Western Eskimo (Yupik)
        *Sirenik (Sirenikski)
        East Cape Yupik (Naukan, Naukanski)
        Central Siberian Yupik
        Central Alaskan Yup'ik
        Pacific Yupik (Alutiiq)
    Eastern Eskimo (Inuit)
        Seward Peninsula Inupiaq
        North Alaska Inupiaq
        Western Canadian Inuktitut
        Eastern Canadian Inuktitut
        West Greenlandic
        East Greenlandic
Aleut(Unangam Tunuu)
    Aleut
    *Copper Island Aleut (Mednyj Aleut) (Aleut-Russian mixed language; See Chapter 8.)

(See also Johns 2021, 524; see Dorais 2010 especially for details on Inuit dialects.)
(Map 2.2. Eskimo-Aleut Languages.)

Languages of the Eskimoan branch of the Eskimo-Aleut language family stretch from Kamchatka in northeast Asia across North America and on to Greenland—it extends beyond North America on both sides, with representatives in both hemispheres. Greenlandic Eskimo was the first Indigenous American language to come into contact with Europeans; Norse settlements in Greenland began in the late tenth century, led by Erik the Red. Later contacts led to loanwords in various Eskimo-Aleut languages from Danish, French, English, and Russian, as well as from other Indigenous languages.

Aleut (Unangan) is the only language of the Aleut branch of the Eskimo-Aleut family. It has two principal dialects, **Eastern Aleut** and **Western Aleut**. Western has two subdialects, **Atkan** and **Attuan** (Woodbury 1984, 49). Its speakers are indigenous to the Aleutian Islands, the Pribilof Islands, and the Alaska Peninsula west of Stepovak Bay. Aleut's autonym is *Unangan*; the name "Aleut" was introduced by Russians, who used the same term for the Pacific Yupik Eskimos. In the early nineteenth century, Russian Orthodox missionaries promoted native literacy and helped foster a remarkably bilingual society. One of them, Ivan Veniaminov, developed a writing system for Aleut and translated religious material into the

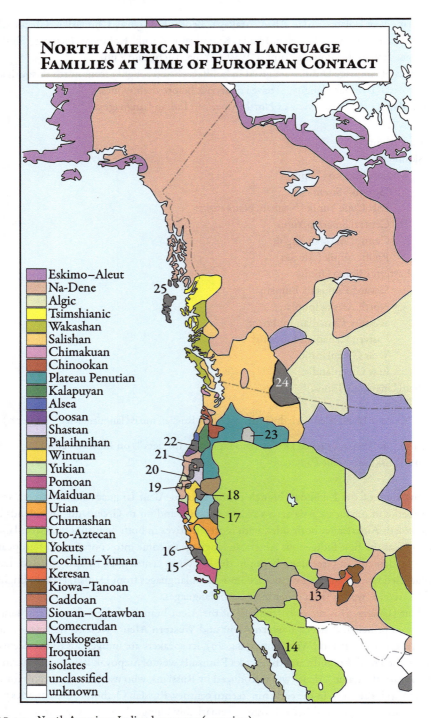

MAP 2.1. North American Indian languages (overview)

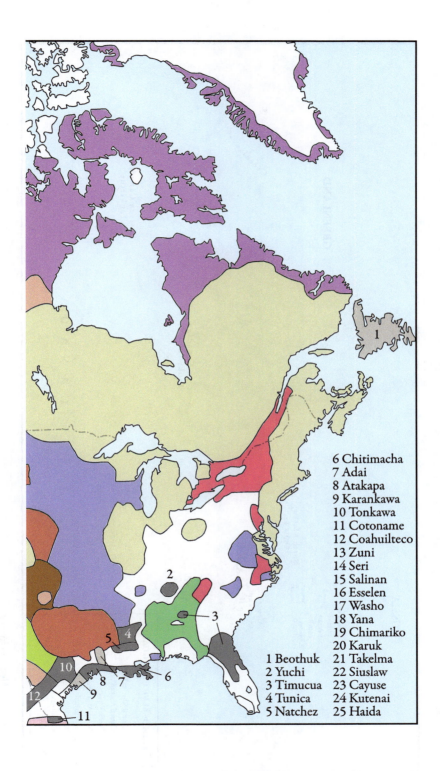

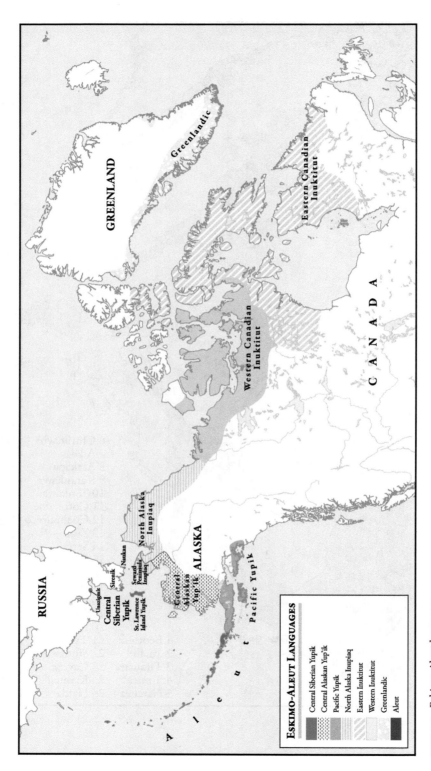

MAP 2.2. Eskimo-Aleut languages

language. Aleut was involved in a considerable amount of language contact that resulted in many loanwords and some structural change (Berge 2020).

Copper Island Aleut (Mednyj Aleut) is a mixed language originally spoken on Copper (Mednyj) Island, Kamchatka Province, Russia. By 1969 the entire community had been relocated to the village of Nikol'skoye on Bering Island. Its lexicon and noun morphology are mostly from Aleut, and its verb morphology is mostly Russian. The language recently became dormant. As a mixed language, it is uncertain whether it can legitimately be classified as an Aleut and Eskimo-Aleut language. (See Chapter 8 for details.)

The **Yupik** branch has five languages, originally located on the coast of the Chukchi Peninsula and from Norton Sound south to the Alaska Peninsula and east to Prince William Sound (Woodbury 1984, 49). Siberian Yupik (also called Asiatic Eskimo or Yuit; including Sirenikski, Naukanski, and Central Siberian Yupik [or Chaplinski]) is not a valid subgroup within Yupik. Now that Naukanski and Sirenikski are better known, it is not possible to find common innovations that unite Asiatic Eskimo and distinguish it from the Alaskan languages.[2]

Sirenik (Sirenikski, also called Old Sirenik to differentiate it from the Sirenik dialect of Central Siberian Yupik) is a recently dormant language of the Yupik branch, formerly spoken in the village of Sireniki, Provideniya County, Chukchi Autonomous District, Russia. Sirenik is quite divergent from the other Yupik languages; it has been influenced by Chukchi. Sirenik was sometimes considered a third branch of Eskimo, alongside Inuit and Yupik. Beginning in the 1950s, the indigenous population of Sireniki shifted first to Central Siberian Yupik, the language of more numerous forced immigrants, and then largely to Russian. The last speaker, Valentina Vyie [Выйе], died in 1997.

East Cape Yupik (or Naukan Yupik, Naukanski) is a severely endangered Western Eskimo language of Siberia. Linguistically it is the link between Central Alaskan Yup'ik and Central Siberian Yupik. It was spoken originally in Naukan, on East Cape (Cape Dezhnev), Chukchi Autonomous District, Russia, facing the Diomede Islands in Alaska. The community was forcibly relocated in 1958 to the nearby villages of Lorino and Lavrentiya. Shift to Russian is taking place rapidly.

Pacific Yupik (Alutiiq) is a distinct language within the Yupik branch, although it is closely related to Central Alaskan Yup'ik. It is spoken on the south coast of Alaska from the Alaska Peninsula to Prince William Sound. Speakers call themselves "Aleuts" in English, reflecting the early Russian use of *Aleuty* to designate all of the native people of the south coast of Alaska. *Alutiiq* is the Pacific Yupik version of the same name, and *Sugpiaq* has also been used for it in recent decades. The two dialects of Pacific Yupik are **Koniag** in the west, on the upper part of the Alaska Peninsula and Kodiak Island, and **Chugach** in the east, on the Kenai Peninsula and Prince William Sound.

The evidence is good, though not conclusive, for grouping Central Alaskan Yup'ik and Pacific Yupik in an Alaskan subgroup (Woodbury 1984, 55–56). Central Alaskan Yup'ik has four principal dialects; a fifth was attested in the nineteenth century.

Inuit (Eastern Eskimo) is a chain of dialects spoken in some 165 settlements from Norton Sound in northwestern Alaska to the East Coast of Greenland, the Inuit-Inupiaq branch of Eskimoan. The dialects at the opposite ends of this chain are not mutually intelligible, but the location of "language" boundaries is largely arbitrary. Mainly for political and cultural reasons three languages are typically distinguished, **Inupiaq** in Alaska, **Inuktitut** in Canada, and **Greenlandic** in Greenland. Each of these is subdivided into dialect clusters or emergent languages of their own.[3]

Inupiaq refers to the dialects of Western Eskimo spoken in Alaska and adjacent parts of Northern Canada. There are two major dialect groups, **Seward Peninsula Inupiaq** (Qawiaraq) and **North Alaskan Inupiaq**. Seward Peninsula Inupiaq includes the dialects of the southern Seward Peninsula and Norton Sound area, and of the villages surrounding Bering Strait and on King and Diomede Islands. North Alaskan Inupiaq includes the **Malimiut** dialect around Kotzebue Sound and the **North Slope** dialect spoken along the Arctic Coast as far east as the Mackenzie Delta. The Seward Peninsula and North Alaskan dialect groups differ from each other, and speakers of the two find it difficult to understand one another without considerable experience interacting.

Inuktitut is the name for the dialects of **Inuit** (Eastern Eskimo) spoken on the northern coast of Canada, from the Mackenzie Delta in the west to Labrador in the east. Inuktitut is also sometimes used for Eastern Eskimo dialects in general, synonymous with Inuit. The dialects of **Western Canadian Inuktitut** are usually distinguished from **Eastern Canadian Inuktitut**, with the boundary between the Central Arctic coast and Baffin Island, but there is no sharp linguistic border. All of the Inuktitut speakers of Nunavut territory, which has dialects belonging to both the Western and Eastern divisions, understand one another's dialects.

Greenlandic is the English name for the **Inuktitut** (Eastern Eskimo) dialects of Greenland (the native name is *Kalaallisut*). Of the 79 Inuit communities in Greenland, all but 17 are on the west coast. There is a significant dialect difference between **West Greenlandic** of the west coast settlements and **East Greenlandic** of those on the east coast. The five **Thule** communities in the far northwest of the island constitute a third dialect cluster, sometimes called **Polar Eskimo**. This dialect is closer to the speech of Baffin Island than to West or East Greenlandic, and is usually considered to be a variety of Eastern Canadian Inuktitut that has been influenced by standard Greenlandic. Many speakers of Greenlandic live in Denmark, most of them in Copenhagen. Greenland officially became Danish territory in 1814; it became an autonomous province associated with the Danish Commonwealth in 1979.

The kinship between Aleut and Eskimoan was recognized already by Rasmus Rask in 1819 (Thalbitzer 1922), even though the two are only very distantly related to each other. Most agree that there appear to be more grammatical similarities, especially in inflectional morphology, while cognate lexical roots appear to be much scarcer. Only about 15 percent of the lexicon is cognate in Knut Bergsland's (1986) count. Bergsland (1986) found Eskimo-Aleut sound correspondences and many cognates. Fortescue, Jacobson, and Kaplan (2010) reconstructed the following phonemes for Proto-Eskimo-Aleut: /p, t (t_1, t_2), c (c_1, c_2), k, q, v, ð, ɣ, ʁ, (ɬ), l, m, n, ŋ, j; i, u, a, ə/. The *t (t_1, t_2)* represents unclear correspondences involving /t/ ~ /c/ ~ /s/. For *c (c_1, c_2)*, Bergsland (1986) reconstructed *č (voiceless alveopalatal affricate) while Fortescue et al. (2010) reconstructed *c (voiceless palatal stop). Anne Berge (2018) points out a number of irregularities in a number of the sound correspondences upon which these reconstructions are based. Together, Bergsland (1986, 1994) and Fortescue et al. (2010) proposed 470 cognates shared by Aleut and Eskimoan, though, as pointed out by Berge (2018, 232), a significant number of them involve irregular or unexplained sound correspondences or wide semantic discrepancies.

The phonemic inventory of Proto-Eskimoan, a branch of Eskimo-Aleut, has been reconstructed with: /p, t, č, k, kʷ, q, qʷ, s, x, xʷ, χ, χʷ, v, ɣ, ɣʷ, ʁ, ʁʷ, m, n, ŋ, ŋʷ, ř y; i, iː, ɜ, a, aː, u, uː/ (Bergsland 1986; see also Krauss 1979; Woodbury 1984). Michael Fortescue (1998, 124–125) reconstructed: /p, t, tʲ, k, q, c, cʲ, v, ð, ɣ, ʁ, m, n, (nʲ), ŋ, l, (ł), j; i, ə, a, u/. His *nʲ may not have been distinct from *n. The *ł may have developed later from l in clusters with stops. Fortescue does not make it clear whether c, cʲ, were considered to be affricates ([ts], [tsʲ]) or fricatives ([s], [sʲ]).

The split up between Eskimoan and Aleut is generally estimated to have occurred about 4,500 years ago, though Berge (2018, 240) sees "no particularly good reason to maintain this date on linguistic grounds." The original homeland of Proto-Eskimo-Aleut appears to have been in western coastal Alaska, perhaps in the Bristol Bay-Cook Inlet area. Greenlandic Eskimo is a relatively recent expansion (Krauss 1980, 7; Woodbury 1984, 62).

Hypotheses of external relationships of Eskimo-Aleut with other language families include Uralic, Indo-European, Chukotko-Kamchatkan, Wakashan, Yukagir, and even the defunct Ural-Altaic. None of these has many followers and the evidence presented so far in their favor is far from persuasive (Bergsland 1959, 1979; Bonnerjea 1978, 1979, 1983; Fortescue 1981, 1988, 1998; Hammerich 1951; Hamp 1976; Koo 1980; Krauss 1973a, 1979; Sauvageot 1924, 1953; Swadesh 1962; Thalbitzer 1928, 1945, 1952; Uhlenbeck 1905, 1942, 1945; Voegelin and Voegelin 1967, 575).

An often-repeated idea is that Eskimo-Aleut may be the result of a later migration across the Bering Strait into North America and that therefore the Eskimo-Aleut languages are quite different from those of all other Native American linguistic groups. Already in the late 1800s, Daniel Brinton (1894, 146–147) could say "the Asiatic origin of the Eskimos has been a favorite subject with several recent writers. They are quite dissatisfied if they cannot at least lop these hyperboreans from the American stem, and graft them on some Asian stock." The archaeological and human genetic evidence seems to support a more recent arrival for Eskimo-Aleut than for speakers of other languages of the Americas (see Willerslev and Meltzer 2021).

Na-Dene (Narrow Sense) (Athabaskan-Eyak-Tlingit [AET])
    Tlingit
    Eyak-Athabaskan
        *Eyak
        Athabaskan[4]
            Ahtna
            Tanaina
            Koyukon-Ingalik
                Ingalik (Deg Hit'an)
                *Holikachuk
                Koyukon
            Tanana
                Upper Kuskokwim (Kolchan)
                Lower Tanana
                Tanacross
                Upper Tanana

Tutchone
   Northern Tutchone
   Southern Tutchone
Kutchin-Han
   Gwich'in (Kutchin)
   Han
Central Cordillera
   *Tagish
   Tahltan
   Kaska
Southeastern Cordillera
   Sekani
   Beaver
Dene
   Slave (South Slavey)
   Mountain Slavey
   Bearlake (North Slavey)
   Hare (North Slavey)
   Dogrib
   Chipewyan (Dene Soun'line)
Babine-Carrier
   Babine
   Carrier
Chilcotin (Tsilhqot'in)
*Nicola
*Tsetsaut
Sarcee (Tsutina)
*Kwalhioqua-Clatskanie (Tlatskanie, Tlatskanai)
*Oregon Athabaskan
   *Upper Umpqua
   *Tututni
   *Galice-Applegate
   *Tolowa
California Athabaskan
   Hupa
   *Mattole
   *Eel River
   *Kato (Cahto)
Southern Athabaskan (Apachean)
   Navajo
   Western Apache
   Mescalero-Chiricahua
   Jicarilla
   *Lipan
   *Plains Apache (Kiowa Apache)

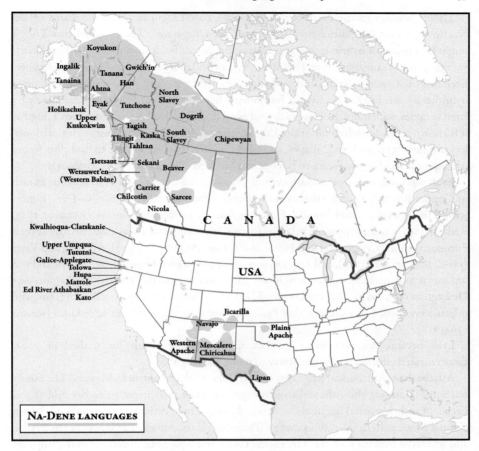

MAP 2.3. Na-Dene languages

Now the claim that Eyak-Athabaskan and Tlingit are distantly related appears to be solidly confirmed (Leer 2010). Edward Sapir's (1915b) original Na-Dene proposal grouped Tlingit and Athabaskan, along with Haida. Eyak had not yet been re-discovered by American linguists then (see below). However, Haida turns out not to be related, at least not demonstrably so (see below). It was removed from Na-Dene and is considered a language isolate. For that reason, *Narrow Sense* is added to the name of today's **Na-Dene** family to clarify that it is without Haida.

Na-Dene (Narrow Sense) is one of the largest language families in the Americas, in terms of both number of languages and the territory involved, from Alaska to Mexico.

Tlingit is spoken along the Alaska panhandle. It has moderate dialect differences, with more dialect differentiation in the south than in the north, leading to the supposition that Tlingit expansion moved from south to north (Krauss and Golla 1981, 67). The **Tongass** dialect is quite conservative and has preserved the internal stem contrasts of /Vh, Vʔ, V:ʔ, and V:/, whereas in the other dialects these have developed into vowels with tonal contrasts (Krauss 1979).

Tlingit belongs to the Northern Northwest Coast Linguistic Area, a subarea of the Northwest Coast Linguistics Area (Leer 1991; see Chapter 7). The proposal that Tlingit might be a mixed or hybrid language is interesting, but difficult to evaluate. Michael Krauss (1973b, 953–963) suggested that Tlingit may be a hybrid of Eyak-Athabaskan and some unrelated language (see also Krauss and Golla 1981, 67). Jeff Leer (1990, 1991) also views Tlingit as hybridized—not the Krauss' hybrid, but rather a hybridization or creolization of closely related varieties, with more than one variety of pre-Tlingit involved in the creation of Tlingit as it is known today. Such hybridization, Leer suggests, may explain such things as lexical doublets and variant phonological shapes, and why it is difficult in some cases to find clear sound correspondences for what seem to be cognates between Tlingit and Eyak-Athabaskan.[5]

Eyak was spoken along the south-central coast of Alaska from Yakutat to near the mouth of Copper River. Eyak and Athabaskan together form one branch of the Na-Dene family, with Tlingit as the other branch. Eyak was known in Russian sources (Rezanov 1805; Radloff 1857), and its possible relationship to other languages was discussed by several European scholars, Alexander von Humboldt (1809–1814[1811], 4:347), Adelung and Vater (1816), Buschmann (1856), and Aurel Krause (1885). However, Eyak fell out of sight and was unknown in American sources until it was rediscover in 1930 by Frederica De Laguna (see De Laguna 1937, 1990a; Birket-Smith and De Laguna 1938). John Wesley Powell (1891) and others were misled by opinions that Eyak was just a Tlingitized form of Eskimo (Krauss 1964, 128).[6]

Eyak became dormant when the last speaker, Marie Smith Jones, died in 2008. Concentrated efforts are now underway to revive the language.

Athabaskan. Athabaskan languages extend from Alaska to northern Mexico.[7] The family relationship among the Athabaskan languages has been recognized since the mid-1800s. Excellent early historical linguistic work was done by Emile Petitot (1876, 1889) and Adrien Gabriel Morice (1891, 1892, 1904, 1907). There are eleven Athabaskan languages in Alaska, and several in western Canada. The Pacific Coast and Apachean (Southern) subgroups are clear; the Pacific Coast subgroup is "more divergent from the [languages of the] North than is Apachean" (Krauss 1973b, 919, see also Thompson and Kinkade 1990, 30). **Kwalhioqua** in southwestern Washington and **Clatskanie** (Tlatskanai, Tlatskanie) in northwestern Oregon (together also called Lower Columbia Athabaskan) seem to have been not separate languages but a single language consisting of two dialects. Its subgrouping position within Athabaskan is not clear. It may not belong to the Pacific Coast subgroup. Thompson and Kinkade (1990, 31) considered Kwalhioqua-Tlatskanai probably an offshoot of the British Columbia languages.

Michael Krauss (1973b, 953) believed that Proto-Athabaskan and Proto-Eyak separated about 1500 BCE. Eyak is no more closely related to its geographically nearest Northern Athabaskan relative, Ahtna, than it is to, say, Navajo in the Southwest (Krauss and Golla 1981, 68). Proto-Athabaskan was unified until 500 BC or later (Krauss 1973b, 953; 1980, 11).

The reconstructed phonemes of Proto-Athabaskan are: /t, tl, d dl, t' tl', ł, ɬ, ts, dz, ts', s, z, č, ǰ, č', š, ž, čʷ, ǰʷ, č'ʷ, šʷ, žʷ, ḵ, g, ḵ', x̣, y̱, q, ɢ, q', χ, ʁ, qʷ, ɢʷ, q'ʷ, χʷ, ʁʷ, ʔ, h, w, y, w̃[m], ỹ[ñ/ŋ]; i, e, a, ə, ʊ, ɑ/ (Krauss and Golla 1981, 71; Krauss 1979; Cook and Rice 1989).

The Proto-Eyak-Athabaskans' homeland was apparently in the interior of eastern Alaska, perhaps also including the Yukon and parts of British Columbia. Many locate the

Proto-Athabaskan homeland along the Yukon River in interior northern British Columbia and in the southern Yukon (Golla 2007, 71). The area of greatest linguistic differentiation is in the Northern Athabaskan territory. The distribution of Athabaskan languages points to an interior origin; in Northern Athabaskan only the Tanaina occupied a coastline. The Eyak were on the coast but they had a land-based economy, contrasting with the maritime orientation of the Tlingit and Eskimoan groups. In Krauss and Golla's (1981, 68) hypothesized diversification and expansion of Athabaskan, Athabaskan spread from this homeland westward into Alaska and southward along the interior mountains to central and southern British Columbia (see also Kinkade 1991b, 152).

The Apachean (Southern Athabaskan) branch represents a relatively recent expansion into the Southwest. Many archaeologists believe Athabaskan arrived in the Southwest late, in the 1400s or early 1500s. That the Apachean languages came from the north was confirmed by Edward Sapir's (1936) famous linguistic proof of a northern origin. Apachean languages share a number of distinct innovations which demonstrate their status as a clear subgroup within the family. For example, Proto-Athabaskan labialized alveopalatal affricates ($\check{c}^w$, $\check{j}^w$, etc.) merged with their plain counterparts ($\check{c}$, $\check{j}$, etc.) in Apachean (see Young 1983, 394–396).

While many Athabaskan languages have tonal contrasts, Proto-Athabaskan lacked tone—a trait that can be shown to have developed from (Pre-)Proto-Athabaskan differences among *V, and *V? (and *V:) (Krauss 1979; see also Cook 1981; Cook and Rice 1989, 7; Krauss and Golla 1981, 69–71).[8] The lack of most labial consonants in Proto-Athabaskan and in most of its daughters is a striking feature. The vowels include the four "full" or long vowels (*i, *e, *a, *u) and the three "reduced" (or short) vowels (*ə, *ʊ, *a). The reduced vowels apparently could appear only in CVC syllables in Proto-Athabaskan stems (though CV syllable prefixes with reduced vowels, normally ə, could also occur). Distributional limitations of this sort have led some scholars to question the status of *ə (Cook and Rice 1989, 12–13).

Some of the more interesting sound changes that some of the Athabaskan languages have undergone include:

*ts > tl in Koyukon
*ts > kʷ in Bearlake (variant of Slavey-Hare) and in Dogrib
*ts > p in Mountain (variant of Slavey-Hare)
*ts > f in Hare
*ts > tθ in several (Holikachuk, Ingalik, Tanacross, Han, Tuchone, Slavey)
*čʷ > pf in Tsetsaut
*t > k in Yellowknife Chipewyan and in Kiowa Apache.

In comparison to these, most other Athabaskan sound changes are natural and mostly unremarkable (Krauss and Golla 1981; Cook 1981; Cook and Rice 1989).

Proto-Athabaskan contrasted nouns, verbs, particles, and postpositions. Nouns could bear possessive prefixes, while verbs were complex, potentially preceded by several inflectional and derivational prefixes. Traditionally, verb prefixes have been divided into two classes: conjunct (all those morphemes that were closer to the verb stem and more tightly bonded phonologically) and disjunct (also called preverbs or proclitics, the ones that were farther from the verb stem).

Ahtna is the language of eight communities along the Copper River and in the upper Susitna and Nenana drainages in south-central Alaska. The language has also been called Copper River and Mednovskiy. Its dialects are: Upper, Central, Lower, and Western.

Tanaina (Dena'ina) is the language of the Cook Inlet area of southern Alaska. Distinct local dialects are associated with the Kenai Peninsula, the Upper Inlet area above Anchorage, and coastal and inland areas of the west side of Cook Inlet.[9]

Tanana is a group of varieties spoken in east-central Alaska and adjacent Canada, from the upper Kuskokwim River to the headwaters of the Tanana River. Four languages are usually distinguished in the Tanana group: **Upper Kuskokwim**, **Lower Tanana**, **Tanacross**, and **Upper Tanana**. Speakers of the neighboring "languages" can usually understand one another, although with difficulty.

Upper Kuskokwim (or Kolchan) belongs to the Tanana group. It is spoken in the villages of Nikolai, Telida, and McGrath in the Upper Kuskokwim River drainage of central Alaska.

Lower Tanana, of the Tanana group, was originally spoken in a number of villages on the Tanana River in the vicinity of Fairbanks but now is spoken only at Nenana and Minto.

Tanacross, also of the Tanana group, is spoken at Healy Lake, Dot Lake, and Tanacross on the middle Tanana River of central Alaska.

Upper Tanana belongs to the Tanana group also. It is spoken primarily in the Alaska villages of Northway, Tetlin, and Tok, but also in the Beaver Creek area of the Yukon. Each of these communities has a different local variety.

Koyukon is the language of eleven villages along the Koyukuk and middle Yukon Rivers of central Alaska. It is the most widespread Athabaskan language in Alaska. It has three dialects, Upper, Central, and Lower. Koyukon was carefully documented in the early 1900s by Jules Jetté, a Jesuit missionary.[10]

Ingalik (Deg Xinag) is spoken in west-central Alaska at Shageluk and Anvik and in the multilingual community at Holy Cross on the lower Yukon River in Alaska.[11]

Holikachuk, also in west-central Alaska, was spoken at Holikachuk on the Innoko River, now located at Grayling on the lower Yukon River. It is intermediate between Ingalik and Koyukon, not identified as a separate language until the 1970s. The last native speaker, Wilson "Tiny" Deacon, died in 2012.

Northern Tutchone and **Southern Tutchone**. Northern Tutchone is spoken in the Yukon in Mayo, Pelly Crossing, Stewart Crossing, and Carmacks. Thomas Canham, Anglican archdeacon, undertook early documentation of the language in the 1890s, but most of his work remains unpublished in manuscript form. **Southern Tutchone** is spoken in the southwestern Yukon, at Aishihik, Burwash Landing, Champagne, Haines Junction, Kloo Lake, Klukshu, and Lake Laberge, as well as in the city of Whitehorse.

Gwich'in (Kutchin) is spoken in northeastern Alaska in Arctic Village, Venetie, Fort Yukon, Chalkyitsik, Circle, and Birch Creek, as well as in Aklavik, Inuvik, Tsiigehtchic (formerly Arctic Red River), and Fort McPherson in the Northwest Territories, and in Old Crow in the Yukon Territory. Western (Alaskan) and Eastern (Canadian) dialects are distinguished; the Canadian varieties are often called **Loucheux**.[12]

Han (Hän, Haen), a Northern Athabaskan language, is spoken in the village of Eagle, Alaska, and in Dawson City, Yukon Territory.[13]

Dene was used synonymously with "Athabaskan" formerly in Canada, but is now used to name a complex of Athabaskan varieties and emergent languages in the Mackenzie River drainage of northwestern Canada, primarily in the Northwest Territories but also extending into parts of northern British Columbia, Alberta, Saskatchewan, and Manitoba. There are three major Dene languages, **Slavey**, **Dogrib**, and **Chipewyan**. Slavey can be further divided into **Bearlake** and **Hare** (together constituting **North Slavey**), **Mountain**, and **Slave** or **South Slavey**. There is a moderate degree of mutual intelligibility across the Dene complex, but this extends as well to some other adjacent Athabaskan languages, particularly to **Beaver**, **Sekani**, and **Kaska**, that are not usually called Dene. This usage of the name "Dene" is based on social and political criteria more than on linguistic grounds.

Tagish is closely related to **Tahltan** and **Kaska**. Tahltan and Kaska are mutually intelligible. Until the mid-nineteenth century Tagish was spoken around the lakes at the head of the Yukon River south of Whitehorse. In the later nineteenth century the Tagish community shifted their language to Tlingit and by the mid-twentieth century only a handful of older people remembered Tagish from their childhood. Lucy Wren, believed to be the last native speaker of Tagish, died in 2008.

Tahltan is the language of remote Telegraph Creek, on the upper Stikine River in northwestern British Columbia. It is also spoken in the mixed Sekani-Tahltan community of Iskut, at Kinaskan Lake.[14]

Kaska (Danezāgé') is spoken in the southeastern Yukon at Ross River, Watson Lake and Upper Liard, and in northern British Columbia at Lower Post, Fireside, Good Hope Lake, Dease Lake, and Muncho Lake. Kaska territory adjoins that of Tahltan and Tagish in the southwest and Sekani on the southeast. There is a high degree of mutual intelligibility among these languages and the adjoining dialects of Kaska.

Sekani (Tse'khene) is spoken in two remote north-central British Columbia communities, Ware and Fort McLeod, and also by some people in the Beaver community of Prophet River and the Tahltan community of Iskut. There is a fair degree of mutual intelligibility between Sekani and Beaver, Kaska, and Tahltan.

Beaver (Dane-Zaa) is spoken in eastern British Columbia in Doig, Blueberry, Hudson Hope, and Prophet River, and in northwestern Alberta in Horse Lakes, Clear Hills, Boyer River, and Rock Lane. Beaver is partially intelligible to speakers of the emergent languages in the Dene dialect complex, but for political and geographical reasons it is usually considered a separate Dene language.

Slavey is the general term for a group of Athabaskan dialects or emergent languages of the Dene complex that includes **Bearlake** and **Hare** (together constituting **North Slavey**), **Mountain**, and **Slave** or **South Slavey**.

The name *Slavey* (also *Slave*, from *Slavé*) is thought to come from attaching the French suffix *-ais* (as in *anglais* 'English', *francais* 'French') to English *slave*. It is believed to be a translation of Cree *awahka:n* 'captive, slave', and sometimes 'stranger'. It was reported that the Cree pejoratively called groups of Athabaskans "slave" whom they had driven out of the Lake Athabasca area in late precontact times (Asch and Goddard 1981, 347–348).

Slave, or **South Slavey**, is an emergent language in the Slavey dialect region of the Dene complex (mentioned above). Slave is one of the official languages of the Northwest Territories. It is spoken in the Northwest Territories and in adjacent parts of northern British

Columbia and Alberta. Its principal Northwest Territories communities include: Fort Liard, Fort Providence, Fort Simpson, Hay River Dene, Jean Marie River, Nahanni Butte, and Trout Lake, and some speakers in Hay River. In northern British Columbia the main community where it is spoken is Fort Nelson. In Alberta Slave is spoken at Meander River, Chateh Lake (Assumption), and at a few other places on the upper Hay River.

Mountain (Mountain Slavey) is an emergent language in the Slavey dialects of the Dene complex. In the Northwest Territories it is principally spoken at Fort Wrigley, and by some people in Tulita (formerly Fort Norman). There are also speakers of Mountain Slavey in the Yukon at Fort Liard and at Ross River.

Bearlake is another emergent language in the North Slavey group of Slavey dialects of the Dene complex. It is spoken in two communities in the Northwest Territories, at Déline (formerly Fort Franklin) and Tulita. At Déline, Bearlake is the lingua franca of a dialectally mixed community, and many speakers are also fluent in Dogrib. At Tulita, there are speakers of Bearlake who also speak Mountain.

Hare is another emergent language in the North Slavey group of Slavey dialects of the Dene complex. It is spoken in Northwest Territories at Colville Lake and Fort Good Hope. The name reflects the Hare people's dependence on hare for food and clothing.

Dogrib is a language of the Dene complex, spoken in the Northwest Territories between Great Slave Lake and Great Bear Lake, in Detah, Rae Lakes, Rae-Edzo, Snare Lake, and Wha Ti. There are also speakers in Yellowknife, as well as speakers in the dialectally mixed community of Déline, where Bearlake is the lingua franca.[15]

Chipewyan (Dene Soun'line) is a language of the Dene complex spoken in communities across a large area in the forest and tundra of northern Alberta, Saskatchewan, Manitoba, and the eastern Northwest Territories. The language has official language status in the Northwest Territories.[16]

Babine (Bulkley Valley/Lakes District Language) is spoken on Bulkley River and in the Lake Babine area of central British Columbia to the north and west of the Carrier dialect complex. Although there is a tradition of grouping Babine with Carrier—and Babine has sometimes been referred to as "Northern Carrier"—there is a sharp linguistic and cultural boundary between the two speech communities. Babine has two clearly differentiated dialects. The western dialect, usually called **Wetsuwet'en**, includes the Bulkley River communities of Hagwilget, Moricetown, Smithers, Houston, and Broman Lake and the Nee-Tahi-Buhn and Skin Tayi bands at Burns Lake. The eastern dialect, "**Babine proper**," includes the Lake Babine and Takla Lake communities, as well as some now in Burns Lake.

Carrier is the general term for a complex of dialects in central British Columbia, adjoining but distinct from Babine on the northwest and Chilcotin on the south. Carrier is called locally **Dakelh**. Its local varieties are traditionally divided into "Upper Carrier" in the communities to the north of Fort St. James, around Stuart and Trembleur Lakes, and "Lower Carrier" in communities to the south. Lower Carrier distinguishes a Fraser/Nechako dialect group (Prince George, Cheslatta, Stoney Creek, Nautley, and Stellakoh) and a Blackwater dialect group (Ulkatcho, Kluskus, Nazko, Red Bluff, and Anahim Lake). A Carrier lingua franca was established by Catholic missionaries, most notably by Father Adrien Gabriel Morice, in the nineteenth century, based on the dialect around Fort St. James, and a syllabic writing system was introduced.[17]

Chilcotin (Tsilhqot'in) is spoken in south-central British Columbia, and in several communities along the Chilco and Chilcotin Rivers in the vicinity of Williams Lake, including Alexis Creek, Anaham, Nemaiah Valley, Stone, and Toosey, as well as at Alexandria on the Fraser River. Although Chilcotin adjoins Carrier on the north and there are several communities in which both languages are spoken, the two languages are quite distinct and are not mutually intelligible.

Nicola is dormant. It was spoken in the Nicola and Similkameen Valleys of south-central British Columbia, adjoining Thompson (Salishan) territory. It is known only from fragmentary wordlists that are not sufficient for determining where it fits within the Athabaskan language family, though it appears to be most closely related to Chilcotin.

Tsetsaut, now dormant, was spoken on Portland Canal, on the north coast of British Columbia adjacent to Nass-Gitksan territory. It is known only from a vocabulary collected by Franz Boas in 1894; these data are, however, sufficient to show that Tsetsaut constituted a distinct subgroup of Athabaskan on its own.

Sarcee (Tsuut'ina) also constitutes a separate subgroup on its own within the Athabaskan family. It is the only northern Athabaskan language spoken by a Plains group. The Tsuut'ina First Nation is located directly east of Calgary, Alberta.

Kwalhioqua-Clatskanie was formerly spoken in two separate areas along the lower Columbia River, with the Kwalhioqua to the north of the river and the Clatskanie to the south, separated by the territory of the Lower Chinook and Cathlamet. The Kwalhioqua, along the Willapa River in southwestern Washington, had two subgroups, the Willapa and the Suwal. The Kwalhioqua-Clatskanie people were dispersed among Coast Salish tribes in the nineteenth century.[18]

Upper Umpqua belongs to the Oregon Athabaskan subgroup. It was spoken in the upper drainage of the Umpqua River, southwestern Oregon. After the Rogue River War of 1855–1856, the Upper Umpquas were forcibly resettled on the Grand Ronde and Siletz Reservations. The last speaker, believed to be John Warren, died in about 1940.

Tututni also is a member of the Oregon Athabaskan subgroup, formerly spoken along the Oregon coast from the Coquille River to just north of the California border. There were several distinct local varieties; best attested of these are **Coquille**, **Euchre Creek**, and **Chasta Costa**. After the Rogue River War of 1855–1856 the Tututnis were resettled on the Grand Ronde and Siletz Reservations. The last fluent speaker died in 1983.

Galice-Applegate, of the Oregon subgroup of Athabaskan, was spoken along Galice Creek and Applegate River, which are tributaries of the Rogue River in southwestern Oregon. Only the Galice Creek dialect is well attested though there was at least one other dialect. After the Rogue River War of 1855–1856, the Galice-Applegate people were also forcibly resettled on the Grand Ronde and Siletz Reservations, where the language became dormant.

Tolowa is a language of the Oregon subgroup of Athabaskan. It was spoken in the Smith River Rancheria near Crescent City, California. Its last native speakers died before 1990.

Hupa belongs to the California subgroup of Athabaskan. It is spoken on the Hoopa Valley Reservation in northwest California. There is only one native speaker, Verdena Parker (born 1936), with a small number of semi-speakers and second-language learners. All of the other California Athabaskan languages are dormant. Victor Golla (2011, 76) spoke of the "Hupa-Chilula" language, saying it had "two shallowly differentiated local dialects: Hupa... and **Chilula-Whilkut**."

Mattole, a California Athabaskan language, was spoken along the Mattole and Bear Rivers near Cape Mendocino. There were two distinct dialects, the **Mattole River** and **Bear River** dialects. The last native speaker died in the 1950s.

Eel River Athabaskan belongs to the California subgroup of Athabaskan. It was a complex of closely related dialects along the Eel River and its major tributaries in Humboldt and Mendocino Counties. Four dialect clusters are often distinguished: **Sinkyone**, **Nongatl**, **Lassik**, and **Wailaki**. There have been no fluent speakers since before 1970.[19]

Kato (Cahto), of the California Athabaskan subgroup, was spoken in Cahto Valley, near Laytonville. Between 1905 and 1910 Pliny Earle Goddard published a grammatical sketch and a volume of narrative texts on the language. The last native speaker died in the 1960s.

Navajo (Diné Bizaad) is a member of the Southern Athabaskan (Apachean) subgroup. This subgroup is actually a dialect complex; there is some degree of mutual intelligibility between Navajo and the other emergent languages of the Southern Athabaskan group, in particular with Western Apache, though the Navajo and Apache communities have been politically and culturally distinct since at least the early eighteenth century. Navajo is the largest Indigenous language of North America in terms of number of speakers, with estimates from 120,000 to 170,000 speakers now.[20]

Western Apache is an emergent language in the Southern Athabaskan (Apachean) subgroup/dialect complex, spoken in several reservation communities in southeastern Arizona: San Carlos Reservation, Ft. Apache Reservation (White Mountain Apache Tribe), Tonto Reservation at Payson, the Camp Verde Reservation (shared with Yavapais), and Ft. McDowell Reservation near Scottsdale (shared with Yavapais and Mojaves).

Mescalero-Chiricahua is another emergent language of the Southern Athabaskan subgroup/dialect complex. There is very little dialect difference among speakers whose tribal identity is Mescalero or Chiricahua. They are now located at the Mescalero Tribe of New Mexico and Ft. Sill in southwestern Oklahoma, the principal Chiricahua community. Geronimo was a famous Chiricahua leader.

Jicarilla (Jicarilla Apache) is also an emergent language of the Southern Athabaskan (Apachean) subgroup/dialect complex. It is spoken on the Jicarilla Reservation in northeastern New Mexico.

Lipan was another emergent language of the Southern Athabaskan subgroup/dialect complex. In the eighteenth century it was spoken by several bands of Plains Apaches in south-central Texas; during the nineteenth century the Lipan amalgamated with other Apache groups; now their descendants are on the Mescalero Reservation in southeastern New Mexico, with the Mescalero and the Chiricahua. Lipan no longer has any native speakers. It is poorly documented.

Plains Apache (Kiowa Apache) is a Southern Athabaskan language, distinct from the other varieties in the Southern Athabaskan subgroup/dialect complex. It was spoken in Caddo County, western Oklahoma, by the descendants of an Apache band that joined the Kiowas in the eighteenth century. The last native speaker of the language passed away in 2008.

Edward Vajda (2010, 2018) argued that Na-Dene and Yeniseian (of central Siberia) are genetically related. Though several linguists look favorably on this classification, it has not held up (see Chapter 6 for an evaluation of it).

Haida (Xaad kil, X̱aat Kíl, X̱aadas Kíl, X̱aayda Kil)

Haida is spoken on Queen Charlotte Island, south of the Tlingit area. An eighteenth-century migration from Masset resulted in a few Haida also living in Alaska, in the villages of Hydaburg, Kasaan, and Craig on the southern half of Prince of Wales Island, as well as in Ketchikan. The two main varieties of Haida, **Masset** and **Skidegate**, are emergent languages; opinion differs concerning whether they constitute distinct languages or are only divergent dialects of a single language. (See Map 7.1.)

Edward Sapir (1915b) proposed joining Haida with Athabaskan and Tlingit in his Na-Dené super-stock hypothesis, but most specialists now find no reliable evidence that would allow Haida to be classified with these other Na-Dené (Narrow Sense) languages. Haida, thus, is considered by most to be a language isolate, or possibly a very small family if Masset and Skidegate are thought to be separate languages (see Leer 1990, 1991; Levine 1979; Campbell 1997a; Campbell and Poser 2008, 280–283). A very few scholars still believe that it may be possible to connect Haida with the Na-Dene languages (Enrico 2004; Pinnow 1985, 2006).

Tsimshianic (Tsimshian) (British Columbia, Alaska)
  Nass-Gitksan (Interior Tsimshianic)
    Nisga'a
    Gitksan
  Maritime Tsimshian
    Southern Tsimshian (Sküüx̱s, Skixs)
    Coast Tsimshian (Sm'algyax)

(See Map 7.1.)

The name *Tsimshian* is often used in two different ways. It is the term used in much of the literature to refer to the entire Tsimshianic language family. At the same time, it is often used as a synonym for Coast Tsimshian (Sm'algyax), an emergent language in the Maritime Tsimshian branch in Tsimshianic.[21]

The Tsimshianic varieties are closely related to one another, and there is some difference of opinion about whether they represent separate languages or merely divergent dialects of the same language. Even with the assumption of separate languages, there is some difference of opinion about whether four, three, or only two Tsimshianic languages are involved. The four would be Coast Tshimsian, Southern Tsimshian, Gitksan, and Nisga'a (Nass). In the view that there are just two languages, Coast Tsimshian and Southern Tsimshian (Sm'algyax) are considered dialects of the single Maritime Tsimshian language, with Gitksan and Nisga'a (Nass) as dialects of Nass-Gitksan (Interior Tsimshianic) (see Thompson arid Kinkade 1990, 33; Tarpent 1997).

Marie-Lucie Tarpent's (1997, 70) tentative reconstruction of Proto-Tsimshianic has the following consonants: /p, t, ts, k, kʷ, q, qʷ, p', t' ts', k', kʷ', q, qʷ', s, ɬ, x, χ, xʷ, χʷ, ɬ, l, w, y, l', w', y', m, n, m', n', h, hʷ, ʔ, ʔʷ/. (The sounds *l'*, *w'*, *y'*, *m'*, *n'*, *m'*, and *n'* are glottalized.)

Tsimshianic has been associated with Edward Sapir's (1929a) Penutian hypothesis. Most scholars do not find the evidence for this convincing, though Tarpent (1996, 1997, 2000, 2002) believes some support can be found.

Nass-Gitksan, the more northerly of the two branches of the Tsimshianic family, consists of two emergent languages. **Nisga'a** (Nisgha, Nishgha) is spoken in four village communities along the Nass River. **Gitksan** is spoken in six villages along the Skeena River upriver from Coast Tsimshian.

Maritime Tsimshian is the more southern branch of the Tsimshianic language family. It has two markedly different dialects or possibly emergent languages. **Southern Tsimshian** (Sküüx̱s, Skixs) was spoken along the coast south of the Skeena River and on a few islands; it is now dormant. **Coast Tsimshian** (Sm'algyax, often referred to simply as Tsimshian) is spoken near Terrace on the lower Skeena River and on the coast near the Skeena estuary, as well as at one location in southern Alaska.

Wakashan
    Northern Wakashan
        Haisla
        Heiltsuk-Oowekyala
        Kwak'wala (Kwakiutl)
    Southern Wakashan (Nootkan)
        Nuu-chah-nulth (Nootka)[22]
        Nitinaht (Ditidaht)
        *Makah

(See Map 7.1.)

Wakashan languages are located in British Columbia on Vancouver Island, and in the northwest corner of the Olympic Peninsula in Washington state. The relationship between Northern Wakashan and Southern Wakashan (Nootkan) was postulated already by Franz Boas (1889a[1888]) and was included in Powell's classification (1891).[23]

The Wakashan languages are in the Northwest Coast Linguistic Area and thus share a number of features with other languages of the area (see Chapter 7). Nitinaht and Makah (but not Nuu-chah-nulth [Nootka]) belong to a smaller linguistic subarea in which the languages of several different families lack primary nasals. Thus Nitinaht and Makah have changed their original nasals to voiced stops (*m > *m' > b'; *n > d, *n' > d')[24] under the influence of the other nasalless languages in the area. Nitinaht and Nuu-chah-nulth have changed certain original uvulars to pharyngeals (*q', *qʷ' > ʕ, and *χ, *χʷ > ħ). The widely diffused sound change of *k > č affected the Wakashan languages, as well as several Salishan, Chimakuan, and other Northwest Coast languages (Sapir 1926; Jacobsen 1979b).

The original homeland of the Wakashan family appears to have been mainly on Vancouver Island, although it is assumed to have also included a part of the mainland to the east and north. Maritime culture is strongly reflected in the specialized vocabulary and grammar of these languages—for example, there are suffixes in Kwak'wala (Kwakiutl) and Nuu-chah-nulth (Nootka) that designate activities located on the beach, rocks, and sea (Lincoln and Rath 1980; Kinkade et al. 1998).

The Mosan hypothesis would have grouped Wakashan, Chimakuan, and Salishan together in a larger putative family, but Mosan is now thoroughly abandoned (see Campbell and Poser 2008, 190–191).

Haisla is the northernmost Northern Wakashan language, spoken in northwestern British Columbia adjacent to Coast Tsimshian. The main Haisla community is Kitamaat. The present population of Kitamaat came from different sources, bringing some language differences with them. The two most notable ones are **Kitimaat** (X̄a'islak'ala) and **Kitlope** (X̄enaksialak'ala).[25]

Heiltsuk-Oowekyala is a Northern Wakashan language, spoken on the coast of British Columbia south of Haisla and Coast Tsimshian and north of Kwak'wala (Kwakiutl). It has two markedly distinct dialects or emergent languages, **Heiltsuk** (a.k.a. Bella Bella) and **Oowekyala**. Heiltsuk is spoken mainly in two communities, Bella Bella and Kitasoo (or Klemtu) —Kitasoo is in former Southern Tsimshian territory.[26]

Kwak'wala (Kwakiutl) is the southernmost of the three Northern Wakashan languages. It has several local varieties on the central coast of British Columbia from Smith Sound to Cape Mudge, and on the northern third of Vancouver Island. The main communities are Campbell River, Cape Mudge, Fort Rupert, Mamaleleqala, Nimpkish (Alert Bay), Nuwitti, Qualicum, Quatsino, Tanakteuk, Tlowitsis-Mumtagilia, Tsawataineuk, and Tsulquate.

Nuu-chah-nulth (Nootka) is a Southern Wakashan (Nootkan) language, spoken on the west coast of Vancouver Island from Cape Cook to Barkley Sound. The name *Nuu-chah-nulth* was adopted in 1985 to represent the fifteen bands formerly known as Nootka. "Nuuchahnulth" is used locally to include also Nitinaht, although Nitinaht is a very different language.[27]

Nitinaht (Ditidaht) is also a member of the Southern Wakashan (Nootkan) subgroup. It is the language of two groups on the west coast of Vancouver Island to the south of Nuu-chah-nulth (Nootka) territory, organized as the Ditidaht and Pacheenaht Bands. Although the Nitinahts were traditionally part of the Nootkan interaction sphere (and the Ditidaht Band is represented on the Nuu-chah-nulth Tribal Council), the Nitinaht language is very different from Nuu-chah-nulth, more closely related to Makah within the Southern Wakashan subgroup.

Makah is the third Southern Wakashan (Nootkan) language, formerly spoken by the Makah Tribe at Neah Bay on the northwest tip of the Olympic Peninsula, Washington state. Within the Southern Wakashan subgroup, Makah is more closely related to Nitanaht than to Nuu-chah-nulth (Nootka). Makah lost its last native speaker in 2002; very active revitalization efforts are underway.

Salishan
  Nuxalk (Bella Coola)
  Central Salish
    Comox (Éy7á7juuthem)
    *Pentlatch
    Sechelt (She shashishalhem; Sháshísháḷh, Shashishalhem)
    Squamish (Sḵwx̱wú7mesh sníchim)
    Halkomelem (Halq'eméylem)
    *Nooksack (Lhéchalosem, Lhéchelesem)
    Northern Straits Salish
    *Klallam (Clallam) (Nəxʷsƛ̕ay̕əmúcən)
    Lushootseed (xʷəlšucid, dxʷləšúcid)
    *Twana (təw'ánəxʷ)

*Tsamosan
    *Quinault
    *Lower Chehalis
    *Upper Chehalis
    *Cowlitz
*Tillamook
Interior Salish
    Lillooet (St'át'imcets)
    Thompson (Nłeʔkepmxcín)
    Shuswap (Secwepemctsin)
    Okanagan (Nsyilxcən)
    Spokane-Kalispel (Flathead) (Kalispel-Spokane-Pend d'Oreille-Salish)
    Coeur d'Alene (Snchitsu'umshtsn)
    Columbian (Nxaʔamxcín)

(See Davis 2019, 452–453) for a more detailed classification of Salishan languages with principal dialects.)
    (See 2.4. Salishan Languages.)

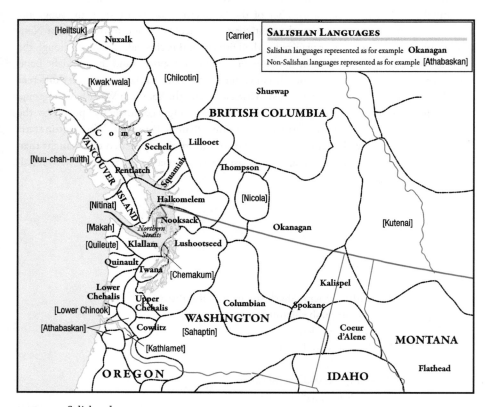

MAP 2.4. Salishan languages

The Salishan family comprised about twenty-two languages with considerable diversification. They extend from the coast and southern interior of British Columbia southward to the central coast of Oregon and eastward to northwestern Montana and northern Idaho.

Nuxalk (Bella Coola) is spoken by members of the Bella Coola Band in Bella Coola on the north-central coast of British Columbia. The term **Nuxalk**, the native name for Bella Coola Valley, was adopted by the Band around 1980 to designate the language and its speakers that are from that place. Nuxalk (Bella Coola) by itself is a subgroup of the Salishan language family. It is isolated geographically from the other Salishan languages and has been heavily influenced by the neighboring Wakashan languages, Haisla and Heiltsuk-Oowekyala.

Comox (Éy7á7juuthem) is a member of the Central Salish subgroup of Salishan. It is spoken at the north end of the Strait of Georgia, British Columbia, both on the mainland and on the east coast of Vancouver Island. **Island Comox** and **Mainland Comox** dialects are recognized, with Mainland Comox divided into three varieties associated, respectively, with the Homalco, Klahoose, and Sliammon Bands.[28]

Pentlatch, a Central Salish language, was spoken on the east coast of Vancouver Island to the south of the Island Comox. The last speaker died in 1940.

Sechelt (She shashishalhem) is a Central Salish language spoken by members of the Sechelt Band, on the north coast of the Strait of Georgia, British Columbia.

Squamish (Sḵwx̱wú7mesh sníchim) is a Central Salish language, spoken on the Squamish reserves at Howe Sound and Burrard Inlet, British Columbia, on the Strait of Georgia just north of the city of Vancouver.

Halkomelem (Halq'eméylem) belongs to the Central Salish subgroup of Salishan. It is spoken in a number of small communities in southwestern British Columbia along the lower Fraser River and on the east coast of Vancouver Island. Three dialects are recognized: **Island Halkomelem**, southeast coast of Vancouver Island, spoken in local varieties at Malahat, Cowichan, Halalt, Chemainus, Penelakut, Nanaimo, and Nanoose; **Downriver Halkomelem**, at the mouth of the Fraser River in and around the city of Vancouver; and **Upriver Halkomelem** (Sto:lo), in the Fraser River Valley.

Nooksack (Lhéchalosem, Lhéchelesem) is a Central Salish language. It was spoken around Bellingham, northwest Washington, between Halkomelem and Lushootseed. The language is said to have become dormant with the death of Sindick Jimmy in 1988.[29]

Northern Straits Salish also belongs to the Central Salish subgroup of Salishan, spoken on the southern tip of Vancouver Island, the San Juan Islands, and the mainland just south of the US-Canadian border. It has three well-known dialects, spoken in a number of small communities: the **Saanich** (Senćoten) dialect on Vancouver Island, the **Samish** (Si, Námeś) dialect of the San Juan Islands, and the **Lummi** (Xwlemi Chosen) dialect of the mainland. Lummi no longer has any first-language speakers.[30]

Klallam (Clallam) (Nəxʷsƛ̕ay̕əmúcən, S'klallam, Na'klallam) is a Central Salish language on the north shore of the Olympic Peninsula in Washington. It is loosely related to Northern Straits Salish, and the two are sometimes grouped together as "Straits Salish." The main Klallam communities are on three small reservations, Port Gamble, Lower Elwha, and Jamestown. There is also a Klallam community on the Becher Bay Reserve on Vancouver Island. Klallam is dormant; there are no first-language speakers now.

Lushootseed belongs to the Central Salish subgroup and is a complex of closely related dialects spoken in the Puget Sound area of Washington state. It was called Puget Sound Salish in older sources. The main modern communities where Lushootseed is the heritage language include the Upper Skagit, Swinomish, Suquamish, Muckleshoot, Puyallup, and Nisqually Reservations, and especially the Tulalip Reservation near Marysville. Lushootseed has had no first-language speakers since 2008.[31]

Twana, also a Central Salish language, was spoken along Hood Canal on the east side of the Olympic Peninsula in Washington. The Twana were concentrated on the Skokomish Reservation in 1859. The last fluent speaker died in 1980.

Quinault is one of the four languages of the Tsamosan subgroup of Salishan. It was spoken on the west coast of the Olympic Peninsula in Washington state, south of Quileute. Much of that territory is now the Quinault Reservation, which the Quinault descendants share with several other tribes, including the closely related Lower Chehalis. The last first-language speaker of Quinault is believed to have been chief Oliver Grover Mason (a.k.a. Tax-o-la Wi-e-le); he died in 1996.

Lower Chehalis, of the Tsamosan subgroup of Salishan, was spoken in several local varieties along the lower Chehalis River and around Grays Harbor and Shoalwater Bay on the coast in southwest Washington. Most Lower Chehalis descendants live on the Shoalwater Bay Reservation; some are on the Quinault Reservation. The language is dormant.[32]

Upper Chehalis is another of the four Tsamosan languages in the Salishan family. It was spoken on the upper Chehalis River, southwestern Washington. Most Upper Chehalis descendants live on the Chehalis Reservation, west of Centralia, which they share with the descendants of several other groups. The last first-language speaker died in 2001.

Cowlitz is the last of the four Tsamosan languages in the Salishan family. It was formerly spoken along the Cowlitz River in southwestern Washington. Cowlitz descendants live in scattered locations in and around their former territory. The language is very poorly documented, and there are no known native speakers.[33]

Tillamook constitutes a Salishan subgroup with only this one member. It was spoken in several varieties along the northwest coast of Oregon, from the Nehalem River to the Siletz River. The last speaker, thought to be Minnie Scovell, died in 1972.

Lillooet (Stʼatʼimcets) is a member of the Interior Salish subgroup, in southwestern British Columbia. It has two major dialect clusters, **Upper Lillooet**, in and around Fountain and Lillooet on the Fraser River, and **Lower Lillooet**, in and around Mount Currie, near Pemberton, on the Lillooet River.

Thompson (Nłeʔkepmxcin) is an Interior Salish language, spoken along the Fraser River Canyon in southwest British Columbia and along the Thompson and Nicola Rivers. There is a dialect distinction between Upper Thompson varieties in northern Thompson territory and Lower Thompson varieties in the south. The principal modern settlements are at Lytton on the Fraser River and at Lower Nicola and Merritt in Nicola Valley.

Shuswap (Secwepemctsin) is an Interior Salish language spoken in east-central British Columbia along the Fraser River and its tributaries, upstream from Lillooet and Thompson, adjoining Chilcotin and Carrier territory in the north. The modern Shuswap are organized into seventeen bands, with the largest settlement at Kamloops on the Thompson River.

Okanagan (Nsyilxcən), of the Interior Salish subgroup of Salishan, is spoken in a number of communities in southern interior British Columbia and northeastern Washington. There are seven Okanagan Reserves in British Columbia: Vernon, Douglas Lake, Westbank, Penticton, Keremeos (Lower Similkameen), Hedley (Upper Similkameen), and Oliver (Osoyoos).

Spokane-Kalispel (Kalispel-Spokane-Pend d'Oreille-Salish) is a Salishan language of the Interior Salish subgroup. It is spoken in Washington, Idaho, and Montana, in three principal dialects. The **Spokane** dialect is spoken on the Spokane Reservation in northeastern Washington. The **Flathead** dialect (also called **Montana Salish**) is spoken on the Flathead Reservation in western Montana, home of the Confederated Salish and Kootenay Tribes. **Kalispel** is sometimes considered distinct from Montana Salish, the language of the **Bitterroot Salish** and the **Pend d'Oreille**. The **Kalispel** dialect primarily survives on the Kalispel Reservation in northeastern Washington. A few speakers live on the Spokane Reservation and in the nearby community of Chewelah. Flathead speakers of **Pend d'Oreille** descent are said to have a subdialect.

Coeur d'Alene (Snchitsu'umshtsn) is a severely endangered Salishan language of the Interior Salish subgroup spoken on the Coeur d'Alene Reservation in northern Idaho.

Columbian (a.k.a. Nxaʔamxcín, Columbia-Moses, Columbia-Wenatchi) is a member of the Interior Salish subgroup, once spoken in a number of local dialects along the Columbia River in north-central Washington. Best known of these varieties are **Columbia** (Sinkiuse, Columbian) and **Wenatchi** (Wenatchee, Entiat, Chelan). The language is severely endangered; most of the remaining speakers are on or near the Colville Reservation.

The inventory of Proto-Salishan phonemes given by Sarah Thomason (2006, 733) has the following sounds: /p, t, c, k, kʷ, q, qʷ, ʔ, p', t', tl', c', k', kʷ', q', qʷ', ɬ, s, x, xʷ, χ, χʷ, (h), m, n, (r), l, y, (r'), l', ŋ'ʷ, y', ʕ, ʕʷ, ʕ', ʕ'ʷ, w, y, w', y'; i, a, ə, u/.[34] Though the system includes *tl' (a glottalized lateral affricate), no plain counterpart tl existed. Dale Kinkade (1998) argued that *ə should not be reconstructed in Proto-Salishan. Salishan languages are well known for long complex consonant clusters.

Proto-Salishan grammar appears to have had several kinds of reduplication, a gender contrast (feminine vs. non-feminine), partly ergative alignment, an elaborate system of suffixation (marking categories of aspect, transitivity, control, voice, person, and causation), "lexical" suffixes (that refer to what in other languages would usually be coded as independent lexical items, referring to body parts, common objects in nature, or culturally salient objects), and a claimed lack of clear contrast between noun and verb as distinct lexical categories (Thompson and Kinkade 1990, 33; Kinkade et al. 1998; Paul Kroeber 1999).

Based on more than 140 reconstructed terms for Proto-Salishan plants and animals, Dale Kinkade argued that they indicate a coastal rather than an interior homeland for Proto-Salishan, but that the speakers of Proto-Salishan "must also have had access to mountains, in particular the Cascade Mountains, because they had names for mountain goats and hoary marmots, both of which are found only at higher elevations" (Kinkade 1991b, 147).

Kinkade suspected that expansion from this homeland area would have been rapid, with little obstruction. While the Interior Salishan split may represent one of the earliest divisions within the Salishan family, expansion into the interior may have been one of later movements by branches of the family. Kinkade et al. (1998) believed that from a homeland along the lower Fraser River, the most likely expansion of Salish into the Plateau would be along the Fraser and Thompson Rivers, then down the Okanogan and Columbia Rivers into eastern Washington. Nuxalk (Bella Coola), the most divergent and most northerly Salishan language, may have had an interior origin, as suggested by the fact that a majority of its terms for coastal species are borrowed from Wakashan languages and it shares uniquely some cognates with Interior Salishan languages (Kinkade 1991b, 149–150).

As mentioned, Edward Sapir (1929a) had proposed to group Salishan, Wakashan, and Chimakuan in the now abandoned Mosan, "effectively debunked" (Davis 2019, 454). Some scholars proposed a possible Salishan-Kutenai connection (see Haas 1965; Morgan 1991; Bakker 2006). Although this is not implausible, it is not a strong hypothesis (Dryer 2007). Various other even broader classifications that include Salishan have been made, though without convincing evidence (see Chapter 6).

*Chimakuan
  *Chemakum
  *Quileute

The small Chimakuan family must have been located in the northern part of the Olympic Peninsula of western Washington before intrusion from the north by Makah (Nootkan) and Klallam (Clallam) (a Central Salish language). The Olympic Peninsula was apparently the homeland of Proto-Chimakuan. Chimakuan speakers in historical times have had a discontinuous distribution, with Chemakum in the northeast corner and Quileute on the northwest coast of the peninsula. Nevertheless, earlier these and perhaps other Chimakuan groups must have occupied a continuous territory as neighbors on the Olympic Peninsula and perhaps elsewhere in northwestern Washington (Collins 1949; Kinkade 1991b, 151). (See Maps 2.4. and 7.1.)

Jay Powell's (1993, 454) inventory of Proto-Chimakuan phonemes is: /p, t, ts, č, k, kʷ, q, qʷ, p̓, t̓, tl̓, ts̓, č̓, k̓, k̓ʷ, q̓, q̓ʷ, ł, s, š, x, xʷ, χ, χʷ, l, l̓, m, n, m̓, n̓, w, y, h, ʔ, w̓, y̓; i, a, o/. The alveopalatals *č, *č̓, and *š appear to have developed from earlier *kʷ, *k̓ʷ, and *xʷ, respectively, before front vowels. Quileute nasals became voiced stops, just as in Nitinaht and Makah (Nootkan), and in some other languages in this linguistic subarea, mentioned above.

Chemakum was spoken in a small territory between Hood Canal and Port Townsend, on the east side of the Olympic Peninsula in northwest Washington state. Franz Boas found three speakers in 1890, and the language was fully dormant by the 1940s.[35]

Quileute was spoken on the west coast of the Olympic Peninsula in northwest Washington, south of the Makah and north of the Quinault. The Quileutes now live on two small reservations, Quileute (at La Push) and Lower Hoh River. The last native speaker died in 1999.[36]

Quileute and Makah (Nootkan) share a homogeneous culture. Because of the many Nootkan loans in Quileute, it seems that Quileute speakers adopted much of the shared culture from Nootkan speakers. However, linguistic evidence from place names, loanwords, diffused sound changes, and the classification and geographical distribution of the languages support the idea that Chimakuan-speaking peoples originally controlled the northern part of the Olympic Peninsula and only later came under influence from Makah (Nootkan) and Klallam (Clallam) (Central Salishan) speakers who immigrated to the peninsula (Kinkade and Powell 1976, 94–99).

Some proposals would link Wakashan and Chimakuan as related (see Powell 1993), and the now no-longer-supported Mosan hypothesis (cf. Jacobsen 1979a) would add Salishan together with these other two. The languages show considerable structural similarity, but much of that appears to be due to diffusion within the Northwest Coast Linguistic Area (see Chapter 7).

*Chinookan
    *Lower Chinook (Coastal Chinook, Chinook)
    *Kathlamet (Katlamat, Cathlamet)
    *Kiksht (Upper Chinook, Columbia Chinook, Wasco-Wishram)

(Silverstein 1974, 1990; Thompson and Kinkade 1990.)

Speakers of Chinookan languages lived on the Pacific Coast from Willapa Bay in Washington to Tillamook Bay in Oregon, on the Willamette and Clackamas Rivers, and along the Columbia River. The two branches of the family are quite distinct. **Kiksht** (Upper Chinookan) includes the closely related language varieties **Cathlamet** (Kathlamet), **Multnomah**, and **Kiksht** (with varieties of its own called **Clackamas, Cascades, Hood River**, and **Wasco-Wishram**).[37] (See Maps 2.4. and 7.1.)

The homeland of the Chinookan family may have been around the confluence of the Willamette River with the Columbia River, since the greatest area of diversification is there, whence the languages spread down the Columbia to the ocean and upriver to just above The Dalles (Kinkade et al. 1998). Thus, Chinookan has representatives in both the Northwest Coast and Plateau linguistic areas (see Chapter 7), and the different dialects and languages show differences that agree with traits shared by other languages in the distinct linguistic areas to which they belong. For example, Lower Chinookan verbal aspects reflect the Northwest Coast areal trait, while varieties of Upper Chinookan have shifted earlier verbal aspect to tense patterns under the influence of neighboring Sahaptian languages in the Plateau Linguistic Area (Silverstein 1974; for other areal traits, see Chapter 7).

Chinookan was also assigned to Sapir's (1929a) broad Penutian hypothesis, though as an outlier. This proposed relationship is mostly doubted today.

Kathlamet (Cathlamet), Chinookan, was spoken along the lower Columbia River in the vicinity of Astoria and upstream for about 50 miles. Franz Boas provided documentation in 1890s, mainly in narrative texts. The language has been dormant since the 1930s. Lewis and Clark interacted with speakers of this language in their famous expedition in 1805–1806. They call them *Cathlamet*, though at one point Clark referred to them as *Calt-har-ma*.

Kiksht (Upper Chinook) is a Chinookan language originally spoken upstream along the Columbia River from Portland to the vicinity of The Dalles, Oregon. It originally included a string of dialects, of which **Wasco-Wishram** is the easternmost. The **Wasco** variety was represented on the Warm Springs Reservation in central Oregon, the **Wishram** variety on the Yakama Reservation in eastern Washington. The language recently lost its last native speaker.

Lower Chinook was spoken at the mouth of the Columbia River from Shoalwater Bay in the north to Tillamook Head in the south, and for about 10 miles upstream. After the establishment of a fur-trading post at Astoria, Oregon, in 1811, they suffered a steep demographic decline. The last speaker died in the 1930s.

*Alsea

Alsea was spoken in two varieties, **Aslea** and **Yaquina**, by adjacent tribes in a small territory on the central coast of Oregon. (See Map 7.1.) In 1875 the remaining people of both the Alsea and Yaquina tribes were removed to the Siletz Reservation. Some Yaquina vocabulary was documented in the 1880s, but it appears to have become dormant soon after that. Alsea was more thoroughly documented, primarily by Leo Frachtenberg in 1910–1913. The last native speaker, John Albert, died in the 1951 (Grant 2018, 8).

Today most scholars believe Alsea and Yaquina to be dialects of a single language and consider Alsea a language isolate, although in the past the two were often considered to be closely related but distinct languages, members of the postulated Alsean family. John Wesley Powell's (1891) classification placed Alsea and Siuslaw together in "Yakonan." This was later abandoned when it did not hold up under closer examination.

Alsea is often associated with Edward Sapir's (1929a) Oregon Penutian, in which he placed Takelma, Kalapuyan, and "Coast Oregon Penutian" (composed of Coosan, Siuslaw, and Alsea) (see for example Hymes 1957; Grant 1997; 2018, 7). M. Dale Kinkade (2005) concluded from his comparisons, "if pressed, I would probably accept a relationship between Alsea and Siuslaw, and leave further relationship with Coosan open, but go no further than that." Kinkade found no credible evidence that Alsea could be related to any other putative Penutian languages. Most scholars have severe reservations about the broader Penutian hypothesis; some are more sympathetic to some form of Oregon Penutian or Coast Oregon Penutian (Grant 1997). (See Chapter 6.)

*Siuslaw

Siuslaw is generally considered a dormant language isolate. Its two varieties, **Siuslaw** and **Lower Umpqua**, were spoken in southern Oregon around present-day Florence, on the lower courses of the Umpqua and Siuslaw Rivers and on the adjacent Pacific Coast. (See Map 7.1.) They may have been either emergent languages or divergent dialects of a single language. Although some Siuslaw people were removed to reservations between 1855 and 1875, most remained in their traditional territory. The Confederated Tribes of Coos, Lower Umpqua, and Siuslaw received federal recognition in 1984, with tribal headquarters at Coos Bay. There is considerable documentation of Siuslaw from several linguists working between 1884 and 1966.[38] The last speaker of Siuslaw was Mae Barrett Elliot, who died in 1960; William Dick, the last speaker of Lower Umpqua, died in 1957 (Grant 2018, 8).

Siuslaw is often associated with Edward Sapir's (1929a) now mostly doubted Penutian hypothesis, though some hold the Oregon Penutian hypothesis as a possibility worthy of more investigation (see Grant 1997). This, however, is unconfirmed. (Thompson and Kinkade 1990, Zenk 1990b.)

*Coosan
  *Hanis
  *Miluk (Lower Coquille)

Coosan is a small family of two closely related languages, **Hanis** and **Miluk**, that were spoken in the Coos Bay and Coos River area of Oregon. **Miluk** (also called Lower Coquille) was spoken on the lower part of the Coquille River; **Hanis** was spoken north of Miluk. Both languages are often referred to as "Coos," although they were very clearly distinct languages. (See Map 7.1.)

Some Hanis and Miluk people were removed to reservations between 1855 and 1875, but most remained in their traditional territory. The Confederated Tribes of Coos, Lower Umpqua, and Siuslaw was recognized officially in 1984, with its tribal headquarters in Coos Bay. Hanis and Miluk both have rather extensive documentation from several linguists, including a number of sound recordings made by Melville Jacobs in the 1930s. The last fluent first-language speaker of Miluk, Annie Miner Peterson, died in 1939; the last speaker of Hanis, Martha Harney Johnson, died in 1972 (Grant 2018, 9).

Coosan is also often assumed to belong to Penutian, part of Sapir's (1929a) Oregon Penutian group, though without sufficient proof. This possibility is left open for further investigation by some scholars (Grant 1997; see Chapter 6).

*Takelma

Takelma, a language isolate, was spoken along the middle portion of the Rogue River in Oregon. The Takelmas were displaced in the Rogue River War of 1855–1856, and survivors settled on the Grand Ronde and Siletz Reservations. (See Map 7.1.) There may have been several local dialects, but only one is reflected in most of the documentation, the largest part of which comes from Edward Sapir's work in 1906, the subject of his doctoral dissertation (Sapir 1909; see also 1922a). The language was extinct by the 1940s.[39]

The Takelman hypothesis, proposed by Leo Frachtenberg (1918), would group Kalapuyan and Takelma together. Some find this proposed relationship very improbable, while others find it possible but unlikely—perhaps most are just agnostic. That the two are very different in morphological structure has been pointed out by those who doubt it most.

Sapir initially thought Takelma was related to Coos, but then later joined Takelma, Kalapuya, and Coast Oregon Penutian—that contained Coos, Siuslaw, and Yakonan (Alsea)—together in the Oregon Penutian branch of his tentative Penutian super-stock (cf. Sapir 1921a, 1929a; Sapir and Swadesh 1953). These proposals have not generally been found persuasive, although a number of scholars believe they are worthy of further investigation (see Swadesh 1965; Shipley 1969; Grant 1997; Kendall 1997; Golla 2011, 129).

Kalapuyan (Kalapuya)
  *Tualatin-Yamhill (Northern Kalapuya)
  *Central Kalapuyan (Santiam)
  *Yoncalla (Yonkalla, Southern Kalapuya)

The three closely related Kalapuyan languages were spoken throughout most of the Willamette Valley of western Oregon. All three languages had well-differentiated local dialects. **Tualatin-Yamhill** had the dialects **Tualatin** and **Yamhill**. **Central Kalapuya** had

Santiam and several other dialects. **Yoncalla** (Yonkalla, Southern Kalapuya) was spoken in the Umpqua River Valley. (See Map 7.1.)

The Kalapuyan people suffered a catastrophic demographic decline after contact with White people; in 1856 the few survivors were settled on the Grand Ronde Reservation, where most shifted from their native language to Chinook Jargon or other local American Indian languages. Most Kalapuyan varieties became dormant before 1940. The last speaker of Tualatin, Louis Kenoyer, died in 1937. Louisa Selky spoke Yamhill; she died in 1918. John B. "Mose" Hudson was the last speaker of Santiam; he died in 1954. William Hartless was the last speaker of Mary's River Kalapuya, a variety of Central Kalapuya; he died in 1920. The last speaker with some knowlede of Yoncalla died in 1964 (Grant 2018, 10).[40]

The Proto-Kalapuyan phoneme inventory has been reconstructed by Howard Berman (1990a, 29–30) with the following sounds: /p, t, c, k, k^w, ʔ, p^h, t^h, c^h, k^h, k^{wh}, h, p', t', c', k', k$^{w'}$, ɸ, s, ɬ, l, m, n, w, y; i, a, (o,) u; vowel length/. The sounds symbolized by c and c' are said to have varied between [ts] and [č]. Berman (1990a, 30–31) did not reconstruct short *e for Proto-Kalapuyan, and short *o is uncertain, given the limited number of cognate sets which seem to suggest it.

As mentioned above, the Takelman proposal would join Takelma and Kalapuyan together. Kalapuyan has also been included in Oregon Penutian and in Penutian generally. None of these is widely accepted now (see Chapter 6).

Plateau (Plateau Penutian)
   *Klamath-Modoc
   Sahaptian
      Sahaptin
      Nez Perce
   *Molala

(See Map 7.2.)

The Plateau family has three branches, Klamath-Modoc, Sahaptian, and Molala (Aoki 1963; DeLancey 1992; DeLancey, Genetti, and Rude 1988; Rude 1987; Berman 1996). The family is also called Plateau Penutian after Sapir's (1929a) Plateau Penutian division of his Penutian super-stock. The name of just *Plateau* is favored by those who are reluctant to associate this family with the controversial and mostly abandoned Penutian macro-family, while Plateau Penutian is preferred by some who believe that maintaining the history behind the name may be useful.

Klamath-Modoc. **Klamath** and **Modoc** are dialects of a single language, perhaps no more divergent than dialects of American English (Barker 1963, 1964).

Klamath was spoken in southeastern Oregon around the lakes from which the Klamath River originates. The southern part of this basin was the territory of the **Modocs**, of the Tule Lake area in adjacent northeastern California, extending toward Pit River. After the Modoc War of 1872–1873 about 150 Modocs were relocated to Oklahoma, the remainder merging into the Klamath community. Today there are no known native speakers of Klamath-Modoc, though ongoing attempts to reclaim the language are strong. The last speaker of Klamath died in 1999; the last Modoc speaker died in 2003 (Grant 2018, 8).

Sahaptian. The Sahaptian subgroup has two languages, **Nez Perce** and **Sahaptin**, spoken throughout the southern Plateau linguistic area. Nez Perce extended from the Bitterroot Mountains on the east to the Blue Mountains on the west, to where Idaho, Oregon, and Washington meet. The Snake River was the boundary between the two main dialects of Nez Perce, **Upper** (Eastern) and **Lower** (Western). Nez Perce and Sahaptin are fairly closely related; this was recognized already by Lewis and Clark in 1805–1806 (Kinkade et al. 1998).

The Proto-Sahaptian consonants, in Noel Rude's (2012) reconstruction, are: /p, t, tl, c, č, k, kʷ, q, qʷ, p', t', tl', c', č', k', kʷ', q', qʷ' s, š, χ, χʷ, ł, l, l', m, n, m', n', w, w', y, y', h, ʔ/. The Proto-Sahaptian vowels are: /i, æ, ɨ, u, o, ɑ/ (Rude 2012), though their analysis has been disputed (see Aoki 1966; Rigsby 1965a; Rigsby and Silverstein 1969).

Sahaptin, spoken along the Columbia River and adjacent Plateau in eastern Oregon and Washington, has marked dialectal diversity, in two main divisions: **Northern** (with Northwest and Northeast dialects) and **Southern**. The **Northwest** dialects were spoken in the Yakima River drainage and included **Klickitat**, **Yakima**, **Taitnapam** (a.k.a. Upper Cowlitz), and **Upper Nisqually** (Mishalpam). The **Northeast** varieties were spoken on the Columbia River above Southern Sahaptin and along the lower Snake River, and included **Wanapam**, **Palouse** (Palus), **Wallawalla** (Waluulapam), and **Lower Snake** (Chamnapam, Wauyukma, and Naxiyampam); these dialects were all influenced by **Nez Perce**. Southern, with the **Columbia River cluster** of dialects, was originally spoken along the Columbia River from The Dalles to the Umatilla River, and included the Columbia River dialect group, **Tygh Valley**, **Tenino**, **Celilo** (Wayampam), **John Day**, **Rock Creek**, and **Umatilla**.

The main communities with speakers today are the Warm Springs Reservation in north-central Oregon, the Umatilla Reservation near Pendleton, Oregon, and Toppenish on the Yakima Reservation in south-central Washington.

Nez Perce is relatively homogeneous. Two dialects are distinguished, **Upriver** and **Downriver**, correlated with the original settlement pattern along the Snake River and its tributaries in eastern Washington and Idaho. Speakers of the Upriver dialect are at Kamiah and Lapwai on the Nez Perce Reservation in north-central Idaho and on the Colville Reservation in eastern Washington. Downriver dialect speakers are on the Umatilla Reservation in Oregon (most of them descendants of **Cayuse** speakers who adopted Nez Perce in the nineteenth century).[41]

Molala (Molale) was spoken along the western slopes of the Cascade Mountains of central Oregon, from the upper Rogue River to the vicinity of Mt. Hood. The Northern Molala occupied the Molalla River drainage system and the southwestern tributaries of the Clackamas River; the Southern Molala (unattested linguistically) were located on the upper Rogue River and upper part of the North and South Forks of the Umpqua River (Kinkade et al. 1998).

The Molala were displaced and suffered a severe decline in population after White people occupied their territory in the mid-1800s. The survivors were settled on the Grand Ronde Reservation, where their language and tribal identity were lost. The last speaker of Molala was Fred Yelkes, who died in 1958 (Grant 2018, 9). However, sometimes Kate Yelkes Chantal (or Chantelle, a.k.a. Molala Kate), who also died in 1958, is reported as the last surviving speaker.

Horatio Hale (1846) had grouped Cayuse and Molala together. Powell (1891a) accepted this, calling it the Waiilatpuan stock. However, Bruce Rigsby (1965b, 1966, 1969) disproved this formerly assumed relationship. Hale had apparently based his classification primarily on nonlinguistic considerations, an observation of Cayuse and Molala communicating with each other in some language, mistakenly taken as evidence of mutual intelligibility (Rigsby 1966; Berman 1981, 249).[42]

*Cayuse** (Cailloux, Willetpoos)

Cayuse is a language isolate, formerly spoken in the Plateau region of northeastern Oregon and southeastern Washington. (See Map 7.2.) In the early nineteenth century, Cayuse territories included the drainage systems of the Butter Creek, the upper Umatilla, the upper Walla Walla, the Touchet, the Tucannon, the upper Grand Ronde, the Burnt, and the Powder Rivers (Silverstein 1979, 680; Kinkade et al. 1998). Already in 1837 Marcus Whitman, famous missionary, wrote that the Cayuse had extensively intermarried with Nez Perce, that all of them spoke Nez Perce, and that younger Cayuse did not understand Cayuse at all. All eventually shifted to Nez Perce. Cayuse is poorly attested. A few people retained some fluency in the language as late as the early 1930s, but by the 1960s Cayuse was fully dormant.

As mentioned above, Horatio Hale (1846) thought Cayuse and Molala were related, included in Powell's (1891a) Waiilatpuan family. However, Bruce Rigsby (1965b, 1966, 1969) showed that the evidence does not support a genetic relationship between the two. As mentioned above, Hale had apparently based his classification primarily on nonlinguistic considerations (Rigsby 1966; Berman 1981, 249).

Kutenai (Kootenay, Kootenai, Ktunaxa, Ksanka)

Kutenai is a language isolate spoken along the border between the United States and Canada, in British Columbia, Idaho, and Montana. The Kutenai territory historically centered around the Kutenai River drainage system, bordering the Plains Linguistic Area, between Interior Salishan and Blackfoot (Algonquian). (See Map 7.2.)

Kutenai is the heritage language of three groups in Montana, Idaho, and British Columbia. The Montana Kootenai are part of the Confederated Salish and Kootenai Tribes, and are concentrated at the northern end of the Flathead Reservation, around Elmo. The Kootenai Tribe of Idaho has a reservation near Bonners Ferry, in northern Idaho. The name Ktunaxa is now official in Canada. The Ktunaxa (Kutenai) communities in British Columbia are represented by the Ktunaxa/Kinbasket Tribal Council and include the Lower Kootenay Band, with a reserve near Creston; the Tobacco Plains Band with a reserve at Grasmere; the St. Mary's Band with a reserve near Cranbrook; and the Columbia Lake Band with a reserve at Windermere.

Proposals of genetic relationship have attempted to link Kutenai with its neighbors, Salishan and Algonquian, and also with Wakashan and others, but these are unsubstantiated (see Salishan above). A number of scholars have looked favorably upon the possibility of a genealogical link between Kutenai and Algonquian. Matthew Dryer (2007) thinks the similarities that the two share seem to be too similar to be due to inheritance from a common ancestor that would have had to have diversified very long ago.

***Wintuan** (Wintun)
   *Northern Wintuan (Wintu-Nomlaki)
   *Patwin (Southern Wintuan)

Wintuan is a family of essentially two languages, each with dialect divisions. Wintuan speakers occupied the west of the Sacramento Valley and the upper Trinity River drainage in northern California. The name is from Wintu *wint^hu-h* 'person'. Patwin, from their word *patwin* 'people', has also been called Southern Wintun. Powell's (1891) Copehan stock's name for the Wintuan family comes from *Copeh*, an early name for Patwin. Wintu has the dialects **Nomlaki** and **Wintu**, a custer of mostly homogeneous varieties. (See Map 2.6.)

Northern Wintuan (Wintu-Nomlaki) was originally spoken in the northern half of the Sacramento Valley, on the upper Sacramento River below Mt. Shasta, in the upper drainage of the Trinity River, and on Hayfork Creek in Trinity County. There were two major dialects, **Nomlaki**, spoken along the Sacramento River south of Red Bluff, and **Wintu**, spoken elsewhere in the territory. There appears to have been no significant difference between the variety of Wintu spoken in the Trinity-Hayfork area and the Sacramento Valley variety. The last fluent speaker of Wintu, the Winnemem shaman Flora Jones, passed away in 2003.

Patwin (Southern Wintuan) had two major dialects or dialect clusters. **River Patwin** was spoken along the Sacramento River in Colusa County. **Hill Patwin** was spoken in the plains and foothills of the Coast Range to the west. **Southern Patwin** is a very poorly attested variety and may be a third dialect of Patwin or possibly a separate, emergent language (Golla 2011, 140). It was spoken from central Yolo County to Suisun Bay and west as far as the Napa River. Patwin descendants live on small rancherias at Cortina and Colusa, and on the Rumsey (Cache Creek) Rancheria west of Woodland.

The spit up of Proto-Wintuan into the two daughter languages has been estimated at circa 1,500–2,000 years ago; the difference between the languages is said to be like the difference of the more distantly related Romance languages from one another (Pitkin 1984, 2, Golla 2011, 140). It is hypothesized that Proto-Wintuan was spoken earlier in interior southwestern Oregon or northwestern California, and that "Wintuans almost certainly entered California from the north" (Moratto 1984, 563; Whistler 1977, 166). Victor Golla (2007, 78) said that the western Oregon homeland for Wintuan "is indicated by the nature of the plant and animal vocabulary that can be reconstructed in proto-Wintuan, which includes no terms for California species that are not found also in western Oregon and many terms for species common to both areas" (Whistler 1977). The Patwins moved south, into Miwok territory, disrupting them.

Proto-Wintuan's phonemic inventory is reconstructed with: /p, t, č, k, q, p^h, t^h, č^h, k^h, q^h, p', t', tl', č', k', q', b, d, s, x, ɬ, l, r, m, n, w, y, h, (ʔ); i, e, a, o, u; vowel length/ (Shepherd 2005, 5–7; cf. Whistler 1980).

Wintuan was considered one of the five branches of Penutian when the hypothesis was first proposed (Dixon and Kroeber 1913, 1913b, 1919), later called California Penutian, which also included Yokuts, Maiduan, Miwok, and Costanoan. California Penutian is now essentially abandoned (see Chapter 6), though Miwokan and Costanoan are clearly related (see below).

*__Maiduan__ (Maidun)
  *Maidu (Northeastern Maidu, Mountain Maidu)
  *Chico Maidu
  *Konkow
  *Nisenan

The four closely related Maiduan languages (also called Maidun, Powell's Pujunan stock) were spoken in the area of the American and Feather River drainages in the northern Sierra Nevada of California, with Nisenan in the valley, Konkow in the foothills, and Maidu in the mountains. (See Map 2.6.) The name "Maidu" is from Maidu (Northeastern Maidu) *maydɨ* 'man, person'. Victor Golla (2011, 136) noted that "some degree of mutual intelligibility existed among all the Maiduan speakers." All of the Maiduan languages are sometimes referred to collectively as "Maidu." All four are now dormant.

It is uncertain whether Chico Maidu is an independent language or a divergent dialect of Konkow (Golla 2011, 138). Maidu (Northeastern Maidu) and Chico Maidu share more lexically, but Maidu differs from the other three in a number of grammatical features. Golla (2011, 136) saw the grammatical differences in the Maiduan languages as more telling than the phonological or lexical differences. He reported them as probably reflecting external influences, Washo and Palaihnihan on Maidu (Northeastern Maidu), Northern Wintuan on Konkow and Chico Maidu, and Eastern Miwok on Nisesan. Russell Ultan (1964) thought that the lexical and phonological similarities as opposed to the morphosyntactic differences among Maiduan languages may be the result of intensive lexical borrowing among these languages.[43] No noteworthy dialect differences were recorded for Maidu (Northeastern Maidu). Nisenan had four major dialects, **Valley Nisenan, Northern Hill Nisenan, Central Hill Nisenan**, and **Southern Hill Nisenan**.

The reconstructed Proto-Maiduan phonemes are: /p, t, c, k, ʔ, p', t', c', k', b, d, s, l, m, n, w, y, h; i, e, a, ɨ, o, u; vowel length; phonemic stress/. The *b* and *d* were often slightly imploded. The *s* was apical and usually retroflexed ([ṣ], IPA [ʂ]). (Ultan 1964, 356–361; cf. Golla 2011, 139).

Kenneth Whistler noted that borrowings among Maiduan plant names and other irregularities seem to be evidence that the group arrived relatively recently in California, probably from northwestern Nevada (reported by Moratto 1984, 562).

Maidu, also known as Northeastern Maidu or Mountain Maidu, is the Maiduan language of the people who traditionally occupied the northern Sierra Nevada and the Honey Lake Valley, east and south of Lassen Peak in northeastern California. Some Maidu descendants are members of the small Susanville and Greenville Rancherias, but most live in scattered locations in Plumas and Lassen counties.

Konkow was spoken in the Feather River and Oroville area in California, at the eastern edge of the Sacramento Valley. The principal modern Konkow community is at the Mooretown Rancheria.

Nisenan, also known as Southern Maidu, was spoken in a number of local village dialects along the Yuba River in the Sierra Nevada foothills east of Sacramento. Nisenan descendants live at Auburn Rancheria in Placer County, Shingle Springs Rancheria in El Dorado County, and in other scattered locations in the area.

Utian (Miwok-Costanoan)
  Miwokan
    Eastern Miwok
      Sierra Miwok
        Southern Sierra Miwok
        Central Sierra Miwok
        Northern Sierra Miwok
      *Plains Miwok
      *Saclan (Bay Miwok)
    *Western Miwok
      *Coast Miwok (Bodega Miwok-Marin Miwok)
      *Lake Miwok
  *Costanoan (Ohlone)
    *Karkin
    *Northern Costanoan
      *San Franciso Bay (*Ramaytush, *Chochenyo [Chocheño], *Tamyen)
      *Chalon
    *Southern Costanoan
      *South Central
        *Awaswas
        *Mutsun
    *Rumsen

(Callaghan 2014, 8, 17.)
(See Map 2.5. Utian languages.)

The relationship between Miwokan and Costanoan languages is not immediately obvious on superficial inspection. A shared kinship for them had been suggested earlier, though Powell (1891) separated them, with Miwokan languages as his Moquelumnan stock and with a distinct Costanoan stock.[44] However, the two are, in spite of Powell's doubts, clearly related. Catherine Callaghan's many publications since 1967 established this beyond any doubt as she worked out the history and reconstruction of the family, which she named Utian, culminating in her 2014 book.

Classifications of Costanoan before Callaghan (2014) relied heavily on the reconstruction of *k^w and *t' and assumed sound changes involving the reflexes of these putative proto sounds in the daughter languages, and it was assumed that Proto-Utian also had these two sounds. However, Callaghan (2014) discovered that there is no reason to reconstruct them for Proto-Costanoan, and so also not for Proto-Utian. It turns out that evidence for *k^w and *t' came only from Southern Costanoan, and the reflexes involving these sounds in the other branches of the family do not need to be derived from reconstruction of these sounds; rather, they are from other sounds that were strengthened to give *k^w and *t' in Southern Costanoan. This recalibration of the reconstruction of these sounds had a significant impact on the classification of the languages, since several now no longer involve changes that before seemed like shared innovations.

MAP 2.5. Utian languages

In the Miwokan branch, the three Sierra Miwok languages are closely related, similar to the relationship among the languages of the Scandinavian branch of Germanic: they are partially but not fully mutually intelligible. **Bodega** and **Marin** Miwok were dialects of a single language. In the Western Miwok branch, the relationship between **Lake Miwok** and **Coast Miwok** is like that of Spanish with Italian (separate branches of the Romance languages), and the difference between Lake Miwok and the **Sierra Miwok** languages is on the order of the difference between English and German (Callaghan 2014, 8–9). Callaghan (2014, 9) estimated the time depth of Proto-Miwok as similar to that of Germanic, at circa 2500–3000 years.

Miwok is the common name for the languages of the Miwokan branch of the larger Utian (Miwok-Costanoan) family, spoken in north-central California from San Francisco Bay to the Sierra Nevada. Seven languages are usually distinguished, subdivided linguistically into **Western Miwok** and **Eastern Miwok**. (See Callaghan 2014.)

Western Miwok has two languages, both now dormant, **Coast Miwok** and **Lake Miwok**. **Coast Miwok** was spoken from the Marin Peninsula to Bodega Bay in Marin County and southern Sonoma County, just north of San Francisco. The Coast Miwoks were brought into the Franciscan missions at San Rafael and Sonoma, and their culture and language were largely extinguished before 1835. There were several local dialects, with the Bodega Bay dialect (**Bodega Miwok**) somewhat divergent from the others (**Marin Miwok**). The last known person to have direct knowledge of the language died in the 1970s.

Lake Miwok was geographically isolated from the other Miwokan languages. Lake Miwok descendants live at the Middletown Rancheria, to the southeast of Clear Lake.

Eastern Miwok is one of the two branches of the Miwok languages. Eastern Miwok languages were formerly found on the western slopes of the Sierra Nevada, extending inland from Ione to Stockton. There are five Eastern Miwok languages, in north-central California.

Saclan (also called **Bay Miwok**), an Eastern Miwok language, is attested in only a single vocabulary of about eighty words from Father Felipe Arroyo de la Cuesta in 1821. The language's traditional area is not well understood but was east of the hills in the east San Francisco Bay area, in parts of Contra Costa County, west of Mt. Diablo.

Plains Miwok, also of the Eastern Miwok branch, was spoken along the lower Cosumnes and Moquelumne Rivers and on the Sacramento River southeast of Sacramento, from Ione to Stockton. Plains Miwok descendants now reside at the Ione Rancheria and the Wilton Rancheria.

Sierra Miwok languages were spoken from the Fresno River to the Cosumnes River on the western slopes of the Sierra Nevada, to the east and south of the Plains Miwok, as far south as Yosemite Valley. The Sierra Miwok descendants refer to themselves as "Mewuk"; they now live in a scattering of small communities, the largest ones on the Jackson and Tuolumne Rancherias.

Three emergent languages are typically distinguished in the Sierra Miwok dialect complex. **Northern Sierra Miwok** traditionally was spoken in the foothills of the Sierra Nevada along the upper Mokelumne and Calaveras Rivers and along the south fork of the Cosumnes River. Today it is spoken by only a few elders at the Jackson Rancheria near Westpoint. **Central Sierra Miwok** was in the foothills of the Sierra Nevada along the Stanislaus and Tuolomne Rivers. It had two dialects, **West** and **East**. **Southern Sierra Miwok** speakers were traditionally in the foothills of the Sierra Nevada between the Merced and Chowchilla Rivers. It also had two dialects: the **Merced River** dialect (which retained *š* for Proto-Sierra Miwok *š*) and the **Mariposa-Chowchilla** dialect (with /h/ for *š*). Sierra Miwok today has very few speakers, although there are very active language revitalization programs underway.

Costanoan (Ohlone), the other main branch of the Utian family, has eight languages that were spoken in a compact area along the coast of California from north of San Francisco to south of Monterey, from Carquinez Strait to Big Sur.[45] The Costanoan languages were apparently all dormant by 1935, most very poorly attested, though fortunately J. P. Harrington was able to record some things for **Mutsun**, **Rumsen**, and **Chocheño** (Callaghan 1988a, 54). Three of the four languages formerly spoken around San Francisco Bay, **Karkin**, **Ramaytush**, and **Tamyen**, have been dormant since the mid-nineteenth century. Tamyen and Chocheño have been shown now to be dialects of a single language, called **San Francisco Bay Costanoan**, and the evidence indicates that very probably **Ramaytush**

also was a dialect of this same language. Mutsun and Rumsen clearly belong together in the same subgroup, Southern Costanoan. San Francisco Bay and **Karkin** diverge from the others and thus are separate branches of their own within Costanoan. The position of **Chalon** and **Awaswas** is less clear. Lexical evidence would seem to place Chalon in the Southern Costanoan subgroup, but phonological evidence would seem to join Chalon and Awaswas with San Franciso Bay Costanoan (Callaghan 2014, 15–16). Callaghan (2014, 22) reached the conclusion that the Awaswas materials represent disparate dialects whose speakers were in the process of language shift from Northern Costanoan to Mutsun. Mutsun was influencing Chalon, too.

Karkin is attested only in a short vocabulary recorded by Father Felipe Arroyo de la Cuesta in 1821. **Ramaytush** (San Francisco Costanoan) was spoken in San Mateo and San Francisco Counties on the San Francisco Peninsula to as far south as Palo Alto and Pescadero. It may also have been spoken just north of the Golden Gate Bridge. During the mission period, Ramaytush was spoken at Mission Dolores. It is only attested in a few wordlists.

Tamyen (Santa Clara Costanoan) was spoken in the lower Santa Clara Valley and around the south end of San Francisco Bay. During the mission period, it was spoken at Mission Santa Clara. Tamyen is attested only in a single wordlist.[46]

Chochenyo (Chocheño, also called East Bay Costanoan) was formerly spoken along the eastern shore of the San Francisco Bay from Richmond to Fremont, and during the mission period at Mission San José. It was moderately well documented by J. P. Harrington early in the twentieth century.

Awaswas was spoken on the north shore of Monterey Bay, along the coast in Santa Cruz County. It is very scarcely attested only in wordlists.

Chalon (Soledad) traditionally was spoken along Chalone Creek to the east of the Salinas River; during the mission period, it was spoken at Mission Nuestra Señora de la Soledad. It became dormant very early and is very scantily attested.

Mutsun was the language of the area around Mission San Juan Bautista, spoken throughout the Pajaro River drainage, and from there west to Monterey Bay, north to Gilroy, east to Hollister, and southeast to the Pinnacles. It survived until the 1930s and is well documented, both from the Mission period and in the twentieth century by J. P. Harrington. The Mission materials have been published, and there is an unpublished grammar and dictionary based on Harrington's materials. Mutsun is attested in the Father Felipe Arroyo de la Cuesta's nineteenth-century publications, in the of J. P. Harrington's fieldnotes, and in works derived from them (Arroyo de la Cuesta 1861a, 1861b [1815]).

The **Rumsen** (Rumsien) language was spoken on the Monterey Peninsula and along the lower Carmel, Sur, and Salinas Rivers, around Salinas and Fort Ord, near Castroville, and from Carmel Valley to Point Sur. It was spoken at Mission San Carlos de Borroméo in Carmel during the mission period. It is moderately well documented, mostly in J. P. Harrington's extensive fieldnotes. Harrington obtained much Rumsen data from Isabelle Meadows, the last speaker; she died in 1939.

The reconstructed Proto-Utian phonemes are: /p, t, ṭ, č, k, kʷ, ʔ, s, ṣ, š, l, m, n, w, y, h; i, e, ɨ, u, o a; vowel length/ (Callaghan 2014, 69).

The Proto-Utian homeland is postulated to have been inland from the San Francisco Bay area (Callaghan 2014, 24). Callaghan found substantial evidence of influence from Esselen (a language isolate), of "an Esselen substrate in current Costanoan territory and contact of some kind with early Miwok speakers," and also a number of probable Rumsen loanwords in Esselen, and Esselen loanwords into Rumsen, Mutsun, and Chalon (Callaghan 2014, 39–56).

While Miwokan and Costanoan are clearly related, the other families in the original Penutian proposal (Dixon and Kroeber 1919), later called California Penutian, with which Utian is usually associated, have not been demonstrated to be related. Most scholars now reject California Penutian, and only a very few hold out hope for better evidence in future research to support Sapir's (1929a) broader Penutian stock (see Chapter 6). The Yok-Utian hypothesis, which would joint Utian and Yokuts together, is also evaluated in Chapter 6.

Yokuts

Yokuts is a complex of emergent languages, in many dialects and subdialects. Powell's (1891) name for Yokuts was Mariposan. Although the classification is unclear, six emergent languages are usually recognized for Yokuts. The Yokuts were divided into nearly forty small tribe-like units ("tribelets"), each with its own dialect, in the southern half of the San Joaquin Valley and the foothills of the Sierra Nevada to the east (Golla 2011, 147). The differences among them are mostly lexical.

Victor Golla's (2011, 148–149) classification of the Yokuts dialects is:

Yokuts
- Poso Creek
- General Yokuts
  - Buena Vista
  - Nim-Yokuts
    - Tule-Kaweah
    - Northern Yokuts
      - King's River
      - Gashowu
      - Valley
      - Delta

(See Map 2.6.)

Poso Creek was the most divergent of the emergent languages in the Yokuts complex. **Palewyami Yokuts** is the only attested variety of Poso Creek; though unattested, the **Kumachisi** tribe is usually also assumed have spoken another Poso Creek dialect. Palewyami Yokuts, spoken along Poso Creek in Kern County, has partial documentation in the form of several wordlists, the longest and most reliable from by J. P. Harrington in the 1920s. There have been no speakers of Palewyami since the 1930s. The other varieties belong to Golla's **General Yokuts**.

Buena Vista Yokuts is another distinctive emergent language in the Yokuts complex; it was spoken in at least two local varieties around Buena Vista Lake in Kern County, California. There are several wordlists of Buena Vista Yokuts. There have been no speakers since the 1930s.

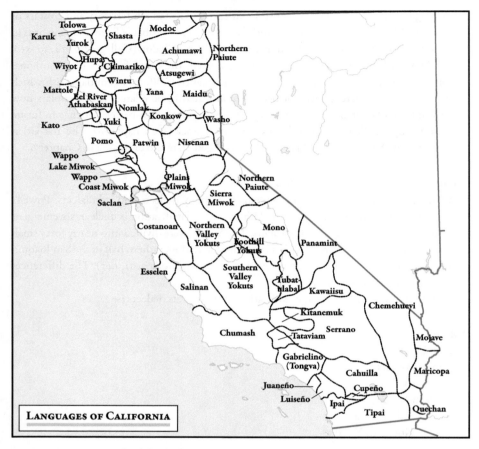

MAP 2.6. Languages of California (pre-contact)

Golla's (2011) **Nim-Yokuts** division has **Tule-Kaweah** and the **Northern Yokuts** varieties. Tule-Kaweah is a cluster of dialects originally spoken in the Sierra Nevada foothills along the Tule and Kaweah Rivers, east of Porterville. Its two best-known dialects are **Yawdanchi** and **Wikchamni** (Wukchumne). There are Tule-Kaweah people today on the Tule River Reservation. The **King's River** dialect cluster was originally spoken in the Sierra Nevada foothills east of Fresno. The group had the dialects **Choynimni** (Choinumne), **Chukaymina**, **Michahay**, and **Aiticha**.

Gashowu territory was in the foothills southeast of Friant Dam near Fresno on Dry Creek and Little Dry Creek.

Valley Yokuts is a large complex of shallowly differentiated dialects spoken mainly in the San Joaquin Valley. It is divided in two networks of subdialects, **Northern Valley** and **Southern Valley**. The remaining speakers Valley Yokuts dialects are of the **Yawelmani** (Yowlumne) variety on the Tule River Reservation, of **Chukchansi** at the Picayune and Table Mountain Rancherias in the foothills northeast of Fresno, and of **Tachi** at the Santa

Rosa Rancheria near Lemoore. The Southern Valley Yokuts subdialect of **Yawelmani** (Yowlumne) is well known in linguistic literature from later publications based on Stanley Newman's (1944) description of Yawelmani.

The classification of poorly attested **Delta** (Far Northern Valley) is uncertain; it may have been an additional division of **Valley Yokuts** or another branch of **Northern Yokuts**. (Golla 2011, 147–154.)

Proto-Yokuts phonemes are: /p, t, (c), (ṭ), k, ʔ, p', ṭ', c', t', k', pʰ, tʰ, cʰ, ṭʰ, kʰ, s, ṣ, x, m, n, ŋ, m', n', (ŋ'), l, l', w, y, w', y', h; i, a, ɨ, o, u; vowel length/. The segments in parentheses may have been marginal. In Proto-Yokuts, plain stops and affricates in syllable-final position were apparently aspirated (Whistler and Golla 1986, 334).

It is argued that the Yokuts entered California from the north, displacing Uto-Aztecan groups into the San Joaquin Valley, after speakers of Miwokan and Costanoan had spread in the San Francisco Bay area (Whistler 1977; Moratto 1984, 554–556, 563).

Yokuts is frequently classified as Penutian; Yokuts, together with Wintun, Maiduan, Miwok, and Costanoan, constituted Dixon and Kroeber's (1913a, 1913b, 1919) originally proposed Penutian, the California kernel to which Sapir and others later proposed many language groups as possible additional relatives (see Chapter 6). Most specialists now hold the view that a relationship uniting all these language families has not been successful and that no faith in the original Penutian hypothesis is warranted, and by implication, certainly none is warranted in the broader, more far-flung Penutian proposals (see Shipley 1980, 1983–1984; Whistler 1977; Callaghan 2014, 2–5, 23; see discussion in Chapter 6).

Karuk (Karok)

Karuk (called Quoratean in Powell's 1891 classification) is a language isolate spoken in northern California along the middle course of the Klamath River, around the communities of Happy Camp, Inam, Katimin, and Panamnik. It is the heritage language of the Karuk Tribe of the Klamath River in northwestern California.[47] (See Map 2.6.)

The Karuk knew almost nothing of the existence of White men until the arrival of gold miners in 1850 and 1851 shattered their existence. The language is now critically endangered.

Karuk was part of Dixon and Kroeber's (1913a, 1913b) original Hokan hypothesis; Hokan is a disputed and mostly abandoned classification (see Chapter 6). Culturally, Karuk speakers differ little from neighboring Yurok (Algic) and Hupa (Athabaskan), and the three together constitute a small culture area, part of the larger Northwestern California culture area (Bright 1957, 1978; see Chapter 7).

*Chimariko

Chimariko (formerly also called Chimalakwe) is a language isolate of northwest California. (See Map 2.6.) It is dormant; already in 1906, Roland Dixon (1910) found only two surviving speakers. In historical times the Chimariko territory was a small region in mountainous northwestern Trinity County, particularly in a 20 mile stretch of a narrow canyon along the Trinity River. Victor Golla (2011, 87–88) recognized "three distinct regional entities,"

New River Chimariko, Trinity River Chimariko, and **South Fork Chimariko.**[48] (See Jany 2009.)

Conflicts with the gold miners resulted in the near annihilation of the Chimariko by the 1860s. The few remaining Chimariko took refuge with the Hupa and Shasta (Silver 1978a). Many Chimarikos were bilingual in Hupa, a neighboring Athabaskan language. Chimariko was extensively documented by J. P. Harrington in the 1920s. The last speaker died around 1950.

Chimariko has long been grouped in Hokan, but the Hokan hypothesis is doubted by most linguists today (see Chapter 6).

*Shastan
 *Shasta
 *New River Shasta
 *Konomihu

Shastan languages (Powell's [1891] Sastean) were spoken in central and western Siskiyou County, California. (Golla 2011, 90; Silver 1978b, 211.) (See Map 2.6.)

Shasta (proper) was spoken in a large territory from the Rogue River in Oregon, across the Siskiyu Mountains, to the upper Klamath River in California, to the Shasta and Scott Rivers. Its four shallow dialects were **Oregon Shasta, Klamath River Shasta, Scott Valley Shasta,** and **Shasta Valley Shasta** (Golla 2011, 91). Shasta was the only Shastan language to have survived into the twentieth century; it lost its last native speakers after 1980. Many modern Shastas have merged their political and cultural identity with the Karuk Tribe and now consider Karuk their heritage language. "Shasta" is often used as the cover term for all of the Shastan languages.

New River Shasta was spoken in a remote area near the headwaters of Salmon River and New River, scattered across the Salmon Mountains. It has been dormant since about 1870 and is poorly attested.

Konomihu was spoken along the lower Salmon River, centered in the area around Forks of Salmon. It, too, has been dormant for many generations and is very poorly attested. (Larsson 1987.)

Okwanuchu may be a fourth Shastan language; its classification is uncertain. It was once spoken along the upper Sacramento River, just south of Mount Shasta. It has long been dormant. It is very poorly attested, with only a wordlist of seventy-five words and seven words extracted from another source. These words divide sharply into one group of words that are nearly identical to Shasta and another group that bear no similarity to Shasta or to any of the other languages of the region. Victor Golla (2011, 94) surmised that this difference in the vocabulary reflects a speech community in the process of undergoing language shift. The unidentified non-Shasta words in the Okwanuchu corpus beg questions about their identity and interpretation.

Shasta was classified as Hokan in the original Hokan proposal (Dixon and Kroeber 1913a, 1913b, 1919) and was part of Sapir's (1929a) Northern Hokan group. These are contested and mostly abandoned proposals (see Chapter 6).

*Palaihnihan
 *Achumawi (Achomawi, Pit River)
 *Atsugewi

Palaihnihan was Powell's (1891) name for the family with these two languages, **Achumawi** and **Atsugewi**, based on the name "Palaihnih" used by Hale (1846), said to be from Klamath *p'laikni* 'mountaineers, uplanders'. Both languages were spoken along the Pit River and its tributaries in northeastern California.[49] (See Map 2.6.)

The two are not closely related to one another. David Olmsted (1964, 1) calculated that the split up of Proto-Palaihnihan into the two languages took place at about 3,500–4,000 years ago, based on glottochronology and archaeology. The two languages may have borrowed significantly from one another, since there was considerable bilingualism among the Atsugewi, as well as frequent intermarriage (Olmsted 1964, 1). Both Achumawi and Atsugewi are heritage languages of the Pit River Tribe's 11 bands representing the tribal groups with traditional territory along the Pit River.

Achumawi, along the Pit River, had nine shallowly differentiated dialects that fall into two clusters, the **Downriver Dialect Group** and the **Upriver Dialect Group**. The Downriver dialects are: **Madesiwi, Itsatawi, Ilmawi**, and **Achumawi**. The Upriver dialects are: **Atwamkwi** (Atwamisini), **Astariwawi, Kosalektawi, Hammawi**, and **Hewisedawi** (Golla 2011, 97).

Atsugewi's traditional territory was south of the Pit River, along Hat Creek to the west and Aporige (Apwaruge) in Dixie Valley to the east. The two Atsugewi dialect groups were **Atsuge** ('pine-tree people'), of the valleys north of Mount Lassen, and **Apwaruge** (Dixie Valley Atsugewi), to the east of the Atsuge on the more barren plain (Garth 1978; Olmsted 1984). There have been no known speakers since 1988.

David Olmsted's (1964, 34–35, 62) incomplete reconstruction of the Proto-Palaihnihan consonant phonemes includes: /p, t, k, q, ʔ, s, š, x, h, w, y, ɪ, L, r, m, n, (N), (ŋ)/. There has generally been doubt about aspects of Olmsted's proposed reconstruction (see for example Nevin 2017; Good et al. 2003).[50] Good et al.'s (2003, 5) revised inventory of reconstructed Proto-Palaihnihan consonants is: /p, t, c, k, q, pʰ, tʰ, kʰ, qʰ, p', t', c', k', q', s, h, m, n, m', n', h', l, r, l', r', w, y, w', y'/.

While most scholars have accepted the classification that Achumawi and Atsugewi are genetically related, the two members of the Palaihnihan family, Bruce Nevin (2017) cast some doubt on this assumption, based on the possibility of complications from many loanwords and from the poor quality of Olmsted's data. Though the relationship appears solid to me, this certainly calls for more intensive investigation.

Palaihnihan's potential broader connections have received a fair amount of attention. Roland Dixon (1905, 1907[1906]) proposed a Shasta-Achomawi "stock." Dixon and Kroeber (1913a, 1913b) included this group, which they called Shastan, in their original Hokan hypothesis, and Sapir (1929a) proposed a Northern Hokan subgroup (called **Kahi** by Bright 1955), which included so-called Shastan, Chimariko, and Karuk. However, Olmsted (1956, 1957, 1959, 1964) has convinced most scholars that the Palaihnihan languages bear no closer relationship to Shasta than to any of the other so-called Kahi or Northern Hokan languages. The Northern Hokan hypothesis now has little if any support from scholars, and broader Hokan is doubted by most scholars (see Chapter 6).

*Pomoan
   *Northeastern Pomo
   *Southeastern Pomo
   *Eastern Pomo
   *Western Pomoan
      *Northern Pomo
      *Southern Group
         *Central Pomo
         *Southern Pomo
         *Kashaya

Pomoan languages were formerly spoken between the Pacific Coast and the Sacramento Valley in north-central California. (See Map 2.6.) Powell's (1891) name for the family was the Kulanapan stock. The seven Pomoan languages have an internal divergence greater than that of Germanic languages (McLendon and Oswalt 1978). Robert Oswalt (1964) judged the time depth of the Southern Group as similar to Western Romance languages, less than 1250 years, with the split between Northern Pomo and Southern Pomo as like that between Romanian and Western Romance, somewhat more than 1,500 years (see Golla 2011, 106).[51]

Northeastern Pomo was spoken along Stony Creek on the eastern slope of the Inner Coast Range in Northern California, around Stonyford, on the west side of the Sacramento Valley north of Clear Lake. The Northeastern Pomo speakers were isolated from speakers of other Pomoan languages by territory belonging to the Patwin (of the Wintuan family), with whom they identified culturally; bilingualism in Patwin was common. Northeastern Pomo speakers controlled large salt deposits and as a result had contacts with speakers of several languages, especially with Nomlaki. The last fluent Northeastern Pomo speaker died in 1961.

Southeastern Pomo was spoken at the eastern end of Clear Lake around East Lake and Lower Lake, and is the heritage language of the Elem Indian Colony at Sulphur Bank and the Lower Lake Rancheria. Southeastern Pomo was strongly influenced by Patwin.

Eastern Pomo was centered on the west side of Clear Lake. The language recently became dormant, but in 2008 it had a handful of semi-fluent speakers at the Robinson and Big Valley Rancherias at the west end of Clear Lake (Golla 2011, 108).

Languages of the **Western** branch of Pomoan were spoken on the Russian River, divided into a Northern Pomo and Southern Pomo groups.

Northern Pomo's territory was larger than that of the other Pomoan languages, and the language had several dialects, linked with Northern Pomo triblets: **Mato**, **Mitom**, **Kacha**, **Masut**, **Balokay**, **Shodakay**, and **Komli**. **Shinal** and **Bowal** appear to have been linguistically mixed groups. Northern Pomo's last known speaker, Elenor Stevenson Gonzalez, died in 2005, at the Sherwood Rancheria near Willits, California (Golla 2011, 109).

Southern Group comprises three languages, Central Pomo, Southern Pomo, and Kashaya.

Central Pomo was spoken on the California coast at Point Arena-Manchester and about 40 miles inland in the Hopland area. It had three triblets, each with their own dialecs: **Yokaya, Shokowa,** and **Yobakeya**. It no longer has native speakers, but revitalization efforts are underway.

Southern Pomo (called Gallinomero in early sources) was spoken on the lower course of the Russian River in Sonoma County, in the Dry Creek Valley, and on the Santa Rosa plain. It is less well known than the other languages of the group. It had identified dialects: **Makahmo, Kale,** and others.

Kashaya (Southwestern Pomo) was spoken on the Sonoma County coast from just north of Bodega Bay to around Stewart's Point and Annapolis (Golla 2011, 109–110).

There is not full agreement among those who have reconstructed Proto-Pomoan phonology. One proposal for the Proto-Pomoan phonemic inventory is: /t, ṭ (c), k, q, ʔ, b, d, pʰ, (tʰ), ṭʰ, kʰ, qʰ, (p'), t', ṭ', c', k', q', s, x, χ, h, l, m, n, w, y; i, e, a, o, u; vowel length; two tones/ (see McLendon 1973, 20–33, 53; Oswalt 1976a, 14; Moshinsky 1976, 57; see also Webb 1971). The sound correspondences upon which these reconstructed phonemes are based are generally clear, though opinions concerning the best reconstruction for some of these sounds have differed. For example, for the correspondence set with x in Southeastern Pomo and $š$ in the other languages, Robert Oswalt (1976a) reconstructed *š while Sally McLendon (1973) reconstructed *x. This is in opposition to the correspondence set of Southeastern χ, Eastern Pomo x, and the other languages h for which McLendon (1973, 18) reconstructed *χ. The Proto-Pomoan velar series, with *k, *kʰ, *k', has for the most part shifted to alveopalatal affricates, č, čʰ, č', respectively, in all the languages except Eastern Pomo, which retains the velar reflexes. Oswalt (1976a) reconstructed the alveopalatals for Proto-Pomoan, while McLendon (1973) and Moshinsky (1976) reconstructed the velars. This is correlated with the shift in all the languages except Eastern Pomo and partly in Kashaya of the uvular series, *q, *qʰ, *q', to the velars, k, kʰ, k', respectively. From the perspective of typical directionality of sound change, McLendon's and Moshinsky's reconstruction seems the more likely to be accurate. Proto-Pomoan had verbal suffixes for imperative, durative, causative, singular, optative, plural active, reciprocal, reflexive, semelfactive, speculative, and sentence connectives, with a series of instrumental prefixes.

The Proto-Pomoan homeland appears to have been around Clear Lake, in the foothill oak woodlands. The reconstructed Proto-Pomoan vocabulary suggests that Proto-Pomoan speakers were hunters and gatherers. The reconstructed vocabulary reveals that Proto-Pomoan speakers subsisted on game, seafood, nuts (and acorns), grains, berries, and tubers; they hunted with bow and arrow, fished with nets and traps, and used baskets for gathering, storing, and cooking. They danced and sang for ritual reasons, played at least one musical instrument, and had beads (McLendon 1973, 63–64; Moratto 1984, 551–552; Whistler 1983–1984).

Margaret Langdon (1979) presented comparisons on the basis of which she argued that Pomoan may be related to Yuman. The broader Hokan hypothesis, with which Pomoan is often linked, is not sustained by most linguists (see Chapter 6).

*Yana

Yana is a language isolate. The Yana territory was in north-central California west of Mt. Lassen, in the hills and canyons at the northeastern corner of the Sacramento Valley, between the Pit River and the Tehama-Butte county line. (See Map 2.6.)

Like other Native American groups in the area, the Yana suffered heavily in the first twenty years of their contact with White people, especially with the gold miners, beginning about 1850. The Yahi band isolated itself and was not rediscovered until 1908, in the vicinity of upper Mill Creek and Deer Creek Canyon. By 1911 all Yahi had perished except, Ishi (c. 1861–1916). Ishi's story is extremely famous, the subject of four movies and more than ten books. The names *Yana* and *Yahi* mean 'people' in these language varieties, *ya:na* and *ya:xi*, respectively.

Yana's three dialects were **Northern Yana**, spoken in a small area around Montgomery Creek; **Central Yana**, on Cow Creek; and **Southern Yana**, spoken in the southern two-thirds of the territory. In Sapir and Swadesh's (1960, 13) words, these varieties were "clearly identifiable dialects, mutually intelligible within limits." Northern and Central Yana differed mostly just in vocabulary and were clearly mutually intelligible. Southern Yana, on the other hand, was more distinct from the other two, with many lexical, phonological, and grammatical differences. Southern Yana "was understood by Northern and Central Yana speakers only with difficulty" (Golla 2011, 101). Southern Yana had a number of sub-dialects. **Yahi**, the best known of these, was Ishi's language. At least one speaker of Yana survived until about 1940.

Yana distinguished between forms of speech used by males and those used by females, although Yana has no grammatical gender. For example, for 'person' males said *yana* (from which the language gets its name) while females said *ya* (see Sapir 1949[1929b], 207).

Yana is often associated with the disputed and largely abandoned Hokan hypothesis (see Chapter 6).

*Salinan
 *Antoniano
 *Migueleño

Salinan, now dormant, was spoken along the south-central coast of California, in the southern part of the Salinas River (the source of Salinan as the language's name) and in the nearby mountain range in San Luis Obispo, Monterey, and perhaps also San Benito Counties in California (Turner 1980, 53; 1987; Golla 2011, 114). (See Map 2.6.) Salinan consisted of two closely related languages or emergent languages/dialect clusters, a northern one, **Antoniano**, primarily associated with Mission San Antonio de Padua, near Jolon in southern Monterey County, and a southern one, **Migueleño**, primarily associated with Mission San Miguel Arcángel, in northern San Luis Obispo County. The last speakers of both died in the late 1950s or early 1960s.

The unknown language of **los playanos**, who lived to the west of the region, has been suspected of being perhaps another dialect of Salinan, an additional Salinan language, Esselen, Chumash, or some unknown "relict" language distinct from all these others (Golla 2011, 115–116; Turner 1987, 1, 5).

Dixon and Kroeber (1913a, 1913b, 1919) originally grouped Salinan and Chumash in their "Iskoman" group, which they subsequently placed in their larger Hokan proposal. For the proposed Iskoman, they presented only twelve presumed cognates, clearly not sufficient evidence. Terrence Kaufman (1988, 2015a, 2015b) removed Chumash from his version of the

Hokan hypothesis, but retained Salinan, thus further challenging the Iskoman proposal. Most other linguists have abandoned Hokan or at least have grave doubts about it (see Chapter 6).

Cochimí-Yuman
  *Cochimí
    *Northern
    *Southern
  Yuman
    Kiliwa
    Core Yuman
      Pai
        Paipai
        Upland Yuman
      River Yuman
        Mojave (Mohave)
        Quechan (Yuma)
        Maricopa (Piipaash)
      Diegueño-Cocopah (Delta-California Yuman)
        Ipai (Northern Diegueño)
        Kumeyaay
        Tipai
        Cocopah (Cocopa, Cucupá)

(Mixco 1978; León-Portilla 1985; also Langdon and Munro 1980, 122; Langdon 1990.) (See Maps 2.6. and 2.1.)

    Cochimí is dormant and poorly documented, but it is clearly related to Yuman (Mixco 1978). Cochimí was a chain of dialects formerly spoken in the central portion of the Baja California peninsula, from about 150 miles south of the US border to about 200 miles north of Cabo San Lucas. The Jesuit missionary Miguel del Barco compared the diversity in Cochimí to that of the languages of the Iberian Peninsula (Mixco 1978, 39). Two dialect clusters or emergent languages can be identified. **Northern Cochimí** was spoken by nomadic bands in the Central Desert and later associated with the missions at Santa María Cabujacamang, Santa Gertrudis, and San Francisco de Borja Adac. It was also called **Borjeño** or **Borjino**, after the San Francisco Borja Adac mission. **Southern Cochimí** was spoken by more settled groups at the oases and in the highlands south of the 28th parallel, best attested from the missions of San Javier de Viggé-Biaundó, San José de Comondú, and San Ignacio Kadakaamán. Most of the scanty documentation of Cochimí comes from the Jesuit missions (1697–1767), although there are some nineteenth-century vocabularies.
    Yuman groups occupy the southernmost part of California and the northern part of Baja California along the Colorado River, as well as part of Arizona and adjacent areas of Sonora, Mexico.

Kiliwa is the most divergent language of the Yuman branch (Mixco 1985, 1996, 2000, 2013). It was spoken on the Baja California peninsula south of Paipai. It is critically endangered; its few speakers are now at Santa Catarina with speakers of Paipai.

Paipai of the Pai subgroup of Yuman is spoken in several small communities in northern Baja California, near San Miguel, Santa Catarina, and San Isidoro. Paipai is closely related to the Upland Yuman languages of western Arizona.

Upland Yuman is a single language with several mutually intelligible dialects, but this can be confusing because the dialects represent groups that have well-known ethnic identities, **Hualapai**, **Havasupai**, and **Yavapai**. The Yavapai traditionally were divided into four regional subtribes. Each community speaks a distinct variety, although all varieties are mutually intelligible with little difficulty. Hualapai (Walapai) is spoken at the Hualapai Indian Reservation in Peach Springs, Arizona. Havasupai is spoken in the village of Supai in Havasu Canyon, at the western end of the Grand Canyon. Yavapai is spoken in four small reservation communities, Prescott, Fort McDowell, Camp Verde, and Clarkdale. Local varieties, however, reflect pre-reservation subtribes and include **Yavepe**, **Tolkapaya**, **Keweevkapaya**, and **Wipukpaya**.[52]

Mojave (Mohave), of the River subgroup of Yuman, is the heritage language of the Fort Mojave Tribe, near Needles, California, and of the Mojave members of the Colorado River Indian Tribes, near Parker, Arizona.[53]

Quechan (Yuma), also of the River subgroup, is spoken by some members of the Quechan Indian Nation of southeastern California, adjacent to Yuma, Arizona.[54]

Maricopa (Piipaash), of the River subgroup, was originally spoken by several small tribes along the lower Gila and Colorado Rivers. It is now spoken by a minority of the members of the Maricopa (or Pee-Posh) tribe of Arizona, most of them located at the Maricopa Colony at Laveen, on the Gila River Reservation south of Phoenix, and in the community of Lehi on the Salt River Reservation northeast of Phoenix.

The name **Diegueño** can be confusing. It refers to Ipai-Kumeyaay-Tipai together, which are sometimes referred to collectively as just *Kumeyaay*. The classification is complicated further by the fact that **Ipai** and **Tipai**—names that are taken from the word for 'person' in each of the groups—are to some extent mutually intelligible, raising the question of whether they should not be classified as just dialects of a single language instead of as separate languages. To add to complications, a third dialect cluster intermediate between Ipai and Tipai was added, called **Kumeyaay**, making "Kumeyaay" confusing because of its use by different people to refer to different things in different contexts.

Three emergent languages are recognized within this dialect complex. **Ipai** (Northern Diegueño) is spoken by a small number of elderly people in four communities in northwestern San Diego County, including Mesa Grande, Santa Ysabel, San Pasqual, and Barona. **Kumeyaay** is spoken in several locations in central and southern San Diego County, the most important being Campo. **Tipai** is spoken in several communities in northern Baja California, as far south as Ensenada and Santa Catarina, and also in California by the Jamul community near San Diego. The distinction between Kumeyaay and Tipai is perhaps more political and social than linguistic, and is greatly influenced by the US-Mexican border.

Cocopah (Cocopa, Cucupá) together with the Diegueño complex belongs to the Diegueño-Cocopah subgroup of Yuman. Cocopah was originally spoken on the lower

Colorado River and its delta. It is spoken today by some of the members of the Cocopah Tribe, whose reservation is near Yuma, Arizona, and by Mexican Cucapás in communities in Baja California and Sonora, Mexico.

The Proto-Yuman area appears to have been the lower Colorado River. The Proto-Yuman phonemes are: /p, t, (t̪), c, kʸ k, kʷ, q, qʷ, ʔ, s, ṣ, x, xʷ, m, n, nʸ, l, lʸ, r, w, y; i, a, u; vowel length/ (Langdon and Munro 1980, 126; cf. Wares 1968). Cochimí-Yuman is one of the largest language families from among those which have often been thought to belong to the controversial Hokan classification. Although Cochimí-Yuman has not definitely been shown to be related to any other languages, Langdon (1979) presented evidence suggestive of a possible Pomoan-Yuman genetic affiliation. (See Chapter 6.)

Washo (Washoe)

Washo is a language isolate. The Washo territory is on the California-Nevada state line, in the drainages of the Truckee and Carson Rivers, centering on Lake Tahoe. (See Map 7.3.) Washo is critically endangered, spoken by a very few elders of the Washoe Tribe, divided among four small reservations in both Nevada and California.

Washo is the only non-Numic (Uto-Aztecan) group in the Great Basin Culture Area and the Great Basin Linguistic Area (see Chapter 7). However, the language also shares areal traits with some neighboring California languages (Jacobsen 1986, 109–111; see also Sherzer 1976, 128, 164, 238–239, 246).

Based on geography, on apparent older loanwords from neighboring languages (Numic, Miwokan, and Maiduan), and on the uncertainty of any external genetic relationships, "one can only assume that Washoe has long been in approximately the same area in which it is now found" (Jacobsen 1986, 107). It has been associated with the Hokan classification, but even Alfred Kroeber (1953, 369) admitted that "the affiliation [of Washo] with other Hokan languages can not be close." Others find the Hokan hypothesis very doubtful and many reject it outright (see especially Jacobsen 1986; see Chapter 6).

*Yukian (Yuki-Wappo)
 *Yuki (Northern Yukian)
 *Wappo (Southern Yukian)

Yukian languages were spoken in the Coast Range of northern California. (See Map 2.6.) Some scholars had some reservations about the Yukian classification (see for example Sawyer 1980, 1991). Wappo and Yuki are said to share less than 20 percent of their basic vocabulary (Golla 2011, 191). Nevertheless, William Elmendorf's (1988) evidence conclusively established that these languages are genetically related, in Victor Golla's (2011, 188) words, "securely demonstrated." Elmendorf's (1981, 1988) evidence for the genetic relationship is extensive, with clear sound correspondences. He said of their degree of relatedness that it is "comparable to that of Italian to German, or of German to Russian" (Elmendorf 1968, 177).

Jesse Sawyer's (1991, 76) doubts involved his seeing the evidence as due to borrowing or shared areal features. For example, he argued that if Wappo and Yuki were genetically related, they should have common terms for 'black', 'white', and 'red' but that these terms are "totally unrelated" in Wappo and Yuki, which to him was evidence of lack of relatedness (Sawyer 1991, 103). However, by this criterion Latin and Greek, both Indo-European languages, with *niger-maúros* 'black', *albus-leuko* 'white', and *ruber/rufus-kókkinos* 'red', would no longer be related either. Elmendorf and Shepherd (1999) also countered that the words which Sawyer claimed were loans constituted only 6.9 percent of the set of resemblant lexical items.

Wappo was spoken north of San Francisco from Napa Valley to Clear Lake, bordered by Pomoan languages on the west, Lake Miwok on the north, and Patwin on the east and south. Wappo had several dialects: **Mishewal**, **Mayacama/Caymus**, **Guilicos** (Guilucos), and **Lile'ek** (Golla 2011, 191), all mutually intelligible. Most of the documentation is from Mishewal and Mayacama. Wappo borrowed from all the languages that surround it—from Lake Miwok, Coast Miwok, Southern Pomo, Eastern Pomo, Southeastern Pomo, and Wintun dialects (Sawyer 1978, 256–257). Wappo became dormant recently.[55]

Wappo was analyzed as having a typologically unusual nominative subject marking clitic *=(y)i* with objects not marked. Its sister language Yuki does not have this. Marianne Mithun (2021b) re-examined the Wappo materials and found that this morpheme apparently instead marked topic shift and that it appears to be due to influence from neighboring Pomoan languages, which have a similar enclitic that marks topic shift.

Yuki (Northern Yukian) was a complex of dialects that were spoken in the mountains of northern Mendocino County, "from the high ridges of the Coast Range bordering the Sacramento Valley to the rocky coast north of Fort Bragg" (Golla 2011, 188). It had three main vaarieties, called "language-like dialects" by Elmendorf (1993, 178). The three were at least partially mutually intelligible (Miller 1978). **Coast Yuki** was spoken along the coast between Fort Bragg and Usal Creek. **Huchnom** was spoken along the lower part of the South Eel River northeast of Willits.[56] **Yuki** (Yuki proper, Round Valley Yuki) was spoken in and around Round Valley in the upper drainage of the Middle Fork of Eel River (Golla 2011, 189).

The name Yuki is said to come from Nomlaki *yuki* 'enemy'; Golla (2011, 193) mentions that Wintu and Nomlaki *yukeh* 'enemy, hostile people' was used to designate any group with which they had hostile relations.

The sound systems of the two Yukian languages are similar, though Wappo lacks the nasalized vowels and uvular consonants found in Yuki, and the Wappo affricates *ts*, *ts'*, and *č* do not appear in Yuki.

The Proto-Yukians may be the only truly autochthonous people of northern California. The Yuki and the Wappo seem to have been separated approximately 3,000 years ago (Elmendorf 1968) by the expansion of Pomoan speakers into their territory. Both Yukian and Pomoan peoples occupied the area before the arrival of Wintuan speakers (Whistler 1977, 1983–1984; Moratto 1984, 538).

Suggestions about possible broader genetic connections for Yukian have included Hokan, Penutian, Siouan, and even Swadesh's (1954b) Hokogian net (proposed to include Hokan, Muskogean, and several other languages of the Gulf region, grouped more closely with Coahuiltecan and Chitimacha) (see Campbell 1997a, 132 for details). None of these has proven acceptable (see Chapter 6).

*Esselen
Esselen is a language isolate. It was spoken by several triblets in the late eighteenth century in the upper Carmel Valley and around Big Sur, on the central California coast south of Monterey, in the northern Santa Lucia Range in Monterey County. They were brought into three missions, San Carlos (in Carmel), Soledad (in the Salinas Valley), and San Antonio. (See Map 2.6.) Esselen was among the first languages of California to become dormant. Already in 1833, Fray Felipe Arroyo de la Cuesta reported that there were very few remaining speakers of the language. Esselen is attested in three vocabularies collected between 1786 and 1832, as well as in a catechism and a short translation. Additional material was obtained between 1830 and 1930 from Costanoan speakers who remembered something of Esselen. The total extant corpus is about 300 words and a few phrases and short sentences (Beeler 1977).

As mentioned above, Catherine Callaghan (2014, 39–56) found substantial evidence of an Esselen substrate in Utian, with a number of loanwords. She interpreted this as Utian Speakers (especially Costanoans) moving into territory where Esselen speakers resided. David Shaul (1988, 2014) also presented a number of "lookalikes" suggestive of borrowing between Esselen and neighboring Costanoan, with a few shared also with certain Miwokan languages. He interprets the pattern of borrowing as indicative of Costanoan spreading south along the coast and absorbing (or at least being in contact with) Esselen or Esselen-related speech communities. Michael Moratto (1984, 558) reported that Esselen territory was greatly reduced by Costanoan expansion, and "archaeologically these developments are seen in the replacement of the older 'Sur Pattern' [Esselen?] by the 'Monterey Pattern' [Costanoan?] between circa 500 BC and 1 AD."

Esselen has usually been mentioned in connection with the mostly abandoned Hokan hypothesis; however, some scholars consider the Esselen data so fragmentary that they defy classification altogether.

*Chumashan
   *Obispeño (Northern Chumash, Tilhini)
   *Southern Chumash
      *Central Chumash (emergent languages or dialects)
         *Purisimeño
         *Ineseño (Samala)
         *Barbareño (Shmuwich)
         *Ventureño (Mitsqanaqa'n)
      *Island Chumash (Isleño [Samala] and Cruzeño)

(Klar 1977, 38; Beeler 1970, 14; Beeler and Klar 1977; Grant 1978, 505; Shipley 1978, 86; Golla 2011, 194–201.)

Chumash is the general term for the six languages or varieties of the Chumashan family once spoken in southern California.[57] (See Map 2.6.) All are now dormant; Mary Yee, the last fluent speaker of Barbareño, died in 1965. Chumashan languages are closely related to one another. They were formerly spoken on the Santa Barbara Islands and in the adjacent coastal territory from just north of San Luis Obispo to approximately Malibu, and they extended inland as far as the San Joaquin Valley. The languages are attested in varying degrees, from quite well for Inezeño, Barbareño, and Ventureño to very poorly for Interior Chumash, for which there is only one wordlist of about sixty items (Klar 1977). After 1913 these languages became the focus of much work by J. P. Harrington. He extensively documented all of the languages that retained speakers then, and continued the work on them until his death in 1961.

Most of the languages are referred to by the name of the Franciscan mission with which they were associated.

Obispeño is named for Mission San Luis Obispo. Obispeño (Northern Chumash) is generally recognized as the most divergent variety of Chumash (Kroeber 1910, 1953; Langdon 1974; Klar 1977).

The Southern Chumash branch has the Central Chumash emergent languages and Island Chumash. Of the four Central Chumash varieties (Purisimeño, Inezeño, Barbareño, and Ventureño), Victor Golla (2011, 195) said, "all were probably mutually intelligible, although communication between speakers at the geographical extremes—Purisimeño and inland varieties of Ventureño—could well have been difficult."

Purisimeño is named for Mission La Purísima Concepción. It was spoken at this mission in the lower the Santa Ynez River valley, near modern Lompoc, California, and in the territory to the north as far as Santa Maria.

Inezeño (Ineseño) is named for Mission Santa Inez (also spelled Ines and Ynez). It was spoken at that mission and throughout the upper valley of the Santa Ynez River.[58]

Barbareño is the Chumash language once spoken at the Santa Barbara mission, from which it takes its name, and along the southern coast of Santa Barbara County from Point Conception to Carpinteria. Barbareño also included the **Emigdiano** variety. Emigdiano was spoken in the nineteenth century in a San Joaquin Valley community. It was a mixture of Barbareño Chumash and Yokuts, the result of mission-era trading and resettlement, not a precontact inland extension of Barbareño (Golla 2011, 196).

Ventureño was spoken at the San Buenaventura mission, whence it gets its name, and in most of Ventura County. There were at least six different dialects, which probably included the **Castac** dialect and apparently also **Alliklik** (see below).

Island Chumash (Isleño) was spoken originally on three islands in the Santa Barbara Channel—San Miguel, Santa Rosa, and Santa Cruz—but with the establishment of the Spanish missions, the Island Chumash communities were relocated to the mainland, primarily at San Buenaventura. The island dialects were different from the Chumash languages of the adjacent mainland. Victor Golla (2011, 194) reported that intercommunication between the Island Chumash and the Barbareño and Ventureño varieties was "apparently difficult," but the degree of difference is difficult to determine because of the paucity of the data.

Cruzeño (Cruceño) and **Roseño**, though often listed as distinct, are considered variants of Island Chumash. Cruzeño is named for Santa Cruz Island, where the speakers lived before they were settled on the mainland around 1824 (Beeler and Klar 1977; Klar 1977, 1). Roseño gets its name from Santa Rosa Island.

Since there is so little data on **Cuyama** (Interior Chumash), it is unclear whether it constituted a distinct variety (Grant 1978, 505).

Kathryn Klar (1977, 32) reconstructed Proto-Chumash with the phonemic inventory: / p, t, k, q, ʔ, p', t', k', q', S, (C), h, (S'), C', m, n, m', n', l, l', w, y, w', y'; i, e, a, ɨ, o, u/. While Proto-Chumash must have had both *q and *x, Klar reconstructed only *q, since these sounds were in alternation in the proto language, seemingly not contrastive sounds. Klar's *S covers both s and the results of regressive assimilation found in most of the varieties. The sibilant harmony of Chumashan makes the sound correspondences irregular. In Chumash sibilant harmony, the regressive assimilation of a final š causes all preceding instances of s in a word to change to š, while final s causes preceding cases of š to change to s (Beeler 1970; Klar 1977, 125–128). For *C/*C' (to represent both dental c/c' [that is, ts/ts'] and alveopalatal č/ č'), Klar has only one cognate set, glottalized in Inezeño and Ventureño, but without glottalization in Obispeño. She tentatively also reconstructed *S', though there are no cognate sets to support its reconstruction. The reconstruction of the sibilants is also complicated by sound-symbolic alternations, significant throughout Chumashan (Klar 1977, 129–133). J. P. Harrington (1974, 8) said of Ventureño that "any part of speech can be diminutivized by changing its consonants as follows: s > č; c [ts] > č; š > č, sometimes c [ts]; č > c [ts]; l > n; x > q ... Although not frequent in the language, it permeates the whole structure and lexicology" (see also Klar 1977, 130). Proto-Chumashan had VOS basic word order (Klar 1977, 133–135).

Chumashan appears to have occupied their coastal region continuously from as early as 2,000 years ago (Moratto 1984, 558).

Chumashan has often been linked with the broader but contested Hokan proposal. Kaufman (1988, 2015a, 2015b) removed Chumashan from his version of the Hokan hypothesis. In any case, Hokan in general is highly contested and rejected by most other linguists working with the languages that have been linked in linguistic discussions with the Hokan hypothesis.

Uto-Aztecan
    Northern Uto-Aztecan
        Eastern Northern Uto-Aztecan
            Numic
                Western Numic
                    Mono
                    Northern Paiute
                Central Numic
                    Panamint
                    Shoshone (Shoshoni)
                    Comanche
                Southern Numic
                    Kawaiisu
                    Ute-Chemehuevi-Southern Paiute
        Hopi

Western Northern Uto-Aztecan
    Takic
        *Serrano-Kitanemuk
            *Serrano
            *Kitanemuk
        *Gabrielino-Fernandeño (Tongva)
        Cupan
            Cahuilla
            *Cupeño
            *Luiseño-Juaneño
    *Tübatulabal (Tubatalabal)
Southern Uto-Aztecan
    Piman
        O'odham (Pima-Papago)
        Pima Bajo
        Tepehuan
            Northern Tepehuan
            Southern Tepehuan
        *Tepecano
Taracahitic
    Tarahumaran
        Tarahumara
        Guarijío
    Tubar
    Cahitan (Yaqui, Mayo, Cahita, Tehueco)
    *Opatan
        *Ópata
        *Eudeve
Corachol-Aztecan
    Cora-Huichol
        Cora
        Huichol
            Nahua (Aztecan) (See Canger 1988)
                *Pochutec
                General Nahua
                      Pipil (Nawat)
                      Nahua main branch
                          Central Nahua
                          Peripheral Nahua
                              Western Group
                              Eastern Group

(Cf. Campbell 1997a, 134–138; Kaufman 1980, 2003; and Hale and Harris 1979. See Haugen 2021, 551–552 for a slightly different classification. See also Greenhill et al. 2023.)

(See Map 2.7. Uto-Aztecan Languages (pre-contact distribution). See also Maps 2.6. and 7.8.)

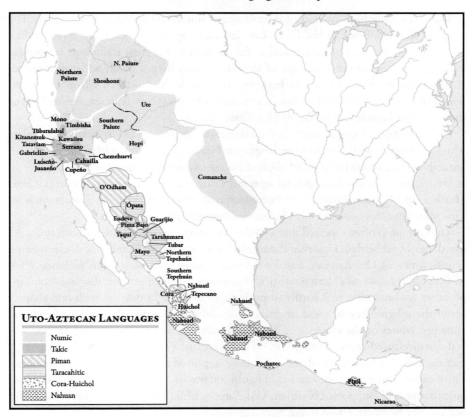

MAP 2.7. Uto-Aztecan languages (pre-contact distribution)

Uto-Aztecan is one of the largest Native American language families in terms of numbers of languages, speakers, and geography, extending from Oregon to Costa Rica. Michael Foster (1996, 90–91) described Uto-Aztecan as one of the best-studied language families of the Americas, providing a model of understanding of how language history can serve the interests of culture history; he said it has the honor of being the first language family in the Americas to which the comparative method was comprehensively applied, by Edward Sapir (1913–1915, 1919).

The classification of Uto-Aztecan languages has had a complicated history (for details see Caballero 2011; Campbell 1997a, 133–139; Dakin 2001; Haugen et al. 2020). Briefly, Daniel Brinton (1891, 118–119) coined the name Uto-Aztecan and classified the languages in three branches: **Shoshonean**, **Sonoran**, and **Nahuatl/Nahuatlecan** (Aztecan [Nahua]). John Wesley Powell (1891a) rejected Uto-Aztecan, listing Shoshonean and Sonoran as belonging to distinct stocks. However, Sapir (1913–1919[1915]) proved the relatedness of the languages of the Uto-Aztecan family conclusively to everyone's satisfaction in one of the first compelling demonstrations of the applicability of the comparative method to languages that do not have a long written tradition.

There is a fairly high amount of diversification among the branches of the family. For example, although Brian Stubbs' (2011) *Uto-Aztecan Comparative Vocabulary* has more than 2,500 cognate sets, only 167 are found in five to eight of the eight traditional subgroups, meaning that only about 6 percent of the sets actually have a family-wide distribution. Another 525 sets have cognates in languages from both the Northern Uto-Aztecan and Southern Uto-Aztecan branches, that is, 27 percent of the sets have representative in both of the two major branches of the family. (See Shaul 2014, 305.)

Eight branches of Uto-Aztecan at the lower levels are recognized by nearly all scholars who have worked with Uto-Aztecan languages: Numic, Takic, Tübatulabal, Hopi, Piman, Taracahitic, Cora-Huichol (Corachol), and Nahua (Aztecan). In the view of Haugen et al. (2020, 3), there has also been general agreement that the subgroups Numic, Piman, Cora-Huichol, and Nahua (Aztecan) are uncontroversial. However, there has not always been agreement about higher-level, more inclusive subgroupings.

The opinion is often repeated that Uto-Aztecan subgroup classification is uncertain, debated, or not yet settled. However, there have been a fairly large number of distance-based classifications of Uto-Aztecan, based on lexical information alone—this includes Wick Miller's often-cited (1984) lexicostatistical classification—and given that distance-based approaches are unreliable, it is hardly surprising that they might disagree with one another about the subgrouping of these languages, particularly since they do not all rely on the same procedures or the same set of data. For example, Haugen et al. (2020) applied several distance-based analyses using UPGM (Unweighted Pair-Group Method), Neighbor-joining, and NeighborNet analyses to the same improved lexical dataset and the resulting classifications differ from one another in significant ways. Cortina-Borja and Valiñas' (1989) quantitative study supported Northern Uto-Aztecan while Haugen et al.'s (2020) study did not support Northern Uto-Aztecan.[59]

However, the studies that have used standard historical linguistic methods (e.g., Kaufman 1980; Campbell 1997a; Hill 2011) and the more reliable character-based quantitative methods (Greenhill et al. 2023) are all largely in agreement with one another, though there has not been complete agreement among classifications. Jane Hill's (2011, 273) classification differs in some significant regards from the general classification given above. She did not accept Southern Uto-Aztecan and had some doubts about the internal classification of Takic and the existence of Taracahitic. Her classification is:

Uto-Aztecan
    Northern Uto-Aztecan
        Hopi
        Numic
        Californian
            Serran
            Gab[rielino]-Cupan
            Tübatulabal
    Tepiman
    Cahitan (Yaqui-Mayo)
    Ópata-Eudeve

Tarahumara-Guarijío
Tubar
Corachol-Aztecan
    Corachol
    Aztecan

Hill's classification would dissolve Takic, replacing it with her Californian subgroup, which has Serran (composed of Serrano and Kitanemuk), and Gab-Cupan (containing Gabrielino [Tongva], and Cupan [composed of Cupeño, Luiseño, and Cahuilla]), with Tübatulabal grouped with these two groups. For Hill, Tubar remains a separate branch of its own.

Jason Haugen (2020, 551–552) accepts Southern Uto-Aztecan as valid, but with Tubar as a separate branch within Southern Uto-Aztecan. Otherwise he follows Hill (2011), though maintaining *Takic* instead of *Californian* as the label for the subgroup containing Serran, Gabrielino-Cupan, and Tübatulabal.

Haugen et al. (2020) compared results from several clustering algorithms (UPGMA [Unweighted Pair-Group Method], Neighbor-Joining, and Neighbor-Net), coming up with results similar to those of Wick Miller (1984) based on lexical evidence, though not supporting Miller's Sonoran grouping. As mentioned, they found support for Southern Uto-Aztecan but not for Northern Uto-Aztecan, and they found only weak evidence for Hill's Californian grouping. Their methods do recognize Numic, but only weakly so. They conclude from this that it "shows that these methods shouldn't be used in isolation, nor in lieu of more traditional historical linguistic methods" (Haugen et al. 2020, 26).

The primary split into Northern and Southern Uto-Aztecan branches is now well established. The unity of the Northern Uto-Aztecan branch was supported in a number of studies. Jeffrey Heath's (1977) morphological evidence and Alexis Manaster Ramer's (1992) demonstration that the Northern Uto-Aztecan languages share the innovation of *$ts > y$ proved influential. This evidence notwithstanding, Northern Uto-Aztecan has not been clearly indicated in some of the lexically based quantitative studies (Haugen et al. 2020). The unity of Southern Uto-Aztecan is generally supported, including by the lexically based studies.

Hale and Harris (1979) supported the unity of the Northern Uto-Aztecan branch, finding additional lexical evidence to support a split in Northern Uto-Aztecan into two branches, one with Numic and Hopi together as Eastern and one with Takic and Tübatulabal together as Western. As seen above, Jane Hill (2011) reached a similar conclusion for Northern Uto-Aztecan, grouping Takic and Tübatalbal in her "Californian" subgroup (see also Golla 2011, 169; Haugen et al. 2020, 3; Shaul 2014, 33).

Wick Miller's (1984) lexicostatistical classification supported Southern Uto-Aztecan, merging traditional Sonoran and Aztecan into a single larger unit. However, Miller did not join the Northern Uto-Aztecan groups together but instead saw them as four independent branches of the family. Northern Uto-Aztecan includes Numic, Takic, Tübatulabal, and Hopi. Southern Uto-Aztecan has Piman, Taracahitic, and Corachol-Aztecan (Cora-Huichol plus Aztecan [Nahua]). All of Haugen et al.'s (2020) different distance-based applications agree with Miller in not supporting Northern Uto-Aztecan as unified subgroup and with subgrouping Southern Uto-Aztecan languages together. For Haugen et al., Hill's

Californian subgroup (joining Tübatulabal and the Takic languages) shows up in only one of their applications (Neighbor-Net), and Miller's Sonoran shows up only in one version of Neighbor-Joining.

The name "**Numic**" is taken from the word for 'man, person', which in these languages has the form *nimɨ* or something very similar to it. Each of the Numic branches is a dialect chain in which some emergent languages are identified.

In **Western Numic**, the difference between **Mono** and **Northern Paiute** is not a sharply defined one; "the degree of intelligibility across the boundary seems largely to be a function of distance" (Golla 2011, 173). **Mono** is spoken in central California both on the western side of the Sierra Nevada, between Yosemite National Park and Kings Canyon National Park, and on the eastern side in Owens Valley from Lone Pine north to Big Pine. **Mono** has the main varieties **Western Mono** (Monachi), **Eastern Mono** (Owens Valley Paiute), **Northeastern Mono**, and **Southeastern Mono**. **Western Mono** is spoken in several communities that are near Yokuts communities and socially connected to them. The most important of these are at North Fork and Auberry (Big Sandy Rancheria). There are also a few speakers at Tollhouse (Cold Springs Rancheria) and Dunlop. **Eastern Mono** (Owens Valley Paiute) is spoken in the Owens Valley communities of Bishop, Big Pine, Lone Pine, and Fort Independence.

Northern Paiute varieties are **Oregon Northern Paiute** and **Nevada Northern Paiute** (Paviotso). Northern Paiute was spoken in the western Great Basin from roughly the John Day River in Oregon south through the western third of Nevada, to the vicinity of Mammoth, California. Today limited numbers of speakers are found in reservation communities and colonies in Oregon, Nevada, California, and Idaho, as well as in urban locations in these states. Principal communities are at Warm Springs and Burns, Oregon; Fort McDermitt, Owyhee, Winnemucca, Pyramid Lake, Reno-Sparks, Lovelock, Fallon, Yerington, and Walker River, Nevada; and Lee Vining and Fort Bidwell, California. The variety called **Bannock** is also spoken by a few elderly persons at Fort Hall, Idaho, where otherwise Shoshone is the heritage language.

Central Numic has **Panamint**, **Shoshone**, and **Comanche** as its members.

Panamint was formerly spoken between the Sierra Nevada in California and the Nevada valleys east of Death Valley. It has two main dialects, **Eastern Panamint** and **Western Panamint**. Eastern Panamint is in the community around Beatty, Nevada. Western Panamint includes groups living in Lone Pine and Darwin, California. **Tümpisa** (Timbisha) is considered transitional between the two. The Timbisha community is in Death Valley and Lone Pine.

Shoshone (Shoshoni) was spoken in a wide band stretching from Lida, Nevada, northeast through Nevada, Utah, Idaho, and Wyoming as far north as Lemhi, Idaho, and as far east as Wind River, Wyoming. Although there are a few large reservations that are predominantly Shoshone, there are many smaller reservations and communities scattered throughout the region. Shoshone is a dialect continuum without rigid isoglosses to separate the dialects. Several major clusters of varieties can be identified, but what separates them is not clear, as they interlock and overlap (Miller 1970; 1986, 99–100). **Western Shoshone** includes the communities throughout Nevada except for the Gosiute and Duck Valley communities. **Northern Shoshone** includes the Duck Valley and Fort Hall communities, as well as the smaller communities of northern Utah and southern Idaho. **Eastern Shoshone** includes the Wind River community in Wyoming. **Gosiute** (Goshute) includes the Gosiute and Skull Valley communities in Utah. The largest Shoshone speech community is at Fort Hall, Idaho.

Comanche is usually treated as a separate language within Central Numic. Before the eighteenth century the ancestors of the Comanches were Shoshone speakers in Wyoming; they acquired horses, took on Great Plains culture, and moved to the southern Plains from Kansas and Colorado to the Rio Grande. With this separation from Shoshone territory, the Comanche dialect developed, and the two "languages" are now mutually intelligible only with difficulty. In the late nineteenth century the Comanches were placed on reservation lands in southwestern Oklahoma, north of Lawton.

Southern Numic has Kawaiisu and Ute-Chemehuevi-Southern Paiute.

Kawaiisu is the language of a small tribe of the Tehachapi region between the Mohave Desert and the San Joaquin Valley in south-central California. It differs from the other Southern Numic varieties, usually treated as a distinct language.

Ute-Chemehuevi-Southern Paiute varieties fall in a dialect chain, with several distinguished local dialect clusters: **Southern Paiute**, **Southern Ute**, **Northern Ute** (Uintah-Ouray Ute), and **Chemehuevi**.

Ute-Chemehuevi is a dialect chain within Southern Numic that extends from central Colorado westward across Utah and southern Nevada to the eastern Mojave Desert in California. There are three major regional varieties, all mutually intelligible. **Ute** is spoken in and around three reservation communities: **Southern Ute** (Ignacio, Colorado), **Ute Mountain Ute** (Towaoc, Colorado), and **Uintah and Ouray Ute** (Northern Ute) (Ft. Duchesne, Utah).

Southern Paiute is spoken in ten widely separated communities in Utah, Arizona, and Nevada. The five Utah communities constitute the Paiute Tribe of Utah. The San Juan Paiute Tribe is located on the Navajo Reservation in Utah and Arizona. The Kaibab Paiute Tribe have a reservation north of the Grand Canyon. The three southern Nevada tribes are at Moapa, Las Vegas, and Pahrump.

Chemehuevi is spoken on the Colorado River Indian Reservation at Parker, Arizona, which Chemehuevis share with Mojaves, Navajos, and Hopis, and on the neighboring Chemehuevi Reservation in California.

Tübatulabal (Tubatulabal) has often been considered a separate branch by itself of Northern Uto-Aztecan. As mentioned above, there is evidence to group it together with Takic, in a Western Northern Uto-Aztecan subgroup.[60] It is the heritage language of the Tubatulabal tribe of Kern County, California. It is reported to have lost its last native speaker with the death of Jim Andreas in 2008.[61]

Takic is a subgroup of Northern Uto-Aztecan with languages spoken in southern California. The name "Takic" is based on words for 'man, person' in these languages. Together with Tübatulabal, it belongs to the Western Northern Uto-Aztecan subgroup (mentioned above).

Serrano-Kitanemuk is a division of the Takic subfamily.

Serrano was originally spoken in much of the Mojave Desert and the San Bernardino Mountains of southern California. Serrano descendants live mainly at the San Manuel Reservation near San Bernardino, also a number of Serranos have intermarried with the

Cahuillas on the Morongo and Soboba Reservations. There are no longer any native speakers of the language.

Kitanemuk is closely related to Serrano. It was formerly spoken in the Tehachapi Mountains and Antelope Valley in the interior of southern California, immediately south of the San Joaquin Valley. The last speakers probably died in the 1940s. Kitanemuk is characteristically considered a separate language of its own, though Serrano speakers understood it well. It and Serrano can be considered dialects of the same language (Golla 2011, 183).

Vanyume was a dialect of Serrano, but also appears to have shared some features with Kitanemuk. It has very little attestation (Golla 2011, 183).

Gabrielino (Tongva, Gabrielino-Fernandeño) is named for Mission San Gabriel near Los Angeles. The Gabrielino were originally a large tribe whose territory included most of Los Angeles and Orange County. The language is dormant. Several local dialects were distinguished including **Gabrielino** (proper), spoken in the Los Angeles basin, **Fernandeño**, spoken in San Fernando Valley, and the variety spoken on Santa Catalina Island. A few speakers survived into the twentieth century, and the language was extensively documented, primarily by J. P. Harrington between 1914 and 1933. **Fernandeño** was named for Mission San Fernando in San Fernando Valley. Gabrielino (Gabrielino-Fernandeño) is clearly a Takic language; some have seen it as aligned with Serrano-Kitanemuk and others group it with Cupan; Victor Golla (2011, 179) considered it "transitional between Serrano-Kitanemuk and Cupan."

Nicoleño was spoken on San Nicolas Island in California. Its last speaker was reported to be Juana María, who died in 1853. The total corpus attested of Nicoleño is four words and two songs, attributed to Juana María. It has generally been assumed that it is a Uto-Aztecan language; some believe it should be grouped with the languages of the Takic subgroup, while others would place it more specifically in the Cupan subgroup. (See Munro 2000[2002].)

Cupan is the Takic subgroup to which **Cahuilla**, **Cupeño**, and **Luiseño-Juaneño** belong.

Cahuilla is the heritage language of several small tribes in the inland area of southern California, including people at Morongo, Agua Caliente (Palm Springs), Cabazon, Augustine, Torres-Martinez, Santa Rosa, Cahuilla, Ramona, and Los Coyotes. Originally there were probably three dialects of Cahuilla: **Mountain Cahuilla**, **Desert Cahuilla**, and **Pass Cahuilla** (Wanikik).

Cupeño was originally spoken near Warner's Hot Springs, in Riverside County, but in 1902 the Cupeños were resettled with speakers of Luiseño on the rancheria at Pala. The last fluent speaker of Cupeño, Roscinda Nolasquez, died in 1987.

Luiseño-Juaneño (Luiseño) was originally spoken on the southern California coast north of the Diegueño and south of the Gabrielino regions, in the area dominated by the missions of San Luis Rey, which gives Luiseño its name, and San Juan Capistrano, that provided the **Juaneño** (Ajachemem) dialect its name. The dialects of the two mission communities differed, but were mutually intelligible; both dialects are now dormant. Both were extensively documented by J. P. Harrington in the 1930s, and considerably later documentation on Luiseño was done. Descendants of the San Luis Rey and San Juan Capistrano communities currently live at the La Jolla, Rincon, Pauma, Pechanga, and Pala Reservations, and in the town of San Juan Capistrano.

Hopi is often considered an independent branch in Northern Uto-Aztecan, though there is evidence to group it together with Numic in an Eastern Northern Uto-Aztecan subgroup (mentioned above). Four dialects are usually distinguished. The First Mesa dialect is in the villages of Walpi and Sichomovi and the town of Polacca. Unrelated **Hano** (Tewa of the Kiowa-Tanoan family) is spoken there by about a third of First Mesa's population. Another dialect is in the Second Mesa village of Shipaulovi, and the third dialect is spoken in the Second Mesa village of Mishongnovi (also called Toreva). The fourth dialect is in the Third Mesa villages of Oraibi, Hotevilla, Bacabi, and New Oraibi, as well as at Moencopi 40 miles to the west.[62]

The **Southern Uto-Aztecan** branch is firmly established (Campbell 1997a, 136–137; Campbell and Langacker 1978; Kaufman 1981; Merrill 2013; Stubbs 2011). William Merrill (2013) presented several sound changes shared by the Southern Uto-Aztecan languages, which he argues supports the Southern Uto-Aztecan classification.

Piman (Tepiman, Pimic) is a subgroup of Southern Uto-Aztecan.

O'odham (Upper Piman) is the northernmost of the languages of the Piman subfamily, the only one spoken in the United States. There are fluent speakers of all ages in Arizona and in Mexico. Two major dialects are distinguished, **Tohono O'odham** (formerly called Papago) and **Akimel O'odham** (or Pima). Most Akimel O'odham speakers live on the Gila River, Salt River, and Ak Chin Reservations, in the vicinity of Phoenix. Most Tohono O'odham speakers in the United States live on the Papago Reservation in southern Arizona west of Tucson; there are also speakers on the San Xavier and Gila Bend Reservations.[63]

Pima Bajo (Nevome, Mountain Pima, Lowland Pima) is spoken in northern Mexico, mainly in three communities Yepachic, Maycoba, and Yécora, with speakers also in small outlying villages and on isolated ranches in the area.

Tepehuan is a small group of two languages in the Piman subgroup. **Northern Tepehuan** is spoken in the north of Durango and the south of Chihuahua, two Mexican states. **Southern Tepehuan** is spoken in southeastern and southwestern Durango.

Tepecano is a member of the Piman subgroup, once spoken in Azquetlán, Jalisco, on the Río Bolaños. The last known speaker of Tepecano, Lino de la Rosa, died sometime after 1980.

Taracahitic is a large subgroup within Southern Uto-Aztecan made up of **Tarahumaran**, **Cahitic**, **Ópatan**, and (less certatinly) **Tubar**. Most Uto-Aztecanists accept the Taracahitic subgroup, though David Shaul (2014, 28) believes that it "has not been established."

Tarahumaran has **Tarahumara** and **Guarijío** as its members.

Tarahumara (Rarámuri) is a large language spoken in the state of Chihuahua, Mexico, mostly in the Sierra Madre Occidental mountains. It has five main dialects or even more by some counts.

Guarijío (Varihío) is spoken in villages in the Sierra Madre Occidental Mountains near the border of the Mexican states of Chihuahua and Sonora. The mountain variety is spoken primarily in the eastern part of Uruachi and around Arechuyvo in Chihuahua. The river variety is in the southwest in the Río Mayo basin and north to San Bernardo in Álamos. Mutual intelligibility between the two varieties is said to be difficult.

Tubar is dormant. It, too, was spoken in Chihuahua, Mexico, in a small valley between Guarajío and the Cahitan languages. Its position within the larger subgroup is difficult to determine (Stubbs 2011, 7).[64]

Cahitan is the name given to the collection of varieties that include **Yaqui** and **Mayo**. Yaqui and Mayo share a considerable degree of mutual intelligibility.

Yaqui (Hiaki, Yoeme) is spoken in northern Sonora, Mexico, and in Arizona.

Mayo is spoken in the south of Sonora and the north of Sinaloa, two Mexican states.

The name **Cahita** can be confusing, since it is sometimes used as a synonym for Mayo and sometimes for Yaqui and Mayo together.[65]

Opatan has two members, Ópata and Eudeve. David Shaul (2014) challenges the classification of Opatan as a subgroup of Taracahitic, though others have generally accepted it. It is often thought that Ópata and Eudeve were dialects of the same language, but that does not hold. They are reasonably different from one another; for example, Wick Miller (1984) found that they share only 73 percent of their basic vocabulary, a smaller amount than Tarahumara and Guarijío's shared 83 percent, for example, and there are grammatical differences (Shaul 2014, 176–177).

Ópata was spoken in central and northeastern Sonora, Mexico, extending to the US border. Most of what is known of Ópata is from the grammar by Jesuit Natal Lombardo (c. 1702[1641?]).

Eudeve (Dohema), also formerly spoken in Sonora, Mexico, had two dialects, **Heve** (Egue) and **Dohema**. What is known of Eudeve comes from two Jesuit sources, from Balthasar Loaysa's grammar (date not known) from the Eudeve of Tonichi and from a grammar of the Eudeve of Batuc (Pennington 1981).

David Shaul (2014, 28, 180) adds **Jova** as a Uto-Aztecan subfamily made up of a single language, between Opatan and Tarahumaran.

Cora and **Huichol** are clearly related to each other more closely than to other Uto-Aztecan groups. The two (often called Corachol) form a subgroup together with Nahua (Aztecan). Cora-Huichol and Nahua share several innovations, for example:

Proto-Uto-Aztecan (PUA) *p- > h (later h- > Ø in Nahua)
PUA initial *wo > ho (later h- > Ø in Nahua)
PUA *u > $ɨ$ ($ɨ$ > i later in Nahua) (see Campbell and Langacker 1978).

Terrence Kaufman (2003:6, 8, 15, 27) thought these changes took place in Nahua as a result of language contact with Cora-Huichol. There is, however, no compelling reason why these shared changes should be thought to be due to later language contact while other similar changes elsewhere in Uto-Aztecan are considered shared innovations and thus indicative of closer subgrouping classification. That Cora-Huichol and Nahua should be subgrouped together seems clear (see Campbell 1997a; Campbell and Langacker 1978; Haugen et al. 2020; Hill 2011, Greenhill et al. 2023, etc.).

Cora is spoken in the mountains of northern Nayarit, a Mexican state whose name comes from Cora's ethnonym, *Naáyarite*. Cora speakers recognize five dialects, **Cora from Jésus María**, **Mesa de Nayar**, **Santa Teresa**, **Corápan**, and **San Francisco**. Speakers find it difficult to understand some of the varieties. For example, the variety from Santa Teresa, spoken in the mountains north of the town of El Nayar, is said to have a low degree of mutual intelligibility with the other varieties.

Huichol is spoken in mountainous regions primarily of Jalisco, but extending also to the Mexican states of Durango, Nayatrit, San Luis Potosí, and Zacatecas. Huichol has many dialects.

Nahua (Aztecan) has **Pochutec** and **General Nahua**. General Nahua has all the other Nahua languages and varieties except Pochutec; it includes Pipil (Nawat) of Central America. (See Chapter 3 for details.)

The many names from colonial sources that are often thought to represent unattested or scarcely attested, dormant Uto-Aztecan languages are considered in Chapter 5.

The most commonly cited reconstruction of the Proto-Uto-Aztecan phonemic inventory has: /p, t, ts, k, kʷ, ʔ, s, h, m, n, (ŋ), (l), (r), w, y; i, a, ɨ, o, u; vowel length/ (see Kaufman 1981; Langacker 1977, 22; Campbell 1997a, 138; Stubbs 2011, 11–34). The controversy about whether the fifth vowel was *ɨ or *e has been resolved: it was *ɨ (Langacker 1970; Campbell and Langacker 1978). The sounds in parentheses in this inventory are the ones for which alternative reconstructions have been proposed. For example, several scholars have favored reconstructions that have *l and *n, where Terrence Kaufman (1981), Campbell and Langacker (1978), and others reconstruct these instead as *n and *ŋ respectively. In the first view, *n and *l are reconstructed and are assumed to have shifted in appropriate contexts to ŋ and n respectively in Northern Uto-Aztecan languages. In the second view, *ŋ and *n are reconstructed instead, and they changed to n and to l, respectively, in appropriate contexts in Southern Uto-Aztecan.⁶⁶ Sapir (1915a, 475) had reconstructed *ŋ, *L, and *n, where Proto-Uto-Aztecan *L changed to n in Northern Uto-Aztecan languages. Brian Stubbs (2011, 20) also favors this view (see also Haugen 2021, 559).

Uto-Aztecan has three well-known phonological processes, spirantization (lenition), nasalization, and gemination (hardening), proposed by Edward Sapir (1913–1919), largely limited to Northern Uto-Aztecan languages. Discussions of them have sometimes made them seem somewhat mysterious. Terrence Kaufman (1981) explained them and thus removed all mystery. Spirantization is the straightforward process that affects obstruents between vowels. Nasalizing stems merely reflect an earlier nasal segment that shows up on the surface only in limited circumstances and otherwise has undergone various sound changes in the different languages. Gemination results from an original consonant cluster with *-hC-. In Southern Uto-Aztecan, *hC, *nC, and plain *C show no distinct reflexes, although Kaufman (2003, 8) thought that word-finally *h# and *n# are reflected as long vowels in Pre-Nahua, though he said this interpretation was unclear. Proto-Uto-Aztecan *p after a vowel is weakened to a fricative or glide (or was lost) in the Southern languages, correlating with spirantization/lenition in Northern Uto-Aztecan. In Proto-Uto-Aztecan, all three processes took place both across morpheme boundaries and morpheme-internally. Thus an obstruent is spirantized between vowels whether within a single morpheme or at the boundary when two morphemes come together where the second morpheme has an initial vowel. Word-final *-n and *-h are lost, except that final n is preserved in Shoshone and Tübatulabal. However, when these two sounds are morpheme-final before another morpheme beginning in a consonant, some Northern Uto-Aztecan languages preserve distinct reflexes of the resulting *nC and *hC clusters. In Northern Uto-Aztecan, the *h in cases of *hC is retained as h in Hopi and Comanche, and partially in Shoshone, Serrano, and Southern Paiute. In the other Northern Uto-Aztecan languages, when the C of these *hC cases is an obstruent, they change by geminating, that is *hC > CC, where the resulting first C is a copy of the second. Obstruents that were not protected by preceding *h or nasal underwent lenition (spirantization). (For details of the correspondences and various sound changes in the individual branches and languages, see Kaufman 1981; Stubbs 2011.)

There are a few Uto-Aztecan languages whose classification within the family has not been certain for lack of sufficient documentation. The position of very poorly known **Tataviam**, from the upper Santa Clara River Valley, California, is unclear. It is a Takic language that may independently represent a fourth branch within Takic or it may belong with Serrano-Kitanemuk, but it is so scarcely attested that clear subgroup classification is not possible (Golla 2011, 179, 183–184). Poorly attested **Giamina** (Onomil) could be another Takic language, but the data are insufficient to determine its classification accurately. These and the many dormant and mostly unattested languages of northern Mexico that are often thought to be Uto-Aztecan are discussed in Chapter 5.

For general information on the classification of Uto-Aztecan and its history, see also Caballero 2011; Campbell 1997a, 133–139; Campbell and Langacker 1978; Greenhill et al. 2023, Hale 1958–1959, 1964; Haugen et al. 2020; Heath 1977; Langacker 1977; Miller 1967, 1983, 1984; Stubbs 2011; and Voegelin, Voegelin, and Hale 1962.

The date of the break-up of Proto-Uto-Aztecan unity is uncertain. Jane Hill (2021, 576) gave the Proto-Northern-Uto-Aztecan branch a time depth of circa 4000–3500 BP. However, Proto-Uto-Aztecan as a whole had been estimated at circa 5,000 BP (Fowler 2083, 235; Hill 2012, 59), and most recently at circa 4100 years ago by Greenhill et al. (2023).

Most Uto-Aztecanists firmly believe that the Proto-Uto-Aztecan speakers were hunter-gatherers whose homeland was in the Southwestern US-northwestern Mexican border area. Catherine Fowler (1983, 231) concluded from the evidence she assembled that the Proto-Uto-Aztecan homeland had "a mixed woodland/grassland setting, in proximity to montane forests," in southern Arizona along the Sierra Madre extending into northern Mexico (Shaul 2014, 73). From here, speakers spread to as far north as Oregon (Northern Paiute), east to the Great Plains (Comanche), and south as far as Costa Rica and maybe Panama (Nahua groups; see W. Fowler 1989). The Proto-Numic homeland was in southern California, near Death Valley (C. Fowler 1972). Wick Miller (1983, 123) suggested that the homeland of the proposed Sonoran grouping (essentially Southern Uto-Aztecan without Nahua) was in the foothill area between the Mayo and the Sinaloa Rivers in northern Mexico. (See Hale and Harris 1979, 176–177.)

Jane Hill (2001, 2002, 2012) proposed a different, controversial Proto-Uto-Aztecan homeland. She argued instead that Proto-Uto-Aztecans were maize cultivators, with their homeland in the south, associated with Mesoamerican maize agriculture—a view influenced by the farming/language dispersal hypothesis that sees agriculture as the driving force behind the dispersal of most larger language families (Bellwood 1997; Renfrew 1994, 2000; see Campbell and Poser 2008, 337–350 and Hammarström 2010 for critiques). More specifically, Hill would locate the Proto-Uto-Aztecan homeland on the northwest edge of Mesoamerica, in the area of Jalisco, Nayarit, Durango, and Zacatecas. There are serious problems with Hill's interpretation.

Most reconstructed Proto-Uto-Aztecan plant and animal terms are consistent with either Hill's southern or the traditional more northerly homeland hypotheses. However, the center-of-gravity model of linguistic diversification (also called linguistic migration theory), based on minimum moves and maximum diversification (see Campbell 2020a, 423–424), supports the traditional northern homeland. A southern homeland view has difficulty explaining the distribution of the languages, with less diversification in the south and more in the north (in terms of the time depth for the individual subgroups in each branch). Similarly, Nahua (Aztecan), the only branch of Uto-Aztecan situated squarely in Mesoamerica, shows every sign of being a late entrant into Mesoamerica, after breaking away from its Uto-Aztecan relatives. Nahua acquired several Mesoamerican structural traits and underwent changes that make it more like its Mesoamerican neighbors but that set it apart from other Uto-Aztecan languages, for example shift from SOV [Subject-Object-Verb] to VSO [Verb-Subject-Object] or VOS [Verb-Object-Subject] basic word order and shift of postpositions to relational nouns (Campbell et al. 1986; see also Kaufman 2003, 21). Nahua is head-marking, while Northern Uto-Aztecan and most other Southern Uto-Aztecan languages are dependent-marking, from which David Shaul (2014, 182) concludes, "so clearly Nahua is intrusive into Mesoamerica." Terrence Kaufman (2003, 23) argued that Nahua verb syntax was restructured, morphologized, into a single word due to contact with Mesoamerican languages; specifically he held that "of all the Meso-American languages, only Mije-Sokean [Mixe-Zoquean] and Totonako [Totonac] could have supplied a clear and full model for the morphologization of the verb word in Nawa [Nahua]" (p. 23; see also 2020a, 56). He also presented a number of other examples with ample discussion of the Mesoamericanization of Nahua syntax (Kaufman 2003, 24–28; 2020, 45, 51–56). Kaufman (2020, 24) observed further that "without doubt many indigenous inhabitants of Central Mexico," speakers of Huastecan, Totonakan, Pamean, Matlatzincan, Otomí-Mazahua, and Chiapanec-Mangue languages, "shifted to Nawa [Nahua]." This language contact presumably helped to push Nahua towards Mesoamerican linguistic structures.

Also, Nahua borrowed much vocabulary that matches the ecology and cultural traits diagnostic of the Mesoamerican area, but that do not reflect the drier areas to the north. These are not the earmarks of a language in its homeland whose sisters marched away to the north. Kaufman (2003, 7) observed that out of about 3,000 root morphemes in Huasteca Nahuatl, "only about 400 or less have UA [Uto-Aztecan] etymologies" —that is, only 13 percent. David Shaul (2014, 181) says of these that beyond these 400 native morphemes, "the rest are borrowed from Mixe-Zoquean, Totonacan, and Huastecan Mayan."

In Jane Hill's (2001, 2002, 2012) view, most of the Northern Uto-Aztecan languages except Hopi lost agriculture, with the result that the argument for Proto-Uto-Aztecan agriculture rests heavily on evidence from Hopi, with little support from other Northern Uto-Aztecan languages. Hill relied principally on thirteen putative Uto-Aztecan cognate sets whose assumed maize associations are limited primarily to Hopi and Southern Uto-Aztecan languages. These comparisons are problematic. Some of these words involve borrowings; for others, the semantic disparities among the forms compared are so wide that it challenges them as being cognates, and several involve exceptions to Uto-Aztecan sound correspondences and thus are questionable again as true cognates (that is, not being reconstructible to Proto-Uto-Aztecan). Nearly all require assumptions of semantic shift, and for most of her cases, it is more plausible that a shift from earlier non-agricultural meanings to later expanded meanings that include association with maize took place. (See Campbell and Poser 2008, 347–350; Kaufman and Justeson 2009, 225–226; Merrill 2013 for detail of the problems with these sets.) As David Shaul (2014, 224) points out, Hill's proposed "cognates either show the expected phonological shape but lack a corn-complex related meaning, or else have a corn-complex-related meaning but do not have a phonological shape predicted by regular sound correspondences (are not regular cognates)." Shaul (2014, 218) declares that "Hill's application of the Farming/Language Dispersal Hypothesis has been disproven."[67]

In short, Hill's reinterpretation of the Uto-Aztecan homeland as southern with agriculture fails to be convincing.

William Merrill et al. (2009, 2010) thought the Proto-Uto-Aztecan homeland was in the Great Basin, though this does not work well for a number of reasons. David Shaul (2014, 309), taking up an earlier idea (discussed by Hill 2021, 581), argued for a Proto-Uto-Aztecan homeland "in the north, including the southern Central Valley [of California] spilling over into the edge of the Great Basin and Arizona." He argued that "both lexical and grammatical linguistic artifacts show that there was contact between PUA [Proto-Uto-Aztecan] and some central California languages (Esselen, Salinan, Chumashan, Wintuan, Costanoan)" (p. 90). There are, however, problems with Shaul's assumed borrowings that leave this homeland interpretation extremely unlikely.

The criteria for showing that something is a loanword are strict. It is necessary in each case to make a stronger case that something is borrowed than that something else can explain the similarity noted, for example, accident, inheritance (from a perhaps undetected common ancestor), onomatopoeia, and nursery forms. Shaul appears to consider loans from Esselen his strong case, though he presents as loanwords or at least as evidence of contact very similar lists involving Uto-Aztecan and the other languages of the southern Central Valley of California that he believes also exhibit evidence of contact with Uto-Aztecan. Suffice it here to mention problems with just the Esselen case. Shaul (2014, 189) gives fifteen Esselen comparisons with Uto-Aztecan. Two are onomatopoeic ('fly' and 'owl'); nine are short forms (possibly explained by accidental similarity); three involve wide semantic disparities among the words compare; two involve common verbs unlikely to be borrowed ('come', 'die'); and so on. Shaul presents similar comparisons from Uto-Aztecan with Salinan (thirteen cases), Mutsun (eighteen cases), Chumashan (sixteen cases), Wintuan (eleven cases), and Yukian (twenty-seven cases), with a few short morphological similarities also. In short, these comparisons alleging contact between Uto-Aztecan and these other languages are not well founded, and therefore the argument for the Proto-Uto-Aztecan homeland being located in Central California based on such assumed language contact fails to be convincing.

The Uto-Aztecan family was often assumed to be more distantly related to Kiowa-Tanoan, in a macro-family called Aztec-Tanoan (Whorf and Trager 1937). This hypothesis is now abandoned (see Campbell 1997a, 269–273 for details). (For other proposals of external connections involving Uto-Aztecan, see Chapter 6.)

Kiowa-Tanoan
  Kiowa
  Jemez (Towa)
  Tiwa
    Northern Tiwa
      Taos
      Picuris
    Southern Tiwa (Isleta-Sandia)

Tewa
　　Tewa
　　Arizona Tewa (Hano)
*Piro

(See Map 7.4. and 7.5.)

It was commonly thought that Kiowa separated first from the other languages of the family, classified together under the name **Tanoan**, and that these Tanoan languages diversified from one another later. The speakers of the "Tanoan" languages inhabit many of the pueblos of the US Southwest. The idea that Kiowa split off first is now challenged. Arguments hold that Kiowa is not demonstrably a more distant relative to all the other Kiowa-Tanoan languages.[68]

Kiowa is the only Kiowa-Tanoan language not spoken in one of the Pueblo communities of the US Southwest. In early historical times the Kiowa were located in western Montana near the headwaters of the Missouri and Yellowstone Rivers (Davis 1979; Shaul 2014, 104). The Kiowa are a Plains tribe; they are now settled in southwestern Oklahoma, mainly in Caddo, Kiowa, and Comanche counties. They have no reservation, but the Kiowa Tribe has its headquarters in Carnegie, Oklahoma.

Jemez, sometimes known as **Towa**, is the language of the Jemez Pueblo (pronounced "Háy-mis"), 45 miles northwest of Albuquerque.[69]

The residents of the former **Pecos** Pueblo, east of Santa Fe, moved to Jemez early in the nineteenth century, and some Pecos descendants retain separate traditions, though their language is essentially undocumented.

Northern Tiwa is spoken at the pueblos of Taos and Picuris. The Taos and Picuris languages are closely related, but they are not mutually intelligible.

Taos, a Northern Tiwa language, is spoken by members of the Pueblo of Taos, 70 miles north of Santa Fe, New Mexico.[70]

Picuris, also a Northern Tiwa language, is spoken in the Pueblo of Picuris, 50 miles north of Santa Fe, New Mexico.

Southern Tiwa is spoken at the Sandia and Isleta pueblos, on the Rio Grande, with Sandia about 15 miles north of Albuquerque and Isleta 15 miles south of Albuquerque.[71]

Tewa is essentially a single language of mutually intelligible though divergent dialects. It is or formerly was spoken at San Juan, Santa Clara, San Ildefonso, Nambe, Pojoaque, and Tesuque in New Mexico, and at Hano on the Hopi reservation in Arizona.[72]

Piro is dormant; it was spoken in a number of now-abandoned pueblos in the Rio Grande Valley south of Isleta. After the Pueblo Revolt of 1680 most of the Piros, together with some Isletas and other Southern Tiwas, moved south to the vicinity of El Paso and established new settlements, only one of which, Ysleta del Sur, still remains. No speakers of Piro survived into the twentieth century, and documentation is sparse. **Tompiro**, mentioned in many of the same early Spanish sources that mention Piro, was probably a dialect of Piro. William Leap (1971) argued that Piro is not a Tanoan language; however, the evidence is more than sufficient to demonstrate its membership in the family. David Shaul (2014, 101), who has investigated Piro, concluded that "initial sound correspondences indicate that Piro is a Tanoan language distinct from the other branches of the family."

The Proto-Kiowa-Tanoan consonants are: /p, t, c, k, kʷ, ʔ, p', t', ts', k', (kʷ'), pʰ, tʰ, tsʰ, kʰ, kʷʰ, b, d, dz, (g), gʷ, m, n, s, w, y, h/ (Hale 1967; Watkins 1978). The classification of the "Tanoan" languages into three branches was made by J. P. Harrington (1910a, 1910b). The linguistic connection between Kiowa and "Tanoan" was first proposed by J. P. Harrington (1910a, 1928) and accepted by subsequent scholars.

About the position of Kiowa in the family, Laurel Watkins (1984, 2) wrote that "it is difficult to point to any constellation of features that might indicate a particularly long period of separation [of Kiowa] from Tanoan before the Tanoan languages split from each other." Paul Kroskrity (1993, 56–57) thought that the common view of the subgrouping of Kiowa versus Tanoan is not supported by the grammatical and other evidence and that "a radical adaptive shift toward a Plains orientation on the part of the Kiowa might have produced linguistic consequences which give an unwarranted impression of great divergence." Kroskrity recommended that "we abandon the notion of Kiowa divergence," though he acknowledged that "the definitive comparative work remains to be done." (See also Shaul 2014, 105). Time depths have been calculated glottochronologically at about 3,000 years of separation between Kiowa from Tanoan and at 2,000 or 2,500 years ago for the breakup of Tanoan (Hale and Harris 1979, 171). This seems to offer support to the original view that Kiowa is more divergent and that Tanoan forms a separate subgroup; however, glottochronology is at best a very rough gauge and is considered invalid by most linguists.

An alternative view of the subgroup classification of the family would group Kiowa and Towa (Jemez) together in a Kiowa-Towa branch against a separate Tewa-Tiwa branch. Another hypothesis is that the family diversified into four equally distinct branches simultaneously (Davis 1979, 400–402). Irvine Davis (1979, 400–402) thought all of these different subgrouping schemes were compatible with the data.

It appears from reconstructible terms that Proto-Kiowa-Tanoan speakers already had agriculture before the family diversified (Shaul 2014, 250).

Kiowa-Tanoan and Uto-Aztecan were frequently assumed to belong together in a more inclusive grouping called Aztec-Tanoan, proposed by Whorf and Trager (1937). This proposal has been widely cited and often repeated, but the evidence it is based on is very weak at best, and the hypothesis has now mostly been abandoned (see Campbell 1997a, 269–273).

Keresan
  Acoma-Laguna (Western Keresan)
  Rio Grande Keresan (Eastern Keresan)

Keresan is spoken in seven varieties, usually assumed to be dialects of a single language, but with significant divergence between the Western and Eastern groups. They are spoken at seven pueblos in New Mexico. Five are Eastern Keresan, in the Rio Grande Valley: Zia-Santa Ana, San Felipe-Santo Domingo, and Cochiti. The other two are Western Keresan: Acoma and Laguna. (See Map 7.4.) The greatest linguistic differences are between Acoma and Cochiti, though the time depth is very shallow. Irvine Davis (1959) thought that the Keresan separation took place no more that 500 years ago.

Acoma-Laguna is the Keresan language spoken in the Acoma and Laguna Pueblos. Acoma-Laguna is partially intelligible to speakers of most Rio Grande Keresan varieties, but is usually considered a separate language.

Rio Grande Keresan is a dialect complex spoken by members of five New Mexico Pueblos located near the Rio Grande or Jemez River north of Albuquerque: Zia, Santa Ana, San Felipe, Santo Domingo, and Cochiti. There is considerable local variation, but all varieties are mutually intelligible, as well as partially intelligible to speakers of Acoma-Laguna.

The reconstructed Proto-Keresan phonemes are: /p, t, c, ç, tʲ, k, ʔ, pʰ, tʰ, cʰ, çʰ, čʰ, kʰ, p', t', c', ç', č', k', s, s̨, š, h, (s'), s̩', š', m, n, m', n', r, r', w, y, w', y'; i, e, a, i̥, o, u; vowel length/ (see Miller and Davis 1963).

Miller and Davis (1963) thought that the reconstructed terms for flora and fauna suggest a Keresan homeland in a forest-mountain biome but with a desert environment suggested by some of the terms. David Shaul (2014, 109) believes, based on ethnohistory, archaeology, and linguistic homeland indicators, that the Keresans were "to the north of the Sonoran Desert area in a large speech community starting on the edge of the Sonoran Desert and going north to Acoma, then to Chaco, and then to Mesa Verde." There is evidence that Keresan had prestige among some languages of the area, since several ceremonial words in Hopi and Zuni are borrowed from Keresan (Shaul 2014, 110–111).

Keresan has no known external relatives. Edward Sapir (1929a) had tentatively put it in Hokan-Siouan, his default super-stock where most unrelated leftovers ended up. Morris Swadesh (1967b) suggested a connection between Keres and Caddo (actually Wichita); David Rood (1973) clarified many of the forms, suggesting tentatively that the evidence "should go a long way toward proof of a Keres-Wichita relationship." Irvine Davis (1979) suggested a possible kinship between Keresan and Uto-Aztecan. This has not been pursued by other scholars. Joseph Greenberg (1987, 163) accepted a part of Sapir's proposal, lumping Keresan, Siouan, Yuchi, Caddoan, and Iroquoian into what Greenberg called Keresiouan, part of his more far flung Almosan-Keresiouan—where Almosan comprises (as in Sapir 1929a) Algic (Algonquian- Ritwan), Kutenai, and so-called Mosan (which joins Chemakuan, Wakashan, and Salish together). All of these groupings have been rejected in consensus classifications of North American Indigenous languages (see Davis 1979; Hale and Harris 1979, 173; see also Chapter 6).

Zuni

Zuni is a well-known language isolate, spoken mostly at Zuni Pueblo in New Mexico (also in eastern Arizona). (See Map 7.4.) Zuni appears to have developed in situ. It has borrowed words, especially ceremonial terms, from Keresan and Hopi. Hopi has borrowed names of kachinas from Zuni.[73]

Edward Sapir (1929a) had tentatively put Zuni in his Aztec-Tanoan phylum, but there is no real evidence for that. Several scholars thought Zuni might be Penutian; however, evidence of a Zuni relationship with any of the languages linked with the Penutian hypothesis is barely suggestive at best, far too inadequate to support any of the proposals (see Swadesh 1954b, 1956, 1967a, 1967b; Newman 1964). Karl-Heinz Gursky's (1966a, 419–420) Keresan-Zuni proposal is also unsupported.[74] (See Chapter 6.)

*Karankawa

Groups collectively called the Karankawa lived on the Texas coast from Galveston Bay to Corpus Christi Bay; they were not a homogeneous group politically and perhaps not even culturally. The language has been dormant since the last Karankawa were slaughtered by Mexican soldiers and Texas Rangers on Padre Island in October of 1858 (Grant 1994, 1). (See Map 2.1.)

Information on these groups comes from Spanish, French, and American explorers, and castaways, missionaries, and soldiers who came into contact with them, including Alvar Núñez Cabeza de Vaca, Robert Cavelier de La Salle, and Jean Laffite (the buccaneer). The Karankawa linguistic corpus amounts to about two hundred words in total. The earliest, twenty-nine words, was provided in 1698 by Jean-Baptiste Talon, a survivor of La Salle's expedition who had been captured by "Clamcoeh" (Karankawa) Indians living near Matagorda Bay in Texas (Troike 1987). A list of 106 words was provided in 1720 by Jean Béranger, a French sea captain sent to explore the Gulf coast (see Villiers du Terrage and Rivet 1919), and another list was given by Jean Louis Berlandier (Swizz-born botanist and physician) in 1828. The most extensive vocabulary was collected by the Mexican geologist Rafael Chowell in 1828–1829 (Grant 1994, 1). Interestingly, a long vocabulary was obtained by Albert Gatschet from Alice W. Oliver, a White woman in Massachusetts who had spent her childhood on the Texas coast in the neighborhood of the last Karankawa speaking band. Anthony Grant (1994, 2) characterizes this as her "memories of apparently xenolectal Karankawa." Gatschet also obtained a few Karankawa forms from two Tonkawa speakers who had learned some of the language. (See Goddard 1979a; Newcomb 1983.) These records seem to suggest that Karankawa had a high degree of internal diversity (Grant 1994, 1).

Karankawa is a language isolate. The earlier proposals to link it with hypothesized "Coahuiltecan" and that with broader putative "Hokan" are now abandoned (see Goddard 1979a; Swanton 1940; Troike 1987; see Chapter 6).

*Tonkawa

Tonkawa is a language isolate. The Tonkawa were first mentioned in 1719; the earliest data are from Chowell and from Berlandier (Berlandier and Chowell 1828–1829), but when and where they were recorded is not known. In 1872 the tribe was at Fort Griffin, Texas. Many bands (for example, Yojuane, Mayeye [Méye, Míyi], and Ervipiame) are associated with the Tonkawa, but these identifications, based on historical sources, are tentative (Goddard 1979a, 358–359; Hoijer 1933, ix–x; 1946b). (See Map 2.1.) One of the Tonkawa speakers whom Albert Gatschet (1891a, 36) interviewed affirmed that the **Méye** (Míyi) spoke a dialect of Tonkawa (Goddard 1979a, 359). The language was fairly well documented by Harry Hoijer (1933, 1946b, 1949, 1972).

Tonkawa was spoken in the eighteenth century at San Gabriel Mission, between Austin and Waco in east-central Texas, and apparently by some other groups in that region. After tangled relations with White people and other American Indian groups in the first half of the nineteenth century, the Tonkawa were removed to Oklahoma, ultimately to a reservation in Kay County.

Ives Goddard (1979a, 361) surmised that extensive "culturally governed vocabulary replacement" in the form of taboo replacement of names and of words similar to names of the dead is behind many differences in the vocabulary between older and later Tonkawa sources. Albert Gatschet had reported in 1884 that "they change the name of individuals who had nearly the same name as one deceased," and he provided several examples of such changes (cited by Goddard 1979a, 361).

Proposals of genetic relationship have attempted to place Tonkawa in the Coahuiltecan and Algonquian-Gulf hypothesized groupings, but these hypotheses are now abandoned; they do not hold up under scrutiny (see Chapter 6).

*Coahuilteco (Pajalate)

Coahuilteco is another language isolate. It was spoken in the area between the Guadalupe River east of San Antonio and the middle course of the lower Rio Grande near Laredo, principally in Texas, extending slightly into present-day Mexico. (See Map 2.1.) The name Coahuilteco, given by Manuel Orozco y Berra (1864, 63), reflects the earlier extension of the Mexican state of Coahuila into what is now Texas. The language was also sometimes called **Pajalate**, the name of one of the bands that spoke it.

Identification of which groups spoke Coahuilteco is a difficult matter. Southern Texas and northeastern Mexico had literally hundreds of small hunting and gathering bands identified by various names in Spanish colonial reports: "For this region and various areas immediately adjacent to it scholars have encountered over 1,000 ethnic group names in documents that cover a period of approximately 350 years" (T. Campbell 1983, 347). There is no linguistic information on most of them. As Thomas Campbell (1983, 343) indicated, "this inability to identify all the named Indian groups who originally spoke Coahuilteco has been a perennial stumbling-block in efforts to distinguish them from their neighbors." Some of the many bands that appear to have spoken Coahuilteco were the Pacoas, Tilijayas, Pausanes, Pacuaches, Mescales, Pampopas, Tacames, and Venados. Extant materials indicate different dialects for those of San Antonio and the Rio Grande, and for the Pajalates of the Purísima Concepción mission. (T. Campbell 1983; Goddard 1979a; Swadesh 1959, 1963a; Swanton 1940, 5; Troike 1967, 82).

Coahuilteco was a lingua franca in the area around Monterrey, Mexico (Troike 1967; Goddard 1979a); it was a second language at least for the Orejones, Pamaques, Alazapas, and Borrados. According to Bartholomé García (1760), all the young people of the Pihuiques, Sanipaos, and Manos de Perro spoke Coahuilteco, which suggests that it was a second language for these groups. There was apparently considerable multilingualism in the area where these languages were spoken. One of Gatschet's Cotoname consultants was a Comecrudo speaker; Tonkawa speakers provided Karankawa vocabularies and the only recorded phrase of Aranama; and Mamulique women were said not to speak "their native language."

Coahuilteco is primarily known from an eighty-eight-page bilingual Spanish-Coahuilteco confessor's manual published in Mexico in 1760, which apparently represents the Pajalate dialect.

Coahuilteco is at the core of the Coahuiltecan hypothesis. This proposed grouping of languages began with Manuel Orozco y Berra's (1864) map and continued through many differing interpretations even to the present. All of Coahuilteco, Cotoname, Aranama-Tamique, Solano, Comecrudan, Tonkawa, and Karankawa were assumed to belong to some larger grouping, usually Coahuiltecan. The smallest proposed grouping assumed that Comecrudo and Cotoname were related, and more commonly Coahuilteco was included with these two as well. The larger version of the Coahuiltecan hypothesis included these three languages plus Tonkawa, Karankawa, Atakapa, and Maratino, with the assumption that Aranama and Solano were varieties of Coahuilteco. Edward Sapir's (1929a) well-known Hokan-Coahuiltecan stock grouped Tonkawa and Karankawa with Coahuilteco, Comecrudo, and Cotoname as Coahuiltecan; he further proposed that Hokan-Coahuiltecan belonged in his broader Hokan-Siouan superstock.

Ives Goddard's (1979a) reexamination, especially in light of the Berlandier materials, indicates that none of these hypotheses has linguistic support. Even the minimum grouping of Comecrudo and Cotoname has no support. The investigation of the Berlandier Cotoname material shows many differences between the two languages where Gatschet's information showed similarities. On the other hand, the Comecrudan family (below), which includes Comecrudo, Garza, and Mamulique, is now confirmed (Goddard 1979a; see Thomas Campbell 1983, 343).

Alexis Manaster Ramer (1996) argued for what he called the Pakawan family, a grouping of Coahuiteco, Cotoname, Comecrudo, Garza, and Mamulique. However, upon closer inspection, the evidence presented in favor of this proposed language family proved problematic and therefore the proposal cannot be embraced (see Campbell 1996).

*Comecrudan
   *Comecrudo
   *Mamulique
   *Garza

Ives Goddard (1979a) presented persuasive evidence that Comecrudo, Mamulique, and Garza, three little-known languages of the lower Rio Grande area of southern Texas and northeast Mexico, are related, members of the Comecrudan family. (See Map 2.1.)

In 1829 Jean Louis Berlandier collected a **Comecrudo** vocabulary of 148 words near Reynosa, Tamaulipas, Mexico; he called the language "Mulato." Adolf Uhde (1861, 185–186) also obtained some Comecrudo data but he called the language "Carrizo," the language of the lower Rio Grande.[75] Remnants of Comecrudo people were at Las Prietas near Camargo, Tamaulipas, when Albert Gatschet obtained his vocabulary in 1886 (Swanton 1940, 55–118) (see Goddard 1979a, 369–370).

Mamulique (Carrizo de Mamulique) is known only from a twenty-two-word list given by Berlandier. It was spoken near Mamulique, Nuevo León, Mexico, between Salinas Victoria and Palo Blanco, south of Villaldama (Goddard 1979a, 370–371).

The only record of **Garza** is Berlandier's twenty-one-word list. In 1828 speakers lived at Mier in northeast Mexico on the lower Rio Grande. In a 1748 manuscript they were called *Atanaguayacam* in Comecrudo; in Cotoname they were called *Meack(n)an* or *Miákan* (Goddard 1979a, 371).[76]

Formerly, the Comecrudan languages were usually associated with one or another version of the Coahuiltecan hypothesis (see discussion of Coahuilteco above). The evidence, however, has not proven convincing for any of these proposed connections.

*Cotoname (Carrizo de Camargo)

Cotoname, generally considered a language isolate, was spoken along the lower Rio Grande River and its delta in southern Texas and northeastern Mexico, adjacent to the Comecrudan languages. (See Map 2.1.) It is known only from Berlandier's vocabulary of 104 words, called "Carrizo de Camargo" (Berlandier and Chowell 1828–1829), and Gatschet's notes taken in 1886 in part from a native speaker of Comecrudo (Swanton 1940, 5, 118–121; Goddard 1979a, 370).[77]

Cotoname, too, has usually been associated with the now no-longer-accepted Coahuiltecan hypothesis (see discussion with Coahuilteco above).

For other languages of the lower Rio Grande area in Texas and northeast Mexico too poorly attested to be able to be classified, see Chapter 5.

Siouan-Catawban (Siouan)
  Siouan
    Missouri River
      Hidatsa (Gros Ventre, Minitari)
      Crow (Upsaroka, Apsáalooke)
    *Mandan
    Mississippi Valley Siouan
      Dakotan
        Sioux
        Assiniboine (Nakon, Nakoda)
        Stoney
      Chiwere-Winnebago
        *Chiwere (Iowa, Oto, *Missouri)
        Winnebago (Ho-Chunk, Hochank)
      Dhegiha
        Omaha-Ponca
        *Osage
        *Kansa
        *Quapaw
    *Southeastern
      *Ofo
      *Biloxi
      *Tutelo
  *Catawban
    *Catawba
    *Woccon

(Rood 1979, 1992b; Rankin 2005, 454, 492. Hollow and Parks' 1980, 76, classification is slightly different.)

(See Maps 2.8. and 7.5.)

Siouan-Catawban languages are or were spoken in central and southeastern North America.

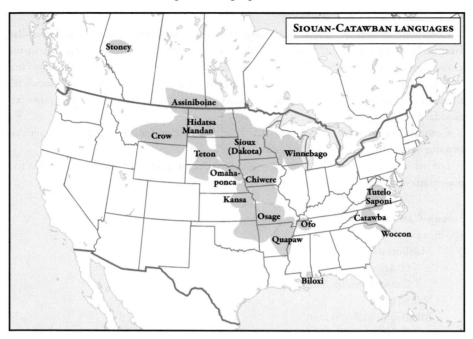

MAP 2.8. Siouan-Catawban languages (pre-contact)

Hidatsa and **Crow** are closely related and together form the Missouri River subgroup of Siouan.

The **Hidatsa** were often called Minitari and are still frequently called Gros Ventre (not to be confused with Algonquian Atsina, also called Gros Ventre). They were located in North Dakota along the Missouri River, upstream from the Mandan villages. In 1845 they moved to their present location in the Fort Berthold area. Today the Hidatsa are part of the Three Affiliated Tribes, sharing the Fort Berthold Reservation of North Dakota with Mandans and Arikaras. Their principal reservation settlement is Mandaree.

The **Crow** (earlier often called Upsaroka) have always, as far as is known, been located near the Yellowstone River in Montana. Crow is spoken on the Crow Reservation on the Big Horn River, a tributary of the Yellowstone in southeastern Montana and in nearby communities off the reservation. Principal Crow towns on the reservation are Crow Agency, Lodge Grass, Pryor, Wyola, and St. Xavier.

Mandan by itself constitutes a separate subgroup of Siouan. It was originally spoken in a cluster of villages along the Missouri River in North Dakota, located between the Hidatsa villages to the north and the Arikara villages to the south. The modern Mandans are one of the Three Affiliated Tribes on the Fort Berthold Reservation in North Dakota, which they share with the Hidatsas and the Arikaras. The Mandans' primary settlement is Twin Buttes. The last first-language speaker of Mandan, Edwin Benson, died in 2016.

Dakotan is a Siouan dialect complex. Intelligibility among its varieties is low, although speakers can communicate with speakers of other varieties after a while with some difficulty. **Sioux** is the cover term for the varieties of the **Dakotan** dialect complex excluding

Assiniboine and Stoney.[78] Europeans first encountered Sioux (Dakota) in the general area of the upper Mississippi River. Three Sioux dialect groups can be distinguished, from east to west: the **Santee-Sisseton** (Dakota) dialect is spoken in at least fifteen widely dispersed reservation communities in Minnesota, Manitoba, and Saskatchewan, and in the eastern parts of Nebraska and the Dakotas. The **Yankton-Yanktonai** dialect is primarily spoken on the Yankton and Crow Creek Reservations in South Dakota, and on the northern part of the Standing Rock Reservation in North Dakota, although it also has speakers on the Devils Lake and Fort Peck Reservations in North Dakota and on a few reserves in Saskatchewan. **Teton** (Lakota) is the dialect of the Cheyenne River, Lower Brule, Pine Ridge, Rosebud, and Sisseton Reservations of South Dakota, as well as of the southern part of the Standing Rock Reservation in South Dakota and of the Wood Mountain Reserve in Saskatchewan. There are also a number Sioux speakers in communities off the reservations, particularly in Rapid City, Minneapolis, and other urban centers in the upper Midwest. (Rood 1979; Chafe 1973). There is a fair degree of mutual intelligibility among these three groups.

Assiniboine (Nakon, Nakoda) is an emergent language in the Dakotan dialect complex, spoken on the Fort Belknap and Fort Peck reservations in Montana and on three Saskatchewan reserves: Whitebear, Carry the Kettle, and Mosquito-Grizzly Bear's Head. Cree is widely spoken on the Saskatchewan reserves, and many Assiniboine speakers are fluent also in Cree. In Montana, Assiniboines share the Fort Belknap Reservation with the Gros Ventre (Atsina), and the Fort Peck Reservation with speakers of Sioux.

Stoney is another emergent language in the Dakotan dialect complex. It is spoken on five reserves in Alberta located along the eastern base of the Rocky Mountains west of Calgary and Edmonton: Alexis, Paul, Bighorn, Morley, and Eden Valley. The main community is Morley, midway between Calgary and Banff.

Dhegiha is another subgroup of Siouan. At the time of the earliest European contact, the Dhegiha were in the central plains, though tradition locates them at an earlier time farther east, near the junction of the Wabash and Ohio Rivers.[79]

Omaha-Ponca, of the Dhegiha subgroup, is a language with two shallowly differentiated dialects, the heritage language of the Omaha Tribe of Nebraska and of the two Ponca tribes, the Northern Ponca of Nebraska and the Southern Ponca of Oklahoma. Formerly they were on the Missouri River in northeastern Nebraska. Most of the remaining speakers of the **Omaha** dialect live in Macy and Walthill in rural southeastern Nebraska. The **Ponca** dialect is spoken in the Red Rock area of south-central Oklahoma.

Osage belongs to the Dhegiha subgroup. It was spoken in the eighteenth century along the Osage River in Missouri and later in northeast Kansas. Since the 1870s the Osage Tribe has been settled in the northeastern corner of Oklahoma, around Pawhuska. Osage and **Kansa** are mutually intelligible.

Kansa is closely related to and mutually intelligible with Osage. It was spoken before the mid-nineteenth century by the Kansa or Kaw tribe on the Kansas River in northeastern Kansas; in 1873 they were removed to a small reservation in Oklahoma. The Kaw Nation was dissolved in 1902, but reconstituted in 1959 with its headquarters at Kaw City, Oklahoma. There have been no first-language speakers of Kansa since the early 1980s.

Quapaw (also sometimes called Arkansas) is a Dhegiha language formerly spoken near the junction of the Arkansas and Mississippi Rivers in eastern Arkansas. The Quapaw occupied places in Arkansas, Kansas, and Oklahoma; they lived briefly in northern Louisiana until 1867, when they were moved to a small area in northeastern Oklahoma. The last first-language speakers died in the 1960s and 1970s (Rankin 2005.) Robert Rankin (2005, 455) reported that Quapaw "can only marginally be considered to share salient features of the Southeastern *Sprachbund*" and what traits of this area it does have are found in the other varieties of Dhegiha as well (see Chapter 7).

Chiwere belongs to the Chiwere-Winnebago subgroup. It is now dormant. Two tribal dialects are distinguished. **Otoe-Missouria** (Jiwere) is the dialect of the Otoe-Missouria Tribe of the Red Rock region of north-central Oklahoma. The **Oto** were first located near the confluence of the Platte and Missouri Rivers. For a time they lived in parts of Nebraska and Kansas, but they moved to Oklahoma in the 1880s. The **Missouri** were once located on the Missouri River near the Grand River in the state of Missouri. They were badly defeated by Sauk and Fox at the end of the eighteenth century and suffered much in a war with the Osage early in the nineteenth century. After that they lived with the Oto, with whom they later moved to Oklahoma. The other dialect of Chiwere was **Iowa** (Ioway). The Iowa occupied several places in Iowa and neighboring states; in 1836 they were given a reservation in Nebraska and Kansas, and some later settled in Oklahoma. Iowa (Baxoje) is the dialect of the Iowa Tribe of Perkins, Oklahoma, and of the Iowa Tribe of Kansas and Nebraska at White Cloud, Kansas.

Winnebago (Ho-Chunk, Hochank) is related to Chiwere but is a separate language within that subgroup. The Winnebago once lived south of Green Bay, Wisconsin, and some remain there; others after many moves eventually settled on a reservation in northeastern Nebraska. They are now divided between the Winnebago Tribe of northeastern Nebraska and the Ho-Chunk Nation of central Wisconsin.[80]

The **Southeastern** subgroup of Siouan has the three languages, Ofo, Biloxi, and Tutelo. This group was called "Ohio Valley Siouan" by Vogelin (1941:247).

John R. Swanton showed that the **Ofo** were the Mo(n)sopelea in earlier French sources and maps, which placed them definitely in the Ohio Valley (though not necessarily Ohio) (Goddard 2005:9). They were first encountered by Europeans in 1673 on the east bank of the Mississippi River below the mouth of the Ohio River in western Tennessee. By 1690, they had withdrawn to the Yazoo River in Mississippi, near the Yazoo and Tunica tribes. They were subsequently absorbed into nearby tribes. Their location between 1784 and 1908 is not recorded. In 1908 John R. Swanton found a single surviving Ofo speaker, a woman living among the Tunica in Louisiana, from whom he obtained the extant linguistic material (see Haas 1969b; Swanton 1946, 165–166).

The **Biloxi** were located on the lower Pascagoula River and Biloxi Bay in Mississippi when they were first encountered by French and Spanish explorers. They subsequently lived in several locations in Louisiana; some were removed to Texas and Oklahoma (Swanton 1946, 96– 98). Ofo and Biloxi are fairly closely related to one another; both are now dormant. James Owen Dorsey provided most of the documentation of Biloxi, obtained in 1892–1893 from members of the tribe living in Rapides Parish, Louisiana. Biloxi is dormant.

Tutelo was encountered by Europeans near Salem, Virginia, in 1671. From there the Tutelo moved eastward and northward. In 1714 they were settled with other tribes at Fort Christianna and on the Meherrin River. After peace was made between the Iroquois and the Virginia tribes in 1722, the Tutelo moved northward before 1744 to settle at Shamokin, Pennsylvania, under Iroquois protection. In 1753 they were formally adopted into the League of the Iroquois. In 1771 they settled near Cayuga Lake in New York State. They moved with the Cayuga to Canada after the American Revolution (Swanton 1946, 199). The last confirmed fluent speaker, Nikonha (a.k.a. Waskiteng), died in Canada in 1870. He supplied most of the fairly extensive documentation, recorded by Horatio Hale (1883).

Catawban is the most divergent branch of the Siouan-Catawban family, though it is definitely related to Siouan, demonstrated by Frank Siebert (1945). Some scholars call the family just Siouan, though others prefer to call it Catawba-Siouan or Siouan-Catawban. Booker et al. (1992, 410) put it this way: "Catawban as a family is distantly related to Siouan, but it is a mistake in modern nomenclature to call Catawba 'Siouan'. (It would be like calling Oscan and Umbrian 'Romance')."

As a political unit the **Catawba** tribe was formed in the first half of the eighteenth century by the consolidation of many small groups of peoples of North and South Carolina. Some of them probably spoke additional Catawban languages while others did not, and they were also joined by refugee groups originally from elsewhere in the southeast. During colonial times the Catawba, together with the Cherokee, were the most important indigenous group of the Carolinas, but after smallpox epidemics—for example, in 1759 nearly half of the Catawba died of the disease—the Catawba ceased to play a prominent role in history. Some fled to the Choctaws in Oklahoma, and others joined the Cherokee. The Catawba Nation is on a small reservation near Rock Hill, South Carolina, near their old homeland, where the language continued to be spoken until the mid-twentieth century.

The last speakers represented two dialects, **Esaw** (Catawba proper) and **Saraw**.

The Esaw and Saraw dialects presumably trace back to two aggregations of small tribes that coalesced after the Tuscarora War of 1711–1713, the Catawba Esaw on the Catawba River and the Cheraw-Saraw on the Pee Dee River. Modern Catawba people descend from these two ethnically and linguistically diverse components (Goddard 2005, 9).

Booker et al. (1992, 410) found that "Catawba grammar and vocabulary show evidence of language mixture."

A number of different names of languages and dialects once spoken in the Carolina Piedmont Region are often grouped as Catawban, though the evidence for this is inconclusive and opinions vary concerning them (Booker et al. 1992, 410). In the Catawban branch there is documentation only for **Catawba** and **Woccon**.

Woccon is known only from a vocabulary of 143 items published by John Lawson (1709) (cf. Carter 1980; Sturtevant 1958). It was spoken in the early eighteenth century in eastern North Carolina. Its relationship with Catawba (proper) is clear but not close.

There were other Siouan (or Siouan-Catawban) languages in Virginia and the Carolinas at the time of first European contact, but practically nothing is known about them. Apart from **Woccon** (of the Catawban branch), three languages that are genuinely identified as Siouan, perhaps more closely related to Tutelo, are **Saponi**, **Occaneechi** (Occaneechee), and **Monyton** (Moniton) (Goddard 2005, 7). (See Chapter 5.)

Rankin et al. (1998, 1) reconstructed Proto-Siouan with the phonemes: /p, t, k, ʔ, p', t', k', pʰ, tʰ, kʰ, hp, ht, hk, s, š, x, s', š', x', w, r, y, h, W, R; i, e, a, o, u; ī, ā, ū; vowel, length; pitch accent (generally, but not always, on second syllable)/. They say of *hp, ht, hk* that "in pre-Proto-Siouan it is possible that there was no pre-aspirated series. The preaspirates pretty clearly arose as regular allophonic variants of plain voiceless stops preceding an accented vowel" (Rankin et al. 1998, 1). They say also that "it may not be necessary to reconstruct postaspirated stops for P[roto-]Si[ouan], at least not for native morphemes ... the postaspirates generally originate from two distinct sources ... they arise morphophonemically when prefixes that have undergone vowel syncope are placed before roots that begin with /h/" and "in a small set of words that often also show abnormal accentuation patterns or other strange features strongly reminiscent of what one would expect from *borrowings*" (p. 2). Further, Rankin et al. "have some qualms" about reconstructing glottalized stops and fricatives. Historically, glottalized consonants can only occur in accented syllables, and where Mississippi Valley Siouan languages have ejectives (seen as *C?V*), in Mandan and Hidatsa the reflexes are *CV?*. In several of the languages long vowels typically have falling pitch, where "the glottalized stops and fricatives could have arisen as all allophonic feature of falling pitch," which automatically gave a syllable-final glottal stop (p. 3). Siouanists have hoped to be able to merge **W* with **w* and **R* with **r*, and thus eliminate **W* and **R* from the Proto-Siouan inventory. The **w* has the reflex [w] or [m] in most of the daughter languages, and **r* usually is reflected as [r, l, ð, y]. However, **W* is reflected by [w, b, mb, p] in some languages, and **R* has reflexes that include [r, ɪ, d, nd, t] in the daughter languages. There is "evidence that **W* usually represents a secondary development from geminated **w+w* (across a morpheme boundary or, in a few instances, a laryngeal plus *w*" (p. 5). The case of **R* is not as clear, but Rankin et al. (1998, 6) said that "it is probably secondary and probably represents an old cluster too—perhaps of **r* with a laryngeal."

No nasal consonants are reconstructed for Proto-Siouan, though the need to reconstruct nasalized vowels is not in doubt. Voiced stops probably had nasals as allophones preceding nasal vowels. This is similar to the behavior of nasals in several South American languages.

If all these features about which there is some doubt and where possible alternative analyses of them exist are removed, then Rankin et al. (1989, 6) end up suggesting that possibly Pre-Proto-Siouan had the phonetic inventory: /p, t, k, ʔ, s, š, x, h, w, r, y; i, e, a, o, u, ĩ, ã, ũ, vowel length/. (See also Larson 2016.)

Proto-Siouan also had active/stative alignment, head-marking, and SOV [Subject-Object-Verb] basic word order (Rankin et al. 1989, 6). A set of positional verbs meaning 'sit', 'lie', and 'stand' "served to classify nouns by shape/position" (p. 8).

Rankin (1993) dated the earliest internal Core Siouan split at approximately 3,000 BP (or 1,000 BCE) and the Catawban split from Siouan at probably 1,000 years earlier.

For a detailed evaluation of the proposed broader grouping of Siouan with Caddoan and Iroquoian, see Campbell (1997a,e 262–269). For possible affiliation with Yuchi, see Yuchi (below).

Caddoan
    Northern Caddoan
        Arikara
        *Pawnee
        *Kitsai
        *Wichita
    Southern Caddoan
        Caddo

(Hollow and Parks 1980, 77; cf. Chafe 1979; Taylor 1963a, 1963b.)

The Caddoan languages were spoken in the heart of the Great Plains, from South Dakota to northeastern Texas and eastward in Arkansas and northwestern Louisiana (Chafe 1979, 213; see also Grant 2017). (See Maps 2.1. and 7.5.)

Arikara and **Pawnee** are closely related.

Arikara, a Northern Caddoan language, was formerly spoken in earthlodge villages along the Missouri River in central and north-central South Dakota, downstream from Mandan. Arikara is one of the Three Affiliated Tribes, sharing Fort Berthold Reservation in North Dakota with Mandan and Hidatsa. The Arikara now live in the Eastern Segment of the reservation, mostly in White Shield and Parshall. The language is critically endangered.

Pawnee was spoken in villages along the Platte River in central Nebraska until 1874, when the tribe was relocated to what is now Pawnee County in north-central Oklahoma, where they reside today. It was spoken in two distinct but similar dialects, **Skiri** and **South Band**. Today no fluent speakers of either dialect remain.

Kitsai formerly was south of the Wichita area in east Texas, but the Kitsai joined the Wichitas in Oklahoma in 1858. Kitsai continued to be spoken alongside Wichita for two or three generations before it became dormant. The language was moderately well documented in 1929–1930 from the last speaker, Kai Kai, who died in 1940.

Wichita is a Northern Caddoan language, spoken by the Wichita Tribe, formerly a confederacy of autonomous bands that until the late nineteenth century lived in an area extending from central Oklahoma through central Texas. **Tawakaru** and **Weku** are associated with Wichita (Taylor 1963b, 113). Today the Wichita live in Caddo County in central Oklahoma, primarily in and around the town of Anadarko, an area in which the Caddo, Delaware, and Kiowa also live. The last native speaker of Wichita, Doris Lamar-McLemore, died in 2016.

Caddo is the only member of the Southern branch of Caddoan still to have native speakers. It was once spoken over a wide area that included parts of Arkansas, northern Louisiana, eastern Texas, and southeastern Oklahoma. Wallace Chafe (2005, 323) reported that "there appear to have been two major clusters of Caddo towns, one constituting the **Hasinai** . . . centered in eastern Texas, the other the **Kadohadaccho**, whose center was the area where the Red River forms the boundary between Texas and Arkansas." The modern Caddo Tribe was formed by aggregations of a number of independent bands that spoke distinct dialects. It was organized into at least three confederacies that were distributed over a vast area of eastern Texas, southeastern Oklahoma, southwestern Arkansas, and northern Louisiana. In the nineteenth century the remnants of those groups settled in present-day Caddo County, Oklahoma, mostly in the vicinity of Anadarko, Binger, and Ft. Cobb.

There may have been other Caddoan groups. The vocabulary of **Yatasi** collected by Albert Gatschet in the 1880s shows it to be a divergent variety of Caddo, with "phonological differences and some differences in basic vocabulary" (cited in Goddard 2005, 15), and Yatasi were remembered in the twentieth century as Caddo speakers (Lesser and Weltfish 1932, 2).[81]

The reconstructed Proto-Caddoan phonemes are: /p, t, c, k, (kw), ʔ, s, r, n, w, y, h; i, a, u/ (Chafe 1979, 218–219; cf. Taylor 1963a). (For information on Proto-Caddoan morphology, see Chafe 1979, 226–232.) Hollow and Parks (1980, 80) presented Park's glottochronological calculations for the number of millennia of separation for Northern Caddoan languages, though they mention that they have no confidence in glottochronology. They report the Arikara-Wichita separation at two millennia, Kitsai-Wichita at 1.95, Pawnee-Wichita at 1.9, Arikara-Kitsai and Pawnee-Kitsai both at 1.2, and Pawnee-Arikara at 0.3 millennia.

Proposals of broader connections for Caddoan have tended to involve Iroquoian and Siouan; these hypotheses have not proven convincing (see Campbell 1997a, 262–269).

*Adai (Adaize)

Adai is dormant and very poorly documented. The Adai lived between the Red and Sabine Rivers in western Louisiana. (See Map 2.1.) They were first encountered by Europeans near Robeline, Louisiana. Adai was a language of the Spanish mission of San Francisco de las Tejas, west of Natchitoches, the first mission in eastern Texas, founded in 1690. After the mission was closed in 1792 the remnants of the tribe apparently joined one or more Caddoan groups. The tribe was reported as almost extinct by 1778. They were last reported in 1805 in a small settlement on Lake Macdon (Swanton 1917).[82]

Adai appears to be a language isolate. The only source is a vocabulary of 275 items recorded by John Sibley in 1806 or 1807 (Sibley 1832). Earlier Sibley (1806, 50–51) had said that Adai "differs from all other [sic], and is so difficult to speak or understand, that no nation can speak ten words of it" (quoted in Goddard 2005, 14). Adai has often been classified with Caddoan (Swanton 1946, 83–84; see Taylor 1963a, 1963b), though some scholars have thought that the Sibley materials are not sufficient for demonstrating an affinity of Adai to Caddoan or to any other language (see, for example, Goddard 1996a; 2005, 14; Campbell 1997a, 143, 400; Mithun 1999:326). However, in the view of other scholars, the recorded 275 words are sufficient for undertaking meaningful comparisons, which have not shown solid evidence of affiliation with any other language. It is for that reason it is now considered, tentatively, a language isolate (Mithun 2018, 195).

*Atakapa

Atakapa is a Choctaw name meaning 'people eater' (*hattak* 'person' + *apa* 'to eat') (Booker 1980, 7)—the Gulf coast tribes practiced cannibalism on their enemies. Atakapa is dormant; it was spoken from Vermillion Bay and lower Bayou Teche in Louisiana to Galveston Bay and Trinity River in Texas, between Karankawa and Tonkawa territories (Gatschet and Swanton 1932, 1). (See Maps 2.1. and 7.7.) Atakapa is considered a language isolate, although some have thought it is a small language family, Atakapan, with sometimes two, sometimes three distinct but closely related languages. Others find relatively little difference among the three and consider them varieties of a single language (see Goddard 2005, 14 and Mithun 2018, 197).

Western Atakapa was extensively documented by Albert Gatschet in 1885, and a dictionary, grammatical sketch, and collection of texts were published. Gatschet collected materials on the language from the last fluent speaker in 1885 at Lake Charles, Louisiana (published in Gatschet and Swanton 1932). Two earlier vocabularies were from Jean Béranger in 1721, from captives who lived at Galveston Bay, and one from Martin Duralde, with 287 entries, collected in 1802 at Poste des Attakapas (now Franklin, in Saint Martinville Parish) in far eastern Atakapa territory (Goddard 2005, 13). These two sources differ in a number of words, especially words for numbers, which led Swanton to classify the language of the Duralde vocabulary as a separate **Eastern Atakapa** language, different from Western Atakapa of other sources. Jack Martin (2004, 79) and others who have examined the data find that the vocabularies are not different enough to qualify as separate languages.

The situation is complicated further, however, by Swanton's belief that the Béranger vocabulary represented **Akokisa**, a group who lived inland from Galveston Bay, sometimes considered possibly a third Atakapa language. Morris Swadesh sometimes classified Atakapa as a family consisting of three languages, with Akokisa as one of them (see for example Swadesh 1954a, 327). However, Jack Martin (2004, 79) points out that no ethnic name is given to the Béranger vocabulary in the source material and therefore there is no justification for assuming an Akokisa association for it (Goddard 2005, 14). Sibley (1806, 511–551) said the Akokisa "have a language peculiar to themselves," but used sign language with others; he mistakenly thought that they spoke Karankawa (Sibley 1806, 53, 60). Essentially nothing is known of the true language of the Akokisa, only *Yesga* 'Spaniards' and *Quiselpoo*, a woman's name (Swanton 1911, 35–36, cited by Goddard 2005, 38). (See Chapter 5.)

John Swanton (1919) thought that Atakapa, Chitimacha, and Tunica were genetically related in a stock he called Tunican. Edward Sapir (1920) included Atakapa in his Coahuiltecan family, but he later removed Atakapa from Coahuiltecan and instead placed it with Tunica and Chitimacha (as in Swanton's Tunican) in a separate division of his Hokan-Siouan superstock (Sapir 1929a). Morris Swadesh (1946, 1947) accepted Swanton's Tunican but compared only Atakapa and Chitimacha because of the availability of information on those two at that time. Several other broader proposals also include Atakapa, for example, Haas' Gulf proposal, but all of these suggested broader affiliations remain doubtful (see Haas 1979; Swanton 1919; Gatschet and Swanton 1932; Troike 1963).[83]

*Chitimacha

Chitimacha is a language isolate. It is the heritage language of the Chitimacha Tribe of Charenton, St. Mary Parish, Louisiana.[84] When they were first encountered by the French in the late 1600s the Chitimacha were living along Bayou La Fourche and on the west side of the Mississippi River below present-day Baton Rouge, Louisiana. (See Map 2.1.) Though linguistically unattested, the **Washa** and **Chawasha** groups, known historically, are generally assumed also to have spoken Chitimacha or something closely related to it (Swanton 1917). Although attested in wordlists in the nineteenth and early twentieth centuries, the primary documentation of Chitimacha is the extensive data collected by Morris Swadesh in 1932–1934 from the last two fluent speakers, Chief Benjamin Paul and Delphine Decloux Stouff, most of which remains unpublished. Mrs. Stouff, the last speaker, died in 1940.

As mentioned above, Swadesh (1946, 1947) had thought Chitimacha and his Atakapan were probably related. Other proposed broader classifications have attempted to group Chitimacha in Tunican (see above), Gulf, and even broader hypotheses. Brown et al. (2014) attempted to relate Chitimacha to Totonacan and Mixe-Zoquean (see Chapter 6 for an evaluation of this). None of these was successful and today they are abandoned.

The Chitimacha tribe today is working vigorously to revive the language.

*Tunica

Tunica is a dormant language isolate. It is a heritage language of the Tunica-Biloxi Tribe of Marksville, Avoyelles Parish, Louisiana. (See Map 7.7.) The Tunica were first encountered by Europeans in 1682 along the Yazoo River, in Mississippi; they were known for trading salt. The language was spoken in the seventeenth and eighteenth centuries along the Mississippi River near Vicksburg, Mississippi. It was also spoken by the neighboring **Tiou**. The **Koroa**, **Yazoo**, and **Grigra** probably spoke other dialects of Tunica or closely related languages, though there are no linguistic data from any of them.

Some materials on Tunica were collected in the late nineteenth and early twentieth centuries, but the primary documentation was provided by Mary R. Haas (1941a, 1946, 1950, 1953), working with Sesostrie Youchigant, the last speaker to learn any of the language from native speakers. There is now a thriving reclamation effort to awaken the language at the Tunica-Biloxi reservation in Marksville.

Various proposals have been made which would classify Tunica together with other languages. As mentioned above, John Swanton (1919) proposed Tunican with Tunica, Chitimacha, and Atakapa. Edward Sapir (1929a) incorporated Swanton's proposed Tunican into his Hokan-Siouan super-stock. Mary Haas (1951, 1952, 1958b) grouped these and other southeastern languages in her proposed Gulf classification. None of these proposals is upheld today. (See Haas 1979.)

*Natchez

Natchez is another language isolate, also dormant. The Natchez lived in scattered villages along St. Catherine's Creek, east of present-day Natchez, Mississippi. Natchez was also spoken by the **Taensa**, who lived across the river, probably in a form that was not too different from what the Natchez people spoke. (See Map 7.7.) Two nicknames learned among the **Colapissa** of southern Mississippi and eastern Louisiana suggest that the Colapissa also spoke a closely similar language. The early 1700s saw the French involved in several missionizing attempts and three wars, which culminated in 1731 with the surrender of about 400 Natchez, who were sent to the West Indies as slaves. Many of the survivors took refuge with the Creeks and the Chickasaws, moving with them to Oklahoma in the 1830s, where they also intermarried with the Cherokees. One band reached South Carolina and ultimately united with the Cherokees there. (See Kimball 2005, 385.)

Four Natchez wordlists were collected in Oklahoma during the nineteenth century, but the most important documentation was done by John R. Swanton in 1907–1915 and by Mary R. Haas in 1934–1936, who between them worked with all the surviving speakers. Much of this material remains unpublished. The last known speaker died in 1965.

Attempts to relate Natchez to other languages have mostly been unsuccessful. Swanton (1924) thought it was related to Muskogean, as did Mary Haas (1956) and Geoffrey Kimball (1994, 2005). Sapir (1929a) included Natchez and Muskogean in the Eastern division of his Hokan-Siouan super-stock. Haas (1951, 1952, 1958b) further combined Swanton's Natchez-Muskogean and Tunican (Tunica, Atakapa, Chitimacha) in her proposed Gulf grouping. Today none of these proposals is considered valid, although the possibility of a connection between Natchez and Muskogean deserves further investigation (see Haas 1979; Kimball 1994, 2005; Swanton 1917, 1919).

Muskogean

There are competing classifications of Muskogean, and the issue of Muskogean subgrouping "will not be easily solved" (Booker 1988, 384). There is general agreement that there are four branches of the family, each composed of a pair of languages (or language varieties), but there is disagreement about higher-order branches of the Mukogean family tree.

Karen Booker and several others favor a scheme like that of Mary Haas (1949, 1979). Booker (1988, 1993) discussed phonological innovations shared by Creek and Seminole, and others shared by Alabama-Koasati and Hitchiti-Mikasuki, which are supportive of Haas' (1949, 1979) view of the subgrouping. Booker's (2005, 246) classification of Muskogean is:

Proto-Muskogean
    Western Muskogean
        Choctaw
        Chickasaw
    Eastern Muskogean
        Central
            Alabama-Koasati
                Alabama
                Koasati
                *Apalachee
            Hitchiti-Mikasuki
                Hitchiti
                Mikasuki
        Creek-Seminole

(See also Booker 1993, 414; Broadwell 2021.)
(See Maps 2.1. and 7.7.)

Martin and Munro (2005, 317) argue that the "historical morphology provides little support for the idea that the first division in the family was an Eastern-Western one ... many morphological developments appear to have originated in the proposed Southern or Southwestern branches of the family." They observe that "there are also phonological developments supporting a Southern grouping" (Martin and Munro 2005, 318.) Martin and Munro's (2005, 299) classification of Muskogean is:

Proto-Muskogean
    Southern
        Hitchiti-Mikasuki
            Hitchiti
            Mikasuki

           Southwestern
                Chickasaw-Choctaw (Western)
                      Choctaw
                      Chickasaw
                Alabama-Koasati
                      Alabama
                      Koasati
     Creek

(Creek includes Muskogee, Oklahoma Seminole, and Florida Seminole dialect of Creek.)

A third proposed classification is that of Geoffrey Kimball, who envisages a three-way split among the languages. His classification (reported in Heather Hardy 2005, 72) is:

Proto-Muskogean
     Western Muskogean
           Choctaw
           Chickasaw
     Central Muskogean
           Alabama-Koasati
                 Alabama
                 Koasati
           Hitchiti-Mikasuki
                 Hitchiti
                 Mikasuki
     Eastern Muskogean (Creek-Seminole)

Before we consider some of the reasons for the disagreements concerning the internal classification of Muskogean, it will be helpful to look at the phonemic inventory of Proto-Muskogean and some of the sound correspondences. The Proto-Muskogean phonemic inventory is: /p, t, ts, č, k, kʷ, ɸ [or xʷ], θ [or n̥], s, (š), x, ɪ, ɬ, m, n, w, y; i, a, o/ (Booker 2005, 248, 259).

Some of the correspondence sets upon which these reconstructed sounds are based are:

*θ (or *N)   WM n: EM ɬ
*c   WM s: EM č
*s   WM š: EM s
*š   WM š: EM č
*kʷ   Creek k: Others b

(WM = Western Muskogean, EM = Eastern Muskogean).

Some of these reconstructed sounds are not straightforward. Mary Haas (1947) reconstructed *kʷ based on the correspondence of k in Creek-Seminole to b in most of the other daughter languages; b is the only voiced obstruent in these languages.[85] Haas (1941b) reconstructed *θ based on the correspondence of n in Western Muskogean (Choctaw-Chickasaw) languages to ɬ in Eastern Muskogean (the other languages). However, as Booker (2005, 286) says, the *θ for this sound is just a symbol of convenience; "the true nature of the reconstructed phoneme is not known." Later, Haas (1956; 1979, 306) changed, reconstructing it as *N̥, based on the observations that Natchez has a voiceless *n*, assuming that the Natchez voiceless *n* corresponds with this Muskogean correspondence set.

Jeoffrey Kimball (1992, 451) challenged this; he believes that Natchez and Muskogean are related to one another and that the *θ of Proto-Muskogean corresponds rather to Natchez š (see Booker 2005, 252). It would seem to me that even if Natchez cannot be shown to be related to Muskogean, phonetic plausibility still makes a voiceless "n" (N, i.e., [n̥]) a better candidate for the reconstruction to represent the correspondence of *n* to ɬ. The existence of voiceless "n" in Natchez lends credibility to the reconstruction by showing that at least such a sound was not unknown in the linguistic area—Natchez has a whole series of voiceless nasals and sonorants (M, N, L, W, Y)[86] (Kimball 2005, 392).

Though "f" is written in the daughter languages, phonetically it represents the voiceless bilabial fricative [ɸ]. In spite of it being ɸ in the daughter languages, Haas (1956) reconstructed this as *x^w, reasoning that labial fricatives are uncommon in American Indian languages and that a *x^w would show pattern congruity with her reconstructed *k^w (see Booker 2005, 254). Nevertheless, if all the daughter languages have ɸ as their reflex, then clearly the best reconstruction for Proto-Muskogean is *ɸ. Also, there are other Indigenous languages of the Americas that have this sound. The existence of voiceless "l" ([ɬ]) and possibly voiceless "n" would make a reinterpretation of *ɸ as voiceless "w" (W, [w̥]), which is nearly equivalent phonetically to [ɸ], very plausible in this sound system. Note that Natchez also has a voiceless "w" (Kimball 2005, 392).

There has been doubt about whether there was a contrast between *s and *š in Proto-Muskogean. The *s has the reflexes š in Choctaw and Chickasaw and *s* in the other languages. Booker (2005, 251) suspects that this Proto-Muskogean "sibilant was in all probability phonetically retroflexed." It seems that perhaps *š can be discarded. Mary Haas (1941b) reconstructed it for a sound correspondence of š in Western Muskogean (Choctaw-Chickasaw) to "č" in Eastern Muskogean (the other daughter languages). She found this correspondence, however, only in two putative cognate sets, one for 'cricket'—clearly onomatopoeic—and one for 'squash', which possibly involves borrowing (the vowels in this putative cognate set do not match expected vowel correspondences). There may, however, be a small handful of additional cognate sets that exhibit this sound correspondence, so Booker (2005, 259) retains *š in her reconstruction.

Taking these considerations into account, I would tentatively propose that Proto-Muskogean had the following phonemes: /p, t, ts, č, k, k^w, W ([w̥]), s, x, ɪ, ɬ, m, n, N ([n̥]), w, y; i, a, o/.

Concerning the different views of Muskogean subgrouping, Haas (1979, 306) believed that "the problem is in part genetic and in part areal or diffusional." She interpreted changes involving all the languages except Creek as diffused areally among her Eastern and Western Muskogean languages. Booker (1988, 384) followed Haas, saying that some of the Muskogean sound changes seem to crosscut subgroups, the result of "'areal' or 'diffusional' phenomena in which overlapping isoglosses cloud the genetic picture." For example, Hitchiti-Mikasuki shows strong influence from Creek. Booker is of the opinion that "until contact phenomena and diffusional patterns throughout the Southeast are better understood, i.e. until diffusion can be separated from inheritance, it is doubtful that the question of [Muskogean] subgrouping will be definitively answered" (Booker 2005, 247).

Pamela Munro (1993, 394) doubts the validity of the Haas-Booker subgrouping. She said:

> It is not clear whether the Eastern languages—despite their great number of similar sound correspondences—actually share any innovations . . . The sibilant correspondences are much more complex than Haas (1941[b]) implies, and the confusion among the proto sibilants may have arisen because of sound symbolic alternations.

(See also Munro 1987a, 3.)

Munro's subgrouping of the family (similar to that of Swanton 1917, 1924) is based on shared lexical and morphological traits (some of them retentions), and it accommodates the sound changes in which Proto-Muskogean *k^w became p/k in Creek-Seminole, but became b in the other languages. In particular, Munro lists several of what she takes to be morphological innovations shared by Southwestern Muskogean languages, a subgroup not recognized in Haas' and Booker's classifications. Munro paid particular attention to pronominals (Munro 1993, 395–396).

A good deal is now clear about Proto-Muskogean grammar. For example, the basic word order was SOV [Subject-Object-Verb]. Its alignment was nominative-accusative and a case suffix for each is reconstructed. There was extensive compounding. Proto-Muskogean morphology includes preverbal markers for direction instrumentality, agentive, non-agentive, person marking, dative functions, reflexivity, reciprocity, location, and adpositional relationships. Postverbal markers include distributive suffixes, voice-related auxiliaries, diminutive, and sentence-final particles. (Martin and Munro 2005, 300–301. (Heather Hardy 2005, 73, Martin and Munro 2005).

T. Dale Nicklas (1994, 16) located the Proto-Muskogean homeland in the middle Mississippi region, whence there was an eastward movement to a new homeland in eastern Mississippi and western Alabama, with subsequent expansion of Choctaw to the west and south, and of Creek and Apalachee to the east and south. Most of the Muskogean groups were forced to move west of the Mississippi River during the Indian removal of 1836–1840, many to Oklahoma.

Broader connections of Muskogean with other language groups of the Southeast have been proposed, but none is sufficiently well supported. Mary Haas' (1951, 1952) Gulf classification was widely cited. It would have connected Muskogean and Natchez, on the one hand, with Tunica, Atakapa, and Chitimacha on the other (Haas 1979; Kimball 1994; Swanton 1917). However, Haas largely abandoned the proposal later (Haas, personal communication, cf. Haas 1979). Pamela Munro (1994) attempted to defend the Gulf classification, although the evidence she presented was unconvincing (see Campbell 1997a, 306–308 for details). The possible connection between Natchez and Muskogean does merit further investigation (Haas 1956; Kimball 1994; 2005, 402).

Choctaw is a Western (or Southwestern) Muskogean language, closely related to Chickasaw. The Choctaw were originally in Mississippi and a small portion of Alabama. In 1830s most of the Choctaws were forced to relocate to Oklahoma. The Mississippi Band of Choctaws has speakers in seven small communities scattered throughout the state; the tribal headquarters is on a reservation near Philadelphia, Mississippi. Speakers associated with the Choctaw Nation of Oklahoma live mostly in southeastern Oklahoma. Dialect differences, however, are minor, though there appear to be three dialects on the Mississippi Choctaw reservation, depending on the community where the different speakers reside (Broadwell 2005, 157).

As mentioned, **Chickasaw** and Choctaw are closely related. Often the two have been considered dialects of the same language, but politically distinct, though most scholars today find sufficient differences to consider them distinct languages. The Chickasaw were originally in a small area of northern Missisipi. Most Chickasaws have some familiarity with Choctaw from the Choctaw Bible and hymnal, but Choctaws do not have knowledge of Chickasaw. Chickasaw was spoken over a large area in Alabama, Mississippi, Tennessee, and Kentucky. Today it is spoken by members of the Chickasaw Nation in south-central Oklahoma. (Munro 1987b; Martin 1994; Heather Hardy 2005, 71; Munro 2005, 114, 152).

The **Mikasuki/Seminole** tribal names and language names do not match well, which is a source of confusion. Mikasuki speakers were found among various southeastern tribes after their resettlement in Indian Territory (Oklahoma), but few, if any, are to be found there today. The majority of the "Seminoles" of Florida, however, speak Mikasuki, and a small number of them speak Seminole.[87]

Mikasuki is the only surviving dialect of the Muskogean language known as **Hitchiti** or **Hitchiti-Mikasuki**. It is spoken in Florida by members of the Miccosukee Tribe, as well as by many members of the Seminole Tribe. There are five Seminole reservation communities, with Mikasuki the dominant language at the Big Cypress, Immokalee, Hollywood, and Tampa reservations, while the Florida Seminole dialect of Creek is dominant at the Brighton Reservation. Though Hichiti is sometimes counted as a separate language, Hitchiti and Mikasuki were dialects of a single language.

Seminole is sometimes used loosely to refer to Oklahoma Seminole Creek, a variety of Creek spoken in the Seminole Nation of Oklahoma. **Florida Seminole** is a variety of Creek that is spoken by some members of the Seminole Tribe of Florida, although most speak Mikasuki. Creek and Seminole are generally thought to be dialects of a single language.

Apalachee is a long-dormant Muskogean language. The Apalachee were first encountered by the Spanish in 1528 between the Aucilla and Apalachicola Rivers in western Florida. The language was spoken in the late 1600s in northern Florida around present-day Tallahassee and Apalachee Bay. Its main attestation is a letter written in 1688 to Charles II of Spain, published in 1860, the original of which is lost. This difficult document has been analyzed in detail by several scholars and a vocabulary of about 120 items recovered from it (see for example Kimball 1988). Haas (1949) and Kimball (1987a) have determined that Apalachee belongs together with Alabama-Koasati in a subdivision of Muskogean.

Alabama (Alibamu) is another Muskogean language. In the sixteenth century, the Alabama (Alibamu) were located in northeastern Mississippi near present-day Starkville; they were tributaries of the Chickasaw. Later they moved to east-central Alabama, where they became allied with the Creek Confederacy. Most of them moved to Spanish Louisiana and Florida with the British takeover in 1763, but some remained behind and were removed to Indian Territory in the 1830s. Alabama is spoken by residents of the Alabama-Coushatta Indian Reservation near Livingston, in the Big Thicket area of East Texas. Some were among members of the Alabama-Quassarte Tribe, a subdivision of the Muskogee Creek Nation, in Okfuskee County, Oklahoma. Alabama appears not to have any significant dialect differences.

Koasati (Coushatta) is closely related to Alabama. Alabama (Alibamu) and Koasati were probably still mutually intelligible in the 1500s (Booker et al. 1992, 411). Koasati was probably the northernmost Muskogean language. In the sixteenth century it was spoken as far north as eastern Tennessee, in the upper Tennessee Valley, but was located in northern Alabama in the eighteenth century (Booker et al. 1992, 411). It moved into Louisiana in the 1700s and is now centered on the Coushatta Reservation at Elton, Louisiana, and the Alabama-Coushatta Reservation near Livingston in southeastern Texas.

Creek (Muskogee) was spoken earlier by groups in Alabama and Georgia. It was taken to Florida in the early 1700s and after the Indian Removal Act of 1830, most of the speakers, Muscogee and Seminole, were forced to Oklahoma. The language is spoken today by members of the Muscogee (Creek) Nation and Seminole Nation in east-central Oklahoma, and by some members of Seminole Tribe of Florida, most of them living on the Brighton Reservation. The dialect of Creek spoken by the Florida Seminoles is somewhat different. There are also some differences between the dialects of the tribal groups in Oklahoma. However, all are mostly mutually intelligible with one another (Donald Hardy 2005, 200).[88]

(For Mobilian Jargon, see Chapter 8.)

Yuchi (Euchee)

Yuchi is a language isolate. In the sixteenth century the Yuchis appear to have been located west of the Appalachian Mountains in Tennessee (Booker et al. 1992, 411). They moved from Georgia to Oklahoma as part of the Indian removal of 1836–1840. (See Map 7.7.) They have been politically associated with the Muscogee Creeks since then, and most live among the Creeks in northeastern Oklahoma, near Sapulpa, Hectorsville, and Bristow.

Many ideas of broader affiliation have been suggested that would combine Yuchi with other languages, but none has been accepted. Edward Sapir (1921a, 1929a) placed Yuchi in his Hokan-Siouan super-stock, closer to Siouan (see also Haas 1964). William Elmendorf (1963) argued for linking Yuchi and Yukian (of California), part of a broader assumed Siouan connection, but the evidence for this is unconvincing. James Crawford (1973, 173) felt that it looked "promising that a genetic relationship can eventually be shown to exist between Yuchi and Siouan," but he also presented similarities shared by Yuchi, Tunica, and Atakapa (Crawford 1979). Robert Rankin (1997, 1998) presented morphological evidence that he thought tentatively might show that Yuchi and Siouan belong together in a higher-order classification. However, Mary Linn (personal communication), expert on the Yuchi language, finds Rankin's evidence unconvincing. Ryan Kasak (2016) took up the question again. He argues "in favor of the morphological similarities found in both Siouan-Catawban and Yuchi to be more than coincidental. Such similarities are most likely due to genetic inheritance" (Kasak 2016, 7). He presents several sound correspondences and several suggestive possible lexical cognates, most of them (eleven out of twenty) are short in Yuchi (CV in shape), however. He relies in particular on inflectional morphology and the sequencing of affixes within the verbal template. Mary Lin (personal communication) also has reservations about his evidence. His findings may be suggestive, but not conclusive.

*****Timucua** (Florida)

Timucua, dormant since at least 1800 (Sturtevant 2005, 14), was spoken in northern Florida from around Tallahassee to St. John's River near Jacksonville, and southward to

Cape Canaveral on the Atlantic and Tampa Bay on the Gulf of Mexico (Swanton 1946, 190–191; cf. Granberry 1990). (See Map 7.7.) It is said to have had a number of dialects; Julian Granberry (1990, 61) listed **Timucua** proper, **Potano, Itafi, Yufera, Mocama, Tucururu, Agua Fresca, Agua Salada, Acuera, Oconi,** and **Tawasa**. The best-known material is from Francisco Pareja (1614, 1886 [1614]); Pareja's various works constitute more than 2000 pages of Timucua text (Granberry 1990, 61). Most of the other extant Timucua materials represent the Mocama and Potano dialects. (About Tawasa, see Chapter 5).

Many broader relationships, all unsuccessful, have been proposed for Timucua. Adelung and Vater (1816, 285) noted a resemblance to **Illinois** (an Algonquian language). Daniel Brinton (1859, 12) at first had expected Timucua eventually to prove to be related to Cariban languages. Edward Sapir (1929a) placed Timucua tentatively in his Hokan-Siouan super-stock, for no evident reason. Morris Swadesh (1964b, 548) compared Timucua with Arawakan. James Crawford (1988) presented twenty-three lexical and morphological similarities shared by Muskogean and Timucua; he viewed eight as probable borrowings and the rest as possible cognates. Julian Granberry claimed to have found a connection with Warao (a language isolate of Venezuela and Guyana), but he also saw "cognates" with "Proto-Arawak[an], Proto-Gulf, Proto-Muskogean, and late Muskogean" (Granberry 1970, 607, quoted in Crawford 1988, 157). Later, Granberry (1991, 204) claimed that Timucua was a "creolized system" that originated in the northwest Amazon, which he thought was probably the "reason that attempts to find the source of Timucua linguistically have been fruitless ... The language has no single provenience." He believed that the basic patterns of Timucua grammar have the closest similarities to Warao (language isolate) and to Cuna (a Chibchan language of Panama and Colombia), but he presented as evidence of multiple lexical sources some similarities he saw in words from Warao, Chibchan, Paezan, Arawakan, Tukanoan, and other (mostly Amazonian) languages; he opted for a "Chibchan-related ultimate origin for the language" (Granberry 1991, 235). None of this is remotely convincing, however. Joseph Greenberg (1987) placed Timucua in his vast Chibchan-Paezan macro-family. Connections have also been suggested with Cherokee (Iroquoian) and Siouan. All of these proposals are highly doubtful.

Iroquoian
    Southern Iroquoian: Cherokee
    Northern Iroquoian
        Tuscarora-Nottoway
            *Tuscarora
            *Nottoway
        Lake Iroquoian
            *Huron-Wyandot
            *Laurentian
        Iroquois Proper (Five Nations Iroquois)
            Seneca-Cayuga
                Seneca
                Cayuga

Onondaga
*Susquehannock (Andaste, Conestoga)
Oneida- Mohawk
    Oneida
    Mohawk

(Mithun 1999, 418; see also Mithun 1979.)
(See Map 2.9. Iroquoian languages.)

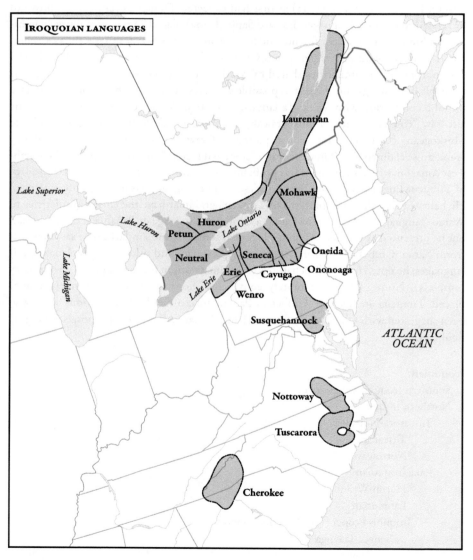

MAP 2.9. Iroquoian languages

*Wenro (east of Lake Erie) and *Erie (southeast of Lake Erie) are also Iroquoian, but their position within Iroquoian subgrouping is uncertain due to limited attestation for them. Charles Julian's (2010, 10) classification of Iroquoian is somewhat different:

Proto-Iroquoian
    Cherokee
    Proto-Northern-Iroquoian
        Proto-Tuscarora-Nottoway
            *Tuscarora
            *Nottoway
        *Susquehannock
        *Laurentian
        Proto-Mohawk-Oneida
            Mohawk
            Oneida
        Onondaga
        Cayuga
        Seneca
        *Huron-Wyandot
            *Huron
            *Wyandot

Julian's classification differs from Mithun's in not having a separate Proto-Lake Iroquoian subgroup or a separate Iroquois Proper (Five Nations Iroquois) subgroup.

When Europeans first came to North America, Iroquoian peoples were found from Quebec to Georgia, and from the coasts of Virginia and Carolina to Ohio, Pennsylvania, and Ontario. **Laurentian** was probably the first North American language recorded by Europeans. What is known of Laurentian was taken down on Jacques Cartier's voyages (1534, 1535–1536, 1541–1542) near what is today the Quebec City (Mithun 1981a, see below).

Tuscarora is a Northern Iroquoian language. It was spoken until the early eighteenth century in eastern North Carolina, in the area of Goldsboro, Kinston, and Smithfield. After 1711–1713 many Tuscaroras moved north and were adopted in about 1723 into the League of the Iroquois in New York, settling near the Seneca. After the American Revolution part of the group fled to Canada, joining other Iroquois peoples on the Six Nations Reserve in Ontario. Tuscarora became dormant in 2020, spoken before that on the Tuscarora Reservation (Lewiston, New York) and at the Six Nations of the Grand River First Nation, near Brantford, Ontario.

Nottoway is closely related to Tuscarora. It was spoken in colonial times and into the nineteenth century along the Nottoway River in southeastern Virginia, adjacent to the original territory of the Tuscaroras in North Carolina. There are two tribes of Nottoway in Virginia: the Nottoway Indian Tribe of Virginia and the Cheroenhaka (Nottoway) Indian Tribe. Other Nottoway descendants live in Wisconsin and Canada, to where some Nottoway fled in the eighteenth century. The last known speaker was Edith Turner, who died in 1838. Nottoway is attested only in two wordlists from the early nineteenth century.[89]

Huron-Wyandot (Wendat) is a Northern Iroquoian language represented by several dialects, originally spoken in the Georgian Bay area near Lake Huron in Ontario. One variety of this language was the lingua franca of the Huron Confederacy in the seventeenth century. After the Huron Confederacy was destroyed by the Iroquois in 1649 in a war over control of the fur trade, some Hurons settled at Lorette, near Quebec City, and others moved to Ohio. From there one group moved to Amherstburg, south of Windsor, Ontario, and the others were removed to Kansas and later to Oklahoma, home of the Wyandotte Tribe of Oklahoma. Huron dialects were documented by French missionaries in Canada in the seventeenth and eighteenth centuries, and Wyandot by Marius Barbeau in Ontario and Oklahoma in the early twentieth century. The last native speaker died around 1980, a member of the Oklahoma group.[90]

Laurentian (also called St. Lawrence Iroquois, Kwedech, Hochelaagan, and Stadaconan) refers to a Northern Iroquoian language spoken in the sixteenth century along the St. Lawrence River in Quebec. It was first recorded in 1534 when Jacques Cartier sailed into the Gaspe Bay; 58 words of the language appear in the account of his first voyage, and another 170 words are in a list appended to the account of his second voyage. In the interval between Cartier's last voyage in 1542 and Samuel de Champlain's visit to this area in 1603, the Laurentians had disappeared. Because of the limited material available and the difficulty of interpreting its orthography, the place of Laurentian in the Iroquoian family has not been settled. The data seem to indicate that perhaps more than one dialect was involved in the recordings, and an uncertainty is whether Cartier's material represents a single Iroquoian language or was obtained from speakers of more than one (see Lounsbury 1978, 335; Mithun 1981a).

Seneca is another Northern Iroquoian language. Senecas were first encountered by Europeans between Seneca Lake and the Genesee River in New York State. During the seventeenth century, they moved toward Lake Erie, and after the American Revolution, some moved to the Six Nations Reserve. Seneca is the westernmost tribe of the Six Nations Iroquois Confederacy, in western New York and adjacent Pennsylvania. Senecas are now in three reservation communities in New York state: Cattaraugus, on Lake Erie; Allegany, in Salamanca; and Tonawanda, near Buffalo.

Cayuga is a Northern Iroquoian language, originally spoken by a tribe of the Iroquois Confederacy (Six Nations), located west of the Onondagas and east of the Senecas, between Cayuga and Owasco Lakes. Cayugas were first encountered by Europeans on the shores of Cayuga Lake in New York State. After the American Revolution many of the Cayugas fled to Canada, where their modern descendants make up part of the population of the Six Nations Reserve at Grand River, Ontario. Other Cayugas joined the Seneca, where their language was replaced by Seneca, and yet others moved westward with other Iroquois, eventually settling in northeastern Oklahoma. Cayuga underwent changes caused by contact with other Iroquoian languages, especially Seneca. A dialect of Cayuga was spoken in Oklahoma as late as the 1980s but it now has no speakers.[91]

Onondaga is spoken in upstate New York by the central tribe, the "firekeepers," of the Iroquois Confederacy (Six Nations). Onondagas were in New York State when Europeans first arrived, and many still live there. After the American Revolution a number moved to Ontario. Most modern Onondagas live on a reservation in their old homeland, south of the city of Syracuse, but there is also a smaller community on the Six Nations Reserve in southern Ontario.[92]

Susquehannock (also called Andaste, Conestoga, Minqua) is a long-dormant Northern Iroquoian language spoken in the seventeenth and eighteenth centuries along the Susquehanna River in southeastern Pennsylvania and northeastern Maryland. It is known only from a single source, the *Vocabula Mahakuassica* written by Johannes Campanius, Swedish Lutheran missionary, during the 1640s, appended to a Delaware catechism. It contains some eighty words and phrases (Campanius 1696; Mithun 1981b).[93]

Oneida is a Northern Iroquoian language. The original home of the Oneidas was south of Oneida Lake, in New York State. After the American Revolution, many Oneidas went to the Six Nations Reserve in Ontario. In 1846 a group of Oneidas left New York for Wisconsin, where their descendants still live. Oneida was a tribe of the Iroquois Confederacy (Six Nations) located east of the Onondagas and west of the Mohawks. Most of the modern Oneidas live in two widely separated reservation communities, on the Thames River near London, Ontario, and at Green Bay, Wisconsin, as well as in upstate New York, some on a small tract of land near the town of Oneida and others dispersed into neighboring communities.[94]

Mohawk was spoken originally by the easternmost tribe of the Six Nations (Iroquois Confederacy) in the Mohawk River Valley of New York state, between present-day Schenectady and Utica. Mohawks were first encountered there by Samuel de Champlain in 1609. Around 1670 many settled near Montreal. Most who stayed in the Mohawk Valley sided with the British during the American Revolution, and afterward were moved to the Six Nations Reserve.[95]

There are modern Mohawk communities in northern New York state and in southeastern Canada. In New York they are Ganienkeh and Kanatsiohareke; in Canada they are Kahnawake and Kanehsatake in the vicinity of Montreal; Ahkwesahsne on the St. Lawrence River at the US-Canadian border; Ohsweken (Six Nations on the Grand River in southern Ontario); Doncaster (Tioweróton), in the Laurentides region of Quebec; the Tyendinaga Reserve on the Bay of Quinté near Kingston; and a small settlement at Gibson (Wahta) east of Georgian Bay. Mohawk ironworkers ("skywalkers") in New York City are well known.

Cherokee is the most divergent of the Iroquoian languages. During the seventeenth century, the Cherokees were in western North Carolina and in very small areas in neighboring states. In 1838–1839, they were forced to march to Oklahoma, an event called the "Trail of Tears," relocated in northeastern Oklahoma, but many hid in the North Carolina mountains until 1849, when they were allowed to settle on land bought there on their behalf.

Cherokee is spoken in three divergent dialects by members of the Cherokee Nation of Oklahoma, of the Eastern Band of Cherokees in North Carolina, and of the United Keetoowah Band of Oklahoma and Arkansas. There were three major dialects of Cherokee spoken in the eighteenth and early nineteenth centuries: **Lower** (Elati), **Middle** (Kituhwa), and **Western** or **Overhill** (Otali). The Lower dialect had /r/ where the others have /l/; that dialect stopped being spoken by the end of the nineteenth century. The Overhill dialect, from the upper Tennessee Valley, is the variety spoken today in northeastern Oklahoma, where most Cherokees were forced to relocate in the late 1830s. The

Middle dialect is used on the Qualla Boundary reservation, North Carolina, by descendants of Cherokees who resisted removal. The modern dialect spoken in the Snowbird community near Robbinsville, North Carolina, combines features of the Western and Middle dialects (Scancarelli 2005, 351).

Cherokee is written in the traditional syllabary, created in the 1820s by Sequoyah (whose English name was alternatively spelled as *George Gist* or *George Guess*). The syllabary remains a badge of Cherokee tribal identity. Sequoyah's creation of the Cherokee syllabary has been called "one of the most remarkable intellectual *tours de force* in American history" (Walker 1969, 150, cited by Sturtevant 2005, 29).

Charles Julian (2010, 20) gives the inventory of reconstructed Proto-Iroquoian phonemes as: /t, ts, k, kʷ, ʔ, s, ɹ, n, j, w, h, i, e, a, o u, ī, ē, ā, ō, ū, vowel length/. The precise phonetic character of *ɹ is uncertain, represented by Julian (2010, 22) as an "alveolar approximant." The *s apparently was always preceded by *h ("unless preceded by another consonant") (p. 31). However, there are cases that require recognition also of the consonant cluster *hts (p. 37), thus eliminating the possibility that *s could be interpreted just as the variant of *ts that occurs after *h. Julian's inventory mostly matches the reconstructed phonemes given in earlier works, with small differences. Iroquoian languages lack labial consonants, something that has prompted a good number of comments in both the professional and the speculative literature.

Proto-Iroquoian split up, according to Marianne Mithun (1981b, 4), about 4,000 years ago (see Lounsbury 1978, 334). Cherokee (Southern Iroquoian) was the first to split off from the rest of family and it is the most divergent. Cognates between languages of the two branches of the family "are not numerous" (Barrie and Uchihara 2021, 424). Floyd Lounsbury (1978, 336) proposed much of New York State, central and northwestern Pennsylvania, and perhaps northeastern Ohio as the Iroquoian "center of gravity" (homeland), from which the languages dispersed. Schillaci et al. (2017) argue for a different interpretation, based on a quantitative analysis of lexical data, with geographic data, applying the much-criticized ASJP (Automated Similarity Judgment Program) approach, which deals with a list of only forty words (see Chapter 6). They date Proto-Iroquoian to 2,624 BCE;[96] they see the Finger Lakes region of west-central New York as the most likely homeland. They present various classifications of Iroquoian languages based on different scholar's data, including a neighbor-joining language tree based on the percent of shared cognates presented in Julian (2010). For the most part, these different family trees based on different people's data and different methods match that of Mithun (1999, 418), given above, and of other linguists established by standard linguistic methods. It is doubtful that the conclusions of Schillaci et al. that rely so strongly on such limited lexical information will be received well by Iroquoianist linguists or others.

Marianne Mithun (1984a) investigated reconstructed lexical material to see what they reveal of Proto-Iroquoian culture. She suggested that the set of words that are reconstructible to Proto-Northern-Iroquoian involving "aquatic subsistence" (for example, 'lake' or 'large river', 'row a boat', 'fishhook') indicates the probability that the Proto-Iroquoians lived near a large river or lake. For hunting little can be reconstructed for Proto-Iroquoian, but Northern Iroquoian contained two terms for 'bow' and terms for 'bowstring', 'arrow', 'arrow/feather', and 'arrowhead'. The total absence of reconstructible terms for corn cultivation or agriculture in Proto-Iroquoian suggests that in Proto-Iroquoian times corn and agriculture were not yet known. Corn, so important to Iroquoian culture, seems to have arrived relatively recently in the Northeast; however, a term for 'bread' is reconstructible at least to Proto-Northern-Iroquoian and perhaps to Proto-Iroquoian. As for other material culture, Proto-Northern-Iroquoian and perhaps Proto-Iroquoian had words for 'leggings', Proto-Northern-Iroquoian 'shoe' or 'moccasin', 'basket', 'wooden trough', 'kettle' or 'pot', 'dish', 'bowl', 'cradleboard', 'knife', and 'axe'.

Algic (Algonquian-Ritwan)
  *Ritwan
    *Wiyot
    *Yurok
  Algonquian
    Blackfoot
    Cree-Innu (Cree-Montagnais)
      Cree
        Plains Cree
        Woods Cree
        Western Swampy Cree
        Eastern Swampy Cree (includes Moose Cree)
        Attikamek
        Michif (Plains Cree-French mixed language)
      Innu-Naskapi-East Cree (Montagnais-Naskapi)
        East Cree
          Southern East Cree
          Northern East Cree
            Northern East Cree
            Western Naskapi (Naskapi)
        Innu (Montagnais)
          Western Innu
          Central Innu
          Eastern Innu
          Eastern Naskapi (Mushuau Innu)
    Arapahoan
      *Gros Ventre (Atsina)
      Arapaho
      *Besawunena
      *Nawathinehena
    Cheyenne
    Menominee
    Ojibwayan
      Northern Ojibwe
        Severn Ojibwe (Oji-Cree)
        Northern Algonquin

Southern Ojibwe
　　　　Saulteaux
　　　　Central Southern Ojibwe (Anishinaabemowin)
　　　　Eastern Ojibwe (includes "Southern Algonquin")
　　　　Ottawa (Odawa)
　　　　*Old Algonquin
　　Potawatomi
　　Sauk-Meskwaki-Kickapoo
　　　　Meskwaki-Sauk
　　　　Kickapoo
　　　　(*Mascouten) (Goddard 1973)
　　Shawnee
　　*Miami-Illinois
　　Eastern Algonquian
　　　Micmac
　　　Abenakian
　　　　Maliseet-Passamaquoddy
　　　　*Eastern Abenaki
　　　　Western Abenaki
　　　*Etchemin
　　　*Southern New England Algonquian
　　　　*Massachusett-Narragansett
　　　　*Loup languages
　　　　*Mohegan-Pequot
　　　　*Quiripi-Unquachog-Shinnecock-Montauk
　　　*Mahican
　　　　*Eastern Mahican
　　　　*Western Mahican
　　　Delaware
　　　　Munsee-Wamapano
　　　　　Munsee
　　　　　*Wamapano
　　　　*Unami complex
　　　　　*Unalachtigo
　　　　　*North Unami
　　　　　*South Unami
　　　*Nanticoke-Conoy
　　　*Virginia Algonquian
　　　*Carolina Algonquian

(See Oxford 2021, 505 for an abbreviated classification, which treats Blackfoot as a sister to Proto-Algonquian.)

　(See Map 2.10. Algonquian languages; see also Maps 2.6. and 7.6.)

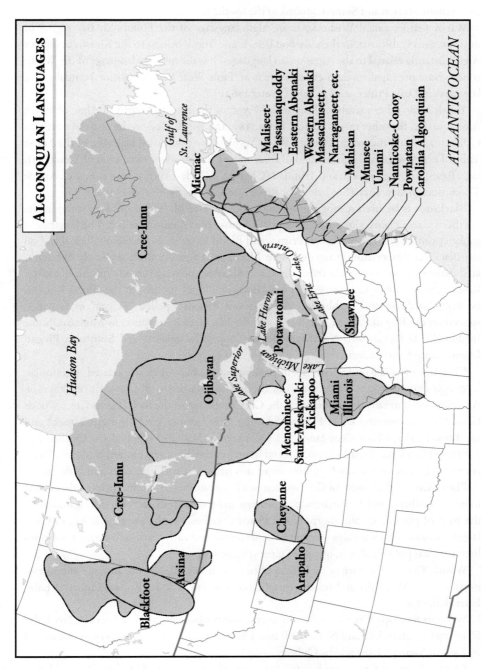

MAP 2.10. Algonquian languages

Algic spans a remarkable geographical expanse, from the northern California coast in the west to the Atlantic seaboard in the east, and from Labrador and the subarctic in the north to northern Mexico and South Carolina in the south.[97]

Wiyot (earlier called Wishosk) is an Algic language of the Humboldt Bay region of northwestern California, in the redwood belt. It and Yurok belong to the Ritwan branch of Algic, distantly related to the Algonquian languages. It is the heritage language of the Wiyot tribe, whose principal modern community is at Table Bluff Rancheria near Ferndale. The last speaker, Della Prince, died in 1962 (Teeter 1964b).[98]

Yurok is the other member, along with Wiyot, of the Ritwan branch of Algic of which Algonquian is the other major branch. Before 1850 the Yurok lived on the coast of northern California and on the lower Klamath River. Yurok is the traditional language of the Yurok Tribe of northwestern California and of three nearby independent rancherias of Yurok heritage, Reseghini, Big Lagoon, and Trinidad (Cher-Ae). The last known native speaker, Archie Thompson, died in 2013. (See below for Ritwan and its place within the family.)[99]

Blackfoot is by itself a subgroup of Algonquian. The Blackfoot speakers were on the northern Great Plains, along with a number of other bison-hunting tribes. The language is spoken primarily on the Blackfoot, Peigan, and Blood Reserves in southern Alberta, and on the Blackfeet Reservation in northwestern Montana. There are three shallowly differentiated dialects, representing old tribal divisions: **Siksika**, spoken primarily on the Blackfoot Reserve, southeast of Calgary, Alberta; **Kainaa**, or Blood, spoken on the Blood Reserve, between Cardston and Lethbridge, Alberta; and **Piegan** (spelled "Peigan" in Canada), spoken on the Peigan Reserve in Alberta and the Blackfeet Reservation in Montana. Some further divide Piegan into **Northern Piegan** (Aapágohsispikani) and **Southern Piegan** (Aamskáápipikani) dialects.

Cree-Innu (Cree-Montagnais) is a large subgroup, a chain of closely related Algonquian languages extending across Canada from the Rocky Mountains to the coast of Labrador. A distinction is usually drawn between the **Cree** languages in the west (Plains Cree, Woods Cree, Western Swampy Cree, Eastern Swampy Cree, Moose Cree, and Attikamek) and the **Innu-Naskapi-East Cree** languages (Montagnais-Naskapi) of northern Quebec and Labrador (East Cree, Western Innu, Central Innu, Eastern Innu, and Eastern Naskapi). There is some degree of mutual intelligibility across this entire chain of languages and dialects.[100]

Plains Cree is the variety of Cree spoken in a large number of communities in the central prairies of Alberta and Saskatchewan. Northern and southern dialects are distinguished on the basis of phonology and morphology. Plains Cree became the prestige dialect of Cree, largely because a considerable amount of nineteenth- and early twentieth-century religious literature was published in it, using the Cree syllabic script.

Woods Cree is the variety of Cree spoken in communities in the forested interior of northwestern Manitoba and north-central Saskatchewan (Lac La Ronge, Montreal Lake, Peter Ballantyne).

Western Swampy Cree is spoken in northeastern Manitoba at York Factory, Fox Lake, Shamattawa, Churchill, and Norway House. The dialect of Fort Severn has been influenced by Eastern Swampy Cree and by Ojibwe.

Eastern Swampy Cree is spoken in Ontario on the west coast of Hudson Bay and James Bay at Fort Albany, Attawapiskat, and Peawanuck, where the Weenusk band moved after being flooded out of their village at Winisk in 1986. **Moose Cree** is the Cree variety spoken at Fort Albany, Kasechewan, and Moose Factory, on the southwestern shore of James Bay in northern Ontario. Moose Cree gradually merges with Eastern Swampy Cree, especially at Kashechewan, where it has been influenced by the Swampy Cree spoken at nearby Albany Post.

Attikamek (Tête de Boule, Atikamekw) is the variety of Cree spoken on the Manouane/Manuan, Obedjiwan/Obidjewan, and Weymontachingue/Wemontachie Reserves, north of Trois-Rivières in south-central Quebec.

Michif (Mitchif) is a mixed language that combines parts from Plains Cree and parts from French (see Chapter 8 for details). It is spoken in Manitoba, Saskatchewan, Alberta, and North Dakota in communities where Métis live, descendants of Cree women and French fur traders who formed a distinct ethnic group on the northern Great Plains. The words, grammar, and pronunciation of nouns and their modifiers are almost entirely from a variety of Canadian French, while the verbs are grammatically complex, fully inflected forms of Plains Cree, with only minor differences. Since it is a mixed language, whether it should be classified as a member of Algonquian is not settled.

Innu-Naskapi-East Cree (Montagnais-Naskapi) is the other large branch of the Cree-Innu subgroup of Algonquian languages.

East Cree is the variety of Innu-Naskapi-East Cree spoken in northwestern Quebec, along the east coast of James Bay and Hudson Bay and inland. There is a distinction between the **Northern East Cree** and **Southern East Cree** subvarieties, the latter with coastal and inland varieties. The northern dialect is spoken in Whapamagostui (Great Whale River), Chisasibi (Fort George), and Wemindji (Paint Hills); southern dialects are spoken in Nemaska (Nemiscau), Waskaganish (Rupert House), Eastmain, Waswanipi, Ouje-bougamau, and Mistissini.

Innu (Montagnais) is a group of languages and emergent languages related closely to East Cree and more distantly to the Cree varieties spoken in Quebec and Labrador.

Western Innu is spoken at Mashteuiatsh (Pointe-Bleue on Lac Saint-Jean) and Betsiamites, Quebec; it was formerly spoken on the Essipit reserve (Les Escoumins).

Central Innu is spoken on the Matimekush and Lac-John reserves near Schefferville and the Uashat and Maliotenam reserves at Sept-Iles.

Eastern Innu is spoken at Ekuanitshit (Mingan), La Romaine (Uanaman-Shipu), Natashquan, and Pakuashipi (St-Augustin) in Quebec and at Sheshatshiu in Labrador.

Eastern Naskapi (Mushuau Innu) is spoken at Davis Inlet, Labrador.

Innu-Aimun is a socio-political designation for the Innu dialects of Labrador, specifically the Eastern Naskapi spoken at Natuashish and the Innu spoken at Sheshatshiu (sometimes called just the Innu language). The term Innu is also sometimes used to refer to all Innu varieties.

Naskapi is a cover term for two varieties of Cree-Innu: Western Naskapi (in Quebec) and Eastern Naskapi (in Labrador).[101]

Western Naskapi is spoken on the Kawawachikamach Reserve, near Schefferville, Quebec. The community moved from Fort Chimo in 1956. The dialect is similar to Eastern Naskapi, but shares features with Northern East Cree.

Eastern Naskapi is an Innu (Montagnais) dialect or emergent language spoken by the Mushuau Innu community of Labrador. It was relocated from Utshimassits (Davis Inlet) to

Natuashish (Sango Bay) in 2002. It is distinct from the Eastern Innu spoken at Sheshatshiu, Labrador, having more features in common with Western Naskapi and Northern East Cree, but like Innu it is often referred to as Innu-Aimun.

Arapahoan is a separate subgroup of Algonquian with three or four languages as its members: Gros Ventre (Atsina), Arapaho, Besawunena, and Nawathinehena.

Gros Ventre (Atsina) is closely enough related to Arapaho that speakers of the two languages could understand each other to some extent. It is the heritage language of the Gros Ventre on the Fort Belknap Reservation, Montana, which they share with Assiniboine (Siouan). The Gros Ventre allied with the Blackfeet in the eighteenth century. Early vocabularies show that by that time the language was already differentiated from Arapaho. There has sometimes been confusion regarding the name, since unrelated Hidatsa were also called Gros Ventre by the French, apparently because the signs for the two tribes in Plains Indian Sign Language are similar. The last first-language speaker of Gros Ventre died in 1981.

Arapaho and its closely related sisters were spoken at the beginning of the nineteenth century by three independent bands on the Great Plains south of the Missouri River. One band soon consolidated with the others, but the Staetan band remained independent for a few decades, and some words of **Besawunena** (the Staetan band), were still remembered in the 1930s. **Besawunena** has sometimes been considered a dialecst of Arapaho; Ives Goddard considers it an independent language. Modern Arapaho, presumably the variety of the dominant band, became the language of the descendants of all three of the bands, as well as of the Nawathinehena (see below). Consequently, Arapaho is the heritage language of both the Northern Arapaho of the Wind River Reservation in central Wyoming and of the Southern Arapaho members of the Cheyenne-Arapaho Tribe in west-central Oklahoma.

Nawathinehena is closely related to Arapaho; it was spoken south of the Arapaho bands in the early nineteenth century. In its phonology it is quite different from Arapaho and shares some innovations with Cheyenne, which was presumably formerly its southern neighbor. The Nawathinehena adopted Arapaho. The Nawathinehena language is known only from a vocabulary collected by Alfred Kroeber in 1899 (Kroeber 1916).

Cheyenne is another Algonquian subgroup of its own. It is spoken on the Northern Cheyenne Reservation in southeastern Montana, and in scattered communities in central Oklahoma. There are some small differences between the Northern Cheyenne and Southern Cheyenne dialects. Cheyenne has undergone considerable sound change from Proto-Algonquian.

Menominee, historically located in northern Wisconsin, is spoken on the Menominee Reservation in the towns of Keshena, Neopit, South Branch, and Zoar, in Wisconsin. The language is severely endangered.[102] Leonard Bloomfield (1962) is a much-celebrated grammar of the language.

The **Ojibwayan** subgroup is a large dialect complex with varieties spoken in many communities in Canada from Alberta to Quebec and in the north-central United States. At least seven emergent languages or regional dialects can be distinguished: Severn Ojibwe, Northern Algonquin, Saulteaux, Central Southern Ojibwe (Anishinaabemowin), Eastern Ojibwe (including Southern Algonquin), Ottawa (Odawa), and Old Algonquin. The first two are classified as Northern Ojibwe, the others as Southern Ojibwe.[103]

Severn Ojibwe (Oji-Cree) is a well-defined variety in Northern Ojibwe of the Ojibwayan dialect complex, spoken in northwestern Ontario in communities on Severn River, Winisk River, and Sandy Lake. First-language use of Severn Ojibwe is high, but Cree also has cultural prominence in these communities.

Northern Algonquin (Algonquin du Nord) is a distinct regional dialect of Northern Ojibwe in the Ojibwayan dialect complex, spoken in southwestern Quebec at Lac Simon, Grand Lac Victoria, La Barriere, and a few other communities.

Saulteaux is an emergent language in the Ojibwayan dialect complex, closely related to Central Southern Ojibwe. The name "Saulteaux" (pronounced [sotó]) refers to the origin of the group from Sault Ste. Marie and around Lake Superior. They moved westward to the prairies with the fur trade in the eighteenth and nineteenth centuries. Today, most varieties of Saulteaux are spoken in southern Manitoba near Lake Winnipeg and in the city of Winnipeg, although there are speakers as far west as British Columbia. The Saulteaux varieties north and east of Lake Winnipeg and into Northern Ontario, sometimes called **Northern Ojibwe**, show considerable influence from Severn Ojibwe, including use of the syllabic writing. Most Saulteaux varieties have a number of borrowings from Cree and other features that show Cree influence.

Central Southern Ojibwe is another emergent language of the Ojibwayan complex. Central Southern Ojibwe is spoken in a large number of communities in Northern Ontario, Michigan, Wisconsin, and Minnesota, as well as on reservations in North Dakota and Montana. These include twenty-five separate tribal groups in the United States and a roughly equal number of communities in Canada. Different groups refer to themselves and their language as Ojibwe, Ojbwa, Ojibway, Chippewa, Chippeway, and Anishinabe, but linguistically local varieties do not differ substantially from one another. Central Southern Ojibwe is closely related to Saulteaux in Manitoba and to Eastern Ojibwe and Ottawa in Michigan and Southern Ontario, a relationship that reflects the historical dispersal of Southern Ojibwe speakers across the Great Lakes and beyond during the fur trade from the seventeenth to the nineteenth century.

Eastern Ojibwe is spoken in southern Ontario and Quebec in two main dialect clusters. The more westerly variety, historically called **Mississauga** in Canada, is spoken east of Georgian Bay, with the largest number of speakers today on Parry Island and at Curve Lake, near Peterborough, Ontario. It was formerly spoken in many other places both in Ontario west of Georgian Bay and in southern Michigan (where it was called **Chippewa**), though in these areas it was generally replaced by the Ottawa language in the nineteenth and early twentieth centuries. The Michigan varieties were not markedly different from Central Southern Ojibwe. The more easterly variety of Eastern Ojibwe is called **Algonquin** at Golden Lake, Ontario, and Maniwaki, Quebec. This was historically the **Nipissing** dialect from north of Lake Huron. The **Southern Algonquin** dialect must be distinguished from **Northern Algonquin**, which is very different.

Southern Algonquin (Nipissing) is an emergent language in the Ojibwayan subgroup, spoken mainly at the River Desert Reserve, on the Gatineau River at Maniwaki, Quebec. Although speakers identify themselves and their language as Algonquin, Southern Algonquin is different from Northern Algonquin, as well as from the long-dormant **Old Algonquin** that was spoken in the Ottawa Valley in the seventeenth century. Southern Algonquin is the eastern part of Eastern Ojibwe.[104]

Ottawa (Odawa) is an Ojibwayan language originally spoken on the north shores of Lake Huron. The most active community of speakers today is at the Wikwemikong Reserve on Manitoulin Island, Ontario. There are also speakers on Walpole Island and other reserves in Ontario, and in Michigan, where the largest community is on Isabella Reservation. A number of Ottawas were relocated to Oklahoma in the nineteenth century, but the language does not survive there now. **Old Ottawa**, the form of the language in the seventeenth and eighteenth centuries, is extensively documented, and there is a variety of Ottawa spoken on Sugar Island and elsewhere on the Upper Peninsula of Michigan. Ottawa has tended to replace Eastern Ojibwe; the eastern varieties of Ottawa and the western subdialect of Eastern Ojibwe are said now to constitute an emergent language, called **Nishnaabemwin**. Some individuals and communities speak forms of the language that merge gradually with Central Southern Ojibwe.

Old Algonquin was the language spoken in the early French missions in the lower Ottawa Valley and along the St. Lawrence. It is attested in a number of seventeenth- and eighteenth-century documents. It ceased to be used in the nineteenth century. Although it was part of the Ojibwayan dialect complex, Old Algonquin was quite distinct from the Ojibwe dialects that are now called Northern Algonquin and Southern Algonquin.

Potawatomi is closely related to the Ojibwayan complex. Historically it was spoken around the Great Lakes in Michigan and Wisconsin and in southern Ontario. It has speakers in several widely separated communities in the United States and Canada, including the Hannahville Indian Community (Upper Peninsula of Michigan), the Pokagon and Huron Bands (southern Michigan), the Forest County Band (northern Wisconsin), the Prairie Band (eastern Kansas), and the Citizen Potawatomi Nation of Oklahoma. A few Potawatomi speakers also live among the Eastern Ojibwe in Ontario, particularly at the Walpole Island Reserve.

Potawatomi has a writing system that uses syllabic signs, based on the Latin alphabet. It was used also by Ottawa, Sauk, Meskwaki, and Winnebago groups.

Sauk-Fox (Meskwaki) is spoken by members of the Meskwaki Tribe in Iowa. It was the heritage language also of the historically separate Sauk tribe, whose descendants today are the Sac and Fox Tribe of central Oklahoma and the Nemaha Sauks on the Kansas-Nebraska border. The **Meskwaki** variety is also called "Fox"; it differs from Sauk in minor ways, and the variation within Meskwaki alone is nearly as much as that between Meskwaki and Sauk. Originally **Kickapoo** was part of the same dialect complex, but for historical and social reasons it is treated as a separate language.[105]

Kickapoo is in part mutually intelligible with Sauk-Fox, but since the earliest contact with Europeans in the seventeenth century the Kickapoo have been a separate political group. The Kickapoos were in southeastern Michigan and northwestern Ohio at that time; after the mid-seventeenth century they were in Wisconsin and later in Indiana. They are now on reservations in Kansas and the Mexican state of Coahuila, and in other communities near McLoud, Oklahoma, and Eagle Pass, Texas.

Shawnee was spoken in the Ohio Valley, in Ohio, and north of the Ohio River in several neighboring states when first recognized in historical sources. Today most of the descendants of the Shawnee live in Oklahoma, in three distinct groups: the Absentee Shawnee Tribe, located in and around the town of Shawnee, near the Citizen Potawatomi Nation;

the Eastern Shawnee Tribe, in Ottawa County near the Oklahoma Seneca community; and the Loyal Shawnee (or "Cherokee Shawnee"), in the Cherokee region of northeastern Oklahoma, mainly around Whiteoak.[106]

Miami-Illinois (Myaamia) is an Algonquian dialect complex that was spoken in the eighteenth century and earlier by groups in Illinois and northern Indiana. The **Illinois** variety is represented in the older Jesuit records. For Miami, at least three dialect clusters were retained after their removal to Kansas in the nineteenth century: **Peoria-Kaskaskia**, **Piankashaw-Wea**, and **Miami**. Eventually the surviving Illinois speakers went to Oklahoma, where they became known as the **Peoria**. About half the Miami remained in Indiana; the other half were relocated to Oklahoma, ending up near the Peoria, and all of the Wea and Piankashaw were also forcibly relocated to Oklahoma, where they merged with the Peoria. There have been no first-language speakers since 1962, though a very active language-recovery program is underway.

Eastern Algonquian is the clearest subgroup of the Algonquian family. Speakers of its numerous languages and varieties occupied the Atlantic coast of North America and adjacent inland areas from the Canadian Maritimes provinces to North Carolina. The available information about individual languages and varieties varies widely. Some are known only from one or two documents containing words and phrases collected by missionaries, explorers, or settlers, and some documents contain fragmentary evidence about more than one language or dialect. Most of the Eastern Algonquian languages are dormant, though **Micmac** (Mi'kmaq) and **Malecite-Passamaquoddy** have a sizeable number of speakers, and **Western Abenaki** and **Munsee** have a few speakers though both are critically endangered. Many of the Eastern Algonquian languages are poorly attested, especially those of southern New England, Virginia, and the Carolinas.

Mi'kmaq (Micmac, Mi'gmaq, Miikmaq) is an Eastern Algonquian language spoken in over twenty-five reserves scattered across the Canadian provinces of Nova Scotia, New Brunswick, Prince Edward Island, and Quebec, and in Boston. The largest speech communities are at Restigouche, Quebec; Big Cove, New Brunswick; and Eskasoni, on Cape Breton Island, Nova Scotia; and there are many Micmacs in the United States, primarily in Boston. A distinctive script called "Micmac Hieroglyphs" was devised by missionaries in the seventeenth century, and is still in use in the Catholic liturgy on the Eskasoni Reserve and in a few other places.

Maliseet-Passamaquoddy is the Eastern Algonquian language spoken in the St. Croix and St. Johns river valleys along the border between Maine and the New Brunswick. Most speakers in Maine are members of the Passamaquoddy tribe, while in Canada they identify themselves as Maliseet; however, there is very little dialect difference between the two. The principal communities in Maine are Pleasant Point and Indian Township. In New Brunswick there are speakers at Tobique, Woodstock, Kingsclear, St. Mary's, and Oromocto. There are also some speakers of both groups living with the Penobscots of Indian Island, in Old Town, Maine, and in Bridgeport, Connecticut.[107]

Eastern Abenaki is a dormant Eastern Algonquian language, spoken formerly in southern and central Maine. The **Penobscot** group of Eastern Abenaki is in Old Town, on Indian Island north of Bangor, Maine; the last native speaker of the Penobscot dialect died in 1993. Another dialect was spoken into the twentieth century at Bécancourt, Quebec. The language was extensively documented by French Jesuit missionaries in the late seventeenth and early eighteenth centuries and by Frank T. Siebert Jr. in the twentieth century.[108]

Western Abenaki is predominantly the language of the people the French called Sokoki, whose old village was Squakheag (Northfield, Massachusetts). Western Abenaki is critically endangered.

Etchemin was spoken along the coast of Maine; it has been dormant since the seventeenth century. Nothing is known of it except a list of numbers, which indicate it was distinct from the neighboring Algonquian languages.

Massachusett-Narragansett is a Southern New England Algonquian dialect complex formerly spoken in eastern Massachusetts and most of Rhode Island, including on Martha's Vineyard and Nantucket. Several local varieties were documented in colonial times. The **Natick** variety is represented in John Eliot's translation of the whole Bible (1663) and his grammatical sketch (1666). The **Narragansett** variety is the dominant one in Roger Williams' (1643) *A Key into the Language of America*. Goddard and Bragdon's (1988) edition of documents written by native speakers includes a grammar prepared by Ives Goddard. The language ceased to be used in most areas during the eighteenth century, but a variety on Martha's Vineyard was spoken until the end of the nineteenth century. There are now vigorous ongoing efforts to revive the language under the name **Wampanoag** (Wôpanâak).[109]

Loup was the collective name used in French sources for the Southern New England Algonquian languages spoken by refugees in Canada from central Massachusetts. These are known mainly from two manuscript vocabularies, called "**Loup A**" and "**Loup B**." They exhibit lexical, grammatical, and phonological differences that point to the existence of at least five distinct languages. One of these can be identified as **Nipmuck**, spoken in east-central Massachusetts, and the others were the languages of the Pocumtuck Confederacy of the central Connecticut River Valley, most likely those spoken by the **Pocumtuck**, **Norwottuck**, **Woronoco**, and **Pojassick** village bands (Goddard 2016).

Mohegan-Pequot is a Southern New England Algonquian language formerly spoken in southeastern Connecticut and southwestern Rhode Island, and on eastern Long Island, where the local variety was called **Montauk**. There is scattered documentation, but the dialect diversity is poorly known. The Eastern **Niantic** dialect of Rhode Island was called "Narragansett" in the eighteenth century. The last known speaker was Fidelia Fielding, a Mohegan; she died in 1908.

Quiripi-Unquachog-Shinnecock-Montauk belongs to the Southern New England group of Eastern Algonquian. It was spoken in western Connecticut and on central Long Island in several varieties and emergent languages, the number of which is unknown. Thomas Jefferson's informants said that three of these were mutually unintelligible (Ives Goddard, personal communication.) The very limited documentation includes a vocabulary of Montauk, a seventeenth-century catechism with words from two varieties, and an **Unquachog** vocabulary collected on Long Island by Thomas Jefferson. These languages/varieties were dormant by the early nineteenth century.

There are two **Mahican** languages, **Western Mahican** spoken in the upper Hudson River Valley from Lake Champlain south to Greene County and the northern edge of Dutchess County, in New York, and **Eastern Mahican** in the upper Housatonic Valley in Massachusetts and northwestern Connecticut. Both shared some features with **Munsee** and with Southern New England languages. Eastern Mahican grammar changed under influence from the languages to the east sufficiently to make Eastern Mahican a separate language. It was the dominant language at the mission village of Stockbridge, Massachusetts, in the eighteenth century. Many Mahicans joined groups of Delawares, and their descendants switched to Munsee or Unami. Some who had remained in upstate New York were removed to Wisconsin in the nineteenth century, where the language ceased being spoken in the 1930s.

Munsee (Canadian Delaware), of the Eastern Algonquian subgroup, was originally spoken from around Minisink Island in the upper Delaware River Valley to the middle Housatonic River in western Connecticut, including northern New Jersey, the lower Hudson River and the New York City area, and western Long Island. There had been speakers of Munsee in several places farther west, the largest groups on the Moraviantown, Caradoc (Munceytown), and Six Nations reserves in Canada. Others ended up in eastern Kansas and among the Unami-speakers of Oklahoma, the Mahicans in Wisconsin, and the Senecas of western New York. **Wampano**, spoken northeast of Manhattan, on the Housatonic River, is attested in three hymn translations. It had taken some features from Mahican and the southern New England languages. The Dutch considered it a separate language; they called it Manhattan (Ives Goddard personal communication). It is not to be confused with **Wappinger**, a separate language, closely related with Munsee. Early in the seventeenth century they lived along the east bank of the Hudson River from Manhattan Island to Poughkeepsie and eastward to the lower Connecticut River valley.

Munsee is critically endangered, with only two native speakers known as of 2018, living among the Delaware First Nation on the Moraviantown Reserve near Thamesville, Ontario.

Unami complex (Oklahoma Delaware, Lenape). **Unami** has been considered an Eastern Algonquian language, spoken originally in southern and central New Jersey, eastern Pennsylvania, and northern Delaware. Ives Goddard (personal communication), however, fnds evidence to consider it really a group of three separate languages, Unalachtigo, North Unami, and South Unami. As the Delawares migrated westward, **Southern Unami** came to be spoken in Ohio, Indiana, and Kansas, and after the American Civil War it ended up in Oklahoma, the heritage language of the Delaware Tribe, near Bartlesville and Dewey, Oklahoma, and the Delaware Tribe of Western Oklahoma, near Anadarko. The last speaker died in 2002. **Northern Unami** has extensive documentation done by German-speaking Moravian missionaries in the late eighteenth century. It survived into the twentieth century among the Canadian Munsees. **Unalachtigo**, originally from the Trenton, New Jersey, area, appears also to be reflected in the Moravians' materials.[110]

Nanticoke-Conoy was the language of Chesapeake Bay and the Delmarva Peninsula. **Conoy** (Piscataway) is known mainly from Roman Catholic prayers translated by Andrew White, an English Jesuit. **Nanticoke** is recorded in a 1792 vocabulary from the Choptank River in Dorset County, Maryland. A few words were also recorded from a group of Nanticokes who joined the Iroquois in the eighteenth century and ended up on the Six Nations Reserve in Canada, where it was spoken until the 1860s. Other Nanticokes lost their language after joining Delaware refugees in the west.

Virginia Algonquian is named for the language attested in two vocabularies collected at Jamestown, Virginia, between 1607 and 1611. It is assumed to be the language of the

Powhatan confederacy in tidewater Virginia. There may have been speakers as late as 1790, but no other documentation exists (Siebert 1975).

Carolina Algonquian, also known as **Pamlico**, was spoken in the vicinity of Pamlico Sound, North Carolina. It is known only from two short wordlists, one from the Roanoke colony in the 1580s, the other published in 1709. The language became dormant in the eighteenth century.

The Proto-Algonquian phonemes are reconstructed as: /p, t, č, k, s, š, h, m, n, θ, r, w, y; i, e, a, o, i:, :, a:, o:/ (Goddard 1979b, 1988, 1990, 1994b).[111] Traditionally, Algonquianists have followed Leonard Bloomfield's (1946) reconstruction for Proto-Central-Algonquian, which has been considered reasonably representative of Proto-Algonquian phonology in general. Ives Goddard (1994a, 1994b) showed that Bloomfield's *l is more accurately reconstructed as *r; r is the reflex that predominates in the earliest branches of the family. Bloomfield's *θ was more controversial, and even Bloomfield said that it may have been a voiceless "l" (ł) in the proto language. These sounds *θ and *r are retained with separate reflexes in Arapaho-Atsina and Cree-Montagnais, and in some clusters in Munsee, but are merged in other branches of Algonquian. Goddard (1994b, 205) also argues cogently that the famous *čk, which Bloomfield reconstructed for Proto-Algonquian, originally largely on the testimony of different reflexes of it in Swampy Cree, is more accurately reconstructed as *rk, and Goddard also reinterpreted Bloomfield's *x as *s in the consonant clusters that Bloomfield reconstructed with *xp and *xk.

The grouping of Wiyot and Yurok in northern California together was called Ritwan by Dixon and Kroeber (1913a), one of their proposed Californian stocks. The connection of Ritwan with Algonquian was first put forward by Edward Sapir (1913); it was very controversial at that time (see Michelson 1914, 1915; Sapir 1915a, 1915c). Nevertheless, the relationship has subsequently been demonstrated to the satisfaction of all (see Haas 1958a, 1966; Teeter 1964a; Goddard 1975, 1979b, 1990; Berman 1982, 1984).

Many scholars commented that although Wiyot and Yurok are neighbors in northern California, they seemed not to have a closer relationship with each other than either has with Algonquian. For this reason, Howard Berman (1982) first urged that the family not be called Algonquian-Ritwan because "Ritwan" would seem to suggest a closer connection between Wiyot and Yurok than had been established. Shortly afterward, however, Berman proposed certain innovations shared by Wiyot and Yurok, which he took as suggesting "that they had a period of common development after the end of Algonquian-Ritwan unity" (Berman 1982, 412), which show them to be more closely related to each other than to Algonquian proper (Berman 1990a). For this reason, he calls the family Algonquian-Ritwan, though Algic is used more frequently. An attempt has been made by Paul Proulx (1984) to reconstruct Proto-Algic phonology, but whether other specialists will accept it or portions thereof remains to be seen. Berman's work has had better reception.

Various possible dates for Proto-Algic and for Proto-Algonquian have been considered in the literature. One possibility has around 4,000 years ago for Proto-Algic and 3,000 years ago for Proto-Algonquian (Golla 2007, 73; 2011, 256). Will Oxford (2021, 506) cites Pentland's (1979, 329) similar date of circa 1000–500 BCE for Proto-Algonquian.

Ives Goddard (1994b) presented Algonquian classification and dispersal as a west-to-east cline, not of genealogical subgroups but of chronological layers, with the greatest time depth found in the west and the shallowest in the east. That is, each layer, in Goddard's view, is distinguished from those to the west by innovations and from those to the east only by archaic retentions, where each wave of innovations took place farther to the east, giving the characteristic clinal configuration that reflects the general west-to-east movement of the family. Blackfoot (in the West) is the most divergent; Arapaho-Atsina and Cree-Montagnais are the second oldest layer. The next oldest includes Arapaho-Atsina, Cree-Montagnais, Cheyenne, and Menominee; next are Core Central Algonquian languages; the final layer is Eastern Algonquian, the only grouping or layer that constitutes a truly valid subgroup in Goddard's view. These "dialect" layers represent innovations shared through diffusion, but this non-genetic shared history in this instance helps to determine the historical location of these languages and the relative age when they were in contact.

Frank Siebert (1967) postulated that the original homeland of the Proto-Algonquian people must have been in the region between Lake Huron and Georgian Bay and the middle course of the Ottawa River, bounded on the north by Lake Nipissing and the Mattawa River and on the south by the northern shore of Lake Ontario. In Siebert's analysis, the various Algonquian groups extended from this area to the various geographical locations where their speakers were first encountered by Europeans. Dean Snow (1976) re-examined the question and concluded that an area considerably larger than that postulated by Siebert was the best candidate for the Proto-Algonquian homeland, but one nevertheless still bounded on the west by Niagara Falls (to accommodate the word for 'harbor seal' and the limits of their geographical distribution). In more recent work, Goddard finds the terms Siebert reconstructed "consistent with the homeland of Proto-Algonquians being somewhere immediately west of Lake Superior," but he points out the circularity of the method—that words for 'harbor seal' would typically survive only in languages in areas where harbor seals are found, thus eliminating languages that lacked a cognate for this term. Goddard (1994b, 207) concluded that "the Algonquians came ultimately from the west." (See also Golla 2011, 256.)

There have been several conjectures about a possible Proto-Algic (Algonquian-Ritwan) homeland. Howard Berman (1982, 419) thought that the homeland is "unknown," but he speculated that the similarity between the "Proto-Algonquian-Ritwan" vowel system, as he reconstructs it, and that of Proto-Salishan, if it were the result of contact rather than coincidence, "would place the Proto-Algonquian-Ritwan homeland near the Proto-Salish homeland ... probably somewhere in the northwest, to the north of the Ritwan languages and to the west of the Proto-Algonquian homeland." Victor Golla (2011, 257) suggested that "the hypothetical Proto-Algic homeland that would best fit the geographical facts would be on the Columbia Plateau, somewhere in the region historically occupied by the Sahaptians and the Interior Salish" (see also Golla 2007, 73). Several scholars locate Wiyot and Yurok originally in Oregon, probably with independent movements into northern California, with Wiyot arriving there earlier than Yurok (Golla 2011, 257).[112]

*Beothuk

Beothuk is a language isolate, formerly spoken in Newfoundland. The Beothuks were among the first natives of the New World with whom Europeans had contact. On his first voyage in 1534, Jacques Cartier reported their custom of covering themselves in red ocher, a trait frequently noted by explorers and writers, and it has been speculated that this may be the origin of why Native Americans came commonly to be called "Red Indians" (Hewson 1978, 3). (See Maps 2.1 and 7.6.)

The last known Beothuk survivor died in 1829. Although the English began settling the island of Newfoundland in the early sixteenth century and were in contact with the Beothuks for over 300 years, only three short vocabulary lists are known, with a combined total of about 325 items. Photographic facsimiles of all of them are published in Hewson (1978). A number of later copies made of these three originals are also extant. As John Hewson (1982, 181) indicated, "the vocabularies are full of errors of every kind." They were taken down in chaotic English spellings, and "none of the native informants knew sufficient English to communicate in any satisfactory manner, so that the only means of interpreting the meaning of Beothuk words was through mime, drawing and pointing." For example, Hewson (1982, 181–182) recounts a revealing instance. Of Albert Gatschet's *stiocena* 'thumb' we learn from Hewson (1982, 181–182):

> This item had started life as *ifweena* "thigh" in the Leigh vocabulary... When Leigh came to copy his vocabulary for John Peyton... he wrote the English *thumb* and then instead of copying the Beothuk word *pooeth*, inadvertently wrote instead the Beothok word *ifweena* which happens to be the next word down the page in the original Leigh vocabulary... Consequently, in the so-called Peyton copy of Leigh, the entry appears as: *Itweena* "thumb." Another copy of this item was made by James P. Howley and sent to Sir William Dawson... who in turn copied it out by hand and sent a copy to the Reverend Dr. Silas Rand... Mr. Rand in turn copied it out and sent a copy to Gatschet. By the time this item had gone through all these varying copyings, the original capital *i* had become an *s*, the following ambiguous *f* [the only example of an *f* in the corpus] had become a *t*, the *w* had become an *i* and an *o*, the double *e* had become *ce* and only the *na* had survived intact.

Of Beothuk prehistory, little can be said with certainty. The Beothuks had a folk tradition of crossing into Newfoundland over the Belle Isle Strait. Archaeological evidence suggests they arrived in Newfoundland in about 500 CE; before that (from 500 BCE to 500 CE) Newfoundland was inhabited by Dorset Eskimos. Culturally, Beothuks were like Algonquians and unlike Eskimos and Iroquoians (Hewson 1982, 184).[113] It has long been conjectured that Beothuk may be related to the Algonquian family, and John Hewson (1968, 1971, 1982, etc.) has argued for this view. However, the material available on Beothuk is so scant and poorly recorded that evaluation of the proposed connection is difficult.

For unclassified languages of North America, see Chapter 5. For proposed but unconfirmed distant genetic relationships involving many of these language families (including language isolates), see Chapter 6. For discussion of loss of diversity in North America, see Chapter 1.

NOTES

1. Eskimo-Aleut has occasionally been called *Eskaleut*, and more recently *Inuit-Yupik-Unangan*. The term *Eskimo* is an exonym. "Eskimo" has often been erroneously assumed to come from an

Algonquian language with a meaning of something like 'raw eaters'. However, early European sources seem to indicate a Montagnais (Algonquian) source: *a-y-askyime-w*, connected in meaning to 'snowshoe-netter' (Goddard 1984, 6). In the earliest sources the name apparently referred to other Algonquian groups, notably Micmac, rather than to Eskimoan speakers (Ives Goddard, personal communication).

Today *Eskimo* is believed to be offensive by some. *Eskimo* is, nevertheless, the preferred term in Alaska (and the United States), though other groups recommend that it be replaced (see Johns 2021, 525).

2. The name *Yupik* is from the Central Alaskan Yupik *yuppik* 'real, genuine person' (Goddard 1984, 7).

3. *Inuit* is the autonym (self-designation); it is the plural of *inuk* 'person, people'. *Inupiaq* is from *iñupiaq* 'real, genuine person' (Goddard 1984, 7). *Inuktitut* is widely used in Eastern Canada as the name for this language.

4. The Athabaskan subfamily is sometimes called *Dene*, but that is confusing, since the name "Dene" is used by different people to refer to several different things.

5. The name *Tlingit* is from the autonym (self-designation) *ɬi:ngít* 'human being, person'. John Wesley Powell (1891) called Tlingit *Koluschan*. The earlier name *Kolusch* is thought to come from Aleut *kalu:* 'wooden dish' in a form with the Russian diminutive, *kalushka*, believed to be in reference to wooden labrets that Tlingit women wore (De Laguna 1990b, 226; Pinnow 1976, 4).

6. The name Eyak apparently comes from the Eyaks' autonym, meaning 'inhabitants of Eyak', the name of the Eyak village, *í:yaq* (*ʔi:ya:G*), borrowed from Chugach Eskimo *iya:q* 'outlet of a lake'. Earlier, Eyak was often called *Ugalach(mute)*, *Ugalents*, or something similar, from the Russian name *Ugalyakhmyut*, which is also from Chugach Eskimo, from *uŋalaɣmiut* 'people of the southeast' (Birket-Smith and De Laguna 1938, 338; De Laguna 1990a, 196).

7. At times Athabaskan has also been spelled variously as *Athapaskan*, *Athapascan*, and *Athabascan*. It is derived from Lake Athabaska in northern Alberta, Canada. Etymologically that name comes from a Cree language (Algonquian), from a form similar to *ahdhap-ask-a-w* that translates roughly as 'where there are plants distributed in a net-like pattern', as in a shallow end of a lake (The Name "Athabaskan," Alaska Native Language Center, https://www.uaf.edu/anlc/research-and-resources/resources/resources/the_name_athabascan.php.)

8. There is general agreement that Athabaskan tonogenesis is linked closely to constricted vowels and that in Pre-Proto-Athabaskan, at least, these vowels derive from *Vʔ*; there is disagreement about whether Proto-Athabaskan itself had constricted vowels (see Leer 1979, 12–13; Cook and Rice 1989, 9–11).

9. The name *Tanaina* is from the Tanaina autonym (self-designation), *danaʔina* 'the people' (Goddard 1981, 638).

10. *Koyukan* is a created name, meant to suggest the names of the Koyukuk and Yukon Rivers. It is related to the Inupiaq word *kuiyuk* 'river that flows' (Goddard 1981, 599).

11. The name *Ingalik* came to English through Russian, borrowed from Yupik Eskimo *iŋqiliq* 'Indian', meaning literally 'having many nits', a reference to the "uncut hair style" of the Athabaskans (Goddard 1981, 613).

12. *Gwich'in* (Kutchin) is derived from the Gwich'in word *gʷičʼin* 'people of, dwellers of'. The name *Loucheux*, commonly used for the Eastern Gwich'in in Canada, is from French *loucheux* 'squinters', a translation of the Chipewyan name for Gwich'in, that means 'squint-eyed' (Goddard and Slobodin 1981, 530).

13. The name *Han* comes from Gwich'in (Kutchin) *han-gʷičʼin* 'people of the river' (*gʷičʼin* 'people') (Goddard 1981, 512).

14. The name *Tahltan* comes from Tlingit *ta:łta:n*, "the name of a low flat at the mouth of the Tahltan River that was in important trading ground" (Goddard 1981, 465).

15. There is a widespread Northern Athabaskan creation story in which a woman mates with a dog. The name *Dogrib* appears to reflect this, assumed to come through Cree, who called the Dogrib people the equivalent of 'dog side' (Helm 1981, 303–304).

16. English got the name *Chipewyan* from Cree, apparently from *či:pwaya:n* '(those who have) pointed skins or hides', thought to refer to "their manner of cutting their hunting shirts or preparing beaver pelts, which the Cree ridiculed" (Goddard and Smith 1981, 283).

17. The name *Carrier* apparently comes from the custom of Carrier widows carrying the cremated remains of their husbands on their backs. English *Carrier* is a translation of French *porteur*, which comes from the translation of a Sekani word that means 'carrier' (Goddard 1981, 430).

18. The names *Kwalhioqua* and *Clatskanie* (*Tlatskanai*) are from the Chinook names for these groups, *tkʷlxiugʷádiks* and *iłáckʼani*, respectively. The *iłáckʼani* form means literally 'those of the region of small oaks' (Krauss 1990, 532).

19. *Wailaki* is from a Wintu word meaning 'north language' (Hinton 1994, 158).

20. The name *Navajo* comes from Spanish *Navajó*, the seventeenth-century name of the territory in northwestern New Mexico inhabited by Navajos. Apaches and Navajos were not distinguished in the earliest sources. There are early references to *Apaches de Nabajú* and *Apaches de Nauajó*; *Nauajó* was said to mean 'large planted fields'. Spanish *Navajó* appears to be borrowed from Tewa *navahu:* composed of *nava* 'field' and *hu:* 'wide arroyo, valley', meaning a large arroyo in which there are cultivated fields (Brugge, Goddard, and De Reuse 1983, 496).

The name *Apache* in English is from Spanish *Apache*, assumed to be from Zuni *ʔa:pačʼu* 'Navajos' (De Reuse 1983, 385).

21. The name *Tsimshian* comes from *tsʼmsyan* 'inside the Skeena River', the self-designation of Coast Tsimshian and Southern Tsimshian speakers. John Wesley Powell's (1891) name for the group, *Chimmesyan*, was a variant spelling of this. *Gitksan* is from the Gitksan speakers' autonym *kitxsan* 'people of the Skeena River'. *Nishga* is from *nisqáʔa*, another autonym, with no clear etymology (Halpin and Seguin 1990, 282).

22. *Nuu-chah-nulth* is said to mean 'along the outside (of Vancouver Island)'. The older name *Nootka* is more widely known, though now not favored by community members.

23. The name *Wakashan* is said to be from the Nuu-chah-nulth (Nootka) word *wa:ka:š* 'bravo, good', which Captain James Cook heard at Nootka Sound and supposed to be the name of the local people (Arima and Dewhirst 1990, 410).

24. The sounds *mʼ, bʼ, nʼ* and *dʼ* are glottalized.

25. The name Haisla is from *Xáʔisəla* '(those) living at the river mouth, (those) living downriver'. *Kitamaat* is from Coast Tsimshian *kitama:t* 'people of the falling snow' (Hamori-Torok 1990, 310).

26. The name *Bella Bella* is from Heiltsuk *pəĺbáĺá*, a term that referred to the site of Fort McLoughlin and the native village that developed around it, said to be based on the Heiltsuk pronunciation of the English name *Milbanke* that then came back into English as the name of the people. The name *Heiltsuk* is from *híldzáqʷ*, whose meaning is unclear (Hilton 1990, 321).

27. The name *Nuu-chah-nulth* was created for the Nootkan tribes from *nuča:nʼuł* 'all along the mountains', in reference to the mountains of Vancouver Island, which are common to all the Nootkan tribes. *Nootka* was the name Captain James Cook gave to Nootka Sound; it came to be used to refer also to the people of the area. Cook thought this was the native name, though it is thought perhaps to come from Cook misunderstanding the verb *nu:tka:* 'circling around' (Arima and Dewhirst 1990, 410).

28. The name *Comox* is from Kwak'wala (Kwakiutl) *q*ʷ*úmux*ʷ*s*, based on *q'wm-* 'rich', applied to the Comox harbor area and later to the people who settled there. *Sliammon* is from Comox *łáʔmin* (Kennedy and Bouchard 1990, 450–451).

29. The name *Nooksack* comes from *(nə)x*ʷ*séʔeq* 'place of bracken roots', the name of a village and prairie at the mouth of Anderson Creek (Suttles 1990, 474).

30. The name *Lummi* is from *x*ʷ*ləməy'* or *x*ʷ*ləmiʔ*, said to be from *x*ʷ*lálməs* 'facing each other', the name of a large L-shaped house at Gooseberry Point (Suttles 1990, 474).

31. The name *Lushootseed* is from *dx*ʷ*-ləṣ̌úcid*, composed of *ləṣ̌* 'Puget Sound region' flanked by the parts *dx*ʷ*- . . . -úcid* 'language' (Suttles and Lane 1990, 501).

32. The name *Chehalis* is from Lower Chehalis *c'x̣íl'əs* 'sand', the name of their principal village, at the site of Westport on Grays Harbor (Hajda 1990, 516).

33. The name *Cowlitz* comes from *káwlic* 'Cowlitz River' and *káwlicq* 'language/people of Cowlitz River' (Hajda 1990, 516).

34. Laurence Thompson's (1979, 725) reconstruction of Proto-Salishan sounds had: /(p), t, c, k, kʷ, q, qʷ, ʔ, (p'), t', c', tl', k', kʷ', q', qʷ', s, ɬ, x, xʷ, χ, χʷ, h, (m), n, (r), l, (ŋ), ŋʷ, ɣ, ɣʷ, (m'), n', (r'), l', ŋ'ʷ, ɣ', ɣʷ', ʕ', w, y, w', y'; i, a, ə, u/. Paul Kroeber's (1999, 7) reconstruction is similar though it has *p, p',* and *(h),* and lacks *(r), (r'), (ŋ), ŋ*ʷ*, ŋ*ʷ*, ɣ*ʷ*, ɣ*ʷ', and ʕ'₂ (The *ʕ'₂ was postulated by Thompson [1979] to handle the unexpected "darkened" reflexes of vowels in Interior Salish normally connected with a following uvular or pharyngeal.) Aert Kuipers (1981) had a similar inventory, but there are some differences; Kuipers disapproved of the reconstruction of *r (but see Kinkade and Thompson 1974), and of the labials and the labialized velars, with doubts about the Coast Salish counterparts of the Interior Salish uvular resonants (ɣ, ɣʷ). The sounds *r* and *r'* contrast with *l* and *l'* respectively only in some of the Southern Interior Salish languages; Kuipers (1981, 324) saw these sounds "either as remnants or as innovations" but not as part of the proto sound system. A ɣ is marginal, found only in Lillooet, Thompson, Shuswap, and northern Okanagan.

The list of reconstructed Proto-Salishan consonants presented by Henry Davis (2021, 457) has /p, t, c, k, kʷ, q, qʷ, ʔ, p', t', c', tl', k', kʷ', q', qʷ', s, ɬ, h, x, xʷ, χ, χʷ, h, m, n, l, ɣ, ɣʷ, m', n', l', ɣ', ɣʷ', ʕ', w, y, w', y'/.

35. *Chemakum* is the English version of a Salishan name for the Chemakum people. Variants of this name are known in several Salishan languages, for example Twana *čəbqəb* (note that Twana has no nasals) (Elmendorf 1990, 440).

36. The name Quileute is from *kʷoʔlí:yot'*, the name of the village at La push (Powell 1990b, 437; Elmendorf 1990, 440).

37. The name *Chinook* is originally from Lower Chehalis *ts'inúk*, the name for a village on Baker Bay and its inhabitants, later applied to all people of the area with related languages. *Cathlemet* (Kathlemet) is from *gałámat*, meaning the people of the village at Cathlamet Head. *Clackamas* is from *gi(t)łáq'imaṣ̌* 'those of Clackamas River' (Silverstein 1990, 544).

The last speaker of Lower Chinook, George Clipp, died in the 1930s.

38. The name *Siuslaw* comes from Siuslaw *šaʔyú:štl'a:*, the Siuslaw name of the Siuslaw River region (Zenk 1990b, 578).

39. The name *Takelma* is from *ta:kelmàʔn* meaning 'person/people from Rogue River', derived from *ta:kelám* 'Rogue River', composed of *ta:-* 'along, beside' + *kelám* 'river' (Kendall 1990, 592).

40. The name *Kalapuya* apparently comes from Chinookan, seen for example in the Upriver Kiksht *igalapúyuiyukṣ̌* and Clackmas *itk'alapúyawaykṣ̌* names for Kalapuya, though its origin in Chinookan is unknown (Zenk 1990a, 552).

41. *Nez Perce* is from French *nez percé* 'pierced nose'. Reportedly some older Nez Perce remembered *cú:pn'itpel'u:* 'with a pointed object-pierce-people' as their self-designation, reflecting their

custom of piercing the nasal septum, presumably also the source of the French name (Kinkade et al. 1998).

42. DeLancey and Golla (1997) and Golla (2007, 77) saw some evidence to link Maiduan with Plateau (Plateau Penutian), and DeLancey and Golla (1997, 85) thought that "all of Wintuan, Plateau Penutian, and Yok-Utian have a common ancestor more recent than Proto-Penutian," though Delancey (2018, 1) concedes that "the inclusion of Wintuan here is dubious." Others generally have not found these proposals convincing.

43. More precisely, Ultan (1964, 356) said: "Although there appears to be a fairly large number of lexical similarities, there are structural differences of both a morphological and a syntactic nature. Thus it would seem that the only plausible hypothesis which could be set forth to account for this apparent paradox would be one which assumes a great deal of convergence, perhaps covering a long period of time, but either particularly active in the more recent past or occasioned by more or less continuous reborrowing of forms."

44. The name *Miwok* is from Central Sierra Miwok *míw:i:k* 'people, Indians'; compare Proto-Miwokan **miw:i* (Callaghan 1988a; 2014, 319).

45. The name *Costanoan* seems to be derived somehow from Spanish *costeño* or *costanero*, terms for someone or something on the coast (from the root *costa* 'coast'); there is, however, no such Spanish word as *costano* or *costaño* from which *Costanoan* could come, in spite of *Costanoan* being thoroughly entrenched in publications in anthropology and linguistics.

46. There may be other wordlists, but it is not clear whether they represent Tamyen (Survey of California and Other Indian Languages, https://cla.berkeley.edu/languages/tamyen.php, accessed May 25, 2021).

47. The name *Karuk* (Karok) is from the Karuk word *káruk* meaning 'upriver' (Hinton 1994, 157).

48. The name *Chimariko* is from the Chimariko autonym (self-designation), *č'imaríkʼo*, based on *čʼimar, čʼimal* 'person' (Silver 1978a, 210).

49. The name *Achumawi/Achomawi* is from the self-designation, *ajuma:wi* 'river people'. *Atsugewi* is from *atsuke*, the native name of a place on Hat Creek in the middle of Atsuge territory (Garth 1978, 243).

50. There appear to be clear sound correspondences that require reconstruction of a number of liquids and nasals. Olmsted's **l* is for the correspondence of Achomawi *l*: Atsugewi *l* (*l/l*), while his **r* represents the *l/r* correspondence. There is also, however, the correspondences that Olmsted symbolizes with the indeterminate reconstruction **L* for *l/n*, with **N* for the *n/r* sound correspondence, and **n* for the *n/n* sound correspondence—all these proto-sounds appear to be in contrast with one another.

51. McLendon and Oswalt (1978, 277) explained that the name *Pomo* appears to derive from a confusion of two different Northern Pomo forms, *pʰo:mo*: (*pʰo*: 'magnesite, red earth or clay' + *mo* 'hole' [which with final vowel length means 'at']), and *pʰoʔmaʔ* (*pʰo-* 'reside, live in a group'), which together mean something like 'those who live at red earth hole'.

52. Hualapai (Walapai) in English apparently reflects the Mojave *huwa:ɬapay* 'pine person'; the term in Hualapai is *hwa:laʔpay* 'ponderosa pine people', originally the name of a single band that lived west of the Hualapai Mountains (McGuire and Goddard 1983, 36).

The name *Havasupai* reflects the Havasupai self-designation *havasúwə ʔəpá* 'person/people of the blue/green water'; here *ha-* represents *ʔəha* 'water' and *vasúwə* 'blue/green color'. The name in English is probably from one of the related Yuman languages that have *-pai* (*pay*) 'person'; several of them have similar names for Havasupai (Goddard 1983, 23).

53. The name *Mojave* is from the Mojave autonym *hàmakhá:v*, which also has a shortened form *makhá:v* (Goddard 1983, 69). The spelling *Mohave* is rejected by the tribe.

54. Quechan comes from $k^w acá:n$, the Quechan self-designation, meaning 'those who descended', thought to refer to their traditional belief concerning their creation on a sacred mountain (Goddard 1983, 97).

55. According to tradition, the name *Wappo* is from the Spanish word *guapo*, one sense of which is 'brave' (also 'harsh, severe, daring'), though it is better known in its meaning of 'handsome'. The 'brave, daring' attribute fits their resistance to the military adjuncts of the Franciscan missions.

56. The name *Huchnom*, given to the Yuki group of Round Valley, means 'tribe outside (the valley)' (Miller 1978, 254).

57. "The name Chumash was arbitrarily chosen by Powell [1891] from the word used by Coastal Chumash for Santa Cruz Island and its inhabitants, *Mi-tcú-mac* [mičúmaš], or *Tcú-mac* [čúmaš]. Each regional group had its own name for itself" (Grant 1978, 507).

58. In modern Spanish, its name would be *ineceño*.

59. Cortina-Borja et al.'s (2002) quantification employed evidence from both the lexicon and phonology.

60. Alexis Manaster Ramer (1992) and Jane Hill (in an unpublished paper) argued that Tübatulabal should be subgrouped together with Gabrielino and Cupan, separate from Serrano-Kitanemuk (reported in Golla 2011, 185).

61. The name *Tübatulabal* means 'pine-nut eaters'; it was applied to some Tübatulabal bands by their Yokuts and Kawaiisu neighbors and by themselves (Smith 1978, 437).

62. The name *Hopi* is the Hopi name for themselves, *hópi*; *hópi* also means 'good in every respect' in the Third Mesa dialect; $hó^b pi$ means 'is good, peaceful' and *hópi* 'is wise, knowing' in the Mishongnovi dialect. The older term *Moki/Moqui* is from the self-designation $mó:k^w i$. From the older Spanish spelling with *moqui* this came into English as *Moki*, but this term was eliminated from official US government usage because it resembles Hopi *móki* 'dies, is dead' (Schroeder and Goddard 1979, 550–551).

63. *Pima* apparently were named by the Spanish for the word for 'nothing', *pimahaitu* in the eighteenth century. A number of languages got their exonyms from their words meaning 'nothing' or 'there are none' (after Spanish *no hay*), as for example Cahita from *kaita* [kaa hita] 'nothing'.

O'odham is now the official name that has replaced former *Papago*. The name *Papago* apparently comes from a form meaning 'bean Pimas', seen in an earlier Spanish version of the name *papabotas*, glossed '*pimas frijoleros*' ('bean Pimas'); compare *bá:bawi-ʔóʔodham* 'bean Piman(s)' (*báwi* 'tepary bean') (Goddard 1983, 134).

64. David Shaul (2014, 180) thinks that both Tubar and Jova had a rather different history from their closest geographical neighbors. He says:

> The geographic positions of both Jova and Tubar suggest UA [Uto-Aztecan] migrations at different times into northwestern Mexico. First in position would be Jova and Tubar, then the expansion of Tarahumaran, Opatan, and Cahitan. A final wave of migration is represented by Tepiman, with some Tepiman speakers developing Eudeve from the imperfect learning of Opata.

Tubar retained Proto-Uto-Aztecan $*k^w$ as k^w where other languages lost or changed the velar part of this sound (with changes of $*k^w$ variously to b^w, b, or w in the other Taracahitic languages). That Tubar does not share this change also raises doubts about its subgroup classification, thought the lexically based quantitative classifications do group Tubar together with the other Taracahitic languages.

65. It is assumed that the name *Cahita* comes from their *kaita* [kaa hita] 'nothing', given to this group by the Spanish.

66. It was sometimes thought that there is a sound correspondence in medial position of Northern Uto-Aztecan -*n*- to Southern Uto-Aztecan -*n*-, reconstructed by some scholars as **-n-*. However, Terrence Kaufman (1981) showed that there are very few putative cognate sets involving this proposed correspondence and that the reflexes are in fact not regular but sporadic, so that this assumed sound correspondence and the proposed reconstruction based on it can be eliminated. (There are ten examples in Stubbs 2011, 24–25). The *r is found only word-medially, and some thought it could be eliminated because it might be just a reflex of *t or maybe of some other sound in that position. However, arguments for its elimination have not been persuasive.

67. There is no need to rehearse the problems with the linguistic evidence Jane Hill presented earlier in favor of her hypothesis (see Campbell and Poser 2008, 347–350; Kaufman and Justeson 2009, 225–226; Merrill 2013; Shaul 2014 for details). However, it will be useful for illustration's sake to mention some of the difficulties with some of the new information given in Hill (2012).

Hill's Proto-Uto-Aztecan (PUA) **paʔtsi/a* (*paCtsi, *paʔtsi [Stubbs 2011, 317]) still appears to have meant 'seed, pit', where various Uto-Aztecan languages later shifted meanings to include new senses, some of them related to maize. Noting Nahuatl *xina:ch-* (/šina:č-/) as related to *ach* (/ač/) does not change the fact that *ač* means 'seed, pit' generally though it could be used to include maize seeds (kernels), too. It is not at all certain that *šina:č* 'seed, seed of garden, seed of vegetables (i.e., non-maize seed)' is derived from *ač* 'seed (in general)' since there is a discrepancy in vowel length between the two (*a:č* is a different form, meaning 'elder brother'). Derived forms mean 'semen, sperm' but 'seed' and 'semen' are connected semantically in many languages, including English. That Classical Nahuatl *xinachioa*, based on *šina:č*, is glossed 'to sow the seeds of corn that had been used to make images of the maize god at the feast of Hue:i Toso:stli' means only that the 'seed' meaning could also extend to include maize seeds in this context, but not that its original source must have included 'maize seed' and thus could be taken as support the existence of PUA maize agriculture.

Hill adds *sura, which she glosses as 'germ of corn kernel, corn kernel', based on Hopi *soona-* 'corn kernel, the edible part of pinyon nuts and other seeds, the germ of corn kernel'—glossed by others as 'edible part of seed' (Stubbs 2011, 215)—Eudeve *surát* 'corn kernel', and Nahuatl *xi:l-o:-tl* (/ši:lo:-/) 'tender ear of green corn', but saying that these come from PUA *sura 'heart', "perhaps parallel development in the three languages" (Hill 2012, 58). This *sura is what has been reconstructed as PUA *suna 'heart' (with *sula in Southern Uto-Aztecan) (Stubbs 2011, 215), with extended meanings in deferent Uto-Aztecan languages that include 'middle of', 'center', 'inside', 'grain/kernel, pit', 'and 'edible part of seed'. There is little reason to believe its original meaning involved maize agriculture; however, extending the original meaning of 'heart' to include also 'center', 'inside', 'edible part of seed', and 'seed' is plausible. It is doubtful that Nahuatl *ši:lo:-* is cognate to the other forms cited here, Since Nahuatl *š* comes from *s before *i but not before PUA *u as in *suna 'heart'.

Hill (2012, 58) added *tawak 'the tender young maize plant, the green ear of maize of such a plant, cornstalk', based on only Hopi *tawak-tzi* 'a type of fresh corn associated with the nadir' and Nahuatl *to:k-tli* 'tender young maize plant, corn stalk' (which in Classical Nahuatl also meant 'fertilized land'). However, Nahuatl *to:k-* did not originally involve maize at all and may not be cognate with the Hopi word; in any case, with only two languages represented, it is not possible to determine that a true PUA etymon is involved here. The Nahuatl form is derived from *to:ka* 'to plant, bury', compare *to:ka-ni* 'planter, one who sows'.

68. Powell's name for the family was *Tañoan*. The name *Tano* (Spanish *Taño*) appears to derive from Tewa *thanuge'in t'owa* 'southern people' (Kroskrity 1993, 59). *Taño* had been a name

for Southern Tiwa; spellings with *Tahano* and *Tagno* also occurred. The Rio Grande Tewa were called *Táno* in Spanish (probably for *tʰáno*); the Hopi-Tewa (Arizona Tewa, Hano Tewa, living among the Hopi) call themselves *tʰá:nu téwa* (borrowed as *háno* in Third Mesa Hopi, hence the name '*Hano*') (see Goddard 1979c, 234–235, 601).

69. *Towa* comes from a mistake made by J. P. Harrington (1909, 594). He thought Jemez (and Pecos) had *tôwa* 'home' and based the name on that. The correct form is *tí:wa* 'at Jemez Pueblo [to the north]' (Goddard 1979c, 235).

70. The name *Taos* comes from Spanish adaptation of Taos *tŏotho* 'in the village', with an *-s* attached that is the Spanish 'plural' *-s* (Goddard 1979c, 267).

71. *Tiwa* was meant as the English equivalent of Spanish *Tigua*, used primarily to designate the Southern Tiwa (Goddard 1979c, 235).

72. The English name *Tewa* appears to be adapted from Spanish *Tegua*, from the Tewa autonym *tewa* (Goddard 1979c, 235).

73. The name *Zuni* earlier was *Zuñi*, from Spanish *Zuñi*. It comes from the Keresan name, seen in Acoma *sî:ni* 'Zuni people, Zuni Pueblo' and Santa Ana *sî:ni* 'Zuni people'. Zunis call themselves *šiwi* and call Zuni Pueblo *šiwiʔna* 'Zuni place' (Goddard 1979c, 479–480). It is unclear whether the Keresan name may be connected in some way to this Zuni name for a Zuni Pueblo.

74. Stanley Newman's (1964) article attempting to establish a Penutian relationship for Zuni has generally been considered unfortunate at best. It has been called a methodologically ill-executed paper (Grant 2018, 14); it has been considered a prime example of how not to compare languages for genealogical relationships; and it has been suggested that Newman was not serious when he wrote it but rather considered it something of a gag. In any event, it was far from convincing. (See Campbell 1997, 321 for evaluation of Newman's data.)

Karl-Heinz Gursky (1966a, 419) thought that he had found fifty "recht deutliche Parallelen" (quite clear [lexical] parallels) between Keresan and Zuni, saying "diese Übereinstimmungen lassen eine genealogische Sprachvervantdschaft durchaus möglich erscheinen; sie reichen aber natürlich keineswegs als Beweis aus" (these correspondences make a genealogical linguistic relationship seem entirely possible, but of course they are by no means sufficient as proof) (p. 420). He adds that Stanley Newman wrote to him about his word comparisons, saying a number of them look good, but that there is the problem of "determining whether or not borrowings may explain some of the lexical similarities, particularly since we know that there has been a great deal of intermarriage and ceremonial interaction between many of the Southwestern pueblos for generations. Zuni has had close relations with Hopi, Acoma, and Laguna, as well as with the non-pueblo Navaho" (p. 420).

75. *Comecrudo* is from Spanish, literally 'raw-eat'. *Carrizo* is the Spanish word for 'reed'.

76. *Garza* is the Spanish word for 'heron'.

77. Because the extant data on Cotoname is so limited, some might prefer to consider it unclassified rather than a language isolate.

78. The etymology of the name *Sioux* is not certain, though plausible suggestions have been offered. In one, English got the name via French from a shortened form of *Nadouessioux*, said by several to be from an Ojibwe name for the Sioux meaning 'little snakes' (the Iroquois were referred to as *nadowe* 'big snakes'). The spelling with final *-x* reflects the plural of French. The name in several other Algonquian languages for 'Northern Iroquoian' refers to a small rattlesnake. A different view derives *Sioux* from the early Ottawa (Algonquian) name *na·towe·ssi* (*na·towe·ssiwak* in the plural), from the Proto-Algonquian verb **-a·towe:*-meaning 'to speak a foreign language'.

There are widespread names among Algonquian languages referring to various Iroquoian groups based on this verb. (See, for example, *Oxford English Dictionary*, entry for Sioux; Dorsey 1885, 919; Goddard 1978c, 320.)

79. J. Owen Dorsey (1885, 919) said that *Ȼegiha* (his spelling of *Dhegiha*) means 'belonging to the people of the land' or 'those dwelling here', that is 'the aborigines or home people'.

80. The name *Winnebago* is from an Algonquian language, perhaps Potawatomi *winpyeko*; etymologically it means 'people of the dirty water', referring to "the muddy water of their river (the lower course of the Fox River of Wisconsin) plus Lake Winnebago" (Golla and Goddard 1978, 706).

Ho-chunk appears to be from Winnebago *ho:čák* meaning 'sacred voice'.

81. Goddard (2005, 14–15) tells us:

> The Yatasi and Natchitoches were reported by Sibley (1806, 50, 58) to speak the same language, which was different from all others, though they also spoke Caddo. Later, in sending Thomas Jefferson a Natchitoches vocabulary, having previously sent him one of Caddo, Sibley explained that "this nation from intermarriages with the Caddos and living so much Amongst them use their language," and he left a blank in Jefferson's printed vocabulary form for the items that "are caddo words" (Sibley 1805). It is possible that Yatasi-Natchitoches became more and more like the emergent Caddo koine in the course of the nineteenth century, and that Gatschet's Yatasi vocabulary has even fewer of the originally distinct words of Yatasi-Natchitoches than the language had in Sibley's day.

82. John Wesley Powell (1966[1891], 121) derived the name *Adai* from Caddo *hadai* 'brushwood'.

83. Swanton suggested that the Han of Núñez Cabeza de Vaca's account, found on the east end of Galveston Island in 1528, were probably Atakapan, where Han may be derived from the Atakapa word *añ* or *ã* (/aŋ/?) 'house' (Gatschet and Swanton 1932, 2; Swanton 1946, 85).

84. The name *Chitimacha* has had several pronunciations. Most common has been [čɪtɪməšá], though [čɪtɪmáčə] is also frequent, especially among non-linguists. In earlier French and other sources in addition to <Chitimacha>, spellings of <Chetimacha> and <Shetimacha>, are encountered. It seems that the earlier pronunciation must have begun with the fricative [š] (IPA [ʃ]) and not the affricate [č] (IPA [tʃ]), with [š] (IPA [ʃ] being the phonetic value of French <ch>. It has been speculated that earlier generations may have changed the initial [š] to [č] in their pronunciation in order to avoid the first part of the name sounding like it had something to do with excrement (in English).

85. The reflexes are actually more nuanced than just a straight *b*: *k* correspondence. As Karen Booker (1993, 414) showed, among its various reflexes of Proto-Muskogean *k^w are *k* initially and *p* intervocalically of Creek-Seminole, which correspond to *b* of the other languages. This makes the *k^w reconstruction seem all the stronger (Booker 2005, 250).

86. M, N, L, W, Y in IPA are [m̥, n̥, ɬ (or l̥), w̥, y̥], respectively.

87. The name *Seminole* is from Creek *simanó:li* 'wild, runaway, fugitive', from earlier Creek *simaló:ni*, a loanword from Spanish *cimarrón* 'wild, unruly' and 'runaway slave' (see *The Random House Dictionary of the English Language*).

88. Aaron Broadwell (1991) has argued that two extinct languages, **Guale** and **Yamasee**, both once spoken in South Carolina and Georgia, are Muskogean languages, belonging to the Northern branch of the family. However, William Sturtevant (1994) showed that the forms Broadwell cited are in fact from Creek and not from Yamasee or Guale. Since the language(s) of the Yamasee and

Guale are known only from early historical records and remain unattested linguistically, they are considered unclassified.

89. The name *Nottoway* is from Algonquian. It is derived from the Proto-Algonquian **na:towe:wa* (connected with the Proto-Algonquian **-a:towe:-* 'speak a foreign language'). This is a widespread Algonquian name for Iroquoians matching the word for rattlesnake in some languages. Ojibwe has /naadowe/ in both meanings referring to various Iroquoian groups (See Goddard 1978c, 320).

90. The name *Huron* was first used by Samuel de Champlain, in July 1623. One idea of its etymology is that it is from French *hure* 'boar's head, bristly head' since the haircut of the Hurons resembled the erect bristles on the head of a boar. Another proposed explanation for the name is that it is from an Old French word meaning 'ruffian, knave, lout, unkempt person' (Heidenreich 1978, 387).

Wyandot comes from the Huron and Wyandot autonym (self-designation) *wę̈ⁿdat*, probably a shortening of something corresponding to Mohawk *skaw:ęnat* 'one language' or *tshaʔtekawę́:nat* 'the same language (word, speech)' (Goddard 1978c, 405).

91. The name *Cayuga* is from the Cayuga autonym, *kayohkhó:noʔ* 'people of Oiogouen'; the entymology of the town name *Oiogouen* is unknown (Goddard 1978c, 503).

92. The name *Onondaga* comes from the Onondaga autonym *onǫtáʔke* 'people of *onǫtáʔke:kàʔ*, the main Onondaga town, which means literally 'on the hill' (Goddard 1978c, 499).

93. The name *Susquehannock/Susquehanna* is believed to come via French from Iroquoian *skahentawaneh* 'big grassy flat', seen in comparison with Mohawk *skahę̀tó:wanę* and Oneida *skahę̀tówanę́* 'great field' (Jennings 1978, 362).

94. The name *Oneida* is from the Oneida self-designation, *onęyoteʔa:kà:* 'people of the erected stone' (see *onęyóteʔ* 'erected stone'), reflecting an Oneida village name that refers to a large syenite boulder, which, according to tradition, always appeared near the main Oneida settlement (Goddard 1978c, 489).

95. The name *Mohawk* is from Algonquian. Ives Goddard (1978c, 478) said that of the various spellings that appeared in earlier sources, Roger Williams' <Mohowawogs> was etymologically the most accurate, with English *-s* 'plural' added to a Narragansett or Massachusett word for 'people-eaters' (compare the Unami cognate *mhuwé:yɔk* 'cannibal monsters').

96. That is, more precisely, Schillaci et al. (2017, 448, 460) give the dating of the initial breakup of Proto-Iroquoian as 4,624 years ago plus or minus 1,341 years, that is, to between 3,965 and 1283 BCE—a very sizeable range.

97. The Algonquian family is named for Algonquin, of the Ottawa River Valley. The French studied this language intensively in their early involvement with the First Nations peoples of Canada. The spelling *Algonquian* reflects the language family's origin, named after the Algonquin language. Some scholars have spelled it as *Algonkian* in English, reflecting French pronunciation, but the spelling *Algonquian* with its historical precedent has predominated. In any case, both spellings have the same pronunciation (with [ki] not [kwi]).

98. The Wiyot name is from *wiyat*, their native name for the Eel River delta; it is also the name of one of the three principal Wiyot groups (Elsasser 1978, 162).

99. The name *Yurok* is from Karuk *yúruk* meaning literally 'downriver'. The Yurok traditional name for themselves is *Puliklah* (Hinton 1994, 157), from *pulik* 'downstream' + *-la* 'people of', thus equivalent in meaning to the Karuk name by which they came to be known in English (Victor Golla, personal communication).

100. The name *Cree* is from Old Algonquin (Ojibwa) *kiristino:*. It comes from the name of a little-known band from an area south of James Bay in the first half of the seventeenth century. The French adopted the name with their plural *-s*, spelled variously *Kristinos, Kiristinous, Christinaux*,

and applied it to all Cree-speaking groups. It became shortened to *Cris* (singular and plural), sometimes *Cri* singular, from which English took it as *Cree* (Pentland 1981, 227–228).

The name *Montagnais* is from French meaning 'mountaineer, people of the mountains', a reference to the mountains of their territory (Goddard 1981, 185).

101. The name *Naskapi* reportedly is a derogatory term signifying 'uncivilized people' or 'those who have no religion', but the etymology is unknown (Goddard 1981, 185).

102. The Menominee name appears to come from Ojibwa *mano:mini:*, meaning 'wild rice people' (see *mano:min* 'wild rice') (Spindler 1978, 723), though the Menominee autonym also relates to 'wild rice'. Wild rice was a staple food for the Menominee.

103. *Ojibwa* is the most frequent form of this name; *Chippewa* is preferred by groups in the United States and southern Ontario, and *Ojibway* is the more common spelling in the rest of Canada. The name Ojibwa/Ojibway/Chippewa reflects the autonym, *očipwe:*. This is explained as meaning 'puckered up', reflecting the form of Ojibwa moccasins (Goddard 1978c, 768–769).

104. The name *Algonquin*—after which the Algonquian language family is named—is thought to be from Maliseet *elakómkwik* 'they are our relatives (or allies)' (Day and Trigger 1978, 792).

105. The Sauk (also spelled *Sac*) are known in French by the name *saki* (with various spellings). An Algonquian form of this name was borrowed into English; perhaps something like the Ojibwa *osa:ki:* was borrowed without the *o-* prefix and was then shortened. Some early spellings reflect *asa:ki:waki* (a plural form, with *a-* from earlier *o-*). Ives Goddard (1978c, 654) interpreted it etymologically as 'people of the outlet', in reference to the mouth of the Saginaw River (Ojibwa *sa:ki:na:nk* '[at] the country of the Sauk').

106. The name *Shawnee* comes from the Shawnee autonym *ša:wanwa* 'person of the south'. There are cognate names in several other Algonquian languages (Callender 1978, 634).

107. The name *Maliseet* comes "from Micmac where it probably means 'lazy speakers'" (Erickson 1978, 135).

The name Passamaquoddy is from Passamaquoddy *muhkat* 'a Passamoquoddy, literally one who spears pollock'. The plural is pestomuhkatíyik (where the <o> is /ə/), the source of the "y" in the name Passamaquoddy (Ives Goddards personal communication; see also Erickson 1978, 135).

108. The name Abenaki is from Western Abename /wôbanakii/ 'easterner; Abenaki' (where /ô/ is the nasalized vowel, unrounded for most speakers, and where /-ii/ is two syllables, with the *-i* making it mean 'person of' (Ives Goddard personal communication).

109. The name *Massachusett* ends with the locative suffix /-ət/); it means 'at Great Blue Hill', literally 'at arrowhead hill', Mâssachusett "an hill in the form of an arrow's head", explained by Josiah Cotton (a speaker of the language, cited in Pilling 1885,112). The initial element appears as <môhsh-> 'flint'. (Ives Goddard personal communication.) "The Narragansett name was Massachuséuck" (Salwen 1978, 174); The Narragansett form in <-êuck> is an animate plural: 'people of the ...' (Goddaard personal communication).

110. The name *Delaware* for these Indigenous groups comes from the name of the Delaware River, which was named for Sir Thomas West, Lord de la Warr, first governor of Virginia.

Lenape was another common name for the Delaware in early publications. It is from the Unami self-designation is *ləná:p:e* 'person'.

The name *Munsee* is from the Delaware term meaning 'person from Minisink'; it is *mwəns:i* in Unami, *mən'si:w* in Munsee.

Unami is the German spelling of the name, from Munsee *wŏná:mi:w* 'downriver person' (Goddard 1978b, 235–237, Goddard personal communication).

111. Will Oxford (2021, 507) lists *ʔ also as a Proto-Algonquian consonant, although Ives Goddard does not reconstruct *ʔ as a phoneme of Proto-Algonquian; it shows up as the first

member in some consonant clusters. Goddard interprets ʔ in these cases as the result of neutralization of *p and *k in this position (see Goddard 1979b, 77–78).

112. Howard Berman (1982, 419) argued that the Ritwan homeland must have been in northern California, since "their [Wiyot's and Yurok's] location adjacent to each other amid a horde of languages unrelated to them is too much a coincidence to be the result of chance." Kenneth Whistler, however, argued on linguistic and archaeological grounds that these languages arrived in California in separate movements from the north—from the Columbia Plateau, perhaps from the middle Columbia River area following the Deschutes River, about 900 CE for Wiyot and about 1100 CE for Yurok (reported in Moratto 1984, 540, 564).

113. It is possible that the Beothuks had contact with the Norse settlement of L'Anse au Meadows on the northernmost tip of Newfoundland, dated to circa 1000 CE; however, there is no evidence in the Beothuk language or culture to suggest any such contact.

3

Middle American Languages (Mexico and Central America)

3.1. INTRODUCTION

This chapter is about the history and classification of the Indigenous languages of Mexico and Central America. Mexico and Central America together are sometimes called "Middle America" in anthropological and linguistic literature.[1] The classification of the languages of Middle America is well established, and the reconstruction of the various proto-languages is advanced. In general, the historical linguistic research on these languages has been of high quality, though more work is needed and further advances are possible, and, of course, not all historical linguistic works concerning these languages have been accurate or of value.

Mexico and Central America together are the home of circa 200 known Indigenous languages, with more than 180 still spoken. They fall into fifteen language families, four of which are language isolates.[2]

"Mesoamerica" is a well-known, cohesive area, important linguistically and culturally, that occupies a large part of Mexico and Central America and is home to the majority of the languages of Middle America. In parts of this chapter, the languages of Mesoamerica are discussed together, with the non-Mesoamerican languages of the Middle America considered separately. "Mesoamerica" refers to a culture area defined by a number of cultural traits shared by the pre-Columbian cultures of the geographical region that extends from the Pánuco River in northern Mexico to the Lempa River in El Salvador, continuing along the Pacific coast of Nicaragua and Costa Rica (first defined by Paul Kirchhoff 1943). Mesoamerica is also a linguistic area; the Mesoamerican Linguistic Area coincides approximately in the territory with the Mesoamerican Culture Area, defined by linguistic traits shared among languages of the area (Campbell, Kaufman, and Smith-Stark 1986). (See Map 7.8.)

The countries of the Middle American region, together with the number of still-spoken Indigenous languages in each, are:

Belize   4 languages
Costa Rica   9 languages
El Salvador   3 languages
Guatemala   26 languages
Honduras   7 languages
Mexico   circa 125 languages
Nicaragua   3 languages
Panama   11 languages

(Note that some languages are spoken in more than one country.)

3.2. CLASSIFICATION AND HISTORY OF MIDDLE AMERICAN LANGUAGES

There is general agreement that Mesoamerica has seven established and mostly uncontroversial language families—Mayan, Mixe-Zoquean, Tequistlatecan, Totonacan (Totonac-Tepehua), Otomanguean, Uto-Aztecan, and Xinkan—and three language isolates: Cuitlatec, Huave, and Purépecha (Tarascan). Middle America beyond Mesoamerica has an additional four language families—Guaicurian (Waikurian), Jicaquean (Tol), Lencan, and Misumalpan—and one more language isolate: Seri. In what follows, these language families (and isolates) with their subgrouping classification are presented and highlights of their history surveyed. The consensus classification presented here represents the culmination of investigations that extend over two centuries. Among the tasks that remain to be done are to improve further the subgrouping of these language families, to seek more complete reconstructions, and to work out more completely the impacts of language contact.

The language families of Middle America (including language isolates) are the following.

(1) Four language isolates:
   *Cuitlatec
   Huave
   Purépecha (Tarascan)
   Seri

The first three are in Mesoamerica; Seri is spoken in the Mexican state of Sonora, north of Mesoamerica.

(2) Seven language families of Mesoamerica:
   Mayan (31 languages)
   Mixe-Zoquean (c. 19 languages)
   Tequistlatecan (3 languages)

Totonacan (Totonac-Tepehua) (c. 6 languages)
Otomanguean (c. 83 languages)
Uto-Aztecan (c. 32 languages in North America, and c.16 in Mexico and Central America)
*Xinkan (4 languages)
(3) Four non-Mesoamerican language families found in Middle America:
*Guaicurian (Waikurian) (Mexico)
Jicaquean (Tol) (Honduras)
*Lencan (Honduras, El Salvador)
Misumalpan (Nicaragua, El Salvador)

Some other language families have representatives both in Middle America and in countries outside the region. The Cochimí-Yuman family has languages both in the US Southwest and in Mexico, principally in Baja California. Algonquian (of the larger Algic family) has one representative—Kickapoo—with speakers both in Mexico and the United States. Several now extinct and poorly documented languages had speakers in both southeastern Texas and northeastern Mexico (see for example Coahuilteco, Comecrudan, and Cotoname, Chapter 2). Uto-Aztecan languages extend from Oregon to Costa Rica. Uto-Aztecan, with Northern Uto-Aztecan languages in North America and Southern Uto-Aztecan languages mostly in Mexico and Central America, is discussed primarily in Chapter 2 on North American languages; the Nahua (Aztecan) branch is discussed in this chapter. The Chibchan family extends from Honduras (with Pech) to Colombia and Venezuela, with several Chibchan languages in Nicaragua, Costa Rica, and Panama. The Arawakan family of South America, with languages from Venezuela and the Guianas to southern Brazil (and Argentina by some interpretations), reached the Caribbean and from there extended on into Central America with Garífuna, spoken in Belize, Guatemala, Honduras, and Nicaragua. The Chocoan languages are spoken in both Colombia and Panama. See Chapter 4 for details concerning these cases.

Some individual languages have speakers in both the United States and Mexico: O'odham, Yaqui, Kickapoo, and several Cochimí-Yuman languages, not to mention the many recent immigrants and refugees to the United States who speak various of the Middle American Indigenous languages. These languages are dealt with in Chapter 2 on North American languages, only because for most of these language families more of their member languages are found in North America, and North America comes up first in this book. Cuna and Teribe (Chibchan), and Waunana, Northern Emberá, and Southern Emberá (Chocoan languages) have speakers in both Panama and Colombia; they are presented in Chapter 4 on South America. Some proposals of broader relationships involving various of the language families of Middle America are mentioned in various cases here and are considered in a more concentrated way in Chapter 6.

I now turn to the classification and history of these languages.

3.2.1. MESOAMERICAN LANGUAGES

Mayan

Languages of the Mayan family are spoken in Guatemala, southern Mexico, Belize, and a small area in Honduras. They occupy about one-third of the territory of Mesoamerica

(Kaufman 2017, 63). The most widely accepted classification of the languages of the family is:

Mayan
    Huastecan
        Huastec[3] Mexico
        *Chicomuceltec[4] (Chicomuselteco) Mexico
    Core Mayan (Southern Mayan)
        Yucatecan
            Mopán Guatemala, Belize
            Itzaj-Yucatec-Lacandón
                Itzaj Guatemala
                Yucatec-Lacandón
                      Yucatec (Yucatec Maya)[5] Mexico
                      Lacandón Mexico
        Central Mayan
            Western Mayan
                Cholan-Tzeltalan (Greater Tzeltalan)
                    Cholan
                        Chol-Chontal
                            Chol (Ch'ol)[6] Mexico
                            Chontal[7] Mexico
                        Choltí-Chortí[8]
                            *Choltí Mexico
                            Chortí (Ch'orti') Guatemala, Honduras
                    Tzeltalan
                      Tzeltal Mexico
                      Tzotzil[9] Mexico
                Greater Q'anjob'alan (Q'anjob'alan-Chujean)
                    Q'anjob'alan
                      Q'anjob'alan Complex
                          Q'anjob'al Guatemala
                          Akateko[10] Guatemala
                          Jakalteko (Popti')[11] Guatemala, Mexico
                          Mocho' (Motocintlec; with Tuzantec)[12] Mexico
                    Chuj-Tojolab'al
                      Chuj[13] Guatemala
                      Tojolab'al[14] Mexico
            K'ichean-Mamean (Eastern Mayan)
                Greater K'ichean
                    Q'eqchi'[15] Guatemala
                    Uspantek[16] Guatemala
                    K'ichean

Poqom
  Poqomam Guatemala
  Poqomchi' Guatemala
Central K'ichean (K'ichean Proper)
  K'iche'[17] Guatemala
  Kaqchikel[18] Guatemala
  Tz'utujil Guatemala
  Sakapultek[19] Guatemala
  Sipacapa (Sipakapense)[20] Guatemala
Mamean (Greater Mamean)
  Mam-Teco (Mamean proper)
    Mam[21] Guatemala
    Teco (Tektiteko) Mexico, Guatemala
  Awakateko-Ixil (Ixilan)
    Awakatek[22] Guatemala
    Ixil Guatemala

(Campbell and Kaufman 1985; Campbell 2017a; Kaufman 2017.)
(See Map 3.1. Mayan Languages.)

In Terrence Kaufman's (2017, 62) words, "Mayan linguistic studies achieved an impressive level of maturity during the early 1960s, and have maintained and beefed up that maturity." As Lauren Clemens (2021, 388) says, "the Mayan language family is one of the best-documented and well-studied language families in the Americas."

The **Huastecan** branch was the first to separate from the rest of the family. Next, **Yucatecan** branched off, and then later the remaining **Central Mayan** groups separated into distinct branches. The subgroups (subfamilies) **Huastecan, Yucatecan, Cholan-Tzeltalan, Greater Q'anjob'alan**, and **Eastern Mayan** (K'ichean-Mamean) are clear and for the most part uncontroversial. It is generally believed that Cholan-Tzeltalan (Greater Tzeltalan) and Greater Q'anjob'alan belong together in a single higher-order branch, although the evidence for this is not strong, and more work is needed to clarify it. Opinions have differed about whether **Tojolab'al** belongs to Greater Q'anjob'alan or to Cholan-Tzeltalan (see Law 2014 for a survey of opinions). Danny Law (2017b) argues that Tojolab'al is a mixed language, with substantial input from both **Tzeltal** and Tojolab'al, accounting for the difficulty in classifying it uniquely as belonging either to Cholan-Tzeltalan or to Greater Q'anjob'alan.

*__Coxoh__, dormant since the colonial period and with essentially no attestation, may be a separate Mayan language as is often reported, though Campbell and Gardner (1988) argued that it in fact belonged with the southeastern dialect of Tzeltzal.

Relationships among Mayan languages have been recognized since early colonial times. Several early scholars of Mayan comparative linguistics utilized methods developed in the study of Indo-European languages at almost the same time that these methods established in Europe.[23]

Abraham M. Halpern (1942) presented the first real reconstruction of several Proto-Mayan sounds, based on a set of sound correspondences. Norman McQuown (1955, 1956b)

Middle American Languages (Mexico and Central America) 151

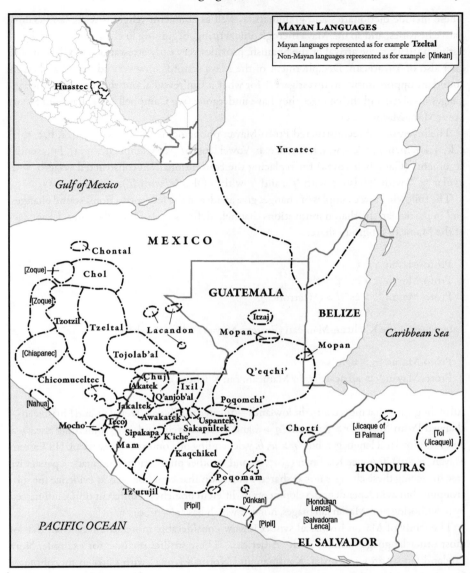

MAP 3.1. Mayan languages

is often credited as founder of modern Mayan comparative linguistics. Several Proto-Mayan phonemes that McQuown postulated were eliminated in later refinements (see Kaufman 1964a, 1969, 2017a; Kaufman and Norman 1984; Kaufman with Justeson 2003; Kaufman 2017; and Campbell 1977, 89–90, 97–101; 1988a, 6–12; 2017a). The classification and the picture of Proto-Mayan reconstruction given in Campbell and Kaufman (1985) still represent the consensus view, for the most part.[24]

Several Mayan languages have extensive attestations beginning shortly after the earliest Spanish contact, written in or about the Indigenous languages using Spanish orthography.

These include dictionaries and grammars, as well as abundant religious texts, land claims, native histories, and so on. Maya hieroglyphic writing, beginning in circa 300 BCE and persisting until after the arrival of the Spanish, provides very early attestations of **Cholan**, and later also of **Yucatecan**. Decipherment of the Maya script is now very advanced and offers abundant opportunities to investigate it for what it can reveal about the history of the languages involved and the changes they have undergone (see Campbell 1984; Law and Stuart 2017; Mora-Marín 2022).

The inventory of reconstructed Proto-Mayan phonemes is /p, t, ṭ, ts, č, k, q, ʔ, ɓ, t', ṭ', ts', č', k', q', l, r, m, n, ŋ, s, š, χ, w, y, h, i, e, a, o, u, Vowel length/ (see Campbell 2017a). I presented arguments (Campbell 2017a) for replacing the conventionally reconstructed velar *x with uvular *χ, *t with *ṭ (also *t' with *ṭ'), and *ṱ with *t (also *ṱ' with *t').

The following few examples of changes give an idea of the reconstructions, sound changes, and in particular, the shared innovations that help define some of the subgroups. Languages of the Mamean subgroup share:

Proto-Mayan *r > t
Proto-Mayan *ṭ > č; *ṭ' > č'
Proto-Mayan *č > ʂ; *č' > ʂ' (retroflex).

Languages of the K'ichean-Mamean (Eastern Mayan) subfamily share:

Proto-Mayan *ŋ > x
Proto-Mayan *t > affricate (*ts* in Mamean, *č* in K'ichean).

All of the groups that moved into the lowlands—Yucatecan, Cholan-Tzeltalan, and Huastecan—changed Proto-Mayan *r > y; *q and *q' > k and k' respectively; and *ŋ to something else, *ŋ > n in most lowland languages, but *ŋ > w, h, y depending on context in Huastecan. (In Eastern Mayan, *ŋ > x.) Terrence Kaufman (2017, 72 and in other publications) has made a persuasive case for seeing these changes not as shared innovation that could be seen as evidence for subgrouping, but as independent developments in different branches at different times, influenced by neighboring non-Mayan languages, none of which has /r/, /q/, or /ŋ/.

The study of Mayan historical syntax is now considerably more advanced than that of most other language families in the Americas.[25] These studies include, for example, Nora England (1991) on word order, Kaufman and Norman (1984) with Ch'olan morphology, David Mora-Marín (2003) on reconstruction of applicative and antidative constructions, William Norman (1978) on "instrumental voice," Norman and Campbell (1978) about Proto-Mayan syntax generally, John Robertson (1992) on tense/aspect/mood/voice in verbs, Thomas Smith-Stark (1976) on aspects of syntax and morphology, and especially Terrence Kaufman's (2002) detailed treatment of Mayan morphosyntax. These studies reveal that Proto-Mayan was an ergative language, with associated antipassive constructions. The subjects of intransitive verbs and the objects of transitive verbs were treated in the same way, both bearing absolutive cross-referencing affixes on verbs, distinct from the marking of subjects of transitive verbs, which bore ergative cross-referencing prefixes. It is argued that Proto-Mayan had VOS (Verb-Object-Subject) basic word order when the subject was higher than the object on the "animacy" hierarchy (where 'human' is highest, 'animate' next highest, and 'inanimate' lowest), in instances such as 'the boy [HUMAN] cured the dog [ANIMATE]', but had VSO word order when subject and object were equal in animacy, in cases such as 'the woman [HUMAN] cured the man [HUMAN]' (see Kaufman 2002).

Kaufman (2017, 71) located the Proto-Mayan homeland around Uspantán in highland Guatemala. He provided dates, mostly based on glottochronology (not thought to be reliable by most linguists), for the diversification of the languages of the Mayan family. As he saw it, Huastecan split off, leaving Core Mayan (Southern Mayan) at 2200 BCE. Yucatecan separated from Core Mayan (Southern Mayan), leaving Central Mayan (Cholan-Tzeltalan and Greater-Q'a'njob'alan) at 1900 BCE. Central Mayan split shortly later into Eastern and Western Mayan at 1600 BCE. Eastern Mayan divided into Greater K'ichean and Mamean at 1400 BCE. Western Mayan broke up into Greater Tzeltalan (Cholan-Tzeltalan) and Greater Q'anjob'alan at 1000 BCE. Greater K'ichean and Mamean (his Greater Mamean) both diversified at 1600 BCE. He saw the first diversification of Greater K'ichean at 600 BCE, when Q'eqchi' split off (p. 175). He dated the spread of Greater Tzeltal into the Mayan lowlands at 500 BCE, though with some of them remaining in the Guatemalan highlands (p. 176). He dated at 500 CE both the break-up of Q'anjob'alan, with the separation of Mocho', and the separation of Mamean-Teco (Mamean Proper) into Mam and Teco (p. 205). Greater Q'anjob'alan and Greater Tzeltalan (Cholan-Tzeltalan) both diversified at about 100 CE. He dated to 600 CE the split-up of Cholan, the separation of Tzeltalan into Tzeltal and Tzotzil, and the break-up of Awakateko-Ixil (Ixilan) into Awakateko and Ixil (p. 207).

The Huastecan branch has two languages, Huastec in Veracruz and San Luis Potosí and Chicomuceltec in Chiapas, near the Guatemalan border. There have been various ideas about how and when these very closely related languages came to be separated by such a distance, over 1,000 kilometers: (1) Huastecan migrated north after separating from the rest of the Mayan family, later diversified, and then Chicomuceltec migrated back to be next to other Mayan languages. (2) Huastecan stayed near the other Mayan languages, diversified, and then Huastec went north and Chicomuceltec remained behind. (3) Huastecan migrated part-way between current Huastec territory and the rest of the Mayan area, split up there, and then Huastec continued on north to its present location while Chicomuceltec migrated back to its location next to other Mayan languages. In Kaufman's view (2003, 6),

> The Wastekos [Huastecs] have probably been in their historically-known location since 1800 BCE, and they (or the Kabils [Chicomuceltecs]) probably occupied the central Veracruz region as well until about 1100 CE, when they were overrun and/or driven out by Totonakos [Totonacs]. (see also Kaufman 2020a, 26)

Whatever the true story was, Huastecan was clearly in contact with languages of the Maya Lowlands, since both of the Huastecan languages share several sound changes and some morphological similarities due to contact with these languages (see Norcliffe 2003; Law 2014; 2017a, 120). Huastecan shares with Lowland Mayan languages (Cholan-Tzeltalan and Yucatecan) and some Greater Q'anjob'alan languages the changes: *r > y, *q > *k (and *q' > *k'), and *k > č (and *k' > č'). However, the complicated conditioning environments for the changes *k > č and *k' > č' in Ch'olan-Tzeltalan languages (see Kaufman and Norman 1984) are different from those in Huastecan and Yucatecan. This change (or at least aspects of the change) had to have happened independently in these different subgroups.

Huastec *tak'in* 'silver, money, precious metal' seems clearly borrowed from a Lowland Mayan language. It is composed of pieces that in Proto Mayan would be **ta:ʔ* 'excrement' + **qʼi:ŋ* 'sun, day', probably connected with a Mesoamerican calque, as in Nahuatl *teōkwitlatl* 'gold, precious metal' (*teō-* 'god' + *kwitlatl* 'excrement') (more on this in Chapter 7). However, Huastecan has *kʼih* 'day', not *kʼin*, which is the form that Cholan-Tzeltalan and Yucatecan have for this cognate. *Takʼin* thus is a borrowing from one of those lowland Mayan languages into Huastecan (see Norcliffe 2003; cf. Campbell 1988, 211; 2017a; Kaufman 1980, 2017; Kaufman and Justeson 2003, 400). Evidence of this sort suggests that contact between Huastecan and lowland Mayan languages took place with Huastecan being nearer other Mayan languages before Huastec migrated to the north.

Terrence Kaufman favored the view that Huastecan arrived in its current location circa 4,000 year ago, when the Mesoamerican Culture Area was still being formed, and then Chicomucelteco split off much later and migrated back to the Grijalva Valley in Chiapas at circa 1100 (Kaufman 2020a, 38; also 1980, 2017). He relied primarily on nine assumed loanwords from Huastec into other languages of central and northeastern Mexico for support of this view (Kaufman 2017, 68, Kaufman and Justeson 2008, 68, 70–72). I mentioned problems with most of them in Campbell (2017a).

A case Kaufman seems to rely heavily on is Pajalat (Coahuilteco) <jat> [*xat*] 'how many?'; he assumes it was borrowed from an earlier stage of Huastecan when it was closer to Proto-Mayan *xar 'how many?', with "Pajalat [t] for Mayan [r]" before Proto-Mayan *t (i.e., *ṭ) shifted to *y* in Huastec (Huastec *xay* 'how many?') (Kaufman 2017, 62). Problems with this involve the fact that borrowing of words meaning 'how much?' are rarely ever found in other languages, particularly in the absence of a number of other loanwords to confirm that there had been contact and that lexical borrowing had taken place. The /t/ here is hardly reliable evidence of an earlier /r/ (Huastec's /y/) in the assumed donor language. Accidental similarity seems to be a stronger possibility for explaining this case.

Kaufman believed the following are borrowed from earlier Huastecan; he compared these assumed loans from other languages not directly with Huastecan words but with Proto-Mayan forms. Four of his proposed loans involve verbs, but borrowing of verbs is extremely rare in the world's languages, especially not verbs with very common meanings.

Yemé *kamaw* 'to kill' and Tarascan (Purépecha) *khamá-* 'to be finished, used up', both compared with Proto-Mayan *kam 'to die' (see Huastec *čem, čam* 'to die'), assumed to be borrowed before the change in Huastecan of *k > *č*.

Nahua *ke:ml-* (*sic*, for *ke:mi-*) 'to wear clothes' compared to Proto-Mayan *kem 'to weave'. While Kaufman and Justeson's (2003, 1023–1025) Mayan etymological dictionary has cognates of this root widely spread across other Mayan languages, it has no Huastecan cognate.

Tarascan (Purépecha) *xanhára-ni* 'to walk' (*xanhá-ri* 'road') compared to Proto-Mayan *xanh (i.e. *šaŋ) 'to walk'.

His other cases that do not involve verbs are:

Tarascan (Purépecha) *khamé-ri* 'bitter' compared with Proto-Mayan *kʼah "bitter."
Tarascan (Purépecha) *kapárhi* 'bumblebee' compared with Proto-Mayan **ka:b* 'bee, honey'.
Proto-Oto-Pamean *tzoatz7 'bat' compared with Proto-Mayan *so7tz (actually **so:ts*'; see Kaufman and Justeson 2003, 570).

Nahua *ahko* 'up' compared with Proto-Mayan *7ahq'ol* 'up, on'.

Probably all of these assumed loans are only accidentally similar to Mayan forms and not borrowed at all. There are problems with most involving the mismatch in semantics of the compared forms and with leftover sounds (unaccounted for sounds) that match no sounds of the Mayan words that are assumed to be the source of the words in the other languages, as in the assumption that Tarascan (Purépecha) *kaphari* 'bumblebee' is borrowed from Mayan **ka:b'* 'honey, bee'. Tarascan (Purépecha) is also not very close to Huastec geographically. Words for 'bitter', 'bat', and 'up', are unlikely to be borrowed, again especially if loans of other sorts are lacking to confirm that language contact had taken place. If Nahua *ahko* 'up' were borrowed, that could have taken place quite late (and **7ahq'ol* is not Proto-Mayan but rather is found in Greater Lowland Mayan languages).

These cases are not convincing. Given the evidence of later contacts with languages of the Mayan lowlands, the case for Huastecan being in Huastec territory early and then Chicomuceltec migrating back later seems unlikely. With a location of Huastecan closer to the body of other Mayan languages, for Chicomuceltec to end up where it did seems much less surprising, less of a coincidence, and does not demand a different explanation for why it got exactly there as the view of a back-migration from present-day Huastec territory would require.

Kaufman (2020, 120) hypothesized that sometime between 1200 and 1000 BCE Pre-Yucatecan speakers left the Guatemalan highlands and moved into the Petén and farther north. The Maya Lowland area was occupied before the arrival of speakers of Mayan languages, clear in the archaeological record, but there is no clue as to what their ethnolinguistic identity may have been.[26] They were all either displaced or assimilated by speakers of the immigrant Mayan languages, though they may have had an impact on the phonology and structure of the Mayan languages that ended up in the lowlands (see Kaufman 2020a, 120).

Many of the Mayan languages participated in the Huehuetenango, Lowland Mayan, or more inclusive Greater Lowland Mayan diffusion zones (contact zones, linguistic areas) (see Chapter 7).

Mixe-Zoquean (Mexico)
    Mixean[27]
        Oaxaca Mixean
            North Highland Mixe (Totontepec)
            South Highland Mixe
                Zempoaltepetl (Tlahuitoltepec, Ayutla, Tamazulapan)
                Non-Zempoaltepetl
            North Midland Mixe
            South Midland Mixe (Juquila, Cacalotepec)
            Lowland Mixe (Coatlán, Camotlán; Guichicovi; Mazatlán
    *Tapachultec[28]
    Sayula Popoluca[29]
    Oluta Popoluca[30]
    Zoquean
        Gulf Zoquean

Texistepec Zoque[31]
Ayapa[32]
Soteapan Zoque[33] (Sierra Popoluca)
Chimalapa (Oaxaca) Zoquean[34]
    Santa María Chimalapa Zoque
    San Miguel Chimalapa Zoque
Chiapas Zoquean
    North Zoque (Magdalena/Francisco León)
    Northeast Zoque
        NE Zoque A. (Tapalapa, Ocotepec, Pantepec, Rayón)
        NE Zoque B. (Chapultenango, Oxolotán)
    Central Zoque (Copainalá, Tecpatán, Ostuacán)
    South Zoque (Tuxtla Gutiérrez, Ocozocuautla)

(See Wichman 1995; Justeson and Kaufman 1993, 1704.)
  (See Map 3.2. Mixe-Zoquean languages.)

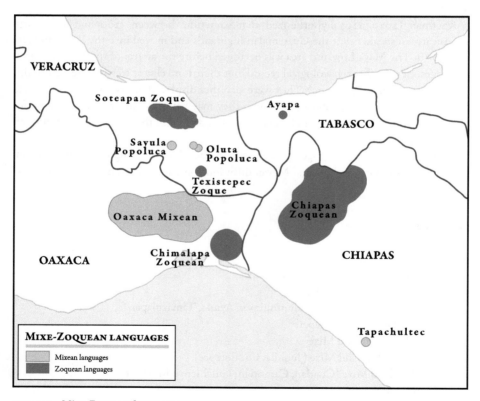

MAP 3.2. Mixe-Zoquean languages

Proto-Mixe-Zoquean had the following phonemes: /p, t, ts, k, ʔ, s, m, n, w, y, h; i, e, a, ɨ, o, u/.

The Olmec civilization appears to have been borne, at least in part, by Mixe-Zoquean speakers, Zoquean in particular (Campbell and Kaufman 1976; Kaufman 2020a; see below for more information). The Epi-Olmec writing system (fully developed by c. 400 BCE) represents an early form of Zoquean (Justeson and Kaufman 1993; 2020, 179; Kaufman and Justeson 2008). The decipherment of Epi-Olmec writing is one of the most stunning intellectual feats in the whole history of decipherments.

Terrence Kaufman (2020, 151, and elsewhere) argued that one possible model of Mixe-Zoquean diversification would not be with just the two major branches, Mixean and Zoquean, but with three, with these two and a separate Northern Mixe-Zoquean branch. He postulated this third branch based on evidence of its existence in central Mexico assumed to reflect Mixe-Zoquean influences on languages there. (See below for more on this.)

Otomanguean (Oto-Manguean)
   Western Otomanguean
      Oto-Pamean-Chinanteco
         Oto-Pamean
            Pamean (Northern Oto-Pamean)
               Chichimeco (Chichimeco, Jonaz)
               Pame
                  Northern Pame virtual language
                  Central Pame virtual language
                  *Southern Pame virtual language
            Southern Oto-Pamean
               Matlatzinca-Ocuilteco
                  Matlatzinca[35]
                  Ocuilteco (Tlahuica)[36]
               Otomían
                  Otomí language area[37]
                      Northeast Otomí emergent language
                      Northwest Otomí emergent language
                      Western Otomí emergent language
                      Tilapa Otomí emergent language
                      Ixtenco Otomí emergent language
                      *Jalisco Otomí [undocumented]
               Mazahua[38]
      Chinantecan[39]
         Ojitlán Chinanteco
         Usila Chinanteco

            Quiotepec Chinanteco
            Palantla Chinanteco
            Lalana Chinanteco
            Chiltepec Chinanteco
        Tlapanecan (Subtiaba-Tlapanec)[40] language area
            Malinaltepec Tlapaneco (Yopi) emergent language
            Azoyú Tlapaneco emergent language
            *Subtiaba[41] emergent language Nicaragua
    Eastern Otomanguean
        Manguean (Chorotegan, Chiapanec-Mangue)
            *Chiapanec[42]
            *Mangue (Chorotega) Nicaragua, Honduras
        Mazatecan-Zapotecan
            Mazatecan
                Mazatec
                    Huautla-Mazatlán Mazatec
                    Ayautla-Soyaltepec Mazatec
                    Jalapa Mazatec
                    Chiquihuitlán Mazatec
            Chochoan
                Ixcateco
                Chocho-Popoloca[43] (Ngigua)
                    Chocho emergent language
                    Northern Popoloca emergent language
                    Western Popoloca emergent language
                    Eastern Popoloca emergent language
            Zapotecan
                Chatino (Eric Campbell 2013; Sullivant 2016; Beam de Azcona 2022)
                    Teojomulcco Chatino
                    Core Chatino
                        Zenzotepec Chatino
                        Coastal Chatino
                            Tataltepec Chatino
                            Eastern Chatino
                Zapotec (Beam de Azcona 2022)
                    Soltec
                    Totomachapa Zapotec
                    Coyachilla Zapotec (dialect continuum)
                    Core Zapotec
                        Southern Zapotec
                            Coatecan
                                San Vincente Coatlán
                                Coateco

Miahuatecan
>Miahuateco Zapotec
>Yautepec Zapotec
>Amatec Zapotec
Monte Albán Zapotec
>Papabuco
>>Texmelucan Zapotec
>>Zaniza Zapotec
>>Elotepec Zapotec
>Nuclear Zapotec
>>Sierra Juárez Zapotec
>>Eastern Zapotec
>>>Cajonos Zapotec
>>>Rincón Zapotec
>>>Central Zapotec
>>>>Ayoquezco Zapotec
>>>>Etla Zapotec
>>>>Zimatlán Zapotec
>>>>Mitla Zapotec
>>>>Albarradas Zapotec
>>>>Quiatoni Zapotec
>>>>Trans-Yautepecan (dialect continuum)
>>>>Tlacolulita Zapotec
>>>>Isthmus Zapotec

Amuzgo-Mixtecan
>Amuzgo[44]
>>Guerrero Amuzgo
>>Oaxaca Amuzgo
>Mixtecan-Cuicatecan
>>Mixtec complex
>>>Central Alta Mixtec
>>>>NIC, SAMV, Ñumi, Santa María Asunción
>>>>>Tlaxiaco; (Santiago Nundichi), Santa Cruz
>>>>>Nundaco; Santo Tomás Ocotepec; San Bartolomé Yucuañe
>>>>San Agustín Tlacotepec
>>>>San Pedro Molinos; San Esteban Atatlahuca; Vera, Santa Cruz Itundujia
>>>>Santa María Yucuhiti, C Alta 14; Santiago Nuyoo
>>>>San Juan Teita; Chalcatongo de Hidalgo; San Miguel el Grande;
>>>>>Santiago Yosondu; Santa María Yolotepec
>>>>San Mateo Sindihui
>>>>San Miguel Piedras
>>>Northeast Alta Mixtec
>>>>San Pedro Tidaa

Santiago Tilantongo
Santo Domingo Nuxaa
San Juan Tamazola; Santa María Peñoles; Santiago Tlazoyaltepec; Santa Catarina Estetla; San Antonio Huitepec
San Juan Coatzospan; Santa Ana Cuauhtémoc; Cuyamecalco Villa de Zaragoza
San Pedro Jocotipac; (Ndua), Apoa; San Miguel Chicahua; Santiago Ixtaltepec; (Santa María Apasco)
San Bartolo Soyaltepec
Santiago Cacaloxtepec
North Baja Mixtec
Santa María Chigmecatitlán
Xaycatlán de Bravo; San Jerónimo Tonahuixtla; Cosoltepec; Santiago Chazumba; Tepejillo
Guadalupe Portezuelo/Villahermosa
South Baja Mixtec
ZAH, TamS, Nuch, YUCT, Aten, Ahue, SilM, IxpN, TIN, Cahuatachi-Cahuatache; Santos Reyes Tepejillo; Santiago Juxtlahuaca; Metlatónoc
San Martín Peras; Coicoyán de las Flores
Cuatzoquitengo
Santa María Yucunicoco; San Juan Mixtepec
Tepango
Coast Mixtec
Santa María Zacatepec
Santiago Ixtayutla
San Cristóbal; San Agustín Chayuco; San Agustín Chayuco; San Agustín Chayuco; Santa Catarina Mechoacán
San Francisco de Asís Sayultepec, Costa; San Antonio Tepetlapa; San Pedro Atoyac; San Juan Colorado; San Lorenzo; Pinotepa De Don Luís; San Pedro Jicayán; Santa María Jicaltepec; Santa María Huazolotitlán; Santiago Jamiltepec
Santa María Acatepec; San Pedro Tututepec
Amoltepec Mixtec (AMOL)
Cuicatec[45]
Trique
San Juan Copala Trique
San Martín Itunyoso Trique
San Andrés-Santo Domingo Chicahuaxstla Trique

(This classification of Otomanguean languages is based primarily on Kaufman 2015c, 2020, 2021. The classification of the Zapotec languages here relies from Beam de Azcona 2022. See also Eric Campbell 2017 and Lillehaugen 2020.)

(See Map 3.3. Branches of the Otomanguean language family. See also Map 7.8.)

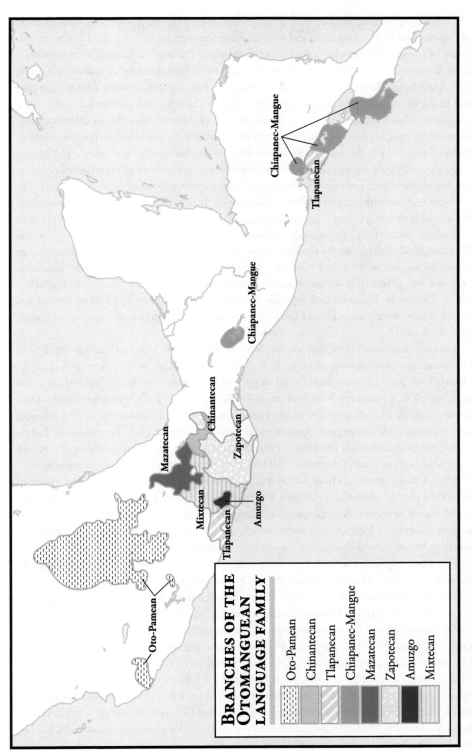

MAP 3.3. Branches of the Otomanguean language family

There is no general agreement on how many Otomanguean languages there are. Classification of Zapotec and Mixtec languages and varieties has been particularly complicated. The classification of Mixtec relies on what is used in the *Catalogue of Endangered Languages* (at www.endangeredlanguages.com). There is considerable uncertainty and diversity of opinion regarding how many distinct languages versus non-independent dialects there are in the Zapotec complex and in the Mixtec complex, and about how to classify the relationships internal to these two complexes. This is also true to a lesser extent of some of the other branches of Otomanguean. Fortunately, progress has been made recently in unraveling the classification complications of Zapotec, especially in the work of Rosemary Beam de Azcona (2022) and others. The Mixtec languages and varieties given here mostly do not have distinct names and are reflected rather by a listing of the various towns or locations where each variety is spoken.[46]

Otomanguean is the largest, oldest, and most widespread language family in Mesoamerica. Relationships among Otomanguean languages were discovered gradually over time. Hervás y Panduro (1800–1805) had already correctly recognized the relationship among Otomí, Mazahua, and Chichimec. By the late 1960s the relatedness of most of the Otomanguean languages to one another had been established (see Rensch 1976), and finally Tlapanec-Subtiaba was definitively demonstrated to belong to Otomanguean (Rensch 1977; Suárez 1986). Previously Tlapanec and Subtiaba had generally been considered to be part of the large but now mostly abandoned Hokan hypothesis (Sapir 1925a) (see Chapter 6 for discussion of Hokan).[47]

Terrence Kaufman's (to appear, see also Kaufman 1988) reconstruction of Proto-Otomanguean phonemes is: /p, t, ts, k, k^w, ʔ, θ, s, x, x^w, h, l, m, n, w, y; i, e, a, o, o, ia, ea, ai, au/. The *p is extremely rare, found in only eight or nine cognates; Chinantecan is the only branch that preserves *p distinct from *k^w. Reconstruction of Otomanguean tones was not attempted, though several Otomanguean languages are infamous for having complex tone systems; all Otomanguean languages are tonal.[48] Kaufman (1988) reconstructed some twenty-seven grammatical markers to Proto-Otomanguean, involving tense, aspect, mood, voice, and nominalization, together with how they fit in the Otomanguean subgroups.

Some Otomangueanists have believed that Otomanguean reconstruction is so advanced as to rival that of Indo-European (see, for example, Longacre 1968, 333), though this view is not shared by others. For example, Eric Campbell (2017) holds that Otomanguean is the language family of Mesoamerica about which the least is known, because of the extensive diversity and structural complexity among its languages.

The Otomanguean homeland has been assumed to be around the Tehuacán Valley, in the state of Puebla, where speakers of Proto-Otomanguean were involved in the early development of agriculture in Mesoamerica (Eric Campbell 2017; Kaufman 2015c), though that homeland is not certain. Terrence Kaufman (2020, 112) gave the date of 3000–1500 BCE for when, in his view, Otomanguean spread out through the Tehuacán Valley, the Valley of Puebla, Oaxaca, Morelos, Guerrero, the Balsas basin, and the basin of Mexico and diversified into its eight principal branches. Earlier, he had given Otomanguean a time depth of circa 6,000 years (Kaufman 2006, 819). He dated the beginnings of Mixtec diversification at 500 CE (p. 205) and the diversification of Zapotec to after 500 CE (p. 186). He believed that at 1200 CE Subtiaba of Nicaragua and Tlapanec of Guerrero Mexico separated, Otomí began to diversify, Matlatzinca-Ocuilteco split into Matlazinca and Ocuilteco, and Chocho-Popoloca began to diversify (p. 228).

Both Zapotec and Mixtec had pre-Columbian writing systems, important in Mesoamerican prehistory. There are a large number of texts in and on many of the Otomanguean languages written during the colonial period.

There have not been many proposals of broader connections for Otomanguean. Swadesh (1959) thought Huave belonged with Otomanguean, a proposal accepted earlier by several scholars but now essentially abandoned. Joseph Greenberg (1987) grouped Otomanguean (aside from Subtiaba-Tlapanec, which he put with "Hokan") together with "Aztec-Tanoan" in the "Central Amerind" branch of his "Amerind." His proposed affiliations have not been accepted by other scholars. Terrence Kaufman (2015a, 2; 2015b, 1) thought that potentially Otomanguean and Hokan might be related (see Chapter 6).

Uto-Aztecan

For the Uto-Aztecan family in general, see Chapter 2. See Chapter 5 for the long list of names identified in colonial sources from northern Mexico that are often thought to represent extinct Uto-Aztecan languages about which little if anything is known. Here, I address only further details that pertain to the languages of the Nahua (Aztecan) branch, the only branch of Uto-Aztecan squarely situated within Mesoamerica. (See Maps 2.7 and 7.8.)

The evidence that sound changes Cora-Huichol and Nahua (Aztecan) belong together in a subgroup is clear, based on several shared sound changes (see Chapter 2).

There are differing views of the internal classification of the Nahua branch, and the position of **Pipil** (Nawat) of Central America within Nahua in particular has been subject to different interpretation. It is certain that the Nahua subfamily (also called Aztecan) first split up into **Pochutec** and **General Nahua**, the latter comprising all the other Nahua languages and varieties excluding Pochutec. I believe that there is good evidence that Pipil (Nawat) is distinct from the other varieties in General Nahua, although not all other classifications agree. Opinions also vary widely on how many languages there are in the General Nahua branch, and about how they are classified. I believe the most accurate classification of these languages probably is:

Nahua
  *Pochutec[49]
  General Nahua
    Pipil (Nawat)
    Nahua main branch
      Central Nahua
      Peripheral Nahua
        Western Group
        Eastern Group

Central Nahua has the varieties: **Huasteca, North Puebla, Valley of Mexico, Morelos, Tlaxcala, Central Puebla**, and **Central Guerrero**. The Western Group of Peripheral Nahua includes the varieties: **Jalisco, Colima, Durango; Michoacán; Almomoloa;** and **North Guerrero**. The Eastern Group of Peripheral Nahua has the varieties: **Sierra de Puebla, East Puebla, South Guerrero**, and **Isthmus**. (See Canger 1988; see also Lastra 1986.)

Terrence Kaufman's (2003, 3; 2020, 23) classification is somewhat different:

Nawan
  Pochuteko
  General Nawa
    Eastern Nawa
      Pipil; Gulf/Isthmus
      Sierra de Puebla; Huasteca
    Central-Western Nawa
      Central Nawa (Valleys of Mexco-Morelos-Puebla; Tlaxcala; C[entral Guerrero]; SE Puebla)
      Western Nawa (Toluca; N Guerrero; SE Guerrero; Michoacán; Guadalajara; Durango)

There are varieties in Veracruz and Tabasco, Mexico, that are sometimes also called "Pipil." Some of them share some linguistic features with the Pipil (Nawat) of Central America. Confusion over this name has sometimes complicated the classification of Nahua.[50] Several scholars have held that Pipil (Nawat) is just a dialect belonging to the Eastern Group of Peripheral Nahua, linked with southern varieties in Veracruz and Tabasco. Comparison of traits in Chart 3.1 shows that Pipil cannot be assigned to the Peripheral group because it shares many traits considered diagnostic in the classification of Nahua both with the Central group and with the Peripheral group. Chart 3.1 marks with a tick (✓) the traits Pipil shares with either Central or Peripheral varieties. As is abundantly clear from this list, it does not align clearly with either group, but shares some traits with one and other traits with the other.

CHART 3.1

Pipil (Nawat) traits shared with Central and with Peripheral Nahua groups

Central Nahua	Peripheral Nahua
✓ Initial *e-* (as in *e-tl* 'bean')	Initial *ye-* (as in *ye-tl* 'bean')
✓ *mochi* 'all'	*nochi* 'all'
totoltetl 'egg'	✓ *teksistli* 'egg'
tesi 'grind'	✓ *tisi* 'grind'
✓ *-h/-ʔ* 'plural suffix on verbs'	*-lo* 'plural suffix on verbs'
	(Pipil has *-t*; all others changed *-t* to *-h/-ʔ*)
-tin 'main plural suffix on nouns'	✓ *-meh/ʔ* 'main plural suffix on nouns'
	(Pipil *-met*)
o- 'past' prefix	✓ 'past' (no prefix)
-nki/-wki 'past participle' forms	✓ *-nik/-wik* 'past participle' forms
✓ *tiltik* 'black'	*yayawik* 'black'
-ki 'agent noun suffix'	✓ *-ket(l)/-kat(l)* 'agent noun suffix'

In one trait, Pipil (Nawat) preserves earlier -*t* 'plural of nouns' while all varieties of Central Nahua share an innovation of *-*t* to -*ʔ* or to -*h*—that is, they and Pipil once shared -*t* for this trait and then later the other varieties change the original -*t* to something else (-*ʔ* or -*h*). This should be sufficient to demonstrate that Pipil was separated already when the ancestor of the other varieties changed, leaving their descendants sharing this innovation, not shared by Pipil. (See Campbell 1985, 6–13, 911–942.) The fact that Pipil shares nearly an equal number of the diagnostic traits with Central Nahua as it does with Peripheral Nahua also suggests that it cannot reliably be assigned to either of these branches. Most of these shared traits are things Pipil retains from Proto-Nahua, not shared innovations that would allow it to be subgrouped with other varieties that also share the retentions.

Terrence Kaufman (2003, 1) argued persuasively that "linguistic facts preclude the presence of Nawa [Nahua] in the Valley of Mexico before 500 CE" (see also Kaufman 2020a, 21). He calculated that Nahua split between Pochutec and General Nawa at 500 CE, with General Nawa starting to diversify in Central Mexico at about 900 CE (Kaufman 2003, 5).

Totonacan (Totonac-Tepehua) (Mexico)
    Proto-Totonac
        Sierra Totonac
        Papantla Totonac
        Northern Totonac
        Misantla Totonac
    Proto-Tepehua[51]
        Tlachichilco Tepehua
        Pisaflores Tepehua
        Huehuetla Tepehua

(Mackay and Trechsel 2018, 54. See Beck 2014 for a different classification.)
(See Map 7.8.)

Totonacan languages are spoken in the Mexican states of northwestern Veracruz, northern Puebla, and southern Hidalgo. At the time of first European contact, Totonacan languages were also spoken along the Gulf coast.

The Totonac languages are closely related to one another, as are the Tepehua languages to each other. Mackay and Trechsel (2018, 54) list the following as the varieties of the Totonacan languages. **Sierra Totonac** has Zapotitlán, Coatepec, Huehuetla (Chilocoyo del Carmen), Caxhuacan, and Ozelonacaxlta. **Papantla Totonac** has El Escolín, El Tajín, El Carbón, and Papantla. **Northern Totonac** varieties are Apapantilla, Patla, Chicontla, Cacahuatlán, Filomeno Mata, San Pedro, and Tlaolantongo. **Misantla Totonac** members are Yecuatla, San Marcos Atexquilapan, and Jilotepec. For **Tlachichilco Tepehua** there are Tlachichilco, Tierra Colorada, Chintipán, and Tecomajapa. **Pisaflores Tepehua** has Pisaflores, El Tepetate, San Pedro Tziltzacuapan, and San José del Salto. Finally, **Huehuetla Tepehua** varieties are Huehuetla (Hidalgo), Barrio Aztlán, Linda Vista (Mirasol), and Mecapalapa (Puebla).

Mackay and Trechsel (2018, 60) reconstruct Proto-Totonacan phonemes as: /p, t, ts, č, k, q, ʔ, p', t', ts', č', k', q', tl, tl', s, š, ɬ, l, m, n, w, y, h, i, a, u, vowel length/.

The most debated issue in Proto-Totonacan phonology is whether the proto language had glottalized (ejective) consonants or so-called glottalized (laryngealized) vowels. Tepehua has glottalized consonants (C'V(C)) that correspond in most environments to Totonac forms with glottal stop in CVʔ(C) —the so-called glottalized vowels. Mackay and Trechsel (2018, 52) argue that the proto language did not have contrastive laryngealized vowels, but rather had contrasting sets of glottalized and non-glottalized stops and affricates. In their analysis the contrast between so-called laryngealized (or glottalized) vowels and plain vowels in the Totonac languages "is a consequence of the diachronic spreading of the laryngeal feature Constricted Glottis [CG] associated with glottalized stops and affricates in Proto-Totonac-Tepehua to adjacent vowel nuclei." They demonstrate "that the reconstruction of a series of glottalized stops and affricates in PTT [Proto-Totonac-Tepehua], and not a series of laryngealized vowels, affords the simplest and most straightforward account of the phonological developments that characterize the linguistic prehistory of the Totonac-Tepehua language family."

Terrence Kaufman (2020, 175) dated the split up of Totonacan into Totonac and Tepehua at 600 BCE.

Totonacan has quite complicated word formation, and this has led to speculation concerning its possible broader relationships, without any definitive results. Totonacan has most often been placed with Mayan and Mixe-Zoquean in a grouping called Macro-Mayan (McQuown 1942, 1956a). While some aspects of this hypothesis are attractive, it remains inconclusive and requires much more investigation (see Chapter 6).

Brown et al. (2011) proposed that the Totonacan languages are genetically related to the Mixe-Zoquean languages and presented a reconstruction of what they refer to as Proto-Totozoquean. Brown et al. (2014) go further and suggest that their Proto-Totozoquean construct is also related to Chitimacha, a dormant language isolate of Louisiana. Both the proposed Totozoquean and the wider connection with Chitimacha are seriously flawed and thus cannot be embraced. (See Chapter 6 for details.)

Ethnohistorical accounts and loanword evidence suggest the Totonacs as the strongest candidates for the builders of Teotihuacan, the most influential Mesoamerican city in its day (200–650 CE). This inference is supported by a small but significant number of Totonacan loanwords in Lowland Mayan languages, Nahuatl, and other Mesoamerican languages (Justeson et al. 1985; Kaufman 2020a). In spite of a frequently voiced opinion, Teotihuacan was not built by Nahua speakers. Nahua speakers' arrival in Mesoamerica was not earlier than 500 BCE and comes closer to the fall of Teotihuacan than to its rise.

For more on Totonac's role in the linguistic prehistory of Mesoamerica, see below.

Tequistlatecan (Chontal of Oaxaca, Oaxaca Chontal) Mexico
    Huamelultec (Lowland Chontal)
    Highland Chontal (Highland Oaxaca Chontal)
    *Tequistlatec proper

(See Turner 1969; Waterhouse 1969; Campbell 1997a, 160.)
(See Map 7.8.)

Tequistlatecan is often called "Chontal of Oaxaca," but this should not be confused with Chontal of Tabasco, a Mayan language. For that reason, many linguists prefer to use the name Tequistlatec(an). Viola Waterhouse (1985), however, recommends that Tequistlatec be used only to refer to the language of Madgalena Tequisistlán and that Oaxaca Chontal be reserved for the family name, although the family name is most often now given as Tequistlatecan. Whatever name is used, it is important to recognize the third language, Tequistlatec (proper), that is often neglected, which was described briefly by De Angulo and Freeland (1925) and by Waterhouse (1985).

Huamelultec (a.k.a. Huamelultec Chontal, Lowland Chontal) is spoken in San Pedro Huamelula, Oaxaca. **Tequistlatec** was spoken in Tequisistlán, Oaxaca, until recently; it is now dormant. **Highland Chontal** is spoken in the mountains, la Sierra de Oaxaca.

The Proto-Tequistlatecan phonemic inventory has been reconstructed with the following phonemes: /p, t, ts, k, ʔ, b, d, g, f', tl', ts', k', ɬ, s, h, l, m, n, w, y, W, N, i, e, a, o, u/ (Turner 1969; Waterhouse 1969). The sounds *W* and *N* are voiceless and can perhaps be analyzed as clusters of *hw* and *hn*, respectively, instead of as separate phonemes (Campbell 1997a, 160).

Daniel Brinton (1891) suggested that Yuman, Seri, and Tequistlatec were genetically related. Alfred Kroeber (1915) accepted this proposal and included them in the Hokan hypothesis. This has been the subject of controversy. Paul Turner (1967, 1972) argued against the proposed Hokan affiliation for Tequistlatecan, and Bright (1970) argued against Turner's methods and thus implicitly for the possibility of the Hokan connection. Campbell and Oltrogge (1980) see promising but inconclusive prospects for a possible genetic relationship between Tequistlatecan and Jicaquean, though they believe the broader Hokan proposal for these two language families is not supported. The Hokan hypothesis in general is mostly rejected (see Chapter 6).

Xinkan Guatemala

Xinkan is a small family of four languages formerly spoken in southeastern Guatemala. They are not especially closely related, differing from one another on the order of Germanic languages. All four of the languages are in effect dormant, though until recently there has been one or two semi-speakers of Guazacapán and one of Jumaytepeque. (See Map 7.8.)

Xinkan (Xincan)
 *Guazacapán (West Xinkan)
 *Chiquimulilla[52] (South Xinkan)
 Northeast Xinka
     *Jumaytepeque[53] (North Xinkan)
     *Yupiltepeque (East Xinkan) (includes Jutiapa, Yupiltepeque)

(See Rogers 2010, 2016, 2022.)

The Proto-Xinkan phoneme inventory is /p, t, č, k, ʔ, p', t', ts', č', k', s, š, h, ɬ, l', r, r', m, m', n, n', w, w', y, y'; i, ɨ, u, e, o, a, vowel length/ (Rogers 2010, 142; 2022, 21). Terrence Kaufman's (2020, 125) reconstruction is nearly the same: / p, t, tl, č, k, ʔ, p', t', tl', ts', č', k', s, š, x, ɬ (or l), l', r, r', m, m', n, n', w, w', y, y'; i, ɨ, u, e, o, a, vowel length/. Notably, Xinkan languages all have glottalized resonants as well as glottalized (ejective) stops and affricates, and nearly all have voiceless "l" ([ɬ]).

Terrence Kaufman (2020, 210) gave the date of 800 CE for the beginning of Xinkan diversification.

The territory of Xinkan languages was once apparently considerably larger than the corner of southeastern Guatemala where it is documented. Colonial accounts report that "Xinka" predomined in Jalapa and Pinula, though Poqomam was also spoken there at the time and came to be the only language of those places. Strong evidence of Xinka's more imposing geography in the past comes from toponyms of Xinkan origin found in the region from near Guatemala City to the Motagua River Valley and the borders of El Salvador and Honduras. Some examples are: (San Pedro) *Ayampuc* (near Guatemala City) (< *a:y-* 'place of' + *ampuki* 'snake'; the archaeological zone of Ayampuc is on a winding ridge in the shape of a snake); *Ayarza* (with *a:y-* 'place of'); *Ipala* (< *ipaʔla* 'bath'; the Ipala Volcano has a crater lake); *Sanarate* (*šan* 'in, place of' + *arat'ak* 'century plant'); *Sanjaje* (< *šan* 'in, place of' + *hahi* 'avocado', equal to the Nahuatl name of *Aguacat(l)án*, from *a:waka-* 'avocado' + *-tla:n* 'place of').

Others with *šan* 'in, place of' include: Sansare, Sansur, Sansirisay, Sanguayaba, Cerro Sansuque, Sanyoyo, Sansupo, Sanjomo, Sansurutate, Sampaquisoy, and Sancash (< *šan* 'in, place of' + *kaš* 'bat', equal to the Nahuatl name Zinacantán, from *tsina:kan* 'bat' + *-tla:n* 'place of'), and Sashico (with *-n* of *šan* lost before certain consonants). Some others are: Alzatate (San Carlos Alzatate, < *al-* 'at, in', later a Poqomam-speaking town), and so on.

There are other toponyms that J. Eric S. Thompson (1970, 98–99) associated with his "*agua* people," based on place names that ended in *-agua, -ahua*, or *-hua*, which he assumed belonged to a non-Mayan group that was displaced by the invasion of lowland Maya (Ch'orti'). Many of these names turn out to be from Xinka *šawɨ* 'town'. The retroflex fricative /š/ explains the cases written with *s, x, j* (from Old Spanish <x> /š/), *ch*, and *r* (retroflex fricatives have an r-like quality to European ears). The following appear to incorporate this Xinka term for 'town': Xagua, Jaguar, Eraxagua (< *ɨra* 'big' + *šawɨ* 'town', i.e., 'big town'), Pasasagua (compare Xinka *šan-pasaʔ* 'Pasaco'), and Sasagua (< *ša-šawɨ* 'in-town'), Conchagua, Comasahua, Manzaragua, Anshagua, Anshigua, Xororagú, and so on.

None of these names has a Mayan or Nahua etymology, and the Xinkan origin is clear for many of them. (See Campbell 1978b, 1997b.) Xinkan and Lencan were often assumed to be related to one another, but the evidence does not support this, and the hypothesis has been abandoned (see Chapter 6).

Xinkan provides a telling exception to the claims of the farming/language dispersal model (Bellwood 1997; Renfrew 1994, 2000). That model sees farming dispersals, the expansion of populations of agriculturalists, as responsible for the dispersal of the languages of many of the world's language families, with agriculturalists pushing out or assimilating their non-agriculturalists neighbors and their languages. However, nearly all Xinkan terms for cultigens are borrowed from Mayan languages (cf. Campbell 1972b, 1997b), showing that Xinkan speakers acquired agriculture from their Mayan neighbors but maintained their identity and language in face of Mayan agriculture, not being swallowed up by their large agriculturalist neighbors as predicted by the model.

Purépecha (Tarascan)

Purépecha is spoken in the highlands of Michoacán state in Mexico. Lake Pázcuaro was the center of the pre-Columbian Tarascan State and is still today an important center for Purépecha speakers. (See Map 7.8.) Though Purépecha (Tarascan) is generally considered a language isolate, it has several different dialects. Paul Friedrich (1971) applied the comparative method to these dialects to arrive at a reconstruction of an earlier stage of the language—a very valuable procedure for obtaining historical information about language isolates. *Ethnologue* 2023, however, considers Tarascan to be a small language family of two languages, Purepecha and Western Highland Purepecha. The former is spoken around Pátzcuaro, the latter in the vicinity of the Parícutin volcano (around Zamora, Los Reyes de Salgado, Paracho de Verduzco, and Pamatácuaro).[54]

Claudine Chamoreau (in press) argues that Purépecha, though in Mesoamerican territory, shares fewer linguistic traits of the Mesoamerican Linguistic Area than other Mesoamerican languages; she considers it a non-Mesoamerican language (see Chapter 7 for discussion of this).

There have been a few attempts, all unsuccessful, to demonstrate a linguistic kinship between Purépecha and other languages. For example, Morris Swadesh's (1966) proposal of a relationship between Mayan and Tarascan failed (see Campbell 1997a, 224–226 for evaluation of the data). Swadesh (1967a) also proposed a Tarascan-Quechua connection, again based on very limited evidence, exhibiting methodological flaws in the extreme (Campbell 1997a, 325–326). Joseph Greenberg (1987, 106–107) included Tarascan as a member of his putative Chibchan-Paezan phylum (a division of his grand "Amerind" macro-family), which also included other groups scattered from Florida to South America. Very little evidence was presented for the grouping and it has numerous methodological shortcomings (see Campbell 1997a, 176).

*Cuitlatec (Cuitlateco) Mexico

Cuitlatec is a dormant language isolate,[55] formerly spoken in San Miguel Totolapan, Guerrero. Juana Can, who died in the 1960s, was the last known native speaker of the language (Escalante Hernández 1962). (See Map 7.8.)

Very little is known about the history of Cuitlatec (see Heaton 2018). There have been a number of proposals attempting to link it to other language families. Walter Lehmann (1920) thought that Cuitlatec and Tlapanec belonged to a "Californian group," which he believed also contained a number of other languages, but he provided no significant evidence. Roberto Weitlaner (1936–1939) considered possible similarities with Otomían languages. Harvey Lemley (1949) repeated the notion that Cuitlatec and Tlapanec might be related. Pedro Hendrichs Pérez (1947, 137–139) proposed that Cuitlatec might be related to Mayan. There is scarcely any worthwhile evidence for any of these hypotheses. Arana Osnaya (1958) compared Cuitlatec to several languages of the Americas in a glottochronological study; her results indicated that Cuitlatec is not closely related to any of the languages she considered, though she speculated that it might be related at a very deep time depth to Nahuatl and

Paya (Pech, now known to belong to the Chibchan family) (Arana Osnaya 1958, 563). This claim, however, has not been accepted, and indeed, most linguists reject glottochronology as invalid. (For a critique of proposed affiliations of Cuitlatec with other languages, see Heaton 2018.)

Huave

Huave is a language isolate, with four principal dialects spoken on the Pacific coast of the Isthmus of Tehuantepec in Oaxaca, Mexico: **San Francisco del Mar**, **San Mateo del Mar**, **San Dionisio del Mar**, and **Santa María del Mar**. (See Map 7.8.) There is mutual intelligibility among the dialects, though speakers from San Francisco del Mar report that "reliable mutual intelligibility with San Mateo del Mar requires significant exposure" (Kim 2008, 3). Yuni Kim (2008, 3) sees the difference between San Mateo del Mar and the other varieties as "perhaps comparable to that between standard spoken Swedish and standard spoken Danish." She notes that "the San Dionisio del Mar dialect is most similar to San Mateo, while the Santa María del Mar dialect bears the most affinities to San Francisco (although its geographical proximity to San Mateo has resulted in influence from that dialect as well" (p. 3). Jorge Suárez (1975) applied internal reconstruction and the comparative method to these four main Huave dialects and reconstructed Proto-Huave. His Proto-Huave phonemic inventory contains: /p, t, c [ts], k, kʷ, mb, nd, nc [nts], ng, gʷ, s, l, r̃, (w), (r), (y), h, (d); i, e, a, ɨ, o, u, tonal contrast (high, low), vowel length/. Segments in parentheses are uncertain and may be eliminated in future work. The *d* is found in only two cognate sets; the *o* was found in only seven cases; Suarez reconstructed two *r* sounds but suggests that there was probably only one in the proto language and that the two were conditioned variants. The tonal contrast exists only in penultimate syllables and is seen fully only in San Mateo, though Suárez thought there was some residue of it reflected in final consonants of other dialects. Since Huave tone has a low functional load, its historical source may also ultimately be explained, eliminating it from Proto-Huave.

Suárez's application of the comparative method to the dialects, along with internal reconstruction, is another significant example, along with Friedrich's (1971) of Purépecha (Tarascan), of what can be done to increase understanding of the history of language isolates, important since it is often claimed that language isolates have no history (see Campbell 2018b).

A number of proposals have tried to relate Huave to other languages, but none has proven well founded. They include proposed kinship with Mixe-Zoquean, Mexican Penutian, Otomanguean, Algonquian, "Gulf" languages, and Uralic. (See Campbell 1997a; see Chapter 6.)

3.2.2. NON-MESOAMERICAN LANGUAGE FAMILIES OF MIDDLE AMERICA

As mentioned, some languages of the Algonquian, Arawakan, Chibchan, and Chocoan language families that extend into the region are discussed in other chapters. **Garífuna**, formerly called Black Carib, spoken in Belize and Guatemala, and to some extent also in Honduras and Nicaragua, is an Arawakan language, with its relatives in South America. It is a late arrival to Central America from the Caribbean. It does not share most of the areal linguistic traits of Mesoamerican languages (but see more in Chapter 7). **Kickapoo** is an Algonquian language. There are speakers in the Mexican state of Coahuila, on reservations in Kansas, and in communities near McLoud, Oklahoma, and Eagle Pass, Texas (see Chapter 2).

Discussion of the other non-Mesoamerican families of Middle America follows.

***Guaicurian** (Waikurian) (?)
  *Guaicura (Waikurí)
  *Pericú
  *Monqui (Monqui-Didiu)
  Perhaps *Uchití (Huchití)

(See Massey 1949; Robles Uribe 1964; Zamponi in press a.)
(See Map 2.1.)

Several now long-dormant languages were spoken on the southern end of the Baja California peninsula. Several of them have been classified at least tentatively as members of the Guaicurian family, although Raoul Zamponi (in press a) argues that Guaicura should be considered an unclassified language (see below). Unfortunately, of the putative Guaicurian languages, only **Guaicura** (Waikuri) has any appreciable attestation. On the basis of mostly non-linguistic information and the observations of similarities and differences among them reported in colonial documents without supporting examples, it is typically assumed that essentially unattested **Pericú** and **Monqui** (Monqui-Didiu) are related to Guaicura, members of the hypothesized Guaicurian family. Some scholars would add also **Uchití** (Huchití), another essentially unattested language, though it may have been just a variant of Guaicura itself.

Guaicura (Guicuri, Waikuri) was spoken in the area of the San Luis Gonzaga mission, in the interior of Baja California between Loreto and La Paz and south across the Magdalena Plain to the coast. The extant attestations consist of translations of the Lord's Prayer, the twelve articles of the Apostles' Creed, a verb paradigm, and a few other words recorded by Alsatian Jesuit Johan Jakob Baegert (1771), who served at the San Luis Gonzaga mission. Raoul Zamponi (in press a) notes that different points of view are possible, that this documentation "may be considered sufficient to determine that Waikuri [Guaicura] is an isolate or too scant to make such a determination, leaving the language unclassified." However, he states further that "the grammatical morphemes and properties we can extract from the documentation of Waikuri are also not suggestive of a relationship with any other attested language, and a conclusion that can legitimately be drawn based on them (and the lack of lexical similarities with other languages) is that Waikuri is a language isolate."

Pericú was spoken at the southern tip of Baja California, in the mountains around the mission of San José del Cabo, on the southeastern coast between Santiago and La Paz, and on islands off the east coast. The Jesuit missionaries said it was different from Guacura (Waikuri). Unfortunately, it is attested in only eleven words, taken down by seafarers/explorers in 1632 and 1638 and by a Jesuit missionary in 1721. None of the eleven appears similar to words with corresponding meanings in any of the other languages of Baja California (León-Portilla 1976; Zamponi in press a).

Monqui (Monqui-Didiu) was spoken in a small area on the east coast of the Baja California peninsula around the missions at Loreto and San Juan Bautista Malibat. It is attested in only six nouns and one sentence from 1702 and in some place names. Raoul Zamponi (in press a) concluded that "any possible relationship of Monqui to other languages and language families can only be speculative and not supported by the available data."

Uchití (Huchití) was spoken by groups in the rough uplands of the southern Sierra de La Giganta, on the shores of the Gulf from La Paz to Las Palmas, and on the northern and western slopes of the Sierra de la Laguna (Zamponi in press a). Donald Laylander (1997, 28) argued based on geography, but against some colonial observations, that "recognition of a distinct Huchití language [different from Waikuri] is not warranted."

Jicaquean Honduras
  Tol (Eastern Jicaque)
  *Jicaque of el Palmar (Western Jicaque)

There are two Jicaquean languages. Dormant Jicaque of El Palmar (Western Jicaque) is known only from a short vocabulary published in Membreño (1897, 195–196, 233–242), reprinted in Lehmann (1920, 654–668). Tol (Eastern Jicaque) is spoken in La Montaña de Flor, near Orica, Honduras, and was spoken until recently in the department of Yoro, Honduras. (See Map 7.8.)

Proto-Jicaque phonology, as reconstructed by Campbell and Oltrogge (1980), has the phonemic inventory: /p, t, c, k, pʰ, tʰ, cʰ, kʰ, p', t', c', k', ɪ, m, n, w, y, h; i, e, ɨ, a, o, u/.

The two Jicaquean languages are not particularly closely related, perhaps on the order of English and Swedish to each other. Jicaque(an) has often been included in the Hokan hypothesis, following Greenberg and Swadesh (1953), though the evidence presented for that was scanty and unpersuasive. Campbell and Oltrogge (1980) presented a few possible cognates and possible sound correspondences suggestive of a possible genetic relationship with Tequistlatecan. This hypothesis is suggestive and merits further investigation, though it is not at present compelling. The possibility of a connection between Jicaquean and Subtiaba (including also Tequistlatecan), put forward by Oltrogge (1977), does not have persuasive support (see Campbell 1979a; Campbell and Oltrogge 1980). Granberry and Vescelius (2004,28–31) speculated that Ciguayo of the Antilles may have Jicaquean connections, but based on only two words of dubious interpretation.

*Lencan
  *Chilanga (Salvadoran Lenca)
  *Honduran Lenca

The small Lencan family has two languages, Honduran Lenca and Salvadoran Lenca, also known as Chilanga, named for the principal town in which it was spoken. Lencan is located just outside the Mesoamerican Linguistic Area. Both languages are dormant. Honduran

Lenca was spoken with some dialect differences in Intibuca, Opatoro, Guajiquiro, Similatón (modern Cabañas), and Santa Elena. (See Map 7.8.) The documentation on both of these languages is limited, most of it reprinted in Lehmann (1920). There appears to be more available on Chilanga and less on Honduran Lenca; in spite of that, Alan King (2017) was able to produce an impressive sketch grammar of Honduran Lenca based on the extant though limited corpus.

The two languages are not closely related. Morris Swadesh (1967a, 98–99) calculated thirty minimum centuries of divergence. Gilda Arguedas Cortés (1987) reconstructed Proto-Lencan with: /p, t, k, p', t', c', k', s, l, r, w, y; i, e, a, o, u/. Terrence Kaufman (2020, 123) listed Proto-Lencan sounds as /p, t, k, p', t', ts', č', k', s, š, l, ɬ, r, m, n, w, y; i, e, a, o, u/.

The Lencan homeland was probably in central Honduras. Salvadoran Lenca speakers were responsible for the archaeological site of Classic Quelepa in El Salvador. Terrence Kaufman (2020, 128) dates the break-up of Lencan into its two branches at 1000 BCE.

There have been numerous hypotheses attempting to classify Lencan in broader groupings (see Chapter 6). Walter Lehmann's (1920, 727) proposal that joins Xinkan and Lencan has often been repeated though is now abandoned (Campbell 1978a; 1979, 961–962; see Chapter 6 for details).

Misumalpan
    Miskito (Mísquito) Honduras, Nicaragua[56]
    Sumo-Matagalpa-Cacaopera
        Sumo (Sumu) Honduras, Nicaragua
            Ulwa (Southern Sumu)
            Mayangna (Northern Sumu)
        *Cacaopera-Matagalpan
            *Cacaopera[57] El Salvador
            *Matagalpa[58] Nicaragua

(Hale and Salamanca 2002, 34)

Miskito is the most divergent of the Misumalpan languages. **Sumo** has considerable dialect diversity; it includes varieties called **Tawahka, Panamaka, Ulua, Bawihka,** and **Kukra**, among others. Most scholars today consider Sumo a language complex with two separate but closely related languages: **Mayangna** (Northern Sumo) and **Ulwa** (Southern Sumo) (Hale and Salamanca 2002). Sumo diversity has been supposed by some to be as great as that between German and Dutch. Hale and Salamanca (2002, 34) report that "of a sample of a hundred basic vocabulary items, Northern and Southern Sumu share [only] between 61 and 71 percent." Twahka and Panamahka are clearly sister dialects of a single language, Mayangna (Northern Sumu). Hale and Salamanca (2002, 34) say of the Northern and Southern branches of Sumu that "there are certain systematic morphosyntactic differences between them whose cumulative effect is substantial enough to impede easy mutual intelligibility. A learning period of some months would be required in order for a Northern Sumu speaker to acquire a reasonable command of Southern Sumu" (Hale and Salamanca 2002, 34).

Cacaopera and **Matagalpa** are very closely related, though separated by considerable distance geographically, about 400 kilometers. Cacaopera and Matagalpa together have been called **Matagalpan** (Brinton 1895) and were sometimes thought to be dialects of a single language, although they are clearly separate languages. An unresolved question is how Cacaopera, spoken in El Salvador, so closely related to Matagalpa in Nicaragua, came to be so separated geographically from the other Misumalpan languages, whose center of gravity seems to be in northern Nicaragua?

That the Misumalpan languages constitute a language family has long been recognized, though rigorous historical linguistic study is still needed (see Campbell 1975a, 1975b, 1976; Constenla Umaña 1987). The branches of the family are not closely related; Morris Swadesh (1959; 1967a, 89) calculated, on the basis of glottochronology, forty-three minimum centuries of divergence.

Adolfo Constenla Umaña (1987, 135) reconstructed the following phonemes for Proto-Misumalpan: /p, t, k, b, d, s, l, m, n, ŋ, w, y, h; i, a, u/.

The Misumalpan family is often grouped with Chibchan or included in some version of the Macro-Chibchan hypothesis (see Constenla Umaña 1987). Hale and Salamanca (2001, 35) say that "if Misumalpan is in fact related genetically to Chibchan, the relation may be too distant to establish. Certainly, it cannot be established on the basis of shared lexicon, in our opinion, and the evidence from morphology is weak as well" (see Craig and Hale 1992, for a study of one putative morphological etymology).

Seri Mexico

Seri is a language isolate, spoken in Punta Chueca and El Desemboque on the coast of Sonora, Mexico, and also in a number of seasonal camps; it was once also spoken on Tiburón Island in the Gulf of California. (See Map 2.1.) It has been extensively documented.

A kinship linking Seri and Tequistlatecan (and Yuman) was proposed early (see Brinton 1891), and they were placed in Hokan soon after its formulation (Kroeber 1915), though that hypothesis has not proven persuasive to most scholars; most doubt Hokan in general. (See Chapter 6 for evaluation of Hokan.)

3.3. MESOAMERICAN LINGUISTIC PREHISTORY

Much is revealed about the prehistory of Mesoamerica from the languages, from their classification and geographical distribution, from the patterns of borrowing among native languages of Mesoamerica, and from other historical linguistic facts. Some of the major hypotheses and conclusions regarding aspects of Mesoamerican prehistory based on linguistic information are mentioned in what follows, most of them formulated in various works by Terrence Kaufman.

The Mixe-Zoquean languages contributed many early loanwords—Kaufman (2020) presented 150 putative Mixe-Zoquean loans into other Mesoamerican languages. These loans, along with some other linguistic facts, are seen as evidence for the Mixe-Zoquean ethnolinguistic identification of the Olmecs, who were responsible for the first highly successful civilization of Mesoamerica (Campbell and Kaufman 1976, 2020; Kaufman and Justeson 2009;

Kaufman 2020a). Kaufman (2020a, 118–119) gave the dates of 1700–1500 BCE for when the Olmec civilization, speaking Pre-Proto-Mixe-Zoquean, started developing in the Olmec heartland, Southern Veracruz Coast, with 1200–400 BCE for the Olmec florescence, and with the florescence of Izapa also at 1200–400 BCE by a Mixe-Zoquean speaking population that diverged linguistically around 1000 BCE into Mixean (in Soconusco) and Zoquean (in the Olmec heartland).

Kaufman further argued that although there were no Mixe-Zoquean speakers in central Mexico at the time of the first European contact, nevertheless the pattern of Mixe-Zoquean loanwords and other influences in languages of that region show that "there was an Olmec-looking presence in Northern and Western MA [Mesoamerica] in Olmec times, from about 1000 to 400 BCE (cf. Chalcatzingo)" (Kaufman 2003, 6). He concluded that "it is unescapable that a Mije-Soquean [Mixe-Zoquean] language constituted a noticeable presence somewhere north of Central Mexico" (Kaufman 2003, 28, also 2020, 57), and that the presence of several early loanwords in Nahua from Mixe-Zoquean is possibly "a result of the presence of Olmec outposts in Central and Western Mexico in the period 1000–400 BCE" (Kaufman 2003, 12), also that "the Northern Olmecoid Mije-Sokean culture engendered/inspired the Tlatilco and Cuicuilco phases of the Valley of Mexico" (Kaufman 2003, 29; 2020, 57). This claim of Olmecs or Mixe-Zoquean speakers in Central Mexico may be controversial, but Kaufman presented considerable linguistic evidence for it (see Kaufman 2020a, 71–76).

A much-contemplated question is, who were the builders of Teotihuacan, the mightiest of ancient Mesoamerican cities, and what was their ethnolinguistic identity? It has been hypothesized that Totonac speakers built Teotihuacan (200 BCE–650 CE). Kaufman (2003, 7; 2020, 28) had repeated many times that "Totonako [Totonac] is in fact the best candidate for the language of the most important group of Teotihuacanos." He believed that his evidence showed "that the base population of Teotihuacán was Totonako [Totonac] and that the elite was Mije-Sokean-speaking [Mixe-Zoquean-speaking]" (Kaufman 2020a, 61; see also Kaufman 2020a, 75, 93).

Totonac speakers also apparently had strong cultural influence, judging from the Totonac words borrowed by other languages (Justeson et al. 1985; Kaufman 2003, 9; 2020). For example, Mayan languages of the Cholan and Yucatecan branches have *pusik'al* or *puksik'al* 'heart, soul', borrowed from Totonac *puːsikuʔlan* 'church, place of holy things' (composed of *pu-* 'locative prefix' + *sikuʔlan* 'holy') (Justeson et al. 1985, 26; Kaufman 2020a, 112). The direction of borrowing is clear, since (1) nearly all Mayan roots are monosyllabic but *pusik'al* is polysyllabic, and (2) *pusik'al* is monomorphemic in Mayan but is polymorphemic in Totonac. The 'heart' — 'holy' association is assumed to reflect the widespread practice of cutting out the hearts of sacrificial victims in ancient Mesoamerica, abundantly documented at the Classic site of El Tajín, Totonac capital in Veracruz.

Not only did Nahua borrow a number of Totonac words, Kaufman (2003, 12) argues that it borrowed the suffix *-tsīn* "'diminutive (reverential)' and the phoneme /tl/ from Totonac, and that Nahua created some seventeen "Totonako-like metaphors [compounds] that replaced morphologically simplex lexemes" (p. 16).

Nahua loanwords are found in languages throughout Middle America, many of them as a result of the cultural impact of the Toltecs and later the Aztecs, both of whom spoke Nahua.

Similarly, the Mayan languages have contributed a number of borrowed words to the languages of their neighbors. For example, as mentioned above, most Xinkan agricultural terms are loanwords from Mayan languages, leading to the inference that Xinkan speakers were probably not agriculturalists before their contact with Mayan speakers. The languages of the Maya Lowlands also borrowed much from one another and contributed significantly to other Mayan languages and to their non-Mayan neighbors, reflecting the fact that Cholan and later Yucatecan speakers were the bearers of Classic Maya culture (Justeson et al. 1985).

For other aspects of the linguistic prehistory of Mayan languages, see the discussion of Mayan languages above. Other aspects of Mesoamerican prehistory are mentioned above in the discussion of the various language families. For the unclassified and spurious languages of Middle America, see Chapter 5. For discussion of proposals of distant genetic relationships involving several languages of Middle America, see Chapter 6.

NOTES

1. Often the Caribbean is linked with Mexico and Central America, joined together as a geographical unit. However, since the Indigenous languages of the Caribbean belong to language families of South America, the Caribbean languages are represented in Chapter 4 on languages of South America, not in this chapter. (See Granberry and Vescelius 2004.)

2. Unless otherwise indicated, the figures, percentages, and the information reported in this chapter about the vitality of languages are based on the *Catalogue of Endangered Languages*, at www.endangered.languages.com (accessed July 15, 2020).

Languages in Middle America also involve several language families, most of whose member languages are located in other regions but that have some languages also in Middle America. These are treated in other chapters. There is (better said was) also a very large number of unclassified languages about which scarcely anything is known, surveyed in Chapter 5. For these reasons, it is difficult to provide an exact number for the languages spoken in Middle America. There are also three Indigenous sign languages in this region.

3. The name *Huastec* is apparently from Nahuatl *waš-* 'gourd, gourd tree' + *-te:ka* 'inhabitant of place of'.

4. The name *Chicomuceltec* is from Nahuatl *čiko:m(e)-* 'seven' + *o:se:lo:-* 'ocelot' + *-te:ka* 'inhabitant of place of'. *O:se:lo:-tl* <ocelotl> 'ocelot' is a day name in the Aztec calendar; 'Seven Ocelot' apparently comes from a calendar date. The town and the river where the Chicomucelecs lived are both named *Chicomuselo*.

Chicomuceltec has at times been called *Cabil* (*Kabil*), a name given to it in some colonial documents, though that name can be confusing.

5. The name *Yucatec* is derived from *Yucatán*, and several etymologies have been proposed for it. One quite plausible one sees *Yucatán* as coming from Nahuatl *yo(?)ka(:)-* 'richness, inheritance' + *-tla:n* 'place of', with *Yucatec* from this Nahuatl root + *-te:ka* 'inhabitant of place of'. An often repeated proposed etymology has it that *Yucatán* comes from something the Maya may have said to the earliest Spanish they encountered from which the Spaniards gave them their name and the name of the whole Yucatán Peninsula, things involving the Yucatec word *t'an* 'language, word, speech', in phrases such as 'I don't understand your words/speech/language' or 'hear how they talk!'. Another, from early Spanish chroniclers, suggested that it is from *yuca* 'sweet manioc' + Nahuatl *-tla:n* 'place of', though this is probably a folk etymology; *yuca* in Spanish is a Taíno

loanword, not found in Nahuatl or Mayan languages. Another sees *Yucatán* as coming from the Chontal (Maya) autonym *yokot'an* (literally 'speaker of Yoko', with *-t'an* 'language, word' in it).

6. The name *Chol* (*Ch'ol*) is from *č'ol* 'Indigenous person' in Cholan languages. It has often been said to be related to *čol* 'cornfield', but the lack of glottalization on the *č* makes that identification highly unlikely.

7. The name *Chontal* comes from Nahuatl *čontal-* 'foreigner'. That is the source of the names for several other groups in Mexico and Central America (see Brinton 1892).

8. The names *Cholti* and *Chortí* both come from Cholan *č'ol* 'Indigenous person' + *ti?* 'mouth, language'.

9. The name *Tzotzil* is from Tzotzil *sots'* 'bat' + *-il* 'nominal suffix', the name of a principal division of the Tzotzils in colonial times. This origin is also reflected in *Zinacantán*, the name of one of the major Tzotzil towns, which reflects the Nahuatl equivalent of the Tzotzil name, from Nahuatl *tsina:kan-* 'bat' + *-tla:n* 'place of'.

10. The name *Akatek* (*Acateco*) is from Nahuatl *a:ka-* 'reed' + *-te:ka* 'inhabitant of place of'. Akatek is sometimes considered a dialect of Q'anjob'al.

11. The name *Jakaltek* (*Jacalteco*) comes from Nahuatl *ša?kal-* 'hut' + *-te:ka* 'inhabitant of place of'. *Popti'* is presumably from *pop* 'woven mat' + *ti?* 'mouth (language)'. The woven mat was a symbol of royalty for the ancient Maya.

12. Apparently *Motocintlec* is from Nahuatl *mo:to?-* 'squirrel' + *-tsin* 'diminutive' + *-tla?* 'place where are abundant' + *-e:ka* 'inhabitant of'.

Tuzantec is somewhat parallel to *Motocintlec*, involving gopher in Nahuat, from *tosan* 'gopher' + *-te:ka* 'inhabitant of place of'.

Mocho' is also known as Motocintlec. The name *Cotoque* in colonial documents may have referred to Mocho', since *qato?k'* is the Mocho' name for the language, literally 'our language'. It has sometimes been called *Cotoque* or *Qato'k* in modern times, but this can be confusing.

13. The name *Chuj* is from *ču:x* 'steambath' in Mayan languages of the Huehuetenango area. It is *tu:x* 'steambath' in most non-Mamean Eastern Mayan languages; Mamean languages have *ču:x*, and some of the non-Mamean languages of the area borrowed that form from Mamean.

14. The name *Tojolab'al* is from Tojolab'al *toh-ol* 'straight, correct' + *ab'al* 'language'.

15. The name *Q'eqchi'* comes from Q'eqchi' *q'eq* 'black' + *či?* 'mouth (language)'.

16. The name *Uspantek* (*Uspanteco*) is from Nahuatl *očpa:n-* (root for 'broom', from 'to sweep') + *-te:ka* 'inhabitant of place of'.

17. The name *K'iche'* (*Quiché*) is from K'iche' *k'i(h)* 'many' + *če:?* 'trees' (that is, 'forest').

Achi is considered a dialect of K'iche', though sometimes, for non-linguistic reasons, it is considered a separate language.

18. The name *Kaqchikel* (*Cakchiquel*) includes Kaqchikel *kaq* 'red' (modern *kyaq*) and *či?* 'mouth (language)'.

19. The name *Sakapultek* (*Sacapulteco*) comes from Nahuatl *saka-* 'grass' + *-po:l* 'augmentative, derogatory' + *-te:ka* 'inhabitants of place of'.

20. This name *Sipakapeño* (*Sipakapa, Sipakapense, Sipacapa*) is from Nahuatl *sipak* 'alligator (cayman), supernatural beast' + *a:pan* 'river'.

21. The name *Mam* is from the word *ma:m* 'grandfather' (also meaning 'grandson') in Eastern Mayan languages. The name of the municipio (city) and department of *Huehuetenango* appears to be a Nahuatl approximation of the Mayan name, from *we:we?-* 'old man' + *tena:mi-* 'wall, fortified town' + *-ko* 'in'.

22. The name *Awakatek* (*Aguacateco*) comes from Nahuatl *a:waka-* 'avocado' + *-te:ka* 'inhabitant of place of'.

Chalchitek (Chalchiteco) is sometimes listed among the names of Mayan languages, though it is a variety of Awakatek.

23. For example, Charles Felix Hyacinthe, Le Comte de Charencey (1870) used sound correspondences to classify and subgroup the languages of Mesoamerica. Charencey's 1872 and 1883 papers include several Mayan sound correspondences and sound changes. Otto Stoll (1885, 257) also presented a number of sound correspondences and associated sound changes among Mayan languages, saying:

> These changes follow regular phonetic laws and bear a strong affinity to the principle of "Lautverschiebung" (Grimm's law), long ago known as an agent of most extensive application in the morphology of the Indo-Germanic languages.

Stoll (1912–1913, 40) added:

> When . . . it concerns . . . on which basis . . . I proposed the diversification of the Mayan language family . . . the following can be mentioned here . . . One of the most striking differences between the individual groups of Mayan languages is the regular sound shift from one group to the other [several examples of which were given. (Stoll 1912–1913, 40)]
>
> [Wenn es sich . . . darum handelt . . . auf deren Grund ich . . . die Zerfällung der Maya-Sprachfamilie . . . so kann hier . . . folgendes erwähnt werden: . . . Einer augenfälligsten Unterschiede zwischen den einzelnen Gruppen der Maya-Sprachen ist die gesetzmässige Lautverschiebung von einer Gruppe zur andern.]

24. It should be noted that Brown and Wichmann's (2004) view of Proto-Mayan phonology has been ignored or rejected by other Mayanists. Many of their proposals in that paper are inconsistent with standard procedures of linguistic reconstruction.

25. Serious comparative syntactic study of Mayan languages was undertaken already by Eduard Seler (1849–1922), the most renowned authority on Mesoamerican antiquities in his day but trained in comparative linguistics. His dissertation on the historical morphology and syntax of Mayan languages at the University of Leipzig, *Das Konjugationssystem der Maya-Sprachen* (Seler 1887), was in the Indo-Europeanist mode of the time, but actually appeared before Delbrück's celebrated work on comparative Indo-European syntax (Delbrück 1888, 1893), which is held by many to be the foundation of historical syntax in the Neogrammarian tradition.

26. Kennett et al. (2022), in their analysis of ancient genomes from southern Belize, concluded that there were multiple migrations into the Maya region. The oldest individuals are from 9600 to 7300 BP. Individuals in a later cluster from 5600 to 3700 BP have a portion of their ancestry from the earlier residents and a portion attributed to Chibchan populations, which Kennett et al. interpret as representing a south-to-north movement into southeastern Yucatan, which "may have been accompanied by improved varieties of maize and other domesticated plants, as well as elements of early Chibchan languages" (p. 7). They report that around 75 percent of the ancestry of the present-day Maya comes from a combination of those two ancient groups, while 25 percent is most closely related to highland Mexican populations. They present "25 phonologically and semantically comparable basic vocabulary items to study the linguistic evidence for interaction between early Chibchan and Mayan languages" (p. 6).

A serious problem with this is that there were no Mayan groups in Belize or Yucatan at those early dates. From linguistics and archaeology it has long been clear that the Mayan homeland was in highland Guatemala and that Mayan speakers did not arrive in Yucatán or the Mayan lowlands until around 1000 BCE. We know nothing linguistically of the people who were there already before Mayan groups arrived. What we can say from Kennett et al.'s findings is that the genes that Mayan groups inherited come from the different directions/sources a very long time before there were "Mayan" groups to identify them with. Chibchan languages are spoken to the south of the Mayan areas, and so some gene flow would be understandable, though apparently from a time long before there were people in the Maya lowlands who could actually be identified as Mayan linguistically or ethnically.

The 'maize' terms they compared in their Table 9 represent a *Wanderwort* shared in several Central American languages in a form like *ayma* (and Proto-Mayan **eʔm*), but its origin and direction and time of borrowing are unknown (see Chapter 9). The linguistic data in their Supplementary Tables 7 and 8 with comparisons of twenty-five Proto-Mayan and Proto-Chibchan words is both irrelevant and flawed. It is irrelevant because the 5600–3700 BP dates attributed to the arrival of Chibchan genes to the area are far too early to have involved direct contact with Mayan-speaking groups. The twenty-five comparisons are inadequate to distinguish accidental similarity from borrowing or from possible inheritance from an earlier common ancestor. Supplementary Table 7 proposes sound correspondences, but does not account for the other sounds in the compared words that are not related to the proposed sound correspondence (for example, Proto-Mayan **qʼab*' 'hand, arm'/Proto-Chibchan **kU* (or **kʷa*) 'finger, digit, hand', with no account for the *b*'). At least sixteen involve short forms. Several involve semantic disparities 'to sleep'/ 'to die', 'rain'/ 'water', 'to give'/ 'causative', 'brush'/ 'tree', 'tongue'/ 'sharp, tooth (molar)'). In short, the twenty-five look like an assembly of just accidentally similar forms. The forms in Supplementary Table 10 "Related terms for 'maize' (either loans or cognates)" with comparisons of terms for 'maize' in several Central American languages and several Chibchan languages suffer from the same problems (except for the repeated *ayma*-like *Wanderwort*), comparing 'maize' terms as disparate as *i-*, *ep-*, *au*, and so forth. There is nothing in the linguistic data that they present that supports any sort of connection between Mayan and Chibchan, and even if some word or words could be taken as borrowings, there is no evidence of who may have borrowed it from whom or whether the word went accompanied by genes or spread without accompanying gene flow.

27. A possible source of the name *Mixe* is seen in the hypothesis that is sometimes repeated that it comes from Nahuatl *mi:ši:-* 'intoxicating herb (maybe jimsomweed?)'.

28. The name *Tapachultec* comes from Nahuatl *tlapačo:l-* 'subject, someone ruled or governed, oppressed, subjugated' + *-te:ka* 'inhabitant of place of'. It is reflected also in *Tapachula*, the name of a town in Mexico on the Guatemalan border, in the area where the Tapachultecs lived.

29. *Sayula* is from Nahuatl *sa:yo:l-* 'fly' + *-la:n* 'place of', that is literally 'place of flies'. *Popoluca* is from Nahuatl *popoloka* 'to speak unintelligibly, speak a foreign language'.

30. The name *Oluta* is from Nahuatl *o:lo:-* 'corncob (without kernels)' + *-tla:n* 'place of.' As seen in several other names, *popoluca* is from Nahuatl *popoloka* 'to speak unintelligibly, speak a foreign language'.

31. *Texistepec* is from Nahuatl *te:ksis-* 'egg shell, conch shell' + *-tepe:-* 'mountain' + *-k* 'in'.

32. Etymologically, *ayapa* appears to be from Nahuatl *a:ya:-* 'cloak or blanket of cotton or henequin' + *-pan* 'on, in'.

33. The name *Soteapan* appears to be from a form meaning 'water snail' (see Spanish *jute* 'water snail', borrowed from a Nahua form not attested in Classical Nahuatl, cf. Pipil *šuti*) + *-apa:n* 'river'.

34. The name *Chimalapa* is from Nahuatl *či:mal-* 'shield' + *a:pan* 'river'.

35. The name *Matlatzinca* is from Nahuatl *ma:tla-* 'net, snare' + *-tsin* 'diminutive' + *-ka* 'inhabitant of'.

36. The name *Ocuilteco* is from Nahuatl *okʷil-* 'worm, caterpillar' + *-te:ka* 'inhabitant of place of'.

37. The name *Otomí* comes from Nahuatl *otomi-tl* 'Otomí'. Its further etymology in Nahuatl is uncertain. It is generally believed that it contains *mi:-tl* 'arrow', though some have assumed it comes from Nahuatl and means 'one who walks with arrows', though 'bird arrowman' has also been suggested.

38. The name *Mazahua* is from Nahuatl *masa:-* 'deer' + *-waʔ* 'pertaining to, having'. *Mazateco* is from Nahuatl *masa:-* 'deer' + *-te:ka* 'inhabitant of the place of' (in this case of the place of "deer").

39. The name *Chinantec* (*Chinanteco*) comes from Nahuatl *čina:mi-* 'fence of cane' (also a term for a division in the social structure) + *-te:ka* 'inhabitant of'.

40. The name *Tlapanec* (*Tlapaneco*) appears to come from Nahuatl *tlalpan* 'roof' + *-e:ka* 'inhabitant of'.

41. The name *Subtiaba* appears to be from a form meaning 'water snail' (see Spanish *jute* 'water snail', borrowed from a Nahua form not attested in Classical Nahuatl, cf. Pipil *šuti*) + *-apa:n* 'river'. The <b> is due to a mistaken addition to the Spanish name.

42. The name *Chiapanec* is from Nahuatl *čiyan* 'chia plant' + *-a:pan* 'river'.

43. The name *Popoloca* is from Nahuatl *popoloka* 'to babble, to speak a language badly'. Several other Mesoamerican languages also have names similar to this that derive from this same Nahuatl root.

44. The name *Amuzgo* is from Nahuatl *amoš-* 'water moss' + *-ko* 'in'.

45. The name *Cuicatec* comes from Nahuatl *kwi:ka* 'song' + *-te:ka* 'inhabitant of place of'. I have always assumed that it reflects the fact that Cuicatec is very noticeably a tonal language.

46. The name *Zapotec* is from Nahuatl *tsapo-* 'zapote fruit (sapota)' + *-te:ka* 'inhabitant of place of'.

Mixtec comes from Nahuatl *miš* 'cloud' + *-te:ka* 'inhabitant of place of'.

Opinions of the number of Mixtec and Zapotec languages have varied much. Lillehaugen (2020, 335–337), for example, following the ISO codes for these languages, lists fifty-seven Zapotec languages, and fifty-two Mixtec languages.

47. The name *Otomanguean* (sometimes spelled "Oto-Manguean") is a blend of *Otomí* and *Mangue*.

48. There had been doubt about whether Chiapanec and Mangue had a tonal contrast, but see Eric Campbell (2017) for evidence that it did have contrastive tone.

49. The name *Pochutec* (*Pochuteco*) is from Nahuatl *po:čo:-* 'silk-cotton tree (ceiba)' + *-te:ka* 'inhabitant of place of'.

50. The name *Pipil* is derived from Nahua *-pil* 'son, boy'. There is a related Pipil (Nawat) word *pi:pil* 'boy'. Because of this, some have thought that the name *Pipil* must be disrespectful or pejorative, but that is not the case, just the opposite. Rather, when reduplicated it could refer also to nobles, as for example in the Classical Nahuatl cognate *pi:l* 'noble' and *pi:pil-tin* 'nobles'. There are other Indigenous groups in Mesoamerica whose names are also derived from a word of their language meaning 'son' or 'child of' that also meant 'noble' (from 'sons of nobles'), quite parallel to Spanish *hidalgo* 'a rank of nobility' that evolved from *hijo de algo/de alguien* 'son of something/someone'. See also Pipil (Nawat) *-pil-tsín* 'boy, son', with the reverential/diminutive suffix *-tsin*.

51. The name *Tepehua* is from Nahuatl *te:-* 'non-specific human object' + *-pe:wa* 'capture', seemingly meaning 'conquered people'.

52. The name *Chiquimulilla* appears to be from Nahuatl *čikimol-* 'goldfinch' + the Spanish feminine diminutive suffix *-illa*.

53. Jumaytepeque was unknown to outsiders until I "discovered" the language in the early 1970s; it is spoken near the top of the Jumaytepeque volcano. The etymology of the name is uncertain. It is from Nahuatl and contains *tepe:-* 'mountain' + *-k* 'in', but the first part is not clear. It may involve Nahuatl *šoma-* 'a bush whose leaves are used to cure fevers' or *šomaʔ-* 'spoon made of clay'.

54. https://www.ethnologue.com/subgroup/1900, accessed December 19, 2023.

55. Perhaps surprisingly, the name *Cuitlatec* (*Cuitlateco*) comes from Nahuatl *kʷitla-* 'excrement' + *-te:ka* 'inhabitants of the place of'.

56. *Misumalpan* is a created name, composed of the parts of the names of the component languages, **Mi**skito, **Su**mo, **Ma**tagalpa**n**.

57. It is frequently said that the name *Cacaopera* is from forms in Lenca that approximate *kakaw* 'cacao' and *pera* 'jaguar'.

58. Matagalpa's name is from Nahuatl *maʔtlak* 'ten' + *-kal* 'house' + *-pan* 'place of'. This name probably reflects a calendar date, 'ten house'; *kal(-li)* 'house' is a day name in the Aztec calendar.

4

Indigenous Languages of South America

4.1. INTRODUCTION

This chapter is about the Indigenous languages of South America and their history. South America is home to 100 language families (including isolates)—47 language families and 53 language isolates. Of the 48 language families, 39 are relatively small, with 6 or fewer languages belonging to them, and 9 are relatively large. These numbers, however, are misleading, for several reasons. While there are circa 326 South American (henceforth SA) languages still spoken today, there are literally hundreds of unclassified languages in SA (see Chapter 5 for details), most long dormant with little or no attestation, although a good number of them have at times been listed among the language isolates or as possible members of various language families (see also Campbell 2012a, 115–130).

In the classification of languages presented in this chapter, there are circa 210 dormant languages. However, that is also misleading—it represents just the dormant languages we actually know something about. There are an additional circa 380 names of unclassified and mostly dormant SA languages listed in Chapter 5 of which little if anything is known; together this comes to nearly 600 dormant languages (or likely languages), nearly twice as many no-longer spoken ones as those still spoken today—and there are others not even included in these lists. (See Chapter 5 for details.)

The exact number of distinct currently spoken languages and language families in SA is just unknown. In SA there are more than 50 indigenous groups that live in isolation (see, for example, https://en.wikipedia.org/wiki/Uncontacted_peoples, accessed July 8, 2020; Douglas Rodrigues 2014). In Brazil alone there are officially at least 40 "uncontacted" indigenous groups. For some of these uncontacted groups, it is not known whether they speak an already identified language, a language currently unknown but which will turn out to belong to a known language family, or a language that represents an as yet unknown language family or language isolate. The identification of SA Indian languages is further complicated, as mentioned in Chapter 1, on the one hand by cases of a single language having a variety of names and on the other hand by instances of a single name referring to multiple languages. Most SA languages have more than one name (see Campbell 2012a, 60–62). In some cases we do not yet know whether a certain named entity refers to some independent language or is just a dialect of a language known by another name.

With circa 397 language families (including language isolates) known in the world, South America's 100 families constitute a quarter of the world's linguistic diversity (25%), calculated in terms of language families. SA was the last continent to become inhabited by human beings and yet has such vast linguistic diversity. SA languages are not only genetically diverse, but are typologically diverse as well (see Campbell 2012b). This gives the indigenous languages of SA a special position in linguistics, which has as one of its main goals to discover the full range of what is possible in human languages.

In addition to the genealogical classification of SA languages, presented in this chapter, a significant part of the history of these languages, as elsewhere, involves language contact (see Chapters 7, 8, and 9). As mentioned, there are also pervasive typological differences among the language families and sometimes among languages within individual language families. This, of course, raises questions about the history behind these differences, about how and why they came about. Moreover, several typological properties are frequent in South America that are much rarer elsewhere in the world. These include, among others: nasal spreading and nasal harmony, classifiers (both nominal and verbal), evidentiality marking, rich demonstrative systems with several semantic dimensions, directional/locative markers on verbs, nominalization for clause subordination, and desiderative and frustrative grammatical morphemes (see for example Muysken and O'Connor 2014). We would like to know to what extent if any these traits may reflect very old genealogical relationships or large-scale diffusion and possible larger linguistic areas, although so far answers to these questions remain mostly in the realms of speculation.

4.2. CLASSIFICATION AND HISTORY OF SOUTH AMERICAN INDIGENOUS LANGUAGES

The documentation of South American indigenous languages has expanded greatly over the past two decades, and this in turn has provided needed information for refinements in the classification of the languages and for understanding of their histories. It can be expected that improvements in the documentation and classification of these languages will continue in the future, though for the most part the language families are established and major revisions or reductions in the classification are not likely.[1]

The history of language classification in South America has been dominated by large-scale, wholesale classifications of all the languages of the continent together, with more attention to distant genealogical relationships than to subgrouping classification within known language families (for example Greenberg 1960, 1987; Kaufman 1990a, 1994, 2007; Loukotka 1968; Mason 1950; Suárez 1974; Swadesh 1959; Tovar 1961; and Tovar and Larrucea de Tovar 1984) —the methods employed in each of these have been criticized, in different ways (see Adelaar 2012a; Campbell 1997a, 2012a; Campbell and Poser 2008; Rowe 1954). Given the sheer number of languages and language families and the lack of information on many of them (and conflicting information on others), these broad classifications often simply repeated portions of previous classifications that contain proposals of linguistic affiliations for which there was little or no real evidence. As Patience Epps (2009, 583) put it, "authors of classifications simply cited preceding classifications for nearly 100 years, creating a kind of snowball effect that produced an illusion of authority. Very recently, new descriptive work on some of these languages has led to efforts to re-evaluate these claims for relationship."

Opinions vary regarding the state of historical linguistic understanding of SA languages. In 2000, Aryon Rodrigues (2000, 23) was of the opinion that "historical-comparative studies of Amazonian languages are in a very incipient stage, and will only progress more decidedly when descriptive studies are intensified and cover the great majority of the region's languages." Patience Epps (2009a, 581–582) held a similar opinion, though recognized that great progress had recently been made:

> Our current understanding of Amazonian languages and their interrelationships represents little more than a single step into this "last frontier" of linguistic discovery. Yet recent years have seen an exponential increase in descriptive and historical work involving these languages, heralding the opening of new vistas on this previously uncharted territory.

It is true that large numbers of languages have poor if any documentation, meaning that the understanding of their history and classification cannot yet be complete. Still, given the significant advances in both the descriptive and historical linguistic investigation of many SA languages and language families in recent years, I believe it is safe to say that we are way beyond the incipient stage and early steps. Though much remains to be done, our knowledge is now far better than even only a dozen or so years ago. (See Adelaar 2012a and Campbell 2012a on the history of language classification in SA.)

Five of the language families involve widespread expansions. **Arawakan** languages are or were spoken in some dozen countries: Belize, Bolivia, Brazil, Colombia, French Guiana, Guatemala, Guyana, Honduras, Nicaragua, Peru, Suriname, Venezuela, and on several Caribbean islands. **Cariban** languages are spoken in Brazil, Colombia, French Guiana, Guyana, Suriname, and Venezuela, and formally also on some Caribbean islands. **Macro-Jê Sensu Stricto** languages are or were spoken widely over the southern half of Brazil. **Quechuan** languages and varieties are in Colombia, Ecuador, Peru, Bolivia, and Argentina. **Tupían** languages are (or were) spoken in Argentina, Bolivia, Brazil, Colombia, French Guiana, Paraguay, Peru, and Venezuela. Though these large families are very widely distributed, in many cases languages from different families appear interspersed in the same regions, with many smaller, local families and language isolates interspersed among them, giving a decidedly patchwork feel to the linguistic map of SA languages.

Not all SA language families are strictly confined to SA territory, either. The Chibchan family extends as far north as Honduras (with Pech [Paya]) in Central America, Cariban languages reach into the Caribbean, and Arawakan is found also as far north as Belize (with Garífuna).[2] Most other SA language families tend to be confined to smaller local areas.

Most of the SA language families listed in the following classification are generally considered established and are not very controversial.

4.2.1. Larger Language Families

The larger established families, with more than 6 language members, are:

1. Arawakan (c. 65–80 languages; 40 still spoken) (Kaufman 2007)[3]
2. Cariban (c. 40–50 languages, c. 100 languages named, c. 25 still spoken) (Gildea 2012)
3. Chapacuran (10 languages) (Birchall et al. 2016)
4. Chibchan (23 languages (Constenla Umaña 2012, Pache 2018)
5. Macro-Jê Sensu Stricto (c. 33 languages) (Ribeiro 2006; Rodrigues 1999; Nikulin 2020)
6. Pano-Takanan (c. 39 languages) (Fleck 2013; Girard 1971a, 145–171; Oliveira 2014, 2023, Valenzuela and Guillame 2017, Valenzuela and Zariquiey 2015)
7. Quechuan (c. 27 languages?) (Cerrón-Palomino 1987, *The Catalogue of Endangered Languages*)
8. Tukanoan (Tucanoan) (c. 29 languages, 8 of which are extinct) (Chacon 2014, Chacon and List 2015)
9. Tupían (c. 55–70 languages) (Rodrigues and Cabral 2012)

4.2.2. Small Language Families

The accepted smaller families (with no more than 6 languages) are:

1. Arawan (Arahuan, Arauan, Arawán) (6 languages?) (cf. Dienst 2008)
2. Aymaran (2 languages) (Cerrón-Palomino 2000)
3. Barbacoan (c. 5 languages) (Curnow and Liddicoat 1998)
4. Boran (Bora-Muinane) (3 languages) (Seifart and Echeverri 2015)
5. Bororoan (3 languages)
6. Cahuapanan (3 languages, possibly only 2)
7. Cañar-Puruhá (Ecuador) (uncertain family of 2 languages)
8. Charrúan (3 languages) (Viegas Barros 2020)
9. Chicham (Jivaroan) (4 languages) (Kohlberger 2020)
10. Chocoan (3 languages?)
11. Cholonan (2 languages) (Adelaar and Muysken 2004, 460–462)
12. Chonan (Chon family) (5–6 languages?) (Viegas Barros 2015)
13. Enlhet-Enenlhet Mascoyan (6 languages) (Elliott 2021; Fabre 2005)
14. Guaicuruan (Waykuruan) (5 languages) (Ceria and Sandalo 1995; Viegas Barros 2013b)
15. Guajiboan (4 languages)
16. Harákmbut-Katukinan (4 languages) (Adelaar 2007)
17. Huarpean (Warpean) (2 languages)
18. Jirajaran (3 languages)
19. Kakua-Nukak (2 languages) (Bolaños Quiñonez 2016)
20. Kariríán (Kariri family) (4 languages)
21. Kaweskaran (Qawasqaran, Alacalufan) (3 languages?) (Viegas Barros 1990; 2005a, 37–43)
22. Lule-Vilelan (2 languages) (Viegas Barros 2001, 2006a)
23. Mapudungun (Mapudungun, Araucanian) (2 languages)
24. Matacoan (4 languages)

25. Nadahup (Nadehup) (4 languages) (Epps and Bolaños. 2017)
26. Nambiquaran (4 languages?) (Eberhard et al. in press)
27. Otomacoan (2 languages)
28. Sáliban (Sálivan) (3 languages?) (Zamponi 2017)
29. Tallán (2 languages) (Urban 2019a)
30. Tikuna-Yurí (3 languages) (Carvalho 2009, Seifart and Echeverri 2014)
31. Timotean (2 languages)
32. Tiniguan (2 languages)
33. Uru-Chipaya (3 languages) (Cerrón-Palomino 2006)
34. Yaguan (3 languages)
35. Witotoan (Huitotoan) (5 languages) (Aschmann 1993; Wojtylak 2017)
36. Yanomaman (4 languages) (Migliazza 1972)
37. Zamucoan (3 languages) (Bertinetto and Ciucci 2020)
38. Zaparoan (3–8 languages?)

4.2.3. Language Isolates

The language isolates (languages with no known relatives) in South America are:

1. Aikanã Brazil
2. Andaqui Colombia
3. Andoque (Andoke) Colombia, Peru
4. Arara do Rio Branco (Arara do Beiradão, Rio Branco Arara) Brazil
5. Arutani (Awaké, Ahuaqué, Uruak) Venezuela, Brazil
6. Atacameño (Cunza, Kunza, Atacama, Lipe) Chile, Bolivia, Argentina
7. Betoi-Jirara Venezuela
8. Candoshi (Candoxi, Maina, Shapra, Murato) Peru
9. Canichana Bolivia
10. Cayuvava (Cayuwaba, Cayubaba) Bolivia
11. Chiquitano Bolivia
12. Chono Chile
13. Cofán (A'ingaé) Colombia, Ecuador
14. Culle Peru
15. Esmeralda Ecuador
16. Guachí Brazil
17. Guamo Venezuela
18. Guató Brazil
19. Iatê (Yaté, Yatê, Fulniô, Furniô, Fornió) Brazil
20. Irantxe (Iranche, Münkü) Brazil
21. Itonama (Saramo, Machoto) Bolivia, Brazil
22. Jotí (Yuwana) Venezuela
23. Kamsá (Camsá, Sibundoy, Coche) Colombia
24. Kanoê (Kapixaná) Brazil
25. Kwaza (Koayá, Koaiá, Arara) Brazil

26. Leco Peru-Bolivia border
27. Máku (Mako) Brazil
28. Matanawí Brazil
29. Mochica (Yunga, Yunca, Chimú, Mochica, Muchic) Peru
30. Mosetén-Chinamé (Mosetén)
31. Movima Bolivia
32. Munichi (Muniche, Munichino, Otanabe) Peru
33. Omurano (Humurana, Numurana; Mayna, Maina, Rimachu) Peru
34. Paezan (possibly a small family, 3 languages?)
35. Payaguá Paraguay (dormant, often attributed to Guaicurúan, but the evidence for this remains unclear) (Viegas Barros 2004)
36. Pirahã (Muran) Brazil (possibly a small family of closely related languages)
37. Puinave (Wãnsöhöt) Colombia, Venezuela
38. Puquina Bolivia
39. Purí-Coroado
40. Sapé (Kaliana, Caliana, Cariana, Chirichano) Venezuela
41. Sechura?
42. Taruma (Taruamá) Brazil, Guyana
43. Taushiro (Pinchi, Pinche) Peru
44. Tequiraca (Aewa, Aiwa, Tekiraka, Aushiri, Auishiri, Avishiri)[4] Peru
45. Trumai (Trumaí) Brazil
46. Urarina (Simacu, Kachá, Itucale) Peru
47. Waorani (Sabela, Huao, Auca, Huaorani, Auishiri) Ecuador
48. Warao (Guarao, Warau, Guaruno) Guyana, Suriname, Venezuela
49. Xukurú
50. Yagan (Yaghan, Yámana) Chile
51. Yaruro (Pumé, Llaruro, Yaruru, Yuapín) Venezuela
52. Yuracaré Bolivia
53. Yurumangui Colombia

(See also unclassified languages in Chapter 5.)

This number of 100 language families that includes 53 language isolates is representative but far from exact. There are a number of cases where opinions differ, where it is uncertain whether we are dealing with a single language with dialects—which could increase the number of language isolates—or whether a small language family with more than one language is involved, which would increase the number of language families and diminish the number of language isolates. For example, Paez may be a language isolate or a family of three related languages; Pirahã (or Muran) may be an isolate or a family of four languages; Moseten(an): one language (isolate) or two related languages (a small family); Mapdungun: one or two languages; Kawesqar: single language or several; Karirían: one language with dialects or four related languages; Kakua-Nukak: Kakua is a dialect of Nukak or the two are separate related languages; Jirajara(n): four languages or a single language; Huarpean: Huarpe and Millcayac are dialects of a single language or are two separate languages; Betoi-Jirara: a single language or a pair of languages; Purí-Coroado: a language isolate or possibly two languages; Sechura: a language isolate or a small family; Tallán: one or two languages; and Timotean two languages or only a single one with two dialects.

In other instances involving languages with limited documentation, opinion has sometimes differed over whether the data available are sufficient to show that a language has no relatives when compared with other languages or whether it is unclassified because too little information was ever recorded to allow it to be classified or shown to lack demonstrable relatives. This may be the case with, for example, Culle, where if the attestations are considered sufficient for comparison with other languages, then it is a language isolate; however, if the data on this language are considered too sparce to determine that, then it belongs in the long list of unclassified languages (see Chapter 5). Questions of the adequacy (sufficiency) of the data come up also in the cases of Kariríán, Huarpean, Gorotoqui, Sechura, Tallán, Betoi-Jirara, Xukurú, Yurumanguí, and several others. A sizeable number of the unclassified languages listed in Chapter 5 are of this sort, where some have thought that the attested information on some of them was sufficient for them to be classified together with other languages in language families or enough to consider some of them language isolates if no relatives could be found. In short, the total number of language families and language isolates could be considerably larger or smaller, depending on judgments about the amount and kind of data available in the records for the various languages in question. And, of course, if more data should show up on some of them, it may become possible to reach more definitive classifications of them, and that, too, could change the numbers.

4.3. SOUTH AMERICAN LANGUAGE FAMILIES (INCLUDING LANGUAGE ISOLATES)

The internal classification (subgrouping) of languages within the SA language families follows, including language isolates that are language families that have only a single member, together with aspects of the historical linguistics of these languages when it is known. Since insufficient comparative linguistic work has been undertaken in several instances, controversies remain about the classification of some languages, and some scholars may favor different subgrouping schemes for some of these language families from what is presented here. In cases where major dialects are known by name, these dialect names are also given, though dialect names are mostly ignored unless they have played a role in discussions of classification or identification of the languages.

Aikanã (Aikaná, Huarí, Warí, Tubarão, Kasupá, Mundé, Corumbiara) Brazil
 Aikanã is a language isolate spoken in Rondônia state, Brazil. An important dialect is **Masaká** (Massaca, Massaka, Masáca), spoken along the Corumbiara River. Čestmír Loukotka (1968, 163) listed "Masaca or Aicana" in his "Huari stock" with several of the alternative names that are listed here in parentheses given as separate languages, including also **Aboba**, **Guajejú**, **Maba**, and **Puxacáze** as additional languages of the "stock" but of which "nothing" was known. (Terrence Kaufman 2007, 74.) (See Map 7.10.)

*__Andaquí__ (Andakí) Colombia
 Andaquí is a dormant language isolate, formerly spoken in Colombia's southern highlands. Proposals to link it with Chibchan or Barbacoan have not worked out. It has sometimes been linked also with Paez(an), but with no convincing evidence of a genealogical

connection there either. Kaufman (2007, 63) included it in his "Paes-Barbakóan stock," closer to the "Paes group."

Loukotka (1968, 245) included in his "Andaquí Group" also **Timaná**, once spoken on the Magdalena and Guarapas Rivers around Timaná city, and **Yalcon** (Cambi), from between the Magdalena and La Plata Rivers. "Nothing" was said to be known of either of them. (The name Andaquí should not be confused with Andoque.)

Andoque (Andoke, Cho'oje, Patsiaehé) Colombia, Peru

Andoque is another language isolate, spoken in the area of the Anduche River in Colombia; it is no longer spoken in Peru. It shares some typological similarities with Arawakan, Tukanoan, and Witotoan, but the evidence does not permit classifying it with any of these other language families (Landaburu 2000, 30). (Not to be confused with Andaquí.)

Arara do Rio Branco (Rio Branco Arara, Arara, Arara do Aripuanã, Arara do Beiradão, Koaia, Koaiá, Koayá) Brazil

This language isolate was spoken in Mato Grosso state, Brazil. It is usually listed as unclassified. Though recently dormant, the language now has enough documentation in several wordlists collected from 1958 to 2007 to show it has no discernible affiliation with any other language or family—it is a language isolate (Zamponi in press b).[5]

Arawakan

Arawakan is the largest language family in the Americas, with more than 65 languages, perhaps as many as 80. It is also the most widespread family; Arawakan languages extend from the Caribbean (with Taíno) and Central America (with Garífuna in Belize, Guatemala, Honduras, and Nicaragua), across Amazonia, to Arawakan languages reportedly as far south as Paraguay and northern Argentina. Its classification is complicated both by the number of internal branches and by the fact that almost half of the languages are dormant, several very poorly attested. Arawakan internal classification is less clear than that of most of the other families of SA, and proposed classifications vary considerably one from another (see Aikhenvald 1999, 67–71; Derbyshire 1992; Kaufman 2007, 65–67; D. Payne 1991; cf. Fabre 2009).

With respect to the name of the language family, two clarifications are in order. The first is about the use of *Maipurean* or *Maipuran* to refer to the whole Arawakan family. "Maipurean" (Maipuran) was considered by some scholars to be just one large branch of a broader Arawakan family, with the name "Arawakan" reserved to mean this "Maipurean" branch plus the other languages hypothesized to be related to the "Maipurean" languages in a higher-order classification. However, the languages that can clearly be established as belonging to the family—whatever it is called—now appear all to fall within the group that was labelled Maipurean (Maipuran). Therefore, now most linguists use the traditional name *Arawakan* to refer to the established language family. The term "Macro-Arawakan" that Lev Michael (2021, 335) recommends is an appropriate and less confusing way to refer to the proposed Arawakan family together with the various languages and small families that have at one time or another been thought to be possibly related to the Arawakan family though without adequate proof—they include Arawan, Guajiboan, Timotean, Tiniguan, Harákmbut, Puquina, Kandoshi, and Yurakaré (see also Kaufman's [2007, 65–67] Macro-Arawakan). As Lev Michael (2021, 335) points out, "none of the[se] ... proposals have significant support among Arawakanists now, and they appear to have arisen from suggestive but misleading morphological similarities or by lexical borrowings that were not identified as such."

The other clarification has to do with "Arawak" versus "Arawakan." In English the official name of the language family is *Arawakan*, though some non-native speakers writing in English and a few others influenced by them sometime call it *Arawak*, writing of "Arawak languages" and the "Arawak family." Names of language families in English typically bear the suffix *-an*, as in *Indo-European, Sino-Tibetan, Mayan, Tupían*, and so on. In many cases this suffix disambiguates the name of the language family from a specific language for which the family was named, for example *Tukanoan* versus *Tukano, Tupían* versus *Tupí*, and so on. The name *Arawak* to refer to the family can be confused with the individual language *Arawak* (Arowak, Aruák), now better known as *Lokono*. The tendency for some scholars to use *Arawak* where *Arawakan* is intended in English comes, I believe, from the fact that language family names in Portuguese and Spanish typically do not carry an equivalent to the suffix *-an*; rather, in Spanish, for example, one writes for 'Chibchan' *lenguas chibchas* or *la familia chibcha*, for 'Tukanoan' *lenguas tukanas* or *la familia tukana* (or *lenguas tucanas, familia tucana*), and so on, to avoid the confusion between the name of the language family and the name of a language after which the family has been named. In short, *Arawak* should be avoided as the name of the family, whose proper name in English is *Arawakan*.

The classification presented here follows most closely that of Kaufman (2007 and personal communication). This classification no longer has the traditional "Northern" versus "Southern" division.

Arawakan
   Upper Amazon branch
      Western Nawiki sub-branch
         *Wainumá group
            *Wainumá (Waima, Yanuma) Brazil
            *Mariaté Brazil.
            *Anauyá Venezuela
         Piapoco group
            Achagua Colombia, Venezuela
            Piapoco Colombia
            *Amarizana Colombia
            Cabiyarí Colombia
         Warekena group
            Warekena (Guarequena) Venezuela, Colombia, Brazil
            *Mandahuaca Venezuela, Brazil
         *Río Negro group
            *Jumana (Yumana) Brazil
            *Pasé Brazil
            *Kawishana (Cawishana, Kayuwishana) Brazil

Yucuna (Jukuna) (dialects or languages)
    Yucuna (Jukuna)
    *Garú (Guarú) Colombia
Eastern Nawiki sub-branch
    Tariana Brazil, Colombia
    Karu (dialects or languages)
        Ipeka-Kurripako (dialects or languages) Brazil, Colombia, Venezuela
        Karútana-Baniwa (Baniva) dialect group Brazil, Colombia, Venezuela
        Katapolítani-Moriwene-Mapanai (dialects or languages) Brazil
    Resígaro Peru, Colombia[6]
Central Upper Amazon sub-branch
    Baré group
        *Marawá Brazil
        Baré Brazil, Venezuela
        *Guinao Venezuela
    Yavitero group
        *Yavitero (Yavitano) Venezuela
        *Baniva Venezuela
        *Maipure Colombia, Venezuela
*Manao group
    *Manao Brazil
    *Kariaí Brazil
Languages that belong to the Upper Amazon branch but where there is not enough data to determine where they fit within that branch include *Waraikú, *Yabaána (Jabaana, Yabarana), and *Wiriná, all in Brazil.
Maritime branch (Caribbean)
    *Aruán (Aruá, Aroã) Brazil
    Wapishana-Mawayana (dialects or languages)
        Wapishana (Wapixana) Guyana, Brazil
        Mawayana (Mapidian) Brazil, Suriname
    Ta-Maipurean sub-branch
        *Taíno Caribbean
    Guajiro group
        Guajiro (Wayuu) Colombia, Venezuela
        Paraujano (Añún) Venezuela (only 1 speaker as of 2009)
        Arawak (Lokono, Aruak) Guyana, Suriname, French Guiana, Venezuela
        *Iñeri (Igneri, Island Carib) Lesser Antilles
        *Kalhíphona (Island Carib) Dominica, St. Vincent
        Garífuna (Black Carib) Honduras, Guatemala, Belize, Nicaragua
Eastern branch
    Palikur (dialects or languages)
        Palikur Brazil, French Guiana
        *Marawán-Karipurá Brazil

Western branch
    Amuesha (Yanesha) Peru
    *Chamicuro Peru
Central branch
    Paresi group
        Paresi (Parese-Haliti) Brazil
        Enawené Nawé (Salumã) Brazil
        *Saraveca (Sarave) Bolivia, Brazil
    Waurá group
        Waurá-Mehinaku (Uara, Aura, Mahinacu) Brazil
        Yawalapití Brazil (8 speakers as of 2008)
        *Custenau (Kustenau) Brazil
Southern Outlier branch
    Terena Bolivia, Brazil, Paraguay
        (dialects: Kinikinau, Etelena, Guaná)
    Mojo group
        Mojo (Morocosi, Mojeño, Moxo) (dialects or languages)
        Ignaciano Bolivia
        Trinitario Bolivia (Dialects: Loreto [Loretano], Javierano)
        Bauré (Chiquimiti, Joaquiniano may be a dialect of Bauré) Bolivia
        Paunaca (Paunaka, Pauna-Paicone [Paiconeca]) Bolivia
    Piro (Purus) group (Carvalho 2021)
        Apurinã (Apuriná) Brazil
        Iñapari Peru, Bolivia, Brazil
        Piro dialect cluster
            Yine (Piro) Brazil, Peru.
            *Kuniba
            *Kanamari (Karamirim, Canamaré) Brazil. (Not to be confused with Kanamarí/Kanamaré of the Katukinan family.)
    Campa branch – (Campa dialects or languages) Peru (Michael 2008)
    Ashéninka (Ashéninga)
    Asháninka (Asháninga) Peru
    Caquinte (Kakinte) Peru
    Pajonal Ashéninka (Pajonal Campa) Peru
    Machiguenga (Matsiguenga) Peru (dialects: Caquinte, Machiguenga)
    Nomatsigenga Peru
    Nanti Peru
Other Arawakan languages too poorly attested to determine to which branch of the family they belong are:
    *Shebaya (Shebayo, Shebaye) Trinidad
    *Lapachu (Apolista, Aguachile) Bolivia
    *Morique (Morike) Peru, Brazil

(For other classifications of Arawakan that have been offered, see Aikhenvald 1999; Nikulin and Carvalho 2019; Ramirez 2020; and Walker and Ribeiro 2011.)

    (See Map 4.1. Languages of the Arawakan family.)

Indigenous Languages of South America

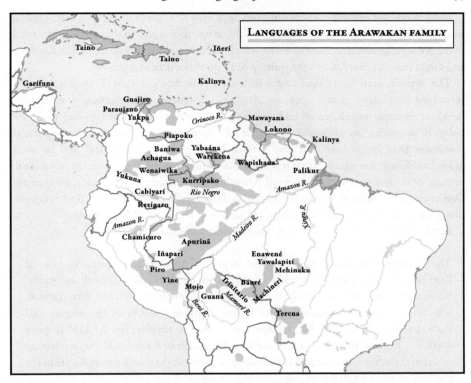

MAP 4.1. Languages of the Arawakan family

Douglas Taylor (1956, 1977) listed "ghost" languages of the West Indies, almost no trace of which remains. For some only the names remain, from seventeenth-century texts. Of **Macorixe** and **Ciboney** only one word of each survives, of **Ciguayo** two words. For **Nepuyo**, **Shebayo**, and **Yao** a few more words are known, the most being for Yao with 52 words recorded in 1640. Taylor's other ghost languages are: **Caquetío, Maisí, Ciguayo, Guaccaierima, Guaikeri,** and **Carinepagoto.** Granberry and Vescelius (2004) believe some of Taylor's "ghost" languages were not distinct languages, mistakenly based only on non-linguistic information. In their interpretation of the sources, the Greater Antilles had, in addition to **Taíno**, possibly three other languages, **Macorís** (with two well-defined dialects), **Ciguayo**, and **Guanahatabey** (which they see as possibly a dialect of Macorís). Ciboney was not distinct, rather, it was the Taíno dialect of Cuba. The languages of the Lesser Antilles, **Iñeri** and **Kalípuna** (Kalhíphona, Island Carib), the source of Garífuna (see above), have more abundant documentation.[7] All these languages are Arawakan, though they may involve different arrivals of distinct Arawakan groups into the Caribbean. There were also speakers of **Kariña** (Kari'nja, Galibi, Kalinya, Kariña, Kariña) (see below), a Cariban language, on Tobago and Grenada when Europeans arrived (Granberry and Vescelius 2004, 62), distinct from Kalípuna (Kalhíphona, Island Carib, an Arawakan language).

Walker and Ribeiro (2011) gave a character-based Bayesian phylogenetic classification of Arawakan. Lev Michael (2021, 334) points out that its reliance on a short concept list (100-word Swadesh list) is problematic; it does not return the higher-level subgroups well (see Carvalho 2020a for a critical assessment of this work).

Ideas about the probable Arawakan homeland vary. It is generally agreed that it was in western Amazonia, but there is uncertainty about whether it was to the north or the south of the Amazon River; structural diversity is high in both regions (Epps 2009, 592). Kaufman and Golla (2000, 52) estimated the split up of Proto-Arawakan at 4500 BP.

The hypothesized "Arawakan linguistic matrix hypothesis" (ALMH) comes from observations that many groups speaking Arawakan languages share certain cultural practices, for example avoidance of endo-warfare, the tendency to form regional trade and political networks, an elaborate set of ritual ceremonies, and so on. The hypothesis postulates that Proto-Arawakan was a trade language or lingua franca used in much of lowland South America and that it was inhibited from diversifying until relatively recently because of its link to a very widespread Arawakan-dominated trade network. Eriksen and Danielsen (2014) propose that Proto-Arawakan began to diversify only after the break-up of that trade network, after 600 CE. (See also Danielsen, Dunn, and Muysken 2011.)

Lev Michael (2021, 334–335) is very critical of the proposal. He says:

> The ALMH thus posits that the time depth of Arawakan is similar to that of Romance, which is highly implausible, given that the internal lexical and grammatical diversity of the family is comparable to language families like Tupian, which is commonly assumed to have a time depth of 5000 years (Rodrigues and Cabral 2012) . . . the linguistic evidence presented to support the ALMH is quite weak . . . Beyond the general weakness of distance based methods for developing internal classifications, there is little reason to suppose that the best explanation for the lack of clear higher-level subgrouping structure in the NeighborNet is the language contact scenario posited by the ALMH, rather than, say, that the chosen features are simply insufficiently informative for higher-level classification purposes. (Michael 2021, 33)

Arawan (Arauán, Arahuan)
   Madi-Madihá
      Madihá
         Kulina (Culina, Madihá, Madija, Corina) Brazil, Peru
         Western Jamamadi Brazil
         Deni Brazil
      Madi Brazil
   Suruwahá (Zuruahá, Suruahá, Sorowahá) Brazil
   Paumari Brazil
   *Arawá Brazil

(Dienst 2008, 62)[8]

The Arawan languages are spoken on the Purus and Juruá Rivers and their tributaries in Amazonas state, Brazil. Esther Matteson (1972) called the family "Madi."

Kulina speakers live on the Jutaí River and on a part of the upper Purus River on the border of Peru and Brazil's Acre state.

Madi has three closely related dialects: **Eastern Jamamadi**, **Banawá**, and **Jarawara**. Eastern Jamamadi speakers of Madi live near the town of Lábrea. **Western Jamamadi** belongs to the Madihá subgroup; its speakers live near the towns of Boca do Acre and Pauini.

Arawá (Arua) is dormant; the last speaker died in 1877. The language is known only from a fifty-two-word list from 1867.

Stefan Dienst (2008) suggests no further subgrouping of Suruwahá, Paumari, and dormant Arawá within the family.

Arawan has often been thought to be linked with Arawakan. Terrence Kaufman (2007, 67) said that "there is no doubt that Arawán is typologically like Arawakan, but that the relationship, if real, is not very close."

Arutani (Awaké, Ahuaqué, Uruák, Urutani) Venezuela, Brazil

Arutani was thought to be dormant; however, one surviving speaker was recently found, living with Ninam speakers in Roraima state, Brazil. It is a language isolate (Migliazza 1978, 1982[1985]; Rosés Labrada et al. 2020; Zamponi in press b). Dixon and Aikhenvald (1999, 20) list Awaké (Arutani) among the "few languages that we say nothing about, for the simple reason that almost nothing is known about them." This is, however, not accurate. Even at that time there was Ernesto Migliazza (1978) documentation of the language, which is more than adequate to determine that this language is a language isolate.

*Atacameño (Kunza, Atacama, Lipe, Lican Antai) Chile, Bolivia, Argentina

Atacameño is a dormant language isolate, formerly spoken in the Atacama Desert region of northern Chile and southern Peru. The last speaker died sometime after 1949. Čestmír Loukotka (1968, 270–271) listed two languages in his Atacama Stock, Atacama (Cunza, Lican Antai), and **Lipe** (Olipe), spoken in Potosí province, Bolivia. Of the second, he said "nothing" is known. (See Map 7.11.)

Aymaran (Jaqi, Aru) Bolivia, Peru
  Southern (Altiplano) Aymaran (Aymara) Bolivia, Peru
  Central Aymaran (Tupe) (with the dialects: Jaqaru and Cauque [Kawki])

(Cerrón-Palomino 2000)

Aymara (Southern Aymara) is spoken primarily in Bolivia and Peru, and also to some extent in northern Chile. It is recognized as an official language in Bolivia and Peru. **Jaqaru** and **Cauque** (Kawki) are mutually intelligible dialects of a single language, Central Aymaran, spoken in the district of Tupe and Catahuasi, Yauyos Valley, in central Peru. (See Map 7.11.)

Quechuan and Aymaran have long been thought possibly to be genetically related, a hypothesis called **Quechumaran**, though this is much debated, denied by many, thought plausible by some. A problem is that clearly the languages of the two families have interacted and influenced one another intensely for a very long time, sharing much vocabulary and many structural traits. This makes it exceedingly difficult, perhaps impossible, to separate what is shared by diffusion from what may be shared by inheritance from a common ancestor. (See Chapter 6 for details.)

Barbacoan
  North Barbacoan
    Guambiano-Totoró
      Guambiano Colombia
      Totoró (Totoro, Polindara) Colombia
    Awa Pit (Cuaiquer) Colombia, Ecuador
  South Barbacoan
    Cha'palaachi (Cayapa, Chachi) Ecuador
    Tsafiqui (Colorado, Tsáchela, Tsachila) Ecuador

(Curnow and Liddicoat 1998, 405; Adelaar and Muysken 2004, 141–142.)
(See Map 7.11.)

Totoró is often considered a dialect of **Guambiano** rather than a separate language (Curnow and Liddicoat 1998, 404). They are often linked with long dormant **Coconuco** (Kokonuko, Cauca, Wanaka) of Colombia in a subgroup called Coconucan, though Adelaar and Muysken (2004, 141) believe that Guambiano-Totoró-Coconuco is best treated as a single language. Alain Fabre (2005) is not convinced of the inclusion of Guambiano-Totoró in Barbacoan, leaving open the possibility that the lexical matches presented could perhaps be due to language contact.

Pasto and **Muellama**, both dormant, are often considered Barbacoan languages, but some do not believe that the evidence for that is very strong. It is possible that Muellama was just the last surviving variety of Pasto. Muellama is attested in a short wordlist from the nineteenth century. Muellama vocabulary is similar to modern Awa Pit. The dormant languages **Barbacoa** (Barbacoas) in Colombia and **Cara** (Kara, Caranqui, Karanki, Imbaya) in Ecuador, are usually associated with Barbacoan. Barbacoa itself is unattested, though the family bears its name. J. Alden Mason (1950, 184) thought that Cara's "affiliation will probably never be certainly known." However, Willem Adelaar (personal communication) sees the Barbacoan affiliation of Cara as very likely based on place names and family names, very close to Pasto-Muellamues and Awa Pit. He says, "the chances of establishing an affiliation are not as desperate as one may assume on the basis of the little that is known of the language."

"**Moguex**" has often mistakenly been classified as a Paezan language, sometimes as Barbacoan. However, the "Moguex" vocabulary turned out to be a mix of Páez and Guambiano (Curnow 1998).

Adelaar and Muysken (2004, 397) see some shared traits in Pasto, which led them to suggest a connection of poorly attested **Cañari-Puruhá** languages with Barbacoan.
Proposed broader affiliations of Barbacoan have linked it with Páez, Paezan languages, Macro-Chibchan, and other postulated groupings. None of these seems very promising. Timothy Curnow (1998) argues that the proposed connection with Páez or so-called Paezan languages is based on misinterpretation of an old document.

*Betoi-Jirara (Betoi, Betoy, Jirarra, Jirarru) Colombia, Venezuela

Betoi consisted of several dialects or related languages once spoken in the area of the Oronoco plains, in Colombia's Arauca and Casanare departments and in Venezuela's Apure state. These Betoi dialects or languages included: **Airico** (Ayrifo), **Anabali, Arauca, Atabaca, Betoi, Ele, Jabúe, Jirara, Lolaca, Lucalia, Quilifay, Situfa** (Citufa), and others (Zamponi 2017, 263). Betoi reportedly was used as a local lingua franca between the Uribante and Sarare Rivers and along the Arauca River. All varieties were dormant by the mid-nineteenth century. Betoi is attested in a number of sources, none of them extensive, but sufficient for Raoul Zamponi (2003a) to write a sketch grammar of the language.

A plausible genealogical relationship between Betoi-Jirara and the Sáliban language family has been proposed but has not been confirmed, perhaps due to the limited attestation of Betoi-Jirara (Zamponi 2017, in press b). A genealogical connection between either of these and Jotí (Hodï) (Rosés Labrada 2019) is more doubtful (see Zamponi 2003, 2017, in press b). In the past several other suggestions of affiliations for Betoi were made. Loukotka (1968, 241–242) placed "languages of the Betoi Group" in his "Chibcha Stock," along with several others now known not to be demonstrably related to Chibchan. Joseph Greenberg (1987, 106) placed Betoi in his Chibchan-Paezan group, but as part of Paezan not Chibchan, along with many other languages generally not thought to be related. In addition to repeated suggestions of Chibchan and Paezan connections, kinship with Tukanoan and Chocoan were also proposed. None of these is accepted today; the evidence presented in their support is not strong. Betoi is considered a language isolate.

Boran (Bora-Muinane)
Bora (Boro, Meamuyna; Miriña/Miranha) Peru, Colombia
Muinane (Muinane Bora, Muinani, Muename) Colombia

Boran languages are spoken in the watershed of the middle Caquetá and Putumayo Rivers in Colombia. Some **Bora** communities have been located also on the Ampiyacu and Yaguasyacu Rivers in Peru since the 1930s. **Muinane** speakers are in Amazonas Department, Colombia. The name "Muinane" can be confusing, used to refer to this Boran language and also as an alternative name for Nipode, a Witotoan language.

Seifart and Echeverri (2015, 280) report that the vocabulary of Bora and Muinane is 75 percent cognate. They reconstruct the Proto-Boran (Proto-Bora-Muinane) phonological inventory with: /p, pp, β, b, d, dʒ, t, tt, ts, tts, tʃ, r, k, kk, g, m, n, h, ʔ, a, e, i, ɨ, o, u, ai/ (Seifart and Echeverri 2015, 282–288). The geminate sounds are based on the correspondence of geminate stops in Muinane to stops preceded by *h* in Bora. It might be preferrable to reconstruct these as clusters of *h* + stop that changed to geminates in Muinane (*hp > pp, *ht > tt, *hts > tts, *hk > kk) instead. A language with no glides (no *w* nor *y* [IPA j]) may seem unusual. Perhaps the *ai* diphthong might be analyzed as *a* + *y*, since otherwise it is odd for a language to have such a diphthong but no phonemic /y/ (IPA [j]).[9] And *β as the only voiced fricative is also odd. The possibility of analyzing it instead as /w/, maybe in Pre-Proto-Boran, could be investigated; the /w/ of numerous other SA languages has [β] as an allophone, leading some to consider it basically /β/ with [w] as an allophone and others to consider it /w/ with [β] as an allophone.

Richard Aschmann (1993) argued that Bora-Muinane belongs to Witotoan, although Seifart and Echeverri (2015) found that much of Aschmann's evidence was due to borrowing and now the two are considered independent families.

Bororoan
  *Umutina (Umotina, Barbado) Brazil (Rodrigues 2007b)
  Bororo group
    Bororo Brazil
    *Otuke group
      *Otuque (Otuke, Otuqui, Louxiru) Bolivia
      *Kovareka-Kuruminaka
        *Kovareka
        *Kuruminaka

Kovareka and **Kuruminaka** are very poorly attested, in small wordlists from Alcide D'Orbigny (1839), nine words of Kovareka and fourteen of Kuruminaka. However, in spite the data being so limited, there is no doubt that they were closely related to **Otuque** (Camargos 2013, 205). Otuque (Otuke) ceased to be spoken at the beginning of the 1900s, but is attested in a vocabulary list from 1831. **Umutina** lost its last speakers after 1995.

Bororo of Cabaçal (Boróro Cabaçais), along the Cabaçal and Jaurú Rivers, has been considered a separate language from Bororo proper (Camargo 2014). It is attested in two wordlists, one from 1825, the other from the 1840s.

Isabelle Combès (2012) believes that **Gorgotoqui** of Bolivia may be another Bororoan language. Loukotka (1968, 61) listed Gorgotoqui simply as an isolated language; others have considered it unclassified for lack of data. During the time of the Jesuit missions in the Chiquitanía region of Bolivia, Gorgotoqui was the largest language of the area in terms of numbers of speakers; it was used as a lingua franca of the Jesuit missions. However, no documentation has survived. It became dormant quite early.

Lidiane Camargos (2013, 188) reconstructs for Proto-Bororoan the phonemes /p, b, t, k, m, n, r, w, y ([j]), i, e, a, o, u, ɨ/.

Bororoan is typically associated with the Macro-Jê hypothesis, though this proposed linguistic kinship is doubted today (see Nikulin 2020; Ribeiro and van der Voort 2010).

Cahuapanan (Jebero, Kawapanan; earlier called Maina, Mainan) Peru
  *Cahuapana (Cuncho, Chuncho, Concho, Chonzo) Peru
  Chayahuita (Chawi, Shawi, Cahuapa) Peru
  Jebero (Xebero, Chebero, Xihuila, Shiwilu) Peru

The Cahuapanan languages are spoken in Peru's northern Amazon basin. Many give Cahuapanan as a family of only two languages, considering **Cahuapana** and Chayahuita dialects of a single language. **Chayahuita** is spoken along the Parapura, Cahuapanas, Sillay, and Shanusi Rivers. **Jebero** is spoken in Jeberos, in the Loreto region of Peru.

Pilar Valenzuela (2011, 282) reconstructed Proto-Cahuapanan with the phonemes /p, t, č [tʃ], k, ʔ, s, š [ʃ], ɾ, m, n, w, y [j], i, a, u, ɘ/. Luis Miguel Rojas Berscia (2019) argues for some refinements of this reconstruction. Valenzuela's *ɾ is based on the sound correspondence of Shawi (Chayahuita) ɾ to essentially Shiwilu (Jebero) l. Shiwilu lʲ also corresponds to Shawi ɾ, but it appears to come from the palatalization of l before i. However, Rojas Berscia (2019) found instances in early texts of Mayna-Chawi, taken to be a predecessor of Shawi, that make it appear that the change was in the other direction, *l > r in Shawi. Rojas Berscia (2019, 174–175) also eliminates *č [tʃ], seeing it as the result of palatalization of *t before front vowels (or in loanwords). Thus Rojas Berscia's (2019, 175) revised Proto-Cahuapanan consonantal inventory is /p, t, k, ʔ, s, l, m, n, w, y/. He would add also a fifth vowel, symbolized as *ɨ, to represent the sound correspondence of Shawi i to Shiwilu ɘr (Rojas Berscia 2019, 175–176, 181–183).

Rojas-Berscia (2019, 2020) argues from onomastics that the otherwise unattested **Chacha** (Chachapuya, Chachapoya) language postulated to have existed in the Amazonas region of northeast Peru "was related to modern Kawapanan [Cahuapanan] languages, or that this was a far understudied area of intense language contact" (Rojas-Berscia 2019, 197). (See Chapter 5.)

Particular caution is needed with regard to the confusing name **Maynas** (Mayna, Maina) that is often also associated with **Omurano**. The language called Mayna (Maynas) in the early sources appears to have been spoken first in the region north of the Marañón, from the east side of the Morona River and both sides of the lower Pastaza River, on to the headwaters of the Nucuray and Chambira Rivers. Loukotka (1968, 155) had two languages, Mayna (Rimachu) and Omurana (Hunurana), in his "Mayna stock." This, however, was based on an error in interpreting the identity of the Mayna/Maynas language. A small handful of Mayna(s) words are found as early as in Saabedra's (1619) account of an expedition (see Hammarström 2011, 2); however, the only early published information ascribed to the name Mayna(s) is the *Pater Noster* in Hervás y Panduro (1787, 4) and a handful of words extracted from other Jesuit sources. Hervás y Panduro (1784, 58) indicated that Maynas was spoken at Misión San Ignazio [Ignacio] (with other languages) and Misión San Giovanni [San Juan]. He presented "Maina" as a 'lingua matrice' (a language family) with the "dialects" (languages) **Chapo**, **Coronado**, **Humarano**, and **Roamaino**. Much later Emilio Teza (1868, 135–136) published a *Pater Noster*, Ave Maria, and Credo found in Cardinal Mezzofanti's *Nachlass*. Though it bore the name "Cahuapana," it was the same language as that of Hervás y Panduro's "Mayna(s)." It seemed plausible that Günther Tessmann's (1930) Omurano from the same general location could be a continuity of Hervás y Panduro's Mayna(s) with its Humurano "dialect." However, Harald Hammarström (2011, 8), upon comparing the sources, discovered that "there is surprisingly little overlap in the meaning between Jesuit-Colonial Maynas and Tessmann's Omurano, but what little there is . . . do[es] not match at all . . . There is no linguistic evidence that Jesuit-Colonial Maynas and Tessmann's Omurano are the same language, and no evidence that they are even genetically related" (Hammarström 2011, 9). Rather, it was clear that the Jesuit-Colonial Mayna(s) and the Cahuapanan languages are genealogically related (Hammarström 2011; Rojas-Berscia 2015).

Nevertheless, Mayna(s) was classified as having various competing genetic affiliations, as a language family of its own, as Jivaroan (Chicham), as related to Jebero in the Cahuapanan family, as related to Cahuapanan but not to Omurano, as Zaparoan, as probably related to Candoshi, and with the Jesuit Mayna(s) together with Omurano as a language family without other connections (Hammarström 2011, 9). Joseph Greenberg (1987, 99, 383) appears to have made the mistake of conflating Omurano with Mayna, which means that by what means he might have classified Omurano is unclear (or just wrong).

Rojas-Berscia's (2015) careful investigation of the Mayna texts leaves no doubt that it was a Cahuapanan language. In his classification of Cahuapanan (Kawapanan), based on phonological changes detected in the documents, he places Mayna together with Shawi as one branch of the family, with Shiwilu as the other branch (Rojas-Berscia's 2015, 404).

Callahuaya (Machaj-Juyai, Kallawaya, Pohena) Bolivia

Callahuaya is a mixed language based predominantly on lexical items mostly from Puquina and morphology from Quechua. It is used as a secret language mostly by male curers who live in a few villages in the provinces of Muñecas and Bautista Saavedra, near Charazani, Bolivia, north of Lake Titicaca, who travel widely in the practice of their curing profession. Their principal language is the local variety of Quechua (Muysken 2009). (See Chapter 8.) (See Map 7.11.)

*Cañar-Puruhá
  *Cañar (Cañari) Ecuador
  *Puruhá (Puruguay, Puruwá) Ecuador

These two languages of the Marañon River Basin in Ecuador are assumed to be related, though both are dormant with very little attestation on which to base comparisons (Adelaar and Muysken 2004, 396–397). **Cañari** is known mostly only from place names. Matthias Urban (2018c) finds lexical parallels to Barbacoan languages in the loanwords assumed to be of Cañari origin in Cañar Quichua, spoken in Cañar Province in Ecuador. This makes a possible Barbacoan affiliation for Cañar-Puruhá plausible.

Loukotka (1968, 263) placed Cañar and **Puruhá** along with several others in his "Chimú stock." Terrence Kaufman (1990, 43; 2007, 69) also placed Cañari, Puruhá, and Yunga in his Chimúan family.

Candoshi (Candoshi-Shapra Candoxi, Maina, Kandoshi, Shapra, Roamaina, "Murato") Peru

Candoshi is a language isolate. It has two principal dialects: **Shapra** [Chapara] and **Candoshi** (Seifart and Hammarström 2018). It is spoken along the Chapuli, Huitoyacu, Pastaza, and Morona River Valleys. It is an official language of Peru.

Paul Rivet (1943) proposed several relatives of Candoshi among now dormant languages of northern Peru, but his propoosals are not convincing.

Loukotka (1968, 156) also had several other languages in his "Murato stock": **Shapra** (Iñuru, Zapa); **Chirino**, of which he says only five words are known; **Pinche** (Llepa, Uchpa, Avaza), of which he reported that nothing is known; **Sacata**, of which he says only five words are known; and **Rabona**, with only a few words known. Antonio Tovar (1984, 69) connected Candoshi with **Taushiro** (Pinche). Greenberg (1987, 384) grouped Esmeralda, Yaruro,

Cofán, Candoshi, and Jívaro in his "Jibaro-Kandoshi" group, part of his larger Equatorial group. Terrence Kaufman (1990, 62) said that "the evidence for Greenberg's Jibaro-Candoshi ... stands as a particularly horrible example."

Terrence Kaufman (2007, 69) placed **Omurano** and **Taushiro** but not Candoshi in his Sparo-Yawan (Záparo-Yaguan) grouping. David Payne (1981) proposed a genetic relationship for Candoshi with Jivaroan (Chicham), which he called Proto-Shuar-Candoshi. Four **Chirino** words are mentioned in *Relación de la tierra de Jaén* (1586), and they seem to favor a Candoshi connection (Adelaar and Muysken 2004, 406; Torero 2002, 280–283). A somewhat longer list of words is given in the same document for **Rabona**, in Ecuador; it includes some plant names that are similar to terms in Candoshi, though they could be borrowed.

*__Canichana__ (Canesi, Canechi, Canisi, Canisiana, Joaquiniano) Bolivia

Canichana is a language isolate of the Beni Department of Bolivia, once spoken on the Mamoré and Machupo Rivers. By the year 2000 it effectively had become dormant. Documentation of Canichana is scarce, including some wordlists, two collections of short conversational sentences, and a few short texts. Still a fair amount is known of the language, enough to assure that it is an isolate, not just unclassified (Zamponi in press b). As Raoul Zamponi (in press b) says, "proposals suggesting [Canichana] relationships to other languages are unconvincing." (See Map 7.10.)

Cariban
    Parukotoan Branch
        Katxúyana (Kaxuiâna) Brazil
            Katxúyana Brazil
            Shikuyana Brazil
            Warikyana Brazil
        Waiwai Subgroup
            Waiwai Brazil, Guyana
            Wabui
            Hixkaryana Brazil
    Pekodian Branch
        Bakairí Brazil
        Arara Group Brazil
            Arara varieties (Not to be confused with Arara do Jiparaná, Tupían.)
                Arara[10]
                Parirí
            Ikpéng Brazil
                Ikpéng
                Txikão
    Venezuelan Branch
        Pemóng-Panare Macro-Group
            Pemóng Group Venezuela, Brazil
                Kapóng cluster (varieties or languages)
                    Kapóng (Akawaio) Venezuela, Brazil

        Patamona Guyana, Brazil
        Ingarikó Venezuela, Brazil
        Makushi Brazil, Venezuela
        Pemón (Taurepang) Venezuela, Brazil[11]
    Panare Venezuela
    Mapoyo-Tamanaku Macro-Group
        *Kumaná
            *Kumaná
            *Chaima
            *Cumanagota
        Mapoyo/Yawarana Venezuela
            Mapoyo
            Wanai
            Yawarana
            Pémono
        *Tamanaku Venezuela
Nahukwa Group (languages or dialects)
    Kuikúro
    Kalapalo
Guianan Branch Venezuela, Guyana, Suriname, Brazil, French Guiana
    Kari'nja
        Carib
        Kalinya
        Cariña
        Galibi
    Makiritare Venezuela, Brazil
        De'kwana
        Maiongong
        Ye'kwana
    Taranoan Group
        Tiriyó Subgroup
            Akuriyo Suriname
            Tiriyó Brazil, Suriname
            Trio Brazil, Suriname
        Karihona Colombia
    Wayana Brazil, French Guiana, Suriname
Residue (Groups and languages still in search of branches, in alphabetical order)
    Apalaí Brazil
    Waimiri Atroari Brazil
    Yukpa Group
        Yukpa (Yucpa) Colombia, Venezuela
        Japréria Venezuela

(Gildea 2012)

As Spike Gildea (2012, 446) points out, "the Venezuelan Branch is still largely an untested hypothesis, but it stands until someone finds a better explanation than shared origin for the combination of phonological and morphological features described in Gildea (2003)." Gildea (2012) does not deal with most of the poorly known dormant languages in his classification. Terrence Kaufman's (2007) classification does include more of the dormant languages. Some of the dormant Cariban languages whose position in Cariban subgrouping is as yet undetermined are:

*Apiaká-Apingi Brazil (Not to be confused with Apiaká, a Tupían language in Mato Grosso)
*Arakajú Brazil
*Boanarí (Bonari) Brazil
*Coyaima (Tupe) Colombia
*Opón-Carare Colombia
*Palmela (Palmella) Brazil
*Paravilhana Brazil
*Patagón (Patagón de Perico) Peru. Only 4 words are known; it perhaps groups with Carijona (Adelaar and Muysken 2004, 405–406).
*Pawixiana Brazil
*Pimenteira Brazil
*Purukotó (Purucotó) Venezuela, Brazil
*Sapará Brazil
*Tivericoto Venezuela
*Wajumará (Wayumará) Brazil
*Yao Trinidad, French Guiana
*Yarumá Brazil

Adelaar and Muysken (2004, 114) list other dormant languages of Colombia that sometimes have been thought perhaps to belong to Cariban: **Muzo-Colima**, **Naruvoto**, **Panche**, **Pantágora**, and **Pijao**.

(See Map 4.2. Languages of the Cariban language family; see also Map 4.7.)

Spike Gildea's (2012, 448) reconstruction of Proto-Cariban phonemes is: /p, t, k, r, m, n, w, j; i, e, a, o, u, ɨ, ô/ (the /ô/ is a mid central vowel).

Meira et al. (2015) gave a computational phylogenetic classification of Cariban. It is a Bayesian analysis of lexical data from thirty-four Cariban varieties, based on Swadesh 100-word lists. It posits five major branches (in decreasing order of confidence): Parukotoan, Pekodian, Venezuelan, Nahukwa, and Guianan, plus a "Residue" group. Only Parukotoan and Pekodian of the higher-order subgroups of the classification based on standard methods (Gildea 2012) are seen in their computational phylogenetic analysis. It does not detect the Venezuelan, Nahukwa, or Guianan branches. Their results separate Pekodian (Arara, Ikpeng, and Bakairi) and Nahukwa (Kuikuro and several co-dialects) of Kaufman's (2007) Southern Branch. (See Michael 2021, 338–339; for difficulties with this classification, see also Michael and Chousou-Polydouri 2019.)

It is generally considered that the Cariban homeland must have been in northeast Amazonia, probably between the Amazon and Orinoco Rivers, where the greatest

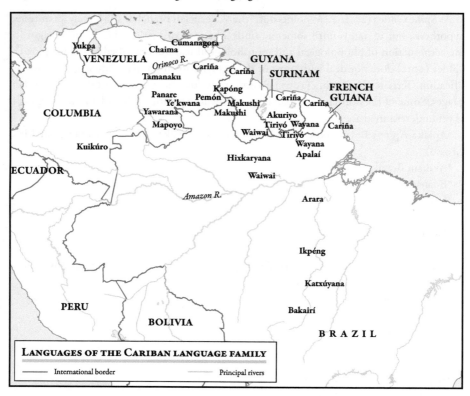

MAP 4.2. Languages of the Cariban language family

concentration in the diversity of the Cariban languages and branches is found (Epps 2009, 592). Kaufman and Golla (2000, 52) estimated that Cariban has a time-depth of 3700 BP.

Several possible connections for the Cariban family have been suggested. Aryon Rodrigues (1985a) thought Cariban and Tupían were related, and that Macro-Jê was related somewhat more distantly to both of these (Rodrigues (2000, 2003, 2009). While there has been some sympathy for these possibilities, the evidence is sparse. (See Chapter 6 for details of these proposals.)

*Cayuvava (Cayubaba, Cayuwaba, Kayuvava) Bolivia

Cayuvava, a language isolate, was spoken in the Beni Department of Bolivia. It is fairly well documented. It appears to have no known speakers now (Seifart and Hammarström 2018).

There have been various proposals to classify Cayuvava with other languages, all as yet not substantiated, for example, Greenberg (1987), Kaufman (1990a, 1994, 2007), and Suárez (1974). (See Map 7.10.)

Chapacuran
  Tapakuric
    *Tapakura (Chapacura, Huachi) Bolivia
    Kitemoka-Napeka
      *Kitemoka (Quitemo, Quitemoca) Bolivia
      *Napeka (Napeca, Nape) Bolivia, Brazil
  Moreic
    *Torá Brazil
    Moré-Cojubim
      Moré (Itene) Bolivia
      Cojubim (Kujubím, Kuyubí) Brazil
  Waric
    Urupá-Jarú
      *Jarú (Yaru) Brazil
    Wanyam-Wari'-Oro Win
      *Wanyam (Wanham, Wañam, Huanyam) Brazil
      Oro Win-Wari'
        Oro Win Brazil
        Wari' (Pakaás-Novos, Orowari) Brazil
  *Rokorona (Rocotona, Ocorona, Orocotona) Brazil.
    Rokorona belongs to Chapacuran but its place within the family is not clear.

Birchall et al.'s (2016, 270) computational phylogenetic analysis based on basic vocabulary gives them the classification:

Chapacuran
  Kitemoka
  Tapakura
    Torá
      Moré
        Cojubim
        Jarú
          Urupá
          Wanyam
            Wari'
            Oro Win

Chapacuran languages are spoken in the upper basin of the Madeira River in Rondônia state in Brazil and in northern Bolivia. (See Map 7.10.)

Names of other dormant languages and their ethnic groups have also been associated with Chapacuran but genealogical relatedness has not been verified for them. They include: **Uomo, Urunamakan, Matawa, Herisobocona,**[12] and **Aricoroni**. Hervás y Panduro (1800, 250) mentioned that the Herisobocona spoke a language similar to **Rokorona**.

Abitana is another variety of **Wanyam** (Pawumwa, Miguelenho); **Kumaná** is a variety of **Kujubim** (Cojubim).[13] Data on these two were collected in the 1930s by Emil Heinrich Snethlage. **Matawa** belongs with **Moré-Kuyubim**. **Cautário** was another name for the Kuyubim (as well as for the river they lived on) (Birchall et al. 2016, 260, Birchall personal communication 2020). Birchall et al. (2016, 260) indicate that the "position of Rokorona within the family still needs further investigation, but it is generally accepted that **Napeka** is the sister language of **Kitemoka**."

Birchall et al. (2016, 262) reconstruct the phonemes for Proto-Chapacuran using the traditional comparative method. They say the easily reconstructible sounds include /*p, *t, *T, *k, *ʔ, *s, *ɾ, *m, *n, *j, and *w; i, e, a, o, u/; however, not everything is straightforward. They find that the nature of specific fricative and affricate segments is somewhat more difficult to reconstruct. Since *t is needed for a straightforward set of sound correspondences, they tentatively reconstruct *T for the regular sound correspondence that has j in Tapakuric languages, z and ʒ in Moreic languages, and t intervocalically in certain cases in the Waric languages. They say that this *T represents a voiceless stop or affricate and most likely had an alveolar place of articulation (pp. 263–264, 269). The phoneme they reconstruct as *s is based on the sound correspondence of /s/ in the Tapakuric languages to /ʃ/ or /tʃ/ in the Moreic languages and to /s/, /ʃ/, or /tʃ/ in the Waric languages (p. 264).

No wider classifications that would include Chapacuran have held out much promise of success. Morris Swadesh (1959) placed Chapacuran in his "Macro-Arawakan." Joseph Greenberg (1987) listed Chapacura in his Equatorial subfamily of Amerind. Terrence Kaufman's (2007, 65) Wamo-Chapakuran stock would include Chapacuran and Wamo.

*Charrúan

*Charrúa Argentina, Brazil, Uruguay
*Güenoa (Guenoa, Minuán) Argentina, Uruguay
Chaná Uruguay

Adelaar and Muysken (2004, 614) and Pedro Viegas Barros (2009) list three separate Charrúan languages: Chaná, Charrúa, and Guenoa (Minuane). Viegas Barros (2020, 236) reports that the almost unknown **Mbeguá** (Mbegua, Begua, Chana-Beguá) language appears also to have belonged to the Charrúan family. Other groups whose language(s) may have been associated with Charrúan and which are sometimes listed with Charrúan include: **Balomar**, **Bohane**, **Calchine** (Calchiné), **Carcarañá** (Caracaná), **Cayastá** (Chayastá), **Colstiné**, **Corondá**, **Guaiquiraré** (Guaiquiaré, Guaiquiraró), **Mepene**, **Mocoreta** (Macurendá, Mocoretá, Mocolete), **Pairindi** (Pairindí), **Quilvazá** (Quiloazá), **Timbú**, and **Yaro** (Yaró) (Adelaar and Muysken 2004, 614; Loukotka 1968, 61–62; Tovar 1961, 29). As Loukotka said, nothing is known of any of these except Charrúa, Chaná, and Güenoa, and very little is known of them.

This **Chaná** is not to be confused with the **Chané** ethnic group who speak **Chiriguano** (Tupí-Guaranían), said to be former speakers of an Arawakan language who switched to a Guaranían tongue (Adelaar and Muysken 2004, 423, 430). Chané is a name applied to several small Arawakan groups (cf. Mason 1950, 216). There is one surviving semi-speaker of Chaná, Blas Wilfredo Omar Jaime, who has been able to provide substantial information on the language (Jaime and Viegas Barros 2013).

In Argentina, at the time of first Spanish contact, the Charrúas lived north in Buenos Aires Province, south of Santa Fe, and in a large part of Entre Ríos. The language is known from two small vocabulary lists collected around 1840 in Uruguay, one of thirty-one words, the other of twenty words and phrases, with a few odd words, personal names, and toponyms scattered in other documents (Viegas Barros 2020, 236). Though all three of the known Charrúan languages are poorly attested, beyond doubt they belong to the same language family. Because of the scarcity of data, there is little that can be said of the grammar of Charrúa or of the Charrúan languages in general (Viegas Barros 2020, 237).

Various suggestions have been made for broader groupings that would include Charrúan. Jorge Suárez (1974) included Charrúan with Guaicurúan in a hypothetical Waikuru-Charrúa stock. Morris Swadesh (1959) included it with Guaicurúan, Matacoan, and Mascoyan (Enlhet-Enenlhet) in his Macro-Mapuche stock. These proposals have mostly been ignored. Hypotheses of distant linguistic kinship for Charrúan include essentially all of the languages and language families of southern South America, Guaraní, Arawakan, Kaingang (and Jêan), Guaicurúan, Matacoan, Lule-Vilela, Zamucoan, Enlhet-Enenlhet, Pano-Takanan, and Chonan. None of these is convincing (Viegas Barros 2020, 237). (See also Blixen 1958.)

Chibchan
    Pech (Paya) Honduras
    Core Chibchan
        Votic
            Rama (Melchora, Voto) Nicaragua
            Guatuso Costa Rica
        Isthmic
            Western Isthmic
                Viceitic
                    Cabécar (Chirripó) Costa Rica
                    Bribri (Viceíta) Costa Rica
                    Teribe (Térraba, Tiribí) Costa Rica, Panama
            *Boruca (Brunca) Costa Rica
            Doracic
                *Dorasque Panama.
                *Chánguena Panama (possibly a dialect of Dorasque)
            Eastern Isthmic
                Guaymíic Panama
                    Guaymí (Movere, Guaymí, Ngäbere) Panama
                    Bocotá Panama
            Cuna (Kuna) Panama, Colombia

Magdalenic
    Southern Magdalenic
        *Chibcha
            Muisca (Mosca, Chibcha) Colombia
            *Duit Colombia
        Tunebo (Uwa, U'wa, Uw Cuwa) Colombia
        Barí (Motilón) Colombia, Venezuela
    Northern Magdalenic
        Arhuacic
            Cogui (Kogi, Cágaba, Kagaba) Colombia
            Eastern-Southern Arhuacic
                Eastern Arhuacic
                    Damana (Guamaca, Sanká) Colombia
                        *Kankuama (Atanques) Colombia
                    Ica (Bíntucua, Ika, Arhuaco) Colombia
                Chimila (Chamila) Colombia
Chibchan languages whose subgrouping is not clear are:
    *Huetar Costa Rica.
    *Antioqueño Colombia

(Constenla Umaña 2012, 417.)
  (Map 4.3. Chibchan languages.)

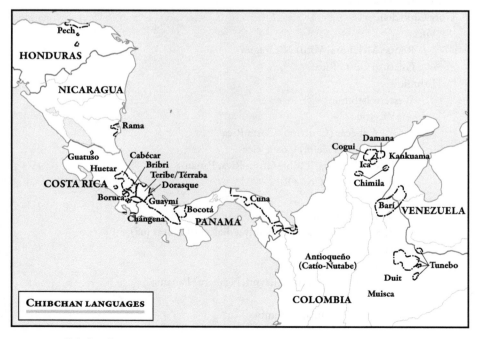

MAP 4.3. Chibchan languages

Chibchan languages are found extended from Honduras to Colombia and Venezuela.

Pech (Paya) is the most divergent Chibchan language. It is spoken in eastern Honduras, in locations mostly around the town of Dulce Nombre de Culmí, Olancho Department, and in three locations in the Department of Gracias a Dios, and one in the Department of Colón.

Rama speakers were once called Votos, Aramas or Arramas, and Melchoras. Rama is found in southeastern Nicaragua, on the mainland south of Bluefields and on Rama Cay. It is critically endangered.

Guatuso (Malecu) is located on the banks of the El Sol River, on the northern plains of Costa Rica. It has three dialects, in the towns of Tonjibe, Margarita, and El Sol.

Cabécar is spoken along the Atlantic slopes of the Talamanca Mountains and adjacent parts of the plains, from Turrialba to the western part of Talamanca.

Bribri was called Viceíta in colonial times. Its original territory was the slopes of the Talamanca range and adjacent plains; at the end of the nineteenth century it extended to the slopes of the Talamanca Mountains in the Pacific watershed. Bribri's three dialects are: the **Western Talamanca**, **Eastern Talamanca**, and the dialect of **Buenos Aires**.

Boruca (Brunka), from Buenos Aires, southwestern Costa Rica, lost its last native speaker in 2004. Adolfo Constenla Umaña (2012, 392) noted that historical evidence suggests that dormant neighboring **Quepo** and **Coto** spoke this same language, Boruca.

Teribe (Térraba) was spoken on the Teribe River in northwest Panama (called Tiribí). Migration at the end of the seventeenth century brought the language to Buenos Aires in southwestern Costa Rica, the variety there called **Térraba**.

Chánguena (Chánguina, Chánguene) is dormant; it was spoken in northwestern Panama, in the area of the Changuinola River, in the Atlantic watershed of the Talamanca Mountains; however, in the eighteenth century its speakers were moved to the area north and west of David, Chiriquí Province.

Dorasque was spoken in northwestern Panama in the Almirante Bay area and on Cristóbal Island. In the seventeenth century, its speakers were moved to the north and northeast of David, Chiriquí Province. Information on the dormant Dorasque language was given under the names Chumulu and Gualaca, two Dorasque towns in Chiriquí.

Guaymí (Ngäbere, Movere) is located in the provinces of Bocas del Toro, Chiriquí, and Veraguas in western Panama. As a result of migration in the twentieth century, it is spoken now also in Corredores, Golfito, and Coto Brus in southwestern Costa Rica. It has been thought that it has three dialects: **Inland Bocas del Toro**, **Coastal Bocas del Toro**, and the **Chiriquí** dialect.

Bocotá (Buglere, Guaymí Sabanero, Murire, Muoi) is spoken in the western Panamanian provinces of Bocas del Toro, Veraguas, and Chiriquí. It has two dialects: **Northern Bocotá** (in Bocas del Toro and northern Veraguas) and **Southern Bocotá** (in Chiriquí and southern Veraguas).

Cuna (Kuna, Tule) was originally in the area of the Urabá Gulf, Colombia. It expanded in the seventeenth century to the mainland and the islands off the northern coast of Panama, the Comarca de San Blas or Kunayala (Guna Yala). It has two dialects: **San Blas Cuna** (Panama) and **Border Cuna** (spoken in Arquía and Caimán Nuevo in Colombia and in Paya and Pucuro in southeastern Panama).

Chimila is spoken south of the Fundación River and the central area of Magdalena Department, Colombia.

Cogui (Cágaba) is spoken on the northern and western slopes of the Sierra Nevada de Santa Marta, Colombia.

Damana (Guamaca, Sanká, Sanhá, Arsario, Malayo, Marocasero, Wiwa) is located on the southern and eastern slopes of the Sierra Nevada de Santa Marta, Colombia.

Atanques (Kankuama) became dormant in the first half of the twentieth century. It was spoken on the eastern slopes of the Sierra Nevada de Santa Marta, Colombia.

Ica (Ika, Arhuaco, Bíntucua) was spoken on the southern slopes of the Sierra Nevada de Santa Marta, Colombia.

Barí (Motilón, Dobocubí, Cunaguasaya) is located in the area of the Oro and Catatumbo Rivers in the Sierra de Perijá in the Colombian departments of César and Norte de Santander and in Zulia state in Venezuela.

Tunebo (Uwa, 'uwa, Tame, Sínsiga, Cobaría) is spoken on the eastern slopes of the Cordillera Oriental and the Sierra Nevada de Cocuy, in the departments of Boyacá, Norte de Santander, Santander, Arauca, and Casanare in Colombia, and in Apure state in Venezuela. Its four reported dialects are: **Western**, **Central**, **Eastern**, and **Angosturas**.

Duit (Chibcha) was spoken in the department of Boyacá, Colombia, probably until the first half of the eighteenth century.

Muisca (Mosca, Chibcha) was spoken in Cundinamarca Department, Colombia, probably until the first half of eighteenth century. Muisca was one of the four languages designated as "lenguas generales" by the Spanish in of the viceroyship of Nueva Granada. **Muisca** and **Duit** were separate languages, but their speakers shared a common culture. Both have been called "Chibcha," but that seemed to refer rather to their shared culture.

Adolfo Constenla Umaña (2012) found sufficient evidence to show that two other dormant languages also belong to the family, though their position in the classification of Chibchan languages is not clear, **Huetar** (Costa Rica) and **Antioqueño** (Antioquian) (Colombia). Huetar, dormant since the eighteenth century, was spoken in central Costa Rica. It is known only from loanwords found in the variety of Spanish used in the former Huetar territory. Antioqueño is known from only thirty-four words and phrases included in early chronicles, which is surprising, since the Spanish considered it a "lengua general" (Constenla 2012, 391, 391). Probably until the eighteenth century it was also spoken in Antioquia Department, Colombia. Colonial sources identify two Antioqueño varieties: **Nutabe** and **Catío** (not to be confused with the Emberá [Chocoan] variety called Catío). Adelaar and Muysken (2004, 49, 614) listed Nutabe (Colombia) among extinct Chibchan languages. Kaufman (2007, 64) grouped Huetar (Wétar) with Guatuso (Watuso) as a branch of his Central Chibchan group.

Tairona is known only from lexical items preserved in the ritual speech of peoples of the Sierra Nevada de Santa Marta, Colombia. It is often listed as probably a Chibchan language, though others doubt this, holding other opinions. For example, J. Alden Mason (1950, 187) saw difficulties with the Chibchan assumption for Tairona:

> The long-extinct Tairona have generally been classified as Chibchan, doubtless because of their close geographical proximity to the Chibchan-speaking Cágaba [Cogui]. The same is true of the living Chimila, sometimes regarded as the modern descendants of the Tairona . . . The language of the Tairona is utterly unknown; they may well have been Cariban or Arawakan. Reichel-Dolmatoff . . . informs me . . . that Chimila is

Arawakan. Arawakan affinities of Tairona would not be unexpected, since they were coterminous with the Arawakan-speaking Goajiro.

Antonio Tovar (1961, 181) was of a very similar opinion. Čestmír Loukotka (1968, 242) held that Tairona (Teyuna) was "now a secret language of the priests of the Cágaba [Cogui] tribe." Adolfo Constenla Umaña (2012, 391) believed it is a variant of still spoken **Damana**." Adelaar and Muysken (2004, 67) say:

> It is not known to what extent the languages spoken by the Kogui and Tairona differed. The religious leaders of the Kogui claim knowledge of a ceremonial language called Téižua, and it is tempting to interpret this as a relic of Tairona.

Terrence Kaufman (2007, 64) included Tairona in his Arawako group of Eastern Chibchan, saying, "Tairona, no longer an ethnic language, is said to be in use as the shamanic/priestly language of the Kogi."

The dormant languages of the **Lache**, **Morcote**, and **Guane** people from the Department of Santander, Colombia, have been assumed to be Chibchan, "but no linguistic evidence has been offered in support of these proposals" (Constenla Umaña 2012, 391).

Mattias Pache's (2018) is the most recent reconstruction of Proto-Chibchan phonology. He reconstructs the following consonants: /p, t, ts, k, k^w, ʔ, ^{m}b, ^{n}d, ^{ŋ}g, ^{ŋ}g^w, s, L, h/ (Pache 2018, 518) (for the vowels see below). Pache indicates that his reconstruction of labialized velar consonants (*k^w, *^{ŋ}g^w) for Proto-Chibchan is tentative (p. 519). Of nasal stops and vowels, Pache says "Proto-Chibchan had nasal vowel phonemes" and "vocalic nasality determined the realization of neighboring voiced stops in Proto-Chibchan as nasal or oral" in line with Constenla Umaña's (2012) analysis (p. 514). In spite of assuming tentatively "that vowel nasality determined the nasality of adjacent (probably preceding) voiced stops" (pp. 518–519), Pache opts for "the representation of Proto-Chibchan voiced stops as prenasalized stops *^{m}b, *^{n}d, *^{ŋ}g, and *^{ŋ}g^w, a solution which solely aims to represent both their voiced character and their ambiguity in terms of nasality" (p. 519). This differs from Adolfo Constenla Umaña's (2012) analysis, which has these as voiced stops that become nasals (have nasal stop allophones) in the environment of nasal vowels, or put differently, the nasal consonants are the result of nasal prosody by which a morpheme has either all oral vowels and oral consonants or all nasal vowels and nasal consonants (where a nasal counterpart of the consonant is possible), as in several other language families of South America, as well as in Siouan of North America. Pre-nasal stops are not found in these languages.

Pache (2018, 511) reconstructs Proto-Chibchan with the vowels: / i, (ĩ), (e), a, ã, (o), (õ), u, ũ/. However, he says that "nasal *ĩ and the mid vowels *e, *o, and *õ seem to be marginal in Proto-Chibchan. Mid vowels are only tentatively reconstructed here in Proto-Chibchan." He would derive modern Chibchan mid-vowels from Proto-Chibchan vowel sequences or diphthongs *ai or *au. Pache (2018, 513–514) does not reconstruct *w or *y (IPA [j]), believing instead that "Proto-Chibchan *i and *u may also have been realized as non-syllabic in the sequences *ai and *au."

Others may not agree with Pache's analysis of the nasal consonants and the lack of glides *w and *y.

Adolfo Constenla Umaña's (2012, 404) reconstruction of Proto-Chibchan phonemes has: /p, t, ts, k, ʔ, b, d, g, s, l, r, h, i, e, a, o, u/ plus nasal prosody, phonemic stress, and three tones.

Constenla Umaña (2012, 419) has the break-up of Proto-Chibchan with Pech (Paya), now spoken in northern Honduras, splitting off first from rest of the Chibchan language, at circa 4676 BCE. Constenla Umaña (2012, 419) located the Chibchan homeland in Central America, specifically in Honduras. However, one of his main reasons for choosing this location was his belief that Chibchan, Misumalpan, and Lencan are related at a remote level, making their center of dispersal Honduras. The evidence for a genetic relationship of these other two families with Chibchan, however, is not strong, weakening the case for this location as the Chibchan homeland. Even so, linguistic migration theory finds the greatest diversity of Chibchan subgroups in Central America, supporting a Central American rather than South American homeland for Chibchan.

Matthias Pache (2018, 656), on the other hand, favors a Chibchan homeland located in eastern South America. His reasons suffer from the same difficulty that confronts Constenla Umaña's Honduras homeland, namely reliance on hypothesized broader genealogical connections that are not supported. Pache cites his own hypothesis of a relationship of Chibchan with Macro-Jê and then mentions further the hypotheses that Macro-Jê, Tupían, and Cariban are genealogically related to one another (Rodrigues 1985a, 2000, 2003, 2009) and that Macro-Jê and Guaicurúan are connected (Viegas Barros 2005b). He says that based on the center-of-gravity approach (linguistic migration theory) a Chibchan homeland in eastern South America fits this better than one located in Central America. Pache mentions also as evidence certain lexical parallels shared by Chibchan and several other South American languages, though this evidence is not strong. He also mentions the shared typology of nasal vowels.

Chibchan has been involved in many proposals of remote genetic relationships, even more than most other language families of the Americas. Matthias Pache (2018, 20–22) presents a chart listing thirty-nine language families (including language isolates) that have been proposed to be affiliated with Chibchan. Constenla Umaña (2012a, 418) proposed a "Lemachí micro-phylum" composed of Chibchan, Misumalpan, and Lencan, which he dated to 7720 BCE. He also proposed "Misulencan," composed of Misumalpan and Lenca, as a branch of this Lemachí. These hypotheses have not been found productive.

Chicham (Jivaroan)
    Aguaruna (Awajún) Peru
    "Shuar" group (?)
        Achuar-Shiwiar
            Achuar (Achual) Ecuador, Peru
            Shiwiar (Mayna, Jívaro) Peru
        Wampis-Shuar
            Wampis (Huambisa) Peru
        Shuar Ecuador

(See Kohlberger 2020, 13, 16.)

The Chicham languages and varieties are reasonably well documented. Chicham has been characterized as a dialect continuum or "language area" with emergent languages (see Kaufman 2007, 67). It is a group of closely related languages and varieties spoken along the border between Ecuador and Peru. A high degree of mutual intelligibility is widespread, especially among neighboring groups. However, "speakers feel very strongly about the differences between the five varieties . . . each corresponding to one of the five ethnic groups that speak them" (Kohlberger 2020, 13–14). Neighboring varieties are especially closely related. For example, **Achuar** and **Shiwiar** are often grouped together as a single language. Loukotka (1968, 157), for example, considered **Huambisa** and "**Achual**" to be dialects of "**Jíbaro**" (Shuar) together with **Antipa, Gualaquiza, Upano, Canelo** (Penday), and **Bolona**.

At the same time, proposed classifications have treated **Aguaruna** as more divergent from the other four, which are seen as more closely related to one another, often placed together in a subgroup called Shuar. This has been based on the view that Aguaruna has conservative traits inherited directly from Proto-Chicham while the varieties in the Shuar subgroup were assumed to have undergone the shared phonological innovation of $*\eta > r$ (where Aguaruna has η, assumed to be a retention). However, it was Aguaruna that underwent a change, $*r > \eta$, and the r of the other four languages/varieties is a shared retention (Kohlberger 2020, 16). Kohlberger gives up on subgrouping, recognizing that "there is ample evidence that Aguaruna is the most divergent of the five" and the "other four languages form a dialect continuum where **Wampis** and **Shuar**, on the one hand, and **Achuar** and **Shiwiar**, on the other hand, are particularly closely related" (Kohlberger 2020, 16–17).

Terrence Kaufman (2007, 69) considered "Hivaro" (Jívaro) a "language area" with two emergent languages, Jívaro [Hivaro] (Jívaro/Achuar-shiwar) and Aguaruna (Awaruna/Awahun [Aguajún]). Adelaar and Muysken (2004, 616) and *Ethnologue* (2023) have the four "Jivaroan" (i.e., Chicham) languages. *Ethnologue* has **Awajún** (Aguaruna) as one branch and another branch that contains Achuar-Shiwiar, Shuar, and Wampís (Huambisa).

Long dormant **Palta, Malacato,** and **Bracamoro** (Pacamuru) in southern Ecuador and northern Peru have frequently been linked to Chicham languages (see for example Adelaar and Muysken 2004, 396–397, 582; Loukotka 1968, 157; Torero 2002, 284–287, etc.). Adelaar and Muysken also list **Xoroca** as Jivaroan, a hypothesis Alfredo Torero (2002, 284–287) favored. Xoroca may be a variety of Palta or an alternative name for Palta.

Palta, once spoken in Loja Province, Ecuador, has often been considered related to Chicham (Jivaroan) languages (Loukotka 1968, 157; Adelaar and Musken 2004, 172, 396). Alfredo Torero (2002, 287) believed in a "Palta-Jíbaro" family, distinguishing two branches, "Palta-Malacata" (perhaps also with **Cumbinamá**) and the Jíbaro branch. Terrence Kaufman (2007, 69), on the other hand, thought that "defunct" Palta "shows little resemblance" to Jivaroan (Chicham). Adelaar and Musken (2004, 396–397) point out that of the four attested words of Palta, three "have been recognized as Jivaroan," and they mention also evidence from place names from the area that appear to have in them a match to a Chicham locative case marker. Kohlberger (2020, 21) shows that three of the Four Palta words, found in the 1586 *Relaciones geográficas de Indias: Perú* (Jiménez de la

Espada 1965 [1586]), appear to have plausible matching words in Chicham; he supplies the following comparisons:

Palta <yumé> 'water': Chicham *yúmi* 'water'
Palta <xeme> (<x> = [ʃ]) 'corn': Chicham *ʃáa* 'corn'
Palta <capal> 'fire': Aguaruna *kapaút* 'burn'

They are not, however, without problems. The first, for 'water', looks attractive; however, the second, for 'corn', lacks any account for the non-matching <me> part; it is short and so it is more difficult to show that pure chance could not account for the similarity; and 'corn' is a culture item that may well be borrowed. The third, comparing 'fire' with 'burn', involves semantic latitude. The fourth Palta word, *let* 'firewood' has no suggested Chicham cognate. Kohlberger (2020, 21) correctly concludes that they "are interesting, but they are not enough evidence to posit a genetic relationship between the Chicham family and Palta, as they may be the result of chance similarity or lexical borrowing."

As with many other South American language families, there have been a number of proposals that would include Chicham (Jivaroan) in larger genetic groupings. Beuchat and Rivet (1909) listed possible lexical similarities between Chicham and Arawakan languages, a classification that a number of later scholars repeated. Greenberg (1960, 1987) grouped Chicham and Candoshi together, part of his broad Equatorial proposal (which is part of his massive Amerind hypothesis). Kaufman (2007, 69) grouped Chicham (his "Hívaro language area") and Kawapanan (Cahuapanan) together in his Hivaro-Kawapánan stock. Others have proposed linking Chicham with Urarina, Puelche, and Huarpe. So far, none of these has significant following.

Chiquitano (Besïro, Chiquito) Bolivia

Chiquitano is spoken in Santa Cruz Department, Bolivia, but it once reached as far as the Beni Department. It is considered a language isolate. (See Map 7.10.) It has distinct dialects: **Besïro** (Lomerío, Lomeriano Chiquitano, Concepción), **San Javier** (Javierano, Piñoco), **San Miguel** (Migueleño Chiquitano), **Santiago** (Santiagueño Chiquitano), **Churapa, Sansimoniano,** and **Tao**.

The Chiquitanía is a reasonably large area in eastern Bolivia; it was the home of a number of indigenous groups before the arrival of the Spanish. Santa Cruz de la Sierra was founded in 1559. Jesuits established a number of mission settlements (also known as reductions) and governed there until their expulsion in 1767. Chiquitano was the lingua franca of the missions and the area. The language is fairly well documented.

Chiquitano is often associated with the Macro-Jé (Sensu Lato) hypothesis. Willem Adelaar (2008b), for example, presented arguments for the relationship, though this is not confirmed, and many others now find a Macro-Jê connection for Chiquitano unlikely (see Nikulin 2020).

Chocoan (Chokóan)
Waunana (Noanamá, Huaunana, Woun Meu, Waumeo) Colombia, Panama
Emberá dialect continuum (Catío, Chamí, Saija, Sambú) Colombia, Panama

Southern Emberá (Epena)
Northern Emberá (Emperã, Eberã, Cholo [Choco])b

Ethnologue (2023) lists six distinct Emberá languages, two Northern Emberá languages (Northern Emberá and Emberá-Catío), and four Southern Emberá languages (Embera-Baudó, Embera-Chamí, Embera-Tadó, and Epena).

Several long-dormant language entities are sometimes classified with Chocoan: **Sinúfana** (Cenufara), **Quimbaya** (Kimbaya), **Anserma** (Anserna), **Arma**, **Cenu**, and **Cauca**. Only eight words are known of Quimbaya; it may not be Chocoan (Adelaar and Muysken 2004, 49, 56–60). *Ethnologue* (2023) considers Anserma to be a Coconuco language, part of its Paezan family. (The status of Coconuco itself is unclear; see Barbacoan above.) *Ethnologue* (2021) considered **Cauca** to be a non-existent language (unless it is the same as Quimbaya), retired from the ISO 639-3 codes in 2020 (https://iso639-3.sil.org/code/cca).

Constenla Umaña and Margery Peña (1991, 137) calculated the breakup of Proto-Chocoan at 2,100 years ago. Their reconstruction of the phonological inventory of Proto-Chocoan includes /p, t, č, k, b, β, s, h, f, ř, r̃, m, n; i, e, a, ɨ, o, u, nasalized vowels/ (Constenla Umaña and Margery Peña 1991, 161, 166).

As with other South American language families, Chocoan has had a number of proposals that would join it in larger language groupings. Several scholars thought it was linked with Cariban (for example Gunn 1980; Suárez 1974). Others would link it with Chibchan (Walter Lehmann 1920 for example). Constenla Umaña and Margery Peña (1991) presented preliminary evidence that they believed indicates a possible genetic connection between Chibchan and the Chocoan families.

The **Cueva** language of Panama has been much misunderstood. The Cueva people were exterminated by about 1535 due to the impact of the Spanish. Later, in the seventeenth and eighteenth centuries, Cuna people (speaking a Chibchan language) settled in the former Cueva area. Loukotka (1968, 238) misidentified a Cuna vocabulary as Cueva (Darien), and a number of others repeated his error; some listed Cueva as a dialect of Cuna. Constenla Umaña and Margery Peña (1991) believed that Cueva belonged with the Chocoan family, not with Chibchan as was often assumed (see also Loewen 1963, who was of the same opinion).

***Cholonan** (Hibito-Cholón) Peru
　　*Cholón (Seeptsá, Tinganés, Cholona)
　　*Híbito (Hibito, Xibito, Xibita, Jibito, Chibito, Zibito, Ibito, Xibitoana)

(Adelaar and Muysken 2004, 460–462; Alexander-Bakkerus 2005, 2006.)

Both **Cholón** and **Híbito** were spoken in the Department of San Martín, in the province of Mariscal Cáceres, Peru. Cholón was in the upper Huallaga Valley in northern Peru. (See Map 7.11.) Their traditional territories partially overlapped and both Cholón and Híbito may have occupied a larger area in the Andean foothills (van de Kerke and Muysken 2014, 144).

Alfredo Torero (2002, 212) came to the conclusion that Cholón and Híbito are not genetically related, but share 20 percent of their vocabulary due to prolonged coexistence in the same basin. Most other scholars consider the Cholonan family with these two languages securely established.

As for possible external relationships, Terrence Kaufman (2007, 69) grouped Cholonan with dormant **Culle** (Kulyi), but said "the hypothesis has not been systematically tested." Connection with poorly attested **Chachapoya** has also been contemplated. It has also been thought that Cholonan might have Chibchan connections. Joseph Greenberg (1987, 383) placed it in the Northern group of the Andean branch of his now rejected Amerind hypothesis.

*****Chonan** (Tehuelchean, Chon family) Argentina, Chile
    Chonan proper
        Island Chonan
            *Ona (Selknam, Selk'nam) Argentina, Chile
            *Haush (Manekenken, Menek'enk) Argentina, Chile
        Continental Chonan
            *Tehuelche (Aoniken, Patagón) Argentina
            *Teushen (Patagón) Argentina
            *Patagón Costero (Sixteenth Century Patagón) (?) Argentina
    *Gününa-Küne (Gennaken, Northern Tehuelche, Puelche, Pampa, Gününa Yajich) Argentina

(Viegas Barros 2005a, 47–72)

Ona (Selknam) was spoken on Isla Grande in Tierra del Fuego. Sources vary, saying its last native speaker died in the 1970s or 1980s.

Haush was spoken on Tierra de Fuego, on the tip of the Mitre Peninsula. Its last speaker died in about 1920.

Tehuelche became dormant in 2019 with the death of Dora Manchado. Tehuelche speakers were in Chilean territory just north of Tierra del Fuego.

Teushen has been dormant since about 1950; it was spoken in Patagonia, Argentina, north of Tehuelche.

Patagón Costero (Sixteenth-Century Patagón) is possibly a third Continental Chonan language, though it may have other explanations. The few sixteenth-century sources collected on the Atlantic coast of Patagonia, the longest with ninety words, suggest this as a language with Chonan affiliation. However, it is also possible that Sixteenth Century Patagón reflects an older stage of Teushen, a stage of Tehuelche, a stage before Teushen and Tehuelche separated, or words from bilinguals, from different languages (Viegas Barros 2005a, 37–40).

Gününa-Küne (also sometimes called Pampa, Serrano, Puelche, Poya, Huillipoya, Dihuihet, Chechehet, Güilliche, Quirquincho, Tehuelche, and Yéonkeshjent) has been dormant since the 1960s or 1970s, formerly spoken in the Río Negro region of the Pampas in Argentina. It is often listed as an isolate, though Pedro Viegas Barros (2005a, 138–152) presents strong evidence of its remote kinship with Chonan, seeing it not as a member of that family per se but as parallel, an "external relative."

Viegas Barros (2005a, 70–71) argues that **Querandí**, a long dormant and scarcely known language of the Buenos Aires region, may be related to Gününa Küne. He also argues for the possibility that **Enoo**, known only from sixteen words taken down by the Dutch sailor Olivier van Noort in 1599, was a "mixed" language, with more of the words belonging to some Chonan language, but with others belonging to Kawesqaran (Viegas Barros 2005a, 68). Viegas Barros (2005a, 78) is of the opinion that **Poya** (Pogya, Huillapoya), known only from some dozen words, was a mixed language with elements from Mapudungun and Gününa Küne. Loukotka (1968, 44) listed Poya (Payo) as a member of his Patagon or Tshon stock, in his Languages of Patagonia division; Mason (1950, 310) and Tovar (1961, 22) considered Poya a dialect of northern Tehuelche.

*Chono Chile

Long dormant Chono from the northern Kawesqaran region of Chile is very poorly attested, principally from an eighteenth-century catechism without Spanish translation. There has been confusion about the language's classification (Viegas Barros 2005a, 83–107). Nevertheless, it appears that enough can be figured out from the extant documentation to determine that it has very little similarity to other languages of the region or elsewhere and is therefore best considered a language isolate (see Adelaar and Muysken 2004, 552–553, 556–558). Some reportedly Chono materials make it appear to be a variant of Qawasqar (Alacaluf), but the material presented by Alessandro Bausani (1975) from the eighteenth-century catechism shows it to be different from Qawasqar (Adelaar and Muysken 2004, 553); it is a distinct language unrelated to others of the region.

Chono is also sometimes equated with **Aksanás**, another confusing term. Aksanás as identified today is one name for Northern Qawasqar. Loukotka (1968, 44) had an Aksanás stock with two languages, Chono (Caucau) and Kaueskar (Aksanás), not connected with his Alacaluf "isolated language" (Loukotka 1968, 43). This Aksaná(s) is not included in this classification on the assumption that Christos Clairis (1978, 32; 1985, 756) is correct in showing that the assumed Aksaná(s) language (not the Qawasqar variety of that name) does not really exist (see Chapter 5 for details).

This "Chono" is not to be confused with Chono of Ecuador, nor with Llaras Samitier's (1967) erroneous "Chono" or Wayteka (see Chapter 5.) It is also not a Chonan language, with which it could be confused (Viegas Barros 2005a, 45–46, 83–107).

Cofán (Kofan, A'ingaé) Colombia, Ecuador

Cofán is spoken in Sucumbíos Province in northeast Ecuador and in southern Colombia. There are two main varieties, **Aguarico**, in Ecuador, and **San Miguel**, primarily in Colombia. Cofán is a language isolate. It has sometimes been grouped with Chibchan, but without justification, though it has borrowed from neighboring Chibchan languages. Terrence Kaufman (200, 68) placed it with Yaruro and Esmeralda (Tacame) in his "Takame-Jarúroan stock," though so far this proposal has not been taken up by others. (See Map 7.11.)

*Culle (Culli) Peru

Culle is dormant and poorly attested. The primary sources on the language are two wordlists, one of nineteen words, the other of forty-three words (Adelaar and Muysken 2004, 401–403). It was spoken in the highlands of northern Peru, originally in parts of the

La Libertad, Cajamarca, and Ancash regions. It is a language isolate. (See Adelaar 1990.) (See Map 7.11.)

Culle has sometimes been thought to be related to Cholonan (for example, Kaufman 2007, 69), but the documentation is too limited to be certain of any genetic affinities. It is usually considered a language isolate, although perhaps it is so poorly attested that it should be shifted to the unclassified languages.

After the mid-twentieth century, it was no longer possible to find speakers of the language.

Enlhet-Enenlhet (Maskoyan, Lengua-Mascoy) Paraguay
    Western[14]
        Enlhet Norte (Lengua Norte)
        Enxet Sur (Lengua Sur, Lengua, Enhlit)
    Eastern
        Southeastern
            Angaité
            Sanapaná
        Northeastern
            Enenlhet (Mascoy, Mascoi, Machicui, Toba-Maskoy)
            Guaná (Cashquiha, Enlhet) (only 4 speakers)

(Elliott 2021, 23; see also Unruh and Kalisch 2003.)
(See Map 7.12.)

Speakers of Enlhet-Enenlhet languages live in the east central Paraguayan Chaco. The languages are closely related: "the whole family, at least historically, likely constitutes something of a non-linear dialect continuum" (Elliott 2021, 20). The family was called "Lengua" or "Mascoy" from the nineteenth century onward, though recognition of its members has been confused. Though mutual intelligibility has not been formally investigated, John Elliott (2021, 24–25) presents some indications that mutual intelligibility between Enxet Sur and Sanapaná is lacking, while at least for some Enxet Sur communities there is a fair degree of mutual intelligibility with Enlhet Norte. Reconstruction of Proto-Enlhet-Enenlhet remains to be done.

Note that **Emok**, formerly listed as a member of this language family, has been retired since 2014 from the ISO 639-3 codes for never having existed (https://iso639-3.sil.org/code/emo) (see Chapter 5).

*****Esmeralda** (Esmeraldeño, Tacame, Atacame) Ecuador

Esmeralda is a dormant language isolate. It was formerly spoken in coastal Ecuador, in particular in western Esmeraldas Province. The only existing data were collected by J. M. Pallares in 1877 for Theodor Wolf, published in full by Eduard Seler (1902).

Seler (1902, 49–64) proposed a connection between Esmeralda and **Yaruro**. Loukotka (1968, 233–234) followed this, grouping Esmeralda together with Yaruro and **Caraque** (a dormant language of which nothing is known) in the Paleo-Chibchan group of his

Chibcha Stock. Kaufman (2007, 68) placed Esmeralda with Yaruro and Cofán in his "Takame-Jarúroan stock." Willem Adelaar (personal communication) finds some interesting similarities between Esmeralda and Yurumanguí, which need to be investigated (see also Adelaar and Muysken 2004, 161); geographically this would be a plausible proposal.

*Guachí (Guasarapo) Argentina, Brazil

Guachí apparently ceased to be spoken by the latter half of the nineteenth century. Its speakers lived near the mouth of the Miranda River, a tributary of the Paraguay River in Mato Grosso do Sul state, Brazil. Guachí is known from only a list of 145 words (only 140 when the 5 words that are repeated in the list are counted only once), collected by Francis de Castelnau in 1845, and another list of 18 words from Johann Natterer from the first half of the nineteenth century (Zamponi in press b). It has been considered both a language isolate and an unclassified language.

It has often been suggested that Guachí is affiliated with Guaicurúan, but the extant data are insufficient to confirm this (Zamponi in press b). Perhaps Guachí should be placed rather in Chapter 5 with unclassified dormant languages. Pedro Viegas Barros (2004, 2006b, 2013a) has presented evidence that he believes supports a Macro-Guaicurúan classification, to which Guacurúan, Matacoan, **Payaguá**, and Guachí would belong. While the case for joining Guaicurúan and Matacoan seems plausible and worthy of more investigation, the case for joining Guachí and Payaguá seems doubtful (see Chapter 6). Nevertheless, Viegas Barros (2004) would place Guachí in his Macro-Guaicurúan but not as a member of the Guacurúan family.

Guaicurúan (Waikuruan, Waykuruan)
    Northern Guaicurúan (Mbayá) Brazil
        *Mbayá proper (Guaicurú)
        Kadiweu (Caduveo)
        *Beakeo
        *Kinikinau-Guaicurú
    Southern Guaicurúan
        *Abipón Argentina
            *Rrikahé
            *Nakaigetergehé
            *Yaaukaniga
    Qom
        Mocoví (Mocobí) Argentina
            Northern Mocoví (Chaco Mocoví)
            Southern Mocoví (Santa Fé Mocoví)
        Pilagá-Toba
            Pilagá Argentina
                Ñachilamole'k
                Pilagá Proper
                    Western Pilagá
                    Eastern Pilagá

Toba (Qom, Namqom) Argentina, Paraguay
   Old Toba
   Eastern Toba
      Paraguayan Toba (Toba-Qom, Emok-Toba)
      Rioverdino
         Rosarino-Cerriteño
           Rosarino
           Cerriteño
   Takshik (Guazú Toba)
   Western Toba
      Lañagashik
      No'olgranak
      Dapigeml'ek

(Viegas Barros 2013b, 26–27; see also Ceria and Sandalo 1995.)
(See Map 7.12.)

Northern Guaicurúan was called "Mbayá" or "Guaicurú," spoken until probably the latter half of the nineteenth century in the northern Chaco region of Paraguay. It survives now in Brazil's Mato Gross do Sul state where it is called **Kadiweu** (Caduveo). The other varieties of Northern Guaicurúan were apparently dialects of that language. Those identified with **Beakeo** (Beaqué, Beaqueo, Beutuebo, Beuquilecho) lived near the city of Miranda, at the headwaters of the Paraguay River. It is known only from forty-five words collected by Loukotka in 1963. The **Kinikinau-Guaicurú** (Quiniquinau, Koinó-Cunó, Guaycury) variety is known only from a wordlist of 136 items compiled near the city of Corumbá in the 1870s. **Kadiweu** is the only still-spoken variety of Northern Guaicurúan, in the area between the Serra de Bodoquena and the Nabileque and Aquidavão Rivers; it is well documented (Viegas Barros 2013b, 12–14).

All the other members of the family belong to the Southern Guaicurúan branch.

Abipón speakers originally lived in the eastern part of Formosa Province in Argentina. In the latter half of the seventeenth century when they got horses their territory expanded greatly to include parts of the Argentinian provinces of Salta, Tucumán, Santiago de Estero, Chaco, Córdova, Corrientes, Entre Ríos, and Santa Fé. The language was dormant by the latter half of the 1800s. The primary documentation is from Austrian Jesuit missionary Martin Dobrizhoffer's 1784 massive book written in Latin: *Historia de Abiponibus, equestri bellicosaque Paraquariae natione, locupletata copiosis barbarorum gentium, urbium, fluminum, ferarum, amphibiorum, insectorum, serpentium praecipuorum, piscium, avium, arborum, plantarum aliarumque ejusdem provinciae proprietatum observationibus*. It was later translated into several other languages, published in three volumes in English in London in 1822 with the title: *An Account of the Abipones, an Equestrial People of Paraguay*. It is an extensive ethnographic description of the Abipón people but also contains a rather ample grammar of the Abipón language, written in the model of Latin grammars of the time. The other source of documentation, of much less significance, is from Dobrizhoffer's colleague Joseph Brigniel (published by Samuel Lafone Quevedo 1894). Dobrizhoffer spoke of three mutually intelligible dialects: **Riikahé** (Riicahè), **Nakaigetergehé** (Nakaikétergehé), and **Yaaukaniga** (Yaukaniga, Jaúcaniga) (Viegas Barros 2013b, 14–15).

Mocoví (Mocobí, Amocovit) is spoken in the south of Chaco Province (Northern Mocoví variety) and in Santa Fé Province (Southern Mocoví variety). Until the beginning of the eighteenth century, Mocoví speakers were in the territory between the Bermejo and Pilcomayo Rivers in Formosa Province (Viegas Barros 2013b, 15).

Piliagá is spoken in the center of Formosa Province, Argentina. Bruno and Najlis' (1965) **Pilagá Abajeño** (Lower Pilagá, or Pilagá 1) has two dialects, **Western Pilagá** (Bañado Pilagá, Las Lomitas Pilagá) and **Eastern Pilagá** (Navagán Pilagá). Their **Pilagá Arribeño** (Upper Pilagá, or Pilagá 2) refers to a somewhat divergent variety of Pilagá whose speakers do not consider themselves Pilagás but rather "Tobas," sometimes called Toba-Pilagá or Tobas of Sombrero Negro; Sombrero Negro is one of their main locations. This causes confusion with the actual Toba language (Viegas Barros 2013b, 16).

Old Toba appears to have been as different from any modern Toba dialect as Pilagá is. It was recorded by the missionary Alonso de Bárcena (or Barzana) in 1595 (published by Samuel Lafone Quevedo 1894–1896), with later sparce data recorded by Francisco de Aguirre in 1792, apparently from near Asunción, Paraguay, and there are a couple of small Jesuit missionary texts.

Modern **Toba** is spoken in the Argentinian provinces of Formosa, Chaco, and Santa Fe, and in the Department of Presidente Hayes in Paraguay, as well as now also in several large cities of Argentina (Viegas Barros (2013b, 17–19). The dialects of Toba are given above in Viegas Barros' classification of the language family (see also Viegas Barros 2013b, 18–19, 26–27).[15]

A number of groups whose names are recorded in sources from the sixteenth and seventeenth centuries have sometimes been thought to have been speakers of Guaicurúan languages, though they are essentially unattested other than as the names of peoples. These names include: **Togacüe**, **Hohoma**, **Hometa**, **Natica**, **Quiloaza**, and **Cocolote**. Some of the names were thought to appear somewhat similar to names for Toba and others (Viegas Barros 2013b, 20). For example, Alfred Métraux (1946, 225) and J. Alden Mason (1950, 205) thought that **Mahoma** or **Hohoma** was possibly related to Toba and Mocoví; this is probably the same name as Loukotka's (1968, 63) **Ohoma**, an unclassified language. (See Chapter 5.)

Pedro Viegas Barros' (2013b, 37–40) reconstruction of Proto-Guaircurúan sounds is: / p, t, ts, ʧ, k, q, ʔ, pʔ, tʔ, tsʔ, ʧʔ, kʔ, qʔ, d, g, ʔd, ʔg, l, ʔl, m, n, ʔm, ʔn, w, j, ʔw, ʔj, i, e, a, o/. (See Ceria and Sandalo 1995 for an earlier reconstruction.) No Guaicurúan language has phonemic glottalized consonants. Viegas Barros (2013b, 37–38) presents several arguments for assuming their presence in the proto language, though none of them strike me as compelling; that is, it seems that they could be explained in other ways without having to assume glottalized consonants in the proto language. Viegas Barros' (2013b, 41) reconstruction of Proto-Southern Guaicurúan (essentially Guaicurúan without Kadiweu) lacks the glottalized consonants (with the sole exception of *ʔd). Much would seem to depend on the nature and origin of certain sounds in Kadiweu. Nonato and Sandalo (2007) say that Kadiweu voiceless geminates are realized as very weakly glottalized, where voiced geminates are phonetically implosive. While the phonetic nature of this "glottalization" needs to be examined carefully, it is not unlikely that these developments may have taken place only in the independent history of Kadiweu and therefore have nothing to do directly with Proto-Guaicurúan.

As for proposed external relationships for Guaicurúan, the dormant and poorly attested **Guachí** and **Payaguá** have both often been classified with Guaicurúan, though the evidence is insufficient to establish such a relationship. Viegas Barros presented some attractive lexical and some morphological comparisons between them and Matacoan and Guaicurúan, but he sums up the evidence for including these two, saying "the similarities from Payaguá and from Guachí with the languages of the Guacurúan family (although some are suggestive) turn out to be—on the whole—scarce, therefore they are insufficient for being able to assure that these languages really belong to the family" (Viegas Barros 2013b, 21).[16] He says further:

> Nevertheless, both [Guachí and Payaguá] are very little-known languages, many of the characteristics that define the Guaicurúan family are not documented in them, and it is very difficult to find regular sound correspondences with the typical Guaicurúan languages, so that membership of these two languages in the family does not seem verifiable. (Viegas Barros 2013b, 25)[17]

As for broader connections, Matacoan has often been claimed to be related to Guaicurúan, and Viegas Barros (2006b, 2013a) has made a very plausible case for this relationship. Other proposed associations with Charrúan, Enlhet-Enenlhet (Mascoyan), Mapudungun, and others do not appear promising. (See Chapter 6 for details.)

Guajiboan (Guahiboan, Guahiban)
  Core Guajiboan
    Guajibo (Guahibo, Sikuani, Sicuani, Hiwi) Colombia, Venezuela
    Cuiva (Cuiba, Cuiba-Wámonae) Colombia, Venezuela
    *Churuya (Bisanigua and Guaigua) Colombia
  Macaguán (Hitnü, Macaguane)
  Guayabero Colombia

(Kaufman 2007, 65, which he spells as Wahivoan; Queixalós 1993)

Guajiboan languages are spoken in the region of the Orinoco River in eastern Colombia and southwestern Venezuela, in the savanna region called the Llanos. **Guajibo** (Guahibo, Sikuani) and **Cuiva** (Cuiba) form a dialect continuum. Guajibo (Guahibo, Sikuani) is spoken in eastern Colombia in most of Vichada Department and in parts of Arauca, Casanare, Guainía, and Meta departments, with many Sikuani also in Venezuela. **Guayabero** is the most divergent of the Guajiboan languages; it is spoken in Meta and Guaviare departments along the Guariare River (Adelaar and Muysken 2004, 162).

Ethnologue (2023) has **Playero** as an additional Guajiboan languages. However, Playero (Río Arauca Guahibo) appears to be the name of a group (subtribe) of Guajibo, with its own dialect. Macaguán (Hitnü, Macaguane) has been considered a dialect of Guajibo by some scholars, but Hitnü (Macaguán, Macaguane), like Guayabero, is a divergent member of the family (Queixalós 1993).

Churuya (Churoya, Churruy) is dormant; it was spoken at El Piñal, in the area of San Martín, Colombia, on the Guaivare River. Churuya seems clearly to be a Guajiboan language, though its place in the family is uncertain. Adelaar and Muysken (2004, 162) do not include it in their classification of Guajiboan, though several others do. There appear to be only two sources on the language, twenty words published by Nicolás Sáenz (1876) and another thirty-two words found by Adolf Ernst (1891) in a manuscript left by Firmin Toro after he died in 1865. Sergio Elías Ortiz (1943, 162) found that twenty-four of fifty of the words match Guahibo words; he believed seven were borrowed from other languages of the Orinoco area, and one was a loanword from Quechua.

Efforts to reconstruct the phonemic system were published by Dana Christian and Esther Matteson (1972), based on Guajibo, Cuiva, and Guayabero; they reconstructed: /p, t, k, b, d, Y, s, x, l, r, m, n, N, w, y, h; i, e, ɨ, a, o, u/. Their reconstruction of *N is based on the sound correspondence of *l: l: n, which contrasts with *n for the correspondence n: n: n and contrasts also with *l for l: l: l. Their *Y is reflected by č in Guayabero and by y/i/Ø in Cuiva and Guajibo.

There have been various attempts to group Guajiboan with other languages, including with Arawakan, Arawan, and Candoshi. Terrence Kaufman (1994, 57) observed that "virtually all major 'lumpers' and classifiers group Wahivoan [Guajiboan] with Arawakan. The hypothesis deserves to be tested or looked into, but I have so far seen no evidence to convince me of the connection," although Kaufman (2007, 65) still has his "Wahívoan family" as a member of his "Macro-Arawakan cluster." Queixalós (1993) was more direct; he assures us that there is no genetic relationship between Guajiboan and Arawakan, though there are loanwords and possibly some areal influences. Miguel Ángel Meléndez-Lozano (2014) reported on loanwords from Arawakan languages, from Piapoco and Achagua in particular, in Guajiboan languages.

*Guamo (Wamo, Guamatey) Venezuela

Guamo speakers were reported to be in the northern Llanos of Venezuela, in the vicinity of the Acarigua, Cojedes, Pao, Guanare, Portuguesa, and Guaparo Rivers. The language has long been dormant. It is known only from a single wordlist recorded in 1788 by a Dominican missionary, signed F. X. C., published in 1928. The list provides 315 translations for the headwords on the 444-word list sent out for Catherine the Great's project of collecting samples of all the world's languages. Many entries have two Guamo equivalents, one from **Santa Rosa** (on the Masparro River) and the other from **San José** (on the Santo Domingo River). Raoul Zamponi (in press b) reports that:

> 182 (58%) of the 315 Spanish headwords have two translations and at least 100 (55%) of the 182 double translations do not appear to involve cognate words . . . the Santa Rosa and San José varieties, apparently sharing about 68% of cognates in their vocabulary, were distinct (but closely related) languages rather than dialects of the same language.

However, Zamponi continues:

> Giving credit to a note included at the end of the wordlist by its author, Guamo was probably a single language with various dialects, all of which were mutually intelligible with each other: "The same Guamo, even though they are of their own nation, constituting various divisions, or the groupings within the same division as well, differ in many words, but they all understand each other." (F. X. C. 1928, 303; Zamponi in press b).[18]

As for attempts to find relatives for Guamo, Joseph Greenberg (1987, 83, 384) provisionally linked Guamo with Arawakan, in his Macro-Arawakan, part of his Equatorial, which is a branch of his Equatorial-Tucanoan, a division of his now rejected Amerind. Terrence Kaufman (2007, 65) included Guamo in his Wamo-Chapakuran stock. Given that no convincing evidence has yet been presented, Guamo is considered a language isolate.

*Guató Brazil

Guató, a language isolate, was spoken until recently in the Pantanal region of Mato Grosso do Sul state in Brazil, on the Paraguay River and up the São Lourenço River.

Guató has typically been associated with the Macro-Jê hypothesis. However, Eduardo Ribeiro (2006) doubted the proposed connection, and Andrey Nikulin (2020, 75), after a thorough comparison, concludes:

> It is possible to observe that Guató shows more technical similarities with Proto-Tupí . . . than with Proto-Macro-Jê . . . or with Chiquitano . . . and even then the observed similarities are not particularly striking and could be fortuitous. We conclude that there is no evidence to classify Guató as a language related to the Macro-Jê stock.[19]

Harákmbut-Katukinan (Adelaar 2000, 2007)
    Harákmbut (Harakmbet, Hate, Tuyoneri, "Mashco") Peru
        Several dialects in two clusters:
            (1) Huachipaeri, Tuyoneri Peru
            (2) Amaracaeri (Amarakaeri), Sapiteri, Arasaeri Peru
    Katukinan (Catuquinan) Brazil
        Katukina (Catuquina, Katukina do Jutaí)
        Kanamarí (Southern Katukina, Tshom-Djapá, Dyapá) (dialects or languages)
        *Katawixí (Catawixi) Brazil (Presumed dormant)

(Kaufman 2007, 68)

Harákmbut is spoken along the Madre de Dios and Colorado Rivers in Peru. Two groups associated with Harákmbut are **Amarakaeri** (Amarakaire, Amaracaire, "Mashco") and **Huachipaeri** (Huachipaire, Wachipaire, also "Mashco"). Terrence Kaufman (2007, 65) listed the two as "emergent languages" in a Tuyoneri "language area." *Ethnologue* (2023) sees them as two separate Harákmbut languages.

    Katukinan languages are closely related to one another. The name Katukina (Catuquina) has been applied to languages of different groups, for example also Arawakan and Panoan, and so care is needed to avoid confusion. Fernando Orphão de Carvalho (2019) believes the name comes from a Piro (Purus, Arawakan) etymology meaning 'speaker of an indigenous language'. *Dyapá* means 'people, clan' and thus is also a possible source of confusion involving the names of languages in this language family. Aikhenvald and Dixon (1999, 343) have as members of Katukinan: Kanamarí, Katukina do Biá, Txunhuã-Djapá, and Katawixí. Willem Adelaar (2007, 180) has two languages, Katawixi and Katukina Lato (which has three varieties: Kanamarí, Katukina do Biá, and Tyohon Dyapa).

Willem Adelaar (2000, 2007) presented persuasive evidence that Harákmbut and Katukinan are genetically related, members of a single language family.

*Huarpean (Warpean) (dialects or languages) Argentina
  *Huarpe (Allentiac)
  *Millcayac

Huarpe (Allentiac) and **Millcayac** are closely related languages of Argentina, sometimes considered dialects of a single language, that have long been dormant. Huarpe (Allentiac) was spoken in the Cuyo region, Mendoza Province; Millcayac was spoken in San Luis Province. Terrence Kaufman (2007, 71) treated both as emergent languages.

In his "Huarpe stock" Loukotka (1968, 277) placed, in addition to these two languages, also **Oico** (Holcotian), **Orcoyan** (Oscollan), **Chiquiyama**, **Tuluyame** (Puelche Algarrobero), **Comechingón**, **Michilenge** (Puntano), and **Olongasto**—saying "nothing" is known of most of these "languages."

Kaufman (2007, 71) had a tentative Macro-Warpean classification, based on the fact that both Swadesh and Greenberg placed Huarpe and Mura-Matanawian languages together under the same higher order grouping. Kaufman (2007, 71) says of it, however, that "no systematic study of this specific connection has so far been made." Other proposals of kinship have also been made, but generally with no supporting evidence.

Iaté (Fulnio, Fulniô, Furniô, Fórnio, Carnijó, Yaathé, Yaté, Yathé) Brazil

Iaté (Fulnio) is a language isolate spoken in Aguas Belas, Pernambuco, in northeastern Brazil. It is well documented (see Seifart and Hammarström 2018 for details). It is said to have two dialects, Iaté and Fulniô. Fulniô is used during the Ouricuri secret ritual, a fourteen-week retreat held in the village of Ouicuri, that reportedly Fulnio are required to participate in to be considered members of the group (https://pib.socioambiental.org/en/Povo:Fulni-ô, accessed January 17, 2022).

Iaté (Fulnio) is usually included in the Macro-Jê hypothesis. However, this hypothesis turns out not to be supported by the evidence, and a Iaté connection with Macro-Jê is now rejected (Nikulin 2020, 69–70). After a comparison of Iaté vocabulary with various putative Macro-Jê language, Nikulin (2020, 70) concludes:

> There is no particularly strong resemblance within this list between Yaathê, Proto-Macro-Jê, Proto-Chiquitano, and Proto-Tupí[an]. This is compatible with the hypothesis that Yaathê is not demonstrably related to these families, unless such relationship takes place at an extremely deep level.[20]

Irantxe (Iranxe, Myky, Mynky, Münkü) Brazil

Irantxe is a language isolate spoken in Mato Grosso state, Brazil, on the Cravari River. (See Map 7.10.)

Dixon and Aikhenvald (1999, 20) listed Irantxe among the "few languages that we say nothing about, for the simple reason that almost nothing is known about them." The language, however, was not that unknown even then; it had considerable documentation in Robert Meader's (1967) grammar and vocabulary notes and in Monserrat and Amarante's

(1995) dictionary of the language. See also Monserrat (2000) for a more recent grammar. Monserrat and Amarante (1995, 48) reported the two dialects of the language as **Irántxe**, spoken in Cravari on the Cravari River, in the município of Diamantino, and **Mỹky** (Mynku), spoken in one isolated village at the headwaters of Escondido Creek, in the município of Brasnorte (see also Monserrat 2000).

Irantxe is generally considered a language isolate, even by those who typically lump things together (for example Loukotka 1968, 98; Kaufman 2007, 74), though Greenberg (1987, 383) placed it in his Macro-Tucanoan branch of Equatorial-Tucanoan.

Itonama (Saramo, Machoto) Bolivia

Itonama is a language isolate, on the Itonamas River and Lake, Beni Department, northeastern Bolivia. (See Map 7.10.) As of 2012 it had only one remaining speaker and may now be dormant.

Although Itonama is considered a language isolate by most scholars, Greenberg (1987, 382) placed it in his large Paezan grouping, a branch of his Macro-Chibchan (a division of his Amerind), and Kaufman (2007, 64) put Itonama loosely in his Macro-Paesan cluster.

*Jirajaran Venezuela
  *Jirajara
  *Ayomán (Ayamán)
  *Gayón (Coyón)

Jirajaran languages were spoken in the mountainous area in Lara and Falcón states in western Venezuela. Some data were collected on the Jirajaran languages, mostly wordlists, in the early years of the 1900s. The languages appear to have become dormant soon after that (Adelaar and Muysken 2004, 129–130). The languages of the family are closely related, sometimes suspected of being varieties of a single language.

Typologically Jirajaran languages seem to be like Chibchan languages. However, "the data are too limited to say anything substantial about their genetic and typological characteristics" (Adelaar and Muysken 2004, 130). Terrence Kaufman (2007, 63) said that "there are no generally accepted hypotheses about outside connections of Hirajaran [Jirajaran]." Greenberg (1987, 382), notwithstanding, placed Jirajara[n] in his Paezan branch of Chibchan-Paezan (part of his Amerind hypothesis).

Jotí (Yuwana, Yoana, Waruwaru, Chicano, Jodi, Hotí, Hodï) Venezuela

Jotí, a language isolate, is spoken in remote, mountainous central Venezuela, between the upper Ventuari and Erebato Rivers in the states of Bolívar and Amazonas, to the east and northeast of San Juan de Manapiare. Its speakers were first contacted by outsiders only in the 1970s.

Dixon and Aikhenvald (1999, 20) listed "Hoti" among the "few languages that we say nothing about, for the simple reason that almost nothing is known about them." The language was not, however, that unknown at that time (see Vilera Díaz 1987). Many proposals suggest possible genetic relationships between Jotí and other languages. These include more recently Sáliban (argued by Rosés Labrada 2019, and earlier also proposed by Walter

Coppens 1983), though the evidence presented for this has not been sufficient to confirm their relatedness (see Zamponi 2017). Henley et al. (1996, 17) argued that what seemed to be cognates between "Hodï" and Piaroa–Sáliban (Sáliban) are instead loanwords; they argued that Jotí may be related to "Puinave-Makúan," that is, to Puinave and the Nadahup languages. Valteir Martins (2005, 341) mentions data that he believes point to a probable "Makúan" (an assumed grouping of Kakua-Nukak with Nadahup) affinity with Hodï, more precisely with the "Kakua." Ernest Migliazza's (1982[1985]) proposed Jotí affinity with Yanomaman appears now to be abandoned. (Seifart and Hammarström 2018, Zamponi in press b.)

Kakua-Nukak (Kakua-Nukakan)
  Kakua (Cacua, Macu de Cubeo, Kakwa) Colombia, Brazil
  Nukak Colombia

Kakua and Nukak are closely related; *Ethnologue* (2021) reported them as mutually intelligible. Martins and Martins (1999, 254) considered Kakua a dialect of Nukak; they said that Nukak and Kakua are mutually intelligible and share around 90 percent of their lexicon in common. (See Map 7.9.)

Kakua (Kakwa) has two dialects: **Vaupés Cacua** and **Macú-Paraná Cacua**. It is spoken in Wacara, near Mitú in the Vaupés Department of Colombia and in Nuevo Pueblo, between the Vaupés and Papurí Rivers (Bolaños Quiñonez 2016).

Nukak is spoken in the departments of Guaviare and Guainia, between the Guaviare River and the Upper Inirida, Colombia. Nukak came to be recognized only after its speakers came into contact with the broader society in the 1980s (Epps and Bolaños 2017).

Though these languages/varieties are related to each other, they are not detectably related to any other languages. Formerly they were linked with the Nadahup ("Makúan," Nadahupan) languages, and all of these together sometimes were joined with **Puinave** (Wãnsöhöt), called the Makú-Puinave family or Puinavean, and *Ethnologue* (2023) has Cacua and Nukak Makú as members of a Cacua subgroup of its Puinavean language family. There appears to be no basis for connecting Kakua-Nukak with any other language group, and Puinave (Wãnsöhöt) is a language isolate. About these hypotheses in general, Epps and Bolaños (2017, 502) conclude:

> Our examination of the new data now available for these languages indicates that we are dealing with what are at this point best understood as three distinct genetic units: the Naduhupan [Nadahup] family (Nadëb, Dâw, Hup, and Yuhup), the small Kakua-Nukakan family, and the isolate Puinave/Wãnsöjöt. Our data reveal no convincing evidence for grouping any of these three units together, although similarities between Puinave and Kakua-Nukakan suggest the possibility of a relationship . . . On the other hand, while their divergent morphosyntactic profiles provide evidence of substantial contact with their Tukanoan and Arawakan neighbors, the seven languages share distinctive phonological and phonotactic characteristics that set them apart from their neighbors, and could perhaps be due to some ancient areal affiliation.

(See also Bolaños Quiñonez 2016.)

Kamsá (camsá, Sibundoy, Coche, Kamentxa, Kamëntšá, Quillacinga, Mocoa) Colombia

Kamsá is spoken in the Sibundoy Valley, Putomayo Department, Colombia. (See May 7.11.) Kamsá is a language isolate. There have been a number of attempts to group it with other languages and language families, especially with Chibchan, but without success. It has also been suggested that it is related to long dormant and unattested **Quillacinga**, from around the nearby city of Pasto. Kamsá could perhaps be related to whatever was spoken in the city of **Mocoa**, but whatever language that may have been is totally unknown. Kamsá has borrowed many words from neighboring Inga (Quechuan), with which it has been in contact for at least five centuries (O'Brien 2018).

Kanoê (Kapixaná, Capixana) Brazil

Kanoê is spoken in southern Rondônia in the eastern Guaporé-Mamoré area near the Bolivian border, on the Brazilian side of the Guaporé River. (See Map 7.10.) There are two groups of speakers, one in the Guaporé River region and another in the Rio Omerê Indigenous Territory. When speakers were first contacted by outsiders in 1995, the Kanoê had already been decimated by violent encroachment from farmers and colonists—only five remained (Seifart and Hammarström 2018, 271, *Povos Indígenas no Brasil*; https://pib.socioambiental.org/en/Povo:Kanoê, accessed July 31, 2021]). As of 2012 there were only three speakers.

Kanoê is a language isolate. Dixon and Aikhenvald (1999, 20) say that Kanoé is among the "few languages that we say nothing about, for the simple reason that almost nothing is known about them." With Laércio Nora Bacelar's (2004) grammar and a dictionary this is fortunately no longer the case. A possible connection with Kwaza has been noted by Hein van der Voort (2005), but needs investigation. David Price (1978) suggested a relationship with Nambikwaran languages and Terrence Kaufman (2007, 63) linked Kanoê with Kunza (Atacameño) in his Kunsa-Kapishaná stock, part of his larger Macro-Paesan Cluster. None of these proposals is confirmed.

*Karirían (Karirí language or language family) Brazil
　*Kipeá (Karirí, Kirirí, Kariri de Mirandela)
　*Dzubukuá (Kiriri, Dzubucua)
　*Sabuyá (Sapoyá)
　*Kamurú (Camurú, Pedra Branca)

These are either closely related separate languages or are dialects of a single language. Most scholars classify them as independent languages, though Raoul Zamponi (in press b) argues strongly that there was only a single Karirí language and that these others are varieties of it. It was once spoken in the Brazilian states of Piauí, Ceará, Paraíba, Pernambuco, and Bahia.

Kipeá (Kirirí) was spoken on Cariris Velhos (Borborema Plateau) in Paraíba and Pernambuco, in Cariris Novo (Paraíba and Ceará), and in the Itaim Valley (Piauí). **Dzubukuá** was spoken on five islands in the São Francisco River between Bahia and Pernambuco. **Sabuyá** (Sapuyá, Sapoyá) was spoken originally in the Serra Chapada and later in Caranguejo (Bahia). **Kamurú** was spoken in the Pardo River area and in Pedra Branca (Bahia).

It is very likely that some of the peoples referred to in the seventeenth-century documents spoke additional dialects of Karirí, though they have disappeared without leaving any documentation behind (see for example Loukotka 1968, 89–90). Raoul Zamponi (in press b) adds also **Moriti** and **Payayá** to the list.

The names *Kariri* and *Kiriri* have been applied to a number of languages and peoples in eastern Brazil, and care is needed not to confuse them.

There is fairly good documentation of Dzubukuá and Kipeá from the end of the 1600s and beginning of the 1700s. For Dzubukuá there is a 1709 bilingual Portuguese-Dzubukuá catechism. For Kipeá there is a 1698 bilingual catechism and a 1699 grammar. Based on the seventeenth- and eighteenth-century material, Márcio de Queiroz (2012) wrote a grammar of Dzubukuá and Gilda de Azevedo (1965) a grammar of Kipeá. For Sabuyá and Kamurú there are only two inaccurately transcribed wordlists published in the nineteenth century. Kamurú has only a list of about 200 words from Carl von Martius (1867, 215–217), and Sabuyá has only Martius' (1867, 218–219) list of about 100 words.

It has been hypothesized that Karirían belongs with languages of the Macro-Jê (Sensu Lato) hypothesis, but any relationship with those languages now looks very doubtful (Ribeiro 2002, 2006; Rodrigues 1986; Nikulin 2020; Zamponi in press b).

Kawesqaran (Alacalufan)
 Qawasqar (Northern Alacaluf, Kaweskar, Kawésqar, Kawaskar, Aksánas) Chile
   (Dialects: Kawésqar, Tawókser)
 Alacaluf (Central Alacaluf, Hekaine) Chile
 Southern Alacaluf (Halakwalup, Pecheré) Chile

The classification of Kawesqaran varies according to the different scholars. Pedro Viegas Barros (1990), after careful analysis of the data, distinguished the two languages, Central Kawesqar and Southern Kawesqar, and then later presented evidence that recognizes three languages in the family (Pedro Viegas Barros 2005a, 37–43). However, Adelaar and Muysken (2004, 617) consider Qawasqar (Alacaluf, Aksanás) a language isolate, and Terrence Kaufman (2007, 71) considered it made up of two emergent languages, Aksaná (Kaweskar) and Hekaine. Viegas Barros (2005a, 44) makes a good case that the language of the **Guaïcaros** (Guaicurúes, Huacurúes, Supalios, Huemules) of the New Brunswick Peninsula, Chile, was a Kawesqaran language, fitting Central Alacaluf best, with Chonan loans, though only nineteen words and some personal names are attested for it (Viegas Barros 2005a, 44).

Several hypotheses of remote linguistic kinship between Kawesqaran and other languages exist. A Yagan-Alacaluf relationship was suggested by several earlier scholars, although generally without evidence (see Viegas Barros 2015, 67, 68). Viegas Barros (2015, 67) considers this quite possible and adds to it Chono, in a Yagan-Alacaluf-Chono proposal (Viegas Barros 2005a, 99–107). This hypothesis merits further attention.

Other proposals of possible remote affiliation seem unlikely. Alfredo Trombetti (1907, 195) added Botocudo (Krenak) to the presumed Yagan-Alakaluf grouping, and he thought these tongues were more remotely related to languages of "eastern Australia, the Torres Strait, and neighboring regions."[21] Jorge Suárez (1974) proposed a relationship between the Alacaluf and the Matacoan family. Joseph Greenberg (1987) included Alacaluf, Yagan, Chon, Gününa Yajüch, and Mapudungun in his "Southern Andean" group, part of larger "Andean," which belongs to the "Andean-Equatorial" part of his massive "Amerind" proposal. None of these is seen as having any reasonable support. (See Viegas Barros 2015, 67–68.) Interestingly, Terrence Kaufman (2007, 71) did not link his "Kaweskar language area" in any broader groupings.

Kwaza (Koayá, Koaiá) Brazil

Kwaza is a language isolate (Van der Voort 2005; Kaufman 2007, 74). It is critically endangered, spoken in southern Rondônia state, Brazil, in the Tubarão-Latundê Indigenous Reserve (Seifart and Hammarström 2018). (See Map 7.10.) In a manuscript from 1913, where "Coaiás" were first mentioned by outsiders, they were located along the São Pedro River, a tributary of the Pimenta Bueno River (Van der Voort 2005, 368, *Povos Indígenas no Brasil* [https://pib.socioambiental.org/en/Povo:Kwazá, accessed July 31, 2021]). Hein van der Voort (2005) provided an extensive grammar of the language.

Van der Voort (2005) observed similarities among Kwaza, Kanoê (Kapixaná), and Aikanã, but believed the evidence was not sufficient to establish a clear genetic link among these three languages.

*Leco (Lapalapa, Leko, Rik'a, Rika, Ateniano) Bolivia

Leco is a dormant language isolate, formerly spoken in La Paz Department east of Lake Titicaca in Bolivia. (See Map 7.10.) Apart from some short vocabulary lists, the main documentation of Leco was a Christian doctrine by Andrés Herrero at the beginning of the 1800s, published by Lafone Quevedo in 1905. Little else was known until Simon van de Kerke located some men in 1994 who were apparently semi-speakers of Leco and in work with them was able to add some additional information beyond that in Lafone Quevedo's analysis (see Van de Kerke 2000, 2013).

As for suggestions of possible relatives, Terrence Kaufman (2007, 69–70) put Leko (Leco) in his Macro-Lekoan cluster, along with Sechura and the Katakaoan family. He said, however, that the Macro-Lekoan cluster "hypothesis has not been systematically tested" (p. 69).

*Lule-Vilelan (Lula-Vilela)
  *Lule Argentina
  *Vilela[22] Argentina

(Viegas Barros 2001, 2006a)

Lule was spoken in the western Chaco and in parts of the Calchaquí Valley in Salta and Tucumán provinces and in the north of Santiago del Estero Province, in Argentina. It was probably dormant before the 1800s. It is known mostly from Antonio Maccioni [Machoni]'s 1732 *Arte y Vocabulario de la Lengua Lule y Tonocoté* (see Badini and Zamponi's introductions to the 2008 edition of Maccioni [Machoni]).

Colonial sources report that **Lule** was spoken by five "nations": Tonocoté, Lule, Ysistiné, Toquistiné, and Oristiné (Adelaar and Muysken 2004, 386). The sources, however, are difficult to interpret, leaving the true linguistic identity of **Tonocoté** and the others unclear. Loukotka (1968, 277) included in his "Lule stock": Lule, Tonocoté, Isistiné, Oristine, Matará (Amualalá), and Jurí, saying nothing was known of any of these except Lule itself. J. Alden Mason (1950, 205) saw Juri (Suri) as "perhaps Guaicurú[an]" (not to be confused with Yurí [Jurí] of Tikuna-Yurí).

Vilela was spoken in a large part of the Chaco plain and in Santiago del Estero, Argentina. There are brief mentions of the language in the eighteenth-century Jesuit missionary writings, and there are some studies of the language from the end of the nineteenth century and the early twentieth century (for example, Ambrosetti 1894, Lafone Quevedo 1895). It is best known, however, from the works of Clemente Balmori (1967; Balmori and Balmori 1998), and Elena Lozano (1964, 1970, 1977, 2006, etc.) (Viegas Barros 2006a).

Chunupí is an alternative name for Vilela, though Loukotka (1968, 53) considered it a distinct language in his Vilela stock. The identity of "Chunupí" in historical sources is unclear, and the name has also been associated with **Nivaclé** (Chulupí, Ashluslay; a Matacoan language), causing confusion.

Pedro Viegas Barros' (2006a, 2) reconstruction of Proto-Lule-Vilela phonemes is: /p, t, ts, č, ky, k, kw, q, qw, ʔ, p', t', č', ky', k', b, g, gw, ɢ, s, xy, x, xw, L, l, m, n, w, y; i, e, a, u, o, ï, ü/. The *ü is based on the sound correspondence of Lule u to Vilela i, while the *ï represents the sound correspondence of Lule u to Vilela e. The other vowels in the chart have the same reflex in both languages, and so their reconstruction is straightforward. There is another set of vowels whose reconstruction Viegas Barros calls "uncertain" (with the correspondences Lule u : Vilela o; u : a; o : u; i : e; e : i; e : a; a : e). These sound correspondences are not found in many cognate sets, but still each is present in multiple sets.

None of the wider connections for Lule-Vilela that have been contemplated offer much hope of success. Kaufman (2007, 72) had his Lule-Vilelan stock in his Macro-Waikuruan cluster, along with most other language families of the Chaco region. Greenberg (1987, 74, 385) placed Lule-Vilela in his massive Macro-Panoan division of Amerind.

Macro-Jê Sensu Stricto
    Jabutían (Yabutían) (Ribeiro and van der Voort 2010)
        Jabutí (Yabutí, Djeoromitxí) Brazil
        Arikapú (Maxubí, Aricapú, Arikapu) Brazil
    Jêan (Gêan, Jê family) (See Ribeiro 2006; Rodrigues 1999)
        Northeastern Jê (Northern Jê)
            Timbíra (Canela [Kanela], Krenjé, Krahó Brazil
            Kreen-Akorore (Creen-Acarore) Brazil
            Apinayé (Apinajé) Brazil
            Kayapó (Cayapó, Mebengokre) Brazil
                (Dialects: Xikrin, Kararaó, Kayapó-Kradaú)
            Suyá Brazil
                (Dialects: Beiço de Pau [Tapayuna], Yaruma [Jarumá, Waiku])
        Central Jê (Akwe branch)
            Xavante (Shavante, Chavante) Brazil
            *Akroá (Akroá-Mirim, Acroá) Brazil
            Xerente (Sherenté) Brazil
            *Xakriabá (Chicriaba, Chakriaba) Brazil
        Southern Jê
            Kaingang (Coroado, Caingang) Brazil
            Xokléng (Shocleng, Botocudo) Brazil

*Ingáin Brazil
*Guayaná (Wayaná) Brazil
Jeikó (Jeicó, Jaikó, Geico) Brazil
***Kamakanan**
    *Kamakán (Camacán) (languages or dialects) Brazil
        *Kamakán (Kamakã, Camacán, Ezeshio)
        *Mongoyó (Mangaló, Monshoko)
        *Kotoxó (Kutaxó, Catashó, Cotoxó)
    *Menién (Manyã)
    *Masakará (Masacará)
Karajá (Caraja) (dialects or languages) Brazil
    (Dialects: Javae, Xambioá, Karajá)
Krenakan (Botocudoan, Aimoré language complex)
    Krenak (Botocudo, Aimoré, Nakrehé) Brazil
    *Guêren (Guerén, Gren, Borun, Borúm) Brazil
Maxakalían
    Maxakalí Brazil
    *Kapoxó (Caposho) Brazil
    *Monoxó Brazil
    *Makoní (Maconí) Brazil
    *Malalí Brazil
    *Pataxó (Pataxó-Háhãhãe [Pataxó-Hanhanhain], Patasho) Brazil
    *Koropó Brazil
        Recent work indicates that ***Koropó** belongs to Maxakalían, not to Purían as previously inaccurately proposed (Nikulin 2020, 19; Zamponi in press b).
Ofayé (Opayé) Brazil
Rikbaktsa (Aripaktsá, Erikbatsa, Erikpatsa, Canoeiro) Brazil

(Nikulin 2020, 25–26; Ribeiro and van der Voort 2010)

Andrey Nikulin (2020, 91) grouped Maxakalían and Krenakan (and possibly also Kamakanan) together within Macro-Jê Sensu Stricto in a branch he calls "Transfranciscanan." His hypothesis for the subgrouping classification of Macro-Jê Sensu Stricto is:

Macro-Jê Sensu Stricto
    Eastern Macro-Jê branch
        Jêan
            Northern Jê-Panará-Akuwẽ
                Northern Jê-Panará
                      Northern Jê
                      Panará
                Akuwẽ
            Ingain-Southern Jê
                Ingain
                Southern Jê

>   Transfranciscanan
>   Maxakalían
>   Nuclear Maxakalí
>   Malalí
>   Krenák
>   Kamakanan
>   Southern Kamakã
>   Masakará
>   Jaikó
> Karajá
> Western Macro-Jê branch
>   Matogrossense-Jabutían
>   Matogrossense
>   Ofayé
>   Rikbáktsa
>   Jabutían
>   Djeoromitxí
>   Chiquitano

(Nikulin 2020, 178)
(See Map 4.4. Macro-Jê Sensu Stricto languages; see also Maps 4.7. and 7.10.)

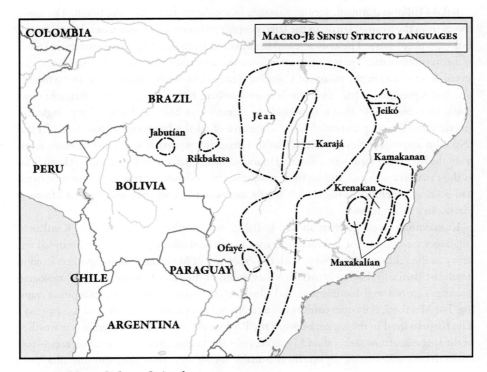

MAP 4.4. Macro-Jê Sensu Stricto languages

Andrey Nikulin (2020) has made a persuasive case for the genetic relationship of the Jê family and several of the language families and isolates that were often associated with the Macro-Jê hypothesis, while at the same time showing that some others that were traditionally thought to be part of that hypothesis actually cannot be shown to be related. This poses a nomenclatural problem—the new more secure classification cannot be called just Jê because it includes more than just the Jê language family, and it cannot be called Macro-Jê without confusion, since it includes less than has often been assumed to belong to "Macro-Jê" in earlier formulations. For that reason I propose to call it Macro-Jê Sensu Stricto. It includes the subfamilies listed above.

Jabutían is composed of two languages, **Djeoromitxí** (Jabutí) and **Arikapú**, both spoken in southern Rondônia state, Brazil. Until the mid-twentieth century, the speakers of both lived on the upper course of the Branco River, with Arikapú upstream from Djeoromitxí (Jabutí). With the expansion of colonization in the twentieth century, the speakers of both languages were forced to move downriver to work on rubber plantations; many fled and were later transferred, living today in the Rio Branco Indigenous Territory and the Rio Guaporé Indigenous Territory in Rondônia. They are both critically endangered; in 2015, Arikapú may have had only two speakers (Nikulin 2014, 27).

Proto-Jabutían has been reconstructed with the following phonemes: /p, t, č, c, k, b, d, ǰ, ɟ, r, m, n, w, i, ɪ, e, a, o, ɔ, ɘ, ə, ɨ, u/ (see Nikulin 2020, 100, 103).

Jêan (Gêan, Jê family) is a subfamily of some dozen languages. Proto-Jê has been reconstructed with the phonemes: /p, t, c, k, r, m, n, ŋ, w, y (j); i, ɪ, e, ɛ, a, o, ɔ, u, ʊ, ə, ɨ, ɨ̥, u, ĩ, ẽ, õ ũ, ə̃, ɨ̃/ (see Nikulin 2020, 84, 87; Ribeiro 2006; Rodrigues 1999).

Jeikó (Jaiko) is dormant, formerly spoken in southeastern Piauí state, Brazil. The name comes from the town of Jaicós, in the Jeikó people's territory, which was around the Canindé and Gurgueia Rivers. The only attested information from the language is extremely sparce and also problematic. There is only a single record, a wordlist from von Martius (1867), collected from a man in the village of Cajueiro. There is, however, doubt about just what the wordlist represents. It has some words from Cariban, Kamakã, and Karirí. Ramirez et al. (2015, 260–261) doubt that it is possible to identify von Martius' list with any single linguistic variety, saying it seemed to be a mixture of all the languages of the state of Piauí (Nikiulin 2020, 16). Nevertheless, Nikulin (2020, 16) reports that at least thirteen items from the list clearly represent a Macro-Jê variety, making Jeikó a real language (at least as far as the thirteen items go), and he finds phonological evidence for treating it not as it often had been, as a member of the Jê (sub)family, but rather as a separate subgroup of Macro-Jê (Sensu Stricto) on its own.

Kamakanan languages were spoken in Bahía state, northeastern Brazil. The Kamkanan languages are all dormant and no longer have recognized ethnic groups. They occupied territory in the southern Bahia State, with the exception of **Masakará**, whose speakers lived in northeast Bahia, in the São Francisco Valley, south of the city of Juazeiro. The Kamakanan languages are not well documented, and all records are from persons lacking linguistic training. For Masakará, only one wordlist exists, collected by von Martius (1867, vol. 2, 144–145). The **Kotoxó** lived in the region between the Pardo and Contas Rivers; there is one wordlist of the language, from 1820, called Mongoió, published in von Martius (1867, vol. 2, 156–158) under the name Kotoxó. Only one list is available for **Menién**, from the Jequitinhonha River.

The speakers of **Kamakã** were also located in the region between the Pardo and Contas Rivers. There is limited lexical information on the language in four sources, from 1892 to 1945 (Nikulin 2020, 22–23).

Karajá (Iny rybè) is spoken on an extensive part of the Araguaia River in the states of Goiás, Tocantins, and Mato Grosso in Brazil. Andrey Nikulin (2020, 23) gives four "co-dialects" for Karajá: Javaé, Xambioá, Northern Karajá, and Southern Karajá.

Karajá has distinct male and female speech registers. One main difference is that women maintain /k/, which is lost from the men's language[23] (https://pib.socioambiental.org/en/Povo:Karajá, accessed January 17, 2022).

Proto-Karajá has been reconstructed with the phonemes: /t, k, b, d, θ, l, r, m, w, h (and *ã* after initial *h*), and other vowels unchanged in the modern languages/ (Nikulin 2020, 95–96).

Krenakan. The Krenák are the last descendants of the **Borum** people (mburuŋ 'people'). In the sixteenth century, the Borum (known by the name of *Aimorés* in colonial sources) occupied territory that stretched from the Recôncavo Baiano region to the Rio Doce. The **Gueren** people are also mentioned, assumed to be related to the Borum people; the Guerens' area extended from Cairu and Camamu on the coast to the vicinity of São Francisco River and Serra do Salitre in the interior. Starting in the seventeenth century, the name Gueren starts to be used as a synonym for **Aimoré**; this was replaced by the name **Botocudo**, because they wore earplugs or lip-plugs (labrets), between the latter half of the 1700s and the first half of the 1800s. The name *Krenak* comes from the name of a chieftain of the Gutkrák subdivision who presided over a separation of the group from others. The contact between the Borum and colonization was of very conflicted and aggressive. Today extremely few speakers survive. Andrey Nikulin (2020, 22) believes the available evidence does not support the idea of an Aimoré (or Krenakan) language family with several members, but rather a single language now labeled Krenak.

Maxakalían. The various Maxakalí groups used to inhabit an area between the Pardo and Doce Rivers, in the Brazilian states of southeastern Bahia, northeastern Minas Gerais, and northern Espírito Santo. The descendants of these groups live in two indigenous areas—Água Boa and Pradinho—which were grouped together to form the Maxakalí Indigenous Territory. It is located in the municipality of Bertópolis, on the headwaters of the Umburanas River, in the Mucuri Valley in northeastern Minas Gerais.

In Nikulin's (2020, 16) view, the Maxakalían subfamily split into two branches: the **Maxakalí** branch and dormant **Malalí**. The Maxakalí branch includes Maxakalí and Ritual Maxakalí (used in ritual chants), plus several dormant languages with little documentation: Pataxó-Háhãhãe, Pataxó, Koropó, and a Makuní dialect complex which is very closely related to the Ritual Maxakalí. Maxakalí speakers were originally in the valleys of the Mucuri, Itanhém, and Jequitinhonha Rivers; today they live in four villages in Minas Gerais: Pradinho, Água Boa, Aldeia Verde, and Cachoeirinha.

Ritual Maxakalí is used by the Maxakalí in their ritual chants, held to be the language of their ancestors. It is a Maxakalían language, but is more closely related to varieties recorded in the 1800s, compiled in von Martius (1867, vol. 2, 169–176) under the names of Machacarí, Macha-culí, Machacalí, Macuni, Capoxô, Cumanachô, and Panháme. Nikulin calls them together the **Makuní** dialect complex (Nikulin 2020, 17).

Of the other Maxakalían languages, **Pataxó-Háhãhãe** (Northern Pataxó), from the coast of southern Bahia, is best documented, with four word lists from 1938 to 1981. The **Pataxó**

(Southern Pataxó) lived to the south of the traditional region of the Pataxó-Háhãhãe, on the coast of Bahia. For this language there is only a vocabulary list collected in the beginning of the 1800s on the Pardo River (Nikulin 2020, 18).

Koropó was spoken in an area next to that of the other Maxakalían languages, on the Rio Pomba, tributary of the Paraío River on the border between the states of Minas Gerais e Rio de Janeiro (Ramirez et al. 2015, 225). Koropó had previously been classified with Purí, but Ramirez et al. (2015) argued persuasively that it belongs to Maxakalían. There are two wordlists of Koropó from the early 1800s, one with 55 words, the other with 127 words. Koropó became dormant probably by the 1930s (Nikulin 2020, 19; Zamponi in press b).

Nikulin (2020, 19) sees **Malalí** as the most divergent language of the Maxakalían sub family, not having undergone innovations shared by all the other Maxakalían languages. The Malalí people lived in the Rio Doce Valley in Minas Gerais. The only data on this language are two wordlists collected in the early 1800s.

Ofayé (Opayé, Ofaié) is spoken on the Ivinhema, Pardo, and Nhandú Rivers in Mato Grosso do Sul, Brazil. Until the beginning of the twentieth century there were thousands of Ofayé speakers, living on the right bank of the Paraná River, from the mouth of the Ivinhema River to the mouth of the Rio Verde, extending westward toward the Rio Negro and Taboco River. They were the victims of genocide by cattle ranchers. They live now in the Ofayé-Xavánte Indigenous Territory. The language is critically endangered. There is some documentation of the language (in publications from 1932 to 2012), though it is sparce (Nikulin 2020, 24–25).

Rikbaktsa (Aripaktsá, Erikbatsa, Erikpatsa, Arikpatsa, Canoeiro) speakers were originally on the middle course of the Juruena River and the lower course of its tributaries, the Arinos and Sangue Rivers, in Mato Grosso state. In the first years of contact with outsiders from the dominant society, 1952–1956, there were violent conflicts with rubber tappers on the Juruena River, which involved incidents of poisoning; the Rikbáktsa population was greatly reduced. Today they live in thirty-four villages in part of their ancestral territory, in the Japuíra and Erikpatsa Indigenous Territories, and in the village of the Escondido (Nikulin 2020, 25–26). Their self-designation *Rikbaktsa* means 'human beings' (*rik* 'person, human being' + *bak* emphasis + *tsa* 'plural'). They are also called *Canoeiros* ('canoe people'), reflecting their canoeing ability, and less commonly *Orelhas de Pau* ('wooden ears'), reflecting their use of large wooden earlobe plugs. There is difference between male and female speech, where endings of many words indicates the gender of the person speaking.

Andrey Nikulin (2020, 108–177) has proposed the following as reconstructed phonemes of Proto-Macro-Jê (Sensu Stricto) with proposed cognate sets to support the sound correspondences upon which they are based: /p, t, r, c, k, m, n, ñ, ŋ, w, y (j); i, e, ɛ, a, o, ɔ, u, ə, ə̦, ɨ, u, ĩ, ẽ, ũ, ɔ̃, ɨ̃/.

See Chapter 6 for more about the several other language groups that have often been associated with the earlier "Macro-Jê" (Sensu Lato) hypothesis, where the evidence has not been considered convincing.

***Maku** (Maco, Mako, Macu, Máku) Brazil

Maku is a language isolate, not to be confused with the "Makúan" [Nadahup] languages or the several other languages with similar names. It was spoken in the Brazil and Venezuela border area, in Brazil's Roraima state along the upper Uraricoera and lower Auari Rivers. The last speaker was Sinfrônio, who died in 2000 (Migliazza 1978, 1982[1985]; Rogers 2020; Zamponi in press b). Various proposals of broader linguistic affiliations for Maku have been made, but none so far has seemed promising.

Mapudungun languages (Araucanian)
Mapudungun (Mapudungu, Mapuzungun, Araucano, Mapuche) Chile, Argentina
Huilliche (Veliche, Huiliche "Beliche") Chile

Mapudungun (Araucanian) appears to be a small language family of two members, although there is not general agreement about whether **Huilliche** is a separate language and not just a dialect of Mapudungun.

Mapudungun has several dialects: **Ranquel, Neuquén, Rucachoroy, Río Negro, Chubut, Cautín, Mapocho** [Mapuchu], **Ngoluche** [Moluche, Nguluche], **Picunche**, and **Pehuenche**. Loukotka (1968, 273–274) listed most of these as separate languages in his Mapuche stock, with **Chilote** [Chauquéz] also included. Robert Croese (1985) gave a much more detailed treatment of Mapudungun dialects, dividing them into eight dialect groups.

Huilliche is often considered just a dialect of Mapudungun (Mapuche), though the weight of current opinion is that it should be treated as a separate language (see though Adelaar and Pache 2022, 165). The other dialects are mutually intelligible; the degree of possible mutual intelligibility between Huilliche and the other varieties has not yet been determined in concentrated investigation. It is spoken in the Los Lagos and Los Ríos regions and in mountain valleys between the city of Valdivia and south toward the Chiloé Archipelago in Chile. Huilliche has at least two varieties, called **Huillichesungun** and **Tsesungun** by their speakers. Huillichesungun is spoken in Wequetrumao, on the island of Chiloé, and Tsesungun is spoken in Choroy Traiguen, on the coast of Osorno province.

Matacoan (Mataco-Mataguayan, Mataguayan)
Chorote-Wichí
Chorote (Manjuy) Argentina, Paraguay
Wichí (Mataco, Weenhayek, Lhamtes) Argentina, Bolivia
Nivaclé-Maká
Nivaclé (Niwaklé, Chulupí, Ashlushlay) Paraguay, Argentina
Maká (Macá) Paraguay

(See Map 7.12.)

Chorote has reasonably divergent varieties: **Chorote Montaraz** (*Wikinawos*), the most distinct variety, from Santa Rosa, Paraguay; the **Iyojwa'ja'** variety (formerly spelled Yofuaha); and the **Iyo'wujwa'** (Manjuy) variety. The latter two varieties are spoken along the Pilcomayo River in Argentina and Paraguay.

Wichí was formerly called Mataco, a term now considered pejorative. It is spoken mostly in northern Argentina, between the Bermejo and Pilcomayo Rivers. The variety spoken in Bolivia is called **Noctén**; two other generally recognized dialects are **Güisnay** and **Vejoz**, and there are several other dialects as well, some considerably different from others (Nercesian 2014, 27–30; 2021; Terraza 2008; Claesson 1994; Alvarsson and Claesson. 2014).

Nivaclé (Niwaklé, Chulupí, Ashlushlay) is spoken in Salta Province in northern Argentina and in southern and western Paraguay in about twenty-five communities primarily in the departments of Boquerón and Hayes. Nivaclé speakers tend to identify with two kinds of Nivaclé, as Arribeños, speakers of the upriver dialect, or as Abajeños, speakers of the downriver dialect. However, these are geographical terms, referring to those living along the Pilcomayo River, and they do not coincide precisely to linguistic varieties. Several writers distinguish three dialect groups: **Chishamne lhavos** (Arribeños), **Shichaam lhavos** (Abajeños), and **Yita' lhavos** (Bush people). Miguel Chase-Sardi (2003, 1, 308–310) distinguished seven varieties: Chishamnee lhavos (upriver people, Arribeños), Jotoi lhavos (savannah people), Tavashai lhavos (country people), Tovoc lhavos (river people), Tuj cuvôyu (literally 'horse eaters'), Yita' lhavos (bush people, also called C'utjaan lhavos 'thorn people'), and Nivaclé c'o'vat (a mythical clan, literally 'place or home of the Nivacle', reported to be north of Mariscal Estigarribia, Paraguay).

Maká is spoken today in a "*colonia*" (suburb) at the northwestern edge of Asunción, Paraguay. It has also been called Macá, Maca, Towolhi, Toothle, Nynaka, Mak'á, Enimaca, and Enimaga.

Matacoan languages are diversified on a scale similar to that of the Germanic languages, that is, clearly related but not closely so. The subgrouping divides into two branches, each with two languages, Chorote-Wichí and Nivaclé-Maká, though this is based primarily on lexical evidence (see Campbell et al. 2020, 5).

My reconstruction of Proto-Matacoan phonemes has: /p, t, ts, k, ʔ, p', t', ts', k', l, ɬ, ɸ, s, m, n, w, j (y), x; i, e, a, ɑ, o, u/ (Campbell 2023). Viegas Barros (2013a, 298) reconstructed some sounds not included here: *q, *q', *hʷ and *ʌ. The languages do have uvular [q] and [q'] and velar [k] and [k'], but the velars do not contrast with the uvulars; [k] and [q] are allophones of a single phoneme, as are [k'] and [q']. Instead of *hw I reconstruct *ɸ; and instead of *ʌ I have *a.

It has long been suspected, often assumed, that the Matacoan and Guaicurúan language families belong together in a larger genetic unit, usually called Macro-Guaicuruan. Until recently the evidence seemed suggestive but insufficient for confidence in the proposal. Pedro Viegas Barros (2013a), however, has presented a very promising case for a genetic relationship between the two families (see Chapter 6 for details).

*Matanawí (Matanauí, Matanauý, Matanaui, Matanaué, Matanaú) Brazil

The dormant language isolate Matanawí was spoken in an area between the Tapajós and Madeira Rivers in Brazil's Amazonas state. Curt Nimuendajú (1925, 166–171) collected the only information on the language, a wordlist of some 300 items with some phrases and sentences. It shows no systematic resemblance to other languages. It is considered a language isolate (Zamponi in press b).

Several scholars have associated Matanawí with geographically nearby Muran (Pirahã). For example, Joseph Greenberg (1987, 107) said that "although Loukotka lists Mura and Matanawi as independent South American stocks, they are so closely related that I include

Matanawi in the Mura family." Terrence Kaufman (2007, 63) put Matanawi and Muran together in his "Mura-Matanawian stock/family." Diego Alves (2019, 76), however, found no convincing evidence to support a genetic relationship between the two.

*Mochica (Yunga, Chimú, Muchic) Peru

Mochica, a dormant language isolate, was spoken on the northern coast of Peru. (See Map 7.11.) It was endangered already in the 1800s and ceased to be spoken around 1920. There is fairly substantial documentation. A major source is Fernando de la Carrera Daza's (1644) *Arte de la lengua Yunga*. Carrera grew up in the Mochica area and learned the language as a boy, and served as a priest in San Martín de Reque. Another important source is Ernst Middendorf (1892), based on his own fieldwork but not completely independent; he had familiarized himself with Carrera's grammar (Adelaar and Muysken 2004, 321; Urban 2019a, 118; Cerrón-Palomino 1995).

Mochica is traditionally associated with the Moche or Chimu culture (100–700 CE) of coastal northern Peru (van de Kerke and Muysken 2014; Urban 2019a).

Mochica has often been linked with dormant **Cañar** (Cañari) and **Puruhá** (Puruguay) of Ecuador. Terrence Kaufman (2007, 69), for example, had a "Chimuan family" made up of Mochica, Kanyari (Cañari), and Puruwá (Puruhá), though he acknowledged that of the latter two "only a few words [of] each are known." Loukotka's (1968, 261–262) "Chimú stock" included in addition to these three languages a number of others: **Ayahuaca**, **Calva**, **Tumbi** (Tumbez), **Puná** (Lapuna), **Colonche**, **Chanduy**, **Tacame** (Atacamez, Esmeralda) (now considered an independent isolate), **Chongón**, **Coaque**, **Manabi** (Manta), and **Huancavilca**. He said nothing is known of any of these other languages with the exception of four words for Huancavilca and "only a few patronyms" for Manabi (Manta). (See Cerrón-Palomino 1995.) Louisa Stark's (1972) proposed Maya-Yunga-Chipayan, which would join Mochica with Mayan and Uru-Chipaya, was not successful and has now been abandoned.

Mosetenan (languages or dialects) (Mosetén-Chiname) Bolivia
  Mosetén (Rache, Muchan, Tucupi, Aparono) emergent language
  Chimané (Tsimane, Chiman, Chumano, Nawazi-Moñtji) emergent language

Mosetén and **Chimané** are spoken along the Beni River in the western Bolivia. (See Map 7.10.) They are said to be mutually intelligible, though they are often treated as separate languages. Together varieties of Mosetén and Chimané constitute a dialect continuum, though Chimané has a separate ethnic identification from Mosetén (Sakel 2004).

Mosetenan has no known external relatives. Jorge Suárez (1969) presented evidence he interpreted as showing a genetic relationship between Mosetén and Pano-Takanan, though others were not convinced. Several others linked Mosetén with Chonan languages. Morris Swadesh (1959, 1962) grouped Mosetén, Chon, and "Hongote" in what he called "Sonchon"—Hongote is a phantom South American language, owed to Daniel Brinton's mistaken identification of a vocabulary from North America (see Chapter 5). Terrence Kaufman (2007, 71) also put Mosetén together with Chonan in his Mosetén-Chon stock, but without comment on what reasons may be behind that decision.

Movima (Mobima, Moyma, Movime) Bolivia

Movima is a language isolate, spoken in the Bolivian Amazon. Katharina Haude (2006, 1) says of the location:

> There are more than 270 ethnically Movima communities and small settlements, mainly located in the districts of Santa Ana del Yacuma, Exaltación, San Joaquín and San Ignacio. The major communities are the villages El Perú and Desengaño. Most of the smaller settlements are located along the rivers Yacuma and Apere, but also along the rivers Rapulo, Mamoré, Matos, and Maniqui.

(See Map 7.10.)

Movima also has no detectable relatives, though there have been a number of suggestions of possible relatives, including Chibchan, Canichana, and Tukanoan (see Haude 2006, 5 for details; Seifart and Hammarström 2018).

*Munichi (Otanave, Otanabe) Peru

Munichi is a language isolate. Munichi has a fairly extensive documentation. The seventeenth-century Jesuit records place Munichi speakers in hills that extend southeastward from the headwaters of the Paranapura River and in the Cachiyacu River basin (Michael et al. 2013, 309). Until recently it was spoken in Munichis settlement in southwestern Loreto Department, Peru. Victoria Huancho Icahuate, the last known native speaker, died in the late 1990s.

Though Munichi has no known relatives, some suggestions have been made. It has been classified with Cahuapanan and "Macro-Tukanoan," and similarities with Arawakan pronoun suffixes have been noted. Terrence Kaufman (2007, 68) put Munichi with Yurí and Tikuna in his "Juri-Tikuna stock" (see Tikuna-Yurí below). Munichi has a considerable number of loanwords from Quechua as well as some from Cahuapanan languages (Michael et al. 2013, 308).

Muran (Pirahã) (a language isolate?, often considered a small family) Brazil
 *Mura
 Pirahã (Pirahá)
 *Bohurá (Buxwaray)
 *Yahahí (Jahahi)

Pirahã is spoken on the Maici River. Muran has typically been considered a small family of closely related languages, but many consider it just a single language with several dialects. Seifart and Hammarström (2018, 272–273) say of Pirahã and its relationship to the other varieties and of their location, "they [the Pirahãs] are the remnants of a once large group, mostly referred to as Mura, probably consisting of various dialects, that moved through a vast territory in Central and Western Amazonia, as far Northwest as the Caquetá River." Daniel Everett (2008, 28–29), for example, believes that "Pirahã and the now extinct related dialect, Mura, form a single language isolate, unrelated to any other known language . . . two very similar dialects of a single language." J. Alden Mason (1950, 285) was of the same opinion. He considered Bohurá, Pirahã, and Yahahí three dialects of "Mura Proper." Loukotka (1968, 95) listed the four "languages" mentioned here as members of his Múra Stock, though saying of **Yaháhi** that nothing was known of this language.

There is general agreement that Muran has no demonstrable relatives, though, as mentioned above, it has often been proposed that Muran is related to geographically nearby **Matanawí**. Kaufman (2007, 71) linked them in his Mura-Matanawian stock/family, though Diego Alves (2019, 76) finds the evidence not convincing for a genealogical relationship between the two languages.

Nadahup (Nadehup, Nadahupan, Makúan, Makú family)
  Nadëb (Kaburi) Brazil
  Vaupés branch
    Dâw Brazil
    Hupda-Yuhup
      Hup (Hupda, Hupdé, Macú de Tucano) Brazil
      Yuhup Brazil, Colombia
  (Epps and Bolaños 2017)

(See Map 7.9.)

The names Makú and Makúan are now avoided, as they are considered pejorative, said to be from Arawakan languages meaning 'without speech'. The name Makú (in variant spellings, Macu, Máku, Mácu, Macú or Maco, Mako, Máko, Macó, Makó) is also very confusing; it has been applied to numerous groups and to languages of a number of different language families (and isolates).

Nadëb is spoken along the Uneiuxi, Japurá, and Río Negro Rivers in Brazil. **Dâw** speakers are in the northwestern part of Amazonas state in Brazil. **Hup** is spoken in the border area between Colombia and Brazil's Amazonas state (Epps 2008a). **Yuhup** speakers are located between the Tiquié and Apaporis Rivers, on the border between Colombia and Brazil. Dormant **Kurikuriaí** (Kurikuriari) appears to be a Dâw dialect, at least partially mutually intelligible with Dâw, though it is sometimes considered a distinct language.

From the 1920s onward, following Paul Rivet (1924), many have classified **Puinave** and the "Makúan" (Nadahup) languages together, often also with Kakua-Nukak, in a presumed Makú-Puinave or Puinavean family. (See, for example, Girón 2008, 428–433.) Epps and Bolaños' (2017, 502) conclusion about these proposals, cited above, is that these are "three distinct genetic units: the Naduhupan family (Nadëb, Dâw, Hup, and Yuhup), the small Kakua-Nukakan family, and the isolate Puinave/Wãnsöhöt." They see no convincing evidence for classifying any of the three together.

The languages **Kakua** and **Nukak** (Kakua-Nukak) were thought to be related to the Nadahup languages, often together with Puinave (Wãnsöhöt) (see Martins 2005, 331–341 and Girón 2008, 428–433). Alexandra Aikhenvald (2002, 145) would have Nadëb as one branch of the postulated family, and Dâw, Hudpa, Yuhup, Kakua, and Nukak as members of the other branch. However, now Kakua, and Nukak connections with these others are no longer thought viable (see Epps and Bolaños 2017).

Henley et al. (1996) presented evidence that he thought would relate **Hodï** (Jotí) to these languages, and Valteir Martins (2005, 341) also mentions data that he thinks point to a probable

"Makúan" affinity for Hodï (Jotí), possibly connected also with Kakua. This, however, has not seemed likely. Valteir Martins (2005, 342–370) grouped Arawakan and Nadahup languages together in a proposed Makúan-Arawakan (Nadahup-Arawakan) family, but this proposal has been challenged. Other broad-scale classifications that include these languages have also been made, though with little credibility.

Nambikwaran (Nambicuaran, Nambikuaran) Brazil
    Sabanê (Sabanés)
    Core Nambikwaran
        Northern Nambikwaran (Mamaindê [Northern Nambiquara, Mamande]); (with dialects: Mamaindé, Negarotê, Tawanxte, Taxmainite, Taxwensite, Yalapmunxte [Lacondê])
        Southern Nambikwaran (languages or dialects)
            Nambiquara (Nambikwara) (with dialects: Manduka, Kitlhaulhú, etc.)
        Sararé emergent language.

All the Nambikwaran languages and varieties are spoken in Mato Grosso state, Brazil. They have been considered dialects of a single language, though there are clearly distinct languages involved. (See Map 7.10.)

The classification of Nambikwaran languages has varied from scholar to scholar, though a consensus seems to have emerged that there are two branches, **Sabanê** versus the others, and that the others all fall into either the Northern Nambikwara branch or the Southern Nambikwara branch (Wetzels and Telles 2011; *Ethnologue* 2023; Eberhard et al. in press; see also Lowe 1999, 269, and; Price 1985). *Ethnologue* (2023) has eight languages in its Nambikwara family. Sabanê, the most divergent, is one branch Northern has six languages, with their Roosevelt Cluster of three. This Northern subgroup has **Alapmunte**, **Mamaindê** and **Yalakalore**; the Roosevelt Cluster, has three languages, (**Lakondê**, **Latundê**, and **Tawandê**. Eberhard et al. (in press) follow the consensus with Sabanê splitting off first and then later Northern Nambikwára and Southern Nambikwára separating from each other. They list as members of Northern Nambikwára: Latundê, Lakondê, Mamaindê, **Negarotê**, and Tawandê. They have as members of Southern Nambikwára: **Hahãintesú**, **Alãntesú**, **Waikisú**, **Wasúsu**, **Nutajensu** (Katithãulhú, Sararé), **Saxuentesú**, **Halotesú**, **Wakalitesú**, **Siwxaisú**, **Nesú**, and **Nambikwara do Campo** (Kithãulhú).[24]

David Price (1978) proposed a broader possible relationship between Nambikwaran and Kanoê (Kapixaná). Greenberg (1987, 93) put "Nambikwara" in his "Macro-Tucanoan stock" (part of Amerind). Others have not followed either of these classifications.

*****Omurano** (Humurana, Numurana, Umurano, Roamaina, "Maina," "Mayna") Peru
Omurano is a dormant language isolate. The traditional Omurano area was the upper Urituyacu River, a tributary of the Marañón River, in Peru's Loreto Province. It is reported that the last productive speaker of Omurano, Esteban Macusi, died in 2006 in the village of Progreso II (O'hagan 2011, 6). The majority of the documentation of Omurano is a wordlist of about 250 items, collected by Günther Tessmann in the 1920s (Tessmann 1930, 455–458)

and some words in Avencio Villarejo (1959) (Zamponi in press b). However, Zachary O'Hagan (2011) was able to obtain some additional information on the language working with rememberers or semi-speakers in 2011.

The confusing name **Maynas** (Mayna, Maina) (see above) has often been associated with Omurano. Luis Miguel Rojas-Berscia's (2015) investigation demonstrates conclusively that Mayna was a Cahuapanan language. He put Mayna together with Shawi as one branch of the Cahuapanan, with Shiwilu as the other branch (Rojas-Berscia's 2015, 404).

Several suggestions for classifying Omurano with other languages have been made. Omurano has been claimed to belong to or with the Záparoan family by several authors, for example, Joseph Greenberg (1960, 794) and Louisa Stark (1985). However, Fernando Carvalho (2013, 108) finds, "given the available evidence, there's no good reason to believe in the hypothesis that Omurano belongs into the Záparoan family." Greenberg's view appears to have shifted, however, since his 1960 publication. In Greenberg (1987, 99, 383) he listed Mayna, identified as "Omurana" in parentheses, in his Andean branch of Amerind, a member of this Itucale-Sabela group (along with Itucale and Sabela [Waorani]); in his 1987 book, Zaparo[an] is still in his Andean branch, but as a member of his Kahuapana-Zaparo group together with Kahuapana [Cahuapanan]). The proposed genealogical links of Omurano with **Taushiro** are not convincing. Terrence Kaufman (2007, 69) grouped Omurano, Taushiro, and **Kandoshi**, saying "on the basis of a certain amount of lexical evidence, it seems that Taushiro may be related to both Omurano and Kandoshi, and more closely to the former."

*Otomacoan (Zamponi in press b) Venezuela
   *Otomaco
   *Taparita

This small language family has two dormant languages as its members, formerly spoken in the Llanos of Apure, Venezuela.

Otomaco was spoken on small islands at the confluence of the Apure River with the Orinoco, along the Apure, Arauca, and Sinaruco Rivers. The language ceased to be spoken in the first half of the twentieth century (Zamponi in press b). There are a few sources on the language, all from the 1700s and 1800s, all with just a few words except for the Capuchin priest Jerónimo José de Luzena's (1788) response to Catherine the Great's 440-word list.

Taparita was spoken along the Cojedes and Portuguesa Rivers. Historical information about the Taparita is very scant. It appears that they were the same as the group called **Amaiba** (or Maiba) in old missionary sources; the names were at times used interchangeably (Zamponi in press b). A long wordlist from Luzena's response to Catherine the Great's wordlist is the only data available on the language (Luzena 1788; Zamponi in press b).

A family relationship between Otomaco and Taparita was first recognized by the Italian Jesuit missionary Filippo Salvatore Gilij (1782, 205). Raoul Zamponi (in press b) makes a detailed comparison of the two.

Among the broader proposed classifications, Terrence Kaufman's (2007, 65) Macro-Otomakoan cluster is representative; it includes the **Tuyoneri** (Harákmbut) language area, with **Huachipaeri** (Harákmbut), Amaracaeri; Otomacoan, with Otomaco and Taparita; and **Trumai**.[25]

Paez (Páez, Nasa Yuwe)
    Paez (Nasa Yuwe, Paisa, Páez) Colombia
    Paniquitá Colombia (possibly a dialect of Paez)
    *Panzaleo (?) (Latacunga, Quito) Ecuador

There is no consensus concerning Paez and its classification. Customarily it has been grouped with at least two other entities in a Paezan language family (Adelaar and Muysken 2004, 619). Adelaar and Muysken (2004, 618) consider Paez a language isolate with **Paniquitá**, **Caldono**, **Munchique**, and **Toribío** as dialects; Seifart and Hammarström (2018) also list Paez as an isolate.

Panzaleo was spoken in the area from Quito in the north to Mocha in the south, throughout the provinces of Cotopaxi and Tungurahua and in the southern part of Pichincha Province (Adelaar and Muysken 2004, 394). It is very poorly attested, with scarcely any data and thus classifying it with Paez is not based primarily on linguistic evidence; the similarities may be due to language contact.

"Paezan," however defined, has in the past been classified with Chibchan and "Macro-Chibchan," Barbacoan, Chocoan, Jirajaran, Andaqui, Betoi, Kamsá, Yaruro, Esmeralda, Mochica, Kunza (Atacameño), Itonama, and Yurumanguí. Terrence Kaufman's (2007, 63) "Macro-Páesan cluster" includes many of these: Kunsa-Kapishana stock (with Kunsa and Kapishana), Betoi, and his Paes-Barbakóan stock (which includes Andaqui, Paes Group (with Paes and Pansaleo), and Kokonuko Group (with Kokonuko, Totoró, and Wambiano [Guambiano]), and the Barbakóan family (with its eight members).

The Coconucan languages (a branch of Barbacoan) have often been associated erroneously with Paezan. Henri Beuchat and Paul Rivet (1910) grouped Coconucan languages and Páez more closely together in their broad version of the Chibchan family. Timothy Curnow (1998) discovered that this is based on misinterpretation of León Douay's (1888) **Moguex** vocabulary, which was actually a mix of Páez and Guambiano/Totoró. Subsequent classifiers followed Beuchat and Rivet's error, grouping Páez with Guambiano and missing the Barbacoan identity of Coconucan. Páez and Guambiano actually share little similar seeming vocabulary.

Pano-Takanan (Pano-Tacanan)
    Panoan (Fleck 2013)[26]
        Mayoruna branch
            Mayo group
                Matses subgroup
                    Matses Peru, Brazil
                    Kulina of the Curuça River Brazil
                        (dialects: Kapishana, Mawi; Chema)
                    *Dëmushbo Brazil
                Korubo Brazil
                    (dialects: Korubo, Chankuëshbo)
                Matis subgroup (similar to Mainline branch)
                    Matis Brazil
                    *Mayoruna of the Jandiatuba River Brazil
                    *Mayoruna of the Amazon River Peru, Brazil
              *Mayoruna of Tabatinga Brazil

Mainline branch
    Kasharari (Kaxararí) Brazil
    Kashibo (Cashibo)
        (dialects: Kashibo, Rubo/Isunubo, Kataibo, Nokaman [Nocaman])
    Nawa group
        Bolivian subgroup
            Chákobo/Pakawara Bolivia
            *Karipuna Bolivia, Brazil
                (maybe a dialect of Chakobo/Pakawara)
            *Chiriba Bolivia
        Madre de Dios subgroup
            *Atsawaka/Yamiaka Peru
            *Arazaire Peru
        *Remo of the Blanco River Peru (also Brazil?)
        *Kashinawa of the Tarauacá River Brazil
        Marubo subgroup
            Marubo (of the Javari Basin) Brazil
            Katukina Brazil
                (dialects: Katukina of Olinda, *Kanamari)
            *Kulina of São Paulo de Olivença Brazil
    Central Panoan Assemblage
        Poyanawa subgroup
            Poyanawa Brazil
            Iskonawa Peru
            Nukini Brazil
            Nawa (of the Môa River) Brazil
                (tentatively classified, lacks data)
            *Remo of the Jaquirana River Brazil
        Chama subgroup
            Shipibo-Konibo Peru
                (dialects: Shipibo-Konibo, Kapanawa of Tapiche River)
            *Pano Peru (probably dormant, uncertain)
            *Sensi Peru
        Headwaters subgroup
            Kashinawa of the Ibuaçu River Peru, Brazil
                (dialects: Kashinawa, *Paranawa)
            Yaminawa Peru, Brazil
                (a large dialect complex: Yaminawa, Shanenawa, Sharanawa, Shawannawa [Arara],Yawanawa, *Nehanawa, etc.)
            Amawaka Peru, Brazil
                (dialects: Amawaka, *Nishinawa, *Yumanawa)
            *Remo of the Môa River Brazil
            *Tuchiunawa Brazil

Takanan (Girard 1971a, 41–42)
    Takanik
        Takana (Tacana) Bolivia

Sapibokona Complex Bolivia
   Sapibkona
   Guarisa
   Maropa
   Reyesano
Araona Bolivia
Mabenaro
Kavinik
   Cavineña Bolivia
   Čamik (Chamik)
      Čama (complex) Bolivia, Peru
         Chama (Tiatinagua)
         Eseʔexa (Eseʔejja, Ese Ejja)
      Warayo (complex)
         Guarayo (Tambopata-Guarayo)

(See Map 4.5. Pano-Takanan languages; see also Map 7.10.)

MAP 4.5. Pano-Takanan languages

The classification and reconstruction given by Sanderson Oliveira (2014, 2023) for the Panoan languages is the most accurate for that branch, based on more data and a careful study of sound correspondences.

Essentially all of the classifications of Panoan recognize a split in the family between a Northern subgroup (Mayoruna branch) and a Main or Principal subgroup, though with disputes over the positions of Kakataibo and Kaxarari in the classification.[27] Oliveira's (2023) careful study based on sound correspondences and shared innovations confirms that Northern was the first to split off from Proto-Panoan, and that formerly disputed Kakataibo and Kaxarari belong to Principal branch as early divergent members of that subgroup. The Northern subgroup includes Matis and Matsés; the other Panoan languages are members of the Principal subgroup. This aligns with Fleck's (2013) classification and partially with that of Valenzuela and Guillaume's (2017). (See Shell 1975 for an earlier classification and reconstruction of Panoan languages.)

Some other names that are sometimes listed as Panoan languages include: **Panavarro, Purus, Mayo** (Maia, Maya, Pisabo, Pisagua) (Brazil, Peru), **Kanamari**, and **Nukuini** (Nucuini, Nuquini) (with dialect **Cuyanawa**) (Brazil) (Adelaar and Muysken 2004, 419; Shell 1975, 14; Migliazza and Campbell 1988, 189–190; Rodrigues 1986, 77–81). *Ethnologue* (2021, 2023) has **Sharanahua** (Acre, Arara) as a distinct language (with dialects: Arinahua [Marináwa] and Chandinahua). Some list **Chirigua** (Bolivia) as a Takanan language (see Girard 1971a, 41–42).

Some of these languages are unattested.

Victor Girard's (1971a, 155–159) reconstructed phonetic inventory for Proto-Pano-Takanan (PPT) is: /p, t, c, č, k, kʷ, ʔ, P, b, d, j, (g), gʷ, r, s, ṣ, š, w, y, h, m, n, M, N, Ṇ; i, e, ɨ, u, a/. The **P has the reflexes Proto-Takanan (PT) *p : Proto-Panoan (PT) *b ([β]). PPT **ṣ has the reflexes PT *c : PP **ṣ̌*; PPT **M has PT *b : PP *m*; PPT **N has PT *r: PP *n; and PPT **Ṇ has PT **d~n*: PP *n.

Oliveira (2014, 349, 385) reconstructed the following Proto-Panoan phonemes: /p, t, k, kw, ʔ, m, n, r, ř, ts, tʃ, tʂ, β, s, ʃ, ʂ, h, w, y, i, ɨ, a, o, ĩ, ɨ̃, ã, õ/. (For earlier reconstructions see Shell 1975.)

Victor Girard's (1971a, 41–42) classification of Takanan languages (and varieties) is seen above. Valenzuela and Guillaume (2017) rely on Girard's classification for the Takanan languages, but include only those currently still spoken. Terrence Kaufman (2007, 70–71) tentatively included **Toromona** (Toromono) in his Chama group of Takanan.[28] Luis Antonio Rodríguez Bazán (2000, 136) considered Toromona an unclassified language whose speakers have not been contacted by non-indigenous people.

Victor Girard's (1971a, 26, 30–31) reconstruction of the Proto-Takanan phonemic inventory has: /p, t, ç, k, kʷ, (ʔ), b, d, j, s, z, x, ř, r, w, y, m, n; i, e, u, a/. The phonetic value of some of the consonants is not straightforward. The *ç appears to be intended to represent a retroflexed affricate ([tʂ], IPA [tʂ]). He says of his *j that it is "meant rather as a symbol for a set of reflexes and not as having any inherent phonetic value" (p. 34). Its reflexes in various languages include ř, š/l, š, c [ts], č, s, θ, h. The *ʔ is uncertain. The *r is retained as *r* only in Cavineña and is lost (is Ø) in all the other languages. Girard says the *r "can be determined as a 'variant' of **n in Proto-Pano-Takanan" (p. 30). The *ř has the reflex *r* in slightly more than half of the languages and is Ø everywhere else, though it has *y* as its reflex in some environments in Eseʔexa. Finally, *z also "should properly be read as a symbol for a set of reflexes. Its status is problematic since in both Ese?xa and Kavineña . . . reflexes to *z appear to be both s and t, sometimes in what appears to be the same root" (p. 35).

Not all scholars are in agreement that Panoan and Takanan are genetically related. Many find the lexical evidence for classifying Panoan and Takanan together in a single larger family stronger, though some have doubted the strength of grammatical evidence (see Zariquiey 2011, 3). However, Valenzuela and Guillaume (2017, 30) list also nineteen structural traits shared by Panoan and Takanan languages. Some scholars suspect that the similarities shared by the two are the result of borrowing and general language contact; some believe more study is needed; and some, including me, believe that very many of the lexical and grammatical matchings are inherited from Proto-Pano-Takanan though at the same time there has been considerable borrowing (see Adelaar with Muysken 2004, 419 and especially Valenzuela and Zariquiey 2015).

Terrence Kaufman's (2007, 70–71) Macro-Panoan cluster is fairly representative of other broadscale classifications that propose connections with these languages. It combines his Pano-Takanan stock and Mosetén-Chon stock (which includes Mosetenan and Chonan). (For an evaluation of Joseph Greenberg's [1987] Macro-Panoan, see Appendix 1 of Chapter 6.)

*Payaguá Paraguay

Payaguá is a dormant language isolate of Paraguay. It was spoken in two regions, in the upper Paraguay River area, near Puerto de la Candelaria, and in an area below Asunción, in the vicinity of the Bermejo River. María Dominga Miranda is recognized as the last speaker of Payaguá; she died in 1943.

The sources of Payaguá, from the end of the 1700s to 1940, provide vocabulary, some sentences, and two short texts, the Act of Contrition (Catholic prayer) with a loose Italian translation in Hervás y Panduro (1787, 228), three verb paradigms, the text of a song (with no translation), and a few sentences. (See Zamponi in press b.)

Payaguá, along with **Guachí**, is often thought to be a Guaicurúan language or related to Guaicurúan. Pedro Viegas Barros (2013b, 20–21) found some attractive lexical similarities and was able to make a few morphological comparisons; his conclusion, however, was that in spite of suggestive similarities, it is not possible to be assured that Payaguá and Guachí belong with the Guacurúan family.

Puinave (Wãnsöhöt, Waipunavi, Guaipunabi, Wanse) Colombia, Venezuela

Puinave (Wãnsöhöt) is spoken in the departments of Guainía and Vichada in Colombia, on the Inírida River and its tributaries, also with some speakers in Venezuela. It is now generally considered a language isolate, although until recently it was commonly thought to be related to so-called Makúan languages and others. Following Rivet and Tastevin (1920), many had classified Puinave and the "Makúan" (Nadahup) languages together, often also with Kakua-Nukak, in a Makú-Puinave or Puinavean family. (See, for example, Girón 2008, 428–433.) As mentioned earlier, Epps and Bolaños (2017, 502) concluded from their investigation of the evidence for these proposals that they are three distinct "genetic units" with no convincing evidence for grouping any of them together, although similarities shared by Puinave and Kakua-Nukakan may be suggestive.

*Puquina (Pukina) Peru, Bolivia

Puquina is a language isolate. It was recognized in 1575 by the Spanish as a *lengua general* ("general language") in colonial Peru, one of three such languages used for administration and mission purposes there. It had great prestige, but in spite of that, it ceased to be spoken by the nineteenth century (Adelaar 2012a, 2020, 239; Torero 2002, 389–404, 408–456).

Puquina played an important role in the Altiplano before the arrival of Aymara and Quechua speakers (Adelaar 2020, 242). It is not entirely clear from colonial records and toponyms where it was spoken. A document called *Copia de curatos* contains an inventory of locations where missionary guidance was required in Puquina. From it, the Puquina-speaking territory around 1600 appears to have been fragmented, with areas along the northwestern, northern, and eastern shores of Lake Titicaca, in a limited area between Sucre and Potosí (Bolivia), northeast of Lake Titicaca in the provinces of Larecaja and Umasuyos, and southeast of the city of Arequipa extending into the Peruvian departments of Moquegua and Tacna and possibly parts of northern Chile (Adelaar 2020, 242; Adelaar and Muysken 2004, 350).

Though there are a limited number of smaller sources on the language, the major reference for Puquina is Luis Gerónimo de Oré's (1607) *Rituale seu Manuale Peruanum*, with translation of Spanish religious texts. It is very poorly attested, in spite of the important role it played. Only some 200 words are identified (Adelaar 2020, 243).

As mentioned in Chapter 1, an error, pointed out long ago and corrected several times, persisted for a long time in which Puquina was said to be related to Uru-Chipaya. Uru and Chipaya each have erroneously been called "Puquina" (Adelaar 1989, 43, 175, 252; Adelaar and Muysken 2004, 175; Campbell 1997a, 189, 210; Cerrón-Palomino 2006, 22–23). However, these languages have next to nothing in common with Puquina.

Puquina is the language commonly associated the pre-Inca Tiahuanaco (Tiahuanacu, Tiwanaku), one of the earliest known civilizations of South American and one of the largest archaeological sites there, 500 CE–1000 CE, concentrated on the Bolivian Altiplano (Adelaar 2020, 239). It is possible that Aymara and Uru were also spoken at Tiahuanaco. Puquina was replaced by Quechua and Aymara. Puquina speakers, it is hypothesized, were known by the term *Colla*, though today it refers to the Aymaran peoples of the altiplano.[29] Puquina may also have been the earlier language of the Incas, later replaced by Quechua (van de Kerke and Muysken 2014, 145–146).

A possible relationship of Puquina with Arawakan has often been mentioned, though there is very little to recommend it except similarities among possessive and personal pronoun prefixes. Puquina has: *no* 'my', *po* 'your', and *chu* 'his/ her', and *ni* 'I', *pi* 'you', and *chu* 'he/ she'. This is compared to such Arawakan languages as Baure, which has, *ni-* 'my' *pi-* 'your', *ro-* 'his' and *ri-* 'her', and *nti'* 'I', *piti'* 'you', *roti'* 'he', and *riti'* 'she' (Adelaar 2020, 245). This, however, is far less impressive than may appear at first glance. Many American Indian languages have *n* in first person pronominal forms; for Puquina and Arawakan to share this similarity means nothing more than that it is widespread and has other explanations (see Campbell and Poser 2008, 215–223 for details). The *p* of the second person forms is similarly seen in several other languages. Greenberg (1987, 277) cites "numerous second-person pronominal forms in *p* and *b* . . . particularly in EQUATORIAL and CHIBCHAN-PAEZAN."[30] If *p* in second-person forms is frequent in these other languages not known to be related to Puquina or Arawakan, then finding it in both Puquina and Arawakan loses its force as evidence exclusively for a relationship between these two. In any case the fact that *p* seems to be shared for second person or *n* for first person may be simply accidental; because they are very short, statistically they are less able to eliminate chance as an explanation for the shared similarity.

No claim has been made that the third person forms are similar, not claimed to be indicative of a possible genetic relationship between these languages. As Adelaar (2020, 245) says, "in other respects, Puquina exhibits no particularly close parallels with the Arawak[an] languages, whether those of the adjacent lowlands or further afield." Typologically it shares much with other Andean languages. The proposed affiliation is very doubtful.

The mixed language **Callahuaya** is composed predominantly of Puquina vocabulary with Quechua morphology (see Chapter 8). The Callahuaya villages are located in a region where Puquina is thought formerly to have predominated.

*Purí-Coroado Brazil

Purí-Coroado is a language isolate. Traditionally **Purí** and **Coroado**, together with **Koropó** (Coropó), were considered members of a Puríān language family. However, recent work has revealed that Purí and Coroado are variants of the same language—the names were used interchangeably for the ethnic group in colonial times—and that Koropó, formerly spoken in the states of Minas Gerais and Rio de Janeiro, is not related to it.

Purí-Coroado appears to have been spoken along the Serra da Mantiqueira from the state of São Paulo to the Rio Doce in Minas Gerais state, an area that included parts of the states of São Paulo (on the upper Paraíba River), Rio de Janeiro (around Campo Alegre), Minas Gerais (from the Peixe River to the middle Rio Doce River), and Espírito Santo (Ramirez et al. 2015, 235). Both Purí and Coroado are attested only in a few wordlists from the 1800s.

Ramirez et al. (2015) show that Purí and Coroado are only slightly differentiated varieties of a single language. They show that the few words shared with Koropó are borrowings from Purí-Coroado, that Koropó seems to belong instead to the Maxakalían languages, and that Purí-Coroado has no detectable genealogical affiliation with languages of eastern Brazil or with others (see also Neto 2007; Nikulin 2020, 19; Zamponi in press b).

The **Guarulhos** and **Goitacás** may also have belonged with Purí-Coroado, but they were exterminated early in the colonial period, and nothing of their language or languages remains (Neto 2007, 14). (See Ramírez et al. 2015 and Zamponi in press b for a summary of this work and for the evidence supporting the conclusions).

The assumed Puríān family was often considered one of the elements joined in the Macro-Jê hypothesis, as in Kaufman's (2007, 73) Macro-Je Cluster. It is not part of Macro-Jê Sensu Stricto (see Chapter 6).

Quechuan (Quechua)

The question of dialects of a single language versus separate languages is particularly vexed in the case of the Quechuan languages and varieties. It is well known that there are a number of distinct languages in the Quechua complex; nevertheless, the tendency to consider them all merely dialects of "Quechua" persists. Much remains to be done to clarify the classification.

Quechuan
  Huaihuash (Quechua I, Quechua B, Central Quechua)
    Pacaraos Peru
    Central Huaihuash
      Huáilay (North)
        Huaylas (Ancash) Peru
        Conchucos Peru
      Ap-Am-Ah
        Alto Pativilca Peru
        Alto Marañón Peru
        Huallaga (Alto Huallaga, Huánuco) Peru
      Huáncay (South)
        Yaru (Tarma, Junín) Peru
        Jauja-Huanca (Huancayo) Peru
        Huangascar-Topará Peru
  Huámpuy (Quechua II, Quechua A, Peripheral Quechua)
    Yúngay (Quechua IIA)
      Central Yúngay
        Laraos Peru
        Lincha Peru
        Apurí Peru
        Chocos Peru
        Madeán Peru
      Northern Yúngay
        Lambayeque (Cañaris-Incahuasi) Peru
        Cajamarca Peru
    Chínchay (Quechua IIB-IIC)
      Northern Chínchay
        Chachapoyas (Amazonas) Peru
        San Martín Peru
        Loreto (Northern Pastaza) Peru
        Ecuador-Colombia Ecuador, Colombia
      Southern Chínchay
        Southern Peruvian Quechua
          Ayacucho Peru
          Cuzco Peru
          Northern Bolivian Quechua (Bolivian Quechua) Bolivia
          Bolivian Quechua Bolivia
          Santiago del Estero Quichua Argentina

(Cf. Cerrón-Palomino 1987; see also Parker 1969a, 1969b, 1969c.)
  (See Map 7.10.)

The Quechuan family has by far the greatest number of speakers of any indigenous language family of the Americas, reported at from 8 to 10 million, spoken in Colombia, Ecuador, Peru,

Bolivia, and Argentina. Its distribution in pre-contact times largely matched that of the Inca Empire. The lowland Quechua-speaking areas apparently came about later, in the Spanish colonial period.

The two primary branches (Huaihuash/Quechua I/Quechua B/Central and Huámpuy/Quechua II/Quechua A/Peripheral) are markedly different from each other. Within these two we are confronted with dialect continua that make it difficult to determine language boundaries, or where or to what degree varieties may be mutually intelligible with one another. There are few sharp language boundaries. It has been suggested that the amount of diversity across the entities that make up the Quechuan family is comparable to that of the Romance languages. It is often suggested that they separated from one another more than 1,500 years ago (van de Kerke and Muysken 2014, 133). I suspect the difference between the two major branches is more than that among the Romance languages.

Willem Adelaar (personal communication) points out that the **Yungay** group in fact is not a unified grouping; it has no common innovations. **Cañaris-Incahuasi** and **Cajamarca** may group together (the former is heavily influenced by Central Quechua), but **Laraos** is quite distinct. **Lincha** and **Madeán** may form a group. Also, **Chachapoyas** and **San Martín** form a group (Chachapoyas is extremely innovative), and the other Northern varieties also group together.

The early expansion of Quechua is thought to be linked with the Huari civilization; the spread of QII varieties has been linked to the Huari culture of the south-central Andes coastal area of Peru, circa 600–11000 CE. Later spread of Quechua was during in the Inca Empire (1200 [or 1438] to 1572), northward into Ecuador and southward into Argentina, linked with population movements (van de Kerke and Muysken 2014, 139).

As mentioned above in connection with Aymaran, disagreements about possible broader connections of Quechuan with other languages, in particular with Aymaran, have been intense. Quechuan and Aymaran have long been thought to be possibly genetically related, in a hypothesis called **Quechumaran**. Many scholars doubt Quechumaran, although some support it. Because Quechuan and Aymaran have interacted and influenced each other intensely over a very long time, they share much vocabulary and many structural traits. This makes it extremely difficult, perhaps impossible, to distinguish what is shared due to diffusion from what may be shared because of being genetically related to one another. (See Chapter 6 for details.) Morris Swadesh (1959) proposed **Quechuachon**, a grouping that would include Quechuan, Aymaran, Chipaya-Uru, Pano-Takanan, Mosetén, and Chonan. This hypothesis is now mostly forgotten.

Sáliban (Sálivan, Sáliba-Piaroan, Piaroa-Saliban)
    Sáliba (Sáliva) Colombia, Venezuela
    Piaroan
        Piaroa (Piaroa-Maco, Wothüha, Wotjuja, Guagua, Quaqua) Venezuela, Colombia
        Mako Venezuela

(Zamponi 2017)

Sáliban is a small family of languages spoken in the middle Orinoco Basin in the area of Venezuela and Colombia called *Llanos* (the plains).

Sáliba (Sáliva) is spoken upstream from the confluence of the Meta and Casanare Rivers, in the Casanare, Vichada, and Meta Departments of Colombia and Cedoño Department, Venezuela.

Piaroa is spoken on the east bank of the Orinoco River, inland from the Paguasa River to the Manapiari River in Amazonas Department, Venezuela, and in the east of Vaupés Department, Colombia, on the border with Venezuela, and several smaller tributaries.

Mako (Maco) is on the mid-Ventuari River and its tributaries in Amazonas Department, Venezuela (Zamponi 2017, 266).

Piaroa and Mako are closely related to each other. Mako was formerly sometimes mistakenly considered a dialect of Piaroa. Terrence Kaufman (2007, 77) says that "Piaroa and Mako may be distinct languages with mutual bilingualism."[31]

Ature is often classified with Sáliban languages, as for example in Loukotka (1968, 151) and Migliazza (1985[1982], 41). Ature was spoken around the Atures Rapids, but had disappeared by 1887, with nothing on the language ever recorded. The assumed Sáliban connection is due to Josef Gumilla (1745), who said that Ature was a derivation or "corruption" of Sáliba (Gumilla 1745, vol. 2, p. 38), that, compared to Sáliba, it is "little different" (Gumilla 1745, vol. 1, p. 212; see also p. 329; Zamponi 2017, 266).

A proposed genealogical relationship between Sáliban and **Betoi-Jirara** is plausible but not confirmed. The proposal of a genetic relationship between **Jotí** (Hodï) and either of these other two appears doubtful (see Rosés Labrada 2019; Zamponi 2017).

*Sapé (Kaliana, Calianá, Chirichano) Venezuela

The Sapé speakers' traditional territory was the mid- and upper Paragua River and the Karún River in Bolívar state, Venezuela, near the border with Brazil. Francia Medina (2008, 740, 744) reported that the last known fully competent speaker of Sapé, Elena Lezama, died in 2004 in the village of Boca de Karún. Her brother, Ramón Quimillo, who could speak reasonably well, died in Kavaimakén village in 2018 (Rosés Labrada and Medina 2019, 173).

Sapé is a language isolate, so recognized by most scholars. Dixon and Aikhenvald (1999, 20) said that Sapé is "among the few languages that we say nothing about, for the simple reason that almost nothing is known about them." This was not the case, however, since there was even then a substantial amount of primary documentation on the language recorded by Ernesto Migliazza (1978, 1982 [1985]) (see also Zamponi in press b). Terrence Kaufman (2007, 68) grouped the three language isolates **Kaliana** (Sapé), **Arutani** (Awaké), and **Maku** (Mako) in his Kalianan stock, apparently composed of a proposed Awaké-Kaliana family and Maku.[32] He gave no indication of what this might be based on; the classification has not been taken up by others.

*Sechura (Sec, Sek) Peru

Sechura (Sek) was spoken in the Piura region near the port of Sechura in northern Peru. (See Map 7.11.) It was probably dormant by the beginning of 1900s. The only documentation is a list of words from bishop Baltazar Jaime Martínez Compañón (1782–1790[1985]) and a wordlist from 1864 collected by Richard Spruce (published in various sources, for example Lehmann 1920, 1084–1085; Urban 2019a, 99–100). Sechura is considered a language isolate.

Olmos, the languages of the oasis of Olmos, may also possibly be connected with Sechura (Adelaar and Muysken 2004, 320, 400); however, the evidence is too sparse to demonstrate that. Matthias Urban (2019a, 62) thinks it is not profitable to speculate about Olmos' possible affinities. (See Chapter 5 for details.)

Paul Rivet (1924, 678, 696) put Sechura and **Tallán** together in a single family that he called "Sek." Čestmír Loukotka (1968, 260) also grouped Sechura ("Sek") with Tallan (or "Atalan"), and a possible relationship between Sechura and Tallán is repeated by several others. Adelaar and Muysken (2004, 400) leave open the question of possible relatedness between Sechura and Tallán because of "the limited number of vocabulary items that are available," and Matthias Urban (2019a, 179) agrees that such a relationship is "not demonstrable based on the available data." Terrence Kaufman (2007, 69–70) placed Sechura inside his Macro-Lekoan cluster. Alfredo Torero (1986, 532), on the other hand, considered Sechura an independent language heavily influenced by Tallán, while Seifart and Hammarström (2018) consider Sechura a language isolate.

*Tallán Peru

Tallán was spoken in the Chira and Piura Valleys, including in the towns of Colán and Catacaos on the north coast of Peru. (See Map 7.11.) **Colán** and **Catacaos** were closely related varieties of the language usually called Tallán. Indications are that it was dormant by the first half of the 1800s. The main source of data on the language is Baltasar Jaime Martínez Compañón's (1985[1782–1790]) wordlists.

Classifications of Tallán with other languages have been varied and often very confused. As mentioned above with Sechura, Tallán has often been linked with Sechura, though several believe the data available are insufficient to demonstrate that possible connection (see Urban 2019a, 79). Much confusion stems from Paul Rivet's (1924, 651) "Atal'an" family, which was followed by several subsequent classifiers though sometimes with or without Colán and Catacaos as members and at times confused with other languages of northern Peru and even Ecuador. As J. Alden Mason (1950, 195) concluded, "apparently *Atalán* and *Tallán* must be distinguished . . . Confusion and disagreement are great." Most scholars in recent discussions now agree that the data available are insufficient to confirm or reject a possible genetic relationship between Tallán and Sechura (see Sechura above). Here Tallán is considered a tentative language isolate.

*Taruma (Taruamá) Brazil, Guyana

Taruma is a recently dormant language isolate. It was presumed extinct until three surviving speakers were found living among the Wapishana, though only one (semi-)speaker remained by 2015 (Carlin 2011, 227; Carlin and Mans 2014, 82–85; Seifart and Hammarström 2018; Zamponi in press b). Taruma was spoken in the Río Negro region, but its speakers migrated to the southern Guianas sometime before 1764. There Taruma speakers came into contact with Wapishana and Manao groups, speakers of Arawakan languages (Carlin 2011, 227; Carlin and Mans 2014, 83). The Taruma were traders who traversed the southern border area of Suriname, Brazil, and Guyana bartering their wares.[33]

There is little published data on Taruma, only two wordlists, from Robert Schomburgk (1848) with 18 headwords and from William Farabee (1918, 277–283) with 233 headwords.

Unpublished things with Taruma material include several words from Jesuit missionary Cuthbert Cary-Elwes from 1919 to 1923 and a wordlist collected in 2015 by Sérgio Meira (see Zamponi in press b for details).

Kaufman (2007, 73) sees Taruma and **Katembri** as genetically related. However, Katembri is very problematic; Raoul Zamponi (in press b) treats it as a "phantom language" (see Chapter 5).

Taushiro (Pinchi, Pinche) Peru

Taushiro is a language isolate of the Peruvian Amazon near the border with Ecuador. In 2015 the probably only surviving speaker, Amadeo García García, lived in Intuto in the Río Tigre basin, Loreto Department, in northeastern Peru (Zachary O'Hagan 2015). Neftalí Ortiz Alicea, SIL missionary, undertook language documentation in the 1970s, with a preliminary sketch grammar, preliminary phoneme analysis, dictionary (*vocabulario*), two short texts, and brief ethnographic notes (see O'hagan 2015 for details). Zachary O'Hagan (2015) obtained additional information from Amadeo García García, who, as the presumed last speaker of the language, was the subject of an expansive story in the *New York Times* by Nicholas Casey (2017).

Various proposals have been made to link Taushiro with other languages. In earlier times it was known more often as **Pinche**. Beuchat and Rivet (1908) classified Pinche as a Zaparoan language, in spite of having no linguistic data on it. Mary Ruth Wise (1999, 312) also believed that Taushiro was connected with Zaparoan. Antonio Tovar (1961, 69) had Pinche as both a dialect of Candoši (**Candoshi**) and as a surviving dialect of **Omurano** (p. 151). Loukotka (1968, 156) placed Pinche in his Murato Stock, which included also Candoshi (Murato), **Shapra**, **Chirino**, **Sacata**, and **Rabona**. He said of Pinche (Llepa, Uchpa, Avaza) that it is the "language of an unknown tribe" of which nothing was known. Terrence Kaufman (2007, 69) said that "on the basis of a certain amount of lexical evidence, it seems that **Taushiro** may be related to both Omurano and Kandoshi, and more closely to the former." He grouped the Zaparoan and Yaguan families together in his "Sáparo-Yawan stock," with Taushiro and Omurano seeming to be in his Yaguan (Yawan) family, though that is probably a printing error where they were intended to be additional members of the stock but not part of Yaguan itself. None of these proposals has been investigated seriously.

*Tequiraca (Tekiraka, Aewa, Aiwa, Aʔɨwa, Aushiri, Auishiri, Ixignor, Vacacocha) Peru

Tequiraca was located in the northern Peruvian Amazon, in Puerto Elvira, near Lake Vacacocha in the Curary River area of Peru. The main sources are the wordlists in Tessmann (1930, 475–485) and Villarejo (1959). It is a language isolate. Tequiraca has not had fluent speakers since the 1980s, although Lev Michael and Christine Beier (2012) located a few semi-speakers in 2008 from whom they collected another wordlist, some short sentences, and made a phonemic analysis. The names Aushiri/Auishiri for Tequiraca should not be confused with Auishiri as a variant name for Waorani. (See Zamponi in press b; Seifart and Hammarström 2018.)

The data available are sufficient to show that the language has no discernible relatives. Loukotka (1968, 156) listed it as a language isolate, as do most other scholars (Adelaar and Muysken 2004, 456; Tovar 1961, 156; etc.). Kaufman (2007, 68) joined Tequiraka (Tekiraka)

together with **Kanichana** (Canichana) in his Macro-Tekirana cluster or Tekiraca-Kanichana Stock, which has these two as its only members. Greenberg (1987, 383, 96, 97) placed "Auixiri" (presumably Tequiraca) in his Macro-Tucanoan, along with Canichana and eighteen other language families and isolates, a branch of the larger Equatorial-Tucanoan branch of his Amerind hypothesis—apparently on what was to him the compelling power of only three look-alike lexical comparisons, one between only Auixiri and Canichana, one with only Kaliana, and one with Canichana, Capixana, Puinave, Dou, Hubde, Tucano, and Coreguaje.

Tikuna-Yurí
  Tikuna (Ticuna, Tukuna, Tucuna) Brazil, Colombia, Peru
  *Yurí (Jurí, Yuri, Xurúpixuna) Colombia, Brazil
  Carabayo Colombia

Tikuna is one of the largest Indigenous languages of South America outside of the Andes, with circa 50,000 speakers in the Amazon Basin in Brazil, Colombia, and Peru. It was generally considered a language isolate until its relationship with Yurí and Carabayo were recently demonstrated.

Yurí (Jurí) is, or was, a language previously spoken on the Puré River in Colombia and the Içá and Japurá Rivers in Brazil. Yurí is poorly known and probably dormant. A small amount of data was collected in 1853 and 1867. Terrence Kaufman (1994, 62, following Nimuendajú 1977[1929], 62) noted that there is good lexical evidence to support a link with Tikuna in a Ticuna-Yurí language family, though the data had never been explicitly compared at that time (Hammarström 2010). Fernando Carvalho (2009) demonstrated that Tikuna and Yurí are genetically related.

In 1969, a military commission contacted the previously uncontacted "**Carabayo**" people and took one family hostage, an adult couple and three children, held in La Pedrera in Colombia for a few weeks before they were "repatriated." All that is known of this language comes from the few words taken down then in 1969 and recovered only in 2013. The name Carabayo is taken from "Bernardo Caraballo," a Colombian boxing champion, given to the Carabayo man by people in La Pedrera because he was feisty when captured. A priest there wrote down fifty words that he heard or that were used in interactions with this man, twenty-five with glosses or context. Several have close parallels in Yurí or Tikuna.

Seifart and Echeverri (2014) were able to demonstrate the connection of Carabayo with Yuri, related to Yurí and Tikuna. Earlier attempts to group Yurí with either Arawakan or Cariban were just speculative, and a proposed grouping of Tikuna with Arawakan has also not held up. Terrence Kaufman (2007, 68) further proposed putting Tikuna and Jurí (Yurí) together with Munichi in his "Juri-Tikuna Stock."

*Timotean (Timote-Cuica) (Language Family or Language Isolate) Venezuela
  *Timote-Cuica (Miguri, Cuica)
  *Mucuchí-Maripú (Mocochí; Mirripú)

The Timotean languages or varieties were spoken in the Venezuelan Andes. They became dormant sometime in the early half of the twentieth century. It is not clear whether Timote and Cuica are separate languages or dialects of a single language (Urban 2018a, 32; Adelaar and Muysken 2004, 124). **Timote** was spoken in the valley of the Motatán and Chama Rivers, from Timote town to the area of La Grita in Táchira state. **Cuica** was spoken from Humocara in Lara state to Jajó at the border of Mérida state with Trujillo state (Adelaar and Muysken 2004, 124).

The status of **Mucuchí** (Mocochí) and **Maripú** (Mirripú) is also not clear; the two together are generally considered dialects, sometimes of a separate language, often as dialects of Timote. Loukotka (1968, 253) has **Mocochó** (Mucuchíe, Torondoy) as "once spoken in the village of Lagunillas, Mérida," and **Mirripú** as "once spoken in the village of El Morro." Adelaar and Muysken's (2004, 125, 127 697) view was apparently that Mucuchí and Mirripú are dialects of Timote. **Miguri** (Chama) is sometimes listed as a separate Timotean language (as in Mason 1950, 188; Loukotka 1968, 253; Greenberg 1987, 385 [where it is spelled "Maguri"]), but is given more often as a dialect of Timote (as in Tovar 1961, 161).

Timote may survive as **Mutú** (Loco, Mutús), an unstudied language (Adelaar and Muysken 2004, 125; Fabre 1998, 803). Migliazza and Campbell (1988, 313) considered Mutú unclassified. Loukotka (1968, 253) included in his Timote Stock all of the languages/varieties mentioned here and also **Mucutu** (Bailadores), "once spoken on the Mucuties River and in the village of Bailadores," of which he said nothing was known.

Most of the extant information on Timote and Cuica, mostly lexical, was collected by local scholars, gathered together and discussed by Paul Rivet (1927). Matthias Urban (2018a, 32) calculates that "the corpus of Timote-Cuica data consists of approximately 900 form-meaning pairs ('words') and 300 phrases and sentences, most just attested for a single doculect."

Broader connections have been suggested for Timotean with Chibchan, Arawakan, and some others. None of them seems promising.

Tiniguan Colombia
  Tinigua (Timigua) (1 speaker in 2013.)
  *Pamigua (Pamiwa)
  *Majigua(?)

Adelaar and Muysken (2004, 620), following Loukotka (1968, 151), include extinct **Majigua** (of which Loukotka said nothing is known) in Tiniguan.

Tinigua was spoken by a single survivor, Sixto Muñoz, in 2013 and may now be dormant. He lived in the rain forest of the La Macarena mountains of Colombia. The language was spoken in the foothills of the Andes, extending into the western Amazon, in Metá Department, Sierra de la Macarena, on the Ariari River and formerly in Llanos de Yarí, Caquetá Department. Seifart and Hammarström (2018) consider **Pamigua** a dialect of Tinigua.

The languages of the family are extremely poorly documented. Some information was given by Marcelino de Castellví (1940). In the 1990s Nubia Tobar Ortiz worked with the last two speakers of Tinigua and published one short article on the language with a phonological description (Tobar Ortiz 1995) and a chapter of a book that summarizes the 1995 article and adds information on noun phrases in Tinigua (Tobar Ortiz 2000).

Unlike many other language families and isolates of South America, there have not been many attempts to join this one with other languages in broader classifications. Earlier attempts to group Tinigua with Sáliban have been abandoned, according to Jon Landaburu (2000, 30). Greenberg (1987, 384) included Tinigua in his Macro-Arawakan, part of his larger Equitorial (within his Amerind), based apparently on a grand total of three look-alikes compared with various languages of his Macro-Arawakan grouping, two words from Tinigua, and one from Pamigua. Terrence Kaufman (2007, 65) left Tiniwan (Tiniguan) as an independent language family, proposing no broader connections.

Trumai (Trumaí, Tramalhy) Brazil

Trumai is a language isolate spoken in the Xingu reserve along the Upper Xingu River in central Brazil. Trumai speakers came to the Upper Xingu from southeastern Brazil in the early 1800s. Trumai is reasonably well documented in Raquel Guirardello's (1999) grammar.

There has been speculation about possible genetic affiliations of Trumai in certain postulated macro-families, but with little evidence and not much sympathy. Joseph Greenberg (1987) adduced eight Trumai words that he judged as similar to certain languages of the sixteen language families that he lumped together in his Equatorial branch of Amerind. He took these eight words as sufficient evidence of Trumai's membership in Equatorial. Terrence Kaufman (2007, 65) put Trumai in his Macro-Otomakoan Cluster, together with Harákmbut (his Tuyoneri Language Area) and the small Otomakoan family.

Tukanoan (Tucanoan)
  Western Tukanoan
    *Kueretú (Cueretú, Coretú, Curetú) Brazil
    Coreguaje (Koreguaje, Caquetá) Colombia
    *Macaguaje (Kakawahe, Secoya, Piojé) Colombia
    *Teteté (Eteteguaje) Ecuador, Colombia
    Maijuna (Máíhɨ̃ki, Orejón, Coto) Peru (Dialect: Nebaji)
    *Tama Colombia
    Secoya-Siona (dialects or separate languages?)
      Secoya (Sekoya) Ecuador
      Siona Colombia, Ecuador
  Eastern Tukanoan
    Southern Eastern Tukanoan
      Tanimuka (Tanimuca) Colombia
      Retuarã Colombia
      *Yahuna (Jaúna, Yauna) Colombia
    Western Eastern Tukanoan
      Barasano-Eduria-Makuna
        Barasano Colombia, Brazil
        Taiwano (Eduria) Colombia

      Makuna (Macuna) Colombia, Brazil
      Desano-Siriano-Yupuá
        Desano-Siriano
          Desano Colombia, Brazil
          Siriano Colombia, Brazil
        *Yupuá-Duriña (Yupua, Duriña) Colombia
    Kubeo (Cubeo) Colombia, Brazil
  Eastern Eastern Tukanoan
    Branch I
      Tukano (Tucano) Brazil, Colombia
      Bará-Tatuyo
        Bará Colombia, Brazil
        Tatuyo Colombia
    Branch II
      Pisamira-Karapana-Tuyuka-Yurutí
        Pisamira-Karapana
          Pisamira Colombia, Brazil
          Karapana (Carapano) Colombia, Brazil
        Tuyuka-Yurutí
          Tuyuka (Tuyuca) Colombia, Brazil
          Yurutí Colombia
      Piratapuya-Wanano
        Pira-Tapuyo (Piratapuya) Brazil, Colombia
        Wanano (Kotiria) Brazil, Colombia
      *Arapaso (Arapaço, Arapasso, Koneá) Brazil, Colombia

(Chacon 2014.)
(See Map 7.9.)

Tukanoan languages are spoken in Colombia, Brazil, Ecuador, and Peru.

Ethnologue (2021) said that **Piratapuyo** is close to **Wanano** linguistically (with 99% lexical similarity) but ethnically distinct; the two groups do not intermarry. Kaufman (2007, 68) listed Wanano and Piratapuyo ("Wanana-Pirá") as a single language.

A major difference of opinion about the classification of Tukanoan has been whether there is a separate "Central Tukanoan" branch, with **Kubeo** (Cubeo) as its principal member. Bruna Franchetto and Elsa Gomez-Imbert (2003, 233) criticized "Central Tukanoan" for grouping the northernmost language (Kubeo) and a southern one (**Tanimuca/Retuarã**) without clear evidence, on pseudo-geographical criteria among others. Thiago Chacon (2014) presented clear evidence that a Central branch of Tukanoan cannot be sustained.

Chacon and List (2015) applied computational phylogenetic methods, including also sound-change characters from Chacon (2014). The result yielded a classification that recognized the Eastern Tukanoan/Western Tukanoan division, but it also had some differences from Chacon's (2014) classification. In particular, it put Kubeo and **Tanimuka** together in a subgroup that is a sister to the rest of Eastern Tukanoan. They conclude by giving a family tree where, taking into account what is known about language contact among Tukanoan languages, they undid some of the subgroups yielded by the computational phylogenetic methods. Chacon and List's (2015) classification with Kubeo as a sister to Eastern Tukanoan in a branch matches Chacon and Michael's (2018) account of the development of the past/perfective verbal subject agreement in Eastern Tukanoan but not in Kubeo. It shows that past/perfective verbal subject agreement in Eastern Tukanoan underwent certain nasal harmony processes in the development of its past/perfective suffixes that did not include Kubeo (Michael 2021, 343).

Thiago Chacon (2014, 281) reconstructs the Proto-Tukanoan consonants as: /p, t, tj, c, k, (k^w), ʔ, p', t', tj', k', (k$^{w'}$), tt, kk, s, h, w, j, m, n/. The consonants /p', t', tj', k', (k$^{w'}$)/ are called "laryngealized stops" (not to be interpreted as ejectives), realized with creaky voice. The *tj and *tj' are alveopalatal stops, and *c is a palatal stop. The alveopalatal and palatal stops "had overlapping realizations in certain contexts; *c was also realized with some amount of affrication, i.e. as [tʃ]" (p. 281).

About the Proto-Tukanoan homeland, Chacon (2014, 315) writes:

Tukanoan languages seem to have begun their major split on the Apaporis and Caquetá/Japurá River hinterlands. While not denying the possibility that Proto-Tukanoan speakers migrated from a different location (possibly more downriver), we can infer that the center of dispersion of Tukanoan languages took place in the region between the Apaporis and the Japurá Rivers.

As for proposed broader connections, Joseph Greenberg (1987, 383–385) classified "Tucanoan" as belonging to his Macro-Tucanoan (along with eighteen other language families and isolates), a part of his massive Equatorial-Tucanoan division of Amerind. Terrence Kaufman's (2007, 68) Tukanoan stock, on the other hand, contains only languages from the Tukanoan family and does not combine it with any others.

Tupían (Rodrigues and Cabral's 2012)
    Western Tupían
        Arikém subfamily
            *Arikém Brazil
            *Kabixiána Brazil
            Karitiána (Caritiana) Brazil
        Mondéan subfamily
            Paitér (Suruí, Suruí do Jiparaná, Suruí de Rondônia, Surui Paiter) Brazil
            Cinta-larga Brazil
            Gavião (Gavião do Jiparaná) Brazil
            Zoró Brazil
            *Mondé (Salamãi) Brazil
            Aruá (Aruaxi, Aruashí) Brazil (5 speakers in 2014)
        Puruborá (Boruborá, Kuyubi, Cujubi) Brazil (only 2 speakers as of 2015)
        Ramaráman subfamily
            Káro (Arara, Urukú) Brazil

*Ramaráma Brazil
*Urumí Brazil
Tuparían subfamily Brazil (see Aragon and Gerardi 2022)
    Tuparí Brazil
    *Kepkiriwát (Quepiquiriuate, Kepikiriwat, Kepkeriwát) Brazil
    Makuráp Brazil
    Mekéns (Mekém, Sakurabiat) Brazil
    Akuntsú Brazil
    *Waratégaya (Amniapé) Brazil
    *Wayoró (Ayurú, Wayru) Brazil
Eastern Tupían
    Awetí (Auetö) Brazil
    Jurúnan subfamily
        Juruna (Yuruna, Yudjá, Djudjá, Jaruna) Brazil
        *Manitsawá (Maritsauá, Manitzula) Brazil (Dialect: Arupai)
        *Xipaya (Shipaya, Shipaja, Xipaia) Brazil
    Mawé (Maué, Sateré, Sateré-Mawé) Brazil
    Mundurukúan subfamily
        *Kuruáya (Caravare, Curuaia, Kuruaia) Brazil (Only rememberers remain.)
        Mundurukú (Mundurucu) Brazil
    Tupí-Guaranían subfamily
        Guaranían Branch
            *Guaraní Antigo (Guaraní, Old Guaraní) Brazil
            Paraguayan Guaraní (Guaraní) Argentina, Brazil, Paraguay
            Kaiwá (Pãi-Tavyterã) Brazil, Paraguay
            Nhandéva (Ñandeva, Chiripá) Argentina, Brazil, Paraguay
            Xetá (Shetá) Brazil (only two speakers as of 2014)
            Chiriguano group (Ava, Simba, Chané, Izoceño, Tapiete) Argentina, Bolívia, Paraguay (Dietrich 2007)
            Aché (Guayakí, Guayaquí, Axe) Paraguay
        Guaráyoan Branch
            Guarayu (Guarayo) Bolivia
            Sirionó Bolivia
            Yuki (Yuqui) Bolivia
        Tupí Branch of Tupí-Guaranían
            *Tupí (Tupí antigo) Brazil
            Nheengatú (Língua Geral Amazônica, Língua Geral) Brazil, Colombia, Venezuela
            *Língua Geral Paulista (Língua Geral, Tupí) Brazil
            *Tupinambá (Língua brasílica, Tupi antigo) Brazil
        Tenetehárán Branch
            Avá (Canoeiro, Avá-Canoeiro) Brazil (16 speakers as of 2012)
            Tapirapé Brazil
            Parakanã (Paracanã, Apiteréwa) Brazil
            Tocantins Asuriní (Assurini, Asuriní do Tocantins) Brazil

    Suruí (Suruí do Tocantins) Brazil
    Tembé (Tenetehára) Brazil
    Guajajára (Tenetehára) Brazil
    *Turiwára (Turiuara) Brazil
  Xingu Branch
    Araweté Brazil
    *Amanayé (Amanajé, Manazo) Brazil
    *Ararandewára Brazil
    *Aurê (Aurá) Brazil
    *Anambé of Cairarí Brazil
    Asuriní of Xingu (Xingu Asuriní, Asuriní do Coatinema) Brazil
  Kawahíb Branch
    Amondáwa (Amundáwa) Brazil
    Uruewawáu (Uru-eu-wau-wau) Brazil
    Karipuna Brazil (10 speakers in 2012)
    Piripkúra Brazil (perhaps 2 speakers, mostly uncontacted group)
    Diahói (Diahui, Jahoi, Jahui, Diarrui) Brazil (4 speakers, 2016)
    Parintintín (Kagwahív) Brazil (possibly a dialect of Tenharim)
    Tenharim (Tenharín) Brazil
    Tupí-Kawahíb (Tupi do Machado, Paranawát, Wiraféd) Brazil
    *Apiaká (Apiacá) Brazil
    Juma (Yuma) Brazil (5 speakers as of 2012.)
    Kayabí (Caiabi) Brazil
  Kamayurá (Kamaiurá, Camaiurá) Brazil
  Northern Tupí-Guaraníán Branch
    *Anambé of Ehrenreich Brazil
    Guajá (Awá, Avá) Brazil
    Kaapór (Urubú, Urubú-Ka'apór, Kaapor)[34] Brazil
    *Takunyapé (Taconhapé) Brazil
    Wayampí (Oyampi, Wajãpi, Waiãpi) Brazil, French Guiana
    Emérillon (Émerillon, Mereo, Teco) French Guiana
    Zo'é (Zoé, Jo'é) Brazil
Kokama/Omagwa (Cocama-Omagua, Kokama-Cocamilla) Peru, Brazil

(See Map 4.6. Tupían Language Family Branches; see also Maps 4.7. and 7.10.)
Galucio et al. (2015) give the following distance-based phylogenetic analysis of Tupían:

Tupían
  Western (40.6% probability)
    Karo; Puruborá
    Mondé
      Suruí
      Nuclear Mondé
        Salamãy

Indigenous Languages of South America

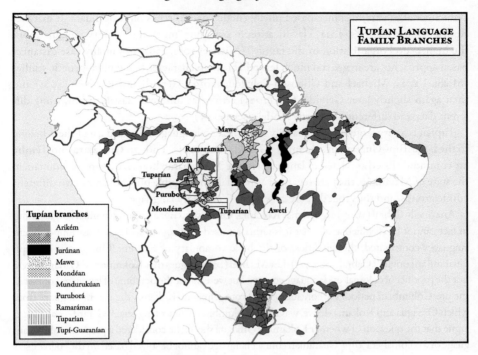

MAP 4.6. Tupían Language Family Branches

        Aruá; Gavião, Zoró
Eastern (40.6% probability)
    Arikém
        Karitiána
    Tuparí
        Makuráp
        Nuclear Tuparí
            Akuntsú, Mekéns
            Wayoró, Tuparí
    Mundurukú
        Mundurukú
        Kuruáya
    Jurúna
        Jurúna
        Xipáya
    Mawetí–Guaraní
        Mawé
        Awetí–Guaraní
            Awetí
            Tupí–Guaraní
                Parintintín
                Tapirapé; Urubú-Ka'apór, Paraguayan Guaraní

Galucio et al.'s (2015) distance-based phylogenetic analysis relies on lexical data. It matches Rodrigues and Cabral's (2012) classification in part, but "much uncertainty remains about the higher-level organization of the family" (Michael 2021, 236), and in any case distance-based approaches are in general much less reliable than character-based phylogenetic studies (Michael 2021; Michael and Chousou-Polydouri 2019). Gerardi and Reichert (2021) and then again slightly later Geraldi et al. (2023) arrived at different classifications, using different data and different phylogeny models (see below).

Tupían is a very large language family with circa 70 languages. Around 49 of them belong to the large Tupí-Guaraníian subfamily (Geraldi et al. 2023). Though **Guajajara** and **Tembé** are commonly listed as related to languages of the Tenetehárran branch of Tupí-Guaraníian, in the state of Maranhão, they are regarded as mutually intelligible but spoken by two different ethnic groups, and thus together are called the **Tenetehára** language.

Ana Suelly Cabral (2007) argued that **Kokáma/Omágwa** is not a Tupí-Guaraníian language and in fact cannot be classified at all, that it is rather a mixed language to which at least four different languages contributed, though "most of the basic vocabulary of Kokáma/Omágwa is of Tupí-Guaraní[an] origin" (Cabral 2007, 375). Lev Michael (2014) argues that **Kokama** and **Omagua** were not the product of colonial-era language contact, but were rather the outcome of language contact in the pre-Columbian period. He concludes that Proto-Omagua-Kokama, the parent language from which Omagua and Kokama derive, was a pre-Columbian contact language.[35] Gerardi et al. (2023) argue that the question of whether Kokamka/Omagua should be considered a pre-Columbian language or a colonial-era Tupí-Guaraníian contact language cannot be solved based on the cognate sets alone. They conclude that Kokama and Omagua belong to the same subgroup as Tupinambá and its descendant Nheengatu (p. 13); their results agree with Michael (2014) that Omagua and Kokama arrived at their historical locations before Tupinambá arrived on the coast.

Rodrigues and Cabral (2012, 502–503) reconstructed Proto-Tupían with the following phonemes: /*p, *pʷ, *t, *tʲ, *c, *č, *k, *kʲ, *kʷ, *pʔ, *pwʔ, *tʔ, *cʔ, *čʔ, *kʔ, *kwʔ, *ʔ, *r, *rʲ, *ᵐp, *ᵑk, *m, *n, *ŋ, *ŋʷ, *w, *j; i, ɨ, u, e, a, o, ĩ, ɨ̃, ũ, ẽ, õ/. The *c represents an alveolar affricate ([ts]).

Rodrigues and Cabral (2012, 500) believe it is "very likely" that Proto-Tupían began to diversify in the area between the Guaporé and the Aripuanã Rivers, in the basin of the Madeira tributary of the Amazon in Brazil's Rondônia state. Most others agree with the Tupían center of dispersal being in Rondônia state (see for example Gerardi and Reichert 2021, 166). Five of the ten Tupían subfamilies are found in this area, including one branch of Tupí-Guaraníian. Rodrigues and Cabral believe, based on archaeological evidence, that the diversification and migrations away from this homeland did not take place before 5,000 years ago. Kaufman and Golla (2000, 52) estimated the time-depth of Tupían at 5500–6000 BP.

Languages of the Tupí-Guaraníian branch extend over 4,000 km in both latitude and longitude, among the few most widely spread language families of the world (Gerardi et al. 2023).

Michael et al. (2015) offer a lexical phylogenetic classification of the Tupí-Guaraníian branch, though the data upon which their classification is based was not presented, making it impossible to check their results. Their classification matches five of the eight subgroups of the Rodrigues and Cabral classification of Tupí-Guaraníian (above) and does not match two of those subgroups. They see **Kamayurá** as sister to the rest of the Tupí-Guaraníian branch (their Nuclear Tupí-Guaraní) (Michael 2021, 337).

Gerardi and Reichert's (2021) character-based Bayesian phylogenetic classification of Tupí-Guaraníian relies on cognate sets that are based on sound correspondences. They consider several different kinds of analysis that display some disagreements regarding the positions of a few of the languages. Their major difference with earlier classifications is that, based on their findings, they believe that "**Tupinambá** should not be considered closely related to the Guaraní[an] languages." They support what they call the "Mawetí hypothesis," a grouping of **Mawé**, **Awetí**, and Tupí-Guaraníian together, also supported in the classifications of several other scholars, and they recognize a major division between "Amazonian" and "non-Amazonian" branches of Tupí-Guaraníian (pp. 155, 159).

Geraldi et al.'s (2023) classification of the Tupí-Guaraníian languages uses Bayesian phylogenetic methods and is based exclusively on lexical data, in part correlated with archaeological and ethnographic information. They argue that the Tupí-Guaraníian branch of Tupían split off at circa 2500 BP, with its homeland in the southeastern Amazaon, in the upper area of the Tapajós-Xingu basins, then splitting into between Southern and Northern branches at circa 1750 BP (p. 1). They rely on archaeological information to establish pre-colonial geography of the Tupí-Guaraníian populations. Differences in their classification from classifications of other scholars are attributed to use of phonological evidence versus lexical evidence, errors in the data, and errors in determining cognates.[36]

They report that "Mawé separates from its ancestor about 3300 ... years ago, while Awetí separates about ca. 2600 ... years ago. It is only at around 1700 BP ... after a stable period of about 850 years that the [core] Tupí-Guaraní group begins to spread" (p. 10).

Geraldi et al.'s basic classification of Tupí-Guaraníian is:

Mawé
Awatí
Group I
    Subgroup Ia
        Tembé
        Guajajara (Tenetehara)
        Guajá
    Subgroup Ib
        Zo'e[37]
        Wayampi
        Tekó
        Ka'apor
    Subgroup Ic
        Kokama-Omagua
            Kokama
            Omagua
        Tupinambá
            Nheengatu
Group II
    Subgroup IIa
        Avá-Canoeiro
        Kamajurá
    Subgroup IIb
        Anambé

Araweté
Subgroup IIc
  Asuriní Xingu
  Tapirapé
  Suruí-Aikewara
  Parakanã
  Asuriní Tocantins
Subgroup IId (Kawahiv clade)
  Kayabi
  Apiaka
  Parintintin
  Urueuwauwau
  Tenharim
  Amondawa
Group III
  Subgroup IIIa Warazu
  Subgroup IIIb Guarayo
  Subgroup IIIc
    Old-Guaraní
    Mbyá
    Kaiowá
    Guaraní
  Subgroup IIId
    Tapiete
    Chiriguano
  Subgroup IIIe Xetá
  Subgroup IIIf
    Yuki
    Sirionó
    Aché

(For greater details of the hierarchical relationships within and among these groups, see their Figure 5, p. 10.)

While Geraldi et al. (2023:16) mention reasons for why they believe that "most phylolinguistic studies should involve exclusively or majorly characters based on lexical innovations," their treatment of the lexical data seems problematic, since apparently what they consider "cognates" does not eliminate borrowings. For example, they say of "the proximity of Ka'apor with subgroup Ic, it can be explained by its many lexical borrowings from Língua Geral" (p. 13). They speak of "borrowings" in several cases, of "admixture" (p. 16, "hybridization" involving Aché and Xetá, Gujajara and Guajá, and "the Urueuwauwau-Parintintin-Tenharim-Amondawa clade ... with a Kayabi-Apiaka hybridization" (p. 12), and of Aché and Xetá going relatively recently "through a process of Guaranization" (p. 15).

Proposals of broader affinity have linked Tupían with Cariban, and both of these with Jê. Several scholars find the Tupían-Cariban and Tupían-Cariban-Jê hypotheses plausible, though few throw unreserved support behind them. (See Chapter 6 for details.) Greenberg

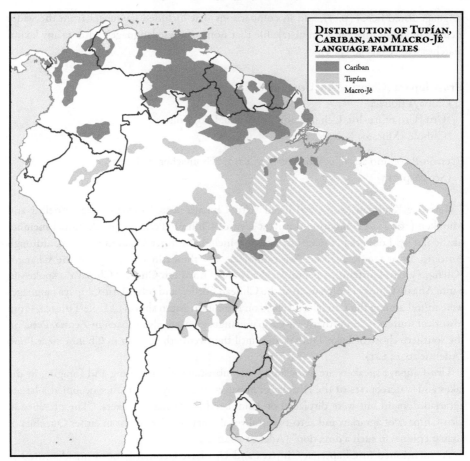

MAP 4.7. Distribution of Tupían, Cariban, and Macro-Jê language families

(1987, 384–385), however, placed Cariban and "Macro-Ge" in his Ge-Pano-Carib division but Tupían in a Kariri-Tupi grouping inside the Equatorial branch of his Equatorial-Tucanoan division of Amerind. Others have not accepted Greenberg's views. (See Map 4.7.)

Urarina (Simacu, Kachá, Itucale, Urariña, Oruarina) Peru

Urarina is a language isolate of Loreto Department, in northwestern Peru, in the Urarinas District along the Chambira River. Urarina is one of the typologically very rare languages that has OVS (Object-Verb-Subject) basic word order.

Speculative classifications have attempted to link Urarina with Panoan (Pano-Takanan), Tupían, Macro-Tukanoan, and "Andean" (as part of Greenberg's Amerind). Terrence Kaufman (2007, 69) placed Urarina in his Hivaro-Kawapanan stock, together with his Hivaro Language Area, Kawapanan (Cahupanan) family, and **Puelche**.[38] None of these proposals has proven at all likely. In comparisons of key terms (mostly basic vocabulary) from Loukotka's lists, Knut Olawsky (2006, 7–9) found in neighboring languages that "remarkably, Urarina words do not even exhibit a single similarity between any lexical items for any language listed here" (p. 7), and in comparisons that included languages from the wider vicinity he found that "it is unmistakable that none of these languages exhibits any lexical matches with Urarina" (p. 9).

Uru-Chipaya (Chipaya-Uru, Uruquilla)
  Chipaya Bolivia
  *Uru (Uru of Iru-Itu, Uchumataqu, Iru-Wit'u, Uro) Bolivia
  *Chholo (Murato) Bolivia.

(Cerrón-Palomino 2006, 25–26; Muysken 2010; Schumacher et al. 2009.)
(See Map 7.11.)

Terrence Kaufman (2007, 70) listed "Uru-Chipaya" as a "language area." Adelaar and Muysken (2004, 622) mention dormant **Uru of Ch'imu** (Peru) as an additional member of the family. Loukotka (1968, 270) had also included extinct **Chango** of Chile, although Antonio Tovar (1961, 49) said "we cannot classify the extinct language of the Changos [Chango y Uru Costeño], a people of the coast of northern Chile."[39] Chipaya is spoken in Santa Ana de Chipaya Bolivian, near the Chilean border, and other Uru-Chipaya languages were found among the Uru lake dwellers on the southeastern shores of Lake Titicaca. From historical sources it seems that Uru-Chipaya languages were also spoken in Zepita, Peru, on the southern shore of Lake Titicaca and until the twentieth century in Ch'imu, near Puno (Adelaar 2020, 241).

Uru-Chipaya speakers are associated with subsistance from fishing and foraging in the lakes and watercourses of the Altiplano; however, they may have earlier occupied a larger, agrarian domain but were displaced or assimilated by Aymara speakers. "The presence in Uru-Chipaya of agrarian and agro-pastoral vocabulary not derived from either Quechua or Aymara points in such a direction" (Adelaar 2020, 242).

As mentioned in Chapter 1, Chipaya and Uru have frequently been misidentified as Puquina, a very different and unrelated language. There have been numerous hypotheses of broader affiliations that would include Uru-Chipaya. Best known is probably Ronald Olson's (1964, 1965) proposal; he argued for a genealogical relationship between Uru-Chipaya and Mayan, which several other scholars had accepted. This proposal has mostly been abandoned (see Campbell 1973a, 1993). Louisa Stark (1972b) accepted Olson's Uru-Chipaya connection with Mayan and added Yunga (Mochica) to it. Stark's (1972a) case for including Yunga is even less convincing than Olson's for Uru-Chipaya with Mayan. Kaufman (2007, 70) placed his Uru-Chipaya "language area" in his Kechumaran stock. (See Chapter 6.)

Alain Fabre (1995) presented some nineteen lexical similarities between Uru-Chipaya and Pano-Takanan languages that could suggest a genetic relationship, though he thought contact was a more likely explanation. They are few and not very convincing. Roberto Zariquiey (2020) showed serious problems with many of Fabre's comparisons. Zariquiey gives eight lexical matchings as possible "cognates," but these are also not very convincing; half of them involve short forms (CV). Zariquiey (2020, 261) presents ten lexical comparisons between Uro (i.e., Uru-Chipaya) and Mosetén together with some possible sound correspondences. Several of these do exhibit interesting similarities, though three of them also involve short forms. While suggestive, this is far too little material upon which to base a viable hypothesis of genetic affiliation for these languages.

Waorani (Sabela, Huao, Wao, Auca, Huaorani, Huarani, Auishiri) Ecuador

Waorani is a language isolate spoken in Ecuador between the Napo and Curary Rivers. There may be a group of Waorani speakers in Peru in an uncontacted group. Waorani has three dialects: **Tiguacuna** (Tiwakuna), **Tuei** (Tiwi Tuei, Tiwi), and **Shiripuno**.

Loukotka (1968, 158) put **Tiwituey** (Tuei) together with Sabela (Waorani) in his Sabela stock. Terrence Kaufman (2007, 69) appears to classify the Yawan (Yaguan) family together with Sabela (Waorani). Other proposals appear to be without foundation, mostly without evidence.

Warao (Guarao, Warau, Warrau, Guaruno, Waraw, Araote, Faraute) Venezuela, Guyana, Suriname

Warao is a language isolate spoken along the Caribbean coast in northern Venezuela, Guyana, and Suriname. Warao is reasonably well documented. It has the typologically extremely rare OVS (Object-Subject-Verb) basic word order.

Loukotka (1968, 27) classified Warao together with **Gunoco**, **Chaguan**, and **Mairusa** in his Uarao Stock, although he says nothing is known of the first two of these languages. J. Alden Mason (1950, 253) added **Waikerí** (Guaiquerí), which he says "may also be related" to the others of his Warrauan (which includes Mariusa and Chaguan). Terrence Kaufman (2007, 64) included Warao in his large Macro-Paesan cluster. Perhaps the least well-received proposal was from Julian Granberry (1993, 15–16), who argued for a Warao connection with **Timucua** of Florida. His views have been challenged and mostly rejected (see Sturtevant 2005, 14, for example).

Witotoan (Huitotoan)
    *Nonuya Colombia, Peru
    Ocaina Peru (Dialects: Dukaiya, Ibo'tsa)
    Witoto (Uitoto)
        Murui (Bue, Murai, Witoto) Colombia, Peru
        Mɨka Colombia
        Mɨnɨka (Meneca) Colombia
        Nɨpode (Nipode, Nɨpode, Muinane) Peru

(Wojtylak 2017, 68)[40]

Katarzyna Wojtylak's classification (above) of the Witotoan family has only three distinct languages, **Nonuya**, **Ocaina**, and "**Witoto**." Witoto is a single language with a dialect continuum composed of **Murui**, **Mɨka**, **Mɨnɨka**, and **Nɨpode**. Wojtylak (2017, 1) says of them, "although all dialects of 'Witoto' are mutually intelligible, Murui and Mɨka are much more similar than Mɨnɨka or Nɨpode." She adds:

> In my view, the four varieties of 'Witoto' could be very well seen as ethnolects, being a distinguishing mark of social identity. It is also important to notice at this point that each 'Witoto' variety has its own clanolects, which are specific to individual clans, and

show minor distinctions in terms of their vocabulary and pronunciation (Wojtylak 2017, 57).

The speakers of Witotoan languages traditionally lived between the middle sections of the Caquetá and Putomayo Rivers in Colombia. They share numerous areally diffused traits of the Caquetá-Putumayo Linguistic Area, as well as shared cultural features (see Chapter 7).

The rubber exploitation from 1900–1930, disease, forced labor, and displacement hit the Witotoan-speaking population and others of the region hard, called the "silent genocide" (Wojtylak 2017, 26). The Nonuya and other groups of the region were taken by force to Peru. The last transport, a tugboat in the early 1930s, sank, and only one Nonuya woman and two boys survived. A very few Nonuya managed to return from Peru in the 1930s. The last three Nonuya native speakers died in 2003; six semi-speakers were reported in 2015 (Wojtylak 2016, 5). The ethnic population of the Murui, Mɨka, Mɨnɨka, and Nɨpode has increased since the 1940s (Wojtylak 2017, 28), though the surviving languages are increasingly endangered.

In the past, several other languages have been thought to belong to the Witotoan family, and a number of classificatory schemes attempted to join Witotoan with other languages in larger family groupings, "Carib stock," "Macro-Cariban," "Macro-Tupi-Guaraní phylum," "Ge-Pano-Carib" (Greenberg 1987), and so on (see Wojtylak 2017, 58). Richard Aschmann (1993) argued that Boran belongs to Witotoan, and Terrence Kaufman (2007, 69) also grouped the Boran Family and the Witotoan Family together in his Bora-Witotan stock. However, Echeverrí and Seifart (2016) refuted Aschmann's evidence for Boran being genetically connected with Witotoan, showing that most of it was rather due to borrowing. Some limited morphological evidence might be suggestive of a genealogical relationship involving the two, but it is by no means conclusive proof. Terrence Kaufman (2007, 69) included in his Witótoan Family: *__Andoquero__, *__Koeruna__ (Coeruna), __Okaina__ (Ocaina), *__Nonuya__, __Murui__[-Witito], __Koihoma__ (Coto, Orejón, [Coixoma]), __Meneka__[-Witoto] (Minica), and __Andoke__ (Andoque).⁴¹ Loukotka (1968, 188–189) included also *__Hairúya__ (Jairuia), said to be a dormant language once spoken on the Tamboryaco River, a tributary of the Putumayo River, in Colombia.

Aschmann (1993, 96) reconstructed the Proto-Witotoan phonemes as: /p, t, k, ʔ, b, d[r], dz, g, x, β, m, n; i, e, a, o, ɨ; nasalized vowels; two tones/. As in a number of other Amazonian languages, voiced stops *b* and *d* become nasals *m* and *n*, respectively, in the environment of nasalized vowels.

*Xukurú

(Shucurú, Xucuru, Ichikile, Shukurú) Brazil (Loukotka 1968, 8–89; Zamponi in press b)

Xukurú was spoken in Serra do Felipe, Serra da Aldeia Velha, Serra do Aió, Serra do Majé (or Pedra Furada), Poço do Mulungú, Serra Isabel Dias, Serra de Gangorra, Serra da Ventania (or do Vento), and probably also Serra do Tiagó, Serra da Porção, Serra da Moça, and Serra dos Xucurú. Xukurú was recorded in several wordlists from 1934 to

1961 (see Zamponi in press b for details). **Paratío** has often been thought to be related to Xukurú, though the evidence is too weak to confirm that (Zamponi in press b).

Xukurú has often been considered a language isolate (Campbell 2012a, 69), though because of its limited documentation some have considered it unclassified (cf. Crevels 2012, 190). Extremely little information is available on Paratío—Loukotka (1968, 89) says "only a few words" are known of it. Loukotka (1968, 89), nevertheless, grouped the two languages in his Shukurú "stock," along with **Garañun**, of which he said nothing is known, formerly spoken in the Serra dos Garanhuns. The evidence for this classification, however, is not compelling (Campbell 2012a, 151). Of Loukotka's six comparisons between Shukurú and Paratió, three are very similar in the two languages, *māzyé/mazya:* 'tobacco', *kiá/kiá* 'sun', and *sheñupre/sheñup* 'man', and three are rather different, *chilodé/vovó* 'tooth', *bandalák/bolúdo* 'ear', and *klari:mon/limolago* 'moon'. A seventh word, Xukurú *krashishi* 'earth', has no Paratío form to compare it with. Clearly no reliable conclusion about classification of these languages is warranted on the basis of such extremely limited information. Some of the similarities in these comparisons may well involve loanwords, for example the words for 'tobacco' and 'sun'. Clearly the case for a Xukurúan family needs to be investigated carefully. I assume that for now it would be best to consider Xukurú itself tentatively a language isolate (or perhaps unclassified) and Paratío an unclassified language. Garañun should also be added to the list of unclassified languages and its status examined (see Chapter 5).

*Yagan (Yagán, Yahgan, Yaghan, Yámana, Yamana, Tequenica, Yapoo) Chile

Yagan (Yámana) is a language isolate of Tierra del Fuego, Chile. Yagan speakers lived on the southern coast of Tierra del Fuego and the archipelago around it, extending to Cape Horn (Adelaar and Muysken 2004, 554). It is relatively well documented, with a number of descriptions, including Thomas Bridges 30,000-word Yamana-English dictionary (Bridges 1933; Adelaar and Muysken 2004, 567–578). The last native speaker, Cristina Calderón, died in 2022.

Although suggestions have been made of possible genetic connections of Yagan with Kawésqar and Chonan, they have not proven convincing to most. Yagan is classified as a language isolate, even by Terrence Kaufman (2007, 71), who factors in most suggestions of broader affiliations for most of the other language isolates of South America. Joseph Greenberg (1987, 383) has Yamana (Yagan) as a member of the Southern branch of his Andean "subgroup" of Amerind.

Yaguan (Peban, Peba-Yaguan Family)
Yagua (Yihamwo, Nijyamïï, Nikyejaada, Yahua, Llagua, Mishara) Peru, Colombia
*Peba (Nijamvo, Peva) Peru
*Yameo (Llameo, Camuchivo, Masamae, Mazan, Parara) Peru

Yaguan (Peba-Yaguan) languages are or were spoken in northwestern Peru and Colombia. **Yagua** is spoken in the Amazon basin of Colombia and northwestern Peru, near the Amazon, Napo, Putumayo, and Yavarí Rivers. **Peba** was spoken in Peba village, Loreto Department, Peru. **Yameo** was spoken along the banks of the Amazon River from the

Tigre River to the Nanay River in Peru. Yameo and Peba are both dormant; Yameo became dormant in the 1960. Neither Yameo nor Peba has much documentation; Yagua is well documented.

There is no solid evidence of possible broader kinship between the Yaguan family and any other languages. Although a link between Yaguan (Peba-Yaguan) and Cariban had been proposed, Gildea and Payne (2007) could find no evidence that supported this claim. Kaufman (2007, 69) grouped the Yaguan and Zaparoan families together in his "Sáparo-Yawan stock," which has also Taushiro and Omurano.

Yanomaman (Yanomamian)
 Ninam (Yanam, Xirianá, Shiriana, Jawaperi, Crichana, Jawari) Brazil, Venezuela
 Sanumá (Sanimá, Sanma, Tsanuma, Guaika, Samatari, Samatali, Xamatari) Brazil, Venezuela
 Yanomam (Waiká, Waicá, Yanomami) emergent language Brazil
 Yanomamö (Yanomamï, Yamomame) emergent language Brazil, Venezuela

(Migliazza 1972)

Ferreira et al.'s (2019) classification differs somewhat from Ernesto Migliazza's (1972); they divide the family into two branches, with Sanumá as the most distinct:

Yanomanan
 Ninam-Yanomam-Yaroamë
  Nimam (Yanami, Yanami-Ninamia) Brazil, Venezuela
  Yanomam-Yaroamë
   Yanomám (Waiká) Venezuela
   Yanomamö (Yanomame, Yanomami) Brazil
   Yaroamë (Jawari) Brazil
   Yãnoma Brazil
 Sanumá (Tsanuma, Sanima) Venezuela

Larger-scale classifiers have not often tried to join Yanomaman with other languages families. Ernesto Migliazza (1982[1985]) contemplated a possible Yanomaman connection with Panoan and Chibchan. Jotí (Hodï) has been suggested as being related to Yanomaman. Joseph Greenberg (1987, 382) grouped Yanomaman and many others in the Chibchan branch of his Chibchan-Paezan division of Amerind.

Yaruro (Pumé, Yuapín) Venezuela
Yaruro is a language isolate, spoken along the Orinoco, Cinaruco, Meta, and Apure Rivers in Venezuela. It is reasonably well documented, though no significant grammar of the language has been published (see for example Mosonyi 1966).

Matthias Pache (2016) argues that Yaruro is related to the Chocoan languages, citing lexical comparisons and sound correspondences as evidence. Terrence Kaufman (2007, 68) places Yaruro with Cofán and Esmeralda in his "Takame-Jarúroan stock." (See Mosonyi and García 2000; Seifart and Hammarström 2018.) Joseph Greenberg (1987,

384) included Yaruro in his Equatorial grouping along with many other language families and isolates, based solely on eight comparisons of lexical look-alikes, each involving matching with just one or a few of the many putative "Equatorial" languages (part of his broader Equatorial-Tukanoan division of Amerind). In three of the eight cases a Yaruro word is compared with a word in only a single language, in one instance only with Taruma, in another with Jíbaro, and in another with Mocochi (Timote). In two examples, the word compared is very short, making chance a greater possible explanation for the similarity: *ak* 'belly', *ea* 'wish'.

Yuracaré (Yuracare, Yurucar, Yuracar, Yurujure, Enete, Cuchi) Bolivia

The language isolate Yuracaré is spoken in the Beni and Cochabamba departments of Bolivia, in particular along Chapare River. (See Map 7.10.) It is reasonably well documented in the grammar written by Rik van Gijn (2006).

Through time, most authors, including Terrence Kaufman (2007, 70), have classified Yuracaré as an unrelated language, a language isolate. The large-scale classifiers did not, however, refrain from suggesting possible relatives for Yuracaré, among them Macro-Quechuan, Equatorial inside of Andean-Equatorial, Mosetén, Chonan, and Pano-Takanan (see van Gijn 2006, 7–8 for details). None of these proposals has enough support to seem believable.

*Yurumanguí (Yurimanguí) Colombia

Yurumanguí is a dormant language isolate once spoken along the Yurumanguí River in Colombia, also on the upper reaches of the Cajambre and Nava Rivers. The only record of Yurumanguí is one wordlist with some phrases recorded by Padre Christoval Romero some time prior to 1768. Romero's list was appended to a report by Captain Sebastián Lanchas de Estrada of his travels in the area in 1768. Fr. Gregorio Arcila Robledo published it and extracts from Lanchas de Estrada's report, presumably with some copying errors. Lanchas de Estrada's original report was rediscovered in the National Archives of Bogota and Romero's wordlist from it was republished by Paul Rivet (1942) with comments and analysis. Rivet argued that Yurumanguí was a Hokan language. Several others accepted and repeated Rivet's claim of Hokan affinity for Yurumangui, including Joseph Greenberg (1987, 132, 381) (see Poser's 1992 critique.) This Hokan connection has, however, now been thoroughly rejected (see Chapter 6). Since the material was collected, the language has disappeared.

Loukotka (1968, 259) included several other languages in addition to "Yurimangui" in his Yurimangui stock: **Timba** (on the Canambre River), **Lili** (near Cali), **Yolo** (Paripazo) (on the San Joaquín River), **Jamundi** (on the Cauca River), and **Puscajae** (Pile) (on the left bank of the Dagila River). However, he says nothing is known of any of them.

Scattered proposals of more distant relatives for Yurumanguí have been made, though none of them has been well received. Most scholars have considered it a language isolate or unclassified. As Adelaar and Muysken (2004, 61) say, "the data on Yurumanguí are very limited and probably unfit to establish genetic connections that are not particularly close."

Zamucoan
  Ayoreo (Ayoré, Moro, Zamuco, Pyeta, Yovai) Bolivia, Paraguay
    (Dialect: Tsiricua, Tsiracua)
  *Zamuco (Old Zamuco) Bolivia
  Chamacoco (Ishiro, Jeywo) Paraguay
    (Dialects: Chamacoco Bravo [Tomaraho, Tomaraxa, Tumarahá], Ebitoso [Ebidoso, Ishiro])

Zamucoan languages are or were spoken in northern Paraguay and in the Santa Cruz Department of Bolivia. (Ciucci and Bertinetto 2015; Bertinetto and Ciucci 2020.) (See Map 7.12.)

Pier Marco Bertinetto's (2021) and Bertinetto and Ciucci's (2020) classification has Proto-Zamucoan dividing into two branches, one with **Old Zamuco** and **Ayoreo** and the other with **Chamacoco** (with two dialects, **Ebitoso** and **Tomaraho**). Old Zamuco was spoken in the 1700s in the Jesuit missions of southeastern Bolivia, relatively well documented by Igace Chomé before 1745 [1958] (Bertinetto and Ciucci 2020). Old Zamuco and Ayoreo are very closely related, while Chamacoco shares only about 30 percent of its lexicon with Ayoreo and Old Zamuco.

Adelaar and Muysken (2004, 623) also list **Guarañoca** (Bolivia) as an extinct language belonging to Zamucoan, possibly a dialect of Ayoreo. In his Zamuco Stock Loukotka (1968, 58–59) listed several additional language names in his Northern Languages division that includes among them Zamuco and "Ayoré." His Southern Languages division had only a single language, Chamacoco, with names of four dialects of the language. J. Alden Mason (1950, 281) listed many other names of languages and dialects in his Zamucoan, six languages in his "North: Zamuco" branch and four in his "South: Chamacoco" branch. Several of his languages are further listed with several dialects.

Terrence Kaufman (2007, 72) placed the "Samukoan family" in his Macro-Waikuruan cluster along with half a dozen other language families and language isolates.

Zaparoan
  Záparo (Zápara, Kayapwe) Peru
  Iquito-Arabela
    Iquito-Cahuarana (Amacacore, Hamacore, Quiturran, Puca-Uma) Peru
    Arabela-Andoa (Chiripuno, Shimigae, Simigae, Gae, Gaye) Peru

(Carvalho 2013, 92)

  Adelaar and Muysken (2004, 623) listed the following as Zaparoan languages:
    *Andoa (Shimigae) Peru (last speaker died in 2012)
    Arabela Peru
    *Cahuarano Peru (last speaker died around the late 1980s)
    Iquito Peru (12 to 15 speakers as of 2015)
    Záparo (Kayapwe) Ecuador (3 speakers as of 2011)
    *Gae (Shimigae, Gay) Peru (Possibly a variant of Andoa?)
    *Coronado Ecuador
    *Oa Ecuador

The Zaparoan languages are spoken in northern Peru and southeastern Ecuador. The precise membership of the family has been complicated, with several scholars assuming that certain languages of the area belonged to the family that have now turned out not to belong.

Fernando Orphão de Carvalho's (2013, 111) classification of Zaparoan has a split first with **Záparo** branching off and then with a second branch that splits into **Iquito** and **Arabela**. Terrence Kaufman (2007, 69) also has three languages in this "Sáparo" family: Sáparo-Konambo (Záparo-Conambo), Arabela-Andoa, and Ikito-Kawarano (Iquito-Cahuarano). *Ethnologue* (2023) has five languages in its Zaparoan family, with two branches. One branch has Iquito and **Cahuarano** as its members; the other branch splits into Záparo and Arabela-Andoa, which splits further into **Andoa** and Arabela.

Carvalho's (2013, 109–110) reconstruction of Proto-Zaparoan sounds has: /p, t, k, ts, s, h, r, m, n, a, i, o, u, ə, aw/.

Classification of Zaparoan languages with others outside the family has been highly varied and quite confused. Terrence Kaufman (2007, 69) grouped the Zaparoan and Yaguan families together in his "Sáparo-Yawan stock." Morris Swadesh (1954a) had also grouped Zaparoan with Yaguan within his Zaparo-Peba phylum. Joseph Greenberg (1987, 384) put Zaparoan and Cahuapanan together in his Kahuapana-Zaparo grouping, part of his Andean division of Amerind. This has not been well received by linguists.

Omurano has sometimes been claimed to belong to Zaparoan (see Omurano above), but the evidence does not support this (Carvalho 2013).

4.4. WRAP-UP

In short, since the earlier classifications in Campbell (1997a) and Campbell (2012a) many previously poorly known and even fully unknown languages have received considerable documentation. This new descriptive material, along with a much larger number of linguistic scholars dedicated to South American linguistics, has resulted in many advances in understanding the classification and history of many languages and language families in South America. And fortunately, we can have every expectation that advances will continue. See Chapter 5 for the unclassified languages of South America, and Chapter 6 for discussion of some of the proposed remote genetic relationships involving various South American linguistic groups. Linguistic areas and contacts involving South American languages are treated in Chapters 7, 8, and 9.

NOTES

1. The classification of South American Indigenous languages presented here relies heavily on Campbell (2012a), extensively corrected and updated to take more recent developments into account.

2. The presence of Garífuna in Central America is not pre-Columbian. African slaves mingled with the indigenous people of Saint Vincent and Dominica, adopting their

language, and later many were deported by British forces to Central America, the bulk arriving around 1832.

3. Lev Michael (2021, 333) gives the number of Arawakan languages as about eighty.

4. Aushiri (Awshiri) and Auishiri (Awishiri) [Waorani, Sabela] should not be confused.

5. *Arara* means 'macaw' ('parrot') in Portuguese, and a few other SA languages also have *Arara* in some version of their names.

6. As of 2018 there was only one surviving speaker of Resígaro, Pablo Andrade. In November of 2016, the only other speaker of the language, Pablo's sister Rosa Andrade, was brutally murdered, beheaded, at the age of sixty-seven (https://www.survivalinternational.org/news/11549, accessed July 23, 2021).

7. Island Carib, the source also of Garífuna, is an Arawakan language that incorporated men's register which has some vocabulary from Cariban. That explains how, in spite of the name that suggests it is a Cariban language, Island Carib (and Garífuna) are nevertheless Arawakan. (See Hoff 1994; Taylor and Hoff 1980.)

8. An earlier classification of Arawan is:

Arawan (Arauán, Arahuan)
Paumarí Brazil
Madi (Jarawara, Jamamadi, Banawá) Brazil
Zuruahá (Suruahá, Sorowahá) Brazil
Dení-Kulina
　Dení Brazil
　Culina (Kulína; Madihá, Madija, Corina) Brazil, Peru
*Arawá (Arua) Brazil

(Cf. Dixon 1999, 295)

9. Both of the Boran languages do have /y/ (IPA [j]) in a small number of words, but Seifart and Echeverri (2015) do not reconstruct this sound to the proto-language.

10. *Arara* is the name or part of the name of a few other SA Indigenous languages; as mentioned earlier, it means 'macaw' ('parrot') in Portuguese.

11. The name *Arekuna* is found in the literature sometimes as a variety of Pemón and sometimes as an alternate name for Pemón (see Derbyshire 1999, 24–25).

12. Herisobocona is Loukotka's (1968, 161) Herisebocon; he said it was once spoken on the Rapulo River, but nothing is known of it.

13. It should be noted that this Chapacuran Kumaná should not be confused with the Kumaná (Cumana) of Cariban, in spite of the names being homophonous.

14. In the past the language names were not always distinguished consistently for the languages of this family. As John Elliott (2021, 19) says, the Enlhet-Enenlhet languages in the linguistic literature suffer "from inconsistent and confusing nomenclature, and ethnolinguistic identity within the E[nlhet-]E[nenlhet] family can at times be a bit fuzzy."

15. The Enlhuet-Enelhet (Mascoyan) language that is also called Toba (or Toba-Emok, Toba-Maskoy) should not be confused with Guaicurúan Toba (Qom).

16. "Las semejanzas del payaguá y el guachí con las lenguas de la familia guaicurú (aunque algunas son sugerentes) resultan – en conjunto – escasas, por lo que son insuficientes para poder asegurar que etas lenguas pertenezcan realmente a esta familia."

17. "Sin embargo, ambos son idiomas muy poco conocidos, muchas de las características que definen a la familia guaicurú no están documentadas en ellos y resulta muy difícil encontrar

correspondencias fonológicas regulares con las lenguas guaicurúes típicas, de manera que la pertenencia de estas dos lenguas a la familia no parece comprobable."

18. "Estos mismos Guamos, aunque sean de propria Nacion, estando en diversos Pueblos, ô las Parcialidades aun en uno, varian bastantes voces, pero se entienden reciprocamente."

19. "É possível observar que o Guató demonstra mais semelhanças técnicas com o Proto-Tupí... do que com o Proto-Macro-Jê... ou com o Chiquitano... do que com o Proto-Macro-Jê... e mesmo nesse caso as semelhanças observadas não são particularmente notáveis e poderiam ser fortuitas. Concluímos que não há evidências para classificar o Guató como uma língua relacionada ao tronco Macro-Jê."

20. "Não há nenhuma semelhança particularmente forte dentro dessa lista entre o Yaathê, o Proto-Macro-Jê, o Proto-Chiquitano e o Proto-Tupí. Isso é compatível com a hipó-tese de que o Yaathê não seja demonstravelmente relacionado a essas famílias, a não ser que tal relação se dê em um nível extremamente profundo."

21. Specifically Trombetti (1907, 195) said:

> It seems to me highly probable that the Botocudo and the Jagan-Alakaluf represent a linguistic group quite distinct from the other American groups . . . Its origin is alleged to be oceanic and the closest linguistic connection seems to be found with the languages of eastern Australia, the Torres Strait, and neighboring regions.
>
> [a me sembra probabilissimo che il Botoccudo e il Jagan-Alakaluf rappresentino un gruppo linguistico ben distinto dagli altri gruppi americani . . . La sua provenienza sarebbe oceanica e la connessione lingüística più sretta sembra trovarsi con le lingue dell'Australia orientale, dello Stretto di Torres e delle regioni cinconvicine.]

22. Vilela, as of 2008, had only one or perhaps two surviving semispeakers (Golluscio and González 2008).

23. The name *Karajá* is from Tupí, meaning roughly 'large monkey'. Sources from the sixteenth and seventeenth centuries that appear to refer to this language have the spellings <Caraiaúnas> and <Carajaúna>.

24. The Latundê were unknown to the outside world until they were contacted by Aikanã speakers in the 1970s; the language is severely endangered (Lüpke et al. 2020, 23).

25. Kaufman (2007, 65) appears to list the language isolate Trumai as a member of the Otomacoan family, though this appears be a printing error. I surmise that it was intended not to be included within Otomacoan but rather as a third entity in his Macro-Otomakoan Cluster.

26. The Panoan branch is named after the Pano language. *Pano* means 'giant armadillo' (*Primodontes maximus*) (Zariquiey 2011, 2).

27. Lanes (2005) had suggested that the distance between the Mayoruna branch and the other Panoan languages is so great that it must be considered a separate language family by itself within the Panoan stock, though this view is not held by other scholars (see Oliveira 2023).

28. Terrence Kaufman's (2007, 70–71) classification of Takanan is:
Takanan
    Takana group
        Tacana Bolivia
        Reyesano Bolivia
        Araona (Carina, Cavina) Bolivia
        Cavineña Bolivia

Chama group
　　Ese'ejja ("Chama") Bolivia, Peru
　　(*?) Toromona (Toromono) Bolivia.

29. The name *colla* [kolya] in northern Argentina refers to Quechua-speakers and to the Indigenous groups from highland Bolivia or Perú.

30. Note also that it is not a large step from labial *p* or *b* to *m* in second-person forms, possibly influenced by the nasal *n* of first person in this pronominal paradigm. Second-person *m* was postulated by Greenberg (1987) as very common in "Amerind" languages, though not as common as Greenberg claimed (see Campbell 1997, 240–253). Note also that the Puquina form alternates between *pi* and *wi* (<ui>) (Adelaar 2020, 245).

31. This Mako (a Sáliban language) should not be confused with the several languages that have been called *Mako* or *Maku*, nor with the Nadahup languages that were formerly called *Makúan*.

32. It appears that Kaufman (2007, 68) intended his Kalianan stock to have two members, his Awaké-Kaliana family and Maku. However, in what appears to be a printing error, Maku is listed together with Awaké and Kaliana under the heading of the Awaké-Kaliana family.

33. Some have thought that **Saluma** was the same language as Taruma. This may be an error or possibly Saluma may be a name that was also sometimes applied to the Taruma (cf. Crevels 2012, 202). However, Saluma (Salumá) is definitely the name of a Cariban language (Gildea 2012, 444; Campbell 2012a, 81, 147), and Salumã is an alternate name of Enawene Nawe, an Arawakan language of Brazil, mentioned by Mily Crevels (2012, 182), see also Aryon Rodrigues (1986, 72).

34. The name *Urubú* is from the Portuguese word *urubú* 'vulture'. There is also a river named *Urubú*, where several languages are spoken.

35. Oddly, Gerardi and Reichert (2021, 153) say that "Omagua and Cocoma . . . are not genetically related to Tupí-Guaraní[an] despite their Tupí-Guaraní[an] lexicon."

36. Geraldi et al. (2023) find that the dispersal of the Tupí-Guaraníán languages is clearly correlated with the spread throughout eastern South America of a particular ceramics type, plant management, and cultivation of a variety of crops. While there seems to be strong support for the correlation of ceramics called "Tupiguarani" and the spread of Tupí-Guaraníán languages, it is important to understand that while non-linguistic evidence can point the way to possible hypotheses of linguistic kinship, non-linguistic information can never be used to demonstrate phylogenetic relationships among languages (see Campbell and Poser 2008, 205–206).

37. Geraldi et al. (2023) mention **Apama**, a presumed Tupían group, said in 1691 to be between the Curua and Maicuru, saying it is unknown whether they are the ancestors of the Zo'e.

38. In Kaufman (2007, 69) Urarina and Puelche appear to be listed as Cahuapanan [Kawapánan] languages, but this appears to be a printing error.

39. "Chango y Uru Costeño. No podemos clasificar la extinguida lengua de los Changos, pueblo de la costa de Chile septentrional."

40. Richard Aschmann's (1993) classification of Witotoan—without the Boran languages which he had classified with Witotoan, but that are now considered members of a separate Boran family—was the following:

Witotoan (Huitotoan, Huitoto-Ocaina)
　　Ocaina Peru (Dialects: Dukaiya, Ibo'tsa)
　　Early Huitoto
　　　　Nipode (Huitoto Muinane, Nipode) Peru
　　　　Minica-Murai

Minica (Huitoto Meneca) Colombia
Murui (Huitoto Murui, Murai, Búe) Colombia, Peru
*Nonuya Colombia, Peru

41. There is potential confusion over some of these names and how they have been presented. Kaufman (2007, 69) has both Andokero (Andoquero) and Andoke (Andoque) listed as Witotoan languages. However, this is probably due to a printing error, where Andoque (a language isolate) was intended to be a member of his Bora-Witotoan stock, but not part of the Witotoan family. Andoquero is also known as Miriña, Miraña-Carapana-tapuyo. Andoque is spoken in the area of the Anduche River in Colombia and was spoken formerly also in Peru.

Koihoma (Coixoma) has been called Coto, Koto, and Orejón as alternative names. However, there is an unrelated Tukanoan language called Orejón (more recently the name Maijuna has become preferred) that is also called Coto, Koto.

5

Unclassified and Spurious Languages

5.1. INTRODUCTION

Some languages are so poorly attested that it is impossible to classify them. They include the presumed languages referred to by the numerous language names mentioned in historical sources about which next to nothing is known, and others about which a little is known but the information is insufficient for adequate classification. In some cases, we lack information even about the location of putative languages mentioned in the records. Possibly some of these names refer to languages that are known today by other names; probably some have to do with names of towns or rivers or clans or ethnic groups applied to languages that are also known by other names, or are the names of dialects of languages that have different names of their own. A number of them appear simply to be the results of errors of various sorts. Some are just false, cases of "phantom" languages, fakes or hoaxes, and spurious "languages" of several sorts that just do not and never did exist. (See Adelaar and Muysken 2004; Campbell 1997a, 2012a; McQuown 1955.)

A sizeable number of cases of formerly unknown languages, languages poorly attested if at all and thus unclassified, have recently been identified from colonial sources (see Adelaar and Muysken 2004; Campbell 2012a; Goddard 2005, 2016; Urban 2019a; and Zamponi 2023, in press a, in press b, among others). Some scholars have at times attempted to classify some of the poorly known and even totally unattested languages based on geographical or cultural (non-linguistic) evidence. It is also generally assumed that numerous real languages disappeared without even their names being recorded. For all these reasons, the total number of Indigenous languages of the Americas will never be known with certainty.

The goal of this chapter is to survey these unclassified and spurious languages and to attempt to provide additional perspective on some of them.

An important question is, what is the difference between an unclassified language and a language isolate, and how is that difference determined? Opinions regarding certain languages with limited attestation have differed over whether the available documentation is sufficient to determine that the particular language in question is a language isolate because it cannot be shown to be related to any other language or whether the available data are too limited to make such a determination or to show relatedness with some other language or languages, leaving the language unclassified. A related question in need of more attention is, for language isolates and very poorly documented languages, how much documentation, and what sort of documentation, is necessary in order to determine whether a language is best considered unclassified or a language isolate?

Hammarström et al. (2021) in *Glottolog* have not answered the question but do employ a heuristic criterion for assigning relatedness or non-relatedness, for distinguishing between different classification proposals. They say:

> There is no universal fixed threshold for how much is sufficient ... An approximate minimal requirement is 50 items or so of basic vocabulary, i.e., not personal names or special domain vocabulary. For example, the extinct language Gamela of northeastern Brazil is known from 19 words only ... hardly enough for a classification. (https://glottolog.org/glottolog/glottologinformation, accessed December 19, January 2023)

This is a useful strategy, but in some cases fifty words may be too few to arrive at satisfying decisions, whereas in other cases, depending on the meanings of the particular words and on the phonological properties of the language compared, fewer than fifty words could be sufficient to make a plausible case for relatedness. Sometimes even a very few words are enough at least to infer possible or even likely linguistic relatives of the language in question, though insufficient for solid confirmation. In the cases of most of the languages considered in this chapter, the amount of extant documentation comes to fewer than fifty words, often far fewer, if any at all.

5.2. UNCLASSIFIED LANGUAGES OF NORTH AMERICA

The unclassified languages of North America are presented here in alphabetical order, with some discussion of what is known or hypothesized about them.

Akokisa was a group who lived inland from Galveston Bay in Texas. John R. Swanton (1946, 85–86) believed that one of the early Atakapa vocabularies represented the Akokisa, but Jack Martin (2004, 79) pointed out that that vocabulary bears no name identifying the language or the group who spoke it, and there is no reason to assume it was Akokisa. Essentially nothing is known of the true language of the Akokisa, just *Yesga* 'Spaniards' and *Quiselpoo*, a woman's name (Swanton 1911, 35–36, cited by Goddard 2005, 38). (See Zamponi 2023:1633; see Chapter 2.)

Amotomanco (Otomoaco) is of uncertain affiliation, perhaps Uto-Aztecan. Hernán Gallegos, chronicler to the 1581 expedition of Francisco "el Chamuscado" Sánchez[1] to New Mexico, reported "Amotomancos" as the name of a people and their language at the confluence of the Rio Grande and the Conchos River on today's Texas-Chihuahua border. This name apparently matches "Otomoacos" given for a people of the area by Diego Pérez de Luxán, chronicler to the 1582 Espejo expedition to New Mexico. William

Griffen (1979, 30, 96) thought that the Amotomanco or Otomoaco were the same people as the group in El Mesquite, Chihuahua, often called just "Mesquites" in the seventeenth and eighteenth centuries.

Very little is known of the Amotomanco (Otomoaco) language, only four words and an untranslated two-word phrase sung with a dance. The four nouns have repeatedly been discussed (see Kroeber 1934, 15; Miller 1983b, 332; and Troike 1988, 238–239). The word *abad* 'water' has been thought possibly to be Uto-Aztecan, compared with Proto-Uto-Aztecan **pa* 'water' (see Mayo *báa'a* and Tarahumara *ba'wi* 'water'). Rudolf Toike (1988, 238) saw the *a-* as a demonstrative prefix and related the final *-d* to the Uto-Aztecan absolutive suffix (from Proto-Uto-Aztecan **-tɨ*). For *teoy* 'corn' Nahua influence has been imagined, perhaps from Nahuatl *tlaol-li, tlayol-li* 'corn' ('maize'), from Proto-Nahua **tlayōl-*; *teoy* is perhaps borrowed from one of the Nahua varieties that has *t* instead of *tl*. The word *ayaguate* 'beans' is very probably borrowed from Spanish that got it from Nahuatl. Varieties of Mexican Spanish have *ayacote, ayocote* 'bean (larger than the common bean)' (Santamaría 1978, 102). This is borrowed into Spanish from Nahuatl *ayeco'tli, ayaco'tli* 'large bean (like fava bean)'. Spanish very often borrowed Nahuatl words that end in *tli* or *tl* with *te* in Spanish. The *te* in *ayeguate* suggests that this is a Spanish loan into Amotomanco, originally taken into Spanish from Nahuatl. With *porba* 'copper', recorded as *payla* in a different source, scholars have found no comparable word in other languages. *Porba*, with *r* and *b* and the cluster *rb*, seems very unlike any of the Indigenous languages of this region, leading to the question, could there have been a scribal error when it was recorded? As for *payla*, it looks suspiciously like Spanish *paila* 'shallow pan'; could this word somehow have associations with this metal and thus be borrowed from Spanish *paila* with the different meaning of 'copper'? This seems a possibility.

As Raoul Zamponi (in press a) concludes, "with one native word that might be Uto-Aztecan but also not, one word that might be an Aztecoid loan but also a native word that has nothing to do with Uto-Aztecan, one patently Aztecoid loan, and one word which looks like nothing else, the only prudent conclusion we may deduce is to leave Amotomanco unclassified."

Aranama (Aranama-Tamique, Jaranames) was spoken in the early 1700s at the Franciscan mission of Espíritu Santo de Zúñiga on the lower Guadalupe River in southeastern Texas. Only two words of Aranama are known,[2] given to Albert Gatschet in 1884 by Old Simon, a Tonkawa speaker who also provided some of Gatschet's Karankawa material. He called the language *Hanama* or *Haname*; other Tonkawas called it *Chaimame* (where <ch> was said to represent Spanish <j> (phonetically [x]). Other known variants of this name or names are *Charinames, Xaranames*, and *Taranames* (Goddard 1979a, 372–373).

The **Tamique** reportedly spoke the same language as the Aranama. The Espiritu Santo de Zúñiga mission was founded for these two groups in 1754, on the lower Guadalupe River in Texas. The language is unclassified. Aranama-Tamique has sometimes been listed as a language isolate; however, obviously it cannot be adequately classified based on its only two attested words and thus it is an unclassified (unclassifiable) language (Goddard 1979a, 372–373).

Bayagoula (Bayogoula). The Bayagoula lived in Mississippi and Louisiana. Due to wars and disease they were in effect destroyed by the early 1700s, and their language remained unattested. It is typically assumed that they must have spoken a Muskogean language; some believe it was perhaps a dialect of Choctaw. By the late 1700s, the surviving Bayagoula had been absorbed by the Houma (Swanton 1911, 278–279). Bayagoula was often written as "Bayoguola," assumed somehow to be associated with *bayou* (Zamponi 2023, 1633).

Bidai (Beadeye, Bedias, Bidey, Viday). The Bidai territory extended from the Brazos River to the Neches River in southeastern Texas. The Bidai suffered an epidemic during 1776–1777, reducing their numbers drastically. The language is known from only nine putative Bidai words. Rufus Grimes, of Navasota, Grimes County, Texas, sent the supposed Bidai words written in English orthography to Albert Gatschet in a letter on November 15, 1887, published in Gatschet (1891a, 39). Andrée Sjoberg (1951, 393) added to them that the Bidai called themselves *Quasmigdo*. The nine words included the Bidai autonym, terms for 'boy', 'corn', and the first six numerals. Anthony P. Grant (1995) pointed out that words similar to *púskus* 'boy' and *tándshai* 'corn' occur in Choctaw *poškoš* ~ *poskos* 'child' and *táci* 'corn', and in Mobilian Jargon *posko(š)* ~ *poškoš* 'baby, child' and *táče* 'corn'—the two words probably represent Mobilian Jargon rather than direct loans from some Muskogean language. Mobilian Jargon is a Muskogean-based pidgin, which was known and used well inside Texas in the mid-nineteenth century (Drechsel 1997, 236; see Chapter 8). As Raoul Zamponi (2023, 1634) observes, "if the words recalled by Rufus Grimes are reflections of Bidai speech, as the numerals may well be, they are surely a testimony of a further language in the Southeast without close genealogical relatives."

Calusa (Calloosa, Caloosa, Caloose, Calos, Carlos) was spoken on the southwest coast of Florida from Tampa Bay to Maro Island. Calusa also has often been considered a language isolate. However, it is known only from some place names and from about a dozen words reported in 1575 by Hernando de Escalante Fontaneda, a Spanish shipwreck survivor who lived from the age of thirteen to thirty as a captive among the Calusa. Escalante Fontaneda (1955[c. 1575]) and other early accounts reported that Calusa was distinct from all other languages of southwestern Florida. The extant record of Calusa is clearly too scant to permit classification (Goddard 2005, 1, 11; see also Zamponi 2023, 1635–1636).

Congaree. John Lawson, an English explorer, visited the Congaree in 1701; they lived in a village in South Carolina on a small creek that flowed into the Santee River. They joined the Catawba but in 1743 reportedly still spoke their own "dialect" (Mooney 1894, 80). Lawson reported that the language was different from the language of their neighbors (Lawson 1709, 27–28, 40–41); he recorded the single word known of Congaree, *Cassetta* 'king' ('chief') (Zamponi 2023, 1636).

Cusabo (Cosabo, Cusabes, Cusabees, Cusaboe, Coosaboys, Corsaboy) is considered an unknown language of the coast of South Carolina. It had been thought to be a Muskogean language, but that is now disputed (Sturtevant 2005, 8). Cusabo is in fact a name applied to several different tribes from 1562 to 1751 in coastal South Carolina from the Santee River to the Savannah River. From accounts at the time, it appears these groups spoke a language or languages distinct from the other languages of the area.

A Cusabo place name from a letter written in 1671 has appeared to be interpretable semantically, and it has resulted in speculation about the possible linguistic identity of the language. The letter reported that the Savannah River was called *Westoe bou* "signifying the enemies' River" (Cheves 1897, 382). *Westoes* was mentioned among the Sewee (see below), who were not speakers of Cusabo; it refers to a native group who were raiding on South Carolina coast when it was settled by the English in 1670 (Waddell 2004, 254). From this, it was therefore assumed that *bou* must be Cusabo for 'river'. Many place names in coastal South Carolina contain *bou* or *boo*. As Zamponi (2023, 1638) says, "with a single word of which we believe to know the meaning no plausible hypothesis about the linguistic affiliation of its language can, of course, be formulated."

Giamina (Oomil) Alfred L. Kroeber (1907, 153) and Sydney Lamb (1964a, 110) thought Giamina of southern California might be a separate branch of Uto-Aztecan, but this is uncertain (Miller 1983, 122). It may belong to Takic (Golla 2011, 179), but the extant data are too scant to determine this. It is known from only nineteen words in a problematic orthography (Hill 2011).

Guale. Guale was possibly first recorded by René de Laudonnière in 1562, who reported that he had "learned to understand the Indians of the South Carolina coast by writing down their words and phrases" (Sturtevant 2005, 8). He was referring to Guale or perhaps **Cusabo**; however, only two putative words of Guale have survived. One is *micoo* 'chief' from 1564 and *Chiluques* 'Indians of Santa Elena' (i.e., 'Cusabo') from 1671. However, *mico* for 'chief' was used in several languages, including in the Catawban area. *Chiluques* is argued also to be probably borrowed among various languages as a word for speakers of a foreign language; it has been compared to Creek *čiló:kki* 'Red Moiety' and *čilo:kk-itá* 'to speak a different language'. The name *Cherokee* also fits this and may be related to it; it is *tsalagi* in modern Cherokee, with no known source in the language itself; Cherokee was *tchalaquei* in a 1775 Spanish spelling. Thus, these two words may be of Muskogean origin and probably are not native words in Guale. (See Zamponi 2023, 1638–1639 for details.)

Aaron Broadwell (1991) argued that Guale and also **Yamasee**, both once spoken in South Carolina and Georgia, are Muskogean languages, belonging to the Northern branch of the family. However, William Sturtevant (1994) showed that the forms Broadwell cited are in fact from Creek and not from Guale or Yamasee. Since Guale and also Yamasee, though mentioned in early historical records, remain essentially completely unattested, they are unclassified.

Jumano (Humano, Jumano, Jumana, Xumana, Chouman [from a French source], Zumana, Zuma, Suma, Yuma). **Suma** may well be the same language as Jumano. Jumanos lived in west Texas, New Mexico, and northern Mexico, in particular near the confluence of the Conchos River with the Rio Grande. It is unclear whether the name applied to a single group or to various different ethnic groups or bands. It is thought that they ceased to exist by about 1750. Though they are most often thought to have spoken a Uto-Aztecan language, other options that have also been suggested include Tanoan and Athabaskan, or that they were a multiethnic group. Rudolf Troike (1988, 237) said of the language, "we have not a single word of Suma or Jumano to judge the linguistic affiliation of these groups, despite two centuries of contact with the Spanish."

Lumbee was retired from ISO 639-3 codes in 2020 as an unattested, non-existent language (https://iso639-3.sil.org/code/lmz). What has been called the Lumbee language is not an American Indian tongue, but rather a local vernacular form of English. It was determined that no separate Indigenous Lumbee language has ever existed as far as can be determined.

Most members of the Lumbee Tribe live in Robeson, Hoke, Cumberland, and Scotland counties, North Carolina. It is a state-recognized tribe but is not recognized federally. The name Lumbee comes from the Lumber River. They have been known officially as the

"Croatan Indians" (in the 1880s) and in 1911 officially as the "Indians of Robeson County." There have been numerous ideas about their origin, some of them quite fanciful. John R. Swanton's account seems likely, that the Lumbee Indians were descendants of some Siouan tribes, Cheraw and Keyauwee in particular, but also with remnants from several other tribes of the region. However, this is considered speculative by some (see Blu 2001, 41). In any case, their language, if they ever had a specific Indigenous language, is utterly unknown.

Nicoleño (San Nicolas) was spoken on San Nicolas Island in California. The total corpus attested for Nicoleño is four words and two songs attributed to Juana María, reportedly its last speaker, who died in 1853. It has generally been assumed that Nicoleño was a Uto-Aztecan language. Some believe it should be grouped with the languages of the Takic subgroup, and Pamela Munro (2000[2002]) argued that it belongs to the Cupan division within the Takic subgroup.

Nansemond. The Nansemond were one of the tribes of the Powhatan confederacy formerly in Nansemond and Norfolk counties on the coast of Virginia. By the early 1900s the Nansemond had lost their native language and differed little from their White neighbors (Mooney 1907, 146). In 1901, James Mooney could find only one old Nansemond man, William W. Weaver, who remembered six words of the language. Significant similarities are not found between these six words and other languages, with the possible exception of a similarity of the word for 'one', *nikkut*, with words of the same meaning in some Algonquian languages. The lack of similarity for the other words could perhaps be because they might have been corrupted in Weaver's memory or in how Mooney wrote them down. In any case they provide no basis for classifying Nansemond with other known languages (Zamponi 2023, 1629).

Playano. As mentioned in Chapter 2, the unknown language of **los playanos** who lived to the west of the Salinas region in California has been suspected of being perhaps a third dialect of Salinas, an additional Salinas language, Esselen, Chumash, or some unknown "relict" language distinct from all these others (Golla 2011, 115–116).

Pamunkey. The Pamunkey were part of the Powhatan confederacy, located on the Virginia coast in King William County around the junction of the Pamunkey and Mattapony Rivers. In 1844 it was said that the Pamunkey no longer used their native language. In that year, clergyman E. A. Dalrymple collected a list of the numerals 'one' to 'eight' and eight other words "found still surviving . . . at the Indian Pamunkey town" (quoted in Zamponi 2023, 1631). Except for *nikkut* 'one'—Nansemond, *nikkut*, Powhatan *nekut*—these words are not similar to any Algonquian language or to other languages. Ives Goddard (1978d, 74) thought that the Pamunkey vocabulary might represent the language of "one of the poorly known inland Virginia groups that have generally been lumped together as Siouan, though often on slender or no evidence." The sparce data do not allow Pamunkey to be classified (Zamponi 2023, 1630–1632).

Sewee. Before 1609 the Sewee lived on or near the Santee River, in South Carolina; in 1670 English colonists visited them on or near Bull's Bay (Waddell 1980, 361). John Lawson (1709, 10–11) reported that the Sewee had been a large tribe, but had been devastated by smallpox and alcohol dependence (Zamponi 2023, 1639). A bare handful of maybe eight words of Sewee were found in two separate accounts from 1670 (Waddel 1980, 31). These words are difficult to interpret, with considerable overlap in some of the forms. One, *comorado* 'comrade', is believed to be borrowed from Spanish *camarada* 'comrade'.

Based on historical accounts, these few words, and some South Carolina toponyms, Gene Waddell (1980, 33) thought that at least two languages were spoken in the low country of South Carolina: one probably Siouan, north of the Ashley River, and another probably spoken by the tribes south of the Ashley River. From this geography, Sewee should belong to Siouan-Catawban, although no Siouan-Catawban morphemes are found in the scraps of the language that were recorded. This may be because Sewee is not related to those languages or just due to the paucity of information available to work with (Zamponi 2023, 1639).

Shoccoree (Shoccoree-Eno). The **Shoccoree** and **Eno** are first mentioned in Virginia in 1654. When Johann Lederer, German explorer, visited them in 1670s, the Shoccoree were on the Eno River, in North Carolina, and the Eno were nearby to the northeast, apparently on the Flat River. John Lederer (1958, 28) reported that the "Shackory" agree with the "Oenocks" in customs and manners, which has been thought to include language as well (Goddard 2005, 26; Zamponi 2023, 1640). In 1701, John Lawson (1709, 56) found the Shoccoree and Eno confederated along with the unknown **Adshusheer**. Their village, that he called Adshusheer, was on the Eno River. The only word recorded of the language is the name of the sport they called *chenco*, to which Lawson (1709, 57) said the Shoccoree and Eno "are much addicted" (Zamponi 2023, 1640). *Chenco* may be a loanword; chunkey was the most popular game among American Indian tribes of the Southeast, with similar names in languages of various language families.

Solano was spoken in the early 1700s, at the Franciscan mission of San Francisco Solano, at Eagle Pass on the Rio Grande in southern Texas. It is attested in only a twenty-one-word vocabulary found at the end of the book of baptisms from that mission, dated 1703–1708; it is presumed to be of the language of the Indians there at that mission. There was no indication with the wordlist of what the language was called; the mission served at least four groups called **Xarame**, **Payuguan**, **Papanac**, and **Siaguan**. Ives Goddard (1979a, 372) reported that Herbert Bolton (1908) thought the list represented the language of the "Terocodame band cluster," associated with the nineteenth-century missions opposite of today's Eagle Pass, Texas. (See also Zamponi 2023, 1643.)

Tanpachoa is unclassified. The expedition to New Mexico led by Francisco "el Chamuscado" Sánchez in 1581 encountered upriver on the Rio Grande a group said to be culturally similar to the Amotomanco (see above) but who spoke a different language. Their name is not given in the account of the expedition, but it is assumed that they must have been the Tanpachoas who were mentioned in the account of another Spanish expedition to New Mexico of about that time led by Juan de Oñate (Troike 1988, 240), thought probably to be the "Manso" ('meek') Indians encountered in the area of El Paso in 1598. They disappeared during the first half of the 1800s. Only one word was preserved, in the account of the 1581–1582 expedition made by Father Agustín Rodríguez and Captain Francisco "el Chamuscado" Sánchez" which says "these people call the arrow 'ocae,' the name given to the bamboo by the Mexicans [Nahuatl speakers]" (Hammond and Rey 1927, 260, cited in Zamponi 2023, 1643–1644). This interpretation of *ocae* 'arrow', however, is quite strained. In Nahuatl 'arrow' is *mī-tl* (related to the verb *mīna* 'to pierce, to prick'). Perhaps the source had Nahuatl *āca-tl* 'reed' in mind, but that is neither phonetically nor semantically very close to *ocae* 'arrow'.

Nahuatl 'bamboo' is *otla-tl*, also not phonetically similar. Rudolf Troike (1996, 240) thought that it might involve a reflex of Proto-Uto-Aztecan **hu* 'arrow, wood' compounded with an unidentified *ka*. However, this too is strained (Zamponi 2023, 1644). It is clearly an unclassified, perhaps unidentified, language.

Tataviam. William Bright interpreted the scant information available on the linguistic history of the upper Santa Clara Valley in Southern California as indicating that two languages were spoken there, and that Tataviam was "a language showing some Takic affinities" (Bright 1975, 230). This interpretation seems reasonable, given that the few words J. P. Harrington identified in his notes as "Tatavyam" look more like Takic and less like Chumash. Beeler and Klar (1977, 301–303) argued that there was no Takic Tataviam, but rather that Tataviam is a misidentified variety of Chumash from the interior, which others called "Castec, Castac" (closely connected with Ventureño). King and Blackburn (1978, 535, citing Bright 1975) believe that Tataviam is "'the remnant, influenced by Takic, of a language family otherwise unknown in Southern California,' or, more likely, that it is Takic (but not, apparently, Serran or Cupan)." The **Alliklik**" that Kroeber (1925, 614) had identified as a Uto-Aztecan language in this same region turns out, on closer inspection, to be Chumash, a form of Ventureño (Beeler and Klar 1977, 296, 299). The Tataviam identification would benefit from further research.

Tawasa was spoken in east-central Alabama. It is attested in a list of only sixty words from 1707. Its classification is unclear and has been disputed. Some have put it in a putative Timucuan language family composed of Timucua and Tawasa. However, as Marianne Mithun (2018, 197) explains, a number of the Tawasa words are so similar to Timucua that they appear possibly to represent the same language. If Tawasa was Timucua or a dialect of Timucua, then Tawasa would not be a separate language and Timucua would be a language isolate. If Tawasa turned out to be a separate, unrelated language, Timucua would still remain an isolate with Tawasa most probably considered unclassified. If Tawasa and Timucua were separate but related languages, then Timucuan would be a small language family. However, given the very limited data representing Tawasa, it is best to consider Tawasa as unclassified and Timucua a language isolate (see Chapter 2) (Mithun (2018, 197).

Tequesta (Tekesta, Tegesta, Chequesta) was spoken to the east of Calusa in southwest Florida, on Biscayne Bay in Miami-Dade County and in Broward County. Possibly one word was recorded of the language in 1743, though it may be a Calusa word (Sturtevant 2005, 8). It has been speculated that Tequesta may be related to Calusa, but without more information on the language this idea must remain just speculation.

Yamasee speakers lived in southeast Georgia, South Carolina, and later in Florida. Aaron Broadwell (1991) argued that **Yamasee, Guale**, and Muskogean are genetically related, though this proved not to be well founded (see Sturtevant 1994). It was sometimes claimed that the Yamasee spoke Hitchiti (a Muskogean language), though the historical sources consistently distinguished between the two (Goddard 2005, 33). The language left no linguistic documentation.

Numerous proposals have been made that attempt to classify various of these unclassified languages of North America. Many of them are summarized and evaluated in Campbell (1997a, 66–80), Goddard (1996a, 308–323), Mithun (1999, 301–310, and Zamponi 2023). None of these proposals, however, has much support among the majority of linguists.

5.3. UNCLASSIFIED LANGUAGES OF MIDDLE AMERICA (MEXICO AND CENTRAL AMERICA)

There are more than a hundred unclassified "languages" in Mexico and Central America whose names are mentioned in historical sources but about which scarcely anything is known. Many are from northern Mexico. There is a long list of names identified in colonial sources that are generally thought probably to represent extinct Uto-Aztecan languages. No information has survived on most of them, and only a very small handful of words is attested for others. It is not certain whether they represent independent languages or just alternative names of languages already known by another name, or are errors of some sort. All of these unclassified languages merit more investigation (see Campbell 1979; 1997a, 133–135; 2012a; Harvey 1972; Longacre 1967; McQuown 1955; Sauer 1934; Swadesh 1968; Zamponi in press a).

The following names have been identified from colonial and other sources. The list is far from exhaustive (see for example Thomas and Swanton 1911, 24–25 for several others). The tentative affinities and alternate names listed here are those given in the sources cited.

Acaxee (Aiage) speakers lived in the Sierra Madre Occidental in eastern Sinaloa and northwest Durango, Mexico. Their language is thought to be closely related to **Tahue**, in the Cahitan group of Southern Uto-Aztecan, linked with **Tebaca** and **Sabaibo**. José Luis Moctezuma Zamarrón (2001, 380) believes it may be a Cahitic variety.

Alagüilac, in Guatemala, is totally unattested linguistically. Historical sources identify San Cristóbal Acasaguastlán with Alagüilac and nearby San Agustín Acasaguastlán with Nahuatl. The Nahuatl of San Agustín Acasaguastlán resulted from the Spanish settling their Nahuatl-speaking auxiliaries from Mexico who had helped them in their invasion of Guatemala. These sources clearly distinguish Alagüilac from both Nahuatl and Ch'orti' (Mayan), also spoken in the region. Daniel Brinton (1887) mistakenly identified Alagüilac as Pipil (Nahua branch of Uto-Aztecan). His evidence was an 1878 wordlist collected in San Agustín Acasaguastlán, the Nahuatl-speaking town, and four manuscript pages dating from 1610 to 1637 written in Nahuatl that he found in the archives of the San Cristóbal Acasaguastlán Parish. He concluded from these that "Alaguilac was a quite pure form of the Nahuatl" (p. 376), closely related to the Pipil of Escuintla, Guatemala (p. 377). However, Nahuatl was a language of colonial administration, and texts written in Nahuatl were encountered in church records in a number of towns in Guatemala where only Mayan languages had ever been spoken. This explains why manuscript pages written in Nahuatl could be found in San Cristóbal Acasaguastlán, which otherwise was identified with Alagüilac, and the resettled Nahuatl speakers explain the presence of Nahuatl in San Agustín Acasaguastlán (Campbell 1972a, 1978b).

It is possible that Alagüilac had Xinkan connections; Xinka was reported in nearby towns and the several place names of Xinkan origin in the region support this possibility (see Chapter 3). However, with absolutely nothing recorded of the Alagüilac language, we will never know for sure whether it was Xinkan or something else altogether. (See Campbell 1972a, 1978b, 1985.)

Baciroa is thought to be closely connected to **Tepahue** in the Taracahitic subgroup. Its speakers were in the middle Mayo drainage, in northwest Mexico. This is in Mayo territory today; Baciroa may just be the name for a local Mayo group (Miller 1983, 329). Moctezuma Zamarrón (2001, 380) believes Baciroa may be a Cahitic variety.

Basopa was mentioned as a language spoken on the Sinaloa River. Thomas and Swanton (1911, 17) says of it:

> The evidence in regard to Basopa, which Orozco y Berra [1864] places in his list of languages is very meager, the only notice, so far as known, being the statement of Zapata ([p.] 408) ... that "the language [of San Ignacio de Chicuris] is in part Tepehuana and in part Basopa, which is that which is commonly spoken." [Juan Ortiz de] Zapata says, further, ([p.] 407) that in Concepción de Chicorato the natives are divided into two parties which speak distinct languages "the Chicurata, and the Basopa." This appears to be the only authority on which Orozco y Berra bases the introduction of these two names into his list of languages. Both are extinct.

Batuc is probably Eudeve, an Ópatan language (Southern Uto-Aztecan). Batuc is a town name. The existence of the Jesuit grammar of Eudeve of Batuc seems strong reason to assume that Batuc is in fact **Eudeve** (see Pennington 1981).

Cahuimeto (Cahuameto), perhaps belongs with **Oguera** (Ohuera) and **Nio**. Manuel Orozco y Berra (1864) apparently took this from Juan Ortiz de Zapata's (1857[1678]) mention that in the vicinity of Ohuera two distinct languages were spoken, Cahuimeto and Ohuera (Thomas and Swanton 1911, 16). Thomas (1902, 212) considered Cahuimeto and "**Macoyahuy**" (Macayahui) dialects of **Tepahue**.

Cazcan (Caxcan), in Mexico's Jalisco and Zacatecas states, is sometimes equated with **Zacateca**. Some scholars have associated it with Nahua; others have thought it was probably connected with **Huichol** or perhaps **Southern Tepehuan**. Wick Miller (1983, 331) refrained from classifying it. Extremely few words of the language are attested, from two sources from the late 1500s, among them *aguano* 'war chief', *yecotl³* 'burner(?)' ('quemedor'),[4] and *cazcan* 'there isn't any' ('*no hay*'). (See https://en.wikipedia.org/wiki/Cazcanlanguage, accessed August 15, 2021.)[5] Cyrus Thomas (1902, 215), who also considered Cazcan unclassified, believed **Tecuexe** and "Teule" (**Teul**) were dialects of Cazcan.

Chínipa was in the headwaters of the Río Mayo and Río Chínipas. It is either closely related to **Ocoroni** or a local name for a variety of **Guarijío**. Chínipa was said to be mutually intelligible with Ocoroni. Miller (1983, 330) listed Chínipa, **Guasapar**, "and probably also **Témori**" together, calling them "Tarahumaran, probably Guarijío." Today the Western dialect of **Tarahumara** is spoken in Chínipas; it is unclear whether or how this might be connected with this reported "Chínipa" language.

Chinarra, see Concho.

Chizo, see Concho.

Coca. Manuel Orozco y Berra (1864) placed Coca on his map to the east and southeast of **Cora**. Thomas and Swanton (1911, 23) says of it, "Coca is extinct if, in fact, it ever existed as a distinct idiom. It could not have been very different from **Tecuexe** if we judge from the slight notices left on record in regard to it; in fact Orozco y Berra includes the two in one area on his map." I wonder, could this "Coca" be a typo or misreading where "Cora" may have been intended?

Colotlan is said to be Piman, closely related to **Tepehuan** or **Teul** and **Tepecano**, or it is just Tepecano itself, though Orozco y Berra (1864, 282) classified it as a dialect of **Cora**. Thomas and Swanton (1911, 23) said, "Colotlan, it seems may also be dismissed, as Orozco y Berra ... identifies it with Tepecano ... It would appear safe from this evidence, which has been gathered from the early statements of the missionaries, to assume that Colotlan and Tepecano were one and the same idiom."[6]

Comanito is said to be closely connected to **Tahue**, belonging to the Taracahitic group. Wick Miller (1983, 330) said of Comanito and **Mocorito**:

Cahitan, perhaps simply a dialect of Tahue or **Mayo**. These two groups lived in the hill and mountain country in and around the headwaters of the Rio Sinaloa. In 1594, the missionary Martín Pérez noted that their speech was close to the Tahue (Sauer 1934, 26). Sauer noted that "Tebaca-Bacapa-Pacaxe and **Comanito** are confusedly mingled in the records" (1934, 37). This may be a clue that there was no real language boundary between **Tebaca** (an **Acaxee** subgroup) and Comanito, and that they were simply intergraded dialects.

(see also Moctezuma Zamarrón 2001, 380)

Concho. **Chinarra**, and **Chizo** were subdivisions of Concho; **Toboso** is also related. Concho speakers lived in the plains of eastern Chihuahua, east of the **Ópata** and **Tarahumara**. Wick Miller (1983, 331) thought Concho was perhaps Uto-Aztecan, "branch unknown." (See also Troike 1988.) Kroeber (1934, 14) thought three Concho words found in the record of the Rodríguez-Chamuscado 1581 expedition (from Hammond and Rey 1928, 275) were Uto-Aztecan, placing Concho in his Cáhita-Opata-Tarahumara subgroup. The words were *bate* 'water', *yolly* 'people', and *sanate* 'corn'. Miller (1983) and others accept *bate* 'water' as possibly Uto-Aztecan (see Proto-Uto-Aztecan *pa: 'water'), but Miller challenges the other two. *Yolly* 'people' appears to be a loanword; terms similar to *yoli* or *yori* 'White man' are found widely in languages of the region. Kroeber (1934, 14) said Concho *sanate* 'maize' corresponded with Ópata *sunut*, though Miller was skeptical because the vowels do not match and agricultural terms are often diffused. I agree with Miller (1983, 332), "[as for] a Uto-Aztecan connection for Concho, I do not think the evidence allows us to say more than maybe."

Conicari. Conicari speakers lived in and near the middle Mayo drainage in northwest Mexico. Conicari may be a name for a local Mayo group (Miller 1983, 319); Moctezuma Zamarrón (2001, 380) believes it may be a Cahitic variety. It may be connected to **Tepahue**.

Guachichil, of the central Mexican states of Nuevo León, San Luis Potosí, and Zacatecas, is assumed to be aligned with **Huichol**, possibly a variety of Huichol (Miller 1983, 331).

Guasave. Guasave speakers lived along the coast in Sinaloa, northwest Mexico. Early accounts report that the **Guasave**, **Comopori**, **Vacoregue** (Vacoregua),[7] **Ahome**, and **Achire** all spoke the same language; they possibly represent dialects of Guasave. It is perhaps a Cahitan language, though it may also not be Uto-Aztecan; it could be linked with the language isolate Seri instead, given its speakers' maritime economy (Miller 1983, 331; Moctezuma Zamarrón 2001, 378).

Guazapar (Guasapar, Guazapare) is possibly either a dialect of **Tarahumara** or is grouped with **Guarijío** and **Chínipa**; perhaps **Guazapar, Pachera,** and **Juhine** are all Tarahumara dialects. It was located on the headwaters of the Río Mayo and Río Chínipas. Wick Miller (1983, 330) listed Chínipa, Guasapar, "and probably also **Témori**" together, calling them "Tarahumaran, probably Guarijío."

Guisca (**Coisa**), a Nahua variety?

Hio (Hios) was possibly a Taracahitic language, possibly an error for *Nio*? Thomas and Swanton (1911, 24) mention Hios but say nothing of them. The mentions of *Ihio* people in Sinaloa in colonial sources may be related.

Huite is unclassified (Miller 1983, 330). Its speakers were in the mountains northwest of the **Zoe** and west of the **Tubar**. Nothing is known of the language other than that it was said to be different from other languages of the region.

Irritila, of Durango state in Mexico, was possibly a **Lagunero** band.[8] Irritla may have been another name for Lagunero.

Jova (Jobal, Ova). Some scholars have classified Jova, in western Chihuahua, as a **Tarahumara** dialect; most link it with **Ópata**; Wick Miller (1983, 329) thought it is "probably Taracahitan." Its speakers lived in rough canyon country surrounded by Ópata. The linguistic data, assembled from colonial sources by Francisco Pimentel (1874, 369–371), is a list of nine words and a translation of the Lord's Prayer. Miller (1983, 329) was of the opinion that this evidence seemed closer to Taracahitan than any other of the Uto-Aztecan languages of that region but that the evidence was too meager to determine to which subgroup it belonged. David Shaul (2014, 28) sees Jova as a distinct subgroup of Uto-Aztecan that has only this single language in it.

Lagunero was said to be like **Nahua** and may be affiliated with **Zacateco** or with **Huichol**. Campbell Pennington (1969, 11–12) had Lagunero as a group located between the **Zacateco** and **Toboso** (see below); he suggested that Lagunero may be affiliated linguistically with Zacateco, and Wick Miller (1983, 332) added that "if Zacateco is aligned with Huichol, then Lagunero is also." **Irritila** may be the same language, another name for Lagunero.

Macoyahui is presumed to be a Cahitan language. Its speakers were located in or near the middle Mayo drainage in northwest Mexico (Miller 1983, 329; see also Moctezuma Zamarrón 2001, 380). Thomas (1902, 212) considered **Cahuimeto** and "**Macoyahuy**" (**Macoyahui**) dialects of **Tepahue**.

Maratino (language of the Maratines) was once spoken in the Sierra de Martines in Tamaulipas, Mexico. Only some fifty-five words and three suffixes are known, where some of these words were extracted from longer phrases (published by Swanton 1940, 122–124), and a supposed war-song with Spanish translation, from Vicente Santa María, Franciscan missionary in the eighteenth century (see Zamponi in press a for a tentative analysis). Morris Swadesh (1963a, 1968) thought Maratino could be classified with Uto-Aztecan; however, the evidence for this hypothesis is not sufficiently reliable to justify it. The word *baah (ka)* 'let us drink!' is suggestively similar to Proto-Uto-Aztecan **pa* 'water' (see Mayo *báa'a* and Tarahumara *ba'wi* 'water'). The Maratino data contain some loanwords from Nahuatl: <peyot> 'peyote' < Nahuatl *peyo-tl* 'peyote'; <tciwat> [tšiwat], <chiguat> 'woman' < Nahuatl *siwa:-tl* 'woman'. The data raise questions about some of the forms and their analysis. For example, why are the words glossed as 'forest', 'mountain', 'to', 'war', and 'woods' all *tamu*? The words for 'forest', 'mountain', and 'woods' could all be responses to Spanish *monte*, and the glosses 'to' and 'war' appear to be extracted from phrases that also have the 'forest/mountain/woods' word in them, suggesting a thorough re-examination of the data is in order. Maratino is unclassified.

Meztitlaneca was spoken in the Sierra de Meztitlán, state of Mexico (Thomas 1902, 211). Thomas and Swanton (1911, 50) thought that Meztitlaneca belonged to the "Nahuatlan family" (Nahua) and "appears to be a dialect of Aztec" (Nahuatl). They say that "the subtribe speaking this dialect inhabited the region north of Tezcuco [Tezcoco], between the Sierra Madre and the Huastecan territory."[9]

Mocorito, see Comanito (above).

Naarinuquia (Themurete?), along the coast of Nayarit state in Mexico, may not be Uto-Aztecan at all, as has been thought, but related to the language isolate Seri, given its speakers' maritime economy (Miller 1983, 331; Moctezuma Zamarrón 2001, 378).

Nacosura has been identified as an Ópata dialect (Uto-Aztecan).

Naolan was spoken in the small village of San Juan de Naola, near Tula in southern Tamaulipas, Mexico. It was very nearly dormant when Roberto Weitlaner (1948) collected forty-three words and phrases, the only known data from the language. Thirty of these words came from Román Rocha. Weitlaner compared his Naolan data with Otopamean, "Hokan," and Uto-Aztecan languages, with the conclusion that he was inclined to consider Naolan as belonging to Uto-Aztecan, nearest to the Cahitan group (Weitlaner (1948, 218). Weitlaner mentioned equating Naolan with **Mazcorros** or maybe with **Pizones** as less likely. William Bright (1955) thought Naolan belonged to "Hokan-Coahuiltecan," possibly identified with **Janambre** (Xanambre) or **Tamaulipec**; Morris Swadesh (1968) also grouped it with "Hokan-Coahuiletecan," closer to **Tonkawa**.

The evidence is so scant that none of these proposals offers much hope of success. Of Weitlaner's forty-three words and phrases, six are loans from Spanish, five are certain loans from other Indigenous languages, and another four are probably also loans (Campbell 1979a, 948–949). This leaves too little native material for reliable linguistic classification. (See Zamponi in press a.)

Nio was spoken along the Sinaloa River, between **Guasave** and **Ocoroni**. Nothing is known about Nio. Perhaps it is affiliated with Ocoroni. Wick Miller (1983, 330) considered Nio as "unclassified," saying "for the Nio, we do not have enough evidence to say it was Uto-Aztecan, though culturally they [its speakers] were like their Cahitan neighbors."

Ocoroni was spoken along the Ocoroni River in northwest Mexico. Ocoroni was reportedly perhaps mutually intelligible with **Nio**; it was said to be similar to **Ópata**. **Huite** and Nio are also perhaps closely connected to Ocoroni, perhaps in the Taracahitic group.

Oguera (Ohuera) is listed on Orozco y Berra's (1864) map. Presumably the name is derived from the town of Ohuera in Sinaloa, Mexico. Orozco y Berra apparently took this from Juan Ortiz de Zapata's (1857[1678]) mention that in the vicinity of Ohuera two distinct languages were spoken, **Cahuimeto** and Ohuera (Thomas and Swanton 1911, 16).[10]

Quinigua (Guinigua, Quinicuane) was spoken by a group called the Borrados[11] in Nuevo León, in the area of Monterrey, Cadereyta, and Cerralvo (Hoyo 1960, 496), spoken between the Sierra Madre Oriental and the Sierra Tamaulipa la Nueva, and between the Rio Grande and the Río del Pilón Grande. What is known of the language was found in several colonial documents in the Municipal Archive of Monterrey by Eugenio del Hoyo (1960). It consists of some ninety words, perhaps only about half of them clear. They are sufficient, however, to show that the language has no obvious kinship with any nearby languages though not enough to assure that it is indeed a language isolate; it is better considered unclassified (Zamponi in press a).

Patarabuey. The linguistic affiliation of the Patarabuey is unknown; their ethnic identity is also uncertain. The Patarabuey speakers lived in the Conchos River Valley in the area of the Junta de los Ríos, junction of the Conchos River with the Rio Grande in Mexico. *Patarabuey* is a Spanish nickname, from *patar-a-buey* 'kick the ox'. Apparently the Patarabuey people were also called Otomoacos (see Amotomanco above), Abriaches, and other names. Early sources say both that the **Jumano** were called Patarabuey (Fowler 2008, 160, 165) and that the Patarabuey were clearly distinct from the Jumano (Troike 1988, 237). Nancy Kenmotsu (2021) says "it is not clear which was the real name for them [the Patarabuey]. In fact, it may well be that there was never a single, all encompassing name for the settled and sometimes-settled peoples who lived at La Junta." (See also Troike 1988, 237.)

Sabaibo. Colonial accounts report that although they were a separate "nation," the Sabaibo spoke the same language as the **Acaxee** (see above) (Thomas and Swanton 1911, 120).

Sayultec, possibly a variety of **Nahua** (Harvey 1972, 301).[12]

Suma, very possibly just another name for **Jumano** (see above).

Tahue may include **Comanito**, **Mocorito**, **Tubar**, and **Zoe**. Tahue speakers lived in central Sinaloa, below **Cahita**. One sixteenth-century source says that speakers of Tahue and Cahita were able to understand each other (Miller 1983, 331). Wick Miller (1983, 331) believed the language belongs to the Cahitan subgroup of Uto-Aztecan (as does Moctezuma Zamarrón 2001, 380).

Tebaca. Carl Sauer (1934, 37) thought that "**Tebaca-Bacapa-Pacaxe** and **Comanito** are confusedly mingled in the records." Wick Miller 1983, 330) adds that "this may be a clue that there was no real language boundary between **Tebaca** (an **Acaxee** subgroup) and **Comanito**, and that they were simply intergraded dialects."

Tecuexe (Tehuexe), in eastern Guadalajara and Jalisco states in Mexico, may have been a **Zacateco** group in dispersal. Thomas and Swanton (1911, 23) believed that Tecuexe and **Coca** "could not have been very different from" each other, placed in the same area on Orozco y Berra's (1864) map.

Teco-Tecoxquin, from Compostela, Nayarit in Mexico, has been suggested to be closely related with **Nahua** (Harvey 1972, 300).

Tecual, on the Tepic plateau of Nayarit, is assumed to be closely related to **Huichol** and connected with **Guachichil** (Miller 1983, 331). Carl Sauer (1934, 14) wrote of **Thequalme** (presumably this is the same as Tecual), that "**Xamaca**, by another name called Hueitzolme [Huichol], all ... speak the Thequalme language, though they differ in vowels."[13]

Témori, of Sinaloa, were mentioned in colonial sources in connection with **Chínipa**, "Guazapare," and "Varohío" (**Guarijío**). They are assumed to be Tarahumaran. (See Miller 1983, 330; Sauer 1934, 32–36.)

Tepahue was in Sonora, Mexico. **Macoyahui**, **Conicari**, and **Baciroa** are said to be close to Tepahue; it is presumably a member of the Taracahitic group (see for example Thomas 1902, 212). Moctezuma Zamarrón (2001, 380) believes it may be a Cahitic variety.

Tepanec. Tepanec is repeatedly mentioned in older sources as an extinct language probably related to **Nahuatl**. The Tepanecs (Tepanecos) were in the Valley of Mexico on the western shore of Lake Texcoco, described as a sister culture of the Aztecs. In the fourteenth century they were very powerful, controlling most of the Valley of Mexico and parts of the valleys of Toluca and Morelos. Then the Aztecs of the Triple Alliance became dominant and the Tepanecos had mostly lost their ethnic identity by the time of the Spanish arrival. It is assumed they spoke Nahuatl or some variety of Nahua. (See Santamarina Novillo 2006.)

Teul (Teul-Chichimeca, Teule, Teúl). Manuel Orozco y Berra (1864, 1.279) said that the "'Teules Chichimecas' used the same idiom as the **Tepecano**" (Thomas and Swanton 1911, 24).

Toboso. Cyrus Thomas (1902, 207) considered Toboso as "Athapascan," in Chihuahua, Sonora, and Durango. The Toboso lived near the **Concho** and are sometimes considered to be connected with them. Wick Miller (1983, 332) noted that Pennington (1969, 12) mentions them in passing as between **Zacatec** and **Concho** groups, but Miller offers no classification of Toboso.

Topia. Earlier sources spoke of Topia as a separate language or dialect, connected with **Acaxee**, but Orozco y Berra (1864) gave Topia as a synonym of Acaxee (Thomas and Swanton 1911, 20). Topia was apparently a toponym for a district in the Acaxee territory.

Topiame. Topiame is listed as another language and is also the name of the "Topiame province," in Acaxee territory. However, *Topiame* looks to be *Topia* (above) with the Nahuatl suffix -*me?/-meh*, plural for people. Given the location of Topia and Topiame, it is probable that they are alternate forms of a name for the same group. The language may not be different from Acaxee.

Totorame. Wick Miller (1983, 331) considered Totorame **Cora**. He said that "this group was known earlier as PINOME. They inhabited the coastal plain between the Tahue and Cora-Huichol. In 1587, Father Ponce noted that they spoke the same language as the Cora."

Xixime (Jijime). **Hine** and **Hume** are subdivisions of Xixime. The speakers of Xixime lived in the Sierra Madre Occidental mountains in the Mexican states of Durango and Sinaloa. Wick Miller (1983, 330–331) considered Xixime unclassified. He said of it, "but for Xixime, we have no clues for its linguistic affiliation. Early observers noted that it was a distinct language. Being surrounded by Uto-Aztecan languages, it would be surprising if it were not Uto-Aztecan, but that hardly proves it to be so." It was repeatedly reported that they practiced ritual cannibalism, though the extent of this may have been exaggerated.

Zacateco (Zacatec) is often equated with **Cazcan**, perhaps in a **Huichol** group (Harvey 1972, 300). Wick Miller (1983, 331–332) classified Zacatec as Cora-Huichol, perhaps specifically Huichol. However, he had doubts concerning the words usually thought to be from this language, saying, "in fact, the words are so much like Huichol, I wonder if the language is not really Huichol rather than Zacatec" (p. 332).

Zoe. Wick Miller (1983, 330) considered Zoe unclassified. He said of the speakers:

> These people occupied a small area in the hill country near the present town of Choix, Sinaloa. Today, this is Mayo country. Carl Sauer says they were probably affiliated with Comanito, but gives no evidence. The missionary Pérez de Ribas noted that they were bilingual in Yecorato (Comanito, hence Cahita) and another language (Zoe) which was totally distinct.

Baimena was a subdivision of **Zoe**. (See also Thomas 1902, 212.)

See Beals 1932; Dávila Garibi 1935, 1942; Escalante Hernández 1963; Harvey 1972; Jiménez Moreno 1943; Kroeber 1934; Mason 1936, 1950; McQuown 1955; Mendizábal and Jiménez Moreno 1944; Miller 1983; Sauer 1934; and Zamponi in press a for more information and greater details on many of these languages.

5.4. UNCLASSIFIED LANGUAGES OF SOUTH AMERICA

The names of many very poorly known "languages" that are repeated in the literature on South American languages follow with some discussion when information is available (see Adelaar and Muysken 2004, 119, 623; Campbell 1997a, 2012a; Fabre 1998, 359; Loukotka 1968, 63, 86–87, 92–93, 165–168, 196–198, 228–230, 259, 272–273; Mason 1950; McQuown 1955; Migliazza and Campbell 1988, 311–316; Zamponi in press b). Many other names could be added to this list.

Aarufi Colombia. "Unknown language from the Quebrada de Oksikgnaná, territory of Caquetá" (Loukotka 1968, 196).

Aburuñe Bolivia. "Once spoken on the Xarayes Lagoon" (Loukotka 1968, 165).

Acarapi Brazil. "Extinct language once spoken on the Parrimé River, territory of Rio Branco" (Loukotka 1968, 196).

Aconipa (Tabancal, Tabacanake, Tabancara) Ecuador. Only five words are known of this language, which reveal no affinity to other languages (Adelaar and Muysken 2004, 406; Torero 2002, 287). J. Alden Mason (1950, 193) said Aconipa was "extinct, the data on it are very few, and insufficient to warrant its classification, at any rate as a distinct family." Čestmír Loukotka (1968, 261) listed it as an extinct isolated language, "once spoken in the village of Aconipa in the department of Cajamarca."

Aguano (Awano, Ahuano, Uguano, Aguanu, Santa Crucino) Peru. Aguano is dormant and unclassified. It was spoken on the lower Huallaga and upper Samiria Rivers. J. Alden Mason (1950, 271) gave a classification for his Aguano group:

Aguano
    Aguano Proper
        Seculusepa
            Chilicawa
    Melikine
        Tivilo
    Cutinana
    Maparina

Loukotka (1968, 146) classified Aguano as a member of the **Chamicuro** Group of his "Awarak Stock," saying nothing was known of the language. Migliazza and Campbell (1988, 311–316) considered it unclassified for lack of data (cf. also Tovar 1961, 67). Different opinions would classify it with Panoan (Pano-Takanan), Cahuapanan, or as independent (unclassified).

Alarua Brazil. "Once spoken between the Japurá and Auati-paraná Rivers, Amazanas state" (Loukotka 1968, 196).

Alon Peru. "Once spoken on the Huambo River, department of San Martín" (Loukotka 1968, 178).

Amasifuin Peru. "Once spoken in the same country [Peru], on the right bank of the Huallaga River" (Loukotka 1968, 178).

Amikoana (Amikuân, Amicuan) Brazil. Amikoana was formerly listed by *Ethnologue* as an unclassified language with "a few speakers," but has been retired from ISO 639-3 as "nonexistent" since 2008 (https://iso639-3.sil.org/code/akn). Loukotka (1968, 201) classified Amicuan as belonging to his Karaib stock (Cariban). He called it an "extinct language once spoken at the source of the Marouini River, French Guiana," of which nothing was known.

Amoeca Brazil. "Language of an unknown tribe living on the Morarô River, state of Amazonas" (Loukotka 1968, 196).

Amuimo Brazil. "Language of an unknown tribe that lived on the Nhamundá River, state of Amazonas" (Loukotka 1968, 228).

Anetine Bolivia. "Once spoken near Mojos" (Loukotka 1968, 165).

Angara Peru. "Once spoken in the ancient Inca province of the same name, department of Ayacucho" (Loukotka 1968, 272).

Anicun Brazil. "Once spoken at the source of the Uruhu and Dos Bois Rivers" (Loukotka 1968, 93).

Anserma (Anserna) Colombia. Adelaar and Muysken (2004, 623) say that Anserma "cannot be classified for absence of data"; they say it includes **Caramanta** and **Cartama**. Loutoktka (1968, 239) placed Anserma (Humbra, Umbra) in his Chibchan Stock, saying "once spoken on the Cauca River around the city of Anserma . . . only a few words." *Ethnologue* (2023) classifies it in the Coconuco subgroup of their in their Paezan family (https://www.ethnologue.com/subgroup/3625, accessed January 11, 2023). (See Chapter 4 for complications with the classification of Coconuno.)

Aparea Argentina. "Unknown language of the ancient mission of Santiago Sánchez in the province of Corrientes" (Loukotka 1968, 63).

Apitupá Brazil. "Unknown language once spoken on the Aquitipi River, Bahia state" (Loukotka 1968, 93).

Apiyipán Bolivia. "Language of an unknown tribe of the Aripuaña River, Amazonas" (Loukotka 1968, 165).

Aracadaini Brazil. "Once spoken on the Corodoá and Aroá Rivers, tributaries of the Cunhuá River, state of Amazonas" (Loukotka 1968, 196).

Arae Brazil. "Unknown language once spoken on the left bank of the Araguaia River south of Bananal Island" (Loukotka 1968, 86).

Aramayu Brazil. "Extinct language once spoken on the Oiapoque River, Amapá territory" (Loukotka 1968, 228).

Aramurú Brazil. "Once spoken in the state of Sergipe on the São Francisco River" (Loukotka 1968, 93).

Arapoá Brazil. "Once spoken around Jaboatão in the state of Pernambuco" (Loukotka 1968, 93).

Ararau Brazil. "Unknown language spoken at the sources of the Nhamundá and Jatapú Rivers, state of Amazonas" (Loukotka 1968, 228).

Arda Peru. Loukotka (1968, 196) said Arda was an "extinct language of a small tribe that once lived between the Nanay River and the upper course of the Mazán River, Loreto, Peru." (See Mason 1950, 234–235 and below for explanation of the confusion with Arda of Africa.)

Arma Colombia. "Once spoken on the Pueblanco River. [Nothing (known of it).]" (Loukotka 1968, 239). Adelaar and Muysken (2004, 623) list Arma-Pozo among the languages that they say "cannot be classified for absence of data." Arma and Pozo are listed by several early classifiers as linked with Chocoan languages in the Cauca basin of Colombia.

Aroásene Brazil. 'Unknown language spoken at the sources of the Nhamundá and Jatapú Rivers, state of Amazonas" (Loukotka 1968, 228).

Artane Bolivia. "Unknown language of Xarayes Lagoon" (Loukotka 1968, 165).

Atavila Peru. "Once spoken in the ancient province of Canta, department of Lima" (Loukotka 1968, 272).

Aticum (Araticum) Brazil. "Extinct language of a tribe that speaks only Portuguese now, in Pernambuco near Carnaubeira" (Loukotka 1968, 93).

Atunceta (Tunceta, Atunseta) Colombia. Loukotka (1968, 257) said of "Tunceta or Atunseta" that it was "once spoken on the right bank of the Dagila River, Valle de Cauca department. [Nothing (known of it).]" Adelaar and Muysken (2004, 623) list Atunceta (Cauca, Valle de Cauca) among the languages that they say "cannot be classified for absence of data" (see also p. 49).

Aueiko Brazil. "Once spoken on the Paranaiuba River, Mato Grosso" (Loukotka 1968, 165).

Avis Brazil. "Unknown language of the state of Pernambuco, once spoken in the valley of the Pajeú River" (Loukotka 1968, 93).

Axata Darpa Paraguay. "Unknown language of an unknown tribe of the Gran Chaco of Paraguay" (Loukotka 1968, 63).

Ayacore Peru. "Once spoken on the Curaray River, Loreto" (Loukotka 1968, 178).

Baenan Brazil. Known from only ten words; Baenan has sometimes been listed as a language isolate but without sufficient evidence to make such a determination (Zamponi in press b). Loukotka (1968, 74) said Baenan was "originally spoken between the Cachoeira and Pardo Rivers, state of Bahia," with only a "few individuals on the Posto Paraguaçú" in 1963.

Bagua Peru. Only three words are known of Bagua; "the evidence is not sufficient to allow any reliable classification" (Adelaar and Muysken 2004, 405). Loukotka (1968, 221) had Bagua only as one of the villages where "Patagon" was spoken, which he put in the "Patagon Group in his "Karaib Stock," noting that "only five words" were known. Alfredo Torero (2002, 278) located Bagua in the Bagua, Chamaya, Lower Tabaconas, and Lower Chinchipe Valleys, and on the banks of the Marañón River. As Torero explained, Paul Rivet linked Patagón with the language of Bagua "in an entirely unfounded way,"[14] referring to one as Patagón de Perico and the other as Patagón de Bagua. As Torero pointed out, Loukotka apparently followed Rivet (p. 279). Torero separated the two languages, noting that actually only four words are known of either of them, but that they coincide in only one similar word, Bagua *tuna* and Patagón *tuná* 'water', which matches words for 'water' in Cariban languages. Torero concludes that Bagua remains unclassifiable because of insufficient linguistic data (p. 279).

Baixóta Brazil. "Extinct language of a tribe that now speaks Portuguese in the Serra Catolé, Pernambuco" (Loukotka 1968, 93).

Bakurönchichi Brazil. "Language of an unknown tribe of the Branco River, Rondônia" (Loukotka 1968, 166).

Barbacoas (Barbácoa, Colima) Colombia. This "language" has generally been thought to be a Barbacoan language. Iso code 639-3, however, retired "Barbacoas" in 2020, finding it "unattested" (https://iso639-3.sil.org/code/bpb). Loukotka (1968, 247) gave "Barbácoa or Colima" as an "extinct language once spoken on the Iscuandé and Patia Rivers, Nariño department, Colombia. [Nothing (is known of it)]," a member of his Barbácoa Group. He, however, also listed **Colima** as a separate "extinct language once spoken on the middle course of the Daule River, Guayas province" (of which he also said "nothing" was known).

Bauá Brazil. "Once spoken on the Motum and Corneg Rivers, Amazonas" (Loukotka 1968, 196).

Bikutiakap Brazil "Unknown language . . . spoken on the right bank of the Pimenta Buena River" in Rondônia state (Loukotka 1968, 166).

Bixarenren Brazil. "Language of an unknown tribe on the Tiucunti River, a tributary of the Jamachiua River, Rondônia" (Loukotka 1968, 166).

Boimé (Poyme) Brazil. "Once spoken in the state of Sergipe near Aracajú on the São Francisco River" (Loukotka 1968, 93).

Bolona Ecuador. Adelaar and Muysken (2004, 397) were of the opinion that "the affiliations of the Bolona language cannot be known for lack of data." Loukotka (1968, 158) had classified it as a member of his Jíbaro Stock (Chicham, Jivaroan), "once spoken in the province of Zamora," though he said "nothing" was known of it. Alfredo Torero (1993, 454) had suggested Bolona was connected with **Cañar**.

Bracamoro (Papamuru) Peru. "Extinct language once spoken near the city of Jaén, department of Cajamarca" (Loukotka 1968, 178).

Buritiguara Brazil. "Unknown language once spoken in the state of Mato Grosso near the confluence of the Araguaia and Manso Rivers" (Loukotka 1968, 86).

Caapina Brazil. "Extinct language once spoken between the Maicuru and Jarí Rivers, state of Pará" (Loukotka 1968, 228).

Cabixi (Kabixi) Brazil. There has been confusion concerning Cabixi. Ricardo Franco de Almeida Serra had written in 1797 that the Cabixi were a nation of the savannas living at the sources of the Guaporé, Sararé, Galéra, Piolho, and Branco (Cabixi) Rivers (cited by Zamponi in press b). Later "Cabixi" came to be used generally to mean wild and aggressive Indians in that region (Zamponi in press b). Loukotka (1968, 166) listed Cabixi as a "language of an unknown tribe from the Steinen River, Mato Grosso." Johann Natterer had obtained about sixty words and a few short sentences from the "Cabixis Indians" in the early half of the 1800s; however, Natterer's Amazonian linguistic materials remained mostly unknown until recently (see Adelaar and Brijnen 2014); his unpublished collection was maintained in the library of the University of Basel, Switzerland. Comparison of Natterer's Cabixi data with other languages does not permit that language to be assigned to any other language family or to be joined with any of the language isolates of Mato Grosso and the region (Zamponi in press b).

Cachipuna Peru. "Once spoken in the Puna de Quillpaco, department of Lima" (Loukotka 1968, 272).

Cafuana Brazil. "Once spoken on the Japurá River south of the Waríwa tribe" (Loukotka 1968, 196).

Cagua Colombia. The ISO 639-3 code for Cagua was retired in 2016, considered nonexistent (https://iso639-3.sil.org/code/cbh).

Caguan (Kaguan) Argentina. "[Kaguan] once spoken at the mission of Santiago Sánchez, Corrientes" (Loukotka 1968, 63).

Cahan Brazil. "Once spoken on the Iguatimí and Espocil Rivers, state of Mato Grosso" (Loukotka 1968, 86).

Caimbé Brazil. "Once spoken in the village of Masacara near Mirandela, state of Bahia" (Loukotka 1968, 93).

Cajamarca Peru. "Once spoken around the city of Cajamarca" (Loukotka 1968, 272). This may have never exited. "Cajamarca" is a name that refers to several different towns and regions.

Cajatambo Peru. "Once spoken around the city of the same name, department of Lima" (Loukotka 1968, 272).

Camana (Maje) Peru. "Once spoken on the Majes River, Arequipa department" (Loukotka 1968, 272).

Camaraxo Brazil. "Once spoken between Ilhéus and Serra dos Aimorés, state of Bahia" (Loukotka 1968, 93).

Camaré Brazil. "Extinct language once spoken on the Camoó River, a tributary of the Trombetas River, Azazonas" (Loukotka 1968, 228).

Cambioá Brazil. "Once spoken in the Serra Negra, Pernambuco state" (Loukotka 1968, 93). Cambioá is probably the same as Kambiwa, as is probably also Quiambioá (see below).

Campaces Ecuador. Barbacoan connections have been suggested, but unconfirmed (Adelaar and Muysken 2004, 392). Loukotka (1968, 248) listed "Campaz" as one of several alternative names for **Colorado** (Tsafiki).

Canelo Ecuador. Adelaar and Muysken (2004, 623) say that Canelo "cannot be classified for absence of data" (cf. Mason 1950, 251–252). Loukotka (1968, 158) placed Canelo (Penday), a language "once spoken on the Canelos River," in his Jíbaro stock. Martin Kohlberger (2020, 14) lists Canelo among the ethnonyms mentioned in the literature that are no longer in use today, identifying it as **Shiwiar** (Chicham [Jivaroan] family).

Cañacure Bolivia. "Once spoken on the Mamoré River" (Loukotka 1968, 166).

Capua Brazil. "Spoken on the Rolim de Moura River, Rondônia" (Loukotka 1968, 166).

Capueni Brazil. "Once spoken on the Japurá River south of the Waríwa tribe" (Loukotka 1968, 196).

Cara (Caranqui, Scyri, Imbaya, Otavalo) Ecuador. Loukotka (1968, 249) said Cara was an "extinct language once spoken in the province of Imbabura and on the Guallabamba River." He, and various others, classified it as Barbacoan (in Loukotka's Barbákoa Group, in his Chibcha Stock). However, Cara (Caranqui) was replaced by **Quechua** and ceased to be spoken before the late 1700s. Due to its lack of documentation "its affiliation will probably never be certainly known" (Mason 1950, 184; see also Adelaar and Muysken 2004, 172).

Caraguata Brazil. "Once spoken between the Amazon River and Lake Anama" (Loukotka 1968, 196).

Carapacho Peru. J. Alden Mason (1950, 272) listed Carapacho as an unclassified language of eastern Brazil. Loukotka (1968, 168) placed Carapacho (Caliseca) in his "Pano Stock" (Panoan), "once spoken on the Carapacho River" in Peru, though he said "nothing" is known of it. Zariquiey Biondi (2011, 43), citing Frank (1994, 131), mentions that missionaries used the name "Carapacho" first around 1733–1734 but by 1765 started calling the ethnic group "Cashibo" and after a period of overlap, "Cashibo" came to dominate and "Carapacho" disappeared from historical accounts. **Cashibo** (Kashibo) is a Pano-Takanan language (see Chapter 4). It appears, then, that Carapacho should be retired from the list of unknown, unclassified languages.

Carára Brazil. "Once spoken at the sources of the Jatapú River, Amazonas" (Loukotka 1968, 228).

Cararí (Carari) Brazil. "Once spoken at the mouth of the Mucoín [Mucuím] River" in Amazonas state (Loukotka 1968, 196; Zamponi in press b). The only attestation of Cararí is a seventy-three-word list collected by Johann Natterer in the first half of the nineteenth century (Zamponi in press b). Raoul Zamponi (in press b) compared Cararí words with those of several languages in the region and somewhat further afield and found that Cararí cannot be linked with any of them. (This Cararí is not to be confused with the names *Kariri* and *Kiriri*, which have been applied to a number of languages and peoples in eastern Brazil.)

Cararú (Cajurú) Brazil. "Once spoken on the Soroabé Island in the São Francisco River, Pernjambuco state" (Loukotka 1968, 93).

Caripó (Curupehe) Brazil. "Once spoken on the São Francisco River near Boa Vista, Pernambuco" (Loukotka 1968, 93).

Cascoasoa Peru (Mason 1950, 272). Loukotka (1968, 154) had "Chasutino or Cascoasoa," "once spoken in the village of Chasuta on the Huallaga River," saying "nothing" is known of it.

Casigara Brazil. "Once spoken at the mouth of the Juruá River" (Loukotka 1968, 196).

Casota Argentina. "Unknown language of the ancient mission of Santa Lucia, Corrientes" (Loukotka 1968, 63).[15]

Catuquinarú (Catinquinarú, Catuquina) Brazil. Catuquinarú speakers lived in the Brazilian state of Acre between the Envira (Embyrá) and Enviraçu (Embyrasú) Rivers, tributaries of the Tarauacá River (Zamponi in press b). The language is known only from a short "vocabulary" of twenty-seven words and two short sentences collected by Argentinian explorer José Bach, who visited the Catuquinarú during his travels of 1896–1897. He gave the information to George Earl Church, who published it in an article in 1898 (Church 1898). As Zamponi (in press b) reports:

> It is unclear whether the Catiquinarú actively spoke their language at the end of the nineteenth century, and no information is given about the informant(s) who supplied Bach the 27 items and two sentences of the wordlist . . . the language of the wordlist does not show any significant similarity to any other known language except Língua Geral Amazônica which appears to be the source of at least 14 of its 27 items. We cannot therefore establish with certainty whether the terms of Língua Geral Amazônica origin . . . are loanwords adopted by the Catuquinarú or, simply, Língua Geral Amazônica words that someone with a limited knowledge of Catuquinarú may have considered to be part of this language.

(For information on Língua Geral Amazônica, see Chapter 8.)

The Catuquinarú employed a "subterranean 'telegraphy,'" described by Bach and published by Church (1898), which involved filling "a cavity in the earth with broken bones, ashes and other solid substances, and by striking this with a club [they] could convey the sound for about a mile to the next *maloca* [longhouse]" (Zamponi in press b).

It should be noted that the name Katukina is seen in the names of several languages of the Amazonia region: Katukina (Panoan), Katukinan (the language family), and a Katukina language retired from Glottolog version 4.8.

Cauacaua (Kawakawa) Brazil. "Once spoken on the Japurá River" (Loukotka 1968, 196).

Cauauri Brazil. "Once spoken south of the Curanave tribe, Amazonas" (Loukotka 1968, 228).

Cauca Colombia. Cauca was presumed to be from the Cauca Valley. *Ethnologue* and *Glottolog* now consider Cauca to be a non-existent language (unless it is the same as **Quimbaya**), retired from ISO code 639-3 since 2020 (https://iso639-3.sil.org/code/cca).

Caucahue (Kakauhua, Kaukaue Caucabue, Caucau, Gaviota) Chile. ISO code 639-3 retired Kakauhua (Caucahue) in 2014, saying it is only an ethnonym, not an attested language (https://iso639-3.sil.org/code/kbf).

Suggested classifications of this "language" would join it with Chonan or with Kawesqaran. Pedro Viegas Barros (2005, 81) suggests that it might be best to consider that the Caucahues were probably actually Chonos, since they were reported to occupy the same territory and to have the same cultural traits as Chonos. Indeed, Loutkotka (1968, 44) equated the two, listing "**Chono** or Caucau" as an "extinct language formerly spoken in the Chonos archipelago and Taitao peninsula, territory of Aisén, Chile," a member of his Aksanás stock.

Cauni Brazil. "Once spoken between the Juruá and Juraí Rivers, Amazonas" (Loukotka 1968, 196).

Caupuna Brazil. "Extinct language once spoken at the mouth of the Purus River" (Loukotka 1968, 196).

Cavana (Maje) Peru. "Once spoken on the middle course of the Majes River, Arequipa department" (Loukotka 1968, 272).

Caxago Brazil. "Once spoken in the state of Sergipe on the São Francisco River" (Loukotka 1968, 93).

Cayú Brazil. "Spoken on the ... Pimenta Bueno River, Rondônia" (Loukotka 1968, 166).

Ceococe Brazil. "Once spoken in São Pedro and Serra Pão de Açúcar, Pernambuco" (Loukotka 1968, 93).

Chachapoya (Chacha, Chachapuya) Peru. This language is dormant and extremely poorly known (Adelaar and Muysken 2004, 407), formerly spoken around Chachapoya city in Amazonas department. Luis Miguel Rojas-Berscia (2019, 2020) argues, on the basis of the extremely limited data available, mostly from onomastics, that it should be grouped with Cahuapanan or that this was "a far understudied area of intense language contact" (Rojas-Berscia 2019, 197). Possible connections that have been suggested for this language include **Hibito-Cholón**, **Copallén**, and even the postulated *-cat(e)* languages (Torero 1989, 236–237; Adelaar and Muysken 2004, 407; see Loukotka 1968, 272).

Chancay Peru. "Once spoken on the Chancay River, department of Lima" (Loukotka 1968, 272).

Chancos Colombia. Located at Chocó in the Cauca Valley, cannot be classified for lack of data (Adelaar and Muysken 2004, 623).

Chango Chile. Loutkotka (1968, 270) placed Chango in his Uro stock, reporting that it was "once spoken on the coast of Chile from Huasco to Cobija, Antofagasta department." Adelaar and Muysken (2004, 176) site its location as in the Tarapacá and Antofagasta regions of northern Chile. They say, "nothing is known about the original language of the Chango, who reportedly became extinct as the result of a tidal wave" (p. 176).

Chechehet ("Pampa") Argentina. (See below.)

Chedua Peru. "Once spoken in the department of San Martín on the Huambo River" (Loukotka 1968, 179). (See also Mason 1950, 272.)

Chicha Bolivia. "Extinct language once spoken in the Cordillera de Chorolque, Potosí province" (Loukotka 1968, 272).

Chincha Peru. "Once spoken on the Chincha River in the department of Ica" (Loukotka 1968, 272).

Chinchipe Peru. "Once spoken in the department of Cajamarca on the Chinchipe River" (Loukotka 1968, 179).

Chipiajes Colombia. *Ethnologue* formerly had Chipiajes as an unclassified extinct language. *Ethnologue* said that Chipiajes is a Sáliba surname and that many Guahibo have that last name. It was retired from ISO 639-3 code in 2016 (https://iso639-3.sil.org/code/cbe).

Chitarero Colombia. Loukotka (1968, 240) had Chitarero as a member of his "Chibcha Group," an "extinct language once spoken around the modern city of Pamplona, department of Santander. [Nothing (known of it).]." Adelaar and Muysken (2004, 623) list it with the languages that they say "cannot be classified for absence of data."

Cholto Peru. Mason (1950, 272) listed Cholto among the unclassified languages of eastern Peru.

Chongo Peru. "Once spoken near the city of Jauja, Junín department" (Loukotka 1968, 272). This may refer to the Chongos Bajo subdialect of Huanca Quechua, spoken in the same general area (see Adelaar and Muysken 2004, 202, 217).

Chono (of Ecuador) Ecuador. Adelaar and Muysken (2004, 623) list this among the languages that "cannot be classified for absence of data." (Not to be confused with the Chono of Chile.) Loukotka (1968, 248) listed it in the Barbákoa Group in his Chibcha stock as an alternate name along with **Colorado**, **Tsáchela**, **Campaz**, **Satxila**, and **Colime**. (See **Tsafiki** [Barbacoan], Chapter 4.)

Chumbivilca Peru. Chumbivilca was probably a variety of **Puquina** (Willem Adelaar, personal communication). Loukotka (1968, 269) considered it a member of his Aymara stock, "once spoken around the city of the same name, department of Cuzco."[16]

Chunanawa Peru. Mason (1950, 272) listed Chunanawa of eastern Peru among the unclassified languages of eastern Peru. Perhaps Chunanawa might be suspected of being Pano-Takanan. Many Panoan ethnonyms end in *-nawa* and names that appear to have this ending have often been assumed to be Panoan based on geography and that ending alone; however, as David Fleck (2013, 15) points out, such names "could just as well be Panoan exonyms for non-Panoans."

Churima Bolivia. "Extinct language once spoken at the ancient mission of San José de Mahanero, Beni province" (Loukotka 1968, 166).

Chusco Peru (Mason 1950, 272; McQuown 1955, 522).

Ciaman Colombia. Loukotka (1968, 257) put Ciaman in his Chocó stock, calling it an "extinct language once spoken on the Cauca River around Ciaman," nothing known of it. Adelaar and Muysken (2004, 623) list it as a language of the Cauca Valley that "cannot be classified for absence of data."

Cognomona Peru. "Once spoken . . . on the upper course of the Huallaga River" (Loukotka 1968, 179; see also Mason 1950, 272).

Colima Colombia, Ecuador(?). There are complications with the name "Colima," and it is not always easy to determine which language is being talked about. Loukotka (1968,

219) listed a Colima in the Pijao Group of his Karaib Stock, an "extinct language once spoken on the right bank of the Magdalena River and on the Negro and Pacho Rivers, Cundimarca department [Colombia]." However, Marshall Durbin (1985[1977], 341) mentioned that Colima and a few other languages "have been proposed as related to Carib[an], but they definitely are not." He mentions that Colima and some other languages exhibit "incontrovertible Carib[an] influence" but are of "unknown affiliation" (p. 349). Adelaar and Muysken (2004, 114) also noted that often a Cariban affiliation is assumed for Colima but they listed it among the languages that "cannot be classified for absence of data" (p. 623). Durbin and Seijas (1973, 51) give ten Colima words found in the available sources.

However, there seems to be confusion about which "Colima" is involved, as Adelaar and Muysken (2004, 623) locate Colima in Ecuador, "Guayas(?)" province. Loukotka (1968, 248–829) also listed a Colima language in his Barbácoa Group as an "extinct language once spoken on the middle course of the Daule River, Guayas province [Ecuador]" of which he also said "nothing" was known. He listed a third Colima "language," as "Barbácoa or Colima," an "extinct language once spoken on the Iscuandé and Patia Rivers, Nariño department, Colombia. [Nothing (known of it)]," also a member of his Barbácoa Group (p. 247). It seems Adelaar and Muysken (2004, 623) may have confused Loukotka's Ecuadoran Colima for Loukotka's Colombian one assumed to be of a Cariban Pijao Group.

Comanahua (Komanawa) Peru. "Once spoken in the department of Huánuco by the neighbors of the Tepqui tribe" (Loukotka 1968, 179). David Fleck (2013, 15) lists Komanawa of the province of Panataguas, Peru, on his table of "Tentative Classification of Possibly Panoan Languages/Dialects Lacking Linguistic Data" (p. 111), with variants of the name as Camunagua, Comanagua, Comanahua, and Comunagua (p. 81).[17]

Comaní Brazil. "Once spoken in the area north of Lake Saracó, state of Para" (Loukotka 1968, 228).

Comechingón Argentina. The language of the Comechingones, once spoken in the mountains of western Córdova, Argentina, is "virtually undocumented" (Adelaar and Muysken (2004, 502). Antonio Tovar (1961, 29) said of it, "this language has not left remains that could give hope of a solution to the problem of classifying it." Nevertheless, Loukotka (1968, 278) put Comechingón, with its presumed dialects **Henia** and **Camiare**, in his Huarpe stock. Adelaar and Muysken (2004, 615) see Comechingón as possibly a cluster of languages, together with *Camiare* and *Henia*; they mention also that a Huarpean affiliation has been suggested.

Copallén (Copallín) Peru. Loukotka (1968, 261 listed Copallén as an extinct isolated language, "once spoken in the villages of Llanque, Las Lomas [del Viento], and Copallén, department of Cajamarca." Alfredo Torero (2002, 287) located "Copallín" in the mountains to the south of the Marañón, in the Peruvian department of Amazonas. He said that "of this language four words remain for us, that do not permit us to establish a secure relationship with any known language or language family" (p. 287).[18] Adelaar and Muysken (2004, 406) concur, saying that apart from some similarities involving the word for 'water', "nothing can be said about the genetic affinities of this language."

Coritanahó Brazil. "Extinct language once spoken on the Ajubacábo River . . . state of Pará" (Loukotka 1968, 228).

Coxima (Koxima) Colombia. Formerly *Ethnologue* had included Coxima as an unclassified extinct language, but it was retired in 2016 from the ISO 639-3 codes for being a "nonexistent" language (https://iso639-3.sil.org/code/kox).

Culaycha Argentina. "Unknown language of the ancient mission of Santa Lucia, Corrientes" (Loukotka 1968, 63).

Cumayari Brazil. "Spoken by an unknown tribe" of the mouth of the Purus River region (Loukotka 1968, 196).

Cumeral Colombia. Cumeral was assumed to be an extinct Arawakan language in earlier editions of *Ethnologue*, but it has now been retired as "non-existent" from the ISO 639-3 codes (https://iso639-3.sil.org/code/cum).

Cumbazá (Belsano) Peru. "Once spoken between Santa Catalina and Yanaycu, department of San Martín" (Loukotka 1968, 179).

Curanave Brazil. "Once spoken west of the Negro River, Amazonas" (Loukotka 1968, 228).

Curi Brazil. "Once spoken in the same region [at the mouth of the Purus River] south of the Pariana tribe" (Loukotka 1968, 196).

Curiane Brazil? "Language of a tribe the location of which is not known exactly" in northeastern South America (Loukotka 1968, 228).

Curierano Venezuela. "Once spoken south of the sources of the Orinoco River, territory of Amazonas" (Loukotka 1968, 228).

Curizeta Peru. "Once spoken on the Cosanga River, Loreto" (Loukotka 1968, 179).

Curubianan Brazil. "Once spoken on the Urubú and Jatapú Rivers, Amazonas" (Loukotka 1968, 228).

Curumiá Brazil. "Once spoken at the source of the Brilhante River, Mato Grosso" (Loukotka 1968, 86).

Curuzirari Brazil. "Once spoken between the mouths of the Juruá and Tefé Rivers" (Loukotka 1968, 196).

Cutaguá Brazil. "Once spoken in the state of Mato Grosso on the Dourados River" (Loukotka 1968, 86).

Cutría Brazil. "Spoken on the middle course of the Branco River, Rondônia" (Loukotka 1968, 166).

Cuximiraíba Brazil. "Spoken at the mouth of the Aripuanã River, Amazonas" (Loukotka 1968, 166).

Cuxiuára Brazil. "Once spoken on the right bank of the Purus River near the mouth" (Loukotka 1968, 196).

Damanivá Brazil. "Spoken on the Igarapé do Pacú ... and in the Serra do Urubú, Rio Branco territory" (Loukotka 1968, 229).

Dawainomol Paraguay. "Unknown language from the Gran Chaco of Paraguay" (Loukotka 1968, 63).

Demacuri Brazil. "Spoken on the Caburi River near São Pedro, state of Amazonas" (Loukotka 1968, 229).

Diaguita (Caca, Cacán, Kakán) Argentina, Chile. In the sixteenth and seventeenth centuries the Diaguita inhabited a wide area of northwestern Argentina, in parts of Catamarca, La Rioja, Salta, Santiago del Estero, and Tucumán, and northern Chile. (See Map 7.11.) Diaguita subtribes included Calchaquí, Capayán, Haulfín, Paccioca, Pular, and Quilme.

Early Spanish sources called the language of the Diaguita **Caca**, soon modified to **Cacán** (Kakán). Nothing is known of the language beyond what can be derived from place names and personal names and a few loanwords presumed to be of Diaguita origin in the Quechua of Santiago de Estero. Colonial sources mention different dialects or possibly closely related languages, for example **Calchaquí, Cayapán**, and **Yacampis** (Adelaar and Muysken 2004, 177, 407–409; Nardi 1979). (See Nardi 1979 and Piispanen 2020 for a synthesis of what is known or can be derived from sources concerning this language.)

Divihet Argentina. Loukotka (1968, 63) listed Divihet as an "extinct language once spoken on the Colorados and Sauce Cuhico Rivers, province of la Pampa." This appears to be the same language as *Dihuihet*. In reality it appears to be one of the alternative names associated with **Gününa Küne** and probably it should be removed from the list of unknown or unclassified languages (see **Chechehet** below for details; Viegas Barros 1992, 2015).

Dokoro Brazil. "Once spoken on the Paranaiuba River, Mato Grosso" (Loukotka 1968, 166).

Duri Brazil. "Spoken on the Paranaiuba River, Mato Grosso" (Loukotka 1968, 166).

Egualo Argentina. "Unknown language of the ancient mission of Santiago Sánchez" (Loukotka 1968, 63).

Eimi Peru. "Language of an unknown tribe that live on the Napo River, department of Loreto" (Loukotka 1968, 179).

Emischata Argentina. "Unknown language of the ancient mission of Santa Lucia, province of Corrientes" (Loukotka 1968, 63).

Emok Paraguay. This name was retired for being a non-existent language from the ISO 639-3 codes in 2014. Emok or Emok-Toba had been said to be the language of a mixed ethnic group, combining Toba (Guaicurúan) with "Maskoy" (Enlhet-Enenlhet). Though people of both Enlhet-Enenlhet and Toba (Guaicurúan) ethnicity live together in the communities once said to have "Emok" as their language, each speaks their own language; they use Guaraní for communication with those who speak the other language and "Emok" never existed. "Emok" is not the name of any language; it is apparently from a word like *emo'ok* or *eemook* 'my neighbor' in Enlhet-Enenlhet languages (Unruh and Kalisch 2003, 13).

Envuelto Colombia. Only eight words are known of this language (Zamponi in press b); "language of an unknown tribe that lived on the Quebrada de Jirijirima, Caquetá territory" (Loukotka 1968, 196).

Erema Brazil. "Once spoken on the Paranaiuba River, Mato Grosso" (Loukotka 1968, 166).

Ewarhuyana Brazil. Ewarhuyana is an unclassified language, possibly extinct, though some recent sources list twelve speakers, in Pará state. The Ewarhuyana live with the Tiriyó. They remained uncontacted by outsiders until late in the twentieth century. The language has sometimes been thought to be Cariban, but for lack of information about it, it is an unclassified language (https://pib.socioambiental.org/pt/Povo:Tiriyó, accessed September 15, 2021).

Foklása Brazil. "Once spoken in the state of Pernambuco in the Serra dos Cavalos" (Loukotka 1968, 93). Geraldo Lapenda (2005, 22) reported that according to Fulniô elders, the "Fo-kh'lá-sas" were a separate group that spoke the same language as the Fulniô, the Iaté (Fulniô) language. This would seem to call Foklása's existence as a separate language from

Iaté (Fulniô) into question. Potentially these people could have earlier spoken something else but shifted from it to later become Iaté speakers. That, of course, is just speculation.

Gadio Brazil. "Once spoken in the state of Espirito Santo, exact locality unknown" (Loukotka 1968, 86).

Galache Brazil. "Once spoken near Macaubas, state of Bahia" (Loukotka 1968, 93).

Gambéla Brazil. "Unknown language once spoken near Ourem and São José, Maranhão state" (Loukotka 1968, 93).[19]

Gamela (Gamela of Viana, Viana Gamela, Gamella, Curinsi, Acobu) Brazil. Known from only nineteen attested words. It is sometimes listed as a language isolate but without sufficient evidence to make such a determination (Zamponi in press b). Loutkotka (1968, 91) located it on the Itapucurú, Turiaçú, and Pindaré Rivers.

Garañun (Garanhun) Brazil. Loukotka (1968, 89) indicated that Garañun was formerly spoken in the Serra dos Garanhuns, saying nothing is known of it. He put it in his Shukurú "stock" (Xucurúan) along with Paratío. The evidence for this classification, however, is very weak (see Chapter 4, Campbell 2012a; 151, Zamponi in press b).

Gorgotoqui Bolivia. Isabelle Combès (2012) believes that **Gorgotoqui** of Bolivia may be another Bororoan language. Loukotka (1968, 61) listed Gorgotoqui simply as an isolated language; others have considered it unclassified for lack of data. During the time of the Jesuit missions in the Chiquitanía region of Bolivia, Gorgotoqui was the largest language of the area in terms of numbers of speakers; it was used as a lingua franca of the Jesuit missions of the region. However, no documentation has survived. It became dormant quite early (Adelaar and Muysken 2004, 623). Terrence Kaufman (1990, 46) suggested that perhaps it should not be listed, since it is completely undocumented, and indeed, it is absent from Kaufman (1994, 2007).

Goyana Brazil. "Extinct language once spoken on the lower curse of the Branco River, territory of Rio Branco" (Loukotka 1968, 229).

Guaca Colombia. Adelaar and Muysken (2004, 623) list Guaca and **Nori** together as languages which "cannot be classified for absence of data."

Guacará Argentina (Mason 1950, 208).

Guadaxo Brazil. "Once spoken on the upper course of the Anhanduí River, Mato Grosso" (Loukotka 1968, 86).

Guaimute Brazil. "Once spoken near the falls of Salto Grande, Espirito Santo" (Loukotka 1968, 86).

Guajarapo (Guasaroca) Bolivia. "Extinct language once spoken around Villa Maria and Santa Ana de Chiquitos, Santa Cruz province" (Loukotka 1968, 166).

Guanaca Colombia. "Cannot be classified for absence of data" (Adelaar and Muysken 2004, 623).

Guane Colombia. Adolfo Constenla Umaña (2012, 391) said it has "been considered Chibchan, but no linguistic evidence has been offered in support of these proposals" (Adelaar and Muysken 2004, 623).

Guanarú Brazil. "Extinct language once spoken on the Juruá River, north of the Marawa tribe, Amazonas" (Loukotka 1968, 196).

Guanavena Brazil. "Once spoken between the Urubú and Jatapú Rivers, Amazonas" (Loukotka 1968, 229).

Guarino Brazil. "Once spoken on the middle course of the Tijuco River, Mato Grosso" (Loukotka 1968, 93).

Guenta Colombia. "Once spoken in the department of Huila" (Loukotka 1968, 259).

Guyarabe Brazil. "Extinct language once spoken between the Amazon and Auatí-paraná Rivers, Amazonas" (Loukotka 1968, 196).

Hacaritama Colombia. Loukotka (1968, 220) had Hacaritama as "once spoken around the modern city of the same name in the department of Santander." However, Adelaar and Muysken (2004, 116) explain that a wordlist once thought to be of this language was from three **Guajiro** workers traveling through the area. "The real affiliation of the Hacaritama language, if it ever existed, remains undetermined."

Harritiahan Brazil. "Extinct language once spoken on the middle course of the Matapi River, Amapá territory" (Loukotka 1968, 229).

Hiauahim (Javaim) Brazil. "Once spoken by a tribe of cannibals on the middle course of the Tapajós River, Pará state" (Loukotka 1968, 166).

Himarimã (Rimarimá, Rimarimã). Brazil. *Ethnologue* (2021) reported forty speakers for this unclassified language of a recently contacted, mixed group; *Ethnologue* (2023) reports the population as "none." *Glottolog* lists it as an unattested Arawan language (https://glotto log.org/resource/languoid/id/hima1247.) R. M. W. Dixon (2004, 3) said:

> A further [Arawán] language has been reported, "Rimarimá." A [youth missionary] ... reports having met a speaker of "Rimarimá" near the Sorowahá village, having taken down a short word list, and having noted that it was an Arawá[n] language; unfortunately she lost the word list. "Rimarimá" could be a separate language, or a further dialect of an already recognized language; we have no way of knowing."[20]

Daniel Everett (1995, 298), on the basis of this information, classified "Rimarimá" in his Arawán family tree.[21] (See M. Carvalho 2016, 309.)

Huancavilca Ecuador. Unclassified extinct language (Adelaar and Muysken 2004, 392); "extinct language spoken in Guayas province around Guayaquil and on the Daule and Yaguachi Rivers" (Loukotka 1968, 262).[22]

Huamachi Peru. "Once spoken on Chongo Alto, department of Junín" (Loukotka 1968, 272).

Humahuaca (Omaguaca) Argentina. Loukotka (1968, 276) has this as an "extinct language once spoken in the valleys of Tilcará and Humahuaca, Jujuy province," in his Humahuaca stock, which also has several other members. Adelaar and Muysken (2004, 410) are much more tentative about it; they say that "the *Quebrada de Humahuaca* ... is believed to have had its own language," citing Loukotka (1968), "usually referred to as *Humahuaca* (or *Omaguaca*). There is hardly any linguistic information on this group."[23]

Huambuco Peru. "Once spoken on the Chinchipe River, Amazonas department" (Loukotka 1968, 272). In colonial documents the Aguaruna (Awajún) were sometimes referred to by different names and Huambuco was one of them (Research team 2010, 14). "The Huambuco, known to the Awajún [Aguaruna] as Wǎmpuku, were according to oral tradition, tall and dark-skinned with curly hair; they were formerly known as Shuwashiwag" (Research team 2010, 14).

Huayana Peru. Mason (1950, 272) placed Huayana with the unclassified languages of eastern Peru on which "there are little or no linguistic data."[24]

Huayla Peru. "Once spoken on the middle course of the Santa River, Ancash department, now Quechuanized" (Loukotka 1968, 272).

Iapama (Apama) Brazil. Iapama was listed in earlier editions of *Ethnologue* as an unclassified language, population unknown. However, it has been retired since 2015 from the ISO 369-3 codes, for being non-existent, said to be of an uncontacted group whose language is likely to be a neighboring language (https://en.wikipedia.org/wiki/Spuriouslanguages, accessed September 15, 2021).

Ibabi Aniji Peru "Language of an unknown tribe" (Loukotka 1968, 179).

Idabaez Colombia. "The only thing known of this language, if it existed as a separate language, is one word, *tubete* 'medicine-man', and a chief's name (*Hijuoba*)" (Adelaar and Muysken 2004, 56).

Imaré Brazil. "Once spoken in Mato Grosso, exact locality unknown" (Loukotka 1968, 86).

Ina Brazil. "Unknown language once spoken on the Paranaíba River, Mato Grosso" (Loukotka 1968, 86).

Iñajurupé Brazil. "Lost language of the ancient mission of Gracioso, Goiás state" (Loukotka 1968, 87).

Irra Colombia. Adelaar and Muysken (2004, 623) put Irra with the languages that "cannot be classified for absence of data." Loukotka (1968, 257) listed "Irrá" with his Chocó Stock, but indicated nothing was known of it.

Iruri Brazil. "Language of an extinct tribe on the right bank of the Madeira River, spoken between the Maiçí and Aripuanã Rivers, Amazonas" (Loukotka 1968, 166).

Isolados do Massaco Brazil. An uncontacted group, in the Guaporé region, Rondônia state, whose language is unknown (Crevels 2012, 181, 189; https://pib.socioambiental.org/pt/ListadesobreposiçõesdeTIseUCs, accessed September 15, 2021). As Mily Crevels (2012, 181) explained, "since the Isolados do Massaco use long bows, like the Sirionó in Bolivia, they have been considered to be Tupí-Guaraní an in the past, but basically nothing is known about them." (See also https://terrasindigenas.org.br/pt-br/terras-indigenas/3920.)

Isolado do Tanarú (Isolado do Buraco) Brazil. This is not about a language per se, but rather about an isolated single survivor of a massacre that started in 1985; his existence was confirmed in 1996, in what is now the Tanarú Indigenous Territory, Rondônia state. He was known as the "Indian of the hole"; he dug deep holes, perhaps to trap animals and for hiding in; it was said that where he slept was a hole that resembled a grave, though his body was found in August 2022 in a hammock covered with macaw feathers. He avoided all contact with others, living alone in isolation for twenty-six years. What language he spoke is unknown. (Crevels 2012, 181, 189; http://g1.globo.com/Amazonia/0,,MUL1635809-16052,00.html, accessed September 15, 2021; https://www.bbc.com/news/world-latin-america-62712318?fbclid=IwAR0lyHtfURfmHAdKGxCJlaOfPWLV_yMWWFbFQpyOP_irMgnhx_SM7NU9r5A.)

Itipuna Brazil. "Once spoken between the Juruá and Juraí Rivers" (Loukotka 1968, 197).

Itucá (Cuacá) Brazil. "Originally spoken in the Serra Negra, Pernambuco state" (Loukotka 1968, 93).

Jacariá Brazil. "Once spoken on the Abuna River, territory of Rondônia" (Loukotka 1968, 197).

Jaguanai Brazil. "Once spoken between the mouth of the Japurá River and the Zuana tribe [Rondônia]" (Loukotka 1968, 197).

Jaguanan Brazil. "Language of a little known tribe from Iguape, Rio Grande do Sul" (Loukotka 1968, 63).

Jamundi Colombia. Adelaar and Muysken (2004, 623) say of Jamundi that it "cannot be classified for absence of data," on the Jamundi-Cauca River. Loukotka (1968) included Jamundi and a number of other purported languages from the same region in a Yurimangui stock in his language classification. However, he noted that nothing is known of any of them.

Jeticó (Jiripancó) Brazil. "Once spoken in the village of Pindaé near Brejo dos Padres, Pernambico" (Loukotka 1968, 93).

Jitirijiti Colombia. Adelaar and Muysken (2004, 623) count this language among those that "cannot be classified for absence of data." Loukotka (1968, 257) listed "Jiritigiti" with his Chocó stock, but indicated nothing was known of the language.

Jurema Brazil. "Unknown language of Piauí state, exact locality unknown" (Loukotka 1968, 87).

Juruena Brazil. "Spoken on the Juruena River, Mato Grosso" (Loukotka 1968, 166).

Jururu Brazil. "Once spoken in the state of Ceará, but exact location is unknown" (Loukotka 1968, 93).

Kaimbé (Caimbé, Caimbe) Brazil. *Ethnologue* (2023) has Kaimbé as an unclassified dormant language. Only seven words that may be from Kaimbé are known. (Zamponi in press b.)

Kamba (Camba) Bolivia. Earlier editions of *Ethnologue* gave Kamba as an unclassified extinct language, possibly Tupían. The name was retired from ISO 369-3 in 2016 (https://iso639-3.sil.org/code/xba). *Camba* historically referred to the Indigenous peoples of eastern Bolivia or to those from the area of Santa Cruz, Beni, and Pando. Today it is a word that refers to the mixed populations born in the eastern lowlands around Santa Cruz de la Sierra.

Kambiwá (Cambiuá, Cambioá) Brazil. *Ethnologue* (2023) lists Kambiwá as a dormant unclassified language. The history of the Kambiwá has been confused with several Indigenous groups that live in rural Pernambuco state. The Kambiwá speakers originally were in the Serra Negra area in Pernambuco, but later were scattered throughout central Pernambuco. In 1935, twenty-seven words were recorded and around 1955, twenty-five words were recorded, some of them overlapping the words gathered in 1935 (Zamponi in press b). The Kambiwá Indigenous Territory is located in the municipalities of Inajá, Ibimirim, and Floresta, in the state of Pernambuco. Currently, the Kambiwá are distributed in eight main villages: Pereiros, Nazário, Serra do Periquito, Tear, Garapão, Americano, Faveleira and Baixa da India Alexandra. For a long time the Kambiwá have spoken only Portuguese (https://pib.socioambiental.org/pt/Povo:Kambiwá, accessed January 19, 2021).[25] The names Cambioá and Quiambioá, also listed here, appear to refer to the same language as Kambiwá.

Kantaruré Brazil (Crevels 2012). *Socioambiental* reports the Kantaruré people as descendants of the **Pankararu**, saying that their start was:

> a little over a century ago, when the Pankararu Indian known as Rosa Baleia left her village in Brejo dos Padres to join Balduíno, a resident of the nearby town of Olho d'Água dos Coelhos, near to Serra Grande. The couple . . . gave birth to 13 children and founded the village of Batida . . . today Kantaruré are also in the Pedras community, both in the Kantaruré Indigenous Territory . . . According to the testimony of a

Kantaruré elder, this ethnonym [Kantaruré] was suggested by a Pankararé Indian, in contrast to the one that had been adopted by the group, "caboclos da Batida," during the process of official recognition.

Currently, the Kantaruré speak Portuguese and cultural losses make their linguistic identification impossible today[26] (https://pib.socioambiental.org/pt/Povo:Kantaruré, accessed November 20, 2021).

It seems that Kantaruré can be removed from the list of unknown or unclassified languages.

Kapinawá Brazil. *Ethnologue* (2023) lists Kapinawá as a dormant unclassified language of Pernambuco state; *Glottolog* has it as "unclassifiable." It is unattested.

Karahawyana Brazil. Earlier editions of *Ethnologue* listed Karahawyana as an unclassified language, though probably Cariban. *Ethnologue* (2023) no longer has a separate entry for Karahawyana, but does list the name as a dialect of **Waiwai**, a Cariban language of Brazil and Guyana. ISO 369-3 retired Karahawyana in 2016 (https://iso639-3.sil.org/code/xkh); *Glottolog* lists it under Cariban as "unattested" (https://glottolog.org/resource/languoid/id/kara1475, accessed January 11, 2023).

Katembri (Catrimbi, Kariri de Mirandela) Brazil. Loukotka (1968, 87–88) had Katembri as a "lost language of the ancient mission of Saco dos Morcegos, now the city of Mirandela, state of Bahia." Several people attempted to obtain data from the people around the town of Mirandela in the last half of the last century, mostly from elderly rememberers of the language. It turns out that much of the data matches that in **Karirí** sources, but another part of the data appears to belong to an entirely different language. This non-Kariri lexical material does not fit with any other language of the zone. Raoul Zamponi (in press b) concludes:

It seems most likely that the non-Kariri native words gathered around Mirandela belong to the unattested language of a disappeared group once living not far from the town, called Katembri or Catrimbí.

Terrence Kaufman (2007, 73) put Katembri and **Taruma** together in his Macro-Katembri cluster, which had only these two languages as its members.

Kiapüre (Quiapyre) Brazil. "Once spoken on the Mequéns River, Rondônia" (Loukotka 1968, 166).

Kohoroxitari Brazil. Earlier, *Ethnologue* had listed Kohoroxitari as an unclassified language, saying it was possibly Tukanoan, maybe the same as **Baniwa**. Kohoroxitari was retired from ISO 639-3 in 2007 (https://iso639-3.sil.org/code/kob). It has been merged with **Sanuma** (Yanomaman), with Kohoroxitari identified as the name of a village and not the name of a language (https://glottolog.org/resource/languoid/id/koho1245, accessed September 15, 2021).

Kokakôre Brazil. "Once spoken in Mato Grosso state along the Tocantins River" (Loukotka 1968, 87).

Komokare Brazil. "Unknown language of Goiás state, exact locality unknown" (Loukotka 1968, 87).

Korubo (Corubo, Caceteiros, Cacetero) Brazil. *Ethnologue* (2021) listed Korubo as unclassified, in Amazonas state in Terra Indígena Vale do Javari, in the Javari River basin near the Itaquai, Ituí, and Quixiti Rivers. They noted that it had twenty-six speakers reported in 2007;

they were first contacted in 1996. However, Korubo has been shown to be clearly a member of the Panoan branch of the Pano-Takanan family, lisited as such now in *Ethnologue* (2023). Sanderson Oliveira (2009, 2014, 2023) classifies Korubo as a member of the Mayoruna subgroup of Panaoan. It is now removed from the list of unclassified languages.

Koshurái Brazil. "Language of an unknown tribe on the lower course of the Jiparaná River, Amazonas" (Loukotka 1968, 166).

Kurumro (Curumro) Paraguay. "Language of an unknown tribe of the Paraguayan Chaco" (Loukotka 1968, 63). Loukotka (1931a, 859) was of the opinion that, although nothing is known of the Kurumro tribe or their language, their language was the same as **Sapuki**, of which seven words were known. Mason (1950, 280) listed Sapuki as a "Mascoi" (Enlhet-Enenlhet) language. John Elliott (2021, 791) notes that the group that some historical sources called *Sapuqui* or *Sapuki* are likely to be the Kelyamok band that generally integrated with the **Sanapaná**, a Enlhet-Enenlhet group.

Kururu Brazil. "Once spoken in the state of Mato Grosso on the Carinhanha River" (Loukotka 1968, 87).

Lache Colombia. Loukotka (1968, 241) listed Lache with the Chibcha Group of his Chibcha Stock, but with the indication that nothing was known of the language. Adelaar and Muysken (2004, 623), however, listed Lache with the languages that "cannot be classified for absence of data," and Adolfo Constenla Umaña (2012, 391) said also that Lache has "been considered Chibchan, but no linguistic evidence has been offered in support of these proposals."

Lambi Brazil. "Extinct language once spoken between the Branco and São Miguel Rivers, Rondônia" (Loukotka 1968, 166).

Lili Colombia. Loukotka (1968, 259) included Lili in his Yurimangui stock with several other purported languages from the same region; he said Lili was once spoken in the region around Cali, but that nothing is known of it. Adelaar and Muysken (2004, 623) included it with the languages that they say "cannot be classified for absence of data."

Llamish Peru. "Once spoken in the department of Lima in the Cordillera de Huantín" (Loukotka 1968, 273).

Macamasu Brazil. "An extinct language the exact location of which is unknown" (Loukotka 1968, 93).

Macarú Brazil. "Once spoken in the village of Brejo dos Padres," Bahia (Loukotka 1968, 94).

Macuani Brazil. "Once spoken on the Oiapoque River, Amapá territory" (Loukotka 1968, 229).

Macuarê Brazil. "Once spoken on the left bank of the Pimenta Bueno River, Rondônia" (Loukotka 1968, 166).

Macuja Brazil. "Spoken by an unknown tribe on the Poré River, Amazonas" (Loukotka 1968, 197).

Macuruné Brazil. "Once spoken on the Mucunis River, state of Minas Gerais" (Loukotka 1968, 87).

Mairajiqui Brazil. "Once spoken on the Bahia de Todos os Santos, state of Bahia" (Loukotka 1968, 94).

Malaba Ecuador. Loukotka (1968, 248) gave Malaba as an "extinct language once spoken on the Mataja River," of which he said nothing was known. Adelaar and Muysken (2004, 623) listed it with the languages that "cannot be classified for absence of data."

Malibú Colombia. Loukotka (1968, 244) had Malibú as an extinct language in a Malibú Group in his Chibcha stock. He located it as once spoken near the Magdalena River between Tamalameque and Tenerife in the department of Magdalena. Adelaar and Muysken (2004, 52) said Loukotka's classification of Malibú was "without any factual basis." They put it among the languages that "cannot be classified for absence of data" (Adelaar and Muysken 2004, 624).

Malquesi Argentina. "Once spoken on the western shore of Laguna Porongos, province of Córdova" (Loukotka 1968, 63).

Manesono (Mopeseano) Bolivia. "Extinct language once spoken at the ancient mission of San Francisco Borja, Beni province" (Loukotka 1968, 166).

Manta or **Manabi** Ecuador. Loukotka (1968, 262) put "Manabi or Manta" in the Northern branch of his Chimú Stock, an "extinct language of Manabí province." However, he indicated that it was unknown except for "only a few patronyms." Adelaar and Muysken (2004, 624) listed Manta as one of the languages that "cannot be classified for absence of data" (see also p. 392).

Maracano Brazil. "Unknown language spoken on the central part of Maracá Island, Rio Branco territory" (Loukotka 1968, 229).

Marapanã Brazil. "Spoken by an unknown tribe on the right bank of the Uaimberê River ... Rondônia" (Loukotka 1968, 166).

Maricoxi Brazil. "Once spoken at the sources of the Branco River, Rondônia" (Loukotka 1968, 166).

Maricupi Brazil. "Extinct language once spoken on the lower course of the Montoura River, Amapá territory" (Loukotka 1968, 229).

Maripá Brazil. "Extinct language once spoken on the Tonantins River, Amazonas" (Loukotka 1968, 197).

Maruquevene Brazil. "Extinct language once spoken between the mouths of the Japurá and Auatí-Paraná Rivers" (Loukotka 1968, 197).

Masa Argentina. "Unknown language of the ancient mission of Santiago Sánchez" (Loukotka 1968, 63).

Masarari Brazil. "Once spoken south of the Juraí River, Amazonas" (Loukotka 1968, 197).

Masaya Colombia. "Once spoken at the sources of the Caguán River, north of the Guaque tribe" (Loukotka 968, 259).

Mashco Peru. Mily Crevels (2012) listed Mashco as an unclassified language spoken by an uncontacted group who reportedly speak a language related to **Piro** (Arawakan). Loukotka (1968, 139–141) had Mashco (Sirineiri, Moeno) in the Preandine Group of his Arawak stock, "spoken on the Pilcopata River, department of Madre de Dios," distinct from "**Inapari** [Iñapari] or Mashco Piro" of the same group, said to be "spoken between the Tacutimani and Amigo Rivers, department of Madre de Dios" (Loukotka 1968, 140). This Mashco is not to be confused with the "Mashco" that is sometimes used as an alternative name for either of the two **Harákmbut** varieties.

Matará Argentina. J. Alden Mason (1950, 208) treated Matará as "best left unclassified," mentioning that others had placed it with **Vilela** and **Mataco** [Wichí]. Loukotka (1968, 277) placed Matará (Amulalá), "once spoken near the city of the same name on the Salado River," in his **Lule** stock, though he conceded that nothing was known of the language.

Maynas (Mayna, Maina, Rimachu) Peru. Harald Hammarström (2011) has shown that "Maynas" is a separate language. It is often mistakenly listed with **Omurano**, due to overlapping names, for example Hervás y Panduro's "Humurano" as a dialect of "Maynas." Loukotka (1968, 155–156) had Mayna (Rimachu), "once spoken between the Nucuray, Chambira and Pastaza Rivers, department of Loreto," in a "Mayna stock," along with Omurana (Humurana) as the only other member. Proposals have tried to link the language also with Jivaroan (Chicham), Cahuapanan, Zaparoan, and Candoshi. It is unclassified. (See Chapter 4 for more details.)

Maxiena (Ticomeri, Majena, Majiena) Bolivia. "Extinct language once spoken on the Mojos plains west of the mission of Trinidad, Beni province" (Loukotka 1968, 166).

Mayu Brazil. Loukotka 1(968, 197) gave Mayu as an "unknown language spoken on the Jaquirana River, tributary of the Javari River, Amazonas." This is perhaps one of the varieties called "Mayo" in the Pano-Takanan languages (see Fleck 2013, 11, 13, 108), although since *mayu* is the Quechua word for 'river, water' found in numerous river names and place names, this "Mayu" language is perhaps a mistaken identity for some other linguistic or geographical entity.

Menejou Brazil. "Extinct language once spoken on the middle course of the Jarí River, Amapá territory" (Loukotka 1968, 229).

Minhahá Brazil. "Once spoken on the Paranaiuba River, Mato Grosso" (Loukotka 1968, 166).

Miranha-Carapana-Tapuya (?) Colombia. Carl Friedrich Philipp von Martius (1867, 277) gave a wordlist from the Caquetá-Putumayo area labeled "Miranha-Carapana-Tapuya." Katarzyna Wojtylak (2017, 19) says that it "does share some similarities with other Witot[o]an languages but the exact affiliation is yet unknown."

Mocana Colombia. Loukotka (1968, 244) classified Mocana in the Malibú Group of his Chibcha Stock, but mentioned that only two words of the language are known. He located it as "once spoken in the region east of Cartagena, department of Bolívar." Adelaar and Muysken (2004, 624) placed it with the languages that "cannot be classified for absence of data."

Mocoa Colombia. Loukotka (1968, 249) gave "Mocoa" as one of the alternative names for **Kamsá**, along with **Sebondoy**, **Sibundoy**, and **Coche**, which he classified as a member of the Sebondoy Group of his Chibcha stock. He called it a "language once spoken at the sources of the (Putumayo) Içá River, Putumayo territory, Colombia," adding that it was "now partly spoken in the villages of Mocoa and Las Cadas only." Kamsá, however, though endangered, has many speakers today. Kamsá is a language isolate (see O'Brien 2018). As Colleen O'Brien (2018, 11) puts it, "Kamsá could theoretically be related to whatever language was once spoken by the Mocoa people (a group who once lived in the area of the current city of Mocoa), but their language is also unknown to us."

Moheyana Brazil. A "language of an unknown, warlike tribe that lived between the Erepecurú and Acapú Rivers, state of Para" (Loukotka 1968, 229).

Morcote Colombia. Loukotka (1968, 240) had Morcote as a member of the Chibcha Group of his Chibcha Stock, but noted that nothing was known of the language. He placed it "on the Tocaría River and in the village of Morcote." Adelaar and Muysken (2004, 624) have it in their list of languages that "cannot be classified for absence of data." Adolfo Constenla

Umaña (2012, 391) said that Morcote and some others have "been considered Chibchan, but no linguistic evidence has been offered in support of these proposals."

Moriquito Brazil. "Once spoken in Alagoas state on the lower course of the São Francisco River" (Loukotka 1968, 94).

Morua Brazil. "Once spoken on the Japurá River south of the Maruquevene tribe" (Loukotka 1968, 197).

Moyobamba (Moyo-Pampa) Peru. "Once spoken around the city of the same name, San Martín department" (Loukotka 1968, 273; see also Mason 1950, 272).[27]

Mure Bolivia. Mure was spoken in the latter half of the 1700s in the Mission of San Simón and by part of the people at San Borja mission in Beni department (Zamponi in press b). Though usually included with Chapacuran, "the available material does not display many typical Chapakuran structural elements, nor does it include Chapakuran basic vocabulary items . . . Neither does this material contain any evidence suggesting a clear genetic relation between Mure and any other known language" (Zamponi in press b). It should not be confused with **Moré** (also called **Itene** or Itoreauhip), a Chapacuran language located around the confluence of the Guaporé (Iténez) and Mamoré Rivers in Bolivia (Birchall et al. 2016, 258), nor with **Mura**, considered either a dormant variety of Pirahã or a separate Muran language (see Chapter 4).

Muriva Brazil. "Once spoken at the mouth of the Jamachim River to the Tapajós River, Para state" (Loukotka 1968, 167).

Muzapa Peru. "Once spoken by the neighbors of the Cognomona tribe in the department of San Martín" (Loukotka 1968, 179).

Muzo Colombia. Loukotka (1968, 219) grouped Muzo in his Karaib (Cariban) stock, in his Pijao Group, indicating that only three words were known from one source and five words from another (see also Durbin and Seijas 1973, 51). He had it as "once spoken at the sources of the Carare River and in the Paima Valley, department of Cundimarca." Adelaar and Muysken (2004, 114) say only that the Muzo nation with several others of the area "have long been extinct" and that "a Cariban linguistic affiliation has often been proposed."

Nacai Brazil. "Extinct language once spoken on the Aquitipi River, Bahia" (Loukotka 1968, 94).

Nambu Bolivia. "Extinct language once spoken on the Guapay River, Santa Cruz province" (Loukotka 1968:167).

Natagaimas (Natagaima) Colombia. Earlier editions of *Ethnologue* listed Natagaimas as an extinct unclassified language of Colombia, but the name has now been dropped depricated from the ISO 639-3 codes in 2015 and merged with Pijao (https://iso639-3.sil.org/code/nts). The general consensus now is that Natagaimas was a variety of **Pijao**, from around the town of Natagaima, in the Magdalena River Valley. It can be removed from lists of unknown South American languages.

Natú (Peagaxinan) Brazil. Raoul Zamponi (in press b) says "nothing is known about the history of the Natú and even their original location is unknown," crediting Loukotka (1955, 1041). Zamponi mentions that in 1935 descendants of this group were in Pôrto Real do Colégio, in Alagoas state. It is sometimes listed as a language isolate but the available material is insufficient for making such a determination; only eighteen words of the language were recorded (Zamponi in press b).

Terrence Kaufman (1990, 48) says "only Gr[eenberg] dares to classify this language." Greenberg (1987, 383) placed it in his Macro-Tucanoan group.

Nauna Brazil. "Extinct language once spoken on the Juraí River south of the Marawa tribe" (Loukotka 1968, 197).

Nindaso Peru. Mason (1950, 272) listed Nindaso among the unclassified languages of eastern Peru. Loukotka (1968, 154) placed it in his **Munichi** stock, "once spoken on the Huallaga River north of the Zapaso tribe," but said nothing was known of it, calling into question his judgment of its classification.

Nocadeth Brazil. "Spoken on the Aripuaná River, state of Amazonas" (Loukotka 1968, 167).

Nomona Peru. Mason (1950, 272) paced Nomona with the unclassified languages of eastern Peru. Loukotka (1968, 154) listed it with his Munichi stock, "once spoken on the ... Saposa [Zaposa?] River," but admitting nothing was known of this language.

Nori Colombia. Adelaar and Muysken (2004, 623) list Nori (of Antioquia) together with **Guaca** as languages that "cannot be classified for absence of data."

Ñumasiara Brazil. "Unknown language spoken on the Giraparaná and Canamari Rivers" (Loukotka 1968, 197).

Ocro Peru. "Once spoken at the sources of the Santa River, Ancash department" (Loukotka 1968, 273). Mason (1950, 194) listed Ocro with the "regions or ethnic groups" that are "of uncertain original language and are left unclassified."

Ocren Brazil. "Extinct language once spoken in Bahia on the São Francisco River near Salitre" (Loukotka 1968, 94).

Ohoma Argentina. This is probably the same as **Hohoma** or **Mahoma**, which Métraux (1946, 225) thought was possibly related to Guaicurúan. Citing Métraux, J. Alden Mason (1950, 205) said they "may have been related to *Toba* or *Mocoví*." Loukotka (1968, 63) gave Ohoma as an "extinct and unknown language once spoken near the ancient mission of Homa or Ohoma, province of Corrientes."

Oivaneca Brazil. "Extinct language once spoken on the Tartarugal River, Amapá territory" (Loukotka 1968, 229).

Olmos (language of the Olmos oasis) Peru. Several early chroniclers mention the language of the oasis town of Olmos in the northeast of the department of Lambayeque on the edge of the Sechura desert. As explained in Chapter 4, extremely scant linguistic material from the language exists, and its interpretation is uncertain. Several have thought that Olmos is possibly connected with **Sechura**, though this cannot be confirmed (see Adelaar and Muysken 2004, 320, 400). Alfredo Torero (2002, 224–226) concluded from chroniclers' comments about the language that it was a mixed language based on Sechura and **Mochica**. Rodolfo Cerrón-Palomino (1995, 27) believed that Olmos might have been a variety of Sechura with a strong Mochica influence, a mochicaized variant of Sechura. Matthias Urban's (2019a, 62) conclusion concerning Olmos is:

> Since the interpretation of the [Olmos] situation must be based to a large extent on casual observations rather than lexical data it seems best to me not to engage in speculation regarding the linguistics of Olmos beyond saying that (i) likely speakers of Mochica and Sechura lived in the region in historical times and that (ii) the sparse linguistic evidence ... and the majority of colonial documents cited do not lend support

to the interpretation that the language of Olmos was completely distinct from either that of Sechura or Mochica... Hence, it is indeed reasonable to assume a close coexistence of Mochica and one or more languages from the Far North in the Olmos region in colonial times.

Omejes Colombia. Omejes was retired from the ISO 639-3 codes in 2015 in 2016 for being non-existent (https://iso639-3.sil.org/code/ome). It had been assumed to be an extinct Arawakan language of Colombia.

Onicoré Brazil. "Once spoken between the mouths of the Manicoré and Marmelos Rivers, state of Amazonas" (Loukotka 1968, 167).

Onoyóro Brazil. "Once spoken on the Paranaiuba River, Mato Grosso" (Loukotka 1968, 167).

Orí Brazil. "Extinct language from Bahia, once spoken between the Itapicurú and Vasa Burris Rivers" (Loukotka 1968, 94).

Ortue Bolivia. "Once spoken on Xarayes Lagoon" (Loukotka 1968, 167).

Otecua Peru. "Spoken on the Sucumbio River, Loreto" (Loukotka 1968, 179).

Otegua Colombia. "Once spoken in the department of Huila" (Loukotka 968, 259).

Otí (Eochavante, Chavante) Brazil. This dormant language, from the Paranapanema basin, is often listed as a language isolate, though so little is known (three wordlists, about 110 total words) that it is unlikely that on that basis it can be determined whether it has no relatives. Terrence Kaufman (1994, 70) said of Otí that of the large-scale classifiers "only Greenberg dares to link this language to anything else"—Greenberg (1987) placed it in his Macro-Ge phylum. Kaufman (2007, 73) listed Otí among the languages of eastern Brazil in his list of "isolates, unclassified, possibly Macro-Je." However, Eduardo Ribeiro (2006, 422) says, "the meagre available data do not support its [Otí's] inclusion into the Macro-Jê stock," and Andrey Nikulin (2020, 77–79) also rejects it from Macro-Jê (Sensu Stricto). (Not to be confused with Jotí [Joti, Jodi, Hotí, Hodï] of Venezuela.) (See Zamponi in press b.)

Pacabuey (Pacabuei) Colombia. Loukotka (1968, 244) called this "an extinct language once spoken around the Zapatoza lagoon." He listed it with the Malibú Group of his Chibcha stock, with the note that nothing is known of the language. Adelaar and Muysken (2004, 624) place it among the languages that they say "cannot be classified for absence of data."

Pacarará (Pakarara) Brazil. "Once spoken in the state of Pernambuco in the Serra Cacaréa and Serra Arapuá" (Loukotka 1968, 94).

Pacimonari Venezuela. "Once spoken on the lower course of the Siapa River, Amazonas territory" (Loukotka 1968, 229).

Paguara Brazil. "Once spoken on the Tefé River" (Loukotka 1968, 197).

Panatagua (Panatahua, Panatawa) Peru. Loukotka (1968, 137) classified Panatahua in the Lorenzo Group of his Arawak stock, spoken on "the Huallaga River between Coyumba and Monzón, now perhaps extinct." Adelaar and Muysken (2004, 422), after mentioning that Arawakan affinities have been proposed, concluded that "the linguistic affiliation of the Panatagua has never been established with certainty" (see also Mason 1950, 272). However, David Fleck (2013, 15, 85) reports Panatawa (Panatagua) in his "tentative classification of possibly Panoan languages/dialects lacking linguistic data," from a 1792 report.

Panche Colombia. Loukotka (1968, 219) placed Panche in his **Pijao** Group of his Karaib stock, calling it an "extinct language once spoken on the Gualí, Mariquita, Guarinó, Coello, Villeta, Seco, Magdalena and Fusagasuga Rivers, Cundinamarca." A Cariban affiliation is often suspected for Panche, though Adelaar and Muysken (2004, 114) agree with Durbin and Seijas (1973) in saying that it "should be left unclassified, because the extremely limited data do not provide enough evidence for a Cariban affiliation." Durbin and Seijas (1973, 51) found only five words of Panche in the sources available. The main reason for suspecting Cariban affiliation has to do with place names that suggest "Cariban toponymy."

Pankararé (Pankaré) Brazil. *Ethnologue* (2023) has Pankararé as a dormant unclassified language. *Glottolog* cites *Ethnologue* but lists it as "unattested" (https://glottolog.org/resource/languoid/id/pank1235). The Pankararé lived near Paulo Afonso in Bahia; originally they lived on the São Francisco River between the Paulo Afonso waterfall, at the mouth of the Pajeú River and the adjacent swamps and mountain (https://pib.socioambiental.org/pt/Povo:Pankararé, accessed August 29, 2021). (Not to be confused with the Pankararu of Pernambuco, Brazil.)

Pankararu (Pancararu, Pancarurú, Brancararu) Brazil. Loukotka (1968, 87–88) considered Pankarurú an "isolated language"; he located it as originally "between the Moxotó and Pajeú Rivers, Pernambuco, now in the villages of Brejo dos Padres and Tacaratú." Known from several short wordlists and a few noun phrases and short sentences, but altogether still very scantly attested. Loukotka (1963, 15) erroneously attributed sixteen **Kambiwá** words collected in Brejo dos Padres to Pankararú (Zamponi in press b). It is sometimes considered a language isolate, but too poorly attested to determine whether it could be classified or not. (Zamponi in press b.) The Pankararu Indigenous Territory is located between the municipalities of Petrolândia, Itaparica, and Tacaratu, in the Pernambuco hinterland, close to the São Francisco River (https://pib.socioambiental.org/pt/Povo:Pankararu).

Pantágora (Palenque, Pantagora) Colombia. Loukotka (1968, 219) listed Pantagora (Palenque) as a member of his **Pijao** Group of his Karaib stock, indicating "nothing" was known of it, "once spoken between the Guarinó and San Bartolomé Rivers, department of Caldas." Adelaar and Muysken (2004, 114) mention the suspected Cariban affiliation, though they, along with Durbin and Seijas (1973), believe that it "should be left unclassified, because the extremely limited data do not provide enough evidence for a Cariban affiliation" (see also Adelaar and Muysken 2004, 624). The status of Pantagora as an independent language is uncertain. As Durbin and Seijas (1973, 47) said, "Pantagora itself has been mentioned as a subgroup within Panche; thus, there is some confusion as to whether Pantagora should be included within Panche and perhaps Pijao, or as a separate group."[28]

Pao Venezuela. "Extinct language spoken on the Pao River, state of Monagas" (Loukotka 1968, 229).

Papamiän Brazil. "Spoken on the São Simão River, Rondônia" (Loukotka 1968, 167). Hein van der Voort (2012, 3) indicates that "The Papamiän probably represent the uncontacted group in what is presently the Massaco reserve."

Papana Brazil. "Once spoken between the Doce and Jequitinhonha Rivers, Minas Gerais" (Loukotka 1968, 87).

Papavô Brazil. Papavô was retired from the ISO 639-3 codes in 2009. It was determined that Papavô was a name given to several uncontacted groups. Previously it had been considered possibly an Arawakan or Panoan language, spoken by some uncontacted group. *Glottolog* lists Papavô as an unattested language under Pano-Tacanan (https://glottolog.org/resource/languoid/id/papa1263, accessed August 30, 2021).

Paragoaru Brazil. "Once spoken on the Capó River" (Loukotka 1968, 229).

Paraparixana Brazil. "Once spoken between the Manicoré and Aninde Rivers, Amazonas" (Loukotka 1968, 167).

Paratío (Prarto) Brazil. Paratío was spoken in the Serra do Ororubá region of Brazil. Only a few words are attested. They were recorded by Curt Nimuendajú in 1934 but his record of the language was lost after his death, although Čestmír Loukotka had a copy. He apparently used it in the seven Xukurú-Paratío comparisons in his book (Loukotka 1968, 89) (Zamponi in press press b). Paratío has often been thought to be related to Xukurú, though the evidence is too weak to confirm that.

Parapicó Brazil. "Once spoken in the Serra Comonati, Pernambuco" (Loukotka 1968, 94).

Patagón Peru. Alfredo Torero (2002, 277) located this Patagón in a small area bordered on two sides by the Chinchipe and Marañón Rivers and on the third side by people of the Chirinos group. He reported that three of the four recorded words appear to belong the Cariban family, citing also Rivet (1934, 246). Torero (2002, 278–280) also sorted out a confusion of Rivet's, followed by Loukotka, who had confused and conflated Patagón and **Bagua**. Torero noted that the two share only a single word and argued that the two were separate languages (see Bagua, above). (This Patagón is not to be confused with the Patagón synonym for **Chon**).[29]

Patiti Brazil. "Once spoken in Rondônia territory on the Mequéns River" (Loukotka 1968, 167).

Payacú Brazil. J. Alden Mason (1950, 302) mentioned Payacú among the little-known languages of the Pernambuco region, saying that "Nimuendajú leaves them unclassified; other authorities ignore them." Loukotka (1968, 91) placed Payacú in his Tarairiú stock as an "extinct language" that was "once spoken in Rio Grande do Norte."

Payanso Peru. "Extinct language once spoken on the Chipurana River, Loreto" (Loukotka 1968, 179; see also Mason 1950, 272). Others place the Payansos on the Huallaga River between the Huayabamba and Chipurana Rivers. David Fleck (2013, 86, 89), however, lists Payanso as a synonym for Shipibo, a Panoan (Pano-Takanan) language.

Pehuenche (Peguenche) Argentina. Adelaar and Muysken (2004, 624) listed Pehuenche, in Nequén province, among the languages that "cannot be classified for absence of data." Though "nothing is known of the original Pehuenche language," early sources are consistent in confirming that the Pehuenche had a separate language of their own (Adelaar and Muysken (2004, 505). (This Pehuenche is distinct from the Pehuenche dialect of **Mapudungun**.) (See also Loukotka 1968, 63.)

Peria (Poria) Brazil. "Extinct language once spoken in the village of Rodelas, Bahia" (Loukotka 1968, 94).

Perovosan Bolivia. "Once spoken to the south of the Xarayes Lagoon" (Loukotka 1968, 167).

Pescadora (Lengua Pescadora, Yunga Pescadora) Peru. The frequent colonial-era mentions of a "fishermen's language" on the Peruvian coast are confusing. The "lengua pescadora" was apparently spoken mostly to the south of the **Mochica** area, in Guañape, Virú,

St. Esteban ("an urban parish in Trujillo"), Mansiche, Guanchaco, Santiago de Cao, and Magdalena de Cao (Urban 2019a, 51). A complication is that **Quingnam** (see below) is also located by several colonial sources in the same area where sources report "lengua pescadora." The two, if they were different, were closely associated geographically. Moreover, one source, the chronicler Antonio de la Calancha (1638, 606), says that Pescadora and Quingnam are basically the same language, but that Pescadora is more "guttural" (cited by Urban 2019a, 54). This has led some to identify the Lengua Pescadora directly as Quingnam or as a sociolect of Quingnam (Adelaar and Muysken 2004, 320; Urban 2019a, 54–55, 226). Urban (2019a, 56) sums up the treatment of Pescadora in the literature as, "at any rate, there is general agreement that there is a close relationship—if not one of identity, one of dialectal variation—between Quingnam and Pescadora."

Piapia Brazil. "Once spoken between the Jamachim and Iriri Rivers, state of Pará" (Loukotka 1968, 167).

Pijao (Piajao, Pixao, Paniquitá, Pinao) Colombia. *Ethnologue* (2021, 2023) has Pijao as a dormant unclassified language of Tolima department, saying "there is not enough data to classify it linguistically" (https://www.ethnologue.com/language/pij, accessed August 30, 2021). A Cariban connection is often assumed for Pijao (Rivet 1943; Adelaar and Muysken 2004, 114). Loukotka (1968, 219) followed Rivet, placing Pijao and ten other unknown or extremely poorly attested language in the Pijao Group of His Karaib stock. Durbin and Seijas (1973, 50) found "perhaps as many as 7 out of 24" of the available Pijao lexical items "resemble Carib[an], but they have several problems," and they concluded that "borrowing could account for the similarities of the lexical items . . . equally as well as genetic relationship" (p. 49).

Pijao was spoken until the 1950s in Ortega, Coyaima, and Natagaima in the Magdalena River Valley. Durbin and Seijas (1973, 48) mention two small vocabularies collected in 1943, unpublished but cited by Loukotka (1968, 219).

Pipipan (Pipipã) Brazil. "Once spoken on the lower course of the Moxotó River, Pernambuco" (Loukotka 1968, 94); historically the Pipipã were inhabitants of the Serra Negra; their territory now is located in Floresta, Pernambuco (https://pib.socioambiental.org/pt/Povo:Pipipã, accessed August 30, 2021).

Pocoana Brazil. "Once spoken between the Amazon River and Lake Maracaparu" (Loukotka 1968, 197).

Ponares Colombia. Ponares was retired in 2016 from the ISO 639-3 codes for being "non-existent" (https://iso639-3.sil.org/code/pod). It was sometimes thought to belong to Arawakan or Sáliban, based on surnames.

Porcá Brazil. "One spoken on Várgea [sic, Várzea] Island in the São Francisco River, Pernambuco" (Loukotka 1968, 94).

Porú (Procáze) Brazil. "Originally spoken in the Serra Nhumarana and Serra Cassuca, later on the Várgea [sic, Várzea] and Nossa Senhora de O [sic, Nossa Senhora?] Islands in the São Francisco River" (Loukotka 1968, 94).

Potiguara Brazil. Earlier *Ethnologue* listed Potiguára as a separate language, but Ethnologue (2023) now has it as a Tupían language. Data potentially attributed to Potiguára in the Dutch National Archives show it to be a variety of Tupinambá (Willem Adelaar personal communication), and Glottolog lists it as a dialect of Tupinambá (https://glottolog.org/resource/languoid/id/poti1237).

Pozo Colombia. "Once spoken on the Pozo and Pacova Rivers" (Loukotka 1968, 239). Adelaar and Muysken (2004, 623) list Arma-Pozo among the languages that they say "cannot be classified for absence of data." Several early classifiers mentioned **Arma** and Pozo as linked with Chocoan languages of the Cauca basin of Colombia.

Pubenza Colombia. Adelaar and Muysken (2004, 624) also put Pubenza among the languages that "cannot be classified for absence of data."

Puná (Lapuna) Ecuador. Loukotka (1968, 262) said nothing was known of this language, "once spoken on the island of Puná"; he nevertheless classified it with the Northern Languages branch of his Chimú stock. Willem Adelaar (2012b, 582) also confirms that the people of Puná Island had their own distinct language.

Puscajae (Pile) Colombia. Loukotka (1968, 259) placed this language, of which he said nothing was known, in his Yurimangui stock, "on the left bank of the Dagila River."

Quelosi Argentina. "Unknown language once spoken to the east of the Mar Chiquita, province of Córdova" (Loukotka 1968, 63).

Querandí (Carendie, Pampa, Serrano, Puelche, Algarrobero, Tubichamint, Bagual, Vilachichí, Diamantino, Taluhet) Argentina. The Querandí lived on the pampas from the Río de la Plata area in the east to the Central Sierras in Argentina's Córdoba, San Luis, and Mendoza provinces. They appear to have ceased to exist by the end of the 1700s. The language is almost unknown. Pedro Viegas Barros (1992, 2005a) argued that Querandí is related to **Gününa Küne**. He based this on (1) the testimony of a German Jesuit missionary, Matías Strobel, from the mid-1700s, who learned what were apparently Querandí and Gününa Küne and said they differed from one another like German from Flamenco (Flemish), closely related; (2) attempted analysis of Querandí material based on similarities from Gününa Küne in two Querandí phrases, apparently insults or curses, recorded by French sailors in around 1555 or 1556; (3) similarities in endings characteristic of proper names in the two languages; and (4) similarities in names. (See also Adelaar and Muysken 2004, 505.)

Quiquidcana (Quidquidcana, Kikidkana) Peru. "Once spoken in the department of Huánuco in the Madgalena valley" (Loukotka 1968, 179; see also Mason 1950, 272).

Quijo (Kijo) Ecuador. Quijo is sometimes associated with **Panzaleo** (Adelaar and Muysken 2004, 394). Adelaar and Muysken (2004, 624) included it in the languages that "cannot be classified for absence of data." Loukotka (1968, 249) had placed it in the Barbácoa Group of his Chibcha stock, though only three words of the language were known. He located it on the Napo and Coca Rivers in Oriente province.

Quillacinga (Quillasinga) Ecuador. Loukotka (1968, 250) called Quillasinga an "extinct language once spoken on the Caquetá and Guaitara Rivers," from around the city of Pasto. Different proposals would classify it with Chibchan, Quechuan, or **Kamsá**. It is unlikely that Quillacinga was Kamsá (O'Brien 2018, 11–12; Adelaar and Muysken 2004, 392). With no records, it remains unclassified, unclassifiable.[30]

Quimbaya Colombia. Adelaar and Muysken (2004, 49) said that "the Quimbaya became extinct as a recognisable group around 1700 ... Their language remains unknown and its affiliations a matter of speculation." Loukotka (1968, 257) identified it as an "extinct language of a tribe of excellent goldsmiths, once spoken on the middle course of the Cauca River ... department of Valle de Cauca." He placed Quimbaya with his Chocó stock, though "only one single word" was known.

Quiambioá Brazil. "Once spoken in the Serra Negra, Pernambuco" (Loukotka 1968, 94).

Quindío (Quindio) Colombia. Adelaar and Muysken (2004, 624) considered Quindío, of Quindío, Colombia, one of the languages that "cannot be classified for absence of data."

Quingnam Peru. Quingnam is a dormant and unclassified language. "There is no linguistic information proper on Quingnam, with the probable exception of a recently discovered list of numerals" (Quilter et al. 2010); "all information on the language is indirect and must be culled from various sources" (Urban 2019a, 149, 150). In spite of this, Matthias Urban (2019a, 147–154) was able to bring together more than fifty probable words from Quingnam and to provide considerable detail on the structure of the language. Nevertheless, it is not even clear from the sources exactly where it was spoken. It was spoken in the early seventeenth century in the "valley" of Trujillo, in the Moche Valley and a wider region, including at San Pedro de Lloc and Jequetepeque, with its southern limit estimated to be at the Nepeña Valley (Urban 2019a, 54, 63). (See Map 7.11.)

A small list of numerals from the early seventeenth century was discovered in 2010 in Magdalena de Cao (Quilter et al. 2010). It is from a previously unknown language. The list does not name the language involved, though it is generally assumed to represent Quingnam (Urban 2019a, 154; Adelaar and Muysken 2004, 620). Several of the number terms involve loanwords from Quechua—Quingnam <tau> : Cuzco Quechua *tawa* 'four'; <sut> : *suqta* 'six'; <canchen> : *qanchis* 'seven'; and < chari pachac> : *pachak* 'one hundred' (<chari> is Quingnam'one'). The other number words are in an otherwise unidentified language (Urban 2019a, 155).

As seen above, the Pescadora (Lengua Pescadora, Yunga Pescadora) of colonial sources is possibly to be equated with Quingnam or was a variety of that language (Adelaar and Muysken 2004, 620; Urban 2019a).

Qurigmã ([Quirigmã]) Brazil. Loukotka (1968, 94) gave Qurigmã [*sic*] as an "extinct language of the first inhabitants of São Salvador Bay, state of Bahia." The source of this seems to be Gabriel Soares de Souza's (1587) description of Brazil, cited in a number of publications, where, speaking of the "Tapuias," he says there are "others called Quirigmã; these were lords of the lands of Bahia and that is why Bahia is called: Quigrigmure. The Tupinambás removed them from their lands and became their lords, and the Tapuias went towards the south" (Souza 1971[1587], 55).[31]

Rabona Ecuador. Loukotka (1968, 156) called Rabona an "extinct language once spoken in the district of Santiago de las Montañas, Loja province." He placed it in his **Murato** stock. Several other classifiers grouped it with **Candoshi**. Adelaar and Muysken (2004, 397) mentioned that some of the few recorded items, mostly plant names, are similar to Candoshi words, but that Rabona also has other similarities with **Aguaruna** (Chicham family). They prefer to leave the classification undecided.

Ramanos Bolivia. The Ramanos were mentioned by Lázaro de Ribera at the end of the 1700s as inhabitants of the missionary settlement of Los Santos Reyes (Reyes de Moxos), now in Beni Department; Lázaro de Ribera recorded eight words of the language (Zamponi in press b; see also Seifart and Hammarström 2018). Raoul Zamponi (in press b) found similarities of four of the eight words with Arawakan words "rather suggestive." As he points out, one of the eight, *quimisa* 'three', is a loan from Quechua or Aymara *kimsa* 'three'. However, two of his four are not convincing; similarities to Ramanos *tatá* 'father' and *naná* 'mother' are found far and wide, examples of the nursery formations that do not necessarily owe their similarities in other languages to a shared common ancestry. With only five words not eliminated as loans or nursery forms, with "no special resemblance to the surrounding languages" (Zamponi in press b) for any of them, Ramanos should definitely be considered unclassified.

Rimarimá. See Himarimá (above).

Roramí (Oramí) Brazil. "Originally spoken in the Serra de Pão de Açucar, state of Pernambuco" (Loukotka 1968, 94).

Runa Colombia. ISO code 639-3 retired Runa in 2016 (https://iso639-3.sil.org/code/rna). It had been thought to be an unattested Chocoan language.[32]

Sácata (Sacata, Zácata, Chillao) Peru. Sácata is a dormant language of which only three words are known. Its speakers inhabited "the Marañon valley near Cujillo, province of Cutervo, and Yamón, province of Utcubamba, Amazonas" (Adelaar and Muysken 2004, 405). Sácata was "spoken in the village of Socota on the Chota River in the department of Cajamarca" (Loukotka 1968, 156). It has been classified with **Candoshi** (for example, by Rivet 1934, and by Loukotka 1968, 156, in what he called his Murato stock) and with Arawakan (Torero 2002, 292), but "the factual basis is insufficient for either conclusion" (Adelaar and Muysken 2004, 405).

Sacosi Bolivia. "Once spoken on the ancient Puerto de los Reyes" (Loukotka 1968, 167).

Sacracrinha (Sequaquirihen) Brazil. "Once spoken in the state of Bahia near the mouth of the Salitre River in the São Francisco River" (Loukotka 1968, 94).

Sanavirón Argentina. "Extinct language formerly spoken in the vicinity of the Salinas Grandes, province of Córdoba" (Loukotka 1968, 48). Loukotka considered it an "isolated language." Only six or seven words can be attributed to Sanavirón (Viegas Barros 2009, 3). Adelaar and Muysken (2004, 502) hold that this "amount of evidence is so small that possible genetic relationship could not be detected, even when [if] it existed." Loukotka (1935) speculated about a possible relationship with **Vilela**. Antonio Tovar (1961, 28) commented that because we do not have much data on the language, that causes difficult problems, but went on to mention possible kinship with **Comechingón, Diaguita**, or **Vilela** (see also Tovar and Larrucea de Tovar 1984, 30). Pedro Viegas Barros (2009) reinvestigated the hypothesis of a possible kinship for Sanavirón with Lule-Vilela, concluding that this hypothesis may never be proven, nor any other involving the classification of Sanavirón, due to how little is known of the language, but that the small number of forms that seem comparable with Lule-Vilela forms is quite significant.

Sapeiné Peru. "Language of an unknown tribe of the Napo River, Loreto" (Loukotka 1968, 179).

Seden Brazil. "Once spoken between the Negro and Uaruma Rivers, Amazonas" (Loukotka 1968, 229).

Shinabo. The name Shinabo appears sometimes in the literature as an alternative name for or possibly a dialect of **Chákobo** (Panoan family). Shinabo was retired from the ISO 639-3 codes in 2017 (https://iso639-3.sil.org/code/snh), as a non-existent Panoan language, according to *Glottolog* (https://glottolog.org/resource/languoid/id/shin1267).

Siberi Bolivia. "Once spoken on Xarayes Lagoon" (Loukotka 1968, 167).

Sintó (Assek, Upsuksinta) Paraguay. "Language of an unknown and warlike tribe in the interior of the Gran Chaco of Paraguay, north of the Choroti [Chorote] tribe" (Loukotka 1968, 63). Loukotka (1931a, 859) mentioned that it is possible that the **Upsucksinta** were just a remnant of the Enimaga Guentuse [Maká], adding that we do not know anything other than their name.

Sinú (Senú, Zenú) Colombia. Loukotka (1968, 257) call Zenú (Senú) an "extinct language once spoken between the Sinú and San Jorge Rivers, department of Bolivar." Though he said nothing was known of the language, he classified it with his Chocó stock. Adelaar and Muysken (2004, 624), however, list it with the languages that "cannot be classified for absence of data." They list as "subgroups" of Sinú (Zenú) **Fincenú, Pancenú, Sinufana,** and **Sutagao.**

Sipisipi Peru. "Once spoken in Peru" (Loukotka 1968, 273).[33]

Socorino Bolivia. "Once spoken in [Bolivia]" (Loukotka 1968, 167).

Stanatevogyet Paraguay. "Unknown language of the Paraguayan Chaco" (Loukotka 1968, 63).

Supeselo Argentina. "Lost language of the ancient mission of Santa Lucia, Corrientes province" (Loukotka 1968, 63).

Surucosi Bolivia. "Once spoken in [Bolivia]" (Loukotka 1968, 167).

Suruim Brazil. Loukotka (1968, 167) listed Suruim as an unknown or unclassified language formerly "spoken on the ... Machado River, Rondônia." This appears to be the same as Suruí (Paiter), a Tupían language of the Mondéan subfamily; the Machado River runs near their territory. They were first officially contacted in 1969, after Loukotka (1968) was written. Probably then, Suruim can be retired from the list of unknown languages.

Sutagao Colombia. Loukotka (1968, 129) placed Sutagao as a language "spoken once on the Pasca and Sumapaz Rivers, Meta territory." He said nothing was known of the language but still classified it as a member of the Caquetío Group in his Arawak stock. Adelaar and Muysken (2004, 624) placed Sutagao with the languages that cannot be classified for lack of data.

Tacunbiacu (Tacumbiacu) Bolivia. "Once spoken between the Guapay River and the Chiquitos plains" (Loukotka 1968, 167).

Taguaylen Argentina. "Lost language of the ancient mission of Santa Lucia, Corrientes province" (Loukotka 1968, 63).

Tacarúba (Tacarua) Brazil. "Once spoken on the island of Soroabé in the São Francisco River, state of Pernambuco" (Loukotka 1968, 94).

Taluhet Argentina. Loukotka (1968, 63) said of this language only that it was "formerly spoken in the plains of the province of Buenos Aires." However, Taluhet's story is part of the account of Chechehet (see below).

Tamacosi Bolivia. "Once spoken on the Guapay River near La Barranca, Santa Cruz province" (Loukotka 1968, 167).

Tamaní Colombia. "Unknown language spoken on the Quebrada de Tamini in Caquetá territory"(Loukotka 1968, 197).

Tamaquéu Brazil. "Once spoken on the São Francisco River in the state of Pernambuco, at the confluence with the Salitre River" (Loukotka 1968, 94).

Tamararé Brazil. "Once spoken at the sources of the Juruena and Galera Rivers, Mato Grosso" (Loukotka 1968, 167).

Tambaruré Brazil. "Once spoken in Rondônia at the mouth of the Apaxoná River" (Loukotka 1968, 167).

Taminani Brazil. "Once spoken on the Uaçá and Curupi Rivers, Amapá territory" (Loukotka 1968, 229).

Tanquihua Peru. "Once spoken around the city of Ayacucho, department of Ayacucho" (Loukotka 1968, 273).

Tapacurá Brazil. This could refer to Chapakurá; Tapacurá is an alternative name for **Chapacura** (a Chapacuran language). Loukotka (1968, 167), however, placed this "once spoken" Tapacurá on the Tapacurá-assú River in the state of Pará, which is a long way from Chapakuran territory.

Tapeba Brazil. Tapeba was listed in earlier editions of *Ethnologue* as extinct and unclassified, but was retired from the ISO 639-3 codes in 2020. The Tapeba people (also called Perna-de-pau) were formed from populations around Nossa Senhora dos Prazeres de Caucaia in Ceará, Brazil. They were federally recognized by FUNAI (National Indian Foundation of Brazil) as "Indians" (indigenous) in 1993, though they had no coherent ethnic identity before that. They speak Portuguese and have no indigenous language (https://pib.socioambiental.org/en/Povo:Tapeba, accessed August 13, 2021).

Tapuisú Brazil. "Once spoken at the mouth of the Maicuru River, Amapá territory" (Loukotka 1968, 229).

Tarairiú (Ochucuyana) Brazil. Tarairuiú was spoken "between the Assú and Apodí Rivers, in the state of of Grande do Norte" (Loutokta 1968, 90). It is sometimes listed as a language isolate, but it is too poorly attested for such a determination to be made (Zamponi in press b). Terrence Kaufman (1994, 70) noted that "not even Gr[eenberg] dares classify this language" (see also Kaufman 2007, 73). Some associated it with Gé or Macro-Jê languages (cf. Mason 1950, 302). Loutokta (1968, 90–91) classified it in his Tarairiú stock also with **Xoró, Janduí, Payacu, Panatí, Miñari, Panahi, Canindé, Genipapo, Camamu, Itañá**, (Baturité), **Candodú, Caratiú, Acriú**, and **Anasé**.

Tarimoxi Brazil. "Language of an unknown tribe to the north of the Guratégaja tribe, Rondônia" (Loukotka 1968, 167).

Taripio Brazil, Suriname. "Unknown language of an unknown tribe that lived to the north of the Reangú tribe in the frontier area of the Brazilian state of Pará and Dutch Guiana [Suriname]" (Loukotka 1968, 229).

Tavúri Brazil. "Once spoken on the Paranaiuba River, Mato Grosso" (Loukotka 1968, 167).

Tchagoyána Brazil. "Unknown language spoken between the Erepecurú and Acapú Rivers, state of Pará" (Loukotka 1968, 229).

Tchicoyna Brazil. "Unknown language spoken in the state of Pará, on the Cuátari River" (Loukotka 1968, 230).

Tegua Colombia. Adelaar and Muysken (2004, 624) place this among the languages that "cannot be classified for absence of data." This is apparently Loukotka's (1968, 129) **Tecua**, "once spoken on the Lengupa River in the village of Teguas, department of Boyacá." It is listed with the Caquetío group of his Arawak stock, though he said nothing is known of it.

Tembey Paraguay. The Tembey lived along the banks of the Tembey River of the Paraná Plateau in eastern Paraguay; they disappeared long ago. Only two words are known, collected in the 1890s. (Zamponi in press b.) (Not to be confused with Tembé, a Tupí-Guaraníian language of Brazil.)

Tepqui Peru. "Once spoken on the Santa María River, Huánuco" (Loukotka 1968, 179; see also Mason 1950, 272).

Tevircacap Brazil. "Spoken on the . . . Pimenta Bueno River, Rondônia" (Loukotka 1968, 167).

Tiboi Bolivia. "Unknown language, exact location unknown" (Loukotka 1968, 167).

Timaná Colombia. Adelaar and Muysken (2004, 624) give Timaná as one of the languages that "cannot be classified for absence of data." Loukotka (1968, 245) thought Timaná (Timine) belonged to the **Andaquí** Group of his Chibcha Stock, though he said nothing was known of it. Loutotka (1968, 245) located it "on the Magdalena and Guarapas Rivers around the city of Timaná."

Timba Colombia. Loukotka (1968, 259) gave Timba as "an extinct language once spoken in the department of Valle de Cauca, on the Canambre River." He included it with several other languages of the region in his Yurimangui stock, though he noted that nothing was known of any of them.

Tingán (Tingan) Peru. "Spoken at the mouth of the Monzón River, Huánuco" (Loukotka 1968, 179; see also Mason 1950, 272).

Tingui-Boto (Tingui, Tingui-Botó, Carapató, Karapató, Dzubukuá) Brazil. *Ethnologue* (2023) lists Tingui-Boto as dormant and unclassified, from Alagoas state. However, *Glottolog* has removed it, saying "there is certainly a corresponding [Tingui-Boto] ethnic group, but this group speaks Portuguese. They retain some of their ancestral language for ritual purposes, but this language is Dzubukuá" (https://glottolog.org/resource/languoid/id/ting1238l, accessed September 1, 2021). **Dzubukuá** belongs to the Karirían family (see Chapter 4; see also *Povos Indígenas no Brasil*, https://pib.socioambiental.org/pt/Povo:Tingui_Botó).

Tobachana Brazil. "Once spoken between the Juruá and Jurí Rivers south of the Itipuna tribe, state of Amazonas" (Loukotka 1968, 197).

Tohazana Venezuela. "Once spoken in Venezuela" (Loukotka 1968, 230).

Tomata Bolivia. "Once spoken near the city of Tupiza, Potosí province" (Loukotka 1968, 273).

Tomedes (Tamudes) Colombia. Tomedes has been presumed to be a dormant Arawakan language; however, it was retired from the ISO 639-3 codes in 2016 (https://iso639-3.sil.org/code/toe), for being non-existent.

Tomina Bolivia. "Once spoken between the Mizque and Pilcomayo Riveres, Chuquisaca province" (Loukotka 1968, 273).

Tonocoté Argentina. Though often identified with **Lule**, the identification is uncertain and disputed. The Tonocoté were commented on with frequency in colonial sources and in works on early Argentinian history, but both their identity and location seem particularly unclear and confused. Though Maccioni [Machoni] (2008[1732]) considered Lule and Tonocoté together, other sources seem to contradict Machoni's view of Tonocoté identity. Different proposals have sought to identify it with several other languages of the Chaco region (Mason 1950, 208; cf. Adelaar and Muysken 2004, 385–386; Tovar 1961, 46). The Tonocoté were associated with a reasonably wide area from the Bermejo River to Santiago de Estero and Tucumán. The language is essentially without any attestation.

Tororí Brazil. "Once spoken on . . . the Madeira River north of the Parintintin tribe, sate of Amazonas" (Loukotka 1968, 167).

Truká [tka]. Brazil. *Ethnologue* (2023) has Truká as a dormant, unclassified language of Bahia and Pernambuco states. *Socioambiental* gives its location as on the island of Assunçao in the middle course of the São Francisco River, in the município of Cabrobó (https://pib.socioambiental.org/pt/Povo:Truká, accessed September 2, 2021). (See also Fabre 1998, 1020.)

Tremembé (Teremembe, Taramembé) Brazil. Loukotka (1968, 94) had Teremembe as "originally spoken by a primitive tribe on the coast between the mouth of the Monim River and the mouth of the Chorro River, state of Ceará." *Ethnologue* (2023) also has Tremembé as unclassified and dormant. Alain Fabre (1998, 1019) gives Tremembé as a language of unknown affiliation, though definitely not Tupían.

Tubichaminí Argentina. Loukotka (1968, 48) had this language as formerly spoken on the Tubichaminí River, province of Buenos Aires, classified as a member of his Chechehet stock, now abandoned (see Chechehet below for details). Pedro Viegas Barros (2015, 76) noted that the name Tubichaminí appears to have been applied to the Querandí or to factions of them.

Tucumanduba Brazil. "Spoken on the upper course of the Canacau River . . . Amazonas" (Loukotka 1968, 197).

Tulumayo Peru. "Once spoken on the Muna, Azul and Aguaytia Rivers, Huánuco" (Loukotka 1968, 179; see also Mason 1950, 272).[34]

Tupijó Brazil. "Once spoken in the state of Bahia by the neighbors of the Maracá tribe" (Loukotka 1968, 94).

Tupiniquim Brazil. Tupiniquim is the name of a group of people; it is not a language name. The Tupiniquim were widespread in the Brazilian states of Espírito Santo, Maranhão, and Bahia. They are descendants of the Tupinambá (Coastal Tupí); they spoke **Tupinambá**, a long dormant Tupían language. The Tupiniquim are very often mentioned but they are one of the least-known Indigenous peoples of Brazil. In Brazilian Portuguese the word *Tupiniquim* is sometimes used as a synonym for 'national', or 'Brazilian'. (https://pib.socioambiental.org/en/Povo:Tupiniquim, accessed August 15, 2021.)

Tupiokón Brazil. "Unknown language spoken on the Paxiuba River, Mato Grosso" (Loukotka 1968, 168).

Tutura Bolivia. "Once spoken around the city of Totora, Cochabamba province" (Loukotka 1968, 273).

Tuxá (Tushá, Tuxa, Rodela) Brazil. Loukotka (1968, 87–88) considered Tuxá an "isolated language," placing it originally "on the São Francisco River near Gloria, now in the village of Rodelas, state of Pernambuco." Others have also sometimes listed Tuxá as a language isolate, but it is too poorly attested to make such a determination. Between 1931 and 1975, when the language was already seriously endangered, some Tuxá material was obtained, fourteen words in 1931 and two short wordlists from the same woman (from 1961 and 1975) with one sentence. An unresolved problem, however, is that many of the words for the same glosses from the earlier list and the later sources are completely different (Zamponi in press b). It is best considered unclassified. Joseph Greenberg (1987, 385) put "Tusha" in his Equatorial grouping despite not presenting a single word from that language in his supposed Equatorial cognates (Alain Fabre, Tuxá, http://www.ling.fi/Entradas%20diccionario/Dic=Tuxa.pdf, accessed March 21, 2022).

Uairua Brazil. "Once spoken between the Juruá and Jaracui Rivers" (Loukotka 1968, 197).

Uauarate Brazil. "Once spoken on the Juraí River north of the Catuquina tribe" (Loukotka 1968, 197).

Unainuman Brazil. This language, of the Paman River, is known only from Johann Natterer's list from the first half of the 1800s of 170 words, only 56 of which are given with translations (Zamponi in press b). "The language recorded by Natterer is not relatable to any known languages of northwest Amazonia" (Zamponi in press b). *Glottolog* has it as "unclassifiable" (https://glottolog.org/resource/languoid/id/unai1234).

Uranaju Brazil. "Once spoken on the middle course of the Araguari River, Amapá" (Loukotka 1968, 230).

Urucuai Brazil. "Once spoken on the Corumbiara River, Rondônia" (Loukotka 1968, 168).

Uruma Brazil. "Once spoken in the state of Sergipe on the São Francisco River" (Loukotka 1968, 95).

Uru-Pa-In Brazil. There is confusion regarding Uru-Pa-In. Sometimes the Uru-Pa-In are considered a mostly uncontacted subgroup of the **Uru-Eu-Wau-Wau**, speakers of a Tupí-Guaraníán language of the Kawahib branch of Tupí-Guaraníán (Tupían family), but occasionally Uru-Pa-In has been given as just an alternate name for Uru-Eu-Wau-Wau. *Ethnologue* (2023) considers Uru-Pa-In a stable Tupí-Guaraníán language of the Kawahib subgroup, of Ariquemes, Rondônia, with fewer than "10k" speakers, spoken by a group with no permanent contact (https://www.ethnologue.com/language/urp/). However, *Glottolog* lists Uru-Pa-In as "unclassifiable," citing *Ethnologue* (2021) as its source (https://glottolog.org/resource/languoid/id/urup1235, accessed September 2, 2021).

Urupuca Brazil. "Once spoken on the Urupuca River, Minas Gerais" (Loukotka 1968, 87).

Ururi Brazil. "Once spoken in the state of Mato Grosso, exact location unknown" (Loukotka 1968, 87).

Vanherei Brazil. "Once spoken at the sources of the Piquiri River, stat of Mao Grosso" (Loukotka 1968, 87).

Vouve Brazil. "Extinct language once spoken on the Piancó River, Pernambuco state" (Loukotka 1968, 95).

Waitaká (Guaitacá, Goyatacá, Goytacaz) Brazil. Loukotka (1968, 68) reported this language together with several others as "extinct or unknown languages that may have belonged to the same linguistic group [his Puri stock], "formerly spoken on the São Mateo River and in the vicinity of Cabo de São Tomé, state of Rio de Janeiro." J. Alden Mason (1950, 300–301) had a Guaitacán family with four subdivisions of Guaitacá: **Mopi**, **Yacorito**, **Wasu**, and **Miri**. He said, however, that "as *Guaitacá* became extinct before a word of it was recorded . . . it cannot be regarded as anything but an unclassified language . . . It very likely, however, was a *Macro-Ge* language." Aryon Rodrigues (1999, 167) agreed; he thought that Waitaká "probably belonged to the Purí family of Macro-Je," but it became "extinct and no record . . . has been preserved." Now Purí (Purí-Coroado) is excluded from Macro-Jê (see Chapters 4 and 6).

Wakoná (Wacona, Aconan) Brazil. Loukotka (1968, 92) had Aconan (Wakona) among unclassified or unknown languages, "originally spoken around Lagoa Comprida and in Penedo; now survivors of the original tribe . . . are found in the city of Pôrto Real do Colégio." *Ethnologue* (2023) has Wakoná an unclassified and dormant.

Walêcoxô Brazil. "Unknown language from the city of Cimbres, Pernambuco" (Loukotka 1968, 95).

Wamoé (Uamué, Huamoé, Uame, Huamoí, Huamâe, Huamué, Humon, Umã, Umâe, Uman, Umão, Urumão) Brazil. "Old accounts of the Uamué . . . locate them in a territory stretching south of the Ceará River until the banks of the São Francisco" (Zamponi in press b).

This language is typically listed as a language isolate in the linguistic literature; however, that is not supported. In 1961 Menno Kroeker collected circa 160 words and some short constructions from three men in different locations, but "this material clearly does not represent a reliable specimen of the old language of the Uamué" (Zamponi in press b). Several of the words appear to be slightly changed Portuguese, several others are Tupí; the three men did not agree upon the words that they gave; and Kroeker suspected that the men gave him wrong forms, trying to protect their culture from outsiders. "It remains unclear if any genuine words from the lost Uamué language have been transmitted to their present-day . . . 'descendants'" (Zamponi in press b).

Wasu (Waçu, Wassu, Wassú) Brazil. *Ethnologue* (2023) has Wasu as dormant and unclassified, in Alagoas state. (See also Fabre 1998, 1203.) As mentioned above, J. Alden Mason (1950, 301) had Wasu as a subdivision of Guaitacá (Waitaká).

Wau Peru. "Language of an unknown tribe on the Coca River, Loreto" (Loukotka 1968, 179).

Xaquese Bolivia. "Once spoken on the Puerto de los Reyes" (Loukotka 1968, 168).

Xaray Boliva. "Extinct and unknown language once spoken on Xarayes Lagoon" (Loukotka 1968, 168).

Xibata Brazil. "Unknown language of a tribe in the state of Ceará. Exact location is unknown" (Loukotka 1968, 95).

Xipará Brazil. "Once spoken between the Urubú and Jatapú Rivers, state of Amazonas" (Loukotka 1968, 230).

Xipináwa (Shipinawa) Brazil. Loukotka (1968, 172) listed Xipináwa as a member of his Pano stock, spoken between the Humaiá and Liberdade Rivers, of which he said nothing was known. However, it was retired in 2016 from the ISO 639-3 codes (https://iso639-3.sil.org/code/xip). *Glottolog* lists is as an unattested, non-existent language (under Pano-Tacanan) (https://glottolog.org/resource/languoid/id/xipi1238, accessed September 2, 2021). David Fleck (2013, 89) lists Shipinawa (with alternative spellings of Chepenagua, Chipinawa, Sipinawa, Šipinawa) among the ethnonyms that have been claimed to be Panoan but for which no linguistic data exist. It was mentioned as a dialect of Shipibo in a source from 1788 (Fleck 2013, 14).

Xiroa Ecuador. Xiroa is mentioned among languages of Ecuador in early sources, but it may be just a variant spelling of Jívaro (Adelaar and Muysken 2004, 393, 397).

Xokó (Xocó, Shoco, Shokó, Chocó, Chocaz) Brazil. This language was originally spoken on the Piancó River, Pernambuco (Loukotka 1968, 88). Only five words are known, collected in 1935 from descendants of Xokó in Pôrto Real do Colégio, in Alagoas state. In classifications of South American languages Xokó has typically been listed among the language isolates, as Loukotka did; however, it really belongs with the languages too poorly known to be classified (Zamponi in press b).

Yalcón Colombia. Loukotka (1968, 245) gave this language as "once spoken between the Madgalena and La Plata Rivers," in the Andaquí Group of his Chibcha stock, though he said nothing was known of it. Adelaar and Muysken (2004, 624) hold that it "cannot be classified for absence of data."

Yamesí Colombia. "Once spoken at the mouth of the Necchi River and on the Porce River" (Loukotka 1968, 239). Loukotka included Yamesi in the Antioquia Group of his Chibcha stock, in spite of saying that "only a single word" was known. Adelaar and Muysken (2004, 624) list it with the languages that "cannot be classified for absence of data."[35]

Yampará Bolivia. "Once spoken on the middle course of the Pilcomayo River, Chuquisaca province" (Loukotka 1968, 273).

Yaperú (Naperú, Apirú) Paraguay. "Once spoken in Paraguay near Asunción" (Loukotka 1968, 87).

Yarí Colombia. Adelaar and Muysken (2004, 623) included Yarí among the languages that "cannot be classified for absence of data" (see also Fabre (1998, 1242). Former editions of *Ethnologue* had Yarí as possibly a dialect of **Carijona** (Cariban). Yarí has been retired as "non-existent" from the ISO 639-3 codes since 2016 (https://iso639-3.sil.org/code/yri, https://glottolog.org/resource/languoid/id/yari1235, accessed September 2, 2021).

Yariguí (Yarigüí) Colombia. Adelaar and Muysken (2004, 624) placed this language among those that "cannot be classified for absence of data." It was often assumed to belong to Cariban, following Loukotka (1968, 220), who put it in the Opone group of his Karaib stock, though he said nothing was known of it. He gave its location as "once spoken on the Sogamosos River and in Barranca Bermeja," Santander department.

Yauei Brazil. "Once spoken on the . . . Madeira River across from the mouth of the Aripuanã River, state of Amazonas" (Loukotka 1968, 168).

Yenmu Colombia. "Unknown language spoken on the Curé River, Amazonas territory" (Loukotka 1968, 197).

Yoemanai Brazil. "Extinct language once spoken on the right bank and at the mouth of the Purus River, Amazonas state" (Loukotka 1968, 198).

Yolo (Paripazo) Colombia. "Once spoken on the San Joaquín River, department of Valle de Cauca" (Loukotka 1968, 259). Loukotka classified this and a number of other purported languages from the same region in his Yurimangui stock, though he noted that nothing is known of any of them.

Yufiua Brazil. "Once spoken south of the Coeruna tribe on the Japurá River" (Loukotka 1968, 19).

Yumbo Ecuador. Loukotka (1968, 248) had Yumbo in the Barbácoa Group of his Chibcha stock (nothing known of it), "once spoken in the Cordillera de Intag and the Cordillera de Nanegal, Pichincha province." Adelaar and Muysken (2004, 624) considered it a language that "cannot be classified for absence of data."

Yurimagua (Zurimagua, Jurimagua, Yoriman) Peru. "Once spoken along the Amazon River to the mouth of the Purus River" (Loukotka 1968, 117). Mason (1950, 240) had Yurimagua (Zurimagua) as an independent language, mentioning that it had generally been considered Tupían.

Zapazo Peru. Loukotka (1968, 154) had Zapazo as an "extinct language... once spoken on the Saposoa River." He said nothing was known of it, but still placed it in his Munichi stock (see also Mason 1950, 272).

Zuana Brazil. "Once spoken on the Amazon River south of the mouth of the Cafuá River, state of Amazonas" (Loukotka 1968, 198).

Zurina Brazil. "Once spoken at the mouth of the Mamorí River, Amazonas" (Loukotka 1968, 168).

As mentioned, other putative language names could be added to this list, while several need to be removed. As Willem Adelaar points out (personal communication), a number of "language" names were originally included in classifications based on the once widespread but mistaken view that Quechua was originally only spoken in the Cuzco area, and so every other area must have had its own language. Thus the following (and others) listed as languages by Loukotka (1968) are doubted and not included in the list above: *Arequipa* Peru (Loukotka 1968, 272); *Cajatambo* Peru (Loukotka 1968, 272); *Camana* (Maje) Peru (Loukotka 1968, 272); *Chancay* Peru (Loukotka 1968, 272); *Chincha* Peru (Loukotka 1968, 272); *Chucurpu* (Chocorvo) Peru (Loukotka 1968, 272); *Chupacho* Peru (Loukotka 1968, 179); *Cutervo* (Huambo) Peru (Loukotka 1968, 272); *Huacho* Peru (Loukotka 1968, 272); *Huamachuco* Peru (Loukotka 1968, 272); *Huamalí* Peru (Loukotka 1968, 272); *Huamanga* (Loukotka 1968:/272); *Huanca* (Wanka) Peru (Loukotka 1968, 272); *Hunacabamba* Peru (*sic*, for Huancabamba, Loukotka 1968, 272); *Ica* Peru (Loukotka 1968, 273) (not to be confused with Chibchan Ica [Ika]); *Lampa* Peru (Loukotka 1968, 273); *Mizque* Bolivia (Loukotka 1968, 273); *Nazca* Peru (Loukotka 1968, 273); *Pocra* Peru (Loukotka 1968, 273); *Rimac* Peru (Loukotka 1968, 273); *Rucana* Peru (Loukotka 1968, 273); *Sora* Peru (Loukotka 1968, 273); *Supe* Peru (Loukotka 1968, 273); *Tarapaca* Chile (Loukotka 1968, 273); and *Yauyo* Peru (Loukotka 1968, 273).

5.5. PHANTOM, FALSE, AND SPURIOUS LANGUAGES

Not only are there many unknown and unclassified languages, and some mistaken ones, but there are also several phantom languages and attempted hoaxes or fakes. They are the subject of this section. Perhaps some of those listed above, particularly many of those that have been retired from the ISO 639-3 codes and so from *Ethnologue* and *Glottolog*, might fit better here.

5.5.1. Phantom, False, and Spurious Languages of North America

Taensa (a.k.a. Tansa, Hastri). The best-known case of what is assumed to be a faked language in the history of North American Indian linguistics is the "curious hoax of the Taensa language" (Brinton 1890, 452). The presumed hoax was perpetrated in the early 1880s by then-nineteen-year-old Jean Parisot, seminary student in Plombières, France, and his friend A. Dejouy. Parisot claimed that after the death of his maternal grandfather, Jean-Dominic Haumonté, he found in his grandfather's library an undated, anonymous manuscript of a grammar and vocabulary, with some texts, of the Taensa language of Louisiana, written in Spanish, which allegedly his grandfather had transcribed (Haumonté et al. 1882).

Parisot's publications on the purported language are Parisot (1880, 1882), Haumonté et al. (1882), and Anonymous (1881). The name Taensa is that of a known Indigenous people, but their language was otherwise undocumented. Authenticity of Parisot's "Taensa language" was vehemently disputed by the leading Americanists of the time. It was defended as genuine by Lucien Adam, Julien Vinson, and initially Albert S. Gatschet; it was rejected by Daniel G. Brinton (1885, 1890), and by John R. Swanton (1911, 1946), among others. Claire Bowern (2019) has recently raised questions about whether the assessment of it as a hoax is actually accurate.

Some of the arguments against the authenticity of this "Taensa" were inaccurate and unpersuasive while others seem more on target. On the mistaken or less persuasive side were arguments of the following sort. Brinton's (1885, 1890) principal reason for calling it a hoax appears to be because the materials did not appear to reflect polysynthesis—a typological trait where single words with their affixes translate as a whole sentence in European languages—something Brinton (like several others before him) believed was a trait true of all American Indian languages (see Campbell 1997a, 26–85). Of course, it is now known that not all Indigenous languages of the Americas are very polysynthetic, though most are— some are even closer to being isolating (languages where each morpheme is an independent word and there is no or at least very little bound morphology). Some other grammatical traits said not to be found in North American Indian languages but seen in the "Taensa" materials turned out to be known in at least some Native American languages. For example, a grammatical gender contrast is actually an areal feature shared by many languages of the Southeast Linguistics Area, and it is also a trait of the Northwest Coast Linguistic Area (see Chapter 7). The Taensa grammar had a "dual" contrast, said to be absent from languages of the Americas, but a grammatical dual category is actually known in several of the Native American languages (see Mithun 1999, 79, 93, 94, 456), and it is an areal trait of the Pueblo Linguistic Area (Bereznak 1995). Swanton erred when he claimed that certain things mentioned in the vocabulary were absent from the region: snow, ice, sugar maples, wild rice, and ox carts. They were not unknown there.

On the side more convincing that it was a hoax, Albert Gatschet (1891b) showed evidence that the Taensa tribe survived at least a good sixty years later than Brinton had assumed to be the case. Importantly, Swanton (1908a, 1946, 239) found contemporary statements that said that the language spoken by the Taensa Indians was Natchez. The Spanish in the materials seemed awkward, and some of it is ungrammatical, unlikely to have been written by a native speaker; there are many errors in the Spanish that reflect French influence. The alleged original documents were never shown by Parisot. (See Auroux 1984; Bowern 2019; see also Parisot 1880, 1882; Hautmonté, Parisot, and Adam 1882; Adam 1885; Brinton 1890; and Sturtevant 2005, 42–44.)

5.5.2. *Phantom, False, and Spurious Languages of Middle America*

A few languages that in fact never existed have been included repeatedly in the literature on languages of Mesoamerica, mistaken for different reasons.

Aguacatec II (of Aguacatán, Guatemala) was made up by Otto Stoll's maid (Stoll 1958[1884], 244). Stoll mentioned 300 words she produced, but he presented only 68, saying the others were too suspicious; many of the published 68 are suspicious also. No one before or after Stoll ever found anything similar to Aguacatec II. Aguacatán is the center of Awakatek (Aguacatec), a Mayan language of the Mamean subgroup. There are no non-Mayan languages near this part of Guatemala.

Corobisi. Corobisi is a name found in Spanish sixteenth- and seventeenth-century sources, but no word of this language is known. Eduard Conzemius (1930), nevertheless, equated a wordlist from Upala, Costa Rica, with the Corobisi language, though Upala is not in the area attributed to the Corobisi. This wordlist turned out to be from **Rama**—the Corobisi of Conzemius' list and Rama are not distinct languages. Nevertheless, Joseph Greenberg (1987, 111, 382) classified Corobisi as distinct, related to Guatuso, Cabécar, and Rama, on the basis of one single cited "Corobisi" word, *kur* 'hear'.

Membreno. Joseph Greenberg (1987) classified *Membreno* as a Lencan language, but there is no "Membreno" language. Greenberg (1987, 194, 293, 382) had mistakenly labelled as "Membreno" material he had taken from Alberto Membreño's (1897) book. He misspelled it as <Membreno> and considered it a language, classifying it as belonging to Lenca, an assumed member of the Chibchan branch of his Chibchan-Paezan division of Amerind (Greenberg 1987, 382).

Pupuluca of Conguaco. Colonial sources say Pupuluca or Populuca was spoken in Conguaco and in nearby towns near the Guatemalan Pacific Coast. But Pupuluca (Popoloca, Popoluca) is a common designation for a number of languages, from Nahuatl *popoloka* 'to babble, speak language badly, unintelligibly'. Otto Stoll (1958[1884]) found a manuscript bearing Popoluca as the name of the language it was written in, and he assumed it was from Conguaco. It turned out to be from Oluta, Veracruz, where the Mixean language Oluta Popoluca is spoken. Whatever Pupuluca of Conguaco may have been, it was not Oluta Popoluca, a Mixe-Zoquean language. Judging from geography, the language of Conguaco was probably a Xinkan language, possibly a variant of one of the four known Xinkan tongues. Other Xinkan languages were sometimes referred to as "Populuca" in some colonial sources, from example "populuca de Guazacapán" for Guazacapán Xinka (see for example Lardé y Larín 1926). However, Pupuluca de Conguaco is utterly unattested and so unless new information should surface, we will never know its linguistic identity for certain.

Subinhá. Catherine the Great's project of collecting samples of all the world's languages received lists from the Audience of Guatemala in 1788–1789, including one entitled "Subinhá," said to be from Socoltenango, Chiapas. Based on this, Subinhá was thought for a long time to be a separate Mayan language. However, examination showed every other word in the list to be Tzeltal alternating with Tojolab'al (Tzeltal for even numbered words, Tojolab'al for odd numbered ones). I found only Tzeltal spoken in Socoltenango (Campbell 1987, 555).

Tapachultec II. Karl Sapper (1912), the "discoverer" of Tapachultec (in Chiapas, Mexico, near the Guatemalan border), was convinced it belonged to Mixe-Zoquean, but he lost his field notes during his return journey to Germany. He attempted to obtain new data through correspondence with A. Ricke, German vice consul in Tapachula. The forms sent by Ricke (obtained from mestizos) so surprised Sapper by their difference from his memory of what he had collected earlier (and lost) that he believed Tapachula to have two distinct languages. Walter Lehmann (1920), a student of Sapper's, later found that in reality only one language was spoken in Tapachula, but he followed his teacher in speaking of two—he separated the Tapachultec vocabulary into two segments, calling Tapachultec I the forms for which he could discover equivalences in other Mixe-Zoquean languages, and calling Tapachultec II the portion of the Tapachultec vocabulary for which he could not find counterparts elsewhere in Mixe-Zoquean. There were never two distinct Tapachultec languages, only one.

5.5.3. Phantom, False, and Spurious Languages of South America

Several phantom languages and false identifications have figured in classifications of South American languages. The main ones follow.

Aksanás. Aksaná(s) as a separate language is now abandoned (Clairis 1978, 32; 1985, 756). It is due to Hammerly Dupuy's misidentification of a variety of Kawesqar as a distinct language. Hammerly Dupuy (1947a, 1947b, 1952) compared fifty words from a 1698 vocabulary taken down by the French pirate Jean de la Guilbaudière with one Hammerly Dupuy himself had taken down and found the two to be different. Christos Clairis (1985, 756) explained the method that resulted in the misidentification:

> Taking the word 'water' for which la Guilbaudière noted *arret* [sic], Hammerly listed *čafalai*... Guilbaudière... showed the Qawasqar a bucket of water... and did not notice that their response was to the receptacle and not to the contents. Thus, *aret* means 'container of liquid'.

Loukotka (1968), following Hammerly Dupuy, considered Aksanas a language isolate distinct from Alakaluf (Kawesqar), and several others followed him in their classifications.[36]

Arda. Arda is a Gbe language of Africa, mistakenly identified with the Arda tribe of Colombia. As J. Alden Mason (1950, 234–235) explained:

> *Arda* was accepted as an independent [South American] linguistic family by all authorities from 1858 to 1924... based on a Doctrina in a language of this name, the Lord's Prayer... published... in 1858... Paul Rivet... examined the original manuscript in Madrid... he compared the words with modern *Dahomean* in Africa and determined their close relationship, especially to the *Popo* dialect. The text was evidently taken in the Slave Coast Kingdom of Arda, and the language has therefore no relation to that of the *Arda* tribe of southeastern Colombia, an extinct group probably related to the *Peba, Yagua,* and *Yameo*.

Chechehet ("Pampa"), **Chechehet family** Argentina. Loukotka (1968, 48) listed Chechehet as a member of his Chechehet stock, which he said was an "extinct language formerly spoken in the Sierra Ventana, Argentine province of Buenos Aires." This stems from a confusion with a long history. In the middle of the 1700s, Jesuit missionary Tomás Falkner distinguished several ethnic groups in the northeast of the pampas region that were apparently not Araucanian (**Mapudungun**); they included Chechehet, Dihuihet, Taluhet, and Tehuelhet. Robert Lehmann-Nitsche (1922) surmised that they must have spoken languages characterized by a demonym (ethnic group name) ending -*het*, and on this basis he postulated a "Het" language family with several members, though he later reduced it to a single language, "Chechehet" (Lehmann-Nitsche 1930), to which he attributed a few words collected by missionaries in the south of Buenos Aires province (Viegas Barros 2015, 40). Loukotka's "Chechehet stock" follows Lehmann-Nitsche, as did several other classifications (see Mason 1950, 309), though Antonio Tovar (1961, 26) thought that it lacked foundation. Pedro Viegas Barros (2015, 77) concluded from his examination of Lehmann-Nitsche's "Het" that:

> It is a phantom linguistic family, since it is based on uncertain data, attributable to the Gününa Yajüch or even to some Chon language . . . However, even in recent works by anthropologists and linguists reference continues to be made from time to time to the languages (or to a linguistic family) "Het."
>
> It is certain that the existing documentation for the language or languages of the pre-Mapuche [pre-Mapudungun] aborigines of the northern Pampas is very sparce and of interpretation (many times) too conjectural to be able to draw definitive conclusions.[37]

Viegas Barros (1992, 3) explained that "Chechehet" is one of the alternative names that **Gününa Küne** has been called.

Hongote. Morris Swadesh (1959, 1962) grouped Hongote with Mosetén and Chon in his "Sonchon" grouping, followed by Greenberg (1987, 105, 383), who listed Hongote as a member of his Patagonian languages (Chonan). Based on a single supposed Hongote word as evidence, *čalas* 'three', Greenberg grouped these languages in the "Andean" branch of his Amerind hypothesis (see Chapter 6). The error comes from Daniel Brinton's (1892b, 1892c, 1892d) reference to two colonial vocabularies with this name, which he included among dialects of Patagonian, but one of the vocabularies was actually from a Salishan language (**Songish**?, Northern Straits Salish), the other from **Tlingit**, both of the northwest coast of North America. The error has been corrected many times, although Hongote has continued to be listed among South American languages (cf. Viegas Barros 2005a, 80–81).

Kukurá (Cucurá, Kokura, Kukura). Kukurá has continued to be listed as a language isolate in classifications of South American languages, stemming from confusion between A. von Frič and Guzmán, his interpreter. Curt Nimuendajú (1932) exposed the misidentification right after Loukotka (1931b) presented Kukura as a new and isolated language (repeated in Loukotka 1968, 83). Von Frič's interpreter had fabricated the wordlist given as Kukurá, about half in badly pronounced **Guaraní** and the other half faked. As Nimuendajú revealed, Guzmán had also falsified wordlists for some other languages where he had been the interpreter (Zamponi in press b).

Wayteka (Chono, Wurk-wur-we). This non-existent language is due to Manuel Llaras Samitier (1967), who believed that a language called "Chono" or Wayteka or Wurk-wur-we was spoken in the north of the **Kawesqar** area, not related to "Alakaluf" (Kawesqar). The "evidence" was a "Wayteka" vocabulary of ninety-seven items, which turned out to be a mixture of words taken from different sources, from **Mapudungu**, **Gününa Küne**, Kawesqar, and **Tehuelche**, with some material added by Llaras Samitier and some that appears to be invented (Viegas Barros 1990, 48; 2005a, 46).[38]

5.5.4. Other Language Fakes

Let me finish this discussion with a note about "fakers," who actually are not speakers of a language of interest but try to fake a language.

In fieldwork in Central America and Mexico scattered over several years, a few times I came upon individuals who attempted to fake a language, to fabricate what they hoped I would take to be an Indigenous language. New, previously unidentified languages are discovered on occasion, but extremely rarely now in Mesoamerica. So it is conceivable though not likely that some language not previously known that is given by someone could turn out to be a new language. Fortunately, the attempted fakings of a language that I have encountered have characteristics that make them really easy to distinguish from real languages.[39] Cases of attempted fake languages that I experienced include what I call:

Fake "Pipil" of Comapa, Guatemala
Fake "Pipil" of Panchimalco, El Salvador
Unidentified "language" of La Trinitaria region, Chiapas, Mexico
Las Cumbres, Chiapas "mystery" language
Guatemala "mystery" language.

Given the large number of potential speakers of various languages that I talked with over the years, this number of actual attempted language deceptions does not strike me as remarkable.

Among whatever motives there might be for why someone would try to forge a counterfeit language, two stand out. In some cases the faker was hoping to make money from his/her deception. Because I paid consultants for their work with me on their languages, some fakers showed up hoping to cash in on the funny gringo's strange language interest. The other main motive was personal status. In two instances, particular individuals were recognized as the repository of local cultural and linguistic knowledge, a symbol of the town's heritage, and this reputation gave them a status in their communities that they clearly enjoyed.

For example, in Comapa, Department of Jutiapa, Guatemala (near the El Salvador border), Pipil (Nawat) used to be spoken. When I visited Comapa to find out whether there might still be any speakers, an elderly woman there enjoyed the position of being a symbol of Comapa's Indigenous heritage. Unfortunately, Pipil had ceased to be spoken there at least two generations before her time. She knew only four or five words of Pipil, learned as a girl from elders who remembered some words from the last speakers. Together in a group, several town leaders took me to visit her with the expectation that she would through her language represent the heritage and pride of the community. To save face, she attempted to fake answers to my questions about "how do you say such-and-such in Pipil." That she did not know the language and that she was attempting to invent answers became apparent almost immediately. I felt for her and definitely did not want to embarrass her, so I quietly suspended the interview and thanked her for allowing me to learn about her language, and paid her for her time. In the cases of sheer fraud that seemed to be based on hopes of payment, I just did not pay; I just politely told them that this was not the language I was looking for and so could not pay for it.

Vocabulary fabrication seems to be the main thing these fakers attempted to do, even if they are unable to keep it up for very long. The fakers soon ran out of steam, unable to continue producing new "words." They would start repeating "words" already given though saying that they had radically different meanings from the meanings offered earlier. They often cribbed from Spanish, sometimes offering archaic or rare Spanish words that they thought I, a foreigner, would not know, or they gave essentially Spanish words but changed them somewhat so as not to be identical to Spanish. For example, when asked for the word for *lechuza* 'barn owl', one faker gave me *avis* [áβis], a slightly modified version of Spanish *aves* [áβes] 'birds'. As interviews went on, the fakers had greater difficulty keeping up the act, with coming up with additional created stuff. In all these attempted fakings of language, the material offered did not differ in pronunciation or structure from that of their main language, Spanish in these cases. The invented forms contained no non-Spanish phonetic material. A characteristic of all these fakers was that when they were asked again for something already elicited earlier in the session, they could almost never repeat what they had given and rather gave something with no connection to what they had said before. The fabricated material never revealed anything of a grammatical nature, and none of the fakers was able to offer whole sentences or even phrases in the made-up language.

So, in all these cases it was very easy to detect the attempts to fake a language (see Campbell 2014 for details).

NOTES

1. "*Chamuscado*" means 'scorched' in Spanish, so named for his red beard.
2. Actually, it is one word and one two-word phrase that also contains the single word in it, 'water' and 'give me water!'
3. The *tl* of *yecotl* suggests Nahuatl or Nahuatl influence, since the lateral affricate *tl* is extremely rare in Mexico. It is found in Classical Nahuatl and closely related varieties of Nahua. However, there is no word in Nahuatl similar to *yecotl* (nor *ecotl*) with this meaning or any other.
4. In Mexican Spanish, *quemador* can mean a 'burner', 'stinging nettle', or 'a kind of stinging caterpillar', making the intended meaning of the gloss given in this case uncertain.
5. Miller (1983, 331) gave "Cazan" as another language but this appears to be a typing error for "Cazcan"; Miller did not list *Cazcan* or *Caxcan*. He said Pennington (1969, 10) mentions the Cazan in connection with defining the limits of the Tepehuan; he said it was located to the south and east of the **Tepehuan** and to the west of the **Guachichil**. Pennington, however, mentions only "Cazcan," and "Cazan" is missing.
6. *Colotlan* is derived from a place name; it means 'place of scorpions' in Nahuatl, from *ko:lo:-* 'scorpion' + *-tla:n* 'place of'.
7. Thomas (1902, 211) puts "Vacoregua" on Río del Fuerte, Sinaloa.
8. Though other sources spell this name "Irritila," Miller (1983) has it as "Iritila."
9. *Meztitlaneca*, like many names of peoples and towns in Mexico and Central America, is Nahuatl in original, apparently from *me:ts-ti-tla:n-eka* 'moon-LIGATURE-place.of-demonym [ethnicity, nationality]', literally 'people of the moon place'. Since vowel length is not shown in most colonial renderings of Nahuatl names, potentially it could be instead with *mets-* 'leg, thigh' and/or with *-tlan* 'below', so 'the under the leg people' or some other combination of these forms—unlikely options.
10. It is possible that Thomas and Swanton's spelling of *Oguera* was perhaps meant to be *Ogüera*, as the variant of *Ohuera* would suggest ([owéra] rather than [ogéra]).

11. Spanish *borrado* means literally 'scratched out, erased', a term applied to a number of groups that practiced facial tatooing.
12. The name *Sayultec* is from Nahuatl *sa:yo:l-* 'fly' + *-te:ka* 'inhabitant of the place of'.
13. The name *Tecual* may well be from Nahua; *T(h)ecualme* may be the same name with the Nahua plural *-meʔ/-meh*, seen here in this quote also in *Hueitzolme*, plural for *Huichol*.
14. "de manera enteramente infundada."
15. *Casota* in Spanish means 'big house'.
16. The name Chumbivilca is from Quechua, presumably from *chumpi* 'belt, sash, (spiritual) belt of energy surrounding the body' and *willca* (/wilʸka/) 'idol, lineage, grandson (and sometime as a boundary marker)'.
17. Many of the Panoan names for tribes and languages end in *-nawa*, many others in *-bo*.
18. "De este idioma nos quedan cuatro palabras, que no permiten establecer una relación cierta con ninguna lengua o familia lingüística conocida."
19. Gambéla and Gamela sound similar and both were located in Marahnão state. This raises the question of whether the same language was implied by both names.
20. Of course there are also other possible explanations, including that the person reporting this as a separate languages was just mistaken, in any of a number of possible ways.
21. FUNAI (Fundação Nacional do Povos Indígenas [National Foundation of Indigenous Peoples]) has adopted the spelling "Himarimá."
22. The name *Huancavilca* is from Quechua, probably from *wankʼa* 'statue, sculpture' and *willca* (/wilʸka/) 'idol, lineage, grandson (and sometime as a boundary marker)'.
23. The name *Humahuaca* is from Quechua, probably from *uma* 'head' + *wakʼa* 'sacred, deity, sanctuary, sacred rock, crevice'. The Quebrada de Humahuaca in Jujuy province of northern Argentina, designated a UNESCO World Heritage site, is a deep mountain valley known for its dramatic rock formations, once home to a number of Quechua villages.
24. It would be easy to confuse this possible language with others that have similar names, though not located in eastern Peru, for example with the Jêan language Wayaná (Guayaná) of the Rio Grande do Sul state in Brazil, or with the Cariban language Wayana of Surinam, French Guiana, and Brazil.
25. Loukotka (1963, 15) extracted sixteen Kambiwá words collected in Brejo dos Padres, which he erroneously attributed to Pankararú (Zamponi in press b).
26. há pouco mais de um século, quando a índia pankararu conhecida como Rosa Baleia deixou sua aldeia no Brejo dos Padres para se unir a Balduíno, morador da localidade de Olho d'Água dos Coelhos, situada junto à Serra Grande. O casal fixou residência e roçados na vertente oposta da serra, onde gerou treze filhos e fundou a aldeia da Batida... hoje os Kantaruré estão também na comunidade de Pedras, ambas na Terra Indígena Kantaruré... De acordo com o depoimento de um ancião kantaruré, esse etnônimo foi sugerido por um índio pankararé, em contraposição ao até então adotado pelo grupo, "caboclos da Batida," quando do processo de reconhecimento oficial. Atualmente os Kantaruré falam o Português e as perdas culturais impossibilitam hoje sua identificação lingüística.
27. The name *Muyubamba* is from Quechua, *muyu* 'circle' + '*pampa* 'plain'.
28. Durbin and Seijas (1973, 47) mentioned that "the name Pantagora may be possibly related to [the name] Patagon, a supposed Carib[an] language of Peru," which they would like to add to the other five unclassified languages of their article that had been considered Cariban by others (p. 50).
29. *Patagón* means 'big foot, big-footed' in Spanish.
30. The name *Quillasinga* appears to be from Quechua *kilʸa* 'moon' + *sinqa* 'nose'.

31. "outros que chamão Quirigmã; estes foram senhores das terras da Bahia e por isso se chama a Bahia: Quigrigmure. Os tupinambás os botarão de suas terras e ficarão senhores dellas, e os Tapuias forão para o sul."

Note that a number of groups have been called *Tapuya*, the Tupí word for 'enemy'.

32. The name *Runa* may be from Quechua *runa* 'man, person'.

33. The name *Sipisipi* may relate to Quechua *sipi* 'feather collar for dances'.

34. The name *Tulumayo* appears to be from Quechua *tullu* [tulʲu] 'bone, skinny' + *mayu* 'river'.

35. It is probably obvious that this Yamesí of Colombia has nothing to do with Yamesee of South Carolina.

36. The name Aksanás is also one name for Northern Kawesqar; this should not be confused with the erroneously claimed independent "Aksanás" language.

37. Se trata de una familia lingüística fantasma, ya que se basa en datos poco ciertos, varios de ellos atribuibles al gününa yajüch o incluso a alguna lengua chon . . . Sin embargo, hasta en trabajos recientes de antropólogos y lingüistas se sigue haciendo referencia de vez en cuando a las lenguas (o a una familia lingüística) "Het"

Lo cierto es que la documentación existente para la lengua o lenguas de los aborígenes pre-mapuches del norte pampeano es muy escasa y de interpretación (muchas veces) demasiado conjetural como para poder extraer conclusiones definitivas.

38. The language of the group traditionally called **Chono** is very poorly attested, and there has been confusion about its classification (see earlier in this chapter), but this is not the same as Llaras Samitier's (1967) "Chono" or Wayteka.

39. I have heard of fakes in other parts of the world, languages created to deceive the investigator, that are reportedly much more elaborate and harder to detect. One example might be "Taensa," discussed earlier in this chapter.

6

Distant Linguistic Relationships

6.1. INTRODUCTION

This chapter is about hypotheses of distant genetic relationship involving the Indigenous languages of the Americas. Numerous proposals have been made that would group various of the language families and language isolates together in assemblages of languages claimed to be remotely related to one another (see Appendix 2 of this chapter for a list of such proposals). These hypothesized groupings vary greatly in terms of their plausibility or lack thereof, some now rejected for lack of supporting evidence, others worthy of further investigation but not at present confirmed. We need to examine the evidence for these hypothesized relationships carefully to eliminate the unsubstantiated ones and to encourage further research on any that prove promising. However, the burden of proof is high (see Campbell and Poser 2008), and at present the unconfirmed proposals remain hypotheses only without sufficient support.

The classifications of families and language isolates in Chapters 2, 3, and 4 are generally accepted and for the most part not controversial. In spite of the trend away from lumping, there have been a number of new proposals for more inclusive, broader genetic groupings. The evidence for most of these hypotheses has not been convincing. Most of the more notable hypotheses of remote relationships involving Indigenous languages of the Americas up to about the year 2000 have been discussed and assessed critically (see Campbell 1997a, 260–329; Campbell and Poser 2008; Goddard 1996a, 308–323; Mithun 1999, 301–310). Therefore, in this chapter I concentrate on some of the more notable hypothesized distant genetic relationships put forth since then and on recent attempts to defend further some previous unconfirmed classificatory schemes. Because of the confusion that some proposals of distant genetic relationship have caused, the better-known ones featured in more recent publications are assessed for their accuracy in this chapter.

6.2. RECENT SUCCESS STORIES

Many proposals of distant genetic relationship have not stood up well when the evidence presented for them has been examined carefully. This might seem to cast a doubt on the likelihood that any as-yet-unproven language family relationships in the Americas will still be discovered or demonstrated. However, there have been a number of relatively recent cases where new phylogenetic connections have been demonstrated (or at least shown to be probable) or where previously proposed but uncertain hypotheses have since come to be confirmed in more recent studies. These include:

Harákmbut-Katukinan (Harákmbut with Katukinan) (Adelaar 2000, 2007; Chapter 4)
Lule-Vilela (with Lule and Vilela) (Viegas Barros 2001, 2006; Chapter 4)
Macro-Je Sensu Sricto (the evidence is now much more convincing for several branches, Nikulin 2020; see Chapter 4)
Mayan—Mixe-Zoquean (Mora-Marín 2016)
Na-Dene (Narrow Sense—minus Haida) (Leer 2010 convincingly demonstrated that Tlingit and Eyak-Athabaskan are genealogically related to each other; Chapter 2)
Pano-Takanan (joining the two former language families of Panoan and Takanan) (Girard 1971a; Valenzuela and Zariquiey 2015)[1]
Pech (Paya) as Chibchan (Holt 1986; Constenla Umaña 2012)
Plateau (Plateau Penutian) (Berman 1996; Golla 2011, 128–129; see Chapter 2)
Tikuna-Yurí (joining Tikuna, Yurí, and Carabayo) (Carvalho 2009; Seifart and Alvaro Echeverri 2014; Chapter 4)
Tlapanec (Subtiaba-Tlapanec) as Otomanguean (not 'Hokan' as previously believed) (Rensch 1977; Suárez 1986; Kaufman 2015a; Chapter 3).

Given these successful cases, we can be confident that new cases of as-yet undiscovered genetic relationships may be found, if proper methodological procedures are followed. Nevertheless, much progress has already been made and it is not expected that future discoveries will change the overall classification of the languages of the Americas in any major ways.

6.3. TERMS AND METHODS

As explained in Chapter 1, the terms stock, phylum, macro-family, and the compounding element 'macro-' (as in Macro-Penutian, Macro-Siouan, etc.) have often been applied to proposed but as yet unconfirmed distant linguistic relationships. However, these terms have been confusing and unnecessary. Any grouping of languages whose members are definitely related, regardless of its age or of the number of branches it may have, is simply a language family, and proposed but unsubstantiated hypotheses of relatedness do not count as language families.

As mentioned, a successful or even just plausible case for genetic relatedness depends crucially on the adequacy of the methods employed and on whether they are applied correctly.

Much has been written about methods for establishing language families, that is, for showing that languages are related to one another (see for example Campbell 1997a, 2020a; Campbell and Poser 2008; Nichols 1996, 1997; Trask 1996, 1999).

Detection of similarities among languages is the usual starting point for attempts to find relationships among languages. However, similarity alone is definitely not proof of genealogical relationship. Unfortunately, some scholars' methods stop at the identification of similarities among compared languages, where they assume mere similarities are sufficient to demonstrate that the languages under comparison are related to one another, descendants of an earlier common ancestor. Detection of similarities is just a beginning. Beside inheritance from a common ancestor, similarities can be due to accident (chance, coincidence), borrowing (language contact), onomatopoeia, sound symbolism, nursery forms, typologically commonplace traits, and language universals. For this reason, careful evaluation of the evidence is called for.

Linguists must identify and set aside those similarities that can be explained by factors other than inheritance in order to make a plausible case for relatedness. Some methods are more successful than others, and even successful ones can be applied inappropriately. The comparative method has always been the basic tool for establishing genetic relationships among languages.

Because of claims about the value of ASJP (Automated Similarity Judgment Program) (Holman et al. 2008, 2011), especially pertaining to Indigenous American languages, it is important to clarify its limitations here. ASJP relies on a list of forty meanings for words claimed to be most stable across languages. The words are subjected to a transcription system for automated comparison for similarities. Harald Hammarström (2014) has claimed that the ASJP method gets about 90 percent of the families established by more traditional methods correct, producing close to the same results as the more standard classifications. He therefore believes ASJP is a useful tool for language classification. However, this is not the case. ASJP results in many errors. It misses several of the larger South American families (Arawakan, Chibchan, Macro-Jê, Tupían), and groups together as families a number of things not accepted as related by others (Aikana-Kwaza, Andaqui-Guajiro, Iranxe-Nambiquaran, Movima-Itonama, Bora-Resígaro, Atacameño-Candoshi-Shapra, Chonan-Payagua, Bororoan-Andoque, Kariri-Araucanian, Fulnio-Leko, Trumai-Guachi, and others).

Even in terms of more traditional classifications, also based primarily on wordlists without the full benefit of application of the comparative method, Terrence Kaufman (1990a) had 118 distinct language families (and isolates) in SA. However, recent advances in the classification of SA languages (many of them relying on sound correspondences and the comparative method), the consensus classification is now reduced to 100 independent language families (including isolates) in SA. Thus even without ASJP, there is an 8.5 percent discrepancy between the 118 of the 1990 classification and the 100 of today.

Hammarström compares Loukotka (1968) with its 117 stocks based on a forty-five-word list (list of meanings) with Campbell's (2012a) 108 families (including isolates). After eliminating Loukotka's stocks where he did not rely on his wordlist and noting family groupings in Campbell (2012a) not combined in Loukotka (1968), Hammarström (2014, 68) concludes that "the correspondence between ASJP ... and C2012 [Campbell 2012a] is very high (as well as with L1968 [Loukotka 1968] ...)." He mentions family groupings in Campbell (2012a) not in Loukotka (1968): Lule-Vilela, Pano-Takanan, Harakmbut-Katukinan and Chon-Puelche, Southern Jê-Central Jê, Purubora-Tupían, Ticuna-Yurí, and Sechura-Catacaoan. He says of them that "curiously, all of these are in fact argued on the basis of basic vocabulary comparison" (p. 67). That, however, is not accurate; most of them depend not just on similarities in wordlists, but on sound correspondences and the comparative method. Actually, thirty-one of ASJP's families do not match Campbell (2012a) by joining entities that the Campbell classification lists as unrelated and by failing to join entities that are related in three other cases—and the ASJP classification does not compare another thirty-four families (and isolates) listed in Campbell.

The ASJP approach involves automated judgments of lexical similarity that rely on Levenshtein distances. Levenshtein distance is defined as the minimum number of successive 'changes' (that is, substitutions) necessary to convert one word into another. How Holman et al. (2011) count 'changes' using ASJP orthographic symbols for Levenshtein distances raises questions. Why is the distance between Spanish <weso> and Italian <osso> 'bone' 3 (for Spanish to Italian: 1 *s* added, 2 *w* deleted, 3 *e* to *o*)? Many see Spanish <we> as a diphthong, a single unit, with *we* to *o* as one not two changes, with a distance then for the word pair of two, not three. The claimed stability of items on the forty-word list is challenged. For example, there are well-known cases of loans involving the items on the list 'dog', 'fish', 'name', 'star', 'sun', 'tongue', and 'tooth' in various languages, and on the list are the items that are borrowings in English: *die, mountain, person,* and *skin*. Words for 'breast' and 'dog' are similar across numerous languages due to onomatopoeia (breasts reflecting nursing or suckling sounds, dog reflecting barking and howling noises).

Unfortunately application of the method does not require real cognates, and complications can enter due to borrowing, accidental similarities, and from comparisons with unrelated languages.

In regard to dating, several cases of higher-order (older) groupings are estimated by ASJP to be younger than some of the branches that are supposed to be their daughters, for example, Algonquian 3343, but Plains Algonquian 5002; 'Hokan' 4915, but 'Northern Hokan' 5666, and Karok-Shasta (given as a branch of Northern Hokan) 5246; 'Penutian' 5522, but 'Oregon Penutian' a whopping 11,886; and Chibchan 4400, but Rama (a branch of Chibchan) 5117. ASJP and its dates are extremely problematic. (See Chapter 1 for discussion of computational phylogenetic methods.)

6.4. HISTORICAL ATTEMPTS TO CLASSIFY THE LANGUAGES OF THE AMERICAS: A CASE STUDY

A brief historical overview of attempts to classify the native languages of the Americas was given in Chapter 1 in which the frenzy to reduce the ultimate number of language families in the Americas was discussed. Here, it may be useful to consider in more detail one case study reflecting that reductionist frenzy to illustrate what things were like in those times in American Indian linguistics, which bequeathed to us various proposals that, though unconfirmed, are still with us today. The Xinca-Lenca hypothesis illustrates this well.

For many years, from the 1920s almost until the present, handbooks and encyclopedias continued to report that "Xinca" (Xinka) and Lenca are related to one another and belong in a single language family. This comes from Walter Lehmann (1920, 767), who thought that the two were linked, though he also included other languages as well, some as far away as California, a fact soon forgotten when the asserted Xinca-Lenca classification was repeated over and over. However, Lehmann's comparison of twelve similar words in the two is all the evidence ever published for this hypothesis. It is instructive to examine Lehmann's evidence against standard criteria for evaluating proposals of genealogical relatedness among languages not yet known to be related (see Campbell and Poser 2008).

"Xinca," by decree of the Guatemalan government, is now officially spelled *Xinka*, pronounced [ˈʃíŋka]. It is actually a language family, Xinkan, composed of four languages in southeastern Guatemala: Guazacapán, Chiquimulilla, Jumaytepeque, and Yupiltepeque-Jutiapa. Lenca is also a small language family, Lencan, composed of two languages, Chilanga (Salvadoran Lenca) and Honduran Lenca. Today, none of these languages has any mother-tongue speakers.

Lehmann's evidence for "Xinca-Lenca" is presented here in its entirety, together with observations to clarify the data and to assess the comparison in each set. Actual, accurate representations of the Xinkan forms are supplied here in Guazacapán Xinka in parentheses.

		Xinka	*Lenca*
1.	'one'	ical (ik'aɫ)	etta, ita

These are not phonetically similar; the sounds do not correspond systematically (neither k': t nor $ɫ$: $\emptyset$ is a recurring sound correspondence).

2. 'two'   bi-al, pi-ar, pi (pi?)   pe

Short forms. Diffused.

3. 'three'   vuaal-al, hual-ar (waɫ, waɫa)   laagua, lagua

Borrowed. These would require metathesis to seem similar.

4. 'four'   iri-ar ((h)irha)   heria, erio (also sa, aria, eslea)

Words for numbers higher than 'two' are widely borrowed in languages of this part of Central America; these include forms similar to those given here for 'two', 'three', and 'four' in these languages. The forms in 3 and 4 involve borrowing.

5. 'water'   uÿ (u:y)   cuy 'winter'

Semantic latitude: 'water'/'winter'
Short forms.
No explanation for why nothing matches the <c>.

6. 'night'   suma (sa-sɨm'a 'in the dark')   ts'ub 'night'
7. 'dark, black' ts'ama (sɨm'a)   ts'ana-uamba 'morning (to dawn)'
8. 'shade'   ti-tzuma (ti-sɨm'a 'in the dark') saba

The Xinkan forms in 6, 7, and 8 all involve the same root, /sɨm'a/ 'dark, black'. Since all three are based on a single Xinkan root, *sɨm'a*, there are not three separate and independent cognate sets as evidence for the hypothesis, but at best only one. This single Xinkan root cannot be cognate with three different words in Lenca (unless they, too, are derived from a single root).

9. 'dog'   xusu (<x> = [š] (IPA [ʃ]))   shushu (<sh> = [š] (IPA [ʃ]))

These languages in effect have no alveopalatal affricate č (IPA [tʃ]). The common colloquial word for 'dog' in Spanish of the area is *chucho*, the loanword source of the word for 'dog' in both Xinkan and Lencan. Probably the original small, hairless, barkless Mesoamerican dog that was eaten was so different from the sorts of dogs introduced by the Spanish that they merited a new term.

10. 'cough'   ojo [<j> = [x]] (oho)   hoo, oiguin

Onomatopoeic. Phonetically similar words for 'cough' are found in languages around the world.

11. 'maize'   au, aima (ayma)   ama, aima

Forms similar to *aima, ama, eima* for 'maize' are found in other languages of this region; they involve borrowings, a *Wanderwort* (see Chapter 9).

12. 'bean'   xinak (šin'ak)   shinag

The term for 'bean' in both languages is a loan from Cholan-Tzeltalan (Mayan) *čenek* 'bean', ultimately from Proto-Mayan *kinaq* 'bean'. Terms for 'bean' are borrowed from Mayan also in some other languages of this part of Central America.

A set of only twelve comparisons is an extremely small amount of evidence upon which to build a hypothesis of genetic relationship to start with. Since nearly all twelve of the comparisons that were offered as supporting evidence are seriously challenged by various standard criteria, the Xinca-Lenca hypothesis is now abandoned. (See the appendix to this chapter for another case study.)

There have been numerous hypotheses attempting to classify Lencan in broader groupings. Penutian, Hokan, Macro-Chibchan, Mayan, and even Uto-Aztecan connections have all been proposed (Mason 1940; Arguedas Cortes 1987, 4), but with little or no supporting evidence. E. Wyllys Andrews' (1970) proposed Mayan connection is rejected, since the data are too weak. Adolfo Constenla Umaña (2002) thought Lenca and Misumalpan were genetically related. Joseph Greenberg (1960, 793) put Lenca together with Misumalpan, Xincan, and Paya in a division of his Macro-Chibchan (in his broad Chibchan-Paezan), and Voegelin and Voegelin (1965, 32) repeated this, including Lenca as one of seventeen divisions in their Macro-Chibchan phylum. There is no solid evidence for connecting Lencan with Chibchan or with any other language outside of Lencan itself, nor for any external relatives of Xinkan, either.

6.5. PROPOSALS OF DISTANT GENETIC RELATIONSHIPS

I turn now to discussion of various of the better-known proposals that have received attention in the last few years, some of them new proposals, others older ones that have received relatively recent reconsideration.

I begin with the Hokan and Penutian hypotheses. Both have been disputed since they were originally proposed and both remain unsubstantiated, now widely abandoned though recent attempts at support for them have been made. Both are still, unfortunately, widely though uncritically cited in formal and typological linguistic works and in non-linguistic publications of many sorts.

6.5.1. The Hokan Hypothesis

I had thought that by about 1980 or so Hokan had been pretty much fully abandoned by linguists who work with languages that had been proposed as members of putative Hokan. However, Terrence Kaufman in work started in 1988 and most recently updated in 2015 (Kaufman 2015a, 2015b) has brought new attention to the hypothesis. Hokan is, in my view, fully deserving of the doubt and skepticism with which the large majority of specialists regard it. However, I also believe that continued attention to the Hokan hypothesis is appropriate, for the hypothesis is interesting and so worthy of not being lost from sight, though it is very tricky and ultimately in my estimation highly unlikely to be confirmed.

Hokan had the shakiest of origins. It began with Dixon and Kroeber's (1913a, 1913b) announcement that they had reduced Powell's twenty-two California stocks to twelve. Their Hokan grouped together six language families or isolates of California: Karok (Karuk), Shasta[n], Chimariko, Palaihnihan (Achomawi-Atsugewi), Pomo[an], and Yana. The name *Hokan* was based on words similar to *hok* meaning 'two' in these languages. Dixon and Kroeber cited as evidence superficial similarities in only five presumed cognate sets, 'eye', 'tongue', 'water', 'stone', and 'sleep'. From this beginning more and more languages were added, and Hokan became one of the most inclusive and most influential proposals of distant genetic relationships in the Americas, though highly disputed.

My own experience and impression from looking at the evidence that has been presented for Hokan affinities among various languages matches Terrence Kaufman's (2015a, 17) comment that "it is a common observation that there is a very small number of etymologies (usually characterized as being 'about thirty') that have reflexes in most of the Hokan families and isolates, and that there do not seem to be any more new and good sets forthcoming," though this is not Kaufman's own view, and I would not call them "etymologies" but rather lexical matches or look-alikes.[2]

By 1919 Esselen, Washo, Chumash, Salinan, Yuman, Seri, and Tequistlatecan (Chontal of Oaxaca) were added to Hokan (Dixon and Kroeber 1919; Harrington 1913). "Thus began an unfortunate tradition in Hokan studies, that of adding to, or subtracting from the group by assertion, without publishing much evidence ... Collection and publication of the data were thereby relegated to a subordinate place for a long period," so David Olmsted (1964, 2) informed us, his point of departure being J. P. Harrington's (1913) announcement of a relationship between Yuman and Chumash, published without data or argumentation. Mary Haas affirmed that the Dixon-Kroeber classification had been accepted without question by most anthropologists without realization of how little proof had been adduced for their amalgamations (Haas 1954, 57; 1964, 74).

Edward Sapir (1917a, 1920, 1925a) assembled many potential cognates and his Hokan papers secured the conviction of most other scholars of that time. Nevertheless, Mary Haas (1964, 75), a student of Sapir's, in her reassessment found that much of the material that Sapir (1917a) had cited as supporting evidence was very poorly recorded, and that "further material of the same or better quality was not forthcoming either from Sapir or anyone else."

Sapir also argued for joining "Coahuiltecan" of northeastern Mexico and southern Texas (which allegedly included Coahuilteco [with Comecrudo and Cotoname], Karankawa, and Tonkawa) together with "Hokan" as coordinate branches of his broader Hokan-Coahuiltecan phylum, and then proposed that Hokan-Coahuiltecan was a branch of a much more far-reaching superstock that he called "Hokan-Siouan" (which contained also Yukian, Keresan, Atakapa, Tunica, Chitimacha, Caddoan, Iroquoian, Muskogean, Natchez, Siouan, and Yuchi) (Sapir 1920, 1921a, 1929a). As Victor Golla (2011, 83) noted, Hokan-Siouan "never enjoyed wide acceptance." (See Voegelin and Voegelin (1973) against Sapir's Hokan-Siouan classification.)

In addition to the languages already mentioned, several others were proposed as also belonging with Hokan: Jicaque (Greenberg and Swadesh 1953), Quechua (Harrington 1943b), Yurumaguí (Rivet 1942), Quinigua (Gursky 1964), Guaicurian (Gursky 1966b), "Gulf" (Gursky 1968), and Subtiaba-Tlapanec (Sapir 1925a). Subtiaba-Tlapanec proved clearly to belong to the Otomanguean family (see Chapter 3). Various of the language families (including isolates) that have been proposed as belonging to Hokan have been challenged with recommendations to remove them from consideration as relatives of other putative Hokan languages. These include: Chumash(an), Karankawa, Tonkawa, Yurumanguí, Seri, Tequistlatecan (Chontal of Oaxaca), and as mentioned Subtiaba-Tlapanec (Jany 2016, 13).

In short, Hokan is a hypothesis not just about all of these various language families (including language isolates) possibly being genealogically related. It would be possible for some of the putative Hokan languages to be related to others without all of them necessarily being related to one another. In effect, there are many hypotheses of relatedness possible within the Hokan complex that would involve only smaller subsets of the languages without the inclusion of others. (See Jany 2016, 2.)

Since the late 1970s, most linguists who have worked with so-called "Hokan" languages have taken a skeptical stand on the Hokan hypothesis, and many reject it outright. Hannah Haynie (2012, 62) speaks of the "quiet consensus in the field that the evidence for a genealogical relationship among the Hokan languages is inadequate," saying that "caveats regarding the general insufficiency of the evidence—and even the certainty of their own findings—have appeared in papers that argue in favor of the Hokan hypothesis." Haynie's (2012) own examination based on statistical evidence found "no evidence" for the grouping. Criticisms have included, among others, that proposals were based on little available data, relying on data that were often inaccurate, taken for some of the languages from semi-speakers with imperfect knowledge of the languages, sometimes confusing vocabulary from other languages with which they were familiar. Also, because of long-term contact among many of the languages, it is very difficult to distinguish between old loanwords and possible cognates. (Jany 2016, 3.) It is claimed that the major problem for the Hokan hypothesis is "that it is based on very little evidence" (Jany 2016, 3). I have not felt that lack of evidence was so serious an obstacle as just the methodological problems with how the data have been handled (see below).

See Langdon (1974) for a detailed historical overview of Hokan until 1974; see also Campbell (1997a, 290–305), Haynie (2012), Jany (2016), Kaufman (2015a), and Poser (1995).

Terrence Kaufman (1988, 2015a, 2015b) took a supportive stance based on his re-examination of the evidence. He favored a broad version of Hokan, with the "probable members": Pomoan, Chimariko, Yanan, Karuk, Shastan, Achumawi-Atsugewi (his "Achu" family), Washo (his "Washu"), Esselen, Salina, Yuman, Cochimí (his "Kochimí"), Seri, Coahuilteco (his "Pajalat"), Comecrudan (his "Yeméan"), Chontalan (Tequistlatecan), and Jicaquean (his "Tol"). He considered as "doubtful members": Chumashan, Guaicurian (his "Waikuri family"), Tonkawa, Karankawa, Cotoname, Quinigua, and Yurimangui (Kaufman 2015a, 5). He did "not think there is any useful distinction to be made between 'Hokan' and 'Coahuiltecan'" (p. 9).

Kaufman's evidence involves several hundred potential cognates, assembled from previous publications, especially from Gursky (1974, 1988), from which he hypothesized sound correspondences. However, Kaufman unfortunately did not present the actual forms from the languages upon which his judgments of cognacy and sound correspondences were based; he said rather, "a presentation of the complete set of data supporting each reconstruction will be made at a later time" (Kaufman 2015a, 17). He gave his phonological formulas representing tentative reconstructions (signaled by "#", not the usual "*" for linguistic reconstructions), along with what he believed their glosses to be, but without the words from the compared languages believed to support these proposed reconstructions. Where relevant each case also indicates alternations and the specific linguistic area where the putative cognates are found. He also gave a list of what he considers Hokan grammatical morphemes in the 2015a paper, and the 2015b paper is fully dedicated to what he sees as Hokan grammar; he believed that "at least 90 grammatical morphemes can be postulated for proto-Hokan" (2015b, 2).

Kaufman (2015a, 65) postulated for the Proto-Hokan phonemic inventory:

Consonants   **Vowels**
p, t, c, k, kʷ, ʔ   i   u
p', t', c', k', kʷ'   a
f, θ, s, x, xʷ, h   vowel length /:/
r
l
m, n
w, y

Kaufman (2015a, 1) considered his Hokan work as "very much 'in progress,'" although he also said that "it is not my aim to prove the Hokan hypothesis. I assume it to be correct" (p. 5). Unfortunately, it is not possible to evaluate Kaufman's Hokan proposal properly since he did not provide the actual forms in the languages upon which the tentative reconstructions are based. That means that essentially the same uncertainty remains that has always attended the Hokan hypothesis—there certainly is enough there to make us curious about the possibility of genetic relationship and to want to know more, and yet the evidence presented to date is not sufficient to confirm the hypothesis, regardless of which set of languages is included in the proposal.

In spite of the lack of the actual data upon which Kaufman's proposed Hokan reconstructions rest, it is still possible to evaluate aspects his Hokan work by checking what is provided against standard criteria. Given the attention that Hokan gets and the confusion around it, it will pay to do that.

Forms with limited distribution. Kaufman recognized several linguistic areas in which languages (both "Hokan" languages and others) have influenced one another due to language contact: Northern California, Coastal California, the Southwest, Texas-Coahuila, and Mesoamerica. He said that he employed as a criterion that "an etymology found only within a [single] given area . . . will not be attributed to proto-Hokan" (p. 8). Nevertheless, 242 of his reconstructions are listed as occurring in only a single linguistic area: 193 only in Northern California, 24 only in the Southwest area, 22 only in Mesoamerica, and 3 only in the Texas-Northeast Mexico area.

Semantic latitude. A good number of Kaufman's proposed cognates appear to exhibit considerable semantic difference in the languages compared, as for example

'badger'; 'porcupine'
'butterfly'; 'bat'
'crooked'; 'basket'
'deer'; 'body'?
'elbow'; 'jaw, chin'
'gopher'; 'coati'?
'mountain'; 'top; on'
'nape; neck'; 'shoulder; arm'
'neck'; 'throat'; 'to swallow'

'to break, split, squeeze, wring'
'to burn'; 'be ripe, cooked'
'to hit'; 'break'
'to jab'; 'nudge, crack'
'to rub'; 'cricket; cicada'
'to move a long object lengthwise'; 'sting, pierce, stab, poke hole'

Note that these are the glosses of Kaufman's reconstructed forms, which lack the actual words from the compared languages that they are based on.

Onomatopoeia. A significant number of Kaufman's examples appear to reflect onomatopoeia and thus may be challenged as cognates:

to shout, cry, bark, weep: 7 cases (with "reconstructred" forms such as *#wa*, *#wo&wo*, *#ifu*, etc.)
breast, milk, suckle, suck: 9 cases (with forms imitative of nursing, sucking, e.g., *#šuʔ*, *#tsots'*, *#itsʰi*, *#ma*, *#itsí(ts) ~ #atsí(ts)*)
to blow, wind, to whistle: 7 cases (with forms such as *#pxú ~ #ipxú, #xu, #pʰusu: ~ #pʰušu: ~ #pʰusu:l ~ #pʰušu:l, #(p)xu(y), #wA*)
to spit (*#qxet'*)
to piss (*#su ~ #tsu*)
to hit, crack, burst, break, crush, pound: 14 cases (with forms such as *#pa, #PaK* [*#pakʸ ~ #paq ~ #fakʸ ~ #faq*], *#PaT* [*#pat ~ #fat ~ #paṭ ~ #fat*], *#(u)Pakʸʰ* [a ~ i] [*#pakʸʰ ~ #fakʸʰ ~ #pikʸʰ ~ #fikʸʰ ~ #upakʸʰ ~ #fuakʸʰ*], *#qʰaw, #Xaw* [*#xaw ~ #xʸaw*], *#X!aw* [w ~ m] [*#xaw ~ #xʸaw ~ #xʷaw, ~ #xam ~ #xʸam ~ #xʷam*], etc.)
fish hawk: 2 cases (with the forms: *#čuKču(K), #čiqxči(qx)* [*#čuqču ~ #čuxʸču ~ #čuqčuq ~ #čuxʸčuq ~ #čuqčuxʸ ~ #čuxʸčuxʸ*], *#čiqxči ~ #čiqxčiqx*)
crow (*#qa:q ~ #qxa:q*)
several other birds with names that appear to be onomatopoeic: sparrowhawk, owl, buzzard, woodpecker, robin, yellowhammer, killdeer, goose, crane, crane/duck, duck, kingfisher, and quail (4 terms)

In speaking of animal terms, Kaufman (2015a, 101) said, "there are many items showing sound symbolism and imitation, irregular phonological relationships, and similarities with forms in non-Hokan languages."

Nursery forms. Of the reconstructions, seventeen forms appear to be nursery forms (of the *ma(ma), na(na), pa(pa), ta(ta), ca(ca)* type) referring to 'mother', 'father', or other elder kin, the kind of meanings that have similar sounding words in many languages around the world.

The problem of alternate reconstructions. Kaufman (2015a, 30) may be correct that in the putative Hokan languages there are "recurrent patterns of alternations between definable sets of phonemes in morph shapes that cannot be explained by any obvious phonological factors but can be correlated with grammatical, semantic, or lexical facts," similar to ablaut (apophony) in Indo-European and other languages. He says that "even with our primitive ideas about comparative Hokan phonology, several good Hokan etymologies require the positing of proto-forms with more than one allomorphic variant in any reasonable reconstruction." However, unless the conditions under which the alternations occur are understood, assuming multiple possible phonological shapes for morphemes just increases the possibility that chance (accident) rather than inheritance from a common ancestor explains similarities among the compared forms.

Kaufman marks cases where he believes the "etymology" involves such alternations with "~". He listed the following kinds of alternations: a ~ u; i ~ a; u ~ i; l ~ n ~ r; and w ~ m, though he also mentioned other sorts of alternations in some examples. He has 183 reconstructions that involve such alternative forms, in some cases multiple alternative forms in a single reconstruction.

This problem of indeterminacy in the reconstructions is compounded greatly by Kaufman's use of "cover symbols." He explains his usage of them as follows:

> In many etymologies the set of languages that the etymon survives in does not allow for complete specificity in the reconstruction. Rather than state all possibilities in such reconstructions, I have devised a set of cover symbols standing for the most frequent specific ambiguous cases, and the reconstructions have been symbolized in those terms. In the instances of ambiguity not covered by these symbols, I have stated the alternative possible reconstructions. (Kaufman 2015a, 67)

His cover symbols are:

*P = *p or *f
*Y = *y or *θ
*R = *l or *r
*L = *l or *lʸ
*N = *n or *nʸ
*C = *ts or *č
*T = *ṭ or *t
*K = *q or *kʸ
*S = *S or *š
*X = *x or *xʸ
*I = *i or *e
*U = *u or *o
*X! = *x, *xʸ, or *xʷ
*K! = *q, *kʸ, or *kʷ
*E = both *e and *i
*O = both *o and *u
*A = both *a and *e
*H = *h and/or *ʔ and/or *:

A great many of Kaufman's Hokan reconstructions have one or more of these cover symbols. This challenges the regularity of proposed sound correspondences and also greatly increases the possibility that chance rather than inheritance explains the similarities in the words that are compared in these sets (though we do not have the actual words, just reconstructions with cover symbols in them).

Some of the examples with alternative forms involve **sound symbolism**, different forms of a root depending on size, shape, intensity, or affect signaled by alternation of certain sounds (pp. 31–32). It is clear that several of the languages do exhibit sound symbolism, which means that greater care must be exercised when assembling potential cognate sets and attempting reconstructions where sound symbolism is involved, but it also increases the risk that sound symbolism and alternating forms will be assumed in cases where the similarities may be due just to accident and not to inheritance. Sound symbolism and onomatopoeia often seem to be related to each other. Kaufman identifies sixteen of his forms as "symbolic" (others could also be included).

Several examples illustrating Kaufman's alternations were seen in the onomatopoeia examples above. Here are a few others to show what is involved.

#ma(s) [s ~ š; a ~ o] 'face; forehead' [N]. This symbolizes that all of the following are possible reconstructions of this: #ma, #mo, #mas, #maš, #mos, #moš. It is found in only the languages of the Northern area.

#mO.. 'worm; centipede' [MA]. This indicates alternatives of #mo or #mu. Apparently the actual words have more sounds in them that are not represented here, indicated by the ".." at the end. This, however, goes against the principle of total accountability, that there needs to be an account of all the sounds in forms that are compared as potential cognates, not just some arbitrarily selected string of similar sounds in words that are compared. This proposed cognate occurs only in languages of the single Mesoamerican area, so by Kaufman's criteria would not be accepted as a reconstruction to Proto-Hokan in any case.

#t.'eK [Sal] ~ #t.eK' [Cho] 'to cut'. This one compares forms from only two languages, Salinan and Chontal. The Salinan forms allow both #t'eq and #t t'ekʸ, compared to Chontal #teq' and #t tekʸ. Not only is the distribution limited, but it also possibly involves onomatopoeia.

#Tu 'turkey' [S]. This reconstruction means either #tu or #ṭu. It is short, possibly involves borrowing, and possibly onomatopoeia. Kaufman indicates that "forms like this are widespread in Meso-America" (p. 114), that is, in only a single linguistic area.

#La [a ~ o] 'leaf' [MA]. This covers the possibilities: #la, #lo, #lʼa, #lʼo. Furthermore, it is a short form and is found only in the Mesoamerican linguistic area.

Errors, doubtful cases, and cases with irregular sound correspondences. Kaufman flagged some of the reconstructions as problematic in other ways, mentioned as doubtful, uncertain, or not fitting the sound correspondences. For example, Kaufman (2015a, 39) said, "the section on vowels, particularly mid vowels, is especially sketchy and somewhat programmatic." He also said:

In a small number of instances, in a given etymology there is evidence for reconstructing more than one phonologically similar proto-Hokan phoneme. Some of the more common types of discrepancy are *plain vs. *glottalized, *plain vs. *aspirated,

*aspirated vs. *glottalized, *s vs. *ts, *š vs. *č. These discrepancies will have to be explained. My current view is that they are probably irregularities that will be explained on a case-by-case basis rather than being clues to a more subtle understanding of proto-Hokan phonology, but time will tell. (p. 63)

There are six cases that Kaufman flagged specifically as irregular among his Hokan reconstructions, in particular among the animal and bird names; he called one of them "very doubtful."

Possible borrowings. Without the actual forms from the compared languages, it is not possible to determine whether forms are borrowed or not. Still, among the glosses for proposed reconstructions, the following designate items that are quite possibly borrowed (known to be borrowed in other languages) and definitely do not belong to basic vocabulary, which is more resistant to borrowing: blanket, bow, spear, bear, otter, coyote, goose, pinole, tobacco (two terms), squash, basket (seven terms), digging stick, bread, fence, net/weir, and shamanry.

Short forms. A great many of Kaufman's reconstructions are short forms, composed of just a consonant and vowel (CV) or of only a vowel and consonant (VC) in form and length. Such forms run a high risk of involving just accidental similarity rather than inheritance.

Found also in languages beyond Hokan. Kaufman indicated with ten of his reconstructions that similar forms are found also in languages outside of Hokan; he called another nine cases "widespread." Such forms potentially involve borrowing rather than inheritance only within Hokan.

In summary, Kaufman's (2015a, 2015b) Hokan papers represent impressive work, but given the many complications with the things he presents as reconstructions for putative etyma, supposedly reflecting cognates in the various languages, and the fact that the data on which they depend were not presented, it seems evident that the doubt and skepticism around the Hokan hypothesis are still warranted.

If Hokan is controversial, it is safe to say that Sapir's (1929a) broader Hokan-Siouan proposal has been completely abandoned, even by Greenberg (1987), who otherwise followed almost all of Sapir's other classifications. Sapir himself referred to Hokan-Siouan as his "wastepaper basket stock" (quoted in Haas 1973a, 679).

Let me also take this opportunity to clarify my own experience with and view regarding "Hokan," since Kaufman (2015a, 9) cited it. He said:

Campbell ca 1976 surveyed the comparative literature on Hokan because he had collected data on Jicaque and wanted to know if it was related to anything. Eventually he decided it was related to Oaxaca Chontal, but not with certainty to anything else. In an unpublished paper written ca 1976 he conceded that Jicaque might also be related to Yemé (Comecrudo) and Pajalat (Coahuilteco), and perhaps also Seri, but he probably would be more cautious than that these days. (p. 9)

I had done brief fieldwork with Tol (Jicaque) (see Campbell and Oltrogge 1980). I did want to see how much merit Greenberg and Swadesh's (1953) claim that Jicaque belonged to Hokan might have, given better data on Jicaque. I did find some similarities between Tol

(Jicaque) and various of the putative Hokan languages—primarily among the thirty or so words mentioned above that seem to pop up among various of the languages hypothesized to be Hokan—but it was difficult if not impossible to know what to make of them, and indeed some of the similarities seemed to go better with Comecrudo or Coahuilteco than with other putative Hokan languages, but there were few such cases.

David Oltrogge and Calvin Rensch (1977, 1) had argued that Subtiaba-Tlapanec, Tequistlatecan, and Jicaque "trace their origins to a single source." Subtiaba-Tlapanec, however, proved not to have "Hokan" affinities but rather to belong to Otomanguean (see Chapter 3). Moreover, in checking further the possible link between Jicaque and Tequistlatecan that Oltrogge and Rensch had proposed, I found additional matchings that made the hypothesis seem plausible, though not demonstrated (see Campbell and Oltrogge 1980, 222–223). Kaufman was right that I would be cautious today. I still think a Jicaque-Tequistlatecan connection is possible, though I also suspect it may perhaps never be possible to demonstrate it adequately; still, it is worthy of further investigation.[3] I, however, remain very skeptical about Hokan in general. Nevertheless, there are those tantalizing recurrent similarities that need explanation, and it would be difficult to reject Kaufman's work entirely, and so research on possible Hokan connections should continue. However, my strong belief is that if there ever was a Hokan genetic unity, it was so far in the past and so much has changed in the languages since then that it will never be possible to confirm a genetic relationship among those languages on the basis of the information that remains today.

Kaufman (2015a, 9) mentioned in this context that in conversation with Victor Golla in 1987, Golla gave the opinion that "Hokan is a residuum of proto-Amerind date." It might be possible to imagine that the thirty or so words mentioned above that seem like possible cognates that turn up across many of the "Hokan" languages might be inherited not from some Proto-Hokan, but from some Ur-American language of long ago, maybe even one spoken by some of the first inhabitants in the New World.[4] However, being able to provide substantive support for such an idea probably is impossible, given the time depth and the great amount of linguistic change that has taken place in all the languages descended from some imaginable Ur-ancestor language, if ever it existed.

Another, possibly related, way to look at it is to suspect that these thirty or so words are not evidence of a Hokan genealogical connection among those particular languages but rather are instead pan-Americanisms (see Campbell 1991a)—although the very mention of pan-Americanisms raises more issues and objections, and misunderstanding, than it is worth. Campbell and Kaufman (1983, 853) spoke of "widespread forms (so-called pan-Americanisms)." Many took this to mean words involving some ancient genetic relationship among the languages, even though by "pan-Americanisms" we meant those seemingly similar forms that appear to pop up repeatedly in broad comparisons of American Indian languages not known to be related to one another, probably a collection of accidentally similar forms, loanwords (maybe including some *Wanderwörter*), unrecognized onomatopoeia, sound symbolism, and the like. Whatever is behind them, it would be great to have an explanation for them, for each of them individually. And, if any of them really are reflexes of inherited things that have persisted from some long-ago ancestor of many of the languages, which we can no longer reach due to the limitations of our methods and the assailable data, so much the better. However, unless we get lucky in intensive future investigation, which seems highly unlikely, we will never know for sure for most of what have been taken to be pan-Americanisms.[5] (See Campbell 1991a; Campbell and Kaufman 1983.)

In short, there are good grounds for remaining skeptical about Hokan, but also good reasons for continued investigation for possible demonstrable links among some if not all of the putative Hokan languages.

6.5.2. Penutian

Penutian, like Hokan, is a highly disputed hypothesis that persists, in spite of widespread rejection of it. (For details of its history, see Callaghan 2014, 1–6; Campbell 1997a, 309–322; DeLancey and Golla 1997; Golla 2011, 128–130; Grant 2018.)

Like Hokan, it began with Dixon and Kroeber's (1913a, 1913b) attempts to reduce diversity among California languages to fewer language family units. Under the label "Penutian" they grouped five Californian "families": Miwok, Costanoan, Yokuts, Maiduan, and Wintun. The name comes from a joining together of *pen*, which resembles words for 'two' in Yokuts, Wintun, and Maiduan, and *uti*, similar to words meaning 'two' in Miwokan and Costanoan. It was soon established that Miwokan and Costanoan really are related to each other, members of a non-disputed language family, Miwok-Costanoan, now usually called Utian. It reduces Dixon and Kroeber's Penutian from five original California families to four. However, the possible unity of the other languages, the "pen" languages, with one another and the "pen" languages with Utian, has been subject to major dispute for a very long time.

For their Penutian, Dixon and Kroeber (1919, 55–69) presented 171 "cognate stems" and other lexical resemblances, along with "an attempt at what would be rather chaotic sound correspondences in the modern sense" (Silverstein 1979, 651).

Edward Sapir (1921c, 1929a) extended Penutian by a lot to include in addition to Dixon and Kroeber's original five (then four) families, which he relabeled "California Penutian," also several other language families and language isolates. His Penutian included Tsimshianic, Chinookan, "Oregon Penutian" (with Takelma, "Coast Oregon Penutian" [Coosan, Siuslawan, Alsea], and Kalapuyan); "Plateau Penutian" (with Sahaptian, Klamath-Modoc, Molala [with Cayuse]), and later "Mexican Penutian" (Mixe-Zoquean and Huave) (Sapir 1929a). Given the impact of Sapir's Penutian superstock, it is somewhat surprising that he actually published very little supporting evidence for it, unlike Hokan, for which he did publish substantial proposed evidence.[6]

Sapir's typological characterization of Penutian languages was:

> The Penutian languages are far less cumbersome in structure than the preceding three [Eskimo-Aleut, Algonkin-Wakashan, Nadene] but are more tightly knit, presenting many analogies to the Indo-European languages; make use of suffixes of formal, rather than concrete, significance; show many types of inner stem change; and possess true nominal cases, for the most part. Chinook seems to have developed a secondary "polysynthesis" form on the basis of a broken down form of Penutian; while Tsimshian and Maidu have probably been considerably influenced by contact with Mosan and with Shoshonean and Hokan respectively. (Sapir 1990[1929a], 101)

As Grant (2018, 3) points out, "typologically, the alleged Penutian languages are very diverse in all respects." Still some general similarities, such as Sapir's, have been considered, though none of them "is without exception" (Grant 2018, 3). They include: no tone or pitch accent; typically a small range of vowel qualities (3–8); at least a few glottalized stops, /h/ and /ʔ/ , and contrastive uvular stops in most of the languages; the California "Penutian" languages tend to have retroflex and dental stops and retroflex sibilants, ablaut and reduplication, preference of suffixes over prefixes, and case-systems, and many have ergativity (Grant 2018, 3).

Today, Sapir's Mexican Penutian is completely abandoned; Oregon Penutian has some defenders; Plateau Penutian is established (with Cayuse removed, see Chapter 2), though often called just "Plateau" to distance it from controversies involving other putative Penutian connections (see Chapter 2); and Californian Penutian is flatly rejected by most linguists, though still seen as possible by a few. As Anthony Grant (2018, 1) put it:

> The validity of Penutian as a single if widely ramified language family . . . covering much of California, Oregon, and part of Washington and British Columbia is a highly contested issue . . . It can hardly be emphasized too strongly that few linguists nowadays regard all the languages . . . as being non-trivially and ultimately related on historical grounds.

Catherine Callaghan's (2014) account of her evolution from a Penutian believer to skeptic or denier parallels that of several other Penutianists (see below). Callaghan (2014, 2) recalls that "initial comparison [among the California families] seemed to confirm Dixon and Kroeber's hypothesis. It was easy to assemble resemblant sets. Finding regular and recurrent sound correspondences, especially non-identical correspondences, was a different matter." She added, "my only surprise had been how easy finding similarities between different languages became under those circumstances" (of "ignoring regular sound correspondences and constancy of meaning") (Callaghan 2014, 2).

Callaghan (1997, 57) had reported that "'Penutian' is now so ill-defined a category that it is difficult to state the criteria for membership." She said:

> Although some comparative scholars believe that Utian, Yokuts, Wintun, and Maidun are ultimately related at a deep level, none of them, so far as I known, still believe that the four families form a genetic subunit apart from other languages. In other words, the Penutian core has either been discredited or it has been shrunk to the level of Yok-Utian. What, then, does it mean to say that a language or a language family is Penutian? It cannot mean a systematic relationship to a non-existent core. The term has become so ill-defined that William Shipley (1983–1984) has called for its abandonment. (Callaghan 2014, 5)

"Evidence has been accumulating since the [19]70s that the Wintun, Maidun, Yokuts, and Utian speakers had separate entries into California, making a California Penutian genetic unit unlikely" (Callaghan 2014, 5; see also Golla 2011; Delancey and Golla 1997, 178; cf. Grant 2018, 2). This was seen as clinching the demise of core Penutian ("California Penutian") as a unit apart from other languages. As DeLancey and Golla (1997, 177–178) put it, "as soon as some of the Oregon languages are brought into the picture, it is immediately clear that there is no evidence that sets all and only the 'California Penutian' stocks off as a distinct unit." They reported that though there may be a few remaining dissenters, the general agreement among Penutianists is that the hypothesis of a "California Penutian kernel [is] dead" (p. 179).[7]

Attempts to expand Penutian did not stop with Sapir's main Penutian classification. Even Sapir (1949[1929a], 178) himself spoke also of wider extensions: "The Penutian languages, centered in Oregon and California, must early have extended far to the south, as they seem to be represented in Mexico and Central America by Mixe-Zoque, Huave, Xinca, and Lenca." The Xinca and Lenca possible connections, however, seem never to have been pursued after this statement.

More far-flung Penutian connections were proposed by Benjamin Whorf (1935, 608, 1943, 7), whose Macro-Penutian included, in addition to the groups in Sapir's Penutian classification, also Uto-Aztecan, Kiowa(-Tanoan), Mayan, Mixe-Zoquean-Huave (with reservations), Totonacan, and reportedly (though not mentioned in Whorf's publications) several other language groups (Mason 1940, 58, 81–86, citing personal communication from Whorf). J. Alden Mason 1940, 104–110) accepted this version of Macro-Penutian. Morris Swadesh's (1954b, 1956) lexicostatistically based "Penutioid" phylum attempted to link many additional groups, twenty in all, with Penutian, including in addition to all of Sapir's and most of Whorf's groups, Coconucan, Paez, Cholonan, Quechua-Aymara, Tarascan, and Zuni. Neither Whorf's nor Swadesh's proposals attained any following, and today both are mostly forgotten.

In 1958, Harvey Pitkin and William Shipley (1958, 175) gave a particularly critical assessment of Penutian:

> Penutian investigations have followed a pattern of supplying to the literature new and bold, but undemonstrated, hypotheses of wider and wider relationships, while those suggestions already in the literature have stood uninvestigated for the last half century. Mere speculation based on the use of imaginative techniques which are themselves open to question is of doubtful value. One cannot use a suspect technique to establish a relationship nor a hypothetical relationship to validate a technique . . . No series of sound correspondences has been published either between or within the Penutian families. Neither phonological nor morphological cognates have been demonstrated. Further, the significant factor of diffusion has remained uninvestigated, even though the borrowing of linguistic material undoubtedly plays an important role.

Then after twenty-two more years of labor and having produced some of the more important publications on Penutian, William Shipley, in a 1980 article entitled "Penutian among the ruins: a personal assessment," ended up declaring Penutian dead:

> Although we have amassed a vastly greater and more accurate amount of lexical data since [Dixon and Kroeber], it is very important to point out that the fundamental characteristics of the sets one finds are much as they were for Dixon and Kroeber. There are many resemblant forms—I believe Pitkin and I accumulated over three

hundred for our 1958 article (Pitkin and Shipley 1958) and there are lots more—but they are irritatingly unsatisfactory. Most of the consonant resemblances are identities, furthermore there is little parallelism from one set to another . . . The Penutian area looks as if it had been subjected to a massive and prolonged process of lexical diffusion, layered in like sedimentary rock . . . It has been very puzzling, and has engendered a steady stream of cautionary statements from people familiar with the situation. (Shipley 1980, 437–438)

Shipley went on to propose the "working principle" that:

The term "Penutian" has no genetic definition at all. The very use of the term prejudges the case and sets us off to working from a kind of axiomatic entity which we have not defined . . . If we ever find real genetic connections somewhere among [any of] these languages, then the term Penutian might be all right to use again, although it is pretty shopworn. I think we should stop misleading everybody and drop the term out of our working vocabulary even though it might produce an identity crisis in some of us. It is not that I feel there are no genetic connections to be found—I just don't want to name something until I have something to name. (Shipley 1980, 440)

Hannah Haynie's (2012) examination of the statistical evidence found "no evidence" for Penutian.

DeLancey and Golla (1997) and Golla (2007, 77) saw some evidence to link Maiduan with Plateau (Plateau Penutian), and they thought that "all of Wintuan, Plateau Penutian, and Yok-Utian have a common ancestor more recent than Proto-Penutian" (DeLancey and Golla (1997, 85), though Delancey (2018, 1) concedes that "the inclusion of Wintuan here is dubious."

Scott DeLancey (2018) presented evidence that he believes shows that Plateau Penutian and Yok-Utian (see below) are linked in what he calls "Inland Penutian."[8] While the evidence he presented is interesting, many linguists will probably not find it compelling. As he mentions, most of the Plateau comparisons are represented by Klamath alone, and in general only two or three languages are involved in the comparisons. He presents evidence that he believes supports a regular sound correspondence between Klamath and Yok-Utian together with two morphological comparisons. It will pay for us to look a bit more closely at this evidence.

Delancey (2018, 1) mentions what he believes is a well-known example of valid comparisons in these languages, Klamath *wlep'al-s*: Proto-Utian **welip* 'lightening'. While the match of three consonants is impressive, a single instance of such is not beyond the possibility of accidental similarity, perhaps aided here by expressive symbolism, or even possible borrowing. Many languages have an "l" in their words for 'lightning'; a good number have both *w* (or *v*) and *p*; several have *w-l-k* (or *v-l-k*). The "regular correspondence" is a list of ten comparisons with Klammath "alvelopalatal *c, c*" matching "retroflex **ṭ, *ṭ'*' in Proto-Yokuts, Proto-Miwok-Costanoan, or both" (p. 2). The ten are not without difficulties, however. For Proto-Miwok-Costanoan **ṭiw(:)ak*: Klamath *c̓ew-s* 'yellowhammer', Callaghan (2014, 422) thought that 'yellowhammer' was a widely borrowed *Wanderwort* (see Chapter 9), and DeLancey concedes it is also onomatopoeic (p. 3). DeLancey also concedes that four of the ten have an "extra initial consonant" in the Klammath word for which he does "not have explanations" (p. 3). The 'break' and 'twist' sets may involve onomatopoeia/expressive symbolism. 'House' involve a short (CV) comparison. Only two cases compare forms in all three, Yokuts, Miwok-Costanoan, and Klammath. Three comparisons involving forms relating to 'shaman' or 'medicine' were also compared. These are not straightforward comparisons, as Delancey's discussion of them indicates, and some have been asserted to involve borrowing. DeLancey also compared unusual behavior of an irregular locative suffix and a plural suffix. The comparisons DeLancey presented are suggestive and interesting, and they indicate that the hypothesis is worthy of further investigation, but I do not think it constitutes persuasive evidence of the proposed relationship, at least not yet.

I agree with Shipley and others (above). Most are skeptical of Penutian at best and many reject outright any classification involving Penutian. Some guises of Penutian are favored in some works by Berman (1983, 2001), Golla (2000, 2011), DeLancey (2018), DeLancey and Golla (1997), and by Marie-Lucie Tarpent (1996, 1997, 2000, 2002). Tarpent's papers suffer from too many methodological shortcomings.[9]

Possible connections among languages associated with the Penutian hypothesis are worthy of more research, but my personal expectation is that the likelihood of significant developments is very low.

6.5.3. *Yok-Utian*

A plausible hypothesis involving three of Dixon and Kroeber's (1913) five originally proposed "Penutian" families in California is Yok-Utian (Yokutian) (Callaghan 1997, 2001, 2014, 26–39; cf. Golla 2011, 129–130), composed of Yokuts and Utian (Miwokan + Costanoan). The hypothesis is unconfirmed, however. As Victor Golla (2011, 130) pointed out, "the resemblant words show many unresolved phonological irregularities, and extensive borrowing cannot be ruled out. A full demonstration of the relationship will need to explain the considerable differences in both phonology and morphosyntax between the two language families." Accordingly, Yok-Utian is not embraced, though it is worthy of more investigation.

6.5.4. *Amerind*

Joseph Greenberg's Amerind classification and his method of multilateral comparison (mass comparison) on which it is based have come and mostly gone since the publication of his 1987 book, leaving considerable turbulence in its wake. There is now an extensive literature criticizing the hypothesis, revealing the reasons for why Amerind has been rejected by nearly all specialists in Native American languages and by most historical linguists. As Paul Heggarty (2020a, 97) puts it, Greenberg's classification has "been unmasked by a rollcall of prominent figures in comparative and historical linguistics."

Greenberg's (1987) Amerind hypothesis proposed to group all Indigenous languages of the Americas except 'Na-Dene' and Eskimo-Aleut into a single "super-macro-family" called Amerind[10] (see also Greenberg and Ruhlen 2007). Perhaps the kindest thing that can be said of this episode in the history of American Indian linguistics is that it led to sharpening understanding of the methods for establishing genealogical relationships among languages and for investigating proposals of remote linguistic relatedness (see Campbell and Poser 2008 for details). Details of the many criticisms of Amerind do not need be rehearsed here, though it is worth referring to some of the kinds of criticisms the hypothesis has received to show why it has been rejected.

Extensive inaccuracies in Greenberg's data were reported, over and over: "the number of erroneous forms probably exceeds that of the correct forms" (Adelaar 1989, 253); "nearly every form [cited for Yurok and Kalapuya] required some sort of emendation" (Berman 1992, 230); "it [Greenberg 1987] is marred by errors in both methodology and data, which make it essentially useless for its intended purpose" (Kimball 1992, 447); "the work [Greenberg 1987] is riddled with mistakes in data interpretation and reproduction" (Muysken and O'Connor 2014, 4), and so on. As Robert Wright (1991, 58) put it, though an exaggeration, "Greenberg's detractors ... almost invariably veer to their favorite subject: his sloppiness."

Greenberg assembled forms that are similar on superficial inspection among the languages he compared, declaring them evidence of common heritage and calling them "etymologies," though they are not etymologies in any normal sense of the word. However, where Greenberg's method stops, after having assembled the similarities, is where others start. Similarities can be due to a number of factors—accident, borrowing, onomatopoeia, sound symbolism, nursery words (the *mama, papa, dada, nana, caca* sort), and general typological tendencies. Therefore, for a plausible proposal of genealogical relationship, attempts must be made to eliminate other possible explanations, leaving a shared common heritage the most likely. Greenberg made no attempt to eliminate these other explanations; his assembled similarities appear to be due mostly to accident and combinations of these other factors.

Frequently, Greenberg equated words with very different meanings, misidentified numerous languages, failed to analyze the morphology of some words and erroneously analyzed that of others, neglected regular sound correspondences, failed to eliminate loanwords, compared only arbitrarily selected sections of words, and misinterpreted or ignored well-established findings. The Amerind "etymologies" he proposed are often limited to only a very few of the many languages included in his language groupings.

Greenberg's method has proven incapable of distinguishing Amerind from implausible and even impossible relationships. For example, as mentioned earlier, Greenberg classified some things that are not languages at all; Membrenan (*sic*), which Greenberg (1987, 194, 293, 382) classified as a Lencan language, is actually just the name of the author of a reference that he consulted (Membreño 1897).

Numerous of his proposed "etymologies" involve *borrowing*. For example, his "Chibchan-Paezan" 'axe' etymology compares Cuitlatec *navaxo* 'knife' (borrowed from Spanish *navajo/navaja* 'knife, razor') and Tunebo *baxi-ta* 'machete' (borrowed from Spanish *machete*), two of the only four languages compared for this example (Greenberg 1987, 108).

Examples of *excessive semantic latitude* among words compared from different languages are rampant, with cases such as the following where the different meanings separated by the slash ("/") are the glosses of words compared from different languages: 'back/wing/shoulder/hand/arm/buttocks/behind'; 'back/behind/kidney/spine/bird's tail'; 'bitter/to rot/sour/sweet/ripe/spleen/gall'; 'body/belly/heart/skin/ meat/be greasy/fat/deer'; 'child/copulate/son/girl/boy/tender/bear/small'; 'deer/dog/animal/ silver fox/lynx'; 'excrement/

night/grass'; 'earth/island/forest/mud/village/town/dust/world/ground'; 'field/devil/bad/underneath/bottom'; 'hole/mouth/ear/listen/chin/nose/smell/blow nose/sniff'; and so on.

Such semantic permissiveness increases the probability that chance explains the compared forms. "Greenberg so relaxes the criteria for a match, on all levels, that the statistical effect, far from excluding chance, is exactly the opposite: opening the floodgates so widely that 'matches' are statistically guaranteed. His 'method' is a machine for generating false positives." "Wherever one might wish to find false positives, multilateral comparison can oblige" (Heggarty 2020a, 98, 99).

Onomatopoeic forms are very frequent, for example: in one "Amerind" set, p^hu-, pu-, $puhi$, pui, are given from different languages with the meaning 'to blow' (Greenberg 1987, 196).

Undetected morpheme divisions can make unrelated forms seem more similar than they actually are, and Greenberg's data exhibit many cases of this. For example, Rama (Chibchan language of Nicaragua) *mukuik* 'hand' is said to be "cognate" with forms in other languages similar to *ma* or *makV* 'hand' (Greenberg 1987, 229); however, 'hand' in Rama is *kwi:k*; the *mu-* is the 'second person possessive prefix' ('your'). The root *kwi:k* is not similar to Greenberg's *ma-kV* target for 'hand'.

Several cases involve insertion of a *morpheme boundary where none is justified*. William Poser (1992) showed that, of Greenberg's Salinan and Yurumanguí forms, eleven of twenty-six have specious morphological analyses. Howard Berman (1992, 232) noted "there is not a single Tualatin [Kalapuya] word in which Greenberg segments any of these prefixes correctly." The example mentioned above of Tunebo *baxi-ta* 'machete,' borrowed from Spanish *machete*, is another case, where the artificially inserted morpheme division makes this mistakenly appear more similar to Cabecar *bak* and Andaqui *boxo-(ka)* 'axe' (Greenberg 1987, 108).[11]

Greenberg ignored well-established findings, for example, grouping Subtiaba-Tlapanec mistakenly with "Hokan," instead of with Otomanguean. For example, it was well known that Sapir's (1925a) linking of Subtiaba-Tlapanec with Hokan was mistaken and rather that Subtiaba-Tlapanec had been demonstrated to belong to Otomanguean. (See Suárez 1983a, 1986, and Kaufman 2015a for details.) The erroneous classification of Uru-Chipaya with Puquina had been pointed out many times, though Greenberg (1987, 384) nevertheless maintained the mistaken classification.

In short, it is with good reason that the Amerind hypothesis has been rejected. As Terrence Kaufman (2015a) put it, "this very careless but heavily hyped piece of work [Greenberg 1987] needed debunking." Jason Haugen's (2021, 550) view of it is widely shared: "The Amerind proposal, and multilateral comarrison as a 'method' specifically, have become textbook examples of how not to do historical linguistics." As Paul Heggarty (2020a, 95) says, "there is no trace of Greenberg's chimeras in [the] standard classifications." (See Campbell 1988b, Campbell and Poser 2008, Heggarty 2020a.)

Although Greenberg's Amerind hypothesis has been rejected, his Amerind classification encompasses within it a number of proposed subordinate groupings, each a massive proposed but unconfirmed macro-family in itself, containing as members other, smaller groupings that are also proposed distant genetic relationships themselves. The major "branches" of his Amerind are:

> Northern Amerind (with Almosan-Kerisiouan [where Almosan and Kerisiouan each contains 5 language families and isolates], Penutian [composed of 28 families and isolates as its units], Hokan [24 units])

Central Amerind (with Kiowa-Tanoan, Oto-Mangue, Uto-Aztecan)
Chibchan-Paezan (with Chibchan [with 7 units], Paezan [with 10 units])
Andean (with Aymara, Itucale-Sabela [3 units], Kahuapana-Zaparo [2 units], Northern [5 units], Quechua, Southern [5 units])
Equatorial-Tukanoan (with Macro-Tucanoan [22 units], Equatorial [with Macro-Arawakan [9units] plus 16 other units)
Ge-Pano-Carib (with Macro-Carib [5 units], Macro-Panoan [6 units], Macro-Ge [17 units)[12]

None of these are recognized today as other than unconfirmed and doubted proposals, and they have been criticized. As Paul Heggarty (2020a, 95) points out, these are essentially just geographical groupings. (See the appendix to this chapter for an additional case study evaluating the evidence for Greenberg's Macro-Panoan grouping, a branch of this Ge-Pano-Carib.)

6.5.5. Dene-Yeniseian

Edward Vajda (2010, 2018) proposed a connection between Na-Dene and the Yeniseian family of central Siberia. Na-Dene is composed of Tlingit and Eyak-Athabaskan, minus Haida of Sapir's (1915b, 1929a) original Na-Dene hypothesis. The languages of the Yeniseian family are Ket, Yugh, Kott, Assan, Arin, and Pumpokol. The hypothesis was received favorably by several scholars and enthusiastically in some media reports.[13] Though initially attractive, much of the evidence presented in its favor turns out to have serious problems, and overall it is inadequate to support the proposed relationship (see Campbell 2011; Starostin 2012).

Vajda's hypothesis appeared attractive because Vajda is a solid scholar whose other work has generally been very good.[14] He attempted to deploy standard methods calling on evidence from proposed cognates, several from basic vocabulary, recurring sound correspondences (not all of them nearly identical), and morphological matchings. On the other hand, the hypothesis seemed unlikely and was criticized for its geographical implausibility (given the great distance separating the Yeniseian and Na-Dene territories), the great time-depth separating the two, grammaticalizations that weaken similarities seen in verb affix patterns, typological mismatches, the limited amount of evidence, little or no support from archaeology and human genetics, lack for the most part of matchings in pronouns and in basic kinship terms, problems with proposed sound correspondences, semantic disparities in meanings of proposed cognates, and poor fit with areal neighbors—not all of these are important; some are discussed in more detail in what follows. Because of the positive attention the hypothesis has received, it deserves scrutiny.

Several scholars have commented on what seemed to them to be the limited amount of lexical evidence, circa 100 proposed cognates between Yeniseian and Na-Dene (cf. Starostin 2012, 128; Vajda 2018, 285). This has not seemed to me to be a particularly telling objection; some 100 proposed cognate sets is not an insignificant number. More important is that many of the word comparisons are challenged based on standard criteria, and there are also problems with the phonological and morphological evidence presented (see below). Vajda (2018, 292) acknowledges difficulties with the lexical evidence; he says, "the lexical evidence remains on the whole insufficient, both in a quantitative (too few cognates) as well as qualitative sense (the need for more rigorous etymologies), arguably because much of the needed research has yet to be completed."

Of the circa 100 proposed cognate sets, some 27 involve significant semantic differences; for example (only the glosses are presented here, Na-Dene first, followed after the back slash ["/"] by the gloss of the Yeniseian form it is compared with): 'black'/'blue, green, grey, brown'; 'cloud'/'dark, darkness'; 'day'/'light'; 'distributional plural proclitic'/'collective suffix'; 'eat (animate object)'/'swallow'; 'fire'/'day, daytime'; 'fly'/'dragonfly'; 'go in a herd'/'in a row, small fish, vee (of birds)'; 'handle'/'kettle'; 'hem, hanging end of garment, breechcloth'/ 'sews'; 'hill'/'cliff, concave edge of riverbank'; 'hook-shaped, hook'/'back, return, half'; 'hot'/ 'molten fat, summer'; 'jump (also fire ignites, burns, blazes; shine)'/'by moonlight, moonlit night, flare up'; 'king salmon'/'burbot'; 'knee'/'waist seam of dress, up to the edge'; 'lower leg, shin'/'thigh, base of tree'; 'point, end'/'fishhook barb'; 'poke'/'dig'; 'rear, back end, rump, buttocks'/'under'; 'ridge, hill'/'pile of small fragments, small pile'; 'robin'/'color, paint'; 'sharp'/'claw, fingernail'; 'shrub, plant'/'willow'; 'stone'/'mountain'; 'thorn'/'penis'; 'undergo pangs'/'die'. When semantically non-equivalent forms are compared, the possibility that chance accounts for the phonetic similarity is greatly increased.

A dozen of the sets involve words that are onomatopoeic; again, only the glosses are given here: breast, teat, milk; breath, breathe, shadow, shade, safety, health, life/soul, vapor; cry; eagle; laugh; medicine song, cure by singing, shaman/shaman; merganser/common goldeneye (duck); robin; spit; spruce hen; spruce grouse; wind blows/wind. Onomatopoeic forms are eliminated from proposals of distant genetic relationship because their similarity may be explained as due to mimicry of sounds in nature rather than as inheritance from a common ancestor.

Some examples involve borrowings: Ket *quˀj* (Yugh *quˀj*) 'birch bark' is a loan from Selkup (a neighboring Uralic language of the Samoyedic branch) *qwā̈*, *küe* (Kulonen 1992, 386), from Proto-Uralic **koxji* 'birch' (Sammallahti 1988, 537); 'wart' is also acknowledged as perhaps a Selkup loan (Vajda 2010, 90); Proto-Yeniseian **dəli* 'willow' appears to be a borrowing from Turkic (mentioned as a possible loan by Vajda; see Proto-Turkic **dal* 'willow') (Starostin 2012, 136). Sets for 'name', 'shaman' (that is, 'medicine song, cure by singing, shaman'/'shaman'), 'son-in-law', and 'canoe' involve terms identified as loans in some other Eurasian languages and might involve borrowing here.

About thirty of the sets involve very short forms, of the shape V or CV. The greater the number of matched segments in a proposed cognate set, the less likely it is that accident may account for the similarity. With short forms such as these, it is difficult to show that it is not accidental similarity rather than shared history that explains the phonetic similarity shared by compared words (Ringe 1999).

In several cases in Vajda (2010) a single form in one family was erroneously considered cognate to multiple forms in the other family. In a couple of instances, three separate proposed cognate sets involved "false doublets." In 2018, Vajda corrects these. Vajda (2018, 291) notes that such cases led him to conflate distinct sound correspondences into a single correspondence, noting that such "false pairings . . . illustrate how easy it is to go astray when searching for cognates based on casual inspection."

There are problems with the sound correspondences that Vajda gave. In George Starostin's (2012, 137) opinion, "Vajda's 'regular correspondences' are not, or, at least, not yet properly 'regular' in the classic comparative-historical sense of the word." Starostin showed several cases of proposed cognates that have exceptions to Vajda's sound correspondences. Most of the sound correspondences occur in only a few cognate sets. For example, the sound correspondences on the basis of which four proto sounds are reconsructed are each found in only a single proposed cognate set; only two proposed cognate sets support the proposed reconstructions for each of sixteen other sounds. Sound correspondences have to recur to be acceptable. Also, Vajda himself pointed out some proposed cognates that do not fit his sound correspondences.

The majority of the proposed cognates have problems, questioned on the basis of standard criteria for investigating proposals of distant genetic relationship. If the proposed cognate sets that are questioned because of excessive semantic latitude, onomatopoeia, borrowing, and so on are set aside, too few proposed cognates remain to support most of Vajda's proposed sound correspondences. The Proto-Yeniseien phonological inventory, with twenty consonants—and Ket with only thirteen—is considerably smaller than that of Proto-Na-Dene, with forty-three consonants. This means that there are multiple consonant targets in Na-Dene from which to seek matchings for each individual Yeniseian consonant, increasing the possibility of chance rather than inheritance from a common ancestor explaining similarities detected, in particular when the correspondence is found in only one or two or a very few potential cognates.

About the criticism of lack of matchings in pronouns, Vajda (2010, 53) himself allowed that "Dene-Yeniseian differs from established families . . . in the relative inscrutability of its pronominal morphology." Vajda (2018) does, however, speculate about assimilations that would make some plausible connections for some pronominal forms.

About the lack of support from human genetics or archaeology, Vajda (2018, 279, 281) believes the hypothesis is now matched by human genetic and archeological data thought to connect the Kets with a population that entered Alaska from Asia about 4,800 years ago. The Ket nuclear genome shows that Ket speakers represent an ancient North Asian population; it was argued that they have a close connection with a population that entered Alaska about 4,800 years ago, which Vajda (2018, 280) believes gives a "scenario whereby a Dene-Yeniseian language family becomes plausible."

About the issue of the amount of time since separation of the languages and the amount of morphological change expected, George Starostin (2012, 127) summarized it this way:

> Complex morphological patterns do not generally tend to be stable over periods of several millennia, and it is possible that either the Yeniseian system, or the Na-Dene system, or both, could have undergone the process of erosion of the original patterns and rebuilding of new ones in the meantime. (Even such closely related languages as Ket and Kott show significantly different patterns of affixation that turn the reconstruction of the original verbal morphology into a serious chore).

It appears that some scholars were most impressed by the seemingly neat matchings in the morphological template of the verbs between Na-Dene and Yeniseian. The semantic/functional content of the verbal affixes and their order relative to one another on verbs appears quite similar in the two families. The "slots" (affix order in the verbal template) that

Vajda presented include several spatial (locative) prefixes, tense/aspect/mood prefixes, and subject-agreement prefixes. Since complex verb morphology typically has changed dramatically over time in well-studied language families, it would be very surprising if both Yeniseian and Na-Dene had managed to retain so much of the original morphology in its original prefix order in such strikingly similar form over such a long time span. In older language families, the morphology has changed much, often resulting in different typological profiles for related languages, and indeed Vajda (2010, 36) pointed out considerable change in Yeniseian structure due to foreign influences, with possibly "a steady effect on realigning Yeniseian morphological typology." Modern Ket verbs have eight prefix slots (the first actually a clitic) and one suffix slot, in contrast to only four prefix slots for Proto-Yeniseian (refined later to five prefix slots). Many of these compared verbal affixes are very short, composed of mostly highly frequent consonants, and some have very general meanings, while others have functions or meanings that do not match that well between the two language families.

The most serious problem in the morphological evidence is the recognition that a number of the affixes and their slots in the order of bound morphemes in verbs are not original, but came about through grammaticalization of formerly independent items. As Vajda (2010, 40) says:

> One must start by considering that the elaborate prefixal strings typical of the modern [Yeniseian and Na-Dene] languages developed out of a more analytic structure. Evidence suggests a bipartite phrasal verb consisting of an auxiliary followed by a lexical verb root, each of which hosted its own prefixes and suffixes.

Vajda speaks of auxiliary verbs with their own affixes that later become combined with lexical verbs with their own affixes as lying behind the verb template he proposes for the Dene-Yeniseian hypothesis. Some of the morphological examples pair suffixes in one branch with prefixes in another, or clitics in one with bound morphemes in the other. Such cases, in order to be cognate, would almost certainly have to be the results of grammaticalizations that attached formerly independent elements onto verbs. Starostin (2012, 138) puts it more strongly: "Verbal morphology is a dead end unless we stop talking in terms of synthetic paradigms and begin talking in terms of grammaticalization."

Some see as an extremely difficult problem for the hypothesis that

> the Yeniseian template contains nothing that could be transparently analyzed as . . . "classifiers," a crucial component in the typical Na-Dene form and, quite likely, one of the oldest sets of morphological markers in the paradigm, since it occupies the slot that is immediately adjacent to the root morpheme itself. (Starostin 2012, 121)

Andrej Kibrik (2010) and Campbell (2011) make the same point. Na-Dene verbs have a morphological slot for 'classifiers', morphemes placed directly before the verb stem to signal changes in grammatical role. However, there is no comparable classifier morpheme slot in the Yeniseian verb complex. Given classifier morpheme's adjacency to the verb root, we would assume it is older (grammaticalized earlier) than other prefix slots that must have been added later. The mismatch, with the absence in Yeniseian of the immediately pre-root 'classifier' affixes so crucial in Na-Dene languages, challenges the asserted broad matchings in the affix patterns in Vajda's verbal template.

If what is compared turns out to be only elements that originally were just very short independent lexical items of general meaning that then later grammaticalized as affixes, which are short and typically made up of mostly unmarked (simpler) phonemes, with strained meaning/function associations, then the morphological evidence ceases to be impressive, or, as Starostin (2012, 121) put it, "it invalidates the idea of an elegant common origin of the *templates*."

Vajda (2018, 281–284) attempted to address aspects of the criticism of the morphological arguments in favor of the hypothesis. Vajda's (2010a) strongest argument had appeared to be that the proposed finite verb template in the two families represented common inheritance. Vajda (2018, 281) attempts to refine this template, though the revision raises questions. His new template represents Pre-Proto-Dene-Yeniseian. He says this "template may have arisen through coalescence of an auxiliary and heavy lexical verb" (p. 281). This single morphological word, he argues, gave rise to a mostly prefixing template where "in Yeniseian the suffixes were mostly lost or reanalyzed" (p. 281). He believes that "many seemingly unrelated idiosyncrasies in Ket, Athabaskan and Tlingit verb structure can be accounted for based on evolution from this model" (p. 282).

Specifically about the serious criticism involving the absence in Yeniseian of the pre-root 'classifier' affixes that are centrally important in Na-Dene languages, Vajda (2018, 282) now believes that the Na-Dene classifier prefixes developed from earlier TAM (Tense-Aspect-Model) affixes that evolved into a system marking valence increase or decrease, with part of it reanalyzed from a generic third-person agreement prefix, part of it "metathesized rightward ahead of the subject slot and was reanalyzed as a valence-increase marker" (p. 282), and so on.

Vajda (2019, 284) believes "some differences can be attributed to differential areal contact on each family after separation." He says, "quite different areal influences shaped how the Ket verb evolved, as it gradually reoriented from prefixing to suffixing" (p. 284), and "divergent phonological evolution reflects in part the starkly different areal influences affecting each separate family. Na-Dene, but not Yeniseian, merged all of its inherited labial obstruents with uvulars" (p. 285). That is, there are "striking incongruities" between the two families, and areal influences are postulated though not demonstrated to have produced them.

The new template and these hypothetical changes are plausible but not very compelling. Much seems to rely on a considerable amount of speculation about what could have been and could have happened but with little direct evidence. Still unanswered are the problem of the morphology remaining so similar over such a long time when morphology in other languages is not stable over long time periods; the problem that the postulated affixes are short forms, easily similar due to change; the problem of grammaticalization of what must have been unbound morphemes; areal influences (language contact); lack of matchings in pronouns (addressed but not really solved in Vajda 2018, see p. 284); and so on. While Vajda (2018) makes a more plausible case for genetic relatedness, it is still far from being stronger than other possible explanations for the similarities detected.

Unfortunately, neither the lexical evidence with putative sound correspondences nor the morphological evidence adduced has proven sufficient to support a genealogical relationship between Na-Dene and Yeniseian.

6.5.6. Mayan-MixeZoquean

This hypothesis would join the Mayan and Mixe-Zoquean families into a single larger family. Some of the evidence that has been presented is less convincing (see, for example, Brown and Witkowski 1979), although the evidence and arguments given by David Mora-Marín (2016) for this hypothesis are now very encouraging. This case is made more difficult by the fact that after long centuries of mutual influence between these two neighboring language families, it is sometimes not possible to distinguish between shared similarities that may be inherited (real cognates) and those that may be due to diffusion (borrowings). Mora-Marín's (2016) investigation, utilizing careful methods, makes this proposal of genetic relatedness much more plausible.

Although Mayan–Mixe-Zoquean now seems quite likely, the broader **Macro-Mayan** hypothesis is doubtful. Several other proposals have attempted to join the Mayan family with others (see below), but none has held up well under closer scrutiny. Attempts to find other remote relatives of Mayan will no doubt continue. It is impossible to anticipate how successful they may be, but it is unlikely that striking breakthroughs are in store.

6.5.7. Chitimacha-Totozoquean

Cecil Brown et al. (2014) argued that Chitimacha, a language isolate of Louisiana, is related to "Totozoquean," a postulated grouping together of the Totonacan and Mixe-Zoquean families (see Brown et al. 2011) that has not been accepted by other linguists. Because of space limitations, I do not give a detailed assessment of the data presented for Chitimacha-Totozoquean, but offer an overview of the kinds of problems involved that make this hypothesis non-viable. Nearly all of the ninety-one sets of lexical comparisons that they present as possible cognates suffer from methodological shortcomings involving standard criteria (see Campbell and Poser 2008).

(1) 26 sets involve compared forms that are not semantically equivalent, as in set 7. below, which compares a Chitimacha word meaning 'shoot, stem' with Mixe-Zoquean 'cornfield'.
(2) 21 sets compare short forms, composed of a single consonant and vowel. These could be true cognates, but they are so short that their similarity with forms in other languages could also easily be due just to chance. Their example 43 illustrates the problem: Chitimacha *pe(h)*: 'auxiliary verb of horizontal position': Totonacan **pa* 'to be lying (second person)' (no Proto-Mixe-Zoquean matching was proposed).
(3) 10 sets involve comparisons that are onomatopoeic and expressive/symbolic, for example, their 82. 'to cry, yell', and 88. 'musical horn'/'blowgun', and so on (with no matching in Totonacan).
(4) 15 sets involve loans or possible loans. Several of the examples contain words that others have identified as loans; in other cases the words have cultural content of the sort that often involves loanwords. For example, example 6. 'pumpkin' is borrowed from Mixe-Zoquean into several other languages (see Campbell and Kaufman 1976, 83–84; Kaufman and Justeson 2009, 224; see below for additional problems with this example).

(5) 59 sets involve proposed cognates in only two of the three language families involved, either Chitimacha with only Mixe-Zoquean or Chitimacha only with Totonacan, but not Chitimacha with both. In spite of having no example from Mixe-Zoquean or alternatively not from Totonacan in these comparisons, Brown et al. nevertheless provide a reconstruction for their hypothetical "Totozoquean" (Totonacan with Mixe-Zoquean) in these cases. An example is their set 43. (below) where a Proto-Totozoquean reconstruction *paʔ 'to be lying' is given, based solely on their Proto-Totonacan *paʔ 'to be lying (second person)'—that is, in the absence of a Proto-Mixe-Zoquean matching, they just promoted their Proto-Totonacan form on up to represent the supposed higher order Proto-Totozoquean. Unjustified Proto-Totozoquean forms were created in this way for most of the 59 cases where only two of the three language families have compared forms.

David Mora-Marín (2016, 172) cites several problems for "Totozoquean" with the data and methodology in Brown et al. (2011), including "narrow distribution of etyma in at least one of the two language families; unmatched segments without morphological justification; possible loanwords; and semantic leeway." For these reasons, in the example sets presented below, I ignore the proposed Proto-Totozoquean reconstructions, citing instead the Totonacan and/or Mixe-Zoquean forms that they give.

(6) 22 sets involved words with unexplained sounds, cases that compare only some of the sounds of a word but not all the sounds of the whole word with sounds in words compared from other languages. Brown et al. accepted as cognates compared words where only two segments of longer forms fit their expected sound correspondences and were similar in the compared languages, ignoring the remaining sounds of the compared words. This goes strongly against the standard etymological principal of total accountability, where there must be an account for all the sounds of a word, not just some arbitrarily selected part of a word. This is seen, for example, in their set 6. below.

(7) At least 3 sets involve irregular sound correspondences. For example, their 68. gives Proto-Mixe-Zoquean *tam 'fruit', but by their sound correspondence rules *tən is expected.

(8) 12 of the alleged sound correspondences lack sufficient examples among the proposed cognates to demonstrate that they recur with regularity, that the sounds actually do correspond. Of the 26 sound correspondences involving vowels given in the paper, one correspondence rests on but a single proposed cognate set (example 27, Chitimacha *a*: Totonacan *u*)—however, to be considered a regular correspondence, it must be found repeated in other proposed cognates. Eight cases of proposed correspondences rest on only two putative cognate sets each.

The following few cases examined in more detail illustrate these kinds of problems in the data, cited by their numbers from the Brown et al. (2014) paper. Their abbreviations are: Ch Chitimacha, PMZ Proto-Mixe-Zoquean (with PM Proto-Mixean, PZ Proto-Zoquean), PTn Proto-Totonacan, PTz Proto-Totozoquean; and /¢/ is [ts].

1. PCh-Tz *ča₁ 'TO SEW' | Ch *čʼuš+i 'to sew'; PTn *ča'pá' 'to sew'; (no PMZ).
   Only the first syllable is compared (čʼu and ča) and the leftover sounds (š and pá') are left unexplained. Only two of the three language families are represented; there is no Mixe-Zoquean comparison.

6. PCh-Tz *či**ʔ** SQUASH | Ch *čiška 'pumpkin'; (no PTn); PM ***či**ʔwa 'squash'.
   Only the boldfaced parts are compared, essentially only the first CV, with no account for the rest of the sounds in the words in these language (ška in Chitimacha and ʔwa of Proto-Mixean). It also lacks a Totonacan comparison. The Mixe-Zoquean word for 'squash' is borrowed into a number of Mesoamerican languages (Kaufman 2020a, 138).

7. PCh-Tz *ka:¹ma₁ or *kya:¹ma₁ or *ka:¹ma₁' or *kʸa:¹ma₁' CORNFIELD, MAIZE STALKS, STEMS | Ch *ka:mu* 'sprout; stem'; (no PTn); PMZ *kama 'cornfield'.
   The semantic difference is very large between 'sprout, stem' and 'cornfield'. Only two of the three language families are represented. Terms for 'cornfield' may involve borrowing. See, for example, Nahuatl *kamāwa* 'for maize to get ripe', Pipil *kamawak* 'ear of corn in a dried-up cornfield', similar enough to suggest possible borrowing involving the PMZ 'cornfield' word.

31. PCh-Tz *ⁿko₁wa:² LEACHED CORN (NIXTAMALIZED MAIZE) | Ch *nowa* 'Indian hominy', PTn *qa'wa: 'nixtamal'; (no PMZ).
    Only two of the three language families are represented. Borrowing is a very real possibility (see for example in Chapter 9 the various borrowed forms in Mesoamerica containing *wa* with meanings involving products from maize).

43. PCh-Tz *pe:2' TO BE LYING, BE IN A HORIZONTAL POSITION | Ch *pe(h)* 'auxiliary verb of horizontal position "to be in horizontal position", familiar, when applied to human in horizontal position'; PTn *pa:' 'to be lying (second person)'; (no PMZ).
    Only short forms, CV in shape, are compared. Though short forms could be cognate, it is difficult to show that the similarity is not due to sheer chance. Only two of the families are represented; there is nothing to represent Mixe-Zoquean. The semantics are not a close match, comparing an auxiliary verb 'to be (horizontal)' with 'you are lying'.

68. PCh-Tz *ntə₁'n FRUIT | Ch *nanu* 'persimmon'; PTn *ti'n 'seed'; PMZ *təm 'fruit' (note: *tən is expected).
    The compared forms are not semantically a good match, 'persimmon', 'seed', and 'fruit'. The Proto-Mixe-Zoquean form does not fit their sound correspondence rules.

85. PCh-Tz *ʔiš or *ʔi:š TO SEE, SEEK | Ch *ʔiš+i-* 'to seek; to collect; to tease'; (no PTn); PMZ *ʔis 'to see'.
    These are short forms. The semantics ('seek, collect, tease' vs. 'see') are not a good match. Only two of the three language families are involved.
    In short, nearly all the data presented in support of this hypothesis are challenged for not measuring up to requirements of standard criteria. The data upon which this proposal

linking of Chitimacha with those Mesoamerican language families are riddled with so many problems that the hypothesis needs to be abandoned.

6.5.8. Macro-Jê Sensu Lato

The Jê (Gê) family is well established (Davis 1966). However, a number of other language families and isolates have been suggested as related to the Jêan languages in various versions of what has been called "Macro-Jê "(Macro-Gê). Loukotka's (1968, 76–83) "Zé or Ge stock" included some of those other families and isolates. Irvine Davis' (1968) Macro-Jê is the most cited of early versions. He included in it, in addition to the Jê family: Maxakalían, Karajá, Jeikó, Ofayé, Kamakanian, Purían (with Purí, Coroado, and Koropó), and Botocudo [Krenak], with even broader possible connections with Borôro, Fulniô, and Tupían. Others proposed other additions to the Macro-Jê complex: Rikbaktsa, Guato, Jabutían, and Chiquitano. Greenberg's (1987, 386) Macro-Ge includes all of these groups plus Otí. Terrence Kaufman's (2007, 72) "Macro-Je cluster" includes Chiquitano in his Chikitano-Bororoan stock, Aimoré language complex (with Krenak), Je stock, Jeikó, Kamakanan, Mashakalian, Purian (with Koropó and Purí), Fulnio, Karajá language area, Ofayé, and Guató, with "unclassified, possibly macro-Je" languages Otí, Baenan, and Kukurá. The evidence presented in Ribeiro and van der Voort (2010) relating Jabutían and Jêan families seems persuasive.

There are problems, however, with the proposed inclusion of several of these languages. Eduardo Ribeiro (2006, 422) reported for Otí "the meager available data do not support its inclusion into the Macro-Jê stock." He argued further that the evidence does not allow Fulniô (Yatê) and Guató to be classified with Macro-Jê (Sensu Stricto) languages (Ribeiro 2012, 263–264). Willem Adelaar (2008b) presented arguments for the inclusion of Chiquitano, which Ribeiro and van der Voort (2010) see as more probable. They conclude, "evidence for the inclusion of different families in the Macro-Jê stock is rather uneven, ranging from the fairly proven (Maxakalí, Krenák, and other, extinct Eastern Macro-Jê languages, Ofayê, Karajá, etc.) to the virtually untested (Guató and, to a lesser degree, Yatê)" (Ribeiro and van der Voort 2010, 548). They hypothesized that Maxakalían, Krenakan, Kamakanan, and Purían may form a subgroup inside Macro-Jê.

Though evidence had been published to make connections among some of the Macro-Jê languages seem attractive, it was not until Andrey Nikulin's (2020) detailed comparisons that the relatedness among these families was satisfactorily established and the extent to which their membership in Macro-Jê was shown to be trustworthy. I have called this more definitive classification Macro-Jê Sensu Stricto. It includes the subgroups (subfamilies): Jabutían, Jêan, Jeikó, Kamakanan, Menién (Manyã), Masakará, Karajá, Krenakan (Botocudoan), Maxakalían, Ofayé (Opayé), and Rikbaktsa. Nikulin (2020, 91) sees Maxakalían and Krenakan (and possibly also Kamakanan) as forming a closer grouping within Macro-Jê Sensu Stricto, a branch he calls "Transfranciscanan." (See Chapter 4 for details.)

Matthias Pache (2018) suggests a distant genetic relationship between Macro-Jê and Chibchan. The evidence for this, however, is not compelling. A possible connection between Macro-Jê and Tupían has been proposed, but Tupían has not been thought of as belonging to Macro-Jê itself (see below).

6.5.9. *The Tupían-Cariban and Tupían-Cariban-Jê hypotheses*

Several possible larger connections involving Tupían, Cariban, and Macro-Jê have been suggested. Irvine Davis (1985[1968], 299–300) presented some potential cognates in similarities shared by Tupían and Jêan and some Macro-Jê languages. Aryon Rodrigues (1985a) suggested that Cariban and Tupían were related to each other, and he later proposed that Macro-Jê was related somewhat more distantly to both of these families (Rodrigues 2000, 2009). For Tupí-Cariban Rodrigues (1985a) presented 121 possible cognate sets and proposed sounds correspondences, and tried to identify and remove loanwords. Meira et al. (2010) think that some morphemes that can be reconstructed to Proto-Tupían and Proto-Cariban appear to be good candidates for cognates linking the two families, but it is not possible to reach firm conclusions either in favor of or against these proposals (Gildea 2012, 446–447).

Joseph Greenberg (1987) proposed Macro-Carib with Cariban, Bora-Witotoan, Peba-Yaguan, Andoke, and Kukura; he joined his Macro-Carib with Macro-Panoan and Macro-Ge in the Ge-Pano-Carib branch of his Amerind Macro-family. However, Gildea and Payne (2007) tested Greenberg's Macro-Carib with more reliable data, finding little support. The grammatical evidence offered by Greenberg cannot be reconstructed to Proto-Cariban, and the lexical data offer almost no support either.

As Lev Michael (2021, 337) explains, the Tupían-Cariban-Jê hypothesis relies very strongly on the idea that languages of all three families have "relation prefixes." The relation(al) prefixes always seemed odd and troubling, maybe even a bit mystical, unlike what is found in other languages of the world. They are a set of elements presumed to be prefixes that supposedly indicate whether a head is preceded by its complement or not, for example, something possessed preceded by its possessor in a possessive noun phrase or a transitive verb preceded by its object. However, Meira and Drude (2013) challenge the analysis for Tupí-Guaranían languages, where the analysis with relational prefixes is best known. Meira and Drude show that the so-called relational prefixes are actually the result of phonological alternations, where root-initial segments change (alternate) when something is put before them, phonologically conditioned by presence or absence of preceding elements that happen to be heads, similar to the initial consonant mutation in Celtic languages and similar changes in various other languages.

Singerman (2021) presents very compelling evidence that the so-called relational prefixes in Tuparí are not prefixes at all, but instead involve a stem-initial segment that gets deleted following a vowel-final pronominal prefix.

Some Macro-Jê Sensu Stricto groups have this linking behavior but Nikulin (2020) does not reconstruct it to the proto-language. Salanova (2011) shows that the core Jê alternations that had been labeled "relational prefixes" are actually the result of phonological processes that adjust syllabe onsets to make them possible (see also Singerman 2021). Such an alternation was present in Cariban, but a number of Cariban languages have lost it.

A number of scholars find the Tupían-Cariban and Tupían-Cariban-Jê hypotheses interesting and perhaps plausible, meaning that further research on them is warranted. However, the hypothesis is considerably weakened to the extent that it relies significantly on the erroneous notion of relational prefixes assumed to be shared in these language groups. "In short, the data invoked are extremely sparse, and this proposal remains firmly outside standard classification" (Heggarty 2020a, 100–101).[15]

6.5.10. Macro-Guaicurúan

It has long been suspected, often assumed, that the Matacoan and Guaicurúan language families belong together in a larger classificatory unit. Alcide Dressalines d'Orbigny (1839, 114) thought some Matacoan languages belonged with the Guaicurúan languages, and the possibility of a Matacoan-Guaicurúan genetic relationship has been repeated since then. Daniel Brinton (1898, 182–183) rejected the possibility of a relationship between Matacoan (a.k.a. Mataco- Mataguayo) and Guaicurúan, as did Theodor Koch-Grünberg (1904, 29). Samuel Lafone Quevedo (1915, xix) later also separated the two families, attributing similarities between them to long contact in the region (see also Lehmann-Nitsche 1936, 122). Jules Henry (1939, 86) noted that "Ashluslay" (Nivaclé, a Matacoan language) and Pilagá (a Guaicurúan language) show "that although lexically Pilaga and Ashluslay are quite different the grammatical structures of the two languages are so similar that an ancient historical relationship should be postulated." Nevertheless, his conclusion was:

> These correspondences [between Nivaclé and Pilagá] do not argue very strongly for a single origin of the two languages, particularly in view of [the] fact that on the whole the vocabularies are extremely divergent. Nevertheless, if some good phonetic transcriptions of the Chaco languages were made it might turn out that d'Orbigny's guess [that the two families might be related] was a good one. (Henry 1939, 91)

This view that the number of comparable lexical items seemed meager though at the same time there were striking morphological similarities in the languages of the two families was shared and repeated by several scholars (e.g. Lafone Quevedo 1896, 122–123; Imbelloni 1936, 197; Tovar 1951, 377–378, 401; etc.)—this also matches my own earlier perceptions.

The name Macro-Guaicuruan was coined by J. Alden Mason (1950, 201–204). Mason (1950, 202) accepted Henry's (1939) grammatical evidence of a relationship that joined the Matacoan (his Mataco-Maca) and Guaicurúan families, saying that "doubtless other families of the region, at present regarded as independent, will eventually be joined to it"; he mentioned as candidates for this Chiquito [Chiquitano] and Lule-Vilela (p. 201). The Matacoan and Guaicurúan families were frequently asserted to be related in the broadscale classifications of South American languages, but on the basis of little or no published evidence (see in addition to Mason 1950; also Swadesh 1959; Greenberg 1987; Kaufman 1994, 2007; etc.). Joseph Greenberg (1987, 73) asserted that "even the most cursory examination will show that these two groups [Matacoan and Guaicurúan] are indeed closely related," although he presented only thirty-five lexical and eight supposed grammatical shared similarities (Viegas Barros 1993–1994, 193; see appendix 1 of this chapter).

Evidence presented earlier for the hypothesis was suggestive but not conclusive. Nevertheless, Pedro Viegas Barros (1993–1994, 2004, 2006b, 2013a) found a very large number of possible cognates; he has presented a very promising case for a genetic relationship between the two families based on these words and on phonological, and morphological evidence, with proposed sound correspondences.

Guachí and Payaguá are often linked with the Macro-Guaicurúan hypothesis. The evidence for including Guachí and Payaguá, however, is not convincing. After comparing a good number of lexical forms, Viegas Barros (2013a, 295) said:

> The similarities of Payaguá and Guachí with the languages of the Guaicurúan and Mataguayan [Matacoan] families (although some may be suggestive) are few and do not seem sufficient to assert with certainty that there is—in this case—kinship. What does seem clear is that, if such a relationship did exist, Guachí and the Payaguá would not belong to either the Guaicurúan or the Matacoan families.[16]

That is, they would be rather branches of a larger genetic unit that included them all. (See also Viegas Barros 2004.)

Viegas Barros (2005b) compared several morphological similarities between Macro-Jê and his Macro-Guaicurúan languages. There are profound differences among these languages; for example Macro-Jê languages tend to have very little bound morphology, while the grammatical morphology of Guaicurúan and Matacoan languages is extensive. Viegas Barros believes, however, that in spite of the differences, there are similarities in at least a dozen important grammatical elements. While these are interesting, they alone do not provide adequate evidence that these languages share a genetic relationship.

6.5.11. Quechumaran

The possible relatedness of Quechuan and Aymaran was noted soon after the earliest contacts between the Spanish and speakers of these languages, and the hypothesis has been persistent, and persistently controversial. The hybrid name *Kechumaran* was created by J. Alden Mason (1950, 196) "to designate the yet unproved but highly probable subphylum consisting of *Quechua* and *Aymara*." The proposal became best known, under the spelling *Quechumaran*, from Orr and Longacre (1968). The proposal had been widely accepted, although it had not received any detailed investigation until the Orr and Longacre paper. After that publication, most Andeanists came out against the hypothesis, arguing that long-term language contact explains the similarities between the two language families in a number of papers that frequently repeated each other's criticisms (see Campbell 1995; 1997a, 273–284 for details). There is no doubt that these two neighboring language families share a great number of similarities in vocabulary, phonology, morphology, and syntax, and they are typologically very similar. It is also beyond doubt that much is shared due to borrowing. At issue is whether they share anything else because they are genetically related. Their situation presents one of the greatest challenges to sorting out traits shared due to borrowing from shared traits due to inheritance from a common ancestor.

Many of the often repeated criticisms of the hypothesis were beside the point. Many of the complaints centered on claims that language contact explains what they share. However, language contact is not at issue; it has to be conceded that there is much similarity shared by the two families that is due to language contact. The criticisms of some aspects of Orr and Longacre (1968) data were accurate. In the end, however, none of these criticisms were sufficient to preclude the possibility that some of the shared similarities could be because the languages were genetically related, even if they may have separated a very long time ago and had undergone many changes because of being in constant contact. In my own investigations (Campbell 1995), I came to believe that Quechuan and Aymaran probably are related to each other, and I tried to point to directions that might help get past the problems of intensive sharing by borrowing. However, it has to be noted, too, that the evidence, at least so far, has been insufficient to guarantee that conclusion. For more informative discussions, both pro and con, see Adelaar 1986, 1987, 2012b, 2012c, 2017; Campbell 1995, 1997a, 273–284; Cerrón-Palomino 1994[2008]; Emlen 2017; Emlen and Dellert 2020; Michael 2021, 333; Torero 2002, 151–160; Van de Kerke and Muysken 2014.). The matter definitely deserves more careful investigation.

APPENDIX I
A CLOSER LOOK AT GREENBERG'S MACRO-PANOAN HYPOTHESIS

As another case study involving proposals of distant genetic relationships, in this appendix all of the evidence presented by Joseph Greenberg (1987, 74–78) for his proposed Macro-Panoan hypothesis (a branch of the Ge-Pano-Carib division of his Amerind proposal) is evaluated based on standard criteria. The purpose for presenting this evaluation of the evidence presented for this classification is to show in greater detail the kinds of problems involved in this and other similar proposals of distant genetic relationships. Other possible explanations (other than that of cognates inherited from some common ancestor) for the similarities among the lexical items compared from the different languages are pointed out. Greenberg's Macro-Panoan hypothesis would group several South American language families and isolates: Panoan, Takanan (actually a single family, Pano-Takanan), Moseten, Mataco[an], Guaicuru[an], Charruan, Lule, Vilela (now recognized as a single Lule-Vilela family), and Mascoy[an] (Enlhet-Enenlhet).

Greenberg's comparisons follow. Some clarifications of some of the names and forms are given in square brackets ([. . .]); this is information that is not present in Greenberg (1987). This is followed by brief discussion of the problems in each comparison set.

1 BE ABLE [Enlhet-Enenlhet] Lengua [Enlhet] *wan(-či), wan(-kje)*. Mataco[an]: Chulupi [Nivaclé] *ha-wanaia* [no such form exists; *xa-* '1ST PERSON ACTIVE'].

Problems: Only two languages are compared from the many in the set of languages involved. The form in one of the two languages is spurious (non-existent). For Chulupi [Nivaclé] *ha-wanaia*, possibly *xa-wan* 'I see/find/have' was somehow involved, but in none of these senses is this close to 'to be able'. Nivaclé has no verb equivalent to 'can, be able'; rather, it uses either a direct assertion (instead of 'I can lift it' the equivalent of 'I lift it' or the equivalent of 'it is good for me that I eat' for 'I can eat') (Campbell et al. 2020, 472–473).

2 ANIMAL Guaicuru[an]: Toba-Guazu *sigiak*. [Enlhet-Enenlhet:] Lengua [Enlhet] *askok*. Mataco[an]: Vejoz [Wichí] *łokue*.

Problems: *łokue* is a spurious form; no such word exists in Wichí. There is *łokʷe*, but it means 'jug'; *lo* is the classifier for possessed domestic animals and that could be involved here, but it shares no similarity to the other two forms compared in this set.

3 ANSWER (v.) Mataco[an]: Choroti [Chorote] *kamtini* 'speak'. Panoan: Cazinaua *køma*. Cavineña *kiema*.

Problems: Semantic latitude: 'answer'/'speak'. Only two language families are represented in the comparisons, and only one Matacoan language and only two Panoan (Pano-Taakanan) languages are represented from each of the two families, though each of them has several other languages in them. (Cazinaua is unknown, at least in that spelling; probably Kashinawa [Caxinahua] is intended.)

4 ANUS Guaicuru[an]: Caduveo *-auio* 'buttocks'. Mataco[an]: Choroti *i-we*, Vejoz [Wichí] *wex* ['tail, backside']. Moseten *jive* 'buttocks, anus'. Panoan [Pano-Tacanan]: Caripuna *wahaa* 'open'. Tacanan [Pano-Takanan]: Huarayo *wexa* 'opening,' Chama *wexa* 'hole'.

Problems: Semantic latitude: 'buttocks, anus'/'tail'/'open/opening/hole'. Short forms: perhaps only *w/v* match across the proposed cognates.

5 AWAKE Charruan: Chana *inambi*. Guaicuru[an]: Toba-Guazu *tom* 'awake, dawn'. Mataco[an]: Vejoz [Wichí]: *nom* (intransitive) [*n-om* 'come, arrive', *n-* 'DIRECTIONAL']. Panoan: Proto-Panoan (S) **nama* 'to dream'.

Problems: Semantic latitude: 'awake, dawn'/'come, arrive'/'dream'. Missed morphological analysis (*n-om*); the root *om* 'come, arrive' is not very similar to most of the other forms and is itself a short form. Only four Charrúan words are seen in all the comparisons for the Macro-Panoan hypothesis.

6 BACK [Enlhet-Enenlhet:] Lengua [Enlhet] *ak-puk*, *(eja-)puk* 'behind'. Panoan: Shipibo *puika*. Tacanan: Cavineña *ebekakwa*, Chama *kiibaaxaxe* 'behind'.

Problems: Only two families involved (Pano-Takanan is a single family). There is some semantic latitude, though not implausible: 'back'/'behind'.

7 BAD Guaicuru[an]: Guachi <oetcho> 'devil'. Mataco[an]: Nocten [Wichí], Vejoz [Wichí] *tsoi* 'devil'. Moseten *ači-tui* 'make dirty'. Tacanan: Tacana *ači*. Cf. Lule *ičelo* 'devil'.

Problems: Semantic latitude: 'devil'/'make dirty'. Phonology: only *ts / č* are matched. Classification problem: Guachí is not Guaicurúan; there are only three words from Guachí in all the proposed cognates purportedly supporting Greenberg's Macro-Panoan classification (see 50 OLD and 57 SON below).

8 BAT Guaicuru [?]: *kahit*. Panoan: Proto-Panoan **kaši*.

Problem: Only two languages are compared from many in the set of languages involved.

9 BE Lengua [Enlhet-Enenlhet]: Mascoy *h-*. [Matacoan:] Mataco [Wichí] *ihi, hi* [*i-* 'to be', *i- hi* 'be-LOCATIVE].

Problems: Only short forms are compared. Phonology: perhaps nothing matches (h: i?). Morphological analysis was missed: Mataco [Wichí] *ihi, hi* is composed of *i-* 'to be' + the locative suffix *-hi*]. Only two languages are compared from many in the set of languages involved.

10 BEAR (v.) Guaicuru[an]: Mocovi *koo*, Toba-Guazu *koe*. Lule *kaa* 'born'. [Matacoan:] Mataco [Wichí] *ko*, Vejoz [Wichí] *ko*. Panoan: Proto-Panoan (S) **kai* 'to bear, mother,' Chacobo *ko* 'born'. Tacanan: Chama *kwaja* 'be born'.

Problems: Short forms. Mataco and Vejoz are a single language; Mataco is now called Wichí; Vejoz is one variety of Wichí.

11 BEFORE Lengua [Enlhet-Enenlhet]: Lengua, Mascoy *nanič*, Lengua *nahno, nahtu* 'mucho anteo' [*anteo* is unclear in Spanish]. Mataco[an]: Chulupi [Nivaclé] *naxeš* 'forward' [no such form exists, Payagua *inahi* [not Matacoan], Moseten <yno>, *xinoje*.

Problems: Semantic latitude: 'much before'(?)/'forward'. Spurious form: no such from as Chulupi [Nivaclé] *naxeš* 'forward' exists. Possibly it is from *nax-* 'to end, terminate'; probably a mixture of *nayiš* 'road' and the verb derived from it, *nayi-n* 'to go on ahead, anticipate, prepare, be first', where one translation in Spanish is *adelantarse* is 'to go forward, go ahead,' similar to *adelante* 'ahead, forward, in front of, before'. The 'mucho anteo' Spanish gloss for the Lengua forms is unclear; it appears to be a typo for *mucho antes* 'long before'. Guachí is not a Guaicurúan language, though it has at times been hypothesized as belonging to Guaicurúan or Macro-Guaicurúan (see above).

12 BLOOD Guaicuruan: Toba *t-auo*, Lule *ewe*. Mataco[an]: Chunupi [Nivaclé] *woi* [woʔoy]. Tacanan: Chama *woʔo* 'red'.

Problems: Semantic latitude: 'blood'/'red'. Phonology: only *w* matches.

13 BODY Lule *toip* [*-p* '3ᴿᴰ ᴘᴇʀs ᴘᴏssᴇssɪᴠᴇ ᴘʀᴏɴᴏᴜɴ']. Mataco[an:] Mataco [Wichí]: *tape* [*t-* '3ʳᵈ ᴘᴇʀs ᴘᴏssᴇssɪᴠᴇ ᴘʀᴏɴᴏᴜɴ']. Tacanan: Cavineña *etibo* 'trunk' [*e-tibu: e-* 'Pronoun', *tibu* 'base'].

Problems: Semantic latitude: 'body'/'base'. Missed (fudged?) morphological analysis: the Lule *toip* is composed of *toi* 'body' + *-p* '3ᴿᴰ ᴘᴇʀsᴏɴᴀʟ ᴘᴏssᴇssɪᴠᴇ ᴘʀᴏɴᴏᴜɴ'—notice that this *-p* is segmented in all the other Lule forms which end in *p* that Greenberg cited. Phonology: with Lule's *-p* segmented off as a separate morpheme, *toi* bears little similarity to the words compared from the other languages.

14 BREAK Lengua [Enlhet-Enenlhet]: Mascoy *pok-* (intransitive). Mataco[an:] Mataco [Wichí] *puhʷoje* [*pux-u* 'break, explode'], Suhin [Nivaclé] *poktoče* (intransitive) [*pakxet-ši*: *pakxet* 'break' + *-ši* 'ɪɴᴅᴇғɪɴɪᴛᴇ ᴅɪʀᴇᴄᴛɪᴏɴ ᴏʀ ʟᴏᴄᴀᴛɪᴏɴ']. Moseten *fok*.

Problems: Onomatopoeic.

15 BREAST Lengua [Enlhet-Enenlhet]: Lengua *namakuk*, Kaskiha *neme* 'nipple'. Lule *ineme* 'milk'.

Problems: Semantics latitude (not severe): 'breast'/'milk/nipple'. Onomatopoeic (cf. nursing, suckling noises). Only two families are compared (two languages from one family, one language from the other). No explanation for the non-matching sounds in these comparisons is offered.

16 BROTHER Charruan: Charrua *inčala*. Lule *kani* 'younger brother'. Mataco[an:] Mataco [Wichí] *čila* 'older brother' [*kʼila*], *činix* 'younger brother' [*kʼinix*], Choroti *kiili* 'older brother' [*-kilia*], *kiini* 'younger brother [*-yini*]'. Vilela *ikelebepe*.

Problems: two separate Matacoan cognate sets are involved—one for 'elder brother' and a separate one for 'younger brother' are conflated into a single one here. Only four Charruan words are seen in all the comparisons for the Macro-Panoan hypothesis.

17 CLOSE (v.) Mataco[an:] Choroti [Chorote] *pone, pione* 'close, cover,' Vejoz [Wichí] *ponhi* 'imprison,' Towothli [Maká] *aponik* 'cover'. Tacanan: Cavineña *pene*.

Problems: Forms from only Matacoan languages and one Tacanan language are compared. Semantic latitude: 'close, cover'/'imprison'. The Chorote form is *-po:-* 'to cover', and the cognates in the other Matacoan languages reflect *-po* 'to cover'; there does not appear to be an *n* associated with this root, which would be needed to make the Chorote root match well the forms cited from other languages.

18 COLD₁ [Enlhet-Enenlhet]: Lengua *math(-kaiyi)* 'be cold'. Panoan: Proto-Panoan (S) **matʲi* 'be cold'.

Problem: only two languages are compared. What is the *-kaiyi* of the Lengua form?

19 COLD₂ Lule *kei*. Mataco[an:] Enimaga [Maká] *koija*, Chunupi [Nivaclé] *kui* [k'uy].

Problems: Only forms from two language families are compared, Lule and two Matacoan languages. (The Maká word is *-k'wi* 'to be cold'. *k'uy-im* 'to feel cold', not *koija*.) In effect it is short forms that are compared, where the only seeming match is between *k* and *k'*.

20 CUT Lengua [Enlhet-Enenlhet]: Guana *čečet* 'cut up'. Mataco[an]: Suhin [Nivaclé] *siči*, Choroti [Chorote] *esita, ešita*. Panoan: Proto-Panoan **šaʔti*.

Problems: Nivaclé has ten distinct verbs which translate as 'to cut'; the one intended here is probably *seʔx* 'to cut up', perhaps *seʔx-ši* 'cut up-INDEFINITE.LOCATION']. The flawed form of Suhin [Nivaclé] makes it appear more similar to the others than it actually is, with nothing to match the *t* of these other languages. The Chorote form is unclear (unknown?). It appears to involve Chorote *-eysaxam* 'to cut by hand'.

21 DARK Guaicuru[an]: Toba, Mocovi *epe, pe* 'night'. Mataco[an]: Choroti [Chorote] *pe* 'shadow' Tacanan: Chama *kea-apo* 'night,' Tacana *apu-* 'dark'.

Problems: Short forms (only *p* matches). Semantic latitude: 'night'/'shadow'/'dark'. The Chorote root is *-pel* 'shade, shadow, image', with a derivative form *-pel-uk*.

22 DIG Mataco[an]: Vejoz [Wichí] *tih,* Mataco [Wichí] *tiho [tix-i* 'dig']. Tacanan: Chama *teo*.

Problems: Only two languages—Wichí and Chama—are compared. Phonology: apparently only *t* is intended to match.

23 DOG Mataco[an]: Suhin [Nivaclé] *nuu* [nuʔu], Choropi [Nivaclé] *nuux* [nuʔu]. Panoan: Proto-Panoan (S) **ʔino, *ʔinaka*.

Problems: Only two "languages" are compared, Nivaclé and Proto-Panoan. (Suhin and Choropi are just alternative names for Nivaclé.) Phonology: Only *n* matches; perhaps *u* / *o* are intended to match, also.

24 DOOR Lule *atʲiki-* <aciqui-p> 'hole'. Panoan: Proto-Panoan **šikʷi* 'doorway'. Tacanan: Proto-Tacanan **t̯ekʷe* 'door, doorway'.

Problems: Semantic latitude: 'hole'/'doorway, door'. Only two entities are compared (Lule and Pano-Tacanan); Panoan and Tacanan belong to a single language family, Pano-Tacanan.

25 DRESS (v.) Lule *tala* 'clothing,' *talaks*. Mataco[an]: Mataco [Wichí] *tula* 'clothing' [the form *tula* is unknown].

Problems: Only two languages are compared. The Wichí form may be spurious ('clothing' in Wichí is *-wuy*).

26 DRY [Enlhet-Enenlhet:] Lengua *jima(-gjaji)* 'be dry'. Mataco[an]: Mataco [Wichí] *jim* 'dry up', Suhin, Chulipi [Nivaclé] *jim*, Macca [Maká] *iim*. Moseten *jiñ* 'bone'.

Problems: Semantic latitude: 'dry'/'bone'. Wichí has no /ɨ/; probably Macato [Wichí] *jɨm* here is a typo. The same root appears in three separate putative cognate sets, again in 27 and 30 (see below).

27 EMPTY Lule *em-p*. Mataco[an]: Mataco [Wichí] *jim,* Chulupi [Nivaclé] *jimši*.

Problems: The same root is compared to different sets of forms in 26 and 27, and 30, as though they involved separate cognate sets instead of just one. Only two language families are compared, Lule (from Lule-Vilelan) and Matacoan (two languages). The Chulupi [Nivaclé] *jimši* is *yim-ši* 'to dry up, to end, run out', composed of *yim* 'dry' + *-ši* 'INDEFINITE LOCATION'. Phonology: The compared parts are short forms; perhaps only *m* is intended to match (or perhaps also *e / i*).

28 FEAR₁ (v.) Guaicuru[an]: Toba-Guazu *nahi*. Mataco[an]: Vejoz [Wichí] *nowai* [the root is *oway*; *n-* is 'MIDDLE VOICE MARKER']. Moseten *nojii* 'frighten'. Panoan: Cashibo *noo* 'frighten,' Nocaman *no* 'enemy,' Panobo, Shipibo *nawa* 'enemy'.

Problems: Semantic latitude: 'fear'/'frighten'/'enemy'. Morphological analysis: with *n-* of Wichí segmented off as a prefix not involved in the meaning of the root, the root is no longer similar phonetically to the forms in the other languages. In Vejoz [Wichí] *nowai*, the root is *oway*, and *n-* is 'MIDDLE VOICE MARKER'. In effect, only short forms are compared in set 28, where other sounds beyond *no* or *na* in these words appear mostly to be ignored.

29 FEAR₂ (v.) Lule *lako* 'be ashamed'. Panoan: Proto-Panoan **rakʷi*.

Problems: Semantic latitude: 'be ashamed'/'fear'. Only two "languages" are compared.

30 FINISH Lule *tum-p* 'be finished'. Mataco[an]: Choroti [Chorote] *temi*, Suhin [Nivaclé] *timš* Cf. Tacanan: Cavineña *tupu* 'enough'.

Problems: Morphological analysis: There is no Suhin [Nivaclé] form *timš*; rather, what is involved is *im* 'to end, run out, dry up'. Perhaps it is based on *t-im-ši* [VERB.CLASS-end-INDEFINITE.LOCATION]. With the verb class morpheme *t-* segmented from the Nivaclé root *im*, little similarity is left. (The same root was compared to other forms also in 26 and 27). If the Cavineña form is intended to be included in this set, then there is the problem of semantic latitude: 'be finished'/'end, run out'/'enough'.

31 FLY (v.) Moseten *naj*. Panoan: Proto-Panoan **noja*.

Problems: Only two "languages" are compared. There are problems with the Proto-Panoan form. Sanderson Soares de Oliveira (2014, 450) reconstructs **[n]o[ya]-* 'to fly' for Proto-Panoan. However, his **[n]* represents the possibility that the proto form had either **n* or **r*, because the data are not available from the language that preserves independent reflexes of the **n-/*r* contrast. That is, if Proto-Panoan 'to fly' was **ro[ya]* instead of **no[ya]*, the comparison with Mosetén would not seem very similar. Moreover, Oliveira uses square brackets in reconstructed forms when there is doubt about the existence of a certain part of the form. In short, for **[n]o[ya]-* the only thing that is not in doubt is **o*.

32 GREEN Lule <za>. Moseten <za>. Panoan: Proto-Panoan (S) **ṣoo* 'green, not ripe.' Tacanan: Proto-Tacanan **zawa*. [Note that Panoan and Tacanan are members of the Pano- Tacanan family.]

Problems: Short forms. Only two entities are compared, Mosetén and Pano-Takanan.

33 HANG Moseten *pina* 'hammock'. Panoan: Conibo *panea* 'be hung,' *pani* 'hang up,' Shipibo *panni* 'hang up'.

Problems: Semantic latitude: 'hammock'/'be hung'/'hang up'. Only two language families are involved in the comparison, Mosetén and Panoan. Possible borrowing: 'Hammock' is a culture item, subject to possible borrowing.

34 HATE Guaicuru[an]: Abipone *n-paak* 'hated'. Moseten *fakoj, fakin* 'be angry'.

Problems: Only two languages are compared; only one of the Guaicurúan languages is represented. Semantic latitude (not serious): 'hated'/'be angry'.

35 HORN Lengua [Enlhet-Enenlhet]: Guana *taša*. Moseten *daš* <dasc>.

Problems: only two languages are compared; only one of the Enlhet-Enenlhet languages, Guaná, is represented; in fact, data from Guaná appear in only two comparison sets, this one and set 20.

36 KNEAD [Matacoan:] Mataco [Wichí] *pʔon*. Moseten *puñe* 'knead, mud'.

Problems: only two languages are compared.

37 KNOW Mataco[an]: Vejoz [Wichí] *hanex* [*han-* 'to know', *-ex* 'APPLICATIVE'], Choroti *hane* 'know, be able' [-xane?]. Moseten *(am)-xeñ* '(no se puede' [it is not possible]). Panoan: Proto-Panoan *onā* 'know, be able', Shipibo *huna*.

Problems: Semantics?: 'to know (be able)'/'it is not possible'

38 LEAF Guaicuru[an]: Toba: *l-awe*. [Enlhet-Enenlhet:] Lengua *wa*.

Problems: Short forms. Only two languages are compared, only one each from Guaicurúan and from Enlhet-Enenlhet.

39 LEAVE (ABANDON) Guaicuru[an]: Toba-Guazu *jane*. Lengua [Enlhet-Enenlhet]: Mascoy *jiño*. Panoan: Proto-Panoan *ini*. Vilela *jane*.

Problems: Phonological match?; just *n* / *ñ* (or also *j* / *j* / Ø / *j*?). (Oliveira's [2014, 303] reconstruction for Proto-Panaoan is *hi[n]iC_c* 'leave, go away', where the *[n]* is uncertain and could be *r or *n.)

40 LOOK Charruan: Chana *sola*. Guaicuru[an]: Pilaga *čelage*, Toba-Guazu *silaha*.

Problems: Only two families are represented in the comparisons (Chana and two Guaicuruan languages).

41 LOSE Moseten *moñi* 'perish, lose, err'. Panoan: Cashibo *mano* 'forget', Cashinahua *manu* 'miss'. Tacanan: Proto-Tacanan **manu* 'die'.

Problems: Semantic latitude: 'perish, lose, err'/'forget'/'miss'/'die'. Only two language families are involved (Pano-Takanan is a single language family).

42 MAKE Guaicuru[an]: Toba-Guazu *uo*. Panoan: Proto-Panoan (S) **wa, *ʔa*. Tacanan: Proto-Tacanan **a* 'make, say'.

Problems: Short forms. Only two families are represented; Toba-Guazu is the only Guaicurúan language involved. Oliveira (2014, 397) reconstructs *ʔak 'to make, to kill' for Proto-Panoan, which makes the compared forms less similar.

43 MANY Guaicuru[an]: Toba-Guazu *lamai*. [Enlhet-Enenlhet:] Lengua *lamo*. Mataco[an]: Payagua [not a Matacoan language] *lehmi* 'all'.

Problems: Semantic latitude(?) 'many'/'all' (not serious). Classification problem: Payaguá does not belong to Matacoan; some have proposed a Guacurúan connection for it, but that is not substantiated (see Chapter 5, see above). Payaguá figures in only four putative cognate sets in Greenberg's

Macro-Panoan data. Only one of the Guaicurúan languages is represented (and Matacoan is not represented at all) in this set.

44 MEAT Guaicuru[an]: Pilaga *niiak* 'fish'. [Enlhet-Enenlhet:] Lengua *nohak* 'wild animal'. Tacanan: Chama *noe*, Tiatinagua, Huarayo *noči*. Vilela *nuhu* 'fish'.
Problems: Semantic latitude: 'fish'/'wild animal'. Phonology: perhaps only *n* matches?

45 MOSQUITO Lengua [Enlhet-Enenlhet]: Mascoy *p-aija*. Mataco[an]: Choroti [Chorote] *eji* [*eye*], Suhin [Nivaclé] *iya* [(*y*)*iya*ʔ].
Problems: These forms are onomatopoeic. Only two entities are compared (one Enlhet-Enenlhet language and two Matacoan languages). The words compared are short forms.

46 MOTHER Mataco[an]: Macca [Maká] *nana*. Tacanan: Proto-Tacanan *nene* 'aunt'. Vilela *nane*.
Problems: These are nursery forms. Similar forms for 'mother' are found in languages all over the world. Semanatic latitude(?): 'mother'/'aunt'.

47 MOUSE Guaicuru[an]: Toba-Guazu *mekahi* 'bat'. Moseten *meče* 'rat'. Panoan: Proto-Panoan **maka* 'rat, mouse'. Cf. Mataco[an]: Mataco [Wichí], Suhin [Nivaclé], Chulupi [Nivaclé] *ama*, Vejoz [Wichí] *ma*.
Problems: Semantic latitude: 'bat'/'rat', 'mouse'. Short forms are involved, at least in the case of Vejoz [Wichí] *ma*.

48 NECK₁ Moseten *tetˢ* <tez>. Panoan: Proto-Panoan **tišo*.
Problems: only two languages are compared. (Oliveira [2014, 280] has **tišo* 'neck'.)

49 NECK₂ Lule *u(-p)*. Mataco[an]: Mataco [Wichí], Choroti, and so on. *wo* [Chorote *-wo*ʔ]. Moseten <huh> 'throat'.
Problems: Short forms. Phonology: perhaps no clear matches in these words (maybe *u*: *o*?, or *u*: *w*?).

50 OLD Guaicuru[an]: Guachi *seera*. Mataco[an]: Payagua *aheri* 'old woman'. Panoan: Proto-Panoan **šini*. Tacanan: Proto-Tacanan **ziri*.
Problems: Semantic latitude?: 'old'/'old woman'. Classification problem: Guachí is unclassified, and Payaguá is a language isolate; very few comparisons from these two are made with other languages in Greenberg's data. Guachí is not a Guaicurúan language and Payaguá is not a Matacoan language, though it has at times been proposed that both are connected with Guaicurúan or Macro-Guaicurúan (see above).

51 RED Guaicuru[an]: Toba, Mocovi *tok*. [Enlhet-Enenlhet:] Lengua *eteig-ma*. Mataco[an]: Macca [Maká] *tek* 'blood'. Tacanan: Proto-Tacanan **čiaka*.
Problems: Semantic latitude: 'red'/'blood'. Spurious form: Macca [Maká] *tek* 'blood', no such form exists in Maká; Maká has *-athits* 'blood', *-atxu*ʔ 'to bleed', and *siyixi*ʔ 'red'.[17] Only one language is represented each from Matacoan and Takanan (Pano-Takanan).

52 RIB Guaicuru[an]: Mocovi <emeneh>. Moseten *mana*.
Problems: Only two languages are compared, only one from the Guiacurúan family.

53 ROTTEN [Enlhet-Enenlhet:] Lengua *abik*. Lule *poko* 'to rot'. Moseten *fokoi*.
Only one Enlhet-Enenlhet language is represented.

54 SHOUT Lule *se* 'cry'. Panoan: Shipibo *sei*, Conibo *sɨje*, Cashinahua *sa*. Tacanan: Proto-Tacanan *ṭʼea*.
Problems: Only languages from two families are compared, Lule and Pano-Takanan. The compared words are short forms. Potentially, 'shout' involves onomatopoeia.

55 SIDE Guaicuru[an]: Toba-Guazu *ai, aji*, Mocovi *ai* 'side,' Abipone *uii*. Lule *je*.
Problems: Only two language families are represented, Guaicuruan and Lule. These are short forms. 'Side' in Lule is *peyuelet* (see also *yecquicsç* 'to lie on one's side') (Maccioni [Machoni] 2008, 108).

56 SMALL Lengua [Enlhet-Enenlhet]: Mascoy *etkok*. Mataco[an]: Churupi [Nivaclé] *tikin* [*tikʼin*], Suhin [Nivaclé] *tika* [no such form exists, perhaps a mistake for *tikʼin* 'small']. Towothli [Maká] *taake* 'short'. Panoan: Culino *tukuča* 'short'.
Problems: Semantic latitude(?): 'small'/'short'. Churupi and Suhin are just alternate names for Nivaclé, a single language. The Nivaclé form is sound symbolic.

57 SON Charruan: Chana, Guenoa *ineu*. Guaicuru[an]: Guachi *inna*. Vilela *ina-hmi* (Pelleschi [source]), *ina-ke* 'son, daughter' (Gilij [source]), *hina-kis* (Fontana [source]).
Problems: Classification: Guachí is not a Guaicurúan language. Both Guachí and Charrúan show up in very few comparisons in Greenberg's data.

58 SOUR Mataco[an]: Choroti [Chorote] *paši* <paxhi>. Moseten *pase*. Panoan: Proto-Panoan *paṣa* 'sour, raw, uncooked,' Tacanan: Proto-Tacanan *paṭʼe*.
Problems: Panoan and Takanan are not from separate families. The Chorote form appears to represent either *paxyiʔ* 'bitter' or *paxhi* 'sour'. Oliveira (2014, 455) has Proto-Panoan *paṣa* but with the gloss 'raw, fresh, new'—not 'sour', nor is 'sour' a gloss of any of the cognates to this form from eleven Panoan languages that he cites.

59 SWIM Guaicuru[an]: Pilaga *ubogai*. Moseten <vigi>. Tacanan: Proto-Tacanan *beṭʼa*.
Only one Guaicurúan language is represented.

60 THIN Lule *kam*. Moseten *kum*. Cf. Mataco[an]: Vejoz [Wichí] *čemsa-* 'small'.
Problems: Semantic latitude(?): 'thin'/'small'. Apparently only two languages are compared.

61 URINE [Enlhet-Enenlhet:] Lengua *jis(-weji)* 'urinate'. Lule <ys> 'urinate'. Mataco[an]: Suhin [Nivaclé] *yuɬ*, Churupi [Nivaclé] <yius, yiusl> 'urinate' (*sl* just represents the voiceless lateral fricative *ɬ* here. Panoan: Proto-Panoan (S) *isõ, *istõ.
Problems: These forms here and in many languages are onomatopoeic or sound symbolic. They are short forms. Suhin and Churupi are both alternate names for Nivaclé; both have the root *-uɬ* 'urine, to urinate, y-uɬ* 'he/she/it urinates', *y-* '3RD PERS PRONOUN'. The morphological analysis failure to segment off Nivaclé *y-* '3RD PERS PRONOUN' made the forms appear similar when there is in fact little similarity. Oliveira (2014, 325) reconstructs *hisor-* 'urine, to urinate' for Proto-Panoan.

62 WEAK Lengua [Enlhet-Enenlhet]: Mascoy *jil, jel-k*. Mataco[an]: Mataco [Wichí] *jel* 'weak, tired' [*y-* "3ʳᴰ PERS PRONOUN," root *-et* 'to tire'].

Problems: Morphological analysis: the failure to segment off Wichí *y-* (Greenberg's *j*) makes the forms appear similar when there is little similarity. Short forms are compared. Only two language families are represented with only one language from each of them.

63. WOMAN Moseten *pen*. Proto-Tacanan **e-pona*.

Problem: Only two languages families are compared. Victor Girard (1971a, 113) reconstructed Proto-Takanan **puna* 'woman'. Takaná and some of the other Takanan languages have *e-puna* 'woman', while a few of have *e-pona* 'woman, female'.

In summary, there are methodological problems of one sort or another with nearly all of Greenberg's proposed Macro-Panoan cognate sets. When one tries to establish sound correspondences across the languages that are proposed as belonging to the grouping, there are insufficient cases, even if we are generous with the data provided, to be able to establish reliably recurring sound correspondences among Panoan, Tacanan (Pano-Takanan), Mosetén, Matacoan, Guaicuruan, Charrúan, Lule, Vilela (Lule-Vilela), and Mascoyan [Enlhet-Enenlhet] (maybe with Payaguá and Guachí slipped in). For example, Charrúan forms (not even all of which are from the same Charrúan language) appear in only four of Greenberg's lexical sets (5, 16, 40, 57), far too few to establish sound correspondences for Charrúan, or to show a genetic relationship. The same story holds for Vilela, represented in only five lexical sets (16, 39, 44, 46, 57), and several of these Vilela words are questionable. In short, given the paucity of data and the many problems with the data that Greenberg did present, it is hardly surprising that linguists have not been convinced.

APPENDIX 2

LIST OF DISTANT GENETIC RELATIONSHIP PROPOSALS

Here, a list of proposals of distant genetic relationships involving Indigenous languages of the Americas is provided. It includes most of the better-known hypotheses but not all of them by a long shot. Several others are mentioned in various earlier chapters; they do not need to be repeated here.

Algonkian-Gulf Mary Haas' Algonkian-Gulf proposal—that there is a relationship between Algic (Algonquian-Ritwan) and the putative Gulf languages—received considerable attention in the past (see for example, Gursky 1966–1967, 1968). For Algonkin-Gulf + Hokan-Subtiaba see Gursky 1965–1966.

Almosan and Beyond Edward Sapir (1929a) combined Algic (Algonquian-Ritwan), Kutenai, and Mosan (see Gursky 1966a, 412).

American Indian languages-Altaic (Ferrario 1933, 1938).

American Indian languages-Asian languages (and Aztec-Sanskrit) (Milewski 1960).

American Indian languages-Polynesian (Key 1984).

American Indian languages-Semitic (Leesberg 1903).

Amerind (Greenberg 1979, 1987, 1989, 1990a, 1994, 1996a, 1996b, 2000a; Greenberg and Ruhlen 1992, 2007; Paul Newman 1991, 1993; Ruhlen 1991, 1994a, 1994b, 1994c).

Andean: Greenberg (1987, 99, 382–383) grouped Alakaluf, Araucanian, Aymara, Catacao, Cholona, Culli, Gennaken (Pehuelche), Itucale (Simacu), Kahuapana, Leco, Mayna (Omurana), Patagon (Tehuelche), Quechua, Sabela (Auca), Sechura, Yamana (Yahgan), and Zaparo. He distinguished a "Northern Andean subgroup" (Catacao, Cholona, Culli, Leco, and Sechura) and a "Southern Andean" (Alakaluf, Araucanian, Gennaken, Patagon, and Yamana).

Arawakan and Cariban (Mason 1950, 209; David Payne 1990, 83).

Atakapa-Chitimacha (Swadesh 1946, 1947).

Athabaskan and Sino-Tibetan (Shafer 1952, 1957, 1969; Swadesh 1952; cf. Na-Dené–Sino-Tibetan, Sapir 1925b).

Athabaskan–Sino-Tibetan, Na-Dene-Basque(-North-Caucasian), and Athabaskan-Tlingit-Yuchi-Siouan (several papers).

Australian with various American Indian languages, for example, Chon–Australian and Malayo-Polynesian (Rivet 1925a, 1925b, 1957[1943]); South American–Australian (Trombetti 1928).

Aztec-Tanoan (Uto-Aztecan + Kiowa-Tanoan) (Whorf and Trager 1937; Davis 1989; Shaul 1985; see Campbell 1997a, 269–273 for a critical appraisal of the evidence).

Basque–American Indian languages (Trombetti 1928[1926], 173; Vinson 1876[1875]).

Beothuk-Algonquian (Hewson 1968, 1971, 1978, 1982; see Campbell 1997a, 289–291).

Bora-Witotoan (Aschmann 1993). Joining Boran and Witotoan. Now doubted, since much of the evidence for joining Boran with Witotoan appears to be due to borrowing (Seifart and Echeverri 2015).

Caddoan-Siouan (see critical evaluation in Campbell 1997a, 262–265).

Cariban-Tupían-Arawakan (de Goeje 1909).

Cayuse–Molala (see critique in Rigsby 1966, 1969).

Central Amerind: Greenberg distinguished "three apparently coordinate branches" of Central Amerind: "Kiowa-Tanoan, Uto-Aztecan, and Oto-Mangue" (Greenberg 1987, 123–131, 381).

Chibchan-Paezan. This large grouping for Greenberg "consists of the following families": Allentiac, Andaqui, Antioquia, Aruak, Atacama, Barbacoa, Betoi, Chibcha, Chimu, Choco, Cuitlatec, Cuna, Guaymi, Itonama, Jirajara, Lenca, Malibu, Misumalpan, Motilon, Mura, Paez, Paya, Rama, Talamanca, Tarascan, Timucua, Warrau, Xinca, and Yanomama (Greenberg 1987, 106–121, 382). It is surprising to find North American Timucua, Mexican Cuitlatec and Tarascan, Central American Lenca and Xinca, and remote South American Chimu, Warrau (Warao), and Yanomama included here with the Chibchan and Paez[an] languages.

Chono-Alacalufan-Yagan (Viegas Barros 2005, 83–107).

Coahuiltecan (Manaster-Ramer 1996; Sapir 1920, 1929a; see Goddard 1979a; Campbell 1996, 1997a, 297–304).

Culle-Cholonan (Kaufman 1994, 64). (Joining Culle and Cholonan.)

Dene-Caucasian, Dene–Sino-Caucasian (cf. Macro-Caucasian phylum: Burushic [Burushaski], Caucasic, Basque) (Bengtson 1991a, 1991b, 1992; Blažek and Bengtson 1995; Catford 1991; Nikolaev 1989, 1991; Ruhlen 1998; Shevoroshkin 1991; Schuhmacher 1989; Starostin 1991; Trask 1995; cf. Sino-Caucasian, Dene–Sino-Tibetan).

DURALJAN (Dravidian, Uralic, Altaic, Japanese-Korean, Andean-Equatorial) (Hakola 1997, 2000).

Equatorial. In 1960 Greenberg had an Equatorial-Andean grouping, but in 1987 he broke this up into three separate groups: Equatorial, Macro-Tucanoan, and Andean. In his later Equatorial he placed Arawa, Cayuvava, Chapacura, Coche, Cofan, Esmeralda, Guahibo, Guamo, Jibaro, Kandoshi, Kariri, Katembri, Maipuran, Otomaco, Piaroa, Taruma, Timote, Tinigua, Trumai, Tupi, Tusha, Uro,Yaruro, Yuracare, and Zamuco (combining into a subgroup that he called Jibaro-Kandoshi, the language groups Cofan, Esmeralda, Jibaro, Kandoshi, and Yaruro) (Greenberg 1987, 83–94, 384–385).

Eskimo and Indo-European (Hammerich 1951; Uhlenbeck 1922–1945; cf. Thalbitzer 1945).

Eskimo-Aleut and Austronesian (Schuhmacher 1974, 1991).

Eskimo-Aleut–Chukotan (American–Arctic-Paleo-Siberian phylum, Luoravetlan) (cf. Fortescue 1994, 1998; Hamp 1976; Krauss 1973a; Swadesh 1962; see also Nikolaev and Mudrak 1989; cf. Boas 1933; Campbell 2000).

Eskimo-Aleut–Yukagir (Fortescue 1988; cf. Campbell 2000).
Eskimo-Uralic (Bergsland 1959, 1979; Sauvageot 1924, 1953; Thalbitzer 1928, 1952; Uhlenbeck 1905).
Eskimo–Ural-Altaic (Koo 1980).
Eurasiatic (Greenberg's 2000b grouping of Indo-European, Uralic, Eskimo-Aleut, Ainu, and several other otherwise unaffiliated languages).
Gê and Old World macro-families (Aikhenvald-Angenot and Angenot 1989).
Gê-Pano-Carib (Greenberg 1987, 385–386).
Gilyak [Nivkh], Chukchi-Kamchatkan, and Almosan-Keresiouan (Mudrak and Nikolaev 1989).
Guaicurian-Hokan (Gursky 1966–1967).
Gulf (Muskogean, Natchez, Tunica, Atakapa, Chitimacha) (Haas 1951, 1952, 1960; Munro 1994; see Campbell 1997a, 306–309; Kimball 1992, 1994; see Swanton's 1919 Tunica, Chitimacha, and Atakapa, and Swanton's 1924 Natchez-Muskogean).
Gulf-Yukian (Yukian-Gulf) (Munro 1994).
Hokan–Malayo-Polynesian, Hokan-Melanesian (Rivet 1957[1943]).
Hokan + Penutian. Kaufman (2015a, 3) suggested that "if, as I suppose, there is a linguistic stock to be called Hokan, and another stock to be called Penutian, it is possible that the two stocks have in turn a common ancestor."
Hokan-Siouan and Haas' Algonquian-Gulf proposals. (See Campbell 1997a, 309–322.)
Hokan–Subtiaba-Tlapanec (Sapir 1929a).
Hokan, Hokan-Coahuiltecan, Hokan-Siouan. (See above in this chapter.)
Huave-Mixe (Radin 1916).
Huave-Uralic (Bouda 1964, 1965).
Jicaque-Hokan (Greenberg and Swadesh 1953).
Jicaque–Subtiaba-Tlapanec (Oltrogge 1977).
Jicaque-Subtiaba(-Tequistlateco) (Oltrogge 1977; Oltrogge and Rensch 1977).
Keresan-Caddoan (Davis 1974; Rood 1973).
Keresan–Uto-Aztecan (Davis 1979).
Keresan-Zuni (Gursky 1966a).
Keresiouan (Greenberg 1987).
Kutenai and Algonquian (Haas 1965).
Lenmichí "micro-phylum" (Lencan, Misumalpan, and Chibchan) (Constenla Umaña [2012, 418] suggested that the proto-language split around 9,700 years ago from a proto-language comprised of these families).
Luoravetlan (see Eskimo-Aleut–Chukotan).
Macro-Carib. Greenberg (1987, 385) followed Loukotka (1968) and Rivet (1924) and included in his Macro-Carib (a subgroup of his Ge-Pano-Carib division of Amerind): Cariban, Andoke, Bora (Miranya), Kukura, Uitoto (Witotoan), and Yagua (Peba).
Macro-Chibchan (Craig and Hale 1992).
Macro-Jê + Chibchan (Pache 2018).
Macro-Jê + Macro-Guaicuruan (Viegas Barros 2006b).
Macro-Mayan (Mayan, Mixe-Zoquean, Totoanacan, sometimes Huave), Mayan-Zoquean (Brown and Witkowski 1979; Kaufman 1964b; McQuown 1942, 1956; Radin 1916, 1924; Wonderly 1953). Although now the Mayan–Mixe-Zoquean hypothesis looks likely (see above), the broader Macro-Mayan hypothesis is doubtful. It includes Mayan, Mixe-Zoquean, Totonacan, and in some versions also Huave. The suggested connection with Huave has been abandoned. A possible Totonacan connection with either Mayan or Mixe-Zoquean is plausible, and proposals have favored both, although the evidence presented so far is unconvincing, not holding to standard methodological procedures (see McQuown 1942, Brown et al. 2011, 2014; cf. Campbell 1997a, 333–334; Kaufman 2020a, 242–242).

Macro-Panoan. Greenberg (1987, 74–78) combines "Panoan, Tacanan, and Mosetén on the one hand and Mataco, Guaicuru, Charruan, Lule, and Vilela on the other," plus Lengua (Enlhet-Enenlhet [Mascoyan]). (See Appendix 1, above.)

Macro-Penutian, see Penutian (above).

Macro-Siouan (Siouan, Iroquoian, Caddoan, sometimes also Yuchi) (Allen 1931; Chafe 1964, 1973, 1976; Rudes 1974; see also Ballard 1978; Rankin 1981; see Campbell 1997a, 262–269 for a critical evaluation of the evidence for this hypothesis).

Macro-Tacanan (Pano-Tacanan, Chon, Mosetén, and Yuracare) (Suárez 1973).

Macro-Tucanoan. Greenberg (1987, 93–99, 383–384) grouped Auake, Auixiri, Canichana, Capixana, Catuquina, Gamella, Huari, Iranshe, Kaliana, Koaia, Maku, Mobima, Muniche, Nambikwara, Natu, Pankaruru, Puinave, Shukuru, Ticuna, Tucano, Uman, and Yuri.

Makúan-Arawakan (Nadahup-Arawakan) (Martins (2005, 342–370) (Arawakan + Nadahup). (See Nadahup-Arawakan below.)

Maya-Chipaya (Mayan + Uru-Chipayan) (Hamp 1967, 1970; Olson 1964, 1965; Stark 1972a; see Campbell 1993[1973a] for critical evaluation).

Maya-Chipaya—Yunga (Mayan–Yunga–Uru-Chipayan) (Stark 1972a).

Mayan-Araucanian (Hamp 1971; Stark 1970).

Maya-Arawakan (Noble 1965, 26; cf. Schuller 1919–1920).

Mayan-Altaic (Wikander 1967, 1970, 1970–1971).

Mayan-Turkic (Frankle 1984a, 1984b).

Mayan-Cariban-Arawakan (Schuller 1919–1920).

Mayan-Lencan (Andrews 1970).

Mayan–Sino-Tibetan (Fahey 2004).

Mesoamerican phylum (Witkowski and Brown 1978, 1981; cf. Campbell and Kaufman 1980, 1983).

Mexican Penutian (see above in this chapter).

Misulencan (Misumalpan + Lenca) (Constenla Umaña 2012, 418).

Misumalpan-Chibchan (Constenla Umaña 1987, 2002, 2012).

Mixe-Penutian (Freeland 1930).

Mixe-Zoquean-Totonacan-Otomí with Caucasian languages (Bouda 1963).

Mosan (Salishan, Wakashan, Chimakuan) (Sapir 1929a; Swadesh 1953a, 1953b).

Mosetén and Pano-Tacanan (Suárez 1969).

Na-Dene (including Haida, see above in this chapter).

Na-Dene (or Dené) with Mongol, Turkish, Chinese, Northeast Tibetan, Tokharian, and Italo-Celtic (Stewart 1991).

Nadahup-Arawakan (Makúan-Arawakan) (Martins 2005, 342–370). Aikhenvald (2006, 237) argues against this hypothesis, saying it is based on "misconception, poor data from Arawak[an] languages, and lack of proper application of the comparative method."

Nahuatl-Greek and Indo-European (Denison 1913).

Natchez-Muskogean (Haas 1956, Kimball 1994, 2005, Swanton (1924).

Nostratic-Amerind. (Mentioned in several papers.)

Ob-Ugric–Penutian (Sadovsky 1981, 1984, 1996). (See also Viitso 1971 on California Penutian, Uralic, and Nostratic languages.)

Otomanguean + Hokan. Terrence Kaufman (2015a, 2) believes that the possibility that "Hokan" and Otomanguean may be related "is quite promising," something to be investigated after Hokan "has been adequately characterized," though he also suggested that it is the case that they are related (Kaufman 2015b, 1).

Otomanguean-Huave (Swadesh 1964b, 1967a; Rensch 1973, 1976; cf. Campbell 1997a, 324).

Paezan-Barbacoan (Kaufman 1990a, 1994, 2007).
Pakawan (Coahuilteco, Comecrudo, Garza, Mamulique, and Cotoname) (Manaster Ramer 1996; see Campbell 1996 for a critique).
Pano-Takanan and Yanomaman (Migliazza and Campbell 1988).
Peruvian languages-Polynesian (Christian 1932).
Proto-Amerindian (Matteson 1972; Radin 1919).
Quechua-Altaic. It is surprising to find Dell Hymes in support of a genetic connection between Quechua and the so-called Altaic languages; he is on record with the statement: "Clearly this attempt [Bouda 1960] . . . confirms the genealogical relationship of Quechua with Altaic, letting one recognize that still another ancient American *Kultursprache* stems from Asia" (Hymes 1961, 362).
Quechua-Aymara-Sumerian-Assyrian (Patrón 1907).
Quechua-Hokan (Hokan-Quechua) (Harrington 1943b; cf. Mason 1950, 197).
Quechua-Māori (Dangel 1930; Palavecino 1926).
Quechua-Oceania (Imbelloni 1926, 1928).
Quechua-Tungusic (Bouda 1960; see also Hymes 1961).
Quechua-Turkish (Dumezil 1955, see also Droixhe 1955, Hymes 1961).
Quechuachon (Quechuan, Aymaran, Uru-Chipaya, Pano-Takanan, Mosetén, and Chonan) (Swadesh 1959).
Quechumaran (Quechuan + Aymaran). (See above in this chapter.)
South American languages and Japanese (Gancedo 1922; Zeballos 1922).
South American-East Asian languages (Koppelmann 1929).
Sumero-Assyrian and Quechua and Aymara (Patrón 1907).
Takelman (Takelma-Kalapuyan). (See above in this chapter.)
Tarascan-Mayan (Swadesh 1966).
Tarascan-Quechua (Swadesh 1967a, 92–93).
Timucua-Muskogean (Crawford 1988).
Timucuan and Amazonian languages (Warao, Cariban, Arawakan, etc.) (see Granberry 1991).
Tonkawa and Algonquian (Haas 1959).
Tonkawa–Na-Dene (Manaster Ramer 1993).
Totozoquean (Totonacan + Mixe-Zoquean) (Brown et al. 2011, 2014).
Tunican (Tunica, Chitimacha, Atakapa) (Swanton 1919).
Tupían-Cariban (Rodrigues 1985a, 2000, 2003, 2007a, 2009).
Ural-Altaic and Eskimo-Aleut (Bonnerjea 1975, 1978, 1979, 1984).
Uto-Aztecan and Mixe-Zoquean (Wichmann 1999).
Uto-Aztecan and Panoan (Wistrand-Robinson 1991).
Uto-Aztecan with Chukchi (Bouda 1952).
Uto-Aztecan–Plateau Penutian (Rude 2000; this proposal is criticized by Haugen 2021).
Yagan-Alacaluf-Chono proposal (Viegas Barros 2005a, 99–107).
Yuchi-Atakapa (Crawford 1979).
Yuchi-Tunica (Crawford 1979).
Yukian-Penutian (Shipley 1957).
Yukian-Siouan (Elmendorf 1963); Yuchi, Siouan, and Yukian (Elmendorf 1964).
Yurumanguí-Hokan. (See above in this chapter.)
Zuni-Penutian (Hamp 1975; Newman 1964; see Campbell 1997a, 321).

In the next three chapters we turn to historical aspects of the Indigenous languages of the Americas that involve language contact.

NOTES

1. Valenzuela and Guillaume (2017) survey scholars who have thought the similarities shared by Panoan and Takanan languages may be due to language contact and scholars who support the genetic relationship between the two. Some scholars acknowledge similarities due to borrowing but at the same time also find the genetic relationship convincing. I find it fully persuasive.

2. It should be mentioned that Victor Golla (2007, 78) saw "the Hokan phylum" as established, "the oldest linguistic relationship among western North American languages that can be established by normal comparative linguistic methods," with a time depth "on the order of 8,000 years ago." As seen in this section, Hokan is far from established to the satisfaction of the majority of linguists who have worked with these languages.

3. Victor Golla (2011, 84) reported that the relationship of Jicaque with Tequistlatecan has been "demonstrated" by Campbell and Oltrogge (1980, 221). We presented a selection of the data we thought supportive of this hypothesis, with thirty proposed cognates and six sound correspondences. This evidence still looks attractive today, but is insufficient for declaring the hypothesized genetic relationship demonstrated.

4. I do not know which thirty or so words that look similar across various of the putative Hokan languages that others might have had in mind, but I suspect they must include at least forms with the following meanings: arm/shoulder, ashes, body/meat/deer, bone, dog, earth/ground, eye, grease/fat, hand/give, knee, many, skin, sleep, stone, tail, tongue, and water.

5. Terrence Kaufman's (1990, 26) ideas about pan-Americanisms later apparently differed from the interpretation that I reported here. Writing of the arrival of the peoples to the Americas and the possibility that all or many of the languages (except Eskimo-Aleut and Na-Dené) may be related, he said:

> My opinion is based on the extremely informal observation that there is a good deal of similarity among American Indian languages overall, and that the similarities I have in mind are not usually due to borrowing. These similarities are often referred to as "pan-Americanisms."

6. As Morris Swadesh (1964a, 182) reported it, it was generally known among Sapir's students and colleagues that "he was waiting for the appearance of ample source material on some of the languages of the [Penutian] complex" (see also Sapir and Swadesh 1953, 292–293).

7. It should be mentioned that DeLancey and Golla (1997) were sympathetic in general to some version of Penutian, unlike most others.

8. Delancey (2019, 1) does not deal with broader possible Penutian relationships here, but does say that he assumes "the validity of the theory that these [Plateau and Yok-Utian] belong in turn to larger Penutian family [sic]."

9. The possibility that things shared among putative Penutian languages could derive from very old areal contacts has also been mentioned (Haugen 2021, 532), but so far not explored.

10. Jason Haugen (2021, 550) refers to Greenberg's Amerind as "one giant megastock (or a macro-macro-phylum)."

11. Tunebo requires morphemes to have either nasal consonants with nasalized vowels or oral consonants with oral vowels; it this case, Spanish *machete* was accommodated by the oral option (*baxita*) rather than the nasal one (with *mã*...); because Tunebo lacks some vowels and consonants that Spanish has, the other substitutions seen here are the expected ones.

12. Kaufman (1990, 62) says of Greenberg's Ge-Pano-Carib grouping, "there is practically no special lexical connexion for linking these in the evidence given by Gr[eenberg]."

13. Starostin (2012, 119) calls it a "mini-consensus."

14. Starostin (2012, 121) mentions the "'admirers' of his [Vajda's] work, who point out that diligence and methodological accuracy of this level are rarely met in the field of long-range comparison."

15. Carvalho and Nikulin (2018) tentatively proposed to join several language families of the Gran Chaco and of the Brasilian plateau to the north of the Chaco in a proposed genetic relationship they call "Macro-Chaco." It would include Tupían, Macro-Ge, Bororoan, Cariban, Kariri, Matacoan, Guaycurúan, Zamucoan, and Chiquitano. They cite as evidence for the proposal several similarities in pronominal affixes and a half dozen lexical roots they believe are probably reconstructible to Proto-Macro-Chaco, and some other twenty lexical roots perhaps reconstructible to various less inclusive configurations of languages within their Macro-Chaco language families. They also identify some similarities as probably diffused areal traits. So far, this hypothesis has not been followed by others. While it is an interesting proposal, it needs much more evidence than presented so far.

16. Las semejanzas del payaguá y el guachí con las lenguas de las familias guaicurú y mataguaya (aunque algunas pueden ser sugerentes) son pocas y no parecen suficientes para aseverar con certeza que haya—en este caso—parentesco. Lo que sí parece claro es que, si efectivamente existiera tal relación, el guachí y el payaguá no pertenecerían ni a la familia guaicurú ni a la mataguaya.

17. The root in Maká appears to be *athi-*, seen also in *-athii* 'to menstruate'.

7

Linguistic Areas of the Americas

7.1. INTRODUCTION

This chapter surveys the linguistic areas of the Americas. Some of the linguistic areas discussed here are fairly well established, for example, the Northwest Coast and Mesoamerica; some are just preliminary hypotheses in need of more extensive research; and still others have been proposed but are unlikely. Areal linguistics is very important to the study of Native American languages, because we want to know what happened, to determine the real linguistic history, whether it is (or parts of it are) due to inheritance from an earlier ancestor or due to contact with other languages. The defining characteristic of a linguistic area, also sometimes called a *Sprachbund* or diffusion area, is the sharing of structural traits among languages of a particular geographical area, where these shared features in the languages of the area are normally assumed to be the result of language contact, diffused across languages.

In some cases different languages from a particular language family participate in distinct linguistic areas. For example, there are Uto-Aztecan languages in the following linguistic areas: Great Basin, Southern California-Western Arizona, Pueblo area, the Plains, and Mesoamerica. The Athabaskan family has language members in the Northwest Coast, Plateau, Northern California, and Pueblo linguistic areas. Representatives of Algic languages are found in Northern California, the Plains, the Southeast, and the Northeast linguistic areas. Similar cases are found also in South America, where languages from one language family are found represented in multiple linguistic areas (see below).

7.2. NORTH AMERICAN LINGUISTIC AREAS

Several linguistic areas have been proposed in North America. (See Campbell 1997a, 331–344 and Mithun 1999, 314–317; 2017.) They are surveyed here.

7.2.1. Northwest Coast Linguistic Area

The Northwest Coast is the best known of the North American linguistic areas. It is also "home of one of the most geographically extensive *Sprachbünde* in the world" (Beck 2000, 147). As most commonly construed, it includes: the Na-Dene languages of the region, Haida, Tsimshianic, Wakashan, Chimakuan, Salishan, Alsea, Coosan, Kalapuyan, Takelma, and Lower Chinook. It also includes most of the languages that Leer (1991) placed in the Northern Northwest Coast Area, with the exception of Aleut, a subarea of the Northwest Coast Linguistic Area. The Northwest Coast Linguistic Area is known for the complexity, both phonological and morphological, exhibited by its languages. It also has more linguistic diversity than other linguistic areas in North America and most other areas of the world, with representatives from ten of the fifty-four language families of North America found in this one linguistic area.

The languages of the Northwest Coast share very similar, highly elaborate phonemic inventories characterized by several typologically unusual consonants. They typically include: glottalized stops and affricates, labiovelars, multiple laterals (*l, ɬ, tl, tl'*) (all have *ɬ*; most have *tl'*, though some lack plain voiced *l*, and some do not have a plain non-glottalized *tl*),[1] *s/š* opposition, *ts/č* opposition, *q*, one fricative series (voiceless), with velar fricatives. A series of "resonants" structure together, in which nasals, lateral resonants, *w*, and *y* function as a single series, often in morphophonemic alternation with obstruent counterparts. The labial consonant series typically contains far fewer consonants than those for points of articulation farther back in the mouth (labials are completely lacking in Tlingit and Tillamook, and are quite limited in Eyak and in most Athabaskan languages). In contrast, the uvular series is especially rich in most of these languages. The vowel systems, however, are limited; there are only three vowels in several languages and usually no more than four in others, though a vowel-length contrast is common. Other well-known shared phonological traits that have a more limited distribution among these languages are pharyngeals and glottalized continuants.

Typical shared morphological traits are: the well-known reduplication processes (often of several kinds in one language, signaling various grammatical functions, such as iteration, continuative, progressive, plural, and collective); numeral classifiers; alienable/inalienable oppositions in nouns; pronominal plural; nominal plural; verbal reduplication signifying distribution, repetition, and so on; suffixation of tense-aspect markers in verbs; verbal evidential markers; locative-directional markers in the verb; masculine/feminine gender contrast; visibility/invisibility opposition in demonstratives; and nominal and verbal reduplication signaling the diminutive. Aspect is generally relatively more important than tense. All the languages except Tlingit have passive-like constructions. The negative appears as the first element in a clause regardless of the usual word order. Tlingit, unlike the many other languages of its family, shares an agent-patient alignment system with neighboring Haida (Mithun 2020, 604). Northwest Coast languages also have lexically paired but phonologically distinct singular and plural verb stems—in effect different, suppletive, lexical roots for verbs with singular versus plural actors. (Leer 1991, 161; Sherzer 1973, 766–771; 1976, 56–83; Thompson and Kinkade 1990, 42–44; Campbell 1997, 332–334).

390   The Indigenous Languages of the Americas

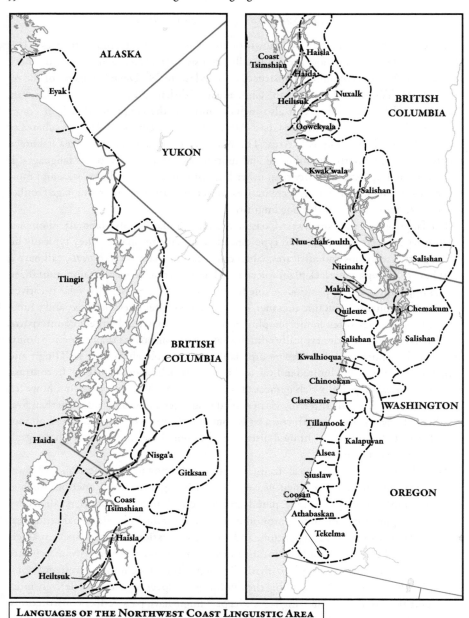

LANGUAGES OF THE NORTHWEST COAST LINGUISTIC AREA

MAP 7.1. Languages of the Northwest Coast Linguistic Area

Some other traits shared by several Northwest Coast languages but more restricted in their distribution across other languages of the area include:

1. A widely diffused sound change of *k > $č$ affected Wakashan, Salishan, Chimakuan, and other Northwest Coast languages (Sapir 1926; Swadesh 1949, 166; Jacobsen 1979b).

2. Tonal (or pitch-accent) contrasts are found in Tlingit, Haida, Heiltsuk, Upriver Halkomelem, Quileute, Kalapuyan, Takelma, and more than half of the Athabaskan languages.
3. Interdental θ and θ', which developed in Halkomelem, in Saanich (a dialect of Northern Straits Salish), and in dialects of Comox; one or both of these sounds exist in Pentlatch and in Chasta Costa (dialect of Tututni).
4. Also, *w* became k^w and *y* became *č* in Northern Straits Salish, Clallam, Makah, and Chemakum.
5. Several languages have ergative alignment, at least in part: Tlingit, Haida, Tsimshianic, some Salishan languages (such as Comox; Interior Salishan is partly ergative), Taitnapam (Sahaptin), Chinookan, and Coosan (Thompson and Kinkade 1990, 44).

"Lexical suffixes" are found in Wakashan, Chimakuan, Tsimshianic, and to a lesser extent in Eskimo-Aleut languages. They designate such familiar objects (normally signaled by full lexical roots in most other languages) as body parts, geographical features, cultural artifacts, and some abstract notions. Wakashan, for example, has some 300 lexical suffixes (Thompson and Kinkade 1990, 40; Campbell 2020b). The grammar of these languages has a severely limited role (some linguists assert that the contrast is totally lacking for some of the languages) for the contrast between nouns and verbs as distinct categories (see Thompson and Kinkade 1990, 33; Beck 2000, 165). There has been extensive debate about whether several languages of the area make a grammatical distinction between nouns and verbs or not. Although a number of linguists have argued against the contrast in these languages, others have presented cogent arguments that confirm that they do have the contrast. (For more discussion and some other traits, see Haas 1969c; Jacobs 1954; Thompson and Kinkade 1990; Beck 2000.)

Some scholars have thought that Wakashan, Chimakuan, and Salishan are genetically related as was proposed in the Mosan hypothesis (Sapir 1929a; Swadesh 1949, 1953a, 1953b, 1953c). These languages have considerable structural similarity, but much of it is due to areal diffusion (Beck 2000; Campbell and Poser 2008, 190–191). The proposed Mosan grouping has no support today (Beck 2000; Jacobsen 1979a, 1979b; Thompson 1979). David Beck (2000) spoke of these three language families as a "central Northwest Coast area" and shows in detail that the traits in them that were attributed to Mosan are in fact not limited to these languages but are found also in other languages of the region and sometimes beyond.

Several of the traits associated with the Northwest Coast Linguistic Area extend beyond also to languages of the Plateau and Northern California Areas, and to the Eskimo-Aleut languages, while others have a more limited distribution within the Northwest Coast, not found in all the languages of the area (Beck 2000; Thompson and Kinkade 1990, 42). In fact, it is difficult to determine what would distinguish the Plateau Linguistic Area and the Northern California Linguistic Area (see below) from the Northwest Coast Linguistic Area.

In a subarea of the Northwest the languages lack primary nasals; this includes Twana and Lushootseed (Salishan), Quileute (Chimakuan), and Nitinaht and Makah (Nootkan, of the broader Wakashan family) (see Haas 1969a; 89, Kinkade 1985; Thompson and Thompson 1972). Nitinaht and Makah, for example, have changed their original *m >

b, **mˁ* > *bˁ*, and **nˁ* > *d*, **nˁ* > *dˁ*, due to areal pressure, but closely related Nuu-chah-nutlh (Nootka) has retained the original nasals. Comox (Salishan) has been described as having *b* and *d* as optional variants of *m* and *n*, respectively, and a similar situation has been observed in Sechelt and Clallam and in two dialects of Halkomelem (three Salishan languages, Kinkade 1985, 479). Franz Boas (1911b, 565) observed that there was much confusion regarding "surds and sonants" in Lower Chinook pronunciation on account of "semiclosure of the nose," and older records of several of the other languages reveal a similar situation (Kinkade 1985, 478–479). Dale Kinkade (1985, 480) reported that "in virtually every littoral language [at least twelve of them] of the Northwest from the 46th to the 50th parallel nasals were at times pronounced without full closure of the velum," and that in recent time many of the languages that had these sounds intermediate between nasals and voiced stops have settled in favor of one or the other of the sounds, eliminating the intermediate variant.

Several individual languages of the Salishan and Wakashan families, and arguably also of some Athabaskan languages in the Northwest Coast Linguistic Area, have pharyngeal segments. Since pharyngeals are among the rarest speech sounds in the world, it is quite possible that those shared among languages of the Northwest Coast are the product of areal diffusion (Colarusso 1985). Melville Jacobs (1954) pointed out several shared features. He reported that Boas' finding of "anterior palatals" such as *gʸ*, *kʸ*, *kʸ'*, and *xʸ* was indicative of two subdistricts in the Northwest—in the adjacent languages Coos, Alsea, Tillamook (Coast Salish), and Lower Chinook (with a *kʸ* allophone of *k* in Upper Chehalis [Coast Salish]), and separately again in Kwakiutl (Kwak'wala) and Tsimshianic in northern British Columbia. Jacobs found that in Tillamook anterior palatals were used only to express the diminutive, derived from the phonemes ɢ, *q*, *q'*, and χ (1954, 48; Thompson and Kinkade [1990, 44] add Nitinaht, Sechelt, Lushootseed, and probably Nuu-chah-nulth [Nootka]). Jacobs (1954, 52–53) also reported that Molala and Kalapuya, neighbors on either side of the northern Oregon Cascade Mountains, share "bilabial continuants" (written *f* and *fʷ* [presumably ɸ and ɸʷ]). Moreover, "Alsea, Molale, and Kalapuya, contiguous to one another, lack the contrast of *s* and *š* of many Northwest languages and use only a retracted *s* that may be transcribed *ṣ* . . . Takelma, a little south of them, also has it" (see also Haas 1969a, 85–88).

Several of the Northwest Coast Linguistic Area traits are found also associated with the Plateau and Northern California linguistic areas (Sherzer 1976, 127; Beck 2000), and since the Northern Northwest Coast Linguistic Area is a subarea of the Northwest Coast Area, traits in the two naturally coincide significantly.

7.2.2. *Northern Northwest Coast Linguistic Area*

The Northern Northwest Coast Linguistic Area in the extreme northwest of the Northwest Coast of North America was proposed by Jeff Leer (1991). It is a subarea of the larger Northwest Coast Linguistic Area. In the Northern Northwest Coast area, Haida and Eyak were in close contact, forming with Aleut a looser contact group. Tlingit was allied with them, but peripherally to Haida and Eyak, constituting something of a bridge between Haida-Eyak and Athabaskan. The area was ultimately broken up by the intrusion of Tlingit and Alutiiq (a.k.a. Pacific Yupik) (Eskimoan). Leer (1991) considered the diagnostic traits of the Northern Northwest Coast area to be:

(1) Lack of labial obstruents, in Aleut, Eyak, Tlingit, and Proto-Athabaskan, and marginally in Haida. Labials are present in other Northwest Coast languages. The lack of labial stops in Aleut was often thought to be due to influence from Athabaskan or Na-Dene (Sensu Stricto) languages.
(2) Promiscuous number marking, in Aleut, Eyak, Haida, and Tlingit. For example, in Tlingit the proclitic *has* signals plural of animate third person pronouns; as a proclitic to a transitive verb with animate third-person subject and object *has* may "promiscuously" pluralize either the subject or the object, or both. In Haida, Eyak, and Aleut, the promiscuous number marking can associate semantically with any pronoun within the clause.
(3) Periphrastic possessive construction, in Eyak and Haida, of the form 'money me-on he.stole-he', meaning ambiguously 'he stole my money' or 'he stole money from me'.
(4) Among weaker traits of the area are the following. The Northern Northwest Coast languages and Eskimo have strict head-final (XSOV) word order and a clear focus-position at the beginning of the sentence (several other Northwest Coast languages have VSO word order). In Northern Northwest Coast and Athabaskan languages, inalienable possession and postpositions are signaled by the same construction. Haida and Tlingit share active/stative alignment. In Haida, Tlingit, and Eyak, there is a distinction between non-human and human (or inanimate and animate) third-person pronouns, and 'plural' is distinguished only for human (or animate) third persons. Finally, there are syllable-initial glottalized sonorants shared by Eyak and Haida, but also in other families of the Northwest Coast Linguistic Area. Thompson and Kinkade (1990, 44) mention the additional trait of noun-classificatory systems shared by Eyak, Athabaskan, and Tlingit, while Haida has a similar system marked by shape prefixes.

7.2.3. Plateau Linguistic Area

The languages commonly thought to belong to the Plateau Linguistic Area are: the Plateau family (with Sahaptian, Klamath-Modoc, and Molala), Upper Chinook (Kiksht), Nicola (Athabaskan), Cayuse, Kutenai, and Interior Salishan (subgroup of the Salishan family). The Plateau is a relatively clearly defined culture area. However, since most of the traits shared by its languages are also found in the Northwest Coast Linguistic Area, it is an open question whether the Plateau constitutes a legitimate linguistic area or whether it should be included in the Northwest Coast area. Kinkade et al. (1998) were of the opinion that no set of language features distinguishes the Plateau as a separate linguistic area and instead that the Plateau should be considered part of the larger Northwest Coast Linguistic Area.

The Plateau area languages are characterized by glottalized stops, contrasting velar and uvular obstruents (for example, k contrasting with q), and multiple laterals ($l, ł, tl, tl'$; but tl' is lacking from Kutenai, Coeur d'Alene, Nez Perce, Cayuse, Molala, and Klamath). Other shared traits, thought to be less salient, include: labiovelars; one fricative series; velar (and

MAP 7.2. Languages of the Plateau Linguistic Area

uvular) fricatives; a series of glottalized resonants (sonorants) contrasting with plain resonants (except in Sahaptin, Cayuse, Molala, and Kiksht); consonant clusters of four or more consonants in length in medial or final position in words (except in Kiksht, and uncertain in Cayuse and Molala); vowel systems of only three or four vowel positions (Nez Perce, with five, is the only exception); a vowel-length contrast; size-shape-affective sound symbolism involving interchanges of consonants; pronominal plural, nominal plural; prefixation of subject person markers of verbs; suffixation of tense-aspect markers in verbs (aspect as basic and tense secondary, except that tense is basic and aspect is secondary in Kiksht, Sahaptin, and Nez Perce); several kinds of reduplication (except in Nicola); numeral classifiers (shared by Salishan and Sahaptian languages); locative-directional markers in verbs; and different roots for the singular and the plural for various actions (for example, 'sit', 'stand', 'take'—except in Kutenai and Lillooet and uncertain in Cayuse and Molala) (Sherzer 1976, 84–102; Kinkade et al. 1998).

Haruo Aoki presented "a preliminary cross genetic linguistic study of the **eastern Plateau area**" that included Nez Perce and eastern members of Interior Salish. He found that the "quinary-decimal" numerical system "is a diffused feature among the languages of Oregon, Washington, and Idaho" and that the bifurcate collateral kinship system shared by Sahaptian and Interior Salish "is probably convergent and brought about by diffusion." The phonology of the Interior Salish languages and Nez Perce also have "some interesting traits, probably attributable to diffusion" (Aoki 1975, 187–188). One of these is labiovelars, which are found in most of the languages, including underlyingly in Nez Perce. Nez Perce (Sahaptian) and Coeur d'Alene (Salish) share a rule that a consonant (other than sibilants) and a glottal stop combine, resulting in a glottalized consonant (as in Nez Perce ʔilp-ʔilp → ʔilp'lip 'red' [reduplicated]). Nez Perce has $a \sim i$ alternations in pairs of related words, which also existed in Proto-Sahaptian; in some instances Coast Salish a corresponds to Interior Salish i; in others Coast Salish i corresponds to Interior Salish a; Aoki (1975, 190) therefore suspects that the Sahaptian rule must have operated "across the Salishan-Sahaptian border." The two groups also share a number of lexical borrowings and similarities in the formation of neologisms. Nez Perce and Coeur d'Alene share linguistic features in the various "abnormal types of speech"; for example, Coyote in folktales changes s to $š$. In fact, there are similarities in the genre of "abnormal speech" (also sometimes called "animal talk" or "baby talk") of a number of Northwest Coast and Plateau languages, including at least in Nuu-chah-nulth (Nootka), Kwak'wala (Kwakiutl), Quileute, Takelma, Nez Perce, and Coeur d'Alene.

Joel Sherzer (1973, 760, 772–773) dealt with the Northwest Coast and Plateau linguistic areas independently, but he also combined them into a larger linguistic area, whose common traits are, he said, a glottalized stop series, pharyngeals, glottalized continuants, nominal and verbal reduplication, and numeral classifiers, plus others. As mentioned above, other researchers would additionally include Northern California in this conjoined larger area. There is also some overlap with the Great Basin, which raises questions about the definition of the Great Basin as a linguistic area (see below). For example, Cayuse and Molala of the Plateau area have a voiceless bilabial fricative (ϕ) and a velar nasal (η) —two traits that they have in common with neighboring Northern Paiute (a Uto-Aztecan language), that belongs to the Great Basin Linguistic Area, but also with some languages of the Northern California and Greater South Coast Range areas (see below), and with nearby Kalapuyan languages of the Northwest Coast Linguistic Area.

Chinookan is particularly interesting in this regard, since it has representatives in both the Northwest Coast and Plateau linguistic areas, and these different varieties exhibit a number of traits in common with the other languages in their respective linguistic areas. While Lower Chinookan is characterized by verbal aspects rather than tenses, Upper Chinookan (Kiksht) has developed complex tense categories as a result of the influence from other Plateau Linguistic Area languages. For example it has a tense distinction between "recent" past and "remote" past, as do Nez Perce and Molala (Silverstein 1974). The Wasco and Wishram varieties of Upper Chinookan have borrowed possessive, instrumental, and locative case endings from Sahaptin, and they may also have borrowed the Molala allative suffix ('to, toward'). Chinookan has ergative syntax, but these borrowed case endings and a borrowed derivational suffix display a rather different nominative-accusative syntax. Upper Chinookan also shares the directional categories of "cislocative" (motion hither) and "translocative" (motion away, thither) with Nez Perce, Sahaptin, and Columbian (Salishan) (Cayuse and Molala apparently also have the cislocative) (Silverstein 1974; Kinkade et al. 1998).

7.2.4. Northern California Linguistic Area

There is considerable doubt about whether Northern California constitutes a legitimate linguistic area, though many accept it. As mentioned, languages of the postulated Northern California Linguistic Area also have several traits in common with the languages of the Northwest Coast, the Plateau areas, and the Great Basin. The Northern California area includes: Yurok and Wiyot (Algic); Hupa, Mattole, and Kato (Athabaskan); Yukian; Lake Miwok and Southern Sierra Miwok (Miwokan); Wintuan; Maiduan; Klamath-Modoc; Pomoan; Chimariko; Palaihnihan; Karuk; Shasta; Yana; and for some scholars also Washo (though Washo is usually assigned to the Great Basin area). (See Dixon and Kroeber's [1903] Northwestern California structural-geographical type, with Yurok as typical, contrasted with their Central Californian type, typified by Maidu.)

Mary Haas, in her investigation of the languages of northern California to ascertain possible areal traits, noted the spotty occurrence in this area of back velar consonants (uvulars such as q), found in Klamath, Wintu, Chimariko, and Pomoan; she observed that they are "highly characteristic of the Northwest Coast area, though rare in Athabaskan languages" (Haas 1976, 352). She also pointed out that the voiceless laterals, ɬ and less frequent tɬ', of the Northwest Coast area and all of Athabaskan languages are also found in this area in Yurok and Wiyot (both with ɬ), Patwin and Lake Miwok (with ɬ and tɬ'), and Wintu (in which tl is an allophone of ɬ). She found retroflexed stops shared by several languages of this area, including Chimariko, Kashaya Pomo, Wappo, Lake Miwok, and Sierra Miwok. In each language there is a retroflexed stop in all the stop series (plain, aspirated, and glottalized) in Chimariko, Kashaya (Pomoan), and Lake Miwok; in two series (plain and globalized) in Wappo, and only one series (plain) in Southern Sierra Miwok. This retroflexion is also shared by Yokuts, farther to the south. A few of the languages of this area have both *l* and *r*: Yurok and Wiyot, Wintu-Patwin, Lake Miwok, and perhaps Yana. (In Yurok and Wiyot, alternations between *r* and *l* are associated with consonant symbolism.) A distinct series of voiced stops is rare but is found in the east-west strip of languages that includes Kashaya (Pomoan), Wintu-Patwin, and Maidu (though with implosion in Maidu) (Haas 1976, 353). Haas (1976, 354–355) also described the areal trait of consonant sound symbolism that is found in Yurok, Wiyot, Hupa, Tolowa, Karuk, and Yana, and formal aspects of the numeral systems. (See Conathan 2004; Haas 1967, 1976; Haynie 2012; Jacobs 1954; O'Neill 2008; Sherzer 1976, 127–128.)

Haynie (2012) examined the traits often thought to be areal traits of the Northern California Linguistic Area, finding difficulties in their distributions that raise questions about several of them and whether they are due to areal diffusion. She found that the pattern of the following traits was not statistically significant nor different from what would be expected by chance:

The three-way contrast of plain, glottalized, and aspirated stops (p. 103).
The pattern of glottalized stops (p. 104).

The five-vowel system trait (p. 105).
Quinary numeral systems (p. 117).
n-initial first person pronoun and *m*-initial second person pronoun: *n*-initial first person pronoun is not statistically significant and not different from what would be expected due to chance (p. 121). *m*-initial second person pronoun, however, is statistically significant and different from what would be expected due to chance (p. 122).
Prefixed possessive markers (p. 123).
Prefixed subject markers (p. 124).
Pre-verbal tense and aspect markers (p. 125).

The distribution of the following traits is statistically significant and unlikely to have arisen due to chance:

The "back velar" (uvular) consonants (pp. 107–109).
The lateral fricatives and affricates (pp. 110–113).
The presence of contrast between *r* and *l* (p. 114).
Velar nasal (p. 115).
The pattern of the "back" apical stops trait; however, this pattern is centered in Central California and extends only into Sierra Miwok and the Clear Lake area in Northern California" (p. 106).[2]
Sound symbolic diminutivization (p. 116).
Reduplication with distributive, iterative, and plural meanings (pp. 118–119).
Nominal case marking (p. 120).
Numeral classifier systems (p. 126).

The traits of this latter set "are likely to have spread through geographic contact between languages" (p. 127). The fact that they are likely to be due to diffusion, however, does not automatically qualify them as areal traits of Northern California. None of these features "has a distribution that coincides with the boundaries of a Northern California area, and none occur entirely within the Northern California area. The vast majority of the traits have a patchy distribution in Northern California and are also found in neighboring regions" (Haynie 2012, 128). Haynie (2012, 134) concludes:

> The findings of this analysis suggest that Northern California is not a linguistic area. No feature distribution is matched well enough to the boundaries of Northern California to serve as a basis for classifying this region as a linguistic area ... And no significant difference is found between the number of "Northern California features" found in Northern California and in the surrounding areas. The conclusion that must be drawn from these findings is that Northern California is not, in fact, a true linguistic area.

It is important to point out that Washo, which is usually assigned to the Great Basin area, also shares a number of traits with Northern California languages. They include the pronominal dual; a quinary/decimal numeral system (similar to one in Maidu); the absence of vowel-initial syllables; and free stress (like that of Maiduan) (Jacobsen 1986, 109–111). This calls into question the existence of, or at least the definition of, the Great Basin as a linguistic area (see below).

The difficulty of distinguishing Northern California as a linguistic area from the Northwest Coast Linguistic Area is mentioned with some frequency in the literature, since several of the traits shared by languages of northern California are also traits of the Northwest Coast Linguistic Area (see, for example, Haynie 2012; Hill 2021, 582, 574). For example, from her careful scrutiny of the traits attributed to the Northern California Linguistic Area, Haynie concluded:

> There is no doubt that linguistic traits have spread across genealogical boundaries in the Northern California region ... it is less clear whether it is most appropriate to classify this exact region as a linguistic area, or to instead think of it in terms of smaller regions of more intense areal diffusion or an extension of some of western North America's larger linguistic areas. (Haynie 2012, 88)
>
> Northern California appears less like a cohesive region of areal feature diffusion and more like a collection of smaller diffusion zones that is overlapped by the fuzzy boundary of the Great Basin area to the east and may be linked to the Northwest Coast linguistic area to the north (Haynie 2012, 89).

7.2.5. Northwest California

Northwest California is a small linguistic area, a subarea of the Northern California Linguistic Area, containing the languages Wiyot, Yurok (Algic), Hupa (Athabaskan), and Karuk (language isolate) (see Blevins 2017, 92, 96–97; Bright and Bright 1965; Hill 2021, 574, 577–578; Conathan 2004; and O'Neill 2008). Speakers of these languages share relative cultural homogeneity, and the languages share several linguistic traits.

7.2.6. Clear Lake Linguistic Area

The languages of the Clear Lake Linguistic Area are: Lake Miwok, Patwin, Eastern Pomo, Southeastern Pomo, and Wappo. This is a very clear linguistic area, centered around Clear Lake, circa 80 miles northeast of the San Francisco Bay. These languages share, among other things, retroflexed consonants, voiceless *l* ([ɬ]), and glottalized glides (see Callaghan 1964; Mithun 1999, 317; Sherzer 1976, 129). Lake Miwok, for example, has three series of stops (plain, aspirated, and glottalized), whereas its sister languages have only one; it also has *r*, *ł*, and the affricates *ts', č, č', tł'*, and word-final *š*, which the others Miwokan languages lack. These are clearly borrowed from neighboring languages—mostly imported with loanwords that contained them, after which they spread to some native Lake Miwok words (Callaghan 1964, 47, 1987; 1991, 52; Berman 1973). Yuki, in the Clear Lake area, shows an agent-patient alignment system like that of its Pomoan neighbors but unlike that of Wappo, Yuki's sister language (Mithun 2020, 605).

7.2.7. South Coast Range and Greater South Coast Range Linguistic Areas

Leanne Hinton (1991) proposed a **South Coast Range Linguistic Area**, which contains Chumash, Esselen, and Salinan. The South Coast Range area is also part of a larger area that can be referred to as the **Greater South Coast Range Linguistic Area**, which includes, in addition to the languages of the South Coast Range, also Yokutsan and several Northern-Uto-Aztecan languages. Dixon and Kroeber's (1903, 8) **Southern Phonetic Group**, which included Chumashan, Yokuts, Salinan, Southern California Uto-Aztecan, and Yuman languages, may perhaps be seen as a precursor to the definition of this linguistic area (compare Dixon and Kroeber's [1903] Southwestern California structural-geographical type, typified by Chumash). Joel Sherzer (1976, 129) had pointed out that languages of what he called the Yokuts-Salinan-Chumash region share traits: three series of stops, retroflexed sounds, glottalized resonants, and prefixation of verbal subject markers. These traits are not unique to this region, however, and some overlap with traits of other areas—for example, the retroflexed sounds and three series of stops in the languages of the Clear Lake Area. The areal traits of the Greater South Coast Range Area include presence of h, i, c [ts], and η, shared widely in the area, but not all these traits are found in every language (for details, see Hinton 1991, 139–140).

Langdon and Silver (1984, 141) discussed the distribution of the /t/-/ṭ/ contrast in California languages, which includes several of these Greater South Coast Range area languages (but not all) and is found in others as well: "We find that their territory [that of retroflex /ṭ/] encompasses about half the state [of California], including a large continuous area extending north and south of San Francisco Bay, with one lone northern outlier (Chimariko) and a set of southern outliers (all Yuman)." Specifically, the languages involved that have this contrast are Salinan, Esselen, Yokutsan (but not all its varieties; it is absent in Chukchansi Yokuts, for example), Utian (Miwok-Costanoan), Yukian, Pomoan, Chimariko, and Yuman (Diegueno, Cocopa, Yuma, Mojave)—not all Yuman languages have a phonemic contrast, though Proto-Yuman is believed to have had the two sounds allophonically (Langdon and Silver 1984, 144). With the recognition that it is actually realized as an affricate in some of these languages, we can add Serrano-Kitanemuk (Uto-Aztecan) and Tolowa (Athabaskan, in the extreme northern corner of California) to the list (Langdon and Silver 1984, 149; see also Hinton 1991). Langdon and Silver (1984, 142) observed that "the distribution of this contrast suggests that we are dealing with a classical case of areal diffusion." They conclude that there are two distinct subareas: the northern subarea (Yukian, Pomoan, and Miwokan) is defined by languages in which there is a contrast between two stops; the southern subarea (Costanoan, Esselen, Salinan, Yokuts, and Serrano-Kitanemuk) consists of languages in which the contrast is between a stop and a retroflexed affricate (Langdon and Silver 1984, 155).

7.2.8. Central California Linguistic Area

Victor Golla (2011, 247–248) listed a number of shared traits among languages of central California that suggest to him "the existence of an ancient linguistic area." More specifically, he said:

> In addition to its lexical connections to Costanoan, Esselen shares a number of typological features with the Utian languages in general, Miwok as well as Costanoan.

These include the absence of a glottalized series, and (late developments in the Eastern Miwok languages aside) a relatively analytic morphosyntax. The general similarity of this typological profile to that of the Uto-Aztecan languages is probably not accidental and suggests the existence of an ancient linguistic area stretching from the central Sierra Nevada through Sacramento—San Joaquin Delta to San Francisco.

David Shaul (2014, 203–207) has also favored a Central California Linguistic Area, involving Esselen, Salinan, Chumashan, some of the Utian languages, and Uto-Aztecan. However, the evidence presented at least for the Uto-Aztecan connection is not very convincing. Catherine Callaghan (2014) also mentioned various similarities among various of these languages.

7.2.9. Southern California-Western Arizona Linguistic Area

Leanne Hinton (1991) has demonstrated that extensive areal linguistic change has affected the Yuman and Cupan languages, and less extensively the Takic languages (the Uto-Aztecan subgroup which includes Cupan among other languages) in general. Some of the more broadly distributed traits within Southern California include a distinction between k and q and the presence of k^w, $č$, x. Traits shared more specifically between Yuman and Cupan include k^w/q^w contrast, $s/ṣ$ contrast, x^w, $ñ$, $ḃ$, r/l contrast, a small vowel inventory, and sound symbolism (see Hinton 1991, 144–147 for details). Several of these characteristics are listed also by Joel Sherzer (1976, 128) as "regional areal traits of southern California." They reflect the strong influence from Yuman on Cupan languages, for each trait diverges from common Takic (or Northern-Uto-Aztecan) in the direction of features in Proto-Yuman (Hinton 1991, 152–154). In addition, several Yuman and Takic languages share v, e, and more marginally $š$, though these are not in the proto language of either group. Though the first, v, is not known in the South Coast Range Area, the latter two are; they may have existed earlier in the South Coast Range and later spread to the Yuman-Takic area. It is the River subgroup of Yuman that shares the most traits in common with Cupan; the specific traits they share are mostly allophonic in one or the other, which suggests very recent contact. Eric Elliott (1994) argued that Cupan has been influenced more directly by Diegueño (Yuman) in that Cupan borrowed (1) the indefinite marker m- and (2) the affixation of definite and indefinite prefixes on verbs that mean 'to be', which results in words for 'thus' and 'how', respectively. (See also Elliot 1994; Hill 2017.)

Shaul and Andresen's (1989) **Southwestern Arizona ("Hohokam") Area** is surely related to the Southern California-Western Arizona Area defined by Hinton (1991). Shaul and Andresen believe that a linguistic area developed in southwestern Arizona through the interaction of Piman (Uto-Aztecan) and Yuman speakers as part of the Hohokam archaeological culture. However, they define this area based on a single shared feature: "the linguistic trait we have found important in defining a prehistoric linguistic area in southwestern Arizona is phonological, i.e., a retroflex stop shared by Pimans [/ḍ/, development from *r] and some Yuman speakers [/ṭ/]" (Shaul and Andresen 1989, 109; see also Sherzer 1976, 151). For other traits and more detail, see also Shaul (2014, 159–164).

Robert Oswalt (1976b, 298) attributes the presence of switch reference in languages of the western United States (in Southern Paiute, Tübatulabal, Hopi, Tohono O'odham, and Zuni, as well as in the Yuman languages) to diffusion. However, William Jacobsen (1983, 172–173) showed that the trait is found in many more languages, though its history is not yet fully understood:

> The history of the development of the device of switch-reference in these languages is not understood in a detailed way ... A consideration of the geographical distribution of switch-reference in North America reveals a striking clustering of the languages in a largely continuous area centering on the Southwest and Great Basin culture areas.... It forms a solid area in the western half of the Southwest.... It also extends westward to a string of languages in the Plateau and California areas which border on these Great Basin languages: from north to south, Klamath, Maidu, Yokuts, and Tübatulabal. Then there is a separate area in coastal northern California constituted by Pomo and Yuki. Outliers are Huichol farther south on the west coast, Tonkawa farther east in the southern Plains, and Muskogean in the Southeast. This Southwestern areal spread ... has become even more salient with the ... additions ... of ... Yuman-Cochimi and Seri, and it stands out by contrast with the larger northern and eastern areas of the continent from which this device seems to be lacking. One naturally thinks of the likelihood of diffusion in at least some cases within this area.

7.2.10. Great Basin Linguistic Area

As defined by Joel Sherzer (1973, 1976), the languages of the Great Basin Linguistic Area are those of the Numic branch of Uto-Aztecan and Washo, a language isolate. He listed as characteristic traits of the Great Basin: voiceless vowels, nasals, and semivowels; k/k^w contrast; bilabial fricatives; x^w; η; and an overtly marked nominal case system (Sherzer 1976, 165). The languages also share an inclusive/exclusive pronominal distinction, and $ɨ$ is present in all of them (Jacobsen 1980).

However, as mentioned above, the Great Basin may not be a legitimately defined linguistic area. The common traits in Washo and Numic are also found in languages of adjacent areas, as well. As William Jacobsen (1986, 110) pointed out:

> [Sherzer's] approach of starting out from culture areas seems to introduce some distortions as applied to Washoe, in that it minimizes the comparably great similarities to the California stocks (some of which Sherzer 1976, 128, 164, 167, 238–239, 246 indeed notes). For example, ... the two striking points of agreement, presence of $ɨ$ and η, are also shared with groups to the west, while the other features of Washoe – presence of glottalized stops, $ɬ$, and a $s/š$ contrast, and absence of k^w—separate it from Numic and unite it with one or more of its western neighbors.

Jacobsen (1986, 110) mentioned other features that are common to Great Basin and California languages. For example, similarities between Washoe and Northern Paiute systems of kinship terminology are shared as well by Miwok and Yokuts; the Washo reduplication pattern is similar to that of Numic but also to that of Maiduan and less so also to that of Sierra Miwok. Instrumental verb prefixes are shared by Washo and Numic and are also found

MAP 7.3. Languages of the Great Basin Linguistic Area

in Maiduan, Shasta, and Achumawi. The pronominal inclusive/exclusive distinction, innovative in both Washo and Numic, is found also in Miwokan. Jacobsen (1980) argued that this distinction diffused in a number of more or less contiguous languages of north-central California, the Great Basin, and their neighbors—in Numic (Uto-Aztecan), Washo (an isolate), Tübatulabal (Uto-Aztecan), Yuki (Yukian), Palaihnihan (primarily in Achumawi), Wintu (Wintuan), Sahaptin (Sahapatian, in the Plateau family, also in the Plateau Linguistic Area, bordering Northern Paiute (Numic), Shuswap (Interior Salish), Kwakiutl (Kwak'wala) (Wakashan), and other languages to the east: Algonquian, Siouan, Iroquoian, Kiowa, Pawnee, and Yuchi. Both the inclusive/exclusive contrast and switch-reference are also found widely in contiguous languages extending across a large area (Jacobsen 1986, 110). Robert Oswalt (1976b) had shown that switch reference exists in several of the languages of the Northern California, including Washo, several Uto-Aztecan languages, Pomoan, and Maiduan (see above). Whistler and Golla (1986, 352–353) suggested that "the presence of *ɨ in the phonemic inventories of the Penutian languages of the Sierra Nevada region [Maiduan, Utian, and Yokutsan] is the result of early diffusion." The presence of this sound is sometimes attributed to Numic contact, but the sound is also found in several of the putative Hokan languages (particularly in Washo and Chumashan; compare also the epenthetic ə in Atsugewi and Pit River) (see also Jacobsen 1980).

Perhaps, then, the whole concept of a Great Basin linguistic area is merely an extension of the Northern California Linguistic Area. In any case, it demonstrates the difficulties that can be created by assuming, as Sherzer (1973, 1976) did, that culture areas and linguistic areas will coincide.

7.2.11. Pueblo Linguistic Area

The languages of the Pueblo Linguistic Area are Keresan, Tanoan, Zuni, and Hopi, with intrusive Apachean (Southern Athabaskan) (Bereznak 1995; Everdell 2013; Shaul 1980, 2014, 156–157).

The Pueblo region is a recognized culture area, characterized by the kachina cult and medicine societies, among other things, and several of its cultural traits (such as loom weaving, agriculture, and moiety systems) have diffused into neighboring Apachean. This culture area also corresponds to a linguistic area. Catherine Bereznak (1995) discussed twenty-eight shared linguistic traits and concluded additionally that at least four of them were very strong areal indicators, since they occur throughout the area but do not extend into neighboring languages (for example, not in Yuman and other Uto-Aztecan languages). They are: (1) glottalized consonants (with the exception of Hopi), (2) tones (absent only from Zuni; present in the Third Mesa dialect of Hopi), (3) final devoicing

MAP 7.4. Languages of the Pueblo Linguistic Area

of vowels and sonorants, and (4) dual number distinction (e.g., 'we [two]' vs. 'we [more than two]'). Everdell (2013) cites several others that he considers diagnostic and strongly supportive of the Pueblo Linguistic Area, different from Bereznak's. For example, he believes that a grouping of several features that may have diffused into only one or two languages can also be strongly supportive of a linguistic area. Other supportive areal features, distributed throughout the area but not beyond, include: (5) k^w—Joel Sherzer (1976, 137) suggested that the development of this sound in Navajo "is perhaps due to contact with neighboring Pueblo languages"; (6) ł (innovative in Tiwa; Sherzer 1976, 140); (7) aspirated consonants (perhaps diffused into Zuni); and (8) shared ceremonial vocabulary, among others.

Acoma (Keresan) and Navajo (Apachean branch of Athabaskan) share glottalized nasals and glides. Sherzer (1976, 141, 142) suggested that Navajo acquired these traits as a result of contact with Keresan. David Shaul (1982) interpreted the partial series of glottalized consonants with low functional yield in Zuni as an areal feature acquired through Zuni contact with Keresan and Tanoan languages, which have a fully integrated glottalic series. There are other shared features, such as SOV word order, which are not strong areal indicators since they are inherited in Apachean from Proto-Athabaskan and in Hopi from Proto(-Northern)-Uto-Aztecan, and are frequent in neighboring languages, as well as in languages spoken elsewhere in the Americas. Sherzer (1976, 151–152) also suggested that the development of a 2-2-1 vowel system (i, e, a, o, u) in some Tanoan languages may be due to contact with Zuni and Keresan; that Santa Clara Tewa retroflexed sounds may be the result of contact with Keresan; that the Santa Clara *ts/č* contrast may be the result of influence from neighboring languages; that the Navajo k/k^w contrast is perhaps the result of contact with its neighbors (mentioned above); that Navajo h^w is perhaps due to Tanoan contact; that Navajo's glottalized nasals and semivowels may be explained by contact with Keresan; and that the development of *r* in dialects of Tewa and Tiwa (to which Hopi *r* can be added) may be due to Keresan contact.

Paul Kroskrity (1982, 1985, 1993, 60–66) argued that some traits diffused from Apachean into Tewa. He found the Tewa passive, which is signaled by prefixes, to be like the passive of Apachean and unlike the passives of other Tanoan languages (in which passives are simply verbs inflected for intransitivity which permit an "agent" argument). This construction includes the semantic foregrounding of patient subjects and a requirement that in certain conditions the subject must be animate (as in Navajo inverse clauses, where, for example, animate objects are obligatorily raised to subject when the logical subject is inanimate; in Southern Tiwa animate goals are obligatorily raised to subject when the logical subject is inanimate). Tewa and Navajo also exhibit similarities in their relative clause constructions; they are the only two languages in the southwest "with a recognizable anaphor as a relativizer" (Kroskrity 1982, 65). There are similarities in the classificatory verbs of Tewa and Navajo. Kroskrity (1982, 66, 1985, 1993, 60–66) also thought that Tewa borrowed its possessive morpheme *-bí* from Apachean languages' third-person possessive *bi-*; although it is a suffix in the former and a prefix in the latter, the positions of these morphemes match in nominal possession constructions—for example, Arizona Tewa *sen-bí khaw* [man-POSSESSIVE song] '(a) man's song', Navajo *bisóódi bi-tsi* [pig POSSESSIVE-flesh] 'the pig's flesh'. Moreover, this matching possessive morpheme is also used in postpositional constructions in both Tewa and Apachean. Other Kiowa-Tanoan languages lack this possessive construction entirely (instead they share a construction with a dative-like prefix on a relativized stative or existential verb, as in Taos Tiwa 'an-'u-k'o-'i [1ˢᵗ SG. POSSESSIVE-son-have/lie-RELATIVE] 'my son'), nor do they have such a postpositional construction.

Evidence of interethnic contacts between Tewa and Apachean that could lead to the sharing of these linguistic traits includes the stable trade networks between the two and the traditional winter settlement of Apachean peoples just outside the boundaries of various pueblos. Finally, the Arizona Tewa (Hano) -*tí* passive construction appears to have converged with the corresponding Hopi construction; Tewa maintained a native construction but borrowed the Hopi passive suffix (Kroskrity 1993, 64, 74–75).

Some of these traits and others not mentioned here were considered by Joel Sherzer (1973, 784; 1976, 132–152) in his areal survey of languages in the Southwest, though he concluded that the Southwest as a whole, centered around the Puebloan cultures, does not constitute a significant linguistic area. Cathy Bereznak's (1995) study, however, was thorough and solidly convincing. David Shaul (1980; 2014, 156–157) also supports the **Puebloan Linguistic Area**, with Keresan, Tanoan, Hopi, and Zuni as its members. He lists as its defining traits: series of ejective consonants, series of aspirated consonants, phonemic tone, subject marking by verb prefix, passive governed by animacy hierarchy, plural for hortative/imperative, verb ergativity based on number, conjunctions suffixed to verb, internal verb reduplication for iterative, subject marking by independent nominal, -*it* inceptive ('to begin') verb suffix, object case marking with -*y(a)* 'one's own', switch reference, dual number. Most of these traits, however, are shared only by two of the language families involved. Moreover, Shaul (2014, 134–135) sees also a **Western Puebloan Linguistic Area** and an **Eastern Pueblo Linguistic Area** within the Pueblo Linguistic Area. His Western Puebloan Linguistic Area, with Keresan, Zuni, and Hopi, is characterized by some grammatical borrowings and borrowed ceremonial vocabulary.

7.2.12. Plains Linguistic Area

Joel Sherzer's (1973, 1976) Plains Area illustrates the problems caused by assuming that culture areas and linguistic areas will coincide. The languages spoken in the Plains Culture Area include representatives of Athabaskan (Sarsi, Kiowa Apache, Lipan Apache), Algonquian (Arapaho, Blackfoot, Cheyenne, and dialects of Cree and Ojibwa), Siouan (Crow, Dakota, Dhegiha, Hidatsa, Iowa-Oto, Mandan), Kiowa-Tanoan (Kiowa), Uto-Aztecan (Comanche and Wind River Shoshone), and Tonkawa (an isolate).

Hollow and Parks (1980, 68) counted thirty-three languages (or distinct dialects) that are known to have been spoken in the Plains in historic times. However, these languages share extremely few linguistic traits that are indicative of mutual influence and borrowing, and the traits that they do have in common are also found widely in languages outside the area. The Plains area is the "most recently constituted of the culture areas of North America (late eighteenth and nineteenth century)" (Sherzer 1973, 773). Thus, as would be expected, strong linguistic indicators of longer-term mutual influence are not abundant here.

Sherzer (1973, 773–775) listed the following as area traits of the Plains Area: prefixation of possessive pronouns on nouns, prefixation of subject person markers in verbs, and pronominal plural. However, these features are not uncommon among languages of North America. Frequent traits in the Plains, but not shared by all the Plains languages,

MAP 7.5. Languages of the Plains Linguistic Area

include: one stop series, *x*, alienable/inalienable opposition in nouns, nominal plural suffix, inclusive/exclusive opposition in first person plural of pronouns, nominal diminutive suffix, animate/inanimate gender, and evidential markers in verbs. These are all found also with some frequency outside of the Plains. Plains languages, other than Comanche (and

Wind River Shoshone) and the languages of the Southern Plains subregion, lack labiovelars. This is an indication of why the definition of a linguistic area's constituency should not be just assumed based on the existence of a culture area, for Comanche is known to be a recent arrival in the area, extremely closely related to Shoshone in the Great Basin. The Comanches crossed into the Plains after having acquired horses, which the Spanish had introduced to the New World. Sherzer points to $ð$ as a regional areal trait of the eastern Plains, and he lists phonemic pitch, k^w, voiced/voiceless contrasting fricatives, and r as regional areal traits of the Southern Plains (Sherzer 1976, 185–186).

Hollow and Parks (1980, 82) list a few other Plains areal features (though most of them are of limited distribution within the area), and they point out that they were missed by Sherzer because of his dependence on a predetermined and limited checklist of traits for which he sought examples as he attempted to define the linguistic areas of all of North American. Hollow and Parks argue persuasively that Arikara (Caddoan) acquired its sound-symbolic consonant alternations involving fricatives from Siouan languages, since this trait is unknown in other Caddoan languages, but it is reconstructible for Proto-Siouan. For example, in Arikara (Caddoan) word-final x and $š$ are replaced by s to signal 'diminutive', as in for example *kunahúx* 'old man', but *kunahús* 'little old man'; and *wi:náxtš* 'boy', but *wi:náxts* 'little boy'. This can be compared with sets that illustrate sound-symbolic alternations in Dakota (*zi* 'yellow', *ži* 'tawny', *yi* 'brown') and in Mandan (*síre* 'yellow', *šíre* 'tawny', *xíre* 'brown'), both Siouan languages. Sound-symbolic alternations are also an areal trait of the Southeast Linguistic Area (see below). Other examples of traits that they attribute to the Plains Linguistic Area are vowel devoicing shared by Arikara (Caddoan), Cheyenne (Algonquian), Comanche (Uto-Aztecan), and Fort Belknap Assiniboine (Siouan); sex differentiation (either according to the speaker's sex, as in Dakota and Arikara, or according to the addressee's sex, as in Mandan)—also a feature of the Southeast Linguistic Area; contrasting kinship terms for siblings depending on the sex of ego (Siouan and Caddoan); and relatively restricted consonantal inventories (Caddoan has few consonants; Mandan, Hidatsa, and Crow have fewer than do their other Siouan relatives). Ives Goddard (1974b, 110) pointed out that "the phoneme inventory of Proto-Arapaho-Atsina [Algonquian] is almost identical to that of Wichita [Caddoan]," perhaps quite significant, since Arapaho-Atsina phonology has undergone very far-reaching changes from Proto-Algonquian (Goddard 1974b).

I conclude from these shared traits that there is evidence of areal borrowing and of at least an incipient linguistic area in the Plains, if not a full-blown one.

7.2.13. Northeast Linguistic Area

The Northeast Linguistic Area as defined by Joel Sherzer (1976, 188–201) includes the following languages: Winnebago (Siouan), Northern Iroquoian, and a number of Eastern Algonquian languages (Abenaki, Delaware, Fox, Malecite-Passamaquoddy, Menominee, Miami, Potawatomi, and Shawnee, plus dialects of Ojibwa and Cree).

Sherzer proposed as central areal traits of the Northeast: a single series of stops, a single series of fricatives, h, nominal plural, and noun incorporation. However, he finds that only the first (a single series of stops) is especially characteristic of the Northeast. That is, based on these traits the Northeast is not a very well-defined area. Sherzer (1976, 201) conceded that "the Northeast can be characterized more for traits which are totally absent in the area than

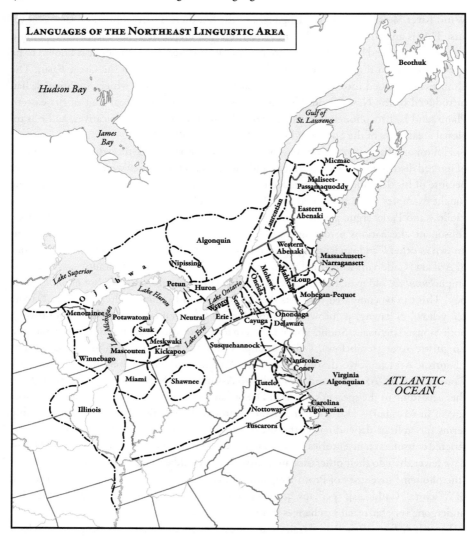

MAP 7.6. Languages of the Northeast Linguistic Area

for traits which are present." Regional areal traits of New England are a vowel system with *i, e, o, a*; nasalized vowel[3]; and a pronominal dual. Sherzer argued that the nasalized vowels and pronominal dual of New England Algonquian languages are the result of influence from Iroquoian languages. The nasalized vowels shared by Iroquoian and Eastern Algonquian languages is the best-known Northeast areal feature (see Goddard 1965, 1971, 2016; Sherzer 1972). Proto-Eastern-Algonquian *a: became a nasalized vowel in Eastern Algonquian due to influence from neighboring Northern Iroquoian languages, which have two nasalized vowels, reconstructed as *ę̃ and *ǫ̃ (Mithun 1979).

In some respects it is difficult to draw a boundary between the Northeast and the Southeast linguistic areas, since some traits seem to extend to languages in both areas.

7.2.14. Southeast Linguistic Area

The Southeast Linguistic Area correlates well with the Southeast Culture Area, which is bounded by the Potomac and Ohio Rivers on the north, the Atlantic on the east, the Gulf of Mexico to the south, and by a line running parallel to the Mississippi River about 200 miles west of it (Crawford 1975, 1; Booker 1980, 1).

As indicated by Ives Goddard (2005, 1), the Southeast of aboriginal North America was linguistically extremely diverse, where "a very large number of the languages spoken by small local populations, and in some cases by larger groups, are undocumented, and it is likely that additional language families were represented among these lost languages." (See Chapter 5.) The more salient languages of the Southeast Linguistic Area are the Muskogean family; Chitimacha, Atakapa, Tunica, Natchez, and Yuchi (language isolates); and Ofo and

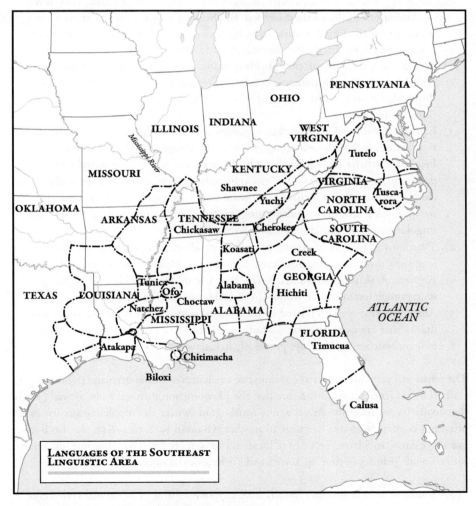

MAP 7.7. Languages of the Southeast Linguistic Area

Biloxi (two Siouan languages). Less centrally the area includes also Timucua (an isolate); Quapaw, Dhegiha, Tutelo and Catawban (Siouan); Tuscarora and Cherokee (Iroquoian); and Shawnee (Algonquian).[4] Several other languages that were spoken in this linguistic area became extinct with little or no documentation, for example, Calusa, Cusabo, Guale, Sewee, Tawasa, and Yamasee (see Goddard 2005). Evidence of this includes the many attested tribal and town names in the Southeast for which at present no linguistic affiliation is known, and historical references to a number of other languages formerly spoken in the area (see Goddard 2005; Haas 1969a, 90–92; 1973b; Rankin 1988; see Chapter 5).

Muskogean subgrouping is made difficult by areal diffusion (see Chapter 2; see also Nicklas 1994).

A summary of proposed areal traits of the Southeast follows.

(1) Bilabial or labial fricatives (ɸ, sometimes *f*) (Haas 1969a, 90) is the only trait Sherzer (1976, 217) found to be especially characteristic of the Southeast area. This shows the limitations of the method he used. By checking only for specific traits from a preset list for all of his linguistic areas, he missed many of the traits that others see as the most relevant in the Southeast Linguistic Area.

(2) The lateral spirant ɬ (voiceless *l*) (Haas 1969a, 90), according to Sherzer (1976, 217), is a trait of the Muskogean-Timucuan region. Nicklas (1994) lists Atakapa, Proto-Muskogean, Yuchi, and Cherokee as other languages of the area that have this sound.

(3) Extensive positional classification of nouns and noun phrases, for example, distinct articles such as those in Quapaw (shared by Quapaw and Dhegiha in general). Inanimate articles include k^he 'long horizontal objects', t^he 'long upright objects', $n\varrho$ 'round or squat objects', $n\iota ke$ 'round or squat objects', and *ke* 'scattered objects, cloth'. Animate articles include ni 'animate singular moving', *(a)pa* 'animate plural moving', $n\iota k^he$ 'animate singular sitting', nik^ha 'animate plural sitting', $t^h\varrho$ 'animate singular standing' (Rankin 1988, 639–640).

(4) 'Positional' classifiers of verbs (for sitting, standing, lying objects) are salient in languages throughout the Southeast, including all Muskogean languages, Tunica, Natchez, Atakapa, Chitimacha, Yuchi, Biloxi, and Dhegiha. The trait is also present, though less salient, in Iroquoian and Algonquian (Rankin 1988, 642).

(5) Auxiliaries that are still related to their lexical source main verbs and other auxiliaries that are now derivational suffixes are found in Proto-Muskogean, Proto-Siouan, Natchez, and perhaps previously in Catawba (Nicklas 1994, 17).

The positional verbs also occur as continuative auxiliaries in Muskogean and in Siouan generally. The evidence seems to indicate that the phenomenon diffused from Siouan (where the auxiliaries are reconstructible) across Muskogean (where the suppletive auxiliaries are often not cognate from one language to another) (Rankin 1988, 642–643; see also Booker 1980, 75). Auxiliaries based on verbs of location ('to be there') that have become inflectional suffixes mark 'priority in time' in Tunica and Yuchi (Nicklas 1994, 14).

(6) Southeast area languages typically have suppletive forms of positional verb stems based on number, as in Choctaw 'to sit': *hinili* 'singular', *hikiya* 'dual', *hinohmaaya*

'plural'. Biloxi has such suppletively related verb-stem forms for at least 'to sit', 'to stand', 'to lie', and 'to be around', though such suppletion for number is unknown elsewhere in Siouan (Rankin 1986, 82–83; Booker 1980, 75, 79–82).

(7) In both Biloxi (Siouan) and Choctaw (Muskogean), possessive constructions are composed of positional verbs (for example, 'to sit/move/be located': 'my dog sits' and 'three children to us sit' are the equivalent of 'I have a dog' and 'we have three children', respectively) (Rankin 1986, 81–82).

(8) Timucua and Natchez share the trait that for a plural possessor, a circumlocution with a copula of the form, for example, 'he who is father to us' is used for 'our father' (Nicklas 1994, 9).

(9) It is claimed that Dhegiha, Algonquian, and some Muskogean languages have pre-aspirated voiceless stops. In Muskogean they are hC clusters; in Dhegiha they are best thought of as single surface phonemes (not clusters); in other Siouan languages they are (post-)aspirated (for example, Dhegiha /hp, ht, hc, hk/ correspond to Dakota, Tutelo, etc. /p^h, t^h, c^h, k^h/) (Rankin 1988, 642; see Chapter 2). The aspirated stops shared by Siouan and Yuchi may fit here too, since Siouan evidence shows that they developed late in Pre-Proto-Siouan (minus Catawban) (see Chapter 2). That is, since aspirated stops are secondary in Siouan, but are shared by Siouan, Yuchi, and to some extent also by some of the Muskogean languages, the pre-aspirated consonants are a good candidate for a possible areal feature.

(10) Retroflexed sibilants (for example, Quapaw [$\underset{\cdot}{s}$] and [$\underset{\cdot}{z}$]) are found in Creek (dialects), Hitchiti, Mikasuki, Alabama (allophonically in the last two), Mobilian Jargon, Natchez, Tunica, and Quapaw. Rankin (1988, 644) says that "sibilant retroflexion is unquestionably a bona fide southeastern areal feature" (see also Nicklas 1994, 18).

(11) Muskogean, Dhegiha, and Algonquian share a quinary counting system that contrasts with the system of more northern Siouan and neighboring Caddoan languages. Dhegiha has clearly adopted something foreign, though whether it was borrowed from Muskogean or from Algonquian is not clear (Rankin 1988, 642).

(12) Koasati (Muskogean) appears to have borrowed its *-na:nan* 'marker of distributive of numerals' from Quapaw *-nana* (same meaning), whereas the Choctaw-Chickasaw apparently borrowed a marker of ordinals for 'second' and 'third', formed with the prefix *hi-* (not the common Muskogean *a-*), which matches Quapaw *hi-* (same meaning). Both of these Quapaw forms have solid Siouan cognates (Rankin 1988, 644). This is more a local borrowing, not an area-wide trait.

(13) A discontinuous negative construction is shared by some languages of the area. For example, Allen (1931, 192) cites Cherokee *ni . . . na* (compare also Mohawk *ya' . . . de*), Tutelo *ki . . . na*, and Biloxi *i . . . na*; modern Muskogean languages have *ak- . . . -o* (Booker 1980, 256).

(14) Crawford (1988, 159) reported that the Hitchiti *-ti* 'negative suffix to verbs', which he says occurs in no other Muskogean language (except possibly Alabama), "undoubtedly was borrowed by Hitchiti from Timucua." Timucua has the same suffix with the same meaning. This also is a local borrowing, not area-wide.

(15) A trait found in many Siouan and Muskogean languages is the use of separate markers, usually post-verbal, to distinguish between male and female speech in

declarative or imperative categories (Rankin 1988). Nicklas (1994, 14) reported that nouns (both inanimate and animate) are marked for gender and number in Tunica, Yuchi, and Quapaw, where most other Southeast languages mark plural only on human nouns. This is also reported as a trait of the Plains Linguistic Area.

(16) Rankin (1986) pointed out that "fricative ablaut"—essentially sound-symbolic alternations among fricatives involving size and intensity—is a possible Southeast area trait. It is shared by Muskogean and Siouan languages, for example, Dakota *zi* 'yellow' / *ži* 'brown' / *yi* 'dark brown'; Winnebago *-sox* 'frying sound' / *-šox* 'bubbling sound' / *-xox* 'breaking sound'; Choctaw *fopa* 'bellow, murmur' / *chopa* 'roar (as water)' / *hompa* 'whoop, bang', *fąma* 'strike, beat' / *samak* 'sound of a bell' / *chamak* 'clink, to clink' / *hąma* 'to stroke'. This is also a trait of the Plains Linguistic Area, seen above.

(17) Rankin (personal communication) noted a very prevalent structural feature in Southeastern languages where a large number of verbs are not themselves directly inflected, but rather an accompanying postposed auxiliary bears the inflectional morphology. This trait is found at least in Muskogean, Natchez, and Catawba, and probably in some other languages of the area.

(18) Sonorants (*m, n, l, r, w*, and *y*) are devoiced word-finally and before a voiceless consonant in Tunica, Natchez, and Chitimacha. In Chitimacha these voiceless sonorants further changed to *h* (Nicklas 1994, 7, 11–19).

(19) It had been claimed that verbs are inflected with nominative-accusative marking in many of the languages of the Southeast, but in fact most of them have active-patient verb alignment (Mithun 2020, 605; see also Heaton 2016). While the active-patient verb trait is widely shared in the area, it also appears in the Plains and the Northeast areas, making it not a very distinctive trait upon which to define a linguistic area involving only languages of the Southeast.

(21) Different pronominal series are used to mark alienable and inalienable possession. In Iroquoian, Cherokee, Catawba, Yuchi, and Biloxi, the inalienable prefix series is identical with the agentive-subject prefixes; in other Siouan languages and Muskogean, it is identical with the non-agentive object prefixes. In Natchez and Timucua, the possessive markers are suffixed (Nicklas 1994, 11, 13).

(22) An inclusive first-person plural category is shared by Proto-Muskogean, Proto-Siouan, and Caddo; it is based at least in part on indefinite third person elements (Nicklas 1994, 17).

(23) In Choctaw, Catawba, and Siouan, demonstratives follow nouns, but they precede the nouns in all other Southeast area languages (Nicklas 1994, 19). This suggests that Choctaw has been influenced by the Siouan pattern.

One difficulty in dealing with the Southeast Linguistic Area is that some features are shared not only across the Southeast but are found also in the Plains Area and throughout eastern North America, particularly in Algonquian and Iroquoian languages, and also in the Siouan languages generally. The possibility of a broader linguistic area, which might include the Southeast Linguistic Area as a subarea, may merit consideration.

It should also be noted that several of the features that were sometimes thought to be evidence of the Gulf hypothesis—a proposed distant genetic relationship which would group several southeastern languages, Natchez, Muskogean, Atakapa, Chitimacha, and Tunica (see Chapter 2) —appear to be diffused areal features in the Southeastern Linguistic Area. These include: SOV basic word order (including postpositions), active-stative alignment, stative verbs inflected by patient affixes and stative verbs inflected by dative affixes (Natchez, Muskogean), nominal alignment markers (active-stative cases), locative cases (Natchez, Chitimacha, Muskogean), independent inflected verbs and inflected auxiliary verbs (Tunica, Muskogean, Natchez, Chitimacha), reference tracking devices (switch-reference [-t/-k/-n] and focus [-o-] in Muskogean, reference tracking [-k] and focus [-o-k] in Natchez, reference tracking [-man] in Tunica, and focus in Chitimacha [-š] and Atakapa [-š]), and possessive suffixes (Tunica, Muskogean, Natchez) (Kimball 1994). Many of these appear to be traits of the Southeast Linguistic Area, not evidence of a genetic relationship. (See also Mithun 1999, 319–320.)

7.3. MESOAMERICAN LINGUISTIC AREA

The Mesoamerican Linguistic Area is one of the best-known linguistic areas in the Americas and elsewhere. It coincides in territory closely though not exactly with the Mesoamerican Culture Area (Kirchhoff 1943). The two probably began to form simultaneously as a result of contact and exchange presumably during the Mesoamerican Preclassic period (c. 1500 BCE– 100 CE), with significant influence from Olmec culture (1200–400 BCE). The languages of this linguistic area are: Cuitlatec, Huave, Mayan, Mixe-Zoquean, Nahua (Aztecan, branch of Uto-Aztecan), Otomanguean (except Chichimeco-Jonaz and some Pame languages beyond the northern frontier of Mesoamerica), Purépecha (Tarascan), Tequistlatecan, Totonacan, and Xinkan. Because they lack some linguistic traits diagnostic of the area, some languages to the north (Cora and Huichol) and to the south (Lenca, Jicaquean, and Misumalpan) of the Mesoamerican Linguistic Area are not included, though some scholars include the societies that speak them in the Mesoamerican Culture Area.

How the Mesoamerican Linguistic Area was defined and what traits characterize it have at times been misunderstood. There had been some expressions of doubt about whether Mesoamerica is a real linguistic area (see for example Suárez 1983b). Because of that, Campbell, Kaufman, and Smith-Stark (1986) emphasized five areal traits that are shared by nearly all of the languages in the Mesoamerican area but not by others beyond the borders of Mesoamerica. These were considered strong cases that even skeptics would have difficulty doubting. However, Campbell et al. also presented a significant number of other traits diffused among languages of the area, some that reach only some of the languages of the area but not all, and others that are widely shared among languages of the area but also extend to some other languages outside of the area. Though we stressed the probative value of the five cases that were shared by almost all of the languages in the region and that bundled at the border and did not extend beyond the linguistic area, such bundling of areal traits is in fact extremely rare in linguistic areas, and other well-known linguistic areas mostly do not exhibit such bundling at their borders. In this respect, linguistic areas are similar to traditional dialects, where typically one trait may extend across a greater range while another trait's territory may be more limited, so that the areas covered by the different traits do not coincide ('bundle'), and often the areal traits crisscross or overlap each other in different ways (Campbell 2017b; 2020a, 245–247). In a situation where a number of strong traits do coincide at a clear boundary, rare

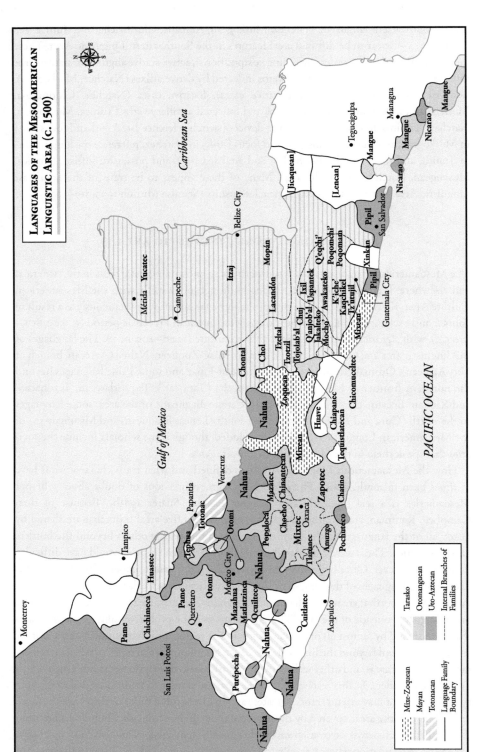

MAP 7.8. Languages of the Mesoamerican Linguistic Area (c. 1500)

though this is, the definition of a linguistic area based on their shared boundary is relatively secure, as is the case with the Mesoamerican Linguistic Area.

The five areal traits that Campbell et al. (1986) found to be common to nearly all Mesoamerican languages and mostly not found in languages just beyond the borders of Mesoamerica are:

(1) Nominal possession of the type *his-noun$_1$ (the) noun$_2$*, illustrated by Pipil (Nawat) (Nahua) *i-pēlu ne tākat*, literally 'his-dog the man', to mean 'the man's dog'. Others have sometimes called this head-marked nominal possession (for example Brown 2011, 272).

(2) Relational nouns, relational expressions equivalent to prepositions or postpositions in other languages, composed of a noun root with possessive pronominal affixes, as in Tz'utujil (Mayan): *(č-)r-i:x* 'behind it, in back of it': *č-* 'at, in', *r-* 'his/her/its', *-i:x* 'back'; *č-w-i:x* 'behind me': *č-* 'at/in', *w-* 'my', *-i:x* 'back'.

(3) Vigesimal numeral system, based on twenty, illustrated by Chol (Mayan): *hun-k'al* '20' (1 X 20), *čaʔ-k'al* '40' (2 X 20), *uš-k'al* '60' (3 X 20), *hoʔ-k'al* '100' (5 X 20), *hun-bahk* '400' (1 X 400), *čaʔ-bahk* '800' (2 X 400), and so on.

(4) Basic word order with the verb before the object, that is, the languages are not verb-final (not SOV). Although Mesoamerica is surrounded on both the north and south by languages with SOV basic word order, languages within the Mesoamerican Linguistic Area have VOS, VSO, or SVO basic orders, but not SOV (nor OSV or OVS).

(5) Mesoamerican languages have many shared calques (semantic loan translations). They include such examples as 'boa' = 'deer-snake' (as in Nahuatl *masākōwatl* 'boa', from *masā-* 'deer' + *kōwa-tl* 'snake'), 'egg' = 'bird-stone/bone', 'lime' = '(stone-)ash', 'knee' = 'leg-head', and 'wrist' = 'hand-neck'. Campbell et al. (1986) presented thirteen calques widely shared in Mesoamerica, selected from Thomas Smith-Stark's (1994) list of fifty-two such calques among Mesoamerican languages.

A sixth feature common to Mesoamerican languages was also mentioned, the absence of switch-reference constructions. While switch-reference is found in the languages just beyond both borders of Mesoamerica—in Coahuilteco, Seri, Yuman, and Jicaquean—it is entirely absent from languages in Mesoamerica. However, this is probably not an independent trait; rather, probably it reflects the fact that switch-reference is found predominantly only in SOV languages, meaning that the absence of switch-reference from Mesoamerican languages is probably correlated with the absence of SOV word order there.

However, it is important not to lose sight of the fact that the Mesoamerican Linguistic area is characterized not only by these five so-called signature or criterial traits, but, as most other linguistic areas are, also by the other traits that are common to several languages but not to all of them and by other traits that also extend to some languages beyond the area's borders. Among features of these two kinds, phenomena distributed among various Mesoamerican languages listed in Campbell et al. (1986), include:

(1) Inalienable possession of body parts and kinship terms. This trait, however, is characteristic of almost all Mesoamerican languages but also of many other languages throughout the Americas.

(2) Numeral classifiers are found in many Mayan languages, Purépecha (Tarascan), Totonacan, Huamelultec (Tequistaltecan), and Nahuatl—for example, Tzeltal *oš lehč teʔ* [three FLAT.CLASS wood] 'three plants', *oš tehk teʔ* [three PLANT.CLASS wood] 'three trees', *oš kʼas siʔ* [three BROKEN.CLASS firewood] 'three chunks of firewood'.

(3) Affix indicting non-specified possessor on inalienably possessed nouns, in Nahua and Mayan, but also in Pech (Paya) and Misumalpan, as for example Kʼiche' *xolom-aːx* '(somebody's) head', contrasted with *a-xoloːm* [your-head] 'your head'.

(4) Noun-incorporation of the sort where a nominal object is incorporated morphologically in the verb, found in some Mayan languages (Yucatec, Mam), Nahua, and Totonac. An example is Yucatec (Mayan) *čʼak-čeʔ-n-ah-en* [cut-wood-INTRANSITIVE-ASPECT-1ABSOLUTIVE] 'I cut wood' ('I wood-cut'); this contrasts with the unincorporated counterpart: *t-in-čʼak-ah čeʔ* [ASPECT-1ERGATIVE-cut-ASPECT wood] 'I cut wood'), or in Nahuatl *ni-tlaškal-čiwa* [I-tortilla-make] 'I make tortillas', with incorporation compared with unincorprated *ni-k-čiwa tlaškal* [I-3OBJECT-make tortillas] 'I make tortillas'. Noun incorporation is also found in a good number of languages elsewhere in the Americas (see Mithun 1984a; 1999, 44–47; Sapir 1911).

There is also a type of noun-incorporation in which specific forms for body parts are incorporated into the verb, usually as instrumentals (in Mixe-Zoquean, Nahua, Purépecha (Tarascan), Tlapanec, and Totonac), as in Pipil (Nawat): *ni-k-tan-kwa* [I-3OBJECT-**tooth**-eat] 'I bite it' and *n-k-ikši-ahsi* [I-3OBJECT-**foot**-arrive] 'I reach it, I overtake him/her/it'. Sometimes the incorporated body part morpheme has a different phonological form from the free-standing body part with the same meaning. For example Nahuatl has **kwā**-*totoniā* 'to get angry' (with **kwā**- 'head' incorporated), but *kwāyi-tl* 'head' (when not incorporated), and *totoniā* 'to heat, warm' without the incorporation; and **mā**-*kwepa* 'to restore, recoup losses' (with **mā**- 'hand' incorporated), but *māyi-tl* 'hand' (unincorporated), and *kwepa* 'to turn, return' (without incorporation). This type of incorporation is found also in a number of languages elsewhere in the Americas.

(5) Directional morphemes (indicating, for example, away from or toward the speaker) are incorporated into the verb in Mayan, Nahua, Tequistlatecan, Purépecha (Tarascan), some Otomanguean languages, and Totonac—for example, Kaqchikel (Mayan) *y-e-bʼe-n-kam-is-ax* [ASPECT-3PL.ABSOLUTIVE-**THITHER**-1SG.ERGATIVE-die-CAUSATIVE-TRANSITIVE] 'I'm going there to kill them'.

(6) Locatives derived from body parts are found in most Mesoamerican languages, though they are also found in languages around the world, as in Yosondúa Mixtec *čii* 'stomach, in(side)', *nuu* 'face, to, in, by, before', *xata* 'back, behind', *yuʔu* 'mouth, beside' (Beaty de Farris 2012).

(7) Noun plural affixes are absent or are largely limited to human referents in most Mesoamerican languages; this, however, is also typical of a number of other languages in the Americas and elsewhere.

(8) Positional verbs differ in form (in morphological class) from intransitives and from transitives in Mayan and Otomanguean.

(9) An inclusive-exclusive contrast in first-person plural pronouns, in Chol, Mam, Akateko, Jakalteko (Mayan languages); Chocho, Popoloca, Ixcatec, Otomi, Mixtec, Trique, Chatino, Yatzachi Zapotec, Tlapanec (Otomanguean languages), Huave, and several Mixe-Zoquean languages—for example, Chol *tsa? letsiy-on loxon* [PAST ascend-1PERSON EXCLUSIVE] 'we (exclusive) go up, ascend' vs. *tsa? letsiy-on-la* [PAST ascend-1PERSON -INCLUSIVE] 'we (inclusive) go up, ascend'.

(10) An overt copula is lacking from equational constructions in most Mesoamerican languages, as for example in K'iche' *saq le: xa:h* [white the house] 'the house is white'. This is also found widely elsewhere in the Americas and around the world. Copular constructions involving noun or adjective roots with pronominal person affixes are found in Mayan, Nahua, Chocho, Chinantec, Mazatec, Otomí, and several Mixe-Zoquean languages. Copular sentences with pronominal subjects are formed with pronominal affixes attached to the complement—for example, Q'eqchi' (Mayan) *išq-at* [woman-2SG.ABSOLUTIVE] 'you are a woman', *winq-in* [man-1SG.ABSOLUTIVE] 'I am a man', and Pipil (Nawat) *ni-tākat* [I-man] 'I am a man', *ti-siwāt* [you-woman] 'you are a woman'. This construction is found elsewhere as well, for example in several Northwest Coast languages and several languages of the Chaco region of South America.

(11) Lack of a specific verb of possession 'to have', characteristic of Mayan (excluding Huastec), Mixe-Zoquean, Tequistlatecan, Xinkan, Chinantecan, Mazatec, and Trique, among others. The most common construction for 'to have' in Mesoamerican languages is equivalent to 'there is' or 'there exists' plus a possessed noun, as in Kaqchikel (Mayan) *k'o xun nu-ts'i:?* [there.is one my-dog] 'I have a dog'.

(12) Some "Sprechbund" traits (ethnography of communication features) are also encountered in several Mesoamerican languages. For example, a stylized form of ritual language and oral literature with shared conventional forms involving, among other things, paired couplets with semantic associations is very widespread and occurs in remarkably similar form in K'iche', Tzeltal, Tzotzil, Yucatec, Nahuatl, Ocuiltec, Amuzgo, Popoloca, Totonac, and others. This is called Huehuetla'tolli in Nahuatl and Ts'ono:x in K'iche' (see Barrett 2017).

Paired couplets are illustrated in the following short prayer from the Popol Vuh (in K'iche', a Mayan language):

at tz'aqool, at b'itool	you shaper, you creator
k-oj-aw-ila', k-oj-a-ta'	see-us, hear-us
m-oj-a-tzoqoh, m-oj-a-pisk'aliij	don't-let-us-fall, don't-abandon-us
chi-kaaj, chi uleew	in-heaven, on earth
u-k'u'x kaaj, u-k'u'x uleew	heart of heaven, heart of earth

(Mondloch 1983, 75).
(See also the discussion in Constenla Umaña 1991.)

Some form of whistle speech is found in Amuzgo, Mazatec, Otomi, several Zapotec groups, Mopán, Chol, Totonac, Tepehua, and some Nahua dialects, also in Mexican Kickapoo.

(13) Among phonological traits shared among Mesoamerican languages that were mentioned in the Campbell et al. (1986) article are:

[1] Devoicing of sonorant consonants (*l, r, w, y*) word-finally, in K'ichean (Mayan); Nahuatl, Pipil (Nawat) (Nahua); Xinkan; Totonac, Tepehua (Totonacan); Purépecha (Tarascan); and Sierra Popoluca (Mixe-Zoquean)—as well as in Sumu and Cacaopera (Misumalpan), as for example in Nahuatl *no-mīl* [no-mi̥ɬ] 'my cornfield' or Kaqchikel (Mayan) *te:w* [te:w̥] 'cold'.

[2] Voicing of obstruents after nasals, in most Otomanguean languages, Purépecha (Tarascan), Mixe-Zoquean, Huave, and Xinkan—as well as in Jicaquean and Lencan—as for example in Copainalá Zoque /n-tik/ [ndik] 'my house'.

[3] Limited vowel harmony (often involving only subsets of suffixes), in Mayan, some varieties of Zoque, Mazahua, Xinkan, and Huave—as well as in Lencan and Jicaquean.

[4] Predictable (non-phonemic) stress in most Mesoamerican languages. Contrastive (phonemic) stress is very rare but is known in Tequistlatecan and Cuitlatec. Some languages share the specific stress rule which places the accent on the vowel before the last (right-most) consonant of the word (V→ V́ /__C(V)#). They include Oluta Popoluca, Totontepec Mixe (Mixe-Zoquean); Xinkan; and most Mayan languages—as well as Lencan and Jicaquean. In Most Mayan languages, stress falls on the final syllable of a word, but since roots do not end in a vowel, they also fit this rule by default (that is, there are V́C# words but no V́CV# words).

[5] General similarities in phonemic inventories:
   (a) Contrasting voiced stops (and affricates) are almost totally absent; they are present in a few Otomangueuan languages, Cuitlatec, and Tequistlatec (where they can be explained historically).
   (b) Contrastive voiced fricatives are lacking. The lenis/non-geminate series in some Zapotec languages appears phonetically to involve voicing of some consonants, but it does not primarily involve a phonemic voicing contrast in Zapotec languages.
   (c) A lateral affricate is generally lacking but is found in some Nahua dialects, Totonac, and Tequistlatecan. In Tequistlatecan, the sound in question is a /tl'/, the glottalized counterpart of /l/ in this language family; Tequistlatecan has no plain *tl*.
   (d) Uvular stops (*q* and *q'*) are found only in Totonacan and Mayan languages.
   (e) Aspirated stops and affricates are rare but occur in Purépecha (Tarascan) and some Otomanguean languages; Jicaquean also has them.
   (f) Glottalized consonants occur in Tepehua, Tequistlatecan, Otopamean, Mayan, and Xinkan—as well as in Lencan, Jicaquean, and Coahuilteco.
   (g) Tonal contrasts are found in all Otomanguean languages, Huave, Cuitlatec, and a few Mayan languages (Yucatec, Uspantek, and marginally in Mocho'). Several languages spoken just outside Mesoamerica (Northern Tepehuan, Cora-Huichol, Paya, Guaymí, and Bribri) have tone or pitch accent contrasts.
   (h) Retroflexed fricatives (and affricates) occur in Mamean, Q'anjob'al, Jakalteko, and Akateko (Mayan); Guazacapan and Chiquimulilla (Xincan); some Mixean languages; and Chocho, Popoloca, Mazatec, Trique, and Yatzachi and Guelavia Zapotec (Otomanguean); they occur allophonically in Purépecha (Tarascan).

(i) A central vowel /ɨ/ (or sometimes /ə/) is found in Mixe-Zoquean, several Otomanguean languages, Huave, Xinkan, Proto-Nahua (Proto-Aztecan), and some Mayan languages (Proto-Yucatecan, Cholan, dialects of Kaqchikel and K'iche', allophonically in Mam), and allophonically also in Purépecha (Tarascan). This vowel is also found in Jicaquean and Northern-Uto-Aztecan languages and in some other languages spoken outside of Mesoamerica.

Finally, it is worth mentioning even more local kinds of diffusion involving only a couple of languages or language families. For example, Robert Zavala (2002) and Danny Law (2017a, 115) mention a number of syntactic traits shared by Mayan and Mixe-Zoquean languages, several borrowed from Mixe-Zoquean into some Mayan languages and others that involve Mayan influence on Mixe-Zoquean languages.

While lexical borrowings are not considered the kind of diffusion that defines linguistic areas, it is worth mentioning that the languages of the Mesoamerican area do share many loanwords. Some are quite widespread, and the meaning of several suggests cultural items that are diagnostic of the Mesoamerican Culture Area (Campbell et al. 1986; Justeson et al. 1985; see Chapter 9).

Since publication of the Campbell et al. (1986) paper, some proposals would add new areal traits to Mesoamerica, some recommend adding additional languages, and others argue for removal of some language from the linguistic area. Some scholars would modify some traits, and some criticisms challenge aspects of some of the traits and which languages exhibit them. On the whole, however, the Mesoamerican Linguistic Area and its traits stand mostly intact as described in Campbell et al. (1986).

Thomas Smith-Stark (1988) proposed adding "Pied-Piping with Inversion" as a Mesoamerican areal trait (see Munro 2017, 347–349). In questions where the object of a preposition (a relational noun in these cases) is questioned, the prepositional phrase is "pied-piped" to the front of the sentence with the preposition and the question word being inverted. English has for example, *'With whom does the woman drink water?'* (where *'with whom'* has been brought to the front of the clause [pied-piping the object along with its preposition]). In many Mesoamerican languages the equivalent to this is of the form, *'Who(m) with does the woman drink water?',* where the equivalent of the prepositional phrase *'with who(m)'* is preposed and then the question word matching *'who(m)'* is inverted, placed before the equivalent of the preposition *'with'*.

Pamela Munro (2017, 350–351) also makes a good case that a number of Mesoamerican languages have what she calls "absence of prepositions with 'large locations.'" Where in most instances these languages have an overt indicator of location or direction (equivalent to 'he went **into** the house', not 'he went house'), with "large locations" such as towns or large buildings they lack such an indicator, the equivalent of 'we live Los Angeles' rather than 'we live in Los Angeles'.

Munro (2017, 351) also argues that Garífuna (an Arawakan language of Belize, Guatemala, Honduras, and Nicaragua) "should perhaps be recognized as Mesoamerican." Garífuna has a partial vigesimal number system, though it was apparently inspired by vigesimal aspects of French counting; in fact Garífuna has French loanwords for 'twenty' and some other numbers (Munro 2017, 341–342). Also, Garífuna has, in Munro's (2017, 342) analysis, five calques from among Smith-Stark's (1994, 52), though only one coincides with the thirteen most typical ones presented in Campbell et al. (1986). She finds in Garífuna two of four features involving phoneme inventories shared among several Mesoamerican language, and eleven of eighteen morphosyntactic features given in Campbell et al. (1986). Several of these are not particularly strong as evidence goes for defining linguistic areas, for example, absence of switch-reference, absence of plural markers on nouns, 'zero' copular', absence of a verb 'to have', intimate (inalienable) possession, locatives derived from body parts—these are quite common in other indigenous New World tongues, and several of them are found also in languages elsewhere around the world. However, she adds to these also the additional traits just mentioned that Garífuna also shares with a number of other Mesoamerican languages, "Pied-Piping with Inversion" and "absence of prepositions with 'large locations'" (Munro 2017, 348, 351).[5]

Claudine Chamoreau (in press), on the other hand, doubts that Purépecha (Tarascan) is a Mesoamerican language; she thinks that it does not share enough Mesoamerican areal traits to be considered a member of the Mesoamerican Linguistic Area. She admits, though, that Purépecha does share several of the Mesamerican traits but asks "whether these features are merely typological coincidences or whether they should be viewed as the result of contact-induced convergence" (p. 36), conceding that "the relations between Purepecha and MA [Mesoamerican] languages remain to be clarified" (p. 36). She suggests that of the five strong Mesoamerican traits, Purépecha has only the vigesimal numeral system (p. 36). Also she indicates that Purépecha does have SVO basic word order (one of the word orders found in some other Mesoamerican languages) but does not have some of the other orders typically associated with SVO typology. This seems not a serious objection, however; even some Mixe-Zoquean languages in some constructions have word orders more typically associated with SOV languages although they are not SOV when it comes to the order of the constituents Subject, Verb, and Object in main clauses. Purépecha has a genitive case marker and locative cases rather than the possessive construction and relational nouns more typical of Mesoamerica. Chamoreau sees Purépecha as predominantly dependent-marking, unlike most Mesoamerican languages, but acknowledges that it also exhibits some head-marking characteristics (p. 25). As seen above, there are also a number of other traits that Purépecha shares with Mesoamerican languages, beyond just the five signature diagnostic traits.

Heriberto Avelino (2006) showed that Northern Pame has a numeral system based on eight while Central and Southern Pame have Mesoamerican vegismal counting. He points out that the numeral systems of these Pamean languages can "contribute to our understanding of historical relations between the north-east of Mesoamerica and northern areas" (p. 58).

There have also been other suggested refinements and some criticisms of some traits and their distribution among the languages, for example whether Zapotec has the Mesoamerican possessive construction or lacks it (Munro 2017).

Ultimately, the question should not be, is Purépecha or alternatively is Garífuna a Mesoamerican language, that is, are they members of the linguistic area, but rather, to what extent do they share traits with other languages of the area? As should be expected from typical linguistic areas, some diffused traits extend further than others and may be found in some languages but be absent in others. Languages on the peripheries of linguistic areas often share fewer of the areally diffused traits found in languages more intimately integrated in the particular linguistic areas (see Campbell 2017b). Ultimately it probably matters little whether we might be able to declare definitively that Purépecha, Garífuna, or certain Pamean languages belong squarely to the Mesoamerican Linguistic Area or whether they are not true member of the linguistic area but are influenced in a certain set of features by the languages of the area. It is the diffused traits themselves more than a yes-or-no categorization of areal membership that matters. Perhaps Cora and Huichol are similar in this regard; they also share some traits with Mesoamerican languages, but they lack several other of the traits that seem important to languages of the Mesoamerican Linguistic Area.

Cecil Brown (2011) provided useful additions to and corrections concerning the distribution of the calques, one of the five Mesoamerican traits considered strong in the Campbell et al. (1986) article. However, Brown believed that most of the areal traits of Mesoamerica developed quite late, possibly after contact with European languages, due to the influence of Nahuatl as an assumed lingua franca, though he concentrated his attention only on the shared calques. Dakin and Operstein (2017, 3–4) also think the possibility that Nahuatl was actually a participant in the creation of a number of areal traits needs to be considered. Brown argued that five of thirteen calques in Campbell et al. (1986) "occur frequently enough in peripheral languages to suggest that these traits may not be diagnostic of a Mesoamerican linguistic area" (p. 174), and he suggested that six of the thirteen "occur relatively frequently across the languages of [his] table 2, suggesting that Amerindians are universally inclined to independently develop them" (p. 178). There certainly are cases of similar calques in languages outside of Mesoamerica as shown in Brown's table 2, though the judgment that they "occur relatively frequently" seems to overstate what the table actually shows (pp. 178–180).

Brown asserted that distributions of these calques can "contribute in a straightforward manner to understanding how MA [Mesoamerica] developed as a linguistic area" (p. 181). He grouped six widespread post-contact borrowings—not considered by anyone as relevant to characterizing Mesoamerica—with five Mesoamerican calques from the original thirteen to which he had no strong objections. He asserted that "native terms for imported items rarely (at a rate of only 14%) have diffused across Amerindian languages when languages involved do not include a lingua franca and do not belong to the same genetic grouping" (p. 190). He then asserted that Nahuatl "served as a widespread lingua franca both before and after contact" (p. 191). He concluded that "since most, if not all, of the six post-contact features diffused from Nahuatl, plausibly, Nahuatl was the primary agent in the diffusion of the five semantic calques . . . as well" (p. 191), and "the five semantic calques . . . could have diffused in post-contact times" (p. 193). True, Nahuatl was a language widely used in Spanish administration in early colonial times, but the evidence is not compelling that it was ever widely used as a lingua franca among many of the Indigenous groups themselves in pre-contact times.

It certainly does not follow from six post-contact widely diffused lexical borrowings that the Mesoamerican calques must have the same source nor that they must be from post-contact times. First, it is far from certain that even a majority of Brown's six are from Nahuatl.[6] Second, lexical items are far easier to borrow than structural traits, and the definition of Mesoamerica as a linguistic area relies on a large number of structural traits shared among the languages (as seen above).

Brown devoted considerable attention to the Mesoamerican calque that has 'gold' or 'silver' as the equivalent of 'god excrement' or 'sun excrement', trying to make a case that it originated in Nahuatl, late, and then diffused to some Mayan and other languages (pp. 192, 198). This, of course, is not the case for 'gold'/'silver', or in fact for most of the other thirteen original calques of Campbell et al. (1986)—most of these are well attested in Maya hieroglyphic texts from at the latest before 900 CE, as demonstrated for example by Christophe Helmke (2013). This includes both the one for 'gold/silver' = 'god excrement/sun excrement', and the one for 'boa/large snake' = 'deer snake', instances singled out for special comment by Brown.[7] That is, the early glyphic evidence conclusively demonstrates that these are not late borrowings under the influence of an assumed Nahuatl lingua franca. Brown went even further, however, to claim that "we can assume that the four [other] linguistic traits mentioned by CKS [Campbell et al. 1986)] as meeting their 'tight constraints' for defining a linguistic area . . . spread from Nahuatl to other languages of MA [Mesoamerica]" (p. 200). This in no way follows. The evidence does not support Brown's conclusion that Nahuatl had a preeminent role in the formation of Mesoamerica as a linguistic area (p. 201). Nahua arrival in Mesoamerica was far too late for that, not earlier than 500 CE (see Kaufman 2003, 2020; Kaufman and Justeson 2009; see Chapter 3). In fact, it was just the opposite. Rather than Nahua influencing the structure of its neighbors in Mesoamerica, Nahua itself was reshaped significantly after its arrival, taking on Mesoamerican traits not shared by its other Uto-Aztecan relatives (see Chapter 2).

There are also some subareas within Mesoamerica. Many of the Mayan languages participated in specific diffusion zones (contact zones, linguistic areas): Lowland Mayan Linguistic Area, the more inclusive Greater Lowland Mayan Linguistic Area (Justeson et al. 1985; Kaufman 2017; Law 2014, 2017a), and the Huehuetenango Diffusion Area (Barrett 2002; Kaufman 1974, 2002, 2017). As Danny Law (2014, 31) points out, changes shared in the Lowland Maya Linguistic Area include phonological borrowings, diffusion of specific sound changes, direct borrowing of several bound morphemes, and much convergence or borrowing of syntactic patterns and morphosyntactic structures. Law (2014, 175) identifies features shared through contact among two or more languages in the Lowlands that range from diffused phonological innovations (phonemic mergers, sound changes, and even new phonemic contrasts), to syntactic and semantic patterns (the loss of the agent focus antipassive, the development of an inclusive/exclusive distinction in person marking, aspect-based split ergativity), to the direct replication of actual morphological forms, linguistic 'matter' (several person markers, voice and aspect suffixes, auxiliaries, plural markers, numeral classifiers). Classic Maya culture and civilization were borne primarily by speakers of Cholan languages. The cultural clout of Cholan accounts for many loanwords among Lowland Mayan languages and others. Terrence Kaufman (2020, 189) dated the spread of several loanwords from Cholan cultural vocabulary to Highland Mayan languages at 100–400 CE.

The Huehuetenango Diffusion Area (a.k.a. the Huehuetenango Sphere) involved Mamean and the Greater Q'anjob'alan languages with the exception of Tojolab'al and Mocho'. (See Barrett 2002; Kaufman 1974, 2002, 2017 for details.)

7.4. LINGUISTIC AREAS OF SOUTH AMERICA

South America has what may seem to be a surprising number of linguistic areas and proposed linguistic areas. Considerable structural diffusion and various areal phenomena have been identified in languages of South America, but most South American linguistic areas have, for the most part, not been the subject of concerted investigation, and hence most are not clearly established or well understood. What Terrence Kaufman (1990a, 21–22) said of this is still true: "There is much to be done here." Studies of language contact and language areas in South America exhibit much overlap and conflict, making it clear that areal linguistic investigation in South America requires extensive attention. (See Campbell, Chacon, and Elliott 2020 for a general survey of SA linguistic areas.)

7.4.1. Proposals of Macro-linguistic Areas in South America

David Payne (1990) pointed out some widely shared traits among South American (henceforth abbreviated SA) languages that he believed indicate either diffusion or an undocumented deep genetic relationship. They include: a negative morpheme of the approximate shape *ma*, a causative affix of the approximate shape *mV*, a causative verbal prefix (signaled by a back vowel), a directional verb suffix (often *pV* or *Vp*), an auxiliary 'to have', 'to do', or 'to be', usually containing *ka*, often coinciding in the same language with the verb 'to say, to work' and often with a valency-changing verbal affix of the same or similar shape. Large-scale contact and areal effects involving phonological patterns in South America are discussed by Michael et al. (2014) and discourse practices by Beier et al. (2002). Guillaume and Rose (2010) found that specific markers of sociative causation (a kind of causation where the causer not only makes the causee do an action, but also participates in it) are very frequent in South American languages and they hypothesized that a marker for sociative causation could be an areal feature of South America.

Other proposals have suggested macro-subdivisions within SA. Doris Payne (1990a, 1990b) and Harriet Klein (1992, 33–34) considered the possibility that all lowland SA languages constitute a linguistic area. An East-West, or Highland-Lowland, division among SA languages has been contemplated since Samuel Lafone Quevedo (1896), who based his division on suffixed pronominal markers (his "Quichua" type languages) versus prefixed ones (his "Guaraní" type). Doris Payne (1990b) and Joshua Birchall (2014a, 2014b) suggest a division between Western and Eastern Amazonian languages. In Payne's and Birchall's proposals, their Eastern area covers Cariban, Macro-Jê, and Tupían languages, where Birchall's also includes the Chaco-Planalto area.[8] Their Western contact areas also mostly agree, except that Birchall also includes Southern Cone and Andean languages in his **Western South American Linguistic Area (WSALA)**. Doris Payne's (1990b) **western group** includes languages from Pano-Takanan, Arawakan, Tukanoan, Saliban (Sálivan), Zaparoan, Yaguan, Witotoan, and Cahuapanan families. It is characterized by high verbal polysynthetsis, verbal directionals (that may also have tense-aspect-modality functions), noun classification systems (missing in Pano-Takanan and some Arawakan languages), and verb-initial and postpositional word orders (found in some Arawakan and Zaparoan languages, and in Taushiro and Yagua). Payne's **eastern group** includes languages belonging to the "Je-Bororo," Tupían, Cariban, and "Makúan" (Nadahup) families. They share a more isolating morphology and minimal (or no) verbal directionals, and they lack noun classification.

Joshua Birchall (2014a, 203) found that ergative alignment, which had been considered an Amazonian feature by some, fits only with the southern Amazon region and his **Eastern**

South American Linguistic Area (ESALA), not with northern or western Amazonia. The inclusive-exclusive distinction, claimed as an Andean feature, is not limited to that area, but is a feature of Birchall's WSALA. Many Cariban and Tupían languages also have a first-person plural inclusive-exclusive distinction, despite belonging to ESALA. Birchall found that several other features that had been associated with particular SA linguistic areas turn out to reflect either WSALA or ESALA (Birchall 2014a, 205–206). His east-west division is seconded by Epps and Michael (2017, 952–953), who report that phonological similarities in SA also cluster in ways consistent with Birchall's WSALA versus ESALA. The east-west linguistic division may pattern well with differences between eastern and western populations seen in both mtDNA and Y chromosome patterns (O'Connor and Kolipakam 2014, 32).

7.4.2. Amazonia as a Linguistic Area?

Amazonia is the lowland region drained by the Amazon and Orinoco Rivers. Its status as a linguistic area is much talked about but "as yet [there is] little consensus on this issue" (Epps 2009, 590). Derbyshire and Pullum (1986, 16, 20) found typological tendencies shared across Amazonia, but they caution that the amount of information available was not enough for certainty. The language families included are: Arawakan, Arawan, Cariban, Chapacuran, Jêan, Pano-Takanan, Puinave, Kakua-Nukak, Tukanoan, and Tupían (Derbyshire and Pullum 1991, 3). The extensive linguistic diversity in Amazonia is especially remarkable given that there are no major physical barriers that would lead to isolating local groups.

Derbyshire and Pullum mentioned the tendency of these languages to have O-before-S word orders (VOS, OVS, OSV); Derbyshire (1987, 313) noted that in the OVS and OSV languages word order tends to be flexible, making it difficult to decide which word order is basic. Other widely shared Amazonian traits include: lack of contrast between l and r; presence of i in numerous languages; typically five vowels (as opposed to the three vowels of several Andean languages); nasal vowels, and nasal spreading; noun classifier systems; ideophones; lack of high numerals; verb agreement with both subject and object (plus null realization of subject and object nominals); nominalizations for relative clauses and other subordinate clauses; nominal modifiers following their heads (Noun-Adjective, Genitive-Noun, Noun-Postposition orders); no agentive passive construction; lack of indirect speech forms (reliance on direct speech constructions); absence of coordinating conjunctions (juxtaposition to express coordination); extensive use of right-dislocated paratactic constructions; extensive use of particles that are phrasal subconstituents syntactically and phonologically but are sentence operators or modifiers semantically; tendency toward ergative or active/stative subject marking; complex morphology; and applicatives (valency-changing morphemes) resembling -*tA*; multiple grammatical cases (Derbyshire 1986, 560–561; Derbyshire and Pullum 1986, 16–19; Derbyshire and Payne 1990; Dixon and Aikhenvald 1999; Crevels and van der Voort 2020; van Gijn and Muysken 2020).

Adolfo Constenla Umaña (1991, 135) questioned some of the linguistic traits listed for Amazonia. He believed that Amazonia is not a single linguistic area, but rather that some of its languages should be assigned to neighboring linguistic areas instead. He believed the following were common also in linguistic areas beyond Amazonia: absence of a passive construction; agreement of transitive verb with subject and object and the correlated null realization of full noun phrases in cases of "given" information; and the predominance of the word orders Noun-Adjective, Genitive-Noun, and postpositions. He noted also that the use of nominalizations for subordinate clauses and the absence of direct-indirect speech indicators have broader distributions. Epps and Michael (2017, 952) also challenge some of these traits (see also Klein 1992, 33–34). Rik van Gijn (2014) also showed that there is not a rigid separation of Andean and Amazonian linguistic features but that rather in the foothill-fringe area, the area where the Amazon basin and the Andes meet, their distribution shows a gradual and complex transition from the Andean to the Amazonian area.

Alexandra Aikhenvald (2012, 68–71) attempted to revise the claim that Amazonia is a linguistic area by introducing the term "language region," in contrast to the more rigorously defined notion of "linguistic area," to characterize Amazonia as a region of recurrent but sporadically attested shared features, such as antipassives and complex classifier systems.

Adam Tallman and Patience Epps' (2020) purpose was not to define or defend any particular linguistic area; rather they focus more on morphological complexity and the possible grammaticalization and diffusion of particular traits in western Amazonian languages. Structural diffusion in the western Amazon, however, is prominent in their paper, and it does seem to lend added support to Joshua Birchall's (2014a, 2014b) Western South American versus Eastern South American linguistic areas (see also Doris Payne 1990b). Their results "lend support to the view that low morphological autonomy is a robust feature of languages in the western Amazon region" (Tallman and Epps 2020, 16). Their results suggest "that a relatively loose distinction between syntax and morphology is an areal feature of western Amazonian languages (perhaps extending into neighboring regions)" (Tallman and Epps 2020, 29). They find that "Amazonian languages tend to display a high degree of morphological elaboration in particular grammatical domains, and that many of these prolific domains show evidence of restructuring and diffusion across unrelated languages in particular geographic regions" (p. 16). With respect to morphological complexity, they show "a tendency toward elaboration in western Amazonian languages" in "nominal classification, tense, evidentiality, and valence-adjustment" (p. 29), and they cite examples involving cases in specific languages where borrowing has taken place in these structural domains.

Specifically about diffusion involving evidentiality, Tallman and Epps (2020, 13) say:

Müller (2013, 227) observes the regional clustering of Amazonian languages exhibiting evidentiality, as for example in the Guaporé-Mamoré (Crevels and van der Voort 2008) and the Vaupés regions, and evidentiality does appear to be relatively prone to diffusion cross-linguistically (see e.g. Aikhenvald 2004, 21). Surveys of Amazonian evidentiality (Aikhenvald and Dixon 1998; Aikhenvald 2004, 292; Müller 2013, 228) suggest multiple points of independent innovation, from which the phenomenon has likely diffused more widely. Probably the clearest examples of contact-driven elaboration of evidential systems come from the Vaupés, in which a number of unrelated languages have undergone the grammaticalization of native forms to fill a regionally defined set of categories; this is the case for Hup (see above), Tariana (Arawakan, see Aikhenvald 2002, 117–129), and Kakua (Kakua-Nukakan; Bolaños 2016), among other languages.

Tallman and Epps (2020) also discuss similar cases involving nominal classification, tense, and valence-adjustment.

7.4.3. The Colombian-Central American Linguistic Area

Adolfo Constenla Umaña (1991, 103, 2012, 421–424) proposed what he called the Colombian-Central American Linguistic Area, composed primarily of Chibchan languages, but also including Lencan, Jicaquean, Misumalpan, and Chocoan. He believed that it "corresponds quite well but not exactly to the Lower Central America archaeological area," in eastern and central Honduras, eastern El Salvador, central and Atlantic Nicaragua, Costa Rica except for the Nicoya Peninsula, Panama, and the northern part of South America (Constenla Umaña 2012, 421). He listed the main features shared within this area as "voicing contrasts in stops, SOV order, postpositions, predominant genitive-noun order, noun-adjective order, noun-numeral order, non-obligatoriness of initial position for question words, negation predominantly expressed by suffixes or postposed particles, absence of gender contrasts in pronouns and inflection, absence of accusative case marking in most languages, [and] predominance of languages without the non-possessed (absolute state)/possessed (construct state) opposition in nouns" (Constenla Umaña 2012, 421).[9]

Constenla Umaña (2012, 424) recognized two subareas in his Colombian-Central American Area. The **Northern Subarea** includes the languages in northern Costa Rica, Nicaragua, Honduras, and El Salvador: those belonging to Jicaquean, Lencan, Misumalpan, Pech (Paya), Rama, and Guatuso. This subarea is characterized by traits such as person inflection in nouns, intransitive verbs, and transitive verbs (for both patient and agent), predominance of nominative-accusative case systems, length contrasts in vowels, presence of /ŋ/ and absence of /ʃ/. His **Central Subarea** includes the languages spoken to the west of the Magdalena River in Colombia, Panama, and southern Costa Rica, that is, the Chocoan and the Isthmian Chibchan languages. It is characterized by predominance of ergative or active case systems, absence of person inflection, and predominance of languages with nasalization and tenseness contrasts in the vowels, and voicing contrasts in alveopalatal affricates.

7.4.4. Northern Amazonia Linguistic Areas

7.4.4.1. The Vaupés (Vaupés-Içana) Linguistic Area

More has been written about language contact in the Vaupés region than anywhere else in SA (see for example Aikhenvald 2002, 2006; Chacon 2013; Díaz Romero 2021; Epps 2007, 2012, 2020; Lüpke et al. 2020; Sorensen 1967; Stenzel 2013; Stenzel and Gomez-Imbert 2009, among others). It involves dozens of languages belonging to the Eastern Tukanoan, Arawakan, Nadahup, and Kakua-Nukak language families, with Nheengatú also in the area.

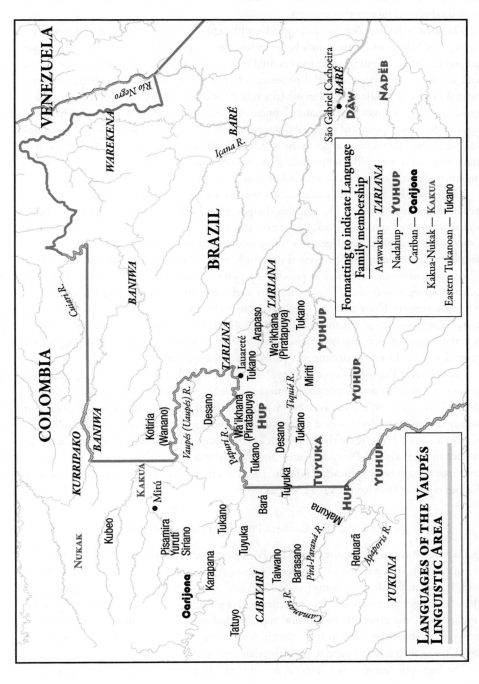

MAP 7.9. Languages of the Vaupés Linguistic Area

Areal traits shared among languages of this linguistic area include systems of nominal classification, evidentiality, serial verb constructions, shared tense-aspect-mode values, and lexical calquing, among other features.

The area is famous for its widespread multilingualism, associated with linguistic exogamy (see below) and a strong link between language and social identity. Language contact among the languages of the area has resulted in a high degree of morpheme-to-morpheme and word-to-word intertranslatability between languages. As Alexandra Aikhenvald has repeated in several publications, Tariana (the sole Arawakan language in the area) has undergone extensive changes in its grammar under Tukanoan influence, for example change in word order, development of nominal cases, reduction of the set of multiple locative markers to a single one, elaborate changes in the nominal classifier system, change of the two evidential categories to five, verb compounding, switch-reference, new complementizer structures, and phonological changes (cf. Epps and Michael 2017, 940).

There has also been areal diffusion among the Eastern Tukanoan languages (Chacon 2013; Gomez-Imbert 1993). The Nadahup languages and Kakua have also changed markedly due to influence from Tukanoan (Epps 2005, 2007, 2008b; Epps and Michael 2017). On the other hand, Arawakan languages have influenced some Eastern Tukanoan languages, for example in the development of aspirated stops in Kotiria (Wanano); development of an alienable versus inalienable distinction; possessive proclitics in Kotiria, Kubeo, Tatuyo, and some other languages; and use of shape classifiers with non-human animates in Kubeo and (to a lesser extent) in Kotiria (Gomez-Imbert 1996; Stenzel and Gomez-Imbert 2009; Stenzel 2013). The influence of Tukanoan on Tariana, as well as on Kakua and Nadahup languages, seems to reflect more recent language contact in the region, where Arawakan languages were more dominant in a more distant past (Chacon 2017; Epps 2017).

Camilo Díaz Romero's (2021, 283, 308) areal-typological survey of the Indigenous languages of Colombia found that the languages of the Vaupés do not form a particularly well-defined territorial unit. That is, it seems better defined based on phonological traits but clearly not supported well based on grammatical properties. This study revealed also that Koreguaje fits the features of the Vaupés area even though it is a Western Tukanoan language spoken in the Caquetá[-Putumayo] area, and that Yukuna fits with languages of the Caquetá area even though geographically it is located between the northern Amazonian and southern Vaupés regions (Díaz Romero 2021, 30, 294).

7.4.4.2. The Caquetá-Putumayo Linguistic Area

A Caquetá-Putumayo Linguistic Area has been proposed for southern Colombia and northern Peru, though it is not well studied yet. Languages of this linguistic area are the Boran and Witotoan families, Resígaro (Arawakan), and Andoke (language isolate). Speakers of these languages refer to themselves together as "People of the Center" and are widely multilingual. All these groups share cultural traits, including ritual ingestion of pounded coca leaves and tobacco in a liquid form (licked by men, not inhaled), common shared origin myth, trade, intermarriage, and so on (Wojtylak 2017, 3, 12–18; Epps 2020).

The linguistic features shared in the area include: first-person plural inclusive/exclusive contrast, second-position tense-aspect-mood clitics, loss of object cross-referencing suffixes, restructuring of verbal morphology, borrowing of classifiers, and inhibition against lexical borrowing (Seifart 2011, 14, 88; Aikhenvald 2001, 189; Wojtylak 2017, 3). Classifier systems are in all languages of this linguistic area but are found widely also in languages of the Vaupés Area and elsewhere in South America. Chang and Michael (2014) argue that these languages have undergone significant convergence in their phonological inventories (Epps and Michael 2017, 944). Resígaro (Arawakan) added new phonemes (/ɸ/, /dʒ/, /ʔ/), syllable structure restrictions, and a two-tone contrast due to influence from other languages of this linguistic area (Aikhenvald 2001; Seifart 2012; Chang and Michael 2014). All the languages of the area have ɨ (high central unrounded vowel), though this trait is found also in many Tukanoan and Cariban languages north of the Caquetá-Putumayo Linguistic Area (Wojtylak 2017, 3). Moreover, Resígaro has, in addition to high central unrounded /ɨ/, also high back unrounded /ɯ/, which it borrowed from Bora (Boran family). This /ɯ/ entered via the many loanwords that Resígaro took from Bora and then later was extended so that it also could occur in native Resígaro lexical items of Arawakan origin. This pattern with both ɨ and ɯ, shared by Bora and Resígaro, is extremely rare elsewhere (Carvalho 2018a).

7.4.4.3. The Venezuelan-Antillean Linguistic Area

Adolfo Constenla Umaña (1991; 2012, 422) proposed a Venezuelan-Antillean Linguistic Area that includes several Arawakan languages (Taino, Island Carib, Caquetío, Lokono), various Cariban languages (Cumanagoto, Chaima, Tamanaco, Cariña), Otomacoan, Guamo, Yaruro, and Warao. The traits common to the languages of the area are: VO basic word order (absence of SOV) and Numeral-Noun orders; Noun-Genitive order, at least as frequent as Genitive-Noun; gender inflection, although not predominant; and languages without voicing contrasts and with a palatal nasal (Constenla Umaña 1991, 125–126; 2012, 422). Constenla Umaña (1991, 136) believed that this area could be extended to the south to include the western part of the Amazonia, where Arawakan languages with VO order predominate (Constenla Umaña 1991, 125–126; Campbell 2012b, 307; Epps and Michael 2017, 948–949).

7.4.4.4. Southern Guiana (Northeastern Amazonian) Linguistic Area

The Northeast Amazon region is located in a wide geographical area encompassing eastern and southeastern Venezuela, Guyana, Suriname, French Guiana, and the Brazilian states of Roraima, Amapá, and northeastern Pará. It is an area predominantly occupied by speakers of Cariban languages, but also by speakers of a number of Arawakan languages, Sálivan languages, languages of the Tupí-Guaraní an branch of Tupían, and Taruma; some scholars also include Yanomaman, Warao, Arutani, Sapé, and Maku (Mako) (see Carlin 2007, 2011; Epps 2020). Five official European languages (English, Portuguese, Spanish, French, and Dutch) are also in use in the region, and numerous creoles developed there or were brought into the region during its colonial history, for example Guyanese English Creole, Haitian Creole, Kheuól, Sranantongo (see Chapter 8 for creole languages of the area involving Indigenous languages). Missionary activities, both Catholic and Protestant, have favored Tiriyó and made it now the dominant indigenous language in the region (Lüpke et al. 2020, 21).

There is intense interaction that resulted in structural diffusion among languages of the southern Guianas region. Eithne Carlin (2007) found grammatical diffusion from Cariban languages (principally Tiriyó [Trió] and Waiwai) into Mawayana (Arawakan), seen in comparison with Wapishana, a sister of Mawayana, that lacks it; it includes creation of a first-person plural exclusive distinction (borrowing from Waiwai), nominal tense marking, marking on nouns or verbs to express 'pity' or 'recognition of unfortunate circumstance', frustrative marker on verbs, 'similative' marker on nominals, and so on (Epps 2020; Epps and Michael 2017, 948–949; Lüpke et al. 2020, 19–21).[10]

7.4.5. Southern Amazonia Linguistic Areas

7.4.5.1. Guaporé-Mamoré Linguistic Area

The Guaporé-Mamoré Linguistic Area is linguistically very diverse. It includes parts of Rondônia state in Brazil and the Amazonian region of Bolivia, with over fifty languages from seventeen different families (Arawakan, Chapacuran, Jabutían, Nambikwaran, Pano-Takanan, Tupían, eleven language isolates, twelve unclassified languages, and one pidgin).

It has many shared structural features among the languages together with shared cultural traits, with considerable morphological borrowing in the Brazilian part of the zone. Some of the shared traits include grammatical gender, evidentiality, classifiers, verbal classification, subordination by nominalization, switch reference, many prefixes, preference for verbal number (alteration of the verb by suppletion, reduplication, or affixation to express the number of the subject or object), accompanied by a general lack of nominal number, presence of verbal cross-reference systems with similar morpheme positions, and complex systems of directional morphemes (see Braga et al. 2011, 224–229; Crevels and van der Voort 2008, 167; Epps 2020; Epps and Michael 2017, 947–948). Diffusion in the Guaporé-Mamoré Linguistic Area also involves cases of direct borrowing of morphological forms, especially in the nominal classifier systems (van der Voort 2005, 397; Crevels and van der Voort 2008, 167)—a parallel to which is known also in the Caquetá-Putumayo Linguistic Area (Epps and Michael 2017, 947–948).

While most recent scholarship accepts the Guaporé-Mamoré Linguistic Area as well established, Lüpke et al. (2020, 21–22) see it differently. They say that the "languages exhibit some shared lexical and grammatical traits that also likely spread through contact, but do not indicate a clearly delineated linguistic area. Rather . . . there are several partially overlapping subareas." This view may be influenced by the fact that the area involves more than one culture area, the Moxos and Guaporé culture areas. However, lack of clear delineation may be characteristic of most linguistic areas (see discussion in Campbell 2006, 2017b, 2020a).

7.4.5.2. Tocantins-Mearim Interfluvium Linguistic Area(?)

Another possible linguistic area is in the land between the Tocantins and Mearim Rivers in northeastern Brazil, with several Tupí-Guaranían and Jêan languages. The Tupí-Guaranían languages include Guajajára and Tembé (Teneteháran Branch), Guajá and Urubú-Ka'apór (Northern Tupí-Guaranían Branch), memory of Anambé and Amanajé (Xingu Branch), and evidence of Ararandewára (Xingu Branch), Turiwára (Teneteháran Branch), and Tupinambá and Língua Geral Amazônica (Tupí Branch of Tupí-Guaranían). Jêan is represented by three dialects of Timbira (Braga et al. 2011, 224). Shared features include change in

Linguistic Areas of the Americas

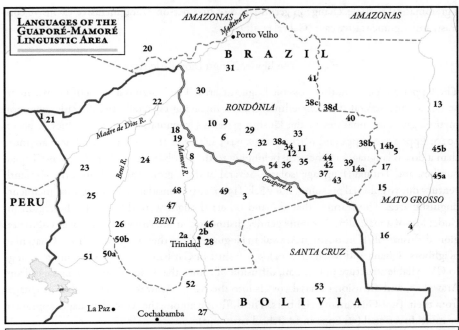

Language		Classification			
1	Machineri Mojo	Mojo, Arawakan	29	Uru-eu-wau-wau	Kawahíb, Guaraníian, Tupían
2a	Trinitario	Mojo, Arawakan	30	Karipuna	Kawahíb, Guaraníian, Tupían
2b	Ignaciano	Mojo, Arawakan	31	Karitiana	Arikém, Tupían
3	Bauré	Arawakan	32	Puruborá	Tupían
4	Paresí	Arawakan	33	Tuparí	Tuparían, Tupían
5	Enawené-Nawé (Salumã)	Arawakan	34	Makuráp	Tuparían, Tupían
6	Cojubim (Kuyubí)	Chapacuran	35	Mekéns	Tuparían, Tupían
7	Wanyam	Chapacuran	36	Wayuru	Tuparían, Tupían
8	Moré (Itene)	Chapacuran	37	Akuntsú	Tuparían, Tupían
9	Oro Win	Chapacuran	38a	Aruá	Mondéan, Tupían
10	Wari'	Chapacuran	38b	Cinta Larga	Mondéan, Tupían
11	Arikapú	Jabutí, Macro-Jê	38c	Gavião	Mondéan, Tupían
12	Djeoromitxi (Jabutí)	Jabutí, Macro-Jê	38d	Zoró	Mondéan, Tupían
13	Rikbaktsá	Macro-Jê	39	Mondé (Salamãi)	Mondéan, Tupían
14a	Latundé	Nambikwaran	40	Suruí-Paitér	Mondéan, Tupían
14b	Lakondé	Nambikwaran	41	Karo (Arara)	Ramarama, Tupían
15	Nambikwara	Nambikwaran	42	Aikanã	Language isolate
16	Sararé	Nambikwaran,	43	Kanoê (Kapixaná)	Language isolate
17	Sabanê	Nambikwaran	44	Kwazá (Koaiá)	Language isolate
18	Chákobo	Panoan, Pano-Takanan	45a	Irantxe	Language isolate
19	Pakawara	Panoan, Pano-Takanan	45b	Mýky	(Irantxe) Language isolate
20	Kaxararí	Panoan, Pano-Takanan	46	Canichana	Language isolate
21	Yaminwa	Panoan, Pano-Takanan	47	Movima	Language isolate
22	Ese Ejja	Takanan Pano-Takanan	48	Cayubaba	Language isolate
23	Araona	Takanan Pano-Takanan	49	Itonama	Language isolate
24	Cavineña	Takanan Pano-Takanan	50a	Mosetén	Language isolate
25	Takana	Takanan Pano-Takanan	50b	Chimane	(Mosetén) Language isolate
26	Maropa (Reyesano)	Takanan Pano-Takanan	51	Leco	Language isolate
27	Yuki	Guaraníian, Tupían	52	Yurakaré	Language isolate
28	Sirionó	Guaraníian, Tupían	53	Chiquitano (Besiro)	Language isolate
			54	(unknown)	(unknown)

MAP 7.10 Languages of the Guaporé-Mamoré Linguistic Area

a grammatical particle, change in gerund, loss of first-person plural inclusive-exclusive contrast, and argumentative case (Cabral et al. 2007).

7.4.5.3. The Upper Xingu Linguistic Area

The Upper Xingu is another possible linguistic area. The Xingu is an area of intense interaction among several different ethnic groups, involving especially ritual, trade, common mythology, commonalities in the kinship systems (Iroquoian type), and values (Chacon 2020; Epps 2020; Epps and Michael 2017, 946; Lüpke et al. 2020, 17–19). There are more than a dozen languages in the area, belonging to the Cariban, Arawakan, Jêan, and Tupían families, and Trumai (language isolate). Several of these groups arrived since the sixteenth century due to colonial pressures. Lucy Seki (1999, 2011) considered the Xingu an "incipient" linguistic area. The features that she and others thought were diffused in the region include: loss of a masculine-feminine gender distinction in the Arawakan languages of the region, diffusion of /ɨ/ into Xingu Arawakan languages from their Cariban or Tupí-Guaraní an neighbors (Chang and Michael 2014), *p* > *h* shift in Cariban and Tupí-Guaraní an, change to CV syllable structure in Cariban, diffusion of *ts* into the Xingu Cariban languages from Arawakan, and diffusion of nasal vowels into the Xingu Arawakan and Cariban languages from their Tupí-Guaraní an neighbors. The diffusion among the Xingu languages appears to be multidirectional (cf. Epps and Michael 2017, 947).

7.4.6. Highlands (West) Linguistic Areas

7.4.6.1. The Andean Area, Central Andean Linguistic Area

The central highland Andean region is considered a linguistic area, though further investigation is needed. It is dominated by Quechuan and Aymaran, though several other languages are also found in the area, several of them long dormant: Atacameño (Kunza), Callahuaya, Candoshian, Chacha, Cholonan (Cholón and Hibito), Culle (Culli), Esmeralda, Mochica (Yunga, Muchik), Puquina, Quingnam, Sechura-Catacaoan (Sechura, Tallán), Uru-Chipaya, and numerous other now extinct languages about which we have little information (Adelaar 2008a, 2012b; Urban 2019b; Van Gijn and Muysken 2020, 179; see also Heggarty 2020b).

Adolfo Constenla Umaña (1991, 123–124) postulated a broad Andean area that also included his Ecuadoran-Colombian subarea (below), containing the languages of highland Colombia, Ecuador, Peru, and Bolivia. He also believed that some languages spoken in the region east of the Andes could additionally be incorporated into the Andean Linguistic Area. Thomas Büttner (1983, 179) included Quechuan, Aymaran, Callahuaya, and Chipaya in the linguistic area he defined based on phonological traits.

Quechuan and Aymaran have tended to dominate views of what an Andean Linguistic Area should look like. They share a large number of structural, phonological, and lexical similarities, constituting "one of the most intriguing and intense cases of language contact to be found in the entire world" (Adelaar 2012a, 575). "Often treated as a product of long-term *convergence*, the similarities between the Quechuan and Aymaran families can best be understood as the result of an intense period of social and cultural intertwinement" (Adelaar 2012a, 575; see also discussion of Quechumaran in Chapter 6).

Linguistic Areas of the Americas 433

MAP 7.11. Languages of the Andes Area

The distribution of the languages appears to have changed over time. Today languages of the Aymaran and Quechuan families dominate the Altiplano, but in Adelaar's view they do not have a long history there; rather their "origin lies further north, in central Peru, from where they must have spread south-eastwards sometime between the Late Intermediate

Period and the Independence Era (c. AD 1300 to 1800)." Adelaar bases this on the fact that the dialect differentiation in both languages "is limited and shallow within this region, but much wider outside it" (Adelaar 2020, 240).

Some of the traits that Adelaar (2008a) lists as having been considered representative of languages of the Andes are presented here, juxtaposed with Alexandra Aikhenvald's (2007) characterization of some Andean traits:

(1) "Complex number system" (Adelaar 2008a, 25). Aikhenvald (2007, 193) "Full set of lexical numbers."
(2) "Agglutinative structure with an exclusive or near exclusive reliance on suffixes for all morphological and morphosyntactic purposes" (Adelaar 2008a, 25). Aikhenvald (2007, 193) "no prefixes"; she speaks of it this way: "Andean languages are synthetic, and combine head and dependent marking; basically agglutinating with some fusion (subject, object, and tense suffixes to the verb may be fused)."
(3) "Constituent order is relatively free in Andean languages, although there seems to be a preference for the order in which subject/actor and object precede the verb (SOV)" (Adelaar 2008a, 26).
(4) In many of the languages, "subordinate clauses are strictly verb-final" (Adelaar 2008a, 26).
(5) In most of the languages, in noun phrases "modifiers must precede the modified" (Adelaar 2008a, 26).
(6) Few vowels, no tone contrasts, and no "nasality spread" (Adelaar 2008a, 26). Aikhenvald (2007, 193) "a three-vowel system i, a, and u, with no contrastive nasalization."
(7) Many of the languages have a contrastive uvular stop (Adelaar 2008a, 27).
(8) "Absence of Amazonian-type classifier systems" (Adelaar 2008, 28). Aikhenvald (2007, 193): "no genders or classifiers."
(9) "Gender distinctions are not expressed morphologically" (Adelaar 2008a, 28). Aikhenvald (2007a, 193): again, "no genders or classifiers."
(10) "Case marking on noun phrases expressed by means of suffixes or postpositions is common" (Adelaar 2008a, 29). Aikhenvald (2007, 193): "Extensive set of core and oblique case markers."
(11) "Accusative case marking is found in several central Andean languages" (Adelaar 2008a, 29). Aikhenvald (2007, 193): "Fully nominative/accusative systems."
(12) "The stative-active distinction, which is attested in eastern lowland languages ... and in languages of the Gran Chaco ... has not been found in the Andes" (Adelaar 2008a, 30). Aikhenvald (2007, 193): again, "fully nominative/accusative systems."
(13) "Verbal morphology is extremely rich and varied" (Adelaar 2008a, 30).
(14) First person plural inclusive-exclusive contrast (Adelaar 2008a, 31).
Aikhenvald (2007, 193) includes as further traits:
"Two or three liquids; fricatives rather than affricates."
"Two core arguments are marked on the verb."

(See also van Gijn's 2014 and van Gijn and Muysken's 2020 comparison of Andean and Amazonian features; see also Heggarty 2020b.)

Several of these traits, however, are seen in other linguistic areas and are not exclusive to languages of the Andean region. Also, as mentioned above, sight should not be lost of the fact that there is not a rigid separation between Andean and Amazonian linguistic features, that in the upper Amazon area there is a gradual and complex transition from the Andean to the Amazonian area (van Gijn 2014; van Gijn and Muysken 2020).

As Willem Adelaar (2008a, 23) mentions, it "has been a common practice among linguists working on South American languages to make an intuitive distinction between 'Amazonian' and 'Andean' languages on the assumption that there would be two different language types corresponding to these labels." Nevertheless, as several linguists have pointed out (e.g. Campbell 2013; Campbell and Grondona 2012b; Dixon and Aikhenvald 1999, 9; Epps and Michael 2017, 952; Urban 2019b; Díaz Romero 2021, 293, 309), the strict separation of the Andean and Amazonian linguistic areas is not supported; rather the evidence speaks for the west-east split (above), where the western area corresponds roughly to the Andes, Southern Cone, and the Western Amazonian region, matching Joshua Birchall's (2014a, 2014b) WSALA (cf. Doris Payne 1990b), while the other large linguistic area to the east consists of the remainder of the continent's languages.

Matthias Urban (2019b) examined in detail each of the putative Andean areal traits presented by Aikhenvald (2007) and finds that many of them are not found in many of the non-Quechuan, non-Aymaran languages of the region. For example, Aikhenvald (2007, 193) was mistaken in saying Andean languages have "fricatives rather than affricates"; all the languages have affricates, usually several affricates (see also Urban 2019b, 285); Aikhenvald was also incorrect in that many of the languages have more than three vowels in their vowel systems. Her assumption of "no genders or classifiers" also does not hold up; for example, as Urban (2019b) shows, Chipaya and Cholón have gender systems, and Mochica and Cholón have a set of numeral classifiers; several of the languages, but not Quechuan and Aymaran, have prefixes; and not all of them are clearly "fully nominative/accusative systems." It is clear that there has been influence from Quechuan and Aymaran on several of the languages, Cholón, Chipaya, Mochica, and Puquina at least, but they also exhibit typological differences from Quechuan and Aymaran.

Urban (2019b, 217) concluded that the evidence does not support a "a clear-cut linguistic area comprising the entire Central Andes narrowly defined, and that perceived homogeneity is partially due to an over-emphasis on the largest and surviving Central Andean language families, Quechuan and Aymaran."

On the other hand, Alfredo Torero (2002, 523–534) proposed the existence of an "extensive **Andean Area**," from southeastern Colombia to the north of the Southern Andes, one sustained by few traits of its own, seen more directly in relief against the Ecuadorian-Colombian Subarea (see below). Torero listed the following as traits shared by all or most of the languages in this broader Andean Area:

Palatal nasal (/ñ/).
Frequent syllable pattern of (C)VC, closed syllables.
Decimal numeral system.
Adjective before noun order.
Possessor before possessed word order.

Presence of the adpositional construction possessor name—determiner / core definite noun when the possessor is non-human. Determining possessor name / Determined nominal nucleus.

Obligatory placement of question element at the beginning of the clause.

Neutralization (absence) of plurality.

He listed also forty other traits whose distribution among the languages is not general, that is, is more limited, but included also some that were considered "very extensive," for example, presence of a velar/uvular contrast in voiceless stops and presence of voiceless retroflex affricate.

Among his subareas of the Andes, Torero (2002, 518–522, 535) defined a **Quechuan-Aymaran Linguistic Area** ("el área lingüística quechua-aru" in his words) or "Nuclear" subarea (subárea quechua-aru), with several of the traits listed above and others. Torero's (2002, 535–536) **Altiplano Subarea** ("Subárea Altiplánica") consisted of the four languages Puquina, Uruquilla (Uru-Chipaya), Cunza, and Huarpe, though he said it is much less uniform than the Quechuan-Aymaran Subárea. For example, there is no single areal trait in Torero's list (p. 530) shared by all four of these languages but not by others in the broader area. Rather, in pairwise comparisons among these four, they share a relatively higher number of the traits than other languages share with these four languages (p. 531).

It is abundantly clear that indeed Quechuan and Aymaran have been too much the focus of most claims about an Andean Linguistic Area. However, it is also clear that a number of traits are shared across different languages of the region. Caution is in order and more investigation is needed.

7.4.6.2. The Ecuadoran-Colombian Subarea

The Ecuadoran-Colombian subarea of the Andean Linguistic Area, as Adolfo Constenla Umaña (1991, 2012, 222) defined it, includes Paez; Guambiano, Cuaiquer [Awa Pit], Cayapa [Cha'palaachi], Colorado [Tsafiqui] (Barbacoan); Kamsá; Cofán; Esmeralda; and Ecuadoran Quichua. Most of these languages share the traits: high-mid opposition in front vowels,[11] presence of the palatal phonemes /lʸ/ (/ʎ/) and /š/ (/ʃ/), absence of glottalized consonants and glottal stop, absence of uvular stops, lack of a rounding contrast in more than one rounded back vowel, lack of person inflection in nouns, prefixes to express tenses or aspects, predominant Adjective-Noun and Numeral-Noun orders, and accusative case marking (Constenla Umaña 1991, 123–125, 2012, 222). The absence of traits from languages, as is the case in many of the traits listed by Constenla Umaña for this linguistic area, generally is not as useful for defining a linguistic area as the presence of traits, leaving this proposed linguistic area perhaps in some doubt.

7.4.7. The Gran Chaco Linguistic Area(?)

The Gran Chaco is the extensive lowland plain of central South America, stretching across northern Argentina, Paraguay, southeastern Bolivia, and southern Brazil. It is also a culture area (Métraux 1946; Murdock 1951) characterized by cultural traits shared among the ethnic groups there. More than twenty languages from some seven language families and a few other languages whose status is not clear are found in the Chaco: Charrúan, Enlhet-Enenlhet (Mascoyan), Guaicurúan, Guachí, Lule-Vilelan, Matacoan, Payaguá, Zamucoan, and some Tupí-Guaraníán languages.

A fair amount has been written about shared traits among these languages and about the possibility of a Chaco Linguistic Area (see Aikhenvald 2011; Campbell 2013, 2017b; Campbell and Grondona 2012b; Carol and Messineo 2012; Ciucci 2014, 2020; Comrie et al. 2010; Fabre 2007; Gerzenstein 2004; Gerzenstein and Gualdieri 2003; Golluscio and Vidal

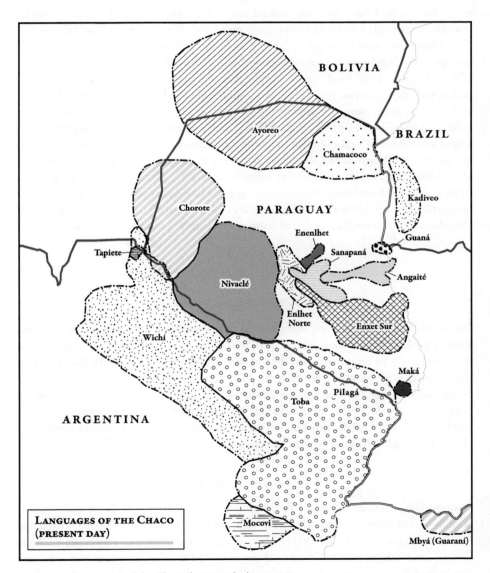

MAP 7.12. Languages of the Chaco (present day)

2009–2010; González 2014, 2015; Kirtchuk 1996; Messineo 2011; Messineo et al. 2016; Rona 1969–1972; and Vidal and Gutiérrez 2010).

A number of linguistic traits are shared among these languages. These include: SVO word order, grammatical gender, possessive noun classifiers, complex set of demonstratives, active-patient alignment, presence of nominal tense, extensive set of directional/locative verbal affixes, shared patterns in pronominal affixes, inclusive/exclusive contrast in pronouns, and resistance to lexical borrowing (See Campbell 2006, 2013, 2017b; Campbell and Grondona 2012b; and Ciucci 2020 for details and for other shared traits).

Most of these shared structural traits in languages of the region are found also in some languages beyond the Chaco, and some traits that were thought possibly to be areal are actually characteristic of only a few of the languages within the region. Few are true of a majority of Chaco languages; none is unique to the area, and some are typologically commonplace (for example, SVO word order). Active-patient verb alignment is shared by most of the languages of the area, but not exclusively so. The Tupí-Guaranían languages of the Chaco share active-patient verb alignment but Tupí-Guaranían extends far beyond the Chaco region; a linguistic area based on this feature or including Tupí-Guaranían languages that have it would hardly reflect a "Chaco" linguistic area geographically. Tupí-Guaranían also shares many traits with languages of the putative Amazonian Linguistic Area (above). Moreover, Michael et al. (2014, 49) assert that "Patagonia and the Chaco constitute an essentially contiguous phonological area with the Southern Andes" (see also Torero 2002, 523, 535; Urban 2019b, 297). This overlapping of shared traits between Chaco languages and languages beyond the Chaco has complicated attempts to define a Chaco linguistic area. (See Campbell 2013, 2017a; Campbell and Grondona 2012b for a full set of shared features involving languages of the Chaco.)

7.4.8. Southern Region Linguistic Areas

7.4.8.1. The Southern Cone Linguistic Area(?)

Harriet Manelis Klein (1992, 35) noted several traits common to languages of the Southern Cone (e.g. Mapudungun, Guaicurúan, and Chonan), including: semantic positions signaled morphologically by means of "many devices to situate the visual location of the noun subject or object relative to the speaker; tense, aspect, and number are expressed as part of the morphology of location, direction, and motion" (Klein 1992, 25); more back consonants than front ones; SVO basic word order (cf. Campbell 1997a, 351). This possible linguistic area has not received much attention, and the traits Klein cited are encountered also in some other regions of SA. Most of what Klien mentioned fits the Chaco as well.

7.4.8.2. "Fuegian" Linguistic Area(?)

The possibility has been raised, in different guises, that the languages of Tierra del Fuego and possibly also of Patagonia form a linguistic area, but this remains inconclusive (Adelaar and Muysken 2004, 578–582). The Tierra de Fuego languages are: Chonan, Kawesqaran, Chono (isolate), and Yahgan (isolate). Enclitizicization, suffixation, compounding, and reduplication are widely shared among these languages. The languages of Tierra del Fuego mostly have OV word order, where the position of the subject varies (Adelaar and Muysken 2004, 579).

NOTES

1. All the language of the Northwest Coast Linguistic Area have the glottalized lateral affricate *tl'* but the plain non-glottalized *tl* is lacking from Nass-Gitksan, Alsea, and Salishan with the exception of Comox, that borrowed it from Wakashan; Quileute also borrowed *tl* from Wakashan (Beck 2000, 157).

2. There has been some confusion about what have been called "retroflex" consonants. Some of the languages, more toward the south, do have true retroflex consonants, while, in several languages more toward the north, the contrast is rather between dental vs. alveolar (Mithun 1999, 316).

3. Also in Mahican, where Western Mahican is outside of New England.

4. Robert Rankin (2005, 455) reported that Quapaw "can only marginally be considered to share salient features of the Southeastern *Sprachbund*" and what traits of this area it does have are found in the other varieties of Dhegiha [Siouan] as well.

5. Munro (2017, 345–346) lists "gapping" in subject extraction constructions as an additional trait, shared by Garífuna and Mayan languages. However, the lack of an overt pronominal subject agreement marker on the transitive verbs in question, focus, and relative clause constructions in the Mayan languages is not due to gapping, as Munro's analysis assumes. Rather, these three constructions in many Mayan languages require the verb to be put in what was traditionally called in Mayan linguistics an antipassive form (a focus construction) that is made intransitive and therefore takes absolutive subject markers rather than the typical ergative pronominal subject agreement markers of transitive verbs. Since the third-person singular (but not the other pronominal persons) has Ø marking for the subject of absolutive (intransitive) verbs, this is not gapping—an overt absolutive pronominal marker would be present if non-third-person subjects of the verbs in these constructions were involved. The absence of an overt third-person singular absolutive affix here is therefore not a case of gapping. That this is a Ø-marked subject is seen in its opposition to the overt non-third-person absolutive pronominal subject markers that are required by verbs in constructions that involve intransitivized (antipassive) verbs, which permit only absolutive subject marking.

6. Brown associated the six post-contact words with Nahuatl, and that may be right, though not necessarily so: two are definitely widespread post-contact borrowing from Nahuatl ('domestic cat', 'goat'). The 'sheep'-'cotton' equation may be just a natural extension of a word for 'cotton' being extended to 'sheep' because wool, like cotton, was used also in production of clothing, or the metaphorical association may just reflect a perceived similarity between sheep's wool and cotton—Nahuatl is not needed to get sheep and cotton associated with one another. The other three cases all involve an adjective of Spanish origin that Brown interpreted as *castillan*, involving Spanish *castilla* 'Castilian': 'chicken' (= Castilian turkey), 'bread' (= Castilian tortilla), and 'wheat' (= Castilian maize). Nahuatl may have somehow been involved in the spread of these, but that is by no means certain. Brown, following some others, interpreted the final *-lan* of this form as being influenced by the Nahuatl suffix *-la:n* 'place of', arguing that if this came directly from Spanish *castellano* 'Castilian' it would not have dropped the final *o* when borrowed. However, even in Spanish in the sixteenth century there was considerable variation, with various masculine adjectives having variants with and without final *-o*.

Brown pointed out that the calque that matches 'thorn-opossum' for 'porcupine' translates as 'thorn pig' in some of the languages, probably based on Spanish *puerco espín*, literally 'thorn pig'. He mentioned that pig is a post-contact introduction in the New World, but did not mention that the word for 'pig' in various of the languages is based on the native name of some other animal whose meaning was extended to or shifted to accommodate the newly introduced 'pig', including peccary, coatimundi, and opossum. Porcupines were certainly known before the arrival of the Spanish, as were, of course, opossums.

The association between 'molar' tooth and 'grindstone' could potentially involve influence form Spanish, where *muela* 'molar' is related to *moler* 'to grind', but the 'molar'-'grindstone' equivalence is far too deeply rooted in the Mesoamerican languages for that to be the case. For example, in Mayan it comes from Proto-Mayan times, **ka:ʔ* 'molar', **ka:ʔ* 'grindstone'; clear examples with these meanings are found in Maya hieroglyphic texts, long before contact with Spanish.

7. While the calque for 'gold' was certainly composed of 'god' or 'sun' + 'excrement', also sometimes applied to 'silver', a term sometimes applied to 'silver' was composed of pieces meaning 'moon' and 'excrement', Nahuatl *metzcuitlatl* (*me:ts-* 'moon' + *kwitlatl* 'excrement'). Siméon (1977, 270) glosses *metzcuitlatl* as ' "excremento de la luna", especie de piedra que se coloca en láminas finas sobre las cuales el fuego ejerce poca acción" ["moon excrement, a kind of stone that is placed on thin pates on which fire exercises little action"]. This was registered as the loanword <mezquitat> 'silver' in the Dionysio de Zúñiga 1608 dictionary of Poqomchi' (a Mayan language).

8. It should be noticed that there have been inconclusive proposals of distant genetic relationship among three major linguistic families grouped within a purported eastern South America linguistic area, namely: Tupían, Cariban and Macro-Jê (Rodrigues 1985, 2000; see Chapter 6).

9. A larger **Orinoco-Amazon Linguistic Area** that would include parts of the Orinoco and northern Amazon watersheds was proposed by Ernesto Migliazza (1985[1982], 20). He viewed the Northern Amazon Culture Area as also constituting a linguistic area, with the languages: Yanomaman; Salivan: Piaroa; Arawakan: Baniwa (Karutiana-Baniwa), Wapishana, Baré, Mandahuaca, Warekena, Baniva (Yaviero); Cariban: Panare, Yabarana (Mapoyo-Yavarana), Mapoyo, Yekuana, Pemon, Kapong, Makuxi, Waiwai, Waimiri, Hixkaryana, Warikyana; language isolates: Joti; Arutani (a.k.a. Uruak, Awake); Sapé (Kaliana); and Maku. Some traits that Migliazza noted as shared are: a pattern of discourse redundancy, ergative alignment (except in a few Arawakan languages), OV (SOV or OVS) order (except in a few Arawakan languages), lack of active-passive distinction, and relative clauses formed by apposition and nominalization. Diffusion from west to east of nasalization, aspiration, and glottalization has also been suggested (Migliazza 1985[1982], 20, 118). As Epps and Michael (2017, 951) point out, Amazonianists today would now see several of these features as having a broader Amazonian distribution; they note that the features that Derbyshire (1987, 311) tentatively proposed as defining an Amazonian linguistic area include most of these. That being the case, it seems best to abandon the idea of an Orinoco-Amazon Linguistic Area.

10. Alexandra Aikhenvald (2000, 383) held a possessed classifier construction in languages in the northeastern part of South America, in Cariban into North Arawakan languages, to be the result of diffusion.

11. The opposition of high vowels with mid vowels may only seem significant in comparison with other Andean languages that have only three or four vowels, but lack /e/ and /o/. In most Quechuan varieties, only /i, a, u/ are phonemic; [e] and [o], however, are allophones of /i/ and /u/ respectively in the presence of uvulars. Borrowings from Spanish have complicated the phonemic status of *e* and *o* in some varieties.

8

Contact Languages

8.1. INTRODUCTION

This chapter is dedicated to the Indigenous contact languages of the Americas. They include pidgins of indigenous origin, mixed languages, and Indigenous languages used as lingua francas. They all involve language contact and communication across languages in some way. Typically such contact languages have not played much of a role in classifications of American Indian languages, though they are a significant part of the overall linguistic history. These Native American pidgins, contact languages, mixed languages, and lingua francas deserve much more attention.

8.2. PIDGINS

A pidgin is traditionally seen as a minimal contact language, for example used to facilitate trade, though it is not the native language of any of the interacting groups. Instead, it is usually based largely on a simplified version of one of the languages, perhaps mixed with elements from the other language or languages in the contact situation. Many pidgins involving Indigenous languages of the Americas were not well known until recent years.

8.2.1. Indigenous Pidgins of North America

The pidgin languages involving Indigenous languages of North American that have been recognized or at least postulated include: Basque-Algonquian Pidgin, Broken Oghibbeway (Broken Ojibwe), Broken Slavey, Chinook Jargon (Chinook Wawa), Eskimo Trade Jargon, Haida Jargon (Haida-English Jargon), Hudson Strait Pidgin Eskimo, Inuktitut-English Pidgin, Labrador Eskimo Pidgin (Labrador Inuit Pidgin French), Loucheux Jargon (Jargon

Loucheux), Mobilian Jargon, Nootka Jargon, Pidgin Delaware, Pidgin Massachusett, and West Greenlandic Pidgin. Discussion of some of these follows. (See also Bakker and Grant 2011; Campbell 1997a, 18–25; de Reuse 1996; Goddard 2000; Mithun 1999, 322–326, 587–605; and Rhodes 1982, 2012 for general discussion.)

Chinook Jargon (Chinook Wawa) was the lingua franca of the Pacific Northwest, used from the Alaska Panhandle to northwestern California and inland from these regions especially in the eighteenth and nineteenth centuries by speakers of over 100 languages (Mithun 2021a, 517). "Jargon," as Chinook Jargon is often called in the area, may have been spoken as a second language by as many as 100,000 people at one time, used widely among Native American groups of northwestern North America, and also eventually by French and English speakers as well (Bakker and Grant 2011; Mithun 2021a, 517). It is thought that initially it was based on Nootka (now called Nuu-chah-nulh) vocabulary.

Though there is some disagreement, Chinook Jargon appears not to have begun with the arrival of Europeans, but was rather already well formed and in use before that, though American and European seafarers and fur traders certainly helped to spread it. William Anderson, surgeon and naturalist on Captain James Cook's third voyage in 1778, compiled a reasonably extensive vocabulary of Nootka (Nuu-chah-nulh), and his vocabulary was used widely by travelers to the Northwest Coast after its publication in 1784, helping to promote the Nootka traders' jargon, which was the lexical base from which Chinook Jargon lexicon was later expanded (Goddard 1996b, 25).

In addition to Nuu-chah-nulh (Nootka, Wakashan family), the vocabulary of Chinook Jargon is largely from Lower Chinook (Chinookan family) and Chehalis (Salishan family), with loans from English and French, for example *pastən, boston* 'white man, American' (borrowed from English *Boston*) and *kinchochman* 'white man, English' (borrowed from English *King George man*). By the time Lewis and Clark arrived at the mouth of the Columbia River in 1805, a number of English words and phrases were in use in Chinook Jargon, including 'musket', 'powder', 'shot', 'knife', 'file', 'damned rascal', and 'son of a bitch' (Silverstein 1996, 128).

Chinook Jargon is by far the best documented of pidgin languages involving Indigenous languages in the Americas. Much has been written about it; see for example Gibbs 1863; Jacobs 1932; Boas 1933; Silverstein 1972, 1996; Thomason 1983; Thomason and Kaufman 1988, 256–263; Powell 1990; Mithun 2021a, 517–519; among many others.

Attempts are underway to revive Chinook Jargon (Chinook Wawa).

Mobilian Jargon (Chickasaw-Choctaw Trade Language) was at one time widely used in the southeastern United States, among numerous American Indian tribes, by Choctaw, Chickasaw, Apalachee, Alabama, and Koasati (Muskogean family); Atakapa, Chitimacha, Natchez, and Tunica (language isolates); Ofo and Biloxi (Siouan family); Caddo (Caddoan family); some Algonquian languages; and by speakers of English, French, and other languages. It developed in the lower Mississippi Valley and eventually spread north into present-day Illinois, east into Florida, and west into Texas. It was always a pidgin, never acquired as a first language. It has been said by different scholars to be primarily based variously on Chickasaw, Choctaw, or Alabama (Muskogean languages), or combinations of these (Crawford 1978; Drechsel 1979, 1983b, 1984, 1987, 1993, 1997, 2001; Munro 1984; Mithun 2021a, 519).

Pidgin Delaware (Delaware Jargon) developed in the 1620s from Unami. It was used among the Delaware, speakers of Unami and Munsee (two closely related Algonquian languages, languages of the central and lower Hudson River Valley, western Long Island, the upper Delaware River Valley, and the northern part of New Jersey), and Dutch, Swedish, and English colonists. The two main sources on Pidgin Delaware are Johannes Campanius' catechism and vocabulary completed in 1656 (Campanius 1696) and the Anonymous (1684) *The Indian Interpreter*, compiled in West New Jersey in the late 1600s. It survived in a book of land records from Salem County, New Jersey. A few other sources contain a few words and phrases. Its last documentation is from 1785 (Goddard 1997, 43–44). In spite of its European users, it is pidginized Unami with no input to the grammar or vocabulary from those Germanic languages. As Ives Goddard (1997, 83–84) points out, it is an exception to claims and expectations by being a pidgin used between Europeans and non-Europeans but based solely on a language of its non-European users. Goddard (1997) provides a detailed analysis and history of Pidgin Delaware (see also Prince 1912; Goddard 1977, 1978a; Goddard at al. 1995; Mithun 2021a, 516; Thomason 1980).

Several other possible Algonquian pidgins have been mentioned, though too little is known about most of them to be certain of their status as pidgins or as something else reported in language contact situations (Goddard 1996b, 18–190).

Peter Bakker in his studies of the historical and linguistic information concerning early language use in northeastern Canada reports evidence of the existence of several pidgins. They include the following.

Labrador Eskimo Pidgin (called **Labrador Inuit Pidgin French** by Norval Smith 1994); this was commented on in a few reports from the late seventeenth and eighteenth centuries and was involved in trade among speakers of Basque, Breton, and Inuit in the Strait of Belle Isle (Bakker 1987, 1989a, 1989b; Bakker and Grant 2011).

Hudson Strait Pidgin Eskimo was "a rudimentary Eskimo pidgin" spoken between 1750 and 1850, which also contained Cree words (Bakker and Grant 2011).

Peter Bakker discussed a possible **Micmac pidgin Portuguese** from the sixteenth century, a **Micmac pidgin Basque**, and **Montagnais pidgin Basque** from the sixteenth and seventeenth centuries (see below), an **Inuktitut French jargon** from the seventeenth and eighteenth centuries, an **Inuktitut English Pidgin** from the seventeenth century, a **Micmac Pidgin English** from the nineteenth century, and **pidginized Inuktitut** used in the twentieth century. Hein van der Voort (1997) described a more or less stable **contact variant of Kalaallisuut** (Greenlandic) used between the Greenlandic Inuit and European whalers and traders from the seventeenth to the nineteenth century. Bakker pointed out that most of these pidgins contain vocabulary from multiple sources and identifies an **Inuit Pidgin French-Inuktitut-Montagnais-Basque**, and an **Inuit Pidgin Inuktitut-Cree**, with terms passed along by middlemen through trade networks. Discovering the true nature of these early contact languages is a challenge, because documentation is sparse and orthographic conventions were not established (Bakker 1987, 1989a, 1989b, 1991, 1996a, 1996b; Bakker and Grant 2011).

Connected with the cases Bakker discussed is what in 1606 and 1607 Marc Lescarbot observed as the kind of communication between Micmacs and French colonists at Fort Royal (later Port Royal). It apparently involved French, Micmac, and the jargon, with lexical items from this **Souriquois Jargon** and Basque. Basque was the language of a good portion of the European fishermen and sailors along the North American east coast (Silverstein 1996, 122).

In 1633 Paul Le Jeune wrote of a *baragouin* ('jargon, gibberish') used in contact between the French and the Montagnais at Tadoussac on the Saint Laurence River—**Montagnais Jargon** (Silverstein 1996, 122). From examples of it, a good portion of its vocabulary is not from either French or Montagnais. It also has lexical items from Basque and from some Eastern Algonquian languages that are not Montagnais. Michael Silverstein (1996, 122) saw it as "a substantially Basque-lexified contact jargon that spread westward from the easternmost mainland coast between the late sixteenth and mid-seventeenth centuries, with two centers of attestation, among the Micmacs and among the Montagnais."

Willem de Reuse (1996) presented what could be determined from the scant information available of the simplified, unstable trade jargons on the Chukotka Peninsula of far eastern Russia, involving Chukchis, Eskimos, and the mostly English-speaking crews of explorers and whaling ships. In the latter half of the 1800s, ships of explorers and commercial whalers often spent winters on the Chukotka coast, which gave rise to an Eskimo jargon, a Chukchi jargon, and an English Jargon. The **Eskimo-based jargon** (Eskimo-Chukchi jargon) was used for communication between Eskimo and Chukchi groups, and other outsiders; it contained many Chukchi loanwords, including especially particles and personal pronouns. The other two are less relevant here, since they were not based on an Indigenous language of the Americas, though used in interactions with speakers of the Siberian Eskimoan languages. The **Chukchi-based jargon**, mostly simplified Chukchi, was used for communication with outsiders. The **whaler's jargon** was probably English based, but had Hawaiian and Portuguese loans, used by and with the ships' crews, mostly the sort of pidgin used on the whaling ships, though it contributed some loanwords to the local languages of Chukotka. (See also Stefánsson 1909, 1922.)

Occaneechi (Occaneechee) is a long dormant language, often assumed to be related to Catawban (Siouan-Catawban) and about which very little is known (see Chapter 2). It was used as a lingua franca by a number of Native American groups in Virginia and the Carolinas in early colonial times (see below). The extent to which it was pidginized for this purpose is not known, though some scholars have asserted that it was a pidgin language.

Apalachee-Spanish. Michael Silverstein (1996, 124) wrote of a possible jargon used by the Spaniards with the indigenous groups of western Florida. For the Apalachee, Apalalchee was their usual language but was mixed with words from Spanish and Alabama before the Apalachee were given a land grant and moved before 1710 from Spanish settlements in Florida to live near the French at Fort Mobile. Silverstein believes this jargon may have influenced later Mobilian Jargon.

Trader Navajo could perhaps be added to this list, though it is apparently spoken only by non-Navajo traders at trading posts, not by Navajos themselves (see).

Other Pidgins and trade languages referred to by Norval Smith (1994), about which I have no additional information, include **Haida Jargon** (based on Haida, used by speakers of English, Haida, Coast Tsimshian, and Heiltsuk on Queen Charlotte Islands in the 1830s), and **Kutenai Jargon** (based on Kutenai and used in communication between Europeans and Kutenai speakers in the nineteenth century).

Broken Slavey, also known as Slavey Jargon, was used in the Mackenzie River district, and **Jargon Loucheux** was in use along the Yukon River. Peter Bakker (1996b) surveyed descriptions of the languages and cited the missionary Emile Petitot (1889), who reported that

Broken Slavey was made up of French, Cree, and Dene Slave, and Jargon Loucheux was made up of French, English, Chipewyan, Slave, and Gwich'in (Loucheux). Cree is an Algonquian language, and the others (except for French and English) are Athabaskan, known for their complex phonologies and verb morphologies. They were apparently used by speakers of Slave and Chipewyan (Athabaskan), Cree, Inuit, French, and other European languages.

8.2.2. Indigenous Pidgins in South America

Akuntsú-Kanoe "pidgin." The so-called Akuntsú-Kanoê pidgin (Crevels and Voort 2008, 156) is a contact language that arose among the surviving speakers of Akuntsú (Tupían) and the Kanoê (Kapixaná) (language isolate) after the Akuntsú were massacred in the 1980s by cattle ranchers, with only six survivors (first officially contacted by FUNAI [National Foundation of Indigenous Peoples of Brazil] in 1995). The two groups were placed in the same indigenous territory on the Omeré River (Aragon 2014, 1–11; 2022, 225–226). The Akuntsú seek communication more often with the Kanoê, and for that purpose they use the grammar of their native language with a mixture of Kanoê and Akuntsú vocabulary (Carolina Aragon, personal communication 2018).

Ndyuka-Trió Pidgin (Carib Pidgin, Ndyuka-Amerindian Pidgin). This pidgin arose for trade and general communication between speakers of Ndyuka and Tiriyó (Trió) (a Cariban language). The Ndyuka language and society arose in the 1700s from large numbers of escaped slaves (called "Maroons") from the Suriname coastal area who fled to east-central Suriname. It came to be used also by Wayana (Cariban) speakers, in Suriname and French Guiana (De Goeje 1906, 1908, 1946; Huttar 1982; Huttar and Velantie 1997).[1] Curt Nimuendajú (1926, 112–113, 124, 140–143) reported it also in Brazilian territory, used there by the Palikur speakers. Its syntax is essentially Tiriyó (Trió), not Ndyuka; its lexicon is from both Ndyuka and Tiriyó, with mainly Ndyuka pronouns, verbs, and adverbs, and with nouns being equally from the two sources, Tiriyó and Ndyuka. It has SOV basic word order, very unexpected for a creole language (Huttar and Velantie 1997, 117).

Wayana-Aluku Trade Jargon. Two other societies in addition to the Ndyuka composed mostly of escaped slaves formed later in eastern Suriname: Paramaccans and Alukus (Bonis). The three groups are ethnolinguistically distinct from one another, but "there is a high degree of linguistic similarity among the three" (Huttar and Velantie 1997, 99). There are also other black groups of central Suriname (Saramaccan, Matawai, Kwinti), all speaking creole languages. At least three languages were reported to be in use between these groups and Native American groups in Suriname and French Guiana. C. H. de Goeje (1939, 10) referred to two "trade languages" used between black groups (Ndyukas) and American Indian groups (Triós [Tiriyós] and Wayanas), and Henri Coudreau (1895, 120) reported yet another used by "créoles" (persons of European descents born in the colonies) with speakers of "Émerillon" (a Tupí-Guaraníanlanguage) in French Guiana, but only one sentence in the language, without translation, was reported (Huttar and Valentie 1997, 102, 120).

Claudius de Goeje (1946, 100–101) provided most of what is known of the Wayana-Aluku Trade Jargon. He said that in the Lawa and Litanim near the Alukus, the language was a very simplified Wayana mixed with Kalinha (Galibi, Kalinya, Kariña, Kari'nja) words and that the Kalinha words and prefixes indicate that it was the remains of a trade jargon formerly used by the French with the Kalinhas of the coastal region (Huttar and Velantie 1997, 118). However, Huttar and Velantie (1997, 119) found that in fact very few of the forms given by de Goeje were from Wayana; rather, far more involved words from Kalinha (Galibi) than Wayana.

Orther Indigenous pidgins or creoles of South America? Pieter Muysken (1980, 69–70) cited numerous references to Spanish-based pidgins among Indigenous groups of the upper Amazon region; he cited examples from different sources, some involving Jívaro (now called Shiwiar) and Záparo speakers. However, he found that it is unclear whether the features he pointed out were conventionalized and thus represent a real pidgin or not. (See also Media Lengua, below, a Quechua-Spanish mixed language.)

Some of the South American languages discussed later in this chapter have at times been considered pidgins (or even creoles) in that, though they are basically Indigenous languages, some of them appear to be simplified as used by some of the groups.

8.2.3. Línguas Gerais of Brazil

Língua geral is a specific term for a particular kind of languages, which emerged in South America in the sixteenth and seventeenth centuries under special conditions of contact between Europeans and indigenous peoples. The name *língua geral* took on a specific meaning in Brazil in the seventeenth and eighteenth centuries (Rodrigues 2010, 6). However, the term *língua geral* can be confusing since it has at times been used to mean a variety of things, sometimes to designate the indigenous languages spoken by the Tupí and the Tupinambá; sometimes to refer to a language created or shaped by the Jesuits in the sixteenth century based on the language of these Indigenous people, or often claimed to be a pidgin or a creole language that originated in the contact between Portuguese and different Indigenous groups. As Aryon Rodrigues (2010, 6) clarified, these concepts lack any historical and linguistic basis. The term is also not to be confused with the Indigenous languages that were designated "general languages," *lenguas generales* and *línguas gerais*, in the sixteenth century to facilitate religious and political administration in the colonial period (see below).

Here, *língua geral* is used to refer in particular to two cases in Brazil—Língua Geral Paulista and Nheengatú—where the large number of unions of European men with indigenous women had as a consequence the rapid formation of mestizo populations whose mother tongue was the indigenous language of the mothers and not the European language of the fathers.

Rodrigues (2010, 10–11) cited as general sociolinguistic characteristics of the *línguas gerais* that they are the special product of language contact that originated with European men and Indígenous women, where initially the two groups lived together and mixed; little by little the indigenous portion of the community became less intense and less frequent in comparison to the mestizo portion. From the beginning there was a situation of partial bilingualism, with a monolingual majority and a bilingual minority. There was at no time an interruption of transmission of the language (no language shift). For a long time the *línguas gerais* prevailed as the main means of contact between indigenous peoples who were reached in colonial expansion by the Europeans and their mestizo descendants, giving new bilinguals who swelled the numbers of speakers, contributing to change in the language. The *línguas gerais* were not written languages.

Over time these languages simplified, which is a principal reason why some have thought they are pidgin or creole languages, though their origins are very different from those of pidgins and creoles. Some of the structural changes, mostly simplifications, that they have undergone from original Tupí and Tupinambá are: change from SOV to SVO basic word order, reduction of distinctions in the deictic system, change of the verbal nominalizer suffix to a particle marking relative clauses, merger of some verb mood markers with the indicative marker, reduction of the morphological case system, with loss of argumentative, predicative, diffuse locative, situational locative cases, and with persistence only of the punctual locative extended to be a generic locative, reduction of the evidential particles, development of a nominal plural particle, addition of several conjunctions from Portuguese, addition of numerals beyond 4 or 5, and addition of many loans and calques from Portuguese (Rodrigues 2010, 12–13).

Língua Geral do Sul (Língua Geral Paulista, Língua Geral of São Paulo, Tupí Austral). Língua Geral do Sul originally was the Tupí language of the region and became the dominant language in São Paulo until it was displaced by Portuguese in the eighteenth century (Rodrigues 1986, 102).

Língua Geral do Sul arose in the mixed population whose mother tongue was the Tupí of the mothers, and continued for more than a hundred years to be the language of the people of São Paulo. The Tupí of São Paulo began to cease to exist as an independent and culturally diverse people, while their language was passed on as the language of the mestizos, that is, of the persons of mixed Portuguese and Indigenous descent. Even after there was no longer any direct incorporation of indigenous people into the families, the linguistic situation of the families of Portuguese married with people of mixed Portuguese-Indigenous descent was basically the same as families made up only of mestizos. The original indigenous language was spoken, and only the husband and, from a certain age, the male children were bilingual in Portuguese. The language that the people of São Paulo spoke no longer served an indigenous society and culture; rather it served the society and culture of the mestizos that more and more became distanced from its indigenous origins and closer to Portuguese culture (Rodrigues 2010, 8). Língua Geral do Sul was spoken by those from São Paulo who in the seventeenth century explored the states of Minas Gerais, Goias, and Mato Grosso, and southern Brazil. As the language of these settlers and adventurers, it penetrated far into the interior. Later, government policy promoted Portuguese and Língua Geral do Sul eventually ceased to be spoken.

Unfortunately, the surviving documentation for Língua Geral o Sul (Língua Geral Paulista) is very sparse. Its last speakers apparently died in the beginning of the twentieth century (Rodrigues 1986, 2010).

Nheengatú (Língua Geral Amazônica, "Língua Boa," Língua Brasílica, Língua Geral do Norte, called Yeral in Venezuela and Colombia). Portuguese colonization in Maranhão, in Pará, and in Amazonia in general had its beginning in the first half of the seventeenth century, after the expulsion of the French. It began in territory where Tupinambá (a Tupían language) was broadly spoken along the coast. The strong interaction of Portuguese colonists and soldiers with the Tupinambás gave rise to a mestizo population there, as in São Paulo above, initially of European fathers and Indigenous mothers, whose language became the Tupinambá of the mothers. Over time, the language progressively became more different from the Tupinambá spoken by the Indigenous Tupinambás, who survived until the mid-eighteenth century. This language was also called *língua geral* in colonial times, also called *Brasiliano*. In the latter half of the nineteenth century it came to be called also *Nheeengatú*, and later also *língua geral amazônica* to make clear its distinction from the *língua geral do sul* (*língua geral paulista*).

From the seventeenth century onward this language accompanied Portuguese expansion in the Amazon. It became the lingua franca for a large region of the Amazon Basin, used by various indigenous groups, also becoming the native language of several of them. It extended its use throughout the entire Amazon Basin and tributaries to the Amazon, going up the Rio Negro, reaching Venezuelan and Colombian Amazon regions. In Venezuela and Colombia it is called *lengua yeral*. It continues to be spoken today by some 20,000 people, extensively along the Rio Negro and in pockets elsewhere in the Amazon region, but it waned with the decline of rubber extraction, with Tukano taking over its lingua franca function throughout the northwest Vaupés region.

Today's Nheengatú differs from both Tupinambá and eighteenth-century Língua Geral. In addition to the changes mentioned above, it simplified the demonstratives from a system that contrasted visible/invisible and three degrees of proximity (like 'this'/'that'/'that yonder') to just two, equivalent to 'this' and 'that'. The personal pronoun system was reduced from various plural forms for 'inclusive' and 'exclusive' to only one. It developed subordinate clause structures that are more like Portuguese (Bessa Freire 1983; Cruz 2011; Moore et al. 1994; Rodrigues 1986, 99–109; 2010; Taylor 1985).

8.3. LINGUA FRANCAS OF THE NEW WORLD

Sources indicate that several Indigenous languages were used as lingua francas, some in wider areas, others among speakers of different languages in more localized regions. Today the lingua franca for indigenous peoples of North America communicating across language lines is English; it is French in some areas of Canada; it is, Spanish, Portuguese, or French in various areas of Latin America. Though some cases of lingua francas are well known, for many we have very little information about the lingua franca and the circumstances of its use.

8.3.1. North American Indigenous Lingua Francas

I turn first to cases of Indigenous languages that have been used as lingua francas in North America. For many of them, few details are known about their use as lingua francas.

Bearlake is the lingua franca in Déline (Fort Franklin), Northwest Territories, used among speakers of several Athabaskan languages there (see Chapter 2).

Carrier was established as a lingua franca by Catholic missionaries, most notably by Father Adrien Gabriel Morice in the nineteenth century, based on the dialect around Fort St. James in British Columbia (see Chapter 2).

One variety of **Huron-Wyandot** was the lingua franca of the Huron Confederacy in the seventeenth century.

Tuscarora was reportedly used as a lingua franca (Drechsel 1983a, 389–390).

Catawba was also reportedly used as a lingua franca (Drechsel 1983a, 389–390).

Occaneechi (Occaneechee), a long-dormant language, typically assumed to be related to Catawban (Siouan-Catawban), was used as a lingua franca by a number of Native American groups in Virginia and the Carolinas in early colonial times. The extent to which it was pidginized for this purpose is not known, though some scholars have asserted that it was a pidgin language. Ives Goddard (2005, 8) reported of it:

> In 1705 ... Beverley [1947] reported that the language of the Occaneechi was used as a regional lingua franca, "understood by the Chief men of many Nations," whose languages differed greatly, "so that Nations at a moderate distance, do not understand one another" (1947, 191). Presumably this was the language of the short vocabulary collected at Fort Christanna in 1716 as Saponi (Alexander 1971), which incorporates some Algonquian and Iroquoian loanwords. (Goddard 1972. See also Silverstein 1996, 119.)

Creek was widely used as a lingua franca in the Southeast, though Mobilian Jargon served that purpose further west in French Louisiana (Crawford 1978, 5–7; Sturtevant 2005, 33).

Shawnee was also widely used as a lingua franca in early colonial times (Goddard 2005, 33).

Virginia Algonquian may have been used as a lingua franca (Goddard 2005, 43).

Coahuilteco of southern Texas and northeast Mexico was a lingua franca in the area around Monterrey, Mexico (Troike 1967; Goddard 1979a). It was a second language for the Orejones, Pamaques, Alazapas, and Borrados groups, and reportedly the young people of the Pihuiques, Sanipaos, and Manos de Perro spoke Coahuilteco in 1760, presumably as a second language for these groups. (See Chapter 2.)

Plains Sign Language is probably the best-known and most extensively used contact language in North America. It was the lingua franca from central Canada to northern Mexico, used among speakers of nearly forty Indigenous languages of the Plains (Mallery 1880; Salwen 1987; Taylor 1978, 1996, 2011).

It appears to have originated in the extreme southern part of the Plains or on the Texas Gulf Coast (Taylor 1996, 275). Ives Goddard (1979a, 356) pointed out a Texas sign language and argued that "it is very likely that the Texas sign language was the ancestor of the Plains sign language of the nineteenth century" (see also Wurtzburg and Campbell 1995, who share Goddard's view).

It was frequently said that the Kiowas were excellent sign talkers. The Comanches, Cheyenne, and Arapahos were also considered to be good sign talkers. It is likely that the Kiowas were centrally involved in the spread of Plains Sign Language in the southern plains (Taylor 1996, 275).

8.3.2. Lingua Francas in Latin America

In Latin America, *Lenguas Generales* (called *Línguas Gerais* in areas where Portuguese is dominant) were established in the sixteenth century to facilitate religious and political administration in the colonial period.[2] These were languages of ethnic groups with strong influence over larger territories; some of them had been in widespread use as lingua francas among speakers of different languages before European contact. The status of these "general languages" was strengthened by King Phillip II of Spain's favorable attitude toward them. In 1580 he ordered university chairs of the "general languages" to be established. The major "lenguas generales" ("línguas gerais") were Aymara, Chibcha (Muisca), Guaraní, Nahuatl, Puquina, Quechua, and Tupinambá (cf. Estenssoro 2015; Itier 2011; Heath 1972; Mannheim 1991).

Nahuatl was indeed a *lengua general* and an important language in Spanish colonial administration, apparently serving as a lingua franca for at least some individuals in some circumstances. How widely spread and widely used it was as a lingua franca are unknown, and opinions have differed about these things. Judging from loanwords of Nahuatl origin in various languages of Mesoamerica, there was also apparently a least some bilingualism involving Nahuatl in some places before first contact with Europeans. However, evidence of Nahuatl serving as a widespread lingua franca in pre-contact times is unclear and in my estimation unlikely, though there is disagreement in the literature about that (see, for example, Brown 2011; Dakin 1982, 2010; Dakin and Operstein 2017).

Epps and Michael (2017, 954) believe cases of lingua francas are "rare or even unattested in ... Amazonian contact zones." Some argue that a confluence of economic and sociolinguistic factors made lingua francas unlikely or at least unstable in some regions of lowland South America prior to changes brought about by colonization (Ball 2011, 95). There are, nevertheless, several reported cases of lingua francas in Amazonia as well as elsewhere in South America, most of them having arisen in colonial times. The use of indigenous lingua francas appears to have been common in the pre-colonial Andes, but less common in the lowlands, although more research on this topic is needed. Several of the Indigenous lingua francas known in South America are listed in what follows.

Betoi reportedly was used as a local lingua franca by peoples between the Uribante and Sarare Rivers and along the Arauca River, in Venezuela. It became dormant by the mid-nineteenth century (Zamponi 2003a, 2017).

Chandul Guaraní, in several provinces of northern Argentina and Uruguay, filled the role of lingua franca, "not only among different Indigenous groups, but also between Indigenous people and Europeans" (Viegas Barros 2020, 238).[3] There are also many loanwords of Guaraní origin in the Spanish of this region and in the indigenous languages there.

Chiquitano was promoted as a lingua franca by Jesuit missionaries, imposed on the groups reduced to and united in Jesuit missions, probably because it was the language of the most numerous indigenous group in its region (Santana et al. 2009, 101).

Gorgotoqui. During the time of the Jesuit missions in the Chiquitanía region of Bolivia, Gorgotoqui was the largest language of its area in terms of numbers of speakers, and it was used as a lingua franca of the Jesuit missions. However, no documentation of this language survived and it became dormant very early. (See Chapter 4.)

Kamayurá (Tupí-Guaraníian branch of Tupían) serves as a kind of lingua franca in the Upper Xingu region (https://pib.socioambiental.org/en/Popular:Trumai).

Kubeo functions as the lingua franca for the northwest Vaupés region. Its role as lingua franca is expanding (Chacon 2013).

Makurap (Tuparían branch of Tupían). At the time of the rubber tappers, Makurap speakers were the first and main interlocutors of rubber bosses and other White people. Makurap became a lingua franca in the Rio Branco region used among several other indigenous groups (https://pib.socioambiental.org/en/Popular:Tupari). Portuguese has taken the place as the lingua franca formerly occupied by Makurap in the Middle Guaporé region (https://pib.socioambiental.org/en/Povo:Wajuru).

Sanavirón. Pedro Viegas Barros (2009) presented evidence that Sanavirón (Córdoba province, Aregntinia), of which very little is actually known, was used as a lingua franca in the Sierra de Córdoba region of Argentina in the earliest colonial times there. (See Chapter 5.)

Tonocoté. Although Tonocoté has long been dormant and essentially nothing is known of the language itself, it was reported as in use as a lingua franca for communication also with Lules and Abipones in the Chaco (Caraman 1975, 192, 209). (See Chapter 5.)

Tukano is the very widespread lingua franca for the southeastern Vaupés region, used by speakers of many languages there. Its role is expanding (https://pib.socioambiental.org/pt/Povo:Tukano).

Waiwai (Cariban) has become a lingua franca, the language predominantly spoken in the indigenous General Assemblies in its region (northern Brazil and Guyana) (https://pib.socioambiental.org/en/Public:Waiwai).

As indicated above, **Língua Geral do Sul** and **Nheengatú** were also widely used as lingua francas.

8.4. MIXED LANGUAGES

A mixed language is one that has different source languages for different components of its grammar and so has no single ancestor. There are very few true mixed languages. Until the early 1980s most linguists believed that no true mixed languages existed; now we know better. Several of the best known of the demonstrated mixed languages are from the Americas. It is believed that a mixed language can arise only in very restricted social circumstances, typically correlated with how newly formed or reorganized ethnic groups see their identity (Thomason 1997).

Copper Island Aleut (Mednyj Aleut) is a mixed language originally spoken in the village of Preobrazhenskoye on Copper (Mednyj) Island, Kamchatka Province, Russia. The first settlers on Copper Island in the early nineteenth century were Russians, soon followed by Aleuts brought from Attu Island. By 1969 the entire community had been relocated to the village of Nikol'skoye on Bering Island.

Copper Island Aleut is a true mixed language. Its lexicon, nominal inflection, and derivational morphology are derived largely from Aleut, while its verbal inflection and syntax are basically Russian. More specifically, from a vocabulary of about 500 words Irinia Sekerina (1994) found that 94 percent of verb roots were from Aleut and 6 percent from Russian; 61.5 percent of nouns were from Aleut and 38.5 percent from Russian (particularly terms for introduced items); and 31.5 percent of function words were from Aleut with 68.5 percent from Russian (Mithun 2021a, 520–521).

The language recently became dormant, with no known speakers today. (See Evgenij Golovko 1994, 1996, 2003; Golovko and Vakhtin 1990; Menovščikov 1968, 1969; Mithun 2021a, 520–521; Sekerina 1994; and Thomason 1997.)

Michif (Mitchif) is a mixed language in which nouns and their modifiers, with their pronunciation and morphology, are almost all from a variety of Canadian French, while the verbs with their pronunciation and morphology are mainly from Plains Cree, with minor differences. Michif is not mutually intelligible with either Cree or French. It is spoken in some communities of Métis, descendants of Cree women and French fur traders who formed a distinct ethnic group on the northern Great Plains. Michif was spoken only by a small minority of Métis families. Métis communities have typically been multilingual, with Cree, Ojibwe, French, and more recently English widely spoken. Michif developed in Saskatchewan and Manitoba in Canada, and North Dakota and Montana in the United States. The most detailed source on the language is Bakker (1997); Laverdure and Allard (1983) is a dictionary of the language (see also Bakker 1994).

Bilingual Navajo emerged when Navajo-speaking children were sent away to boarding school during the first half of the twentieth century and forbidden to speak their language. When they returned to their Navajo communities, they brought a different language back with them. Neither Navajo nor English monolinguals understand it, and fluent Navajo-English bilinguals cannot automatically speak it. Bilingual Navajo draws most of its grammatical and discourse structure from Navajo, but from English some vocabulary, primarily nouns, some adjectives and adverbs, and a few verbs. It is described by Schaengold (2004) (see also Mithun 2021a, 522–523).

Tojolab'al. There have been disagreements over the classification of Tojolab'al within the Mayan family (see Chapter 3). Danny Law (2017b) argues that Tojolab'al is a mixed language, with substantial input from both Tzeltal (of the Cholan-Tzeltalan branch) and Tojolab'al (of the Greater Q'anjob'alan branch), and this accounts for the difficulty of determining its position in Mayan subgrouping. In fact, Law (2017b, 122) argues that Tojolab'al is a "unique type of contact language":

> Unlike prototypical mixed languages, [Tojolab'al] is not consistent about which donor language contributed material to which part of the grammar. Instead Tojolab'al appears to have thoroughly intermixed forms from both contributing languages throughout its grammar and lexicon.

Callahuaya (Machaj-Juyai, Kallawaya). Callahuaya is a mixed language based predominantly on lexical items from long-dormant Puquina (language isolate, see Chapter 4) with Quechua morphology. It is used only for curing ceremonies by mostly male curers from Charazani and a few villages in the provinces of Muñecas and Bautista Saavedra, Department of La Paz, Bolivia. These curers travel widely to practice their profession. They also speak Quechua, Aymara, and Spanish.

Louisa Stark (1972b) found that 70 percent of Callahuaya words in the Swadesh 200-word list are from Puquina, 14 percent from Quechua, 14 percent from Aymara, and 2 percent from Uru-Chipaya; Muysken (1994a) reported that some Callahuaya words are also from Takana. The grammatical morphology, however, is almost wholly from Cuzco Quechua, for example: 'accusative' -*ta* (Callahuaya *usi-ta*, Quechua *wasi-ta* 'house'), 'imperative' -*y* (Callahuaya *tahra-y*, Quechua *l'ank'a-y* 'work!'), 'plural' -*kuna* (Callahuaya *simi-kuna*, Quechua *ñan-kuna* 'roads'). The possessive pronominal suffixes are of Quechua origin and are identical in Callahuaya and Cuzco Quechua (-*y* 'my', -*yki* 'your', -*n* 'his/her/its', -*nčis* 'our [inclusive], -*yku* 'our [exclusive]'). The locative suffixes are also identical (-*man* 'to', -*manta* 'from', -*pi* 'in', -*wan* 'with', -*rayku* 'because of'). The verb morphology is also from Quechua (for example, *-a* 'causative', *-na* 'reciprocal', *-ku* 'reflexive', *-mu* 'hither', *-rqa* 'past', *-sqa* 'narrative past') (see Büttner 1983, 23; Muysken 1994a, 2011; Oblitas Poblete 1968; Stark 1972b).

Guajiro-Spanish mixed language. Norval Smith (1994) reported an unnamed Guajiro-Spanish mixed language that is replacing Guajiro (Wayuu) in parts of Colombia and Venezuela. More information is needed to determine whether it actually is a true mixed language and what its characteristics may be.

Kokama. Kokama (a.k.a Kokama-Cocamilla, Kukama-Kukamiria, Kokáma/Omágua) is endangered, spoken in the Peruvian Amazon (Loreto and Ucayali provinces). The Kokama lexicon is mostly from Tupinambá, but contains also words of Portuguese, Spanish, Arawakan, and Panoan origin, with a substantial number from Quechua.

In Ana Suelly Cabral's (1995) analysis, Kokama began when a group of Tupinambá speakers migrated in the late fifteenth century from the Atlantic coast to the upper Amazon and came in contact with speakers of other languages. Cabral argued that the large number of lexical elements from Tupinambá, coupled with an almost complete absence of morphological and grammatical features from Tupinambá, and a number of phonological changes untypical of Tupían languages, indicate that Tupinambá was learned imperfectly as a second language by other groups, meaning that Kokama is a mixed language (see also Braga et al. 2011, 223; , 2007; Vallejos Yopán 2005, 2010).

Lev Michael (2014) argues that Kokama and Omagua were not the product of colonial-era language contact, that they are the outcome of language contact in the pre-Columbian period. He concludes that Proto-Omagua-Kokama, the parent language from which Omagua and Kokama derive, was a pre-Columbian contact language.

Media Lengua and related varieties. Media Lengua is a mixed language in Salcedo (Cotopaxi province, Ecuador). Its name is Spanish meaning 'half language'. Pieter Muysken (1980, 75) defined *Media Lengua* as "a form of Quechua with a vocabulary almost completely derived from Spanish, but which to a large extent preserves the syntactic and semantic structures of Quechua," where "all Quechua words, including all core vocabulary, have been replaced" by Spanish (Muysken 1994b, 203).

Muysken speculated that Media Lengua probably originated with acculturated Quechua who did not identify completely with either rural Quechua culture or Spanish culture, and Media Lengua served the role of ethnic self-identification (Muysken 1981, 1994b, 1997). It began around 1967 when many young men started working in construction in a nearby town and began learning Spanish. Muysken (1997, 376) claims that this occurred "because acculturated Indians could not completely identify with the traditional Quechua culture or the urban Spanish culture."

The mixture is seen in the following example, where the lexical roots are all of Spanish origin, in boldface, with the grammatical morphology from Quechua, in italics:

(1) **Unu** **fabur**-*ta* **pidi**-*nga-bu* **bini**-*xu-ni*
 one favor-ACC ask-NMLZ-BEN come-PROG-1SG
 'I come to ask a favor' (Muysken 1997, 365)

(ACC = accusative, NMLZ = nominalization, BEN = benefactive, PROG = progressive)

The lexical roots, all from Spanish, are: /unu/ 'one' < Spanish *uno* 'one, a'; /fabur/ < Sp. *favor* 'favor'; /pidi/ < Sp. *pedi(r)* 'to ask for'; and /bini/ < Sp. *veni(r)* 'to come'.

The Media Lengua of Salcedo may no longer be spoken. There are other "media lenguas," **Catalangu**, **Saraguro Media Lengua** (Muysken 1980), and **Imbabura (Pijal) Media Lengua** (Gómez Rendón 2005, 2008). Catalangu, also a mixed language, is said to be "much closer to Spanish than [Salcedo] Media Lengua" (Muysken 1980, 78) (see also Lipski 2017; Muysken 1981).

Jopara (Yopara) is spoken in Asunción, Paraguay, and in Corrientes Province, Argentina, and by Paraguayan immigrants in Buenos Aires, Argentina (Muñoz 1993). The name *Jopara* is from a Guaraní word for 'mixture'. It is not in danger of loss in the foreseeable future (Lustig 1996, 39). It is typically considered a variety of Guaraní, generally held in low esteem, but has also been called the third language of Paraguay (with Spanish and Guaraní as the other two). Alternatively, Jopara has been considered a mixed language, a nascent pidgin or creole language, just Guaraní with heavy borrowing from Spanish, a new linguistic system different from Guaraní, a low-level sociolect, not a language proper but a style of speaking, a linguistic behavior, or just a kind of speech with extensive code-switching (Dietrich 2010, 40–41). It is characterized by a high degree of code-switching used by speakers—"Continuous code switching is the main characteristic of this phenomenon called 'Jopara'" (Dietrich 2010, 39). Wolf Dietrich (2010, 40) is of the opinion that "Jopara may only be described in an adequate way if we succeed in describing how code switching functions." He considers Jopara one of the two levels of Guaraní, spoken Guaraní "with lots of social and stylistic variants" (p. 40), "the only existing form of modern spoken Guaraní"; "it is simply modern Guaraní"; "Jopara is colloquial Guaraní and there is no other spoken Guaraní than Jopara" (p. 44); "Jopara as the low level variant of [Guaraní] which implies the partial use of Spanish by the method of frequent code switching" (p. 45). However, Dietrich also says that "Jopara is based on the bilingualism of the speakers. Speakers of Jopara have a more or less active and passive command of both Guaraní and Spanish" (p. 49).

As Wolf Lustig (1996, 39) sees it:

> It is not that there is a third language in Paraguay, but rather that there is an increasingly important part of the Paraguayan people that has no place either in the world of peasant tradition (Guaraní) or in the civilization of progress (Spanish). They use a spurious dialect that, because it is "impure," "disorderly" and "abnormal" does not deserve the attention of philologists, writers and educators. Those who speak Jopara are those who live on the fringes of two worlds, stranded between two languages, between two cultures, on the shifting ground between the city and the river that, to top it all, does not belong to them.[4]

This does sound like the attribute of mixed languages involving how newly formed ethnic groups see their identity. This view of Jopara and its role in the population, however, contrasts markedly with Wolf Dietrich's view (above) of Jopara as just spoken Guaraní with lots of code switching.

It seems, then, that Jopara is not a true mixed language, though questions of its nature and use remain and should be investigated.

8.5. SOCIO-CULTURAL-POLITICAL FACTORS IN SOUTH AMERICA LANGUAGE CONTACT

It is sometimes said that language contact in some regions of South America is different from the kinds of language contact that are characteristic of languages elsewhere in the world, for example, with less lexical borrowing, less code-switching, and different patterns of language shift (long-term language maintenance), often involving extensive multilingualism (see for example Epps and Michael 2017, 936–937; Epps 2020). This appears to be relatively true, though only to a degree. Any differences in the language contact in regions of South America from cases known elsewhere need careful investigation (Epps 2017; Epps and Michael 2017, 950).

For instance, it has repeatedly been claimed that there is a marked absence of code-switching, in particular in the upper Amazon region (Aikhenvald 2002, 95; Epps and Michael 2017, 937, 954; Epps and Stenzel 2013, 36). Code-switching or code mixing has even been characterized as criminal and strongly condemned culturally by some groups of the area (Epps and Stenzel 2013, 36; Lüpke et al. 2020, 28). This notwithstanding, cases of code-switching have been observed involving speakers of some languages of this region. For example, Wilson Silva (2020) recorded code-switching among speakers of several languages in a Desano-Siriano community in Colombia, and Stenzel and Williams (2021) report code-switching among speakers of Kotiria (Wanano) and Wa'ikhana (Piratapuya). For another case, see Paula (2001).

It has been claimed that in small-scale societies in general the following are typically missing or only weakly developed: lingua francas, social dialects, prestige languages, societal bilingualism, honorifics, and writing (see for example Miller 1996, 228). This may be true of many small-scale societies in the Americas, but there certainly are telling exceptions, some seen here.

Neither restricted lexical borrowing nor limited code-switching seems restricted only to particular regions of South America. Preferences for new words to be formed from native language resources over lexical borrowing have long been reported for numerous North American languages (for example by Boas 1911a, 50; Brown 1999). It is also claimed that languages that have complex verbal morphology—as many South America languages do and as do others scattered all over the world—tend to have restrictions involving the adoption of loanwords (Bakker and van der Voort 2017, 421). There are, of course, numerous cases of South American languages with complex verb morphology that have also undergone considerable lexical borrowing, for example, Amuesha, Aymara, Cholón, Kamsá, and Quechua, among various others (see Chapter 9; Muysken 2012). Consequently, potential differences between language contact in regions of South America and those known elsewhere in the world need investigation, and claims of great difference need to be approached with considerable caution.

Work on language contact in South America has shown how social, political, and economic factors affect the diffusion of linguistic traits among languages (Epps 2012, 2017). Linguistic exogamy is an important example and serves well to illustrate this point.

8.5.1. Marriage Patterns, Multilingualism, Linguistic Exogamy

Some of the best-known and most intensive forms of language contact in South America occur in communities with a tradition of linguistic exogamy, where marriage is between speakers of different languages. The extensive multilingualism and linguistic exogamous marriage patterns of speakers of many languages in the Vaupés region are famous, not matched elsewhere in the world (Chacon and Cayón 2013; Epps 2007, 2012; Jackson 1983; Sorensen 1967; and many others). Another unusual case is that of Misión La Paz, Argentina (henceforth MLP) (Campbell and Grondona 2010). A comparison of the two cases is instructive.

In MLP three indigenous languages, Chorote, Nivaclé, and Wichí (members of the Matacoan family, not closely related), are spoken, as well as Spanish. MLP practices linguistic exogamy. Each spouse speaks his/her own language and is addressed in/understands the other spouse's language in return—a spouse does not accommodate by speaking the other spouse's language; each maintains and uses his or her own. People "identify" with a single language and speak it with all others. Most interactions in MLP are multilingual— each participant in the conversation typically speaks his or her own language, and the other participants in the conversation each speak their own particular language in return. People communicate regularly with speakers of different languages, but commonly not in the same language as the one addressed to them. This sort of non-reciprocal language use where each speaker speaks his or her own language but understands the other's language in return has been called "dual-lingualism" (Lincoln 1979; Campbell and Grondona 2010).

The Vaupés area's linguistic exogamy and extensive multilingualism are well known (see Chapter 7). The situations in the Vaupés and Misión La Paz are similar in that spouses marry someone who speaks a different language, and they avoid borrowings from other languages. Both involve small populations with low population density and the languages are considered of equal status (Jackson 1983, 164, 175). However, the two also differ in fundamental ways. In the Vaupés area, one identifies with and is loyal to the father's language. Wives were expected to learn and use the language of the husband's longhouse, and people learn and use other languages eagerly. In MLP the language a person identifies with can be either the father's or the mother's, and it is a personal choice. People typically use only their own language, not shifting to the language others speak, resulting in multiple languages used in single conversations. Men exchange women in the Vaupés; in MLP women select the men they marry. Residence is patrilocal in the Vaupés; Vaupés patrilocality with residential exogamy contributes somewhat automatically to linguistic exogamy. In MLP the man usually lives with the wife's family initially until the first child is born, and then the couple typically goes to live with the husband's family. Women are community outsiders in the Vaupés (who come to the longhouse because of patrilocal residence rules); this is not the case in MLP. Linguistic exogamy in the Vaupés is a major principle of social organization, residence patterns, kinship, and regional interactions; failure to conform is considered incest. In MLP there is linguistic exogamy, but the practice is not talked about as a necessary rule. The dual-lingualism sometimes practiced in the Vaupés is sporadic and short term; in MLP, dual-lingualism is the predominant kind of verbal interaction and is institutionalized.

Interestingly, these examples of intensive long-term contact and multilingualism do not conform to some assumptions about convergence in language contact. Linguists agree with Leonard Bloomfield's (1933, 476) declaration, "when two speech communities are in continuous communication, linguistic convergence is expected, and any degree of divergence requires an explanation." The expectation is that in intensive language contact, languages become more similar to one another and should not undergo changes that make them less similar. For example, in famous cases from India, different languages in intensive long-term contact became so structurally similar that rather exactly matching morpheme-by-morpheme translations became possible (Gumperz and Wilson 1971; Nadkarni 1975). However, examples of multilingualism and linguistic exogamy in South America give us examples of the opposite phenomenon: languages tenaciously maintaining structural distinctions or actively diverging in situations of intensive contact.

For example, the three indigenous languages of MLP, though in intensive contact, have diverged structurally in several traits and are not converging as expected. They have undergone several structural changes in both morphosyntax and phonology that make the languages more different from one another, not more similar (see Campbell and Grondona 2010; Campbell 2017b; Campbell et al. 2020). It would be expected that the intensive multilingual interactions of MLP would influence these languages not to undergo changes in which they diverge further from one another but rather that they should keep traits that the other languages spoken there have. On the other hand, in the Vaupés Linguistic Area, languages have converged in semantic and structural features; although speakers may actively avoid code-switching and lexical borrowing, borrowing of grammatical structures has occurred (Epps 2012, 224).

All three of the indigenous languages of MLP had phonemic /ɬ/, voiceless "l". However, Chorote speakers have changed voiceless "l" to a consonant cluster of /x/ + voiced /l/, which alternates, especially word-initially and word-finally, with just plain /l/, as in the following (spelled phonetically):

xlop / lop 'its nest' (cf. Nivaclé *ɬup*)
xlaʔa / laʔa 'fruit' (cf. Nivaclé *ɬaʔ*)
axlu 'iguana' (cf. Nivaclé *aɬu*)
samexl / samel 'we'

This change has taken place in spite of these Chorote speakers being in constant intensive contact with speakers of the other two languages, which preserve unaltered their unitary voiceless /ɬ/. This goes against expectations of languages in such close, intensive contact. We would expect the very frequent voiceless "l" of Nivaclé and Wichí in such intensive, constant contact to cause Choroté to resist changing a sound that these other languages have.

In another example, both Nivaclé and Wichí have very frequent contrastive first-person plural inclusive and exclusive pronominal forms, as seen in Nivaclé:

(1a) kas-waʔatša [1PL.POSSESSIVE.INCLUSIVE-pronominal.root] 'we' (inclusive, all of us)
(1a) yi-waʔatša-ʔelh [1SG.POSSESSIVE-pronominal.root-PL.EXCLUSIVE] 'we' (exclusive, we but not you)
(2a) katsi-tata [1PL.POSSESSIVE.INCLUSIVE-father] 'our father' (of all of us)
(2b) yi-tata-ʔeɬ [1SG.POSSESSIVE-father-PL.EXCLUSIVE] 'our father' (but not yours)
(3a) šta-sekkis [1ACT.PL.INCLUSIVE-scrape] 'we scrape it' (all of us)
(3b) xa-sekkis-eɬ [1ACT.SG-scrape-PL.EXCLUSIVE] 'we scrape it' (but not you)

However, Chorote has lost this contrast and now has only a single first person plural category (for both inclusive and exclusive):

(4) sam, sameł (samel) 'we'
(5) si-ʔleh 'our language'
(6) a-lan-a [1PL-kill-SUFFIX] 'we killed it'

Contrast Chorote (5) with Nivaclé corresponding forms in (7a) and (7b):

(7a) kas-kliʔiš [1PL.POSSESSIVE.INCLUSIVE-language] 'our language' (inclusive)
(7b) xa-kliʔiš-eł [1SG.POSSESSIVE-language-PL.EXCLUSIVE] 'our language' (exclusive).

Contrast the verb form in Chorote (6) with the Nivaclé forms in (8a) and (8b):

(8a) šta-klɑn [1ACTIVE.PL.INCLUSIVE-kill] 'we kill it' (inclusive)
(8b) xa-klɑn-eł 'we kill it' [1SG.ACTIVE-kill-PL.EXCLUSIVE][5]

Thus, Chorote has only 'we' with no distinction for inclusive or exclusive. Again, we would not expect one of the languages to lose a morphological contrast that is so salient in the other two languages, a contrast that speakers of Chorote hear and understand constantly in the other two languages of MLP. (For other examples, see Campbell et al. 2020, 490–493.)

These examples show that pressure toward conformity (convergence) among the three languages in MLP due to their intensive interaction has not been as compelling as expected, since they are undergoing some changes that result in greater structural difference, rather than greater similarity, among the three. We see in these two contact situations, in the Vaupés and in MLP, a range of results. Although both the Vaupés and MLP have intensive language contact as a result of linguistic exogamy, the linguistic outcomes of contact differ in the two. It is mistaken to insist that languages in intensive contact must necessarily change only in the direction of more convergence, as we see in the MLP instances of structural divergence and in the explicit avoidance of lexical borrowing in both the Vaupés and MLP (and in other Chaco languages).

In the next chapter we turn attention to loanwords and lexical change.

NOTES

1. Ndyuka is an English-based creole language of Suriname and French Guiana. Maroons (once called *Bushinengues*, also formerly called *Bushnegroes*) are descendants of escaped slaves of African origin who fled to the interior, some of whom joined with indigenous tribes. Ndyuka is a language of some of the Maroon tribes (Huttar and Huttar 1994).

2. As indicated earlier in this chapter, there is another sense of *língua geral* (*línguas gerais* in the plural) in Brazil, meaning an Indigenous language that came to be extensively used by mixed colonial populations, that over time became reduced in some ways, different from the original form of the language. See the discussion of Língua Geral do Sul and Nheengatú in this chapter.

3. Los guaraníes que vivían en esta zona fueron llamados **chandules**. Su habla cumplió el papel de **lingua franca**, no solo entre distintos grupos indígenas, sino también entre aborígenes y europeos.

4. No es que haya una tercerea lengua en Paraguay, sino que hay una parte cada vez más importante del pueblo paraguayo que no tiene cabida ni en el mundo de la tradición campesina (guaraní) ni en la civilización del progreso (español). Se sirven de un dialecto espurio que por "impuro", "desordenado" y "anormal" no merece la atención de filólogos, literatos y educadores. Los que hablan *jopara* son los que viven al margen de los mundos, encallados entre dos lenguas, entre dos culturas, en el terreno movedizo entre la ciudad y el río que para colmo no les pertenece.

5. Notice in these examples that although they are not obviously similar at first glance, the roots are cognate in the two languages, Chorote *leh*: Nivaclé *kliʔiš* 'language' (< Proto-Matacoan **lix*), and Chorote *-lan*: Nivaclé *-klan* 'kill, hit' (< (< Proto-Matacoan **-lan*).

9

Loanwords and Other New Words in the Indigenous Languages of the Americas

9.1. INTRODUCTION

There has been no wholesale study of loanwords in Indigenous languages of the Americas, though many loanwords of various kinds have been identified in studies of particular languages, and much has been written about loanwords of different kinds involving these languages. Some of the languages are known to have borrowed many words from other Indigenous languages, especially, for example, languages in contact with Nahuatl and Quechua. This chapter is about lexical borrowing and ways new words are created in the lexicons of the Native American languages under the influence of other languages. Clearly, it is not possible here to treat all instances of such borrowings and neologisms. The goal of this chapter is rather to explore recurrent themes involving loanwords and creation of new words in these languages through examination of representative and interesting cases, and to give some sense of the borrowings involving a number of languages. Many other kinds of changes that come about due to language contact are described in Chapters 7 and 8.

9.2. WANDERWÖRTER

Wanderwörter are loanwords that are found widely diffused in a number of languages but where the original donor language is usually unknown. A number of individual *Wanderwörter* have been identified (and others have been proposed) in different regions of the Americas, and there has been some discussion of what their implications might be for the broader prehistory of certain regions, especially in Amazonia.

One case is the terms for '**buffalo**' (actually 'bison') among a number of North American languages, in particular in the US Southeast, seen for example in Choctaw *yaniš*, Alabama-Koasati *yanasa*, Hitchiti *yanas-i*, Creek *yanása* (Muskogean); Cherokee (Iroquoian) *yahnsā*; Natchez *yanasah*; Tunica *yániši*; Biloxi *yinisa'/yanasa/yunisa'*, Catawba *yunnaus/yanas* (Siouan-Catawba). Compare also Santee *wana'sa* 'to hunt buffalo' and Ponka *wana'se* 'to hunt buffalo' (Siouan) (Haas 1951, 78; 1969a, 81–82; Taylor 1976).[1]

Words for '**bean**' are widely borrowed, particularly in languages of the southwestern United States and western and central Mexico: Hopi *móri-*, Southern Paiute *muurii*, Tohono Oodham *muni* (*muuñ*), Tarahumara *muní*, Guarijío *mu?uní*, *muuní*, Mayo *muúni*, *muúnim*, Yaqui *múuni*, Eudeve *mun(i)*, Cora *múhume*, Huichol *múume* (Uto-Aztecan languages); Mandan *ó:mīnīe*, Lakota *omníčka*, Kansa *hōbrlige* (Siouan); Proto-Chiapanec-Mangue **(nu-)mu*, Tlapanec *ni¹-ma²* 'bean plant', Mazatec *yu⁴hmã̃ʔ²*, Proto-Popolocan **hmaʔ³*, Proto-Mazatec **na⁴hma¹*, Ixcatec *hmaʔ* (Otomanguan languages), Proto-Otomanguean **mɔ*, Eastern Otomanguean **mau*; and a form approximating *marík* among Yuman languages.

Terms for '**cedar**' are diffused among several languages of the southeastern United States. In the case of Creek *ačína* and Cherokee *acina* ([a̧²ji²na]), the direction of borrowing is not clear, though Hitchiti *ačin-i* is probably borrowed from Creek. The *čuwahla* 'cedar' in Choctaw, Alabama, and Koasati may reflect a Proto-Muskogean form; Biloxi (Siouan) *čuwahna*, however, is borrowed from Muskogean, since Muskogean languages have both *l* and *n*, but Biloxi has only *n* (Haas 1969a, 81–82).

Catherine Callaghan (2014, 422) thought that '**yellowhammer**' (red-shafted flicker) involved wide-scale borrowing in several languages. She compared Proto-Utian **ṭiw(:)ak* and Proto-Yokuts **ṭiwis(a)*, noting that "the feathers of this bird were a much traded item." Woodpecker scalps were considered like money among peoples of northern California, so culturally salient that Wiyot and Yurok have numeral classifiers exclusively for counting woodpecker scalps.

Words for '**dog**' and '**tobacco**' are widespread among Californian languages (Hill 2021, 579). Jane Hill (2021, 579) cites what she calls a "spectacular *Wanderwort*" with forms like *əl-* or *al-* with meanings involving '**bad**', '**evil**', '**ghost**', '**ugly**', seen in languages along eastern California, in the Great Basin, and reaching as far as Hopi.

A very well-known widespread loanword from Mesoamerica is '**cacao**'. Its ultimate source is from Proto-Mixe-Zoquean **kakawa* 'cacao'. It was borrowed into many Middle American languages, for example Nahuatl *kakawa-tl*; pan-Mayan *kakaw*; Purépecha (Tarascan) *khékua* 'cacao, chocolate'; Jicaque *kʰaw*; Lenca *kaw*; Pech (Paya) *kaku*, Guatuso *kaxu*, and Boruca *káu*.[2] The 'cacao' term is spread throughout the Mayan family, though it probably involves internal diffusion at least in some of the languages. If it went back to Proto-Mayan we would expect some of the languages, especially of the Cholan-Tzeltalan subgroup, to have changed the two instances of *k* in *kakaw* to *č* via the regular sound changes in these languages, but that did not happen—all have only cases of *k*, none has *č*. It is, however, definitely not a recent loan in Mayan languages, since it is spelled out phonetically as <ka-ka-wa> in Maya hieroglyphic texts. (See Kaufman and Justeson 2007.)

This word traveled far beyond the territory of its Mesoamerican origin, borrowed as *cacao* into Spanish (from Nahuatl *kakawa-tl*), and then from Spanish on to English *cacao* and *cocoa*, and to many other languages around the world, for example French *cacao*, Russian *kakao*, Finnish *kaakao*, Japanese *kakao*, Mongolian *kakao*, Swahili *kakao*, and many more.

Another *Wanderwort* of Middle America is '**corn**, maize'. Similar terms for 'corn' are shared by several languages there, for example Jumaytepeque, Guazacapán *ayma*, Chiquimulilla *eyma* (Xinkan); Proto-Mayan **eʔm*; perhaps Proto-Otopamean **hme* 'corn' (Kaufman to appear), Proto-Otopamean **hmē* 'tortilla', and so on.³ The original source is unknown.

Another possible *Wanderwort* involves something **made of corn**: Proto-Mayan **wah* 'tortilla', Tuzanteco *wayuʔ* 'to grind corn coarsely'; Proto-Mixe-Zoquean **way* 'to grind corn', **way-e* 'corn dough, pozole'; Proto-Otomanguean **(H)wi(h)(n)* (Rensch 1976), **hme* (Kaufman to appear) 'corn', Proto-Otopamean **hmē* 'tortilla' (note that in some branches of Otomanguean *m* is an allophone of /w/ before a nasalized vowel); Cuitlatec *veye* 'leached corn' (*nixtamal*); Naolan *wii* 'tortilla'; Xinkan **iwa* 'to make tortillas'; Tol (Jicaque) *we* 'tortilla, leached corn (*nixtamal*)', *we pim* 'corn dough' (see also Kaufman 2020a, 240). These forms very probably involve a considerable amount of borrowing, although the sources and directions are unclear, and some of them may be only accidentally similar. It is possible that some of the forms of this set are related in some way to verbs meaning basically 'to eat', as in Proto-Mayan **waʔ*, **weʔ* 'to eat (bread-like things)'.⁴

Another widespread loan involves words for '**turkey**': Proto-Zoquean **tu(ʔ)nuk* (Proto-Mixean **tu:tuk*); Proto-Chinantec **tuL*, ProtoTrique **toʔlo:* / **teʔlo:*; Proto-Otomangeuan **tu*, Juchitán Zapotec *touʔ*; Totonac *taʔhnaʔ*, Tepehua *t'ahniʔ*; Tzeltal, Tzotzil *tuluk'*, Chuj, Jakalteko, Mocho' *tunuk'* (the native Mayan etymon is **ak'*); Tol (Jicaque) *tol-i-*; Tequistlatec *-dulu* /tulu/; Proto-Huave **túli* 'turkey'; Proto-Nahua **tōtol-* 'turkey', Nahuatl *tōtol-* 'chicken', Pochutec *tutul* 'turkey'; Seri *too*. Some of these could be accidentally similar, but most appear to involve borrowing. Terrence Kaufman (2020, 19) noted that some Mixe-Zoquean loanwords with /n/ show /l/ in the recipient languages, Mixe-Zoquean **tu(ʔ)nuk* 'turkey' being a prime example of that; he suggests that this indicates that pre-Proto-Mixe-Zoquean "may have had both *n and *l, or that /n/ had an allophone [l]."

Most of the *Wanderwörter* in South America involve items of salient cultural significance (as they tend to do elsewhere, as well), terms for 'gourd dipper', 'bean' (Tupí-Guaraníán originally?), 'coca' (originated in Boran or Witotoan?), 'maize', 'signal drum' (with connections to 'canoe', 'bench', 'laurel tree', and 'shaman/curer'), iguana' (possibly originally from Cariban?), and 'spider monkey' (perhaps originally from Arawakan?) (Haynie et al. 2014; Epps 2012; Zamponi 2020).

Raoul Zamponi (2020) reported five *Wanderwörter* in many languages belonging to numerous language families in greater Amazonia. They are, with their approximate shapes: *jawi ~ jawar* 'jaguar', probably from Proto-Tupí-Guaraníán; *mana ~ nama* 'path, road'; *mapa* 'bee' (sometimes 'honey'); *masiki*, 'maize (corn)', probably ultimately of Arawakan origin; and *puC(u)* 'termite'.

Martin Kohlberger (2020, 22) notes that while there are few indigenous loanwords in Shiwiar (Chicham, a.k.a. Jívaroan), many of them are *Wanderwörter*. Among the *Wanderwörter* he mentions are words with the following meanings: 'chicken', 'canoe', 'pineapple', 'pig', 'banana', 'piranha', 'fish poison', 'signal drum', 'silvery woolly monkey', 'outsider/white person', and several bird species (Kohlberger 2020, 25–26). The words for 'pig' and 'banana' are ultimately Spanish in origin, though widely spread from language to language;

some other words also diffused widely after contact with Spanish, 'chicken', for example, though the form is ultimately from Quechua (see below).[5]

Epps and Michael (2017, 940) see a connection in Amazonia between the presence of the *Wanderwörter* in the languages there and the "remarkably low levels of lexical borrowing despite the intense, long-term contact among them." They believe this is linked to speakers' conscious efforts to avoid language mixing. They have "the impression that *if* a lexical item is to be borrowed, it is likely to travel widely, possibly because it loses an association with a particular language in the process and thus becomes 'fair game'." (See also Muysken 2012, 252.) Perhaps the distinction between *Wanderwort* and ordinary loanword as well as the motivation they contemplate may be difficult to pin down, leaving room for much more investigation to determine the extent to which such things are in play.

The languages of the Gran Chaco in general resist lexical borrowing, but nevertheless there are a few *Wanderwörter* shared among various languages of the region.

One is '**algarrobo**': Wichí *hʷaʔay*, Chorote *waʔay*, Nivaclé *ɬaʔay* (Matacoan languages); Proto-Guaicurúan **waʔye-k*; Lule <*vaya*> 'algarrobo tree', 'algarrobo fruit'. Algarrobo seeds were a major source of food. Maká does not have an attested cognate to these words in the other Matacoan languages; however, Maká *iniq-ak* 'algarrobo' does appears to involve borrowing from (or perhaps to) Proto-Guaicurúan **inaqa* 'algarrobo', though this may refer to a different species of algarrobo (algarrobo blanco?). There is more to the story, too. Different seasons of the year were named for the principal food plant obtained during that season. Proto-Guaicurúan **inaqá* 'summer, year' (based on Kadiweu *nika:Ga-pi* 'year' and Proto-Southern Guicurúan **inyaGá* 'year, summer') appears to reflect its connection with 'algarrobo' (Proto-Guaicurúan **inaqa*), as does also Maká *iniqap* 'summer, year', and this Maká word does appear to have cognates (or at least similarities) in the other Matacoan languages: Nivaclé *inkaʔap* 'year, autumn, algarrobo season', Chorote *nahkap* 'year', Wichí *nekčaʔ* 'year'. The Matacoan forms bear the -**-Vp* suffix for seasons (Viegas Barros 2013b, 172; Campbell et al. 2020, 128–129, 149).

'**Sweet potato**'/'**manioc**': Nivaclé *pejaya* 'sweet potato', Maká *peXeyeʔ* 'sweet potato', Wichí *piʔyok* 'manioc' (Matacoan); Pilagá *piyók* 'manioc', Kadiweu *-biogo* 'manioc bread' (Guaicurúan); Ayoreo *pehey, pehek* 'manioc' (Zamucoan); Enlhet *pehēyi* or *pehayaʔ* 'sweet potato', Angaité *pexēyé* or *piya ~ pihiya*, Enxet Sur *piheyi* (Enlhet-Enenlhet) (Sušnik 1962; Viegas Barros 2013a, 300; Ciucci 2014, 40). In Enlhet-Enenlhet languages, most masculine nouns begin in /p/, which appears to be a frozen former gender/class marker (Elliott 2021:199). That the Enlhet-Enenlhet words for 'sweet potato' begins in /p/ suggests it has this frozen morpheme in it and that therefore the direction of borrowing was from Enlhet-Enenlhet to the other languages, where the words are monomorphemic, though it does not prove that. It is possible that these forms involve two different sets of borrowings, one for 'sweet potato' and another for 'manioc', though that does not appear to be the case.

'**Parrot** (species)': Wichí *eleʔ*, Chorote *eleʔ*, Nivaclé *ekle* (Matacoan languages); Lule <*elé*>. For other loans in languages of the Chaco, see below.

Adelaar and Pache (2022, 177–179) consider a number of *Wanderwörter* and potential *Wanderwörter* that involve Mapudungun. These include widespread words for 'lightning', 'maize', 'chili pepper'; words relating 'dog', 'jaguar', and 'puma'; and terms approximating *kaka* and *kuku* in numerous languages most frequently referring "to parents' opposite-sex siblings (mother's brother, father's sister) or grandmother, and one may venture that originally %kaka and %kuku may have meant 'father-in-law' and 'mother-in-law', respectively" (p. 178).

9.3. OTHER LOANWORDS AMONG INDIGENOUS LANGUAGES

Native American languages have borrowed from one another, in some areas rather extensively (see Bright 1973), though others have been resistant to lexical borrowing. From the great many examples of loanwords in many languages, only a few cases are considered directly here to give a general idea of the kinds of things that are involved.

Steven Jacobson (1984) identified a number of borrowings in Central Alaskan Yup'ik from Aleut (words for 'albatross', 'dish', 'liquor' [from Aleut for 'water'], 'wooden bowl'), and from Inupiaq (words for 'doll' [from the Inupiaq word for 'person'], 'mother', 'rich man' [from an Inupiaq word meaning 'boat captain, rich man']) (see Mithun 1999, 311).

Pharris and Thomason (2005) identified over fifty loanwords from Southern Interior Salish (Montana Salish-Spokane-Kalispel) to Molala-Sahaptian (or Plateau, mostly to Nez Perce). A sizeable number of them are morphologically complex in Salishan but not in Nez Perce, indicative of borrowing from the former into the latter.

There are Rumsen loanwords in Esselen, and Esselen loanwords into Rumsen, Mutsun, and Chalon (Callaghan 2014, 39–56; see also Shaul 2014, 203–207). Several ceremonial words in Hopi and Zuni are borrowed from Keresan, evidence of Keresan prestige among languages of the Pueblo Area (Shaul 2014, 110–111). Navajo borrowed some words from Tewa: Tewa *bæ:h* (Proto-Tanoan **pe*) 'deer' > Navajo *bi:h* 'deer' and Tewa *aše:h* 'salt' > Navajo *áših* [sic] 'salt' (Shaul 2014, 152). Natchez *kamʔeh* 'huckleberry' (with -*eh* suffix) is borrowed from Chitimacha *kamʔ* 'hackberry' (Kimball 2005, 393, 452).

Although Northern Iroquoian languages resisted borrowing from non-Iroquoian languages, Charles Julian (2010, 8) reported some borrowings among neighboring Iroquoian languages. For example, he cited the following items from the Swadesh hundred-word list of core vocabulary that appear to be have been borrowed into Cayuga from Seneca or another Northern Iroquoian language: -*hsoht*- 'hand', -*ējōhs*- 'heart', -*hskwa*- 'stone', and -*nehs*- 'sand'. He explains that they have irregular reflexes, evidence that they are borrowed; if they had been inherited directly from Proto-Northern Iroquoian in Cayuga, the reflexes would be expected to be -*ʔsoht*-, -*enjahs*-, -*ʔskwa*-, and -*ʔnehs*-, respectively.

Loanwords in the native languages of Mesoamerica have been investigated in more detail than those in North American or South American languages (see for example Campbell 1972b, 1976, 1977, 1978a, 1978b, 1997b; Campbell and Kaufman 1976, 1980; Campbell et al. 1986; Justeson et al. 1985; Kaufman 1976, 2003, 2017, 2020; Kaufman and Justeson 2009; Thompson 1943; Whorf 1943; etc.). Terrence Kaufman (2020) listed several hundred loanwords and possible loanwords in languages of Mesoamerica and their neighbors.

For example, more than a dozen Mayan languages borrowed a word for **town** from Nahuatl *tenāmi-tl* 'wall, fortified town', for example K'iche and Kaqchikel *tinamit*, Q'eqchi' *tenamit*. The direction of borrowing is certain, since Mayan roots are almost all monosyllabic, though this word is polysyllabic in the languages that have borrowed it, and it is morphologically complex in Nahuatl, where the final -*tl* is the bound 'absolutive' suffix (for noun stems in isolation that have no other bound morphology), seen reflected in the final *t* in the monomorphemic loanwords in these languages. The loan reflects the fortification of highland Guatemalan towns during the Post-Classic period with its increased warfare, where previously native Mayan *a:ma:q' was the common term for 'town' in these languages.

In Campbell (1977, 103–109) I identified over seventy loanwords from Nahua into K'ichean languages, many presumably from Gulf Coast Nahua reflecting Toltec influence, and others from colonial times.

Wichmann and Hull (2009) listed some sixty-eight loans in Q'eqchi' from Cholan or Yucatecan, three from Yucatecan, one from Q'anjob'alan, and many from Spanish. While the ones from Spanish are clear, many of their decisions about what to consider loans from the other Mayan languages are questionable on standard criteria for identifying loanwords and for dealing with etymologies. In particular, most of their twenty verbs assumed to be borrowed from other Mayan languages are doubtful, as are a number of the other words, though many others are clearly borrowed.

The proposed loanwords in Wichmann and Brown (2003) are even more questionable for methodological reasons. They listed as possible loanwords from other Mayan languages 50 in Ixil, 134 in Q'eqchi', and 35 in Chicomuceltec. A good number of these are indeed loans (several recognized in Justeson et al. 1985), identifiable as such based on phonological or morphological criteria. For example, in Q'eqchi' *čakmut* 'great curassow (faisán)' is borrowed from some Greater Lowland Mayan language, probably Cholan. In Q'eqchi' it is monomorphemic but has the morphological composition in Cholan of *čak* 'red' and *mut* 'bird'. These are not the Q'eqchi's native morphemes, which are in Q'eqchi' *kaq* 'red' and *ts'ik(n)* 'bird'. Moreover, *čak* 'red' (from Proto-Mayan *kaq) has undergone the Cholan sound changes of *k > č, and *q > k that Q'eqchi' did not undergo. However, a large number of Wichmann and Brown's putative loans are doubtful.

In two Mayan languages, the word for 'dog'—Huastec *pik'oʔ* and Yucatec *pèːkʼ*—is borrowed from Zapotec *biʔku* 'dog' (Otomanguean family) (Kaufman 1980), for unexplained reasons.

Languages of Mesoamerica and beyond have a number of loanwords of Nahuatl origin. Several of these reflect the influence of Spanish in the transmission of vocabulary of Nahuatl origin (Dakin and Operstein 2017). Several were also acquired not directly from Nahuatl but from some other language that had borrowed the Nahuatl term earlier.

Many other examples from Mesoamerican languages could be mentioned.

In South America, some languages have borrowed many words from other Indigenous languages. Terms for numerals are borrowed in many languages. Numerals above 'three' or 'four' were borrowed widely from Quechua and Aymara in pre-Andine languages. Chipaya replaced all of its native numerals above four with Aymaran numerals (van Gijn and Musken 2020, 205). Aymara *pataka* 'hundred' was borrowed into Mapudungun, and then from there into Allentiac, Tehuelche, and Gününa Yajich. Cavineño (Pano-Takanan) borrowed its numerals above two from Aymara (Muysken 2012, 252.) Chamicuro (Arawakan), in the Amazonian lowlands of northern Peru, took its numerals above four from Quechua.

Amuesha (a.k.a. Yanesha', Arawakan family), for example, borrowed extensively from Quechua, with numerous Panoan loans, too (Adelaar 2006; Wise 1976). Most other languages of the Andes and adjoining regions also have loanwords from Quechua and Aymara. Some words have been borrowed widely into several languages. For example, the Quechua word for 'chicken', *atawalʼpa* or *walʼpa*, diffused far and wide after European contact, "through 35 pre-Andine Amazonian languages" and well beyond (Adelaar and Muysken

2004, 500–501; see Carpenter 1985; Hamp 1964; Nordenskiöld 1922; Zamponi 2017, 271; Kohlbrerger 2020, 25). Quechua and Aymara have borrowed a great many words from each other. Aymara has loans from Puquina, for example Aymara *imilla* 'girl' derived from Puquina *imi* 'mother' and *layqa* 'witch' from Puquina *reeqa* (Adelaar 2020, 243).

Raoul Zamponi (2003b, 11) identified loans from Cariban languages in Maipure (a long-dormant Arawakan language). Esmeralda borrowed heavily from Barbacoan languages (Adelaar 2012b, 583). Shiwiar (Chicham family, a.k.a. Jivaroan) overall has few indigenous loanwords, but those that are there seem overwhelmingly to be terms for animals (Kohlberger 2020, 22). Victor Girard (1971a, 138–140) identified several loans into Takanan languages from others, with over thirty loans from Aymara and Quechua mostly into Takana, but also in Cavineña and others, for example Aymara (and Quechua) *kimsa* 'three' > Takana and Cavineña *kimiša* 'three', and Aymara (or Quechua) *walʼpa* 'chicken' > Takana *waripa* and Eseʔexa *waʎipa* 'chicken'.

A. M. Meléndez-Lozano (2014) has reported a number of loanwords from Arawakan languages, from Piapoco and Achagua in particular, in Guajiboan languages. Katarzyna Wojtylak (2017, 110–111) lists several loanwords in Witoto (Murui variety) from Boran, Quechuan, and Tukanoan languages, as well as from Spanish and a few scattered possible loans from a few other Indigenous languages.

Pedro Viegas Barros (2001, 28–40) identified numerous loans and probable loans in Lule and Vilela from various neighboring languages. Fernando de Carvalho (2018b) found loans from Guaicurúan languages into Terena (Arawakan). Although languages of the Chaco generally resist lexical borrowing, Luca Ciucci (2014) found a small but significant number of loanwords in Zamucoan languages, a number from Kadiweu and others shared with Guaykurúan and Matraacoan languages.

A number of loans have been identified between Tupí-Guaraní and some Cariban languages of the northern Amazonian area, and Língua Geral has contributed a number of loans to many of these same Cariban languages (Rodrigues 1985a, 389–392). A few of these were borrowed also into European languages, for example Tupinambá *kwati*, Galibi *kuasi* 'coatimundi' and Tupinambá *naná*; Galibí (and others) *nana* 'pineapple (borrowed as *ananas* in several European languages). Fernando Orphão de Carvalho (2017), on the other hand, rejects proposed cases of Tupí-Guaraní loanwords in Southern Arawakan languages, finding other explanations for them. He does, however, find in Terena, one Southern Arawakan language, "a set of forms that can be reliably traced to a source in one or more Guarani varieties, with Old or 'Jesuitic' Guarani having a fair share of importance in the processes behind the diffusions of these loanwords" (Carvalho 2017, 63–64). Yanomaman has borrowed from Cariban languages (for example from Pemón); Resígaro has borrowed much from Witotoan. Cariña (Carib [Galibi], a Cariban language) and Lokono (Arawakan) in the Antilles and northern South America share many loanwords, while Cariña and Tupí (unrelated languages) also share many lexical items, apparently as a result of diffusion (Taylor 1977, 4). (See also Carpenter 1985; Girard 1971b; D. Payne 1991). Harákmbut and Arawan exhibit lexical borrowings from their Arawakan neighbors (for Arawakan-Arawan borrowings, see Facundes and Brandão 2011). Pedro Viegas Barros (2015) listed quite a number of loans from Yagan to Selknam and Haush, from either Selknam or Haush to Yagan, Haush loans to Selknam, from Kawesqaran (Alacalufan) languages to Chonan languages, from

Chonan languages to Kawesqaran (Alacalufan) languages, from Gününa Yajüch and from Mapudungun to Tehuelche and Teushen, from Tehuelche or Teushen to Gününa Yajüch, from Teushen to Tehuelche, and many loans diffused in languages of Patagonia.

Numerous other cases could be cited.

9.4. LOANWORDS FROM INDIGENOUS LANGUAGES INTO EUROPEAN LANGUAGES

Indigenous American languages have contributed numerous words and place names to the colonial languages that they have been in contact with, and much has been written about them (for some broader treatments see for example Alvar 1997; Carriazo Ruiz 2014; Cutler 1994; Galasso 2007; Kettunen 2021; Morínigo 2008; see references in Dakin and Operstein 2017). English has abundant loanwords from different Native American languages. These are not centrally concerned with the history of the Indigenous languages themselves. (See Silva and Campbell in press for numerous examples and discussion.)

9.5. LOANWORDS FROM EUROPEAN LANGUAGES INTO INDIGENOUS AMERICAN LANGUAGES

Unsurprisingly, most Indigenous languages of the Americas have borrowed words from the dominant colonial languages of their regions, some with only a few, but many others have many such loans (see for example Brown 1999). Native American languages have borrowed words from a number of European languages: from **Basque** (a few Basque loans in Micmac and in some other languages of Canada's Maritime Provinces are the a result of early contact with fishing vessels; Bakker 1987, 1989a, 1989b); from **Dutch** (Goddard 1974a; Swiggers 1985); from **French** (Cuoq 1886; Bloomfield 1962, 23); from **Swedish** (Goddard 1974a); from **English** (many examples; see Bright 1960); from **Russian** (Oswalt 1958; Bright 1960l Jacobson 1984; Bergsland 1986); and from **Spanish** (called hispanisms). Hispanisms are seen in Indigenous languages in California, the US Southwest, and all over Latin America, and there is a huge literature on them. Some better-known or more representative examples are: Bright 1960, 1979, 2000b; Bright and Thiel 1965; Boas 1930; Campbell 1976, 1991b; Canfield 1934; Clark 1977; Fernández Garay 1996; Friederici 1947; Giraldo Gallego 2013; González Casanova 1933; Jara Murillo 2012; Karttunen and Lockhart 1976; Kiddle 1968; Kroskrity 1993, 67–71; Lenz 1940; Morínigo 1931; Muñoz 1993; Parodi 1987, 2017; Shipley 1962; several chapters in Stolz et al. 2008; among many others. (See Dakin and Operstein (2017) and Karttunen and Lockhart (1976) for additional discussion.)

Haspelmath and Tadmor (2009) have chapters on loans in particular South American languages: Epps (2009b) on loans in **Hup** (Nadahup), Golluscio (2009) for **Mapudungun**, Gómez Rendón and Adelaar (2009) for **Imbabura Quichua**, Renault-Lescure (2009) for **Kali'na** (Cariban), and Vidal and Nercesian (2009) for **Wichí** (Matacoan). Most of the loans identified in these chapters are not from other indigenous languages; for example, for Imbabura Quichua 95.3 percent are from Spanish.

9.6. CALQUING

Cases of calques (semantic borrowings) are found in various of the Indigenous languages of the Americas. Many of the ones that have been identified involve semantic influences from colonial languages on various of the Indigenous languages. For example, Tunica (language Isolate of Louisiana) *čukirisa* 'grey oak' (*čuki* 'oak' + *risa* 'gray') is calqued from French *chêne gris* 'gray oak', literally 'oak gray' (Heaton and Anderson 2017, 355). Vincent Collette (2017, 148) lists several calques in Nakota (Siouan) from English, among them *šúga káda* 'hot dog' (*šúga* 'hot' + *káda* 'dog'); *wamnúška wiyą* 'ladybug' (*wamnúška* 'insect, bug' + *wiyą* 'woman'); and *hąwíwiyakpa* 'moonshine' (*hąwí* 'moon' + *wiyakpa* 'to be shiny').

Several of the widespread calques in the Mesoamerican Linguistic Area were mentioned in Chapter 7. As mentioned, examples in numerous languages of Mesoamerica words for 'boa' are compounds based on DEER + SNAKE (seen for example in Nahuatl *masākōwatl* 'boa' [from *masā-* 'deer' + *kōwa-tl* 'snake'), 'egg' calque based on BIRD + STONE, 'lime' based on STONE + ASH (or on ASH alone), 'wrist' based on HAND + NECK, and so on (See also Kaufman 2020a, 244–245; Smith-Stark 1994.)

Though lexical borrowing is largely avoided in several South American languages (as seen above), calquing is frequent in the Vaupés area, "pervasive in place names and ethnonyms, binomial names for flora and fauna, and items of material and ritual culture" (Epps and Michael 2017, 940), as for example in the name of "a regional culture hero": Tukano *o'ã-kó* 'Bone-Son', Tariana *yapi-riku-ri* 'One on the Bone', Hup *g'ə̃g tə̃h* 'Bone Son'; see Aikhenvald (2002, 229), Epps (2013), Floyd (2013)." Alcionílio Silva (1962, 57) and Simeon Floyd (2013, 275–291) show systematic calquing among languages in contact in the Vaupés area, particularly in the domains of place names, ethnonyms, and cosmology.

There are a number of polysemous words in languages of the Chaco where the multiple meanings appear to involve calques that are shared across a number of languages. Some examples are:

fish (the word for generic 'fish') / *sábalo* (a fish species, *Prochilodus lineatus*)
hair / feather / leaf
husband / wife (spouse)
see / find
shirt / dress < 'enter'
trousers < 'step'

9.7. TABOO AND MULTILINGUAL OBSCENITY AVOIDANCE

Words can be avoided and even totally replaced because they sound like other words that are obscene. For example, English *ass* 'donkey, jackass' has largely been replaced by *donkey* or *burro* to avoid sounding like *ass* 'buttocks, backside, the part of the body one sits on', because *ass* 'backside' is obscene (from *arse*). Sometimes, speakers of one language will avoid a word of their language because it sounds like an obscene word in another language in multilingual situations, a process of bilingual taboo avoidance. For example, Spanish *puta* 'whore' is quite obscene. In Nivaclé (Matacoan language) *puta* means 'forest cottontail'

(*Sylvilagus brasiliensis*)', but because this sounds like obscene Spanish *puta*, many Nivaclé speakers replaced this native Nivaclé word with *nanxatetax*, derived from *nanxate* 'Chaco Mara (*Dolichotis salinicola*)' + *-tax* 'similar to' (literally 'the thing like a mara [hare-like]').

Not often but occasionally in language contact the obscene senses of a word in one language can get transferred to another language's word that is equivalent in meaning except for lacking the obscene sense that the foreign word additionally has. In some cases, after a word in the influenced language takes on the obscene meaning from the influencing language, that word goes on to be replaced to avoid the obscenity. For example, in Latin American Spanish *pájaro* 'bird' got extended to include also an obscene sense of 'penis', and for that reason *pájaro* is now often avoided in the sense of 'bird' in Spanish, often replaced by *pajarito* (originally the diminutive form of 'bird', like 'birdy' in English). The taboo 'penis' sense in Spanish of the word that originally meant only 'bird' was taken on by K'iche' (Mayan) and added to the meaning of its native words for 'bird', which originally had no obscene senses. *Ts'ikin*, originally only 'bird', became obscene with the added 'penis' sense, and was then replaced by *čikop*, originally meaning 'small animal', but now meaning 'bird', to avoid the obscenity that is due to influence from Spanish.

9.8. RETICENCE TOWARD LOANWORDS

While it is often assumed that vocabulary is the first feature to be affected in contact situations, resulting in loanwords, as mentioned above many languages have surprisingly few loanwords, but nevertheless do exhibit significant structural parallelisms to other languages. "In these areas speakers often put special efforts into keeping their languages distinct, working to avoid transferring what they are most conscious of: words" (Mithun 2021a, 503; see also Epps 2009, 589; Epps and Michael 2017). Whatever the explanation may be, numerous languages in both North America and South America have been reported to avoid lexical borrowing, instead relying on native material for creation of new words.

Charles Julian (2010, 7–8) reports that "generally speaking, the Northern [Iroquoian] languages have not borrowed vocabulary from non-Iroquoian languages," although he cites "the exception of a very few recent loanwords from European languages, all of which are nouns (e.g. Modern Mohawk /tsihs/ 'cheese' from English *cheese*, and /akwaˈtəht/ 'my aunt', from French '*(ma) tante*')."

Resistance to lexical borrowing is true of most languages in the Gran Chaco area of South America (Campbell and Grondona 2012a; 2012b, 653, 657; Ciucci 2020). Relatively little lexical borrowing occurs in languages of the Upper Xingu Linguistic Area, though some loans exist (Seki 1999, 2011; cf. Epps and Michael 2017, 946), and in languages of the Southern Guiana area there are relatively few loanwords (Carlin 2007). Though Resígaro (Arawakan) was in intense contact with the Bora people, it borrowed very few lexical items, but was nevertheless influenced structurally and morphologically by Bora (Seifart 2011, 182–190; Wojtylak 2017, 19). (See also Epps 2020.)

However, even in the Vaupés region, known for being particularly resistant to direct borrowing, there are nevertheless some lexical borrowings. For instance, Kubeo (Tukanoan) borrowed a good number of words from Baniwa (Arawakan) (Chacon 2013); Alexandra Aikhenvald (2002) mentions borrowings, particularly of verbs, from Tukano into Tariana (an Arawakan language). Rose et al. (2017) report borrowings in Tanimuka-Retuarã (Tukanoan) from different Arawakan sources. Thiago Chacon (2017) analyzes several cases of lexical and grammatical borrowings from Arawakan languages into Proto-Tukanoan and its daughter languages throughout the long history of contact between these families. Epps and Michael (2017, 940–941) report that a "systematic lexical study of ten different Vaupés languages reveals only 2-4 per cent loans in basic vocabulary" (see Bowern et al. 2011, 2014; Epps 2009b). Epps and Michael found "slightly higher levels in flora-fauna and material/ritual culture terms (around 10–12 per cent in Nadahup and Kakua-Nukak languages, lower in Tukanoan and Arawak[an])." In spite of low levels of lexical borrowing, they did find calquing of lexical items across languages (p. 940).

9.9. NEW WORDS THAT RELY ON NATIVE RESOURCES

Though numerous languages have been reported to be intolerant of lexical borrowing, it is nevertheless not the case that the lexicon in these languages is not affected in language contact. The effects of contact are seen, for example, in new words created from native resources involving processes of derivation, compounding, calquing, metaphoric extension, onomatopoeia, and so on.

For new words, various languages of the Gran Chaco rely on a derivational suffix meaning 'similar to' (SIMULATIVE), compounding, and sometimes onomatopoeia. For example, in Nivaclé (Matacoan) the suffix -tax / -itax 'similar to' derives new words for introduced concepts, as in tašinš-tax 'goat' (< tašinša 'grey brocket deer' + -tax 'similar to'), and katis-itax 'flashlight, lantern, lightbulb' (< katiʔis 'star' + -itax 'similar to'). Some new words are created by metaphorical extension of the meaning of existing words. For example Nivaclé siwaklak 'spider' was extended (or drafted) to mean also 'bicycle', and tukus 'ant' to mean 'soldier'. Some other examples created by metaphor include 'flour' < 'dust'; 'lemon' < 'sour;' 'needle' < 'thorn'; and 'wristwatch' < 'bracelet'. Compounding and lexical items formed by lexicalizing phrases gave 'glass' < 'sight goes through it', 'guitar' < 'horse's tail', 'hair of horse's tail'; 'radio' < 'it sings'; 'scissors' < 'knife's legs'; and so on. New words based on onomatopoeia include, for example, Nivaclé k'ututut, Chorote pohpoh, and Maká qofqof, all meaning 'motorcycle' (Campbell and Grondona 2012a).

The following is a sample of terms, listed by their English gloss, for items of acculturation in Nivaclé that use only resources native to the language (Campbell and Grondona 2012a; Campbell et al. 2020, 487–488). The Spanish word from which borrowing might be expected (based on the equivalents of these words in numerous other Latin American indigenous languages that are loanwords, see Brown 1999) is listed in parentheses after the English gloss.

accordion (acordeón): *akloxeš ɬtasxey* < *aklox* 'many' + *-eš* 'VALENCY.INCREASE', *ɬ-* 'ITS' *tasx-* 'seed/eye' + *-ey* 'PLURAL' (= 'buttons'); literally 'many buttons'

bed sheet (*sábana*): *kliminiɬ* < *klim* 'white' + *-iniɬ* 'MADE.OF '

Bible (*Biblia*): *watasinak ɫašiy* (literally 'container of words') < *wat-* 'UNPOSSESSED' + *asina-* 'word' + *-k* 'PLURAL' *ɫ-*'its' + *ašiy* 'container'

bicycle (*bicicleta*): *siwaklak* < *siwaklak* 'spider'
brick (*ladrillo*): *kotsxatitax* < *kotsxaʔ-* 'ground, earth' + *-itax* 'SIMILAR'
donkey (*burro*): *kuwayutax* < *kuwayu-* 'horse' + *-tax* 'SIMILAR' (*kuwayu* is borrowed from Spanish *caballo* 'horse')
flour (*harina*): *klimshi* < *klim* 'white' + *-shi* 'INTENSIVE'
guitar (*guitarra*): *kuwayu łakaʔas* < *kuwayu* 'horse' *ła-* 'ITS' + *kaʔas* 'tail' (literally 'horse's tail')
light bulb, flashlight (*bombita de luz, linterna*): *katisitax* < *katiʔis-* 'star' + *-itax* 'SIMILAR'
machete (*machete*): *klesatax* < *klesa-* 'knife' + *-tax* 'SIMILAR'
motorcycle (*moto*): *k'utuṭuṭ* (onomatopoeic)
needle (*aguja*): *k'utxaʔan* < *k'utxaʔan* 'thorn' (metaphor)
Note: the "needles" used for traditional weaving were long cactus thorns from the cardon cactus (*cardón*) (*Cactaceae, Stetsonia coryne*).
ox, bull (*buey, toro*): *wakatax* < *waka-* 'cow' + *-tax* 'cow' + 'SIMILAR' (*waka* is borrowed from Spanish *vaca* 'cow').
radio, tape recorder (*radio, grabador/grabadora*): *tišxan* < *t-* '3PERSON.ACTIVE *iš-* 'sing' + *-xan* 'UNSPECIFIED OBJECT MARKER' (literally 'it sings').
scissors (*tijeras*): *klesa łkaʔklay* < *klesa* 'knife', *ł-* 'ITS' + *kakla-* 'leg' + *-y* 'PLURAL' (literally 'knife's legs')
table (*mesa*): *yitsakkunjaʔwat* < *itsakkun-* 'eat' + *-ja* 'LIGATURE' + *-ʔwat* 'PLACE.OF'.
table, desk (*mesa*): *watwankʼisxawa*t < *wat-* 'UNPOSSESSED' *wank'-* 'INTRANSITIVE' *-is* 'mark/write' + *-ja-* 'LIGATURE' + *-wat* 'PLACE.OF'.

Some languages extensively use nominalization of verbs to develop new nouns, for example Enxet Sur (Enlhet-Enenlhet) *sēlpextetamo* 'soldier' is literally from 'those who tie us up', from underlying *seg-el-pextet-amo* [1PLURAL.INVERSE-DISTRIBUTIVE-tie-NOMINALIZATION] (Elliott 2021, 162, 645).

It is significant also that the numerous cases of New World languages with resistance against lexical borrowing but with fairly abundant structural borrowing go against the claim that structural borrowing is only possible if connected with lexical borrowing (e.g., Labov 2007).

NOTES

1. Loanwords meaning 'buffalo' ('bison') appear in several other languages as well. For example the similarity between Proto-Kiowa-Tanoan **kon* / **koʔo-n* (Hill 2008, 180) and Atakapa <cokō´ñ, coko´m, coko´n, cokoⁿ´, ciko´m> (Gatschet and Swanton 1932, 115), presumably /šokón/ or something like it, suggests possible borrowing (Campbell 1997a, 271; Hill 2008, 180–181). Haruo Aoki (1975, 191) pointed out the borrowing involving Nez Perce (Sahaptian) *tsú:lim* 'bull, bison' and Interior Salish languages Coeur d'Alene *tsúłum* 'buffalo', Kalispel, Spokane, Colville *stsúłəm* 'bull', and Flathead *stsúłəm* 'bull'. The Sahaptin word for 'buffalo', *talayi*, is a derivative of *tala* 'testes'. Nez Perce also has *qoqá:lx̣*, "a possibly indigenous word for *bison*" (Aoki 1975, 191). This word bears similarity to Kiowa *kɔl* 'buffalo (cow), herd of buffalo', from Proto-Kiowa-Tanoan

*kV⁷,²l 'buffalo (bison)', reflected in Tanoan forms such as Taos kòn and Kiowa kɔl 'buffalo, bison' (Hill 2008, 181).

Incidentally, Comanche has *kuhtsuʔ* 'cow' from Proto-Numic *kuhtsuⁿ-* 'buffalo, cow', but for 'buffalo' ('bison'); according to Swanon (1940, 88, 98) it has *wakate' papi'* (*wakate'* a loan from Spanish *vaca* 'cow' and *papi'* 'wild'—'buffalo' is literally 'wild cow'), which again shows terms for 'buffalo' being borrowed.

2. It is borrowed with the meaning 'peanut' in Xicotepec Totonac and Zapotitlán *kakaw*, Mazahua *kakawa*, and a few others. This appears to be borrowed from Nahuatl, where 'peanut' is *tla:l-kakawa-tl*, literally 'ground cacao'.

3. The Taíno *mahiz* 'maize' could perhaps be suspected of also being connected to this *Wanderwort*, though perhaps it is only accidentally similar. This is the source, through borrowing, of Spanish *maíz* 'maize', from which English borrowed *maize*.

4. It is also possible that some of these forms involve words in languages of Central America that relate to planting (planting corn), e.g., Proto-Mayan **aw* 'to plant (corn)', Proto-Otomanguan **wan* 'to plant corn', Xinkan *a:w'u, a:w'i* 'corn kernel', and several others.

5. Matthias Urban (2018b) compared three similar-looking terms for kinds of shellfish that look plausibly like *Wanderwörter* along parts of the Pacific coast of Mexico, Central America, and South America. Clearly there was active trading of certain shells that were culturally salient for numerous peoples of these zones and beyond, and the phonetic similarities that the languages share do make the hypothesis that they are *Wanderwörter* plausible. Still, there appear also to be other possible explanations, including accidental similarity, meaning that the final decision about the status of these forms as possible borrowings should remain open for the present.

REFERENCES

Adam, Lucien. 1882. *Les Classifications, l'Objet, la Méthode, les Conclusions de la Linguistique.* Paris: Maisonneuve.
Adam, Lucien. 1885. *Le Taensa a-t-il été Forgé de Toutes Pièces? Response à M. Daniel G. Brinton.* Paris: Maisonneuve Frères et Ch. Leclerc.
Adelaar, Willem F. H. 1986. La relación quechua-aru: perspectivas para la separación del léxico. *Revista Andina* 4.379–426.
Adelaar, Willem F. H. 1987. La relación quechua-aru en debate. *Revista Andina* 5.83–91.
Adelaar, Willem F. H. 1989. Review of *Language in the Americas*, by Joseph H. Greenberg. *Lingua* 78.249–255.
Adelaar, Willem F. H. 1990. En pos de la lengua culle. *Temas de Lingüística Amerindia*, ed. by Rodolfo Cerrón-Palomino and Gustavo Solís Fonseca, 83–105. (*Actas del Primer Congreso Nacional de Investigaciones Lingüístico-Filológicas.*) Lima: CONCYTEC/GTZ.
Adelaar, Willem F. H. 2000. Propuesta de un nuevo vínculo genético entre dos grupos lingüísticos indígenas de la Amazonia occidental: harakmbut y katukina. *Actas I Congreso de Lenguas Indígenas de Sudamérica*, vol. 2, ed. by Luis Miranda Esquirre, 219–236. Lima: Editorial Universitaria.
Adelaar, Willem F. H. 2006. The Quechua impact in Amuesha, an Arawak language of the Peruvian Amazon. *Grammars in Contact: A Cross-Linguistic Typology*, ed. by Alexandra Y. Aikhenvald and Robert M. W. Dixon, 290–312. Oxford: Oxford University Press.
Adelaar, Willem F. H. 2007. Ensayo de clasificación del Katawixí dentro del conjunto Harákmbut-Katukina. *Lenguas Indígenas de América del Sur: Estudios Descriptivo-Tipológicos y sus Contribuciones para la Lingüística Teórica*, ed. by Andrés Romero-Figueroa, Ana Fernández Garay, and Ángel Corbera Mori, 159–169. Caracas: Universidad Católica Andrés Bello, Venezuela.

Adelaar, Willem F. H. 2008a. Towards a typological profile of the Andean languages. *Studies in Slavic and General Linguistics* 33.23–33.
Adelaar, Willem F. H. 2008b. Relações externas do Macro-Jê: o caso do chiquitano. *Topicalizando Macro-Jê*, ed. by Stella Telles and Aldir Santos de Paula, 9–28. Recife: NECTAR.
Adelaar, Willem F. H. 2012a. Historical overview: Descriptive and comparative research on South American Indian languages. *The Indigenous Languages of South America: A Comprehensive Guide*, ed. by Lyle Campbell and Verónica Grondona, 1–57. Berlin: Mouton de Gruyter.
Adelaar, Willem F. H. 2012b. Languages of the middle-Andes in areal-typological perspective. *The Indigenous Languages of South America: A Comprehensive Guide*, ed. by Lyle Campbell and Verónica Grondona, 575–624. Berlin: Mouton de Gruyter.
Adelaar, Willem F. H. 2012c. Modeling convergence: Towards a reconstruction of the history of Quechuan-Aymaran interaction. *Lingua* 122.461–469.
Adelaar, Willem F. H. 2017. A typological overview of Aymaran and Quechuan language structure. *The Cambridge Handbook of Linguistic Typology*, ed. by Alexandra Y. Aikhenvald and R. M. W. Dixon, 651–682. Cambridge: Cambridge University Press.
Adelaar, Willem F. H. 2020. Linguistic connections between the Altiplano region and the Amazonian lowlands. *Rethinking the Andes-Amazonia Divide: A Cross-disciplinary Exploration*, ed. by Adrian J. Pearce, David G. Beresford-Jones, and Paul Heggarty, 239–249. London: UCL Press (University College London).
Adelaar, Willem F. H. and Hélène B. Brijnen. 2014. Johann Natterer and the Amazonian languages. *Revista Brasileira de Linguística Antropológica* 6.333–352.
Adelaar, Willem F. H. and Pieter C. Muysken. 2004. *The Languages of the Andes*. Cambridge: Cambridge University Press.
Adelaar, Willem F. H. and Mathias Pache. 2022. Are all language isolates equal?: The case of Mapudungun. *Language Change and Linguistic Diversity: Studies in Honour of Lyle Campbell*, ed. by Thiago Costa Chacon, Nala H. Lee, and W.D.L. Silva, 164–186. Edinburgh: Edinburgh University Press.
Adelung, Johann Christoph and Johann Severin Vater. 1816. *Mithridates oder allgemeine Sprachenkunde mit dem Vater Unser als Sprachprobe in bey nahe fünfhundert Sprachen und Mundarten*. (Dritten Theil, dritte Abtheilung.) Berlin: Voss.
Aikhenvald, Alexandra Y. 1999. The Arawak language family. *The Amazonian Languages*, ed. by R. M. W. Dixon and Alexandra Y. Aikhenvald, 65–106. Cambridge: Cambridge University Press.
Aikhenvald, Alexandra Y. 2000. *Classifiers: A Typology of Noun Categorization Devices*. Oxford: Oxford University Press.
Aikhenvald, Alexandra Y. 2001. Areal diffusion, genetic inheritance, and problems of subgrouping: A North Arawak case study. *Areal Diffusion and Genetic Inheritance: Problems in Comparative Linguistics*, ed. by Alexandra Y. Aikhenvald and Robert M. W. Dixon, 167–194. Oxford: Oxford University Press.
Aikhenvald, Alexandra Y. 2002. *Language Contact in Amazonia*. Oxford: Oxford University Press.
Aikhenvald, Alexandra Y. 2004. *Evidentiality*. Oxford: Oxford University Press.
Aikhenvald, Alexandra Y. 2006. Semantics and pragmatics of grammatical relations in the Vaupés linguistic area. *Grammars in Contact: A Cross-Linguistics Typology*, ed. by Alexandra Y. Aikhenvald and R. M. W. Dixon, 237–266. Oxford: Oxford University Press.

Aikhenvald, Alexandra Y. 2007. Languages of the Pacific Coast of South America. *The Vanishing Languages of the Pacific Rim*, ed. by Miyaoka Osahito, Osamu Sakiyama, and Michael E. Krauss, 183–205. Oxford and New York: Oxford University Press.

Aikhenvald, Alexandra Y. 2011. The wonders of the Gran Chaco: Setting the scene. *Indiana* 28.171–181.

Aikhenvald, Alexandra. 2012. *The Languages of the Amazon*. Oxford: University of Oxford Press.

Aikhenvald-Angenot, Alexandra Y. and Jean-Pierre Angenot. 1989. The South-American Proto-Ge and the Old World. *Explorations in Language Macrofamilies: Materials from the First International Interdisciplinary Symposium on Language and Prehistory*, ed. by Vitaly Shevoroshkin, 403–418. Bochum: Brockmeyer.

Aikhenvald, Alexandra Y. and Robert M. W. Dixon. 1998. Evidentials and areal typology: A case study from Amazonia. *Language Sciences* 20.241–257.

Aikhenvald, Alexandra Y. and Robert M. W. Dixon. 1999. Other small families and isolates. *The Amazonian Languages*, ed. by Robert M. W. Dixon and Alexandra Y. Aikhenvald, 341–384. Cambridge: Cambridge University Press.

Alexander, Edward P. 1971. An Indian vocabulary from Fort Christanna, 1716. *The Virginia Magazine of History and Biography* 79.303–313.

Alexander-Bakkerus, Astrid. 2005. *Eighteenth-century Cholón*. Utrecht: LOT.

Alexander Bakkerus, Astrid. 2006. Phonological interpretation of de la Mata's *Cholón* (1748). *Lenguas Indígenas de América del Sur: Estudios Descriptivo-Tipológicos y sus Contribuciones para la Lingüística teórica*, ed. by Andrés Romero-Figueroa, Ana Fernández Garay, and Ángel Corbera Mori, 61–74. Carácas: Universidad Católica Andrés Bello.

Allen, Louis. 1931. Siouan and Iroquoian. *International Journal of American Linguistics* 6.185–193.

Alvar Ezquerra, Manuel. 1997. *Vocabulario de Indigenismos en las Crónicas de Indias*. Madrid: Editorial CSIC-CSIC Press.

Alvarsson, Jan-Åke and Kenneth Claesson. 2014. 'Weenhayek. *Lenguas de Bolivia*, vol. 3: *Oriente*, ed. by Mily Crevels and Pieter Muysken, 415–465. La Paz: Plural Editores

Alves, Diego Valio Antunes. 2019. *Langue Matanawí: Description Phonologique et Proposition de Classification Linguistique*. MA thesis, Université de la Sorbonne.

Ambrosetti, Juan B. 1894. Apuntes sobre los indios chunupíes (Chaco austral) y pequeão vocabulario. *Anales de la Sociedad Científica* 37.151–160.

Andrews, E. Wyllys, V. 1970. Correspondencias fonológicas entre el lenca y una lengua mayanse. *Estudios de Cultura Maya* 8.341–387.

Anonymous. 1684. The Indian interpreter. Trenton. Salem Town Records book B.64-68, in the State Archives of New Jersey.

Anonymous. 1881. *Taensagini-Tyañgagi / Cancionero Americano en Lengua Taensa*. Em Epinal: Imprenta V. Collot.

Aoki, Haruo. 1963. On Sahaptian-Klamath linguistic affiliations. *International Journal of American Linguistics* 29.107–112.

Aoki, Haruo. 1966. Nez Perce vowel harmony and Proto-Sahaptian vowels. *Language* 42.759–767.

Aoki, Haruo. 1975. The East Plateau linguistic diffusion area. *International Journal of American Linguistics* 41.183–199.

Aragon, Carolina. 2014. *A Grammar of Akuntsú, a Tupian Language*. PhD dissertation, University of Hawai'i at Mānoa.

Aragon, Carolina and Fabricio Ferraz Gerardi. 2022. The typology of grammatical relations in Tuparian languages with special focus on Akuntsú. *Language Change and Linguistic Diversity: Studies in Honour of Lyle Campbell*, ed. by Thiago Costa Chacon, Nala H. Lee, and W. D. L. Silva, 224–241. Edinburgh: Edinburgh University Press.

Arana Osnaya, Evangelina. 1958. Afinidades lingüísticas del cuitlateco. *International Congress of Americanists* 33.560–572.

Arguedas Cortés, Gilda Rosa. 1987. *Los Fonemas Segmentales del Protolenca: Reconstrucción Comparativa*. MLit thesis, Universidad ed Costa Rica.

Arima, Eugene and John Dewhirst. 1990. Nootkans of Vancouver Island. *Handbook of North American Indians*, ed. by William C. Sturtevant, vol. 7: *Northwest Coast*, ed. by Wayne Suttles, 391–411. Washington DC: Smithsonian Institution.

Arroyo de la Cuesta, Felipe. 1861a[1815]. *Extracto de la Gramatica Mutsun, ó de la Lengua de los Naturales de la Mission San Juan Bautista: Grammar of the Mutsun Language Spoken at the Mission of San Juan Bautista, Alta California*. (Shea's Library of American Linguistics, 4.) New York: Cramoisy Press.

Arroyo de la Cuesta, Felipe. 1861b[1815]. *A Vocabulary or Phrase Book of the Mutsun Language of Alta California*. (Shea's Library of American Linguistics, 8.) New York: Cramoisy Press. (Original manuscript 1815: Jesus, Maria et Josp. Alphab^s. Rivulus Obeundus, exprimationum causa horum Indorum Mutsun missionis sanct. Joann. Baptiste.)

Asch, Michael I. and Ives Goddard. 1981. Synonymy. *Handbook of North American Indians*, ed. by William C. Sturtevant, vol. 6: *Subarctic*, ed. by June Helm, 347–348. Washington DC: Smithsonian Institution.

Aschmann, Richard P. 1993. *Proto-Witotoan*. (Summer Institute of Linguistics and the University of Texas at Arlington Publications in Linguistics, publication 114.) Arlington: Summer Institute of Linguistics and The University of Texas at Arlington.

Auroux, Sylvain. 1984. L'Affaire de la langue Taensa. *Amerindia* 6.145–179.

Avelino, Heriberto. 2006. The typology of Pamean number systems and the limits of Mesoamerica as a linguistic area. *Linguistic Typology* 10.41–60.

Azevedo, Gilda Maria Correa de. 1965. *Língua Kariri: Descrição do Dialeto Kipeá*. MA thesis, Universidade de Brasília.

Bacelar, Laércio Nora. 2004. *Gramática da Língua Kanoê*. PhD dissertation, Katholieke Universiteit Nijmegen.

Badini, Riccardo. 2008. Introduzione. *Arte y Vocabulario de la Lengua Lule y Tonocoté*, ed. by Riccardo Badini, Tiziana Deonertte, Stefania Pineider, introzione di Riccardo Badini, Raoul Zamponi, vii–xx. Calgliari: Centro di Studi Filologici Sardi, Operativa Universitaria Editrice Cagliaritana.

Baegert, Johann Jakob. 1771. *Nachrichten von der Amerikanischen Halbinsel Californien*. Translated with introduction and notes by M. M. Brandenburg and Carl L. Baumann, 1952, as *Observations in Lower California*. Berkeley and Los Angeles: University of California Press.

Bakker, Peter. 1987. A Basque nautical pidgin: A missing link in the history of fu. *Journal of Pidgin and Creole Languages* 2.1–30.

Bakker, Peter. 1989a. Two Basque loanwords in Micmac. *International Journal of American Linguistics* 55.258–260.

Bakker, Peter. 1989b. The language of the coast tribes is half Basque: A Basque-Amerindian pidgin in use between Europeans and Native Americans in North America, ca. 1540–ca.1640. *Anthropological Linguistics* 31.117–147.

Bakker, Peter. 1991. Trade languages in the Strait of Belle Isle. *Journal of the Atlantic Provinces Linguistic Association* 13.1–19.
Bakker, Peter. 1994. Michif, the Cree-French mixed language of the Métis buffalo hunters in Canada. *Mixed Languages: 15 Case Studies in Language Intertwining*, ed. by Peter Bakker and Maarten Mous, 13–33. Amsterdam: IFOTT.
Bakker, Peter. 1996a. Language contact and pidginization in Davis Strait, Hudson, Strait, and the Gulf of Saint Lawrence (northeast Canada). *Language Contact in the Arctic: Northern Pidgins and Contact Languages*, ed. by Ernst Håkon Jahr and Ingvild Broch, 261–310. Berlin: Mouton de Gruyter.
Bakker, Peter. 1996b. Broken Slavey and Jargon Loucheux: A first exploration. *Language Contact in the Arctic: Northern Pidgins and Contact Languages*, ed. by Ernst Håkon Jahr and Ingvild Broch, 317–320. Berlin: Mouton de Gruyter.
Bakker, Peter. 1997. *A Language of Our Own: The Genesis of Michif, the Mixed Cree-French Language of the Canadian Métis*. New York: Oxford University Press.
Bakker, Peter. 2006. Algonquian-Ritwan, (Kutenai) and Salish: Proving a distant genetic relationship. *The Forty-first International Conference on Salish and Neighbouring Languages*, ed. by Masaru Kiyota and Noriko Yamane-Tanaka, 1–32. Victoria, British Columbia.
Bakker, Peter and Anthony P. Grant. 2011. Interethnic communication in Canada, Alaska, and adjacent areas. *Atlas of Interethnic Communication in the Pacific*, ed. by Stephen A. Wurm, 1107–1170. Berlin: De Gruyter Mouton.
Bakker, Peter and Hein van der Voort. 2017. Polysynthesis and language contact. *The Oxford Handbook of Polysynthesis*, ed. by Michael Fortescue, Marianne Mithun, and Nicholas Evans, 408–427. Oxford: Oxford University Press.
Ball, Christopher. 2011. Pragmatic multilingualism in the Upper Xingu speech community. *Alto Xingu: uma Sociedade Multilíngue*, ed. by Bruna Franchetto. 87–113. Rio de Janeiro: Museo do Índio—FUNAI.
Ballard, William L. 1978. More on Yuchi pronouns. *International Journal of American Linguistics* 44.103–112.
Balmori, Clemente Hernando. 1967. Ensayo comparativo lule-vilela: sufijos -p y -t, con un breve texto vilela. *Estudios de área lingüística indígena*, produced by Clemente Herbando Balmori, 9–32. Universidad de Buenos Aires: Centro de Estudios Lingüísticos.
Balmori, Clemente Hernando and Diana Balmori. 1998. *Clemente Hernando Balmori: Textos de un Lingüista*. Sada (A Coruña): do Castro.
Barker, M. A. R. 1963. *Klamath Dictionary*. (University of California Publications in Linguistics, 31.) Berkeley: University of California Press.
Barker, M. A. R. 1964. *Klamath Grammar*. (University of California Publications in Linguistics, 32.) Berkeley: University of California Press.
Barrett, Rusty. 2017. Poetics. *The Mayan Languages*, ed. by Judith Aissen, Nora C. England, and Roberto Zavala Maldonado, 433–457. London: Routledge.
Barrie, Michael and Hiroto Uchihara. 2020. Iroquoian languages. *The Routledge Handbook of North American languages*, ed. by Daniel Siddiqi, Michael Barrie, Carrie Gillon, Jason Haugen, and Eric Mathieu, 424–451. London: Routledge.
Bausani, Alessandro. 1975. Nuovi materiali sulla lingua chono. *Atti del XL Congresso Internazionale degli Americanisti*, ed. by Ernesta Cerulli and Gilda Della Ragione, vol. 3: *Linguistica—Folklore—Storia Americana—Sociologia*, 107–116. Rome and Genoa: Tilgher.
Beals, Ralph L. 1932. *The Comparative Ethnology of Northern Mexico before 1750*. (Ibero-Americana, 2.) Berkeley and Los Angeles: University of California Press.

Beam de Azcona, Rosemary G. 2022. The historical dialectology of stative morphology in Zapotecan. *Journal of Historical Linguistics* 13.115–172. https://doi.org/10.1075/jhl.21008.bea.

Beaty de Farris, Kathryn. 2012. *Diccionario Básico del Mixteco de Yosondúa, Oaxaca* (3rd edition). Tlalpán, Mexico: Instituto Lingüístico de Verano.

Beck, David. 2000. Grammatical convergence and the genesis of diversity in the Northwest Coast Sprachbund. *Anthropological Linguistics* 42.147–213.

Beck, David. 2014. Totonacan languages. Presented by invitation at Workshop on the State of the Arts in Mesoamerican Languages, Max Planck Institute for Evolutionary Anthropology. Leipzig, December 6–7. https://d1wqtxts1xzle7.cloudfront.net/39799049/Totonacan_languages-with-cover-page-v2.pdf?Expires=1631395901&Signature=gSMLk-W~Lt2rlBVZmdslwksY~A-VWls9AAUgx9wdw2~W-lApDhwT81RNWNCVc1pISpt-TlKAi5zDoUEZ1aN8zjUbD~S27Dlx2607x9kB5YzJ-VodbR5INDABgoUuKTxjVPwnpT7fTBhLHdQ3ezm1WQm8zU5bahvgzi9PfXJarUbukSa6tZYr9KmD1jSbkPCThlUn54j~WOyioUPV30znToubK6O-FTYwm2uJWw1XIP7Co8CdZZVymscdsVxyBAcW7v2a0-KS-4zMsz7scod-~qdag4mVKegrRBrB30~EwBTFq7Qrr7jkeqN1WP2J4keaY84aFzhoOncCfIz-b6Fxsv7qXA__&Key-Pair-Id=APKAJLOHF5GGSLRBV4ZA.

Beeler, Madison S. 1970. Sibilant harmony in Chumash. *International Journal of American Linguistics* 36.14–17.

Beeler, Madison S. 1977. The sources for Esselen: A critical review. *Berkeley Linguistic Society* 3.37–45.

Beeler, Madison S. and Kathryn A. Klar. 1977. Interior Chumash. *Journal of California Anthropology* 2.287–305.

Beier, Christine, Lev Michael, and Joel Sherzer. 2002. Discourse forms and processes in indigenous lowland South America: An area-typological perspective. *Annual Review of Anthropology* 31.121–145.

Bellwood, Peter. 1997. The prehistoric cultural explanations for the existence of widespread language families. *Archaeology and linguistics: Aboriginal Australia in global perspective*, ed. by P. McConvell and N. Evans, 123–134. Melbourne: Oxford University Press.

Benediktsson, Hreinn. 1980. Discussion: Rask's position in genetic and typological linguistics. *Typology and genetics of language: Proceedings of the Rask-Hjelmslev symposium*, ed. by Torben Thrane, Vibeke Winge, Lachlan Mackenzie, Una Canger, and Niels Ege, 17–28. (Travaux du Cercle Linguistique de Copenhague, 20.) Copenhagen: The Linguistic Circle of Copenhagen.

Bengtson, John. 1991a. Notes on Sino-Caucasian. *Dene–Sino-CaucasianLlanguages: Materials from the First International Interdisciplinary Symposium on Language and Prehistory*, ed. by Vitaly Shevoroshkin, 67–157. Bochum: Brockmeyer.

Bengtson, John. 1991b. Notes on Sino-Caucasian. *Dene–Sino-Caucasian Languages: Materials from the First International Interdisciplinary Symposium on Language and Prehistory*, ed. by Vitaly Shevoroshkin, 67–129. Bochum: Brockmeyer.

Bengtson, John. 1992. The Macro-Caucasian phonology: The Dene-Caucasian macrophylum. *Nostratic, Dene-Caucasian, Austric and Amerind: materials from the First International Interdisciplinary Symposium on Language and Prehistory*, ed. by Vitaly Shevoroshkin, 342–51. Bochum: Brockmeyer.

Bereznak, Cathy. 1995. *The Pueblo Region as a Linguistic Area*. PhD dissertation, Louisiana State University.

Berge, Anna. 2018. Re-evaluating the reconstruction of Proto-Eskimo-Aleut. *Journal of Historical Linguistics* 8.230–272.

Berge, Anna. 2020. Language contact in Unangam Tunuu (Aleut). *The Oxford Handbook of Language Contact*, ed. by Anthony P. Grant, 643–659. Oxford: Oxford University Press.

Bergsland, Knut. 1959. The Eskimo-Uralic hypothesis. *Journal de la Société Finno-Ougrienne* 61.1–29.

Bergsland, Knut. 1979. The comparison of Eskimo-Aleut and Uralic. *Finno-Ugrica Suecana* 2.7–18.

Bergsland, Knut. 1986. Comparative Eskimo-Aleut phonology and lexicon. *Journal de la Société Finno-Ougrienne* 80.63–137.

Bergsland, Knut. 1994. *Aleut Dictionary (Unangam Tunudgusii): An Unabridged Lexicon of the Aleutian, Pribilof, and Commander Islands Aleut Language*. Fairbanks: Alaska Native Language Center, University of Alaska.

Berlandier, Jean Louis and Rafael Chowell. 1828–1829. [Vocabularies of languages of South Texas and the Lower Rio Grande.] Additional manuscripts no. 38720, in the British Library, London. [Cited in Goddard 1979b.]

Berman, Howard. 1973. Review of Lake Miwok dictionary, by Catherine A. Callaghan. *International Journal of American Linguistics* 39.260–261.

Berman, Howard. 1982. Two phonological innovations in Ritwan. *International Journal of American Linguistics* 48.412–420.

Berman, Howard. 1984. Proto-Algonquian-Ritwan verbal roots. *International Journal of American Linguistics* 50.335–342.

Berman, Howard. 1990a. An outline of Kalapuya historical phonology. *International Journal of American Linguistics* 56.27–59.

Berman, Howard. 1990b. New Algonquian-Ritwan cognate sets. *International Journal of American Linguistics* 56.431–414.

Berman, Howard. 1992. A comment on the Yurok and Kalapuya data in Greenberg's *Language in the Americas*. *International Journal of American Linguistics* 58.320–348.

Berman, Howard. 1996. The position of Molola in Plateau Penutian. *International Journal of American Linguistics* 62.1–30.

Berman, Howard. 2001. Notes on comparative Penutian. *International Journal of American Linguistics* 67.346–349.

Bertinetto, Pier Marco. 2021. Zamucoan person marking as a perturbed system. *Studia Linguistica* 75.265–288. https://onlinelibrary.wiley.com/doi/epdf/10.1111/stul.12163.

Bertinetto, Pier Marco and Luca Ciucci. 2020. Reconstructing Proto-Zamucoan: Evidence (mostly) from verb inflection. https://www.researchgate.net/publication/337784892ReconstructingProto-ZamucoanEvidencemostlyfromverbinflection/link/5e66364e299bf1744f-6bae88/download (accessed August 10, 2021).

Bessa Freire, Jose. 1983. Da "fala boa" ao portugues na amazonia brasileira [from the "good speech" to Portuguese in the Brazilian Amazon]. *Amerindia* 8.39–83.

Beuchat, Henri and Paul Rivet. 1909. La langue Jíbaro ou Šiwora. *Anthropos* 4.805–822.

Beuchat, Henri and Paul Rivet. 1910. Affinités des langues du sud de la Colombie et du nord de l'equateur. *Le Mouséon* 11.33–68, 141–198.

Beverley, Robert. 1947[1705]. *The History and Present State of Virginia*, ed. by Louis B. Wright. Chapel Hill: University of North Carolina Press.

Birchall, Joshua. 2014a. *Argument Marking Patterns in South American Languages*. PhD dissertation, Radboud Universiteit.

Birchall, Joshua. 2014b. Verbal argument marking patterns in South American languages. *The Native Language of South America: Origins, Development, Typology*, ed. by Loretta O'Connor and Pieter Muysken, 223–249. New York: Cambridge University Press.

Birchall, Joshua, Michael Dunn, and Simon Greenhill. 2016. A combined comparative and phylogenetic analysis of the Chapacuran language family. *International Journal of American Linguistics* 82.255–284.

Birket-Smith, Kaj and Frederica De Laguna. 1938. *The Eyak Indians of the Copper River Delta, Alaska*. Copenhagen: Levin and Munksgaard.

Blevins, Juliette. 2017. Areal sound patterns: from perceptual magnets to stone soup. *The Cambridge Handbook of Areal Linguistics*, ed. by Raymond Hickey, 88–121. Cambridge: Cambridge University Press.

Blixen, Olaf. 1958. *Acerca de la supuesta filiación arawak de las lenguas indígenas del Uruguay*. Montevideo: Editorial Elea. Universidad de la República, Facultad de Humanidades y Ciencias.

Blažek, V. and John Bengtson. 1995. Lexica Dene-Caucasica. *Central Asiatic Journal* 39.11–50.

Bloomfield, Leonard. 1933. *Language*. New York: Holt, Rinehart and Winston.

Bloomfield, Leonard. 1946. Algonquian. *Linguistic structures of Native America*, ed. by Harry Hoijer, 85–129. (Viking Fund Publications in Anthropology, 6.) New York: The Viking Fund.

Bloomfield, Leonard. 1962. *The Menomini Language*. New Haven, CT: Yale University Press.

Blu, Karen I. 2001. *The Lumbee Problem: The Making of an American Indian People*. Lincoln: University of Nebraska Press.

Boas, Franz. 1886. Mittheilungen über die Lilxûla-Indianer. *Mittheilungen aus dem Kaiserlichen Museum für Völkerkunde* 1.177–182. Berlin.

Boas, Franz. 1889a[1888]. The Indians of British Columbia. *Transactions of the Royal Society of Canada for 1888*. 6/2.47–57.

Boas, Franz. 1911a. Introduction. *Handbook of American Indian Languages*, ed. by Franz Boas, 5–83. Bureau of American Ethnology, Bulletin 40, part 1.5–83. Washington DC: Government Printing Office.

Boas, Franz. 1911b. Chinook. *Handbook of American Indian Languages*, ed. by Franz Boas, 559–677. Bureau of American Ethnology Bulletin no. 40, pt. 1. Washington DC: Government Printing Office.

Boas, Franz. 1930. Spanish elements in modern Nahuatl. *Todd Memorial Volume: Philological Studies*, ed. by John D. Fitz-Gerald and Pauline Taylor, 1.85–89. New York: Columbia University Press.

Boas, Franz. 1933. Relations between north-west America and north-east Asia. *The American Aborigines: Their Origin and Antiquity*, ed. by Diamond Jenness, 357–370. [Reprinted 1973, New York: Cooper Square Publishers.]

Bolaños Quiñonez, Katherine Elizabeth. 2016. *A Grammar of Kakua*. Amsterdam: LOT (Netherlands Graduate School of Linguistics / Landelijke).

Bolnick (Weiss), Deborah A., Beth A. (Schultz) Shook, Lyle Campbell, and Ives Goddard. 2004. Problematic use of Greenberg's linguistic classification of the Americas in studies of Native American genetic variation. *American Journal of Human Genetics* 75.519–523.

Bolton, Herbert E. 1908. The native tribes about the east Texas missions. *Texas State Historical Association Quarterly* 11.249–276.

Bonnerjea, René. 1975. Some probable phonological connections between Ural-Altaic and Eskimo-Aleut. *Orbis* 24.251–275.

Bonnerjea, René. 1978. A comparison between Eskimo-Aleut and Uralo-Altaic demonstrative elements, numerals, and other related semantic problems. *International Journal of American Linguistics* 44.40–55.

Bonnerjea, René. 1979. Some probable phonological connections between Ural-Altaic and Eskimo-Aleut II. *Orbis* 28.27–44.
Bonnerjea, René. 1984. Some probable phonological connections between Ural-Altaic and Eskimo-Aleut III. Orbis 33.256–272.
Booker, Karen M. 1980. *Comparative Muskogean: Aspects of Proto-Muskogean Verb Morphology*. PhD dissertation, University of Kansas.
Booker, Karen M. 1988. The loss of preconsonantal *k in Creek/Seminole. *International Journal of American Linguistics* 54.371–86.
Booker, Karen M. 1993. More on the development of Proto-Muskogean *kw. *International Journal of American Linguistics* 59.405–15.
Booker, Karen M. 2005. Muskogean historical phonology. *Native Languages of the Southeastern United States*, ed. by Janine Scancarelli and Heather Kay Hardy, 246–298. Lincoln: University of Nebraska Press.
Booker, Karen M., Charles M. Hudson, and Robert L. Rankin. 1992. Place name identification and multilingualism in the sixteenth-century Southeast. *Ethnohistory* 39.399–451.
Bouda, Karl. 1952. Die Tschuktschische Gruppe und das Utoaztekische. Die Verwandtschaftsverhältnisse der tschuktschischen Sprachgruppe, by Karl Bouda. *Acta Salmanticensia, Filosofía y Letras* 5/6.69–78.
Bouda, Karl. 1960. Tungusisch und Ketschua. *Zeitschrift der Deutschen Morgenländischen Gesellschaft* 110.99–113.
Bouda, Karl. 1963. Zoque, ein mittelamerikanischer Brückpfeiler zwischen Westasien (Kaukasus) und Peru. *Zeitschrift der Deutschen Morgenländischen Gesellschaft* 113.144–167.
Bouda, Karl. 1964. Huavestudien I: Uralisches im Huave. *Études Finno-Ougriennes* 1.18–28.
Bouda, Karl. 1965. Huavestudien II. *Études Finno-Ougriennes* 2.167–175.
Bowern, Claire. 2019. The mysterious Taensa grammar: imaginative fiction or poor description? (Harvard Whatmough Lecture, 2918.) https://campuspress.yale.edu/clairebowern/talk-on-taensa/.
Bowern, Claire, Patience Epps, Russell Gray et al. 2011. Does lateral transmission obscure inheritance in hunter–gatherer languages? *PLoS ONE* 6/9.e25195.
Bowern, Claire, Hannah Haynie, Catherine Sheard, et al. 2014. Loan and inheritance patterns in hunter–gatherer ethnobiological nomenclature. *Journal of Ethnobiology* 34.195–227.
Braga, Alzerinda, Ana Suelly Arruda Câmara Cabral, Aryon Dall'Igna Rodrigues, and Betty Mindlin. 2011. Línguas entrelaçadas: uma situação sui generis de línguas em contato [intertwined languages: a sui generis situation of languages contact]. *PAPIA-Revista Brasileira de Estudos do Contato Linguístico* [PAPIA-Brazilian Journal of Language Contact Studies] 21.221–230.
Bridges, Thomas. 1933 [from 1879 ms]. *Yamana-English: A Dictionary of the Speech of Tierra del Fuego*, ed. by D. Hestermann and M. Gusinde. Mödling: Verlag der Internationalen Zeitschrift *Anthropos*.
Bright, Jane O. and William Bright. 1965. Semantic structures in Northwestern California and the Sapir-Whorf hypothesis. *American Anthropologist* 67.249–258.
Bright, William. 1955. A bibliography of the Hokan-Coahuiltecan languages. *International Journal of American Linguistics* 21.276–285.
Bright, William. 1957. *The Karok Language*. (University of California Publications in Linguistics, 13.) Berkeley and Los Angeles: University of California Press.
Bright, William. 1960. *Animals of acculturation in California Indian Languages*. (University of California Publications in Linguistics, 4.) Berkeley and Los Angeles: University of California Press.

Bright, William, ed. 1964. *Studies in Californian linguistics.* (University of California Publications in Linguistics, 34.) Berkeley and Los Angeles: University of California Press.

Bright, William. 1970. On linguistic unrelatedness. *International Journal of American Linguistics* 36.288–290.

Bright, William. 1973. North American Indian language contact. *Current Trends in Linguistics*, vol. 10: *North America*, ed. by Thomas A. Sebeok, 713–26. The Hague: Mouton.

Bright, William. 1975. The Alliklik mystery. *Journal of California Anthropology* 2.228–230.

Bright, William. 1978. Karok. *Handbook of North American Indians*, ed. by William C. Sturtevant, vol. 8: *California*, ed. by Robert F. Heizer, 180–189. Washington DC: Smithsonian Institution.

Bright, William. 1979. Notes on Hispanisms. *International Journal of American Linguistics* 45.267–288.

Bright, William. 2000b. Hispanisms in southwest Indian languages. *Romance Philology* 53.259–288.

Bright, William and Robert A. Thiel. 1965. Hispanisms in a modern Aztec dialect. *Romance Philology* 18.444–452.

Brinton, Daniel G. 1859. *Notes on the Floridian Peninsula, Its literary history, Indian Tribes and Antiquities.* Philadelphia: Joseph Sabin.

Brinton, Daniel G. 1885. The Taensa grammar and dictionary. *The American Antiquarian and Oriental Journal (1880–1914)* 7/2.108.

Brinton, Daniel G. 1887. On the so-called Alagüilac language of Guatemala. *Proceedings of the American Philosophical Society* 24.366–377.

Brinton, Daniel G. 1890. The curious hoax of the Taensa language. *Essays of an Americanist*, by Daniel G. Brinton, 452–467. Philadelphia: Porter and Coates. (A compilation [with commentary] of (1) The Taensa grammar and dictionary: a deception exposed. *American Antiquarian*, March 1885, and (2) The Taensa grammar and dictionary. *The American Antiquarian*, September 1885.)

Brinton, Daniel G. 1891. *The American Race.* New York: DC Hodges.

Brinton, Daniel G. 1892a. Chontales and Popolucas, a contribution to Mexican ethnography. *International Congress of Americanists* 8.556–564. Paris.

Brinton, Daniel G. 1892b. Studies in South American native languages (VII): The Hongote language and the Patagonian dialects. *Proceedings of the American Philosophical Society* 3.83–90.

Brinton, Daniel G. 1892c. Further notes on Fueguian languages (IV): The Hongote vocabularies. *Proceedings of the American Philosophical Society* 3.249–254.

Brinton, Daniel G. 1892d. The "Hongote" language. *Science*, May 13, 1892: 277.

Brinton, Daniel G. 1894. On the various supposed relations between the American and Asian races. *Memoirs of the International Congress of Anthropology*, ed. by C. Staniland Wake, 145–151. Chicago: Schulte Publishing Co.

Brinton, Daniel G. 1895. The Matagalpan linguistic stock of Central America. *Proceedings of the American Philosophical Society* 34.403–404.

Brinton, Daniel G. 1898. The linguistic cartography of the Chaco region. *Proceedings of the American Philosophical Society* 37.178–205.

Broadwell, George Aaron. 1991. The Muskogean connection of the Guale and Yamasee. *International Journal of American Linguistics* 57.267–270.

Broadwell, George Aaron. 2005. Choctaw. *Native Languages of the Southeastern United States*, ed. by Janine Scancarelli and Heather Kay Hardy, 157–199. Lincoln: University of Nebraska Press.

Broadwell, George Aaron. 2020. Muskogean languages. *The Routledge Handbook of North American Languages*, ed. by Daniel Siddiqi, Michael Barrie, Carrie Gillon, Jason Haugen, and Eric Mathieu, 397–423. London: Routledge.

Brown, Cecil H. 1999. *Lexical Acculturation in Native American Languages*. Oxford and New York: Oxford University Press.

Brown, Cecil H. 2011. The role of Nahuatl in the formation of Mesoamerica as a linguistic area. *Language Dynamics and Change* 1.171–204.

Brown, Cecil H., David Beck, Grzegorz Kondrak, James K Watters, and Søren Wichmann. 2011. Totozoquean. *International Journal of American Linguistics* 77.323–372.

Brown, Cecil H. and Søren Wichmann. 2004. Proto-Mayan syllable nuclei. *International Journal of American Linguistics* 70.128–186.

Brown, Cecil H., Søren Wichmann, and David Beck. 2014. Chitimacha: A Mesoamerican language in the Lower Mississippi Valley. *International Journal of American Linguistics* 80.425–474.

Brown, Cecil H. and Stanley R. Witkowski. 1979. Aspects of the phonological history of Mayan-Zoquean. *International Journal of American Linguistics* 45.34–47.

Brugge, David M., Ives Goddard, and Willem J. de Reuse. 1983. Synonymy. *Handbook of North American Indians*, ed. by William C. Sturtevant, vol. 10: *Southwest*, ed. by Alfonso Ortiz, 496–498. Washington DC: Smithsonian Institution.

Bruno, Lida and Elena L. Najlis. 1965. *Estudio comprativo de vocabularios tobas y pilagás*. Buenos Aires: Univeresidad de Buenos Aries, Facultad de Filosofía y Letras, Centro de Estudios Lingüísticos.

Buschmann, Johann Carl Eduard. 1856. Der athapaskische Sprachstamm. *Abhandlungen der Königliche Akademie der Wissenschaften zu Berlin* 1855.149–319.

Büttner, Thomas T. 1983. *Las Lenguas de los Andes Centrales: Estudios sobre la Clasificación Genética, Areal y Tipológica*. Madrid: Ediciones Cultura Hispánica del Instituto de Co-operación Iberoamericana, Magerit.

Caballero, Gabriela. 2011. Behind the Mexican mountains: recent developments and new directions in research on Uto-Aztecan languages. *Language and Linguistics Compass* 5.485–504. (10.1111/j.1749-818x.2011.00287.x)

Cabral, Ana Suelly Arruda Câmara. 1995. *Contact-Induced Language Change in the Western Amazon: the Non-genetic Origin of the Kokama Language*. PhD dissertation, University of Pittsburgh.

Cabral, Ana Suelly Arruda Câmara. 2007. New observations on the structure of Kokáma/Omágwa. *Language Endangerment and Endangered Languages: Linguistics and Anthropological Studies with Special Emphasis on the Languages and Cultures of the Andean-Amazonian Border Area*, ed. by W. Leo Wetzels, 365–379. Leiden: CNWS Publications.

Cabral, Ana Suelly Arruda Câmara, Ana B. Corrêa da Silva, Marina M. S. Magalhães, and Maria R. S. Julião. 2007. Linguistic diffusion in the Tocantins-Mearim area. *Línguas e Culturas Tupí* [Tupían Languages and Cultures] 1.357–374.

Cáceres, Natalia. 2011. *Grammaire fonctionnelle-typologique du Ye'kwana, Lange caribe du Venezuela*. PhD dissertation, Université Lumière Lyon 2.

Callaghan, Catherine A. 1964. Phonemic borrowing in Lake Miwok. *Studies in Californian Linguistics*, ed. by William Bright, 46–53. (University of California Publications in Linguistics, 34.) Berkeley and Los Angeles: University of California Press.

Callaghan, Catherine A. 1987. Lake Miwok naturalization of borrowed phonemes. *A Festschrift for Ilse Lehiste*, ed. by Brian D. Joseph and Arnold M. Zwicky, 84–93. (The Ohio State

University Working Papers in Linguistics, 35.) Columbus: Department of Linguistics, Ohio State University.

Callaghan, Catherine A. 1988a. Proto Utian stems. *In Honor of Mary Haas: From the Haas Festival Conference on Native America Linguistics*, ed. by William Shipley, 53–75. Berlin: Mouton de Gruyter.

Callaghan, Catherine A. 1991. Climbing a low mountain. *A Festschrift for Willaim F. Shipley*, ed. by Sandra Chung and Jorge Hankamer, 47–59. Santa Cruz: Syntax Research Center, University of California, Santa Cruz.

Callaghan, Catherine A. 1997. Evidence for Yok-Utian. *International Journal of American Linguistics* 63.18–64.

Callaghan, Catherine A. 2001. More evidence for Yok-Utian: a reanalysis of the Dixon and Kroeber sets. *International Journal of American Linguistics* 67.313–345.

Callaghan, Catherine A. 2014. *Proto Utian Grammar and Dictionary with Notes on Yokuts*. Berlin: Mouton de Gruyter.

Callender, Charles. 1978. Shawnee. *Handbook of North American Indians*, ed. by William C. Sturtevant, vol. 15: *Northeast*, ed. by Bruce G. Trigger, 622–635. Washington DC: Smithsonian Institution.

Camargo, Gonçalo Ochoa. 2014. *Boe ewadaru = A língua bororo: breve histórico e elementos de gramática*. Campo Grande, Mato Gross do Sul: Universidade Católica Dom Bosco.

Camargos, Lidiane Szerwinsk. 2013. *Consolidando uma proposta de Família Linguística Boróro: contribuição aos estudos histórico-comparativos do Tronco Macro-Jê*. PhD dissertation, Universidade de Brasília.

Campanius, Johannes. 1696. *Lutheri Catechismus Öfwersatt på American-Verginiske Språket*. Stockholm: Burchardi. [Reprinted 1937, Stockholm: Almqvist and Wiksell.]

Campbell, Eric W. 2017. Otomanguean historical linguistics: exploring the subgroups. *Language and Linguistics Compass* 11.1–23. (e12240.)

Campbell, Eric W. 2013. The internal diversification and subgrouping of Chatino. *International Journal of American Linguistics* 79.395–420. https://doi.org/https://doi.org/10.1086/670924.

Campbell, Lyle. 1972a. A note on the so-called Alagüilac language. *International Journal of American Linguistics* 38.203–207.

Campbell, Lyle. 1972b. Mayan loan words in Xinca. *International Journal of American Linguistics* 38.187–190.

Campbell, Lyle. 1973a. Distant genetic relationships and the Maya-Chipaya hypothesis. *Anthropological Linguistics* 15/3.113–135.

Campbell, Lyle. 1975a. Cacaopera. *Anthropological Linguistics* 17/4.146–153.

Campbell, Lyle. 1975b. El estado actual y la afinidad genética de la lengua indígena de Cacaopera. *La Universidad (Revista de la Universidad de El Salvador)* January–February 1975: 45–54.

Campbell, Lyle. 1976. Kekchí linguistic acculturation: a cognitive approach. *Mayan Linguistics*, ed. by Marlys McClaran, 90–99. Los Angeles: American Indian Studies Center, University of California Los Angeles.

Campbell, Lyle. 1977. *Quichean Linguistic Prehistory*. (University California Publications in Linguistics, 81.) Berkeley and Los Angeles: University of California Press.

Campbell, Lyle. 1978a. Distant genetic relationship and diffusion: a Mesoamerican perspective. *International Congress of Americanists* 52.595–605. Paris.

Campbell, Lyle. 1978b. Quichean prehistory: Linguistic contributions. *Papers in Mayan Linguistics*, ed. by Nora C. England, 25–54. (Miscellaneous Publications in Anthropology, 6, Studies in Mayan Linguistics, 2.) Columbia: Department of Anthropology, University of Missouri.

Campbell, Lyle. 1979. Middle American languages. *The Languages of Native America: An Historical and Comparative Assessment*, ed. by Lyle Campbell and Marianne Mithun, 902–1000. Austin: University of Texas Press.

Campbell, Lyle. 1984. The implications of Mayan historical linguistics for glyphic research. *Phoneticism in Mayan Hieroglyphic Writing*, ed. by John Justeson and Lyle Campbell, 1–16. (Institute for Mesoamerican Studies, pub. 9.) Albany: SUNY.

Campbell, Lyle. 1985. *The Pipil Language of El Salvador*. Berlin: Mouton de Gruyter.

Campbell, Lyle. 1987. Tzeltal dialects: New and old. *Anthropological Linguistics* 29.549–70.

Campbell, Lyle. 1988a. *The Linguistics of Southeast Chiapas*. (Papers of the New World Archaeological Foundation, 51.) Provo, Utah: New World Archaeological Foundation.

Campbell, Lyle. 1988b. Review of *Language in the Americas*, by Joseph Greenberg. *Language* 64.591–615.

Campbell, Lyle. 1991a. On so-called pan-Americanisms. *International Journal of American Linguistics* 57:394–399.

Campbell, Lyle Richard. 1991b. Los hispanismos y la historia fonética del español en América. *El Español de América: Actas del tercer congreso internacional de el español de América*, ed. by César Hernández, H. de Granda, C. Hoyos, V. Fernández, D. Dietrick, and Y. Carballera, 171–80. Valladolid: Junta de Castilla y León, Consejería de Cultura y Turismo.

Campbell, Lyle. 1993. Distant genetic relationships and the Maya-Chipaya hypothesis. Special Issue: A Retrospective of the Journal of Anthropological Linguistics: Selected papers, 1959-1985. *Anthropological Linguistics* 35.1–4:66–89. (Reprinted from 1973, *Anthropological Linguistics* 15.3:113–35.)

Campbell, Lyle. 1995. The Quechumaran hypothesis and lessons for distant genetic comparison. *Diachronica* 12.157–200.

Campbell, Lyle. 1996. Coahuiltecan: A closer look. *Anthropological Linguistics* 38.620–634.

Campbell, Lyle. 1997a. *American Indian Languages: The Historical Linguistics of Native America*. New York: Oxford University Press.

Campbell, Lyle. 1997b. The Linguistic prehistory of Guatemala. *Papers in Honor of William Bright*, ed. by Jane Hill, P. J. Mistry, and Lyle Campbell, 183–192. Berlin: Mouton de Gruyter.

Campbell, Lyle. 2000. Review of *Language relations across Bering Strait: Reappraising the archaeological and linguistic evidence* by Michael Fortescue. *Anthropological Linguistics* 42.572–579.

Campbell, Lyle. 2006. Areal linguistics: A closer scrutiny. *Linguistic Areas: Convergence in Historical and Typological Perspective*, ed. by Yaron Matras, April McMahon, and Nigel Vincent, 1–31. Houndmills, Basingstoke, Hampshire: Palgrave Macmillan.

Campbell, Lyle. 2011. Review of *The Dene-Yeniseian Connection*, ed. by James Kari and Ben A. Potter. *International Journal of American Linguistics* 77:445–451.

Campbell, Lyle. 2012a. The classification of South American indigenous languages. *The Indigenous Languages of South America: A Comprehensive Guide*, ed. by Lyle Campbell and Verónica Grondona, 59–166. Berlin: Mouton de Gruyter.

Campbell, Lyle. 2012b. Typological characteristics of South American indigenous languages. *The Indigenous Languages of South America: A Comprehensive Guide*, ed. by Lyle Campbell and Verónica Grondona, 259–330. Berlin: Mouton de Gruyter.

Campbell, Lyle. 2013. Language contact and linguistic change in the Chaco. *Encontro Internacional Arqueologia e Linguística Histórica das Línguas Indígenas Sulamericanas* [International Meeting Archeology and Historical Linguistics of the South American Indigenous Languages], ed. by Ana Suelly Arruda Câmara Cabral and Jorge Domingues Lopes. Special issue of *Revista Brasileira de Linguística Antropológica* 5.259–291.

Campbell, Lyle. 2014. How to "fake" a language. *Estudios de Lingüística Chibcha* 33.63–74.

Campbell, Lyle. 2017a. History and reconstruction of the Mayan languages. *The Mayan Languages*, ed. by Judith Aissen, Nora C. England, and Roberto Zavala Maldonado, 43–61. London: Routledge.

Campbell, Lyle. 2017b. Why is it so hard to define a linguistic area? *Handbook of Areal Linguistics*, ed. by Raymond Hickey, 19–39. Cambridge: Cambridge University Press.

Campbell, Lyle. 2018b. Language isolates and their history. *Language Isolates*, edited by Lyle Campbell, 1–18. Abingdon and New York: Routledge.

Campbell, Lyle. 2020a. *Historical Linguistics: an Introduction* (4th edition). Edinburgh: Edinburgh University Press, and Cambridge, MA: MIT Press.

Campbell, Lyle. 2020b. Lexical suffixes in Nivaclé and their implications. *Contact, Structure, and Change: A Festschrift for Sarah G. Thomason*, ed. by Anna Babel and Mark Sicoli, 277–315. Ann Arbor, MI: Maize Books.

Campbell, Lyle. 2021. The historical study of American Indian languages: A forty-year retrospective. *Web of Relationships and Words from Long Ago: A Festschrift Presented to Ives Goddard on the Occasion of his 80th Birthday*, ed. by Lucy Thomason, David J. Costa, and Amy Dahlstrom, 45–61. Petoskey, MI: Mundart Press.

Campbell, Lyle. 2023. Proto-Matacoan reconstruction. (Manuscript submitted for publication).

Campbell, Lyle and Anna Belew. 2018. *Cataloguing of Endangered Languages*. London: Routledge.

Campbell, Lyle, Thiago Chacon, and John Elliott. 2020. Contact and South American indigenous languages. *Handbook of Language Contact* (2nd edition), ed. by Raymond Hickey, 625–648. Hoboken, NJ: Wiley-Blackwell.

Campbell, Lyle, Luis Díaz, and Fernando Ángel. 2020. *Nivaclé Grammar*. Salt Lake City: University of Utah Press.

Campbell, Lyle and Brant Gardner. 1988. Coxoh. *The Linguistics of Southeast Chiapas*, by Lyle Campbell, 315–338. (Papers of the New World Archaeological Foundation, 51.) Provo, Utah: New World Archaeological Foundation.

Campbell, Lyle, Ives Goddard, Victor Golla, and Marianne Mithun. In press. Languages of North America. *Atlas of the World's Languages*, ed. by J. Moseley and Ronald E. Asher. London: Routledge.

Campbell, Lyle and Verónica Grondona. 2010. Who speaks what to whom?: Multilingualism and language choice in Misión La Paz—a unique case. *Language in Society* 39.1–30.

Campbell, Lyle and Verónica Grondona. 2012a. Linguistic acculturation in Nivaclé (Chulupí) and Chorote. *International Journal of American Linguistics* 78.335–67.

Campbell, Lyle and Verónica Grondona. 2012b. Languages of the Chaco and Southern Cone. *The Indigenous Languages of South America: A Comprehensive Guide*, ed. by Lyle Campbell and Verónica Grondona, 625–668. Berlin: Mouton de Gruyter.

Campbell, Lyle and Terrence Kaufman. 1976. A linguistic look at the Olmecs. *American Antiquity* 41.80–89.

Campbell, Lyle and Terrence Kaufman. 1980. On Mesoamerican linguistics. *American Anthropologist* 82.850–857.

Campbell, Lyle and Terrence Kaufman. 1983. Mesoamerican historical linguistics and distant genetic relationship: Getting it straight. *American Anthropologist* 85.362–372.
Campbell, Lyle and Terrence Kaufman. 1985. Mayan linguistics: where are we now? *Annual Review of Anthropology* 14.187–198.
Campbell, Lyle, Terrence Kaufman, and Thomas Smith-Stark. 1986. Mesoamerica as a linguistic area. *Language* 62.530–570.
Campbell, Lyle and Ronald Langacker. 1978. Proto-Aztecan vowels: Parts I, II, and III. *International Journal of American Linguistics* 44/2.85–102, 44.3:197–210, 44.4:262–279.
Campbell, Lyle and Marianne Mithun, eds. 1979. *The Languages of Native America: An Historical and Comparative Assessment*. Austin: University of Texas Press.
Campbell, Lyle and David Oltrogge. 1980. Proto-Tol (Jicaque). *International Journal of American Linguistics* 46.205–223.
Campbell, Lyle and William J. Poser. 2008. *Language Classification: History and Method*. Cambridge: Cambridge University Press.
Campbell, Thomas N. 1983. Coahuiltecans and their neighbors. *Handbook of North American Indians*, ed. by William C. Sturtevant, vol. 10: *Southwest*, ed. by Alfonso Ortiz, 343–358. Washington DC: Smithsonian Institution.
Canfield, Delos Lincoln. 1934. *Spanish Literature in Mexican Languages as a Source for the Study of Spanish Pronunciation*. New York: Instituto de las Españas en los Estados Unidos.
Canger, Una. 1988. Nahuatl dialectology: A survey and some suggestions. *International Journal of American Linguistics* 54.28–72.
Caraman, Philip. 1975. *The Lost Paradise: the Jesuit Republic in South America*. New York: The Seabury Press.
Carlin, Eithne. 2007. Feeling the need: The borrowing of Cariban functional categories into Mawayana (Arawak). *Grammars in Contact: A Cross- Linguistic Perspective*, ed. by Alexandra Aikhenvald and Robert M. W. Dixon, 313–332. Oxford: Oxford University Press.
Carlin, Eithne. 2011. Nested identities in the southern Guyana-Suriname corner. *Ethnicity in Ancient Amazonia*, ed. by Alf Hornborg and Jonathan D. Hill, 225–236. Boulder, CO: University of Colorado Press.
Carlin, Eithne B. and Jimmy Mans. 2014. Movement through time in the Southern Guianas: Deconstructing the Amerindian kaleidoscope. *In and Out of Suriname: Language, Mobility and Identity*, ed. by Eithne B. Carlin, Isabelle Léglise, Bettina Migge, and Paul B. Tjon Sie Fat, 76–100. (Caribbean Series 34.) Leiden: Brill.
Carol, Javier, and Cristina Messineo. 2012. La negación y la formación del léxico en tres lenguas del Chaco. *Lenguas Indígenas de América del Sur I. Fonología y Procesos de Formación de Palabras*, ed. by Hebe A. González, and Beatriz Gualdieri, 115–133. Mendoza: Facultad de Filosofía y Letras, Universidad Nacional de Cuyo; Sociedad Argentina de Lingüística.
Carpenter, Lawrence K. 1985. How did the 'chicken' cross the Andes? *International Journal of American Linguistics* 51.361–364.
Carrera Daza, Fernando de la. 1644. *El arte de la lengva yvnga de los valles del obispado de Truxillo del Peru, con vn confessonario, y todas las oraciones christianas, traducidas en la lengua, y otras cosas*. Lima: Joseph Contreras.
Carriazo Ruiz, José Ramón. 2014. Los indigenismos en el "Diccionario crítico etimológico castellano e hispánico" de Joan Corominas y José Antonio Pascual. *Epos: Revista de filología* 30.147–160.
Carter, Richard T. 1980. The Woccon language of North Carolina: Its genetic affiliations and historical significance. *International Journal of American Linguistics* 46.170–182.

Carvalho, Fernando Orphão de. 2009. On the genetic kinship of the languages Tikúna and Yurí. *Revista Brasileira de Linguística Antropológica* 1.247–68.

Carvalho, Fernando Orphão de. 2013. On Záparoan as a valid genetic unity: Preliminary correspondences and the status of Omurano. *Revista Brasileira de Linguística Antropológica* 5.91–116.

Carvalho, Fernando Orphão de. 2017. Tupi-Guarani loanwords in Southern Arawak: Taking contact etymologies seriously. *Revistas Lingüística* 13.41–74.

Carvalho, Fernando Orphão de. 2018a. Diachronic split and phoneme borrowing in Resígaro. *Canadian Journal of Linguistics* 63.339–358.

Carvalho, Fernando Orphão de. 2018b. Arawakan-Guaicuruan language contact in the South American Chaco. *International Journal of American Linguistics* 84.243–263.

Carvalho, Fernando O. de. 2019. On the etymology of the ethnonym Katukina. *Revista Brasileira de Línguas Indígenas* 2.5–16.

Carvalho, Fernando O. de. 2020a. Evaluation of cognation judgments undermines computational phylogeny of the Arawakan language family. *Journal of Language Relationship* 18.87–110.

Carvalho, Fernando O. de. 2020b. Tocantins Apiaká, Pariri and Yarumá as members of the Pekodian branch (Cariban). *Revista Brasileira de Línguas Indígenas* 3.85–93.

Carvalho, Fernando O. de. 2021. A Comparative Reconstruction of Proto-Purus (Arawakan) Segmental Phonology. *International Journal of American Linguistics* 87.49–108.

Carvalho, Mateus Cruz Maciel de. 2016. Imperatives in Arawá languages. *Línguas Indígenas Americanas* (LIAMES) 16.307–322.

Casey, Nicholas. 2017. Thousands once spoke his language in the Amazon. Now, he's the only one. *New York Times* December 26, 2017. https://www.nytimes.com/2017/12/26/world/americas/peru-amazon-the-end.html (accessed August 6, 2021).

Castellví, Marcelino de. 1940. La Lengua Tinigua. *Journal de la Société des Américanistes* 32.93–101.

Castro, Marcos Araújo, Tiago Ferraz, Maria Cátira Bortolini, David Comas, and Tábita Hünemeier. 2021. Deep genetic affinity between coastal Pacific and Amazonian natives evidenced by Australasian ancestry. *Proceedings of the National Academy of Sciences* 118/14. https://doi.org/10.1073/pnas.2025739118.

Catalogue of Endangered Languages. www.endangeredlanguages.com (accessed September 17, 2021).

Catford, J. C. 1991. The classification of Caucasian languages. *Sprung from some Common Source: Investigations into the Prehistory of Languages*, ed. Sydney M. Lamb and E. Douglas Mitchell, 232–268. Stanford: Stanford University Press.

Ceria, Verónica G. and Filomena Sandalo. 1995. A preliminary reconstruction of Proto-Waikuruan with special reference to pronominals and demonstratives. *Anthropological Linguistics* 37.169–192.

Cerrón-Palomino, Rodolfo. 1987. *Lingüística quechua*. Cuzco: Centro de Estudios Regionales Andinos "Bartolomé de las Casas."

Cerrón-Palomino, Rodolfo. 1994. *Quechumara: estructuras paralelas de las lenguas quechua y aymara*. La Paz: Editorial Plural. (Republished 2008: Cochabamba: Universidad Mayor de San Simón; La Paz, Bolivia: Plural Editores.)

Cerrón-Palomino, Rodolfo. 1995. *La lengua de naimlap: reconstrucción obsolescencia del mochica*. Lima: Fonda Editorial de la Pontificia Universidad Católica del Peru.

Cerrón-Palomino, Rodolfo. 2000. *Lingüística aimara*. Cuzco: Centro de Estudios Regionales Andinos "Bartolomé de las Casas."
Cerrón-Palomino, Rodolfo. 2006. *El chipaya o la lengua de los hombres del agua*. Lima: Pontificia Universidad Católica del Peru.
Chacon, Thiago. 2013. Kubeo: Linguistic and cultural interactions in the Upper Rio Negro. *Upper Rio Negro: Cultural and Linguistic Interaction in Northwestern Amazonia*, ed. by Patience Epps and Kristine Stenzel, 403–440. Rio de Janeiro: Museu do Índio-FUNAI.
Chacon, Thiago. 2014. A revised proposal of Proto-Tukanoan consonants and Tukanoan family classification. *International Journal of American Linguistics* 80.275–322.
Chacon, Thiago. 2017. Arawakan and Tukanoan contacts in Northwest Amazonia prehistory. *PAPIA: Revista Brasileira de Estudos Crioulos e Similares* [Brazilian Journal of Criollo and Similar Studies] 27.237–265.
Chacon, Thiago. 2020. Migration, trade and language contact in Latin America. *The Cambridge Handbook of Language Contact, Vol 1: Population and Language change*, ed. by Salikoko Mufwene and Anna María Escobar, 261–298. Cambridge: Cambridge University Press.
Chacon, Thiago C., and Luis A. Cayón. 2013. Considerações sobre a exogamia linguística no noroeste. *Revista de Letras* 6:6–20 (Taguatinga).
Chacon, Thiago and Johann-Mattis List. 2015. Improved computational models of sound change shed light on the history of the Tukanoan languages. *Journal of Language Relationship* 13.177–203.
Chacon, Thiago and Lev Michael. 2018. The evolution of subject-verb agreement in Eastern Tukanoan. *Journal of Historical Linguistics* 8:59–94.
Chafe, Wallace L. 1964. Another look at Siouan and Iroquoian. *American Anthropologist* 66.852–862.
Chafe, Wallace L. 1973. Siouan, Iroquoian, and Caddoan. *Current Trends in Linguistics*, vol. 10: *Linguistics in North America*, ed. by Thomas A. Sebeok, 1164–1209. The Hague: Mouton.
Chafe, Wallace L. 1976. *The Caddoan, Iroquoian, and Siouan languages*. The Hague: Mouton.
Chafe, Wallace L. 1979. Caddoan. *The Languages of Native America: Historical and Comparative Assessment*, ed. by Lyle Campbell and Marianne Mithun, 213–235. Austin: University of Texas Press.
Chafe, Wallace. 2005. Caddo. *Native Languages of the Southeastern United States*, ed. by Janine Scancarelli and Heather Kay Hardy, 323–350. Lincoln: University of Nebraska Press.
Chase-Sardi, Miguel. 2003 *¡Palavai nuu! Etnografía Nivaclé*, 2 vols. (Biblioteca Paraguaya de Antropología, 45.) Asunción: Centro de Estudios Antropológicos Universidad Católica (CEADUC).
Chamberlain, Alexander Francis. 1910. The Uran: A new South American linguistic stock. *American Anthropologist* 12.417–424.
Chamoreau, Claudine. In press. Purepecha: A non-Mesoamerican language in Mesoamerica. *The Languages of Middle America: A Comprehensive Guide*, ed. by Søren Wichmann. Berlin: Mouton de Gruyter. https://www.academia.edu/27822117/Chamoreau_Forthc_Purepecha_a_non_Mesoamerican_language_in_Mesoamerica.
Chang, Will and Lev Michael. 2014. A relaxed admixture model of language contact. *Language Dynamics and Change* 4.1–26.
Charencey, [Charles Felix] Hyacinthe, [Le Comte] de. 1870. *Notice sur quelques familles de langues du Mexique*. Havre: Imprimerie Lepellatier.
Charencey, [Charles Felix] Hyacinthe, [Le Comte] de. 1872. *Recherches sur les lois phonètique dans les idiomes de la famille mame-huastèque*. Paris: Maisonneuve.

Charencey, [Charles Felix] Hyacinthe, [Le Comte] de. 1883. *Mélanges de philologie et de paléographie américaines*. Paris: Ernest Leroux.

Cheves, Langdon, ed. 1897. *The Shaftesbury Papers and Other Records Relating to Carolina and the First Settlement on Ashley River prior to the Year 1676.* (Collections of the South Carolina Historical Society, 5.) Charleston: South Carolina Historical Society.

Chomé, Ignace. Before 1745 [1958]. *Arte de la Lengua Zamuca*. Published by Suzanne Lussagnet. 1958. *Journal de la Société des Américanistes de Paris* 47.121–178.

Christian, Dana R. and Esther Matteson. 1972. Proto Guahiban. *Comparative Studies in Amerindian Languages*, ed. by Esther Matteson, 150–159. (Janua Linguarum, Series Practica, 127.) The Hague: Mouton.

Christian, F. W. 1932. Polynesian and Oceanic elements in the Chimu and Inca languages. *Journal of the Polynesian Society* 41.144–156.

Church, George E. 1898. Notes on the visit of Dr. Bach to the Catuquinarú Indians of Amazonas. *The Geographical Journal* 12.63–67.

Ciucci, Luca. 2014. Tracce di contatto tra la famiglia zamuco (ayoreo, chamacoco) e altre lingue del Chaco: prime prospezioni. *Quaderni del Laboratorio di Linguistica della Scuola Normale Superiore di Pisa* 13.1–52.

Ciucci, Luca. 2020. Matter borrowing, pattern borrowing and typological rarities in the Gran Chaco of South America. *Morphology* 30.283–310.

Ciucci, Luca and Pier Marco Bertinetto. 2015. A diachronic view of the Zamucoan verb inflection. *Folia Linguistica Historica* 36.19–87.

Claesson, Kenneth. 1994. A phonological outline of Mataco-Noctenes. *International Journal of American Linguistics* 60.1–38.

Clairis, Christos. 1978. La lengua qawasqar. *Vicus Cuadernos: Lingüística* 2.29–44.

Clairis, Christos. 1985. Indigenous languages of Tierra del Fuego. *South American Indian Languages: Retrospect and Prospect*, ed. by Harriet E. Manelis Klein and Louisa R. Stark, 753–783. Austin: University of Texas Press.

Clark, Jorie, Anders E. Carlson, Alberto V. Reyes, Elizabeth C. B. Carlson, Louise Guillaume, Glenn A. Milne, Lev Tarasov, Marc Caffee, Klaus Wilcken, and Dylan H. Rood. 2022. The age of the opening of the Ice-Free Corridor and implications for the peopling of the Americas. *PNAS* |119 (14) e2118558119. https://doi.org/10.1073/pnas.2118558119.

Clark, Lawrence E. 1977. Linguistic acculturation in Sayula Popoluca. *International Journal of American Linguistics* 43.128–138.

Clemens, Lauren. 2020. Mayan languages. *The Routledge Handbook of North American Languages*, ed. by Daniel Siddiqi, Michael Barrie, Carrie Gillon, Jason Haugen, and Eric Mathieu, 365–396. London: Routledge.

Colarusso, John. 1985. Pharyngeals and pharyngealization in Salishan and Wakashan. *International Journal of American Linguistics* 51.366–368.

Collette, Vincent. 2017. Nakota linguistic acculturation. *Anthropological Linguistics* 59.17–162.

Collins, June M. 1949. Distribution of the Chemakum language. Indians of the urban Northwest, ed. by Marian W. Smith, 147–160. New York: Columbia University Press.

Combès, Isabelle. 2012. Susnik y los gorgotoquis: Efervescencia étnica en la Chiquitania (Oriente boliviano). *Indiana* 29.201–220. https://doi:10.18441/ind.v29i0.201-220.

Comrie, Bernard, Lucía A. Golluscio, Hebe González, and Alejandra Vidal. 2010. El Chaco como área lingüística. *Estudios de Lenguas Amerindias 2: Contribuciones al Estudio de las Lenguas Originarias de América*, ed. by Zarina Estrada Fernández and Ramón Arzápalo Marín, 85–132. Hermosillo, Sonora, Mexico: Editorial Universidad de Sonora.

Conathan, Lisa. 2004. *The Linguistic Ecology of Northwestern California: Contact, Functional Convergence and Dialectology*. PhD dissertation, University of California, Berkeley.
Constenla Umaña, Adolfo. 1987. Elementos de fonología comparada de las lenguas misumalpas. *Filología y Lingüística* 13.129–61.
Constenla Umaña, Adolfo. 1991. *Las lenguas del área intermedia: introducción a su estudio areal*. San José: Editorial de la Universidad de Costa Rica.
Constenla Umaña, Adolfo. 2002. Acerca de la relación genealógica de las lenguas lencas y las lenguas misumalpas. *Revista de Filología y Lingüística* 28.189–205.
Constenla Umaña, Adolfo. 2012. Chibchan languages. *The Indigenous Languages of South America: A Comprehensive Guide*, ed. by Lyle Campbell and Verónica Grondona, 391–440. Berlin: Mouton de Gruyter.
Constenla Umaña, Adolfo and Enrique Margery Peña. 1991. Elementos de fonología comparada Chocó. *Filología y Lingüística* 17.137–191.
Conzemius, Eduard. 1930. Une tribu inconnue de Costa-Rica: Les indiens Rama du Rio Zapote. *L'Anthropologie* 40.93–108.
Cook, Eung-Do. 1981. Athapaskan linguistics: Proto-Athapaskan phonology. *Annual Review of Anthropology* 10.253–273.
Cook, Eung-Do and Keren D. Rice. 1989. Introduction. *Athapaskan Linguistics: Current Perspectives on a Language Family*, ed. by Eung-Do Cook and Keren D. Rice, 1–61. Berlin: Mouton de Gruyter.
Coppens, Walter. 1983. Los Hoti. *Los Aborigenes de Venezuela*, vol. 2 (Monografía / Fundación la Salle 29), ed. by Walter Coppens, 243–302. Caracas: Fundación la Salle.
Cortina-Borja, Mario, Jane Stuart-Smith, and Leopoldo Valiñas-Coalla. 2002. Multivariate classification methods for lexical and phonological dissimilarities and their application to the Uto-Aztecan family. *Journal of Quantitative Linguistics* 9.97–124.
Cortina-Borja, Mario and Leopoldo Valinas C. 1989. Some remarks on Uto-Aztecan classification. *International Journal of American Linguistics* 55.214–239.
Craig, Colette and Kenneth Hale. 1992. A possible Macro-Chibchan etymon. *Anthropological Linguistics* 34.173–201.
Crawford, James M. 1973. Yuchi phonology. *International Journal of American Linguistics* 39.173–179.
Crawford, James M. 1975. Southeastern Indian languages. *Studies in Southeastern Indian Languages*, ed. by James M. Crawford, 1–120. Athens: University of Georgia Press.
Crawford, James M. 1978. *The Mobilian Trade Language*. Knoxville: University of Tennessee Press.
Crawford, James M. 1979. Timucua and Yuchi: Two language isolates of the Southeast. *The Languages of Native America: Historical and Comparative Assessment*, ed. by Lyle Campbell and Marianne Mithinn, 327–354. Austin: University of Texas Press.
Crawford, James M. 1988. On the Relationship of Timucua to Muskogean. *In Honor of Mary Haas: From the Haas Festival Conference on Native America Linguistics*, ed. by William Shipley, 157–164. Berlin: Mouton de Gruyter.
Créqui-Montfort, G. de and Paul Rivet. 1925–1927. La langue uru ou pukina. *Journal de la Société des Américanistes de Paris* 17.211–244, 18.111–139, 19.57–116.
Crevels, Mily. 2012. Language endangerment in South America: The clock is ticking. *The Indigenous Languages of South America: A Comprehensive Guide*, ed. by Lyle Campbell and Verónica Grondona, 167–234. Berlin: Mouton de Gruyter.

Crevels, Mily and Hein van der Voort. 2008. The Guaporé-Mamoré region as a linguistic area. *From Linguistic Areas to Areal Linguistics*, ed. by Pieter Muysken, 151–179. Amsterdam: John Benjamins.

Crevels, Mily and Hein van der Voort. 2020. Areal diffusion of applicatives in the Amazon. *Advances in Contact Linguistics: In Honour of Pieter Muysken*, ed. By Norval Smith, Tonjes Veenstra, and Enoch Oladé Aboh, 180–216. Amsterdam: John Benjamins.

Croese, Robert A. 1985. Mapuche dialect survey. *South American Indian Languages: Retrospect and Prospect*, ed. by Harriet Manelis Klein and Louisa R. Stark, 784–801. Austin, Texas: University of Texas Press.

Cronhamn, Sandra. 2013. *The spread of cultural vocabulary in Rondônia: a study of borrowability in the semantic fields of religion and agriculture.* BA thesis, Lund University.

Cruz, Aline da. 2011. *Fonologia e gramática do Nheengatú: a língua geral falada pelos povos Baré, Warekena e Baniwa*. Utrecht: LOT.

Cuoq, Jean-André. 1886. *Lexique de la Langue Algonquine*. Montreal: J. Chapleau et Fils.

Curnow, Timothy J. 1998. Why Paez is not a Barbacoan language: The non-existence of "Moguex" and the use of early sources. *International Journal of American Linguistics* 64.338–351.

Curnow, Timothy J. and Anthony J. Liddicoat. 1998. The Barbacoan languages of Colombia and Ecuador. *Anthropological Linguistics* 40.384–408.

Cutler, Charles L. 1994. *O Brave New Words!: Native American Loanwords in Current English*. Norman: University of Oklahoma Press.

Dakin, Karen. 1982. The characteristics of a Nahuatl Lingua Franca. *Texas Linguistic Forum* 18.55–67.

Dakin, Karen. 2001. Isoglosas e innovaciones yutoaztecas. *Avances y Balances de Lenguas Yutoaztecas*, ed. By Jose Luis Moctezuma Zammarrón and Jane H. Hill, 313–344. Mexico City: Instituto Nacional de Antropología e Historia.

Dakin, Karen. 2010. Lenguas francas y lenguas locales en la época prehispánica. *Historia sociolingüística de México*, Vol. 1: *México prehispánico y colonial*, ed. By Rebeca Barriga Villanueva and Pedro Martín Butragueño, 161–183. Mexico City: El Colegio de México.

Dakin, Karen and Natalie Operstein. 2017. Language contact in Mesoamerica and beyond. *Language Contact and Change in Mesoamerica and Beyond*, ed. by Karen Dakin, Claudia Parodi and Natalie Operstein, 1–28. Amsterdam: John Benjamins

Danielsen, Swintha, Michael Dunn, and Pieter Muysken. 2011. The role of contact in the spreading of Arawak languages. *Ethnicity in Ancient Amazonia: Reconstructing Past Identities from Archaeology, Linguistics, and Ethnohistory*, ed. by Alf Hornborg and Jonathan D. Hill, 173–196. Boulder: University Press of Colorado.

Dangel, Richard. 1930. Quechua and Maori. *Mitteilungen der Anthropologische Gesellschaft in Wien* 60.343–51.

Darnell, Regna. 1969. *The development of American anthropology 1879–1920: From the Bureau of American Ethnology to Franz Boas*. PhD dissertation, University of Pennsylvania.

Dávila Garibi, J. I. 1935. Recopilación de datos acerca del idioma coca y de su posible influencia en el lenguage folklórico de Jalisco. *Investigaciones Lingüísticas* 3.248–302.

Dávila Garibi, J. I. 1942. Algunas afinidades de las lenguas coca y cahita. *El México Antiguo* 6.47–60.

Davis, Henry. 2019. Salish languages. *The Routledge Handbook of North American Languages*, ed. by Daniel Siddiqi, Michael Barrie, Carrie Gillon, Jason Haugen, and Eric Mathieu, 452–472. London: Routledge.

Davis, Irvine. 1959. Linguistic clues to northern Rio Grande prehistory. *El Palacio* 66.73–84.

Davis, Irvine. 1966. Comparative Jê phonology. *Estudos Lingüísticos* 1/2.10–24.
Davis, Irvine. 1968. Some Macro-Jê relationships. *International Journal of American Linguistics* 34.42–47. [Reprinted 1985, in: *South American Indian Languages: Retrospect and Prospect*, ed. by Harriet E. Manelis Klein and Louisa R. Stark, 287–303. Austin: University of Texas Press.]
Davis, Irvine. 1979. The Kiowa-Tanoan, Keresan, and Zuni languages. *The Languages of Native America: Historical and Comparative Assessment*, ed. by Lyle Campbell and Marianne Mithun, 390–443. Austin: University of Texas Press.
Davis, Irvine. 1989. A new look at Aztec-Tanoan. *General and Amerindian Ethnolinguistics: In Remembrance of Stanley Newman*, ed. by Mary Ritchie Key and Henry M. Hoenigswald, 365–790. Berlin: Mouton de Gruyter.
Day, Gordon M. and Bruce G. Trigger. 1978. Algonquin. *Handbook of North American Indians*, ed. by William C. Sturtevant, vol. 15: *Northeast*, ed. by Bruce G. Trigger, 792–797. Washington DC: Smithsonian Institution.
De Angulo, Jaime and L. S. Freeland. 1925. The Chontal language (dialect of Tequixistlan). *Anthropos* 20.1032–1052.
de Goeje, Claudius Henricus. 1906. Handelsdialekt, tussen Aucaners en Indianen gebruikelijk (Handelsdialekt, gebrauchlich zwischen Aucanern und Indianern). *Bijdrage tot de ethnographie der surinaamsche Indianen*. Supplement to *Internationales Archiv fur Ethnographie* 17.109–111.
de Goeje, Claudius Henricus. 1908. De "handelstaal" der Joeka's met de Trio's en de Ojana's. Appendix to *Verslag van Toemoekhoemak-expeditie*, 204–219. Leiden: Brill.
de Goeje, Claudius Henricus. 1909. Etudes linguistiques Caraïbes. *Verhandelingen der Koninklijke Nederlandse Akademie van Wetenschappen te Amsterdam*, Afdeeling Letterkunde, nieuwe reeks 10, no. 3, 316–317. Amsterdam: J. Müller.
de Goeje, Claudius Henricus. 1946. *Études linguistiques Caraïbes*, vol. 2: *Verhandelingen der Koninklijke Nederlandse Akademie van Wetenschappen te Amsterdam*, Afdeeling Letterkunde n.s. 40/2.101–102.
De Laguna, Frederica. 1937. *A Preliminary Sketch of the Eyak Indians, Copper River Delta, Alaska*. (Publications of the Philadelphia Anthropological Society, 1.). Twenty-fifth anniversary studies, ed. by D. S. Davidson. Philadelphia: University of Pennsylvania Press.
De Laguna, Frederica. 1990a. Eyak. *Handbook of North American Indians*, ed. by William C. Sturtevant, vol. 7: *Northwest Coast*, ed. by Wayne Suttles, 189–196. Washington DC: Smithsonian Institution.
De Laguna, Frederica. 1990b. Tlingit. *Handbook of North American Indians*, ed. by William C. Sturtevant, vol. 7: *Northwest Coast*, ed. by Wayne Suttles, 203–228. Washington DC: Smithsonian Institution.
De Reuse, Willem J. 1983. Synonymy. *Handbook of North American Indians*, ed. by William C. Sturtevant, vol. 10: *Southwest*, ed. by Alfonso Ortiz, 385–392. Washington DC: Smithsonian Institution.
de Reuse, Willem J. 1996. Chukchi, English, and Eskimo: A survey of jargons in the Chukotka Peninsula area. *Language Contact in the Arctic*, ed. by Ernst Hakon Jahr and Ingvild Broch, 47–62. Berlin: De Gruyter Mouton.
del Hoyo, Eugenio. *See* Hoyo, Eugenio del.
de la Fuente, Constanza, J. Víctor Moreno-Mayar, and Maanasa Raghavan. 2021. Early peopling of the Americas. *Human Migration: Biocultural Perspectives*, ed. by Maria de Lourdes Muñoz-Moreno and Michael H. Crawford, 32–46 Oxford: Oxford University Press.

DeLancey, Scott. 1992. Klamath and Sahaptian numerals. *International Journal of American Linguistics* 58.235–230.
DeLancey, Scott. 2018. Evidence for Inland Penutian. *Anthropological Linguistics* 60.95–109.
DeLancey, Scott, Carol Genetti, and Noel Rude. 1988. Some Sahaptian-Klamath-Tsimshianic lexical sets. *In Honor of Mary Haas: From the Haas Festival Conference on Native America Linguistics*, ed. by William Shipley, 195–224. Berlin: Mouton de Gruyter.
DeLancey, Scott and Victor Golla. 1997. The Penutian hypothesis: Retrospect and prospect. *International Journal of American Linguistics* 63.171–202.
Delbrück, Berthold. 1888. *Altindische Syntax*. (Syntaktische Forschungen, no. 5.) Halle an der Saale: Niemeyer.
Delbrück, Berthold. 1893–1900. *Vergleichende Syntax der Indogermanischen Sprachen.* (Teil 3, Karl Brugmann and Berthold Delbrück. 1900. *Grundriss der vergleichenden Grammatik der indogermanischen Sprachen*.) Strassburg: K.J. Trübner.
Denison, Thomas S. 1913. *Mexican Linguistics: Including Nauatl or Mexican in Aryan Phonology, the Primitive Aryans of America, a Mexican-Aryan Comparative Vocabulary, Morphology and the Mexican Verb, and the Mexican-Aryan Sibilants, with an Appendix on Comparative Syntax*. Chicago: T. S. Denison and Company.
Derbyshire, Desmond C. 1986. Comparative survey of morphology and syntax in Brazilian Arawakan. *Handbook of Amazonian Languages*, ed. by Desmond C. Derbyshire and Geoffrey K. Pullum, vol. 1, 469–566. Berlin: Mouton de Gruyter.
Derbyshire, Desmond C. 1987. Morphosyntactic areal characteristics of Amazonian languages. *International Journal of American Linguistics* 53.311–326.
Derbyshire, Desmond C. 1992. Arawakan languages. *International Encyclopedia of Linguistics*, ed. by William Bright, 1.102–105. New York: Oxford University Press.
Derbyshire, Desmond C. 1999. Carib. *The Amazonian Languages*, ed. by R. M. W. Dixon and Alexandra Y. Aikhenvald, 23–64. Cambridge: Cambridge University Press.
Derbyshire, Desmond C. and Doris L. Payne. 1990. Noun classification systems of Amazonian languages. *Amazonian Linguistics: Studies in Lowland South American Languages*, ed. by Doris L. Payne, 243–271. Austin: University of Texas Press.
Derbyshire, Desmond and Geoffrey Pullum. 1986. Introduction. *Handbook of Amazonian Languages*, ed. by Desmond Derbyshire and Geoffrey Pullum, vol. 1, 1–28. Berlin: Mouton de Gruyter.
Derbyshire, Desmond and Geoffrey Pullum. 1991. Introduction. *Handbook of Amazonian Languages,* ed. Desmond C. Derbyshire and Geoffrey K. Pullum, vol. 3, 3–18. Berlin: Mouton de Gruyter.
Díaz Romero, Camilo Enrique. 2021. *Atlas Tipológico-Holístico de Lenguas Indígenas de Colombia*. Bogotá: Palma Arismendi Editor, ebookvuh. https://ebookvuh.com/.
Dienst, Stefan. 2008. The internal classification of the Arawan language. *LIAMES (Línguas Indígenas Americanas)* 8.61–67.
Dietrich, Wolf. 2007. Nuevos aspectos de la posición del conjunto chiriguano (Guaraní del Chaco Boliviano) dentro de las lenguas tupí-guaraníes bolivianas. *Lenguas indígenas de América del Sur: estudios descriptivo-tipológicos y sus contribuciones para la lingüística teórica*, ed. by Andrés Romero-Figuera, Ana Fernández Garay, and Ángel Corbera Mori, 9–18. Caracas: Universidad Católica Andrés Bello.
Dietrich, Wolf. 2010. Lexical evidence for a redefinition of Paraguayan "Jopara." STUF [*Language Typology and Universals*] 63.39–51.
Dixon, R. M. W. 1999. Arawá. *The Amazonian Languages*, ed. by R. M. W. Dixon and Alexandra Y. Aikhenvald, 293–306. Cambridge: Cambridge University Press.

Dixon, R. M. W. 2004. Poto-Arawá phonology. *Anthropological Linguistics* 46.1–83.
Dixon, R. M. W. and Alexandra Y. Aikhenvald. 1999. Introduction. *The Amazonian Languages*, ed. by Robert M. W. Dixon and Alexandra Y. Aikhenvald, 1–21. Cambridge: Cambridge University Press.
Dixon, Roland B. 1905. The Shasta-Achomawi: A new linguistic stock, with four new dialects. *American Anthropologist* 7.213–217.
Dixon, Roland. 1907[1906]. Linguistic relationships within the Shasta-Achomawi stock. *International Congress of Americanists* 15/2.255–263 [1906 meeting]. Quebec.
Dixon, Roland. 1910. The Chimariko Indians and language. *University of California Publications in American Archaeology and Ethnology* 5.295–380.
Dixon, Roland B. and Alfred L. Kroeber. 1903. The native languages of California. *American Anthropologist* 5.1–26.
Dixon, Roland and Alfred L. Kroeber. 1913a. Relationship of the Indian languages of California. *Science* 37.225.
Dixon, Roland B. and Kroeber, A. L. 1913b. New linguistic families in California. *American Anthropologist* 15.647–655.
Dixon, Roland and Alfred L. Kroeber. 1919. Linguistic families of California. *University of California Publications in American Archaeology and Ethnology* 16.47–118.
Dobrizhoffer, Martin. 1784. *Historia de Abiponibus, equestri bellicosaque Paraquariae natione, locupletata copiosis barbarorum gentium, urbium, fluminum, ferarum, amphibiorum, insectorum, serpentium praecipuorum, piscium, avium, arborum, plantarum aliarumque ejusdem provinciae proprietatum observationibus*. Vienna: Joseph Nob. De Kuzbek.
D'Orbigny, Alcide Dressalines. 1839. *L'Homme Américain (de l'Amérique Méridionale) consideré sous ses rapports physiologiques et moraux*. 2 volumes. Paris: Pitois-Levrault. (Spanish translation: 1944. *El hombre americano: considerado en sus aspectos fisiológicos y morales* [translated by Alfredo Cepeda]. Buenos Aires: Editorial Futuro.)
Dorais, Louis-Jacques. 2010. *The Language of the Inuit: Syntax, Semantics and Society in the Arctic*. Montreal: MccGill-Queen's University Press.
Dorsey, J. Owen. 1885. On the comparative phonology of four Siouan languages. *Annual Report of the Board of Regents of the Smithsonian Institution* [1883], 919–929. Washington DC: Government Printing Office.
Douay, León. 1888. Contribution a l'américanisme du Cauca (Colombie). *Compte-Rendu du Congrès International des Américanistes* 7. 763–786.
Drechsel, Emanuel J. 1979. *Mobilian Jargon: Linguistic, sociocultural, and historical aspects of an American Indian lingua franca*. PhD dissertation, University of Wisconsin, Madison.
Drechsel, Emanuel J. 1983a. The question of the lingua franca Creek. *Proceedings of the 1982 Mid-America linguistics conference*, ed. by Frances Ingemann, 388–400. Lawrence: Departement of Linguistics, University of Kansas.
Drechsel, Emanuel J. 1983b. Towards an ethnohistory of speaking: the case of Mobilian Jargon, an American Indian pidgin of the lower Mississippi Valley. *Ethnohistory* 30.165–176.
Drechsel, Emanuel J. 1984. Structure and function in Mobilian Jargon; indications for the pre-European existence of an American Indian pidgin. *Journal of Historical Linguistics and Philology* 1/2.141–185.
Drechsel, Emanuel J. 1987. On determining the role of Chickasaw in the history and origin of Mobilian Jargon. *International Journal of American Linguistics* 53.21–29.
Drechsel, Emanuel J. 1993. Basic word order in Mobilian jargon: Underlying SOV or OSV? *American Indian Linguistics and Ethnography in Honor of Laurence C. Thompson*, ed. by

Anthony Mattina and Timothy Montler, 343–367. (University of Montana Occasional Papers in Linguistics, 10.) Missoula: University of Montana.

Drechsel, Emanuel. 1997. *Mobilian Jargon: Linguistic and Sociohistorical Aspects of a Native American Pidgin*. Oxford: University Press.

Drechsel, Emanuel. 2001. Mobilian Jargon in Southeastern Indian anthropology. *Anthropologists and Indians in the New South*, ed. by Rachel A. Bonney and J. Anthony Paredes, 175–183. Tuscaloosa: University of Alabama Press.

Droixhe, Daniel. 1955. Remarques complémentaires sur les six premiers noms du nombres de turc et du quechua. *Journal de la Société des Américanistes de Paris* 44.17–37.

Dryer, Matthew S. 2007. Kutenai, Algonquian, and the Pacific Northwest from an areal perspective. *Proceedings of the Thirty-Eighth Algonquian Conference*, ed. by Christoph H. Wolfart, 155–206. Winnipeg: University of Manitoba.

Dumézil, George. 1955. Remarques sur les six premiers noms du nombres de turc et du quechua. *Journal de la Société des Américanistes de Paris* 44.17–37.

Durbin, Marshall. 1977[1985]. A survey of the Carib language family. *Carib-Speaking Indians: Culture, Society and Language*, ed. by Ellen B. Basso, 23–38. Tucson: University of Arizona Press. [Reprinted 1985, in: South American Indian languages: Retrospect and prospect, ed. by Harriet E. Manelis Klein and Louisa R. Stark, 325–371. Austin: University of Texas Press.]

Durbin, Marshall and Haydée Seijas. 1973. A Note on Panche, Pijao, Pantagora (Palenque), Colima and Muzo. *International Journal of American Linguistics* 39.47–51.

Eberhard, David M., Gary F. Simons, and Charles D. Fennig, eds. 2021. *Ethnologue: Languages of the World*. (24th edition). Dallas, TX: SIL International. (Online version: http://www.ethnologue.com.)

Eberhard, David M., Gary F. Simons, and Charles D. Fennig, (eds.). 2023. Ethnologue: Languages of the World. (26th edition). Dallas, Texas: SIL International. (Online version: http://www.ethnologue.com.)

Eberhard, David, Stella Telles, Leo Wetzels. In press. The Nambiwara languages. *Amazonian Languages: An International Handbook*, ed. by Patience Epps and Lev Michael. Berlin: Walter de Gruyter.

Elliot, Eric. 1994. "How" and "thus" in (Uto-Aztecan) Cupan and Yuman: A case of areal influence. *Survey Reports, Survey of California and Other Indian Language*, 145–169. https://escholarship.org/content/qt4fb2x0g4/qt4fb2x0g4.pdf.

Eliot, John. 1663. *The Holy Bible, Containing the Old Testament and the New, Translated into the Indian Language and Ordered to Be Printed by the Commissioners of the United Colonies in New-England*. Cambridge, MA: Samuel Green and Marmaduke Johnson.

Eliot, John. 1666. *The Indian Grammar Begun: A Grammar of the Massachusetts Indian Language*. Cambridge, MA: Samuel Green and Marmaduke Johnson. (New edition, 1822, *A Grammar of the Massachusetts Indian Language*, ed. by John Pickering. Boston: Phelps and Farnham, Collections of the Massachusetts Historical Society, 2nd series, 9:223–312, 1822.)

Elliott, John. 2021. *A Grammar of Enxet Sur*. PhD dissertation, University of Hawai'i at Mānoa.

Elliott, Eric. 1994. "How," and "thus" in UA: Cupan and Yuman: A case of areal influence. *Proceedings of the Meeting of the Society for the Study of the Indigenous Languages of the Americas July 2–4, 1993 and the Hokan-Penutian Workshop*, July 3, 1993, ed. by Margaret Langdon, 145–169. (Survey of California and Other Indian Languages, survey report 8.) UC Berkeley.

Elmendorf, William W. 1963. Yukian-Siouan lexical similarities. *International Journal of American Linguistics* 20.300–309.

Elmendorf, William W. 1964. Item and set comparison in Yuchi, Siouan, and Yukian. *International Journal of American Linguistics* 30.328–340.
Elmendorf, William W. 1968. Lexical and cultural change in Yukian. *Anthropological Linguistics* 10/7.1–41.
Elmendorf, William W. 1981. Features of Yukian pronominal structure. *Journal of California and Great Basin Anthropology—Papers in Linguistics* 3.3–16.
Elmendorf, William W. 1988. Wappo agreements with Northern Yukian—summary. Unpublished paper.
Elmendorf, William W. 1990. Chemakum. *Handbook of North American Indians*, ed. by William C. Sturtevant, vol. 7: *Northwest Coast*, ed. by Wayne Suttles, 438–440. Washington DC: Smithsonian Institution.
Elmendorf, William W. 1993. Lexical and cultural change in Yukian. *Anthropological Linguistics* 35.171–242.
Elmendorf, William W., and Alice Shepherd. 1999. Another look at Wappo-Yuki loans. *Anthropological linguistics* 41.209–229.
Elsasser, Albert B. 1978. Wiyot. *Handbook of North American Indians*, ed. by William C. Sturtevant, vol. 8: *California*, ed. by Robert F. Heizer, 236–243. Washington DC: Smithsonian Institution.
Emlen, Nicholas Q. 2017. Perspectives on the Quechua–Aymara contact relationship and the lexicon and phonology of Pre-Proto-Aymara. *International Journal of American Linguistics* 83.307–340.
Emlen, Nicholas Q. and Johannes Dellert. 2020. On the polymorphemic genesis of some Proto-Quechua roots. *Diachronica* 37.318–367.
England, Nora C. 1991. Changes in basic word order in Mayan languages. *International Journal of American Linguistics* 57.446–486.
Enrico, John. 2004. Toward Proto-Na-Dene. *Anthropological Linguistic*s. 46/3.229–302.
Epps, Patience. 2005. Areal diffusion and the development of evidentiality: Evidence from Hup. *Language* 29.617–650.
Epps, Patience. 2007. The Vaupés melting pot: Tukanoan influence on Hup. *Grammars in Contact: A Cross-Linguistic Typology*, ed. by Alexandra Aikhenvald and Robert M. W. Dixon, 267–289. Oxford: Oxford University Press.
Epps, Patience. 2008a. *A Grammar of Hup*. Berlin: Mouton de Gruyter.
Epps, Patience. 2008b. Grammatical borrowing in Hup. *Grammatical Borrowing: A Cross-linguistic Survey*, ed. by Yaron Matras and Jeanette Sakel, 551–565. Berlin: Mouton de Gruyter.
Epps, Patience. 2009a. Language classification, language contact, and Amazonian prehistory. *Language and Linguistics Compass* 3.581–606.
Epps, Patience. 2009b. Loanwords in Hup, a Nadahup language of Amazonia. *Loanwords in the World's Languages: A Comparative Handbook*, ed. by Martin Haspelmath and Uri Tadmor, 992–1014. Berlin: De Gruyter Mouton.
Epps, Patience. 2012. On form and function in language contact: A case study from the Amazonian Vaupés region. *Dynamics of Contact-Induced Language Change*, ed. by Isabelle Léglise and Claudine Chamoreau. 195–230. Berlin: de Gruyter Mouton.
Epps, Patience. 2013. Inheritance, calquing, or independent innovation? Reconstructing morphological complexity in Amazonian numerals. *Contact Among Genetically Related Languages*, ed. by Patience Epps, Na'ama Pat-El, and John Huehnergard. Special edition of *Journal of Language Contact* 6.2: 329–357. Leiden: Brill.

Epps, Patience. 2017. Subsistence pattern and contact-driven language change. *Language Dynamics and Change* 7.47–101.

Epps, Patience. 2020. Amazonian linguistic diversity and its sociocultural correlates. *Language Dispersal, Diversification, and Contact: A Global Perspective*, ed. by Mily Crevels and Pieter Muysken, 275–290. Oxford: Oxford University Press.

Epps, Patience and Katherine Bolaños. 2017. Reconsidering the "Makú" language family of northwest Amazonia. *International Journal of American Linguistics* 83.509–537.

Epps, Patience and Lev Michael. 2017. The areal linguistics of Amazonia. *The Cambridge Handbook of Areal Linguistics*, ed. by Raymond Hickey, 934–963. Cambridge: Cambridge University Press.

Epps, Patience and Kristine Stenzel. 2013. Introduction. *Upper Rio Negro: Cultural and Linguistic Interaction in Northwest Amazonia*, ed. by Patience Epps and Kristine Stenzel, 13–52. Rio de Janeiro: Museu Nacional / Museu do Índio-FUNAI.

Erickson, Vincent O. 1978. Maliseet-Passamaquoddy. *Handbook of North American Indians*, ed. by William C. Sturtevant, vol. 15: *Northeast*, ed. by Bruce G. Trigger, 123–136. Washington DC: Smithsonian Institution.

Eriksen, Love and Swintha Danielsen. 2014. The Arawakan matrix. *The Native Language of South America: Origins, Development, Typology*, ed. by Loretta O'Connor and Pieter Muysken, 152–176. New York: Cambridge University Press.

Ernst, Adolf. 1891. Über einige weniger bekannte Sprachen aus der Gegend des Meta und oberen Orinoco. *Zeitschrift für Ethnologie*. 23.1–13.

Escalante Fontaneda, Hernando d'. 1944[c. 1575]. *Memoir of Do. d'Escalente Fontaneda respecting Florida, written in Spain, about the Year 1575. Trans. From the Spanish with notes by Buckingham Smith (Washington, 1854)*, ed. by David O. True. (University of Miami and the Historical Association of Southern Florida Miscellaneous Publications, 1.) Miami. Miami: University of Miami.

Escalante Hernández, Roberto. 1962. *El Cuitlateco*. Mexico: Instituto Nacional de Antropología e Historia.

Escalante Hernández, Roberto. 1963. Material lingüístico del oriente de Sonora: Tonichi y Ponida. Anales del *Instituto Nacional de Antropología e Historia* 16.149–178.

Estenssoro, Juan Carlos. 2015. Las vías indígenas de la occidentalización: lenguas generales y lenguas maternas en el ámbito colonial americano (1492–1650). *Mélanges de la Casa de Velázquez* 45.15–36.

Ethnologue. 2021. See Eberhard et al. 2021.

Ethnologue. 2023. See Eberhard et al. 2023.

Everdell, Michael. 2013. *Reconsidering the Puebloan Languages in a Southwestern Areal Context*. BA thesis, Oberlin College.

Everett, Daniel L. 1995. Sistemas Prosódicos da Família Arawá. *Estudos Phonológicos das Línguas Indígenas Brasileiras*, edited by Leo Wetzels, 297–339. Rio de Janeiro: Editora Universidade Federal de Rio de Janeiro.

Everett, Daniel L. 2008. *Don't Sleep, There are Snakes: Life and Language in the Amazonian Jungle*. New York: Pantheon Books.

F. X. C. 1928. Traduccion de algunas voces de la lengua guama. Año de M. DCC. LXXXVIII. *Catálogo de la Real Biblioteca*, vol. 6: *Lenguas de América*, 381–393. Madrid: Real Biblioteca.

Fabre, Alain. 1995. Lexical similarities between Uru-Chipaya and Pano-Takanan languages: Genetical relationship or areal diffusion? *Opción: Revista de Ciencias Humanas y Sociales* 11.45–73.

Fabre, Alain. 1998. *Manual de las lenguas indígenas sudamericanas I*. Munich: Lincom Europa.

Fabre, Alain. 2005. Los pueblos del Gran Chaco y sus lenguas, primera parte: enlhet-enenlhet del Chaco Paraguayo. *Suplemento Antropológico* 40.503–569.

Fabre, Alain. 2007. Morfosintaxis de los clasificadores posesivos en las lenguas del Gran Chaco (Argentina, Bolivia y Paraguay). *UniverSOS* 4.67–85.

Fabre, Alain. 2009. *Diccionario etnolingüístico y guía bibliográfica de los pueblos indígenas sudamericanos: Arawak*. http://butler.cc.tut.fi/~fabre/BookInternetVersio/Dic=Arawak.pdf.

Facundes, Sydney and Ana Paula B. Brandão. 2011. Comparative Arawak linguistics: Notes on reconstruction, diffusion and Amazonian prehistory. *Ethnicity in Ancient Amazonia: Reconstructing Past Identities from Archaeology, Linguistics, and Ethnohistory*, ed. by. Alf Hornborg and Jonathan D. Hill, 197–210. Boulder: University Press of Colorado.

Fagundes, Nelson J. R., Ricardo Kanitz, Roberta Eckert, Ana C. S. Valls, Mauricio R. Bogo, Francisco M. Salzano, David Glenn Smith, Wilson A. Silva Jr, Marco A. Zago, Andrea K. Ribeiro-dos-Santos, and Sidney E.B. Santos, Maria Luiza Petzl-Erler, and Sandro L. Boatto. 2008. Mitochondrial population genomics supports a single pre-Clovis origin with a coastal route for the peopling of the Americas. *American Journal of Human Genetics* 82.583–592.

Fahey, Bede. 2004. Mayan, a Sino-Tibetan language? A comparative study. *Sino-Platonic Papers* 130.1–62, ed. by Victor H. Hair. www.sino-platonic.org/abstracts/ spp130 mayan chinese.html.

Farabee, William C. 1918. *The Central Arawaks*. Philadephia: University Museum.

Fehren-Schmitz, Lars. 2020. Genetics. 2020. *Rethinking the Andes-Amazonia Divide: a Cross-disciplinary Exploration*, ed. by Adrian J. Pearce, David G. Beresford-Jones, and Paul Heggarty, 48–57. London: UCL Press.

Fernández Garay, Ana. 1996. Hispanismos en el ranquel, dialecto mapuche en extinción. *Signo y Seña* 6.277–293.

Ferrario, Benigno. 1933. La investigación lingüística y el parentesco extra-continental de la lengua "qhexwa". *Revista de la Sociedad "Amigos de la Arqueología"* 7.89–120.

Ferrario, Benigno. 1938. Della possible parentela fra le indue "altaiche" en alcune americaine. *Congresso Internazionale degli Orientalisti* 19.210–23. Rome: Tipographia della Reale Accademia dei Lincei del Dott.

Ferreira, Helder Perri, Ana Maria Antunes Machado, and Estevão Benfica Senra. 2019. *As Línguas Yanomami no Brasil: Diversidade e Vitalidade*. São Paulo: Instituto Socioambiental (ISA) and Instituto do Patrimônio Histórico e Artístico Nacional (IPHAN).

Fleck, David W. 2013. *Panoan Languages and Linguistics*. (Anthropological papers, 99.) New York: American Museum of Natural History.

Flegontov, Pavel, N. Ezgi Altınışık, Piya Changmai, Nadin Rohland, Swapan Mallick, Nicole Adamski, Deborah A. Bolnick, Nasreen Broomandkhoshbacht, Francesca Candilio, Brendan J. Culleton, Olga Flegontova, T. Max Friesen, Choongwon Jeong, Thomas K. Harper, Denise Keating, Douglas J. Kennett, Alexander M. Kim, Thiseas C. Lamnidis, Ann Marie Lawson, Iñigo Olalde, Jonas Oppenheimer, Ben A. Potter, Jennifer Raff, Robert A. Sattler, Pontus Skoglund, Kristin Stewardson, Edward J. Vajda, Sergey Vasilyev, Elizaveta Veselovskaya, M. Geoffrey Hayes, Dennis H. O'Rourke, Johannes Krause, Ron Pinhasi, David Reich, and Stephan Schiffels. 2019. Paleo-Eskimo genetic ancestry and the peopling of Chukotka and North America. *Nature* 570.236–240. https://doi.org/10.1038/s41586-019-1251-y.

Floyd, Simeon. 2013. Semantic transparency and cultural calquing in the Northwest Amazon. *Upper Rio Negro: Cultural and Linguistic Interaction in Northwestern Amazonia*, ed. by Patience Epps and Kristine Stenzel, 271–308. Rio de Janiero: Museu do Indio.

Fortescue, Michael. 1981. Endoactive-exoactive markers in Eskimo-Aleut, Tungus and Japanese—an investigation into common origins. *Etudes/Inuit/Studies* 5.3–41.

Fortescue, Michael. 1988. The Eskimo-Aleut-Yukagir relationship: An alternative to the genetic/contact dichotomy. *Acta Linguistica Hafniensia* 21.21–50.

Fortescue, Michael. 1994. The role of typology in the establishment of the genetic relationship between Eskimo and Aleut—and beyond. *Languages of the North Pacific Rim*, ed. by Osahito Miyaoka, 9–36. (Hokkaido University Publications in Linguistics, 7.) Sapporo, Japan: Department of Linguistics, Hokkaido University.

Fortescue, Michael. 1998. *Language Relations across Bering Strait: Reappraising the Archaeological and Linguistic Evidence.* London and New York: Cassell.

Fortescue, Michael, Steven Jacobson, and Lawrence Kaplan. 2010. *Comparative Eskimo Dictionary with Aleut Cognates* (2nd edition). Fairbanks: Alaska Native Language Center, University of Alaska.

Foster, Michael K. 1996. Language and culture history of North America. *Handbook of North American Indians*, vol. 17, ed. by Ives Goddard, 64–110. Washington DC: Smithsonian Institution.

Fowler, Catherine S. 1972. Some ecological clues to Proto-Numic homelands. *Great Basin cultural ecology: A symposium*, ed. by D. D. Fowler, 105–121. (Desert Research Institute publications in the social sciences, 8.) Reno: University of Nevada.

Fowler, Catherine S. 1983. Some lexical clues to Uto-Aztecan prehistory. *International Journal of American Linguistics* 49.224–257.

Fowler, William C. 2008. *Historic Native Peoples of Texas.* Austin: University of Texas Press.

Fowler, William R., Jr. 1989. *The Cultural Evolution of Ancient Nahua Civilizations: The Pipil-Nicarao of Central America.* Norman: University of Oklahoma.

Frachtenberg, Leo J. 1918. Comparative studies in Takelman, Kalapuyan and Chinookan lexicography, a preliminary paper. *International Journal of American Linguistics* 1.175–182.

Franchetto, Bruna and Elsa Gomez-Imbert. 2003. Review of *The Amazonian Languages*. *International Journal of American Linguistics* 69.232–238.

Frank, Erwin H. 1994. Los Uni. *Guía Etnográfica de la Alta Amazonía*, ed. by Fernando Santos and Frederica Barclay, vol. 2, 129–237. Quito: Ediciones Abya-Yala.

Frankle, Eleanor. 1984a. Las relaciones externas entre las lenguas mayances y altaicas. Investigaciones recientes en el área maya. *La 17ª Mesa Redonda, Sociedad Mexicana de Antropología* 1.209–225.

Frankle, Eleanor. 1984b. Los morfemas vocálicos para derivaciones verbales en los grupos mayance y túrquico. Investigaciones recientes en el área maya. *La 17ª Mesa Redonda, Sociedad Mexicana de Antropología* 2.517–524.

Freeland, L.S. 1930. The relationship of Mixe to the Penutian family. *International Journal of American Linguistics* 6.28–33.

Friederici, Georg. 1947. *Amerikanistisches Wörterbuch.* (2nd edition, 1960.) Hamburg: Cram de Gruyter.

Friedrich, Paul. 1971. Dialectal variation in Tarascan phonology. *International Journal of American Linguistics* 37.164–187.

Galasso, Bruno José Betti. 2007. Indigenismos e Americanismos na Conquista das Américas. *Brazilian Journal of Latin American Studies* 6.57–72.

Galucio, Ana Vilacy, Sérgio Meira, Joshua Birchall, Denny Moore, Nilson Gabas Júnior, Sebastian Drude, Luciana Storto, Gessiane Picanço, Carmen Reis Rodrigues. 2015. Genealogical relations and lexical distances within the Tupian linguistic family. *Boletim do Museu Paraense Emílio Goeldi. Ciências Humanas* 10.229–274. https://doi.org/10.1590/1981-81222015000200004. hdl:11858/00-001M-0000-0028-D677-B.

Gancedo, A. 1922. El idioma japonés y sus afinidades con lenguas americanas. *Revista de Derecho, Historia y Letras* 73.114–122. Buenos Aires, Argentina.

García, Bartholomé. 1760. Manual para administrar los santos sacramentos . . . a los indios de las naciones: Pajalates, Orejones, Pacaos, Pacoas, Tilijayas, Alasapas, Pausanes, y otras muchas diferentes que se hallan en las misiones del Rio San Antonio, y Rio Grande . . . Mexico: Imprenta de los Herederos e doña María de Rivera.

Garth, Thomas R. 1978. Atsugewi. *Handbook of North American Indians*, ed. by William C. Sturtevant, vol. 8: *California*, ed. by Robert F. Heizer, 236–243. Washington DC: Smithsonian Institution.

Gatschet, Albert S. 1891a. *The Karankawa Indians, the coast people of Texas*. Cambridge, MA: Peabody Museum of American Archaeology and Ethnology.

Gatschet, Albert S. 1891b. Removal of the Taensa Indians. *American Antiquarian and Oriental Journal* 13/5.252–254.

Gatschet, Albert S. and John R. Swanton. 1932. *A Dictionary of The Atakapa Language: Accompanied by Text Material*. (Smithsonian Institution, Bureau of American Ethnology, Bulletin 108.) Washington DC: United States Government Printing Office.

Gerardi, Fabrício Ferraz and Stanislav Reichert. 2021. The Tupí-Guaraní language family: A phylogenetic classification. *Diachronica* 38.151–188.

Gerardi, Fabrício Ferraz, Tiago Tresoldi, Carolina Coelho Aragon, Stanislav Reichert, Jonas Gregorio de Souza, and Francisco Silva Noelli. 2023. Lexical phylogenetics of the Tupí-Guaraní family: language, archaeology, and the problem of chronology. *PLoS ONE* 18(6): e0272226. https://doi.org/10.1371/journal.pone.0272226.

Gerzenstein, Ana. 2004. Las consonantes laterales y las labializadas en lenguas mataguayas del Chaco argentino-paraguayo. *Estudios en Lenguas Amerindias: Homenaje a Ken L. Hale*, ed. by Zarina Estrada Fernández, Ana Fernández Garay y Albert Álvarez González, 183–197. Hermosillo: Universidad de Sonora.

Gerzenstein, Ana and Beatriz Gualdieri. 2003. La armonía vocálica en lenguas chaqueñas de las familias Guaicurú y Mataguaya. *LIAMES (Línguas Indígenas Americanas)* 3.97–111.

Gibbs, George. 1863. *Dictionary of the Chinook Jargon*. New York: Cramoisy Press.

Gildea, Spike. 2003. Proposing a new branch for the Cariban language family. *Amerindia* 28.7–32.

Gildea, Spike. 2012. Linguistic studies in the Cariban family. *The Indigenous Languages of South America: A Comprehensive Guide*, ed. by Lyle Campbell and Verónica Grondona, 441–494. Berlin: Mouton de Gruyter.

Gildea, Spike and Doris Payne. 2007. Is Greenberg's "Macro-Carib" viable? *Boletim do Museu Paraense Emílio Goeldi* 2.19–72.

Gilij, Filippo Salvatore. 1780–1784. *Saggio di storia americana; o sia, storia naturale, civile e sacra de regni, e delle provincie spagnuole di Terra-Ferma nell' America Meridionale descritto dall' abate F.S. Gilij*. 4 volumes. Rome: Perigio. (1965[1782], *Ensayo de historia americana*, Spanish translation by Antonio Tovar. [Fuentes para la Historia Colonial de Venezuela, 3 volumes, 71–73.] Caracas: Biblioteca de la Academia Nacional de la Historia.)

Giraldo, Gallego and Diana Andrea. 2013. Hispanicisms in the Muisca language, Vocabulario de la lengua chibcha o mosca, manuscrito ii/2922. *Forma y Función* 26.77–97.

Girard, Victor. 1971a. Proto-Takanan phonology. *University of California Publications in Linguistics*, 70. Berkeley and Los Angeles: University of California Press.

Girard, Victor. 1971b. *Proto-Carib phonology*. PhD dissertation, University of California, Berkeley.

Girón, Jesús Mario. 2008. *Una Gramática del Wãnsöhöt (Puinave)*. Utrecht: LOT

Goddard, Ives. 1965. The eastern Algonquian intrusive nasal. *International Journal of American Linguistics* 31.206–220.

Goddard, Ives. 1971. More on the Nasalization of PA *a· in Eastern Algonquian. *International Journal of American Linguistics* 37.139–145.

Goddard, Ives. 1972. Three New Algonquian languages. *Algonquian Linguistic News* 1/2–3 (June–September).5–6.

Goddard, Ives. 1973. Historical and philological evidence regarding the identification of the Mascouten. *Ethnohistory* 19.123–134.

Goddard, Ives. 1974a. Dutch loanwords in Delaware. *A Delaware Indian symposium*, ed. by Herbert C. Kraft, 153–160. (Anthropological Series, 4.) Harrisburg: The Pennsylvania Historical and Museum Commission.

Goddard, Ives. 1974b. An outline of the historical phonology of Arapaho and Atsina. *International Journal of American Linguistics* 40.102–116.

Goddard, Ives. 1975. Algonquian, Wiyot, and Yurok: Proving a distant genetic relationship. *Linguistics and anthropology in honor of C. F. Voegelin*, ed. by M. Dale Kinkade, Kenneth Hale, and Oswald Werner, 249–262. Amsterdam: John Benjamins.

Goddard, Ives. 1977. Some early examples of American Indian Pidgin English from New England. *International Journal of American Linguistics* 43.37–41.

Goddard, Ives. 1978a. A further note on pidgin English. *International Journal of American Linguistics* 44.73.

Goddard, Ives. 1978b. Delaware. *Handbook of North American Indians*, ed. by William C. Sturtevant, vol. 15: *Northeast*, ed. by Bruce G. Trigger, 213–239. Washington DC: Smithsonian Institution.

Goddard, Ives. 1978c. Synonymy. *Handbook of North American Indians*, ed. by William C. Sturtevant, vol. 15: *Northeast*, ed. by Bruce G. Trigger, 320, 404–406, 478–479, 489–490, 499, 503, 524, 654–655, 768–770. Washington DC: Smithsonian Institution.

Goddard, Ives. 1978d. Eastern Algonquian languages. *Handbook of North American Indians*, ed. by William Sturtevant, vol. 15: *Northeast*, ed. by Bruce D. Trigger, 70–77. Washington DC: Smithsonian Institution.

Goddard, Ives. 1979a. The languages of south Texas and the lower Rio Grande. *The Languages of Native America: Historical and Comparative Assessment*, ed. by Lyle Campbell and Marianne Mithun, 355–389. Austin: University of Texas Press.

Goddard, Ives. 1979b. Comparative Algonquian. *The Languages of Native America: Historical and Comparative Assessment*, ed. by Lyle Campbell and Marianne Mithun, 70–133. Austin: University of Texas Press.

Goddard, Ives. 1979c. Synonymy. *Handbook of North American Indians*, ed. by William C. Sturtevant, vol. 9: *Southwest*, ed. by Alfonso Ortiz, 234–235, 267, 479–481, 601. Washington DC: Smithsonian Institution.

Goddard, Ives. 1981. Synonymy. *Handbook of North American Indians*, ed. by William C. Sturtevant, vol. 6: *Subarctic*, ed. by June Helm, 185–187, 412, 430, 465, 512, 599–600, 613–615, 638–639, 661–662. Washington DC: Smithsonian Institution.

Goddard, Ives. 1983. Synonymy. *Handbook of North American Indians*, ed. by William C. Sturtevant, vol. 10: *Southwest*, ed. by Alfonso Ortiz, 23–24, 69, 97, 134–135. Washington DC: Smithsonian Institution.

Goddard, Ives. 1984. Synonymy. *Handbook of North American Indians*, ed. by William C. Sturtevant, vol. 5: *Arctic*, ed. by David Damas, 5–7. Washington DC: Smithsonian Institution.

Goddard, Ives. 1988. Pre-Cheyenne *y. *In Honor of Mary Haas: From the Haas Festival Conference on Native American Linguistics*, ed. by William Shipley, 345–360. Berlin: Mouton de Gruyter.

Goddard, Ives. 1990. Algonquian linguistic change and reconstruction. *Linguistic Change and Reconstruction Methodology*, ed. by Philip Baldi, 99–114. Berlin: Mouton de Gruyter.

Goddard, Ives. 1994a. A new look for Algonquian. Paper presented at the Comparative Linguistics Workshop, University of Pittsburgh, April 9.

Goddard, Ives. 1994b. The west-to-east cline in Algonquian dialectology. *Papers of the 25th Algonquian Conference*, ed. by William Cowan, 187–211. Ottawa: Carleton University

Goddard, Ives. 1995. The Delaware Jargon. *New Sweden in America*, ed. by Carol E. Hoffecker, Carol E. Hoffecker, Richard Waldron, Lorraine E. Williams, and Barbara E. Benson, 137–149. Newark: University of Delaware.

Goddard, Ives. 1996a. The classification of the native languages of North America. *Handbook of North American Indians*, vol. 17, ed. by Ives Goddard, 290–323. Washington DC: Smithsonian Institution.

Goddard, Ives. 1996b. The description of the native languages of North America before Boas. *Handbook of North American Indians*, vol. 17, ed. by Ives Goddard, 17–63. Washington DC: Smithsonian Institution.

Goddard, Ives. 1997. Pidgin Delaware. *Contact Languages: A Wider Perspective*, ed. by Sarah G. Thomason, 43–98. Amsterdam: Benjamins.

Goddard, Ives. 2000. The use of pidgins and jargons on the East Coast of North America. *The Language Encounter in the Americas 1492–1800*, ed. Edward G. Gray and Norman Fiering, 61–78. New York: Berghahn Books.

Goddard, Ives. 2005. The indigenous languages of the southeast. *Anthropological Linguistics* 47.1–60.

Goddard, Ives. 2016. The "Loup" languages of Western Massachusetts: The dialectal diversity of Southern New England Algonquian. *Papers of the Forty-Fourth Algonquian Conference: Actes du Congrès des Algonquinistes*, ed. by Monica Macaulay, Margaret Noodin, and J. Randolph Valentine, 104–138. Albany: SUNY Press.

Goddard, Ives and Kathleen Joan Bragdon. 1988. *Native Writings in Massachusett*. Philadelphia: American Philosophical Society.

Goddard, Ives and James G. E. Smith. 1981. Synonymy. *Handbook of North American Indians*, ed. by William C. Sturtevant, vol. 6: *Subarctic*, ed. by June Helm, 283. Washington DC: Smithsonian Institution.

Goddard, Ives and Richard Slobodin. 1981. Synonymy. *Handbook of North American Indians*, ed. by William C. Sturtevant, vol. 6: *Subarctic*, ed. by June Helm, 530–532. Washington DC: Smithsonian Institution.

Golla, Susan and Ives Goddard. 1978. Synonymy. *Handbook of North American Indians*, ed. by William C. Sturtevant, vol. 15: *Northeast*, ed. by Bruce G. Trigger, 706. Washington DC: Smithsonian Institution.

Golla, Victor. 2000 The history of the term "Penutian." *Proceedings of the Meeting of the Hokan-Penutian workshop*, June 17–13, 2000. Report 11, ed. by Laura Buszard-Welcher, 22–32. Berkeley: Survey of California and Other Indian Languages.

Golla, Victor. 2007. Linguistic prehistory. *California Prehistory: Colonization, Culture, and Complexity*, ed. by Terry L. Jones and Kathryn Klar, 71–82. Lanham: Rowman and Littlefield.

Golla, Victor. 2011. *California Indian Languages*. Berkeley: University of California Press.

Golla, Victor, Ives Goddard, Lyle Campbell, Marianne Mithun, and Mauricio Mixco. 2008. North America. *Atlas of the World's Languages*, ed. by Chris Moseley and Ron Asher, 7–41. London: Routledge.

Golluscio, Lucía. 2009. Loanwords in Mapudungun, a language of Chile and Argentina. *Loanword in the World Languages: A Comparative Handbook*, ed. by Martin Haspelmath and Uri Tadmoor, 1035–1071. Berlin: Mouton de Gruyter.

Golluscio, Lucia and Hebe González. 2008 Contact, attrition and shift in two Chaco languages: The cases of Tapiete and Vilela. *Lessons from Documented Endangered Languages*, ed. by K. David Harrison, David S. Rood, and Arienne M. Dwyer, 196–294. Amsterdam: John Benjamins.

Golluscio, Lucía A. and Alejandra Vidal. 2009–2010. Recorrido sobre las lenguas del Chaco y los aportes a la investigación lingüística. *Amerindia* 33/34.3–40.

Golovko, Evgenij. 1994. Mednyj Aleut or Copper Island Aleut: An Aleut-Russian mixed language. *Mixed Languages: 15 Case Studies in Language Intertwining*, ed. by Peter Bakker and Maarten Mous, 113–121. Amsterdam: IFOTT.

Golovko, Evgeniy V. 1996. A case of non-genetic development in the Arctic area: The contribution of Aleut and Russian to the formation of Copper Island Aleut. *Language Contact in the Arctic: Northern Pidgins and Contact Languages*, ed. by Ernst Håkon Jahr and Ingvild Broch, pp. 63–77. Berlin: Mouton de Gruyter.

Golovko, Evgeniy. 2003. Language contact and group identity: The role of "folk" linguistic engineering. *The Mixed Language Debate: Theoretical and Empirical Advances*, ed. by Yaron Matras and Peter Bakker, pp. 177–208. Berlin: Mouton de Gruyter.

Golovko, Evgeniy and Nikolai Vakhtin. 1990. Aleut in contact: The CIA enigma. *Acta Linguistica Hafniensia* 72.97–125.

Gómez Rendón, Jorge. 2005. La media lengua de Imbabura [the Media Lengua of Imbabura]. *Encuentros y Conflictos: Bilinguismo y Contacto de Lenguas en el Mundo Andino*, ed. by Hella Olbertz and Pieter Muysken, 39–58. Frankfurt: Vervuert.

Gómez Rendón, Jorge A. 2008. *Mestizaje Lingüístico en los Andes: Génesis y Estructura de una Lengua Mixta* [Linguistic mixing in the Andes: genesis and structure of a mixed language]. Quito, Ecuador: Abya-Yala.

Gómez Rendón, Jorge and Willem Adelaar. 2009. Loanwords in Imbabura Quichua. *Loanwords in the World's Languages: A Comparative Handbook*, ed. by Martin Haspelmath and Uri Tadmor, 944–967. Berlin: Mouton de Gruyter.

Gomez-Imbert, Elsa. 1993. Problemas en torno a la comparación de las lenguas Tukano orientales. *Estado Actual de la Clasificación de las Lenguas Indígenas de Colombia*, ed. by Maria Luisa Rodríguez de Montes, 235–267. Bogotá: Instituto Caro y Cuervo.

Gomez-Imbert, Elsa. 1996. When animals become "rounded" and "feminine": Conceptual categories in a multilingual setting. *Rethinking Linguistic Relativity*, ed. by John J. Gumperz and Stephen C. Levinson, 438–469. Cambridge: Cambridge University Press.

González, Hebe A. 2014. Procesos fonológicos como rasgos areales: el caso de la palatización en las lenguas chaqueñas. *LIAMES (Línguas Indígenas Americanas)* 14.11–40.

González, Hebe A. 2015. El Chaco como área lingüística: una evaluación de los rasgos fonológicos. *Language Contact and Documentation*, ed. by Bernard Comrie and Lucía Golluscio, 165–203. Berlin: Mouton de Gruyter.

González Casanova Pablo. 1933. Los hispanismos en el idioma azteca. *Anales del Museo Nacional de México* 8.693–742.

González-José, Maria Catira Bortolini, Fabricio R. Santos, and Sandro L. Bonatto. 2008. The peopling of America: craniofacial shape variation on a continental scale and its interpretation from an interdisciplinary view. *American Journal of Physical Anthropology* 137.175–187.

Good, Jeff, Teresa McFarland, and Mary Paster. 2003. Reconstructing Achumawi and Atsugewi: Proto-Palaihnihan revisited. Paper presented at the Annual Meeting of the Society for the Study of the Indigenous Languages of the Americas, Austin, Georgia, January 2–5. https://d1wqtxts1xzle7.cloudfront.net/65840406/Reconstructing_Achumawi_and_Atsugewi_Pro20210301-7821-14sm418-with-cover-page-v2.pdf?Expires=1663536769&Signature=UesHYxZL7XSv5FLv4L-~QdImTLIjHekWUIEIa1HeVwnN2rmY2SRRpKz10H-1Kq3a0W-1bb2d4TfqJUpOne47MVMNMe5VBnn6dL-U0tiiXJTTN8ksySXlU73bnKciz WyrSotsoLs9B~dyOdic6QlLRWF~3ILpAR9NIr7-6Xkhuhef4tJuwXc74UsfivyXSGpJ9P Y1mQ8pzGkKLiCZ6s5UQYcWSHsjMGCUfIrkM7GMAnK2EIsKclhUqUkBJcXmHvEb KvlGXOO8qul4fhNbH6-FSBOzxrv6iRquxDSXqwn006sHcsEPOv~9d-QMK1m5E5H-GIRm9VMt6p~XdF9gojk1Mm5A__&Key-Pair-Id=APKAJLOHF5GGSLRBV4ZA.

Granberry, Julian. 1970. [Abstract of Granberry's work on Timucua.] *American Philosophical Society Yearbook*, 606–607.

Granberry, Julian. 1990. A grammatical sketch of Timucua. *International Journal of American Linguistics* 56.60–101.

Granberry, Julian. 1991. Amazonian origins and affiliations of the Timucua language. *Language Change in South American Indian Languages*, ed. by Mary Ritchie Key, 195–242. Philadelphia: University of Pennsylvania Press.

Granberry, Julian. 1993. *A Grammar and Dictionary of the Timucua Language* (3rd edition). Tuscaloosa: University of Alabama Press.

Granberry, Julian and Gary S. Vesscilius. 2004. *Languages of the Pre-Columbian Antilles*. Tuscaloosa: University of Alabama Press.

Grant, Anthony P. 1994. Karankawa linguistic materials. *Kansas Working Papers in Linguistics* 19.1–56. https://doi.org/10.17161/KWPL.1808.318.

Grant, Anthony P. 1995. A note on Bidai. *European Review of Native American Studies* 9.45–47.

Grant, Anthony P. 1997. Coast Oregon Penutian: Problems and possibilities. *International Journal of American Linguistics* 63.144–156.

Grant, Anthony P. 2017. Caddoan languages. *Oxford Bibliographies*. https://doi.org/10.1093/OBO/9780199772810-0106.

Grant, Anthony P. 2018. Penutian languages. *Oxford Research Encyclopedia of Linguistics*. https://oxfordre.com/linguistics/view/10.1093/acrefore/9780199384655.001.0001/acrefore-9780199384655-e-358.

Grant, Campbell. 1978. Chumash: Introduction. *Handbook of North American Indians*, ed. by William C. Sturtevant, vol. 8: *California*, ed. by Robert F. Heizer, 505–508. Washington DC: Smithsonian Institution.

Grasserie, Raoul de la. 1890[1888 meeting]. De la famille linguistique Pano. *International Congress of Americanists* 7.438–449.

Greenberg, Joseph H. 1960[1956]. General classification of Central and South American languages. *Men and Cultures: 5th International Congress of Anthropological and Ethnological Sciences (1956)*, ed. by Anthony Wallace, 791–794. Philadelphia: University of Pennsylvania Press.

Greenberg, Joseph H. 1979. The classification of American Indian languages. *Papers of the 1978 Mid-America Linguistics Conference at Oklahoma*, ed. by Ralph E. Cooley, 7–22. Norman: University of Oklahoma Press.

Greenberg, Joseph H. 1987. *Language in the Americas*. Stanford: Stanford University Press.
Greenberg, Joseph H. 1989. Classification of American Indian languages: A reply to Campbell. *Language* 65.107–114.
Greenberg, Joseph H. 1990a. The American Indian language controversy. *The Review of Archaeology* 11.5–14.
Greenberg, Joseph H. 1994. On the Amerind affiliation of Zuni and Tonkawa. *California Linguistic Notes* 24.4–6.
Greenberg, Joseph H. 1996a. In defense of Amerind. *International Journal of American Linguistics* 62.131–164.
Greenberg, Joseph H. 1996b. The linguistic evidence. *American Beginnings: The Prehistory and Palaeoecology of Beringia*, ed. by Frederick Hadleigh West, 525–536. Chicago: University of Chicago Press.
Greenberg, Joseph H. 2000a. From first and second person: the history of Amerind *k(i). *Functional Approaches to Language, Culture, and Cognition: Papers in Honor of Sydney B. Lamb*, ed. by David G. Lockwood, Peter H. Fries, and James E. Copeland, 413–426. Amsterdam: John Benjamins.
Greenberg, Joseph H. 2000b. *Indo-European and Its Closest Relatives: The Eurasiatic Language Family*. Stanford: Stanford University Press.
Greenberg, Joseph H. and Merritt Ruhlen. 1992. Linguistic origins of Native Americans. *Scientific American* 267/5.94–99.
Greenberg, Joseph H. and Merritt Ruhlen. 2007. *An Amerind Etymological Dictionary*. Palo Alto, CA: Stanford University Department of Anthropological Studies.
Greenberg, Joseph H. and Morris Swadesh. 1953. Jicaque as a Hokan language. *International Journal of American Linguistics* 19.216–222.
Greenhill, Simon J., Hannah J. Haynie, Robert M. Ross, Angela M. Chira, Jonathan-Mattis List, Lyle Campbell, Carlos A. Botero, and Russell D. Gray. 2023. A ancient northern origin for the Uto-Aztecan family. *Language* 99.1–23. https://doi.org/10.1353/lan.0.0276.
Griffen, William B. 1979. *Indian Assimilation in the Franciscan Area of Nueva Vizcaya*. Tucson: University of Arizona Press.
Guillaume, Antoine and Françoise Rose. 2010. Sociative causative markers in South American languages: A possible areal feature. *Essais de typologie et de linguistique générale. Mélanges offerts à Denis Creissels*, ed. by Franck Floricic, 383–402. Lyons: ENS Éditions.
Guirardello, Raquel. 1999. *A Reference Grammar of Trumai*. Houston, TX: Rice University. http://scholarship.rice.edu/handle/1911/19387.
Gumilla, Joseph. 1745. *El Orinoco Ilustrado, y Defendido: Historia Natural, Civil, y Geographica Deeste Gran Río y de sus Caudalosas Vertientes* (2nd edition), 2 vols. Madrid: Manuel Fernandez.
Gumperz, John J. and Robert Wilson. 1971. Convergence and creolization: A case from the Indo-Aryan/Dravidian Border in India. *Pidginization and Creolization of Languages*, ed. by Dell Hymes, 151–167. Cambridge: Cambridge University Press.
Gunn, Robert D., ed. 1980. *Clasificación de los idiomas indígenas de Panamá, con un vocabulario comparativo de los mismos* (prepared by Michael Kopesec). (Lenguas de Panamá, 7.) Panama: Instituto Nacional de Cultura, ILV.
Gursky, Karl-Heinz. 1964. The linguistic position of the Quinigua Indians. *International Journal of American Linguistics* 30.325–327.
Gursky, Karl-Heinz. 1965–1966. Ein lexikalischer Vergleich der Algonkin-Golf- und Hoka-Subtiaba-Sprachen. *Orbis* 14.160–215.

Gursky, Karl-Heinz. 1966–1967. Ein Vergleich der grammatischen Morpheme der Golf-Sprachen und der Hoka-Subtiaba-Sprachen. *Orbis* 15.511–537.
Gursky, Karl-Heinz. 1966a. Der augenblickliche Stand der Erforschung der nordamerikanischen Sprachen. *Anthropos* 61.401–454.
Gursky, Karl-Heinz. 1966b. On the historical position of Waikuri. *International Journal of American Linguistics* 32.41–45.
Gursky, Karl-Heinz. 1968. Gulf and Hokan-Subtiaban: New lexical parallels. *International Journal of American Linguistics* 34.21–41.
Gursky, Karl-Heinz. 1974. Der Hoka-Sprachstamm: eine Bestandsaufnahme des lexikalischen Beweismaterials. *Orbis* 23.170–215.
Gursky, Karl-Heinz. 1988. *Der Hoka-Sprachstamm: Nachtrag I*. (Abhandlungen der völkerkundlichen Arbeitsgemeinschaft, 58.) Nortorf: Völkerkundliche Arbeitsgemeinschaft.
Haas, Mary R. 1941a. Tunica. *Handbook of American Indian Languages*, ed. by Franz Boas, vol. 4, pp. 1–143. New York: J. J. Augustin.
Haas, Mary R. 1941b. The classification of the Muskgoean languages. *Language, Culture, and Personality: Essays in Memory of Edward Sapir*, ed. by Leslie Spier, A. Irving Hallowell, and Stanley S. Newman, 41–56. Menasha, WI: Sapir Memorial Publication Fund.
Haas, Mary R. 1946. A grammatical sketch of Tunica. *Linguistic structures of Native America*, ed. by Harry Hoijer, 337–366. (Viking Fund Publications in Anthropology, 6.) New York: The Viking Fund.
Haas, Mary R. 1947. The development of Proto-Muskogean *kw. *International Journal of American Linguistics* 13.135–137.
Haas, Mary R. 1949. The position of Apalachee in the Muskogean family. *International Journal of American Linguistics* 15.121–127.
Haas, Mary R. 1950. Tunica texts. *University of California Publications in Linguistics* 6.1–174.
Haas, Mary R. 1951. The Proto-Gulf word for *water* (with notes on Siouan-Yuchi). *International Journal of American Linguistics* 17.71–79.
Haas, Mary R. 1952. The Proto-Gulf word for *land* (with a note on Siouan-Yuchi). *International Journal of American Linguistics* 18.238–240.
Haas, Mary R. 1953. Tunica dictionary. *University of California Publications in Linguistics* 6.175–332.
Haas, Mary R. 1954. The Proto-Hokan-Coahuiltecan word for "water." *Papers from the Symposium on American Indian Linguistics*, ed. by Murray B. Emeneau, 57–62. (University of California Publications in Linguistics, 10.) Berkeley and Los Angeles: University of California Press.
Haas, Mary R. 1956. Natchez and Muskogean languages. *Language* 32.61–72.
Haas, Mary R. 1958a. Algonkian-Ritwan: The end of a controversy. *International Journal of American Linguistics* 24:159–173.
Haas, Mary R. 1958b. A new linguistic relationship in North America: Algonkian and the Gulf languages. *Southwestern Journal of Anthropology* 14.231–264.
Haas, Mary R. 1959. Tonkawa and Algonkian. *Anthropological Linguistics* 1/2.1–6.
Haas, Mary R. 1960. Some genetic affiliations of Algonkian. *Culture in History: Essays in Honor of Paul Radin*, ed. by Stanley Diamond, 977–992. New York: Columbia University Press.
Haas, Mary R. 1964. California Hokan. *Studies in Californian linguistics*, ed. by William Bright, 73–87. (University of California Publications in Linguistics, 34.) Berkeley and Los Angeles: University of California Press.

Haas, Mary R. 1965. Is Kutenai related to Algonkian? *Canadian Journal of Linguistics* 10.77–92.
Haas, Mary R. 1966. Wiyot-Yurok-Algonkian and problems of comparative Algonkian. *International Journal of American Linguistics* 32.101–107.
Haas, Mary R. 1967. Language and taxonomy in northwestern California. *American Anthropologist* 96.358–362.
Haas, Mary R. 1969a. *The Prehistory of Languages*. The Hague: Mouton.
Haas, Mary R. 1969c. Swanton and the Biloxi and Ofo dictionaries. *International Journal of American Linguistics* 35.286–290.
Haas, Mary R. 1969c. Internal reconstruction of the Nootka-Nitinaht pronominal suffixes. *International Journal of American Linguistics* 35.108–124.
Haas, Mary R. 1973a. American Indian linguistic prehistory. *Current Trends in Linguistics*, vol. 10: *Linguistics in North America*, ed. by Thomas Sebeok, 677–712. The Hague: Mouton.
Haas, Mary R. 1973b. The Southeast. *Current Trends in Linguistics*, vol. 10: *Linguistics in North America*, ed. by Thomas Sebeok, 1210–1249. The Hague: Mouton.
Haas, Mary R. 1976. The Northern California linguistic area. *Hokan studies*, ed. by Margaret Langdon and Shirley Silver, 347–359. The Hague: Mouton.
Haas, Mary R. 1979. Southeastern languages. *The Languages of Native America: Historical and Comparative Assessment*, ed. by Lyle Campbell and Marianne Mithun, 299–326. Austin: University of Texas Press.
Hajda, Yvonne. 1990. Southwestern Coast Salish. *Handbook of North American Indians*, ed. by William C. Sturtevant, vol. 7: *Northwest Coast*, ed. by Wayne Suttles, 503–517. Washington DC: Smithsonian Institution.
Hakola, Hannu Panu Aukusti. 1997. *Duraljan Vocabulary: Lexical Similarities in the Major Agglutinative Languages*. Kuopio: H. P. A. Hakola. (Kuopio University Printing Office.)
Hakola, Hannu Panu Aukusti. 2000. *1000 Duraljan Etyma: An Extended Study in the Lexical Similarities in the Major Agglutinative Languages*. Kuopio: H. P. A. Hakola. (Kuopio University Printing Office.)
Hale, Horatio. 1846. *United States Exploring Expedition, during the Years 1838, 1839, 1840, 1841, 1842, under the Command of Charles Wilkes, U.S. Navy*, vol. 6: *Ethnography and Philology*. Philadelphia: Lea & Blanchard.
Hale, Horatio. 1883. Indian migrations, as evidenced by language, part I: The Huron-Cherokee stock. *American Antiquarian* 5.18–28.
Hale, Kenneth. 1958–1959. Internal diversity of Uto-Aztecan I and II. *International Journal of American Linguistics* 24.101–107, 25.114–121.
Hale, Kenneth. 1964. The sub-grouping of Uto-Aztecan languages: Lexical evidence for Sonoran. *International Congress of Americanists* 35/3.511–517.
Hale, Kenneth. 1967. Toward a reconstruction of Kiowa-Tanoan phonology. *International Journal of American Linguistics* 33:112–120.
Hale, Kenneth and David Harris. 1979. Historical linguistics and archaeology. *Handbook of North American Indians*, vol. 9: *Southwest*, ed. by Alonso Ortiz, 170–177. Washington DC: Smithsonian Insititution.
Hale, Kenneth and Danilo Salamanca. 2002. Theoretical and universal implications of certain verbal entries in dictionaries of the Misumalpan languages. *Making Dictionaries: Preserving indigenous Languages of the Americas*, ed. by William Frawley, Kenneth C. Hill, and Pamela Munro, 25–59. Berkeley and Los Angeles: University of California Press.

Halpern, Abraham M. 1942. A theory of Maya tš-sounds. *Notes in Middle American Archaeology and Ethnology* 13.51–62. Carnegie Institute of Washington.
Halpin, Margorie M. and Margaret Seguin. 1990. Tsimshian peoples: Southern Tsimshian, Coast Tsimshian, Nishga, and Gitksan. *Handbook of North American Indians*, ed. by William C. Sturtevant, vol. 7: *Northwest Coast*, ed. by Wayne Suttles, 267–284. Washington DC: Smithsonian Institution.
Hammarström, Harald. 2010. A full-scale test of the language farming dispersal hypothesis. *Diachronica* 27.197–213.
Hammarström, Harald. 2011. The identity of the Maynas language. Unpublished manuscript.
Hammarström, Harald. 2014. Basic vocabulary comparison in South American languages. *The Native Language of South America: Origins, Development, Typology*, ed. by Loretta O'Connor and Pieter Muysken, 56–70. New York: Cambridge University Press.
Hammarström, Harald, Robert Forkel, Martin Haspelmath, and Sebastian Bank. 2021. *Glottolog 4.4*. Leipzig: Max Planck Institute for Evolutionary Anthropology. https://doi.org/10.5281/zenodo.4761960; http://glottolog.org (accessed August 8, 2021).
Hammerich, Louis L. 1951. Can Eskimo be related to Indo-European? *International Journal of American Linguistics* 17.217–223.
Hammerly Dupuy, Daniel. 1947a. Clasificación del nuevo grupo lingüístico Aksánas de la Patagonia occidental. *Ciencia e investigación* 3/12.492–501. Buenos Aires.
Hammerly Dupuy, Daniel. 1947b. Redescubrimiento de una tribu de indios canoeros del sur de Chile. *Revista Geográfica Americana* 28/168.117–122.
Hammerly Dupuy, Daniel. 1952. Los pueblos canoeros de Fuegopatagonia y los límites del habitat Alakalúf. *Runa* 5.1–2: 134–170. Buenos Aires.
Hammond, George P. and Agapito Rey. 1927. The Rodríguez expedition to New Mexico, 1581–1582. *New Mexico Historical Review* 2.239–268, 334–362.
Hamori-Torok, Charles. 1990. Haisla. *Handbook of North American Indians*, ed. by William C. Sturtevant, vol. 7: *Northwest Coast*, ed. by Wayne Suttles, 306–311. Washington DC: Smithsonian Institution.
Hamp, Eric P. 1964. "Chicken" in Ecuadorian Quichua. *International Journal of American Linguistics* 30.298–299.
Hamp, Eric P. 1967. On Maya-Chipayan. *International Journal of American Linguistics* 33.74–76.
Hamp, Eric P. 1970. Maya-Chipaya and typology of labials. *Chicago Linguistics Society* 6.20–22.
Hamp, Eric P. 1971. On Mayan-Araucanian comparative phonology. *International Journal of American Linguistics* 37.156–159.
Hamp, Eric P. 1976. On Eskimo-Aleut and Luoravetlan. *Papers on Eskimo and Aleut Linguistics*, ed. by Eric Hamp, 81–92. Chicago: Chicago Linguistic Society.
Hardy, Donald E. 2005. Creek. *Native Languages of the Southeastern United States*, ed. by Janine Scancarelli and Heather Kay Hardy, 200–245. Lincoln: University of Nebraska Press.
Hardy, Heather K. 2005. Introduction. *Native Languages of the Southeastern United States*, ed. by Janine Scancarelli and Heather Kay Hardy, 69–74. Lincoln: University of Nebraska Press.
Harms, Phillip Lee. 1994. *Epena Pedee Syntax*. (Studies in the Languages of Colombia, 4.) Arlington: Summer Institute of Linguistics and University of Texas at Arlington.
Harrington, John Peabody. 1909. Notes on the Piro language. *American Anthropologist* 11.563–594.
Harrington, John Peabody. 1910a. On phonetic and lexic resemblances between Kiowa and Tanoan. *American Anthropologist* 12.119–123.
Harrington, John Peabody. 1910b. Introductory paper on the Tiwa language, dialect of Taos, New Mexico. *American Anthropologist* 12.11–48.

Harrington, John Peabody. 1913. [Announcement of the relationship of Yuman and Chumash.] *American Anthropologist* 15.716.

Harrington, John Peabody. 1928. *Vocabulary of the Kiowa language*. (Bureau of American Ethnology, Bulletin 84.) Washington DC: Government Printing Office.

Harrington, John Peabody. 1943b. Hokan discovered in South America. *Journal of the Washington Academy of Sciences* 33/11.334–344.

Harrington, John Peabody. 1974. Sibilants in Ventureño, ed. by Madison S. Beeler and Mary R. Haas. *International Journal of American Linguistics* 40.1–9.

Harvey, H[erbert] R. 1972. The Relaciones Geográficas, 1579–1586: Native languages. *Handbook of Middle American Indians*, ed. by Robert Wauccope, vol. 12: *Ethnohistorical Sources*, ed. by Howard Cline, 279–323. Austin: University of Texas Press.

Haspelmath, Martin and Uri Tadmor, eds. 2009. *Loanwords in the World's Languages: A Comparative Handbook*. Walter de Gruyter.

Haude, Katharina. 2006. *A Grammar of Movima*. Zetten: Manta.

Haugen, Jason D. 2020. Evaluating proposals for long-distance genetic relationships: Uto-Aztecan vs. Plateau Penutian. *The Routledge Handbook of North American Languages*, ed. by Daniel Siddiqi, Michael Barrie, Carrie Gillon, Jason Haugen, and Eric Mathieu, 549–571. London: Routledge.

Haugen, Jason D., Michael Everdell, and Benjamin A. Kuperman. 2020. Uto-Aztecan lexicostatistics 2.01. *International Journal of American Linguistics* 86.1–30.

Haumonté, Jean-Dominic, Jean Parisot, and Lucien Adam. 1882. *Grammaire et vocabulaire de la langue taensa avec texts traduits et commentés*. (Bibliotéque Linguistique Américain, 9.) Paris: Maisonneuve.

Haynie, Hannah Jane. 2012. *Studies in the History and Geography of California Languages*. PhD dissertation, University of California, Berkeley.

Haynie, Hannah, Claire Bowern, Patience Epps, Jane Hill, and Patrick McConvell. 2014. Wanderwörter in languages of the Americas and Australia. *Ampersand* 1.1–18.

Heath, Jeffrey. 1977. Uto-Aztecan morphophonemics. *International Journal of American Linguistics* 43.27–36.

Heath, Shirley Brice. 1972. *Telling Tongues: Language Policy in Mexico*. New York: Teachers College Press.

Heaton, Raina. 2016. Active-stative agreement in Tunica. *Anthropological Linguistics* 58.299–326.

Heaton, Raina. 2018. Language Isolates of Mesoamerica and Northern Mexico. *Language isolates*, ed. by Lyle Campbell, 229–259. London: Routledge.

Heaton, Raina and Patricia Anderson. 2017. When animals become humans: Grammatical gender in Tunica. *International Journal of American Linguistics* 83.341–363.

Heggarty, Paul. 2020a. Deep time and first settlement: What, if anything, can linguistics tell us? *Rethinking the Andes-Amazonia Divide: a Cross-disciplinary Exploration*, ed. by Adrian J. Pearce, David G. Beresford- Jones, and Paul Heggarty, 94–102. London: UCL Press (University College London).

Heggarty, Paul. 2020b. Broad-scale patterns across the languages of the Andes and Amazonia. *Rethinking the Andes-Amazonia Divide: A Cross-disciplinary Exploration*, ed. by Adrian J. Pearce, David G. Beresford- Jones, and Paul Heggarty, 164–177. London: UCL Press (University College London).

Heidenreich, Conrad E. 1978. Huron. *Handbook of North American Indians*, ed. by William C. Sturtevant, vol. 15: *Northeast*, ed. by Bruce G. Trigger, 368–388. Washington DC: Smithsonian Institution.

Helm, June. 1981. Dogrib. *Handbook of North American Indians*, ed. by William C. Sturtevant, vol. 6: *Subarctic*, ed. by June Helm, 291–309. Washington DC: Smithsonian Institution.

Helmke, Christophe. 2013. Mesoamerican lexical calques in Ancient Maya writing and imagery. *PARI (Pre-Columbian Art Research Institute) Journal* 14.1–15.

Henley, Paul, Marie-Claude Mattéi Müller, and Howard Reid. 1994–1996. Cultural and linguistic affinities of the foraging people of North Amazonia: A new perspective. *Antropológica* 83.3–38.

Hendrichs Pérez, Pedro R. 1947. Breve informe del idioma cuitlateco. *International Congress of Americanists* 27.289–295.

Henry, Jules. 1939. The linguistic position of the Ashluslay Indians. *International Journal of American Linguistics* 10.86–91.

Hervás y Panduro, Lorenzo. 1784–1787. *Idea dell'universo: che contiene la storia della vita dell'uomo, elementi cosmografici, viaggio estatico al mondo planetario, e storia de la terra e delle lingue*. Cesena: Biasini.

Hervás y Panduro, Lorenzo. 1800–1805. *Catálogo de las lenguas de las naciones conocidas y numeracion, division, y clases de estas segun la diversidad de sus idiomas y dialectos*, vol. 1 (1800): *Lenguas y naciones Americanas*. Madrid: Administracion del Real Arbitrio de Beneficencia.

Hewson, John. 1968. Beothuk and Algonkian: Evidence old and new. *International Journal of American Linguistics* 37.244–249.

Hewson, John. 1971. Beothuk consonant correspondences. *International Journal of American Linguistics* 37.244–249.

Hewson, John. 1978. *Beothuk Vocabularies: A Comparative Study*. (Technical papers of the Newfoundland Museum, 2.) St. John's, Newfoundland: Department of Tourism, Historic Resources Division.

Hewson, John. 1982. Beothuk and the Algonkian Northeast. *Languages in Newfoundland and Labrador*, ed. by Harrold J. Paddock, 176–187. St. John's, Newfoundland: Department of Linguistics, Memorial University.

Hill, Jane H. 2001. Proto-Uto-Aztecan: A community of cultivators in central Mexico? *American Anthropologist* 103.913–914.

Hill, Jane H. 2002. Proto-Uto-Aztecan cultivation and the northern devolution. *Examining the Farming/Language Dispersal Hypothesis*, ed. by Peter Bellwood and Colin Renfrew, 331–340. Cambridge: McDonald Institute for Archaeological Research.

Hill, Jane H. 2008. Northern Uto-Aztecan and Kiowa-Tanoan: Evidence of contact between the proto-languages? *International Journal of American Linguistics* 74.155–188.

Hill, Jane H. 2011. Subgrouping in Uto-Aztecan. *Language Dynamics and Change* 1.241–278.

Hill, Jane H. 2012. Proto-Uto-Aztecan as a Mesoamerican language. *Ancient Mesoamerica* 23.57–68.

Hill, Jane H. 2017. Historical linguistics. *Oxford Handbook of Southwest Archaeology*, ed. by Barbara Mills and Severin Fowles, 121–135. Oxford: Oxford University Press.

Hill, Jane H., 2020. Areal linguistics and linguistic areas in California. *The Routledge Handbook of North American Languages*, ed. by Daniel Siddiqi, Michael Barrie, Carrie Gillon, Jason Haugen, and Eric Mathieu, 572–586. London: Routledge.

Hilton, Susanne F. 1990. Haihais, Bella Bella, and Oowekeeno. *Handbook of North American Indians*, ed. by William C. Sturtevant, vol. 7: *Northwest Coast*, ed. by Wayne Suttles, 312–322. Washington DC: Smithsonian Institution.

Hinton, Leanne. 1991. Takic and Yuman: A study in phonological convergence. *International Journal of American Linguistics* 57.133–157.

Hinton, Leanne. 1994. *Flutes of Fire: Essays on California Indian Languages*. Berkeley, CA: Heyday Books.

Hoff, Berend J. 1994. Island Carib, an Arawakan language which incorporated a lexical register of Cariban, used to address men. *Mixed Languages: Fifteen Case Studies in Language Intertwining*, ed. Peter Bakker and Maarten Mous, 161–168. Amsterdam: Institute for Functional Research into Language and Language Use.

Hoijer, Harry. 1933. Tonkawa: An Indian language of Texas. *Handbook of American Indian Languages*, vol. 3, ed. by Franz Boas, i–x, 1–148. New York: Columbia University Press.

Hoijer, Harry. 1946b. Tonkawa. *Linguistic Structures of Native America*, ed. by Harry Hoijer, 289–311. (Viking Fund Publications in Anthropology, 6.) New York: The Viking Fund.

Hoijer, Harry. 1949. *An Analytical Dictionary of the Tonkawa Language*. (University of California Publications in Linguistics, 5). Berkeley and Los Angeles: University of California Press.

Hoijer, Harry. 1972. *Tonkawa Texts*. (University of California Publications in Linguistics, 73.) Berkeley and Los Angeles: University of California Press.

Hollow, Robert C. and Douglas R. Parks. 1980. Studies in Plains linguistics: A review. *Anthropology of the Great Plains*, ed. by W. Raymond Wood and Morgot Liberty, 68–97. Lincoln: University of Nebraska Press.

Holman, Eric W., Cecil H. Brown, Søren Wichmann, André Müller, Viveka Velupillai, Harald Hammarström, Sebastian Sauppe, Hagen Jung, Dik Bakker, Pamela Brown, Oleg Belyaev, Matthias Urban, Robert Mailhammer, Johann-Mattis List, and Dmitry Egorov. 2011. Automated dating of the world's language families. *Current Anthropology* 52.841–875.

Holman, Eric W., Søren Wichmann, Cecil H. Brown, Viveka Velupillai, André Müller, and Dik Bakker. 2008. Explorations in automated language classification. *Folia Linguistica* 42.331–354.

Holt, Dennis. 1986. *History of the Paya sound system*. PhD dissertation, UCLA.

Hoyo, Eugenio del. 1960. Vocablos de la lengua quinigua de los Indios Borrados del noreste de México. *Humanitas: Anuario del Centro de Estudios Humanísticos, Universidad de Nuevo León* 1/1.489–515.

Humboldt, Alexander von. 1811[1809–1814]. *Essai politique sur le royaume de la Nouvelle-Espagne*. Paris: Schell.

Huttar, George L. 1982. *A Creole-Amerindian Pidgin of Suriname*. (Society for Caribbean Linguistics Occasional Paper no. 15.) St. Augustine, Trinidad: School of Education, University of the West Indies.

Huttar, George L. and Mary L. Huttar. 1994. *Ndyuka*. London: Routledge.

Huttar, George L. and Frank J. Velantie. 1997. Ndyuka-Trio Pidgin. *Contact Languages: A Wider Perspective*, ed. by Sarah G. Thomason, 99–124. Amsterdam: Benjamins.

Hymes, Dell H. 1957. Some Penutian elements and the Penutian hypothesis. *Southwestern Journal of Anthropology* 13.69–87.

Hymes, Dell H. 1961. Review of Tungusisch und Ketschua, by Karl Bouda. *International Journal of American Linguistics* 27.362–364.

Ibarra Grasso, Dick E. 1958. *Lenguas indígenas americanas*. Buenos Aires: Editorial Nova.

Ibarra Grasso, Dick E. 1964. *Lenguas indígenas de Bolivia*. Cochabamba, Bolivia: Universidad Mayor de San Simón, Museo Arqueológico.

Imbelloni, José. 1926. *La esfinge indiana: antiguos y nuevos aspectos del problema de los orígenes americanos*. Buenos Aires: Buenos Aires: Imprenta Mercatali.

Imbelloni, José. 1928[1926]. L'idioma Kichua nel sistema linguistico dell'Oceano Pacifico. *International Congress of Americanists* 22/2.495–509.

Imbelloni, José. 1936. *Lenguas Indígenas del Territorio Argentino*. Buenos aires: Imprenta de la Universidad de Buenos Aires.

Itier, César. 2011. What was the Lengua General of colonial Peru? *History and Language in the Andes*, ed. by Paul Heggarty and Adrian J. Pearce, 63–85. New York: Palgrave Macmillan.

Jackson, Jean. 1983. *The Fish People: Linguistic Exogamy and Tukanoan Identity in Northwest Amazonia*. Cambridge: Cambridge University Press.

Jacobs, Melville. 1932. Notes on the structure of Chinook Jargon. *Language* 8.27–50.

Jacobs, Melville. 1954. The areal spread of sound features in the languages North of California. *Papers from the Symposium on American Indian Linguistics*, ed. by Murray B. Emeneau, 46–56. (*University of California Publications in Linguistics*, 10.) Berkeley and Los Angeles: University of California Press.

Jacobsen, William H., Jr. 1979a. Wakashan comparative studies. *The Languages of Native America: An Historical and Comparative Assessment*, ed. by Lyle Campbell and Marianne Mithun, 766–791. Austin: University of Texas Press.

Jacobsen, William H., Jr. 1979b. Chimakuan comparative studies. *The Languages of Native America: An Historical and Comparative Assessment*, ed. by Lyle Campbell and Marianne Mithun, 792–802. Austin: University of Texas Press.

Jacobsen, William H., Jr. 1980. Inclusive/exclusive: a diffused pronominal category in native Western North America. *Papers from the Parasession on Pronouns and Anaphora*, ed. by Jody Kreiman and Almerindo E. Ojeda, 204–227. Chicago: Chicago Linguistic Society.

Jacobsen, William H., Jr. 1983. Typology and genetic notes on switch-reference systems in North American Indian languages. *Switch-reference and Universal Grammar*, ed. by John Haiman and Pamela Munro, 151–183. Amsterdam: John Benjamins.

Jacobsen, William H., Jr. 1986. Washoe language. *Handbook of North American Indians*, ed. by William C. Sturtevant, vol. 11: *Great Basin*, ed. by Warren L. D'Azevedo, 107–112. Washington DC: Smithsonian Institution.

Jacobson, Steven A. 1984. *Yup'ik Eskimo dictionary*. Fairbanks: Alaska Native Language Center.

Jaime, Blas W. Omar and Pedro Viegas Barros. 2013. *La lengua Chaná: patrimonio cultural de Entre Ríos*. Paraná: Dirección Editorial de Entre Ríos.

Jaker, Alessandro, Nicholas Welch, and Keren Rice. 2020. The Na-Dene languages. *The Routledge Handbook of North American Languages*, ed. by Daniel Siddiqi, Michael Barrie, Carrie Gillon, Jason Haugen, and Eric Mathieu, 473–503. London: Routledge.

Jany, Carmen. 2009. *Chimariko Grammar: Areal and Typological Perspective*. (University of California Publications in Linguistics, 142.) Berkeley: University of California Press.

Jany, Carmen. 2016. Hokan Languages. *Oxford Research Encyclopedia of Linguistics*. http://oxfordre.com/linguistics/view/10.1093/acrefore/9780199384655.001.0001/acrefore-9780199384655-e-19 (accessed September 22, 2022).

Jara Murillo, Carla Victoria. 2012. Hispanismos en el discurso bribri. *Revista Káñina* 6.111–124.

Jennings, Francis. 1978. Susquehannock. *Handbook of North American Indians*, ed. by William C. Sturtevant, vol. 15: *Northeast*, ed. by Bruce G. Trigger, 362–367. Washington DC: Smithsonian Institution.

Jiménez de la Espada, Marcos. 1965 [1586]. *Relaciones geográficas de Indias: Perú*. (Biblioteca de Autores Españoles 185, ed. by José Urbano Martínez Carreras, 3 vols.) Madrid: Ediciones Atlas.

Jiménez Moreno, Wigberto. 1943. Tribus e idiomas del norte de México. *Revista Mexicana de Estudios Antropológicos* 3.131–133.

Johns, Alana. 2020. Eskimo-Aleut. *The Routledge Handbook of North American Languages*, ed. by Daniel Siddiqi, Michael Barrie, Carrie Gillon, Jason Haugen, and Eric Mathieu, 524–548. London: Routledge.

Julian, Charles. 2010. *A History of the Iroquoian Languages*. PhD dissertation, University of Manitoba. https://mspace.lib.umanitoba.ca/xmlui/bitstream/handle/1993/4175/julian_charles.pdf?sequence=1&isAllowed=y.

Justeson, John S. and Terrence Kaufman. 1993. A decipherment of Epi-Olmec hieroglyphic writing. *Science* 259.1703–1711.

Justeson, John S., William Norman, Lyle Campbell, and Terrence Kaufman. 1985. *The Foreign Impact on Lowland Mayan Languages and Script*. (Middle American Research Institute, publication 53.) New Orleans: Tulane University.

Karttunen, Frances and James Lockhart. 1976. *Nahuatl in the Middle Years: Language Contact Phenomena in Texts of the Colonial Period*. (University of California Publications in Linguistics, 85.) Berkeley and Los Angeles: University of California Press.

Kasak, Ryan M. 2016. A distant genetic relationship between Siouan-Catawban and Yuchi. *Advances in the Study of Siouan Languages and Linguistics*, ed. by Catherine Rudin and Bryan James Gordon, 5–37. Berlin: Language Science Press. https://doi.org/10.17169/langsci.b94.120. https://library.oapen.org/bitstream/handle/20.500.12657/32373/611691.pdf?sequence=1#page=83.

Kaufman, Terrence. 1964a. Materiales lingüísticos para el estudio de las relaciones internas y externas de la familia de idiomas Mayanos. *Desarrollo Cultural de los Mayas*, ed. by Evon Vogt, 81–136. Mexico: Universidad Nacional Autónoma de México.

Kaufman, Terrence. 1964b. Evidence for the Macro-Mayan hypothesis. Unpublished paper.

Kaufman, Terrence. 1969. Teco—a new Mayan language. *International Journal of American Linguistics* 35.154–174.

Kaufman, Terrence. 1976. Archaeological and linguistic correlations in Mayaland and associated areas of Meso-America. *World Archaeology* 8.101–118.

Kaufman, Terrence. 1980. Pre-Columbian borrowing involving Huastec. *American Indian and Indo-European Studies: Papers in Honor of Madison S. Beeler*, ed. by Kathryn Klar, Margaret Langdon, and Shirley Silver, 101–112. The Hague: Mouton.

Kaufman, Terrence. 1981. *Comparative Uto-Aztecan phonology*. [Unpublished monograph.]

Kaufman, Terrence. 1988. A research program for reconstructing Proto-Hokan: First gropings. *Papers from the 1988 Hokan–Penutian Languages Workshop*, ed. by Scott DeLancey, 50–168. Eugene, Oregon: Department of Linguistics, University of Oregon.

Kaufman, Terrence. 1990a. Language history in South America: what we know and how to know more. *Amazonian Linguistics: Studies in Lowland South American Languages*, ed. by Doris L. Payne, 13–67. Austin: University of Texas Press.

Kaufman, Terrence. 1994. The native languages of South America. *Atlas of the World's Languages*, ed. by Christopher Moseley and R. E. Asher, 46–76. London: Routledge.

Kaufman, Terrence. 2002. *Reconstructing Mayan Morphology and Syntax*. Unpublished ms. University of Pittsburgh.

Kaufman, Terrence. 2003. The history of the Nawa language group from earliest times to the sixteenth century: Some initial remarks. https://www.albany.edu/pdlma/Nawa.pdf.

Kaufman, Terrence, with Brent Berlin. 2007. The native languages of South America. *Atlas of the World's Languages* (2nd edition), ed. by Christopher Moseley and R. E. Asher, 61–93. London: Routledge.

Kaufman, Terrence. 2015a. A research program for reconstructing Proto-Hokan: First gropings (revised 2015). https://www.albany.edu/ims/pdlma/2015%20Publications/Kaufman-reconstructing%20protoHokan-first%20gropings-revd2015.pdf.

Kaufman, Terrence. 2015b. Some Hypotheses Regarding Proto-Hokan Grammar. https://www.researchgate.net/profile/Terrence-Kaufman/publication/340925991_Some_hypotheses_regarding_proto-Hokan_grammar_Kaufman_2015/links/5ea49e72299bf112560e7106/Some-hypotheses-regarding-proto-Hokan-grammar-Kaufman-2015.pdf.

Kaufman, Terrence. 2015c. Early Oto-Manguean homelands and cultures: Some premature hypotheses. Institute for Mesoamerican Studies, University at Albany, State University of New York. http://www.albany.edu/ims/PDLMA_publications_new.html.

Kaufman, Terrence. 2017. Aspects of the lexicon of Proto-Mayan and its earliest descendants. *The Mayan Languages*, ed. by Judith Aissen, Nora C. England, and Roberto Zavala Maldonado, 62–111. London: Routledge.

Kaufman, Terrence. 2020a. Olmecs, Teotihuacaners, and Toltecs: Language history and language contact in Meso-America. https://www.researchgate.net/profile/Terrence-Kaufman/publication/340721651_MALP_2020/links/5e9a4336299bf13079a24ec9/MALP-2020.pdf.

Kaufman, Terrence. 2020b. Comparative Oto-Mangean grammar research: phonology, aspect-mood marking, valency changers, nominalizers on verbs, numerals, pronouns, deictics, interrogatives, adpositionoids, noun classifiers, noun inflexion, compounds, word order, and diversification model. Unpublished paper.

Kaufman, Terrence. 2021. *Oto-Mangean Etymological Dictionary*. https://www.researchgate.net/publication/348311264_OtoMangean_Etymological_Dictionary/link/5ff7965e299b-f140887d744c/download?_tp=eyJjb250ZXh0Ijp7ImZpcnN0UGFnZSI6InBiYmxpY-2FoaW9uIiwicGFnZSI6InBiYmxpY2FoaW9uIn19.

Kaufman, Terrence and Victor Golla. 2000. Language groupings in the New World: Their reliability and usability in cross-disciplinary studies. *America Past, America Present: Genes and Languages in the Americas and Beyond*, ed. by Colin. Renfrew, 47–57. Cambridge: McDonald Institute for Archaeological Research.

Kaufman, Terrence, with John Justeson. 2003. *A Preliminary Mayan Etymological Dictionary*. Los Angeles: FAMSI. www.famsi.org/reports/01051/pmed.pdf.

Kaufman, Terrence and Justeson, John. 2007. The history of the word for cacao in ancient Mesoamerica. *Ancient Mesoamerica* 18.193–237. https://doi.org.10.1017/S0956536107000211.

Kaufman, Terrence and John Justeson. 2008. The Epi-Olmec language and its neighbors. *Classic Period Cultural Currents in Southern and Central Veracruz*, ed. by Philip J. Arnold III and Christopher A. Pool, 55–83. Washington DC: Dunbarton Oaks Research Library and Collection.

Kaufman, Terrence and John Justeson. 2009. Historical linguistics and pre-Columbian Mesoamerica. *Ancient Mesoamerica* 20.221–231.

Kaufman, Terrence and William Norman. 1984. An outline of Proto-Cholan phonology, morphology, and vocabulary. *Phoneticism in Maya Hieroglyphic Writing*, ed. by John S.

Justeson and Lyle Campbell, 77–166. (Institute for Mesoamerican Studies, Publication 9.) Albany: State University of New York.

Kendall, Daythal L. 1990. Takelma. *Handbook of North American Indians*, ed. by William C. Sturtevant, vol. 7: *Northwest Coast*, ed. by Wayne Suttles, 589–592. Washington DC: Smithsonian Institution.

Kendall, Daythal L. 1997. The Takelma verb: Towards Proto-Takelma-Kalapuyan. *International Journal of American Linguistics* 63.1–17.

Kenmotsu, Nancy A. 2021. The native peoples of the Trans-Pecos mountains and basins. https://texasbeyondhistory.net/trans-p/peoples/farmers.html (accessed August 17, 2021).

Kennedy, Dorothy I. D. and Randall T. Bouchard. 1990. Northern Coast Salish. *Handbook of North American Indians*, ed. by William C. Sturtevant, vol. 7: *Northwest Coast*, ed. by Wayne Suttles, 441–452. Washington DC: Smithsonian Institution.

Kennett, Douglas J., Mark Lipson, Keith M. Prufer, David Mora-Marín, Richard J. George, Nadin Rohland, Mark Robinson, Willa R. Trask, Heather H. J. Edgar, Ethan C. Hill, Erin E. Ray, Paige Lynch, Emily Moes, Lexi O'Donnell, Thomas K. Harper, Emily J. Kate, Josue Ramos, John Morris, Said M. Gutierrez, Timothy M. Ryan, Brendan J. Culleton, Jaime J. Awe, and David Reich. 2022. South-to-north migration preceded the advent of intensive farming in the Maya region. *Nature Communications* 13.1–10. https://doi.org/10.1038/s41467-022-29158-y.

Kettunen, Harri. 2021. New World words and things in the Old World: How the Americas conquered the world. *Contributions in New World Archaeology*, vol. 14: *Proceedings of the 24th European Maya Conference Cracow, November 11–16, 2019*, part 2, ed. by Chistophe Helmke, Harri Kettunen, and Jarosław Źrałka, 97–200. Kraków: Jagiellonian University, Institute of Archaeology.

Key, Mary Ritchie. 1984. *Polynesian and American Linguistic Connections*. (Edward Sapir Monograph Series in Language, Culture, and Cognition, 12; supplement to Forum Linguisticum 8:3.) Lake Bluff, IL: Jupiter Press.

Kibrik, Andrej. 2010. Transitivity indicators, historical scenarios, and sundry Dene-Yeniseian notes. *The Dene-Yeniseian Connection*, ed. by James Kari and Ben A. Potter, 316–319. (Anthropological Papers of the University of Alaska, New Series, 5.1–2. A special joint publication of the UAF.) Fairbanks: Department of Anthropology and the Alaska Native Languages Center.

Kiddle, Lawrence B. 1968. Hispanismos en las lenguas indígenas de América. *Actas del XI Congreso Internacional de Lingüística y Filología Románicas*, ed. by Antonio Quilis, Ramón Blanco Carril, and Margarita Cantarero, 2069–2084. Madrid: Revista de Filología Española.

Kim, Yuni, 2008. *Topics in the Phonology and Morphology of San Francisco del Mar Huave*. PhD dissertation, University of California, Berkeley.

Kimball, Geoffrey. 1987a. A grammatical sketch of Apalachee. *International Journal of American Linguistics* 53.136–174.

Kimball, Geoffrey. 1988. An Apalachee vocabulary. *International Journal of American Linguistics* 54.387–398.

Kimball, Geoffrey. 1992. A critique of Muskogean, "Gulf," and Yukian material in Language in the Americas. *International Journal of American Linguistics* 58.447–501.

Kimball, Geoffrey. 1994. Comparative difficulties of the "Gulf" languages. *Proceedings of the Meeting of the Society for the Study of the Indigenous Languages of the Americas and the Hokan-Penutian Workshop*, ed. by Margaret Langdon, 31–39. (Survey of California and Other Indian Languages, report 8.) Berkeley and Los Angeles: University of California.

Kimball, Geoffrey. 2005. Natchez. *Native Languages of the Southeastern United States*, ed. by Janine Scancarelli and Heather Kay Hardy, 385–453. Lincoln: University of Nebraska Press.

King, Alan R. 2017. *Lenca for Linguists: Sketch of an Indigenous Language of Honduras*. http://tushik.org/wp-content/uploads/Lenca-for-Linguists.pdf.

King, Chester and Thomas C. Blackburn. 1978. Tataviam. *Handbook of North American Indians*, ed. by William C. Sturtevant, vol. 8: *California*, ed. by Robert F. Heizer, 535–537. Washington DC: Smithsonian Institution.

Kinkade, M. Dale. 1985. More on nasal loss on the Northwest Coast. *International Journal of American Linguistics* 51.478–480.

Kinkade, M. Dale. 1991b. Prehistory of the native languages of the Northwest Coast. *The North Pacific to 1600*, vol. 1, 137–158. Portland: The Oregon Historical Society Press.

Kinkade, M. Dale. 1998. How much does a schwa weigh? *Salish Languages and Linguistics: Theoretical and Descriptive Perspectives*, ed. by Ewa Czaykowska-Higgins and M. Dale Kinkade, 197–216. New York: Mouton de Gruyter.

Kinkade, M. Dale. 2005. Alsea pronouns. *Anthropological Linguistics* 47.61–76.

Kinkade, M. Dale, William W. Elmendorf, Bruce Rigsby, and Haruo Aoki. 1998. Plateau languages. *Handbook of North American Indians*, ed. by William C. Sturtevant general editor, vol. 12: *Plateau*, ed. by Edward E. Walker, Jr., 49–72. Washington DC: Smithsonian Institution.

Kinkade, M. Dale and J. V. Powell. 1976. Language and the prehistory of North America. *World Archaeology* 8.83–100.

Kinkade, M. Dale and Laurence C. Thompson. 1974. Proto-Salish *r. *International Journal of American Linguistics* 40.22–28.

Kirchhoff, Paul. 1943. Mesoamérica. *Acta Americana* 1.92–107.

Kirtchuk, Pablo. 1996. Lingüística areal: deixis y clasificación nominal en lenguas del Gran Chaco. *Lenguas indígenas de Argentina 1942–1992*, ed. by Eusebia H. Martín and Andrés Pérez Diez, 19–32. (Instituto de Investigaciones Lingüísticas y Filológicas "Manuel Alvar".) San Juan: Editorial Fundación Universidad Nacional de San Juan.

Klar, Kathryn. 1977. *Topics in historical Chumash grammar*. PhD dissertation, University of California, Berkeley.

Klein, Harriet E. Manelis. 1992. South American languages. *International Encyclopedia of Linguistics*, ed. by William Bright, 4.31–35. New York: Oxford University Press.

Koch-Grünberg, Theodor. 1904. *Zwei Jahre unter den Indianern: Reisen in Nordwest-Brasilien*. Stuttgart: Strecker & Schröde.

Kohlberger, Martin. 2020. *A grammatical description of Shiwiar*. PhD dissertation, Leiden University. https://scholarlypublications.universiteitleiden.nl/handle/1887/123115.

Koo, J. H. 1980. Eskimo as a member of the Uralo-Altaic family: Some structural similarities. *Congressus Quintus Internationalis Fenno-Ugristarum* 7.216–224. Turku: Suomen Kielen Seura.

Koppelmann, Heinrich L. 1929. Ostasiatische Zahlwörter in süd-amerikanischen Sprachen. *International Archiv für Ethnographie* 30.77–118.

Krause, Aurel. 1885. *Die Tlinkit-Indianer*. Jena: Constenoble. (1956, *The Tlingit Indians: Results of a trip to the Northwest Coast of America and the Bering Straits*, translated by Erna Gunther. Seattle: University of Washington Press.)

Krauss, Michael E. 1964. Proto-Athapaskan-Eyak and the problem of Na-Dene I: the phonology. *International Journal of American Linguistics* 30.118–131.

Krauss, Michael E. 1973a. Eskimo-Aleut. *Current Trends in Linguistics*, vol. 10: *Linguistics in North America*, ed. by Thomas A. Sebeok, 796–902. The Hague: Mouton.

Krauss, Michael E. 1973b. Na-Dene. *Current Trends in Linguistics*, vol. 10: *Linguistics in North America*, ed. by Thomas Sebeok, 903–978. The Hague: Mouton.

Krauss, Michael E. 1979. Na-Dene and Eskimo-Aleut. *The Languages of Native America: An Historical and Comparative Assessment*, ed. by Lyle Campbell and Marianne Mithun, 803–901. Austin: University of Texas Press.

Krauss, Michael E. 1980. *Alaska Native Languages: Past, Present, and Future*. (Alaska Native Language Center, research paper 5.) Fairbanks: University of Alaska.

Krauss, Michael E. 1990. Kwalhioqua and Clatskanie. *Handbook of North American Indians*, ed. by William C. Sturtevant, vol. 7: *Northwest Coast*, ed. by Wayne Suttles, 530–532. Washington DC: Smithsonian Institution.

Krauss, Michael E. and Victor K. Golla. 1981. Northern Athabaskan languages. *Handbook of North American Indians*, ed. by William C. Sturtevant, vol. 6: *Subarctic*, ed. by June Helm, 67–85. Washington DC: Smithsonian Institution.

Kroeber, Alfred L. 1907. Shoshonean dialects of California. *University of California Publications in American Archaeology and Ethnology* 4.65–165.

Kroeber, Alfred L. 1910. The Chumash and Costanoan languages. *University of California Publications in American Archaeology and Ethnology* 9.237–271.

Kroeber, Alfred L. 1915. Serian, Tequistlatecan, and Hokan. *University of California Publications in American Archaeology and Ethnology* 11.279–290.

Kroeber, Alfred L. 1916. Arapaho dialects. *University of California Publications in American Archaeology and Ethnology* 12.73–74.

Kroeber, Alfred L. 1925. *The Indians of California*. (Bureau of American Ethnology, Bulletin 78.) Washington DC: US Government Printing Office.

Kroeber, Alfred L. 1934. *Uto-Aztecan languages of Mexico*. (Ibero-Americana, 8.) Berkeley and Los Angeles: University of California Press.

Kroeber, Alfred L. 1940a. The work of John R. Swanton. *Smithsonian Miscellaneous Collections* 100.1–9.

Kroeber, Alfred L. 1940b. Conclusions: The present status of Americanistic problems. *The Maya and Their Neighbors: Essays on Middle American Anthropology and Archaeology*, ed. by Clarence L. Hay, Ralph L. Linton, Samuel K. Lothrop, Harry L. Shapiro, and George C. Vaillant, 460–487. New York: D. Appleton-Century. [Re-issued 1970, New York: Dover.]

Kroeber, Alfred L. 1953. Concluding review (chapter 20). *An Appraisal of Anthropology Today*, ed. by Sol Tax, 357–376. Chicago: University of Chicago Press.

Kroeber, Paul. 1999. *The Salish Language Family: Reconstructing Syntax*. Lincoln: University of Nebraska Press.

Kroskrity, Paul V. 1982. Language contact and linguistic diffusion: the Arizona Tewa speech community. *Bilingualism and Language Contact: Spanish, English, and Native American Languages*, ed. by Florence Barkin, Elizabeth A. Brandt, and Jacob Ornstein-Galicia, 51–72. New York: Teacher's College Press, Columbia University.

Kroskrity, Paul V. 1985. Areal-historical influences on Tewa possession. *International Journal of American Linguistics* 51.486–489.

Kroskrity, Paul V. 1993. *Language, History, and Identity: Ethnolinguistic Studies of the Arizona Tewa*. Tucson: University of Arizona Press.

Kuipers, Aert H. 1981. On reconstructing the Proto-Salish sound system. *International Journal of American Linguistics* 47.323–335.

Kulonen, Ulla-Maija, ed. 1992. *Suomen Sanojen Alkuperä: Etymologinen Sanakirja* [The Origin of Finnish Words: Etymological Dictionary]. 3 vols. (Suomalaisen Kirjallisuuden Seuran Toimituksia, 556; Kotimaisten Kielten Tutkimuksen Julkasuja, 62.) Jyväskylä: Gummerus.
Labov, William. 2007. Transmission and diffusion. *Language* 83.344–338.
Lafone Quevedo, Samuel A. 1894. Idioma Abipón: Ensayo fundado sobre el DE Abonibus de Dobrizhoffer y los Manuscritos del P[adre] J[oseph] Brigniel, S. J., con Introducción, Mapa, Notas y Apéndices. *Academia Nacional de Ciencias* 15/5.200, 253–423.
Lafone Quevedo, Samuel A. 1895. Lengua vilela ó chulupí: estudio de filología chaco- argentina fundado sobre los trabajos de Hervás, Adelung y Pelleschi. *Boletín del Instituto Geográfico Argentino*, 16.39–86, 87–125.
Lafone Quevedo, Samuel A. 1894–1896. Arte de la lengua toba por el padre Alonso Bárcena Soc. Jes. (MS propiedad del General B. Mitre) con vocabularios facilitados por los Sres. Dr. Angel Carranza, Pelleschi, y otros. *Revista del Museo de La Plata* 5.93–184 and 7:191–227.
Lafone Quevedo, Samuel A. 1896. Grupo matacomataguayo del Chaco: dialecto Vejoz. *Boletín del Instituto Geográfico Argentino* 17.121–176.
Lafone-Quevedo, Samuel A. 1905. *La lengua leca: de los Ríos Mapirí y Beni Según los MSS. de los PP. Cardús y Herrero*. Buenos Aires: Coni Hermanos.
Lafone-Quevedo, Samuel A. 1915. Lenguas guaicuras y mataguayas. *Boletín del Instituto Geográfico Argentino* 31.11–25.
Lamb, Sydney. 1959. Some proposals for linguistic taxonomy. *Anthropological Linguistics* 1/2.33–49.
Lamb, Sydney. 1964. The classification of Uto-Aztecan languages: A historical survey. *Studies in Californian linguistics*, ed. by William Bright, 106–125. (*University of California Publications in Linguistics*, 34.) Berkeley and Los Angeles: University of California Press.
Landaburu, John. 2000. Clasificación de las lenguas indígenas de Colombia. *Lenguas Indígenas de Colombia: una visión descriptiva*, ed. by María Stella González de Pérez and María Luisa Rodríguez de Montes, 25–48. Bogotá: Instituto Caro y Cuervo.
Lanes, Elder José. 2005. *Aspectos da mudança lingüística em um conjunto de línguas Amazônicas: as línguas Pano*. PhD dissertation, Universidade Federal do Rio de Janeiro, Rio de Janeiro.
Langacker, Ronald W. 1970. The vowels of Proto Uto-Aztecan. *International Journal of American Linguistics* 36.169–180.
Langacker, Ronald W. 1977. *An Overview of Uto-Aztecan Grammar, 1. Studies in Uto-Aztecan Grammar 1*. Arlington, TX: Summer Institute of Linguistics.
Langdon, Margaret. 1974. *Comparative Hokan-Coahuiltecan Studies: A Survey and Appraisal*. (Janua Linguarum, series critica, 4.) The Hague: Mouton.
Langdon, Margaret. 1979. Some thoughts on Hokan with particular reference to Pomoan and Yuman. *The Languages of Native America: An Historical and Comparative Assessment*, ed. by Lyle Campbell and Marianne Mithun, 592–649. Austin: University of Texas Press.
Langdon, Margaret. 1990. Diegueño: how many languages? *Proceedings of the 1990 Hokan-Penutian Languages Workshop, Occasional Papers on Linguistics*, ed. by James E. Redden, 15.184–190. Carbondale: University of Southern Illinois, Linguistics Department.
Langdon, Margaret and Pamela Munro. 1980. Yuman numerals. *American Indian and Indoeuropean studies: Papers in honor of Madison S. Beeler*, ed. by Kathryn Klar, Margaret Langdon, and Shirley Silver, 121–135. The Hague: Mouton.
Langdon, Margaret and Shirley Silver. 1984. California t/t̪. *Journal of California and Great Basin Anthropology, Papers in linguistics* 4.139–165.

Lardé y Larín, Jorge. 1926. Lenguas indianas de El Salvador: su distribución geográfica. *Revista de El Salvador, Arqueología y Lingüística* 1.281–286.

Larson, Rory. 2016. Regular sound shifts in the history of Siouan. *Advances in the Study of Siouan Languages and Linguistics*, ed. by Catherine Rudin and Bryan James Gordon, 63–83. Berlin: Language Science Press. https://doi.org/10.17169/langsci.b94.122. https://library.oapen.org/bitstream/handle/20.500.12657/32373/611691.pdf?sequence=1#page=83.

Larsson, Lars J. 1987. Who were the Konomihu? *International Journal of American Linguistics* 53.232–235.

Lastra de Suárez, Yolanda. 1986. *Las áreas dialectales del náhuatl moderno*. (Instituto de Investigaciones antropológicas, Lingüística, serie antropológica, 62.) Mexico: Universidad Nacional Autónoma de México.

Laverdure, Patline and Ida Rose Allard. 1983. *The Michif Dictionary Turtle Mountain-Chippewa-Cree*, ed. by John C. Crawford. Winnipeg, Manitoba: Pemmican Publications Inc.

Law, Danny. 2014. *Language Contact, Inherited Similarity and Social Difference: The Story of Linguistic Interaction in the Maya Lowlands*. Amsterdam: John Benjamins.

Law, Danny. 2017a. Language contacts with(in) Mayan. *The Mayan Languages*, ed. by Judith Aissen, Nora C. England, and Roberto Zavala Maldonado, 112–127. London: Routledge.

Law, Danny. 2017b. Language mixing and genetic similarity: The case of Tojol-ab'al. *Diachronica* 34.40–78.

Law, Danny and David Stuart. 2017. Classic Mayan: An overview of language in ancient hieroglyphic script. *The Mayan Languages*, ed. by Judith Aissen, Nora C. England, and Roberto Zavala Maldonado, 128–172. London: Routledge.

Lawson, John. 1709. *A New Voyage to Carolina; Containing the Exact Description and Natural History of that Country: Together with the Present State Thereof. And a Journal of a Thousand Miles, Travel'd thro' Several Nations of Indians. Giving a Particular Account of Their Customs, Manners, &c*. London. (New edition, 1967, edited by Hugh Talmage Leffler. Chapel Hill: University of North Carolina Press.)

Laylander, Donald P. 1997. The linguistic prehistory of Baja California. *Contributions to the Linguistic Prehistory of Central and Baja California*, ed. by Gary S. Breschini and Trudy Haversat, 1–94. Salinas, CA: Coyote Press.

Leap, William L. 1971. Who were the Piro? *Anthropological Linguistics* 13/7.321–330.

Lederer, John. 1958. *The Discoveries of John Lederer*, ed. by William P. Cumming. Charlottesville: University of Virginia Press.

Leer, Jeff. 1979. Proto-Athabaskan verb stem variation, part one: Phonology. (Alaska Native Language Center, research paper 1.) Fairbanks: University of Alaska.

Leer, Jeff. 1990. Tlingit: A portmanteau language family? *Linguistic Change and Reconstruction Methodology*, ed. by Philip Baldi, 73–98. Berlin: Mouton de Gruyter.

Leer, Jeff. 1991. Evidence for a Northern Northwest Coast language area: Promiscuous number marking and periphrastic possessive constructions in Haida, Eyak, and Aleut. *International Journal of American Linguistics* 57.158–193.

Leer, Jeff. 2010. The palatal series in Athabascan-Eyak-Tlingit, with an overview of the basic sound correspondences. *The Dene-Yeniseian Connection*, ed. by James Kari and Ben A. Potter, 168–193. (Anthropological Papers of the University of Alaska, New Series, 5.1–2; a special joint publication of the UAF.) Fairbanks: Department of Anthropology and the Alaska Native Languages Center.

Leesberg, Arnold C. M. 1903. *Comparative Philology: A Comparison between Semitic and American Languages*. Leiden: E. J. Brill.

Lehmann, Walter. 1920. *Zentral-Amerika*, 2 vols. Berlin: Museum für Völkerkunde zu Berlin.
Lehmann-Nitsche, Robert. 1922. El grupo lingüístico het de la pampa argentina. *Revista del Museo de La Plata* 27.10–84.
Lehmann-Nitsche, Robert. 1930. El idioma Chechehet [Pampa bonaerense]: Nombres propios. *Revista del Museo de La Plata* 32.277–291.
Lehmann-Nitsche, Robert. 1936. Die Sprachliche Stellung der Choropí (Gran Chaco). *Zeitschrift für Ethnologie* 68.118–124.
Lemley, Harvey V. 1949. Three Tlapaneco stories from Tlacoapa, Guerrero. *Tlalocan* 3.76–82.
Lenz, Rodolfo. 1940. Hispanismos léxicos en araucano. *El español en Chile*: Traducción, notas y apéndices de Amado Alonso y Raimundo Lida, ed. by R. Lenz, R., A. Bello, and R. Oroz, 244–258. Buenos Aires: Instituto de Filología, Facultad de Filosofía y Letras de la Universidad de Buenos Aires.
León-Portilla, Miguel. 1976. Sobre la lengua pericú de la Baja California. *Anales de Antropología* 12.87–101.
León-Portilla, Miguel. 1985. Ejemplos de la lengua califórnica, cochimí—reunidos por Franz B. Ducrue (1778–1779). *Tlalocan* 10.363–374.
Lapenda, Geraldo. 2005. *Estrutura da língua Iatê: falada pelos índios Fulniôs em Pernambuco* (2nd edition). Recife: Editora Universitária Universidade Federal de Pernambuco.
Lesser, Alexander and Gene Weltfish. 1932. Composition of the Caddoan linguistic stock. *Smithsonian Miscellaneous Collections* 87/6.1–15.
Levine, Robert D. 1979. Haida and Na-Dene: A new look at the evidence. *International Journal of American Linguistics* 45.157–170.
Lillehaugen, Brook Danielle. 2020. Otomanguean languages. *The Routledge Handbook of North American Languages*, ed. by Daniel Siddiqi, Michael Barrie, Carrie Gillon, Jason Haugen, and Eric Mathieu, 331–364. London: Routledge.
Lincoln, Neville J. and John C. Rath. 1980. *North Wakashan Comparative Root List*. (Canadian Ethnology Service, paper 68.) Ottawa: National Museum of Man, Mercury Series.
Lincoln, Peter C. 1979. Dual-lingualism: passive bilingualism in action. *Te Reo* 22.65–72.
Lipski, John M. 2017. Ecuadoran Media Lengua: More than a "half" language? *International Journal of American Linguistics* 83.233–262.
Llamas, Bastien, Lars Fehren-Schmitz, Guido Valverde, Julien Soubrier, Swapan Mallick, Nadin Rohland, Susanne Nordenfelt, Christina Valdiosera, Stephen M. Richards, et al. 2016. Ancient mitochondrial DNA provides high-resolution time scale of the peopling of the Americas. *Science Advances* 2/4.e1501385. https://www.science.org/doi/full/10.1126/sciadv.1501385.
Llaras Samitier, Manuel. 1967. El grupo chono o wayteka y los demás pueblos [de] Fuegopatagonia. *RUNA* 10.123–194.
Loewen, Jacob A. 1963. Chocó II: Phonological problems. *International Journal of American Linguistics* 29.357–371.
Lombardo, Natal. 1702[1641?]. *Arte de la lengua tegüima vulgarmente llamada ópata*. Mexico: Miguel de Ribera.
Longacre, Robert E. 1967. Systemic comparison and reconstruction. *Handbook of Middle American Indians*, vol. 5, ed. by Norman McQuown, 117–160. Austin: University of Texas Press.
Longacre, Robert E. 1968. Comparative Reconstruction of Indigenous languages. *Current Trends in Linguistics*, vol. 4, ed. by Thomas Sebeok, 320–360. The Hague: Mouton.
Loukotka, Čestmír. 1931a. Die Sprache der Zamuco und die Verwandtschaftsverhältnisse der Chaco-Stämme. *Anthropos* 26.843–861.

Loukotka, Čestmír. 1931b. Les indiens kukurá du Rio Verde, Mato Grosso. *Journal de la Société des Américanistes de Paris* 23.121–125.
Loukotka, Čestmír. 1935. *Clasificación de las lenguas sudamericanas.* (Lingüística sudamericana, 1.) Prague: Published by the author.
Loukotka, Čestmír. 1955. Les langues non-Tupí du Brésil du Nord-Est. *Anais do XXXI Congresso Internacional de Americanistas: São Paulo, 23 a 28 de agôsto de 1954*, vol. 2, ed. by Herbert Baldus, 1029–1054. São Paulo: Anhembi.
Loukotka, Čestmír. 1963. Documents et vocabulaires inédits de langues et de dialectes sudaméricains. *Journal de la Société des Américanistes* 52.7–60.
Loukotka, Čestmír. 1968. *Classification of South American Indian languages.* Los Angeles: Latin American Studies Center, UCLA.
Lounsbury, Floyd G. 1978. Iroquoian languages. *Handbook of North American Indians*, ed. by William C. Sturtevant, vol. 15: *Northeast*, ed. by Bruce G. Trigger, 335–43. Washington DC: Smithsonian Institution.
Lowe, Ivan. 1999. Nambikwara. *The Amazonian Languages*, ed. by R. M. W Dixon and Aleksandra Y. Aikhenvald, 269–291. Cambridge: Cambridge University Press.
Lozano, Elena. 1964. Estudios sobre el vilela. *Boletín de Filología* 10.61–62: 151–157. Montevideo.
Lozano, Elena. 1970. *Textos Vilelas.* Buenos Aires: Ediciones de la Universidad Nacional de La Plata.
Lozano, Elena. 1977. Cuentos secretos *vilelas*: I. La mujer tigre. *VICUS Cuadernos Lingüística* 1.93–115.
Lozano, Elena. 2006. *Textos vilelas*, edición y prólogo de Lucía A. Golluscio. (Serie Archivo de Lenguas Indoamericanas, Colección Nuestra América.) Buenos Aires: Facultad de Filosofía y Letras de la Universidad de Buenos Aires.
Lüpke, Friederike, Kristine Stenzel, Flora Dias Cabalzar, Thiago Chacon, Aline da Cruz, Bruna Franchetto, Antonio Guerreiro, Sérgio Meira, Glauber Romling da Silva, Wilson Silva, and Luciana Storto. 2020. Comparing rural multilingualism in Lowland South America and Western Africa. *Anthropological Linguistics* 62.3–57.
Lustig, Wolf. 1996. Mba'éichapa oiko la guaraní? Guaraní y jopara en el Paraguay. *PAPIA-Revista Brasileira de Estudos do Contato Lingüístico* 4.19–43. https://www.staff.uni-mainz.de/lustig/guarani/art/jopara.pdf.
Luzena, Gerónimo Josef de. 1788. Traducion de la lengua española à la otomaca, taparita y yarura. Manuscript II/2927, Biblioteca del Palacio Real de Madrid. https://realbiblioteca.patrimonionacional.es/cgi-bin/koha/opac-detail.pl?biblionumber=84451.
Maccioni [Machoni], Antonio. 2008 [1732]. *Arte y Vocabulario de la Lengua Lule y Tonocoté, a cura di Riccardo Baddini, Tiziana Deonertte, Stefania Pineider, introzione di Riccardo Badini, Raoul Zamponi*. Calgliari: Centro di Studi Filologici Sardi, Operativa Universitaria Editrice Cagliaritana.
MacKay, Carolyn J. and Frank R. Trechsel. 2018. An Alternative Reconstruction of Proto-Totonac-Tepehua. *International Journal of American Linguistics* 84.51–92.
Malaspinas, Anna-Sapfo, Oscar Lao, Hannes Schroeder, Morten Rasmussen, Maanasa Raghavan, Ida Moltke, Paula F. Campos, et al. 2014. Two ancient human genomes reveal Polynesian ancestry among the indigenous Botocudos of Brazil. *Current Biology* 24/21.R1035–R1037. www.sciencedirect.com/science/article/pii/S0960982214012743.
Mallery, Garrick. 1880. *Introduction to the Study of Sign Language Among the North American Indians as Illustrating the Gesture Speech of Mankind.* Washington DC: US Government Printing Office.

Manaster Ramer, Alexis. 1992. A Northern Uto-Aztecan Sound Law: *-c-→-y-[1]. *International Journal of American Linguistics* 58.251–268.
Manaster Ramer, Alexis. 1993. Is Tonkawa Na-Dene? A case study of the validity of the Greenbergian classification. *California Linguistic Notes* 24.21–25.
Manaster Ramer, Alexis. 1996. Sapir's classifications: Coahuiltecan. *Anthropological Linguistics* 38.1–38.
Mannheim, Bruce. 1991. *The Language of the Inka since the European Invasion.* Austin: University of Texas Press.
Martin, Jack B. 1994. Implications of plural reduplication, infixation, and subtraction for Muskogean languages. *Anthropological Linguistics* 36.27–55.
Martin, Jack B. 2004. Southeastern languages. *Handbook of North American Indians*, ed. by William C. Sturtevant, vol. 14: *Southeast*, ed. by Raymond D. Fogelson (volume editor), 68–86. Washington DC: Smithsonian Institution.
Martin, Jack B. and Pamela Munro. 2005. Proto-Muskogean morphology. *Native Languages of the Southeastern United States*, ed. by Janine Scancarelli and Heather Kay Hardy, 299–320. Lincoln: University of Nebraska Press.
Martínez Compañón, Baltasar Jaime. 1985[1782–1790]. *Trujillo del Perú en el siglo XVIII*, vol. 2. Madrid: Ediciones Cultura Hispánica.
Martins, Valteir. 2005. *Reconstrução fonológica do protomaku oriental.* Utrecht: Landelijke Onderzoekschool Taalwetenschap.
Martins, Silvana and Valteir Martins. 1999. Makú. *The Amazonian Languages*, ed. by R. M. W. Dixon and Alexandra Y. Aikhenvald, 251–268. Cambridge: Cambridge University Press.
Martius, Carl Friedrich Philipp von. 1867. *Beiträge zur Ethnographie und Sprachenkunde Amerika's, zumal Brasiliens* (vol. 1: *Zur Ethnographie Amerika's zumal Brasiliens, mit einem Kärtschen über die Verbreitung der Tupis und die Sprachgruppen*; vol. 2: *Wörtersammlung brasilianischen Sprachen*). Leipzig: Friedrich Fleischer / Erlangen: Junge & Sohn.
Mason, J. Alden. 1936. The classification of the Sonoran languages. *Essays in anthropology Presented to A. L. Kroeber in Celebration of His Sixtieth Birthday, June 11, 1936*, ed. by Robert H. Howie, 183–198. Berkeley: University of California Press.
Mason, J. Alden. 1940. The native languages of Middle America. *The Maya and Their Neighbors: Essays on Middle American Anthropology and Archaeology*, ed. by Clarence L. Hay, Ralph L. Linton, Samuel K. Lothrop, Harry L. Shapiro, and George C. Vaillant, 52–87. New York: D. Appleton-Century.
Mason, J. Alden. 1950. The languages of South America. *Handbook of South American Indians*, ed. by Julian Steward, 6.157–317. (Smithsonian Institution, Bureau of American Ethnology Bulletin 143). Washington DC: Government Printing Office.
Massey, William C. 1949. Tribes and languages of Baja California. *Southwestern Journal of Anthropology* 5.272–307.
Matteson, Esther. 1972. Towards Proto Amerindian. *Comparative Studies in Amerindian Languages*, ed. by Esther Matteson, 21–89. (Janua Linguarum, Series Practica, 127.) The Hague: Mouton.
McGuire, Thomas R. and Ives Goddard. 1983. Synonymy. *Handbook of North American Indians*, ed. by William C. Sturtevant, vol. 10: *Southwest*, ed. by Alfonso Ortiz, 36. Washington DC: Smithsonian Institution.
McLendon, Sally. 1973. *Proto Pomo.* (University of California Publications in Linguistics, 71.) Berkeley and Los Angeles: University of California Press.

McLendon, Sally and Robert L. Oswalt. 1978. Pomo: Introduction. *Handbook of North American Indians*, ed. by William C. Sturtevant, vol. 8: *California*, ed. by Robert F. Heizer, 274–288. Washington DC: Smithsonian Institution.

McQuown, Norman A. 1942. Una posible síntesis lingüística macro-mayance. *Mayas y Olmecas*, 37–38. Tuxtla Gutiérrez: Sociedad Mexicana de Antropología, Reunión de Mesa Redonda sobre problemas antropológicos de México y Centro América.

McQuown, Norman A. 1955. The indigenous languages of Latin America. *American Anthropologist* 57.501–569.

McQuown, Norman A. 1956a. Evidence for a synthetic trend in Totonacan. *Language* 32.78–80.

McQuown, Norman A. 1956b. The classification of the Mayan languages. *International Journal of American Linguistics* 22.191–195.

Meader, Robert E. 1967. *Iranxe: Notas grammaticais e lista vocabular.* (Publicações Série Diversos, Lingüística, 2.) Rio de Janeiro: Universidade Federal do Rio de Janeiro, Museu Nacional.

Medina, Francia. 2008. Los Sapé: notas sobre su situación presente y actualización bibliográfica. *Los Aborígenes de Venezuela* (2nd edition), ed. by Miguel Ángel Perera, 739–746. Caracas: Monte Ávila Editores Latinoamericana.

Meira, Sérgio, Joshua Birchall, Natalia Chousou-Polydouri. 2015. A character-based internal classification of the Cariban family. Talk presented at the 48th Annual Meeting of the Societas Linguisticae Europaea, Leiden, Neth., Sept. 4. https://www.academia.edu/15980095/A_character-based_internal_classification_of_the_Cariban_language_family.

Meira, Sérgio and Sebastian Drude. 2013. Sobre a origem histórica dos "prefixos relacionais" das línguas Tupí-Guaraní. *Cadernos de Etnolingüística* 5.1–31.

Meira, Sérgio, Spike Gildea, and B. J. Hoff. 2010. On the origin of ablaut in the Cariban family. *International Journal of American Linguistics* 76.477–515.

Meléndez-Lozano, Miguel Ángel. 2014. Préstamos arawak (achagua, piapoco y piapoco-achagua) a la familia lingüística guahibo (sikuani). *LIAMES (Línguas Indígenas Americanas)* 14.173–218.

Membreño, Alberto. 1897. *Hondureñismos: vocabulario de los provincialismos de Honduras* (2nd edition). Tegucigalpa: Tipografía Nacional.

Mendizábal, Manuel Othon de and Wigberto Jiménez Moreno. 1944. *Mapas lingüísticos de la República Mexicana.* Mexico: Instituto Panamericano de Geografía e Historia.

Menovščikov, G. A. 1968. Aleutskij jazyk. *Jazyki narodov SSSR*, series ed. by V. V. Vinogradov et al., vol. 5: *Mongol'skie, tunguso-man'czurskie i paleoaziatskie jazyki*, ed. by Ja. Skorik, 386–406. Leningrad: Nauka.

Menovščikov, G. A. 1969. O nekotoryx social'nyx aspektax ėvoljucii jazyka. Voprosy social'noj, 110–134. Leningrad: Nauka.

Merrill, William L. 2013. The genetic unity of southern Uto-Aztecan. *Language Dynamics and Change* 3.68–104.

Merrill, William L., Robert J. Hard, Jonathan B. Mabry, Gayle J. Fritz, Karen R. Adams, John R. Roney, and A. C. MacWilliams. 2009. The diffusion of maize to the southwestern United States and its impact. *PNAS (Proceedings of the National Academy of Sciences)* 196.21019–21026. www.pnas.orgcgidoi10.1073pnas.0906075106.

Merrill, William L., Robert J. Hard, Jonathan B. Mabry, Gayle J. Fritz, Karen R. Adams, John R. Roney, and A. C. MacWilliams. 2010. Reply to Hill and Brown: Maize and Uto-Aztecan cultural history. *PNAS (Proceedings of the National Academy of Sciences)* 107/11.E35–E36.

Messineo, Cristina. 2011. Aproximación tipológica a las lenguas indígenas del Gran Chaco. Rasgos compartidos entre toba (familia guaycurú) y maká (familia mataco- mataguayo). *Indiana* 28.183–225.
Messineo, Cristina, Javier Carol, Harriet Manelis E. Klein. 2016. Deíxis contacto el la región del Gran Chaco: los demostrativos en las lenguas guaycurúes y mataguayas. *International Journal of the Sociology of Language* 240.119–157.
Métraux, Alfred. 1946. Ethnography of the Chaco. *Handbook of South American Indians*, vol. 1: *The Marginal Tribes*, ed. by Julian H. Steward, 197–370. (Smithsonian Institution Bureau of American Ethnology, bulletin 143.) Washington DC: Government Printing Office.
Michael, Lev. 2008. *Nanti evidential practice: language, knowledge, and social action in an Amazonian society*. PhD dissertation, University of Texas, Austin.
Michael, Lev. 2014. On the pre-columbian origin of Proto-Omagua-Kokama. *Journal of Language Contact* 7.309–344.
Michael, Lev. 2021. The classification of South American languages. *Annual Review of Linguistics* 7.329–349.
Michael, Lev and Christine Beier. 2012. Phonological sketch and classification of Aʔɨwa [ISO 639: ash]. Unpublished paper, University of California, Berkeley.
Michael, Lev, Will Chang, and Tammy Stark. 2014. Exploring phonological areality in the circum-Andean region using a naive Bayes classifier. *Quantifying Language Dynamics*, ed. by Søren Wichmann and Jeff Good, 7–66. Brill: Leiden.
Michael, Lev and Natalia Chousou-Polydouri. 2019. Computational phylogenetics and the classification of South American languages. *Language and Linguistics Compass* 13:e12358.
Michael, Lev, Natalia Chousou-Polydouri, Keith Bartolome, Erin Donnelly, Sérgio Meira, Vivian Wauters, and Zachary O'Hagan. 2015. A Bayesian phylogenetic classification of Tupí-Guaraní. *LIAMES (Línguas Indígenas Americanas)* 15.193–221.
Michael, Lev, Stephanie Farmer, Greg Finley, Christine Beier, and Karina Sullón Acosta. 2013. A sketch of Muniche segmental and prosodic phonology. *International Journal of American Linguistics* 79.307–347.
Michelson, Truman. 1914. Two alleged Algonquian languages of California. *American Anthropologist* 16.361–3367.
Michelson, Truman. 1915. Rejoinder (to Sapir). *American Anthropologist* 17.4–8.
Middendorf, Ernst W. 1892. *Das Muchik oder die Chimu-Sprache, mit einer Einleitung über die Culturvölker, die gleichzeitig mit den Inkas und Aimaras in Südamerika lebten, und einem Anhang über die Chibcha-Sprache*. Leipzig: F.A. Brockhaus.
Migliazza, Ernest C. 1972. *Yanomama grammar and intelligibility*. PhD dissertation, Indiana University.
Migliazza, Ernest C. 1978. Maku, Sape and Uruák language: Current status and basic lexicon. *Anthropological Linguistics* 20.133–140.
Migliazza, Ernest C. 1982. Languages of the Orinoco-Amazon region: Current status. *Antropológica* (Caracas) 53.95–162. [Reprinted 1985, in: *South American Indian Languages: Retrospect and Prospec*t, ed. by Harriet E. Manelis Klein and Louisa R. Stark, 17–139. Austin: University of Texas Press.]
Migliazza, Ernest and Lyle Campbell. 1988. *Panorama general de las lenguas indígenas en América*. (*Historia general de América*, 10.) Caracas, Venezuela: Instituto Panamericano de Geografía e Historia.
Milewski, Tadeusz. 1960. Similarities between the Asiatic and American Indian languages. *International Journal of American Linguistics* 26.265–274.

Miller, Virginia. 1978. Yuki, Huchnom, and Coast Yuki. *Handbook of North American Indians*, ed. by William C. Sturtevant, vol. 8: *California*, ed. by Robert F. Heizer, 249–255. Washington DC: Smithsonian Institution.

Miller, Wick R. 1967. *Uto-Aztecan cognate sets*. (University of California Publications in Linguistics, 48.) Berkeley and Los Angeles: University of California Press.

Miller, Wick R. 1970. Western Shoshoni dialects. *Languages and Cultures of Western North America: Essays in Honor of Sven S. Liljeblad*, ed. by Earl H. Swanson, Jr., 17–36. Pocatello: Idaho State University Press

Miller, Wick R. 1983. A note on extinct languages of northwest Mexico of supposed Uto-Aztecan affiliation. *International Journal of American Linguistics* 49.328–333.

Miller, Wick R. 1984. The classification of the Uto-Aztecan languages based on lexical evidence. *International Journal of American Linguistics* 50.1–24.

Miller, Wick R. 1986. Numic languages. *Handbook of North American Indians*, ed. William C. Sturtevant, vol. 11: *Great Basin*, ed. by Warren L. D'Azevedo, 98–106. Washington DC: Smithsonian Institution.

Miller, Wick R. 1996. The ethnography of speaking. *Handbook of North American Indians*, vol. 17, ed. by Ives Goddard, 222–243. Washington DC: Smithsonian Institution.

Miller, Wick R. and Irvine Davis. 1963. Proto-Keresan phonology. *International Journal of American Linguistics* 29.310–330.

Mithun, Marianne. 1979. Iroquoian. *The Languages of Native America: An Historical and Comparative Assessment*, ed. by Lyle Campbell and Marianne Mithun, 133–212. Austin: University of Texas Press.

Mithun, Marianne. 1981a. The mystery of the vanished Laurentians. *Papers from the 5th International Congress on Historical Linguistics*, ed. by Anders Ahlquist, 230–242. Amsterdam: John Benjamins.

Mithun, Marianne. 1981b. Stalking the Susquehannocks. *International Journal of American Linguistics* 47.1–26.

Mithun, Marianne. 1984a. The Proto-Iroquoians: Cultural reconstruction from lexical materials. *Extending the Rafters: Interdisciplinary Approaches to Iroquoian Studies*, ed. by Michael K. Foster, Jack Campisi, and Marianne Mithun, 259–281. Albany: SUNY Press.

Mithun, Marianne. 1984b. The evolution of noun incorporation. *Language* 60.847–894.

Mithun, Marianne. 1999. *The Languages of Native North America*. Cambridge: Cambridge University Press.

Mithun, Marianne. 2017. Native North American languages. *The Cambridge Handbook of Areal Linguistics*, ed. by Raymond Hickey, 878–933. Cambridge: Cambridge University.

Mithun, Marianne. 2018. Language isolates of North America. *Language Isolates*, ed. by Lyle Campbell, 193–228. London: Routledge.

Mithun, Marianne. 2020. Language contact in North America. *Handbook of Language Contact* (2nd edition), ed. by Raymond Hickey, 593–612. Oxford: Wiley-Blackwell.

Mithun, Marianne. 2021a. Language contact in North America. *The Routledge Handbook of Language Contact*, ed. by Evangelia Adamou and Yaron Matras, 503–527. London: Routledge.

Mithun, Marianne. 2021b. Typology, contact, and explanation: The surprising Wappo Case. *Contact, Structure, and Change: A Festschrift in Honor of Sarah G. Thomason*, ed. by Anna M. Babel and Mark A. Sicoli, 165–187. Ann Arbor: Michigan Publishing, Masize Books.

Mixco, Mauricio J. 1978. *Cochimí and Proto-Yuman*. (University of Utah, Anthropology papers, 101.) Salt Lake City: University of Utah Anthropology Papers.

Mixco, Mauricio J. 1985. Kiliwa dictionary. Salt Lake City: University of Utah Press.

Mixco, Mauricio J. 1996. *Kiliwa del Arroyo León, Baja California*. Mexico: El Colegio de México.
Mixco, Mauricio J. 2000. *Kiliwa*. Munich: Lincom Europa.
Mixco, Mauricio J. 2013. Introduction to the Kiliwa Language. *Amerindia* 37.53–86.
Moctezuma Zamarrón, José Luis. 2001. El aporte de Wick Miller a los estudios comparativos de lenguas yutoaztecas. *Avances y balances de lenguas yutoaztecas: homenaje a Wick R. Miller*, ed. by José Luis Moctezuma Zamarrón and Jane H. Hill, 375–384. Mexico: Instituto Nacional de Antropología e Historia.
Mondloch, James L. 1983. Una comparación entre los estilos de habla del quiché moderno y los encontrados en el Popol Vuh. *Nuevas Perspectivas sobre el Popol Vuh*, ed. by Robert M. Carmack and Francisco Morales Santos, 87–108. Guatemala: Editorial Piedra Santa.
Monserrat, Ruth Maria Fonini. 2000. *A língua do povo Mỹky*. Rio de Janeiro: Universidade Federal do Rio de Janeiro.
Monserrat, Ruth Maria Fonini and Elizabeth R. Amarante. 1995. *Dicionário Mỹky-Português*. Rio de Janeiro: Editora Separei, Universidade Federal do Rio de Janeiro.
Mooney, James. 1894. *The Siouan Tribes of the East*. (Bureau of American Ethnology Bulletin 22.) Washington DC: Government Printing Office.
Moore, Denny, Sidney Facundes, and Nadia Pires. 1994. Nheengatu (Lingua Geral Amazonica): Its history and the effects of language contact. *Proceedings of the Meeting of the Society for the Study of the Indigenous Languages of the Americas, July 2–4, 1993, and the Hokan-Penutian Workshop, July 3, 1993*, ed. Margaret Langdon, 93–118. (Survey of California and Other Indian Languages, report no. 8.) Berkeley: Department of Linguistics, University of California.
Mora-Marín, David F. 2003. Historical reconstruction of Mayan applicative and antidative constructions. *International Journal of American Linguistics* 69.186–228.
Mora-Marín, David F. 2016. Testing the Mayan-Mijesokean hypothesis. *International Journal of American Linguistics* 82.125–80.
Mora-Marín, David F. 2022. Evidence, new and old, against the late *k(') > *ch(') areal shift hypothesis. *Language Change and Linguistic Diversity: Studies in Honour of Lyle Campbell*, ed. by Thiago Costa Chacon, Nala H. Lee, and W. D. L. Silva, 130–163. Edinburgh: Edinburgh University Press.
Moratto, Michael J. 1984. *California Archaeology*. New York: Academic Press.
Moreno-Mayar, J. Victor, Simon Rasmussen, Andaine Seguin-Orlando, Morten Rasmussen, et al. 2014. Genome-wide ancestry patterns in Rapanui suggest pre-European admixture with Native Americans. *Current Biology* 24/21.2518–2525. https://doi.org/10.1016/j.cub.2014.09.057.
Morgan, Lawrence. 1991. *A description of the Kutenai language*. PhD dissertation, University of California at Berkeley.
Morice, [Père] Adrien Gabriel, O.M.I. 1891. The Déné languages, considered in themselves and in their relations to non-American idioms. *Transactions of the Canadian Institute* 1.170–212. Toronto.
Morice, Adrien Gabriel. 1892. Déné roots. *Transactions of the Canadian Institute* 3.145–164. Toronto.
Morice, Adrien Gabriel. 1904. Les langues dénées. *Année linguistique* 2.205–247. Paris.
Morice, Adrien Gabriel. 1907. The unity of speech among the Northern and Southern Déné. *American Anthropologist* 9.721–737.

Morínigo, Marcos Augusto. 1931. *Hispanismos en el guaraní*. (Instituto de Filología, Colección de Estudios Indigenistas, 1.) Buenos Aires: Universidad de Buenos Aires.

Morínigo, Marcos Alberto. 2008. *Nuevo diccionario de americanismos e indigenismos*. Buenos Aires: Claridad.

Moseley, Christopher J. and Ronald E. Asher, eds. 2008. *Atlas of the World's Languages*. London: Routledge.

Moshinsky, Julius. 1976. Historical Pomo phonology. *Hokan Studies*, ed. by Margaret Langdon and Shirley Silver, 55–75. The Hague: Mouton.

Mosonyi, Esteban Emilio. 1966. *Morfología del verbo Yaruro*. Caracas: Universidad Central de Venezuela.

Mosonyi, Esteban Emilio and Jorge Ramón García. 2000. Yaruro (Pumé). *Manual de Lenguas Indígenas de Venezuela*, ed. by Esteban Emilio Mosonyi and Jorge Carlos Mosonyi, 544–593. Caracas: Fundación Bigott.

Mudrak, Oleg and Sergei Nikolaev. 1989. Gilyak and Chukchi-Kamchatkan as Almosan-Keresiouan languages: Lexical evidence. *Explorations in Language Macrofamilies: Materials from the First International Interdisciplinary Symposium on Language and Prehistory*, ed. by Vitaly Shevoroshkin, 67–87. Bochum: Brockmeyer.

Müller, Neele. 2013. *Tense, Aspect, Modality, and Evidential Marking in South American Indigenous Languages*. Amsterdam: LOT (Netherlands Graduate School of Linguistics).

Muñoz, Nora Isabel. 1993. La influencia del español en el léxico del guaraní "yopará": un análisis cuantitativo. *Actas: Primeras Jornadas de Lingüística Aborigen, 6 y 7 de octubre de 1992*, ed. by J. Pedro Viegas Barros, 201–209. Buenos Aires: Facultad de Filosofía y Letras, Universidad de Buenos Aires.

Munro, Pamela. 1984. On the Western Muskogean source for Mobilian. *International Journal of American Linguistics* 50.438–450.

Munro, Pamela. 1987a. Introduction: Muskogean studies at UCLA. *Muskogean Linguistics: A Volume of Papers Begun at UCLA on Comparative, Historical, and Synchronic Muskogean Topics*, ed. by Pamela Munro, 1–6. (UCLA occasional papers in linguistics, 6.) Los Angeles: Department of Linguistics, University of California.

Munro, Pamela. 1987b. Some morphological differences between Chickasaw and Choctaw. *Muskogean Linguistics: A Volume of Papers Begun at UCLA on Comparative, Historical, and Synchronic Muskogean Topics*, ed. by Pamela Munro, 119–133, 179–185. (UCLA occasional papers in linguistics, 6.) Los Angeles: Department of Linguistics, University of California.

Munro, Pamela. 1993. The Muskogean II prefixes and their significance for classification. *International Journal of American Linguistics* 59.374–404.

Munro, Pamela. 1994. Gulf and Yuki-Gulf. *Anthropological Linguistics* 36.125–222.

Munro, Pamela. 2000[2002]. Takic foundations of Nicoleño vocabulary. *Proceedings of the Fifth California Islands Symposium*, ed. by D. R. Brown, K. C. Mitchell, and H. W. Chaney, 659–668. Santa Barbara: US Department of the Interior.

Munro, Pamela. 2005. Chickasaw. *Native Languages of the Southeastern United States*, ed. by Janine Scancarelli and Heather Kay Hardy, 114–156. Lincoln: University of Nebraska Press.

Munro, Pamela. 2017. The Mesoamerican linguistic area revisited. *Language Contact and Change in Mesoamerica and Beyond*, ed. by Karen Dakin, Claudia Parodi, and Natalie Operstein, 335–353. Amsterdam: John Benjamins.

Murdock, George Peter. 1951 South American culture areas. *Southwestern Journal of Anthropology* 7.415–436.

Muysken, Pieter. 1980. Sources for the study of Amerindian contact vernaculars in Ecuador. *Amsterdam Creole Studies 3*, ed. by Pieter Muysken and Norval Smith, 66–82. (*Publikaties van het Instituut voor Algemene Taalwetenschap* [Publications of the Institute for General Linguistics], no. 31.) Amsterdam: Universiteit van Amsterdam.

Muysken, Pieter. 1994a. Callahuaya. *Mixed Languages: Fifteen Case Studies in Language Intertwining*, ed. by Peter Bakker and Maarten Mous, 207–211. Amsterdam: Institute for Functional Research into Language and Language Use.

Muysken, Pieter. 1994b. Media Lengua. *Mixed Languages: Fifteen Case Studies in Language Intertwining*, ed. by Peter Bakker and Maarten Mous, 201–205. Amsterdam: Institute for Functional Research into Language and Language Use.

Muysken, Pieter. 1997. Media Lengua. *Contact Languages: A Wider Perspective*, ed. by Sarah G. Thomason, 365–426. Amsterdam: John Benjamins.

Muysken, Pieter. 2009. Kallawaya. *Lenguas de Bolivia*, ed. by Mily Crevels and Pieter Muysken vol. 1, 147–167. La Paz: Plural editores.

Muysken, Pieter. 2010. The demise and attempted revival of Uchumataqu (Uru): values and actors. *New Perspectives on Endangered Languages: Bridging Gaps between Sociolinguistics, Documentation and Language Revitalization*, ed. by José Antonbio Flores Farfán and Fernando Ramallo, 93–118. Amsterdam: John Benjamins.

Muysken, Pieter. 2011. Callahuaya in Bolivia. *Atlas of Languages of Intercultural Communication in the Pacific, Asia, and the Americas*, ed. by Stephen A. Wurm, Peter Mühlhäusler, and Darrell T. Tryon, 1339–1342. Berlin: Mouton de Gruyter Mouton.

Muysken, Pieter. 2012. Contacts between indigenous languages in South America. *The Indigenous Languages of South America: A Comprehensive Guide*, ed. by Lyle Campbell and Verónica Grondona, 235–258. Berlin: Mouton de Gruyter.

Muysken, Pieter and Loretta O'Connor. 2014. South American indigenous languages: Genealogy, typology, contacts. *The Native Language of South America: Origins, Development, Typology*, ed. by Loretta O'Connor and Pieter Muysken, 1–26. New York: Cambridge University Press.

Nadkarni, Mangesh V. 1975. Bilingualism and syntactic change in Konkani. *Language* 51.672–683.

Nardi, Ricardo L. J. 1979. El kakán, lengua de los diaguitas. *Sapiens* 3.1–33.

Nercesian, Verónica. 2014. *Wichi lhomtes: Estudio de la gramática y la interacción fonología-morfología-sintaxis-semántica*. Munich: LINCOM.

Nercesian, Verónica. 2021. Isoglosas fonológicas wichi/weenhayek (mataguaya): consonantes eyectivas, glotalizadas y aspiradas. *Lingüística* 37.79–101 (Montevideo). http://dx.doi.org/10.5935/2079-312x.20210006.

Neto, Ambrósio Pereira da Silva. 2007. *Revisão da Classificação da Família Lingüística Puri*. MA thesis, University of Brasília. Brasília: Universidade de Brasília.

Nevin, Bruce. 2017. Achumawi-Atsugewi cognates: a triage. Paper presented at the Annual Meeting of the Society for the Study of the Indigenous Languages of the Americas, Austin, Texas, January 5–8. https://d1wqtxts1xzle7.cloudfront.net/65840406/Reconstructing_Achumawi_and_Atsugewi_Pro20210301-7821-14sm418-with-cover-page-v2.pdf?Expires=1663527086&Signature=ccNB9EvSpzUBeNGUIr74s~U-wAv8lkGhdajw-5D3osZ1iOkQFQRE9vGh3~sov4TDcX7VhojGZoY18AyFVcEYpCYUmZ5pSASec5ff-BievzgECRD~grmS8ZM~wQGdAdo6qrcE7MkSnm3Q3S9DOhIl6i5pwbKn2swg-DRiZyu9Nmg~ehW~9QorKwqN8OdOG4oib4cyGmqJWuD5jFZBNU~Xgv3uRvBD-S75h1CCo5T1KdDnRaqsmIZUYDD2VpF6gtLJmN2gj-HLt6doYCBlOfo4LwLtwR-

jpXvOqRk44Sfu7SLCJBOL9-8gPQjpTwoMQoIdvjQfGqQs1UTlJ7mKAo2kUmBIX-AA__&Key-Pair-Id=APKAJLOHF5GGSLRBV4ZA.

Newcomb, W. W., Jr. 1983. Karankawa. *Handbook of North American Indians*, ed. by William C. Sturtevant, vol. 10: *Southwest*, ed. by Alfonso Ortiz, 359–367. Washington DC: Smithsonian Institution.

Newman, Paul. 1991. An interview with Joseph Greenberg. *Current Anthropology* 32.453–467.

Newman, Paul. 1993. Greenberg's American Indian classification: A report on the controversy. *Historical Linguistics 1991: Papers from the Tenth International Conference on Historical Linguistics*, ed. by Jaan van Marle, 229–242. Amsterdam: John Benjamins.

Newman, Stanley. 1944. *Yokuts language of California*. (Viking Fund Publications in Anthropology, 2.) New York: Wenner-Gren Foundation for Anthropological Research.

Newman, Stanley. 1964. Comparison of Zuni and California Penutian. *International Journal of American Linguistics* 30.1–13.

Nichols, Johanna. 1996. The comparative method as heuristic. *The Comparative Method Revised*, ed. by Mark Durie and Malcolm Ross, 39–71. Oxford: Oxford University Press.

Nichols, Johanna. 1997. Modeling ancient population structures and movement in linguistics. *Annual Review of Anthropology* 26.359–384.

Nicklas, T. Dale. 1994. Linguistic provinces of the Southeast at the time of Columbus. *Perspectives on the Southeast: Linguistics, Archaeology, and Ethnohistory*, ed. by Patricia B. Kwachka, 1–31. Athens: University of Georgia Press.

Nikolaev, Sergei. 1989. Eyak-Athapascan—North Caucasian sound correspondences. *Reconstructing Languages and Cultures: Materials from the First International Interdisciplinary Symposium on Language and Prehistory*, ed. by Vitaly Shevoroshkin, 63–65. Bochum: Brockmeyer.

Nikolaev, Sergei. 1991. Sino-Caucasian languages in America. *Dene-Sino-Caucasian Languages: Materials from the First International Interdisciplinary Symposium on Language and Prehistory*, ed. by Vitaly Shevoroshkin, 42–66. Bochum: Brockmeyer.

Nikolaev, Sergei L. and O. Mudrak. 1989. Gilyak and Chukchi-Kamchatkan as Almosan Keresiouan languages: Lexical evidence. *Explorations in Language Macrofamilies: Materials from the First International Interdisciplinary Symposium on Language and Prehistory*, ed. by Vitaly Shevoroshkin, 67–87. Bochum: Brockmeyer.

Nikulin, Andrey. 2020. *Proto-Macro-Jê: um estudo reconstrutivo*. PhD dissertation, University of Brasília.

Nikulin, Andrey and Fernando Orphão de Carvalho. 2018. Prehistoria de las lenguas y familias lingüísticas del Gran Chaco, de la meseta brasileña y cercanías: Propuesta de base de datos léxicos y resultados preliminares. *IV Encuentro de Lenguas Indígenas Americanas–ELIA: libro de actas*, 4.545–560.

Nikulin, Andrey and Fernando Orphão de Carvalho. 2019. Estudos diacrônicos de línguas indígenas brasileiras: um panorama. *Macabéa—Revista Eletrônica do Netlli* 8.255–305.

Nimuendajú, Curt. 1925. As Tribus do Alto Madeira. *Journal de la Société des Américanistes* 17.137–172.

Nimuendaju, Curt. 1926. *Die Palikur-Indianer und ihre Nachbarn*. (Göteborgs Kungliga Vetenskaps- och Vitterhets-samhälles Handlingar [Acts of the Gothenburg Royal Society of Science and Letters], vol. 31, no. 2.) Göterborg: Elanders.

Nimuendajú, Curt. 1932. A propos des Indiens Kukura du Rio Verde (Brésil). *Journal de la Société des Américanistes* 24.187–189.

Nimuendajú, Curt. 1977[1929]. *The Tükuna*. Berkeley and Los Angeles: University of California Press, 1977 [1929].
Noble, G. Kingsley. 1965. *Proto-Arawakan and its Descendants*. Bloomington: Indiana University Press.
Nonato, Rafael and Filomena Sandalo. 2007. Uma comparação gramatical fonológica e lexical entre as famílias Guaicurú, Mataco e Bororo: un caso de difusão areal? *Boletim do Museo Paraense Emílio Goeldi,Ciéncias Humanas* 2.91–107.
Nordenskiöld, Erland. 1922. *Deductions Suggested by the Geographical Distribution of some Post-Columbian Words Used by the Indians of South America*. (Comparative Ethnographical Studies, no. 5.) Göteborg: Elanders.
Norman, William. 1978. Advancement rules and syntactic change: The loss of instrumental voice in Mayan. *Berkeley Linguistics Society* 4.458–476.
Norman, William M. and Lyle Campbell. 1978. Toward A Proto-Mayan syntax: A comparative perspective on grammar. *Papers in Mayan linguistics*, ed. by Nora C. England, 136–156. (Studies in Mayan Linguistics, 2, Miscellaneous Publications in Anthropology, 6.) Columbia: Museum of Anthropology, University of Missouri.
O'Brien, Colleen Alena. 2018. *A Grammatical Description of Kamsá, a Language Isolate of Colombia*. PhD dissertation, University of Hawai'i at Mānoa. https://scholarspace.manoa.hawaii.edu/bitstream/10125/62512/1/OBrienhawii0085A10111.pdf.
O'Connor, Loretta and Vishnupriya Kolipakam. 2014. Human migrations, dispersals, and contacts in South America. *The Native Language of South America: Origins, Development, Typology*, ed. by Loretta O'Connor and Pieter Muysken, 29–55. New York: Cambridge University Press.
Oblitas Poblete, Enrique. 1968. *El Idioma Secreto de los Incas*. La Paz: Editorial "Los Amigos del Libro."
O'Hagan, Zachary J. 2011. Informe de campo del idioma omurano. http://www.cabeceras.org/ohaganomuranofw2011report.pdf (accessed August 6, 2021).
O'Hagan, Zachary. 2015. Taushiro and the status of language isolates in Northwest Amazonia, fieldwork forum. http://linguistics.berkeley.edu/~zjohagan/pdflinks/ohaganfforumtaushiroisolatesv1.pdf (accessed August 6, 2021).
Olawsky, Knut J. 2006. *A Grammar of Urarina*. Berlin, New York: Mouton de Gruyter.
Oliveira, Sanderson Castro Soares de. 2009. Preliminares sobre a fonética e a fonologia da língua falada pelo primeiro grupo de indios korúbo recémcontatados. MA thesis, Universidade de Brasília.
Oliveira, Sanderson Castro Soares de. 2014. *Contribuições para a Reconstrução do Protopáno*. PhD dissertation, Universidade de Brasília, Brazil. https://repositorio.unb.br/bitstream/10482/17129/1/2014SandersonCastroSoaresdeOliveira.pdf.
Oliveira, Sanderson Castro Soares de. 2023. Las primeras escisiones en la familia pano: Una propuesta de subagrupamiento en una familia de la amazonía occidental. *International Journal of American Linguistics* 89.289–331.
Olmsted, David L. 1956. Palaihnihan and Shasta I: Labial stops. *Language* 32.73–77.
Olmsted, David L. 1957. Palaihnihan and Shasta II: Apical stops. *Language* 33.136–138.
Olmsted, David L. 1959. Palaihnihan and Shasta III: Dorsal stops. *Language* 35.637–644.
Olmsted, David L. 1964. *A History of Palaihnihan Phonology*. (University of California Publications in Linguistics, 35.) Berkeley and Los Angeles: University of California Press.
Olmsted, David L. 1984. *A Lexicon of Atsugewi*. (Survey of California and Other Indian Languages, report 5.) Berkeley: Department of Linguistics, University of California.

Olson, Ronald D. 1964. Mayan affinities with Chipaya of Bolivia I: Correspondences. *International Journal of American Linguistics* 30.313–324.

Olson, Ronald D. 1965. Mayan affinities with Chipaya of Bolivia II: Cognates. *International Journal of American Linguistics* 31.29–38.

Oltrogge, David F. 1977. Proto Jicaque-Subtiaba-Tequistlateco: a comparative reconstruction. *Two Studies in Middle American Comparative Linguistics*, ed. by David Oltrogge and Calvin R. Rensch, 1–52. Arlington: University of Texas at Arlington Press, Summer Institute of Linguistics.

Oltrogge, David F. and Calvin Rensch. 1977. *Two Studies in Middle American Comparative Linguistics*. Arlington: University of Texas at Arlington Press, Summer Institute of Linguistics.

O'Neill, Conor. 2019. Evidence for the first human colonisation of the Americas: A review. *Journal of the Dublin University Geographical Society* 20.20–31. https://www.tcd.ie/Geography/assets/pdf/Atlas%202019.pdf#page=20.

O'Neill, Sean, 2008. *Cultural Contact and Linguistic Relativity among the Indians of Northwestern California*. Norman: University of Oklahoma Press.

Orozco y Berra, Manuel. 1864. *Geografía de las lenguas y carta etnográfica de México, precedidas de un ensayo de clasificación de las mismas lenguas y de apuntes para las inmigraciones de las tribus*. Mexico: J. M. Andrade and F. Escalante.

Orr, Carolyn and Robert Longacre. 1968. Proto-Quechumaran. *Language* 44.528–555.

Ortiz, Sergio Elías. 1943. Lingüística Colombiana: familia goahibo. *Revista Universidad Pontificia* 9.30–31: 155–181.

Ortiz de Zapata, Juan. 1857 [1678]. Relación de las Misiones que la Compañía de Jesus tiene en el Reino y Provincia de la Nueva Vizcaya. *Documentos Históricos de México*, 4th series, vol. 3.301–419.

Oswalt, Robert L. 1958. Russian loanwords in Southwestern Pomo. *International Journal of American Linguistics* 24.245–247.

Oswalt, Robert L. 1964. The internal relationships of the Pomo family of languages. *Actas y Memorias del XXXV Congreso Internacional de Americanistas* 2.413–427.

Oswalt, Robert L. 1976a. Comparative verb morphology of Pomo. *Hokan studies*, ed. by Margaret Langdon and Shirley Silver, 13–28. The Hague: Mouton.

Oswalt, Robert L. 1976b. Switch reference in Maiduan: an areal and typological contribution. *International Journal of American Linguistics* 42.297–304.

Oxford, Will. 2020. Algonquian languages. *The Routledge Handbook of North American Languages*, ed. by Daniel Siddiqi, Michael Barrie, Carrie Gillon, Jason Haugen, and Eric Mathieu, 504–523. London: Routledge.

Pache, Matthias J. 2016. Pumé (Yaruro) and Chocoan: Evidence for a new genealogical link in northern South America. *Language Dynamics and Change* 6.99–155. https://doi.org/10.1163/22105832-00601001.

Pache, Matthias J. 2018. *Contributions to Chibchan Historical Linguistics*. PhD dissertation, Leiden University.

Palavecino, Enrique. 1926. Glosario comparado Kičua-Maori. *International Congress of Americanists* 22/2.517–525.

Pareja, Francisco. 1886. *Arte de la lengua timuquana, compuesto en 1614*. Ed. by Lucien Adam and Julien Vinson. (Bibliothèque linguistique américaine, 11.) Paris: Maisonneuve.

Pareja, Fray Francisco. 1614. *Arte y pronunciacion en lengua timvquana y castellana*. Mexico: Emprenta de Ioan Ruyz.

Parisot, Jean. 1880. Notes sur la langue des Taensas. *Revue de Linguistique et de Philologie Comparée* 13.166–186.
Parisot, Jean. 1882. Du genre dans la langue Hastri ou taensa. *International Congress of Americanists* 4/2.310–335. Madrid.
Parker, Gary J. 1969a. Comparative Quechua phonology and grammar I: Classification. *University of Hawaii Working Papers in Linguistics* 1.65–87.
Parker, Gary J. 1969b. Comparative Quechua phonology and grammar IV: The evolution of Quechua A. *University of Hawaii Working Papers in Linguistics* 1.149–204.
Parker, Gary J. 1969c. Comparative Quechua phonology and grammar V: The evolution of Quechua B. *University of Hawaii Working Papers in Linguistics* 3.1–109.
Parodi, Claudia. 1987. Los hispanismos de las lenguas mayances. *Studia humanitatis: homenaje a Rubén Bonifaz Nuño*, ed. by A. Ocampo, 339–349. Mexico City: Universidad Nacional Autonoma de México.
Parodi, Claudia. 2017. Spanish loanwords in Amerindian languages and their implication for the reconstruction of the pronunciation of Spanish in Mesoamerica. *Language Contact and Change in Mesoamerica and Beyond*, ed. by Dakin, Karen, Claudia Parodi, and Natalie Operstein, 155–169. Amsterdam and Philadelphia: John Benjamins.
Patrón, Pablo. 1907. *Nuevos estudios sobre lenguas americanas: origen del kechua y del aimará/Nouvelles études sur les langues Américaines: origine du kechua et de l-aimará*. Leipzig: Brockhaus.
Paula, Luiz Gouvêa de. 2001. *Mudanças de Código em Eventos de Fala na Língua Tapirapé durante Interações entre Crianças*. MA thesis, Universidade Federal de Goiás, Faculdade de Letras.
Payne, David L. 1981. Bosquejo fonológico del Proto-Shuar-Candoshi: evidencia para una relación genética. *Revista del Museo Nacional Lima* 45.323–377.
Payne, David L. 1990. Some widespread grammatical forms in South American languages. *Amazonian Linguistics: Studies in Lowland South American Languages*, ed. by Doris L. Payne, 75–87. Austin: University of Texas Press.
Payne, David L. 1991. A classification of Maipuran (Arawakan) languages based on shared lexical retentions. *Handbook of Amazonian Languages*, vol. 3, ed. by Desmond C. Derbyshire and Geoffrey K. Pullum, 355–499. Berlin: Mouton de Gruyter.
Payne, Doris. 1990a. Introduction. *Amazonian Linguistics: Studies in Lowland South American Languages*, ed. by Doris Payne, 1–10. Austin: University of Texas Press.
Payne, Doris L. 1990b. Morphological characteristics of lowland South American languages. *Amazonian Linguistics: Studies in Lowland South American Languages*, ed. by Doris L. Payne, 213–241. Austin: University of Texas Press.
Pennington, Campbell W. 1969. *The Tepehuan of Chihuahua: Their Material Culture*. Salt Lake City: University of Utah.
Pennington, Campbell W. 1981. *Arte y vocabulario de la lengua dohema, heve o eudeva*. Mexico: Universidad Nacional Autónoma de México.
Pentland, David H. 1979. *Algonquian Historical Phonology*. PhD dissertation, University of Toronto.
Pentland, David H. 1981. Synonymy. *Handbook of North American Indians*, ed. by William C. Sturtevant, vol. 6: *Subarctic*, ed. by June Helm, 227–230. Washington DC: Smithsonian Institution.
Petitot, Emile. 1876. *Dictionaire de la langue Dènè-Dindjié*. Paris: Leroux.
Petitot, Emile. 1889. *Quinze ans sous le cercle polaire: Mackenzie, Anderson, Youkon*. Paris: E. Dentu.

Pharris, Nicholas and Sarah G. Thomason. 2005. Lexical transfer between Southern Interior Salish and Molalla-Sahaptian. Papers from the *40th International Conference on Salish and Neighboring Languages*, 184–209. Vancouver: University of British Columbia. https://lingpapers.sites.olt.ubc.ca/files/2018/02/Pharris_Thomason_2005.pdf.

Piispanen, Peter Sauli. 2020. Diaguitan etymologies. *Academia.* https://d1wqtxts1xzle7.cloudfront.net/63834701/Manuscript_83_Diaguitan_etymologies_rev220200705-110330-x54spi-with-cover-page-v2.pdf?Expires=1641679257&Signature=Aotw~UTHjmyCk~UYAsWd42eVXYPwcDpxRud7NJdGBjkntjZ4mKN9a6fDaU~bogu~5zprdjjfHC9Qa6SodL8jE9yh3y~pE9VgdGqc8zlu2U-QB1MJIw9ojXHjUdJN5SWnGwI~OliL62FHfEPMVuoQiK1~HTrMDIMjo4BavbJYpuwLv8hOnY23ZsVDq~zoiKdlj-3qIMoNoGcCa9TCoOCtZICrzUR5RICeYGlef5RhUX9acmVcFfYmAl9x6mO~4qg-kXsuEFR6c9WRwZuxOiUiVBAEOoSseG8-~JW~4xzxjdneGtJZ11AsNxLKtOkvqb7uqzWl85qlDGMn8sP8hB4PB8XA__&Key-Pair-Id=APKAJLOHF5GGSLRBV4ZA.

Pilling, James Constantine. 1885. Proof-sheets of a bibliography of the languages of the North American Indians. Washington: Government Printing Office. [Reprinted 1967, Brooklyn: Central Book Co.]

Pimentel, Francisco. 1862–1865[1874]. Cuadro descriptivo y comparativo de las lenguas indígenas de México. (vol. 1: 1862, vol. 2: 1865.) (2nd edition 1874.) Mexico: Andrade y Escalante.

Pinnow, Heinz-Jürgen. 1976. *Geschichte der Na-Dene Forschung.* (*Indiana*, Supplement 5.) Berlin: Mann.

Pinnow, Heinz-Jürgen. 1985. *Das Haida als Na-Dene-Sprache: Materialen zu den Wortfeldern und zur Komparation des Verbs.* (Abhandlungen der Völkerkundlichen Arbeitsgemeinschaft, Heft 43, 44, 45, and 46.) Nortorf: Völkerkundliche Arbeitsgemeinschaft.

Pinnow, Heinz-Jürgen. 2006. *Sprachhistorische Untersuchung zur Stellung des Haida als Na-Dene-Sprache.* (Unveränderte Neuausgabe aus Indiana 10, Gedenkschrift Gerdt Kutscher, vol. 2.) Berlin.

Pitkin, Harvey. 1984. *Wintu grammar.* (University of California Publications in Linguistics, 95.) Berkeley and Los Angeles: University of California Press.

Pitkin, Harvey and William Shipley. 1958. Comparative survey of California Penutian. *International Journal of American Linguistics* 24.174–188.

Poser, William J. 1992. The Salinan and Yurumangui data in *Language in the Americas.* *International Journal of American Linguistics* 58.202–209.

Poser, William J. 1995. Binary comparison and the history of Hokan comparative studies. *International Journal of American Linguistics* 61.135–144.

Potter, Ben A., James F. Baichtal, Alwynne B. Beaudoin, Lars Fehren-Schmitz, C. Vance Haynes, Vance T. Holliday, Charles E. Holmes, et al. 2018. Current evidence allows multiple models for the peopling of the Americas. *Science Advances* 4(8), eaat573. DOI: 10.1126/sciadv.aat5473.

Powell, J[ay] V. 1990a. Chinook jargon vocabulary and the lexicographers. *International Journal of American Linguistics* 56.134–151.

Powell, J[ay] V. 1990b. Quileute. *Handbook of North American Indians,* ed. by William C. Sturtevant, vol. 7: *Northwest Coast,* ed. by Wayne Suttles, 431–437. Washington DC: Smithsonian Institution.

Powell, J[ay] V. 1993. Chimakuan and Wakashan—the case for remote common origin: another look at suggestive sound correspondences. *American Indian Linguistics and Ethnography in Honor of Laurence C. Thompson,* ed. by Anthony Mattina and Timothy Montler, 451–470.

(University of Montana Occasional Papers in Linguistics, 10.) Missoula: University of Montana.

Powell, John Wesley. 1891. *Indian Linguistic Families of America North of Mexico*. Seventh annual report, Bureau of American Ethnology, 1–142. Washington DC: Government Printing Office. [Reprinted 1966, in: *Franz Boas: Introduction to Handbook of American Indian Languages*; J. W. Powell: *Indian Linguistic Families of America North of Mexico*, ed. by Preston Holder. Lincoln: University of Nebraska Press.]

Price, David P. 1978. The Nambiquara linguistic family. *Anthropological Linguistics* 20.14–39.

Price, David P. 1985. Nambiquara languages: Linguistic and geographical distance between speech communities. *South American Indian Languages: Retrospect and Prospect*, ed. by Harriet E. Manelis Klein and Louisa R. Stark, 304–324. Austin: University of Texas Press.

Prince, J. Dyneley. 1912. An ancient New Jersey Indian jargon. *American Anthropologist* 14.508–524.

Proulx, Paul. 1984. Proto-Algic I: Phonological sketch. *International Journal of American Linguistics* 50.165–207.

Queixalós, Francisco. 1993. Lenguas y dialectos de la familia lingüística guahibo. *Estado Actual de la Clasificación de Las Lenguas Indígenas de Colombia*, ed. by María Luisa Rodríguez de Montes, 189–217. Bogotá: Instituto Caro y Cuervo.

Queiroz, Márcio Correia de. 2008. *Aspectos da fonologia Dzubukuá*. MA thesis, Universidade Federal de Pernambuco.

Queiroz, José Márcio Correia de. 2012. *Um Estudo Gramatical da Língua Dzubukuá, Família Karirí*. PhD dissertation, Universidade Federal da Paraíba.

Quilter, Jeffrey, Marc Zender, Karen Spalding, Régulo Franco Jordán, César Gálvez Mora, and Juan Castañeda Murga. 2010. Traces of a lost language and number system discovered on the North Coast of Peru. *American Anthropologist* 112.357–369. http://onlinelibrary.wiley.com/doi/10.1111/j.1548-1433.2010.01245.x/abstract (10.08.2017).

Radin, Paul. 1916. On the relationship of Huave and Mixe. *American Anthropologist* 18.411–421. (Also 1919, *Journal de La Société des Américanistes* 11.489-499.)

Radin, Paul. 1919. The genetic relationship of the North American Indian languages. *University of California Publications in American Archaeology and Ethnology* 14.489–502.

Radin, Paul. 1924. The relationship of Maya to Zoque-Huave. *Journal de la Société des Américanistes de Paris* 16.317–324.

Radlof[f], Leopold [Radlov, Lev Fedorovich]. 1857. Über die Sprache der Ugalachmut. *Bulletin de la classe des sciences historique, philologique et politiques de l'Académie Imperiale des sciences de Saint Petersbourg* 15.26–38: 48–63, 126–139. [Reprinted 1859, *Mélanges tirés du Bulletin historico-philologique de l'Académie Imperiale des sciences de Saint Pétersbourg*, vol. 3. St. Petersbourg.]

Raff, Jennifer. 2022. *Origin: A Genetic History of the Americas*. New York: Twelve, Hachette Book Group.

Raghavan, Maanasa, Matthias Steinrücken, Kelley Harris, Stephan Schiffels, Simon Rasmussen, Michael DeGiorgio, Anders Albrechtsen, et al. 2015. Genomic evidence for the Pleistocene and recent population history of Native Americans. *Science* 349/6250.aab3884. http://dx.doi.org/10.1126/science.aab3884.

Ramirez, Henri. 2020. *Enciclopédia das línguas Arawak: acrescida de seis novas línguas e dois bancos de dados*. Curitiba: Editora CRV. https://doi.org/10.24824/978655578892.1.

Ramirez, Henri, Valdir Vegini, and Maria Cristina Victorino de França. 2015. Koropó, puri, kamakã e outras línguas do leste Brasileiro: revisão e proposta de nova classificação. *LIAMES (Línguas Indígenas Americanas)* 15.223–277.

Rankin, Robert L. 1981. Review of The Caddoan, Iroquoian, and Siouan languages, by Wallace Chafe. *International Journal of American Linguistics* 47.172–178.

Rankin, Robert L. 1986. Review of a grammar of Biloxi, by Paula Einaudi. *International Journal of American Linguistics* 52.77–85.

Rankin, Robert L. 1988. Quapaw: genetic and areal affiliations. *In Honor of Mary Haas: From the Haas Festival Conference on Native America Linguistics*, ed. by William Shipley, 629–650. Berlin: Mouton de Gruyter.

Rankin, Robert L. 1993. On Siouan chronology. Paper presented at the annual meeting of the American Anthropological Association, Washington DC.

Rankin, Robert L. 1997. Grammatical evidence for genetic relationship and the Macro-Siouan hypothesis. *Actes du 21ième Colloque Annuel de L'Association de Linguistique des Province Altantiques*, ed. by Marie-Lucie Tarpent, 20–44. Halifax: Mt. St. Vincent University.

Rankin, Robert L. 1998. Siouan-Catawban-Yuchi genetic relationship: With a note on Caddoan. Paper presented at the 18th annual Siouan and Caddoan Languages Conference, Indiana University, Bloomington.

Rankin, Robert L. 2005. Quapaw. *Native Languages of the Southeastern United States*, ed. by Janine Scancarelli and Heather Kay Hardy, 454–498. Lincoln: University of Nebraska Press.

Rankin, Robert L., Richard T. Carter, and A. Wesley Jones. 1998. Proto-Siouan Phonology and Grammar. *Papers from the 1997 Mid-America Linguistics Conference*, ed. by Xingzhong Li, Luis Lopez, and Tom Stroik, 366–375. Columbia: University of Missouri-Columbia. https://csd.clld.org/static/RankinCarterJonesProto-SiouanPhonology.pdf.

Rehg, Kenneth and Lyle Campbell. 2018. *Handbook of Endangered Languages*. Oxford: Oxford University Press.

Reich, David, Nick Patterson, D. Campbell, Arti Tandon, Andés Ruiz-Linares, et al. 2012. Reconstructing Native American population history. *Nature* 488.370–374. http://dx.doi.org/10.1038/nature11258.

Renault-Lescure, Odile. 2009. Loanwords in Kali'na, a Cariban language of French Guiana. *Loanwords in the World's Languages: Comparative Handbook*, ed. by Martin Haspelmath and Uri Tadmor, 968–991. Berlin: de Gruyter Mouton.

Renfrew, Colin. 1994. World linguistic diversity. *Scientific American* 270.116–123.

Renfrew, Colin. 2000. At the edge of knowability: Towards a prehistory of languages. *Cambridge Archaeological Journal* 10.7–34.

Rensch, Calvin R. 1973. Otomanguean isoglosses. *Current Trends in Linguistics*, vol. 11: *Diachronic, Areal, and Typological Linguistics*, ed. by Thomas Sebeok, 295–316. Mouton: The Hague.

Rensch, Calvin R. 1976. *Comparative Otomanguean Phonology*. (Language Science Monograph 14.) Bloomington: Indiana University Press.

Rensch, Calvin R. 1977. Classification of the Otomanguean languages and the position of Tlapanec. *Two Studies in Middle American Comparative Linguistics*, ed. by David Oltrogge and Calvin R. Rensch, 53–108. (SIL Publications in Linguistics, 55.) Arlington: Summer Institute of Linguistics and University of Texas at Arlington Press.

Research team of the Organization for the Development of the Border Communities of El Cenepa (ODECOFROC). 2010. *A Chronicle of Deception: Attempts to Transfer the*

Awajún Border Territory in the Cordillera del Cóndor to the Mining Industry. (Report 5.) Copenhaguen: International Work Group for Indigenous Affairs (IWGIA).

Rezanov, Nikoai Petrovich. 1805. [Tanaina vocabulary.] (Manuscript no.118, Fond Adelunga, Academy of Sciences, Leningrad.)

Rhodes, Richard. 1982. Algonquian trade languages. *Papers of the Thirteenth Algonquian Conference*, ed. by William Cowan, 1–10. Ottawa: Carleton University.

Rhodes, Richard. 2012. Algonquian trade languages revisited. *Papers of the Fortieth Algonquian Conference*, ed. by K. Hele and J. R. Valentine, 358–369. Albany, NY: SUNY Press.

Ribeiro, Eduardo Rivail. 2002. O marcador de posse alienavel em Kariri: um morfema macro-je revisitado. *LIAMES (Línguas Indígenas Americanas)* 2.31–48.

Ribeiro, Eduardo Rivail. 2006. Macro-Jê. *Encyclopedia of Languages and Linguistics* (2nd edition), ed. by Keith Brown, 7.422–26. Oxford: Elsevier.

Ribeiro, Eduardo Rivail. 2012. *A Grammar of Karajá*. PhD dissertation, University of Chicago.

Ribeiro, Eduardo Rivail and Hein van der Voort. 2010. Nimuendajú was right: The inclusion of the Jabutí language family in the Macro-Jê stock. *International Journal of American Linguistics* 76.517–570.

Ribeiro-dos-Santos, André M., Amanda Ferreira Vidal, Tatiana Vinasco-Sandoval, João Guerreiro., Sidney Santos, Ândrea Ribeiro-dos-Santos, and Sandro J. de Souza. 2020. Exome sequencing of native populations from the Amazon reveals patterns on the peopling of South America. *Frontiers in Genetics* 11. https://www.ncbi.nlm.nih.gov/pmc/articles/PMC7660019.

Rigsby, Bruce J. 1965a. Continuity and change in Sahaptian vowel systems. *International Journal of American Linguistics* 31.306–311.

Rigsby, Bruce J. 1965b. *Linguistic Relations in the Southern Plateau*. PhD dissertation, University of Oregon, Eugene.

Rigsby, Bruce J. 1966. On Cayuse-Molala relatability. *International Journal of American Linguistics* 32.369–378.

Rigsby, Bruce. 1969. The Waiilatpuan problem: More on Cayuse-Molala relatability. *Northwest Anthropological Research Notes* 3/1.68–146.

Rigsby, Bruce and Michael Silverstein. 1969. Nez Perce vowels and Proto-Sahaptian vowel harmony. *Language* 45.45–59.

Ringe, Don. 1999. How hard is it to match CVCC- roots? *Transactions of the Philological Society* 97.213–244.

Rivet, Paul. 1924. Langues americaines. *Les Langues du Monde*, ed. by Antoine Meillet and Marcel Cohen, 597–712. (Collection linguistique, 16.) Paris: Champion.

Rivet, Paul. 1925a. Les Australiens en Amérique. *Bulletin de la Société Linguistique de Paris* 26.23–63.

Rivet, Paul. 1925b. Les mélanéso-polynésiens et les australiens en Amérique. *Anthropos* 20.51–54.

Rivet, Paul. 1927. La famille linguistique timote (Venezuela). *International Journal of American Linguistics* 4.137–167.

Rivet, Paul. 1934. Population de la province de Jaén, Equateur. *Congrés International des Sciences Anthropologiques et Ethnologiques, compte-rendu de la première session* 245–247. London: Royal Institute of Anthropology.

Rivet, Paul. 1942. Un dialecte Hoka Colombien: le Yurumangí. *Journal de la Société des Américanistes* 34.1–59.

Rivet, Paul. 1943. La influencia karib en Colombia. *Revista del Instituto Etnológico Nacional* 1/1.55–93. Bogotá.

Rivet, Paul. 1957[1943]. *Les origines de l'homme Américain* (8th edition). Paris: Gallimard. (Spanish translation 1960[1943], *Los orígenes del hombre americano*. Mexico: Fondo de Cultura.)

Rivet, Paul and Constant Tastevin. 1920. Affinités du Makú et du Puinãve. *Journal de la Société des Américanistes* 12.69–82.

Robertson, John S. 1992. *The History of Tense/Aspect/Mood/Voice in the Mayan Verbal Complex*. Austin: University of Texas Press.

Robles Uribe, Carlos. 1964. Investigación lingüística sobre los grupos indígenas del Estado de Baja California. Anales del *Instituto Nacional de Antropología e Historia* 17.275–301.

Rodrigues, Aryon Dall'igna. 1985a. Evidence for Tupi-Carib relationships. *South American Indian Languages: Retrospect and Prospect*, ed. by Harriet E. Manelis Klein and Louisa R. Stark, 371–404. Austin: University of Texas Press.

Rodrigues, Aryon Dall'igna. 1985b. The present state of the study of Brazilian Indian languages. *South American Indian Languages: Retrospect and Prospect*, ed. by Harriet E. Manelis Klein and Louisa R. Stark, 405–439. Austin: University of Texas Press.

Rodrigues, Aryon Dall'igna. 1986. *Línguas Brasileiras: para o Conhecimento das Línguas Indígenas*. São Paulo: Edições Loyola.

Rodrigues, Aryon Dall'igna. 1999. Macro-Jê. *The Amazonian languages*, ed. by R. M. W. Dixon and Alexandra Y. Aikhenvald, 165–206. Cambridge: Cambridge University Press.

Rodrigues, Aryon Dall'igna. 2000. Ge-Pano-Carib x Jê-Tupí-Karíb: sobre relaciones prehistóricas em Sudamérica. *Actas del I Congreso de Lenguas Indígenas de Sudamérica*, vol. 1, ed. by Luis Miranda, 95–105. Lima: Universidad Ricardo Palma.

Rodrigues, Aryon Dall'igna. 2003. Evidências de relações Tupí-Karíb. *Saudades da língua*, ed. by Eleonora Albano, Maria Irma Hadler Coudry, Sírio Possenti, and Tania Alkmim, 393–410. Campinas: Mercado de Letras.

Rodrigues, Aryon Dall'igna. 2007a. Linguística comparativa e pré-história dos povos indígenas sul-americanos: a hipótese Tupí-Karíb e as relações genéticas entre Tupí, Karíb e Macro-Jê. *Conferências do V Congresso Internacional da Associação Brasileira de Lingüística*, ed. by Thays Cristófaro Silva and Heliana Mello, 165–176. Belo Horizonte: FALE/UFMG.

Rodrigues, Aryon Dall'igna. 2007b. O parentesco genético das línguas Umutína e Boróro. *Línguas e culturas Macro-Jê*, ed. by Aryon D. Rodrigues and Ana Suelly Arruda Câmara Cabral, 9–18. Brasília: Universidade de Brasília.

Rodrigues, Aryon Dall'igna. 2009. A case of affinity among Tupí, Karíb, and Macro-Jê. *Revista Brasileira de Linguística Antropológica* 1.137–162.

Rodrigues, Aryon Dall'igna. 2010. As línguas gerais sul-americanas. *PAPIA-Revista Brasileira de Estudos do Contato Lingüístico* 4.6–18.

Rodrigues, Aryon Dall'igna and Ana Suelly Arruda Câmara Cabral. 2012. Tupían. *The Indigenous Languages of South America: A Comprehensive Guide*, ed. by Lyle Campbell and Verónica Grondona, 495–574. Berlin: Mouton de Gruyter.

Rodrigues, Douglas A. 2014. Proteção e assistência à saúde de povos indígenas isolados e de recente contato no Brasil. *Organización del Tratado de Cooperación Amazónica*. São Paulo, Brasil. https://www.academia.edu/12865129/ Prote%C3%A7%C3%A3oeAssist%C3% AAncia%C3%A0Sa%C3%BAdedePovosInd% C3%ADgenasIsoladosedeRecente ContatonoBrasil.

Rodríguez Bazán, Luis Antonio. 2000. Estado de las lenguas indígenas del oriente, Chaco y Amazonía Bolivianos. *As Línguas Amazónicas Hoje*, ed. by Francesc Queixalós and Odile Renault-Lescure, 129–149. São Paulo: Instituto Socioambiental.

Rogers, Chris. 2010. *A Comparative Grammar of Xinkan*. PhD dissertation, University of Utah.

Rogers, Chris. 2016. *The Use and Development of the Xinkan Languages*. Austin: University of Texas Press.

Rogers, Chris. 2020. *Máku: A Comprehensive Grammar*. London: Routledge.

Rogers, Chris. 2022. Using the acoustic correlates of voice quality as explanations for the changes in the descriptions of Xinkan glottalized consonants. *Language Change and Linguistic Diversity: Studies in Honour of Lyle Campbell*, ed. by Thiago Costa Chacon, Nala H. Lee, and W. D. L. Silva, 19–46. Edinburgh: Edinburgh University Press.

Rojas-Berscia, Luis Miguel. 2015. Mayna, the Lost Kawapanan Language. *LIAMES (Línguas Indígenas Americanas)* 15.393–407.

Rojas-Berscia, Luis Miguel. 2019. *From Kawapanan to Shawi: Topics in Language Variation and Change*. PhD dissertation, Radboud University Nijmegen.

Rojas-Berscia, Luis Miguel. 2020. The Chachapuya language and Proto-Kawapanan: Lexical affinities and hypothetical contact scenarios. *Indiana* 37.155–188.

Rona, José Pedro. 1969–1972. Extensión del tipo chaqueño de lenguas. *Revista de Antropología* 17.93–103.

Rood, David S. 1973. Swadesh's Keres-Caddo comparison. *International Journal of American Linguistics* 39.189–190.

Rood, David S. 1979. Siouan. *The Languages of Native America: An Historical and Comparative Assessment*, ed. by Lyle Campbell and Marianne Mithun, 236–298. Austin: University of Texas Press.

Rood, David S. 1992b. Siouan languages. *International Encyclopedia of Linguistics*, ed. by William Bright, vol. 3, 449–451. Oxford: Oxford University Press.

Rose, Françoise, Thiago Costa Chacon, Magdalena Lemus, and Natalia Eraso. 2017. A new look into Arawak-Tukanoan contact: The Yukuna-Tanimuka bidirectional hypothesis. Paper presented at the SSILA annual meeting, Austin, Texas.

Rosés Labrada, Jorge Emilio. 2019. Jodï-Sáliban: A linguistic family of the Northwest Amazon. *International Journal of American Linguistics* 85.275–311.

Rosés Labrada, Jorge Emilio, and Francia Medina. 2019. Sapé (Venezuela)—language snapshot. *Language Documentation and Description* 16.169–17. London: EL Publishing.

Rosés Labrada, Jorge Emilio, Thiago Chacon, and Francia Medina. 2020. Arutani (Venezuela and Brazil)—language snapshot. *Language Documentation and Description* 17.170–177. London: EL Publishing.

Roullier, Caroline, Laure Benoit, Doyle B. McKey, and Vincent Lebota. 2013. Historical collections reveal patterns of diffusion of sweet potato in Oceania obscured by modern plant movements and recombination. *PNAS (Proceedings of the National Academy of Sciences)* 110.2205–2210.

Rowe, John Howland. 1954. Linguistic classification problems in South America. *Papers from the Symposium on American Indian Linguistics*, ed. by Murray B. Emeneau, 10–26. (University of California Publications in Linguistics, 10.) Berkeley and Los Angeles: University of California Press.

Rowe, Timothy B., Thomas W. Stafford Jr., Daniel C. Fisher, Jan J. Enghild, J. Michael Quigg, Richard A. Ketcham, J. Chris Sagebiel, Romy Hanna, and Matthew W. Colbert. 2022. Human occupation of the North American Colorado Plateau

37,000 years ago. *Frontiers in Ecology and Evolution* 10.1–22. |www.frontiersin.org,| Article 903795.
Rude, Noel. 1987. Some Klamath-Sahaptian grammatical correspondences. *Kansas Working Papers in Linguistics* 12.67–83.
Rude, Noel. 2000. Some Uto-Aztecan-Plateau grammatical comparisons. *Uto-Aztecan: Structural, Temproal, and Geographic Perspectives: Papers in Memory of Wick R. Miller by the Friends of Uto-Aztecan*, ed. by Eugene H. Casad and Thomas L. Willett, 309–318. Hermosillo, Sonora: Editorial Unison.
Rude, Noel. 2012. Reconstructing Proto-Sahaptian sounds. *Papers for the Forty-seventh International Conference on Salish and Neighbouring Languages*, edited by Joel Dunham, John Lyon and Natalie Weber, 292–324. University of British Columbia.
Rudes, Blair A. 1974. Sound changes separating Siouan-Yuchi from Iroquois-Caddoan. *International Journal of American Linguistics* 40.117–119.
Ruhlen, Merritt. 1991. The Amerind phylum and the prehistory of the New World. *Sprung from Some Common Source: Investigations into the Prehistory of Languages*, ed. Sydney M. Lamb and E. Douglas Mitchell, 328–350. Stanford: Stanford University Press.
Ruhlen, Merritt. 1994a. *On the Origin of Languages: Studies in Linguistic Taxonomy*. Stanford: Stanford University Press.
Ruhlen, Merritt. 1994b. Linguistic evidence for the peopling of the Americas. *Method and Theory for Investigating the Peopling of the Americas*, ed. by Robson Bonnichsen and D. Gentry Steele, 177–188. Corvallis: Oregon State University, Center for the Study of the First Americans.
Ruhlen, Merritt. 1994c. On the origin of the Amerind pronominal pattern. In *Honor of William S-Y. Wang: Interdisciplinary Studies on Language and Language Change*, ed. by M. Y. Chen and O. J-L. Tzeng, 405–407. Taipei: Pyramid Press.
Ruhlen, Merritt. 1998. The origin of Na-Dene. *Proceedings of the National Academy of Science* 95.13994–13996. [Communicated by Joseph H. Greenberg.]
Saabedra, Cristóbal de (1619[1897]). Relación de la entrada que hizo el gobernador d. Diego Vaca de Vega al descubrimiento y y pacificación de las provincias de los indios maynas, cocamas y gibaros, por comisión y poderes del excmo. sr. principe de Esquilache, virrey de estos reinos del Pirú y la descripción de la tierra, calidad della y de los indios que la habitan, ansí en los rio que entran al famoso del Marañón, como á las riberas dél, por donde entró desembocando el estrecho del pongo del dicho rio Marañón por el mes de septiembre de 1619. *Relaciones Geogrficas de Indias*, vol. 4, 139–162. Madrid: Los Hijos de M. G. Hernández.
Sadovsky, Otto J. 1981. Ob-Ugrian elements in the adverbs, verbal prefixes and postpositions of California Wintuan. *Congressus Quintus Internationalis Fenno-Ugristarum* 6.237–643. Turku: Suomen Kielen Seura.
Sadovsky, Otto J. 1984. *The discovery of California, breaking the silence of the Siberia-to-America migrators*. Anaheim, CA: Grizzly Bear Publishing Co.
Sadovsky, Otto J. 1996. *The Discovery of California: A Cal-Ugrian Comparative Study*. Budapest: Akadémiai Kiadó. (International Society for Trans-Oceanic Research, Los Angeles.)
Sáenz, Nicolás. 1876. Memoria sobre algunas tribus del territorio de San Martín en los Estados Unidos de Colombia. *Zeitschrift für Ethnologie* 8.336–342.
Sakel, Jeanette. 2004. *A Grammar of Mosetén*. Berlin: Mouton de Gruyter.
Salanova, Andrés Pablo. 2011. A flexão de terceira pessoa nas línguas Jê. *LIAMES (Línguas Indígenas Americanas)* 11.75–114.

Salwen, Bert. 1978. Indians of southern New England and Long Island: early period. *Handbook of North American Indians*, ed. by William C. Sturtevant, vol. 15: *Northeast*, ed. by Bruce G. Trigger, 160–176. Washington DC: Smithsonian Institution.
Salwen, Bert. 1987. Demythologizing plains Indian sign language history. *International Journal of American Linguistics* 53.63–73.
Sammallahti, Pekka. 1988. Historical phonology of the Uralic languages: With special reference to Samoyed, Ugric, and Permic. *The Uralic Languages: Description, History, and Foreign Influences*, ed. Denis Sinor, 478–554. Leiden: E. J. Brill.
Santamaría, Francisco J. 1978. *Diccionario de Mejicanismos* (3rd edition). Mexico City: Porrua.
Santamarina Novillo, Carlos. 2006. *El Sistema de Dominación Azteca. El Imperio Tepaneca.* Madrid: Fundación Universitaria Española.
Santana, Áurea Cavalcante and Ema Marta Dunck-Cintra. 2009. Estudos da língua Chiquitano do Brasil: trajetória e perspectivas. *Polifonia* 15/17.91–109.
Sapir, Edward. 1909. *The Takelma language of southern Oregon*. PhD dissertation, Columbia University.
Sapir, Edward. 1911. The problem of noun incorporation in American languages. *American Anthropologist* 3.250–282.
Sapir, Edward. 1913. Wiyot and Yurok, Algonkin languages of California. *American Anthropologist* 15.617–646.
Sapir, Edward. 1913-1919. Southern Paiute and Nahuatl, a study in Uto-Aztecan. *Journal de la Société des Américanistes* 10.379–425, 11.443–488. (Also published in 1915, *American Anthropologist* 17.98–120, 306–328.)
Sapir, Edward. 1915a. Algonkin languages of California: A reply. *American Anthropologist* 17.188–194.
Sapir, Edward. 1915b. The Na-Dené languages: A preliminary report. *American Anthropologist* 17:534–538.
Sapir, Edward. 1915c. Epilogue [to Michelson's rejoinder to Sapir 1915a]. *American Anthropologist* 17.198.
Sapir, Edward. 1917a. The position of Yana in the Hokan stock. *University of California Publications in American Archaeology and Ethnology* 13.1–34.
Sapir, Edward. 1920. The Hokan and Coahuiltecan languages. *International Journal of American Linguistics* 1.280–290.
Sapir, Edward. 1921a. A bird's-eye view of American languages north of Mexico. *Science* 54.408.
Sapir, Edward. 1921b. A characteristic Penutian form of stem. *International Journal of American Linguistics* 2.58–67.
Sapir, Edward. 1922a. The Takelma language of southwestern Oregon. *Handbook of American Indian Languages, Bulletin 40, Bureau of American Ethnology*, ed. by Franz Boas, 1–296. Washington, DC: US Government Printing Office.
Sapir, Edward. 1925a. The Hokan affinity of Subtiaba in Nicaragua. *American Anthropologist* 27.402–435, 491–527.
Sapir, Edward. 1925b. The similarity of Chinese and Indian languages. *Science* 62.12.
Sapir, Edward. 1926. A Chinookan phonetic law. *International Journal of American Linguistics* 4.105–110.
Sapir, Edward. 1929a. Central and North American languages. *Encyclopaedia Britannica* (14th edition), vol. 5, 138–141. [Reprinted1949, *Selected Writings of Edward Sapir*, ed. by David G. Mandelbaum, 169–178. Berkeley and Los Angeles: University of California

Press. Also reprinted 1990, *Collected Writings of Edward Sapir*, vol. 5: *American Indian Languages*, first part, ed. by William Bright, 95–104. Berlin: Mouton de Gruyter.]

Sapir, Edward. 1929b. Male and female forms of speech in Yana. *Donum Natalicium Schrijnen*, ed. by St. W. J. Teeuwen, 79–85. Nijmegen-Utrecht: Dekker and van de Vegt. [Reprinted 1949, *Selected Writings of Edward Sapir in Language, Culture, and Personality*, ed. by David Mandelbaum, 206–212. Berkeley and Los Angeles: University of California Press.]

Sapir, Edward. 1931. The concept of phonetic law as tested in primitive languages by Leonard Bloomfield. *Methods in Social Science: A Case Book*, ed. by S. Rice, 297–306. Chicago: University of Chicago Press. [Reprinted 1949, *Selected Writings of Edward Sapir in Language, Culture, and Personality*, ed. by David Mandelbaum, 73–82. Berkeley and Los Angeles: University of California Press.]

Sapir, Edward. 1936. Internal linguistic evidence suggestive of the Northern origin of the Navajo. *American Anthropologist* 38.224–225.

Sapir, Edward and Morris Swadesh. 1946. American Indian grammatical categories. *Word* 2.103–112.

Sapir, Edward and Morris Swadesh. 1953. Coos-Takelma-Penutian comparisons. *International Journal of American Linguistics* 19.132–137.

Sapir, Edward and Morris Swadesh. 1960. *Yana Dictionary*, ed. by Mary R. Haas. (University of California Publications in Linguistics, 22.) Berkeley: University of California Press.

Sapper, Karl Theodor. 1912. Über einige Sprachen von Sud-Chiapas. *Proceedings of the Seventeenth International Congress of Americanists* 17/1.295–320.

Sauer, Carl. 1934. *The Distribution of Aboriginal Tribes and Languages in Northwest Mexico*. (Ibero-Americana, 5.) Berkeley and Los Angeles: University of California Press.

Sauvageot, Andrés. 1924. Eskimo et Ouralien. *Journal de la Société des Américanists de Paris* 16.279–316.

Sauvageot, Andrés. 1953. Caractère ouraloïde du verbe eskimo. *Bulletin de la Société de Linguistique de Paris* 49.107–121.

Sawyer, Jesse O. 1978. Wappo. *Handbook of North American Indians*, ed. by William C. Sturtevant, vol. 8: *California*, ed. by Robert F. Heizer, 256–263. Washington DC: Smithsonian Institution.

Sawyer, Jesse O. 1980. The nongenetic relationship of Wappo and Yuki. *American Indian and Indo-European Studies: Papers in Honor of Madison S. Beeler*, ed. by Kathryn Klar, Margaret Langdon, and Shirley Silver, 209–219. The Hague: Mouton.

Sawyer, Jesse O. 1991. *Wappo Studies*, ed. by Alice Shepherd, with annotations by William W. Elmendorf. (Survey of California and Other Indian Languages, report 7.) Berkeley: Department of Linguistics, University of California.

Scancarelli, Janine. 2005. Cherokee. *Native Languages of the Southeastern United States*, ed. by Janine Scancarelli and Heather Kay Hardy, 351–384. Lincoln: University of Nebraska Press.

Schaengold, Charlotte C. 2004. *Bilingual Navajo: Mixed Codes, Bilingualism, and Language Maintenance*. PhD dissertation, Ohio State University. http://etd.ohiolink.edu/view.cgi?osu1092425886.

Schillaci, Michael A., Craig Kopris, Søren Wichmann, and Genevieve Dewar. 2017. Linguistic clues to Iroquoian prehistory. *Journal of Anthropological Research* 73.448–485.

Schomburgk, Robert H. 1848. Remarks to accompany a comparative vocabulary of eighteen languages and dialects of Indian Tribes inhabiting Guiana. *Simmond's Colonial Magazine* 15.46–64.

Schroeder, Albert and Ives Goddard. 1979. Synonymy. *Handbook of North American Indians*, ed. by William C. Sturtevant, vol. 9: *Southwest*, ed. by Alfonso Ortiz, 550–553. Washington DC: Smithsonian Institution.

Schuhmacher, W. W. 1974. B ~ C? (A = Indo-European, B = Austronesian, C = Eskimo). *Anthropos* 69.625–637.

Schuhmacher, W. W. 1989. Basque and the other Dene-Caucasian languages. *Le Langage et l'Homme* 24/71.262–263.

Schuhmacher, W. W. 1991. "Ado about nothing" or "evidence": Austronesian and Eskaleut. *Zeitschrift für Phonetik, Sprachwissenschaft und Kommunikationsforschung* 44.290–294.

Schuller, Rodolfo R. 1919–1920. Zur sprachlichen Verwandtschaft der Maya-Qu'itsé mit der Carib-Aruác. *Anthropos* 14.465–491.

Schumacher, Achim, Nathalie Böcker, and Francisca Condori Mollo. 2009. Chholo. *Lenguas de Bolivia*, ed. by Mily Crevels and Pieter Muysken, 117–123. La Paz: Plural Editores.

Sekerina, Irinia. 1994. Copper Island (Mednyj) Aleut: A mixed language. *Languages of the World* 8.14–31.

Seifart, Frank. 2011. Bora Loans in Resígaro: Massive morphological and little lexical borrowing in a moribund Arawakan language. *Cadernos de Etnolingüística* (Série Monografías 2).

Seifart, Frank. 2012. The principle of morphosyntactic subsystem integrity in language contact: Evidence from morphological borrowing in Resígaro (Arawakan). *Diachronica* 29.471–504.

Seifart, Frank and Juan Álvaro Echeverri. 2014. Evidence for the identification of Carabayo, the language of an uncontacted people of the Colombian Amazon, as belonging to the Tikuna-Yurí linguistic family. *PLoS One* 9/4e.94814.

Seifart, Frank and Juan Álvaro Echeverri. 2015. Proto Bora-Muinane. *LIAMES* (*Línguas Indígenas Americanas*) 15.279–311.

Seifart, Frank and Harald Hammarström. 2018. Language isolates in South America. *Language Isolates*, ed. by Lyle Campbell, 260–322. London: Routledge.

Seki, Lucy. 1999. The Upper Xingu as an incipient linguistic area. *The Amazonian Languages*, ed. by Robert M. W. Dixon and Alexandra Aikhenvald, 417–430. Cambridge: Cambridge University Press.

Seki, Lucy. 2011. Alto Xingu: Uma sociedade multilíngue? *Alto Xingu: uma Sociedade Multilíngue*, ed. by Bruna Franchetto, 57–86. Rio de Janeiro: Museu do Indio/Funai.

Seler, Eduard. 1887. *Das Konjugationssystem der Mayasprachen*. Berlin: Unger. [Reprinted 1902, in: Eduard Seler, *Gesammelte Abhandlungen zur Amerikanischen Sprach- und Altertumskunde*, vol. 1, 65–126. Berlin: Ascher. Reissued, 1960, Graz: Akademische Druck- und Verlagsanstalt.]

Seler, Eduard. 1902. Die Sprache der Indianer von Esmeraldas. *Gesammelte Abhandlungen zur Amerikanischen Sprach- und Alterthumskunde*, vol. 1: *Sprachliches, Bilderschriften, Kalender und Hieroglyphenentzifferung*, 49–64. Berlin: A. Asher & Co.

Siméon, Rémi. 1977. *Diccionario de la lengua náhuatl o mexicana*. Mexico: Siglo Veintiuno. (Spanish translation of 1885 *Dictionaire de la langue Nahuatl ou Mexicaine*. Paris: Imprimérie Nationale).

Shafer, Robert. 1952. Athapaskan and Sino-Tibetan. *International Journal of American Linguistics* 18.12–19.

Shafer, Robert. 1957. Note on Athapaskan and Sino-Tibetan. *International Journal of American Linguistics* 23.116–117.

Shafer, Robert. 1969. A few more Athapaskan and Sino-Tibetan comparisons. *International Journal of American Linguistics* 35.67.

Shaul, David L. 1982. Glottalized consonants in Zuni. *International Journal of American Linguistics* 48.83–107.

Shaul, David L. 1985. Azteco-Tanoan ***-l/r-. *International Journal of American Linguistics* 51.584–586.

Shaul, David L. 1988. Esselen: Utian onomastics. In *Honor of Mary Haas: from the Haas Festival Conference on Native America Linguistics*, ed. by William Shipley, 693–703. Berlin: Mouton de Gruyter.

Shaul, David L. 2014. *A Prehistory of Western North America: The Impact of Uto-Aztecan Languages*. Albuquerque: University of New Mexico Press.

Shaul, David L. and John M. Andresen. 1989. A case for Yuman participation in the Hohokam regional system. *Kiva* 54.105–126.

Shell, Olive A. 1975. *Las Lenguas Pano y su Reconstrucción*. (Serie Lingüística Peruana, 12.) Yarinacocha, Peru: Instituto Lingüístico de Verano (ILV).

Shepherd, Alice. 2005. *Proto-Wintun*. (University of California Publications in Linguistics, 137.) Berkeley and Los Angeles: University of California Press.

Sherzer, Joel. 1972. Vowel nasalization in Eastern Algonquian: An areal-typological perspective on linguistic universals. *International Journal of American Linguistics* 38.267–268.

Sherzer, Joel. 1973. Areal linguistics in North America. *Current Trends in Linguistics*, vol. 10: *Linguistics in North America*, ed. by Tomas A. Sebeok, 749–795. The Hague: Mouton.

Sherzer, Joel. 1976. *An Areal-Typological Study of American Indian Languages North of Mexico*. Amsterdam: North-Holland.

Shevoroshkin, Vitaly. 1991. Introduction. *Dene-Sino-Caucasian Languages: Materials from the First International Interdisciplinary Symposium on Language and Prehistory*, ed. by Vitaly Shevoroshkin, 1–11. Bochum: Brockmeyer.

Shipley, William. 1957. Some Yukian-Penutian lexical resemblances. *International Journal of American Linguistics* 23.269–274.

Shipley, William. 1962. Hispanisms in indigenous California. *Romance Philology* 16.1–21.

Shipley, William. 1969. Proto-Takelman. *International Journal of American Linguistics* 35.226–230.

Shipley, William. 1978. Native languages of California. *Handbook of North American Indians*, ed. by William C. Sturtevant, vol. 8: *California*, ed. by Robert F. Heizer, 80–90. Washington DC: Smithsonian Institution.

Shipley, William. 1980. Penutian among the ruins: a personal assessment. *Berkeley Linguistics Society* 6.437–441.

Shipley, William. 1983–1984. Penutian among the ruins: A personal assessment. *Journal of the Steward Anthropological Society* 15.59–63.

Sibley, John. 1805. [Letter, December 14, 1805, to Thomas Jefferson.] *MS, Thomas Jefferson Papers Series*, vol. 1: *General Correspondence*. Washington DC: Library of Congress.

Sibley, John. 1806. Historical Sketches of the Several Indian Tribes in Louisiana, South of the Arkansa River, and between the Mississippi and River Grand [April 5, 1805]. *Message from the President of the United States Communicating the Discoveries Made in Exploring the Missouri, Red River, and Washita*, by Thomas Jefferson, 48–62. New York: G. F. Hopkins.

Sibley, John. 1832[c. 1804]. Historical sketches of the several Indian tribes in Louisiana, south of the Arkansas River, and between the Mississippi and River Grande. *American State Papers, Class II, Indian Affairs* 1.721–731. Washington.

Siebert, Frank. 1945. Linguistic classification of Catawba. *International Journal of American Linguistics* 11.100–104, 211–218.

Siebert, Frank T., Jr. 1967. The original home of the Proto-Algonquian people. *Contributions to Anthropology: Linguistics 1. National Museum of Canada Bulletin* 214.13–47.

Siebert, Frank T., Jr. 1975. Resurrecting Virginia Algonkian from the dead. *Studies in Southeastern Indian languages*, ed. by James M. Crawford, 285–453. Athens: University of Georgia Press.

Silva, Alcionílio Bruzzi Alves da. 1962. *A Civilização Indígena do Uaupés*. São Paulo: Centro de Pesquisas de Iauareté, Missão Salesiana do Rio Negro.

Silva, Wilson de Lima. 2020. Multilingual interactions and code-mixing in Northwest Amazonia. *International Journal of American Linguistics* 86.133–154.

Silva, Wilson and Lyle Campbell. In press. Etymology in the study of the Indigenous languages of the Americas. *Oxford Handbook of Etymology*, ed. by Philip Durkin. Oxford: Oxford University Press.

Silver, Shirley. 1978a. Chimariko. *Handbook of North American Indians*, ed. by William C. Sturtevant, vol. 8: *California*, ed. by Robert F. Heizer, 205–210. Washington DC: Smithsonian Institution.

Silver, Shirley. 1978b. Shastan peoples. *Handbook of North American Indians*, ed. by William C. Sturtevant, vol. 8: *California*, ed. by Robert F. Heizer, 211–224. Washington DC: Smithsonian Institution.

Silverstein, Michael. 1972. Chinook Jargon: Language contact and the problem of multilevel generative systems. *Language* 48.378–406, 596–625.

Silverstein, Michael. 1974. *Dialectal Developments in Chinookan Tense-Aspect Systems: An Areal-Historical Analysis*. (Indiana University Publications in Anthropology and Linguistics, Memoir 29.) Bloomington.

Silverstein, Michael. 1979a. Penutian: An assessment. *The Languages of Native America: An Historical and Comparative Assessment*, ed. by Lyle Campbell and Marianne Mithun, 650–691. Austin: University of Texas Press.

Silverstein, Michael. 1990. Chinookans of the lower Columbia. *Handbook of North American Indians*, ed. by William C. Sturtevant, vol. 7: *Northwest Coast*, ed. by Wayne Suttles, 533–546. Washington DC: Smithsonian Institution.

Silverstein, Michael. 1996. Dynamics of language contact. *Handbook of North American Indians*, vol. 17, ed. by Ives Goddard, 117–136. Washington DC: Smithsonian Institution.

Singerman, Adam Roth. 2021. There are no 'relational prefixes' in the Tuparí language: Synchronic and diachronic consequences. Talk given at the Harvard GSAS Indo-European and Historical Linguistics Workshop, September 24, 2021.

Sjoberg, Andrée F. 1951. The Bidai Indians of southeastern Texas. *Southwestern Journal of Anthropology* 7.391–400.

Skoglund, Pontus and David Reich. 2016. A genomic view of the peopling of the Americas. *Current Opinion in Genetics and Development* 41.27–35.

Skoglund, Pontus, Sapan Mallick, Maria CátoraBortolini, Niru Chennagiri, Tábita Hünemeier, Maria Luiza Petzl-Erler, Francisco Mauro Salzano, Nick Patterson, and David Reich. 2015. Genetic evidence for two founding populations of the Americas. *Nature* 525.104–108. www.nature.com/nature/journal/v525/n7567/abs/nature14895.html.

Smith, Charles R. 1978. Tubatulabal. *Handbook of North American Indians*, ed. by William C. Sturtevant, vol. 8: *California*, ed. by Robert F. Heizer, 437–445. Washington DC: Smithsonian Institution.

Smith, Norval. 1994. An annotated list of creoles, pidgins, and mixed languages. *Creoles and Pidgins: An Introduction*, ed. by Jacques Arends, Pieter Muysken, and Norval Smith, 331–374. Amsterdam: John Benjamins.

Smith-Stark, Thomas C. 1976. Some hypotheses on syntactic and morphological aspects of Proto-Mayan (*PM). *Mayan Linguistics I*, ed. by Marlys McClaran, 44–66. Los Angeles: American Indian Studies Center, UCLA.

Smith-Stark, Thomas. 1988. Pied-piping 'con inversión en preguntas parciales. Unpublished manuscript, Centro de Estudios Lingüísticos y Literarios, Colegio de México y Seminario de Lenguas indígenas.

Smith-Stark, Thomas. 1994. Mesoamerican calques. *Investigaciones lingüísticas en Mesoamérica*, ed. by Carolyn J. Mackay and Verónica Vázquez, 15–50. Mexico City: Seminario de Lenguas Indígenas del Instituto de Investigaciones Filológicas, UNAM.

Snow, Dean R. 1976. The archaeological implications of the Proto-Algonquian Urheimat. *Papers of the Seventh Algonquian Conference*, ed. by William Cowan, 339–346. Ottawa: Carleton University.

Snow, Dean R. 1978. Eastern Abenaki. *Handbook of North American Indians*, ed. by William C. Sturtevant, vol. 15: *Northeast*, ed. by Bruce G. Trigger, 137–147. Washington DC: Smithsonian Institution.

Sorensen, Arthur P. 1967. Multilingualism in the northwest Amazon. *American Anthropologist* 69.670–684.

Souza, Gabriel Soares. 1971[1587]. *Tratado Descritivo do Brasil*. São Paulo: Editora Nacional e Editora da Univeridade de São Paulo.

Spindler, Louis S. 1978. Menominee. *Handbook of North American Indians*, ed. by William C. Sturtevant, vol. 15: *Northeast*, ed. by Bruce G. Trigger, 708–724. Washington DC: Smithsonian Institution.

Stark, Louisa R. 1970. Mayan affinities with Araucanian. *Chicago Linguistics Society* 6.57–69.

Stark, Louisa R. 1972a. Maya-Yunga-Chipayan: A new linguistic alignment. *International Journal of American Linguistics* 38.119–135.

Stark, Louisa R. 1972b. Machaj-Juyai: Secret language of the Callahuayas. *Papers in Andean Linguistics* 2.199–227.

Stark, Louisa R. 1985. Indigenous languages of lowland Ecuador: History and current status. *South American Indian languages: Retrospect and prospect*, ed. by Harriet E. Manelis Klein and Louisa R. Stark, 157–193. Austin: University of Texas Press.

Starostin, George. 2012. Dene-Yeniseian: A critical assessment. *Journal of Language Relationship* 8.117–138.

Starostin, Sergei A. 1991. On the hypothesis of a genetic connection between the Sino-Tibetan languages and the Yeniseian and North-Caucasian languages. *Dene-Sino-Caucasian Languages: Materials from the First International Interdisciplinary Symposium on Language and Prehistory*, ed. by Vitaly Shevoroshkin, 12–41. Bochum: Brockmeyer.

Stefánsson, Vilhjálmur. 1909. The Eskimo trade jargon of Herschel Island. *American Anthropologist* 11.217–32.

Stefánsson, Vilhjálmur. 1922. *Hunters of the Great North*. New York: Harcourt, Brace and Co.

Stenzel, Kristine. 2013. Contact and innovation in Vaupés possession-marking strategies. *Upper Rio Negro: Cultural and Linguistic Interaction in Northwestern Amazonia*, ed. by Patience Epps and Kristine Stenzel, 353–400. Rio de Janeiro: Museo do Índio.
Stenzel, Kristine and Elsa Gomez-Imbert. 2009. Contato linguístico e mudança linguística no noroeste amazônico: o caso do Kotiria (Wanano). *Revista da ABRALIN* 8.1–100.
Stenzel, Kristine and Nichols Williams. 2021. Towards an interactional approach to multilingualism: Ideologies and practices in the northwest Amazon. *Language and Communication* 80.136–164.
Stewart, Ethel G. 1991. *The Dene and Na-Dene Indian Migration—1233 A.D.: Escape from Genghis Khan to America*. Columbus, GA: Institute for the Study of American Cultures.
Stoll, Otto. 1884. *Zur Ethnographie der Republik Guatemala*. Zurich: Füssli. (Spanish translation 1958, *Etnografía de Guatemala*, translated by Antonio Goubaud Carrera. [Seminario de Integración Social Guatemalteca, publicación 8.] Guatemala: Ministerio de Educación Pública.)
Stoll, Otto. 1885. Supplementary remarks to the grammar of the Cakchiquel language, ed. by Daniel G. Brinton. *Proceedings of the American Philosophical Society* 22.255–268.
Stoll, Otto. 1912–1913. Zur Psychologie der indianischen Hochlandsprachen von Guatemala. *Jahresbericht der Geographisch-ethnographischen Gesellschaft in Zürich* 1912–1913.34–96. Zürich: Kommissions-Verlag von Beer & Cie.
Stolz, Thomas, Dik Bakker, and Rosa Salas Palomo, eds. 2008. *Hispanisation: The Impact of Spanish on the Lexicon and Grammar of the Indigenous Languages of Austronesia and the Americas*. Berlin: De Gruyter Mouton.
Stubbs, Brian D. 2011. *Uto-Aztecan: a comparative vocabulary*. Blanding: Rocky Mountain Books and Productions. https://utoaztecan.blogspot.com/.
Sturtevant, William C. 1958. Siouan languages in the East. *American Anthropologist* 60.738–743.
Sturtevant, William C. 1994. The misconnection of Guale and Yamasee with Muskogean. *International Journal of American Linguistics* 60.139–148.
Sturtevant, William C. 2005. History of research on the native languages of the Southeast. *Native languages of the Southeastern United States*, ed. by Heather K. Hardy and Janine Scancarelli, 8–65. Lincoln: University of Nebraska Press.
Suárez, Jorge. 1969. Moseten and Pano-Tacanan. *Anthropological Linguistics* 11/9.255–266.
Suárez, Jorge. 1973. Macro-Pano-Tacana. *International Journal of American Linguistics* 39.137–154.
Suárez, Jorge. 1974. South American Indian languages. *Encyclopaedia Britannica* (15th edition), Macropaedia 17.105–112.
Suárez, Jorge. 1975. *Estudios Huaves*. (Colección Científica, Lingüística, 22). Mexico: Instituto Nacional de Antropología e Historia, Departamento de Lingüística.
Suárez, Jorge. 1983a. *La Lengua Tlapaneca de Malinaltepec*. Mexico: Universidad Nacional Autónoma de México.
Suárez, Jorge. 1983b. *The Mesoamerican Indian Languages*. Cambridge: Cambridge University Press.
Suárez, Jorge. 1986. Elementos gramaticales otomangues en tlapaneco. *Language in Global Perspective: Papers in Honor of the 50th Anniversary of the Summer Institute of Linguistics, 1935–1985*, ed. by Benjamin Elson, 267–284. Dallas: Summer Institute of Linguistics.
Sušnik, Branislava J. 1962. Algunas palabras culturales del área chaqueña. *Boletín de la Sociedad Científica del Paraguay y del Museo Etnográfico* 6.33–68. Asunción: Museo Etnográfico "Andrés Barbero."

Suttles, Wayne. 1990. Central Coast Salish. *Handbook of North American Indians*, ed. by William C. Sturtevant, vol. 7: *Northwest Coast*, ed. by Wayne Suttles, 453–475. Washington DC: Smithsonian Institution.

Suttles, Wayne and Barbara Lane. 1990. Southern Coast Salish. *Handbook of North American Indians*, ed. by William C. Sturtevant, vol. 7: *Northwest Coast*, ed. by Wayne Suttles, 485–502. Washington DC: Smithsonian Institution.

Swadesh, Morris. 1946. Phonologic formulas for Chitimacha-Atakapa. *International Journal of American Linguistics* 12.113–132.

Swadesh, Morris. 1947. Atakapa-Chitimacha *kw. *International Journal of American Linguistics* 13.120–121.

Swadesh, Morris. 1949. The linguistic approach to Salish prehistory. *Distribution of the Chemakum language. Indians of the urban Northwest*, ed. by Marian W. Smith, 160–173. New York: Columbia University Press.

Swadesh, Morris. 1952. Review of *Athapaskan and Sino-Tibetan*, by Robert Shafer [1952]. *International Journal of American Linguistics* 18.178–181.

Swadesh, Morris. 1953a. Mosan I: A problem of remote common origin. *International Journal of American Linguistics* 19.26–44.

Swadesh, Morris. 1953b. Mosan II: Comparative vocabulary. *International Journal of American Linguistics* 19.223–236.

Swadesh, Morris. 1953c. Salish-Wakashan lexical comparisons noted by Boas. *International Journal of American Linguistics* 19.290–291.

Swadesh, Morris. 1954a. Perspectives and problems of Amerindian comparative linguistics. *Word* 10.306–332.

Swadesh, Morris. 1954b. Time depth of American linguistic groupings. *American Anthropologist* 56.361–364.

Swadesh, Morris. 1956. Problems of long-range comparison in Penutian. *Language* 32.17–41.

Swadesh, Mauricio [Morris]. 1959. *Mapas de clasificación lingüística de México y las Américas.* (Instituto de Historia, 51.) Mexico: Universidad Nacional Autónoma de México.

Swadesh, Morris. 1962. Linguistic relations across the Bering Strait. *American Anthropologist* 64.1262–1291.

Swadesh, Mauricio [Morris]. 1963a. El tamaulipeco. *Revista Mexicana de Estudios Antropológicos* 19.93–104.

Swadesh, Morris. 1964a. Comparative Penutian glosses of Sapir. *Studies in Californian Linguistics*, ed. by William Bright, 182–191. (University of California Publications in Linguistics, 34.) Berkeley and Los Angeles: University of California Press.

Swadesh, Morris. 1964b. Linguistic overview. *Prehistoric Man in the New World*, ed. by Jesse D. Jennings and Edward Norbeck, 527–556. Chicago: University of Chicago Press.

Swadesh, Morris. 1965. Kalapuya and Takelma. *International Journal of American Linguistics* 31.237–240.

Swadesh, Mauricio [Morris]. 1966. Porhé y Maya. *Anales de Antropología* 3.173–204. Mexico: Universidad Nacional Autónoma de México.

Swadesh, Morris. 1967a. Lexicostatistic classification. *Handbook of Middle American Indians*, ed. by Robert Wauchope, vol. 5: *Linguistics*, ed. by Norman A. McQuown, 79–115. Austin: University of Texas Press.

Swadesh, Morris 1967b. Linguistic classification in the Southwest. *Studies in Southwestern Ethnolinguistics: Meaning and History in the Languages of the American Southwest*, ed. by Dell Hymes and William E. Bittle, 281–309. The Hague: Mouton.

Swadesh, Mauricio [Morris]. 1968. Las lenguas indígenas del noroeste de México. *Anales de Antropología* 5.75–86. Mexico: Universidad Nacional Autónoma de México.

Swanton, John R. 1908a. The language of the Taensa. *American Anthropologist* 10.24–32.

Swanton, John R. 1911. *Indian Tribes of the Lower Mississippi Valley and Adjacent Coast of the Gulf of Mexico.* (Bureau of American Ethnology Bulletin 43.) Washington DC: Government Printing Office.

Swanton, John R. 1917. Unclassified languages of the Southeast. *International Journal of American Linguistics* 1.47–49.

Swanton, John R. 1919. *A Structural and Lexical Comparison of the Tunica, Chitimacha, and Atakapa Languages.* (Bulletin of the Bureau of American Ethnology, 68.) Washington DC: Government Printing Office.

Swanton, John R. 1924. The Muskhogean connection of the Natchez language. *International Journal of American Linguistics* 3.46–75.

Swanton, John R. 1940. *Linguistic Material from the Tribes of Southern Texas and Northeastern Mexico.* (Bureau of American Ethnology, Bulletin 127.) Washington DC: U.S. Government Printing Office.

Swanton, John R. 1946. *The Indians of the Southeastern United States.* (Bureau of American Ethnology Bulletin, 137.) Washington DC: U.S. Government Printing Office.

Swiggers, Pierre. 1985. Munsee Borrowings from Dutch: Some Phonological Remarks. *International Journal of American Linguistics* 51.594–597.

Tallman, Adam J. R. and Patience Epps. 2020. Morphological complexity, autonomy, and areality in western Amazonia. *The Complexities of Morphology*, ed. by Peter Arkadiev and Francesco Gardani, 230–264. Oxford: Oxford University Press.

Tamm, Erika, Toomas Kivisild, Maere Reidla, Mait Metspalu, David Glenn Smith, Connie J. Mulligan, Claudio M. Bravi, Olga Rickards, Cristina Martinez-Labarga, Elsa K. Khusnutdinova, Sardana A. Fedorova, Maria V. Golubenko, Vadim A. Stepanov, Marina A. Gubina, Sergey I. Zhadanov, Ludmila P. Ossipova, Larisa Damba, Mikhail I. Voevoda, Jose E. Dipierri, Richard Villems, Ripan S. Malhi. 2007. Beringian standstill and spread of Native American founders. *PLoS ONE* 2(9).e829. https://doi.org/10.1371/journal.pone.0000829.

Tarazona-Santos, Eduardo and Fabricio R. Santos. 2008. The peopling of the Americas: a second major migration? *American Journal of Human Genetics* 70.1377–1380.

Tarpent, Marie-Lucie. 1996. Reattaching Tsimshianic to Penutian. *Proceedings of the Hokan-Penutian Workshop: July 8–9, 1994, University of Oregon, Eugene, and July 5–6, 1995, University of New Mexico, Albuquerque*, no. 9, ed. by Victor Golla, 91–112. Berkeley: Survey of California and Other Indian Languages.

Tarpent, Marie-Lucie. 1997. Tsimshianic and Penutian: Problems, methods, results, and implications. *International Journal of American Linguistics* 63.65–112.

Tarpent, Marie-Lucie. 2000. Tsimshianic l-initial Plurals: Relics of an Ancient Penutian Pattern. *Proceedings of the Meeting of the Hokan-Penutian Workshop*, June 17–13, 2000. Report 11, ed. by Lisa Conathan and Teresa McFarland, 88–108. Berkeley: Survey of California and Other Indian Languages.

Tarpent, Marie-Lucie. 2002. A Pan-Penutian database of materials for comparison and reconstruction: its organization, uses and current results. *Proceedings of the 50th Anniversary Conference, June 8–9, 2002, University of California at Berkeley.* Report 12, ed. by Laura Buszard-Welcher, 119–136. Berkeley: Survey of California and other Indian Languages.

Taylor, Allan R. 1963a. The classification of the Caddoan languages. *Proceedings of the American Philosophical Society* 107.51–59.

Taylor, Allan R. 1963b. Comparative Caddoan. *International Journal of American Linguistics* 29.113–131.
Taylor, Allan R. 1976. Words for *buffalo*. *International Journal of American Linguistics* 42.165–166.
Taylor, Allan R. 1978. Nonverbal communication in aboriginal North America: The Plains sign language. *Aboriginal Sign Languages of the Americas and Australia*, vol. 2: *The Americas and Australia*, ed. by D. Jean Umiker-Sebeok and Thomas A. Sebeok, 223–244. New York: Plenum Press.
Taylor, Allan R. 1996. Nonspeech communication systems. *Handbook of North American Indians*, vol. 17, ed. by Ives Goddard, 275–289. Washington DC: Smithsonian Institution.
Taylor, Allan R. 2011. The plains Indian sign language. *Atlas of Languages of Intercultural Communication in the Pacific, Asia, and the Americas*, ed. by Stephen A. Wurm, Peter Mühlhäusler, and Darrell T. Tryon, 1241–1252. Berlin: De Gruyter Mouton.
Taylor, Douglas R. 1956. Languages and ghost-languages of the West Indies. *International Journal of American Linguistics* 22.180–183.
Taylor, Douglas. 1977. *Languages of the West Indies*. Baltimore: John Hopkins University Press.
Taylor, Douglas R. and Berend J. Hoff. 1980. The linguistic repertory of the Island Carib in the seventeenth century: The men's language—a Carib pidgin? *International Journal of American Linguistics* 46.301–312.
Taylor, Gerald. 1985. Apontamentos sobre o nheengatu falado no Rio Negro, Brasil. *Amerindia* 10.5–23.
Teeter, Karl V. 1964a. Algonquian languages and genetic relationship. *Proceedings of the 9th International Congress of Linguists*, ed. by Dwight L. Bolinger and Horace G. Lunt, 1026–1033. The Hague: Mouton.
Teeter, Karl V. 1964b. *The Wiyot Language*. (University of California Publications in Linguistics, 37.) Berkeley and Los Angeles: University of California Press.
Tessmann, Günther. 1930. *Die Indianer Nordost-Perus: Grundlegende Forschungen für Eine Systematische Kulturkunde*. Hamburg: Friederichsen, de Gruyter & Co.
Terraza, Jimena. 2008. *Gramática del wichí: fonología y morfosintaxis*. PhD dissertation, Université du Québec à Montréal.
Teza, Emilio. 1868. Saggi inediti di lingue americane. *Annali delle Università Toscane*, Parte prima: *Scienze Neologiche* 10.117–143.
Thalbitzer, William. 1922. The Aleutian languages compared with Greenlandic: A manuscript by Rasmus Rask, dating from 1820, now in the Royal Library at Copenhagen. *International Journal of American Linguistics* 2.40–57.
Thalbitzer, William. 1928[1926]. Is there any connection between the Eskimo language and the Uralian? *International Congress of Americanists* 22.2.551–567.
Thalbitzer, William. 1945[1944]. Uhlenbeck's Eskimo-Indoeuropean hypothesis: A critical revision. *Travaux du Cercle Linguistique de Copenhague* 1.66–96. Copenhagen: Einar Munksgaard.
Thalbitzer, William. 1952. Possible contracts between Eskimo and Old World languages. *Indian Tribes of Aboriginal America*, ed. by Sol Tax. *Proceedings of the 29th International Congress of Americanists* 3.50–54. Chicago.
The Catalogue of Endangered Languages. www.Endangeredlanguages.com.
Thomas, Cyrus. 1902. Provisional list of linguistic families, languages, and dialects of Mexico and Central America. *American Anthropologist* 4.207–216.

Thomas, Cyrus and John R. Swanton. 1911. *Indian Languages of Mexico and Central America and Their Geographical Distribution*. (Bureau of American Ethnology, Bulletin 44.) Washington DC: Government Printing Office.

Thomason, Sarah G. 1980. On interpreting 'The Indian Interpreter'. *Language in Society* 9.167–193.

Thomason, Sarah G. 1983. Chinook Jargon in areal and historical context. *Language* 59.820–870.

Thomason, Sarah G. 1997. Mednyj Aleut. *Contact Languages: A Wider Perspective*, ed. Sarah G. Thomason, by 449–468. Amsterdam: John Benjamins.

Thomason, Sarah G. 2006. Salishan languages. *Encyclopedia of Language and Linguistics* (2nd edition), ed. by Keith Brown, vol. 10, 732–733. Oxford: Elsevier.

Thomason, Sarah G. and Terrence Kaufman. 1988. *Language Contact, Creolization, and Genetic Linguistics*. Berkeley and Los Angeles: University of California Press.

Thompson, J. Eric S. 1943. *Pitfalls and Stimuli in the Interpretation of History through Loan Words*. (Philological and Documentary Studies 1: Middle American Research Institute, publication 11.) New Orleans: Tulane University.

Thompson, J. Eric S. 1970. *Maya history and religion*. Norman: University of Oklahoma Press.

Thompson, Laurence C. 1979. Salishan and the Northwest. *The Languages of Native America: An Historical and Comparative Assessment*, ed. by Lyle Campbell and Marianne Mithun, 692–761. Austin: University of Texas Press.

Thompson, Laurence C. and M. Dale Kinkade. 1990. Languages. *Handbook of North American Indians*, ed. by William C. Sturtevant, vol. 7: *Northwest Coast*, ed. by Wayne Suttles, 30–51. Washington DC: Smithsonian Institution.

Thompson, Laurence C. and M. Terry Thompson. 1972. Language universals, nasals, and the Northwest coast. *Studies in Linguistics in Honor of George L. Trager*, ed. by M. Estellie Smith, 441–456. The Hague: Mouton.

Tobar Ortiz, Nubia. 1995. Los tinigua, en el umbral de una muerte inevitable. *Lenguas Aborígenes de Colombia, Serie Memorias, III*, 62–74. Bogotá: CCELA [*Centro Colombiano de Estudios de Lenguas Aborígenes*], Universidad de los Andes.

Tobar Ortiz, Nubia. 2000. La Lengua Tinigua: Anotaciones fonológicas y morfológicas. *Lenguas Indígenas de Colombia: Una Visión Descriptiva*, ed. by María Stella González de Pérez and María Luisa Rodríguez de Montes, 669–679. Bogotá: Instituto Caro y Cuervo.

Torero Fernández de Córdova, Alfredo A. 1986. Deslindes lingüísticos en la costa norte peruana. *Revista Andina* 4.523–548.

Torero Fernández de Córdova, Alfredo A. 1989. Áreas toponímicas e idiomas en la sierra norte peruana: un trabajo de recuperación lingüística. *Revista Andiana* 7.217–257.

Torero Fernández de Córdova, Alfredo A. 1993. Lenguas del nororiente Peruano: La hoya de Jaén en el siglo xvi. *Revista Andina* 22.447–472.

Torero Fernández de Córdova, Alfredo A. 2002. *Idiomas de los Andes: lingüística e historia*. Lima: Editorial Horizonte.

Tovar, Antonio. 1951. Un capítulo de lingüística general: los prefijos posesivos en lenguas del Chaco y la lucha entre préstamos morfológicos en un espacio dado. *Boletín de la Academia Argentina de Letras* 20.360–403.

Tovar, Antonio. 1961. *Catálogo de las lenguas de América del Sur: enumeración, con indicaciones tipológicas, bibliografía y mapas*. Buenos Aires: Editorial Sudamericana. (1st edition; cf. Antonio Tovar and Larrucea de Tovar 1984, 2nd edition.)

Tovar, Antonio and Consuelo Larrucea de Tovar. 1984. *Catálogo de las lenguas de América del Sur*. (New edition [cf. Tovar 1961, first edition].) Madrid: Gredos.

Trask, R[ichard] L[arry]. 1995. Basque and Dené-Caucasian: A critique from the Basque side. *Mother Tongue* 1.3–82.

Trask, R[ichard] L[arry]. 1996. *Historical Linguistics*. London: Arnold.

Trask, R[ichard] L[arry]. 1999. Why should languages have any relatives? *Nostratic: Examining a Linguistic Macrofamily*, ed. Colin Renfrew and Daniel Nettle, 157–176. Cambridge: McDonald Institute for Archaeological Research.

Troike, Rudolf C. 1963. A contribution to Coahuilteco lexicography. *International Journal of American Linguistics* 29.295–299.

Troike, Rudolf C. 1967. Review of El cuadernillo de la lengua de los indios Pajalates (1732), por Gabriel de Vergara, y el confesonario de indios en lengua coahuilteca, ed. by Eugenio del Hoyo. *International Journal of American Linguistics* 33.78–81.

Troike, Rudolf C. 1978. The date and authorship of the Pajalate (Coahuilteco) Cuadernillo. *International Journal of American Linguistics* 44.329–330.

Troike, Rudolf C. 1987. Karankawa linguistics data. *Three Primary Documents: La Salle, the Mississippi, and the Gulf*, ed. by Robert S. Weddle, 288–301. College Station: Texas A and M University Press.

Troike, Rudolf C. 1988. Amotomanco (Otomoaca) and Tanpachoa as Uto-Aztecan languages, and the Jumano problem once more. *International Journal of American Linguistics* 54.235–241.

Troike, Rudolph C. 1996. Sketch of Coahuilteco, a language isolate of Texas. *Handbook of North American Indians*, ed. William Sturtevant, vol. 17: *Languages*, ed. by In Ives Goddard, 644–665. Washington DC: Smithsonian Institution.

Trombetti, Alfredo. 1907. *Come si fa la critica di un libro: Con nuovi contributi alla dottrina della monogenesi del linguaggio e alla glottologia generale comparata*. Bologna: Libreria Treves di Luigi Beltrami.

Trombetti, Alfredo. 1928[1926]. Origine asiatica delle lingue e popolazioni americane. *International Congress of Americanists* 22/1.169–246.

Turner, Katherine. 1980. The reconstituted phonemes of Salinan. *Journal of California and Great Basin Anthropology, Papers in Linguistics* 2.53–92.

Turner, Katherine. 1987. *Aspects of Salinan Grammar*. PhD dissertation, University of California, Berkeley.

Turner, Paul R. 1967. Seri and Chontal (Tequistlatec). *International Journal of American Linguistics* 33.235–239.

Turner, Paul R. 1969. Proto-Chontal phonemes. *International Journal of American Linguistics* 35.34–37.

Turner, Paul R. 1972. On linguistic unrelatedness—A rejoinder. *International Journal of American Linguistics* 38.146–147.

Uhde, Adolf. 1861. *Die Länder am untern Rio Bravo del Norte*. Heidelberg: Mohr.

Uhlenbeck, Christianus Cornelius. 1905. Uralische Anklänge in den Eskimosprachen. *Zeitschrift der deutschen morgenländischen Gesellschaft* 59.757–765.

Uhlenbeck, Christianus Cornelius. 1942–1945. Ur- und altindogermanische Anklänge im Wortschatz des Eskimos. *Anthropos* 37–40.133–148.

Ultan, Russell. 1964. Proto-Maidun phonology. *International Journal of American Linguistics* 30.355–370.

Unruh, Ernesto and Kalisch, Hannes. 2003. Enlhet-Enenlhet: una familia lingüística chaqueña. *Thule, Rivista italiana di studi americanistici* 14/15.207–231. https://enlhet.org/pdf/nne28-enlhet-enenlhet.pdf.

Urban, Matthias. 2018a. A new approach to the reconstitution of the pronunciation of Timote-Cuica (Venezuelan Andes). *Cadernos de Etnolingüística* 6.31–50.
Urban, Matthias. 2018b. Maritime loanwords in languages of Pacific Meso- and South America? An exploratory study. *New Perspectives on the Peopling of the Americas*, ed. by Katerina Harvati, Gerhard Jäger, Hugo Reyes-Centeno, 27–60. (Words, Bones, Genes, Tools: DFG Center for Advanced Studies Series.) Tübingen: Kerns.
Urban, Matthias. 2018c. The lexical legacy of substrate languages: a test case from the 1333 southern Ecuadorian Highlands. *Transactions of the Philological Society* 116.435–459. https://doi.org/10.1111/1467-968X.12129.
Urban, Matthias. 2019a. *Lost Languages of the Peruvian North Coast*. (Estudios Indiana, 12.) Berlin: Mann Verlag, Ibero-Amerikanisches Institut Preussischer Kulturbesitz.
Urban, Matthias. 2019b. Is there a Central Andean Linguistic Area? A View from the Perspective of the "Minor" Languages. *Journal of Language Contact* 12.271–304.
Vajda, Edward. 2010. A Siberian link with Na-Dene languages. *The Dene-Yeniseian Connection*, ed. by James Kari and Ben A. Potter, 33–99. (Anthropological Papers of the University of Alaska, n.s., 5, nos. 1–2: A Special Joint Publication of the University of Alaska, Fairbanks.) Fairbanks: Department of Anthropology and Alaska Native Language Center.
Vajda, Edward. 2018. Dene-Yeniseian: progress and unanswered questions. *Diachronica* 35.277–295.
Valenzuela Bismarck, Pilar. 2011. Contribuciones para la reconstrucción del proto-cahuapana: comparación léxica y gramatical de las lenguas jebero y chayahuita. *Aru, Simi, Taqu, Lengua: Estudios en homenaje a Rodolfo Cerrón-Palomino*, ed. by Willem F. H. Adelaar, Pilar Valenzuela Bismarck, and Roberto Zariquiey Biondi, 271–304. Lima: Fondo Editorial, Pontificia Universidad Católica del Perú.
Valenzuela, Pilar and Antoine Guillaume. 2017. Estudios sincrónicos y diacrónicos sobre lenguas Pano y Takana: una introducción. *Amerindia* 39.1–49.
Valenzuela, Pilar M. and Roberto Zariquiey. 2015. Advances in favor of the Pano-Takanan Hypothesis. *Annual Meeting of the Societas Linguistica Europeae* 48.2–5.
Vallejos Yopán, Rosa. 2005. Entre flexión y derivación: examinando algunos morfemas en Kokama-Cocamilla. *Memorias del Congreso de Idiomas Indígenas de Latinoamérica-II*, October 27–29. University of Texas at Austin.
Vallejos Yopán, Rosa. 2010. *A grammar of Kokama-Kokamilla*. PhD dissertation, University of Oregon.
Van de Kerke, Simon. 2000. Case marking in the Leko language: essays on indigenous languages of Lowland South America. *Contributions to the 49th International Congress of Americanists in Quito 1997*, 25–37. Leiden: University of Leiden.
Van de Kerke, Simon. 2013. Verb formation in Leko: Causatives, reflexives and reciprocals. *Typology of Verbal Categories*, ed. by Mily Crevels, Simon van de Kerke, Sérgio Meira, and Hein van der Voort, 241–254. Leiden: Research School of Asian, African, and Amerindian Studies (CNWS).
Van de Kerke, Simon and Pieter Muysken. 2014. The Andean matrix. *The Native Language of South America: Origins, Development, Typology*, ed. by Loretta O'Connor and Pieter Muysken, 126–151. New York: Cambridge University Press.
Van der Voort, Hein. 1997. New light on Eskimo pidgins. *The Structure and Status of Pidgins and Creoles*, ed. by Arthur K. Spears and Donald Winford, 373–394. Amsterdam: John Benjamins.

Van der Voort, Hein. 2005. Kwaza in a comparative perspective. *International Journal of American Linguistics* 71.365–412.
Van der Voort, Hein. 2012. Whatever happened to Mashubi? Taking a new look at Fawcett's vocabulary. *Cadernos de Etnolingüística* 4.1–20. http://www.etnolinguistica.org/issue:vol4n1.
Van Gijn, Rik. 2006. *A Grammar of Yurakaré*. Nijmegen: Radboud Universiteit. http://webdoc.ubn.ru.nl/mono/g/gijnevan/gramofyu.pdf.
Van Gijn, Rik. 2014. The Andean foothills and adjacent Amazonian fringe. *The Native Language of South America: Origins, Development, Typology*, ed. by Loretta O'Connor and Pieter Muysken, 102–125. New York: Cambridge University Press.
Van Gijn, Rik and Pieter Muysken. 2020. Highland-lowland relations: A linguistic view. *Rethinking the Andes-Amazonia Divide: A Cross-Disciplinary Exploration*, ed. by Adrian J. Pearce, David G. Beresford-Jones, and Paul Heggarty, 178–210. London: UCL Press (University College London).
Vidal, Alejandra and Analía Gutiérrez. 2010. La categoría de "tiempo nominal" en las lenguas chaqueñas. *La renovación de la palabra en el bicentenario de la Argentina*, ed. by Victor M. Castel and Liliana Severino de Cubo, 1348–1355. Mendoza: Universidad Nacional de Cuyo.
Vidal, Alejandra and Verónica Nercesian. 2009. Loanwords in Wichí, a Mataco-Mataguayan language of Argentina. *Loanwords in the World's Languages: Comparative Handbook*, ed. by Martin Haspelmath and Uri Tadmor, 1015–1034. Berlin: de Gruyter Mouton.
Viegas Barros, J. Pedro. 1990. Dialectología qawasqar. *Amerindia* 15.43–73.
Viegas Barros, J. Pedro. 1992. La familia lingüística tehuelche. *Revista Patagónica* 13/54.39–46.
Viegas Barros, J. Pedro. 1993–1994. ¿Existe una relación genética entre las lenguas mataguayas y guaycurúes? *Hacia una Nueva Carta Étnica del Gran Chaco* 5.193–213. Las Lomitas: Centro del Hombre Antiguo Chaqueño.
Viegas Barros, J. Pedro. 2001. *Evidencias del parentesco de las lenguas Lule y Vilela*. (Colección Folklore y Antropología 4.) Santa Fe: Subsecretaría de la Provincia de Santa Fe.
Viegas Barros, J. Pedro. 2004. *Guaicurú no, Macro-Guaicurú sí: una hipótesis sobre la clasificación de la lengua Guachí (Mato Grosso do Sul, Brasil)*. Goiânia: Biblioteca Virtual do Grupo Etnolingüística.
Viegas Barros, J. Pedro. 2005a. *Voces del viento: raíces lingüísticas de la Patagonia*. Buenos Aires: Mondragón.
Viegas Barros, J. Pedro. 2005b. Algunas semejanzas gramaticales macro-guaicurú–macro-jê. *Encontro de pesquisadores de línguas e Culturas Macro-Je, Universidade Federal de Pernambuco, Recife* 4.3–5. http://www.adilq.com.ar/MACRO-GUAICURU-MACRO-JE.pdf.
Viegas Barros, J. Pedro. 2006a. Proto-Lule-Vilela: una reconstrucción fonológica preliminar. Comisión "Lenguas Chaqueñas." *Congreso Internacional de Americanistas 52*. Sevilla: Universidad de Sevilla. https://www.adilq.com.ar/PROTO-LULE-VILELA.pdf (accessed January 8, 2021).
Viegas Barros, J. Pedro. 2006b. La hipótesis macro-guaicurú: semejanzas gramaticales guaicurú-mataguayo. *UniverSOS: revista de lenguas indígenas y universos culturales* 3.183–212.
Viegas Barros, José Pedro. 2009. Avances en la hipótesis de parentesco lingüístico sanavirón–lule-vilela. *Tercer Congreso de Culturas originarias: Córdoba recuperando la conciencia indígena*. Córdoba. https://d1wqtxts1xzle7.cloudfront.net/50724322/SANAVIRON-LULE_VILELA-libre.pdf?1480950635=&response-content-disposition=inline%3B+filename%3DAvances_en_la_hipotesis_de_parentesco_Sa.pdf&Expires=1688403880&Signature=L-mzyR~FUorvOf4KfHdt-GdkauRoDv3wd7gtGnp9mR-BZlmeB58VBhHLLnfVwzOdioVzpFCLoEBxkycApz

OFgCxt4~4E1eENY1MuFT3WwZHdmwYnnSeHGgCV8Sd42dci2udIsoLyAWO-qpriyfwgG4wkC-9p19051SOuzlbF7bf3I-cFEjVoQCJuEgkUKN3tcRr4g2AibWfo4n-hbn55KFFjgw-gAtzJo7fxFrczHFxdmvBd9z-sF4Oud5IcLtq29KrEQDuWCv9zoqr-a32 7hyzxKx54RsGE7i5jdk4WL8C~AvoddY8X15pyytQSDZgJFgbcNWgbfc zQQ-r3dRpXszbw__&Key-Pair-Id=APKAJLOHF5GGSLRBV4ZA.

Viegas Barros, J. Pedro. 2013a. La hipótesis de parentesco Guaicurú-Mataguayo: estado actual de la cuestión. *Revista Brasileira de la Lingüística Antropológica* 5.293–333.

Viegas Barros, J. Pedro. 2013b. *Proto-Guaicurú: Una Reconstrucción Fonológica, Léxica y Morfológica.* Munich: LINCOM Europa.

Viegas Barros, J. Pedro. 2015. *Proto-Chon: Fonología, Morfología y Léxico.* PhD dissertation, Universidad de Buenos Aires. http://repositorio.filo.uba.ar:8080/bitstream/handle/filodigital/3013/ubaffylt2015903656v1.pdf?sequence=1&isAllowed=y.

Viegas Barros, J. Pedro. 2020. Antropónimos Charrúas de Cayastá (1758–1760): Algunas Observaciones Lingüísticas. *Filología y Lingüística* 46.235–265. https://doi.org/10.15517/rfl.v46i2.43279; https://revistas.ucr.ac.cr/index.php/filyling/index (accessed July 24, 2021).

Vilera Díaz, Diana. 1987. Introducción a morphosintaxis de la lengua Hoti: el lexema nominal. *Boletín de lingüística* 6.79–99.

Villarejo, Avencio. 1959. *La selva y el hombre.* Lima: Ausonia.

Villiers du Terrage, Marc de and Paul Rivet. 1919. Les indiens du Texas et les expéditions françaises de 1720 et 1721 à la "Baie Saint-Bernard." *Journal de la Société des Américanistes de Paris* 11.403–442.

Vinson, Julien. 1876[1875]. Basque et les langues Americaines. *International Congress of Americanists* 1875.377.

Voegelin, Carl F. 1941. Internal relationships of Siouan languages. *American Anthropologist* 43.246–249.

Voegelin, Charles F. and Florence M. Voegelin. 1965. Classification of American Indian languages. (Languages of the World, Native American fascicle 2, section 1.6.) *Anthropological Linguistics* 7/7.121–150.

Voegelin, Charles F. and Florence M. Voegelin. 1967. Review of *Die nordamerikanischen Indianersprachen*, by Heinz-Jürgen Pinnow. *Language* 43.573–583.

Voegelin, Charles F. and Florence M. Voegelin. 1973. Map of North American Indian Languages. *Annual Review of Anthropology* 2.139–151.

Voegelin, Charles F., Florence M. Voegelin, and Kenneth L. Hale. 1962. Typological and comparative grammar of Uto-Aztecan: I (phonology). (Indiana University Publications in Anthropology and Linguistics, memoir 17.) Bloomington: Indiana University.

Waddell, Gene. 1980. *Indians of the South Carolina Low Country 1562–1751.* Columbia: Southern Studies Program, University of South Carolina.

Waddell, Gene. 2004. Cusabo. *Handbook of North American Indians*, vol. 14: *Southeast*, ed. by Raymond D. Fogelson, 254–264. Washington DC: Smithsonian Institution.

Walker, Robert S., and Lincoln A. Ribeiro. 2011. Bayesian phylogeography of the Arawak expansion in lowland South America. *Proceedings of the Royal Society B: Biological Sciences* 278.2562–2567. https://www.ncbi.nlm.nih.gov/pmc/articles/PMC3136831.

Wares, Alan C. 1968. A comparative study of Yuman consonantism. (Janua linguarum, series practica, 57.) The Hague: Mouton.

Waterhouse, Viola. 1969. Oaxaca Chontal in reference to Proto-Chontal. *International Journal of American Linguistics* 35.231–233.

Waterhouse, Viola. 1985. True Tequistlateco. *International Journal of American Linguistics* 51.612–614.
Watkins, Laurel. 1978. On *w and *y in Kiowa-Tanoan. *Berkeley Linguistics Society* 4.477–484.
Watkins, Laurel. 1984. *A Grammar of Kiowa*. Lincoln: University of Nebraska Press.
Webb, Nancy M. 1971. *A Statement of Some Phonological Correspondences among the Pomo Languages*. (Supplement to *International Journal of American Linguistics*, vol. 37, no. 3.) Bloomington, Indiana.
Weitlaner, Roberto J. 1936–1939. Notes on the Cuitlatec language. *El México Antiguo* 4.363–373.
Weitlaner, Roberto J. 1948. Un idioma desconocido del norte de México. *International Congress of Americanists* 28.205–227.
Werner, Oswald. 1963. *A Typological Comparison of Four Trader Navaho Speakers*. PhD dissertation, Indiana University.
Wetzels, W. Leo M. and Stella V. Telles. 2011. La famille Nambikwara. *Dictionnaire des Langues*, ed. by E. Bonvini, E. Busuttil, and A. Peyraube, 1460–1474. Paris: Presses Universitaires de France.
Whistler, Kenneth W. 1977. Wintun prehistory: An interpretation based on linguistic reconstruction of plant and animal nomenclature. *Berkeley Linguistics Society* 3.157–174.
Whistler, Kenneth W. 1980. *Proto-Wintun Kin Classification: A Case Study in Reconstruction of a Complex Semantic System*. PhD dissertation, University of California, Berkeley.
Whistler, Kenneth W. 1983–1984[appeared 1988]. Pomo prehistory: A case for archaeological linguistics. Archaeology and linguistics. Special issue of the *Journal of the Steward Anthropological Society* 15.64–98.
Whistler, Kenneth W. and Victor Golla. 1986. Proto-Yokuts reconsidered. *International Journal of American Linguistics* 52.317–358.
Whorf, Benjamin L. 1935. The comparative linguistics of Uto-Aztecan. *American Anthropologist* 37.600–608.
Whorf, Benjamin L. 1943. Loan-words in ancient Mexico. Philological and documentary studies 1.3–14. (Middle American Research Institute Publications, II.) Tulane University, New Orleans. [Reprinted in: *Studies in Linguistics* 5.49–64.]
Whorf, Benjamin L. and George L. Trager. 1937. The relationship of Uto-Aztecan and Tanoan. *American Anthropologist* 39.609–624.
Wichmann, Søren. 1995. *The Relationship Among the Mixe-Zoquean Languages of Mexico*. Salt Lake City: University of Utah Press.
Wichmann, Søren and Cecil H. Brown. 2003. Contact among some Mayan languages: Inferences from loanwords. *Anthropological Linguistics* 45.57–93.
Wichmann, Søren and Kerry Hull. 2009. Loanwords in Q'eqchi', a Mayan language of Guatemala. *Loanwords in the World's Languages*, ed. by Martin Haspelmath and Uri Tadmor, 873–896. Berlin: Mouton de Gruyter.
Wikander, Stig. 1967. Maya and Altaic: Is the Maya group of languages related to the Altaic family? *Ethnos* 32.141–148.
Wikander, Stig. 1970. Maya and Altaic II. *Ethnos* 35.80–88.
Wikander, Stig. 1970–1971. Maya and Altaic III. *Orientalia Suecana* 19–20.186–204.
Willerslev, Eske and David J. Meltzer. 2021. Peopling of the Americas as inferred from ancient genomics. *Nature* 594/7863.356–364. https://www.nature.com/articles/s41586-021-03499-y.
Williams, Roger. 1643. *A Key into the Language of America*. London: Gregory Dexter.

Wise, Mary Ruth. 1976. Apuntes sobre la influencia inca entre los amuesha: factor que oscurece la clasificación de su idioma. *Revista del Museo Nacional* 42.355–366.

Wise, Mary Ruth. 1999. Small language families and isolates in Peru. *The Amazonian Languages*, ed. by R. M. W. Dixon and Alexandra Y. Aikhenvald, 307–340. Cambridge: Cambridge University Press.

Witkowski, Stanley R. and Cecil H. Brown. 1978. Mesoamerican: A proposed language phylum. *American Anthropologist* 80.942–944.

Wojtylak, Katarzyna (Kasia). 2016. Some notes on aspects of Nonuya (Witotoan) grammar. https://researchonline.jcu.edu.au/52759/1/After_PresentationDraft12.pdf.

Wojtylak, Katarzyna Izabela. 2017. *A Witotoan Language of Northwest Amazonia*. PhD dissertation, James Cook University, Australia.

Woodbury, Anthony C. 1984. Eskimo and Aleut languages. *Handbook of North American Indians*, ed. by William C. Sturtevant, vol. 5: *Arctic*, ed. by David Damas, 49–63. Washington DC: Smithsonian Institution.

Wright, Robert. 1991. Quest for the mother tongue. *The Atlantic Monthly* 267.39–68.

Wurtzburg, Susan and Lyle Campbell. 1995. North American Indian Sign Language: Evidence of its existence before European contact. *International Journal of American Linguistics* 61.153–167.

Yellow Bird, Michael. 1999. What we want to be called: Indigenous peoples' perspectives on racial and ethnic identity labels. *American Indian Quarterly* 23.1–12.

Young, Robert W. 1983. Apachean languages. *Handbook of North American Indians*, vol. 10: *Southwest*, ed. by Alonso Ortiz, 393–400. Washington DC: Smithsonian Institution.

Zamponi, Raoul. 2003a. *Betoi*. Munich: LINCOM Europa.

Zamponi, Raoul. 2003b. *Maipure*. Munich: LINGCOM Europa.

Zamponi, Raoul. 2008. Sulla fonoloogia e la rappresentazione ortografica del lule. *Arte y Vocabulario de la Lengua Lule y Tonocoté*, ed. by Riccardo Badini, Tiziana Deonertte, Stefania Pineider, introzione di Riccardo Badini, Raoul Zamponi, xxi–lviii. Calgliari: Centro di Studi Filologici Sardi, Operativa Universitaria Editrice Cagliaritana.

Zamponi, Raoul. 2017. Betoi-Jirara, Sáliban, and Hodĩ: Relationships among three linguistic lineages of the Mid-Orinoco region. *Anthropological Linguistics* 59.263–321.

Zamponi, Raoul. 2020. Some precontact widespread lexical forms in the languages of Greater Amazonia. *International Journal of American Linguistics* 86.527–573.

Zamponi, Raoul. 2023. Unclassified languages. *The Languages and Linguistics of Indigenous North America: a Comprehensive Guide*, ed. by Carmen Datostino, Marianne Mithun, and Keren Rice, 1627–1648. Berlin and Boston: de Gruyter Mouton.

Zamponi, Raoul. In press a (2023). Extinct isolates and unclassified languages of Mexico. *Languages and Linguistics of Mexico and Northern Central America: A Comprehensive Guide*, ed. by Søren Wichmann. Berlin and Boston: de Gruyter Mouton.

Zamponi, Raoul. In press b (2023). Extinct lineages and unclassified languages of Greater Amazonia. *Amazonian Languages: An International Handbook*, vol. 2: *Smaller Language Families*, ed. by Patience Epps and Lev Michael. Berlin and Boston: de Gruyter Mouton.

Zapata. See Ortiz de Zapata, Juan. 1857.

Zariquiey Biondi, Roberto. 2011. *A Grammar of Kashibo-Kakataibo*. PhD dissertation, LaTrobe University.

Zariquiey, Roberto. 2020. Hypothesized language relationships across the Andes-Amazonia divide: The cases of Uro, Pano-Takana and Mosetén. *Rethinking the Andes-Amazonia*

Divide: A Cross-disciplinary Exploration, ed. by Adrian J. Pearce, David G. Beresford-Jones, and Paul Heggarty, 250–262. London: UCL Press (University College London).

Zavala, Roberto. 2002. Calcos sintácticos en algunos complejos verbales Mayas y Mixe-Zoques. *Pueblos y Fronteras* 4.169–187.

Zeballos, Estanisláo S. 1922. Consultas: etimologías araucanas. *Revista de Derecho, Historia y Letras* 73.770–771.

Zenk, Henry B. 1990a. Alseans. *Handbook of North American Indians*, ed. by William C. Sturtevant, vol. 7: *Northwest Coast*, ed. by Wayne Suttles, 568–571. Washington DC: Smithsonian Institution.

Zenk, Henry B. 1990b. Siuslawans and Coosans. *Handbook of North American Indians*, ed. by William C. Sturtevant, vol. 7: *Northwest Coast*, ed. by Wayne Suttles, 572–579. Washington DC: Smithsonian Institution.

Zúñiga, Dionysio de. Circa 1608. *Diccionario pocomchi-castellano y castellano-pocomchí de San Cristobal Cahcoh*. (Manuscript in the Berendt collection at the University of Pennsylvania library, Philadelphia.)

INDEX OF LANGUAGES

Index: Names of languages, language families, proposed linguistic relationships, linguistic areas, ethnolinguistic groups, and cultures

For the benefit of digital users, indexed terms that span two pages (e.g., 52–53) may, on occasion, appear on only one of those pages.

Figures are indicated by *f* following the page number

Aarufi, 295
Abenakian, 122
Abipón, 219, 220–21, 451
Aburuñe, 295
Acarapi, 295
Acaxee, 288, 290, 293, 294
Achagua, 190, 223, 466
Aché (Guayakí, Guayaquí), 261, 266
Achire, 290. *See also* Guasave
Achuar (Achual), 212, 213
Achuar-Shiwiar, 212, 213
Achumawi (Achomawi, Pit River), 69, 138n.49
Acoma, 94, 95, 404
Acoma-Laguna (Western Keresan), 94, 95
Aconipa (Tabancal), 295
Adai (Adaize), 29, 106, 142n.82
Adshusheer, 286
Aguacatec, Aguacateco. *See* Awakatek
Aguacatec II, 331–32
Aguano (Awano, Ahuano, Aguanu), 295

agua people, 168
Aguaruna (Awajún), 212, 213, 214, 307, 321
Ahome, 290. *See also* Guasave
Ahtna, 35, 38, 40
Aikanã (Aikaná), 186, 188, 230, 341
Aimoré, 235. *See also* Krenak
A'ingaé. *See* Cofán
Akatek, Akateko, 149, 177n.10, 417, 418
Akimel O'odham, 87
Akokisa, 107, 281
Akroá (Akroá-Mirim, Acroá), 231
Aksanás, 217, 301, 333
Aksanás (spurious language), 333
Akuntsú, 261, 263, 445
Akuntsú-Kanoe pidgin, 445
Akuriyo, 202
Akuwẽ, 232
Alabama (Alibamu), 109, 110, 112–14, 287, 411, 442, 444, 461
Alabama-Koasati, 109, 110, 113

Alacaluf, 217, 229–30. *See also* Qawasqar
Alagüilac, 288
Alarua, 296
Alaska Native languages, 2–4
Albarradas Zapotec, 159
Aleut, 29–33, 34, 35, 389, 392–93, 451, 464–29
Algic, 11, 13, 28, 95, 121–33, 148, 381, 388
Algonkian-Gulf, Algonquian-Gulf, 97, 381, 383
Algonkian. *See* Algonquian
Algonkin-Wakashan, 12, 354
Algonquian, 5–6, 9, 11, 13, 58, 100, 121–33, 123*f*, 134, 141–42n.78, 143n.89, 143n.95, 143n.97, 144n.105, 144n.106, 148, 170–71, 285, 342, 382, 383, 385, 401–3, 405, 407, 410, 411, 412, 442–43, 444–45, 449
Algonquian-Gulf, 97, 383
Algonquian-Ritwan, 132. *See also* Algic
Alliklik, 78, 287
ALMH. *See* Arawakan linguistic matrix hypothesis
Almosan, 95, 360, 381
Almosan-Keresiouan, 95, 360, 383
Alon, 296
Alsea, 29, 54, 354, 389, 392
Altaic, 381, 382, 383, 384, 385
Altiplano Subarea, 436
Alto Marañón, 251
Alto Pativilca, 251
Aluku (Boni), 445
Alutiiq. *See* Pacific Yupik
Amaiba (Maiba), 243
Amanayé (Amanajé, Manazo), 262
Amaracaeri (Amarakaeri), 224, 243
Amarizana, 190
Amasifuin, 296
Amatec Zapotec, 159
Amawaka, 245
Amazonian languages
Amazonian Linguistic Area, 424–26, 435, 438
Amerind, 3, 14, 21, 163, 169, 206, 214, 216, 224, 229–30, 231, 243, 255–56, 258, 260, 266–67, 271, 272, 275, 278n.29, 332, 334, 358–61, 370, 373, 381, 383, 384, 386n.9, 421
Amikoana, 296
Amoeca, 296
Amoltepec Mixtec (AMOL), 160
Amondáwa (Amundáwa, Amondawa), 262, 266
Amotomanco (Otomoaco), 281–82, 286–87, 293
Amuesha (Yanesha), 192, 455, 465–66

Amuimo, 296
Amuzgo, 159, 180n.44, 417
Amuzgo-Mixtecan, 159
analogical change, 22
Anambé, 265, 430–32
Anambé of Cairarí, 262
Anambé of Ehrenreich, 262
Anauyá, 190
ancestral East Asians, 15
Ancient Northern Siberians, 15
Andaquí (Andakí), 186, 188, 189, 244, 325, 329, 341, 360, 382
Andean-Equatorial, 229–30, 273, 382
Andean Linguistic Area, 432–36, 433*f*
Andoa, 274, 275
Andoque (Andoke), 186, 189, 270, 341
Andoquero, 270, 279n.41
Anetine, 296
Angaité, 218, 463
Angara, 296
Anicun, 296
Anserma (Anserna), 215, 296
Antioqueño, 208, 210, 382
Antoniano, 72
Ap-Am-Ah, 251
Apalachee, 109, 112, 113, 442, 444
Apalachee-Spanish, 444
Apalaí, 202
Aparea, 296
Apiaká (Apiacá, Apiaka), 203, 262, 266
Apiaká-Apingi, 203
Apinayé (Apinajé), 231
Apitupá, 296
Apiyipán, 296
Apurí, 251
Apurinã (Apuriná), 192
Arabela, 274, 275
Arabela-Andoa, 274, 275
Aracadaini, 296
Arae, 256
Arakajú, 203
Aramayu, 296
Aramurú, 296
Aranama (Jaranames), 97–98, 282
Aranama-Tamique, 97–98
Araona, 246
Arapaho, 121, 126, 132–33, 405, 407, 449
Arapahoan, 121, 126
Arapaso, 259

Index of languages

Arapoá, 296
Arara, 201
Arara Group, 201
Arara do Rio Branco (Rio Branco Arara, Arara, Arara do Aripuanã, Arara do Beiradão, Koayá), 186, 189
Arará, Arara, 6–7, 201, 276n.5, 276n.10
Ararandewára, 262, 430–32
Ararau, 296
Araucanian. *See* Mapudungun
Arawá, 195
Arawak, 190. *See also* Arawakan
Arawakan, 7, 115, 148, 170–71, 184, 185, 189–90, 193f, 195, 206–7, 210–11, 214, 223, 224, 227, 240, 241–42, 254, 256, 257, 258, 304, 316, 317–18, 319, 321–22, 325, 341, 382, 384, 385, 423, 424, 425–26, 428–29, 432, 453, 465–67, 469–70
Arawakan linguistic matrix hypothesis (ALMH), 194
Arawak stock, 312, 316, 323, 324
Arawan (Arauán, Arahuan), 185, 189–90, 194, 195, 223, 307, 424, 466–67
Araweté, 262, 266
Arazaire, 245
Arda (of Africa), 297, 333
Arda (of Peru), 297, 333
Arhuacic, 208
Aricoroni, 205–6
Arikapú (Maxubí, Aricapú, Arikapu), 231, 234
Arikara, 100, 104, 105–6, 407
Arikém, 260, 263
Arikém subfamily, 260
Arin, 361
Arizona Tewa, 87, 93, 405. *See also* Hano
Arma, 215, 297
Arm-Pozo, 297, 320
Aroásene, 297
Artane, 297
Aru. *See* Aymaran
Aruá (Aruaxi, Aruashí), 260, 263
Aruán (Aruá, Aroã), 191
Arutani (Awaké, Ahuaqué, Uruák, Urutani), 186, 195–85, 253, 429
Asháninka (Ashánínga), 192
Ashéninka (Ashéninga), 192
Ashluslay, Ashlushlay. *See* Nivaclé
Asiatic Eskimo. *See* Siberian Yupik
Assan, 361

Assiniboine, 99, 100–1, 126, 407
Asuriní of Xingu (Xingu Asuriní, Asuriní do Coatinema), 262, 266
Atacameño (Kunza, Cunza, Atacama), 186, 195, 228, 244, 341, 432, 436
Atakapa, 29, 97–98, 106–7, 108–9, 112, 114, 281, 346, 382, 383, 385, 409–10, 412–13, 442
Atakapan. *See* Atakapa
Atalán, 254
Atanques (Kankuama), 208, 210
Atavila, 297
Athabaskan, 35, 37, 38–39, 40, 41, 43, 45, 68, 135n.7, 284, 365, 382, 388, 389, 391, 392–93, 396, 404, 405, 444–45, 448
Aticum (Araticum), 297
Atsawaka/Yamiaka, 245
Atsina, 5–6, 100, 121, 126, 132–33, 407. *See also* Gros Ventre
Atsugewi, 69, 401–3
Attikamek, 121, 124, 125
Atunceta (Tunceta, Atunseta), 297
Ature, 253
Aueiko, 297
Auré (Aurá), 262
Australasian, 18, 19, 20
Avá (Canoeiro, Avá Canoeiro), 261
Avis, 297
Awajún. *See* Aguaruna
Awakatek, 150, 153, 177–78n.22, 331–32
Awakateko-Ixil (Ixilan), 150, 153
Awaké, 195, 253. *See also* Arutani
Awa Pit (Cuaiquer), 196, 436
Awarak Stock, 295
Awaswas, 61, 63–64
Awetí (Auetö), 261, 263
Axata Darpa, 297
Ayacore, 297
Ayacucho, 251
Ayapa, 156, 179n.32
Ayautla-Soyaltepec Mazatec, 158
Aymara, 195, 249, 268, 302, 321–22, 361, 372, 381–82, 385, 449–50, 452–53, 455, 465. *See also* Southern Aymaran
Aymaran, 185, 195–96, 249, 252, 372–73, 385, 432–34, 435, 436, 465–66
Ayomán (Ayamán), 226
Ayoquezco Zapotec, 159
Ayoreo (Ayoré, Moro), 274, 463
Azoyú Tlapaneco, 158

Index of languages

Aztec, 6, 175, 176n.4, 181n.58, 292, 294, 381
Aztecan, 80, 81, 82, 83–84, 88, 89, 90–91, 163, 413. *See also* Nahua
Aztec-Tanoan, 12, 92, 94, 95, 163, 382

Babine, 36, 42
Babine-Carrier, 36
Baciroa, 289, 293
Bagua, 297, 318
Baimena, 295. *See also* Zoe
Baixóta, 297
Bakairí, 201
Bakurönchichi, 297
Baniva, 7, 191
Baniwa, 7, 469–70
Baniwa (Baniva, Karutana- Baniwa), 7
Baniwa of Guainia (Baniva, Avani, Abane), 7
Baniwa of Içana (Kurripako), 7
Bannock, 84
Bará, 259
Barasano, 258
Barasano-Eduria-Makuna, 258
Bará-Tatuyo, 259
Barbacoa, 196, 303, 382
Barbacoa Group, 298, 303, 320, 329
Barbacoan, 185, 188–89, 196–97, 200, 215, 244
Barbacoas, Barbacoa (Barbócoa, Colima), 196, 298
Barbareño, 77–78
Baré, 191
Baré group, 191
Barí (Motilón), 7, 208, 210
Basopa, 289
Basque, 382, 443–44, 467
Basque-Algonquian Pidgin, 441–42
Batuc, 88, 289
Bauá, 298
Bauré (Chiquimiti), 192, 249–50
Bawihka, 173
Bayagoula (Bayogoula), 282–83
Bay Miwok. *See* Saclan
Beakeo, 219, 220
Bearlake, 36, 39, 41, 42, 448
Beaver, 36, 41
Beothuk, 29, 133–34, 382
Beringia, 15, 16, 19, 25n.11
Bering land bridge, 14, 15, 16, 25n.11
Besawunena, 121, 126
Besïro. *See* Chiquitano

Betoi (Betoy). *See* Betoi-Jirara
Betoi-Jirara (Betoi, Betoy), 186, 187–88, 197, 244, 253, 382, 450
Bidai, 283
Bikutiakap, 298
bilingualism, 69, 253, 446, 450, 454, 455
Bilingual Navajo, 452
Biloxi, 99, 102, 108, 409–11, 412, 442, 461
Bixarenren, 298
Blackfoot, 58, 121, 122, 124, 132–33, 405
Boanarí (Bonari), 203
Bocotá, 207, 209
Bodega Miwok, 62, 63. *See also* Coast Miwok
Bohurá, 240–41
Boimé, 298
Bolivian Quechua, 251
Bolivian subgroup, 245
Bolona, 298
Bora (Boro, Miriña/Miranha), 185, 197, 341, 383, 428–29
Boran (Bora-Muinane), 185, 197–98, 270, 382, 428
Bora-Witotoan, 270, 370, 382
Borjeño, Borjino. *See* Northern Cochimí
Bororo, 198, 369, 423
Bororo group, 198
Bororo of Cabaçal (Boróro Cabaçais), 198
Bororoan, 185, 198–200, 306, 341, 369
Boruca (Brunca), 207, 209, 461
Botocudo, 6–7, 229–30, 235, 369. *See also* Krenakan
Bracamoro, 213, 298
Branch I (Tukanoan), 259
Branch II (Tukanoan), 259
Bribri, 207, 209, 418
Broken Oghibbeway (Broken Ojibwe), 441–42
Broken Slavey, 441–42, 444–45
Buena Vista Yokuts, 65
Bureau of Indian Affairs, 2
Buritiguara, 298

Caapina, 298
Cabécar (Chirripó), 207, 209, 332, 360
Cabixi (Kabixi), 7, 298
Cabiyarí, 190
Cacán (Kakán). *See* Diaguita
Cacaopera, 5, 173, 174, 181n.57, 418
Cacaopera-Matagalpan, 173
Cachipuna, 298
Caddo, 93, 95, 104, 105, 412, 442

Caddoan, 28, 95, 104–6, 346, 382, 383, 384, 407, 411, 442
Caddoan-Siouan, 382
Cafuana, 298
Cagua, 298
Caguan, 299
Cahan, 299
Cahita, 80, 88, 139n.65, 290, 293, 294
Cahitan, 80, 82, 87–88, 288, 290, 291, 292, 293
Cahto. *See* Kato
Cahuapana, 198, 199
Cahuapanan (Jebero, Kawapanan), 185, 198, 199–200, 214, 240, 243, 275, 295, 301, 313, 423
Cahuarano, 274, 275
Cahuilla, 80, 83, 85–86
Cahuimeto, 289, 291, 292
Caimbé, 299
Cajamarca (Quechua), 251, 252
Cajamarca (unclassified language), 299
Cajatambo, 299
Cajonos Zapotec, 159
Cakchiquel. *See* Kaqchikel
Calchaquí. *See* Diaguita
California Athabaskan, 36–, 44–
Californian group (Walter Lehmann's), 169–70
California Penutian, 59, 65, 354, 355–56, 384
California Uto-Aztecan, 399
Callahuaya (Kallawaya), 200, 250, 432, 452–53
Calusa, 283, 287, 409–10
Čama (complex), 246
Camana, 299
Camaraxo, 299
Camaré, 299
Cambioá, 299, 309
Čamik (Chamik), 246
Campa branch, 192
Campaces, 299
Cañacure, 299
Canamarí. *See* Kanamarí
Cañar (Cañari), 200, 239, 298
Cañaris-Incahuasi, 252
Cañar-Puruhá, Cañari-Puruhá, 185, 196, 200–1
Candoshi, 186, 200–1, 214, 223, 255, 313, 321, 341, 432
Canelo, 213, 299
Canichana (Kanichana), 201, 255–56
Capixana, 255–56, 384. *See also* Kanoê
Capua, 299
Capueni, 299

Caquetá-Putumayo Linguistic Area, 270, 428–29, 430
Caquetío, 193, 323, 324, 429
Caquinte (Kakinte), 192
Cara (Kara, Caranqui, Karanki), 196, 299
Carabayo, 256, 340
Caraguata, 299
Carapacho, 299–300
Caraque, 218–19
Carára, 300
Cararí (Carari), 300
Cararú (Cajurú), 300
Carayá, 6–7
Carib, 202
Cariban, 7, 115, 184, 185, 193, 201–4, 210–11, 215, 234, 256, 266–67, 267f, 272, 297, 302–3, 305, 310, 314, 317, 318, 319, 329, 370, 382, 383, 384, 385, 423–24, 428–30, 432, 445, 466–67
Cariban-Tupían-Arawakan, 382
Cariña, 202
Caripó (Curupehe), 300
Caripuna, 6–7
Carnijó, 6. *See also* Iaté
Carolina Algonquian, 122, 132
Carrier, 36, 42–43, 50, 136n.17, 448
Carrizo de Camargo. *See* Cotoname
Cascoasoa, 300
Cashibo. *See* Kashibo
Casigara, 300
Casota, 300
Castac, 78, 287
Catacaos, 254
Catawba, Catawban, 11, 99, 103, 283, 284, 409–10, 412, 444, 449, 461
-*cat(e)* languages, 301
Cathlamet. *See* Kathlamet
Catuquinarú (Catinquinarú, Catuquina), 300
Cauacaua (Kawakawa), 301
Cauauri, 301
Cauca, 215, 301
Caucahue (Kakauhua, Kaukaue Caucabue, Caucau, Gaviota), 301
Cauni, 301
Caupuna, 301
Cauque (Kawki), 195
Cautário. *See* Moré-Cojubim, Moré-Kuyubim
Cavana, 301
Cavineña, Cavineño (Kavineña), 246, 247–48, 465, 466

Caxago, 301
Cayú, 301
Cayuga, 102–3, 115, 117, 118, 143n.91, 464
Cayuse, 29, 57, 58, 354, 355, 382, 393–96
Cayuse–Molala, 382
Cayuvava (Cayubaba, Cayuwaba, Kayuvava), 186, 204, 382
Cazcan (Caxcan), 289, 294
Celtic, 9, 370, 384
Central Alaskan Yup'ik, 29, 33, 135n.2, 464
Central Alta Mixtec, 159
Central Amerind, 163, 361, 382
Central Andean Linguistic Area, 432–36
Central Aymaran (Tupe), 195
Central branch (Arawakan family), 192
Central California Linguistic Area, 399–400
Central Chumash, 77, 78
Central Cordillera, 36
Central Huaihuash, 251
Central Innu, 121, 124, 125
Central Jê (Akwe branch), 231, 341–42
Central Kalapuyan, 55–56
Central K'ichean (K'ichean Proper), 150
Central Mayan, 149, 150, 153
Central Muskogean, 109, 110
Central Nahua, 80, 163, 164*f*, 165
Central Numic, 79, 84, 85
Central Pame, 420
Central Panoan Assemblage, 245
Central Pomo, 70–71
Central Quechua, 252. *See also* Huaihuash (Quechua I, Quechua B)
Central Salish, 47, 49–50, 52
Central Siberian Yupik, 29, 33
Central Sierra Miwok, 61, 63, 138n.44
Central Southern Ojibwe (Anishinaabemowin), 122, 126, 127, 128
Central Upper Amazon subbranch, 191
Central Yúngay, 251
Central Zapotec, 159
Central Zoque, 156
Cenu, 215. *See also* Sinú; Zenu
Ceococe, 301
Chacha (Chachapuya, Chachapoya), 199
Chachapoyas (Amazonas), 251, 252, 301
Chaco Linguistic Area, Gran Chaco Linguistic Area, 436–38, 437*f*, 469
Chaguan, 269
Chaima, 202

Chákobo (Chákobo/Pakawara, Chacobo), 245, 322
Chalon, 61, 63–65, 464
Chama (Tiatinagua), 246
Chamacoco, 274
Chama subgroup, 245, 247
Chamicuro, 192, 465
Chaná, 206
Chancos, 301
Chandul Guaraní, 450
Chané, 206–7, 261
Chango, 268, 301
Chánguena, 207, 209
Chapacuran, 205–6, 314, 324, 424, 430
Cha'palaachi (Cayapa, Chachi), 196, 436
Charrúa, 206, 207
Charrúan, 206–7, 373, 381, 384, 436–37
Chatino, 158
Chawasha, 107
Chayahuita (Chawi, Shawi), 198–99
Chechehet ("Pampa"), 216, 302, 333–34
Chechehet family, Chechehet stock, 323, 326, 333–34
Chedua, 302
Chehalis, 442
Chemakum, 52, 137n.35, 391
Chemehuevi, 85
Cheraw, 103, 284–85
Cheyenne, 121, 126, 132–33, 405, 407, 449
Chholo, 268
Chiapanec, 158, 180n.42
Chiapanec-Mangue, 90–91, 158
Chiapas Zoquean, 156
Chibcha, 208, 210, 302, 311, 313–14, 382, 449–50
Chibchan, 115, 148, 170–71, 174, 178–79n.26, 184, 185, 188–89, 190, 197, 207–12, 208*f*, 215, 216, 217, 218–19, 226, 228, 240, 244, 257, 272, 296, 306, 311, 313–14, 320, 332, 340, 341, 342, 345, 369, 382, 383, 384, 426
Chibchan-Paezan, 169, 249–50, 332, 345, 359, 361, 382
Chibcha Stock, 210, 218–19, 299, 302, 311, 312, 313–14, 316, 320, 325, 329
Chicha, 302
Chicham (Jivaroan), 185, 200, 201, 212–14
Chichimeco (Chichimeco, Jonaz), 157, 413
Chickasaw, 108, 109, 110, 111, 112–13, 442
Chickasaw-Choctaw Trade Language. *See* Mobilian Jargon

Index of languages

Chickasaw-Choctaw. *See* Choctaw-Chickasaw
Chico Maidu, 60
Chicomucelrec (Chicomuselteco), 149, 153, 154, 155, 176n.4, 465
Chilanga (Salvadoran Lenca), 172–73, 343
Chilcotin (Tsilhqot'in), 36, 42–43, 50, 393–95
Chilicawa, 295
Chilote, 237
Chiltepec Chinanteco, 158
Chimakuan, 28, 46, 52–53, 384, 389, 390, 391
Chimalapa Zoquean, 137n.34, 156
Chimané (Tsimane), 239
Chimariko, 29, 67–68, 69, 138n.48, 345, 347, 399
Chimila (Chamila) Colombia, 208, 209, 210–11
Chimu stock, 200, 239, 312, 320
Chimú, Chimu, 382. *See also* Mochica
Chimu culture, 239
Chimuan, 200, 239
Chinantec, 180n.39, 417
Chinantecan, 157, 162
Chinarra, 290. *See also* Concho
Chincha, 302
Chínchay (Quechua IIB-IIC), 251
Chinchipe, 302
Chínipa, 289, 291, 293
Chinookan, 28, 53, 354, 391, 395–96
Chinook Jargon (Chinook Wawa), 56, 441–42
Chipaya, 5, 249, 268, 384, 435, 465
Chipaya-Uru. *See* Uru-Chipaya
Chipewyan, 5–6, 36, 39, 41, 42, 136n.16, 444–45
Chipiajes, 302
Chippewa, 127, 144n.103, *See also* Ojibwa
Chiquihuitlán Mazatec, 158
Chiquimulilla (South Xinkan), 167, 180n.52, 343, 418, 462
Chiquitano, 186, 214, 224, 233, 369, 371, 450
Chiriba, 245
Chiricahua, 44
Chirigua, 247
Chiriguano, 206–7, 261
Chirino, 200–1, 255, 318
Chitarero, 302
Chitimacha, 107, 108–9, 112, 142n.84, 166, 346, 366–69, 382, 383, 385, 409–10, 412–13, 442, 464
Chitimacha-Totozoquean, 366–69
Chiwere, 99, 102
Chiwere-Winnebago, 99, 102
Chizo, 290

Chocheño, Chochenyo, 61, 63–64
Chocho, 158, 417, 418
Chochoan, 158
Chocho-Popoloca (Ngigua), 158, 162
Chocoan (Chokóan), 148, 170–71, 185, 197, 214–15, 244, 272–73, 297, 320, 322, 426
Chocos, 251
Choctaw, 103, 106, 109, 110, 111, 112–13, 282–83, 410–11, 412, 442, 461
Choctaw-Chickasaw, 110–11, 411
Chol (Ch'ol), 149, 177n.6, 415, 417
Chol-Chontal, 149
Cholan, 149, 151–52, 153, 175, 176, 419, 422, 465
Cholan-Tzeltalan (Greater Tzeltalan), 149, 150, 152, 153–54, 344, 452, 461
Cholón, 215–16, 301, 381–82, 432, 435, 455
Cholonan (Hibito-Cholón), 185, 215–17, 218, 356, 382, 432
Choltí, 149, 177n.8
Choltí-Chortí, 149
Cholto, 302
Chon, 7, 229–30, 239, 318, 334, 341–42, 382, 384
Chonan (Tehuelchean, Chon family), 7, 185, 207, 216–17, 229, 239, 248, 252, 271, 273, 301, 334, 341, 385, 438, 466–67
Chongo, 302
Chono (of Chile), 7, 186, 229, 301, 302, 334, 382, 385, 438
Chono of Ecuador, 217, 302
Chontal, 6, 149, 177n.7
Chontal of Oaxaca (Oaxaca Chontal), 6, 166–67, 346, 352. *See also* Tequistlatec
Chontal of Tabasco, 6, 167. *See also* Chontal (Mayan family)
Choropí (Tšoropí). *See* Nivaclé
Chorote, 237, 322–23, 456, 457, 458, 463, 470
Chorote-Wichí, 237, 238
Chorotega. *See* Mangue
Chorotegan. *See* Chiapanec-Mangue
Chortí (Ch'orti'), 177n.8
Chugach, 33
Chuj, 149, 177n.13, 462
Chuj-Tojolab'al, 149
Chukchansi, 66–67, 399
Chukchi, 33, 383, 385, 444
Chukchi jargon, Chukchi-based jargon, 444
Chukotko-Kamchatkan, 35
Chulupí. *See* Nivaclé

Chumash, Chumashan, 8, 28, 72–73, 77–78, 92, 139n.57, 285, 287, 346, 347, 399, 400, 401–3
Chumbivilca, 302
Chunanawa, 302
Chunupí, 6, 231
Churima, 302
Churuya, 222–23
Chusco, 302
Ciaman, 302
Ciboney, 193
Ciguayo, 172, 193
Cinta-larga, 260
Clallam. See Klallam
Classic Maya culture, 176, 422
Clatskanie (Tlatskanie, Tlatskanai), 38, 43, 136n.18
Clear Lake Linguistic Area, 397, 398, 399
Clovis (Clovis culture), 14, 16–17, 25n.10
Coahuiltecan, 76, 96, 97–98, 99, 107, 346, 382
Coahuilteco, 29, 97–98, 148, 154, 346, 347, 352–53, 385, 415, 418, 449
Coastal Chatino, 158
Coastal Chinook. See Lower Chinook
Coast Chehalis. See Upper Chehalis
Coast Miwok, 61, 62, 63, 76
Coast Mixtec, 160
Coast Oregon Penutian, 54, 55, 354
Coast Tsimshian (Sm'algyax), 45, 46, 47, 444
Coast Yuki, 76
Coatecan, 158
Coateco, 158
Cochimí, 73, 347
Cochimí-Yuman, 28, 73–75, 148, 401
Cochiti, 94, 95
Coconucan, 196, 244, 356
Coconuco, 196, 215, 244, 296
Cocopah (Cocopa, Cucupá), 73, 74–75
Coeur d'Alene, 48, 51, 393–95
Cofán (Kofan, A'ingaé), 8, 186, 200–1, 217, 218–19, 272–73, 382, 436
Cognomona, 302
Cogui (Kogi, C.gaba, Kagaba), 208
Cojubim (Kujubím, Kuyubí), 205
Colán, 254
Colapissa, 108
Colima, 298, 302–3
Colla, 249
Colombian-Central American Linguistic Area, 426

Colotlan, 290
Columbian (Nxaʔamxcín), 8, 48, 51, 395–96
Comanahua (Komanawa), 303
Comanche, 5, 79, 84, 85, 89, 90, 93, 405–7, 449
Comaní, 303
Comanito, 290, 293, 294
Comechingón, 303
Comecrudan, 97–98
Comecrudo, 98
Comopori, 290. See also Guasave
Comox (Éy7á7juuthem), 47, 49, 137n.28, 391–92
Concho, 290, 294
Conchucos, 251
Conestoga. See Susquehannock
Congaree, 283
Conicari, 290, 293
Conoy, 131
Continental Chonan, 216
Coosan, 28, 54–55, 389, 391
Copallén (Copallín), 303
Copper Island Aleut (Mednyj Aleut), 8, 29, 33, 451
Cora, 80, 82, 88, 289–90, 294, 420–21, 461
Cora-Huichol, 80, 82, 83–84, 88, 294, 418
Corachol-Aztecan, 80, 83–84, 163
Corachol. See Cora-Huichol
Core Chatino, 158
Core Chibchan, 207
Core Guajiboan, 222
Core Mayan (Southern Mayan), 149, 153
Core Nambikwaran, 242
Core Siouan, 104
Core Yuman, 73
Core Zapotec, 158
Coreguaje (Koreguaje, Caquetá), 255–56, 258
Coritanahó, 303
Coroado, 6–7, 250, 369
Corobisi, 332
Coronado, 199, 274
Costanoan, 4, 7, 11, 59, 61–65, 67, 77, 92, 138n.45, 354, 357–58, 399–400. See also Ohlone
Costanoan (Ohlone), 59, 61, 65, 67, 358
Cotoname, 97–98, 99
Coushatta. See Koasati
Cowlitz, 48, 50, 137n.33
Coxima (Koxima), 304
Coxoh, 150
Coyachilla Zapotec, 158
Coyaima (Tupe), 203

Index of languages 567

Cree, 41, 101, 121, 124–25, 127, 132, 143–44n.100, 405, 407, 443, 444–45, 451–52
Cree-Montagnais
Cree-Innu (Cree-Montagnais), 121, 124, 125
Cree-Montagnais, 5–6, 132–33
Creek, 108, 109, 110, 111, 112, 113, 114, 142n.86, 284, 411, 449, 461
Creek Confederacy, 113
Creek-Seminole, 109, 110–11, 112
Crow, 99, 100, 405, 407
Cruzeño, 77, 78
Cuatzoquitengo, 160
Cueva, 215
Cuica, 256–57
Cuicatec, 160, 180n.45
Cuitlatec, 147, 169–70, 181n.55, 359, 382, 413, 418, 462
Cuiva (Cuiba), 222, 223
Culaycha, 304
Culle, 186, 188, 216, 217–18, 382, 432
Cumanagota, 202
Cumayari, 304
Cumbazá (Belsano), 304
Cumbinamá, 213–14
Cumeral, 304
Cuna (Kuna), 115, 148, 207, 209, 215, 382
Cupan, 80, 82, 83, 86, 285, 287, 400
Cupeño, 80, 83, 86
Curanave, 304
Curi, 304
Curiane, 304
Curierano, 304
Curizeta, 304
Curubianan, 304
Curumiá, 304
Curuzirari, 304
Cusabo, 283–84, 409–10
Custenau (Kustenau), 192
Cutaguá, 304
Cutinana, 295
Cutría, 304
Cuximiraíba, 304
Cuxiuára, 304
Cuyama, 79
Cuzco (Quechua), 251, 321, 452–53

Dahomean, 333
Dakotan, 99, 100–1
Damana (Guamaca, Sanká), 208, 210, 211
Damanivá, 304

Dâw, 241
Dawainomol, 304
De'kwana, 202
Delaware, 6, 105, 119, 122, 130–31, 144n.110, 407, 442–43
Delta Yokuts, 65, 67
Delta-California Yuman. *See* Diegueño-Cocopah
Demacuri, 304
Dëmushbo, 244
Dene, 36, 41–42, 135n.4
Dene Soun'line. *See* Chipewyan
Dene-Yeniseian, 361–65
Deni, 194
Desano, 259
Desano-Siriano, 259, 455
Desano-Siriano-Yupuá, 259
Dhegiha, 99, 101–2, 142n.79, 405, 409–10, 411
Diaguita (Cacán, Kakán), 304–5
Diahói (Diahui, Jahoi), 262
Diegueño, 74–75, 86, 399, 400
Diegueño-Cocopah, 73, 74–75
Diné. *See* Navajo
Divihet, 305
Djeoromitxí, 233, 234. *See also* Jabutí
Dogrib, 36, 39, 41, 42, 136n.15
Dohema, 88
Dokoro, 305
Doracic, 207
Dorasque, 207, 209
Dorset Eskimos, 134
Duit, 208, 210
DURALJAN, 382
Duri, 305
Dzubukuá (Kiriri, Dzubucua), 228, 229, 325

East Cape Yupik (Naukan, Naukanski), 29, 33
East Cree, 121, 124, 125
East Greenlandic, 29, 34
Easter Island. *See* Rapa Nui
Eastern Abenaki, 122, 129–30
Eastern Algonquian, 122, 129–30, 131, 132–33, 407–8, 443–44
Eastern Arhuacic, 208
Eastern Atakapa, 106–7
Eastern branch (Arawakan family), 191
Eastern Canadian Inuktitut, 29, 34
Eastern Chatino, 158
Eastern Chibchan, 211
Eastern Eastern Tukanoan, 259

Eastern Enlhet-Enenlhet, 218
Eastern Eskimo (Inuit), 29, 33–34
Eastern Group Nahua, 80, 163, 164
Eastern Innu, 121, 124, 125–26
Eastern Isthmic, 207
Eastern Macro-Jê, 232, 369
Eastern Mahican, 122, 130–31
Eastern Mayan, 149, 150, 152, 153. See also K'ichean-Mamean
Eastern Miwok, 60, 61, 62, 63, 399–400
Eastern Muskogean (Creek-Seminole), 109, 110–11
Eastern Naskapi (Mushuau Innu), 121, 124, 125–26
Eastern Nawiki sub-branch, 191
Eastern Northern Uto-Aztecan, 79, 87
Eastern Ojibwe, 122, 126, 127–28
Eastern Otomanguean, 158, 461
Eastern Plateau Area, 395
Eastern Pomo, 70, 71, 76, 398
Eastern Popoloca, 158
Eastern Pueblo Linguistic Area, 405
Eastern South American Linguistic Area (ESALA), 423–24, 425
Eastern Swampy Cree, 124
Eastern Tukanoan, 258, 259–60, 426, 428
Eastern Tupían, 261
Eastern Zapotec, 159
Eastern-Southern Arhuacic, 208
Ecuador-Colombia (Quechua), 251
Ecuadoran-Colombian Subarea, 432, 436
Eel River, 8, 36, 44
Egualo, 305
Eimi, 305
Elotepec Zapotec, 159
Emberá (Catío), 210, 214, 215
Emérillon (Émerillon, Mereo, Teco), 262, 445
Emischata, 305
Emok, 218, 305
Enawené Nawé (Salumã), 192
Enenlhet, 218
Enenlhet (Mascoy, Mascoi, Machicui, Toba-Maskoy), 218
English, 8, 29, 33, 41, 56, 62, 134, 172, 283, 284, 342, 419, 429, 442, 444–45, 448, 451–52, 461–62, 467, 468–69, 470
Enimaga, 238, 322–23. See also Maká
Enlhet Norte (Lengua Norte), 218, 463
Enlhet-Enenlhet (Maskoyan, Lengua-Mascoy), 7, 185, 207, 218n.14, 218–24, 305, 311, 373, 381, 384, 436–37, 463

Eno, 286
Enoo, 216–17
Envuelto, 305
Enxet Sur (Lengua Sur, Lengua), 218, 463, 471
Epi-Olmec writing, 157
Equatorial, 200–1, 206, 214, 224, 249–50, 266–67, 272–73, 326, 361, 382
Equatorial-Tucanoan, 224, 226, 255–56, 258, 260, 266–67, 272–73, 361
Erema, 305
Erie, 117
Esaw, 103
Eseʔexa (Eseʔejja, Ese Ejja), 246, 247–48, 466
Eskimo Trade Jargon, 441–42
Eskimo-Aleut, 12, 14, 21, 28, 29–46, 32f, 134–35n.1, 354, 358–59, 382–83, 385, 391
Eskimo-Aleut–Chukotan, 382
Eskimo-Aleut–Yukagir, 383
Eskimo-based jargon (Eskimo-Chukchi jargon), 444
Eskimo-Uralic, 383
Eskimo, Eskimos, 38, 134, 134–35n.1, 382, 383, 393, 444
Eskimoan, 1, 3, 29, 33–35, 38–39, 134–35n.1, 392–93, 444
Esmeralda (Esmeraldeño, Tacame, Atacame), 186, 200–1, 217, 218–19, 239, 244, 272–73, 382, 432, 436, 466
Esselen, 29, 64–65, 72, 77, 92, 285, 346, 347, 399–400, 464
Etchemin, 122, 130
Etehua. See Nivaclé
Etla Zapotec, 159
Eudeve, 80, 82, 88, 289, 461
Eurasiatic, 383
Ewarhuyana, 305
Eyak, 11, 35, 37, 38–39, 135n.6, 389, 392–93
Eyak-Athabaskan, 35, 37, 38–39, 340, 361

Fake "Pipil" of Comapa, 335
Fake "Pipil" of Panchimalco, 335
Fernandeño, 86
Finnish, 461–62
First Nations, 2, 3, 143n.97
First Peoples, 2, 3, 15, 16–17, 19, 20–21
Flamenco (Flemish), 320
Flathead, 48, 51
Foklása, 305–6
Fornio
Fox, 6, 102, 124, 407. See also Meskwaki; Sauk-Fox

Index of languages

French, 29, 41, 125, 331, 419–20, 429, 442, 443–45, 448, 451–52, 461–62, 467, 468, 469
Fuegian Linguistic Area, 438
Fulniô, 305., –41, 369. *See also* Iaté

Gabrielino, 83, 86
Gabrielino-Cupan, 82, 83
Gabrielino-Fernandeño (Tongva), 80, 86
Gadio, 306
Gae (Shimigae, Gay), 274
Galache, 306
Galibi, 202
Galice-Applegate, 8, 36, 43
Gambéla (Gambela), 306
Gamela, 306
Garañun, Garanhun, 271, 306
Garífuna, 148, 170–71, 184, 189, 191, 193, 275–76n.2, 419–21
Garú (Guarú), 191
Garza, 98, 385
Gashowu, 65, 66
Gavião (Gavião do Jiparaná), 260, 263
Gayón (Coyón), 226
Gbe, 333
Gê (Jê), 8, 234
Ge-Pano-Carib, 266–67, 270, 361, 370, 373, 383
General Nahua, 80, 89, 163
General Yokuts, 65
German, 9, 62, 75, 173, 178n.23, 320
Germanic, 9, 62, 70, 167, 238, 442–43
Giamina (Onomil), 90, 284
Gitksan, 45, 46
Goajiros (Guajiro)
Goitacás, 250
Gorgotoqui, 198, 306, 450
Gosiute, 84–85
Goyana, 306
Gran Chaco culture area, 436–37
Great Basin Culture Area, 75, 401
Great Basin Linguistic Area, 75, 388, 395, 396, 397–98, 401–3, 402*f*
Greater K'ichean, 149, 153, 465
Greater Lowland Mayan diffusion zone, Greater Lowland Mayan languages, 155, 422, 465
Greater Mamean. *Xee* Mamean
Greater Q'anjob'alan (Q'anjob'alan-Chujean), 149, 150
Greater South Coast Range Linguistic Area, 395, 399

Greater Tzeltalan, 153. *See also* Cholan-Tzeltalan
Greenlandic, Geenlandic Eskimo, 29, 33–34, 35, 443
Grigra, 108
Gros Ventre, 5–6, 99, 100, 101, 121, 126. *See also* Atsina and Hidatsa
Gros Ventre (Atsina), 5–6, 101, 121, 126
Gros Ventre (Hidatsa), 5–6, 99, 100
Guaca, 306, 315
Guacará, 306
Guachí, 186, 219, 222, 248, 341, 372, 381, 436–37
Guachichil, 290, 293
Guadalupe Portezuelo/Villahermosa, 160
Guadaxo, 306
Guahibo. *See* Guajibo
Guaïcaros, 229
Guaicura (Waikurí), 171–72
Guaicurian (Waikurian), 147, 148, 346, 347, 383
Guaicurúan (Waikuruan, Waykuruan), 185, 207, 212, 219, 221–22, 238, 248, 305, 315, 371, 372, 374, 375, 381, 436–37, 438, 466
Guaimute, 306
Guaitacán family, 327
Guajá (Awá, Avá), 262, 265, 266, 430–32
Guajajára (Tenetehára), 262, 264, 265, 430–32
Guajarapo, 306
Guajibo (Guahibo, Sikuani), 222–23
Guajiboan (Guahiboan, Guahiban), 185, 189–90, 222–23, 466
Guajiro, 6–7, 191, 307, 341, 453
Guajiro group, 191
Guajiro-Spanish mixed language, 453
Guale, 284, 287, 409–10
Guambiano, 196, 244, 436
Guambiano-Totoró, 196
Guamo, 186, 206, 223–24, 382, 429
Guaná (Enlhet), 6–7, 192, 218
Guanaca, 306
Guanarú, 306
Guanavena, 306
Guane, 211, 306
Guaporé culture area, 430
Guaporé-Mamoré Linguistic Area, 425–26, 430, 431*f*
Guaraní Antigo, Old Guaraní, 261, 266, 466–67
Guaranían Branch, 261
Guarañoca, 274
Guarayo (Tambopata-Guarayo), 246
Guaráyoan Branch, 261, 266

Guarayu (Guarayo), 261, 266
Guarijío, 80, 83, 87, 88, 289, 291, 461
Guarino, 307
Guarisa, 246
Guarulhos, 250
Guasave, 290, 292
Guatemala "mystery" language, 335
Guató, 186, 224–37, 369
Guatuso, 207, 209, 210, 332, 426, 461
Guayabero, 222, 223
Guayaná (Wayaná), 6–7, 232
Guaymí (Movere, Ngäbere), 207, 209, 382, 418
Guaymíic, 207
Guazacapán (West Xinkan), 167, 332, 343, 418, 462
Guazapar (Guasapar, Guazapare), 289, 291, 293
Guelavia Zapotec, 418
Güenoa (Guenoa, Minuán), 206
Guenta, 307
Güentusé (Wentusix). *See* Nivaclé
Guêren (Guerén, Gren, Borun, Borum), 232
Guerrero Amuzgo, 159
Guianan Branch, 202, 203
Guinao, 191
Guisca (Coisa), 291
Güisnay, 237–38. *See also* Wichí
Gulf [Gulf hypothesis, Gulf proposal] 107, 108–9, 112, 170, 346, 381, 383, 412–13
Gulf Zoquean, 155
Gulf-Yukian, 383
Gunoco, 269
Güňüna-Küňe (Gennaken, Northern Tehuelche, Puelche, Pampa, Güňüna Yajich), 216–17, 229–30, 305, 320, 334, 465, 466–67
Guyanese English Creole, 429
Guyarabe, 307
Gwich'in, 36, 40, 135n.12, 444–45

Hacaritama, 307
Haida Jargon (Haida-English Jargon), 441–42, 444
Hairúya (Jairuia), 270
Haisla, 46, 47, 49, 136n.25
Haitian Creole, 429
Halkomelem, 47, 49, 391
Han, 36, 39, 40, 135n.13
Hanis, 54, 55
Hano, 87, 93, 140–41n.68, 405. *See also* Arizona Tewa

Harákmbut (Harakmbet, Tuyoneri, "Mashco"), 185, 189–90, 224, 225, 258, 312, 340
Harakmbut-Katukinan, 185, 224, 340, 341–42
Hare, 36, 39, 41, 42
Harritiahan, 307
Hasinai, 105
Haush, 216, 466–67
Havasupai, 74, 138n.52
Hawaiian, 3, 26n.18, 444
Headwaters subgroup, 245
Heiltsuk, 47, 136n.26, 391, 444
Heiltsuk-Oowekyala, 46, 47, 49
Hekaine, 229
Herisobocona, 205–6
Het language family, 333–34
Heve (Egue), 88
Hiauahim, 307
Híbito (Hibito, Xibito), 215–16, 301
Hidatsa, 5–6, 99, 100, 103–4, 105, 126, 405, 407
Hidatsa, 5–6, 99, 100, 103–4, 105, 126, 405, 407
Highland Chontal (Highland Oaxaca Chontal), 166
Himarimã (Rimarimã, Rimarimá), 307
Hine. *See* Xixime
Hio, 291
Hitchiti, 6, 109, 110, 113, 287, 411, 461
Hitchiti, 6, 109, 110, 113, 287, 411, 461
Hitchiti-Mikasuki, 109, 110, 111, 113
Hitnü 222. *See also* Macaguán
Hixkaryana, 201
Ho-Chunk (Hochank). *See* Winnebago
hoax language, 280, 330–31
Hodï. *See* Jotí
Hohoma, 221, 315
Hokan, 67, 68, 69, 71, 72–73, 75, 76, 77, 79, 96, 162, 163, 167, 172, 174, 273, 292, 340, 342, 345–54, 360, 381, 383, 384, 385
Hokan-Coahuiltecan, 97–98, 292, 346, 383
Hokan-Siouan, 12, 95, 97–98, 107, 108–9, 114, 115, 346, 352, 383
Holikachuk, 35, 39, 40
Honduran Lenca, 172–73, 343
Hongote, 239, 334
Hopi, 79, 82, 83–84, 85, 87, 89, 91–92, 95, 139n.62, 400–1, 403–4, 405, 461, 464
Huachipaeri, 224, 243
Huaihuash (Quechua I, Quechua B, Central Quechua), 251, 252

Index of languages

Huáilay (North), 251
Hualapai, 74, 138n.52
Huallaga (Alto Huallaga, Huánuco), 251
Huamachi, 307
Huambisa. *See* Wampis
Huambuco, 307
Huamelultec (Lowland Chontal), 166, 167
Huámpuy (Quechua II, Quechua A, Peripheral Quechua), 251, 252
Huancavilca, 239, 307, 337n.22
Huancavilca, 307
Huáncay (South), 251
Huangascar-Topará, 251
Huari, 384. *See also* Aikanã; Wari
Huari culture, Huari civilization, 252
Huari stock, 188
Huarpe (Allentiac), 187, 214, 225, 436
Huarpe stock, 225, 303
Huarpean (Warpean), 185, 187, 188, 225, 303
Huastec, 8, 149, 153, 154, 155, 176n.3, 465
Huastecan, 90–91, 149, 150, 152, 153–54, 155, 292
Huautla-Mazatlán Mazatec, 158
Huave, 147, 163, 170, 354, 356, 383, 384, 413, 417, 418, 419, 462
Huayana, 308
Huayla, 308
Huaylas (Ancash), 251
Huchití. *See* Uchití
Huchnom, 76, 139n.56
Hudson Strait Pidgin Eskimo, 441–42, 443
Huehuetenango diffusion area, Huehuetenango diffusion zone, 155, 422
Huehuetenango Sphere. *See* Huehuetenango diffusion area
Huehuetla Tepehua, 165
Huehuetla'tolli, 417
Huetar, 208, 210
Huichol, 80, 82, 83–84, 88, 289, 290, 291, 293, 294, 401, 413, 420–21, 461
Huilliche, 237
Huite, 291, 292
Humahuaca (Omaguaca), 307
Hume. *See* Xixime
Hup (Hupda), 227, 241, 425–26, 467, 468
Hupa, 36, 43–44, 67, 68, 396, 398
Hupda-Yuhup, 241
Huron, 117, 118, 128, 143n.90
Huron Confederacy, 118, 448
Huron-Wyandot, 115, 117, 118, 448

Iapama (Apama), 308
Iaté (Fulnio, Fulniô, Furnió, Yaathé, Yaté), 6, 225
Ibabi Aniji, 308
Ica (Bíntucua, Ika, Arhuaco), 208, 210, 330
Idabaez, 308
Ignaciano, 192
Ikpéng, 201
Illinois, 115, 129. *See also* Miami; Myaamia
Imaré, 308
Imbabura Quichua, 467
Ina, 308
Iñajurupé, 308
Iñapari, 192, 312
Inca, 251–52, 296
Indo-European, 35, 75–76, 150, 162, 178n.25, 190, 349–50, 354, 382, 383, 384
Iñeri (Igneri, Island Carib), 191, 193
Inezeño, 77–78, 79
Ingain, 232
Ingain-Southern Jê, 232
Ingalik (Deg Hit'an), 35, 39, 40, 135n.11
Ingarikó, 202
Inland Penutian, 357
Innu (Montagnais), 5–6, 121, 125–26
Innu-Naskapi-East Cree (Montagnais-Naskapi), 121, 124, 125
Interior Chumash. *See* Cuyama
Interior Salish, 48, 50–52, 58, 133, 391, 393, 395, 401–3, 464
Interior Tsimshianic). *See* Nass-Gitksan
Inuit, 29, 33–34, 135n.3, 443, 444–45. *See also* Eastern Eskimo
Inuit Pidgin French-Inuktitut-Montagnais-Basque, 443
Inuit Pidgin Inuktitut-Cree, 443
Inuit Thule, 17–18
Inuktitut, 34
Inuktitut French jargon, 443
Inuktitut-English Pidgin, 441–42, 443
Inupiaq, 34
Iowa (Ioway) [Siouan] 99, 102, 405
Ipai (Northern Diegueño), 73, 74
Ipeka-Kurripako, 191
Iquito, 274, 275
Iquito-Arabela, 274
Iquito-Cahuarana (Amacacore), 274
Irantxe (Iranxe, Myky, Mynky, Mỹky, Mu̇nku̇), 186, 225–26

Iroquoian, 28, 95, 104, 106, 115–21, 116f, 134, 346, 384, 401–3, 407–8, 410, 412, 432, 449, 464
Iroquois Proper (Five Nations Iroquois), 115, 117
Irra, 308
Irritila, 291
Iruri, 308
Iskoman, 72–73
Iskonawa, 245
Island Chonan, 216
Island Chumash, 77, 78
Isleño. *See* Island Chumash
Isolado do Tanarú (Isolado do Buraco), 308
Isolados do Massaco, 308
isolate, language isolate, 9, 11, 25n.8, 28, 29, 146, 147, 169, 170, 182–83, 184, 186–88, 280–81, 339
Isthmic, 207
Isthmus Zapotec, 159
Italian, 62, 75, 248, 342
Itipuna, 308
Itonama, 186, 226, 244, 341, 382
Itucá (Cuacá), 308
Itzaj, 149
Itzaj-Yucatec-Lacandón, 149
Ixcateco, 158
Ixil, 150, 153, 465
Ixtenco Otomí, 157
Izapa, 174–75

Jabutí (Yabutí), 231
Jabutían (Yabutían), 231, 233, 234, 369, 430
Jacariá, 308
Jaguanai, 309
Jaguanan, 309
Jaikó, 233. *See also* Jeikó
Jakalteko, Jakaltek (Popti'), 149, 177n.11, 417, 418, 462
Jalapa Mazatec, 158
Jalisco Otomí, 157
Jamundi, 273, 309
Janambre (Xanambre), 292
Japanese, 382, 385, 461–62
Japréria, 202
Jaqaru, 195
Jaqi. *See* Aymaran
Jarú (Yaru), 205
Jauja-Huanca (Huancayo), 251
Jêan (Géan, Jê family), 207, 231, 232, 234, 369, 370, 424, 430–32

Jebero (Xebero, Shiwilu, Xihuila), 198–99, 200
Jeikó (Jeicó, Jaikó, Geico), 232, 234, 369
Jemez (Towa), 92, 93
Jeticó (Jiripancó), 309
Jíbaaro. *See* Shuar
Jibaro-Kandoshi, Jibaro-Candoshi, 200–1, 382
Jicaque of el Palmar, 172
Jicaque–Subtiaba-Tlapanec, 383
Jicaquean, 147, 148, 167, 172, 347, 413, 415, 418, 419, 426
Jicarilla, 36, 44
Jirajara, 187, 226
Jirajaran, 185, 187, 226, 244
Jitirijiti, 309
Jívaro, 6–7, 200–1, 213, 328, 446. *See also* Chicham; Shiwiar
Jivaroan, 313. *See also* Chicham
Jopara (Yopara), 454
Jotí (Yuwana, Yoana, Waruwaru, Chicano, Jodi, Hotí, Hodï), 186, 197, 226–27, 241–42, 253, 272
Jova, 88, 139n.64, 291
Juaneño, 86
Juchitán Zapotec, 462
Juhine, 291
Juma (Yuma), 262
Jumana (Yumana), 190, 284
Jumano (Humano, Jumano, Jumana, Xumana, Chouman, Zumana, Zuma, Suma, Yuma), 284, 293
Jumaytepeque (North Xinkan), 167, 181n.53, 343, 462
Jurema, 309
Juri (Suri), 230
Jurí (unknown language), 230
Juruena, 309
Juruna (Yuruna), 261
Jurúnan subfamily, 261
Jururu, 309
Jutiapa (Xinkan), 167, 343

K'iche' 8, 150, 177n.17, 416, 417, 419, 469
K'ichean, 149, 152, 418
K'ichean-Mamean, 149, 150, 152. *See also* Eastern Mayan
Kaapór (Urubú, Urubú-Ka'apór, Kaapor, 262, 263, 430–32
Kabil, 153, 176n.4, *See also* Chicomucelec
Kabixiána, 260

Index of languages

Kadiweu (Caduveo), 219, 220, 221, 463
Kadohadaccho, 105
Kahi. *See* Northern Hokan
Kaimbé (Caimbé, Caimbe), 309
Kaingang (Coroado, Caingang), 207, 231
Kaiwá (Pãi-Tavyterã), 261
Kakua (Cacua, Macu de Cubeo, Kakwa), 187, 226–27, 241–42, 425–26, 428
Kakua-Nukak (Kakua-Nukakan), 185, 187, 226–27, 241, 248, 424, 425–26, 469–70
Kalaallisuut. *See* Greenlandic Eskimo
Kalapalo, 202
Kalapuya, 55–56, 137n.40, 359, 392
Kalapuyan, 28, 54, 55–56, 354, 385, 389, 391, 395
Kalhíphona (Kalípuna, Island Carib), 185, 191
Kaliana. *See* Sapé
Kalinya (Galibi, Kalinya, Kariña, Kari'nja), 202, 445–46
Kalípuna, Kalhíphona (Island Carib), 191, 193
Kalispel, 51
Kamakán (Camacán, Kamakã), 232
Kamakanan, 232, 233, 234–35, 369
Kamayurá (Kamaiurá, Camaiurá), 262, 264, 450
Kamba (Camba), 309
Kambiwá (Cambiuá, Cambioá), 309
Kamsá (Camsá, Sibundoy), 186, 228, 244, 313, 320, 436, 455
Kamurú (Camurú, Pedra Branca), 228, 229
Kanamarí (Kanamari, Canamarí), 6–7, 8, 192, 247
Kanamarí (Southern Katukina, Tshom-Djapá, Dyapá), 8, 192, 224
Kankuama (Atanques), 208, 210
Kanoê (Kapixaná, Capixana), 186, 228, 230, 242, 445
Kansa, 99–101, 409–10
Kantaruré, 309
Kapinawá, 310
Kapóng (Akawaio), 201
Kapóng cluster, 201
Kapoxó (Caposho), 232
Kaqchikel, 4, 5, 8, 150, 177n.18, 416, 417, 418, 419, 464–65
Karahawyana, 310
Karaib stock, 296, 297, 302–3, 317, 319, 329
Karajá (Caraja), 232, 233, 235, 369
Karankawa, 29, 96, 97–98, 106, 107, 282, 346, 347
Karapana (Carapano), 259
Kari'nja (Kariña), 193, 202, 445–46
Kariaí, 191

Karihona, 202
Karipuna (Panoan), 245
Karipuna (Tupían family), 262
Karirían, 185, 187–88, 228, 229, 325
Karitiána (Caritiana), 260, 263
Karkin, 61, 63–64
Káro, Karo (Arara, Urukú), 260, 262
Karu, 191
Karuk (Karok), 29, 67, 68, 69, 138n.47, 345, 347, 396, 398
Karútana-Baniwa (Baniva), 191
Kasharari (Kaxararí), 245
Kashaya, 70, 71, 396
Kashibo (Cashibo), 245, 299–300
Kashinawa of the Ibuaçu River, 245
Kashinawa of the Tarauacá River, 245
Kaska, 36, 41
Katapolítani-Moriwene-Mapanai, 191
Katawixí (Catawixi), 224
Katembri (Catrimbi), 255, 310, 382
Kathlamet (Katlamat, Cathlamet), 53
Kato, 36, 44, 396
Katukina (Catuquina, Katukina do Jutaí), 224
Katukina (Panoan language), 245
Katukinan (Catuquinan), 224–25, 340
Katxúyana (Kaxuiâna), 201
Kavinik, 246
Kawahíb Branch, 262
Kawaiisu, 79, 85
Kawesqaran (Qawasqaran, Alacalufan), 185, 216–17, 229, 301, 466–67
Kawishana (Cawishana, Kayuwishana), 190
Kayabí, Kayabi (Caiabi), 262, 266
Kayapó (Cayapó), 231
Kechumaran. *See* Quechumaran
Kepkiriwát (Quepiquiriuate, Kepkeriwát), 261
Keres-Wichita, 95
Keresan, 28, 94–95, 346, 383, 403, 404, 405, 464
Keresan-Caddoan, 383
Keresan–Uto-Aztecan, 383
Keresiouan, 95, 383
Ket, 361, 362, 363–64, 365
Keyauwee, 284–85
Kheuól, 429
Kiapüre (Quiapyre), 310
Kickapoo, 122, 128, 148, 170–71, 417
Kiksht (Upper Chinook, Columbia Chinook, Wasco-Wishram), 53, 393–96
Kiliwa, 73, 74

King's River, 65, 66
Kinikinau-Guaicurú, 219, 220
Kiowa, 5, 44, 92, 93, 94, 105, 356, 401–3, 405, 449, 471–72n.1
Kiowa Apache, 6, 39, 44, 405. See also Plains Apache
Kiowa-Tanoan, 5, 28, 87, 92–94, 356–61, 382, 404–5
Kipeá (Karirí, Kirirí, Kariri de Mirandela), 228, 229
Kitanemuk, 80, 83, 86
Kitemoka (Quitemo, Quitemoca), 205–6
Kitemoka-Napeka, 205
Kitsai, 104, 105–6
Klallam, 47, 49, 52
Klamath, 56, 69, 357–58, 393–95, 396, 401. See also Klamath-Modoc
Klamath-Modoc, 13, 56, 354, 396
Koasati, 109–10, 113–14, 411, 442, 461
Koeruna (Coeruna), 270, 329
Kohoroxitari, 310
Kokakôre, 310
Kokama, 264, 265, 453
Kokama-Omagwa (Kokama/Omagwa, Cocama-Omagua, Kokama-Cocamilla), 262, 264, 265, 453
Kokonukan. See Coconucan
Kokonuko. See Coconuco
Komokare, 310
Koniag, 33
Konkow, 60
Konomihu, 68
Korean, 382
Koroa, 108
Koropó (Koropó), 232, 250, 369
Korubo, 244, 310–11
Koshurái, 311
Kotiria, 428, 455. See also Wanano
Kotoxó (Kutaxó, Cotoxó), 232, 234–35
Kott, 361, 363
Kovareka, 198
Kovareka-Kuruminaka, 198
Koyukon, 35, 39
Koyukon-Ingalik, 35, 40
Kreen-Akorore (Creen-Acarore), 231
Krenak (Botocudo, Aimoré, Nakrehé), 232, 233, 235, 369
Krenakan (Botocudoan, Aimoré), 232, 369
Kubeo (Cubeo), 259–60, 428, 450, 469–70

Kueretú (Cueretú, Coretú, Curetú), 258
Kuikúro, 202
Kukra, 173
Kukurá (Cucurá, Kokura, Kukura), 334, 369, 370, 383
Kulanapan stock, 70
Kulina (Culina) (Arawan family), 194
Kulina of São Paulo de Olivença, 245
Kulina of the Curuça River, 244
Kumachisi, 65
Kumaná, 202, 205–6
Kumeyaay, 73, 74
Kuniba, 192
Kunsa-Kapishaná stock, 228, 244
Kunza. See Atacameño
Kurikuriaí (Kurikuriari), 241
Kurripako. See Baniwa of Içana
Kuruáya (Caravare, Curuaia, Kuruaia), 261, 263
Kuruminaka, 198
Kurumro, 311
Kururu, 311
Kutchin. See Gwich'in
Kutchin-Han, 36
Kutenai, 52, 58–60, 95, 381, 383, 393–95, 444
Kutenai Jargon, 444
Kwak'wala, 4, 6, 46, 47, 137n.28, 392, 395, 401–3
Kwakiutl. See Kwak'wala
Kwalhioqua, 38, 43, 136n.18
Kwalhioqua-Clatskanie, 36, 38, 43
Kwalhioqua-Tlatskanai. See Kwalhioqua-Clatskanie
Kwaza (Koayá, Koaiá), 186, 228, 230, 341
Kwinti, 445

Labrador Eskimo Pidgin (Labrador Inuit Pidgin French), 441–42, 443
Lacandón, 149
Lache, 211, 311
Laguna, 36, 94–95
Lagunero, 291
Lake Iroquoian, 115
Lake Miwok, 62, 63, 76, 396–93, 398
Lakondê, 242
Lakota, 6, 100, 461. See also Sioux; Teton
Lalana Chinanteco, 158
Lambayeque (Cañaris-Incahuasi), 251
Lambi, 311
language area, 7, 157, 158, 213, 224, 229–30, 243, 267–68, 369, 422–23

Index of languages

Lapachu (Apolista, Aguachile), 192
Laraos, 251, 252
Las Cumbres, Chiapas "mystery" language, 335
Latundê, 242
Laurentian, 8, 115, 117, 118
League of the Iroquois, 117
Leco (Lapalapa, Leko, Rik'a, Rika, Ateniano), 187, 230, 341, 381–82
Leko. *See* Leco
Lemachí, 212
Lenape, 6, 131, 144n.109
Lenca, 5, 181n.56, 212, 332, 343, 344, 345, 356, 382, 384, 413, 461. *See also* Lencan
Lencan, 147, 148, 168, 172–73, 212, 332, 343, 344, 345, 359, 383, 384, 418, 426
Lengua, 6–7, 218. *See also* Enxet Sur; Enlhet-Enenlhet
lengua general, 210, 249, 450
lengua yeral, 448. *See also* Língua geral; Nheeengatú
Lenni-Lenape, 6
Lili, 273, 311
Lillooet, 8, 48, 50, 393–95
Lincha, 251, 252
lingua franca, 24, 42, 118, 194, 197, 198, 214, 306, 421–22, 441, 442, 444, 448–51, 455
Língua geral, 266, 446–48, 466–67. *See also* Nheengatú
Língua Geral do Sul, 447–48. *See also* Língua Geral Paulista
Língua Geral Paulista (Língua Geral), 446, 447–48. *See also* Língua Geral do Sul
linguistic area, 7, 24, 38, 46, 146, 183, 347, 348, 388–440
Lipan, 36, 44, 405
Lipe. *See* Atacameño
Llamish, 311
Lokono (Arawak, Aruak), 190, 191, 429, 466–67
Loreto (Northern Pastaza)
Loucheux Jargon (Jargon Loucheux), 441–42, 444–45
Loup A, 130
Loup B, 130
Loup languages, 122, 130
Lower Chehalis, 8, 48, 50, 137n.32
Lower Chinook, 43, 53, 389, 391–92, 395–96, 442
Lower Coquille. *See* Miluk
Lower Tanana, 35, 40
Lower Umpqua. *See* Siuslaw

Lowland Mayan diffusion zone, Lowland Mayan Linguistic Area, Lowland Mayan languages, 153–54, 155, 166, 422
Lowland Mixe, 155
Luiseño, 83, 86
Luiseño-Juaneño, 80, 86
Lule, 230, 231, 312, 325, 340, 373, 375, 381, 384, 451, 463, 466
Lule-Vilela (Lula-Vilelan), 6, 185, 207, 230, 231, 312–22, 340, 341–42, 371, 373, 381, 436–37
Lumbee, 284
Luoravetlan, 382, 383
Lushootseed, 47, 49, 50, 137n.31, 391–92

Mabenaro, 246
Macaguaje, 258
Macaguán (Hitnü, Macaguane), 222
Macamasu, 311
Macaru, 311
Machacarí, 235
Machiguenga (Matsiguenga), 192
Macorís, 193
Macorixe, 193
Macoyahui (Macoyahuy), 289, 291, 293
Macro Panoan, 231, 248, 267–68, 361, 370, 373, 384
macro-. *See* macro-family
Macro-Arawakan, 189–90, 206, 223, 224, 258, 361
Macro-Carib, Macro-Cariban, 270, 361, 370, 383
Macro-Chibchan, 174, 196, 226, 244, 345, 383
macro-family, 9–10, 21, 56, 92, 115, 340, 360
Macro-Guaicurúan, 219, 238, 371–72, 375, 383
Macro-Jê (Macro-Jê Sensu Lato), 198, 204, 212, 214, 224, 225, 229, 234, 250, 316, 324, 327, 341, 369–70, 372, 383, 423
Macro-Jê Sensu Stricto, 184, 185, 231, 232, 233–34, 233*f*, 236, 250, 316, 340, 369, 370
Macro-Katembri, 310
Macro-Leko, Macro-Lekoan, 230, 254
Macro-Mayan, 9–10, 166, 366, 383, 461
Macro-Paesan, 226, 228, 244, 269
Macro-Panoan, 248, 361, 370, 373, 384
Macro-Penutian, 340, 356, 384
Macro-Siouan, 9–10, 340, 384
Macro-Tacanan, 384
Macro-Tucanoan, Macro-Tukanoan, 226, 240, 242, 255–56, 260, 267–68, 315, 361, 382, 384
Macro-Waikuruan, 231
Macro-Warpean, 225
Macú. *See* Makú

Macuani, 311
Macuare, 311
Macuja, 311
Macuruné, 311
Madeán, 251, 252
Madi, 194, 195
Madi-Madihá, 194
Madihá, 194, 195
Madre de Dios subgroup, 245
Magdalenic, 208
Mahican, 122, 130–31
Mahoma, 221, 315
Maidu (Northeastern Maidu, Mountain Maidu), 60, 354, 396, 397–98, 401
Maiduan (Maidun), 28, 59–60, 67, 75, 354, 355–56, 357, 396, 397–98, 401–3
Maijuna (Orejón), 258, 279n.41
Mainline branch, 245
Maiongong, 202
Maipure, 191, 466
Maipurean (Maipuran), 7, 189–90, 382. *See also* Arawakan
Mairajiqui, 311
Mairusa, 269
Majigua, 257
Maká (Macá), 237, 238, 322–23, 463, 470
Makah, 46, 47, 52, 391–92
Makiritare, 202
Mako (Sáliban), 252, 253
Makoní (Maconí)
Makú (Maco, Mako, Macu, Maku), 187, 236–37, 241, 253, 384, 429
Makú-Puinave, 227
Makú-Puinave, 227
Makúan, 7, 24n.5, 187, 226–27, 236–37, 241–42, 278n.31, 384, 423. *See also* Nadahup
Makuna (Macuna), 259
Makuní dialect complex, 235
Makuráp, Makurap, 261, 263, 450–51
Makushi, 202
Malaba, 311
Malacato, 213
Malalí, 232, 233, 235, 236
Malayo-Polynesian, 382, 383
Malibú, 312
Malinaltepec Tlapaneco (Yopi), 158
Maliseet, 129, 144n.107
Maliseet-Passamaquoddy, 122, 129, 407
Malquesi, 312

Mam, 5, 150, 153, 177n.21, 416, 417, 419
Mam-Teco (Mamean proper), 150
Mamean (Greater Mamean), 150, 152, 153, 331–32, 418, 422
Mamulique, 97, 98, 385
Manabi. *See* Manta
Manao, 191
Manao group, 191, 254
Mandahuaca, 190
Mandan, 99, 100, 103–4, 105, 405, 407, 461
Manesono (Mopeseano), 312
Mangue, 158, 180n.47
Manguean. *See* Chiapanec-Mangue
Manitsawá (Maritsauá, Manitzula), 261
Manta, 312
Māori, 18, 385
Maparina, 295
Mapoyo, 202
Mapoyo-Tamanaku Macro-Group, 202
Mapoyo/Yawarana, 202
Mapudungun (Mapudungu, Mapuzungun, Araucano, Mapuche), 4, 7, 185, 216–17, 222, 229–30, 237–39, 293, 341, 381–82, 384
Mapudungun languages (Araucanian), 237–39
Maracano, 312
Maraparná, 312
Maratino, 97–98, 291–92
Marawá, 191
Marawán-Karipurá, 191
Mariaté, 190
Maricopa (Piipaash), 73, 74
Maricoxi, 312
Maricupi, 312
Marin Miwok, 62, 63. *See also* Coast Miwok
Maripá, 312
Maritime branch (Caribbean), 191
Maritime Tsimshian, 45, 46
Maropa, 246
Marubo (of the Javari Basin), 245
Marubo subgroup, 245
Maruquevene, 312
Masa, 312
Masaká, 188
Masakará (Masacará), 232, 233, 234–35, 369
Masarari, 312
Masaya, 312
Mascouten, 122
Mascoyan (Maskoyan). *See* Enlhet-Enenlhet
Mascoyan. *See* Enlhet-Enenlhet

Index of languages

Mashco, 312
Maskoyan. *See* Enlhet-Enenlhet
Massachusett-Narragansett, 122, 130
Mataco, 4, 237–38, 312. *See also* Wichí
Mataco-Mataguayan. *See* Matacoan
Mataco. *See* Wichí
Matacoan (Mataco-Mataguayan, Mataguayan), 4, 7, 185, 207, 219, 222, 229–30, 231, 237, 238, 371, 372, 373, 381, 384, 436–37, 456, 463
Matagalpa, 173, 174
Mataguayan. *See* Matacoan
Matanawí (Matanauí), 225, 238–39, 241
Matará (Amualalá), 230, 312
Matawa, 205–6
Mathlela. *See* Nivaclé
Matis, 244
Matis subgroup, 244
Matlatzinca, 157, 179n.35
Matlatzinca-Ocuilteco, 157, 162
Matlatzincan, 90–91
Matogrossense, 233
Matogrossense-Jabutían, 233
Matses, 244
Matses subgroup, 244
Mattole, 8, 36, 44, 396
Mawayana (Mapidian), 191
Mawé (Maué, Sateré, Sateré-Mawé), 261, 263, 264–65
Maxakalí, 232, 233, 235–36
Maxakalían, 232, 233, 235–36, 250, 369
Maxiena (Ticomeri, Majena, Majiena), 313
Maya-Chipaya, 384
Maya-Yunga-Chipayan, 239
Mayan-MixeZoquean, 366
Mayan, Mayan languages, 5, 8, 147, 148–55, 151f, 166, 167, 168–70, 175, 176, 178n.23, 178n.25, 178–79n.26, 190, 239, 268, 288, 331–32, 340, 345, 356, 366, 383, 384, 385, 413, 416, 417, 418–19, 421–22, 439n.5, 452, 461, 462, 464–65
Mayangna (Northern Sumu), 173
Mayna (Maynas, Maina), 187, 199–200, 212, 242–43, 313, 381–82
Mayna-Chawi, 199
Mayo (Uto-Aztecan family), 80, 82, 88, 90, 282, 289, 290, 291–92, 294
Mayo (Maia, Maya, Pisabo, Pisagua), 247
Mayo group, 244, 289
Mayoruna branch (Mayoruna subgroup), 244, 247, 310–11

Mayoruna of Tabatinga, 244
Mayoruna of the Amazon River, 244
Mayoruna of the Jandiatuba River, 244
Mayu, 313
Mazahua, 157, 162, 180n.38, 418
Mazatec, 158, 417, 461
Mazatecan, 158
Mazatecan-Zapotecan, 158
Mazcorros, 292
Mbayá (Guaicurú), 219, 220
Mbeguá (Mbegua, Begua), 206
Media Lengua, 446, 453, 454
Mednyj Aleut. *See* Copper Island Aleut
Mejicano (Mexicano). *See* Nahuatl
Mekéns, 261, 263
Melikine, 295
Membreno. *See* Membreño
Membreño, 332, 359
Menejou, 313
Menién (Manyã), 232, 234–35, 369
Menominee, 121, 126, 132–33, 144n.102, 407
Mescalero, 44
Mescalero-Chiricahua, 36, 44
Meskwaki, 128
Meskwaki-Sauk, 6, 122
Mesoamerica, Mesoamerican, 20, 90–91, 146, 147, 148–76, 331, 335, 344, 348, 351, 368–69, 384, 413–22, 414f, 450, 461–62, 464–61, 465, 468
Mesoamerican Culture Area, 146, 154, 413, 419
Mesoamerican Linguistic Area, 146, 169, 172–73, 351, 388, 413–22, 414f
Mesoamerican phylum, 384
Mexican Penutian, 170, 354, 355, 384
Méye (Méyi), 96. *See also* Tonkawa
Meztitlaneca, 292
Mi'kmaq. *See* Micmac
Miahuatecan, 159
Miahuateco Zapotec, 159
Miami, 129, 407
Miami-Illinois, 122, 129
Michif, 121, 125, 451–52
Micmac, 122, 129, 443–44, 467
Micmac Hieroglyphs, 129
Micmac pidgin Basque, 443
Micmac Pidgin English, 443
Micmac pidgin Portuguese, 443
Migueleño, 72
Miguri (Chama), 257. *See also* Timote-Cuica

Mije-Soquean. *See* Mixe-Zoquean
Mikasuki, 6, 109, 110, 113, 411
Mikasuki Seminole,
Millcayac, 187, 225
Miluk, 54–55
Minhahá, 313
Minitari
Miranha-Carapana-Tapuya, 313
Miri, 327
Mirripú. *See* Mucuchí
Misantla Totonac, 165
Miskito (Mísquito), 173
Mississauga, 127
Mississippi Valley Siouan, 99, 103–4
Missouri (Missouia) [Siouan] 99, 102
Missouri River Siouan, 99, 100
Misulencan, 212, 384
Misumalpan, 5, 147, 148, 173–74, 181n.56, 212, 345, 382, 383, 384, 413, 416, 426
Mitla Zapotec, 159
Miwok, 59–62, 63, 64–65, 67, 354, 399–400, 401–3
Miwok-Costanoan, 7, 354, 357–58. *See also* Utian
Miwokan, 59, 61, 62, 63, 65, 67, 75, 77, 138n.44, 354, 358, 398, 399, 401–3
Mixe-Zoquean, 6, 90–91, 147, 155–57, 156f, 166, 170, 174–75, 332–33, 340, 354, 356, 366–67, 368, 383, 384, 385, 413, 416, 417, 418, 419, 420, 462
Mixe-Zoquean-Huave, 356
Mixean, 155, 157, 174–75, 332, 418
mixed language, 24, 29, 33, 121, 125, 150, 200, 216–17, 250, 264, 315, 441, 446, 451–54
Mixtec complex, 159, 162
Mixtecan-Cuicatecan, 159
Mika, 269, 270
Minika (Meneca), 269, 270
Mobilian Jargon (Chickasaw-Choctaw Trade Language), 114, 280, 283, 411, 441–42, 444, 449
Mocana, 313
Moche culture, 239
Mochica (Yunga, Chimú, Muchic), 239, 244, 268, 315–16, 318–19, 432, 435
Mocho' (Motocintlec), 149, 153, 177n.12, 418, 422, 462
Mocoa, 228, 313
Mocoa, 313
Mocochí. *See* Mucuchí

Mocorito, 290, 292, 293
Mocoví (Mocobí), 219, 221, 315
Modoc, 56. *See also* Klamath-Modoc
Moguex, 196, 244
Mohave. *See* Mojave
Mohawk, 116, 117, 119, 143n.95, 411, 469
Mohegan, 130
Mohegan-Pequot, 122, 130
Moheyana, 313
Mojave, 44, 73, 74, 85, 138n.53, 399
Mojo (Morocosi, Mojeño, Moxo), 192, 296
Mojo group, 192
Molala, 13, 56, 57–58, 354, 382, 392, 393–96, 464
Monachi (Western Mono), 84
Mondé (Salamãi), 260, 262
Mondéan subfamily, 260, 323
Mongolian, 461–62
Mongoyó (Mangaló), 232
Mono, 79, 84
Monoxó, 232
Monqui (Monqui-Didiu), 171, 172
Montagnais Jargon, 443–44
Montagnais pidgin Basque, 443
Montagnais-Naskapi
Montana Salish, 51, 464
Monte Albán Zapotec, 159
Monyton (Moniton), 103
Moose Cree, 121, 124–25. *See also* Eastern Swampy Cree
Mopár, 149, 417
Mopi, 327
Moquelumnan stock, 61
Morcote, 211, 313–14
Moré (Itene), 205, 314
Moré-Cojubim, Moré-Kuyubim, 205–6
Moreic, 205, 206
Moricue (Morike), 192
Moriquito, 314
Morití, 228–29
Morua, 314
Mosan, 46, 52–53, 95, 354, 381, 384, 391
Mosetén, 187, 239, 252, 268–69, 273, 334, 373, 381, 384, 385
Mosetén-Chon, 239, 248
Mosetenan, 187, 239, 248
Motocintlec. *See* Mocho'
Mountain Slavey, 36, 39, 41, 42
Movima (Mobima), 187, 240, 341
Moxos culture area, 430

Moyobamba, 314
Mucuchí-Maripú (Mocochí; Mirripú), 256, 257
Mucutu (Bailadores), 257
Muellama, 196
Muinane, 197
Muisca (Mosca, Chibcha), 208, 210
Mundurukú (Mundurucu), 261, 263
Mundurukúan subfamily, 261
Munichi, 187, 240–42, 256, 315, 330
Munichi stock. *See* Munichi
Munsee, 122, 129, 130–31, 132, 144n.110, 442–43
Munsee-Wamapano, 122
Mura, 238–39, 240–41, 314, 382. *See also* Pirahã
Mura-Matanawian, 225, 238–39, 241
Muran (Pirahã), 187, 238–39, 240–41, 314
Murato stock, 200–1, 255, 321, 322
Murato. *See* Candoshi
Mure, 314
Muriva, 314
Murui (Bue, Murai), 269, 270, 466
Muskogean, 28, 76, 108–14, 115, 282–83, 284, 287, 346, 383, 384, 385, 401, 409–10, 411–13
Mutsun, 61, 63–65, 92, 464
Mutú (Loco, Mutús), 257
Muzapa, 314
Muzo, 314
Muzo-Colima, 203

Na-Dene, 11, 12, 14, 21, 28, 35, 37, 37*f*, 38, 44, 45, 340, 358–59, 361–62, 363–65, 382, 384, 385, 389, 393
Naarinuquia (Themurete), 292
Nacai, 314
Nacosura, 292
Nadahup (Nadehup, Nadahupan, Makúan, Makú family), 7, 186, 226–27, 236–37, 241–42, 248, 278n.31, 384, 423, 426, 428, 469–70
Nadëb (Kaburi), 227, 241
Naduhupan. *See* Nadahup
Nahua (Nahuan) ix, 6, 80, 82, 83–84, 88, 89, 90–91, 148, 154, 155, 163–65, 164*f*, 168, 175, 180n.40, 180n.50, 282, 288, 289, 291, 292, 293, 294, 336n.3, 337n.13, 413, 416, 417, 418, 421–22, 465
Nahua main branch, 80, 163
Nahuatl, 6, 80, 81, 91, 140n.67, 154, 165, 168, 169–70, 180n.49, 180n.50, 282, 286–87, 288, 291–92, 294, 332, 336n.3, 336n.6, 336n.9, 337n.12, 384, 415, 416, 417, 418, 421–22,
439–40n.6, 440n.7, 449–50, 460, 461–62, 464–65, 468, 472n.2
Nahuatlan. *See* Nahua
Nahuatlecan, 81. *See also* Nahua
Nahukwa, 202, 203
Nakoda. *See* Assiniboine
Nambikwaran (Nambicuaran, Nambikuaran), 228, 242, 430
Nambiquara (Nambikwara), 242
Nambu, 314
Nansemond, 285
Nanti, 192
Nanticoke, 131
Nanticoke-Conoy, 122, 131
Naolan, 292, 462
Napeka (Napeca, Nape), 205–6
Narragansett, 130
Naruvoto, 203
Nass-Gitksan, 43, 45, 46
Natagaimas (Natagaima), 314
Natchez, 29, 108–9, 110–11, 112, 331, 346, 383, 384, 409–10, 411, 412–13, 442, 461, 464
Natchez-Muskogean, 108–9, 383, 384
Natick, 130
Natú (Peagaxinan), 314
Naukan. *See East Cape Yupik*
Naukanski. See *East Cape Yupik*
Nauna, 315
Navajo, 4, 36, 38, 44, 47, 85, 136n.20, 403–5, 444, 452, 464
Nawa (of the Môa River) (Panoan), 245
Nawa group (Panoan), 245
Nawathinehena, 121, 126
Ndyuka-Trió Pidgin (Carib Pidgin, Ndyuka-Amerindian Pidgin), 445
NE Zoque A, 156
NE Zoque B, 156
Nepuyo, 193
New River Shasta, 68
Nez Perce, 56, 57, 58, 137–38n.41, 393–96, 394*f*, 464
Nhandéva (Ñandeva, Chiripá), 261
Nheengatú, 264, 265, 426, 446, 447–48, 451. *See also* (Língua Geral Amazônica, Língua Geral)
NIC, SAMV, Ñumi, Santa María Asunción, 159
Nicola, 36, 43, 393–95
Nicoleño, 285
Nim-Yokuts, 65, 66

Ninam (Yanam, Xirianá, Shiriana), 195, 272
Nindaso, 315
Nio, 289, 292
Nipissing, 127, 133
Nipmuck, 130
Nisenan, 60
Nisga'a (Nass), 45
Nishnaabemwin, 128
Nitinaht (Ditidaht), 47, 52, 391–92
Nivaclé (Chulupí, Ashlushlay), 6, 24n.4, 231, 237, 238, 371, 456, 457, 458, 459n.5, 463, 468–69, 470
Nivaclé-Maká, 237, 238
Nipode (Nipode, Muinane), 197, 269, 270
Nocadeth, 315
Noctén, 237–38. See also Wichí
Nomatsigenga, 192
Nomlaki, 59, , 70, 76
Nomona, 315
Non-Zempoaltepetl, 155
Nonuya, 269, 270
Nooksack, 47, 49, 137n.29
Nootka, 4, 46, 47, 136n.27, 442. See also Nuu-chah-nulth
Nootka Jargon, 441–42
Nootka. See Nuu-chah-nulth
Nori, 315
North Alaska Inupiaq, North Alaskan Inupiaq, 29
North Baja Mixtec, 160
North Barbacoan, 196
North Highland Mixe (Totontepec), 155
North Midland Mixe, 155
North Slavey, 41, 42. See also Bearlake; Hare
North Unami, 122, 131
North Zoque (Magdalena/Francisco León), 156
Northeast Alta Mixtec, 159
Northeast Linguistic Area, 388, 407–8, 408f, 412
Northeast Otomí, 157
Northeast Xinka, 167
Northeast Zoque, 156
Northeastern Enlhet-Enenlhet, 218
Northeastern Jê (Northern Jê), 231
Northeastern Pomo, 70
Northern Algonquin, 121, 126, 127, 128
Northern Amerind, 360
Northern Athabaskan, 38, 40
Northern Bolivian Quechua (Bolivian Quechua), 251
Northern Caddoan, 104, 105–6

Northern California Linguistic Area, 391, 392, 398, 403
Northern Chínchay, 251
Northern Cochimí, 73
Northern Costanoan, 61, 63–64
Northern Diegueño. See Ipai
Northern East Cree, 121, 125–26
Northern Emberá, 148, 215
Northern Guaicurúan (Mbayá), 219, 220
Northern Hokan, 68, 69, 342
Northern Iroquoian, 115, 117, 118, 119, 120–21, 407, 464
Northern Jê, 231, 232
Northern Jê-Panará, 232
Northern Jê-Panará-Akuwẽ, 232
Northern Kalapuya. See Tualatin-Yamhill
Northern Magdalenic, 208
Northern Namabikwaran, 242
Northern Northwest Coast Linguistic Area, 38, 389, 392
Northern Ojibwe, 121, 126–27–
Northern Paiute, 79, 84, 90, 395, 401–3
Northern Pame, 420
Northern Pomo, 70, 138n.51
Northern Popoloca, 158
Northern Qawasqar, 217
Northern Sierra Miwok, 61, 63
Northern Straits Salish, 24n.2, 47, 49, 334, 391
Northern Tepehuán, 80, 87, 418
Northern Tiwa, 92, 93
Northern Totonac, 165
Northern Tupí-Guaraníian Branch, 262, 430–32
Northern Tutchone, 36, 40
Northern Uto-Aztecan, 79, 82, 83–84, 85, 89, 90–92, 148, 399, 400, 419
Northern Wakashan, 46, 47
Northern Wintuan (Wintu-Nomlaki), 59, 60
Northern Yokuts, 65, 66, 67
Northern Yukian. See Yuki
Northern Yúngay, 251
Northwest California Linguistic Area, 398
Northwest Coast Linguistic Area, 38, 46, 52–53, 331, 388, 389–92, 390f, 393, 395–96, 398
Northwest Otomí, 157
Northwestern California culture area, 67
Nostratic, 384
Nottoway, 8, 115, 117, 143n.89
Nuclear Maxakalí, 233
Nuclear Mondé, 262

Nuclear Zapotec, 159
Nukak, 187, 227, 241
Nukini, 245
Nukuini (Nucuini, Nuquini), 247
Ñumasiara, 315
Numic, 75, 79, 82, 83–84, 87, 90, 401–3
Nuu-chah-nulth, 4, 46, 47, 136n.22, 136n.23, 136n.27, 391–92, 395, 441–42. *See also* Nootka
Nuxalk (Bella Coola), 47, 49, 51–52

O'odham, 4, 36, 80, 139n.63, 148
Oa, 274
Oaxaca Amuzgo, 159
Oaxaca Mixean, 155
Ob-Ugric–Penutian, 384
Obispeño, 77, 78, 79
Ocaina, 269, 270
Occaneechi (Occaneechee), 103, 444, 449
Ocoroni, 289, 292
Ocren, 315
Ocro, 315
Ocuilteco (Tlahuica), 4, 157, 162, 180n.36, 417. *See also* Tlahuica
Ofayé (Opayé), 232, 233, 236, 369
Ofo, 99, 102, 409–10, 442
Oguera (Ohuera), 289, 292
Ohio Valley Siouan, 102. *See also* Southeastern Siouan
Ohlone, 4, 61, 63–64. *See also* Costanoan
Ohoma, 221, 315
Oivaneca, 315
Ojibwayan, 121, 126, 127–28
Ojitlán Chinanteco, 157
Okaina. *See* Ocaina
Okanagan, 48, 50–51
Oklahoma Apache. *See* Kiowa Apache
Oklahoma Delaware, 6, 131
Okwanuchu, 68
Old Algonquin, 122, 126, 127, 128
Old Guaraní. *See* Guaraní Antigo
Old Toba, 220, 221
Olmec, 157, 174–75, 413
Olmos, 254, 315–16
Oluta Popoluca, 6, 155, 179n.30, 332, 418
Omagua, Omagwa, 264, 265, 453
Omaha, 101
Omaha-Ponca, 99, 101
Omejes, 316

Omurano (Humurana, Umurano, Roamaina), 187, 199–200, 201, 242–43, 255, 272, 275, 313
Ona (Selknam, Selk'nam), 216, 466–67
Oneida, 116, 117, 119, 143n.94
Oneida-Mohawk, 116
Onicoré, 316
Onondaga, 116, 117, 118–19
Onoyóro, 316
Ópata, 80, 88, 290, 291, 292
Ópata-Eudeve, 82
Ópatan, 80, 87, 88, 289
Opón-Carare, 203
Oregon Athabaskan, 36, 43
Orejón, 6–7, 279n.41, *See also* Maijuna
Orejones, 97
Orí, 316
Oristine, 230
Oro Win, 205
Oro Win-Wari' 205
Ortue, 316
Osage, 99, 101, 102
Oscan, 103
Otecua, 316
Otegua, 316
Otí, 316
Oto (Otoe), 99, 102, 405
Oto-Pamean, 157
Oto-Pamean-Chinanteco, 157
Otomaco, 243, 382
Otomacoan, 186, 243, 429
Otomanguean (Oto-Manguean), 147, 148, 157–63, 161f, 170, 180n.47, 340, 346, 353, 360, 361, 382, 384, 413, 416–17, 418, 419, 462
Otomanguean-Huave, 384
Otomí, 157, 162, 180n.37, 384, 417
Otomí-Mazahua, 90–91
Otomían, 157, 169–70
Otomnguean-Huave, 384
Otomoaco. *See* Amotomanco
Ottawa (Odawa), 122, 126–., 27–, 128
Otuke group, 198
Otuque (Otuke), 198
Ouricuri (ritual), 225
Owens Valley Paiute (Eastern Mono), 84

Pacabuey (Pacabuei), 316
Pacaraos, 251
Pacarará, 316
Pachera, 291

Index of languages

Pacific Coast subgroup, 38
Pacific Yupik (Alutiiq), 29–33, 392–93
Pacimonari, 316
Paes-Barbakóan stock, 188–89, 244
Paez (Páez, Nasa Yuwe), 187, 188–89, 196, 244–48, 356, 382, 436
Paezan, 115, 187, 188–89, 196, 197, 215, 226, 244, 296, 361, 382, 385
Paguara, 316
Pai, 73, 74
Paipai, 73, 74
Paitér (Suruí, Surui Paiter), 260, 323
Pajalate, Pajalat. See Coahuilteco
Pajonal Ashéninka (Pajonal Campa), 192
Pakawan, 98, 385
Palaeo-Inuit, 17–18
Palaihnihan, 28, 60, 69, 345, 396, 401–3
Palantla Chinanteco, 158
Paleo-Chibchan group, 218–19
Palewyami Yokuts, 65
Palikur, 191, 445
Palmela (Palmella), 203
Palta, 213–14
Pame, 157, 413
Pamean (Northern Oto-Pamean), 90–91, 157–421
Pamigua (Pamiwa), 257, 258
Pamlico. See Carolina Algonquian
Pamunkey, 285
Panamaka, 173
Panamint, 79, 84
Panará, 232
Panare, 202
Panatagua (Panatahua, Panatawa), 316
Panavarro, 247
Panche, 203, 317
Paniquitá, 244, 319
Pankararé (Pankaré), 317
Pankararu (Pancararu, Pancarurú, Brancararu), 309–10, 317
Pano, 245
Pano-Takanan (Pano-Tacanan), 185, 207, 239, 244, 246f, 247, 248, 252, 267–69, 273, 295, 299–300, 302, 310–11, 313, 318, 340, 341–42, 373, 381, 385, 423, 424, 430
Panoan, 244, 247, 248, 272, 295, 299–300, 302, 303, 310–11, 318, 322, 328, 340, 373, 381, 384, 385, 453, 465–66
Pantágora, 203, 317
Pantágora (Palenque, Pantagora), 317

Panzaleo, 244, 320
Pao, 317
Papabuco, 159
Papago. See Tohono O'odham
Papago. See O'odham
Papamiän, 317
Papana, 317
Papantla Totonac, 165
Papavô, 317–18
Paragoaru, 318
Paraguayan Guaraní (Guaraní), 261, 263
Parakanã (Paracanã), 261, 266
Paramaccan, 445
Paraparixana, 318
Parapicó, 318
Paratío, 270–71, 306
Paraujano (Añún), 191
Paravilhana, 203
Paresi, 192
Paresi group, 192
Parintintín (Parintintin, Kagwahív), 262, 263, 266, 325
Parirí, 201
Parukotoan, 201, 203
Pasé, 190
Passamaquoddy, 129, 144n.107
Pasto, 196, 228
Pasto-Muellamues, 196
Patagón (Patagon), 6–7, 216–17, 297, 318, 381–82
Patagón (Patagón de Perico), 203, 216–17
Patagón Costero, 216
Patagón de Bagua, 297
Patamona, 202
Patarabuey, 293
Pataxó (Pataxo-Háhãhãe, Patasho), 232, 235–36
Patiti, 318
Patwin, 59, 70, 76, 396, 398
Paumari, 194
Paunaca (Paunaka), 192
Pawixiana, 203
Pawnee, 104, 105–6, 401–3
Paya. See Pech
Payacú, 318
Payaguá, 187, 219, 222, 248, 341, 372, 381, 436–37
Payanso, 318
Payayá, 228–29
Peba (Peva), 271–72, 333. See also Yaguan
Pech, 148, 169–70, 184, 207, 209, 212, 340, 416, 426, 461

Pehuenche, 318
Pehuenche (dialect of Mapudungun), 237
Pekodian, 201, 203
Pemón (Taurepang), 202
Pemóng Group, 201
Pemóng-Panare Macro-Group, 201
Pémono, 202
Pend d'Oreille, 51
Pentlatch, 47, 49, 391
Penutian, 12, 45, 53, 54, 55, 56, 59, 65, 67, 76, 95, 342, 345, 354–58, 360, 383, 384, 385, 401–3
Peria, 318
Pericú, 171–72
Peripheral Nahua, 80, 163–64, 164f, 165
Perovosan, 318
Pescadora (Lengua Pescadora), 318–19
phantom language, 239, 255, 280, 330–36
Piapia, 319
Piapoco, 18, 190, 223, 466
Piapoco group, 190
Piaroa, 252, 253, 382
Piaroa–Sáliban, 226–27. *See also* Sáliban
Piaroan, 252
Picuris, 92, 93
Pidgin Delaware (Delaware Jargon), 441–43
Pidgin Massachusett, 441–42
pidginized Inuktitut, 443
Piegan (spelled "Peigan, 124
Pijao, 203, 302–3, 314, 317, 319
Pilagá, 219, 221, 371, 463
Pilagá-Toba, 219
Pima, 4, 5, 80
Pima Bajo, 80, 87
Pima-Papago, *See* O'odham
Pima. *See* Akimel O'odham
Piman, 82, 83–84, 87, 139n.63, 290, 400
Pimenteira, 203
Pimic. *See* Piman
Pinche, 200–1, 255. *See also* Taushiro
Pipil (Nawat), 89, 163, 164, 164f, 165, 180n.50, 288, 335, 368, 415, 416, 417, 418
Pipipan (Pipipã), 319
Pira-Tapuyo (Piratapuya), 259
Pirahã, 187, 240–41, 314
Piratapuya-Wanano, 259
Piripkúra, 262
Piro (Purus), 192, 224, 312
Piro (Purus) group, 192
Piro (Arawakan family), 192, 224, 312

Piro (Kiowa-Tanoan family), 93
Pisaflores Tepehua, 165
Pisamira, 259
Pisamira-Karapana-Tuyuka-Yurutí, 259
Pisamira-Karapana, 259
Pizones, 292
Plains Apache, 6, 36, 44. *See also* Kiowa Apache
Plains Cree, 121, 124, 125, 451–52
Plains Culture Area, 405
Plains Indian Sign Language, 5–6, 126, 449
Plains Linguistic Area, 58, 405–7, 406f, 411–12
Plains Miwok, 61, 63
Plateau, Plateau Penutian, 13, 28, 56–58, 138n.42, 355, 357, 385, 388, 401–3, 464
Plateau Culture Area, 393
Plateau Linguistic Area, 53, 57, 340, 354, 391, 392, 393–98, 394f, 401–3
playano, los playanos, 72, 285
Playero, 222
Pochutec, 80, 89, 138n.43, 163, 165, 462
Pocoana, 319
Polar Eskimo, 34
Polynesian, Polynesia, 19–20, 26n.16, 26n.18, 381, 383, 385
Pomo. *See* Pomoan
Pomoan, 28, 70–71, 75, 76, 138n.51, 345, 347, 396, 398, 399, 401–3
Ponares, 319
Ponca, 101
Popoloca, 6, 158, 180n.43, 332, 417, 418
Popti'. *See* Jakalteko
Population Y, 17–19
Poqom, 150
Poqomam, 150, 168
Poqomchi' 150
Porcá, 319
Portuguese, 8, 190, 229, 297, 309, 310, 324, 325, 326, 328, 429, 444, 446, 447–48, 449–51, 453
Porú (Procáze), 319
Poso Creek, 65
Potawatomi, 122, 128, 407
Potiguara, 319
Powhatan Confederation, 131–32, 285
Poya (Huillapoya), 216–17
Poyanawa, 245
Poyanawa subgroup, 245
Pozo, 320
Pre-Proto-Siouan, 411

Index of languages

Proto-Eskimo-Aleut, 34, 35
Proto-Eyak-Athabaskan, 38–39
Proto-Algic, 132, 133
Proto-Algonquian, 122, 126, 132, 133, 407
Proto-Algonquian-Ritwan, 133
Proto-Amerindian, 385
Proto-Arawakan, 194
Proto-Athabaskan, 38–39, 393, 404
Proto-Boran (Proto-Bora-Muinane), 197
Proto-Bororoan, 198
Proto-Caddoan, 105–6
Proto-Cahuapanan, 199
Proto-Cariban, 203
Proto-Central-Algonquian, 132
Proto-Chapacuran, 206
Proto-Chiapanec-Mangue, 461
Proto-Chibchan, 178–79n.26, 211, 212
Proto-Chicham, 213
Proto-Chimakuan, 52
Proto-Chinantec, 462
Proto-Chocoan, 215
Proto-Chumash, 79
Proto-Enlhet-Enenlhet, 218
Proto-Eyak, 38
Proto-Germanic, 9
Proto-Guaicurúan, 221, 463
Proto-Gulf, 115
Proto-Hokan, 347–48, 351–52, 353
Proto-Huave, 170, 462
Proto-Indo-European, 9
Proto-Iroquoian, 117, 120–21
Proto-Jabutían, 234
Proto-Jicaque, 172
Proto-Kalapuyan, 56
Proto-Karajá, 235
Proto-Keresan, 95
Proto-Kiowa-Tanoan, 94
Proto-Lake Iroquoian, 117
Proto-Lencan, 173
Proto-Lule-Vilela, 231
Proto-Macro-Jê, 224, 225, 236
Proto-Maiduan, 60
Proto-Matacoan, 238, 459n.5
Proto-Mayan, 150–51, 152–53, 154–55, 178n.24, 344, 462, 465
Proto-Mazatec, 461
Proto-Misumalpan, 174
Proto-Miwok, 62, 357–58
Proto-Mixe-Zoquean, 157, 166, 367, 368, 461, 462

Proto-Mixean, 367, 368, 462
Proto-Mohawk-Oneida, 117
Proto-Muskogean, 109, 110, 111, 115, 410, 412, 461
Proto-Nahua, 165, 282, 419, 462
Proto-Northern-Iroquoian, 117, 120–21
Proto-Northern-Uto-Aztecan, 90, 404
Proto-Omagua-Kokama, 264, 453
Proto-Oto-Pamean, 154
Proto-Otomanguean, 162, 461, 462
Proto-Otopamean, 462
Proto-Palaihnihan, 69
Proto-Pano-Takanan, 247–48
Proto-Panoan, 247
Proto-Pomoan, 71
Proto-Popolocan, 461
Proto-Sahaptian, 57, 395
Proto-Salishan, 51, 133, 137n.34
Proto-Shuar-Candoshi, 201
Proto-Sierra Miwok, 63
Proto-Sierra Popoluca, 63
Proto-Siouan, 103–4, 407, 410, 412
Proto-Southern Guaicurúan, 221
Proto-Takanan, 247–48
Proto-Tepehua, 165
Proto-Tequistlatecan, 167
Proto-Totonac, 165
Proto-Totonac-Tepehua, 166. See also Proto-Totonacan
Proto-Totonacan, 165–66, 367
Proto-Trique, 462
Proto-Tsimshianic, 45
Proto-Tukanoan, 260, 469–70
Proto-Tupían, Proto-Tupí, 224, 225, 264
Proto-Turkic, 362
Proto-Tuscarora-Nottoway, 117
Proto-Utian, 61, 64–65, 357, 461
Proto-Wintuan, 59
Proto-Witotoan, 270
Proto-Xinkan, 167–68
Proto-Yokuts, 67, 357, 461
Proto-Yucatecan, 419
Proto-Yuman, 75, 399, 400
Proto-Zaparoan, 275
Proto-Zoquean, 367, 462
Pubenza, 320
Pueblo Culture Area, 403–4
Pueblo Linguistic Area, 331, 388 , –405, 403f, 464
Puinave (Wãnsöhöt), 7, 187, 226–27, 248, 255–56, 384, 424

Puinave-Makúan, 226–27
Puinavean, 7, 227, 248. See also Puinave
Pujunan stock, 60
Pumé. See Yaruro
Pumpokol, 361
Puná, 320
Pupuluca of Conguaco, 6, 332
Puquina, 5, 187, 189–90, 200, 249–50, 268, 302, 360, 432, 435, 436, 449–50, 452–53, 465–66
Purépecha (Tarascan), 4–147, 154, 155, 169, 170, 356, 382, 385, 413, 416, 418–19, 420–21, 461. See also Tarascan
Purí, 236, 250, 327, 369
Purí-Coroado, 187, 250
Purían (Purí family, Puarí stock), 250, 327
Purisimeño, 77, 78
Puruborá (Boruborá, Kuyubi, Cujubi), 260, 262, 341–42
Puruhá, 200, 239
Purukotó (Purucotó), 203
Purus, 247
Puscajae (Pile), 273, 320

Q'anjob'al, 149, 418
Q'anjob'alan, 149, 153, 465
Q'anjob'alan Complex, 149
Q'eqchi' 149, 153, 177n.15, 417, 464–65
Qawasqar (Alacaluf), 217, 229, 333
Qom, 219
Quapaw, 99, 101–2, 410, 411–12
Quechan (Yuma), 5, 73, 74, 139n.54
Quechua, 7, 200, 222–23, 240, 249, 250, 313, 321–22, 330, 346, 356, 361, 381–82, 385, 446, 449–50, 452–53, 455, 460, 462–63, 465–66. See also Quechuan
Quechua-Altaic, 385
Quechuachon, 252
Quechuan, 250–53, 268, 273, 299, 320, 372–73, 385, 432–34, 435, 436, 466. See also Quechua.
Quechuan-Aymaran Linguistic Area, 436
Quechumaran, 195–96, 252, 268, 372–73, 385, 432
Quelosi, 320
Querandí, 216–17, 320, 326
Quiambioá, 321
Quiatoni Zapotec, 159
Quiché. See K'iche'
Quijo (Kijo), 320
Quileute, 50, 52, 137n.36, 391–92, 395

Quillacinga, 320
Quillacinga (Quillasinga), 228, 320
Quimbaya (Kimbaya), 215, 301, 320
Quinault, 48, 50, 52
Quindío (Quindio), 321
Quingnam, 318–19, 321, 432
Quinigua, 292–93, 346, 347
Quiotepec Chinanteco, 158
Quiquidcana (Quidquidcana, Kikidkana), 320
Quiripi-Unquachog-Shinnecock-Montauk, 122, 130
Qurigmã (Quirigmã), 321

Rabona, 200–1, 255, 321
Rama, 207, 209, 332, 342, 360, 382, 426
Ramanos, 321–22
Ramaráma, 261
Ramaráman subfamily, 260
Ramaytush, 61, 63–64
Ranquel, 237. See also Mapudungun
Rapa Nui (Easter Island), 19
Red Indians, 133–34
Remo of the Blanco River, 245
Remo of the Jaquirana River, 245
Remo of the Móa River, 245
Resígaro, 191, 276n.6, 428–29, 466–67, 469
Retuará, 258, 259
Reyesano, 246
Rikbáktsa, 232, 233, 236, 369
Rimarimá. See Himarimã
Rincón Zapotec, 159
Rio Grande Keresan (Eastern Keresan), 94, 95
Río Negro group, 190
Ritual Maxakalí, 235
Ritwan, 121, 124, 132, 133, 145n.112
River Yuman, 73
Rokorona (Rocotona), 205–6
Romance languages, 59, 62, 70, 103, 194, 252
Roramí (Oramí), 322
Roseño, 78
Rumsen, 61, 63–65, 464
Runa, 322
Russian, 29, 33, 38, 75

Sabaibo, 288, 293
Sabanê (Sabanés), 242
Sabela. See Waorani
Sabuyá (Sapoyá), 228, 229
Sacata (Sacata, Zácata), 200–1, 322

Saclan (Bay Miwok), 61, 63
Sacosi, 322
Sacracrinha, 322
Sahaptian, 13, 53, 56, 57, 133, 354, 393–95, 464
Sahaptin, 56, 57, 391, 393–96, 401–3
Sakapultek, 150, 177n.19
Salamây, 262
Sáliba (Sáliva), 252, 253, 302
Sáliban (Sálivan, Sáliba-Piaroan, Piaroa-Sáliban), 186, 197, 226–27, 252, 253, 258, 319, 423
Salina. *See* Salinan
Salinan, 28, 72–73, 92, 346, 347, 351, 360, 399, 400
Salishan, 11, 28, 46, 47–53, 48f, 58, 334, 384, 389, 390, 391–92, 393–95, 464
Samoan, 3, 26n.18
Samoyedic branch, 362
San Agustín Tlacotepec, 159
San Andrés-Santo Domingo Chicahuaxstla Trique, 160
San Bartolo Soyaltepec, 160
San Cristóbal; San Agustín Chayuco; San Agustín Chayuco; San Agustín Chayuco; Santa Catarina Mechoacán, 160
San Felipe, 94, 95
San Francisco Bay Coastanoan, 61–64
San Francisco de Asís Sayultepec, 160
San Juan Coatzospan; Santa Ana Cuauhtémoc; Cuyamecalco Villa de Zaragoza, 160
San Juan Copala Trique, 160
San Juan Tamazola, 160
San Juan Teita, 159
San Martín (Quechua), 251, 252
San Martín Itunyoso Trique, 160
San Martín Peras; Coicoyán de las Flores, 160
San Mateo Sindihui, 159
San Miguel Chimalapa Zoque, 156
San Miguel Piedras, 159
San Pedro Jocotipac, 160
San Pedro Molinos, 159
San Pedro Tidaa, 159
San Vincente Coatlán, 158
Sanapaná, 218, 311
Sanavirón, 322
Santa Ana (Pueblo), 95
Santa María Acatepec, 160
Santa María Chigmecatitlán, 160
Santa María Chimalapa Zoque, 156
Santa María Yucuhiti, 159
Santa María Yucunicoco, 160

Santa María Zacatepec, 160
Santee, 461
Santee-Sisseton, 100–1
Santiago Cacaloxtepec, 160
Santiago del Estero Quichua, 251
Santiago Ixtayutla, 160
Santiago Tilantongo, 160
Santiam, 55–56. *See also* Central Kalapuyan
Santo Domingo, 94, 95
Santo Domingo Nuxaa, 160
Sanumá, 272, 310
Sapará, 203
Sáparo-Yawan (Záparo-Yaguan), 201, 255, 272, 275
Sáparo-Yawan stock, 201, 255, 272, 275
Sapé (Kaliana, Calianá), 187, 253, 255–56, 384, 429
Sapeiné, 322
Sapibkona, 246
Sapibokona Complex, 246
Saponi, 103, 449
Sapuki, 311
Sararé, 242, 298
Saraveca (Sarave), 192
Saraw, 103
Sarcee, 36, 43
Sauk, 102, 128, 144n.105
Sauk-Meskwaki-Kickapoo, 122
Saulteaux, 122, 126, 127
Sayula Popoluca, 6, 155, 179n.29
Sayultec, 293
Scandinavian, 62
Sechelt, 47, 49, 391–92
Sechura (Sec, Sek), 187–88, 230, 253–54, 315–16, 381–82, 432
Secoya (Sekoya), 258
Secoya-Siona, 258
Seculusepa, 295
Seden, 322
Sek. *See* Sechura
Sekani, 36, 41
Selknam (Selk'nam). *See* Ona
Selkup, 362
Seminole, 6, 109, 110, 113, 114, 142n.86
Semitic, 381
Seneca, 115, 117, 118, 128–29, 131, 464
Seneca-Cayuga, 115
Sensi, 245
Seri, 5, 147, 167, 174, 290, 292, 346, 347, 352, 401, 415, 462
Serran, 82, 83, 287

Serrano, 80, 83, 85–86, 89
Serrano-Kitanemuk, 80, 85, 86, 90, 399
Severn Ojibwe (Oji-Cree), 121, 126–27
Seward Peninsula Inupiaq, 29, 34
Sewee, 283–84, 285–86, 409–10
Shapra, 200–1, 255, 341
Sharanahua (Arara), 247
Shasta, 28, 68, 69, 342, 396, 401–3
Shastan, 28, 68, 69, 345, 347
Shawi (Chawi), 199, 200, 243. *See also* Chayahuita
Shawnee, 122, 128–29, 144n.106, 407, 409–10, 449
Shebayo (Shebaya, Shebaye), 192, 193
Shikuyana, 201
Shinabo, 322
Shipibo-Konibo, 245, 318, 328
Shiwiar (Mayna, Jívaro), 212, 213, 299, 446, 462–63, 466
Shoccoree, 286
Shoshone (Shoshoni), 79, 84–85, 89, 405–7
Shoshonean, 81, 83–84, 354
Shuar, 212, 213
Shukurú, 271, 384. *See also* Xukurú
Shukurú stock, 271, 306
Shuswap, 48, 50, 401–3
Siberi, 322
Siberian Yupik, 29, 33
sibilant harmony, 79
Sierra Juárez Zapotec, 159
Sierra Miwok, 61, 62, 63, 396, 397, 401–3
Sierra Popoluca, 6, 418–156. *See also* Soteapan Popoluca
Sierra Totonac, 165
Sign Language, 25n.7, 107, 176n.2, 449
Sino-Tibetan, 190, 382, 384
Sintó (Assek, Upsuksinta), 322–23
Sinú, 20, 26n.17, 323. *See also* Zenú, Zenu
Sinúfana, 215
Siona, 258
Siouan, 5–6, 76, 95, 99, 100–1, 102, 103–4, 114, 115, 126, 211, 284–85, 286, 382, 384, 385, 401–3, 405, 407, 409–12, 442, 461, 468
Siouan-Catawban, 11, 28, 99–104, 100f, 114, 286, 444, 449
Sioux, 6, 99, 100–1, 141–42n.78
Sipacapa (Sipakapense, Sipakaño), 150, 177n.20
Sipisipi, 323
Sirenik (Sirenikski), 29, 33
Siriano, 259

Sirionó, 261, 266, 308
Siuslaw, 29, 54, 55, 137n.38, 354
Six Nations, 117, 118–19, 131
Slave, 36, 41–42, 444–45. *See also* South Slavey
Slavey, 39, 41–42
Slavey Jargon. *See* Broken Slavey
Socorino, 323
Sogciagay (Sotygraik, Sotegraik, Sotegai, Sotsiagay, Chotiagagais, Sotiagay). *See* Nivaclé
Solano, 97–98, 286
Soltec, 158
Sonchon, 239, 334
Sonoran, 81, 83–84, 90
Soteapan Popoluca, 6. *See also* Sierra Popoluca
Soteapan Zoque, 156, 179n.33, *See also* Sierra Popoluca
Souriquois Jargon, 443–44
South Baja Mixtec, 160
South Barbacoan, 196
South Central (Costanoan), 61
South Coast Range Linguistic Area, 399, 400
South Highland Mixe, 155
South Midland Mixe, 155
South Slavey, 41–42. *See also* Slave
South Unami, 122, 131
South Zoque, 156
Southeast Culture Area, 409
Southeast Linguistic Area, 331, 407, 408, 409–13, 409f
Southeastern (Siouan), 99, 102
Southeastern Cordillera, 36
Southeastern Enlhet-Enenlhet, 218
Southeastern Pomo, 70, 71, 76, 398
Southeastern subgroup of Siouan, 102
southeastern Tzeltzal, 150
Southern Alacaluf, 229
Southern Athabaskan, 36, 39, 44, 403. *See also* Apachean
Southern Aymaran (Aymara), 195
Southern Caddoan, 104
Southern California-Western Arizona Linguistic Area, 400–1
Southern Chínchay, 251
Southern Chumash, 77, 78
Southern Cochimí, 73
Southern Cone Linguistic Area, 423, 435, 438
Southern Costanoan, 61, 63–64
Southern East Cree, 121, 125

Southern Eastern Tukanoan, 258
Southern Emberá (Epena), 148, 215
Southern Group (Pomoan), 70
Southern Guaicurúan, 219, 220
Southern Guiana (Northeastern Amazonian) Linguistic Area, 429–30
Southern Iroquoian. See Cherokee
Southern Jê, 231, 232, 341–42
Southern Kalapuya. See Yoncalla (Yonkalla)
Southern Kamakã, 233
Southern Magdalenic, 208
Southern Maidu. See Nisenan
Southern Nambikwaran, 242
Southern New England Algonquian, 11, 122, 130
Southern Numic, 79, 85
Southern Ojibwe, 122, 126, 127
Southern Oto-Pamean, 157
Southern Outlier branch (Arawakan family), 192
Southern Paiute, 85, 89, 400–1, 461
Southern Pame, 420
Southern Peruvian Quechua, 251
Southern Phonetic Group, 399
Southern Pomo, 70, 71, 76
Southern Sierra Miwok, 61, 63, 396
Southern Tepehuan, 80, 87, 289
Southern Tiwa (Isleta-Sandia), 92, 93, 404–5
Southern Tsimshian, 45, 46, 47, 136n.21
Southern Tutchone, 36, 40
Southern Uto-Aztecan, 80, 82, 83–84, 87, 89, 90–92, 140n.66, 148, 288, 289
Southern Wakashan, 46, 47, See also Nootkan
Southern Wintuan, Southern Wintun. See Patwin
Southern Yukian. See Wappo
Southern Zapotec, 158
Southwestern Arizona ("Hohokam") Area, 400
Southwestern Muskogean, 112
Sówa. See Nivaclé
Spanish (language), 4–5, 8, 62, 93, 97, 151–52, 168, 190, 217, 223, 249, 282, 284, 285–86, 291–92, 293, 304–5, 330–31, 332, 335–36, 342, 344, 359, 360, 372, 429, 444, 446, 448, 450, 452, 453, 454, 456, 461–63, 465, 466, 467, 468–69, 470, 471
Spokane, 51
Spokane-Kalispel (Flathead) (Kalispel-Spokane-Pend d'Oreille-Salish), 48, 51, 464
Squamish, 47, 49
Sranantongo, 429
Stanatevogyet, 323

stock, 9–10, 12, 340, 341–42, 352
Stoney, 99, 100–1
Subinhá, 332
Subtiaba, 158, 162, 172, 180n.41, 381, 383
Subtiaba-Tlapanec, 162, 340, 346, 353, 360, 383
Sugpiaq, 33
Suhín (Sujín, Súxen, Suhin-Chunupi). See Nivaclé
Suma, 284, 293. See also Jumano
Sumo (Sumu), 173
Sumo-Matagalpa-Cacaopera, 173
Supeselo, 323
Surucosi, 323
Suruí (Suru. do Tocantins), 18, 262
Suruim, 323. See also Suruí (Paiter)
Suruwahá (Zuruahá, Suruahá, Sorowahá), 194, 195
Susquehannock (Andaste, Conestoga), 8, 116, 117, 119, 143n.93
Sutagao, 323
Suyá, 231
Swahili, 461–62

Ta-Maipurean sub-branch, 191
Tacame. See Esmeralda
Tacarúba (Tacarua), 323
Tachi Yokuts, 66–67
Tacunbiacu (Tacumbiacu), 323
Taensa, 330–31
Taensa (people), 108, 331
Tagish, 36, 41
Taguaylen, 323
Tahltan, 36, 41, 136n.14
Tahue, 288, 290, 293, 294
Taíno, 189, 191, 193, 429
Tairona, 210–11
Taiwano (Eduria), 258
Takana (Tacana), 245, 452–53, 466
Takanan, 245, 247, 248, 340, 373, 466
Takanik, 245
Takelma, 29, 54, 55, 137n.39, 354, 389, 391, 392
Takelman, 55, 56, 385
Takic, 80, 82, 83–84, 85, 86, 90, 284, 285, 287, 400
Takunyapé (Taconhapé), 262
Tallán, 186, 187–88, 254, 432
Taluhet, 323
Tama, 258
Tamacosi, 323
Tamanaku, 202

Tamaní, 323
Tamaquéu, 323
Tamararé, 323
Tamaulipec, 292
Tambaruré, 323
Taminani, 324
Tamique, 282
Tamyen, 61, 63–64
Tanacross, 35, 40
Tanaina, 35, 38–39, 40, 135n.9
Tanana, 35, 40
Tanimuka (Tanimuca), 258, 259–60
Tanimuka-Retuará, 469–70
Tanoan, 93–94, 140–41n.68, 141n.69, 284, 403, 404–5
Tanpachoa, 286–87
Tanquihua, 324
Taos, 92, 93, 141n.70, 404–5
Tapachultec, 155, 179n.28, 332–33
Tapachultec II, 332–33
Tapacurá, 324
Tapakura (Chapacura, Huachi), 205
Tapakuric, 205, 206
Taparita, 243
Tapeba, 324
Tapiete, 6, 7, 261, 266
Tapirapé, 261, 263, 266
Tapuisú, 324
Taracahitic, 80, 82, 83–84, 87, 88, 289, 290, 291, 292, 293
Tarahumara, 80, 87, 88, 282, 289, 290, 291–92, 461
Tarahumara-Guarijío, 83
Tarahumaran, 80, 87, 88, 289, 291, 293
Tarairiú (Ochucuyana), 324
Taranoan Group, 202
Tarascan, 4, 154, 155, 169, 356, 382, 385. *See also* Purépecha
Tarascan-Quechua, 169, 385
Tariana, 191, 425–26, 428, 468, 469–70
Tarimoxi, 324
Taripio, 324
Taruma (Taruamá), 187, 254–55, 272–73, 310, 382, 429
Tataltepec Chatino, 158
Tataviam, 90, 287
Tatuyo, 259, 428
Taushiro, 187, 200–1
Taushiro (Pinche), 187, 200–1, 243, 255–56, 272, 423

Tavúri, 324
Tawahka, 173
Tawakaru, 105
Tawandê, 242
Tawasa, 114–15, 287, 409–10
Tchagoyána, 324
Tchicoyna, 324
Tebaca, 288, 290, 293
Teco (Tektiteko), 5, 150, 153
Teco-Tecoxquin, 293
Tecua, 324
Tecual, 293
Tecuexe (Tehuexe), 289–90, 293
Tegua, 324. *See* Tecua
Tehueco, 80
Tehuelche (Aoniken, Patagón), 216–17, 334, 381–82, 465, 466–67
Tembé (Tenetehára), 262, 264, 265
Tembey, 324
Témori, 289, 291, 293
Tenetehárán Branch, 261, 264
Tenharim (Tenharín), 262, 266
Teojomulcco Chatino, 158
Teotihuacan, 166, 175
Tepahue, 289, 290, 291, 293
Tepanec, 294
Tepango, 160
Tepecano, 80, 87, 290, 294
Tepehua, 165, 166, 180n.51, 417, 418, 462
Tepehuan, 80, 87, 289, 290
Tepiman, 82, 87. *See also* Piman
Tepqui, 325
Tequesta (Tekesta), 287
Tequiraca (Tekiraka, Aewa, Aiwa, Aushiri, Auishiri, Vacacocha), 7, 187, 255–56
Tequistlatec, 6, 167, 418, 462
Tequistlatec proper, 166
Tequistlatecan, 6, 147, 166–67, 172, 174, 346, 347, 353, 383, 413, 416, 417, 418
Terena, 192, 466–67
Teribe (Térraba, Tiribí), 148, 207
Tetetê (Eteteguaje), 258
Teton, 100–1. *See also* Sioux, Lakota
Teul, 289, 290, 294
Teushen (Patagón), 216, 466–67
Tevircacap, 325
Tewa, 87, 93, 405, 464
Tewa-Tiwa, 94, 404–5
Texas sign language, 449

Texistepec, Texistepec Zoque, 156, 179n.31
Texmelucan Zapotec, 159
Thequalme. *See* Tecual
Thompson, 8, 43, 48, 50–51
Thule, 17–18, 34
Tiahuanaco (Tiahuanacu, Tiwanaku), 249
Tianyuan Cave, 19
Tiboi, 325
Tikuna (Ticuna), 240, 256, 340
Tikuna-Yurí, 186, 230, 240, 256, 340
Tilapa Otomí, 157
Tillamook, 48, 50, 389, 392
Timaná, 189, 325
Timana, 325
Timba, 273, 325
Timbíra (Canela, Krahó), 231, 430–32
Timote, 256–57, 382
Timote-Cuica (Miguri, Cuica), 256
Timotean (Timote-Cuica), 186, 187, 189–90, 256–57
Timucua, 29, 114–15, 269, 287, 382, 385, 409–10, 411, 412
Timucuan. *See* Timucua
Tingán, 325
Tingui-Boto (Tingui, Tingui-Botó), 325. *See also* Dzubukuá
Tinigua (Timigua), 257–58, 382
Tiniguan, 186, 189–90, 257–58
Tiou, 108
Tipai, 73, 74
Tiriyó, 202, 305, 429–30, 445
Tiriyó Subgroup, 202
Tivericoto, 203
Tivilo, 295
Tiwa, 92, 93, 141n.71, 403*f*, 404–5
Tiwanaku. *See* Tiahuanaco (Tiahuanacu)
Tlachichilco Tepehua, 165
Tlacolulita Zapotec, 159
Tlahuica, 4, 157. *See also* Ocuilteco
Tlapanec, Tlapaneco, 162, 163, 169–70, 180n.40, 340, 360, 383, 416, 417, 461
Tlapanecan, 158. *See also* Tlapanec-Subtiaba
Tlaxiaco; Santa Cruz Nundaco; Santo Tomás Ocotepec; San Bartolomé Yucuañe, 159
Tlingit, 35, 37–39, 41, 45, 135n.5, 334, 340, 361, 365, 382, 389, 391, 392–93
Toba (Qom), 220, 221, 305, 315
Tobachana, 325
Toboso, 290, 291, 294

Tocantins Asuriní (Assurini, Asuriní do Tocantins), 261, 266
Tocantins-Mearim Interfluvium Linguistic Area, 430–32
Tohazana, 325
Tohono O'odham, 87, 400–1
Tojolab'al, 149, 150, 177n.14, 332, 422, 452
Tol, 172, 347, 352–53, 462
Tolowa, 36, 43, 396, 399
Toltec, 175, 465
Tomata, 325
Tomedes (Tamudes), 325
Tomina, 325
Tompiro, 93
Tongass, 37
Tongva. *See* Gabrielino
Tonkawa, 29, 36, 96–98, 106, 282, 292, 346, 347, 385, 401, 405
Tonocoté, 230, 325
Topia, 294
Topiame, 294. *See also* Topia
Toquistiné, 230
Torá, 205
Toromona (Toromono), 247
Tororí, 325
Totomachapa Zapotec, 158
Totonac, 90–91, 153, 165, 166, 175, 391, 416, 417, 418, 462
Totonac-Tepehua. *See* Totonacan
Totonacan, 91, 147, 148, 165–66, 356, 366, 367, 368, 383, 384, 385, 416, 418
Totonako. *See* Totonac
Totorame, 294
Totoró, 196, 244
Totozoquean, 166, 366, 367, 385
Towa. *See* Jemez
Trader Navajo, 444
Trans-Yautepecan, 159
Transfranciscanan, 232, 233, 369
Tremembé (Teremembe, Taramembé), 326
Trinitario, 192
Trió. *See* Tiriyó
Trique, 160, 417, 418
Truká, 326
Trumai, 187, 243, 258–68, 341, 382, 432
Ts'ono:x, 417
Tsafiqui (Colorado, Tsáchela, Tsachila), 196, 436
Tsamosan, 11, 48, 50
Tsetsaut, 36, 39, 43

Tsimshianic (Tsimshian), 28, 45–46, 136n.21, 354, 389, 391, 392
Tsutina. *See* Sarcee
Tualatin, 55–56, 360
Tualatin-Yamhill, 55–56
Tubar, 80, 83, 87, 291, 293
Tübatulabal (Tubatalabal), 80, 82, 83–84, 85, 89, 139n.61, 400–3
Tubichaminí, 326
Tuchiunawa, 245
Tuchiunawa, 245
Tucumanduba, 326
Tukano (Tucano), 259, 448, 451, 468, 469–70
Tukanoan (Tucanoan), 115, 185, 189, 190, 197, 227, 240, 258, 259–60, 310, 423, 424, 426, 428–29, 466, 469–70
Tule-Kaweah, 65, 66
Tulumayo, 326
Tümpisa (Timbisha), 84
Tunebo (Uwa, U'wa, Uw Cuwa), 208, 210, 359, 360
Tungusic, 385
Tunica, 29, 102, 107, 108–9, 112, 114, 346, 383, 385, 409–10, 411–13, 442, 461, 468
Tunican, 107, 108–9, 385
Tuparí, 261, 263, 370
Tuparían subfamily, 261
Tupí (Tupí antigo), 6–7, 190, 328, 382, 446, 447, 466–67
Tupí Branch (of Tupí-Guaranían), 261, 430–32
Tupí-Guaranían subfamily, 261, 264
Tupí-Kawahíb (Tupi do Machado, Paranawát, Wiraféd), 262
Tupían, 184, 185, 190, 194, 203, 204, 212, 260, 262, 263f, 264, 265, 266–68, 309, 323, 326, 329, 341–42, 369–85, 423–24, 429, 430, 432, 453
Tupían-Cariban, 266–67, 370, 385
Tupían-Cariban-Jê, 266–67, 370
Tupijó, 326
Tupinambá (Língua brasílica, Tupí antigo), 261, 264–65, 319, 321, 326, 430–32, 446, 447–48, 449–50, 453, 466–67
Tupiniquim, 326
Tupiokón, 326
Turiwára (Turiuara), 262, 430–32
Turkic, 362, 384
Tuscarora, 115, 117, 409–10, 448
Tuscarora-Nottoway, 115
Tutchone, 36, 40

Tutelo, 99, 102–3, 409–10, 411
Tutura, 326
Tututni, 36, 43, 391
Tuxá (Tushá, Tuxa), 326
Tuyoneri Toyoneri, 224, 243, 258. *See also* Harákmbut
Tuyuka (Tuyuca), 259
Tuyuka-Yurutí, 259
Twana, 47, 50, 391–92
Txikão, 201
Tz'utujil, 150, 415
Tzeltal, 149, 150, 153, 332, 416, 417, 452, 462
Tzeltalan, 149, 153
Tzotzil, 149, 153, 177n.9, 417, 462

Uairua, 326
Uarao Stock, 269
Uauarate, 327
Uchití (Huchití), 171, 172
Ulua. *See* Ulwa
Ulwa (Southern Sumu), 173
Umbrian, 103
Umutina, 198
Unainuman, 327
Unalachtigo, 122, 131
Unami, 6, 38, 122, 130–31, 144n.110, 442–43
Unami complex, 122, 131
Unangan. *See* Aleut
unclassified language, 10, 11, 24, 134, 171, 176, 182, 188, 189, 198, 201, 218, 219, 221, 247, 257, 271, 273, 275, 280–338, 369, 379, 430
uncontacted group, 25n.8, 182–83, 256, 262, 269, 305, 308, 312, 317–18, 327
Unidentified "language" of La Trinitaria region, 335
Unquachog, 130
Uomo, 205–6
Upland Yuman, 73, 74
Upper Amazon branch, 190, 191
Upper Chehalis, 8, 48, 50, 392
Upper Chinook. *See* Kiksht
Upper Kuskokwim (Kolchan)
Upper Paleolithic, 15
Upper Piman. *See* O'odham
Upper Tanana, 35, 39, 40
Upper Umpqua, 8, 36, 43
Upper Xingu Linguistic Area, 432, 469
Upsaroka. *See* Crow
Ural-Altaic, 35, 383, 385

Uralic, 35, 170, 362, 382, 383, 384
Uranaju, 327
Urarina, 187, 214, 267–68
Uru, 5, 249, 268
Uru Costeño, 268
Uru of Ch'imu, 268
Uru-Chipaya, 5, 186, 249, 252, 268–70, 360, 384, 385, 432, 436, 452–53
Uru-Pa-In, 327. *See also* Uruewawáu (Uru-eu-wau-wau)
Urubú-Ka'apór. *See* Kaapór
Urucuai, 327
Uruewawáu (Uru-eu-wau-wau), 262, 327
Uruma, 327
Urumí, 261
Urunamakan, 205–6
Urupá, 205
Urupá-Jarú, 205
Urupuca, 327
Uruquilla. *See* Uru-Chipaya
Ururi, 327
Usila Chinanteco, 157
Uspantek, Uspanteko, 149, 177n.16, 418
Ute, 85
Ute-Chemehuevi, 85
Ute-Chemehuevi-Southern Paiute, 79, 85
Utian, 7, 11, 28, 61–65, 62f, 77, 354, 355–56, 358, 399–400, 401–3
Uto-Aztecan, 5, 6, 9, 21–22, 28, 67, 75, 79–92, 81f, 94, 95, 147, 148, 163, 281–82, 284, 285, 287, 288, 290, 291–92, 293, 294, 345, 356–61, 382, 383, 385, 388, 395, 399–400, 401 , –4, 405, 407, 413, 421–22, 461

Vacoregue (Vacoregua), 290. *See also* Guasave
Valley Yokuts, 65, 66–67
Vanherei, 327
Vanyume, 86
Varihío. *See* Guarijío
Vaupés branch (of Nadahup), 241
Vaupés Linguistic Area, Vaupés-Içana Linguistic Area, 425–29, 427f, 455–56, 457, 468, 469–70
Vaupés-Japura, 7
Vejoz, 237–38. *See also* Wichí
Venezuelan Branch, 201
Venezuelan-Antillean Linguistic Area, 429
Ventureño, 77–78, 79–287
Viceitic, 207

Vilela, 6, 230, 231, 277n.22, 312–22, 340, 373, 381, 384, 466
Virginia Algonquian, 122, 131–32, 449
Votic, 207
Voto. *See* Rama
Vouve, 327

Wa'ikhana, 455. *See also* Piratapuya
Wabui, 201
Waiilatpuan stock, 58
Waikerí (Guaiquerí), 269
Waikurí. *See* Guaicura
Waikuru-Charrúa stock, 207
Waimiri, 202
Wainumá (Waima, Yanuma), 190
Wainumá group, 190
Waitaká (Guaitacá), 327
Waiwai, 201, 310, 429–30, 451
Waiwai Subgroup, 201
Wajumará (Wayumará), 203
Wakashan, 28, 35, 46–47, 49, 51–53, 58, 95, 136n.23, 384, 389, 390, 391–92
Wakon. (Wacona, Aconan), 327
Walapai. *See* Hualapai
Walêcoxô, 328
Wamo. *See* Guamo
Wamoé (Uamué, Huamoé), 328
Wampano, 122, 131
Wampanoag (Wôpanâak), 130
Wampis (Huambisa), 212, 213
Wampis-Shuar, 212
Wanai, 185
Wanano (Kotiria), 259
Wanyam (Wanham), 205–6
Wanyam-Wari'-Oro Win, 205
Waorani (Sabela, Auca, Huaorani, Auishiri), 7, 187, 243, 255, 269
Wapishana (Wapixana), 191, 254, 429–30
Wapishana-Mawayana, 191
Wappinger, 131
Wappo, 75–76, 139n.55, 396, 398
Waraikú, 191
Warao (Guarao, Warau), 115, 187, 269, 382, 385, 429
Waratégaya (Amniapé), 261
Warayo (complex), 246
Warekena (Guarequena), 190
Warekena group, 190
Wari' (Pakaás-Novos, Orowari), 205

Waric, 205, 206
Warikyana, 201
Warpean. *See* Huarpean
Wasco. *See* Kiksht
Washa, 107
Washo (Washoe), 75, 346, 347, 396, 397–98, 401–3
Wasteko. *See* Huastec
Wasu (Waçu, Wassu), 327, 328
Wau, 328
Waunana (Noanamá), 148, 214
Waurá group, 192
Waurá-Mehinaku, 192
Wayampí (Wayampi, Oyampi), 262, 265
Wayana, 202, 445–46
Wayana-Aluku Trade Jargon, 445
Wayoró (Ayurú, Wayru), 261, 263
Wayteka, 217, 334
Wayuu. *See* Guajiro
Weku, 105
Wenro, 117
West Greenlandic, 29, 34
West Greenlandic Pidgin, 441–42
Western Abenaki, 122, 129, 130
Western Apache, 36, 44
Western Atakapa, 106–7
Western branch (Arawakan family), 192
Western Canadian Inuktitut, 29, 34
Western Eastern Tukanoan, 258
Western Enlhet-Enenlhet, 218
Western Eskimo (Yupik), 29, 33, 34
Western Group Nahua, 80, 163
Western Innu, 121, 124, 125
Western Isthmic, 207
Western Jamamadi, 194, 195
Western Macro-Jê, 233
Western Mahican, 122, 130–31
Western Mayan, 149, 153
Western Miwok, 61, 62–63
Western Muskogean, 109, 110–11
Western Naskapi (Naskapi), 121, 125–26
Western Nawiki sub-branch, 190
Western Northern Uto-Aztecan, 80, 85
Western Numic, 79, 84
Western Otomanguean, 157
Western Otomí, 157
Western Pomoan, 70
Western Popoloca, 158
Western Puebloan Linguistic Area, 405

Western South American Linguistic Area (WSALA), 423–24, 425, 435
Western Swampy Cree, 121, 124
Western Tukanoan, 258, 259–60, 428
Western Tupían, 260, 262
whaler's jargon, 444
Wichí (Mataco, Lhamtes, Weenhayek), 4, 237–38, 312, 456, 457, 463, 467
Wichita, 95, 104, 105–6, 407
Wikchamni, 66
Winnebago (Ho-Chunk, Hochank), 99, 102, 128, 142n.79, 407, 412
Wintu, 59, 76, 396, 401–3
Wintuan (Wintun), 28, 59, 67, 70, 76, 92, 354, 355–56, 357, 396
Wiriná, 191
Wishram. *See* Kiksht
Witoto (Uitoto), 269–70, 466
Witotoan (Huitotoan), 186, 189, 197, 198, 269–70, 382, 423, 428, 466–67
Wiyot, 13, 121, 124, 132, 133, 143n.98, 396, 398, 461
Woccon, 99, 103
Woods Cree, 121, 124
Wyandot, 117, 118, 143n.90

Xakriabá (Chicriaba, Chakriaba), 231
Xamaca, 293
Xaquese, 328
Xaray, 328
Xavante (Shavante, Chavante), 18, 231, 236
Xaycatlán de Bravo; San Jerónimo Tonahuixtla; Cosoltepec; Santiagoc Chazumba; Tepejillo, 160
Xerente (Sherenté), 231
Xetá (Shetá), 261, 266
Xibata, 328
Xinca-Lenca, 342–43, 344–45
Xinca-Lenca hypothesis, 342–43, 344–45
Xinca. *See* Xinka
Xingu Branch, 262, 430–32
Xinka, 168, 288, 343
Xinkan, 147, 148, 167–69, 176, 288, 332, 343, 344, 345, 413, 417, 418, 419, 462
Xipará, 328
Xipaya (Shipaya), 261
Xipináwa (Shipinawa), 328
Xiroa, 328
Xixime (Jijime), 294
Xokléng (Shocleng, Botocudo), 231

Xokó (Xocó, Shoco), 328
Xoroca, 213
Xukurú, 188, 270–71
Xukurúan. *See* Xukurú

Yabaána (Jabaana, Yabarana), 191
Yacorito, 327
Yagan (Yahgan), 1, 187, 229–30, 271, 381–82, 466–67
Yagan-Alacaluf, 229
Yagan-Alakaluf, 229–30, 382, 385
Yagan-Alacaluf-Chono, 229, 385
Yagua, 271–72, 333, 383, 423
Yaguan (Peban, Peba-Yaguan Family), 186, 255, 269, 271–72, 370, 381–82, 423
Yahahí (Jahahi), 240–41
Yahi, 72
Yahuna, 258
Yakonan, 54, 55
Yalcon, 189
Yalcón, 329
Yámana. *See* Yagan
Yamasee, 284, 287, 409–10
Yameo, 271–72, 333
Yamesí, 329
Yamhill, 55–56
Yaminawa, 245
Yampará, 329
Yana, 29, 71–72, 345, 347, 396
Yanan. *See* Yana
Yanesha. *See* Amuesha
Yankton-Yanktonai, 100–1
Yanomam (Waiká, Waicá, Yanomami, Yanomam), 272
Yanomaman (Yanomamian), 186, 226–27, 272, 385, 429, 466–67
Yanomamö (Yanomamï), 272
Yao, 193, 203
Yaperú (Naperú, Apirú), 329
Yaqui, 5, 80, 88, 148, 461
Yaqui-Mayo, *See* Cahitan
Yaquina, 54
Yarí, 329
Yariguí (Yariguí), 329
Yaru (Tarma, Junín), 251
Yarumá, 203
Yaruro (Pumé), 187, 200–1, 217, 218–19, 244, 272–73, 382, 429
Yatasi, 105

Yathe (Yaathé)
Yatzachi Zapotec, 417, 418
Yauei, 329
Yautepec Zapotec, 159
Yavapai, 44, 74
Yavitero (Yavitano), 7, 191
Yavitero group, 191
Yawalapití, 192
Yawarana, 202
Yawdanchi, 66
Yawelmani, 66–67
Yazoo, 108
Ye'kwana, 202
Yemé, 154, 347, 352. *See* Comecrudo
Yeméan. *See* Comecrudan
Yeniseian, 44, 361–65
Yenmu, 329
Yine (Piro), 192
Yoemanai, 329
Yok-Utian, 65, 138n.42, 355, 357, 358
Yokuts, 28, 59, 65–67, 78, 84, 354, 355–56, 357–58, 396, 399, 401–3
Yokutsan. *See* Yokuts
Yolo, 273, 329
Yoncalla (Yonkalla), 55–56
Ypykuéra population. *See* Population Y
Ysistiné, 230
Yucatec (Yucatec Maya), 149, 176–77n.5, 416, 417, 413, 465
Yucatec-Lacandón, 149
Yucatecan, 149, 150, 151–52, 153–54, 175, 176, 465
Yuchi (Euchee), 29, 95, 104, 114, 346, 382, 384, 385, 401–3, 410, 411–12
Yucuna (Jukuna), 191
Yufiua, 329
Yugh, 361, 362
Yuhup, 227, 241
Yuit. *See* Siberian Yupik
Yukagir, 35, 383
Yuki (Yukian family), 75–76, 398, 401–3
Yuki (Yuqui), 261, 266
Yuki-Wappo. *See* Yukian
Yukian, 28, 75–76, 92, 114, 346, 383, 385, 396, 399, 401–3
Yukpa (Yucpa), 7, 202
Yuma. *See* Quechan
Yuman, 5, 71, 73–75, 167, 174, 346, 347, 399, 400–1, 403–4, 415, 461
Yumbo, 329

Yunga. *See* Mochica
Yúngay (Quechua IIA), 251, 252
Yupik, 20, 33, 135n.2
Yupiltepeque (East Xinkan), 167, 343
Yupuá-Duriña (Yupua, Duriña), 259
Yuracaré (Yuracare, Yurucar, Yuracar), 187, 273, 382, 384
Yurí (Jurí), 230, 240, 256, 340, 384
Yurimagua (Zurimagua, Jurimagua, Yoriman), 329
Yurok, 13, 67, 121, 124, 132, 133, 143n.99, 359, 396, 398, 461
Yurumanguí (Yurimanguí), 273–75
Yurumanguí-Hokan, 385
Yurutí, 259

Zacateco, 291
ZAH, TamS, Nuch ... 160
Zamuco (Old Zamuco), 274, 382
Zamucoan, 186, 207, 274, 436–37, 466
Zaniza Zapotec, 159
Záparo, 243, 274, 275, 361, 381–82, 446

Zaparoan, 186, 200, 243, 255, 272, 274, 275, 313, 423
Zapazo, 330
Zapotec, 158, 160, 162–63, 180n.46, 417, 418, 420, 465
Zapotecan, 158
Zempoaltepetl, 155
Zenu, Zenú, Sinú, 20, 26n.17, 323
Zenzotepec Chatino, 158
Zia, 95
Zia-Santa Ana, 94
Zimatlán Zapotec, 159
Zo'é (Zoé), 262
Zoe, 291, 293, 294–95
Zoquean, 155, 157, 174–75, 213–14
Zoró, 260, 263
Zuana, 330
Zuni, 29, 95, 124, 141n.73, 356, 383, 403, 404, 405, 464
Zuni-Penutian, 385
Zurina, 330

INDEX OF PERSONAL NAMES

For the benefit of digital users, indexed terms that span two pages (e.g., 52–53) may, on occasion, appear on only one of those pages.
Figures are indicated by *f* following the page number

Adam, Lucien, 330–31
Adelaar, Willem F. H., 5, 196, 203, 206, 211, 213–14, 218–19, 222–23, 224–25, 229, 244, 250, 252, 254, 257, 268, 273, 274, 296, 297, 298, 299, 301, 302–3, 306, 307, 308, 309, 311–12, 313–14, 315, 316–17, 318, 320, 321, 322, 323, 324, 325, 329, 330, 369, 433–34, 435, 463–64
Adelung, Johann, Christoph, 38, 115
Aikhenvald, Alexandra Y., 195, 224, 225–27, 228, 241, 253, 384, 425, 428, 434, 435, 469–70
Alves, Diego Valio Antunes, 238–39, 241
Aoki, Haruo, 395
Aragon, Carolina, 261, 445
Arroyo de la Cuesta, Felipe, 63, 64, 77
Aschmann, Richard P., 198, 270
Avelino, Heriberto, 420

Baegert, Johann Jakob, 171
Bakker, Peter, 443, 444–45, 451–52
Balmori, Clemente H., 231
Beam de Azcona, Rosemary G., 160, 162

Beck, David, 391
Beeler, Madison S., 287
Bereznak, Cathy, 403–4, 403*f*, 405
Berge, Anna, 34, 35
Bergsland, Knut, 34
Berlandier, Jean Louis, 96, 98, 99
Berman, Howard, 13, 56, 132, 133, 358, 360
Bertinetto, Pier Marco 274
Beuchat, Henri, 214, 244, 255
Beverley, Robert, 449
Birchall, Joshua, 23, 205–6, 423–24, 425, 435
Bloomfield, Leonard, 126, 132, 456–57
Boas, Franz, 43, 46, 52, 53, 391–92
Bolaños Quiñonez, Katherine Elizabeth, 227, 241, 248
Booker, Karen M., 103, 109, 110–12
Bridges, Thomas, 271
Bright, William, 167, 287, 292
Brinton, Daniel G. 35, 81, 115, 167, 239, 288, 330–31, 334, 371
Broadwell, George Aaron, 284, 287
Brown, Cecil H., 166, 366, 367, 421–22, 465

Cabeza de Vaca. *See* Núñez Cabeza de Vaca, Alvar
Cabral, Ana Suelly Arruda Câmara, 264, 453. *See also* Rodrigues, Aryon Dall'igna
Callaghan, Catherine A., 61–62, 63–65, 355, 400, 461
Campanius, Johannes, 119, 442–43
Campbell, Eric W., 158, 160, 162
Campbell, Lyle, 13, 150–51, 152–53, 154, 167, 172, 257, 275, 287, 332, 341–42, 352, 353–54, 364–65, 413–22, 465
Campbell, Thomas, 97
Captain James Cook. *See* Cook, Captain James
Caraballo, Bernardo (Colombian boxing champion), 256
Carlin, Eithne, 254, 429–30
Cartier, Jacques, 118
Carvalho, Fernando Orphão de, 23, 224, 243, 256, 275, 466–67
Casey, Nicholas, 255
Cerrón-Palomino, Rodolfo, 315
Chacon, Thiago, 259–60, 469–70
Chafe, Wallace L., 105
Chamoreau, Claudine, 169, 420
Champlain, Samuel de 118
Chase-Sardi, Miguel, 238
Chief Benjamin Paul, 107
Chomé, Ignace, 274
Chowell, Rafael, 96
Christian, Dana R., 223
Church, George Earl, 300–1
Ciucci, Luca, 274, 466
Clairis, Christos, 217, 333
Clark, Jorie, 16
Clark, Willaim, 53. *See also* Lewis and Clark
Constenla Umaña, Adolfo, 174, 209, 210, 211, 212, 215, 306, 311, 313–14, 345, 424–25, 426, 429, 432, 436
Conzemius, Eduard, 332
Cook, Captain James, 442
Coppens, Walter, 226–27
Crawford, James M., 114, 115, 411
Crevels, Mily, 308, 312
Curnow, Timothy J., 196, 244

Dakin, Karen, 421
Davis, Irvine, 94, 95, 369, 370
de Goeje, Claudius Henricus, 445–46
De Laguna, Frederica, 38
DeLancey, Scott, 355–56, 357–58

Delphine Decloux Stouff, 107
Derbyshire, Desmond C., 424
De Reuse, Willem J., 444
Diego Pérez de Luxán 281–82
Dienst, Stefan, 195
Dietrich, Wolf, 454
Dixon, R.M.W., 195, 224, 225–27, 228, 253, 307
Dixon, Roland B., 12, 67–68, 69, 72–73, 132, 345, 346, 354, 355, 356–57, 358, 399
Dobrizhoffer, Martin, 220–21
D'Orbigny, Alcide Dressalines, 198, 371
Dorsey, J. Owen, 102
Douay, León, 244
Dryer, Matthew S., 58
Durbin, Marshall, 302–3, 317, 319

Eliot, John, 130
Elliott, Eric, 400
Elliott, John, 218, 311
Elmendorf, William W., 75–76, 114
England, Nora C., 152–53
Epps, Patience, 183–84, 227, 241, 248, 423–25, 426, 450, 455, 463, 467, 469–70
Erik the Red, 29
Ernst, Adolf, 222–23, 239
Escalante Fontaneda, Hernando de, 283
Everdell, Michael, 403*f*
Everett, Daniel L., 240–41

F. X. C., 223
Fabre, Alain, 196, 268–69, 326
Farabee, William C., 254–55
Ferreira, Helder Perri, 272
Fleck, David W., 247, 302, 303, 313, 316, 318, 328
Fortescue, Michael, 34–35
Foster, Michael K., 81
Fowler, Catherine S. 90
Frachtenberg, Leo J., 54, 55
Franchetto, Bruna, 259
Francisco "el Chamuscado" Sánchez, 281–82, 286–87
Frič, A. von, 334
Friedrich, Paul, 169, 170

Galucio, Ana Vilacy, 262, 264
García García, Amadeo, 255
García, Bartholomé, 97
Gatschet, Albert S., 96–97, 98, 99, 105, 106–7, 134, 282, 283, 330–31

Index of Personal Names

Gerardi, Fabricio Ferraz, 21–22, 264–65
Gibbs, George, 442
Gildea, Spike, 203, 272, 370
Gilij, Filippo Salvatore, 243
Girard, Victor, 247–48, 466
Goddard, Ives, 13, 96–97, 98, 126, 130, 131, 132–33, 285, 286, 407, 409–10, 442–43, 449
Goddard, Pliny Earle, 44
Golla, Victor, 38–39, 43–44, 59, 60, 65, 66, 67–68, 75, 78, 86, 133, 194, 203–4, 264, 346, 353, 355–56, 357, 358, 399, 401–3
Gomez-Imbert, Elsa, 259
Gonzalez, Elenor Stevenson, 70
Granberry, Julian, 114–15, 172, 193, 269
Grant, Anthony P., 96, 283, 355
Greenberg, Joseph H., 3, 14, 21, 95, 115, 163, 169, 172, 197, 200–1, 204, 206, 214, 216, 224, 225, 226, 229–30, 231, 242, 243, 249–50, 255–56, 257, 258, 260, 266–67, 271, 272–73, 275, 315, 316, 326, 332, 334, 345, 352–53, 358–61, 369, 370, 371, 373, 381
Greenhill, Simon J., 21–22, 80, 90
Guilbaudière, Jean de la, 333
Guillaume, Antoine, 247, 248, 423
Guirardello, Raquel, 258
Gumilla, Joseph, 253
Gursky, Karl-Heinz, 95, 347

Haas, Mary R., 13, 107, 108–9, 110–12, 113, 346, 396
Hale, Horatio, 58, 69, 102–3
Hale, Kenneth, 83, 90, 173, 174
Halpern, Abraham M., 150–51
Hammarström, Harald, 199, 240–41, 244, 254, 257, 281, 312, 341–42
Hammerly Dupuy, Daniel, 333
Harrington, John Peabody, 63–64, 65, 68, 77–78, 79, 86, 94, 287, 346
Haspelmath, Martin, 467
Haude, Katharina, 240
Haugen, Jason D., 82, 83–84, 360
Haynie, Hannah Jane, 347, 357, 396, 397, 398
Heggarty, Paul, 358, 360, 361
Helmke, Christophe, 421–22
Hendrichs Pérez, Pedro R., 169–70
Henley, Paul, 226–27, 241–42
Henry, Jules, 371
Hervás y Panduro, Lorenzo, 162, 199, 205–6, 248, 313
Hewson, John, 134

Hill, Jane H., 83, 90, 91–92, 461
Hinton, Leanne, 399, 400
Hoijer, Harry, 96
Hollow, Robert C., 105–6, 405, 407
Hoyo, Eugenio del, 292–93
Humboldt, Alexander von, 38
Huttar, George L., 445–46
Hymes, Dell H., 385

Ishi, 72

Jacobs, Melville, 55, 392
Jacobsen, William H., Jr., 400–3
Jacobson, Steven A., 464
Jacques Cartier. *See* Jacques Cartier
Jean de la Guilbaudière. *See* Guilbaudière, Jean de la
Jefferson, Thomas, 130
Jones, Marie Smith, 38
Julian, Charles, 117, 120, 464, 469

Kasak, Ryan M., 114
Kaufman, Terrence, 7, 8, 72–73, 79, 88, 89, 90–91, 150–51, 152–53, 154, 155, 157, 160, 162, 163, 164, 165, 166, 167–68, 173, 174–75, 188–90, 194, 195, 200–1, 203–4, 206, 210, 211, 213–14, 216, 217, 218–19, 223, 224, 225, 226, 228, 229–30, 238–39, 240, 241, 243, 244, 247, 248, 250, 253, 254, 255–56, 258, 259, 260, 264, 267–68, 269, 270, 271, 272–73, 274, 275, 306, 310, 315, 316, 324, 340, 341, 345, 346, 347–48, 349–51, 352, 353–54, 360, 369, 413–15, 422–23, 462, 464
Kim, Yuni, 170
Kimball, Geoffrey, 108–9, 110, 111, 113
King, Alan R., 172–73
Kinkade, M. Dale, 38, 51–52, 54, 391–92, 393
Klar, Kathryn, 79, 287
Klein, Harriet E. Manelis, 423, 438
Koch-Grünberg, Theodor, 371
Kohlberger, Martin, 213–14, 299, 462–63
Krauss, Michael E., 38–39
Kroeber, Alfred L., 12, 67, 69, 72–73, 75, 132, 167, 284, 287, 290, 345, 346, 354, 355, 356–57, 358, 399
Kroeker, Menno, 328
Kroskrity, Paul V., 94, 404–5

Laffite, Jean, 96
Lafone Quevedo, Samuel A., 230, 371, 423

Lamb, Sydney, 284
Lanchas de Estrada, Captain Sebastián, 273
Landaburu, John, 258
Langdon, Margaret, 71, 75, 347, 399
Lapenda, Geraldo, 305–6
La Salle, Robert Cavelier de, 96
Law, Danny, 150, 419, 422
Lawson, John, 103, 283, 285–86
Laylander, Donald P., 172
Leap, William L., 93
Lederer, John, 286
Leer, Jeff, 38, 389, 392–93
Lehmann-Nitsche, Robert, 333–34
Lehmann, Walter, 169–70, 172–73, 332–33, 343
Lemley, Harvey V., 169–70
Lewis and Clark, 53, 57, 442
Lewis, Merriwether. See Lewis and Clark
Lombardo, Natal, 88
Longacre, Robert E., 372–73
Loukotka, Čestmír, 189, 195, 197, 198, 199, 200–1, 211, 213, 215, 216–17, 218–19, 220, 225, 230, 231, 237, 238–39, 240–41, 253, 254, 255–56, 257, 268, 269, 271, 273, 274, 295, 297, 298, 299–300, 302–3, 305, 307, 310, 311, 312–13, 314, 317, 318, 319, 321, 322, 323, 326, 327, 328, 330, 333–34, 341–42, 369
Lounsbury, Floyd G., 120
Lozano, Elena, 231
Lustig, Wolf, 454
Luzena, Gerónimo Josef de, 243

Maccioni [Machoni], Antonio, 230, 325
MacKay, Carolyn J., 165–66
Manaster Ramer, Alexis, 83, 98
Martin, Jack B., 106–7, 281
Martínez Compañón, Baltasar Jaime, 253, 254
Martins, Valteir, 226–27, 241–42
Martius, Carl Friedrich Philipp von, 229, 234–35, 313
Mason, Chief Oliver Grover (a.k.a. Tax-o-la Wi-e-le), 50
Mason, J. Alden, 196, 210, 216–17, 221, 230, 240–41, 254, 269, 274, 295, 299–300, 302, 308, 311, 312, 315, 318, 327, 328, 329, 333, 356, 371, 372
Matteson, Esther, 194, 223
McLendon, Sally, 71
McQuown, Norman A., 150–51
Meira, Sérgio, 203, 254–55, 370
Membreño, Alberto, 172, 332, 359

Merrill, William L.
Métraux, Alfred, 221, 315
Michael, Lev, 189–90, 193, 194, 255, 264, 370, 423–25, 428–29, 438, 450, 453, 463, 469–70
Middendorf, Ernst W. 239
Migliazza, Ernest C., 195, 226–27, 253, 257, 272, 295
Miller, Wick R., 82, 83–84, 88, 90, 95, 289, 290, 291, 292, 293, 294
Mithun, Marianne, 12, 76, 117, 120–21, 287
Moctezuma Zamarrón, José Luis, 288, 289, 290, 293
Mooney, James, 285
Mora-Marín, David F., 152–53, 366, 367
Moratto, Michael J., 77
Morice, Adrien Gabriel, 38, 42, 448
Moshinsky, Julius, 71
Müller, Neele, 425–26
Muñoz, Sixto, 257
Munro, Pamela, 109, 112, 285, 419–20
Muysken, Pieter, 446, 452–53. See also Adelaar, Willem F. H.

Natterer, Johann, 219, 298, 300, 327
Nevin, Bruce, 69
Nicklas, T. Dale, 112, 410
Nikulin, Andrey, 224, 225, 232, 234, 235, 236, 316, 369, 370
Nimuendajú, Curt, 238, 256, 318, 334, 445
Norman, William, 152–53
Núñez Cabeza de Vaca, Alvar, 96

O'Brien, Colleen Alena, 313
O'Hagan, Zachary J., 242–43, 255
Olawsky, Knut J., 267–68
Old Simon, 282
Oliveira, Sanderson Castro Soares de, 247
Oliver, Alice W., 96
Olmsted, David L., 69, 346
Olson, Ronald D., 268
Oltrogge, David F., 167, 172, 353
Oñate, Juan de, 286–87
Orozco y Berra, Manuel, 97–98, 289–90, 292, 293, 294
Orr, Carolyn, 372–73
Ortiz de Zapata, Juan, 289, 292
Oswalt, Robert L., 70, 71, 400–3
Oxford, Will, 132

Pache, Matthias J., 211, 212–73, 369, 463–64
Pareja, Francisco, 114–15

Index of Personal Names

Parisot, Jean, 330–31
Parker, Verdena, 43–44
Paul, Chief Benjamin. *See* Chief Benjamin Paul
Payne, David L., 201, 423
Payne, Doris, 272, 370, 423
Pennington, Campbell W., 291, 294
Petitot, Emile, 38, 444–45
Pharris, Nicholas, 464
Pimentel, Francisco, 291
Pitkin, Harvey, 356–57
Poser, William J., 13, 360
Powell, J[ay] V., 52
Powell, John Wesley, 12, 38, 46, 54, 58, 59, 61, 65, 67, 69, 70, 81, 345
Price, David P., 228, 242
Prince, Della, 124
Proulx, Paul, 132

Queiroz, [José] Márcio Correia de, 229
Queixalós, Francisco, 223

Raff, Jennifer, 13–14, 15–16, 18
Raghavan, Maanasa, 17
Ramirez, Henri, 234, 236, 250
Rankin, Robert L., 101–2, 103–4, 114, 411, 412
Rask, Rasmus, 34
Reich, David, 17–18
Rensch, Calvin R., 353
Ribeiro, Eduardo Rivail, 224, 316, 369
Rigsby, Bruce J., 58
Rivet, Paul, 5, 200, 214, 241, 244, 248, 254, 255, 257, 297, 318, 319, 333
Robertson, John S., 152–53
Rodrigues, Aryon Dall'igna, 184, 204, 264, 327, 370, 446
Rodríguez Bazán, Luis Antonio, 247
Rogers, Chris, 167–68
Rojas-Berscia, Luis Miguel, 199, 200, 243, 301
Romero, Padre Christoval 273
Rood, David S., 95
Rose, Françoise, 423, 469–70
Rowe, Timothy B., 17–18, 19
Rude, Noel, 57

Saabedra, Cristóbal de, 199
Sáenz, Nicolás, 222–23
Salanova, Andrés Pablo, 370
Sánchez, Francisco "el Chamuscado". *See* Francisco "el Chamuscado" Sánchez

Sapir, Edward, 2, 12, 25n.9, 37, 39, 45, 52, 53, 54, 55, 56, 65, 67, 68, 69, 72, 81, 89, 95, 97–98, 107, 108–9, 114, 115, 132, 346, 352, 354–55, 356, 360, 361, 381, 382, 383, 384, 386n.6
Sapper, Karl Theodor, 332–33
Sauer, Carl. 290, 293, 294
Sawyer, Jesse O., 75–76
Schillaci, Michael A., 120
Schomburgk, Robert H., 254–55
Seifart, Frank, 197–98, 240–41, 244, 254, 256, 257, 270
Sekerina, Irinia, 451
Seki, Lucy, 432
Seler, Eduard, 218–19
Sequoyah (George Gist, George Guess), 120
Sesostrie Youchigant, 108
Shaul, David L., 77, 87, 88, 90–92, 93, 95, 291, 400, 404, 405
Shepherd, Alice, 75–76
Sherzer, Joel, 395, 399, 400, 401, 403–4, 405–8, 410
Shipley, William, 355, 356, 357, 358
Sibley, John, 106, 107
Siebert, Frank, 103, 129–30, 133
Silva, Alcionílio Bruzzi Alves da, 468
Silva, Wilson de Lima, 455
Silver, Shirley, 399
Silverstein, Michael, 443–44
Sinfrônio, 236–37
Singerman, Adam Roth, 370
Sjoberg, Andrée F., 283
Skoglund, Pontus, 18
Smith, Norval, 444, 453
Smith-Stark, Thomas, 152–53, 413–15, 419–20
Snow, Dean R., 133
Souza, Gabriel Soares, 321
Stark, Louisa R., 243, 268, 452–53
Starostin, George, 362–63, 364, 365
Stoll, Otto, 331–32
Stubbs, Brian D., 82, 89
Sturtevant, William C. 284
Suárez, Jorge, 170, 207, 229–30, 239
Swadesh, Morris, 1–2, 7, 22, 27n.20, 72, 76, 95, 107, 115, 163, 169, 172, 173, 174, 183–84, 193, 203, 206, 207, 225, 239, 252, 275, 291–92, 334, 346, 352–53, 356, 382, 383, 384, 385, 386n.6, 452–53, 464
Swanton, John R., 102, 106–7, 108–9, 281, 284–85, 289, 330–31

Tallman, Adam J.R., 425, 426
Talon, Jean-Baptiste, 96
Tarpent, Marie-Lucie, 45
Taylor, Douglas R., 193
Teeter, Karl V., 13
Tessmann, Günther, 199, 242–43, 255
Teza, Emilio, 199
Thomason, Sarah G., 442, 464
Thompson, Archie, 124
Thompson, J. Eric S., 168
Thompson, Laurence C., 38, 392
Tobar Ortiz, Nubia, 257
Tomás Falkner, 333–34
Torero Fernández de Córdova, Alfredo A., 213–14, 215–16, 254, 297, 298, 303, 315, 318, 435, 436
Tovar, Antonio, 200–1, 211, 216–17, 255, 268, 303, 322, 333–34
Troike, Rudolf C., 284, 286–87
Trombetti, Alfredo, 229–30
Turner, Edith, 117
Turner, Paul R., 167

Uhde, Adolf, 98
Ultan, Russell, 60
Urban, Matthias, 200, 254, 257, 318–19, 321, 435

Vajda, Edward, 44, 361–65
Valenzuela, Pilar M., 199, 247, 248
Van de Kerke, Simon, 230
Van der Voort, Hein, 228, 230, 317, 369, 443
Van Gijn, Rik, 273, 424–25
Vater, Johann Severin, 115
Viegas Barros, J. Pedro, 206, 216–17, 219, 221–22, 229, 231, 238, 248, 301, 320, 322, 326, 333–34, 371–72, 451, 466–67
Vinson, Julien, 330–31
Voegelin, Charles F., 12, 345

Waddell, Gene, 286
Walker, Robert S., 193
Waterhouse, Viola, 167
Watkins, Laurel, 94
Weitlaner, Roberto J., 169–70, 292
Whistler, Kenneth W., 60, 401–3
Whorf, Benjamin L., 94, 356
Wichmann, Søren, 465
Willerslev, Eske, 17–18, 19
Williams, Roger, 130
Wise, Mary Ruth, 255
Wojtylak, Katarzyna, 269, 313, 466
Wright, Robert, 359

Zamponi, Raoul, 171, 172, 197, 201, 223, 228–29, 243, 255, 282, 283–84, 300, 310, 314, 321–22, 466
Zariquiey Biondi, Roberto, 268–69, 299–300
Zavala, Roberto, 419

SUBJECT INDEX

For the benefit of digital users, indexed terms that span two pages (e.g., 52–53) may, on occasion, appear on only one of those pages.

Figures are indicated by *f* following the page number

admixture, 19–20, 266
agriculture, agricultural, 90, 91–92, 94, 120–21, 140n.67, 162, 168–69, 176, 290, 403–4
ASJP (Automated Similarity Judgment Program), 23, 120, 341–42
avoidance of homophony, 22

basic vocabulary, 22, 27n.20, 75, 88, 105, 173, 205, 264, 267–68, 281, 314, 341–42, 352, 361, 469–70
Bayesian (analysis), 23, 193, 203–65
Beringian standstill (Beringian incubation model, Beringian Pause), 15
bilingualism, 69, 253, 446, 450, 454, 455
Bureau of Indian Affairs, 2

calque, 154, 415, 419–20, 421–22, 447, 468
Catalogue of Endangered Languages, 10–11, 24n.2, 162, 176n.2
center-of-gravity approach, center-of-gravity model, 90–91, 212
chain shift, 22

character-based (analysis), 23, 82, 193, 264–65
classifier, 183, 364–65, 373, 389, 410, 425, 428–29, 430, 434
code-switching, 454, 455, 457
consensus classification, 28
Cordilleran ice sheets, 14, 16
corn 91–92, 120–21, 214, 282, 283, 290, 368, 462. *See also* maize
creole, creolization, 38, 115, 429, 445, 446, 447, 454

decipherment, 151–52, 157
dialect chain, 84, 85
dialect cluster, 34, 66, 74, 192
dialect complex, 41, 42, 44, 74, 95, 100–1, 126–27, 128, 129, 130, 235, 245
dialect continuum (dialect continua), 7, 84–85, 158, 159, 213, 214, 218, 222, 239, 252, 269
directionality of change, 22
distance-based (analysis), 23, 82, 83–84, 262, 264
distant genetic relationship, 9–10, 12, 24, 339–87, 412–13

diversification, 20–21, 23, 38–39, 49, 53, 82, 90–91, 153, 157, 162, 168, 264
diversity, linguistic diversity, 1, 2, 10–11, 12, 13, 17, 20–21
DNA, 15, 16. *See also* mitochondrial (mtDNA); Y chromosome
dual-lingualism, 456

emergent language, 7, 33–34, 41–42, 44, 45, 46, 47, 54, 59, 63, 65, 72, 73, 74, 77, 78, 84, 101, 125–26, 127–28, 157, 158, 213, 224, 225, 229, 239, 242, 272
ergative, ergativity, 51, 152–53, 355, 391, 395–96, 405, 422, 423–24
ethnohistory, ethnohistorical, 95, 166
Ethnologue, 169, 213, 215, 222, 224, 242, 247, 259, 275, 296, 301, 302, 304, 307, 308, 309, 310–11, 314, 317, 319, 324, 325, 326, 327, 328, 329, 330
evidential, evidentiality 183, 389, 405–7, 425–26, 428, 430, 447

farming/language dispersal hypothesis, farming/language dispersal model, 90, 91–92
founding population, 17–18

gemination, 89
genetics, human genetics, 13–14, 16, 21, 23, 361, 363
genome, genomic, 14–15, 16, 17–19, 178–79n.26, 363
glottochronology, glottochronological, 69, 94, 105–6, 153, 169–70, 174
grammaticalization, grammaticalized, 22, 364–65, 425–26

homeland, linguistic homeland, 15, 35, 36, 38–39, 46, 51–52, 53, 59, 64–65, 71, 90–36, 92, 95, 103, 112, 118–19, 120, 133, 145n.112, 153, 162, 173, 178–79n.26, 194, 203–4, 212, 260, 264, 265
hybridization, 38, 266

Indian Territory, 113
isolate, language isolate, 9, 11, 25n.8, 28, 29, 146, 147, 169, 170, 182–83, 184, 186–88, 280–81, 339

Kelp Highway hypothesis, 16

labret (lip-plug), 6–7, 135n.5, 235
language area, 7, 157, 158, 213, 224, 229–30, 243, 267–68, 369, 422–23

Last Glacial Maximum (LGM), 15, 16–17, 19, 25n.11, 25–26n.13
Laurentide ice sheets, 14
lexical suffix, 51, 391
linguistic area, 7, 24, 38, 46, 146, 183, 347, 348, 388–440
linguistic prehistory, 166, 174–76
lip-plug. *See* labret

maize, 90, 91–92, 140n.67, 178–79n.26, 282, 290, 344, 368, 462, 463–64, 472n.3, *See also* corn
mitochondrial (mtDNA), 14–16, 17–18
mixed language, 24, 29, 33, 121, 125, 150, 200, 216–17, 250, 264, 315, 441, 446, 451–54
mutual intelligibility, mutually intelligible, 7, 9, 33–34, 41, 43, 44, 58, 60, 62, 72, 74, 76, 84, 85, 86, 87, 88, 93, 95, 100–1, 113–14, 124, 128, 130, 170, 173, 195, 213, 218, 220–21, 223, 227, 237, 239, 241, 252, 264, 269, 289, 292, 451–52

nasal harmony 183, 259–60
nasalizing, 89
nasal spreading, 183, 424
Neighbor-Joining, 82, 83–84, 120
Neighbor-Net, 82, 83–84, 194
neologism, 22, 395, 460
nominal tense, 429–30, 438
noun classifier, nominal classifier, 424, 428, 430, 438
noun-incorporation, 416
numeral classifier, 389, 394f, 395, 397, 416, 422, 435, 461

onomatopoeia, onomatopoeic, 92, 111, 341, 342, 349, 351, 353–54, 357–58, 359, 360, 362, 363, 366, 470, 471
orthography, 5, 8, 118, 151–52, 283, 284

paired couplet, 417
pan-Americanism, 353–54
phantom language, 239, 255, 280, 330–36
phylogenetic methods, computational phylogenetic methods, 21–23, 27n.21, 193, 203, 259–60, 264–65
phylum, 9–10, 340
positional verb, 104, 410–11, 416
Powhatan confederacy, 131–32, 285

quantitative method, quantitative analysis, 22, 82, 120
quinary numeral system, 395, 397–98, 411

reanalysis, 22, 361
relational noun, 90–91, 415, 419, 420
relational prefixes, 370
revitalization, 1–2, 11, 47, 63, 70–71

semantic change, 22
semantic discrepancies, semantic disparities, semantic latitude, semantic permissiveness, 34, 91–92, 183, 214, 344, 348, 359–60, 361, 362, 363, 367
semi-speaker, 43–44, 167, 230, 242–43, 255, 270
shared innovation, 22–23, 61, 88, 152, 165, 247
sibilant harmony, 79
sound correspondence, 22, 71, 75, 79, 91–92, 93, 110, 114, 150–51, 172, 199, 206, 222, 223, 231, 236, 247, 264–65, 268–69, 272–73, 341–42, 347, 350–51, 354, 355, 356, 357, 359, 361, 362–63, 365, 367, 368, 371, 381
sound symbolism, 341, 349, 351, 353–54, 359, 393–95, 396, 400
spirantization, 89
Sprachbund, 101–2, 388, 389. *See also* linguistic area
Sprechbund traits, 417

stock, 9–10, 12, 340, 341–42, 352
subgrouping, 21, 22, 24, 28, 38, 82, 83–84, 88, 94, 109, 111–12, 117, 147, 152, 183–84, 188, 194, 195, 203, 208, 213, 232, 238, 410, 452
switch-reference, 401–3, 412–13, 415, 419–20, 428

taboo, 96–97, 468–69
Trail of Tears, 119
trans-Pacific migration, 19

unclassified language 10, 11, 24, 134, 171, 176, 182, 188, 189, 198, 201, 218, 219, 221, 247, 257, 271, 273, 275, 280–338, 369, 379, 430
uncontacted group, 25n.8, 182–83, 256, 262, 269, 305, 308, 312, 317–18, 327
Unweighted Pair-Group Method. *See* UPGM
UPGM (Unweighted Pair-Group Method), 82, 83
Upper Paleolithic, 15

vigesimal numeral system, 415, 419–20

Wanderwort, Wanderwörter, 344, 353–54, 460–64
writing system, 25n.6, 29–33, 42, 128, 157, 163

Y chromosome DNA, 14, 423–24